THE LAW OF HEALTH CARE ORGANIZATION AND FINANCE

Sixth Edition

By

Barry R. Furrow
*Professor of Law and Director, the Health Law Program,
Drexel University*

Thomas L. Greaney
*Chester A. Myers Professor of Law and
Director, Center for Health Law Studies,
Saint Louis University*

Sandra H. Johnson
*Professor Emeritus of Law and Health Care Ethics,
Saint Louis University*

Timothy Stoltzfus Jost
*Robert L. Willett Family Professor of Law,
Washington and Lee University*

Robert L. Schwartz
*Henry Weihofen Professor of Law and Professor of Pediatrics,
University of New Mexico*

AMERICAN CASEBOOK SERIES®

Mat #40647822

American Casebook Series and West Group are trademarks
registered in the U.S. Patent and Trademark Office.

COPYRIGHT © 1987, 1991 WEST PUBLISHING CO.
© West, a Thomson business, 1997, 2001, 2004
© 2008 Thomson/West
     610 Opperman Drive
     St. Paul, MN 55123
     1–800–313–9378

Printed in the United States of America

ISBN: 978–0–314–18477–1

 TEXT IS PRINTED ON 10% POST CONSUMER RECYCLED PAPER

To Donna Jo, Elena, Michael, Nicholas, Eva, Robert and Hayden

B.R.F.

To Nancy, T.J. and Kati

T.L.G.

To Bob, Emily, Kathleen, Colin, Nicholas and Zachary

S.H.J.

To Ruth, Jacob, Micah, and David

T.S.J.

To Jane, Mirra and Elana

R.L.S.

This book is also dedicated to the memory of Nancy Rhoden and Jay Healey, great teachers, wonderful colleagues and warm friends.

*

Preface

The speed at which the health care industry has changed over the past twenty years is staggering. It seems that every passing year and each new session of Congress results in increasingly complex regulations, expansive structural developments, and shifting public opinions regarding health care. 2008 political opinion polls rank health care as a top concern for voters. Economically, politically, and socially, health care is a driving force in many aspects of the contemporary American dialogue. Who has a right to health care? How should we pay for it? How can the health care system be improved? How can barriers to access be eliminated?

In some ways the dynamic nature of the industry poses problems for creating learning tools in forms such as a textbook. This 6th edition of *The Law of Health Care Organization and Finance,* however, incorporates current case law, statutes, and regulations in conjunction with insightful notes and hypothetical problems to provide a sophisticated, up-to-date inquiry into the field. Recent changes regarding ERISA, false claims, antitrust, the Medicare Modernization Act of 2003, and tax regulations are skillfully addressed in this newest edition. Derived from the comprehensive material contained in West's seminal casebook, *Health Law: Cases, Materials, and Problems*, this book is custom made for students of health law interested in the structure and finance of the modern health care enterprise.

This book begins with a broad introduction of essential topics and fundamental concepts of health law, theories of sickness and wellness, and the policy debates regarding each. It then addresses issues of quality control and regulation of health care. The book moves on to issues surrounding access to health care and the controls placed on the cost of care. Finally, it looks at the structure of the health care system including professional relationships, fraud and abuse, and antitrust problems.

The Law of Health Care Organization and Finance is uniquely broad enough to be used in courses outside of law schools and sufficiently detailed to provide meaningful instruction to future health law practitioners. By presenting nuanced notes and examples, this book offers realistic situations for students to begin grappling with problems similar to those they may encounter in practice. *Health Law*, 6th Edition, has also been divided into two other focused course books, one dealing with bioethics and the other with quality of care and liability.

Barry R. Furrow
Thomas L. Greaney
Sandra H. Johnson
Timothy S. Jost
Robert L. Schwartz

June, 2008

*

v

Acknowledgements

Annas, George J., A National Bill of Patients' Rights, 338 New England Journal of Medicine 695 (1998). Copyright 1998 George Annas. Reprinted with permission.

Donabedian, Avedis, The Definition of Quality and Approaches to its Assessment, 1st ed., 4-6, 7, 13, 14, 27, 79-84, 102, 119 (Health Administration Press, Ann Arbor, MI, 1980). Reprinted from Avedis Donabedian, The Definition of Quality and Approaches to its Assessment, in Explorations in Quality Assessment and Monitoring, Volume 1. Copyright 1980. Reprinted with permission.

Enthoven, Alain, Health Plan: The Only Practical Solution to the Soaring Costs of Health Care 1-12 (1980). Copyright 1980 Alain Enthoven. Reprinted with permission.

Hacker, Jacob S., and Theodore R. Marmor, How Not to Think About "Managed Care," 32 University of Michigan Journal of Law Reform 661 (1999). Copyright University of Michigan Journal of Law Reform. Used with permission.

Hager, Christie, The Massachusetts Health Care Plan. Copyright 2008, Christie Hager. Used with permission.

Hyman, David A., Regulating Managed Care: What's Wrong with a Patient Bill of Rights, 73 Southern California Law Review 221 (2000). Copyright 2000, Southern California Law Review. Reprinted with permission.

Jost, Timothy Stoltzfus, Why Can't We Do What They Do? National Health Reform Abroad, 32 Journal of Law, Medicine, and Ethics 432 (2004). Copyright 2004. Reprinted with permission of the American Society of Law, Medicine and Ethics.

Jost, Timothy S, and Mark A. Hall, The Role of State Regulation in Consumer-Driven Health Care, 31 American Journal of Law and Medicine 395 (2005). Copyright 2005. Reprinted with permission of the American Society of Law, Medicine and Ethics.

Leape, Lucian L., Error in Medicine, 272 JAMA 1851 (1994). Copyright 1994, American Medical Association. Reprinted with permission of the American Medical Association.

Morreim, E Haavi, Redefining Quality by Reassigning Responsibility, 20 American Journal of Law and Medicine 79-104 (1994). Reprinted with permission of the American Society of Law, Medicine, and Ethics and Boston University School of Law.

Neuman, Patricia, Medicare Advantage: Key Issues and Implications for Beneficiaries, (#7664), The Henry J. Kaiser Family Foundation (June 2007). This information was reprinted with permission from the Henry J. Kaiser Family Foundation. The Kaiser Family Foundation, based in Menlo Park, California, is a nonprofit, private operating foundation focusing on the major health care issues facing the nation and is not associated with Kaiser Permanente or Kaiser Industries.

Stone, Deborah, The Struggle for the Soul of Health Insurance, 18 Journal of Health Politics, Policy and Law 287 (1993), copyright Duke University Press, 1993. Reprinted with permission.

Summary of Contents

ix

Table of Contents

Table of Cases

The principal cases are in bold type. Cases cited or discussed in the text are roman type. References are to pages. Cases cited in principal cases and within other quoted materials are not included.

*

THE LAW OF HEALTH CARE ORGANIZATION AND FINANCE

Sixth Edition

*

Chapter 1

INTRODUCTION TO HEALTH LAW AND POLICY

Part I of this chapter considers the definition of illness and the nature of health care. Part II examines the definition of quality and its measurement. Part III analyzes the problem of medical error, including its definition and origins and strategies for reducing its incidence. Part IV looks at scarce resources and organ transplantation. Finally, Part V introduces public health.

I. DEFINING SICKNESS

Before examining the meaning of quality in health care, consider the meaning of health and of sickness. We all have an operational definition of health and sickness. I know when I am depressed, have a broken leg, a headache or a hangover. In these circumstances I consider myself to be in ill health because I am not functioning as well as I usually do, even though I may lack a scientific medical explanation of my malaise. But am I in poor health because my arteries are gradually becoming clogged, a process that probably began when I was a teenager? Am I sick or in poor health if I am obese, or addicted to alcohol or drugs, or if I am very old and enfeebled?

We need some definition of health in order to assess the quality of care needed to promote or restore it. A malpractice suit or medical quality audit depends on an ability to distinguish a bad from a good medical care outcome. An understanding of the nature of sickness and health is required to determine what health care society should provide the poor and how much society ought to spend on health care. Should Medicaid (a federal/state health care program for the poor) or a commercial insurer, for example, cover in vitro fertilization or abortions? Does the possibility of organ transplantation mean that replacement hearts should become the normal treatment for a condition that formerly inevitably ended in death? Should organ transplantation be available to all, without regard to the ability to pay? If the state of being old becomes a state of sickness (and particularly if that sickness must be "cured" at public expense), what will be the cost? Is this cost justified? Finally, the definition of health raises questions of autonomy, responsibility and personhood. Should health be defined by the doctor as scientist or the patient as person, or both? Is the drunkard or serial killer diseased or sinning or both or neither?

1

The Constitution of the World Health Organization defines health as "[a] state of complete physical, mental and social well-being and not merely the absence of disease or infirmity." When did you last feel that way? Can health ever be achieved under this definition, or is everyone always in a state of ill health? How much can physicians and hospitals contribute to health under this definition? A further provision of the WHO Constitution provides that "Governments have a responsibility for the health of their peoples which can be fulfilled only by the provision of adequate health and social measures." What are the political ramifications of these principles?

Health can be viewed in a more limited sense as the performance by each part of the body of its "natural" function. Definitions in terms of biological functioning tend to be more descriptive and less value-laden. As Englehardt writes, "The notion required for an analysis of health is not that of a good man or a good shark, but that of a good specimen of a human being or shark." H. Tristam Englehardt, "The Concepts of Health and Disease," in Concepts of Health and Disease 552 (Arthur Caplan, H. Tristam Engelhardt, and James McCartney, eds. 1981) (hereafter Concepts). Boorse compares health to the mechanical condition of a car, which can be described as good because it conforms to the designers' specifications, even though the design is flawed. Disease is then a biological malfunction, a deviation from the biological norm of natural function. C. Boorse, "On the Distinction Between Disease and Illness," in Concepts, *supra* at 553.

Illness can be defined as a subset of disease. Boorse writes:

> An illness must be, first, a reasonably *serious* disease with incapacitating effects that make it undesirable. A shaving cut or mild athlete's foot cannot be called an illness, nor could one call in sick on the basis of a single dental cavity, though all these conditions are diseases. Secondly, to call a disease an illness is to view its owner as deserving special treatment and diminished moral accountability * * *. Where we do not make the appropriate normative judgments or activate the social institutions, no amount of disease will lead us to use the term "ill." Even if the laboratory fruit flies fly in listless circles and expire at our feet, we do not say they succumbed to an illness, and for roughly the same reasons as we decline to give them a proper funeral.

> There are, then, two senses of "health". In one sense it is a theoretical notion, the opposite of "disease." In another sense it is a practical or mixed ethical notion, the opposite of "illness."

Illness is thus a socially constructed deviance. Something more than a mere biological abnormality is needed. To be ill is to have deviant characteristics for which the sick role is appropriate. The sick role, as Parsons has described it, exempts one from normal social responsibilities and removes individual responsibility. See Talcott Parsons, The Social System (1951). Our choice of words reflects this: an alcoholic is sick; a drunkard is not.

A sick person can be assisted by treatment defined by the medical model. He becomes a patient, an object of medical attention by a doctor. The doctor has the right and the ability to label someone ill, to determine whether the lump on a patient's skin is a blister, a wart or a cancer. The doctor can thus decide whether a patient is culpable or not, disabled or malingering. Illness also enjoins the physician to action to restore the patient to health.

Illness thus has many ramifications. First, it affects the individual. It relieves responsibility. The sick person need not report for work at 8:00; the posttraumatic stress syndrome or premenstrual syndrome victim may be declared not guilty of an assault. It means loss of control. The mild pain may have disproportionate effects on the individual who sees it as the harbinger of cancer or a brain tumor. The physician can restore control by providing a rational explanation for the experience of impairment. Illness costs the patient money, in lost time and in medical expenses. And someone receives that money for trying to treat that patient's illness.

Our understanding of illness also affects society. Defining a condition as an illness to be aggressively treated, rather than as a natural condition of life to be accepted and tolerated, has significant economic effects. Medical care is an object of economic choice, a good that many perceive to be different from other goods, with greater, sometimes immeasurable value. Some people are willing to pay far more for medical care than they would for other goods, or, more typically, to procure insurance that will deliver them from ever having to face the choice of paying for health care and abandoning all else. Society may also feel a special obligation to pay for the medical expenses of those who need treatment but lack resources to pay for it.

KATSKEE v. BLUE CROSS/BLUE SHIELD OF NEBRASKA

Supreme Court of Nebraska, 1994.
245 Neb. 808, 515 N.W.2d 645.

WHITE, JUSTICE.

This appeal arises from a summary judgment issued by the Douglas County District Court dismissing appellant Sindie Katskee's action for breach of contract. This action concerns the determination of what constitutes an illness within the meaning of a health insurance policy issued by appellee, Blue Cross/Blue Shield of Nebraska. We reverse the decision of the district court and remand the cause for further proceedings.

In January 1990, upon the recommendation of her gynecologist, Dr. Larry E. Roffman, appellant consulted with Dr. Henry T. Lynch regarding her family's history of breast and ovarian cancer, and particularly her health in relation to such a history. After examining appellant and investigating her family's medical history, Dr. Lynch diagnosed her as suffering from a genetic condition known as breast-ovarian carcinoma syndrome. Dr. Lynch then recommended that appellant have a total abdominal hysterectomy and bilateral salpingo-oophorectomy, which involves the removal of the uterus, the ovaries, and the fallopian tubes. Dr. Roffman concurred in Dr. Lynch's diagnosis and agreed that the recommended surgery was the most medically appropriate treatment available.

After considering the diagnosis and recommended treatment, appellant decided to have the surgery. In preparation for the surgery, appellant filed a claim with Blue Cross/Blue Shield. Both Drs. Lynch and Roffman wrote to Blue Cross/Blue Shield and explained the diagnosis and their basis for recommending the surgery. Initially, Blue Cross/Blue Shield sent a letter to appellant and indicated that it might pay for the surgery. Two weeks before the surgery, Dr. Roger Mason, the chief medical officer for Blue Cross/Blue Shield, wrote to appellant and stated that Blue Cross/Blue Shield would not cover the cost of the surgery. Nonetheless, appellant had the surgery in November 1990.

Appellant filed this action for breach of contract, seeking to recover $6,022.57 in costs associated with the surgery. Blue Cross/Blue Shield filed a motion for summary judgment. The district court granted the motion. It found that there was no genuine issue of material fact and that the policy did not cover appellant's surgery. Specifically, the court stated that (1) appellant did not suffer from cancer, and although her high-risk condition warranted the surgery, it was not covered by the policy; (2) appellant did not have a bodily illness or disease which was covered by the policy; and (3) under the terms of the policy, Blue Cross/Blue Shield reserved the right to determine what is medically necessary. Appellant filed a notice of appeal to the Nebraska Court of Appeals, and on our motion, we removed the case to the Nebraska Supreme Court.

Appellant contends that the district court erred in finding that no genuine issue of material fact existed and granting summary judgment in favor of appellee.

* * *

Blue Cross/Blue Shield contends that appellant's costs are not covered by the insurance policy. The policy provides coverage for services which are medically necessary. The policy defines "medically necessary" as follows: The services, procedures, drugs, supplies or Durable Medical Equipment provided by the Physician, Hospital or other health care provider, in the diagnosis or treatment of the Covered Person's Illness, Injury, or Pregnancy, which are: 1. Appropriate for the symptoms and diagnosis of the patient's Illness, Injury or Pregnancy; and 2. Provided in the most appropriate setting and at the most appropriate level of services[;] and 3. Consistent with the standards of good medical practice in the medical community of the State of Nebraska; and 4. Not provided primarily for the convenience of any of the following: a. the Covered Person; b. the Physician; c. the Covered Person's family; d. any other person or health care provider; and 5. Not considered to be unnecessarily repetitive when performed in combination with other diagnoses or treatment procedures. We shall determine whether services provided are Medically Necessary. Services will not automatically be considered Medically Necessary because they have been ordered or provided by a Physician. (Emphasis supplied.) Blue Cross/Blue Shield denied coverage because it concluded that appellant's condition does not constitute an illness, and thus the treatment she received was not medically necessary. Blue Cross/Blue Shield has not raised any other basis for its denial, and we therefore will limit our consideration to whether appellant's condition constituted an illness within the meaning of the policy.

The policy broadly defines "illness" as a "bodily disorder or disease." The policy does not provide definitions for either bodily disorder or disease.

An insurance policy is to be construed as any other contract to give effect to the parties' intentions at the time the contract was made. When the terms of the contract are clear, a court may not resort to rules of construction, and the terms are to be accorded their plain and ordinary meaning as the ordinary or reasonable person would understand them. In such a case, a court shall seek to ascertain the intention of the parties from the plain language of the policy. [ ]

Whether a policy is ambiguous is a matter of law for the court to determine. If a court finds that the policy is ambiguous, then the court may employ rules of construction and look beyond the language of the policy to ascertain the intention of the parties. A general principle of construction, which we have applied to ambiguous insurance policies, holds that an ambiguous policy will be construed in favor of the insured. However, we will not read an ambiguity into policy language which is plain and unambiguous in order to construe it against the insurer. [ ]

When interpreting the plain meaning of the terms of an insurance policy, we have stated that the " ' "natural and obvious meaning of the provisions in a policy is to be adopted in preference to a fanciful, curious, or hidden meaning." ' "[ ] We have further stated that " '[w]hile for the purpose of judicial decision dictionary definitions often are not controlling, they are at least persuasive that meanings which they do not embrace are not common.' "[ ]

Applying these principles, our interpretation of the language of the terms employed in the policy is guided by definitions found in dictionaries, and additionally by judicial opinions rendered by other courts which have considered the meaning of these terms. Webster's Third New International Dictionary, Unabridged 648 (1981), defines disease as an impairment of the normal state of the living animal or plant body or of any of its components that interrupts or modifies the performance of the vital functions, being a response to environmental factors ... to specific infective agents ... to inherent defects of the organism (as various genetic anomalies), or to combinations of these factors: Sickness, Illness. The same dictionary defines disorder as "a derangement of function: an abnormal physical or mental condition: Sickness, Ailment, Malady." Id. at 652. [ ]

These lay definitions are consistent with the general definitions provided in Dorland's Illustrated Medical Dictionary (27th ed. 1988). Dorland's defines disease as any deviation from or interruption of the normal structure or function of any part, organ, or system ... of the body that is manifested by a characteristic set of symptoms and signs and whose etiology [theory of origin or cause], pathology [origin or cause], and prognosis may be known or unknown. Id. at 481. [ ] Dorland's defines disorder as "a derangement or abnormality of function; a morbid physical or mental state." Id. at 495. [ ]

* * *

The court looked at similar definitional disputes in other jurisdictions, noting that hemophilia, aneurysms, and chronic alcoholism had been held to be diseases or illnesses under insurance policies.]

We find that the language used in the policy at issue in the present case is not reasonably susceptible of differing interpretations and thus not ambiguous. The plain and ordinary meaning of the terms "bodily disorder" and "disease," as they are used in the policy to define illness, encompasses any abnormal condition of the body or its components of such a degree that in its natural progression would be expected to be problematic: a deviation from the healthy or normal state affecting the functions or tissues of the body; an inherent defect of the body; or a morbid physical or mental state which deviates from or interrupts the normal structure or function of any part, organ, or system of the body and which is manifested by a characteristic set of symptoms and signs.

The issue then becomes whether appellant's condition—breast-ovarian carcinoma syndrome—constitutes an illness.

Blue Cross/Blue Shield argues that appellant did not suffer from an illness because she did not have cancer. Blue Cross/Blue Shield characterizes appellant's condition only as a "predisposition to an illness (cancer)" and fails to address whether the condition itself constitutes an illness. Brief for appellee at 13. This failure is traceable to Dr. Mason's denial of appellant's claim. Despite acknowledging his inexperience and lack of knowledge about this specialized area of cancer research, Dr. Mason denied appellant's claim without consulting any medical literature or research regarding breast-ovarian carcinoma syndrome. Moreover, Dr. Mason made the decision without submitting appellant's claim for consideration to a claim review committee. The only basis for the denial was the claim filed by appellant, the letters sent by Drs. Lynch and Roffman, and the insurance policy. Despite his lack of information regarding the nature and severity of appellant's condition, Dr. Mason felt qualified to decide that appellant did not suffer from an illness.

Appellant's condition was diagnosed as breast-ovarian carcinoma syndrome. To adequately determine whether the syndrome constitutes an illness, we must first understand the nature of the syndrome.

The record on summary judgment includes the depositions of Drs. Lynch, Roffman, and Mason. In his deposition, Dr. Lynch provided a thorough discussion of this syndrome. In light of Dr. Lynch's extensive research and clinical experience in this particular area of medicine, we consider his discussion extremely helpful in our understanding of the syndrome.

According to Dr. Lynch, some forms of cancer occur on a hereditary basis. Breast and ovarian cancer are such forms of cancer which may occur on a hereditary basis. It is our understanding that the hereditary occurrence of this form of cancer is related to the genetic makeup of the woman. In this regard, the genetic deviation has conferred changes which are manifest in the individual's body and at some time become capable of being diagnosed.

At the time that he gave his deposition, Dr. Lynch explained that the state of medical research was such that detecting and diagnosing the syndrome was achieved by tracing the occurrences of hereditary cancer throughout the patient's family. Dr. Lynch stated that at the time of appellant's diagnosis, no conclusive physical test existed which would demonstrate the presence of the condition. However, Dr. Lynch stated that this area of research is progressing toward the development of a more determinative method of identifying and tracing a particular gene throughout a particular family, thus providing a physical method of diagnosing the condition.

Women diagnosed with the syndrome have at least a 50–percent chance of developing breast and/or ovarian cancer, whereas unaffected women have only a 1.4–percent risk of developing breast or ovarian cancer. In addition to the genetic deviation, the family history, and the significant risks associated with this condition, the diagnosis also may encompass symptoms of anxiety and stress, which some women experience because of their knowledge of the substantial likelihood of developing cancer.

The procedures for detecting the onset of ovarian cancer are ineffective. Generally, by the time ovarian cancer is capable of being detected, it has already developed to a very advanced stage, making treatment relatively unsuccessful. Drs. Lynch and Roffman agreed that the standard of care for treating women with breast carcinoma syndrome ordinarily involves surveillance methods. However, for women at an inordinately high risk for ovarian cancer, such as appellant, the standard of care may require radical surgery which involves the removal of the uterus, ovaries, and fallopian tubes.

Dr. Lynch explained that the surgery is labeled "prophylactic" and that the surgery is prophylactic as to the prevention of the onset of cancer. Dr. Lynch also stated that appellant's condition itself is the result of a genetic deviation from the normal, healthy state and that the recommended surgery treats that condition by eliminating or significantly reducing the presence of the condition and its likely development.

Blue Cross/Blue Shield has not proffered any evidence disputing the premise that the origin of this condition is in the genetic makeup of the individual and that in its natural development it is likely to produce devastating results. Although handicapped by his limited knowledge of the syndrome, Dr. Mason did not dispute the nature of the syndrome as explained by Dr. Lynch and supported by Dr. Roffman, nor did Dr. Mason dispute the fact that the surgery falls within the standard of care for many women afflicted with this syndrome.

In light of the plain and ordinary meaning of the terms "illness," "bodily disorder," and "disease," we find that appellant's condition constitutes an illness within the meaning of the policy. Appellant's condition is a deviation from what is considered a normal, healthy physical state or structure. The abnormality or deviation from a normal state arises, in part, from the genetic makeup of the woman. The existence of this unhealthy state results in the woman's being at substantial risk of developing cancer. The recommended surgery is intended to correct that morbid state by reducing or eliminating that risk.

Although appellant's condition was not detectable by physical evidence or a physical examination, it does not necessarily follow that appellant does not suffer from an illness. The record establishes that a woman who suffers from breast-ovarian carcinoma syndrome does have a physical state which significantly deviates from the physical state of a normal, healthy woman. Specifically, appellant suffered from a different or abnormal genetic constitution which, when combined with a particular family history of hereditary cancer, significantly increases the risk of a devastating outcome.

We are mindful that not every condition which itself constitutes a predisposition to another illness is necessarily an illness within the meaning of an insurance policy. There exists a fine distinction between such conditions, which was recognized by Chief Justice Cardozo in Silverstein v. Metropolitan Life Ins. Co., 254 N.Y. 81, 171 N.E. 914 (1930). Writing for the court, Chief Justice Cardozo explained that when a condition is such that in its probable and natural progression it may be expected to be a source of mischief, it may reasonably be described as a disease or an illness. On the other hand, he stated that if the condition is abnormal when tested by a standard of perfection, but so remote in its potential mischief that common speech would not label it a disease or infirmity, such a condition is at most a predisposing tendency. The Silverstein court found that a pea-size ulcer, which was located at the site of damage caused by a severe blow to the deceased's stomach, was not a disease or infirmity within the meaning of an exclusionary clause of an accident insurance policy because if left unattended, the ulcer would have been only as harmful as a tiny scratch.

Blue Cross/Blue Shield relies upon our decision in Fuglsang v. Blue Cross, 235 Neb. 552, 456 N.W.2d 281 (1990), and contends that we have already supplied a definition for the terms "disease," "condition," and "illness." Although we find that reliance on Fuglsang is somewhat misplaced, the opinion is relevant to our determination of the meaning of "disease," "illness," and "disorder," and whether the condition from which appellant suffered constitutes an illness.

The issue raised in Fuglsang was whether the disease from which the plaintiff suffered constituted a preexisting condition which was excluded from coverage by the terms of the policy. Blue Cross/Blue Shield relies on the following rule from Fuglsang as a definition of "disease": A disease, condition, or illness exists within the meaning of a health insurance policy excluding preexisting conditions only at such time as the disease, condition, or illness is manifest or active or when there is a distinct symptom or condition from which one learned in medicine can with reasonable accuracy diagnose the disease. [ ]

This statement concerns when an illness exists, not whether the condition itself is an illness. If the condition is not a disease or illness, it would be unnecessary to apply the above rule to determine whether the condition was a preexisting illness. In the present case, Blue Cross/Blue Shield maintains that the condition is not even an illness.

Even assuming arguendo that the rule announced in Fuglsang is a definition of "disease," "illness," and "condition," the inherent problems with the argument put forth by Blue Cross/Blue Shield undermine its reliance on that rule. Blue Cross/Blue Shield emphasizes the fact that appellant was never diagnosed with cancer and therefore, according to Blue Cross/Blue Shield, appellant did not have an illness because cancer was not active or manifest. Appellant concedes that she did not have cancer prior to her surgery. The issue is whether the condition she did have was an illness. Blue Cross/Blue Shield further argues that "[n]o disease or illness is 'manifest or active' and there is no 'distinct symptom or condition' from which Dr. Lynch or Dr. Roffman could diagnose a disease." Brief for appellee at 13. We stated above that lack of a physical test to detect the presence of an illness does not necessarily indicate that the person does not have an illness.

When the condition at issue—breast-ovarian carcinoma syndrome—is inserted into the formula provided by the Fuglsang rule, the condition would constitute an "illness" as Blue Cross/Blue Shield defines the term. The formula is whether the breast-ovarian carcinoma syndrome was manifest or active, or whether there was a distinct symptom or condition from which one learned in medicine could with reasonable accuracy diagnose the disease. The record establishes that the syndrome was manifest, at least in part, from the genetic deviation, and evident from the family medical history. The condition was such that one learned in medicine, Dr. Lynch, could with a reasonable degree of accuracy diagnose it. Blue Cross/Blue Shield does not dispute the nature of the syndrome, the method of diagnosis, or the accuracy of the diagnosis.

In the present case, the medical evidence regarding the nature of breast-ovarian carcinoma syndrome persuades us that appellant suffered from a bodily disorder or disease and, thus, suffered from an illness as defined by the insurance policy. Blue Cross/Blue Shield, therefore, is not entitled to judgment as a matter of law. Moreover, we find that appellant's condition did constitute an illness within the meaning of the policy. We reverse the decision of the district court and remand the cause for further proceedings. [ ]

Notes and Questions

1. Why did the court hold that Katskee was ill when she had no symptoms and no cancer? Can we have a variable definition of illness? For example, could Katskee be "ill" for purposes of payment for the surgery but not ill for purposes of pre-existing condition exclusions or excusal from work? What about treatment for high blood pressure or arteriosclerosis? The medications to prevent heart attacks are expensive, and are typically covered by health insurance plans.

Couch on Insurance defines "disease" as follows:

> an alteration in the state of the body or of its organs or tissues, interrupting or disturbing the performance of its vital functions, and causing or threatening pain or weakness. While the words "disease" and "sickness" are technically synonymous, when given their popular meaning, as required in construing a contract of insurance, "sickness" is a condition interfering with one's usual activities, whereas disease may exist without such result. The term "disease" connotes a serious ailment. Consequently, an ailment such as impacted wisdom teeth, or a sickness resulting from their removal, does not constitute a disease.

Third Edition § 144:33. Disease (2007 Updated).

2. The syndrome in *Katskee*, if it materializes, is a medical problem for which the patient bears no responsibility. A more difficult problem area in defining "disease" involves those conditions or syndromes within the control of the individual. Consider for example alcoholism as a "disease". What difference does such a label make? What characteristics of alcohol consumption justify the label "disease"? See H. Thomas Milhorn, The Diagnosis of Alcoholism, AFP 175 (June 1988) ("... alcoholism can be defined as the continuation of drinking when it would be in the patient's best interest to stop.") See Traynor v. Turnage, 485 U.S. 535, 108 S.Ct. 1372, 99 L.Ed.2d 618 (1988) (considering alcoholism as attributable to "willful misconduct" under Veterans' Administration rules). See also Herbert Fingarette, Heavy Drinking: The Myth of Alcoholism as a Disease (1988); contra, see George Vaillant, The Natural History of Alcoholism (1983).

3. What other emerging clinical "syndromes" or diseases can you think of that raise troubling problems for the medical model of disease? How about anorexia? Obesity? "Battered wife" syndrome? "Restless leg" syndrome? "Parental alienation" syndrome? What forces have led to the proliferation of these new syndromes or diseases?

Problem: The Couple's Illness

You represent Thomas and Jill Henderson, a couple embroiled in a dispute with their health insurance plan over coverage of infertility treatments. The Hendersons have been having trouble getting pregnant. Thomas has a low sperm count and motility, while Jill has irregular ovulation. They have undergone infertility treatment successfully in the past and have one child. They again sought further treatment, in order to have a second child. A simple insemination procedure failed. The health and disability group benefit plan of Thomas's employer, Clarion, paid their health benefits for this procedure.

They were then advised to try a more complex and expensive procedure, called Protocol I, which involved treating Thomas' sperm to improve its motility. Drug therapy was prescribed for Jill to induce ovulation. Semen was then taken from Thomas, and put through an albumin gradient to improve its mobility. The semen was then reduced to a small pellet size and injected directly into the uterine cavity at the time of ovulation.

The Hendersons underwent Protocol I and submitted a bill to Clarion, which refused to pay it. Clarion cited a provision in its plan, Article VI, section 6.7, which provided:

> If a covered individual incurs outpatient expenses relating to injury or illness, those expenses charged, including but not limited to, office calls and for diagnostic services such as laboratory, x-ray, electrocardiography, therapy or injections, are covered expenses under the provisions of [the plan].

Under section 2.24 of the plan, "illness" was defined as "any sickness occurring to a covered individual which does not arise out of or in the course of employment for wage or profit." Clarion denied the Hendersons' claim on the grounds that the medical services were not performed because of any illness of Jill, as required under section 6.7. No provisions in the plan specifically excluded fertilization treatments like Protocol I.

What arguments can you make on behalf of the Hendersons that their situation is an "illness"? What arguments can you make for the insurance company that it is not?

ALAIN ENTHOVEN, PH.D., WHAT MEDICAL CARE IS AND ISN'T

In Alain Enthoven, Health Plan: The Only Practical Solution
to the Soaring Costs of Health Care (1980).

[Some] Misconceptions About Medical Care

* * * In order to establish a conceptual framework that fits the realities, we must clear away seven popular misconceptions that underlie the acceptance of these inappropriate models.

1. "The doctor should be able to know what condition the patient has, be able to answer patient's questions precisely, and prescribe the right treatment. If the doctor doesn't, that is incompetence or even malpractice."

Of course, in many cases the diagnosis is clear-cut. But in many others there is a great deal of *uncertainty* in each step of medical care. Doctors are confronted with patients who have symptoms and syndromes, not labels with their diseases. A set of symptoms can be associated with any of several diseases. The chest pains produced by a gall bladder attack and by a heart attack can be confused by excellent doctors. Diagnostic tests are not 100 percent reliable. Consider a young woman with a painless lump in her breast. Is it cancer? There is a significant probability that a breast X-ray (mammogram), will produce a false result; that is, it will say that she does have cancer when she does not, or vice versa. There is less chance of error if a piece of the tissue is removed surgically (biopsy) and examined under a microscope by a pathologist. But even pathologists may reach different conclusions in some cases.

There are often no clear links between treatment and outcome. If a woman is found to have breast cancer, will she be better off if the whole breast and supporting tissue are removed (radical mastectomy), only the breast (simple mastectomy), or only the lump (lumpectomy)? There is considerable disagreement among doctors because there is, in fact, a great deal of uncertainty about the answer. Because of these uncertainties, there is wide variation among doctors in the tests ordered for similar cases and in the treatments prescribed * * *

2. *"For each medical condition, there is a 'best' treatment. It is up to the doctor to know about that treatment and to use it. Anything else is unnecessary surgery, waste, fraud, or underservice."*

Of course, in many cases there is a clearly indicated treatment. But for many other medical conditions there are *several possible treatments*, each of which is legitimate and associated with different benefits, risks, and costs. Consider a few examples.

A forty-year-old laborer's chronic lower-back pain sometimes requires prolonged bed rest and potent pain medication. One doctor may recommend surgery; another, hoping to avoid the need for surgery, may recommend continued bed rest and traction followed by exercises. Whether one treatment is "better" than the other depends in part on the interpretation of the diagnostic tests (how strong the evidence is of a surgically correctable condition), but also in considerable part on the patient's values and the surgeon's judgment (how large a surgical risk the patient is willing to accept for the predicted likelihood of improvement).

* * *

What is "best" in a particular case will depend on the values and needs of the patient, the skills of the doctor, and the other resources available. The quality of the outcome depends a great deal on how the patient feels about it. What is an annoyance for one patient may mean the inability to keep a job for another with the same condition. There is nothing wrong with the fact that doctors disagree. There is plenty of room for honest differences based on these and other factors. There are more and less costly treatments, practice patterns, and styles of medical care that produce substantially equivalent medical outcomes.

Medical care differs in important ways from repair of collision damage to your car. If you have a smashed fender, you can get three bids and make a deal to have it fixed. You can tell when it is fixed. There is one "correct treatment." Ordinarily, it should not be an open-ended task. But caring for a patient can be open-ended, especially when there is a great deal of uncertainty or when the patient has a chronic disease. Walter McClure, an analyst with

InterStudy, a leading health policy research institute, put the point effectively when he wrote:

> The medical care system can legitimately absorb every dollar society will give it. If health insurance is expanded without seriously addressing the medical care system itself, cost escalation is likely to be severe and chronic. For example, why provide $50 of tests to be 95% certain of a diagnosis, if $250 of tests will provide 97% certainty. [ ]

Although there are generally accepted treatments for many diseases, and doctors can agree that there has been bad care in some cases, for many others there are no generally agreed standards of what is "the best" care. Physicians reject suggestions of what they refer to as "cookbook medicine"; recognizing the infinite variety of conditions, values, and uncertainties, they are understandably reluctant to impose such standards on one another.

The misconception that best-treatment standards exist for most cases underlies much of the belief in the feasibility of an insurance system like Medicare and the hope that regulatory schemes such as Professional Standards Review Organizations can control costs. If we understand that often there is no clear-cut best course of action in medical care, we will think in terms of alternatives, value judgments, and incentives rather than numerical standards.

3.   *"Medicine is an exact science. Unlike 50 or 100 years ago, there is now a firm scientific base for what the doctor does. Standard treatments are supported by scientific proof of efficacy."*

In fact, medicine remains more of an art than a science. To be sure, it uses and applies scientific knowledge, and to become a physician, one must have command of a great deal of scientific information. But the application of this knowledge is a matter of judgment.

To prove beyond reasonable doubt that a medical treatment is effective often requires what is called a "randomized clinical trial (RCT)." In an RCT a large sample of patients is assigned randomly to two or more treatment groups. Each group is given one of the alternative treatments and then is evaluated by unbiased observers to see which treatment produced the better results. One of the "treatments" may be no treatment. (Of course, RCTs may not be needed in the case of "clear winners" such as penicillin, treatment of fractures, and congenital anomalies.) However, many practical difficulties stand in the way of doing a satisfactory clinical trial. As a result, RCTs are the exception, not the rule.

When medical or surgical innovations have been evaluated in this way, more often than not the innovation has been found to yield no benefit or even to be inferior to previous methods of treatment. Even when a clinical trial has established the value of a given treatment, judgment must be used in deciding whether a particular patient or set of circumstances is enough like those in the trial that the same good results can be expected in this particular case.

There are shifting opinions in medical care. Many operations have been invented and enjoyed popularity, only to be subsequently discarded when systematic testing failed to demonstrate their value. * * * Whether or not the coronary artery bypass graft operation that has recently become a billion-dollar-a-year industry will continue indefinitely at its present scale is uncertain. One good reason for not having national standards of care established by government is to avoid either imposing unsubstantiated treatments or freezing them into current practice.

Scientific and balanced analysis of the costs, risks, and benefits of different treatments is still the exception, not the rule.

4. Medical care consists of standard products that can be described precisely and measured meaningfully in standard units such as "inpatient days", "outpatient visits", or "doctor office visits".

In fact, medical care is usually anything but a standard product. Much of it is a uniquely personal interaction between two people. The elements of personal trust and confidence are an integral part of the process. Much of the process consists of reassurance and support—*caring* rather than *curing*. What doctors do ranges from the technical marvels of the heart surgeon to marriage counseling by the family doctor, each of which may fill a legitimate human need. A "doctor office visit" might last a few minutes or more than an hour. An "inpatient day" might be accompanied by the use of the most costly and complex technology or be merely a quiet day of rest, with an occasional visit by a nurse.

* * *

5. "Much of medical care is a matter of life and death or serious pain or disability."

This view may come from watching television programs that emphasize the dramatic side of medicine. It is a foundation for the assertion that "health care is a right." As a society, we have agreed that all people should have access to life-saving care without regard to income, race, or social status.

Of course some medical care is life-saving, and its benefits are obvious and clear-cut. But most medical care is not a life-or-death matter at all. Even in the case of care for life-threatening diseases, the effectiveness of much care is measured in terms of small changes in life expectancy (for example, changes in the probability of surviving another year), as opposed to complete cures. Most medical care is a matter of "quality of life." Much of it is concerned with the relief of pain or dysfunction, with caring and reassurance.

All this is not to diminish the importance or value of medical care. But it does suggest that we are dealing with matters of darker or lighter shades of grey, conflicting values, and not clear-cut cases of life or death. Recognizing this makes it much less clear what it is that people have a "right" to or what is "necessary" as opposed to "unnecessary."

6. "More medical care is better than less care."

There is a tremendous amount of bias in favor of more care versus less. For example, the observation that physicians in group practices hospitalize their patients much less than do their fellow doctors in traditional solo practice is much more likely to cause suspicion that they are denying their patients necessary care than that the solo-practice doctors are providing too much care.

* * *

More medical care may actually be harmful. There is such a thing as physician-caused (known as "iatrogenic") disease. People do die or are seriously injured on the operating table, and some are injured or die from the complications of anesthesia. * * *

* * *

To observe that financial incentives play an important role in the use of medical services is not to imply that they are the only, or even the most important, factor. Physicians are concerned primarily with curing their sick patients, regardless of the cost. That ethic has been instilled in them through years of arduous training. Many take a failure to cure a sick patient as a personal defeat. When we are sick, we want our doctors to be concerned with curing us and nothing else. Physicians and other health professionals are also motivated by a desire to achieve professional excellence and the esteem of their peers and the public. But their use of resources is inevitably shaped by financial incentives. Physicians who survive and prosper must ultimately do what brings in money and curtail those activities that lose money.

* * *

These insights also help explain why qualitative distinctions such as one finds in legal usage are not very helpful. One simply cannot divide all medical care into the categories "necessary" and "unnecessary." What is "necessary" care? Is "necessary" care limited to treatment of serious pain or life-threatening conditions? If it were, a great deal of care would not be "necessary." Even in life-and-death cases, the concept of "necessary" poorly describes many situations. Suppose that a patient with terminal cancer has 99-to-1 odds of dying within a year. Suppose that treatment costing $20,000 will reduce those odds to 97 to 1. Would that be "necessary" or "unnecessary" care? There are doubtless examples that most observers would judge to be "unnecessary." But the fact that two doctors disagree and that the doctor offering the "second opinion" says that the operation is "unnecessary" does not make it so.

Similarly, forceful assertions that "health care is a right" do not help in this large grey zone. In view of the variety of systems and styles of care and treatments, exactly what is a *right?* A *right* to *anything* health care providers can do to make you feel better? That interpretation would make "health care is a right" mean "money is no object." Our society cannot afford and will not support such a generous definition.

The concepts and language most useful for analyzing the problem of health care costs are concepts that have been developed for decision making under uncertainty and for choices of "a little more or a little less."

We need to think in terms of judgments about probabilities and in terms of the balancing of various costs, risks, and benefits. The issues are not, for example, "complete care vs. no care for a heart-attack patient." Rather, they are more of the character "seven vs. fourteen or twenty-one days in the hospital after a heart attack." What is the medical value of the extra days? How do they affect the probability that the patient will be alive a year later? What do they cost, not only in resources measured in money, but also in other terms? Are the extra benefits worth the extra costs? These are the kinds of questions we must keep asking if we want to make sense out of the problem and to get good value for the money we spend on health care. They are matters of judgment, possibly aided by calculation.

Notes and Questions

1.   What are the implications of Enthoven's discussion for the regulation of health care quality? What strategies might you develop to improve quality in health care organizations? What are the merits and drawbacks of a market in health care? Does Enthoven's analysis raise problems for the operation of a market in health care? What kind of problems? Consider these questions again as you study Section II, below, and Chapters 2 and 3.

2.   Enthoven talks about the importance of both the institutional and the financial setting. The fee-for-service mode of paying physicians has been blamed for much of the rapid inflation in health care costs over the past two decades. Physicians control up to 70% of the spending for health care, as agents for their patients. As a result, with few external controls on their ability to order health care tests and treatments, health care costs have risen much faster than the general rate of inflation of the Gross Domestic Product over the past two decades. What ideas might you propose to shift physician incentives toward a more cost-sensitive style of practice? Has managed care been successful in doing so? Are other inflationary forces at work? See Chapters 4, 5, and 6, infra. For a useful discussion of the nature of the health care market, see David A. Wells et al., What Is Different About the Market for Health Care? 298 J.A.M.A. 2785 (2007).

3.   Scholars debate the fundamental question of what health policy should be. Can we agree upon basic goals that health care regulation and policy should see to achieve? Are there unified principles and values that underpin health law generally? For an argument that no single goal can be found, and that we must settle for more modest goals, see M. Gregg Bloche, The Invention of Health Law, 91 Cal.L.Rev. 247, 321 (2003). For further discussion of the nature of health law generally, see Symposium, Rethinking Health Law, 41 Wake Forest L. Rev. 341 (2006).

II.   QUALITY IN HEALTH CARE

Lawyers become involved with quality of health care issues through a variety of routes. They file, or defend against, malpractice suits when a patient is injured during the course of medical treatment. They handle medical staff privilege cases that frequently turn on the quality of the staff doctor's performance. They represent the government in administering programs that aim to cut the cost of health care and improve its quality and providers that must adjust to these programs. Quality is a central concern in health care politics and law.

A.   DEFINING THE NATURE OF QUALITY IN HEALTH CARE

AVEDIS DONABEDIAN, THE DEFINITION OF QUALITY AND APPROACHES TO ITS ASSESSMENT

(Vol. 1) (1980) 4–6.

The search for a definition of quality can usefully begin with what is perhaps the simplest complete module of care: the management by a physician, or any other primary practitioner, of a clearly definable episode of illness in a given patient. It is possible to divide this management into two domains: the technical and the interpersonal. Technical care is the application of the science and technology of medicine, and of the other health sciences, to the management of a personal health problem. Its accompaniment is the management of the social and psychological interaction between client and practitioner. The first of these has been called the science of medicine and the second its art * * *.

There may also be a third element in care which could be called its "amenities". * * * In a way, the amenities are properties of the more intimate aspects of the settings in which care is provided. But the amenities sometimes seem to be properties of the care itself * * *.

* * * At the very least, the quality of technical care consists in the application of medical science and technology in a manner that maximizes its benefits to health without correspondingly increasing its risks. The degree of quality is, therefore, the extent to which the care provided is expected to achieve the more favorable balance of risks and benefits.

What constitutes goodness in the interpersonal process is more difficult to summarize. * * * All these postulates lead us to a unifying concept of the quality of care as that kind of care which is expected to maximize an inclusive measure of patient welfare, after one has taken account of the balance of expected gains and losses that attend the process of care in all its parts.

Notes and Questions

1.   Donabedian is a leader in the theory of health care assessment. Does his definition capture most of what you find important in thinking about quality health care?

The Institute of Medicine, in assessing the Medicare program, has developed its own definition:

> ... quality of care is the degree to which health services for individuals and populations increase the likelihood of desired health outcomes and are consistent with current professional knowledge.

Institute of Medicine, Medicare: A Strategy for Quality Assurance, Vol. I, 20 (K. Lohr, Ed.1990).

Does this definition differ from Donabedian's? If so, what is the difference? Does the difference matter?

See generally LM Rogers, Meeting the Center for Medicare & Medicaid Services Requirements for Quality Assessment and Performance Improvement: A Model for Hospitals, 21 J. Nurs. Care Qual. 325 (2006); Edward L. Hannan, The Continuing Quest for Measuring and Improving Access to Necessary Care, 284 JAMA 2374 (2000); Avedis Donabedian, A Primer of Quality Assurance and Monitoring in Medical Care, 20 Toledo L.Rev. 401 (1989); A. Donabedian, The Criteria and Standards of Quality (1982); A. Donabedian, The Methods and Findings of Quality Assessment and Monitoring: An Illustrated Analysis (1985).

2.   Unnecessary care that causes harm, by Donabedian's criteria, is poor in quality, since such care that causes harm unnecessarily is not counterbalanced by any expectation of benefit. How about care that is unnecessary yet harmless, like over-the-counter medicines that contain no therapeutic ingredients? Or medical

interventions that have no proven value? Donabedian argues that such care should be judged as poor in quality.

> First, such care is not expected to yield benefits. Second, it can be argued that it causes reductions in individual and social welfare through improper use of resources. By spending time and money on medical care the patient has less to use for other things he values. Similarly, by providing excessive care to some, society has less to offer to others who may need it more. Finally, the use of redundant care, even when it is harmless, indicates carelessness, poor judgment, or ignorance on the part of the practitioner who is responsible for care. (Id. at 6–7).

Courts have generally deferred to a doctor's medical judgment as to the benefit of a particular treatment to a patient. Where the diagnostic or treatment modality is found to have no value, the physician may be negligent if a bad outcome results. In Riser v. American Medical International, Inc., 620 So.2d 372 (La.App. 5th Cir., 1993), the doctor performed a femoral arteriogram on the patient, who suffered a stroke and died. The court found that the physician had breached the standard of care by subjecting the patient to a technology which he should reasonably have known would be of "no practical benefit to the patient".

3.   Effectiveness is rapidly becoming the test for a medical treatment or test. The "effectiveness initiative" in modern medicine is based on three premises: (1) many current medical practices either are ineffective or could be replaced with less expensive substitutes; (2) physicians often select more expensive treatments because of bias, fear of litigation, or financial incentives; and (3) patients would often choose different options from those recommended by their physicians if they had better information about treatment risks, benefits and costs.

Much of American medical practice does not improve health. In controlled trials, many cherished practices have been found unhelpful and even harmful. Treatments effective for one indication are frequently extended to other indications where effectiveness data do not exist. Higher quality care may cost more, raising the question of cost-effectiveness. But higher quality care may also be obtained for less money, as by cutting out ineffective services. Medicare reforms designed to contain the system's escalating costs have been based on the assumption that the costs of caring for the elderly can be cut without affecting quality, that the corpus of health care delivery has substantial fat that can be trimmed. Empirical evidence to date supports this hypothesis. In order for "health services for individuals and populations to increase the likelihood of desired health outcomes," they must be used appropriately and effectively. Poor quality care can be caused by underuse, overuse, or misuse. Mark R. Chassin et al., The Urgent Need to Improve Health Care Quality, 280 JAMA 1000 (1998); Steven F. Jencks, Edwin D. Huff, and Timothy Cuerdon, Change in the Quality of Care Delivered to Medicare Beneficiaries, 1998–1999 to 2000–2001, 289 JAMA 305 (2003).

4.   What is the role of the patient and her values in the delivery of medical care? Donabedian's definition of quality combines the doctor's technical management with the patient's expectations and values, as well as cost considerations. An "absolutist" medical view, on the other hand, might define quality as a doctor's management of a patient's problems in a way that the doctor expects will best balance health benefits and risks. Donabedian characterizes this position as follows: "[i]t is the responsibility of the practitioner to recommend and carry out such care. All other factors, including monetary costs, as well as the patient's expectations and valuations, are thereby regarded as either obstacles or facilitators to the implementation of the standard of quality." (Donabedian, *supra* at 13).

A second view, also reflected in the judicial discussions of informed consent, is described by Donabedian as an "individualized" definition of quality:

> A long and honorable tradition of the health professions holds that the primary function of medical care is to advance the patient's welfare. If this is so, it is inevitable that the patient must share with the practitioner the responsibility for defining the objectives of care, and for placing a valuation on the benefits and risks that are expected as the results of alternative strategies of management. In fact, it can be argued that the practitioner merely provides expert information, while the task of valuation falls on the patient or on those who can, legitimately, act on his behalf. Donabedian, *supra* at 13–14.

This shared decision making model of the doctor-patient relationship certainly maximizes patient autonomy. The common law of battery has been applied in cases where a doctor performed a procedure on a patient against the patient's will or without his or her consent. What if the doctor's decision was correct, in the technical sense of achieving a good outcome for the patient? Should the legal system allow an individual to rank a value higher than his or her health, or than life itself?

5. How do cost considerations fit into this individualized definition of quality? If the patient has no insurance and probably cannot pay for an expensive surgical procedure, or if the patient decides to forego a treatment after making his or her own cost tradeoffs, how should the doctor respond? Must the doctor be satisfied with giving the patient less medical care than would be possible, and than would in fact help the patient?

> [I]n real life, we do not have the option of excluding monetary costs from the individualized definition of quality. Their inclusion means that the practitioner does for each patient what the patient has decided his circumstances allow. In so doing, the practitioner has discharged his responsibility to the patient, provided that he has helped the patient to discover and use every available means of paying for care. Donabedian, *supra* at 27.

Even in a society with comprehensive social benefits, such as a national health insurance program, costs must be considered by the practitioner, who is still constrained by the resources available for health care. The doctor as citizen must choose whether to help the patient as much as possible, with the taxpayers absorbing the costs; or to stop short of giving the individual the maximum help.

6. A third definition of quality adds a social dimension, looking at the distribution of benefits within a population. Patients' insurance status significantly affects the procedures they receive to treat various medical problems. Lack of insurance can reduce the length of one's life: mortality studies suggest a reduction in the uninsured's mortality as high as 20% to 25%. The uninsured receive fewer preventive and diagnostic services, tend to be more severely ill when diagnosed, and receive less therapeutic care. Other literature suggests that improving health status from fair or poor to very good or excellent would increase both work effort and annual earnings by approximately 15% to 20%. Jack Hadley, Sicker and Poorer—The Consequences of Being Uninsured: A Review of the Research on the Relationship between Health Insurance, Medical Care Use, Health, Work, and Income, 60 The Urban Institute Medical Care Research and Review, 2 suppl, 3S–75S (2003).

Underuse of health care is a significant social problem in the United States, the result of lack of insurance, poor access to providers, and social attitudes by both patients and providers. Minorities in particular suffer from a lack of access to good health care. Vernellia Randall writes in her book, Dying While Black, Chapter 2 (2006):

> Black Americans have shorter life expectancy, more deaths, more illness, more disease and more disability; by most measures of health. Black Americans are sicker than White Americans. We are quite literally "dying while Black."

> * * *

> The lack of good health is perhaps the most significant deprivation based on color. Certainly, full participation in a society requires money, education, contacts, know-how, it also requires good health. In fact, health is not only significant in itself, but one's health also affects the availability of choices and the decisions regarding those choices throughout one's life. Lack of prenatal care leads to greater likelihood of infant death, neurological damage, or developmental impairment. Childhood illnesses and unhealthy conditions can reduce learning potential. Adolescent childbearing, substance abuse and injuries affect long-term health and access to educational and vocational opportunities. Impaired health or chronic disability in adults contributes to low earning capacity and unemployment. Chronic poor health among older adults can lead to premature retirement and loss of independence and self-sufficiency.

> Thus, health status is an important ingredient in a person's "social position, ... present and future well-being,' especially for Black Americans.

See discussion of health disparities in Chapter 5.

As a society, we appear to value different segments of our population differently, based on our political choices, indifference, or social values. For example, various federal cutbacks in maternity and child care benefits in the early 1980s disproportionately affected minorities and lower class families, reflecting political choices that seriously reduced the quality of health care received by a significant percentage of the U.S. population. Organ transplantation practices may have unduly disadvantaged African–Americans and other minorities in terms of access to organs. See discussion of allocation of kidney transplants in Section IV, below.

See generally Institute of Medicine, Unequal Treatment: Confronting Racial and Ethnic Disparities in Health Care 30 (Brian D. Smedley et al. eds., 2003).

7. Finally, international comparisons of the quality of care in national health care systems reveal national strengths and weaknesses, and point to flaws in the U.S. health care system. Consider the Executive Summary of the Commonwealth Fund report on the comparative performance of the U.S health care system.

KAREN DAVIS, ET AL., MIRROR, MIRROR ON THE WALL: AN INTERNATIONAL UPDATE ON THE COMPARATIVE PERFORMANCE OF AMERICAN HEALTH CARE

http://www.commonwealthfund.org/

MAY 2007

The U.S. health system is the most expensive in the world, but comparative analyses consistently show the United States underperforms relative to other countries on most dimensions of performance. This report, which includes information from primary care physicians about their medical practices and views of their countries' health systems, confirms the patient survey findings discussed in previous editions of *Mirror, Mirror*. It also includes information on health care outcomes that were featured in the U.S. health system scorecard issued by the Commonwealth Fund Commission on a High Performance Health System.

Among the six nations studied—Australia, Canada, Germany, New Zealand, the United Kingdom, and the United States—the U.S. ranks last, as it did in the 2006 and 2004 editions of *Mirror, Mirror*. Most troubling, the U.S. fails to achieve better health outcomes than the other countries, and as shown in the earlier editions, the U.S. is last on dimensions of access, patient safety, efficiency, and equity. The 2007 edition includes data from the six countries and incorporates patients' and physicians' survey results on care experiences and ratings on various dimensions of care.

The most notable way the U.S. differs from other countries is the absence of universal health insurance coverage. Other nations ensure the accessibility of care through universal health insurance systems and through better ties between patients and the physician practices that serve as their long-term "medical home." It is not surprising, therefore, that the U.S. substantially underperforms other countries on measures of access to care and equity in health care between populations with above-average and below-average incomes.

With the inclusion of physician survey data in the analysis, it is also apparent that the U.S. is lagging in adoption of information technology and national policies that promote quality improvement. The U.S. can learn from what physicians and patients have to say about practices that can lead to better management of chronic conditions and better coordination of care. Information systems in countries like Germany, New Zealand, and the U.K. enhance the ability of physicians to monitor chronic conditions and medication use. These countries also routinely employ non-physician clinicians such as nurses to assist with managing patients with chronic diseases.

The area where the U.S. health care system performs best is preventive care, an area that has been monitored closely for over a decade by managed care plans. Nonetheless, the U.S. scores particularly poorly on its ability to promote healthy lives, and on the provision of care that is safe and coordinated, as well as accessible, efficient, and equitable.

For all countries, responses indicate room for improvement. Yet, the other five countries spend considerably less on health care per person and as a percent of gross domestic product than does the United States. These findings indicate that, from the perspectives of both physicians and patients, the U.S. health care system could do much better in achieving better value for the nation's substantial investment in health.

Notes and Questions

1. What is the purpose of a health care system? One study describes the overarching goal of national health systems as "its capacity to contribute to long, healthy, and productive lives." The scorecard includes potentially preventable mortality, life expectancy, and the prevalence of health conditions that limit the capacity of adults to work or children to learn. See Steven A. Schroeder, We Can Do Better–Improving the Health of the American People, 357 N.E.J.M. 1221 (2007); Cathy Schoen, et al., U.S. Health System Performance: A National Scorecard, Health Affairs w.457 (2006).

2.   An earlier study by the World Health Organization systematically ranked all the countries of the world in terms of their health care systems. WHO's *World Health Report, 2000* placed the U.S. health system 37th in the world. The U.S. ranked 24th in terms of "health attainment," even lower (32nd) in terms of "equity of health outcomes" across its population, and lower still (54th) in terms of "fairness of financial contributions" toward health care. http://www.who.int/whr/2000/en/whr00_en.pdf

B.   ASSESSING QUALITY

Thus far we have attempted to give some content to a definition of "quality" in health care. The next step is to examine how to evaluate quality. We need to take the definition of quality and particularize it to describe acceptable medical procedures, and institutional structures and processes.

The elements of such an evaluation have again been provided by Donabedian, whose quality trichotomy is generally accepted as a starting point for thinking about the evaluation of health care.

1.   *Structure, Process and Outcome Measures of Quality*

AVEDIS DONABEDIAN, THE DEFINITION OF QUALITY AND APPROACHES TO ITS ASSESSMENT

Vol. 1 (1980) 79–84.

[T]he primary object of study is a set of activities that go on within and between practitioners and patients. This set of activities I have called the "process" of care. A judgment concerning the quality of that process may be made either by direct observation or by review of recorded information * * *. But, while "process" is the primary *object* of assessment, the *basis* for the judgment of quality is what is known about the relationship between the characteristics of the medical care process and their consequences to the health and welfare of individuals and of society, in accordance with the value placed upon health and welfare by the individual and by society.

With regard to technical management, the relationship between the characteristics of the process of care and its consequences is determined, in the abstract, by the state of medical science and technology at any given time. More specifically, this relationship is revealed in the work of the leading exponents of that science and technology; through their published research, their teachings, and their own practice these leaders define, explicitly or implicitly, the technical norms of good care.

Another set of norms governs the management of the interpersonal process. These norms arise from the values and the ethical principles and rules that govern the relationships among people, in general, and between health professionals and clients, in particular. * * *

It follows, therefore, that the quality of the "process" of care is defined, in the first place, as normative behavior. * * *

* * *

I have argued, so far, that the most direct route to an assessment of the quality of care is an examination of that care. But there are * * * two other, less direct approaches to assessment: one of these is the assessment of "structure", and the other the assessment of "outcome."

By "structure" I mean the relatively stable characteristics of the providers of care, of the tools and resources they have at their disposal, and of the physical and organizational settings in which they work. The concept of structure includes the human, physical, and financial resources that are needed to provide medical care. The term embraces the number, distribution, and qualifications of professional personnel, and so, too, the number, size, equipment, and geographic disposition of hospitals and other facilities. [Donabedian goes on to include within structure the organization of financing and delivery, how doctors practice and how they are paid, staff organization, and how medical work is reviewed in institutions] * * * The basic characteristics of structure are that it is relatively stable, that it functions to produce care or is a feature of the "environment" of care, and that it influences the kind of care that is provided.

* * * Structure, therefore, is relevant to quality in that it increases or decreases the probability of good performances. * * * But as a means for assessing the quality of care, structure is a rather blunt instrument; it can only indicate general tendencies.

* * *

I believe that good structure, that is, a sufficiency of resources and proper system design, is probably the most important means of protecting and promoting the quality of care. * * * As a source of accurate current information about quality, the assessment of structure is of a good deal less importance than the assessment of process or outcome.

* * *

The study of "outcomes" is the other of the indirect approaches that I have said could be used to assess the quality of care. [Outcome is] * * * a change in a patient's current and future health status that can be attributed to antecedent health care. * * * I shall include improvements of social and psychological function in addition to the more usual emphasis on the physical and physiological aspects of performance. By still another extension I shall add patient attitudes (including satisfaction), health-related knowledge acquired by the patient, and health-related behavioral change.

* * *

* * * [T]here are three major approaches to quality assessment: "structure," "process," and "outcome." This three-fold approach is possible because there is a fundamental functional relationship among the three elements, which can be shown schematically as follows:

Structure → Process → Outcome

This means that structural characteristics of the settings in which care takes place have a propensity to influence the process of care so that its quality is diminished or enhanced. Similarly, changes in the process of care, including variations in its quality, will influence the effect of care on health status, broadly defined.

Notes and Questions

1.   Quality assurance strategies depend on evaluation tools that apply the definition of quality to a health care professional or institution. Structure evaluation is the easiest to do. Personnel, equipment, and buildings can be counted or described; internal regulations and staff organization measured against specific criteria; and budgets critiqued. Structure evaluation is the least useful, however, since the connection between structural components and quality of care is not necessarily direct. See discussion of staffing levels and standard setting in Chapter 3.

2.   Process evaluation of health care has several advantages over structural evaluations. It allows doctors to specify criteria and standards of good care or to establish a range of acceptable practice before all the research evidence is in; it assures documentation in the medical record for preventive and informative purposes; and it permits attribution of responsibility for discrete clinical decisions.

The process perspective has three major drawbacks, however. First, "[t]he major drawback * * * is the weakness of the scientific basis for much of accepted practice. The use of prevalent norms as a basis for judging quality may, therefore, encourage dogmatism and help perpetuate error." Donabedian, *supra* at 119. Second, the emphasis on the need for technical interventions may lead to high cost care. Third, the interpersonal process is slighted, since process evaluation focuses on the technical proficiency of the doctor.

How should process review take place within a medical practice? Within a hospital? Should surgeons or internists assess each other's work? What if an errant colleague is spotted?

3.   Outcome evaluation has substantial advantages over both process and structure measures. It provides a flexible approach that focuses on what works and on integrated care that includes consideration of the patient's own contribution. The goal of all health care is, after all, the best possible outcome for the patient.

Outcome measures also have their problems, however: the duration, timing, or extent of outcomes of optimal care are often hard to specify; it is often hard to credit a good outcome to a specific medical intervention; and the outcome is often known too late to affect practice. See Katherine L. Kahn, et al., Measuring Quality of Care With Explicit Process Criteria Before and After Implementation of the DRG–Based Prospective Payment System, 264 NEJM 1969 (1990).

Are outcome measures useful for comparing hospitals? Consider the Department of Health and Human Services' release of mortality figures for various medical procedures at hospitals around the country. Hospitals had widely differing mortality and morbidity rates and success rates for different procedures. This seems to be a pure outcome indicator, a kind of Consumer Reports rating of hospitals to be used comparatively for purposes of consumer information. Is release of such statistics desirable? Does it benefit the health care consumer? Does the consumer care? Provider quality of care can be accurately measured and compared; short term mortality rates following a heart attack, for example, are excellent indicators of quality of care, varying dramatically across hospitals.

It appears that even before such explicit data became available, the relative quality of hospitals played a part in the choices made by admitting physicians and their patients. It is likely that the admitting physicians were aware of hospital differences, and chose selectively for their patients. The proliferation of specific comparative data might accelerate these tendencies to stratify hospitals by their mortality and morbidity records. Harold Luft et al., Does Quality Influence Choice of Hospital? 263 J.A.M.A. 2899 (1990); Donald M. Berwick & David L. Wald, Hospital Leaders' Opinions of the HCFA Mortality Data, 263 J.A.M.A. 247 (1990).

4. A concept of outcomes management has been articulated for the health care industry, as a reaction to the increasing volume of outcomes data that is currently being produced. It has been defined by Ellwood as based on a "permanent national medical data base that uses a common set of definitions for measuring quality of life to enable patients, payers, and providers to make informed health choices ..." Paul Ellwood, Shattuck Lecture—Outcomes Management: A Technology of Patient Experience, 318 NEJM 1549, 1555 (1988). Ellwood writes that outcomes management:

> ... consists of a common patient-understood language of health outcomes; a national data base containing information and analysis on clinical, financial, and health outcomes that estimates as best we can the relation between medical interventions and health outcomes, as well as the relation between health outcomes and money; and an opportunity for each decision-maker to have access to the analyses that are relevant to the choices they must make. Id. at 1551.

Outcomes management systems are being developed to track the effects of medical care on patients over time, measuring patient clinical condition, functional status, and satisfaction with care. See generally David J. Brailer & Lorence H. Kim, From Nicety to Necessity: Outcome Measures Come of Age, Health Systems Review 20 (Sept./Oct. 1996).

Such approaches are currently primitive, given deficiencies in studies and information gathering. One of the risks of such systems is that deceptively objective measures can be easily misapplied. In assessing hospital based care, particularly mortality, the severity of the patient's illness at admission needs to be considerably refined before many such outcome comparisons can be trusted. Jesse Green, et al., The Importance of Severity of Illness in Assessing Hospital Mortality, 263 J.A.M.A. 241 (1990). Patient satisfaction, as measured through a survey, is a central part of the outcome assessment.

5. Possible indicators of good or bad quality health care include:

a. hospital mortality and morbidity rates;

b. adverse events that affect patients, such as nosocomial infections in hospitals;

c. formal disciplinary actions taken by state medical boards against physicians;

d. malpractice awards;

e. process evaluation of physicians' performance in treating a particular condition, such as hypertension screening and management;

f. physician specialization;

g. patient self-assessment of their own care;

h. scope of hospital services, evaluated by external guidelines like those of the Joint Commission.

See Steven J. Jencks et al., Change in the Quality of Care Delivered to Medicare Beneficiaries, 289 JAMA 305 (2003); Meredith B. Rosenthal and Richard G. Frank, What Is the Empirical Basis for Paying for Quality in Health Care? 63 Med. Care. Res.Rev. 135 (2006).

Which of these indicators are structure measures? Which are process or outcome based?

These indicators could be used in a variety of ways, but one common proposal is to give health care consumers information about comparative performance of providers using several of these measures. This market approach would then allow the consumers to select higher quality providers. What kinds of problems do you foresee with consumer report cards? Are individual patients likely to be good consumers? How can individuals be helped to process the kind of quantitative comparative information that can be produced? Might the other consumers of health care, such as insurers and employers, be better able to use such information than individual patients? How?

See generally Kristin Madison, Regulating Health Care Quality in an Information Age, 40 U.C. Davis L. Rev. 1577 (2007). See also Harlan M. Krumholz et al., Evaluation of a Consumer–Oriented Internet Health Care Report Card, 287 JAMA 1277 (2002); William M. Sage, Regulating Through Information: Disclosure Laws and American Health Care, 99 Colum. L. Rev. 1701 (1999); Timothy S. Jost, The Necessary and Proper Role of Regulation to Assure the Quality of Health Care, 25 Houston L.Rev. 525 (1988); Mark R. Chassin, Achieving and Sustaining Improved Quality: Lessons from New York State and Cardiac Surgery, 21 Health Aff. 40, 42–45 (2002); Judith H. Hibbard et al., Does Publicizing Hospital Performance Stimulate Quality Improvement Efforts?, 22 Health Aff. 84, 84 (2003); Ashish K. Jha & Arnold M. Epstein, The Predictive Accuracy of the New York State Coronary Artery Bypass Surgery Report–Card System, 25 Health Aff. 844, 844 (2006) ("Surgeons with the highest mortality rates were much more likely than other surgeons to retire or leave practice after the release of each report card.").

6. *Data Mining.* Searching through medical data using computer programs now provides another approach to detecting bad outcomes in health care institutions. Sources of patient injury in hospitals are often hard to detect in some cases. Hospitals are busy chaotic places with constant turnover of patients, and constant staff changes. Searching for patterns of bad outcomes may require more systematic computer searches, known as data mining. It may find hidden patterns that may be invisible on a case-by-case basis. This approach is especially appropriate for medical data, which often exists in vast quantities in an unstructured format.

Data mining is potentially a powerful new addition to outcomes measurement, moving beyond tracking a particular patient to a satellite view of the whole population of a hospital over time. Using pattern recognition algorithms, data mining can be set to search databases to investigate particular problems. It can spot trends in infections using infection surveillance results, or it can be used in a broad search strategy to mine for hidden problems, trends or other patterns that are fixable. A Florida Hospital, using data mining software, found that pneumonia patients who were not given medication immediately upon admittance suffered significantly worse outcomes than those who were. At another facility, data mining showed that patients with cardiovascular disease were not always prescribed beta-blockers because the discharge process did not include a crucial step to ensure the prescription was ordered and that an easy solution was to change work processes.

These undiscovered sources of patient harm—the connections, system processes or provider missteps that create risks to patients—are negative outcomes waiting to be discovered. Does a provider owe a patient a duty not only to reveal and fix dangerous problems within his or her walls, but also to affirmatively mine his or her data relentlessly to ensure that other sources of patient harm do not exist, or are detected and fixed? The standard of practice may come to include an obligation on health care institutions to discover sources of human error and patterns of harm creation with the goal of reducing and eliminating them.

See generally Barry R. Furrow, Data Mining and Substandard Medical Practice: The Difference Between Privacy, Secrecy and Hidden Defects, 51 Vill. L. Rev. 803, 816–818 (2006).

2. *Medical Practice Variation and the Nature of Quality in Medicine*

The phenomenon of medical practice variation highlights the role of uncertainty in the setting of medical standards. John Wennberg, whose studies in this area are often cited, has analyzed states and regions within states for variation in surgical and other practices:

> [I]n Maine by the time women reach seventy years of age in one hospital market the likelihood they have undergone a hysterectomy is 20 percent while in another market it is 70 percent. In Iowa, the chances that male residents who reach age eighty-five have undergone prostatectomy range from a low of 15 percent to a high of more than 60 percent in different hospital markets. In Vermont the probability that resident children will undergo a tonsillectomy has ranged from a low of 8 percent in one hospital market to a high of nearly 70 percent in another.

John E. Wennberg, Dealing with Medical Practice Variations: A Proposal for Action, 3 Health Affairs 6, 9 (1984). Wennberg is the author of the Dartmouth Atlas, which uses Medicare data to track medical practice variation over the country, by procedure, http://www.dartmouthatlas.org/atlases. Physician variation in treatment approaches is greatest with aging-related conditions, where the outcomes of conservative treatment are unknown. Procedures least subject to variation are those for which there is a professional consensus on the preferred place or style of treatment. Wennberg gives the example of patient time in intensive care units in the last six months of life in selected teaching hospitals. The number of days ranged from 11.4 at UCLA Medical Center to as low as 2.8 at Massachusetts General Hospital.

Wennberg's studies of medical practice variation are based on studies of three categories of care: effective care, preference-sensitive care, and supply-sensitive care.

(1) "Effective Care": interventions that are viewed as medically necessary on the basis of clinical outcomes evidence and for which the benefits so outweigh the risks that virtually all patients with medical need should receive the them.

(2) "Preference-sensitive Care": treatments, such as discretionary surgery, for which there are two or more valid treatment alternatives, and the choice of treatment involves tradeoffs that should be based on patients' preferences. Variation in such care is typified by elective surgeries, such as hip fracture, knee replacement, or back surgery. Surgeons in adjoining coun-

ties in Florida, for example, may operate at very different levels for the same condition and patient.

(3) "Supply-sensitive Care": services such as physician visits, referrals to specialists, hospitalizations and stays in intensive care units involved in the medical (non-surgical) management of disease. In Medicare, the large majority of these services are for patients with chronic illness.

Wennberg has found that "system" causes of unwarranted variation include misuse of preference-sensitive care; poor communication between the doctor and patient regarding the risks and benefits of alternative treatments; patient dependency on a physician's opinion in sorting out preferences; inadequate evaluation of (evolving) treatment theory; and the effects of our health care finance "system" that rewards procedures, not time spent with patients or the quality of decision making.

See generally John E. Wennberg, Variation in Use of Medicare Services Among Regions and Selected Academic Medical Centers: Is More Better?, Commonwealth Fund Pub. No. 874, at 4 (Dec. 2005) (noting "striking regional variations in the proportion of early stage breast cancer patients who undergo lumpectomy" and identifying "idiosyncratic practice style" as the "major source of such widely varying discretionary surgery rates"). For a graphic depiction of the variation, see John E. Wennberg, Understanding Practice Patterns: A Focus on What the Quality Movement Can Do to Reduce Unwarranted Variations. The Institute for Healthcare Improvement Orlando, Fl. (2005), http://www.dartmouthatlas.org/atlases/IHI_lecture_December05. pdf. See also John E. Wennberg, et al., Evaluating The Efficiency Of California Providers In Caring For Patients With Chronic Illnesses, Health Affairs (November 16, 2005) Web Exclusive 10.1377/hlthaff.w5.526; Lars Noah, Medicine's Epistemology: Mapping the Haphazard Diffusion of Knowledge in the Biomedical Community, 44 Ariz. L. Rev. 373, 382 (2002) (recognizing physicians' traditional reliance on personal experience and anecdotal information).

The attitudes of individual doctors influence the range of variation where consensus is lacking; Wennberg has termed this the "practice style factor." This style can exert its influence in the absence of scientific information on outcomes; in other cases it may be unrelated to controversies. Physicians in some hospital markets practice medicine in ways that have extremely adverse implications for the cost of care, motivated perhaps by reasons of their own or their patients' convenience, or because of individualist interpretations of the requirements for defensive medicine. See John E. Wennberg, The Paradox of Appropriate Care, 258 J.A.M.A. 2568 (1987). See generally John Eisenberg, Doctors' Decisions and the Cost of Medical Care (1986).

Doctors make mistakes, and some of these errors injure patients. The frequency of medical misadventures in the nation's hospitals and clinical settings is substantial. Much health care is of unproven value, but consumes patient and governmental resources. We have a definition of quality, we have criteria and standards for its evaluation. How do we translate the criteria into a strategy to modify behavior and performance to improve the quality of care delivered?

Several approaches to quality improvement can be pursued. We can rely on the traditional forces of professional ethics and socialization. We can expand the role of the marketplace, using dissemination of quality information to consumers and buyers of health, on the theory that prudent buyers will reject lower quality providers. We can improve the current modes of self-regulation of the medical profession and the industry, which include accreditation, medical staff privileges, and medical licensing actions. The process by which a patient sues for malpractice can be improved. And the government, as a primary source of financing for much health care in the United States, can intervene, setting standards and demanding better processes and outcomes. We will examine each of these methods of quality improvement in later sections and chapters.

The combined problems of variation in medical practice and lack of evidence of efficacy of many treatment approaches have launched a movement toward practice guidelines. Specialty societies and now the Medicare program have moved to study practices, to articulate consensus on acceptable practice, and to disseminate information on the consensus. The development of practice parameters or protocols has intensified in recent years, as the medical profession attempts to sift through the available research knowledge and reduce variation in medical practice. A new agency within the Public Health Service, the Agency for Health Care Policy and Research, was created to further such research efforts. 42 U.S.C.A., Title ix, section 901. Promotion of quality work is done within this Agency by the Office of the Forum for Quality and Effectiveness in Health Care. 42 U.S.C.A. 201, § 911.

Measuring appropriateness and developing parameters has its problems: it is easier to study overuse than underuse because of difficulties in defining relevant populations; the scientific evidence is always incomplete, requiring reliance on expert judgment; and parameters are slow and expensive to develop in many areas of medical practice. Robert Brook, Practice Guidelines and Practicing Medicine: Are They Compatible? 262 J.A.M.A. 3027 (1989). Consider the *Berry* case and its lessons for emerging standards of practice.

3. *Clinical Standards of Practice*

BERRY v. CARDIOLOGY CONSULTANTS, P.A.

Superior Court of Delaware 2006.
909 A.2d 611.

DEL PESCO, J.

After a jury verdict in favor of the defendants, cardiologist Andrew Doorey, M.D. ("Dr. Doorey"), and his employer, Cardiology Consultants, P.A., in this medical negligence case, the plaintiffs filed a motion for post-trial relief. They present two arguments. First, that the Court erred in admitting into evidence an algorithm offered through a defense expert witness. Second, that the verdict was against the weight of the evidence. I conclude that the algorithm was properly admitted, and the evidence—while hotly contested—supports a defense verdict.

FACTS

Howard Scott Berry Sr. ("Mr. Berry" or "decedent") had been a patient of the defendant, Dr. Doorey, for twelve years prior to his death. Dr. Doorey's care of the decedent began when he had an acute heart attack in April, 1990. Mr. Berry was forty-eight years old at the time. After his admission, he had a second heart attack involving a different area of his heart. At that time, it was discovered that one of his vessels had a 100% blockage which was not cured by angioplasty.

Mr. Berry had another heart attack fourteen months later, in June 1991, involving a different area of the heart. The treatment after that episode was a blood thinner, Coumadin, for life. In 1996, another blockage occurred in a different artery. That was treated with a stent. Over the ensuing years, decedent developed diabetes, high blood pressure, and high cholesterol, all risk factors for heart disease.

In November 2002, a catheterization was performed because of symptoms reported to the cardiologist. The test revealed that the decedent had "triple vessel disease" which required immediate bypass surgery on November 21, 2002. The record reflects that in spite of the surgery, some portions of the decedent's heart were not revascularized.

The events which underpin this litigation occurred at about midnight on November 23, 2002. At that time, Mr. Berry experienced an episode of atrial fibrillation which resulted in the administration of Amiodarone under the direction of surgical staff. That decision was reviewed by Dr. Doorey the next day, after a further incident of atrial fibrillation. Eventually there were three recurrences of atrial fibrillation over the next couple of days. The danger associated with atrial fibrillation is a stroke. Administration of the Amiodarone continued beyond the time of decedent's discharge on November 27, 2002.

Mr. Berry and his wife appeared for a scheduled post-operative appointment with Dr. Doorey on December 9, 2002. He was given a prescription for Amiodarone, which was never filled. Dr. Doorey testified that he explained the appropriate dosage going forward, including a reduction in the medication to commence after a month, and dictated those instructions in a letter to Mr. Berry's treating physician while he and his wife were present.

Mr. Berry returned to the hospital some fifty days later, on February 1, 2003. He had pulmonary complaints A different cardiologist, Dr. Ashish B. Parikh, noted in the medical record: "[t]here is no sign of Amiodarone toxicity at this point ... I hear the 'Velcro' sound in the lungs. Therefore, I believe that this may be suggestive of early Amiodarone effect." Erring on the side of caution, Dr. Parikh directed Mr. Berry to terminate the use of Amiodarone, and discharged him, with a referral to Dr. Gerald M. O'Brien, a pulmonologist.

Mr. Berry returned to the hospital on February 6, 2003, with pulmonary complaints. A pulmonary biopsy was performed. He was discharged on February 24, 2003. The specimens were sent to the hospital's pathology department. The pathologist sought a second opinion from a physician at Harvard Medical School, Eugene J. Mark, M.D. Dr. Mark's letter opinion is incorporated in the hospital's record. It states, *inter alia,* that it is a "difficult case," and he "prefers the diagnosis of Amiodarone pneumonitis." He also mentions Lipitor pneumonitis as "less well established." Mr. Berry was discharged again. He was again admitted on March 4, 2003, and died on March 23, 2003. The certificate of death says that the immediate cause of death was Acute Pneumonitis, and Amiodarone Toxicity.

Plaintiffs' Theory of Liability

Use of Amiodarone

The plaintiffs' theory of the case was that Amiodarone should not have been prescribed. This argument is based on the fact that the Physicians Desk Reference ("PDR") indicates that Amiodarone was approved for ventricular tachycardia, not atrial fibrillation. [This theory was dropped by plaintiff in closing]

Dosage

At trial, plaintiffs' principal argument was that the amount of Amiodarone administered to Mr. Berry was more than double what would be permitted by the standard of care. In support of that argument, the plaintiffs produced expert testimony, as well as evidence that the hospital had a Cardiac Surgery Service Manual ("CSSM") which contained an algorithm[5] for post cardiac surgery atrial fibrillation. The CSSM algorithm provides that when there is post cardiac surgery atrial fibrillation, the appropriate dosage of Amiodarone is 400 mg TID for 5–7 days then 200 mg a day. The amount administered to Mr. Berry was greater than that indicated in the CSSM algorithm. The algorithm was admitted in evidence as Plaintiff's Exhibit 5 and relied upon by plaintiffs as the standard of care for the administration of Amiodarone.[]

Plaintiffs' theory was supported by two experts. Dr. H. Brandis Marsh testified that Amiodarone was an appropriate drug for the treatment of atrial fibrillation, but that the amount of medication administered was excessive. Dr. Robert M. Stark testified that Amiodarone was an inappropriate medication for atrial fibrillation, and he concurred that the amount was excessive and prescribed for too long.

Plaintiffs raised an issue as to the clarity of the communications to Mr. Berry regarding the dosage to be taken, arguing that the dosage on the prescription was different than what Dr. Doorey testified the decedent was to take.

Informed Consent

Plaintiffs argue that the decedent was not informed regarding the risks associated with the usage of Amiodarone, particularly the risks of pulmonary damage. The argument is that Mr. Berry was a compliant, cautious man who would have sought more information before taking Amiodarone, and, had he known of the pulmonary risk, he would have reacted differently to the onset of symptoms.

Defendants' Evidence

Use of Amiodarone

Defendants agreed that the PDR reflects usage of Amiodarone for ventricular arrhythmia. Defense experts explained that Amiodarone was approved

---

5. The chart is not labeled algorithm, I attach that name as an algorithm is defined as "[a] systematic process consisting of an ordered sequence of steps, each step depending on the outcome of the previous one. In clinical medicine, a step-by-step protocol for management of a health care problem...." Stedman's Medical Dictionary 45 (27th ed.2000).

for ventricular arrhythmia in 1985. Subsequent to that time and after the drug was off patent protection, it began to be used for other purposes, known as "off list usage." Because there was no financial incentive to go through the process of FDA approval for a different usage, the PDR does not reflect that expansion in the usage of the drug. In addition to Dr. Doorey, one of plaintiffs' experts and both of the defense experts testified that Amiodarone is well accepted and widely used for the treatment of atrial fibrillation.

Dosage

The CSSM algorithm states a dosage less than that prescribed by Dr. Doorey for Mr. Berry for atrial fibrillation. Dr. Doorey explained that when a patient has cardiac surgery, the patient is under the care of the cardiac surgeon, not the cardiologist. While the cardiologist and other specialists may be consulted on problems, only the surgeon has the ability to issue orders. During the time that the surgeons are off, or unavailable, there are numerous hospital employees including nurses, physician's assistants, and others, who are involved 24/7 in the care of patients. In order to have a prompt response to a problem arising when the surgeon is not available, the cardiac surgeons prepare guidelines for the treatment of certain conditions. Those guidelines e.g. the CSSM algorithm, are designed to enable the support team to get something started at a time when a specialist is not available. The guidelines are not provided to cardiologists such as Dr. Doorey, and do not set a standard to which the specialist is bound.

Creation of Guidelines for Treatment of Atrial Fibrillation

Defendants presented testimony primarily through the testimony of Eric N. Prystowsky, M.D., about the unusual circumstances related to the establishment of a dosage regimen for Amiodarone. Dr. Prystowsky testified that a specific dosage of Amiodarone has not been established.[7] After usage of the drug gained acceptance as a treatment for atrial fibrillation, the American College of Cardiology, the American Heart Association, and the European

---

7.   * * * What typically happens is the drug gets developed in animal models, then goes to clinical testing, goes to phase one. Normal volunteers. They give the drug. They decide what's called pharmocokinetics; how much dose do you need to get? What is the half life? How long is it in the body? It goes through this whole very rigorous drug development process. That s how you get a dosing scheme. How is it that the doctor knows when a new drug comes out to give two twice a day? What I tell you is what someone else is telling me. I haven't done the research of some drug for pneumonia or something, someone else has. The guidance we get is based on all this arduous process that companies are forced to go through; not so Amiodarone. Now you have a scenario where there are literally hundreds of investigators ... publishing papers, trying to figure it all out, everyone is using different regimens. No one made up their minds, and I was invited to Washington, DC with a lot of other people who are very involved, FDA involved, and, frankly, around 1985 the FDA did something they have never done before in our area and never done since, they approved the drug without any formal testing. They realized they simply couldn't deal with this anymore, better to at least approve it, and they put a big black box around it, they restricted its use, frankly scared it was going to be, once it was approved, anyone could get it, that people were going to abuse it, had a lot of down sides. It had a huge upside advantage; it was often the only drug that would work to save someone's life. So they were stuck. So from the very beginning, no one, still today, no one has agreed on what is the typical dose of this drug. No one knows the minimal effective dose. No one knows what the legitimate blood level should be, although many of us have published on it.

.   .   .   .

What happened was when we finally wrote the guidelines to reflect a consensus of a drug dose, a consensus of what is being used, realizing that there is clearly around the margins legitimate other people's opinion.

Society of Cardiology formed a committee to develop guidelines for the treatment of atrial fibrillation. Dr. Prystowsky was a member of the committee. The committee's work was published and distributed by the American College of Cardiology ("ACC") in a pamphlet. Dr. Prystowsky testified that the publication represented a consensus of what is being used, but there are other legitimate opinions "around the margins." [] Dr. Prystowsky personally prepared the ACC algorithm which was included in the publication resulting from the joint effort.[] He was questioned about the ACC algorithm, and the relevant pages were displayed to the jury at the time of his testimony. The displayed pages were admitted, over plaintiff's objection, as Defendant's Exhibits 20, 21 and 22. They are pages 14, 15, 20 and 40 of the pamphlet. Dr. Prystowsky testified that the level of medication prescribed by Dr. Doorey was consistent with the standard of care.

Informed Consent

Dr. Doorey testified that he explained to Mr. Berry the risks associated with the use of Amiodarone the morning after the medication was administered, although the hospital record does not reflect that conversation. His normal practice is to discuss pulmonary risks, along with other side effects associated with the use of Amiodarone. One such risk relates to the thyroid. Dr. Doorey recalls a discussion about thyroid function; and the chart reflects that certain tests were performed at that time to check thyroid function. With regard to dosages, Dr. Doorey testified, and the record confirms, that a letter outlining future dosages was dictated in front of Mr. Berry when he met with Dr. Doorey on December 9, 2002. That letter reflects a reduction of the dosages to 200 mg twice a day, and after a month, once a day.

Discussion

Admissibility of the Algorithm

The first issue in plaintiffs' post-trial motion is whether the Court erred in admitting into evidence the algorithm prepared by Dr. Prystowsky. Plaintiff cites Delaware Rule of Evidence 803(18) in support of the argument that the documents admitted were in the category of a learned treatise, and as such it was error to admit the pages shown to the jury.

The plaintiff's argument is two-pronged. First, they contend that the ACC algorithm was misleading as it did not pertain to Mr. Berry due to the fact that his condition was transient and, according to the medical record, resolved spontaneously. Therefore, use of a chart designed for "Recurrent Paroxysmal or Persistent Atrial Fibrillation" is irrelevant to a patient with first onset, post-operative atrial fibrillation. Whether or not Mr. Berry's condition was within the scope of the algorithm was one of many fact questions left for the jury. Extensive testimony supported the conclusion that Mr. Berry's atrial fibrillation was recurrent.[]

The second prong of plaintiffs' argument is that the algorithm should not have been admitted in evidence because it was a learned treatise.

* * *

Plaintiffs argue that admission of the ACC algorithm is inconsistent with the Delaware Supreme Court's ruling in Timblin v. Kent General Hosp.

(Inc.).[] Timblin was a medical negligence case. The defense presented statistical evidence concerning the percentage of patients who die or suffer brain damage following a cardiac arrest. The allegation of negligence in the case was that a twenty-five minute delay in intubating the decedent after cardiac arrest was the cause of his neurological deficit. The Court noted that in a medical negligence case the defendant may introduce evidence "to show that the applicable standard of care was met or that any departure therefrom did not cause the plaintiff's injury."[] The Court then concluded that the proffered statistical evidence was not probative of either issue.

The ACC algorithm was relevant on the issue of standard of care, in that it provided an analytical path which demonstrated that Amiodarone was an appropriate medication, and a description of an appropriate dosage regimen. This case is readily distinguishable from *Timblin*.

* * *

All the plaintiffs' contentions of negligence and causation were met with counter evidence. The Defendant, and experts called by the defense, did not accept Amiodarone toxicity as the cause of death. [] The evidence was clear that the use of Amiodarone for atrial fibrillation was appropriate. The evidence as to the appropriate dosage was contested. The plaintiffs relied primarily on the CSSM algorithm as the statement of the standard of care. The defendants provided testimony which demonstrated that since the medication had not been through the FDA approval process for atrial fibrillation there was no set dosage; that various practitioners have differing ideas, but that the consensus was as set forth in the ACC algorithm. The jury performed its function. It considered the evidence and reached a verdict which is based on competent evidence, as outlined above. I do not find that the verdict is against the weight of the evidence.

The motion for a new trial is DENIED.

Notes and Questions

1. *Berry* illustrates the real problem facing physicians in many areas of practice: it is often not clear exactly what the best practice is, or the best drug, or the best dosage of the drug. Physicians want as much certainty as they can find in treating patients, and authoritative guidelines are one way to provide guidance. *Berry* involves a drug that has a real clinical benefit, but lacks the kind of rigorous testing that the FDA requires for new drugs. So the FDA appears to have thrown up its hands and said, "Let's let practitioners use it, with warnings, and watch it." Is this a reasonable regulatory approach in the face of clinical uncertainty? See discussion of regulation of physician prescribing, including off-label prescribing, in Chapter 2.

2. The standard of care applied in a tort suit or a hospital peer review process does not normally derive from an external authority such as a government standard. As *Berry* shows, in the medical profession, as in other professions, standards develop in a complicated way involving the interaction of leaders of the profession, professional journals and meetings, and networks of colleagues. Neither the Food and Drug Administration, the National Institutes of Health, the Department of Health and Human Services, nor state licensing boards have had much to do with shaping medical practice. Most clinical policies derive from a flow of reports in the literature, at meetings, and in peer discussions. Over a period of

time, hundreds of separate comments come together to form a clinical policy. If this becomes generally accepted, we can call it "standard practice." See generally David Eddy, Clinical Policies and the Quality of Clinical Practice, 307 NEJM. 343 (1982). One doctor has termed such standards "eminence-based medicine." Dan Mayer, Evidence–Based Medicine, 36 New Eng. L. Rev. 601 (2002).

This decentralized process of policy setting has some advantages, as Eddy notes: the individual doctor benefits from collective wisdom; unwarranted bursts of enthusiasm are dampened; the policies are tested by the best minds (through statistical and other tools); and it provides flexibility by allowing adaptation to local skills and values. Such a policy making process also has drawbacks: oversimplification may ignore side-effects, costs and risks; overly broad conclusions may be drawn from a few observations; examples may be chosen that tend to support the expected result; incentives may favor overuse rather than underuse; an advocacy system may arise in which proponents push and counterarguments may be ignored; the policy consensus may be based upon little more than repetition by the largest or loudest voices; and the inertia inherent in the status quo may dominate.

The diffusion of new medical technologies of diagnosis and treatment poses special problems for the individual physician. Most doctors will note new ideas as they show up in the literature. But they may not be appropriately skeptical. In spite of insufficient evidence of efficacy, doctors in various specialties have been quick to adopt new technologies such as respirator therapy, gastric freezing of ulcers, and other now-discredited techniques. Other tools, such as the CT scan and magnetic resonance imaging, have proliferated rapidly before the evidence on their efficacy was in. The adoption of what has been termed "slam-bang" technologies often precedes careful evaluation.

Even if a cautious and conscientious doctor is skeptical, the data and opinions available are often inadequate to allow evaluation of research findings. The studies may have defects; they may fail, for example, to explain how to translate limited clinical research into practice or may inadequately evaluate controversy over earlier studies. Or the doctor may not be aware of the unique nature of clinical trials. In addition, clinical research is currently inadequate. See Sandra H. Johnson, Polluting Medical Judgment? False Assumptions in the Pursuit of False Claims Regarding Off–Label Prescribing, 9 Minn. J.L.Science & Tech. 61 (2007).

3. Quality improvement requires the development of tools such as (1) evidence-based standards that provide a baseline for measuring the quality of a provider's practice; (2) electronic medical records to better track and manage patient care in light of these baselines of proven good practices; (3) mechanisms for constant feedback and evaluation of practice within health care institutions.

Advances in information processing technology have enhanced the ability of the health care industry to collect, process, and analyze data. These advances allow the analysis of the outcomes of health care processes. Data describing large numbers of patients can be studied to determine the efficacy of alternative diagnostic and treatment modalities. This information can be used to construct practice guidelines, which can in some cases be reduced to algorithms used to enable computer review of the quality of the practices of individual practitioners or institutions. Outcome data can also be used to support pattern analysis, comparing the outcome of the care provided by individual practitioners or institutions with average or optimal practice as revealed by outcome analysis.

These new developments in information technology and industry structure have allowed the development of methods of comparing practitioners and institutions, increasingly enabling consumers to evaluate their physicians, hospitals, and managed care organizations. Several attempts have been made in recent years to enable consumers to comparatively evaluate quality in health care markets. From 1986 until 1992 the federal Health Care Financing Administration published annual data comparing the mortality experience of hospitals for certain procedures. Several states, most notably Pennsylvania, New York, and California, have begun to assemble and release comparative outcome data, permitting prospective patients to compare the performance of various health care institutions and professionals. Other information initiatives have also been proposed, such as the Joint Commission's new disclosure policy, which includes hospital report cards.

Information processing technology and industry reorganization enable lay managers to monitor physicians. The use of algorithms or profiles allows lay managers to assess physician quality. This has led to new industry-originated practices of continuous quality improvement (CQI) or total quality management (TQM). The application of these principles is described in the following excerpt.

TIMOTHY S. JOST, OVERSIGHT OF THE QUALITY OF MEDICAL CARE: REGULATION, MANAGEMENT, OR THE MARKET?

37 Ariz. L. Rev. 825, 837 (1995).

The continuous quality improvement or total quality management movement is based on quality improvement strategies developed in the industrial setting. The ideas of Deming, Juran Shewhart and others had a significant impact on Japanese, and then American industrial production. Within the past few years these ideas have begun to be applied widely in health care as well. Lay managers (sometimes in conjunction with physicians) are using their new-found power within reorganized health care institutions and their new and greatly enhanced access to and ability to manipulate data to improve the quality of medical care delivered in institutional settings.

The quality improvement philosophy is based on several principles:

1) Quality is defined in terms of meeting the needs of "customers," defined broadly to include not only patients but also others who consume the services of the institution, including physicians themselves. This orientation is immediately appealing to managers who are increasingly oriented toward regarding patients as consumers. While this definition short-circuits debates over the true nature of quality, as quality is viewed as what consumers want, it is inherently problematic. If patients as consumers cannot recognize or assess the quality of medical care, as the law has assumed since Dent, how can they define quality?

2) Energy is better directed toward improving the system through which care is delivered than toward looking for "bad apples." Most quality deficiencies are caused by faulty systems, not by incompetents working within those systems. One can accomplish more, therefore, by raising the mean of the performance curve than by chopping off the tail. This emphasis on improving the average performance rather than punishing the bad actor is perhaps the clearest distinction between quality improvement and traditional quality assurance, which has tended to be preoccupied with looking for "bad apples." This orientation gives quality improvement a more positive tone than quality

assurance, thus making it more palatable to hospital employees and medical staff. It also results in a heavy emphasis on process and on systems.

3) Data are very important for driving and shaping systems improvement. Outcomes data are particularly useful for identifying areas where improvement is possible or necessary. Not only must systems be monitored continuously, but improvements in systems must also be monitored to assure that they in fact effective. Much of the arcanity of the quality improvement movement (Ishikawa diagrams, Pareto diagrams, histograms, etc.) results from attempts to organize, make sense out of, and devise rational responses to patterns revealed by data.

4) Management and staff must be involved at all levels in the process of improvement. This is a particular focus of total quality management. The culture of the organization must be molded to emphasize quality.

5) Quality improvement is never finished. This is the primary insight of continuous quality improvement. There is always room for further progress. This should be reassuring, however, and not lead to discouragement.

This newfound confidence in the market and in internal management has been accompanied by a decline in confidence in external public regulation. The cost of health care quality regulation programs has long been recognized, and criticism of the high cost of regulation has become increasingly shrill. The whole range of federal and state regulatory programs, including the PRO program, CLIA, nursing home regulation, and even professional licensure, have been criticized for their direct costs and for the costs they impose on the industry. Increasingly, the benefits of traditional forms of regulation that focus on competence and error have been questioned. The continuous quality improvement/total quality management program poses a serious challenge to traditional regulatory programs that focus on "bad apples." The view of TQM is that such programs depress morale, discourage innovation, and do little to improve the care provided in the vast majority of instances.

Notes and Questions

1. This approach to improving the processes of health care delivery is modeled after Japanese management practices, adopting managerial principles to improve quality:

(1) active visible support from clinical and managerial leadership for the continuous improvement of quality;

(2) focus on processes as the objects of improvement;

(3) elimination of unnecessary variation; and

(4) revised strategies for personnel management.

This ethic of continuous improvement, termed in the parlance of the industry either Continuous Quality Improvement (CQI) or Total Quality Management (TQM), assumes that processes are complex and frequently characterized by unnecessary rework and waste, whose reduction might both improve quality and reduce cost. It combines outcome measures with process technology and emphasis on personnel management, treating staff as resources central to quality improvement. The methodology was developed for use by industrial organizations by W. Edwards Deming, in Quality, Productivity, and Competitive Position (1982) and Joseph M. Juran, Managerial Breakthrough (1964). The techniques have been widely applied in health care as well as American industry. See, e.g., Donald M.

Berwick et al., Curing Health Care: New Strategies for Quality Improvement (1991); Ellen J. Gaucher & Richard J. Coffey, Total Quality in Healthcare: From Theory to Practice (1993). Its application in health care was suggested by Donald Berwick, Continuous Improvement as an Ideal in Health Care, 320 NEJM 53 (1989). Physicians typically resist such TQM/CQI programs and the high level of administrative intervention they often appear to threaten. Can you see any reason why physicians might object to the application of these management strategies to their professional services? See generally Curtis P. McLaughlin & Arnold D. Kaluzny, Continuous Quality Improvement in Health Care: Theory, Implementations, and Applications (3rd ed. 2006) for a history and current applications.

2. *Evidence-based-medicine (EBM)*. Evidence-based-medicine is a movement that is a natural outgrowth of the CQI developments in health care, and is related to the developed of clinical practice guidelines as well. EBM is typically defined as "the conscientious, explicit, and judicious use of current best evidence in making decisions about the care of individual patients." David L. Sackett et al., Evidence–Based Medicine: What It Is and What It Isn't, 312 Brit. Med. J. 71, 71 (1996). EBM incorporate clinical expertise and patient values as well, but the emphasis is on the use of current best evidence. While CPGs can take years to be accepted, EBM assumes that the physician will keep up and incorporate the best evidence into his practice in advance of the development of a clinical practice guidelines. See generally Carter Williams, Evidence–Based Medicine in the Law Beyond Clinical Practice Guidelines: What Effect Will EBM Have on the Standard of Care? 61 Wash. & Lee L. Rev. 479 (2004).

4. Electronic Medical Records

The United States lags behind most European countries in the use of electronic medical records or EMRs, even though such records can provide physicians with immediate lab results and other necessary information for treating patients under critical conditions. The U.S. health care industry has been described as the "world's largest, most inefficient information enterprise." It has been estimated that as of 2006, fewer than 10% of American hospitals have adopted EMRs and other health information technology, such as computer physician order entry (CPOE). Less than 20% of primary care physicians use EMRs. It is still a paper world in health care. The Institute of Medicine called for an electronic medical record years ago, but little progress has been made. See Institute of Medicine, Crossing the Quality Chasm: A New Health System for the 21st Century (2001). Health care spends only 2% of its gross revenues on HIT; contrast this to the finance industry and other information intensive business, where up to 10% is spent. The average hospital runs more than 200 different computer application systems, and most cannot talk to one another. Often different vendors have developed the hospital's individual applications for billing, laboratory work, radiology, and patient charting and the applications don't work together within a single hospital or in systems with other organizations.

Congress enacted the Health Insurance Portability and Accountability Act of 1996 ("HIPAA"). HIPAA had at least two purposes: one was to provide a federal framework for developing electronic medical records; a second was to develop rules to protect the privacy of an individual's personal health information ("PHI"). [] Under HIPAA, "covered entities," including (1) health plans; (2) health care clearinghouses; and (3) health care providers, are required to follow specific regulations (45 CFR §§ 160–164) relating to the collection, use, or disclosure of an individual's personal health information. Generally, a covered entity may not disclose health information of persons without their consent.

Health Information Technology (HIT) is a large category that includes several subcategories of computer-driven tools. HIT includes:

a. Electronic medical records (EMRs) (or EHRs). These are computer patient records containing all medical information from tests or interviews with physicians.

b. Computerized Physician Order Entry (CPOE). These are clinical information technology tools that physicians and other providers can use to enter orders, such as prescription drugs or lab tests, into a computer system for further patient action. Designed for hospitals, they are similar to eRx technology.

c. Electronic Prescribing (eRx), where electronic devices such as Personal Digital Assistants (PDAs) are used to create, process, and communicate prescriptions for medication. These eRx tools can allow physicians to write and manage prescriptions using a computer instead of a paper prescription pad, and more elaborate versions may include treatment advice and communication across organizations.

d. Clinical Decision Support Systems (CDSS). These are software tools to help providers by offering "best practice" recommendations for a patient's situation, using information about the individual patient and a database of recommended procedures.

In a 1997 case, *Johnson v. Hillcrest Health Center, Inc.*, 70 P.3d 811 (Okla. 2003), hospital lab results suggested that the patient, Johnson, had had a heart attack; the raw data from the lab tests was available on computer terminals located throughout the hospital, including Johnson's floor, but the pathologist's report was not on the computer. The results were placed in the wrong patient chart. The treating physician did not check the computer and discharged Johnson, who later died of a heart attack. The court held that the standard of care required that the critical information be placed in the chart, even though it was available on the computers in the hospital.

A hospital's duty requires such care and protection to its patients as the patient's condition requires. Charting provides a record to assist the physician in properly treating the patient. Physicians depend on the reliability and trustworthiness of the chart and as far as a hospital is concerned, there is no more important record than the chart for indicating the diagnosis, the condition, and for treating patients.

The court noted the possible impact of EMRs on hospital standards of care:

(" * * * [W]e refrain from commenting on whether the standard of care would be different today, given the increased implementation of computer technology in the medical profession since that time. We recognize that medical literature reflects and supports the advent of electronic medical records and even advocates the movement towards the elimination of handwritten clinical data in the foreseeable future.")

See Amy Jurevic Sokol & Christopher J. Molzen, The Changing Standard of Care in Medicine: E–Health, Medical Errors, and Technology Add New

Obstacles, 23 J. Legal Med. 449 (2002); See also Charles Safran, M.D., Electronic Medical Records: A Decade of Experience, 285 J.A.M.A. 1766 (2001); Dena E. Rifkin, Electronic Medical Records: Saving Trees, Saving Lives, 285 J.A.M.A. 1764 (2001).

The benefits of health information technology are substantial. A California legislative report summarizes them as follows:

1. Fewer Medical Tests. Access to a patient's electronic health records (EHR) at the point of care through a regional health information organization (RHIO) network would reduce the possibility that a physician would order redundant medical tests. Without such access, a physician would not know whether another physician had ordered a similar test recently. Also, paper records that are lost or located at another facility can result in tests being needlessly repeated at increased cost and inconvenience to the patient.

2. Higher Quality Patient Care. Clinical decision support tools incorporated into electronic prescribing, EHR, or computerized physician order entry systems, can alert physicians to potential treatment risks such as adverse drug interactions, avoiding costly and potentially harmful medical errors. Physicians could receive electronic reminders to take certain standard actions in caring for patients—such as indicating that a diabetes patient is due for a blood test. Case management is improved by ease of tracking patient care for complex chronic diseases. One result of the health care system using more specialists to take care of sicker patients is that physicians are often missing important pieces of clinical information, In one study, researchers found that clinical information such as laboratory and radiology results, letters and medical history was missing during 13.6% of 1,614 patient visits analyzed at 32 Colorado primary care clinics. Peter C. Smith, et al., Missing Clinical Information During Primary Care Visits, 293 JAMA 565 (2005).

3. Improved Emergency Care Outcomes. A hospital emergency room that is linked to a RHIO can quickly access a patient's medical history to inform decisions at the point of care. Accounting for this information helps the physicians avoid potentially dangerous adverse treatment reactions.

4. More Efficient Prescription Drug Processing. When prescriptions are issued electronically to pharmacies, the pharmacist receives the order almost immediately and can begin filling it prior to the patient's arrival. Possible confusion resulting from a doctor's illegible handwriting, a common administrative hurdle with paper prescriptions, can be avoided.

5. Fewer Patient Burdens. Patients in a hospital would not need to repeatedly describe their situation to different doctors and nurses who come to check on them. Instead, up-to-date information in EHR would be available nearby the patient, possibly through a wireless laptop or handheld computer. Also, patients would only need to provide their personal and family medical history once to establish an EHR. From then on, the primary care physician, or other care providers, could access the record through a RHIO and update it, maintaining a comprehensive medical history in one file, rather than in numerous paper files scattered around doctor's offices, laboratories, hospitals, and other locations.

6.   Better Disaster Preparation. Medical histories stored on EHRs would be less likely to be lost during a natural disaster in any particular area, assuming that appropriate precautions were taken to back up electronic records. For instance, a fire or earthquake that destroyed a physician's office might not result in the loss of that practice's records if that physician participated in a RHIO. If the practice kept all its records onsite in paper folders, all records could be lost in such an event.

7.   Increased Public Health Monitoring. Public health monitoring would be improved by the ability to review diagnostic information on a confidential basis from a wide variety of patients. Trends in disease and other medical conditions could be detected faster and, thus, addressed more rapidly.

California Legislative Analyst's Office, A State Policy Approach: Promoting Health InformationTechnologyinCalifornia (2007), http://www.lao.ca.gov/2007/health_info_tech/health_info_tech_021307.aspx.; David F. Doolan and David W. Bates, Computerized Physician Order Entry Systems in Hospitals: Mandates and Incentives, 21 Health Affairs 180 (2002); Richard Hillestad, James Bigelow, Anthony Bower, Federico Girosi, Robin Meili, Richard Scoville, and Roger Taylor, Can Electronic Medical Record Systems Transform Health Care? Potential and Health Benefits, Savings, and Costs, 24 Health Affairs 1103 (2005); Kateryna Fonkych and Roger Taylor, The State and Pattern of Health Information Technology Adoption (Rand 2005) http://www.rand.org/pubs/monographs/2005/RAND_MG409.pdf.

Adoption has been slow in spite of the putative advantages of electronic medical records. First, implementation is expensive. The software, and new hardware in some cases, requires not only acquisition costs but substantial staff training. The administrative structure is different from creating and maintaining paper records. Patient records have to be entered into the system. Staff time is spent learning the system, reducing patient contact time. And who profits from these systems? The incentives are not designed so that implementation leads to higher returns in the health care industry. Evidence suggests however that the economic savings are substantial once the systems are in place. A recent study concluded that "[a]n EHR can rapidly demonstrate a positive return on investment when implemented in ambulatory offices associated with a university medical center, with a neutral impact on efficiency and billing." Dara L Grieger, Stephen H Cohen, and David A Krusch, A Pilot Study to Document the Return on Investment for Implementing an Ambulatory Electronic Health Record at an Academic Medical Center, 205 J. Am. Coll. Surg. 89, 96 (2007).

Second, the products available suffer from a lack of interoperability—i.e. they don't work together because of competing proprietary formats. The marketplace has not yet produced standardization. Without the ability of products to link together, health data cannot be shared across networks. See generally Nicolas P. Terry, Electronic Health Records: International, Structural, and Legal Perspectives, 12 J.Leg. Med. 26 (2004).

Third, the ease of access that electronic records permit may create greater privacy risks for patients.

III. THE PROBLEM OF MEDICAL ERROR

A. MEDICAL IATROGENESIS: DEFINITIONS AND EXTENT

Injury caused by doctors and health care institutions, or iatrogenesis, is the inverse of quality medicine. It is thus helpful to refine our understanding of injury, medical error, and medical fault, as part of our inquiry into the meaning of quality in health care. The literature on iatrogenesis is surprisingly sparse, considering the importance of the subject.

The law has historically focused on physician "error". Until recently, malpractice cases were brought against the treating physician and not his institution because of a variety of legal rules that shielded the hospital. State licensing boards brought disciplinary actions against the individual errant doctor. Staff privilege cases involved the individual doctor's qualifications. The narrow focus on individual error facilitated a clear definition of "bad medicine." Bad medicine was what bad doctors did, "bad apples," doctors whose incompetence was obvious and offensive.

This focus on individual responsibility for error has been the starting point for quality assessment, even though it misses many causes of poor quality health care. Such a concept of error provides a necessary starting point, but bad outcomes at the individual physician level typically occur too infrequently to identify poor or good physicians. The larger problem of quality in medical care must also address systemic failures, poor administrative design for review of health care, inadequacies in training of physicians, and the nature of practice incentives. See generally Joanna K. Weinberg, Medical Error and Patient Safety: Understanding Cultures in Conflict, 24 Law & Policy 93 (2002). The choice of "error" often misses the point of quality improvement, which requires a look at many other facets of health care delivery. For example, surgical volume improves patient outcomes. See John D. Birkmeyer et al., Regionalization of High–Risk Surgery and Implications for Patient Travel Times, 290 JAMA 2703 (2003).

B. THE EXTENT OF MEDICAL MISADVENTURES

PATIENTS, DOCTORS, AND LAWYERS: MEDICAL INJURY, MALPRACTICE LITIGATION, AND PATIENT COMPENSATION IN NEW YORK

The Report of the Harvard Medical Practice.
Study to the State of New York (1990).

[The Harvard Medical Practice Study in New York looked at the incidence of injuries resulting from medical interventions, "adverse events," beginning with a sample of more than 31,000 New York hospital records drawn from the study year 1984. The review was conducted by medical record administrators and nurses in the screening phase, and by board certified physicians for the physician-review phase.]

* * *

We analyzed 30,121 (96%) of the 31,429 records selected for the study sample. After preliminary screening, physicians reviewed 7,743 records, from which a total of 1,133 adverse events were identified that occurred as a result of medical management in the hospital or required hospitalization for treatment. Of this group, 280 were judged to result from negligent care. Weighting these figures according to the sample plan, we estimated the incidence of adverse events for hospitalizations in New York in 1984 to be 3.7%, or a total of 98,609. Of these, 27.6%, 27,179 cases, or 1.0% of all hospital discharges, were due to negligence.

Physician confidence in the judgments of causation of adverse events spanned a broad range, but only 1.3% of all discharges were in the close-call range (defined as a confidence in causation of just under or just over 50–50). An even smaller fraction, 0.7% of discharges were close-call negligent adverse events, but they constituted a larger proportion of total negligent adverse events.

The majority of adverse events (57%) resulted in minimal and transient disability, but 14% of patients died at least in part as a result of their adverse event, and in another 9% the resultant disability lasted longer than 6 months. Based on these figures, we estimated that about 2,500 cases of permanent total disability resulted from medical injury in New York hospitals in 1984. Further, we found evidence that medical injury contributed at least in part to the deaths of more than 13,000 patients in that year. Many of the deaths occurred in patients who had greatly shortened life expectancies from their underlying diseases, however. Negligent adverse events resulted, overall, in greater disability than did non-negligent events and were associated with 51% of all deaths from medical injury.

RISK FACTORS

The risk of sustaining an adverse event increased with age. When rates were standardized for DRG level, persons over 65 years had twice the chance of sustaining an adverse event of those in the 16–44 years group. Newborns had half the adverse event rate of the 16–44 years group. The percent of adverse events resulting from negligence was increased in elderly patients. We found no gender differences in adverse event or negligence rates. Although the rates were higher in the self-pay group than in the insured categories, the differences were not significant. Blacks had higher rates of adverse events and adverse events resulting from negligence, but these differences overall were not significant. However, higher rates of adverse events and negligent events were found in hospitals that served a higher proportion of minority patients. At hospitals that cared for a mix of white and minority patients, blacks and whites had nearly identical rates.

Adverse event rates varied 10–fold between individual hospitals, when standardized for age and DRG level. Although standardized adverse event and negligence rates for small hospitals (fewer than 8,000 discharges/year) were less than for larger hospitals, these differences were not significant. Hospital ownership (private, non-profit, or government) also was not associated with significantly different rates of adverse events. The fraction of adverse events due to negligence in government hospitals was 50% higher than in non-profit institutions, however, and three times that in proprietary hospitals. These differences were significant. The standardized rate of adverse events in upstate, non–MSA hospitals was one-third that of upstate metropolitan hospitals and less than one-fourth that in New York City. These differences were highly significant. The percent of adverse events due to negligence was not significantly different across regions. Non-teaching hospitals had half the adverse event rates of university or affiliated teaching hospitals, but university teaching hospitals had rates of negligence that were less than half those of the non-teaching or affiliated hospitals.

The Nature of Adverse Events

Nearly half (47%) of all adverse events occurred in patients undergoing surgery, but the percent caused by negligence was lower than for non-surgical adverse events (17% vs 37%). Adverse events resulting from errors in diagnosis and in non-invasive treatment were judged to be due to negligence in over three-fourths of patients. Falls were considered due to negligence in 45% of instances.

The high rate of adverse events in patients over 65 years occurred in three categories: non-technical postoperative complications, complications of non-invasive therapy, and falls. A larger proportion of adverse events in younger patients was due to surgical failures. The operating room was the site of management for the highest fraction of adverse events, but relatively few of these were negligent. On the other hand, most (70%) adverse events in the emergency room resulted from negligence.

The most common type of error resulting in an adverse event was that involved in performing a procedure but diagnostic errors and prevention errors were more likely to be judged negligent, and to result in serious disability.

The more severe the degree of negligence the greater the likelihood of resultant serious disability (moderate impairment with recovery taking more than six months, permanent disability, or death).

2. Litigation data

We estimated that the incidence of malpractice claims filed by patients for the study year was between 2,967 and 3,888. Using these figures, together with the projected statewide number of injuries from medical negligence during the same period, we estimated that eight times as many patients suffered an injury from negligence as filed a malpractice claim in New York State. About 16 times as many patients suffered an injury from negligence as received compensation from the tort liability system.

These aggregate estimates understate the true size of the gap between the frequency of malpractice claims and the incidence of adverse events caused by negligence. When we identified the malpractice claims actually filed by patients in our sample and reviewed the judgments of our physician reviewers, we found that many cases in litigation were brought by patients in whose records we found no evidence of negligence or even of adverse events. Because the legal system has not yet resolved many of these cases, we do not have the information that would permit an assessment of the success of the tort litigation system in screening out claims with no negligence.

Notes and Questions

1. The Harvard Study was designed to produce empirical data to better inform the debate about reform of the tort system, including no-fault reforms. Do

the findings of the study, as to level of patient injury attributable to medical error, surprise you? The Study is generally acknowledged as one of the first to take an epidemiological approach to medical errors. It has also been criticized on a number of grounds. See generally Tom Baker, Reconsidering the Harvard Medical Practice Study Conclusions about the Validity of Medical Malpractice Claims, 33 J. L., Med. & Ethics 501 (2005). A second study, the Utah–Colorado Medical Practice Study (UCMPS), found that adverse events connected to surgery accounted for about half (44.9%) of adverse events across both states, with only 16.9% of the surgical adverse events involving negligence. Drug related adverse events comprised the second most prevalent group. The authors concluded that the UCMPS produced results similar to the earlier New York Harvard Study. That is, three to four percent of hospitalizations give rise to adverse events. "Together, the two studies provide overwhelming evidence that the burden of iatrogenic injury is large, enduring, and an innate feature of hospital care in the United States." David M. Studdert, et al., Beyond Dead Reckoning: Measures of Medical Injury Burden, Malpractice Litigation, and Alternative Compensation Models from Utah and Colorado, 33 Ind. L. Rev. 1643, 1662 (2000).

2.   Recent studies have confirmed that most malpractice claims do involve medical errors, and those claims that lack evidence of error are usually denied compensation. David M. Studdert et al., Claims, Errors, and Compensation Payments in Medical Malpractice Litigation, 354 N.E.J.M. 2024 (2006).

3.   Do these study results support the existing tort system's value as a quality control system in detecting and deterring error? Or do they support the need for reform? For an exploration of the role of the tort system in insuring against inadvertent negligence or accidents not caused by a professional failure, see Mark F. Grady, Why Are People Negligent? Technology, Nondurable Precautions, and the Medical Malpractice Explosion, 82 Nw.Univ.L.Rev. 293 (1988).

4.   The hospital setting exposes patients to significant risks of iatrogenic illness. One study found that more than 36% of the patients admitted to a hospital developed iatrogenic injury, either a major or minor complication. Nine percent had major complications, and 2% of all patients died for reasons related to the iatrogenic illness. Exposure to drugs was an important factor in patient complications. Knight Steel et al., Iatrogenic Illness on a General Medical Service at a University Hospital, 304 NEJM 638, 641 (1981). See David C. Classen et al., Adverse Drug Events in Hospitalized Patients: Excess Length of Stay, Extra Costs, and Attributable Mortality, 277 J.A.M.A. 301 (1997) (adverse drug events associated with significantly prolonged lengths of stay, increased economic costs, and an almost 2–fold increased risk of death); David W. Bates et al., The Costs of Adverse Drug Events in Hospitalized Patients, 277 J.A.M.A. 307 (1997) (found that an adverse drug event was associated with about $2,600 of additional costs to the hospital, and for preventable ADEs the figure was almost twice as high); Timothy S. Lesar, et al., Factors Related to Errors in Medication Prescribing, 277 J.A.M.A. 312 (1997) (risks of adverse drug events can be reduced by improving focus of organization, technological, and risk management educational and training efforts).

For an excellent summary of studies of medical errors, see Sheila Leatherman & Douglas McCarthy, Quality of Health Care in the United States: A Chartbook, 2002–Patient Safety, www.cmwf.org/programs/pub_hightlight.asp?ID=1 & CastegoryID=3.

5.   Early studies concluded that patients experiencing care on a surgical ward experienced about a 1% incidence or mishap rate. Diagnostic errors, and delay in performing a procedure, were major contributors to the mishaps. More than half

the medical errors surveyed were errors of commission, including unnecessary or contraindicated surgery, defective execution of an indicated operation, and performance of an improper surgical procedure. The authors of the study concluded that " * * * in 31 instances, or 90 per cent of the errors of therapeutic commission, the mistakes were those of unnecessary, contraindicated, or technically defective surgical activity." Nathan P. Couch et al., The High Cost of Low–Frequency Events, 304 N.Eng.J.Med. 634, 635 (1981).

6. Errors in office-based surgery are a significant problem, as surgical procedures have migrated from hospitals to surgicenters and physician offices. One study of surgical procedures performed in doctors' offices and ambulatory surgery centers in Florida found that there was a 10–fold increased risk of adverse events and death in the office setting. See Hector Vila, et al., Comparative Outcomes Analysis of Procedures Performed in Physician Offices and Ambulatory Surgery Centers, 138 Arch.Surg. 991 (2003).

7. A sophisticated look at the practice of medicine, and how errors occur, is found in Atul Gawande, Complications: A Surgeon's Notes on An Imperfect Science 45–46 (2002). He writes:

> ... [C]ompassion and technology aren't necessarily incompatible; they can be mutually reinforcing. Which is to say that the machine, oddly enough, may be medicine's best friend. On the simplest level, nothing comes between patient and doctor like a mistake. And while errors will always dog us—even machines are not perfect—trust can only increase when mistakes are reduced. Moreover, as "systems" take on more and more of the technical work of medicine, individual physicians may be in a position to embrace the dimensions of care that mattered long before technology came—like talking to their patients.

The book gives good examples of how young physicians learn medicine, and how errors are dealt with in the hospital setting. See also Atul Gawande, Better: A Surgeon's Notes on Performance (2007), analyzing quality and safety issues using narratives.

C. STRATEGIES FOR REDUCING MEDICAL ERRORS

LUCIAN L. LEAPE, ERROR IN MEDICINE

272 JAMA 1851 (1994).

* * *

WHY IS THE ERROR RATE IN THE PRACTICE OF MEDICINE SO HIGH?

Physicians, nurses, and pharmacists are trained to be careful and to function at a high level of proficiency. Indeed, they probably are among the most careful professionals in our society. It is curious, therefore, that high error rates have not stimulated more concern and efforts at error prevention. One reason may be a lack of awareness of the severity of the problem. Hospital-acquired injuries are not reported in the newspapers like jumbo-jet crashes, for the simple reason that they occur one at a time in 5000 different locations across the country. Although error rates are substantial, serious injuries due to errors are not part of the everyday experience of physicians or nurses, but are perceived as isolated and unusual events—"outliers." Second, most errors do no harm. Either they are intercepted or the patient's defenses prevent injury. (Few children die from a single misdiagnosed or mistreated urinary infection, for example.)

But the most important reason physicians and nurses have not developed more effective methods of error prevention is that they have a great deal of difficulty in dealing with human error when it does occur. The reasons are to be found in the culture of medical practice.

Physicians are socialized in medical school and residency to strive for error-free practice. There is a powerful emphasis on perfection, both in diagnosis and treatment. In everyday hospital practice, the message is equally clear: mistakes are unacceptable. Physicians are expected to function without error, an expectation that physicians translate into the need to be infallible. One result is that physicians, not unlike test pilots, come to view an error as a failure of character—you weren't careful enough, you didn't try hard enough. This kind of thinking lies behind a common reaction by physicians: "How can there be an error without negligence?"

Cultivating a norm of high standards is, of course, highly desirable. It is the counterpart of another fundamental goal of medical education: developing the physician's sense of responsibility for the patient. If you are responsible for everything that happens to the patient, it follows that you are responsible for any errors that occur. While the logic may be sound, the conclusion is absurd, because physicians do not have the power to control all aspects of patient care. Nonetheless, the sense of duty to perform faultlessly is strongly internalized.

Role models in medical education reinforce the concept of infallibility. The young physician's teachers are largely specialists, experts in their fields, and authorities. Authorities are not supposed to err. It has been suggested that this need to be infallible creates a strong pressure to intellectual dishonesty, to cover up mistakes rather than to admit them. The organization of medical practice, particularly in the hospital, perpetuates these norms. Errors are rarely admitted or discussed among physicians in private practice. Physicians typically feel, not without reason, that admission of error will lead to censure or increased surveillance or, worse, that their colleagues will regard them as incompetent or careless. Far better to conceal a mistake or, if that is impossible, to try to shift the blame to another, even the patient.

Yet physicians are emotionally devastated by serious mistakes that harm or kill patients. Almost every physician who cares for patients has had that experience, usually more than once. The emotional impact is often profound, typically a mixture of fear, guilt, anger, embarrassment, and humiliation. However, as Christensen et al. note, physicians are typically isolated by their emotional responses; seldom is there a process to evaluate the circumstances of a mistake and to provide support and emotional healing for the fallible physician. Wu et al. found that only half of house officers discussed their most significant mistakes with attending physicians.

Thus, although the individual may learn from a mistake and change practice patterns accordingly, the adjustment often takes place in a vacuum. Lessons learned are shared privately, if at all, and external objective evaluation of what went wrong often does not occur. As Hilfiker points out, "We see the horror of our own mistakes, yet we are given no permission to deal with their enormous emotional impact.... The medical profession simply has no place for its mistakes."

Finally, the realities of the malpractice threat provide strong incentives against disclosure or investigation of mistakes. Even a minor error can place the physician's entire career in jeopardy if it results in a serious bad outcome. It is hardly surprising that a physician might hesitate to reveal an error to either the patient or hospital authorities or to expose a colleague to similar devastation for a single mistake.

The paradox is that although the standard of medical practice is perfection—error-free patient care—all physicians recognize that mistakes are inevitable. Most would like to examine their mistakes and learn from them. From an emotional standpoint, they need the support and understanding of their colleagues and patients when they make mistakes. Yet, they are denied both insight and support by misguided concepts of infallibility and by fear: fear of embarrassment by colleagues, fear of patient reaction, and fear of litigation. Although the notion of infallibility fails the reality test, the fears are well grounded.

The Medical Approach to Error Prevention

Efforts at error prevention in medicine have characteristically followed what might be called the perfectibility model: if physicians and nurses could be properly trained and motivated, then they would make no mistakes. The methods used to achieve this goal are training and punishment. Training is directed toward teaching people to do the right thing. In nursing, rigid adherence to protocols is emphasized. In medicine, the emphasis is less on rules and more on knowledge.

Punishment is through social opprobrium or peer disapproval. The professional cultures of medicine and nursing typically use blame to encourage proper performance. Errors are regarded as someone's fault, caused by a lack of sufficient attention or, worse, lack of caring enough to make sure you are correct. Punishment for egregious (negligent) errors is primarily (and capriciously) meted out through the malpractice tort litigation system.

Students of error and human performance reject this formulation. While the proximal error leading to an accident is, in fact, usually a 'human error,' the causes of that error are often well beyond the individual's control. All humans err frequently. Systems that rely on error-free performance are doomed to fail.

The medical approach to error prevention is also reactive. Errors are usually discovered only when there is an incident—an untoward effect or injury to the patient. Corrective measures are then directed toward preventing a recurrence of a similar error, often by attempting to prevent that individual from making a repeat error. Seldom are underlying causes explored.

For example, if a nurse gives a medication to the wrong patient, a typical response would be exhortation or training in double-checking the identity of both patient and drug before administration. Although it might be noted that the nurse was distracted because of an unusually large case load, it is unlikely that serious attention would be given to evaluating overall work assignments or to determining if large caseloads have contributed to other kinds of errors.

It is even less likely that questions would be raised about the wisdom of a system for dispensing medications in which safety is contingent on inspection by an individual at the end point of use. Reliance on inspection as a mechanism of quality control was discredited long ago in industry. A simple procedure, such as the use of bar coding like that used at supermarket checkout counters, would probably be more effective in this situation. More imaginative solutions could easily be found—if it were recognized that both systems and individuals contribute to the problem.

It seems clear, and it is the thesis of this article, that if physicians, nurses, pharmacists, and administrators are to succeed in reducing errors in hospital care, they will need to fundamentally change the way they think about errors and why they occur. Fortunately, a great deal has been learned about error prevention in other disciplines, information that is relevant to the hospital practice of medicine.

* * *

PREVENTION OF ACCIDENTS

* * *

The primary objective of system design for safety is to make it difficult for individuals to err. But it is also important to recognize that errors will inevitably occur and plan for their recovery. Ideally, the system will automatically correct errors when they occur. If that is impossible, mechanisms should be in place to at least detect errors in time for corrective action. Therefore, in addition to designing the work environment to minimize psychological precursors, designers should provide feedback through instruments that provide monitoring functions and build in buffers and redundancy. Buffers are design features that automatically correct for human or mechanical errors. Redundancy is duplication (sometimes triplication or quadruplication) of critical mechanisms and instruments, so that a failure does not result in loss of the function.

Another important system design feature is designing tasks to minimize errors. Norman has recommended a set of principles that have general applicability. Tasks should be simplified to minimize the load on the weakest aspects of cognition: short-term memory, planning, and problem solving. The power of constraints should be exploited. One way to do this is with "forcing functions," which make it impossible to act without meeting a precondition (such as the inability to release the parking gear of a car unless the brake pedal is depressed). Standardization of procedures, displays, and layouts reduces error by reinforcing the pattern recognition that humans do well. Finally, where possible, operations should be easily reversible or difficult to perform when they are not reversible.

Training must include, in addition to the usual emphasis on application of knowledge and following procedures, a consideration of safety issues. These issues include understanding the rationale for procedures as well as how errors can occur at various stages, their possible consequences, and instruction in methods for avoidance of errors. Finally, it must be acknowledged that injuries can result from behavioral problems that may be seen in impaired physicians or incompetent physicians despite well-designed systems; methods for identifying and correcting egregious behaviors are also needed.

THE AVIATION MODEL

The practice of hospital medicine has been compared, usually unfavorably, to the aviation industry, also a highly complicated and risky enterprise but one that seems far safer. Indeed, there seem to be many similarities. As Allnutt observed,

> Both pilots and doctors are carefully selected, highly trained professionals who are usually determined to maintain high standards, both externally and internally imposed, whilst performing difficult tasks in life-threatening environments. Both use high technology equipment and function as key members of a team of specialists . . . both exercise high level cognitive skills in a most complex domain about which much is known, but where much remains to be discovered.

While the comparison is apt, there are also important differences between aviation and medicine, not the least of which is a substantial measure of uncertainty due to the number and variety of disease states, as well as the unpredictability of the human organism. Nonetheless, there is much physicians and nurses could learn from aviation.

* * *

There are strong incentives for making flying safe. Pilots, of course, are highly motivated. Unlike physicians, their lives are on the line as well as those of their passengers. But, airlines and airplane manufacturers also have strong incentives to provide safe flight. Business decreases after a large crash, and if a certain model of aircraft crashes repeatedly, the manufacturer will be discredited. The lawsuits that inevitably follow a crash can harm both reputation and profitability.

Designing for safety has led to a number of unique characteristics of aviation that could, with suitable modification, prove useful in improving hospital safety.

First, in terms of system design, aircraft designers assume that errors and failures are inevitable and design systems to "absorb" them, building in multiple buffers, automation, and redundancy. * * *

Second, procedures are standardized to the maximum extent possible. Specific protocols must be followed for trip planning, operations, and maintenance. Pilots go through a checklist before each takeoff. Required maintenance is specified in detail and must be performed on a regular (by flight hours) basis.

Third, the training, examination, and certification process is highly developed and rigidly, as well as frequently, enforced. Airline pilots take proficiency examinations every 6 months. Much of the content of examinations is directly concerned with procedures to enhance safety.

Pilots function well within this rigorously controlled system, although not flawlessly. For example, one study of cockpit crews observed that human errors or instrument malfunctions occurred on the average of one every 4 minutes during an overseas flight. Each event was promptly recognized and corrected with no untoward effects. Pilots also willingly submit to an external authority, the air traffic controller, when within the constrained air and ground space at a busy airport.

Finally, safety in aviation has been institutionalized. * * *. The FAA recognized long ago that pilots seldom reported an error if it led to disciplinary action. Accordingly, in 1975 the FAA established a confidential reporting system for safety infractions, the Air Safety Reporting System (ASRS). If pilots, controllers, or others promptly report a dangerous situation, such as a near-miss midair collision, they will not be penalized. This program dramatically increased reporting, so that unsafe conditions at airports, communication problems, and traffic control inadequacies are now promptly communicated. Analysis of these reports and subsequent investigations appear as a regular feature in several pilots' magazines. The ASRS receives more than 5000 notifications each year.

THE MEDICAL MODEL

By contrast, accident prevention has not been a primary focus of the practice of hospital medicine. It is not that errors are ignored. Mortality and morbidity conferences, incident reports, risk management activities, and quality assurance committees abound. But, as noted previously, these activities focus on incidents and individuals. When errors are examined, a problem-solving approach is usually used: the cause of the error is identified and corrected. Root causes, the underlying systems failures, are rarely sought. System designers do not assume that errors and failures are inevitable and design systems to prevent or absorb them. There are, of course, exceptions. Implementation of unit dosing, for example, markedly reduced medication dosing errors by eliminating the need for the nurse to measure out each dose. * * *.

Second, standardization and task design vary widely. In the operating room, it has been refined to a high art. In patient care units, much more could be done, particularly to minimize reliance on short-term memory, one of the weakest aspects of cognition. On-time and correct delivery of medications, for example, is often contingent on a busy nurse remembering to do so, a nurse who is responsible for four or five patients at once and is repeatedly interrupted, a classic set up for a "loss-of-activation" error.

On the other hand, education and training in medicine and nursing far exceed that in aviation, both in breadth of content and in duration, and few professions compare with medicine in terms of the extent of continuing education. Although certification is essentially universal, including the recent introduction of periodic recertification, the idea of periodically testing performance has never been accepted. Thus, we place great emphasis on education and training, but shy away from demonstrating that it makes a difference.

Finally, unlike aviation, safety in medicine has never been institutionalized, in the sense of being a major focus of hospital medical activities. Investigation of accidents is often superficial, unless a malpractice action is likely; noninjurious error (a "near miss") is rarely examined at all. Incident reports are frequently perceived as punitive instruments. As a result, they are often not filed, and when they are, they almost invariably focus on the individual's misconduct.

One medical model is an exception and has proved quite successful in reducing accidents due to errors: anesthesia. Perhaps in part because the effects of serious anesthetic errors are potentially so dramatic—death or brain damage—and perhaps in part because the errors are frequently transparently clear and knowable to all, anesthesiologists have greatly emphasized safety. The success of these efforts has been dramatic. Whereas mortality from anesthesia was one in 10,000 to 20 000 just a decade or so ago, it is now estimated at less than one in 200,000. Anesthesiologists have led the medical profession in recognizing system factors as causes of errors, in designing fail-safe systems, and in training to avoid errors.

Systems Changes to Reduce Hospital Injuries

Can the lessons from cognitive psychology and human factors research that have been successful in accident prevention in aviation and other industries be applied to the practice of hospital medicine? There is every reason to think they could be. Hospitals, physicians, nurses, and pharmacists who wish to reduce errors could start by considering how cognition and error mechanisms apply to the practice of hospital medicine. Specifically, they can examine their care delivery systems in terms of the systems' ability to discover, prevent, and absorb errors and for the presence of psychological precursors.

Discovery of Errors

The first step in error prevention is to define the problem. Efficient, routine identification of errors needs to be part of hospital practice, as does routine investigation of all errors that cause injuries. The emphasis is on "routine." Only when errors are accepted as an inevitable, although manageable, part of everyday practice will it be possible for hospital personnel to shift from a punitive to a creative frame of mind that seeks out and identifies the underlying system failures.

Data collecting and investigatory activities are expensive, but so are the consequences of errors. Evidence from industry indicates that the savings from reduction of errors and accidents more than make up for the costs of data collection and investigation. * * *.

Prevention of Errors

Many health care delivery systems could be redesigned to significantly reduce the likelihood of error. Some obvious mechanisms that can be used are as follows:

Reduced Reliance on Memory.—Work should be designed to minimize the requirements for human functions that are known to be particularly fallible, such as short-term memory and vigilance (prolonged attention). * * * Checklists, protocols, and computerized decision aids could be used more widely. * * *.

Improved Information Access.—Creative ways need to be developed for making information more readily available: displaying it where it is needed, when it is needed, and in a form that permits easy access. Computerization of the medical record, for example, would greatly facilitate bedside display of patient information, including tests and medications.

Error Proofing.—Where possible, critical tasks should be structured so that errors cannot be made. The use of "forcing functions" is helpful. For example, if a computerized system is used for medication orders, it can be designed so that a physician cannot enter an order for a lethal overdose of a drug or prescribe a medication to which a patient is known to be allergic.

Standardization.—One of the most effective means of reducing error is standardizing processes wherever possible. The advantages, in efficiency as well as in error reduction, of standardizing drug doses and times of administration are obvious. Is it really acceptable to ask nurses to follow six different "K-scales" (directions for how much potassium to give according to patient serum potassium levels) solely to satisfy different physician prescribing patterns? Other candidates for standardization include information displays, methods for common practices (such as surgical dressings), and the geographic location of equipment and supplies in a patient care unit. There is something bizarre, and really quite inexcusable, about "code" situations in hospitals where house staff and other personnel responding to a cardiac arrest waste precious seconds searching for resuscitation equipment simply because it is kept in a different location on each patient care unit.

Training.—Instruction of physicians, nurses, and pharmacists in procedures or problem solving should include greater emphasis on possible errors and how to prevent them. * * *.

Absorption of Errors

Because it is impossible to prevent all error, buffers should be built into each system so that errors are absorbed before they can cause harm to patients. At minimum, systems should be designed so that errors can be identified in time to be intercepted. The drug delivery systems in most hospitals do this to some degree already. Nurses and pharmacists often identify errors in physician drug orders and prevent improper administration to the patient. As hospitals move to computerized records and ordering systems, more of these types of interceptions can be incorporated into the computer programs. * * *.

Psychological Precursors

Finally, explicit attention should be given to work schedules, division of responsibilities, task descriptions, and other details of working arrangements where improper managerial decisions can produce psychological precursors such as time pressures and fatigue that create an unsafe environment. While the influence of the stresses of everyday life on human behavior cannot be eliminated, stresses caused by a faulty work environment can be. Elimination of fear and the creation of a supportive working environment are other potent means of preventing errors.

INSTITUTIONALIZATION OF SAFETY

Although the idea of a national hospital safety board that would investigate every accident is neither practical nor necessary, at the hospital level such activities should occur. Existing hospital risk management activities could be broadened to include all potentially injurious errors and deepened to seek out underlying system failures. Providing immunity, as in the FAA ASRS system, might be a good first step. At the national level, the Joint Commission on Accreditation of Healthcare Organizations should be involved in discussions regarding the institutionalization of safety. Other specialty societies might well follow the lead of the anesthesiologists in developing safety standards and require their instruction to be part of residency training.

––––––––––

Leape's analysis became the seminal analysis of the need for a systems focus in reducing adverse patient events in health care institutions. It led to a new federal focus on patient safety, which was marked in 1999 by the first in a series of Institute of Medicine publications dealing with medical errors.

TO ERR IS HUMAN: BUILDING A SAFER HEALTH SYSTEM

Committee on Quality of Health Care In America Institute of Medicine, 1999.
www.nap.edu/readingroom

EXECUTIVE SUMMARY

* * *

When extrapolated to the over 33 6 million admissions to U.S. hospitals in 1997, the results of the study in Colorado and Utah imply that at least 44,000 Americans die each year as a result of medical errors. The results of the New York Study suggest the number may be as high as 98,000. Even when using the lower estimate, deaths due to medical errors exceed the number attributable to the 8th leading cause of death. More people die in a given year as result of medical errors than from motor vehicle accidents (43,458), breast cancer (42,297), or AIDS (16,516).

Total national costs (lost income, lost household production, disability and health care costs) of preventable adverse events (medical errors resulting in injury) are estimated to be between $17 billion and $29 billion, of which health care costs represent over one half.

In terms of lives lost, patient safety is as important an issue as worker safety. Every year, over 6,000 Americans die from workplace injuries. Medication errors alone, occurring either in or out of the hospital, are estimated to account for over 7,000 deaths annually.

Medication-related errors occur frequently in hospitals and although not all result in actual harm, those that do, are costly. One recent study conducted at two prestigious teaching hospitals, found that about two out of every 100 admissions experienced a preventable adverse drug event, resulting in average increased hospital costs of $4,700 per admission or about $2.8 million annually for a 700 bed teach hospital If these findings are generalizable, the increased hospital costs alone of preventable adverse drug events affecting inpatients are about $2 billion for the nation as a whole.

These figures offer only a very modest estimate of the magnitude of the problem since hospital patients represent only a small proportion of the total population at risk, and direct hospital costs are only a fraction of total costs. More care and increasingly complex care is provided in ambulatory settings.

Outpatient surgical centers, physical offices and clinics serve thousands of patients daily. Home care requires patients and their families to use complicated equipment and perform follow-up care. Retail pharmacies play a major role in filling prescriptions for patients and educating them about their use. Other institutional settings, such as nursing homes, provide a broad array of services to vulnerable populations. Although many of the available studies have focused on the hospital setting, medical errors present a problem in any setting, not just hospitals.

Errors are also costly in terms of opportunity costs. Dollars spent on having to repeat diagnostic tests or counteract adverse drug events are dollars unavailable for other purposes. Purchasers and patients pay for errors when insurance costs and copayments are inflated by services that would not have been necessary had proper care been provided. It is impossible for the nation to achieve the greatest value possible from the hundreds of millions of dollars spent on medical care if the care contains errors.

But not all the costs can be directly measured. Errors are also costly in terms of loss of trust in the system by patients and diminished satisfaction by both patients and health professionals. Patients who experienced a longer hospital stay or disability as a result of errors pay with physical and psychological discomfort. Health care professionals pay with loss of morale and frustration at not being able to provide the best care possible. Employers and society, in general, pay in terms of lost worker productivity, reduced school attendance by children, and lower levels of population health status.

Yet silence surrounds this issue. For the most part, consumers believe they are protected. Media coverage has been limited to reporting of anecdotal cases. Licensure and accreditation confer, in the eyes of the public, a "Good Housekeeping Seal of Approval." Yet, licensing and accreditation processes have focused only limited attention on the issue, and even these minimal efforts have confronted some resistance from health care organizations and providers. Providers also perceive the medical liability systems as a serious impediment to systematic efforts to uncover and learn from errors.

The decentralized and fragmented nature of the health care delivery system (some would say "nonsystem") also contributes to unsafe conditions for patients, and serves as an impediment to efforts to improve safety. Even within hospitals and large medical groups, there are rigidly-defined areas of specialization and influence. For example, when patients see multiple providers in different settings, none of whom have access to complete information, it is easier for something to go wrong than when care is better coordinated. At the same time, the provision of care to patients by a collection of loosely affiliated organizations and providers makes it difficult to implement improved clinical information systems capable of providing timely access to complete patient information. Unsafe care is one of the prices we pay for not having organized systems of care with clear lines of accountability.

* * *

In this report, safety is defined as freedom from accidental injury. This definition recognizes that this is the primary safety goal from the patient's perspective. Error is defined as the failure of a planned action to be completed as intended or the use of a wrong plan to achieve an aim. According to noted expert James Reason, errors depend on two kinds of failures: either the correct action does not proceed as intended (an error of execution) or the original intended action is not correct (an error of planning). Errors can happen in all stages in the process of care, from diagnosis, to treatment, to preventive care.

Not all errors result in harm. Errors that do result in injury are sometimes called preventable adverse events. An adverse event is an injury resulting from a medical intervention, or in other words, it is not due to the underlying condition of the patient. While all adverse events result from medical management, not all are preventable (i.e., not all are attributable to errors). For example, if a patient has surgery and dies from pneumonia he or she got postoperatively, it is an adverse event. If analysis of the case reveals that the patient got pneumonia because of poor hand washing or instrument cleaning techniques by staff, the adverse event was preventable (attributable to an error of execution). But the analysis may conclude that no error occurred and the patient would be presumed to have had a difficult surgery and recovery (not a preventable adverse event).

* * *

RECOMMENDATIONS

* * *

The recommendations contained in this report lay out a four-tiered approach:

- establishing a national focus to create leadership, research, tools and protocols to enhance the knowledge base about safety;

- identifying and learning from errors through immediate and strong mandatory reporting efforts, as well as the encouragement of voluntary efforts, both with the aim of making sure the system continues to be made safer for patients;

- raising standards and expectations for improvements in safety through the actions of oversight organizations, group purchasers, and professional groups; and

- creating safety systems inside health care organizations through the implementation of safe practices at the delivery level. This level is the ultimate target of all the recommendations.

Notes and Questions

1.   What are the implications of a focus on system errors? Does the physician as a virtuoso disappear from the model of the health care system as we move toward a model of organizations that deliver care, rather than physicians that treat patients? Are we better off acknowledging the inevitability of the changes that Leape, Jost, and Enthoven describe? See Lucian L. Leape and Donald M. Berwick, Five Years After To Err Is Human: What Have We Learned? 293 JAMA 2384 (2005). Larry I. Palmer, Patient Safety, Risk Reduction, and the Law, 36 Houston L. Rev. 1609 (1999).

2.   If we focus on system errors and system excellence, what happens to the traditional tort suit that starts with physician error? If errors are preventable by

attention to the overall organization, then physicians should no longer be viewed as at "fault" when a patient is injured. What about medical licensing? The merits of discipline for physician errors should be reconsidered, if most errors are due to failures of an organization to provide resources, support, or other structures. What about differential pay for physicians in different practice areas? As health care is integrated and outcomes used to evaluate the overall benefits to a population of patients, why should we pay differentials that reflect the older model of the physician as craftsperson or artist? Perhaps this new model suggests a salary approach to compensation, with bonuses at best for compliance with institutional norms. Or should pervasive federal regulation of safety be developed, along the lines of the regulation of workplace safety through OSHA?

3. Hospitals are complicated institutions, making error reduction more difficult than industrial enterprises. Hospitals have been described as one of the most complex organizations possible, integrating hierarchical bureaucracy and informal professional decision making under one roof. See Odin W. Anderson, Health Services as a Growth Enterprise in the United States Since 1875 309 (1990). The concepts of total quality management and continuous quality improvement are ideas borrowed from industry to foster quality in health care institutions. Other more traditional methods of quality control include the quality assurance systems that exist within hospitals and other health care institutions. Most hospitals employ two distinct but closely related systems to oversee the quality of care: risk management and quality assurance. The goals of an effective risk management program are to eliminate the causes of loss experienced by the hospital and its patients, employees, and visitors; lessen the operational and financial effects of unavoidable losses; and cover inevitable losses at the lowest cost. As such, risk management is concerned not only with the quality of patient care delivered by a hospital but also with the safety and security of the hospital's employees, visitors, and property. The risk manager also administers claims against the hospital if injuries occur and oversees the hospital's insurance programs, determining which risks the hospital ought to insure against and which it ought to retain through self-insurance or high deductibles. Finally, the risk manager must be concerned with public and patient relations, as dissatisfied patients are more likely to sue for medical errors.

4. The incident report has traditionally been the most important tool of the risk manager. Hospitals require incident reports on occurrences not consistent with routine patient care or hospital operation that have resulted or could have resulted in hospital liability or patient dissatisfaction. Examples include sudden deaths, falls, drug errors or reactions, injuries due to faulty equipment, threats of legal action, and unexplained requests from attorneys for medical records. The filing of incident reports (usually prepared by nurses) is the responsibility of department heads or supervisors. Incident reports are directed to the hospital risk manager, who investigates them as necessary. The risk manager also informs appropriate administrative and medical staff about the incident. By compiling data from incident reports, the risk manager can identify problem areas within the hospital and thus help prevent errors and injuries. Incident reports also assist in claims management, permitting the hospital to avoid costly lawsuits by quickly coming to terms with injured patients where liability seems clear and facilitating early coordination with an attorney to plan a defense where litigation seems unavoidable. Some malpractice insurance contracts include reservation of rights clauses, which permit the insurer to refuse to pay claims based on unreported incidents, underscoring the importance of incident reports.

5.   Hospital quality assurance programs are directly concerned with assessing and improving patient care. Quality assurance focuses more narrowly on patient care than does risk management. It is broader than risk management, however, in that it considers a wide range of quality concerns, not just discrete mishaps. Incident reports play a major role in quality assurance, as they permit the hospital to identify serious quality deficiencies. The most significant tools of hospital quality assurance, however, are the hospital committees that oversee the quality of various hospital functions. These committees carry out functions mandated by Joint Commission accreditation standards, and are in some states required by state law or regulation. See West's Ann.Cal.Admin.Code tit. 22, § 70703(e); N.Y.—McKinney's Pub.Health Law § 2805–j. Common hospital committees include a tissue committee, which oversees the quality and necessity of surgery; an infections committee, which evaluates patients' infections and oversees the disposal of infectious material and the use of antibiotics; a pharmacy and therapeutics committee, which monitors the use and handling of drugs; a medical records committee, which assures the quality and completeness of medical records; a utilization review committee, which assures that patients are not admitted inappropriately or hospitalized too long; and medical audit committees, which review the quality of care provided in the hospital as a whole or in certain departments. Some hospitals also have an overall quality control committee, which coordinates quality assurance efforts throughout the hospital. Two other very important committees are the executive and credentials committees. The former serves as the cabinet of the medical staff, and in this capacity oversees all efforts of the medical staff to ensure quality. The credentials committee passes on applications for medical staff appointments and reappointments, and establishes and reviews physician clinical privileges; i.e., it determines which doctors can practice in the hospital and what procedures they may perform. As such, it has a vital role in assuring the quality of care provided by the hospital.

Some committees, such as the credentials or executive committee, are medical staff committees; i.e., they are composed of and answerable to physicians who practice in the hospital. Others, such as the quality assurance or infections control committees, are likely to be hospital committees, answerable to the hospital administration and including other professionals besides physicians. In many hospitals, committees play an active role in assuring the quality of care; in others, they exist primarily to meet accreditation requirements and do little.

6.   Risk management is outcome oriented—it operates primarily by reacting to bad outcomes. Quality assurance is more process oriented. Some quality assurance activities involve concurrent review of the care process, such as the proctoring of doctors with probationary staff privileges. Quality assurance may also include retrospective review of care, another form of process review. Risk management is a managerial function, while quality assurance is predominantly a clinical function.

7.   Government regulation concerned with the quality of medical services and patient safety takes several forms, including market enhancing efforts (such as collection and dissemination of quality information) and command-and-control efforts (through which the government sets and enforces quality standards). See discussion in Chapter 3. Private efforts such as internal quality assurance efforts by health care organizations and private accreditation, also play a significant role.

Problem: Why Operate?

Bonnie Bowser, eighty-two years old, fell and severely injured her elbow. She was examined at the Emergency Department of the Mercy Regional Health

System and diagnosed with a fractured olecranon process, and referred to an orthopedic surgeon. The surgeon who examined Mrs. Bowser scheduled her for corrective surgery the next day. He noted in his examination that she had a past medical history of hypertension, diabetes mellitus, two myocardial infarctions with quadruple bypass surgery, and a cerebrovascular accident affecting her left side. She was taking several medications including Lasix (a diuretic), Vasotec (for treatment of hypertension and symptomatic congestive heart failure), Klotrix (potassium supplement), and Glyburide (for the treatment of hyperglycemia related to diabetes). He noted that she smoked an average of one pack of cigarettes per day; that she had abnormal chest x-rays, suggesting congestive heart failure; an EKG that indicated ischemic heart disease; and signs of edema, indicating congestive heart failure. She was a high risk candidate for any kind of surgery. After the anesthesia was administered, she deteriorated rapidly, had cardiopulmonary failure and stroke, and died a few days later from complications of the stroke. The anesthesia was the cause of her death, as she was severely "medically compromised" and an elbow operation did not justify the obvious risks. Bonnie had consented to the operation. Her health insurance paid for the procedure. The hospital allowed the operation to proceed.

What do you propose to reduce this kind of risk to patients, as Vice–President and General Counsel of the System?

What system-wide rules will you propose to avoid a repetition of such cases, as the head of your state's Department of Health?

As a congressman from your state, what legislation might you propose?

D.   REGULATORY RESPONSES TO MEDICAL RISKS

Regulation of medical errors or adverse events is risk regulation, aimed at improving patient safety when encountering drugs, hospital care, or other forms of medical treatments. The menu of patient safety approaches has rapidly increased since the IOM Report in 1999. The general strategies include legislative initiatives to force disclosure of hospital adverse events and "near misses" to patients along with an apology; publication of performance data about relative risks; "Pay For Performance" initiatives from corporate groups that have spread to Medicare payment; and legal tools ranging from warranties of performance by some providers to patients to improvements in tort liability rules of disclosure of physician performance. The field of Patient Safety is rapidly growing as a subspecialty within health law as a result of this burst of regulatory activity. See generally Barry Furrow, Regulating Patient Safety: Toward a Federal Model of Medical Error Reduction, 12 Widener L. Rev. 1 (2005).

1.   *Error Tracking and System Improvements*

The Institute of Medicine reports, beginning with **To Err Is Human**, focused attention on medical systems and the level of errors they produced. Hospitals and other providers were asked to respond by developing error tracking systems and strategies for improvement including disclosure of both errors and so-called "near misses", events that could have resulted in patient injury but were detected in time. This is not a new idea; as early as 1858 Florence Nightingale developed the use of statistical methodology to show the effects of unsanitary conditions in military field hospitals. Her approach laid the groundwork for standard statistical approaches for hospitals. Florence

Nightingale, Notes on Matters affecting the Health, Efficiency and Hospital Administration of the British Army (1858). See also John Maindonald and Alice M. Richardson, This Passionate Study: A Dialogue with Florence Nightingale, 12 J. Stat. Ed. (2004), www.amstat.org/publications/jse/v12n1/maindonald.html.

The idea of systematically tracking errors in hospitals is also not new. The first systematic approach was developed by Dr. Ernest Codman, a Boston doctor who wanted hospitals and doctors to track their practices and evaluate outcomes of their patients, an ideal he developed around 1920.

To Codman, patient harm due to infections or unnecessary or inappropriate operations was a hospital "waste product". Such performance measurement was a clear threat to physicians, and when the American College of Surgeons (ACS) developed its program of hospital standardization after World War I, the analysis of patient outcomes and reporting of preventible errors was omitted—and these were Codman's most central ideas for error reduction. His work did however lay the foundation for the Joint Commission, which has slowly moved toward a more outcome-based accreditation system. See Virgina A. Sharpe and Alan I. Feden, Medical Harm: Historical, Conceptual, and Ethical Dimensions of Iatrogenic Illness 31 (1998).

Reporting errors or adverse events is essential to system approaches, but it has been a concern for health care providers, who are afraid that disclosure of an error will come to plaintiff lawyers' attention. Voluntary reporting of mistakes has been argued to be the preferable approach to uncovering errors and correcting them. States that have mandatory reporting requirements for errors have found that underreporting is too often the norm. But the fact that underreporting occurs does not mean that performance cannot be improved. The reasons for such poor performance are several. Mandatory systems lack support from physicians, who are worried about liability, damage to reputation, and the hassle factor of any reporting system. Brian Liang, Promoting Patient Safety Through Reducing Medical Error, 22 J.L.Med & Ethics 564 (2002); J. Rosenthal et al., Current State Programs Addressing Medical Errors: An Analysis of Mandatory Reporting and Other Initiatives (2001). Mandatory reporting is resisted by providers, even though it was recommended by the IOM report. A movement toward mandatory reporting models is observable, however. The Joint Commission Sentinel Events policy, the new CMS rules on hospital error, and the new Pennsylvania statute all require disclosure of errors.

a. Sentinel Events and the Joint Commission

The Joint Commission (formerly the Joint Commission on Accreditation of Healthcare Organizations) is a private accreditor, granted authority by federal and state governments to accredit hospitals. See Chapter 3, Section III *infra*. The Joint Commission Sentinel Event Policy has adopted the view of medical errors of the Institute of Medicine report **To Err is Human**. It requires reporting on two levels: first to Joint Commission of serious events, and second to patients.

A sentinel event is defined as "an unexpected occurrence involving death or severe physical or psychological injury, or the risk thereof," including unanticipated death or major loss of functioning unrelated to the patient's condition; patient suicide; wrong-side surgery; infant abduction/discharge to the wrong family; rape; and hemolytic transfusion reactions. Joint Commission, "Sentinel Event Policy and Procedures", online at www.Joint Commission.org.

Hospitals must report serious events to the Joint Commission, and if they do not and Joint Commission learns of the events from a third party, the hospital must conduct an analysis of the root cause or risk loss of accreditation. Loss of accreditation is rarely exercised, however. Sentinel Event Alert, Joint Commission on Accreditation of Healthcare Organizations, 2002, www.JointCommission.org/about+us/news+letters/sentinel+event+alert/index.htm.

The Joint Commission disclosure standard also requires that "[p]atients, and when appropriate, their families, are informed about the outcomes of care, including unanticipated outcomes." Joint Commission on Accreditation of Healthcare Organizations, Revisions to Joint Commission Standards in Support of Patient Safety and Medical/Health Care Error Reduction, at www.Joint Commission.org/standard/fr_ptsafety.html (July 1, 2001)(Joint Commission Revisions) at RI.1.2.2

The intent statement provides: "The responsible licensed independent practitioner or his or her designee clearly explains the outcomes of any treatments or procedures to the patient and, when appropriate, the family, whenever those outcomes differ significantly from the anticipated outcomes". Id.

Notes and Questions

1. The Joint Commission is a private accreditation organization, and its primary weapon for hospital improvement is the threat that accreditation will be revoked, or the hospital placed on the "Accreditation Watch List". Given the infrequency of revocation of hospital accreditation, how does the Joint Commission have a significant effect on hospital behavior?

2. Does the Joint Commission standard suffer from any infirmities? What does "significantly" mean? Is it self-defining? How might hospitals interpret it to reduce their disclosure obligations? Joint Commission indicates that they are the same as "sentinel events" or "reviewable sentinel events". A "sentinel event" is defined in Joint Commission standards as: ". . . an unexpected occurrence involving death or serious physical or psychological injury, or the risk thereof. Serious injury specifically includes loss of limb or function. The phrase 'or the risk thereof' includes any process variation for which a recurrence would carry a significant chance of a serious adverse outcome." Joint Commission on Accreditation of Healthcare Organizations, Hospital Accreditation Standards 53 (2001) (Joint Commission Standards).

3. Where does the disclosure obligation repose? The intent statement specifies that "the responsible licensed independent practitioner or his or her designee" must clearly explain "the outcomes of any treatments or procedures." This practitioner is someone with clinical privileges, typically the patient's attending physician. Since the attending physician typically has the informed consent responsibility, he or she is the logical person to conduct such a conversation. But physicians are not subject to Joint Commission requirements. Are they therefore likely to resist such disclosures out of fear of liability, stigma, loss of hospital credentials, or other motivations? See, e.g. Nancy LeGros & Jason D. Pinkall, The

New Joint Commission Patient Safety Standards and the Disclosure of Unanticipated Outcomes, 35 J. Health L. 189, 205 (2002). See generally Timothy S. Jost, Medicare and the Joint Commission on Accreditation of Healthcare Organizations: A Healthy Relationship? 57 Law & Contemp. Probs. 15 (1994); Eleanor Kinney, Private Accreditation as a Substitute for Direct Government Regulation in Public Health Insurance Programs: When Is It Appropriate?, 57 Law & Contemp. Probs. 47, 52–55 (1994); Douglas C. Michael, Federal Agency Use of Audited Self–Regulation as a Regulatory Technique, 47 Admin. L. Rev. 171, 218–22 (1995); Barry R. Furrow, Regulating the Managed Care Revolution: Private Accreditation and A New System Ethos, 43 Vill. L. Rev. 361 (1998).

b. *"Never" Events*

ELIMINATING SERIOUS, PREVENTABLE, AND COSTLY MEDICAL ERRORS—NEVER EVENTS

CMS Office of Public Affairs.
May 18, 2006.

OVERVIEW:

As part of its ongoing effort to pay for better care, not just more services and higher costs, the Centers for Medicare & Medicaid Services (CMS) today announced that it is investigating ways that Medicare can help to reduce or eliminate the occurrence of "never events"–serious and costly errors in the provision of health care services that should never happen. "Never events," like surgery on the wrong body part or mismatched blood transfusion, cause serious injury or death to beneficiaries, and result in increased costs to the Medicare program to treat the consequences of the error.

BACKGROUND:

According to the National Quality Forum (NQF), "never events" are errors in medical care that are clearly identifiable, preventable, and serious in their consequences for patients, and that indicate a real problem in the safety and credibility of a health care facility. The criteria for "never events" are listed in Appendix 1. Examples of "never events" include surgery on the wrong body part; foreign body left in a patient after surgery; mismatched blood transfusion; major medication error; severe "pressure ulcer" acquired in the hospital; and preventable post-operative deaths. * * *

* * *

Some states have enacted legislation requiring reporting of incidents on the NQF list. For example, in 2003, the Minnesota legislature, with strong support from the state hospital association, was the first to pass a statute requiring mandatory reporting of "never events". The Minnesota law requires hospitals to report the NQF's 27 "never events" to the Minnesota Hospital Association's web-based Patient Safety Registry. The law requires hospitals to investigate each event, report its underlying cause, and take corrective action to prevent similar events. In addition, the Minnesota Department of Health publishes an annual report and provides a forum for hospitals to share reported information across the state and to learn from one another.

During the first year of Minnesota 's mandatory reporting program, 30 hospitals reported 99 events that resulted in 20 deaths and four serious disabilities. In the second year, 47 hospitals reported 106 events that resulted in 12 deaths and nine serious injuries. These included 53 surgical events, and 39 patient care management events. * * *

In 2004, New Jersey enacted a law requiring hospitals to report serious, preventable adverse events to the state and to patients' families, and Connecticut adopted a mix of 36 NQF and state-specific reportable events for hospitals and outpatient surgical facilities. An Illinois law passed in 2005 will require hospitals and ambulatory surgery centers to report 24 "never events" beginning in 2008. Several other states have considered or are currently considering never event reporting laws.

* * *

NEXT STEPS:

From its beginning, the Medicare program has generally paid for services under fee-for-service payment systems, without regard to quality, outcomes, or overall costs of care. In the past several years, CMS has been working with provider groups to identify quality standards that can be a basis for public reporting and payment. This includes the efforts of the Hospital Quality Alliance, which has developed an expanding set of quality measures. As a result of the Medicare Modernization Act and the Deficit Reduction Act, hospitals that publicly report these quality measures receive higher Medicare payment updates. In addition, CMS has launched a number of demonstrations aimed at improving quality of care, including by tying payment to quality. These include the Physician Group Practice Demonstration, the Premier Hospital Quality Incentive Demonstration, the Health Care Quality Demonstration, and the Care Management Performance Demonstration. As the results of these demonstrations become available, CMS expects to work with Congress on legislation that would support adjusting payments based on quality and efficiency of care.

Clearly, paying for "never events" is not consistent with the goals of these Medicare payment reforms. Reducing or eliminating payments for "never events" means more resources can be directed toward preventing these events rather than paying more when they occur. The Deficit Reduction Act represents a first step in this direction, allowing CMS, beginning in FY 2008, to begin to adjust payments for hospital-acquired infections. CMS is interested in working with our partners and Congress to build on this initial step to more broadly address the persistence of "never events."

In particular, CMS is reviewing its administrative authority to reduce payments for "never events," and to provide more reliable information to the public about when they occur. CMS will also work with Congress on further legislative steps to reduce or eliminate these payments. CMS intends to partner with hospitals and other healthcare organizations in these efforts.

Notes and Questions

1. What regulatory weapon does CMS threaten for failures of hospitals to comply with their new rule? If you represent a hospital, what will you advise hospitals to do to achieve compliance and retain their Medicare status?

2. This CMS position on "never events" and payment is a significant step toward "Pay for Performance". Tying Medicare payments to quality is a signifi-

cant incentive for providers to reduce the levels of adverse events, but the CMS description of demonstration projects still suggests it is moving very slowly as it decides how to calibrate payment to quality.

CMS, like HFCA before it, has traditionally viewed itself as a funding agency, not a regulatory one. As Michael Astrue has described CMS and its historical roots, it is a reluctant regulator: "... HCFA [now CMS] has attempted to minimize its role as regulator through liberal use of private contractors and private accrediting agencies." Michael J. Astrue, Health Care Reform and the Constitutional Limits on Private Accreditation as an Alternative to Direct Government Regulation, 57 Law & Contemp. Prob. 75 (1994). Perhaps however this use of payment/quality linkages fits within the regulatory culture and history of CMS.

3. CMS has announced that it is implementing a final rule that will deny payment where hospital "never events" occur. The rule implements a provision of the Deficit Reduction Act of 2005 (DRA) that takes the first steps toward preventing Medicare from giving hospitals higher payment for the additional costs of treating a patient who acquires a condition (including an infection) during a hospital stay. Already the feature of many state health care programs, the DRA requires hospitals to begin reporting secondary diagnoses that are present on the admission of patients, beginning with discharges on or after October 1, 2007. Beginning in FY 2009, cases with these conditions will not be paid at a higher rate unless they are present on admission. The rule identifies eight conditions, including three serious preventable events (sometimes called "never events") that meet the statutory criteria.

2. *Disclosure of Errors to Patients*

The "never events" development in twenty odd states is a major step, forcing providers to disclose adverse outcomes on the list to the state department responsible, with the goal of improving their operations. It is more than just information disclosure. It allows for systematic recording and tracking of errors, for purpose of analysis of patterns of adverse events, feedback to hospitals, and in some states, information for consumers as to th e relative performance of hospitals and other providers.

Adverse event reporting is often coupled with disclosure of classes of bad outcomes to patients and their families. This disclosure idea developed as the result of a program begun by a Veterans Administration hospital, and has been adopted by the VA system. It served as the model for Pennsylvania's legislation creating the Patient Safety Authority.

DISCLOSURE OF ADVERSE EVENTS TO PATIENTS
VHA DIRECTIVE 2005–049.
October 27, 2005.

1. WHAT ADVERSE EVENTS WARRANT DISCLOSURE?

a. Patients and/or their representatives must be informed of the probable or definite occurrence of any adverse event that has resulted in, or is expected to result in, harm to the patient, including the following:

(1) Adverse events that have had or are expected to have a clinical effect on the patient that is perceptible to either the patient or the health care team. For example, if a patient is mistakenly given a dose of furosemide (a diuretic that dramatically increases urine output), disclosure is required because a perceptible effect is expected to occur.

(2) Adverse events that necessitate a change in the patient's care. For example, a medication error that necessitates close observation, extra blood tests, extra hospital days, or follow-up visits that would otherwise not be required, or a surgical procedure that necessitates further (corrective) surgery.

(3) Adverse events with a known risk of serious future health consequences, even if the likelihood of that risk is extremely small. For example, accidental exposure of a patient to a toxin associated with a rare, but recognized serious long-term effect (e.g., HIV infection or increased incidence of cancer).

(4) Adverse events that require providing a treatment or procedure without the patient's consent. For example, if an adverse event occurs while a patient is under anesthesia, necessitating a deviation from the procedure the patient expected, the adverse event needs to be disclosed. Patients have a fundamental right to be informed about what is done to them and why.

* * *

2. WHEN SHOULD DISCLOSURE OF AN ADVERSE EVENT OCCUR?

Optimal timing of disclosure of adverse events varies with the specific circumstances of the case. * * *

3. HOW SHOULD ADVERSE EVENTS BE COMMUNICATED?

a. Disclosure of an adverse event needs to occur in an appropriate setting and be done face-to-face. The location needs to be a quiet, private place and adequate time needs to be set aside, with no interruptions.

b. In general, communication about the adverse event needs to be done through a clinical disclosure of adverse events, when one or more members of the clinical team provides preliminary factual information to the extent it is known, expresses concern for the patient's welfare, and reassures the patient or representative that steps are being taken to investigate the situation, remedy any injury, and prevent further harm. Social workers, chaplains, patient advocate, or other staff may be present to help the patient or representative cope with the news and to offer support, if needed. The patient's treating practitioner is responsible for determining who shall communicate this information.

c. Sometimes, given the nature, likelihood, and severity of injury, and the degree of risk for legal liability, there will be a need for institutional disclosure of adverse events either instead of, or in addition to, clinical disclosure. Institutional disclosure includes the following elements:

(1) Institutional Leaders (e.g., the Chief of Staff or facility Director) invite the patient or personal representative to meet for an Institutional Disclosure of Adverse Event Conference. Institutional leaders may only invite the representative if he or she is involved in the patient's care (and the patient does not object), or the representative is the personal representative as outlined in VHA Handbook 1605.1. NOTE: The facility Risk Manager, treating physician, or other VHA personnel deemed appropri-

ate, may be included in this conference at the discretion of facility leadership.

(2) Institutional disclosure of adverse events should not take place until organizational leaders, including, as appropriate, the facility Director, Chief of Staff, and members of the treatment team, have conferred with Regional Counsel and addressed what is to be communicated, by whom and how.

(3) Any request by a patient or personal representative to bring an attorney must be honored, but may influence whether providers will participate.

(4) The Risk Manager or organizational leaders need to engage in ongoing communication with the patient or personal representative to keep them apprised, as appropriate, of information that emerges from the investigation of the facts.

* * *

(5) Institutional disclosure of adverse events must include:

(a) An apology including a complete explanation of the facts.

(b) An outline of treatment options.

(c) Arrangements for a second opinion, additional monitoring, expediting clinical consultations, bereavement support, or whatever might be appropriate depending on the adverse event.

(d) Notification that the patient or representative has the option of obtaining outside legal advice for further guidance.

(e) After complete investigation of the facts, the patient or representative is to be given information about compensation under Title 38 United States Code (U.S.C) Section 1151 and the Federal Tort Claims Act claims processes, including information about procedures available to request compensation and where and how to obtain assistance in filing forms. In the event that the investigation is not complete, information about compensation may be given based on the current understanding of the facts or information may be deferred until the investigation is competed. There should be no assurance that compensation will be granted, as the adverse event may not give rise to and meet legal criteria for compensation under 38 U.S.C. Section 1151 and the Federal Tort Claims Act.

(f) If a patient or personal representative asks whether an investigation will be conducted and whether the patient or representative will be told of the results of an investigation, the patient or representative is to be informed that only the results of an administrative board of investigation (AIB) may be released.

Notes and Questions

1. Pennsylvania created a Patient Safety Authority that mandates reports to the Authority by hospitals of all "serious events". Fines may be levied for failures to report, and that statute provides for whistleblower protections among other things.

Pennsylvania also adopted a patient notification requirement:

A patient must be notified if he or she has been affected by a serious event. The statute provides:

308(b) Duty to notify patient.—A medical facility through an appropriate designee shall provide written notification to a patient affected by a serious event or, with the consent of the patient, to an available family member or designee, within seven days of the occurrence or discovery of a serious event. If the patient is unable to give consent, the notification shall be given to an adult member of the immediate family. If an adult member of the immediate family cannot be identified or located, notification shall be given to the closest adult family member. For unemancipated patients who are under 18 years of age, the parent or guardian shall be notified in accordance with this subsection. The notification requirements of this subsection shall not be subject to the provisions of section 311(a). Notification under this subsection shall not constitute an acknowledgment or admission of liability.

2.   The patient notification requirements of the Joint Commission and the Veterans Administration raise the risk that patients will become aware of errors for the first time. Will the incidence of malpractice claims increase? Or will disclosure and an apology reduce litigation? The patient disclosure requirements of Joint Commission and the Pennsylvania statute have the potential to not only reduce medical errors but also the frequency of malpractice litigation, if done well. There is evidence that disclosure and apology is desired by patients, and it may even serve to reduce patient inclinations to sue for malpractice when they have experience a bad outcome. See Thomas H. Gallagher et al., Patients' and Physicians' Attitudes Regarding the Disclosure of Medical Errors, 289 J.A.M.A. 1001 (2003) (finding that patients are troubled by the unwillingness of physicians to discuss the cause and future prevention of medical errors).

The Sorry Works! Coalition has been heavily involved in promoting the benefits of an apology approach, www.sorryworks!.com.

3.   The literature on apology is growing rapidly. Jonathan R. Cohen, Advising Clients to Apologize, 72 S. Cal L. Rev. 1004 (1999); Douglas N. Frenkel and Carol B. Liebman, Words That Heal, 140 Ann. Inern. Med. 482 (2004); Peter Geier, Emerging Med–Mal Strategy: "I'm Sorry", The National Law Journal, No. 96, p. 1 (July 17, 2006); G.B. Hickson et al., Factors That Prompted Families to File Medical Malpractice Claims Following Perinatal Injuries, 267 JAMA 1359 (1992); Bryan A. Liang & LiLan Ren, Medical Liability Insurance and Damage Caps: Getting Beyond Band Aids to Substantive Systems Treatment to Improve Quality and Safety in Healthcare, 30 Am. J. L. & Med. 501 (2004); Carol B. Liebman & Chris Stern Hyman, Medical Error Disclosure, Mediation Skills, and Malpractice Litigation (July 2005); K.M. Mazor, et al., Communicating with Patients about Medical Errors: A Review of the Literature, 164 Arch. Intern. Med. 1690 (2003); K. M. Mazor, et al., Health Plan Members' Views about Disclosure of Medical Errors, 140 Ann. Intern. Med. 409 (2004); Erin Ann O'Hara, Apology and Thick Trust: What Spouse Abusers and Negligent Doctors Might Have in Common, 79 Chi.-Kent L. Rev. 1055 (2004); Lee Taft, Apology Subverted: The Commodification of Apology, 109 Yale L.J. 1135 (2000); Lee Taft, Apology and Medical Mistake: Opportunity or Foil?, 14 Ann. Health L. 55 (2005).

Problem: Disclosing Errors

You represent St. Jude Hospital in Pennsylvania, which has implemented a new error management policy in light of the new Joint Commission, CMS, and Pennsylvania rules. How should the hospital handle the following medical misadventures?

1.   Joseph Banes entered the hospital for surgery on a cervical disk to relieve his chronic back pain. During the surgery a nerve was severed at the base of his

spine, causing severe pain and limitations in mobility in his left leg and foot. The injury is likely to be permanent. This is a rare risk of lower back surgery generally, but in this case the surgeon made a slip of the scalpel and cut the nerve. Your investigation reveals that the surgeon and the nurses in the operating room were aware of the surgical error. What steps should the hospital take to comply with Joint Commission sentinel event requirements? The CMS rules? The Pennsylvania MCare law requirements?

2. Sally Thomas, a 45 year old woman with a history of abdominal pain, was found lying on the floor of her home in severe pain. She was taken to the emergency room of St Jude, admitted for diagnosis, and tested to determine the source of the problem. After several days of diagnostic uncertainty, the physicians considered an exploratory laparoscopy suspecting an abnormality in her small intestine. Before surgery an anesthesiologist inserted a central venous catheter (central line) in Sally. She then underwent surgery, and her right fallopian tube and ovary were removed because of infection. She was taken to the Post Anesthesia Care Unit (PACU) with the central line still in place. A surgical resident who had assisted during the surgery wrote out post-operative orders. These orders included a portable chest x-ray to be taken in the PACU. The purpose of the chest x-ray was to check the placement of the central line. The x-ray was completed by approximately 1:45 p m. Sally continued to have pain, and was given pain medications. Finally the x-ray, taken four hours earlier, was checked and it revealed that the central line was inserted incorrectly, and the tip went into the pericardial sac of Thomas' heart. The doctors successfully resuscitated her. She recovered after a week in the hospital, narrowly escaping a cardiac tamponade, in which her heart would have been crushed by fluid pressure, leading to cardiac arrest. What steps do you advise the hospital to take?

3. Wilhelm Gross entered St. Jude to have surgery on his left leg to repair an artery. The surgical team prepped Wilhelm, preparing his right leg for the procedure. Minutes before the surgeon was to make the first incision, nurse Jost noticed on the chart that the procedure was to be done on his left leg. The team then prepped the correct leg and the operation went smoothly. What reporting obligations does the hospital have?

3. *Absorption of Losses: "Pay for Performance"*

THOMAS H. LEE, PAY FOR PERFORMANCE, VERSION 2.0

357 NEJM 531 (2007).

Geisinger, an integrated healthcare delivery system in northeastern Pennsylvania, has begun a new "warranty" program. It promises that 40 key processes will be completed for every patient who undergoes elective CABG—even though several of the "benchmarks" are to be reached before or after hospitalization. And although Geisinger cannot guarantee good clinical outcomes, it charges a standard flat rate that covers care for related complications during the 90 days after surgery.

* * *

For patients who have surgery as part of this program, Geisinger will not charge for related care within 90 days. For example, there are no additional charges for treatment of sternal wound infections or heart failure due to a perioperative infarction, as long as patients receive their care at a Geisinger facility. On the other hand, the usual charges would apply to care for preexisting heart failure or unrelated problems, such as diverticulitis or a hip fracture.

* * *

The real question for Geisinger and for the rest of the health care system is whether this case rate approach might emerge as a new form of pay for performance. Many current models of pay for performance (involving, for example, quality-of-care measures for patients with diabetes) focus on populations of patients whose care is managed by primary care physicians. For most specialists and hospitals, existing incentive systems put only a modest amount of revenue at stake, and as would be expected, resulting changes in care have been modest as well. But the drumbeat is growing stronger for health care financing models that go beyond rewarding volume alone. Case rates and critical pathways are not foreign concepts at many hospitals—they just have not been married so explicitly before. Geisinger is actively working to extend this approach to other surgical procedures, and diseases treated on an outpatient basis, such as diabetes and hypertension, could be next. A reasonable guess is that models that work for organized delivery systems such as Geisinger will spread over time to the rest of U.S. health care. So this experiment bears watching.

Notes and Questions

1.   Treatment costs induced by errors and adverse events are usually either covered by insurance or absorbed by patients, families, insurers, employers and state and private disability and income-support programs. This means that the adverse outcomes are externalized to other payors and not internalized by providers best able to reduce these hazards or prevent them. The added costs of a failed intervention caused either by error or by a failure to use an effective approach include added acute care costs, lost income, lost household production, and extra pain. As Leape and Berwick note,

> . . . [P]ayers often subsidize unsafe care quite well, although unknowingly. In most industries, defects cost money and generate warranty claims. In health care, perversely, under most forms of payment, health care professionals receive a premium for a defective product; physicians and hospitals can bill for the additional services that are needed when patients are injured by their mistakes.

Lucian L. Leape and Donald M. Berwick, Five Years After To Err Is Human: What Have We Learned? 293 JAMA 2384, 2388 (2005). Only tort suits have traditionally imposed these excess costs on the hospital or provider that was responsible for the patient's injury. Haavi Morreim, Holding Health Care Accountable: Law and the New Medical Marketplace (Oxford University Press 2001).

2.   It costs money to generate and mine data, produce useful feedback and finally implement new quality measures. Computer software is needed, new personnel must be hired or retrained, and an institution would like to be able to recapture those costs from its payers or through greater efficiencies that increase its margins. But perverse incentives dominate, and poor care is reimbursed at the same level as high quality care. Use of market power through purchasing concentrations to increase consumer and purchaser knowledge about providers has been one attempted solution to poor quality care. The Leapfrog Group is the most visible current example of this manifestation. Leapfrog members are encouraged to refer patients to hospitals with the best survival odds, that staff intensive care

units with doctors having credentials in critical care, and use error prevention software to prescribe medications. Leapfrog Initiatives to Drive Great Leaps in Patient Safety (2002c). Www.leapfroggroup.org/safety1.htm.

3.   CMS launched a national Quality Initiative in 2002, starting with the Nursing Home Quality Initiative, adding the Home Health Quality Initiative and Hospital Quality Initiative in 2003. The Hospital Quality Initiative has several components. First, the Hospital Quality Alliance is intended to improve and standardize hospital data, data transmission, and performance measures. The goal is to create and validate one set of standardized quality measures with which to evaluate hospital quality that will be reported to the public. The Premier Hospital Quality Incentive Demonstration will reward hospitals that perform well on certain quality measures with monetary bonuses and public recognition of their performance on the CMS website. Thirty four measures relating to five medical conditions common to the Medicare population, Acute Myocardial Infarction, Coronary Artery Bypass Graft, Heart Failure, Pneumonia, and Hip and Knee Replacement, are the criteria of this initiative. These measures are evidence-based and have been extensively validated through research. See generally Centers for Medicare & Medicaid Services, Rewarding Superior Quality Care: The Premier Hospital Quality Incentive Demonstration Fact Sheet (Nov. 2004), *at* http://www. cms.hhs.gov/quality/hospital/PremierFactSheet.pcf. The hospitals will be separated into deciles by performance. The top performers will be in the first and second decile (top 10 and 20%). Those hospitals who perform in the top decile will receive a 2% bonus payment. (2% of the Diagnosis Related Group based prospective payment) If hospital performance falls below the payment adjustment threshold by year 3, the hospital will receive reduced Medicare reimbursement. The Medicare payment could be reduced by one or two percent. If all hospitals improve by year three above the payment adjustment threshold, then no hospital would receive a reduced payment. The average quality performance of all of the hospitals is expected to increase each year.

Hospitals performing in the top fifty percent will have their name and rank published on the CMS website. Those hospitals performing in the top two deciles will be recognized for superior quality. The performance and rank of all other hospitals will not be reported. It is clear that as the percent of payments rises, the interest of providers in developing better quality care will increase.

4.   *Shopping for Quality: Information for Consumers*

Will consumers pay for quality? Should employers as well as consumers shop on the basis of evidence of higher quality care? Can consumer choice be based on different levels of care, representing different levels of resources? The hope of consumer choice advocates is that the proliferation of information about quality will promote improvements in quality as consumer demand selects higher quality providers. There has also been a shift toward evaluating providers based on efficiency. See generally Arnold Milstein and Thomas H. Lee, Comparing Physicians on Efficiency, 357 N.E.J.M. 264 (2007).

The New York Cardiac Surgery reports appear to be effective: information about a surgeon's quality published in the reports influences provider selection by patients and referring physicians. Hospitals also take public reporting seriously, often changing their practices to improve their rank. Critics note however that physicians and hospitals may seek to avoid sicker and more complicated patients in order to improve their ratings. This adverse selection is a real risk of public reporting.

A healthy skepticism toward consumer shopping is needed. Can we expect individual consumers to shop for their care on the basis of quality? A Rand review of health care report cards, provider profiles, and consumer reports concluded that few are influenced by this information: "consumers' choice of hospitals relied more on anecdotal press reports of adverse events than on the comparative assessments that were available." Is the public simply discounting this information, on the theory, so often probably true, that health information is usually aimed to sell a product? In a media environment full of advertising pretending to be scientific, and where medical journals get fooled, even the most intelligent laymen may not easily distinguish hype from information they need. It may also be that quality information—presented in terms of what a patient might reasonably expect—might create a new set of pressures on providers to guarantee their work. One recent study concluded that "... there is limited evidence that public report cards improve quality through this mechanism, and there is some evidence that they paradoxically reduce quality." R.M. Wserner and D.A. Asch, The Unintended Consequences of Publicly Reporting Quality Information, 293 J.A.M.A. 1239 (2005). See also Mark A. Hall and Carl E. Schneider, Patients as Consumers: Courts, Contracts, and the New Medical Marketplace, 106 Mich. L. Rev. 643 (2008).

It may be best for physicians to be the only audiences for such report cards to avoid the problem of adverse selection of higher risk patients, for example. Another study of hospital ratings found to the contrary that quality improvement can be stimulated by the publication of performance information. Dana B. Mukamel, et al., Quality Report Cards, Selection of Cardiac Surgeons, and Racial Disparities: A Study of the Publication of the New York State Cardiac Surgery Reports, 41 Inquiry 435, 443 (Winter 2004/2005).Z.G. Turi, The Big Chill–The Deleterious Effects of Public Reporting on Access to Health Care for the Sickest Patients, 45 J.Am.Coll.Cardiol 1766 (2005). Judith H. Hibbard, et al., Does Publicizing Hospital Performance Stimulate Quality Improvement Efforts? 22 Health Affairs 84 (2003).

Shopping by employers is not likely to fare much better. As employers face large and escalating premium increases over the next few years, it is likely to continue to be cost containment and not quality that is again the primary concern of purchasers. Employer purchasers—in 2003 only 6% of employers in small firms (<200 employees) and 24% of employers in large firms (200–5000 employees) were familiar with the HEDIS data (Health Plan Employer Data and Information Set), the national benchmark for measuring and comparing managed care plans. Less than 5% even thought quality was very important. And should we expect employers to make judgments about quality of care? Should they now have to play complex private contractual compliance games with providers to protect their workers? LeapFrog and other corporate quality groups hope so, but Gabel et al. note that only 3% of employers in small firms and only 18% in large firms were even aware of the LeapFrog Group's national quality effort. Leapfrog Initiatives to Drive Great Leaps in Patient Safety (2002). www.leapfroggroup.org/safety1.htm. Sheila Leatherman, et al, The Business Case for Quality: Case Studies and An Analysis, 22 Health Affairs 17, 25 (2003).

Informed consumerism is harder than it looks, and it may be that generating more information will have little effect on quality. Patients may not use the information, and employers are likely to disregard it. It provides a market driven ideological justification for shifting responsibility from government oversight to the forces of the market, although the consequences are that bad practices increase and patients suffer. Let the consumers suffer the consequences of their bad choices, the free marketeers argue. And the government agency is let off the hook for developing tough new rules to govern a complex health care system that will fight back, tooth and claw.

IV. DISTRIBUTIVE JUSTICE AND THE ALLOCATION OF HEALTH CARE RESOURCES— THE EXAMPLE OF HUMAN ORGAN TRANSPLANTATION

A. INTRODUCTION

We in the United States struggle politically, socially, and ethically over the design and impact of our health care system which depends in large part on wealth as a distributive mechanism. As you will read in later chapters in this text, the publicly financed health care programs in the U.S. tend to provide health care financing for only certain segments of the population. Medicare provides public financing for individuals who fit the age criterion regardless of financial need, although its requirements for copayments and deductibles still make access to benefits dependent on ability to pay; and serious limitations on coverage (e.g., long-term care and gaps in pharmaceutical coverage) leave substantial health care needs unfunded. Other public programs, such as Medicaid, provide health care financing for the poor, but limit themselves to specific categories of poor persons and exclude others. With the exception of public programs such as these and a few others, we rely on private funding of health care, whether through health insurance or out-of-pocket payments. Health care professionals may extend charity toward those without the funds to pay for needed medical care, and there are some narrow legal obligations toward persons in emergency situations as well. See discussion in Chapter 5.

Our debates over our health care system encounter basic political and moral principles. Is it just for certain individuals to suffer with treatable illness that may disable them or shorten their lives for the lack of personal wealth? Is it just or fair to require that persons who pay their own way through hard work pay also for those who do not or cannot? Would "free" health care encourage overconsumption; and if it would, how do we fairly and justly set limits on what is available? Would a strong safety net for health care simply encourage individuals to avoid saving for medical needs or buying health insurance? Do personal decisions that may have a negative impact on an individual's future health and functioning implicate any notion of justice or fairness?

We don't worry so much about the wealth-based distribution of consumer goods or services, such as iPods or automobiles. Some argue that health care has a special status because good health is the *sine qua non* of life as a human being. Without some measure of health, without "normal species functioning," in the words of philosopher Norman Daniels, productive life is nearly impossible. People do not have the opportunity to participate in life in our society without some minimal level of health. We cannot expect citizens to meet their civic and social duties, including supporting themselves, unless they enjoy the health to do so. Some argue that because illness and disability are unevenly distributed, adequate health care levels the playing field for those so burdened in relation to the healthy. Further, some argue, we all benefit from the general good health of the rest of society, so we should be willing to commit our social resources to attain this end. The rest of us will be less subject to disease if others are healthy, and our economy will generate more for all of us if the work force is healthy. Finally, others argue that we have a moral duty to address the human suffering caused by poor health. For a very helpful account of the reasons that health care might be different from other kinds of goods and services, and a response to each of those arguments, see Einer Elhauge, Allocating Health Care Morally, 82 Cal. L. Rev. 1449 (1994). One of the earliest and most often cited applications of the principles of distributive justice to health care resources is found in Norman Daniels, Just Health Care (1985). See also Normal Daniels, Just Health: Meeting Health Needs Fairly (2007); Tom Beauchamp & James Childress, Principles of Medical Ethics (5th ed. 2001).

Approaches to distributive justice that might be applied to health care (and to anything else of which there is a scarce supply) cover a wide spectrum. One approach, the libertarian approach, would accept the current distribution of resources as a general matter, and allow for a change only if willing participants in the market were to trade for one. Under this approach, anyone who wants more health care or more health insurance than that person has now should buy it from any willing seller; but the government should not redistribute resources from those who now have them to those who do not. Such redistribution would constitute an unjust taking from those who have earned their wealth to those who have been unwilling or unable to be productive or have chosen to spend their resources for other purposes.

In contrast, some theories of distributive justice, when applied to health care, do permit or require some redistribution of resources. An egalitarian and communitarian theorist, at the other extreme from the libertarian marketeers, might argue that justice requires equality. Those who take the communitarian approach are more likely to distribute health care so that each person has access to the same range of health care resources whenever those resources are required. Many national health care systems outside of the United States are based, at least in part, on this "equal opportunity" theory.

Virtually all arguments in favor of redistributing wealth in the form of access to health care require the identification of a package of basic services that would be made available to every person. The health resources included in such a package of basic services could be defined as a "minimum package," that is, the resources required by those in the society with the least health care needs. Alternatively, every person could be provided a "generally adequate package," which would include the resources required by most people in society. Each person could instead be provided something greater than that— perhaps a package sufficient to provide for the health care needs of nearly all members of society.

Of course, it is not so easy to decide what, exactly, ought to be in a guaranteed package of health services, or even how that package should be defined. Should it be defined in terms of particular goods and health care services; in terms of patients' desires; in terms of needs defined by primary care physicians; in terms of boundaries set by the community through some process; or in some other way? Some kinds of services—for example, mental health services or infertility services—are deemed to be necessary by some people and to be luxuries by others. The development of such a package of basic health care services has been fundamental to most efforts at systematic health care reform in the U.S. over the past several years. The difficulty in defining such a package may be one reason such reform has failed. Newer proposals, such as the Massachusetts plan and those offered in the context of the 2008 presidential campaign, have emerged. See discussion in Chapter 4.

Unequal distribution of health care resources may manifest itself in many different ways. Beyond the question of wealth, many people are especially concerned by distinctions based on race and gender in the distribution of those resources. There is little question that African Americans have less access to many kinds of health care than do others, even after adjusting for differences in income. Similarly, people residing in rural areas, women, and other minorities may confront less access to some forms of necessary health care services than their urban, male, and nonminority counterparts. See discussion in Chapter 8. Are these, too, questions of justice?

Allocation and Rationing

Through allocation, a society determines what portion of its resources to devote to a particular purpose. For example, how much money should be allocated to Medicare or Medicaid as compared to education or defense? How much federal support should be devoted to medical research and for which diseases or conditions? How many long-term care or hospital facilities should a state approve through its certificate-of-need program? Within Medicare or Medicaid, how much should be allocated to dialysis or transplantation as compared to long-term care?

In an uncommon occurrence in the U.S. health care system, the Medicare program has created nearly universal entitlement for dialysis and kidney transplantation for any person with end-stage renal disease. Covering dialysis leads almost unavoidably to covering kidney transplantation as a matter of cost savings if nothing else. Ability to pay both for the initial costs of the transplantation surgery as well as the long-term medical treatment required to maintain the transplant is required for other transplants. Public benefit programs, like Medicaid, cover some but not all transplants needed by beneficiaries, but payment levels may make coverage less effective. See, e.g., Devantier v. Sherman, 2006 WL 3163053 (W.D. Mo.), reviewing Missouri's decision to cover a particular patient's transplant at an arguably inadequate level. Is payment for transplants a good allocation of health care dollars for public programs? Transplant success rates have been rising. Nearly 63% of persons receiving lung transplants between 2000 and 2003 had survived for three years as compared with 56% of those who had received lung transplants between 1988–1994. Marc Estenne & Robert Kotloff, Update in Transplantation 2005, 173 Am. J. Respiratory & Critical Care Med. 593 (2006). Does that survival rate justify the spending? Should quality of life during the post-transplant years be considered; and if so, how should it be measured and who should measure it? What other values might support, or reject, spending on lung or other organ transplants? Should organ transplants be treated differently than other health care? See Albert R. Jonsen, The God Squad and the Origins of Transplantation Ethics and Policy, 35 J. L. Med. & Ethics 238 (2007):

> The problem that looms behind transplantation medicine is the incessant desire, or rather, demand, that life must be salvaged at all costs.

But see, Gil Siegal & Richard Bonnie, Closing the Organ Gap: A Reciprocity-based Social Contract Approach, 34 J. L. Med. & Ethics 415 (2006):

> Organ transplantation remains one of modern medicine's remarkable achievements. It saves lives, improves quality of life, diminishes health-care expenditures in end-stage renal patients, and enjoys high success rates.

> Through rationing, a community decides which specific individuals receive available resources. Allocation decisions affect rationing decisions: if more resources are allocated to a particular purpose or legal restrictions on supply are removed, rationing may become less pressing or less frequent. Rationing decisions also affect allocation decisions: uncomfortable public rationing decisions may stimulate a greater allocation to increase the supply of the scarce resources. In fact, the Medicare entitlement to kidney transplantation and dialysis may have emerged initially from the experience of allocating the limited dialysis services available in the 1960s. The Admissions and Policy Committee of the Seattle Artificial Kidney Center (sometimes known as the "God Squad") was reported to have selected patients for hemodialysis partly on the basis of age, gender, marital status, number of dependents, emotional stability, education, and occupation among other characteristics. Albert R. Jonsen, supra; Maxwell Mehlman, Rationing Expensive Lifesaving Medical Treatments, 1985 Wisc. L. Rev. 239, 256 (identifying criteria used).

> Allocation and rationing decisions often treat the loss of human life inconsistently, with greater tolerance for "statistical lives" lost and much less tolerance for the loss of "identifiable lives." A classic scenario illustrates the difference: cost-sensitive decisions concerning mine safety that increase the statistical risk of death are accepted even when the predicted loss is quite precise and clear, while at the same time the expense of rescue is of very little concern when an individual miner is trapped in a collapsed mine. Allocation deals mostly with statistical lives, while rationing most often deals with identifiable lives. Whether the individual has a name, a face, and a personality or is just a number may alter decisions.

> Many processes can be used to ration health care resources. As already noted, the U.S. relies on the market to ration most, but not all, health care resources. A second option is to allocate resources and establish rationing rules through a political process. Allocation decisions are often made through political processes, including federal and state budgeting processes. "A responsible" or "black box" committees that are not required to provide reasons for the selection of one recipient over another and that cannot be subject to effective public scrutiny may be used to ration scarce resources. Expert panels may ration scarce resources and may do so under a mantle of scientific or medical or financial expertise. Bureaucratic organizations shield rationing decisions from broad public scrutiny. For a classic and influential analysis of allocation and rationing in several contexts, see Guido Calabresi & Philip Bobbitt, Tragic Choices (1978).

Increased concern about health care costs have stimulated a debate over whether or how extensively and on what principles medical professionals and health care institutions should ration care among patients. Rationing health care "at the bedside" is a substantial departure from the physician's traditional role as determined advocate for each individual patient. Are physicians in the best position to ration care among patients? How might their decisions differ, if at all, from black box committees or bureaucracies, for example? Will physician decisions be more or less reviewable than decisions by others? What impact would such a change in role identification have on physician-patient relationships? See, Mark Hall, Rationing Health Care at the Bedside, 69 N.Y.U.L. Rev. 693 (1994); David Mechanic, Models of Rationing: Professional Judgment and the Rationing of Medical Care, 140 U. Pa. L. Rev. 1713 (1992); Edmund Pellegrino, Rationing Health Care: The Ethics of Moral Gatekeeping, 2 J. Contemp. Health L. & Pol'y 23 (1986); E. Haavi Morreim, Balancing Act: The New Medical Ethics of Medicine's New Economics (1991); Susan Wolf, Health Care Reform and the Future of Physician Ethics, 24 Hastings Ctr. Rep. 28 (1994). The physician's decision whether to list a patient for a transplant can be the equivalent of bedside rationing in the transplantation world, as discussed below.

B. RATIONING SCARCE HUMAN ORGANS

For most health care services and goods, scarcity could be resolved if enough funds were provided. Funding also has an effect on the availability of organ transplantation. For example, access to funding certainly determines whether an individual will receive a transplant; and funding can support research to maximize the success of human organ transplants or the use of non-human organ sources. In the case of organ transplantation, however, even unlimited funding is not likely to resolve the shortage of human organs available for transplantation. In 2006, there were 17,090 kidney transplants (up from 13,613 in 2000); 6,650 liver transplants (up from 4,997 in 2000), and 2,192 heart transplants (compared to 2,199 in 2002). The number of reported deaths on the waiting list for kidney transplants increased from 2000 to 2006 (from 3,346 to 4,439) despite the increase in the number of transplants; but declined for liver transplants (1,822 to 1,704) and for heart transplants (635 to 368). See OPTN Data at http://www.optn.org/latestData/step2.asp. Demand for organs continues to outstrip supply. On December 15, 2007, 98,159 persons were on the wait lists for organs, compared to 43,854 in 1995. United Network for Organ Sharing (UNOS) posts a daily waitlist and donor count. http://unos.org

What criteria should be used to ration available organs? Should we resurrect the God Squad and their criteria? Would other standards be more neutral? Are medical indications relating to survivability with and without transplant neutral standards? Would a lottery or a "first come-first served" system be more acceptable? How should the pool for these latter two methods be defined: should there be regional pools; should it matter whether the patient is a resident of the state where the organ was donated or of the United States; who should decide where the line starts and who is allowed to get in line? Does this decision belong to individual transplant surgeons and hospitals? To public or nonprofit agencies? To the government?

Problem: Selecting an Organ Transplant Recipient

Consider this problem as you read the materials in this section.

You are awakened in the middle of the night by an urgent phone call from an administrative staff member of the large urban teaching hospital that you represent. The hospital is a transplant center. The hospital has encountered the following problem tonight, but the others described are also on your desk.

For the last few weeks, two patients have been under treatment at the hospital for acute liver failure. One, James Patterson, is a 65–year-old retired CEO of a major computer software company. He has two children, a 40–year-old daughter with a child of her own and a 24–year-old son. James is an alcoholic and has been in and out of the hospital for the past few years for problems secondary to his alcoholism. Although he has been through detoxification programs several times, he always has returned to his drinking. This time, though, he has abstained from alcohol for more than six months and so meets the minimum criterion for former alcoholics for liver transplant. James is active in his church and is a financial supporter of the local university athletics department. He is still on his employer's health insurance plan, which has a cap on transplant coverage which James will exceed within six months of post-transplant care and medications required for the rest of his life. The second patient is Antonia Friedman, a 30–year-old attorney with two children, ages 2 and 4. She is an active member of the local city council and has contributed generously in the past year to the hospital's building fund. She recently was exposed to Hepatitis A, which has quickly destroyed most of her liver. Friedman has full coverage health insurance. Within the last week, both patients have taken a turn for the worse; and both will die within the next few weeks if they do not receive a liver transplant.

A few hours ago, a patient was admitted to the hospital with massive head trauma caused by an automobile accident. The patient is brain dead but is being kept on support systems to preserve his organs for transplantation. The liver is undamaged, and it will be donated for transplantation. Tissue matching shows that it is an acceptable organ for either Patterson or Friedman. Patterson's physician was the first to list his patient on the transplant list, which he did three days earlier than did Friedman's physician.

Who should receive the organ and why? Assume that the hospital is prohibited under federal funding requirements from discrimination on the basis of gender, race, age, or disability. How would such a prohibition operate in this situation?

See, V.H. Schmidt, Selection of Recipients for Donor Organs in Transplant Medicine, 23 J. Med. & Phil. 50 (1998); UNOS Policy 3.6; Alvin Moss & Mark Siegler, Should Alcoholics Compete Equally for Liver Transplantation?, 265 JAMA 1295 (1991); Carl Cohen, et al., Alcoholics and Liver Transplantation?, 265 JAMA 1299 (1991); Alan Zarembo, Priority: Doctors Send Young to the Front of the Line–While Older Patients Wait, Often in Vain for Their Chance, San Jose Mercury News (Dec. 4, 2006) at A3; Type of Insurance Affects Speed of Transplantation, Transplant News (June 14, 2003), reporting that persons with private insurance get on transplant lists more quickly than those with Medicare or Medicaid.

Suppose instead that Antonia Friedman is a convicted felon serving two years for insider trading or health care fraud. Should she be excluded from consideration? See, Limited Organ Supply Raises Allocation Concerns, Ethics Forum,

Am.Med. News, July 1, 2002, for a debate between two medical ethicists over the issue (at http://www.ama-assn.org/amednews/2002/07/01/prca701.htm); Carrie Frank, Must Inmates be Provided Free Organ Transplants: Revisiting the Deliberate Indifference Standard, 15 George Mason U. Civ. Rts. J. 341 (2005); Mark Thiessen, Convicted Killer May Get Liver Transplant, Cin. Post (Feb. 28, 2003) at A7; Ed Fletcher, Bill Aims to Limit Organs to Prisoners; The Debate Over a Heart Transplant Spurs the Effort to Let Donors Choose, Sacramento Bee (Jan. 24, 2003) at A3.

Here are some of the other problems on your desk:

The decision to place a patient on the transplant list is made by the individual transplant surgeon. Your transplant team regularly assesses candidates on psychosocial criteria. For example, they won't list patients who have no means of paying for transplant care or patients who have been disruptive or noncooperative during dialysis or patients who have a history of serious depression. The question presented to you is: Should your hospital establish a procedure in which the patient is formally notified that listing is being considered; the patient is given an opportunity to respond; and a record is created documenting the reasons not to list? See discussion of listing practices, below.

The family of a newly-deceased person or a patient making a pre-mortem declaration sometimes wants to designate the organs for particular uses or particular recipients. For example, the family may want to specify that the organs must be used for patients at your hospital instead of being placed in the ordinary distribution network. Such a decision has benefits for your hospital as some of your patients may receive organs sooner than otherwise. Your hospital also will do more transplants, producing more revenue and improving its performance on quality indicators relating to the volume of transplants. Should your hospital encourage or discourage such designations? What implications does the designation of donor organs have for rationing decisions? See discussion of designated donations in notes following *Newman*, below.

A patient awaiting a heart transplant at your hospital has begun an intensive media campaign, complete with billboards and television appearances, to get an organ. He is hoping that a donor family will designate him as a recipient. Some members of the transplant team are concerned about providing services to this patient as his actions are likely to push him ahead of other patients who have a more urgent need. Should they transfer him elsewhere? Should they require patients to agree not to engage in such efforts as a condition of admission to your hospital's transplant program? See UNOS Policy 3.4; Jim Warren, Commentary, 2004 Will Go Down as the Year the Rules for Getting a Life–Saving Organ Transplant Changed Forever, Transplant News, Dec. 15, 2004, commenting that "[P]atients and families decide playing by the rules is stupid if it is an automatic death sentence"; Daniel Stimson, Private Solicitation of Organ Donors: A Threat to the Fairness of the U.S. Organ Transplant System, or a Solution to the National Organ Shortage?, 10 J. Med. & L. 349 (2006), arguing that it is the latter and advocating the adoption of the National Marrow Donor Program for solid organs; Sheldon Zink, et al., Examining the Potential Exploitation of UNOS Policies, 5 Am. J. Bioethics 6 (2005), arguing that a campaign by a "young and attractive couple" advantages wealth and encourages discrimination against particular groups.

Note: The Organ Procurement Transplant Network

The National Organ Transplant Act (NOTA) requires the Department of Health and Human Services (HHS) to establish an Organ Procurement Transplant Network (OPTN) to organize the retrieval, distribution, and transplantation of human organs. HHS contracts with the United Network for Organ Sharing (UNOS), a private nonprofit organization, for management of the federal OPTN.

The effectiveness of UNOS management became a concern in the early 1990s. See e.g., GAO, Organ Transplants: Increased Effort Needed to Boost Supply and Ensure Equitable Distribution of Organs, GAO/HRD–93–56 (Apr. 1993) finding that nearly every Organ Procurement Organization was noncompliant with UNOS policy for distribution of organs. As a result, HHS promulgated new regulations in 1999 through which the federal government took a more active role in organ policy and practice. The federal government intended the new regulation to ensure consistency between OPTN policies (as implemented by UNOS) and the NOTA. See 64 Fed. Reg. 16296 codified at 42 C.F.R. pt. 121 (1998). After the 1999 rule, UNOS no longer enjoyed the deference that had been accorded to its policies; however, the regulation allows OPTN, and thus UNOS, to propose policies that must be agreed upon by an HHS oversight committee. Special Section: Organ Transplantation: Shaping Policy and Keeping Public Trust, 8 Cambridge Quarterly of Healthcare Ethics 269 (1999); Institute of Medicine, Organ Procurement and Transplantation: Assessing Current Policies and the Potential Impact of the DHHS Final Rule (2000).

UNOS revised a good number of significant policies concerning the distribution of organs, some of which are described below, after the 1999 regulation went into effect. In addition, UNOS established a more active system to monitor the quality of transplant centers, penalizing several transplant centers (through probation or exclusion) and causing some centers to voluntarily discontinue transplant services. See reports of actions in Jim Warren, California Transplant Center Woes, OPTN/UNOS Board of Directors' Response Major News Event in 2006, Transplant News, Jan. 1, 2007. But see Tracy Weber & Charles Ornstein, No Transplant Data Improvement: The Number of Federally Funded Programs that Fail to Meet U.S. Survival Standards Doesn't Budge, L.A. Times, July 29, 2006, at A14; Charles Ornstein & Tracy Weber, Transplant Monitor Lax in Oversight: U.S. Organ Network Routinely Fails to Detect Problems; L.A. Times, Oct. 22, 2006, at A1.

Should UNOS, as an expert in the field, be able to establish organ distribution policies without federal government intrusion; or is UNOS so dominated by the transplant industry that it naturally promotes their interests? See Dulcinea Grantham, Transforming Transplantation: The Effect of the Health and Human Services Final Rule on the Organ Allocation System, 35 U.S.F.L. Rev. 751 (2001); Laura E. McMullen, Equitable Allocation of Human Organs: An Examination of the New Federal Regulation. 20 J. Legal Med. 405 (1999). See also Wisconsin v. Shalala, 2000 WL 34234002 (W.D.Wis.), for a discussion of NOTA, OPTN, UNOS, and transplant center and state opposition to the 1999 federal rule.

1. *Geographic Distribution of Organs*

Prior to the 1999 regulation, UNOS policy was to retain organs in the geographic area where they were recovered if a transplant candidate with the appropriate medical status was in that area even if patients with a more urgent need or who presented better survival prospects waited in other regions. Under that system, median waiting times varied considerably by region. The median waiting time for a liver, for example, was 20–78 days in Region 3, while the wait in Region 9 amounted to 279–443 days. 59 Fed. Reg. 46482, 46486 (Sept. 8, 1994). The rationale behind the old UNOS policy was to reduce damage to organs from preservation during transport; to improve organ quality and survival outcomes; to reduce the costs incurred by the patient; and to increase donations.

With the exception of thoracic organs which are still allocated locally, regionally, and then nationally, all other organs are now allocated based on medical urgency rather than geography. UNOS Policy 3.2. With the implementation of a national rather than regional distribution policy, HHS hoped that wait times would become less disparate throughout the country. HHS Office of Inspector General, Racial and Geographic Disparity in the Distribution of Organs for Transplantation, OEI–01–98–00360 (June 1998). Serious geographic wait time differentials persisted, however. In 2003–2004, the average wait time for a liver transplant for a person in Status 1 was 4 days in the Midwest region; 12 days in the Northwest region; and 8 days in the Southwest region (including California). For persons in the next two status levels (MELD/PELD of 25+ and MELDPELD of 19–24) the differences in wait times were quite pronounced: 24 days and 126 days, respectively, in the Midwest; 9 and 39 days in the Northwest; and 34 and 489 days in the Southwest. OPTN Data at http://www.optn.ort/latestData/rptData.asp. For a history of the development of national distribution rules and an excellent analysis of the ethical and legal issues in organ allocation, see Neal Barshes, et al., Justice, Administrative Law, and the Transplant Clinician: The Ethical and Legislative Basis of a National Policy on Donor Liver Allocation, 23 J. Contemp. Health L. & Pol'y 200 (2007). See also Daniel Geyser, Organ Transplantation: New Regulations Alter Distribution of Organs, 28 J. L. Med. & Ethics 95 (2000); David L. Weimer Public and Private Regulation of Organ Transplantation: Liver Allocation and the Final Rule, 32 J. Health Pol. Pol'y & L 9 (2007), arguing that HHS's mandate of national distribution served the interests of liver transplant centers facing increasing competition in certain cities.

The persistent difference in regional wait times for organs encourages the practice of "multiple listing," in which patients with the means to travel at a moment's notice get listed at more than one transplant center. See Gabrielle Glaser, Oregon is a Model in Organ Transplant World, Houston Chronicle (Aug. 26, 2007) at A15, describing Oregon as a destination location for kidney transplantation due to the high rate of organ donation among Oregonians, including a high rate of living donors; the higher Oregon death rates from stroke and suicide which result in more transplantable organs; and the relatively low rates of diabetes or other disease that lead to need for kidney transplants. Several states have enacted laws which favor intra-state distribution by placing restrictions on out-of-state organ transfers. In effect, these state laws attempt to perpetuate the policy as it was before the promulgation of the federal regulations. See, e.g., La. Rev. Stat. Ann. § 17:2353. Roderick Chen, Organ Allocation and the States: Can States Restrict Broader Organ Sharing?, 49 Duke L.J. 261 (1999). What is the rationale for such statutes—possessiveness; protection of citizens in need of organs; encouragement for organ donation; economic development?

Organ transplantation is not only a matter of interstate commerce. There is a global market in organs and in transplantation as well. UNOS has adopted a statement on "transplant tourism," defined as the "purchase of a transplant organ abroad," which states that it "remains a refuge for desperate recipients of means" and "is predicated on the desperation of vendors, recipients and their families." The UNOS Ethics Committee condemns the practice. UNOS Statement on Transplant Tourism, June 26, 2007, at http://www.unos.org/news/newsDetail.asp?id=891 See also Michele Goodwin, Black Markets: The Supply and Demand of Body Parts (2006), for an analysis of the international market with its flow from poor nations to rich.

2. *Listing Patients for Transplantation*

Individual doctors and hospitals decide who gets on the UNOS registry and when. Patients receive priority points for some organs for the length of time they have been on the list, among other criteria, so getting on the list earlier rather than later is quite significant. Once a patient is on the waiting list, the patient data is placed in the UNOS national databank and the patient's medical status places them in line for an organ. Under UNOS Policy 3.6.3, for example, position on the liver wait list is based on a point system which combines both how long a patient has been on the list and the patient's medical status. Time on the wait list, at least for those awaiting livers, does not correlate with mortality, and ranking by hospitalization status (e.g., whether the patient needed ICU care) has been found to be subject to manipulation. See Barshes, et al., supra. In 2004, UNOS eliminated time on the wait list as a factor in the allocation of lungs for transplant into adult recipients but not for some other organs. Selection of a lung recipient is to balance urgency of need (in terms of risk of death without transplant) and greatest survival benefit (the difference between the expected days lived during the first year following a transplant and the expected days lived during an additional year on the waitlist). UNOS Policy 3.7.6. See also, Gundeep Dhillon & Ramona Doyle, The New UNOS Lung Transplantation Allocation System, 4(2) Advances in Pulmonary Hypertension 12 (2005).

Patient listing practices vary substantially among transplant centers around the country. An investigation of listing practices at the University of Illinois and University of Chicago hospitals revealed that physicians there may have exaggerated their patients' medical condition to move them up higher on the list and pump up the volume of liver transplants performed at those facilities. The federal government pursued the issue after a whistleblower faculty member filed a lawsuit. The hospitals involved denied all of the allegations, but settled with the government, with Illinois paying the largest amount of $1 million. A Man of Principle, Chicago Tribune Magazine, Jan. 25, 2004. See also, E. Haavi Morreim, Another Kind of End-run: Status Upgrades, 5 Am. J. Bioethics 11 (2005), describing False Claims Act litigation against another hospital for its transplant listing practices.

A study of the categorization of the medical status of potential transplant recipients found that transplant centers located in high-competition areas were more likely to list patients as being in more urgent categories although the study concluded that this practice was not necessarily deliberate and may have been an unconscious reaction to competition. The study also concluded that more specific listing criteria implemented under the new regulations diminished variation in listing practices. Dennis P. Scanlon, et al., Does Competition For Transplantable Hearts Encourage "Gaming" of the Waiting List?, 23 Health Affairs 191 (2004). UNOS has developed specific national policies for patient listing for some types of transplants, including liver, kidney, thoracic organ, intestine, and pancreas, and a general policy for those organs not specifically addressed. Federal regulations also establish some standardized criteria for placing patients on transplant waiting lists and for distribution of donated organs. Under the 1999 HHS regulation, UNOS listing policies are reviewed by the Advisory Committee on Organ Transplantation which advises the Secretary of HHS. See http://www.organdonor.gov/research/acot.html.

Psychosocial factors traditionally have played a large role in considering which patients receive donated organs, including in physician listing decisions. The UNOS Ethics Committee has expressed concern over the use of non-medical transplant candidate criteria. The Committee, however, justified the use of certain non-medical criteria based on the shortage of available organs for transplantation. Examples of non-medical criteria currently used by physicians and other health care providers include whether organ failure was caused by the patient's behavior; compliance/adherence with medical recommendations; repeat transplantation; and the availability of alternative therapies. According to the UNOS Ethics Committee, the non-medical criteria used to evaluate transplant candidates should be constantly reassessed and modified to reflect changes that occur in technology, medicine, and other related fields and should be examined for excessive subjectivity. UNOS Ethics Committee, General Considerations in Assessment of Transplant Candidacy, http://www.unos.org/resources/bioethics.asp?index=5 See also Denise M. Dudzinski, Shifting to Other Justice Issues: Examining Listing Practices, 4 Am. J. Bioethics 35 (2004), reviewing studies of listing practices that conclude that standards and procedures tended to be informal and disadvantage racial minorities and women. For a compelling narrative of the effect of race on listing decisions, see Vanessa Grubbs. Good for Harvest, Bad for Planting, 26 Health Affairs 232 (2007).

3. *Kidney Matching and Disparate Impact by Race*

Matching of kidneys to recipients is done by analysis of the kidney's antigens. "Zero antigen mismatch" occurs when a recipient patient and a donated kidney have no antigen mismatches, even though all six antigens on which kidneys and recipients would be matched for a "perfect match" may not have shown up in testing a particular kidney. A partial match occurs when a mismatch for one or more of the six antigens has been detected. Transplantation is significantly more likely to succeed where there is a perfect six-antigen match. Data on zero antigen mismatch also show significantly better survival rates. In contrast, partial antigen mismatch shows much smaller differences in survival rates across differences in the numbers of antigens matched. Data from 2001, for example, indicated one-year survival rates for cadaveric kidney transplants of 86.1% for mismatch of 5 antigens; 87.5% for 4; 89.2% for 3; 90.4% for 2; and 91.4% when there is only 1 mismatch. UNOS 1999 Annual Report (September 1999). Are any of these differences significant?

UNOS kidney allocation policies do not uniformly prefer survivability. "Presensitized" patients, who have previously received a kidney that failed within a short time after transplant, receive priority. Presensitized patients have this priority for transplant even though the presensitization caused by the earlier transplant diminishes the chances for successful transplant significantly. In addition, UNOS policy now provides that a person who has earlier donated a kidney receives priority in receiving a transplanted kidney should the need arise in the future. UNOS Policy 3.5.11.6. UNOS policy also provides that kidneys from donors under the age of 35 are to be offered first to children before any adult patients, even those with greater need, with a few exceptions including the priority given to living organ donors who now need an organ. UNOS Policy 3.5.11.5.1.

Data indicate that the priority for zero antigen mismatch and lower partial mismatch has had a disparate impact on the distribution of kidneys by race. For more on health disparities, see Chapter 8. African Americans may be disadvantaged in the rationing of kidneys by the zero antigen mismatch standard and by the partial match standard because antigens are distributed differently among different racial groups. At the same time, end-stage renal disease is much more prevalent among African Americans, occurring at nearly four times the rate of the white population. In December 2007, for example, African–American transplant candidates constituted 34.6% of the kidney waiting list (compared to representation in the general population of approximately 13%); and whites comprised 39.3%. OPTN Data, supra. See also Ian Ayres, et al., Unequal Racial Access to Kidney Transplantation, 46 Vand. L. Rev. 805 (1993).

UNOS altered its kidney antigen mismatch policy in May, 2003, in response to evidence that the policy was having an adverse racial impact. While blacks and whites were represented on the wait lists in roughly equal proportions, whites received more than double the number of available kidneys for transplant as did blacks. The distribution was reflected in comparative wait times, with the median wait time for white candidates in 2003 at 1,284 days and for black candidates at 1,842 days. OPTN, Annual Report 2003. Blacks donated 14.4% of cadaveric kidneys in 2006, a donation rate that exceeds representation in the general population (despite the higher incidence of kidney disease that excludes potential donors); and whites donated 68.5%. To meet the higher need for kidneys solely through increasing donations, African–American rates would have to increase nearly three-fold. See Michele Goodwin, The Body Market: Race Politics & Private Ordering, 49 Ariz. L. Rev. 599 (2007), using this data to argue in favor of compensation to incentivize organ donations.

The proportion of kidney transplants going to African–American recipients has been increasing. In 2007, African Americans received 24.5% of transplanted kidneys; whites received 54.8%; and Hispanic recipients, 14.1%, compared to 23%, 59.3%, and 11.9%, respectively, in 2001. Whether wait times reflect these changes is not clear. OPTN Data, *supra.*

What is a fair basis for allocation? Should race be relevant, so that the proportion of organs received by individual groups is a justice concern? If so, what is the appropriate measure that should be used? Should the proportion allocated be compared to representation in the general population; to the proportion donated; to the need (i.e., the proportion on the wait list)? Or, is race irrelevant as an independent factor so that the concern is that the criteria that are used for allocation are actually race-neutral, both in design and in impact? If so, what is the relevance of distribution data?

Problem: Setting Priorities

Do you agree that policies should give absolute priority for relative efficacy, however you might define that concept? If not, what values might lead you to conclude otherwise? If you do favor departures from relative efficacy, under what terms would you accept them? Whom would you authorize to make those departures? The physician in deciding to list the patient? The individual transplant centers? UNOS? HHS? A "black box" committee?

Transplant survival rates vary widely among hospitals doing transplants. Should this variation be added to the calculation of who gets priority for transplant by shifting organs away from transplant centers with poorer records?

How would you resolve the policy issues regarding these standards if you were the Secretary of HHS; a member of Congress; or UNOS? Is organ allocation subject to equal protection claims? Benjamin Mintz, Analyzing the OPTN Under the State Action Doctrine—Can UNOS's Organ Allocation Criteria Survive Strict Scrutiny?, 28 Colum. J.L. & Soc. Probs. 339 (1995).

C. INCREASING THE SUPPLY OF ORGANS FOR TRANSPLANTATION: THE IMPACT OF LEGAL RESTRAINTS

There is probably an absolute limit in the number of human organs that will be available for transplant, and so an organ shortage will always exist. Ellen Sheehy, et. al., Estimating the Number of Potential Organ Donors in the United States, 349 NEJM 674 (2003). Legal restraints on the collection of human organs for transplantation set limits, however, that are arguably well within that absolute number. Over the past several decades, many attempts to improve the yield from potential donors have met with often disappointing levels of success. These included efforts to encourage larger numbers of people to sign organ donor cards; requiring hospitals to ask families of the newly deceased to consider organ donation and more recently, creating web-based organ donor registries in the states.

These efforts to increase the supply of organs all stay within the current framework of organ donation; i.e., that organ donation is a free gift to the community. Some efforts, such as organized mutual donor-designation initiatives, may retain the notion that organ donation is a gift, but reconceptualize it as a gift to specific individuals rather than the community at large.

Other efforts to increase the supply of human organs reject the notion that organ transfers must be free gifts. On the one hand, some argue that organs are a public resource that should be viewed as available upon death. In contrast, others argue that human organs should be viewed as property and that a market that marshals financial incentives for organ transfers would increase the supply significantly. Some argue that the donor-designation initiatives, in fact, facilitate trades for mutual advantage rather than a gift.

Debate over the appropriate limits on the donation or transfer of human organs and tissue is very rich as new initiatives emerge and arguments that were previously marginalized gain traction. For an overview and analysis, see Institute of Medicine, Organ Donation: Opportunities for Action (2006).

NEWMAN v. SATHYAVAGLSWARAN

United States Court of Appeals, Ninth Circuit, 2002.
287 F.3d 786.

Parents, whose deceased children's corneas were removed by the Los Angeles County Coroner's office without notice or consent, brought this 42 U.S.C. § 1983 action alleging a taking of their property without due process of law. The complaint was dismissed by the district court for a failure to state a claim upon which relief could be granted. We must decide whether the longstanding recognition in the law of California, paralleled by our national common law, that next of kin have the exclusive right to possess the bodies of their deceased family members creates a property interest, the deprivation of which must be accorded due process of law under the Fourteenth Amendment of the United States Constitution. We hold that it does. * * *

* * *

Robert Newman and Barbara Obarski (the parents) each had children, Richard Newman and Kenneth Obarski respectively, who died in Los Angeles County in October 1997. Following their deaths, the Office of the Coroner for the County of Los Angeles (the coroner) obtained possession of the bodies of the children and, under procedures adopted pursuant to California Government Code § 27492.47 as it then existed, removed the corneas from those bodies without the knowledge of the parents and without an attempt to notify them and request consent. The parents became aware of the coroner's actions in September 1999 and subsequently filed this § 1983 action alleging a deprivation of their property without due process of law in violation of the Fourteenth Amendment.

II.   PROPERTY INTERESTS IN DEAD BODIES

[T]he Supreme Court repeatedly has affirmed that "the right of every individual to the possession and control of his own person, free from all restraint or interference of others," [ ] is "so rooted in the traditions and conscience of our people," [ ] as to be ranked as one of the fundamental liberties protected by the "substantive" component of the Due Process Clause. [ ] This liberty, the Court has "strongly suggested," extends to the personal decisions about "how to best protect dignity and independence at the end of life." [ ] The Court has not had occasion to address whether the rights of possession and control of one's own body, the most "sacred" and "carefully guarded" of all rights in the common law, [ ] are property interests protected by the Due Process Clause. Nor has it addressed what Due Process protections are applicable to the rights of next of kin to possess and control the bodies of their deceased relatives.

A.   History of Common Law Interests in Dead Bodies

* * *

Many early American courts adopted Blackstone's description of the common law, holding that "a dead body is not the subject of property right."

[ ] The duty to protect the body by providing a burial was often described as flowing from the "universal ... right of sepulture," rather than from a concept of property law. [ ] As cases involving unauthorized mutilation and disposition of bodies increased toward the end of the 19th century, paralleling the rise in demand for human cadavers in medical science and use of cremation as an alternative to burial, [ ] courts began to recognize an exclusive right of the next of kin to possess and control the disposition of the bodies of their dead relatives, the violation of which was actionable at law. Thus, in holding that a city council could not "seize upon existing private burial grounds, make them public, and exclude the proprietors from their management," the Supreme Court of Indiana commented that "the burial of the dead can [not] ... be taken out of the hands of the relatives thereof" because "we lay down the proposition, that the bodies of the dead belong to the surviving relations, in the order of inheritance, as property, and that they have the right to dispose of them as such, within restrictions analogous to those by which the disposition of other property may be regulated." [ ] * * *

B. Interests in Dead Bodies in California Law

[The court traces the history of California law concerning the disposition of dead bodies. California courts referred to "quasi-property" rights in cases disputing the handling of cadavers, including cases in which the courts held that civil litigants had no right to demand an autopsy; next-of-kin could exclude the decedent's friends from the funeral; and permitted an action for retaining organs after autopsy.]

C. The Right to Transfer Body Parts

The first successful transplantation of a kidney in 1954 led to an expansion of the rights of next of kin to the bodies of the dead. In 1968, the National Conference of Commissioners on Uniform State Laws approved the Uniform Anatomical Gift Act (UAGA), adopted by California the same year, which grants next of kin the right to transfer the parts of bodies in their possession to others for medical or research purposes. [ ] The right to transfer is limited. The California UAGA prohibits any person from "knowingly, for valuable consideration, purchas[ing] or sell[ing] a part for transplantation, therapy, or reconditioning, if removal of the part is intended to occur after the death of the decedent." Cal. Health & Safety Code § 7155, as does federal law, 42 U.S.C. § 274e (prohibiting the "transfer [of] any human organ for valuable consideration"). * * *

In the 1970s and 1980s, medical science improvements and the related demand for transplant organs prompted governments to search for new ways to increase the supply of organs for donation. [ ] Many perceived as a hindrance to the supply of needed organs the rule implicit in the UAGA that donations could be effected only if consent was received from the decedent or next of kin. [ ] In response, some states passed "presumed consent" laws that allow the taking and transfer of body parts by a coroner without the consent of next of kin as long as no objection to the removal is known. [ ] California Government Code § 27491.47, enacted in 1983, was such a law.

III. DUE PROCESS ANALYSIS

"[T]o provide California non-profit eye banks with an adequate supply of corneal tissue," S. Com. Rep. SB 21 (Cal.1983), § 27491.47(a) authorized the coroner to "remove and release or authorize the removal and release of corneal eye tissue from a body within the coroner's custody" without any effort to notify and obtain the consent of next of kin "if . . . [t]he coroner has no knowledge of objection to the removal." The law also provided that the coroner or any person acting upon his or her request "shall [not] incur civil liability for such removal in an action brought by any person who did not object prior to the removal . . . nor be subject to criminal prosecution." § 27491.47(b).[1]

* * *

In two decisions the Sixth Circuit, the only federal circuit to address the issue until now, held that the interests of next of kin in dead bodies recognized in Michigan and Ohio allowed next of kin to bring § 1983 actions challenging implementation of cornea removal statutes similar to California's. *Whaley v. County of Tuscola*, 58 F.3d 1111 (6th Cir. 1995)(Michigan); *Brotherton v. Cleveland*, 923 F.2d 477 (6th Cir. 1991)(Ohio). * * *

The supreme courts of Florida and Georgia, however, have held that similar legal interests of next of kin in the possession of the body of a deceased family member, recognized as "quasi property" rights in each state, are "not . . . of constitutional dimension." *Georgia Lions Eye Bank, Inc. v. Lavant*, 255 Ga. 60, 335 S.E.2d 127, 128 (1985); *State v. Powell*, 497 So.2d 1188, 1191 (Fla. 1986)(commenting that "[a]ll authorities generally agree that the next of kin have no property right in the remains of a decedent"). The Florida Supreme Court recently rejected the broad implications of the reasoning in *Powell* distinguishing that decision as turning on a balance between the public health interest in cornea donation and the " 'infinitesimally small intrusion' " of their removal. *Crocker v. Pleasant*, 778 So.2d 978, 985, 988 (Fla. 2001)(allowing a § 1983 action to go forward for interference with the right of next of kin to possess the body of their son because "in Florida there is a legitimate claim of entitlement by the next of kin to possession of the remains of a decedent for burial or other lawful disposition").

We agree with the reasoning of the Sixth Circuit and believe that reasoning is applicable here. Under traditional common law principles, serving a duty to protect the dignity of the human body in its final disposition that is deeply rooted in our legal history and social traditions, the parents had exclusive and legitimate claims of entitlement to possess, control, dispose and prevent the violation of the corneas and other parts of the bodies of their deceased children. With California's adoption of the UAGA, Cal. Health and Safety Code § 7151.5, it statutorily recognized other important rights of the parents in relation to the bodies of their deceased children_the right to transfer body parts and refuse to allow their transfer. These are all important components of the group of rights by which property is defined, each of which carried with it the power to exclude others from its exercise, "traditionally . . . one of the most treasured strands in an owner's bundle of property rights." [ ]

* * *

1. For body parts other than corneas, California adopted the 1987 version of the UAGA authorizing transfer when no knowledge of objection is known and after "[a] reasonable effort has been made to locate and inform [next of kin] of their option to make, or object to making, an anatomical gift." Cal. Health & Safety Code § 7151.5(a)(2).

Nor does the fact that California forbids the trade of body parts for profit mean that next of kin lack a property interest in them. The Supreme Court has "never held that a physical item is not 'property' simply because it lacks a positive economic or market value." [ ]

Because the property interests of next of kin to dead bodies are firmly entrenched in the "background principles of property law," based on values and understandings contained in our legal history dating from the Roman Empire, California may not be free to alter them with exceptions that lack "a firm basis in traditional property principles." [ ] We need not, however, decide whether California has transgressed basic property principles with enactment of § 27491.47 because that statute did not extinguish California's legal recognition of the property interests of the parents to the corneas of their deceased children. It allowed the removal of corneas only if "the coroner has no knowledge of objection," a provision that implicitly acknowledges the ongoing property interests of next of kin.

* * *

* * * The property rights that California affords to next of kin to the body of their deceased relatives serve the premium value our society has historically placed on protecting the dignity of the human body in its final disposition. California infringed the dignity of the bodies of the children when it extracted the corneas from those bodies without the consent of the parents. The process of law was due the parents for this deprivation of their rights.

* * *

The scope of the process of law that was due the parents is not a question that we can answer based on the pleadings alone. This question must be addressed in future proceedings.

* * *

We do not hold that California lacks significant interests in obtaining corneas or other organs of the deceased in order to contribute to the lives of the living. Courts are required to evaluate carefully the state's interests in deciding what process must be due the holders of property interests for their deprivation. [ ] An interest so central to the state's core police powers as improving the health of its citizens is certainly one that must be considered seriously in determining what process the parents were due. [ ] But our Constitution requires the government to assert its interests and subject them to scrutiny when it invades the rights of its subjects. Accordingly, we reverse the district court's dismissal of the parents' complaint and remand for proceedings in which the government's justification for its deprivation of parents' interests may be fully aired and appropriately scrutinized.

Notes and Questions

1. The court uses the concept of property as a source of rights on the part of the families in this case. See also Moore v. Regents, 51 Cal.3d 120, 271 Cal.Rptr. 146, 793 P.2d 479 (Ca.1990), in which the court rejected John Moore's conversion claim against the researcher who had removed tissue from his body without his knowledge and used it for research and product development. The court held that Moore did not have a cognizable property right in his body. Is *Newman* inconsis-

tent with *Moore*? Could the body be property in one circumstance and not in another? In resolving the plaintiff's claims in *Newman*, has the court set the stage for the sale of organs? See Michele Goodwin, Formalism and the Legal Status of Body Parts, 2006 U.Chi. Legal F. 317 (2006). See note on markets below.

2.   The Ninth Circuit leaves open the possibility that the State could justify its taking of the corneas. How could the State justify its taking of the corneas without consent? Does it matter that tissue may be used (and perhaps sold) for research instead of transplantation? That some is used for cosmetic surgery instead of life-saving surgery? Would legislation that required a reasonable attempt to contact next-of-kin as opposed to actual consent satisfy due process requirements? Many states have statutes similar to that at issue in *Newman*. For example, some states allow for the removal of any organ without consent after an attempt to contact the family is made. See, e.g., Haw. Rev. Stat. § 327–4. Other states allow for the removal of corneas or specified other tissue without an attempt to notify family when there is no objection known. See, e.g., Mo.Stat. § 58–770, Ark. Code § 12–12–320, and Colo. Rev. Stat. § 30–10–621, which allow for the removal of the pituitary gland under such circumstances. Should the type of tissue involved be relevant to whether consent is required? See, e.g., Carrie O'Keeffe, When an Anatomical "Gift" Isn't a Gift: Presumed Consent Laws As an Affront to Religious Liberty, 7 Texas F. C.L. & C.R. 287 (2002).

3.   The California legislature had amended the statute at issue in *Newman* prior to the Ninth Circuit's consideration of the case. The 1998 amendment requires that the coroner obtain written or telephonic consent of the next of kin prior to removing corneas.

Did the legislature strike the right balance on the second try, or should it have stood behind its original legislation? What are we balancing in presumed consent? Respect for dead bodies? Respect for families? Preservation of life and health? Should other states follow California's lead? The new version of the Uniform Anatomical Gift Act (UAGA), published in 2006, deleted the section that allowed removal of tissue after the coroner had made a "reasonable effort" to contact persons authorized to consent to donation and now provides that no part can be removed unless there is an anatomical gift. The comments to the Act state that this provision was deleted because of "a series of § 1983 lawsuits" in which such actions were held to violate private property rights. Should the states with statutes like those in note 2 repeal those statutes? Revise them?

4.   Before the decision in *Newman,* the L.A. County coroner's office discontinued the practice of harvesting corneas without consent after a series of news articles demonstrated that the practice had a disproportionate impact on people of color. At the time, 80% of autopsies were performed on African–American or Latino individuals and only 16% on whites. Ralph Frammolino, Harvest of Corneas at Morgue Questioned, L.A. Times, Nov. 2, 1997. Would this data alter your analysis of the advisability of relying on presumed consent for organ or tissue harvesting? See, Michele Goodwin, Rethinking Legislative Consent Law, 5 DePaul J. Health Care L. 257 (2002) and Deconstructing Legislative Consent Law: Organ Taking, Racial Profiling and Distributive Justice, 6 V.J.L. & Tech. 2 (2001). Presumed consent assumes that it reflects the choice most people would make if given the opportunity. Is that a persuasive claim in this situation? See, e.g., Gil Siegel & Richard Bonnie, Closing the Organ Gap: A Reciprocity–Based Social Contract Approach, 34 J. L. Med. & Ethics 415 (2006). See also, AMA, Presumed Consent and Mandated Choice for Organs from Deceased Donors, Policy 3–2.155, June 2005.

5. Should cadavers be considered "commons" available for public use for compelling reasons? See, e.g., D. Micah Hester, Why We Must Leave Our Organs to Others, 6 Am. J. Bioethics W23 (2006). For an analysis of individual control of body parts under the mainstream theories of legal thought, see Guido Calabresi, An Introduction to Legal Thought: Four Approaches to Law and to the Allocation of Body Parts, 55 Stan. L. Rev. 2113 (2003).

6. It had been hoped that "routine inquiry" or "required request" mandates in which the hospital is required to ask families about organ donation at the time the option became imminent would increase the number of organs donated. That has not been the case. Why do people refuse at the point of the death of a family member? Some facilities have found that who asks the family makes a difference. See e.g., Pulling Together, UNOS Update, July/August 1996, p. 10, reporting on comparative donation rates for requests made by doctors, nurses, or bereavement staff in ascending order in terms of positive response. "Mandated choice," requiring that individuals identify as an organ donor or not at prescribed common events such as getting a driver's license, is gaining some support, although there is some concern that individuals may be more likely to refuse to be identified as a potential donor if pushed. See AMA Report, supra, note 4.

7. The UAGA allows the donor to designate an individual or organization as a recipient, and some believe that this provision can incentivize more donations. LifeSharers is a non-profit organization that has set up a national network for mutual designation of organ donation. Its web site states:

> If you ever need an organ for a transplant operation, chances are you will die before you get one. You can improve your odds by joining LifeSharers. Membership is free. LifeSharers is a non-profit national network of organ donors. LifeSharers members promise to donate upon their death, and they give fellow members first access to their organs. As a LifeSharer member, you will have access to organs that otherwise may not be available to you. As the LifeSharers network grows, more and more organs may become available to you—if you are a member.

LifeSharers argues that a membership network in which members get priority for organs donated by members is justified because "it's not fair to give organs to non-donors when there are donors who need them. But people who have agreed to donate their organs when they die get only about 50% of the organs transplanted in the United States." In order to qualify for priority for LifeSharers donated organs, an individual must be a member for 180 days prior to transplantation. LifeSharers organs that are not suitable for any LifeSharers member would be made available for distribution as an undesignated donation. As of December 2007, LifeSharers claimed over 10,000 members, a 59% increase over the previous year. See http://www.lifesharers.com/. Should LifeSharers be encouraged? See, Elisa Gordon, Haunted by the "God Committee": Reciprocity Does No Justice to Eliminating Social Disparities, 4 Am. J. Bioethics 23 (2004), arguing that these systems disadvantage people with hereditary diseases such as polycystic kidney disease who would be excluded from donating and who are most likely to need a kidney; Adam J. Kolber, A Matter of Priority: Transplanting Organs Preferentially to Registered Donors, 55 Rutgers L. Rev. 671 (2003), arguing that registered donors should have preferential access to organs to increase registration and donation; Michael T. Morley, Increasing the Supply of Organs for Transplantation Through Paired Organ Exchanges, 21 Yale L. & Pol'y Rev. 221 (2003). Designated donations don't always go as planned, however. See Colavito v. New York Organ Donor Network, 438 F.3d 214 (2006).

Note: The "Dead Donor Rule" and Organ Supply

The "dead donor rule," under which life-sustaining organs may be removed only from persons who have died, has been a central principle in ethics, law, and policy concerning organ recovery. The current legal standard for determination of death as performed in the typical organ-donation case, is the whole-brain death standard. The standard has been adopted by the states in part to allow for removal of organs while the person is still attached to a ventilator so that the organs remain oxygenated and transplantable. There have also been efforts to expand the legal standard for determination of death in order to increase the supply of organs, including neocortical or "higher brain death" standard, "brain absence," and donation after cardiac death.

Note: Market Solutions to Organ Shortage

Federal law provides that it is illegal for "any person to knowingly acquire, receive, or otherwise transfer any human organ for valuable consideration for use in human transplantation if the transfer affects interstate commerce." The federal statute defines human organ as "human (including fetal) kidney, liver, heart, lung, pancreas, bone marrow, cornea, eye, bone, and skin or any subpart thereof." Federal law provides that "valuable consideration" does not include "reasonable payments associated with the removal, transportation, implantation, processing, preservation, quality control, and storage of a human organ or the expenses of travel, housing, and lost wages incurred by the donor of a human organ in connection with the donation . . .". 42 U.S.C.A. § 274(e). The UAGA provides that "a person that for valuable consideration, knowingly purchases or sells [an organ, eye, or tissue] for transplantation or therapy if removal of a part from an individual is intended to occur after the individual's death" commits a crime except that "a person may charge a reasonable amount for the removal, processing, preservation, quality control, storage, transportation, implantation, or disposal" of the organ, eye, or tissue. (§ 16) How does the sale of blood, semen, and ova proceed under these statutes? Is the sale of these items different in kind from the sales prohibited under the UAGA or the federal act?

Could an unemployed living kidney donor be paid "lost wages" for the time spent on the removal of the organ and recovery? What should the hourly rate for organ transplantation be? If the donor earns minimum wage, is that the amount that should be paid? Should the lawyer-donor and the cook-donor be paid differently for the same labor? Are ova donors, who are paid several thousand dollars, being paid for their ova or for expenses or for their time? Should this compensation be allowed? Required? Regulated?

Pennsylvania has established a public trust fund to supply funds to families of decedents who donate organs. Payments would be limited to $3,000 and could be used to cover funeral expenses and incidental expenses borne by the family in relation to the donation. 20 Pa.C.S.A. § 88622. See discussion in John Zen Jackson, When It Comes to Transplant Organs, Demand Far Exceeds Supply, 170 N. J. L. J. 910 (2002). Other states have implemented income tax incentives allowing living donors to deduct expenses related to donation. Wis. Stat.Ann. § 71.05. The federal Organ Donation and Recovery Improvement Act of 2004 provides reimbursement for living donors for travel and certain living expenses. 42 U.S.C. § 274f. Donees matched with donors through matchingdonors.com pay donors for travel and living expenses, as well as lost wages and "walking around money." First Ever Organ Transplant Brokered by an Internet Company Causes Stir in US Transplant Community, Transplant News, Oct. 30, 2004. A subcommittee of the Secretary's Advisory Committee has recommended that the NOTA be amended to allow the Secretary to specify what counts as prohibited "valuable consideration" with an eye toward expanding the allowable payments to donors. HHS Advisory Committee on Organ Transplantation, Recommendation 36, November 2004.

In light of the prohibition on sales and the requirement of consent, is the scarcity of human organs any less a result of policy decisions than is the scarcity of other health care services or goods? If it could be proven that allowing the sale of non-life-sustaining organs (such as a single kidney or a part of the liver) by living persons or the sale of any organs by or on behalf of the estate (or creditors) of cadavers would substantially increase the number of organs available, would you support legalization of such sales? If so, under what circumstances?

Historically, the legal boundaries established in the UAGA and in the NOTA have been strong enough to deter the development of a market system even though there are legal gaps that give some room for such a market. Support for financial incentives for "donation" seems to be increasing, however. In June, 2002, the AMA House of Delegates adopted a report from the Association's Council on Ethical and Judicial Affairs (CEJA) recommending that financial incentives for the donation of cadaveric organs be tested on an experimental basis. Cadaveric Organ Donations: Encouraging the Study of Motivation, Report of the Council on Ethical and Judicial Affairs, available in proceedings of the 2002 Annual Meeting of the AMA posted on the AMA's web site at www.ama-assn.org. The AMA has supported limited financial incentives for cadaveric organ donation since 1993. (See Financial Incentives for Organ Donation, Policy E-2.15). The 2002 report recommends rigorous study of the impact of certain financial incentives under the following circumstances: consultation and advice is sought from the population to be studied; written protocols with sound study design are approved by institutional review boards and are available to the public; incentives are modest and set at the lowest level that can reasonably be expected to increase donations; no study should include payment to living donors and should be limited to cadaveric organs only; organs so donated should be allocated by UNOS under medical need standards so that purchases between specific individuals do not occur.

Major concerns about moving to a market in human organs include the commodification and demeaning of the human body; the desperation of the poor which would undermine autonomy and consent for the sale; and the disparate impact on poor populations who would become objects for the rich. It is also feared that the introduction of financial incentives would destroy altruistic donations, increasing the expense of transplants and would introduce elements of fraud undercutting any boundaries that might be set. The counterweights to these arguments include the need for life-saving organs; respect for human individualism and autonomy; and recognition that there is wealth being made in the current transplant industry that is not shared with the donors.

Do the limitations in the AMA proposal respond to these concerns? Do you think that ultimately the sale of organs will be legalized? If so, what limitations do you expect to see, if any? Would the form of compensation or incentive make a difference; i.e., are tax credits or discounted insurance premiums or donations to charities in the name of the organ source more acceptable than direct payments?

For an excellent symposium on public policy and legal issues, see Symposium, Precious Commodities: The Supply & Demand of Body Parts, 55 DePaul L. Rev. 793 (2006). See also, Michele Goodwin, Black Markets: The Supply and Demand of

Body Parts (2006), arguing in favor of a market and challenging conventional wisdom about the potential negative impact on minorities; Mark Cherry, Kidney for Sale by Owner: Human Organs, Transplantation, and the Market (2005), arguing in favor of markets; and Institute of Medicine, Organ Donation: Opportunities for Action (2006), rejecting market exchanges. For a good discussion of these issues from an ethical perspective, see the March 2003 issue of the Kennedy Institute of Ethics Journal, including, Robert Veatch, Why Liberals Should Accept Financial Incentives for Organ Procurement; Amitai Etzioni, Organ Donation: A Communitarian Approach; and Jeffrey Kahn, Three Views of Organ Procurement Policy: Moving Ahead or Giving Up?

Problem: Organ Donation and the UAGA

Laurel Singer, age 17, and her friend Peter Klaus, age 21, were brought to General Hospital after an extremely serious car accident. Although they were alive when treated by the emergency medical technicians in the ambulances, they have since each suffered cardiac arrest. Efforts by the emergency room doctors to resuscitate them have failed. Both Laurel and Peter have died, and the physicians have initiated procedures to preserve their organs for transplantation. Time is critical. Laurel's and Peter's friends have tried to contact their parents. Laurel's parents have arrived at the ER, but Peter's parents are on vacation somewhere in Asia. Laurel signed the organ donor card on the back of her driver's license; however, Laurel's parents have told the hospital to discontinue the organ maintenance procedures and objected to removal of her organs. Peter didn't have a driver's license, but his friends all agree that he was clear about his intentions to be an organ donor.

Assume that the following provisions of the UAGA have been adopted in your state:

§ 4. Who May Make Anatomical Gift Before Donor's Death

(1) [T]he donor, if the donor is an adult or if the donor is a minor and is:

(A) emancipated; or

(B) authorized under state law to apply for a driver's license because the donor is at least [insert the youngest age at which an individual may apply for any type of driver's license] years of age;

. . .

(3) a parent of the donor, if the donor is an unemancipated minor. . . .

(4) the donor's guardian.

§ 8. Preclusive Effect of Anatomical Gift, Amendment, or Revocation.

(a) Except as otherwise provided in subsection (g) . . . , in the absence of an express, contrary indication by the donor, a person other than the donor is barred from making, amending, or revoking an anatomical gift of a donor's body or part if the donor made an anatomical gift of the donor's body or part under Section 5. . . .

(g) If a donor who is an unemancipated minor dies, a parent of the donor who is reasonably available may revoke or amend an anatomical gift of the donor's body or part.

(h) If an unemancipated minor who signed a refusal dies, a parent of the minor who is reasonably available may revoke the minor's refusal.

§ 9. Who May Make Anatomical Gift of Decedent's Body or Part.

(a) Subject to subsections (b) and (c) and unless barred by Section ... 8, an anatomical gift of a decedent's body or part for purpose of transplantation, therapy, research, or education may be made by any member of the following classes of persons who is reasonably available, in the order of priority listed:

(1) an agent [appointed by the decedent prior to death];

(2) the spouse of the decedent;

(3) adult children of the decedent;

(4) parents of the decedent;

(5) adult siblings of the decedent;

(6) adult grandchildren of the decedent;

(7) grandparents of the decedent;

(8) an adult who exhibited special care and concern for the decedent;

(9) the persons who were acting as the [guardians] of the person of the decedent at the time of death; and

(10) any other person having the authority to dispose of the decedent's body.

§ 14. Rights and Duties of Procurement Organization and Others.

(f) Upon the death of a minor who was a donor or had signed a refusal, unless a procurement organization knows the minor is emancipated, the procurement organization shall conduct a reasonable search for the parents of the minor and provide the parents with an opportunity to revoke or amend the anatomical gift or revoke the refusal.

(i) Neither the physician who attends the decedent at death nor the physician who determines the time of the decedent's death may participate in the procedures for removing or transplanting a part from the decedent.

§ 18. Immunity.

(a) A person that acts in accordance with this [act] or with the applicable anatomical gift law of another state, or attempts in good faith to do so, is not liable for the act in a civil action, criminal prosecution, or administrative proceeding.

May a surgeon remove Laurel's and Peter's transplantable organs? Under the UAGA, what must the doctor do in order to proceed? Do Laurel's parents have the right to stop the removal of her organs? If Peter's parents arrive after the surgery has been completed and they object to the removal of their son's organs, do they have any action against the emergency room doctor, the surgeon, or the hospital? How far does the good faith immunity provision of the UAGA extend? Would the hospital and surgeon be entitled to summary judgment on the parents' claim under this immunity clause? What would the parents' damages be if they did have a claim?

A surprising number of cases have been filed against hospitals and transplant centers for actions taken in the harvesting of organs. See, for example, Schembre v. Mid–America Transplant Assn., 135 S.W.3d 527 (Mo. Ct. App. 2004), denying summary judgment in favor of the defendant because negligence of the nurse in explaining procurement of bone is a question of fact; Sattler v. Northwest Tissue Ctr., 110 Wash.App. 689, 42 P.3d 440 (Ct. App. 2002), holding that the question of good faith in the immunity provision precluded summary judgment where the surviving husband claimed that he had authorized harvesting of bone and skin but not the eyes and the hospital's agent claimed that he had; Perry v. Saint Francis Hosp., 886 F.Supp. 1551 (D. Kan. 1995), holding the hospital liable; Jacobsen v. Marin Gen. Hosp., 192 F.3d 881 (9th Cir. 1999), holding that the hospital was not liable for negligence in a failed effort to reach next of kin; Ramirez v. Health Partners of S. Ariz., 193 Ariz. 325, 972 P.2d 658 (Ct.App. 1998), where the hospital was held to have immunity.

Note: Organs from Living Donors

Living donors who are legally competent may donate non-life-sustaining organs and frequently do so for family members in need. In addition, transplant centers are arranging kidney "paired donations" (KPD) in which a living donor whose kidney is incompatible with a family member is matched with others in the same situation and the kidneys are exchanged across family lines. See, e.g. Dept. of Justice, Legality of Alternative Organ Donation Practices under 42 U.S.C. 274e (Mar. 28, 2007), at www.usdoj.gov/olc/2007/organtransplant.pdf, concluding, inter alia, that paired donations do not violate the federal prohibition against the payment of consideration for organ transplants. Some transplant centers also have seen an increase in the number of persons who offer to donate a nonvital organ to anyone who needs it. See Lainie F. Ross, Solid Organ Donation Between Strangers, 30 J.L. Med. & Ethics 440 (2002), for a discussion of the ethical issues arising in intervivos donation; Sally Satel, Desperately Seeking a Kidney, N.Y. Times Magazine (Dec. 16, 2007), for a first-person narrative of the search for a kidney donor.

As living donors have become more common, concerns over safety and outcomes for donors have emerged. See, e.g., Secretary's Advisory Committee on Organ Transplantation, Recommendation 1–7; Medicare Program, Conditions of Participation: Requirements for Approval and Re-approval of Transplant Centers to Perform Organ Transplants, 72 Fed. Reg. 15,198 (Mar. 30, 2007). The Transplantation Society has adopted international standards for recovery of organs from living donors. The Ethics Comm. of the Transplantation Soc'y, Consensus Statement of the Amsterdam Forum on the Care of the Live Kidney Donor, 79 Transplantation 491 (Aug. 27, 2004).

Although ethical issues relating to coercion and consent arise in any intervivos donation, especially those within families, legal issues arise primarily when the donor is legally incompetent. The principles discussed in these cases are the same as those that govern other medical treatment decisions for incompetent patients.

In Strunk v. Strunk, 445 S.W.2d 145 (Ky. Ct. App. 1969), for example, the court decided that it would permit a kidney to be removed from an incompetent ward of the state, upon petition of his mother, to be transplanted into the body of his brother who was dying of kidney disease. The court concluded that the court should use "substituted judgment;" that is, it should decide as the incompetent would if he were capable. In addition, the court stated that the best interests of the incompetent brother were served by allowing the transplant, because in donating a kidney to save his brother's life, the incompetent brother's mental well-being was ensured.

The court in In re Guardianship of Pescinski, 67 Wis.2d 4, 226 N.W.2d 180 (1975), explicitly rejected the substituted judgment rule of *Strunk* in favor of examining exclusively whether the organ donation was in the "best interests" of the incompetent. In *Pescinski*, the court concluded that there was "absolutely no evidence here that any interests of the ward will be served by the transplant." The court appeared to base its conclusion on Pescinski's mental illness which was characterized by "marked indifference" and "flight from reality." The court described the lack of a relationship between Pescinski and his sister who needed the kidney. Would *Pescinski* have been decided differently under the best interests test if the facts were the same as those in *Strunk?* Should the court have been more concerned about the sibling donee? See, John Robertson, Organ Donations by Incompetents and the Substituted Judgment Doctrine, 76 Colum. L. Rev. 48 (1976); Michael T. Morley, Proxy Consent to Organ Donation by Incompetents, 111 Yale L.J. 1215 (2002).

In *Strunk* and *Pescinski*, a sibling donor already existed. What if he had not? In 1989, the parents of Anissa Ayala, who suffered from leukemia and needed a bone marrow transplant, decided to have another child. They hoped that the new sibling could donate bone marrow to Anissa, but they realized that there was only a one in four chance she would be a match. Anissa's sister, Marissa, was born in 1990, and she qualified as a match. She was physically able to donate marrow at six months. Extracting bone marrow can be risky and painful. Should the hospital require court approval before proceeding, or is this the kind of decision parents should ordinarily make for their children? How should the court rule in the case of an infant donor? A survey of 15 bone marrow transplant centers indicated that at least forty children donors had been conceived knowing of the need for a bone marrow donation to a sibling. Reported in, Vicki G. Norton, Unnatural Selection: Nontherapeutic Preimplantation Genetic Screening and Proposed Regulation, 41 UCLA L. Rev. 1581 (1994). See also, Curran v. Bosze, 141 Ill.2d 473, 153 Ill.Dec. 213, 566 N.E.2d 1319 (1990), refusing order for blood testing of toddlers for potential transplant to half-sibling. See also Michele Goodwin, My Sister's Keeper?: Law, Children, and Compelled Donation, 29 W. New Eng. L. Rev. 357 (2007).

Chapter 2

QUALITY CONTROL REGULATION: LICENSING OF HEALTH CARE PROFESSIONALS

The overarching concerns treated throughout this casebook—quality, cost, access, and choice—are at stake in the debate over whether the licensure and disciplinary system produces overall negative or positive outcomes for patients. Take, for example, the restrictions concerning the provision of health services by unlicensed providers. Does the prohibition against the provision of birthing assistance by lay midwives produce higher quality outcomes for mothers and babies? And, even if it were so, is the gain worth the probable cost in terms of access to prenatal care for impoverished women or in terms of individual choice of attendant or site for childbirth? These questions aren't confined to non-physician providers. What standards should the boards use in disciplining physicians or nurses for particular practices? In aggressively monitoring and investigating prescribing practices of doctors treating patients for chronic pain, do the boards contribute to the quality of care available to patients or do they drive physicians away from treating such patients and thus decrease access to treatment? Who should decide whether particular modes of treatment should be used—individual doctors (or nurses or homeopaths) with their patients or a regulatory board? If nurse practitioners practicing in drug-store clinics can provide care more cheaply than doctors, are restrictions on their scope of practice worth the increased cost of care?

Although this debate over professional licensure is an old one, it has been reenergized by changes in the health care system. Among these are a strong movement for alternative or complementary medicine; the growth of non-physician licensed health care professions; and fundamental changes in medical practice itself, including, for example, the movement to increase access to controlled substances for pain relief or the movement back toward midwifery for assistance in childbirth.

Perhaps the most significant change that challenges the conventional operation of state licensure and discipline is the development of more robust data banks formed from electronic patient medical records, pharmacy records, payment records, and other electronic health services information. The traditional rationale for health care quality regulation is the imperfect information available to consumers to make their own risk-benefit balance in selecting provider or treatment as well as limitations on the capacity of patients to evaluate the information that is available. As data becomes cheaper and more accessible—although not equally accessible across all patient populations—health care quality regulation will be challenged:

> [W]hat implications will the health information revolution have for the health care regulatory framework? One possible answer is that the health information revolution should prompt us to regulate less. A patient with access to information about individual providers' quality of care, for example, would have less need for state medical boards' assistance in rooting out poor quality providers. . . . A second possible answer is that the health information revolution should prompt us to regulate more. Information imperfections will persist forever, so regulation can at least potentially benefit some patients. Because information about quality is an input into the regulation process, and technological innovation has reduced the cost of such information, we can regulate more cheaply than we once could. Kristin Madison, Regulating Health Care Quality in an Information Age, 40 U.C. Davis L Rev. 1577 (2007).

Professor Madison offers a third alternative to this either-or option. She argues that the less-or-more dichotomy doesn't entirely capture the reorientation of health care regulation that better information technology makes possible. She categorizes regulatory responses into three types: market-restricting interventions such as restrictive licensure; market-facilitating responses such as the mandates for report cards and increased disclosure of information (including disciplinary actions or malpractice settlements or patient satisfaction surveys or outcomes) to the public; and market-channeling efforts (such as certification) which influence provider behavior without restrictive governmental control mandates.

As you read the materials in this chapter, ask the questions we have discussed in this introduction. Does the particular regulation improve the quality of health care, and what evidence exists that this is or is not so? Does the particular regulatory intervention diminish access to care, either by raising the cost or by confining personal choice? Are laypersons, especially those who are ill, capable of assessing the risks and benefits of all health care services or only those within a universe confined by the professional licensure boards? What systems, standards, or processes best position the state licensure boards to achieve their goals of protecting the health and safety of the states' citizens? Finally, what potential impact do you see in particular cases from increased production and dissemination of medical or health information?

To the extent that discipline seeks to protect the public safety by removing incompetent practitioners, how might a licensure board use the data now being produced through electronic medical records? In other cases, such as those involving nonconforming practices, would you be more or less satisfied with, regulation that simply required that a patient receive particular information before choosing the provider or the specific treatment rather than prohibiting the practice altogether or requiring that only licensed individuals provide that treatment? For more on the implications of information developments on medical licensure and discipline, see Timothy S. Jost,

Oversight of the Quality of Medical Care: Regulation, Management or the Market, 37 Ariz. L. Rev. 825 (1995); William M. Sage, Regulating Through Information: Disclosure Laws and American Healthcare, 99 Colum. L. Rev. 1701 (1999).

A second focus in the critique of the operation of licensure boards goes to the structure of these boards. State law controls licensure of health care professionals under the state's police power. Licensing statutes govern entry into the licensed professions and disciplinary actions against licensed health care professionals. Licensure also regulates the scope of health care services that licensed professionals may provide and prohibits unlicensed persons from providing services reserved for the licensed professions. These statutes are implemented by boards that operate as state agencies but which generally are dominated by members of the licensed profession. Licensure in the U.S., thus, is often described as a system of professional self-regulation, even though the boards act as state agencies; usually include lay members; are governed by procedures and standards set in the state's licensing statute and administrative procedures act; and are subject to judicial review in both their adjudicatory and rulemaking decisions.

Professional participation in licensure may further the public interest by bringing expertise to the evaluation of professionals' competency and behavior. Professional domination of licensure has been strongly criticized, however, as serving the interests of the professions at the expense of their competitors and of the public. For analyses of the debate over professional control of licensure, see Carl F. Ameringer, State Medical Boards and the Politics of Public Protection (1999); Frances H. Miller, Medical Discipline in the Twenty–First Century: Are Purchasers the Answer?, 60 L. & Contemp. Probs. 31 (1997); and E. Clarke Ross, Regulating Managed Care: Interest Group Competition for Control of Behavioral Health Care, 24 J. Health Pol., Pol'y & L. 599 (1999). For a historical perspective on the dominance of licensure by allopathic physicians, see Paul Starr, The Social Transformation of American Medicine (1982); and for the classic study of medical licensure and discipline, see Robert C. Derbyshire, Medical Licensure and Discipline in the United States (1978).

I. DISCIPLINE

IN RE WILLIAMS

Supreme Court of Ohio, 1991.
60 Ohio St.3d 85, 573 N.E.2d 638.

Syllabus by the Court

* * *

... Between 1983 and 1986, Dr. Williams prescribed Biphetamine or Obetrol for fifty patients as part of a weight control treatment regimen. [Both drugs are controlled substances.]

On November 17, 1986, appellant, the Ohio State Medical Board ("board"), promulgated Ohio Adm.Code 4731–11–03(B), which prohibited the use of [drugs such as Biphetamine and Obetrol] for purposes of weight control. Dr. Williams ceased prescribing Biphetamine and Obetrol for weight control upon becoming aware of the rule.

By letter dated March 12, 1987, the board charged Dr. Williams with violating R.C. 4731.22(B)[2] by prescribing these stimulants without "reasonable care," and thereby failing to conform to minimal standards of medical practice. The crux of the board's charge was that Dr. Williams had departed from accepted standards of care by using these drugs as a long-term, rather than a short-term, treatment.

A hearing was held before a board examiner. The parties stipulated to the accuracy of the medical records of the patients in question, which detailed the use of Biphetamine and Obetrol for periods ranging from nearly seven months to several years. The board also introduced into evidence the Physician's Desk Reference entries for Biphetamine and Obetrol, which recommend that these drugs be used for only "a few weeks" in the treatment of obesity. The board presented no testimony or other evidence of the applicable standard of care.

Dr. Williams presented expert testimony from Dr. John P. Morgan, the director of the pharmacology program at the City University of New York Medical School, and Dr. Eljorn Don Nelson, an associate professor of clinical pharmacology at the University of Cincinnati College of Medicine. These experts stated that there are two schools of thought in the medical community concerning the use of stimulants for weight control. The so-called "majority" view holds that stimulants should only be used for short periods, if at all, in weight control programs. The "minority" view holds that the long-term use of stimulants is proper in the context of a supervised physician-patient relationship. Both experts testified that, though they themselves supported the "majority" view, Dr. Williams's application of the "minority" protocol was not substandard medical practice.

The hearing examiner found that Dr. Williams's practices violated R.C. 4731.22(B). The examiner recommended subjecting Dr. Williams to a three-year monitored probation period. The board modified the penalty, imposing a one-year suspension of Dr. Williams's license followed by a five-year probationary period, during which he would be unable to prescribe or dispense controlled substances

Dr. Williams appealed to the Court of Common Pleas of Franklin County pursuant to R.C. 119.12. The court found that the board's order was ". . . not supported by reliable, probative and substantial evidence and . . . [was] not in accordance with law." The court of appeals affirmed.

HERBERT R. BROWN, JUSTICE.

In an appeal from an administrative agency, a reviewing court is bound to uphold the agency's order if it is ". . . supported by reliable, probative, and substantial evidence and is in accordance with law. . . ."[ ]. In the instant

---

2. R.C. 4731.22(B) provides in pertinent part:

"The board, pursuant to an adjudicatory hearing. . . . shall, to the extent permitted by law,. . . . [discipline] the holder of a certificate [to practice medicine] for one or more of the following reasons:

. . . .

"(2) Failure to use reasonable care, discrimination in the administration of drugs, or failure to employ acceptable scientific methods in the selection of drugs or other modalities for treatment of disease;

"(3) Selling, prescribing, giving away, or administering drugs for other than legal and legitimate therapeutic purposes. . . .

. . . .

"(6) A departure from, or the failure to conform to, minimal standards of care. . . . [.]"

case, we must determine if the common pleas court erred by finding that the board's order was not supported by sufficient evidence. For the reasons, which follow, we conclude that it did not and affirm the judgment of the court below.

In its arguments to this court, the board contends that Arlen v. Ohio State Medical Bd. (1980), 61 Ohio St.2d 168, 15 O.O.3d 190, 399 N.E.2d 1251, is dispositive. In *Arlen*, the physician was disciplined because he had written prescriptions for controlled substances to a person who the physician knew was redistributing the drugs to others, a practice prohibited by R.C. 3719.06(A). The physician appealed on the ground that the board failed to present expert testimony that such prescribing practices fell below a reasonable standard of care.

We held that the board is not required in every case to present expert testimony on the acceptable standard of medical practice before it can find that a physician's conduct falls below this standard. We noted that the usual purpose of expert testimony is to assist the trier of facts in understanding "issues that require scientific or specialized knowledge or experience beyond the scope of common occurrences. . . ."[ ] The board was then made up of ten (now twelve) persons, eight of whom are licensed physicians. [ ] Thus, a majority of board members are themselves experts in the medical field who already possess the specialized knowledge needed to determine the acceptable standard of general medical practice.

While the board need not, in every case, present expert testimony to support a charge against an accused physician, the charge must be supported by some reliable, probative and substantial evidence. It is here that the case against Dr. Williams fails, as it is very different from *Arlen*.

Arlen involved a physician who dispensed controlled substances in a manner that not only fell below the acceptable standard of medical practice, but also violated the applicable statute governing prescription and dispensing of these drugs. In contrast, Dr. Williams dispensed controlled substances in what was, at the time, a legally permitted manner, albeit one which was disfavored by many in the medical community. The only evidence in the record on this issue was the testimony of Dr. Williams's expert witnesses that his use of controlled substances in weight control programs did not fall below the acceptable standard of medical practice. While the board has broad discretion to resolve evidentiary conflicts [ ] and determine the weight to be given expert testimony [ ], it cannot convert its own disagreement with an expert's opinion into affirmative evidence of a contrary proposition where the issue is one on which medical experts are divided and there is no statute or rule governing the situation.

It should be noted, however, that where the General Assembly has prohibited a particular medical practice by statute, or where the board has done so through its rulemaking authority, the existence of a body of expert opinion supporting that practice would not excuse a violation. Thus, if Dr. Williams had continued to prescribe Biphetamine or Obetrol for weight control after the promulgation of Ohio Adm.Code 4731–11–03(B), this would be a violation of R.C. 4731.22(B)(3), and the existence of the "minority" view supporting the use of these substances for weight control would provide him no defense. Under those facts, *Arlen* would be dispositive. Here, however, there is insufficient evidence, expert or otherwise, to support the charges against Dr. Williams. Were the board's decision to be affirmed on the facts in this record, it would mean that a doctor would have no access to meaningful review of the board's decision. The board, though a majority of its members have special knowledge, is not entitled to exercise such unbridled discretion.

WRIGHT, JUSTICE, dissenting.

The message we send to the medical community's regulators with today's decision is one, I daresay, we would never countenance for their counterparts in the legal community. We are telling those charged with policing the medical profession that their expertise as to what constitutes the acceptable standard of medical practice is not enough to overcome the assertion that challenged conduct does not violate a state statute. * * *

HOOVER v. THE AGENCY FOR HEALTH
CARE ADMINISTRATION

District Court of Appeal of Florida, 1996.
676 So.2d 1380.

JORGENSON, JUDGE.

Dr. Katherine Anne Hoover, a board-certified physician in internal medicine, appeals a final order of the Board of Medicine penalizing her and restricting her license to practice medicine in the State of Florida. We reverse because the board has once again engaged in the uniformly rejected practice of overzealously supplanting a hearing officer's valid findings of fact regarding a doctor's prescription practices with its own opinion in a case founded on a woefully inadequate quantum of evidence.

In March 1994, the Department of Business and Professional Regulation (predecessor in these proceedings to the Agency for Health Care Administration) filed an administrative complaint alleging that Dr. Hoover (1) inappropriately and excessively prescribed various ... controlled substances to seven of her patients and (2) provided care of those patients that fell below that level of care, skill, and treatment which is recognized by a reasonably prudent similar physician as being acceptable under similar conditions and circumstances; in violation of sections 458.331(1)(q) and (t), Florida Statutes, respectively. All seven of the patients had been treated by Dr. Hoover for intractable pain arising from various non-cancerous diseases or ailments.

Dr. Hoover disputed the allegations of the administrative complaint and requested a formal hearing. * * *

The agency presented the testimony of two physicians as experts. Neither had examined any of the patients or their medical records. The sole basis for the opinions of the agency physicians was computer printouts from pharmacies in Key West where the doctor's patients had filled their prescriptions. These printouts indicated only the quantity of each drug filled for each patient, occasionally referring to a simplified diagnosis. Both of these physicians practiced internal medicine and neither specialized in the care of chronic pain. In fact, both doctors testified that they did not treat but referred their chronic pain patients to pain management clinics. The hearing officer found that this was a common practice among physicians—perhaps to avoid prosecutions like this case.[5] Both doctors "candidly testified that without being

---

5. Referral to a pain management clinic was not an option for Dr. Hoover's indigent Key West resident patients.

provided with copies of the medical records for those patients they could not evaluate Respondent's diagnoses or what alternative modalities were attempted or what testing was done to support the use of the medication chosen by Respondent to treat those patients." Despite this paucity of evidence, lack of familiarity, and seeming lack of expertise, the agency's physicians testified at the hearing that the doctor had prescribed excessive, perhaps lethal amounts of narcotics, and had practiced below the standard of care.

Dr. Hoover testified in great detail concerning the condition of each of the patients, her diagnoses and courses of treatment, alternatives attempted, the patients' need for medication, the uniformly improved function of the patients with the amount of medication prescribed, and her frequency of writing prescriptions to allow her close monitoring of the patients. She presented corroborating physician testimony regarding the appropriateness of the particular medications and the amounts prescribed and her office-setting response to the patients' requests for relief from intractable pain.

Following post-hearing submissions, the hearing officer issued her recommended order finding that the agency had failed to meet its burden of proof on all charges. The hearing officer concluded, for instance, "Petitioner failed to provide its experts with adequate information to show the necessary similar conditions and circumstances upon which they could render opinions that showed clearly and convincingly that Respondent failed to meet the standard of care required of her in her treatment of the patients in question."

The agency filed exceptions to the recommended findings of fact and conclusions of law as to five of the seven patients. The board of medicine accepted all the agency's exceptions, amended the findings of fact in accordance with the agency's suggestions, and found the doctor in violation of sections 458.331(1)(q) and (t), Florida Statutes. The board imposed the penalty recommended by the agency: a reprimand, a $4,000 administrative fine, continuing medical education on prescribing abusable drugs, and two years probation. This appeal follows.

For each of the five patients, the hearing officer found the prescribing practices of Doctor Hoover to be appropriate. This was based upon (1) the doctor's testimony regarding the specific care given, (2) the corroborating testimony of her physician witness, and (3) the fact that the doctor's prescriptions did not exceed the federal guidelines for treatment of intractable pain in cancer patients, though none of the five patients were diagnosed as suffering from cancer.

The board rejected these findings as not based on competent substantial evidence. As particular reasons, the board adopted the arguments of the agency's exceptions to the recommended order that (1) the hearing officer's findings were erroneously based on irrelevant federal guidelines, and (2) the agency's physicians had testified that the doctor's prescription pattern was below the standard of care and outside the practice of medicine. * * *

First, the board mischaracterizes the hearing officer's reference to the federal guidelines. The board reasoned in its final order that "[t]he record reflects that the federal guidelines relied upon by the Hearing Officer for this finding were designed for cancer patients and [the five patients at issue were] not being treated for cancer." It is true, as the hearing officer noted,

"Respondent presented expert evidence that there is a set of guidelines which have been issued for the use of Schedule II controlled substances to treat intractable pain and that although those guidelines were established to guide physicians in treating cancer patients, those are the only guidelines available at this time. Utilizing those guidelines, because they exist, the amount of medication prescribed by Respondent to the patients in question was not excessive or inappropriate."

In so finding, however, the hearing officer did not, as the board suggests, rely solely upon the federal guidelines in its ruling that the doctor's prescribing practices were not excessive. Rather, the federal guidelines merely buttressed fact findings that were independently supported by the hearing officer's determination of the persuasiveness and credibility of the physician witnesses on each side. For example, though he admitted he had not even reviewed the federal guidelines, one of the agency physicians asserted that the amounts prescribed constituted a "tremendous number of pills" and that the doses involved would be lethal. That Dr. Hoover's prescriptions fell within the guidelines for chronic-pained cancer patients may properly be considered to refute this assertion. Such a use of the federal guidelines was relevant and reasonable.

Second, Dr. Hoover testified in great detail concerning her treatment of each patient, the patient's progress under the medication she prescribed, and that the treatment was within the standard of care and practice of medicine. The hearing officer, as arbiter of credibility, was entitled to believe what the doctor and her physician expert opined. [ ] The agency's witnesses' ultimate conclusions do not strip the hearing officer's reliance upon Dr. Hoover of its competence and substantiality. The hearing officer was entitled to give Dr. Hoover's testimony greater weight than that of the agency's witnesses, who did not examine these patients or regularly engage in the treatment of intractable pain.

[T]he hearing officer explicitly recognized that the 1994 [Florida] intractable pain law was not in effect at the time of Dr. Hoover's alleged infractions but cited it for a permissible purpose—to rebut any claim that there is a strong public policy mandate in favor of the board's draconian policy of policing pain prescription practice. [ ] * * *

Reversed.

Note: State and Federal Regulation of Prescribing Practices

Both *Williams* and *Hoover* involve disciplinary action by a state medical board based on a physician's prescribing practices. Physician prescribing is also constricted by the Food and Drug Administration and the Drug Enforcement Administration, two powerful federal agencies. Public and private payers (such as Medicare and Medicaid on the one hand and private insurers on the other) also influence prescribing through coverage and payment policies.

In our federal system, the regulation of the practice of medicine traditionally has belonged to the states through the police power. As you know, our federal government is a government of limited powers, and the authority it has exercised in health care regulation is based primarily upon several enumerated powers; e.g., the taxing power, the spending power, and the power to regulate interstate commerce.

Congress did not intend that either the FDA or the DEA would engage in the regulation of the *legitimate* practice of medicine. The boundary between the agencies' statutory authority and the restraint on their regulation of medical practice is blurry, however, both because of inherent problems in the interaction of law and medicine as well as because of conflicts over appropriate health policy. See Lars Noah, Ambivalent Commitments to Federalism in Controlling the Practice of Medicine, 53 U. Kan. L. Rev. 149 (2004).

The FDA has the authority to approve and monitor the safety of drugs and devices; and this certainly makes the FDA an important gatekeeper of access to drugs. Once a drug is approved for prescribing, however, the FDA does not have the authority to restrict physicians in their prescribing of the drug for particular purposes. Thus, once a drug is approved for a particular purpose (e.g., for the treatment of a particular sort of cancer), a physician may prescribe the drug for other purposes (e.g., for the treatment of another type of cancer). Prescribing drugs for a different purpose, in a higher or lower dose, or for a different population (e.g., children) than those for which the FDA approved the medication is called "off-label" prescribing. You'll see in *McDonagh*, the principle case in the next section, that his prescription of chelation therapy was "off-label." Off-label prescribing is common and necessary in the practice of medicine and may be the standard of care in particular circumstances, although such prescribing raises issues of medical judgment, evidence-based medicine, and the relations between pharmaceutical firms and prescribing physicians. See, e.g., Sandra H. Johnson, Polluting Medical Judgment? False Assumptions in the Pursuit of False Claims Regarding Off-Label Prescribing, 9 Minn. J. L. Sci. Tech. 61 (2008). Off-label prescribing can also raise liability concerns.

The DEA more directly regulates the individual physician's prescribing practices through its authority under the Controlled Substances Act. 21 U.S.C. § 801. Under the CSA, the federal government governs the production and distribution of drugs that have the potential for abuse or addiction. Such drugs are categorized as controlled substances and placed on a "schedule" that rates a drug by its abuse potential from Schedule V (the lowest potential) to Schedule I and II (the highest potential). Schedule I drugs, including heroin and marijuana, are those that are believed to have a very high potential for abuse and no therapeutic benefit. Doctors may not prescribe Schedule I drugs. Schedule II medications have known therapeutic value and are available for prescribing.

Doctors must have a permit issued by the DEA to prescribe drugs on Schedules II through V. The DEA may revoke a permit or pursue criminal action against physicians whose prescription or distribution of these drugs falls outside of the DEA's view of legitimate medical practice. In recent years, DEA policies have conflicted directly with state health policy on several fronts.

One of the areas in dispute is the legalization of marijuana for medical use. At least eight states have enacted legislation to allow physicians or patients access to marijuana for the treatment of medical conditions. See, e.g., Cal. Health & Saf. Code § 11362.5. The federal government has actively opposed such efforts by aggressively enforcing federal prohibitions under the CSA, stimulating significant challenges to federal authority. In United States v. Oakland Cannabis Buyers' Cooperative, 532 U.S. 483, 121 S.Ct. 1711, 149

L.Ed.2d 722 (2001), the Supreme Court held that the CSA did not contain an implied "medical necessity" defense that would prevent the DEA from enforcing the prohibition on prescribing or using marijuana for medical purposes. Advocates then moved to a Constitutional challenge to the CSA. In Gonzales v. Raich, 545 U.S. 1, 125 S.Ct. 2195, 162 L.Ed.2d 1 (2005), the Supreme Court rejected the argument that the CSA exceeded the federal government's authority under the Commerce Clause. During the course of the litigation over federal authority in regard to marijuana, however, the Ninth Circuit held that physicians had a First Amendment right to discuss medical marijuana with their patients in the face of federal threats to prosecute doctors who did so. Conant v. Walters, 309 F.3d 629 (9th Cir. 2002), *cert. denied,* 540 U.S. 946, 124 S.Ct. 387, 157 L.Ed.2d 276 (2003). See Randy E. Barnett, The Presumption of Liberty and the Public Interest: Medical Marijuana and Fundamental Rights, 22 Wash. U. J.L. & Pol'y 29 (2006). For further discussion of marijuana, see discussion in Section II of this Chapter. There has also been considerable federal-state conflict over the legalization of physician-assisted suicide.

Doctors treating patients in pain also confront an area of conflict between state and federal drug policy. At the time of the *Hoover* case, there was strong evidence that medical boards had not adjusted their standards to reflect medical evidence that supported the use of opioids for treatment over the long term and in higher doses than had been customary. This meant that doctors who treated their patients' chronic pain effectively were at risk of disciplinary action while those doctors who provided inadequate treatment faced no legal risk at all. In an attempt to balance legal risks, nearly half of the states enacted legislation generally referred to as "intractable pain treatment acts" which limit state agencies from taking action against physicians in certain circumstances, as discussed in the notes below. The Federation of State Medical Boards also adopted a model policy that specifically recognizes that opioids are essential to the treatment of pain and that state medical boards should be equally concerned about the neglect of pain as they are about prescribing abuse. FSMB, Model Policy for the Use of Controlled Substances for the Treatment of Pain (2004); Sandra H. Johnson, Providing Relief to Those in Pain: A Retrospective on the Scholarship and Impact of the Mayday Project, 31 J.L. Med. & Ethics 15 (2003); Diane Hoffmann & Anita Tarzian, Achieving the Right Balance in Oversight of Physician Opioid Prescribing for Pain: The Role of the State Medical Boards, 31 J.L. Med. & Ethics 21 (2003).

The DEA initially followed the pattern established in the states and issued a statement in 2001 advocating a balanced regulatory policy for prescription of controlled substances for pain management that would account both for concerns over addiction and diversion and concerns for patients needing treatment for chronic pain. In 2003, the DEA issued an FAQ that described its policies in enforcing the CSA, policies that were consistent with the FSMB policy for medical boards. In late 2003, however, the DEA issued a press release entitled "The Myth of the Chilling Effect" in which it claimed that "doctors operating within the bounds of accepted medical practice have nothing to fear." In 2004, the agency withdrew the FAQ document citing "misstatements" and signaling an enforcement policy that departed from that developed by the FSMB. The National Association of Attorneys General expressed concern that as state medical boards took steps to ensure access to pain treatment, the DEA was moving to criminalize physician prescribing, commenting that "the state and federal policies are diverging with respect to the relative emphasis on ensuring the availability of prescription pain medications to those who need them." Available at http://www.naag.org/news/pdf/so–20050119–prescription-pain-med.pdf See Dispensing Controlled Substances for the Treatment of Pain, 71 Fed. Reg. 52,716–23 (Sept. 6, 2006), (codified at 21 C.F.R. pt. 1306). On criminal prosecutions of physicians, see Diane Hoffmann, Legitimate Prosecution or Unnecessary Persecution? The Investigation, Arrest, and Prosecution of Physicians for Opioid Prescribing, 1 St. L. U. J. Health L. & Pol'y ___ (2008). For more on the legal issues relating to the treatment of patients in pain, see Symposium, Legal and Institutional Constraints on Effective Pain Relief, 24 J. L. Med. & Ethics (1997), Symposium, Legal and Regulatory Issues in Pain Management, 26 J. L. Med. & Ethics (1998); Symposium, Pain Management in the Emergency Department: Current Landscape and Agenda for Research, 33 J. L. Med. & Ethics (2005); Ben A. Rich, The Politics of Pain: Rhetoric or Reform?, 8 DePaul J. Health Care L. 519 (2005).

Notes and Questions

1.   Both *Williams* and *Hoover* involve disputes within the medical profession concerning appropriate medical treatment during a transition in professional standards. When the literature on health care regulation references "information failure" as a justification for licensure and discipline, it usually refers to the lack of information available to the patient or the limited capacity of the patient to use available information. Is that the only type of information problem we have in these first two cases? What evidence-based standards existed in the *Hoover* case, if any? Did access to increased health data (e.g., the computerized pharmacy records of her prescriptions) enhance or detract from regulatory decision making?

2.   The Ohio State Medical Board promulgated an administrative rule, cited in *Williams*, requiring that physicians meet the majority standard of practice regarding the prescription of controlled substances. Should licensure boards establish standards of practice or practice guidelines that prefer one approach over another; or should they simply recognize the full range of medical practices, including minority views? Would your answer depend on whether the board was acting in a rulemaking or in an adjudicatory role? Should they consider requiring physicians to inform their patients that the particular recommended treatment is not accepted by the majority of physicians and then allow patients to decide what course of treatment to follow? Do *Williams* and *Hoover* present identical issues in that regard? Do *Hoover* and *Williams* present special challenges because the medications may have a risk of use or diversion for nontherapeutic uses? How should state boards account for the gatekeeper role of physicians in such cases? Where does concern for the public health lie in such cases?

3.   The court in *Hoover* implies that disciplinary actions by a state medical board against individual physicians have an effect on other physicians' practices. Beyond penalizing or removing the "bad apple" from practice, this is actually a core objective of professional discipline. In the case of treatment for pain, however, this deterrence has been called the "Chilling Effect" because the threat of legal sanction seems to lead doctors to avoid legitimate and effective treatments. Judge Kozinski of the Ninth Circuit noted this impact as well, quoting an expert:

Physicians are particularly easily deterred by the threat of governmental investigation and/or sanction from engaging in conduct that is entirely lawful and medically appropriate.... [A] physician's practice is particularly dependent upon the physician's maintaining a reputation of unimpeachable integrity. A physician's career can be effectively destroyed merely by the fact that a governmental body has investigated his or her practice.... Concurring Opinion in Conant v. Walters, 309 F.3d 629 (9th Cir. 2002), *cert. denied,* 540 U.S. 946 (2003).

If this perception of physician reactions to the threat of investigation is accurate, what are the implications for medical boards that want to encourage quality care? Should disciplinary boards refrain from investigations? Should the standards for beginning an investigation be higher because of this impact? Or, does the public health demand active investigations whenever physician prescribing appears questionable? Can anything be done in the investigatory process that could diminish the unintended consequence of driving doctors away from treating chronic pain patients? Similar concerns arise whenever the boards investigate physician practices, including for example, physicians who collaborate with nonphysician providers or provide expert testimony for plaintiffs in malpractice litigation. See discussion in notes following *Sermchief* below.

4. The Florida statute referenced in *Hoover* provides:

Notwithstanding any other provision of law, a physician may prescribe or administer any controlled substance to a person for the treatment of intractable pain, provided the physician does so in accordance with the level of care, skill, and treatment recognized by a reasonable prudent physician under similar conditions and circumstances.

Would this statute provide adequate protection to physicians such as Dr. Hoover? Should it be more specific? Is it appropriate for legislatures to enact statutes concerning permissible medical practices, or should they leave that to rulemaking by the licensure boards?

5. The rationale for physicians' dominance of the membership of state medical boards is that practitioners of the regulated profession are in the best position to judge the practices of their peers. What, then, is at the heart of the dispute over expert testimony in *Williams*? See Huff v. North Dakota State Bd. Of Med. Examiners, 690 N.W.2d 221 (N.D. 2004). On what basis did the Florida court reject the testimony of the agency's experts in *Hoover*?

6. In 2006, 2,916 serious disciplinary actions were taken by state medical boards against physicians, with 0.318% of physicians being disciplined. States varied widely in the rates of discipline. For a state-by-state ranking, see The Public Citizen, Ranking of State Medical Boards' Serious Disciplinary Actions, 2004–2006 available at www.citizen.org/publications. Is 0.318% of physicians too many or too few? How would you measure whether the number of disciplinary actions in your state was too many, too few, or just right? A study of disciplinary actions levied between 1994 and 2002 concludes that somewhere between 25% and 30% of actions were taken for incompetence or negligence or other quality concerns, but that it is hard to analyze the data accurately. Darren Grant & Kelly C. Alfred, Sanctions and Recidivism: An Evaluation of Physician Discipline by State Medical Boards, 32 J. Health Pol. Pol'y & L. 867 (2007). This study also found a high repeat rate among physicians disciplined. Of those physicians receiving a "medium or severe" sanction in one period (1994–1998), 20% were sanctioned at least once again in the second period (1999–2004).

7. If the boards must set priorities due to limited resources, what should those priorities be? Should they focus on the more easily proven cases? Should they respond first to consumer complaints? See Timothy S. Jost, et al., Consumers, Complaints, and Professional Discipline: A Look at Medical Licensure Boards,

3 Health Matrix 309 (1993). Should they affirmatively seek outcomes data on individual physicians from hospitals and medical practice organizations and make it a priority to pursue doctors with poorer outcomes? How would the board's funding levels and staffing configuration influence its effectiveness in relation to this priority? For an excellent study of the operation of medical boards, see Randall R. Bovbjerg, et al., State Discipline of Physicians: Assessing State Medical Boards through Case Studies, U.S. Dept. of Health and Human Services (2006).

8. Following the lead of Massachusetts, most states have established publicly accessible web sites where they post physician profiles. The Massachusetts site posts background information on the physician (such as education, specialties, insurance plans) as well as malpractice claims paid, hospital credentialing actions, criminal convictions, and board disciplinary actions. Mass. Bd. of Reg. in Med., On–Line Physician Profile Site, http://profiles.massmedboard.org Should these sites expand to include complaints filed with the medical board? Malpractice suits filed? Deselection by health plans? See Anonymous v. Bureau of Prof'l Med. Conduct, 2 N.Y.3d 663, 781 N.Y.S.2d 270, 814 N.E.2d 440 (2004), holding that board abused discretion in posting all disciplinary charges against a disciplined physician who had been exonerated of all charges but one. See also Szold v. Med. Bd. of California, 127 Cal.App.4th 591, 25 Cal.Rptr.3d 665 (Ct. App. 2005), interpreting statute requiring posting of disciplinary actions. If an open book on physicians is created, at what point could it replace the disciplinary system?

9. Congress established the National Practitioner Data Bank (NPDB) in part to create an effective system for preventing doctors with disciplinary history in one state from moving to another and practicing until detected, if ever. 42 U.S.C. §§ 11101–11152. State disciplinary and licensure boards are required to report certain disciplinary actions against physicians. Hospitals and other entities engaging in peer review processes are required to report adverse actions as well. Licensure boards have access to the Data Bank to check on licensees, and hospitals must check the Data Bank for physicians applying for staff privileges and periodically for physicians who hold staff privileges. The general public is not allowed access to the information in the Data Bank although there have been several proposals for allowing increased access. The General Accountability Office has issued a report that is quite critical of the accuracy of the information contained in the Data Bank, however, including the information that is reported by state medical boards. National Practitioner Data Bank: Major Improvements Are Needed to Enhance Data Bank's Reliability, GAO–01–130 (Nov. 2000). For arguments for and against public access, see Kristen Baczynski, Do You Know Who Your Physician Is?: Placing Physician Information on the Internet, 87 Iowa L. Rev. 1303 (2002); Laura A. Chernitsky, Constitutional Arguments in Favor of Modifying the HCQIA to Allow the Dissemination of Information to Healthcare Consumers, 63 Wash. & Lee L. Rev. 737 (2006).

10. Most states have established programs to provide rehabilitative, non-punitive interventions for impaired nurses, doctors, and other health professionals. The rehabilitative approach to impairment naturally emerges from the recent emphasis on chemical dependency as an illness rather than a failure in character. It also responds to perceived concerns that a punitive disciplinary approach pushes impaired health care providers undercover, risking greater injury to the public. It is hoped that the availability of a program of non-punitive rehabilitation encourages a higher rate of reporting and self-reporting of impaired physicians. Carol K. Morrow, Doctors Helping Doctors, 14 Hastings Ctr. Rep. 32 (1984). Still, reporting impaired colleagues to health care organizations much less to the

medical board is not common. Ken Terry, Impaired Physicians: Speak No Evil? 19 Med. Econ. 110 (2002).

Physicians who are disciplined for impairment due to drug or alcohol abuse are more likely to have their licenses restored than those disciplined for other reasons, but they are also more likely to be subject to repeat disciplinary action. M.C.Holtman, Disciplinary Careers of Drug-Impaired Physicians, 64 Soc.Sci.Med. 543 (2007). Most studies of physician treatment programs indicate relapse rates of 15% to 25%, some indicating lower rates than the general population. M. F. Fleming, Physician Impairment: Options for Intervention, 50 Am. Fam. Physician 41 (1994); Patrick G. O'Connor & Anderson Spickard, Physician Impairment by Substance Abuse, 81 Med. Clinics N.A. 1037 (1997). Other studies indicate relapse rates ranging from 30% to 57%, although the severity and duration of relapse may vary. Kathryn L. Sprinkle, Physician Alcoholism: A Survey of the Literature, 81 J. Med. Lic. & Disc. 113 (1994).

Should voluntary enrollment in an impaired professional program be confidential, or should the program be required to notify the board of the enrollment? Should boards allow impaired professionals to choose a rehabilitative program with discipline stayed and then expunged upon successful completion? Can rehabilitation be coerced? Should physicians who are abusing alcohol or drugs or who are participating in a state-sanctioned rehabilitation program be required to inform their patients? Would this protect the public? See Barry R. Furrow, Doctors' Dirty Little Secrets: The Dark Side of Medical Privacy, 37 Washburn L.J. 283 (1998), arguing that informed consent is inadequate protection in such a case.

11. The federal Americans with Disabilities Act prohibits discrimination against persons who have a physical or mental disability; a record of disability; or are viewed as having a disability. 42 U.S.C. § 12101. Title II of the ADA applies to licensure and discipline by the professional licensure boards of the States. 28 C.F.R. § 35.130(b)(6) (1991). See, e.g., Colorado State Bd. of Med. Examiners v. Ogin, 56 P.3d 1233 (Colo. Ct. App. 2002). See also Yuri N. Walker, The Impact of the Americans with Disabilities Act on Licensure Considerations Involving Mentally Impaired Medical and Legal Professionals, 25 J. Legal Med. 441 (2004), concluding that the ADA does not seriously constrict the ability of the boards to enforce licensure requirements. There has been significant litigation (including two Supreme Court cases) over the issue of whether the states are immune under the Eleventh Amendment from Title II ADA damages claims in their governmental functions, but that question seems to have settled against immunity for state medical boards. See, e.g., Guttman v. Khalsa, 446 F.3d 1027 (10th Cir. 2006).

Problem: Three Strikes and You're Out?

Medical boards report that disciplinary actions for substandard care or incompetency are the most difficult in terms of requirements of time, expert witnesses, legal representation, and expense. Although some studies point out the vagaries of the malpractice litigation system, studies are consistent on one point: the filing of a malpractice claim against a physician, even if no payment is made on the claim, is predictive of future malpractice claims. See, e.g., Randall R. Bovbjerg & Kenneth R. Petronis, The Relationship Between Physicians' Malpractice Claims History and Later Claims: Does the Past Predict the Future? 272 JAMA 1421(1994); Grant & Alfred, supra, note 6.

Some states are beginning to integrate malpractice actions into their disciplinary processes. Almost all states require that liability carriers report claims paid to the board, and some states require reporting of claims filed. State medical boards can access the NPDB, where 70% of the reports are of malpractice payouts. A study by Public Citizen, however, found that only 33% of doctors who had paid out on ten or more malpractice claims were disciplined in any way by their state boards. Public Citizen, The Great Medical Malpractice Hoax: NPDB Data Continue to Show Medical Liability System Produces Rational Outcomes, Jan. 2007, available at http://www.citizen.org/documents/NPDBReport_Final.pdf. State boards report that they received "far too many reports of malpractice payouts to investigate them all," and some boards don't even list these payouts as "complaints" against the defendant licensee. Randall R. Bovbjerg, et al., supra, note 7. Some states require investigation of physicians with multiple malpractice settlements or judgments. See, e.g., Mich. Comp.Laws Ann. § 333.16231.

Consider the following two problems:

1) In 2004, Florida voters approved by an overwhelming majority the following amendment to the state constitution:

> (a) No person who has been found to have committed three or more incidents of medical malpractice shall be licensed. . . .

> (b)(1) The phrase "medical malpractice" means the failure to practice medicine . . . with that level of care, skill, and treatment recognized in general law related to health care providers' licensure. . . .

> (b)(2) The phrase "found to have committed" means that the malpractice has been found in a final judgment of a court of law, final administrative agency decision, or decision of binding arbitration.

Thereafter, the Florida legislature codified the amendment in the medical licensure statute but added the following provision:

> [T]he board shall not license or continue to license a medical doctor found to have committed repeated medical malpractice, the finding of which was based upon clear and convincing evidence. In order to rely on an incident of medical malpractice to determine whether a license must be denied or revoked under this section, if the facts supporting the finding of the incident of medical malpractice were determined on a standard less stringent than clear and convincing evidence, the board shall review the record of the case and determine whether the finding would be supported under a standard of clear and convincing evidence.

Did the legislature significantly alter the impact of the amendment? Why might they have made this change? See Roy Spece & John Marchalonis, Sound Constitutional Analysis, Moral Principle, and Wise Policy Judgment Require A Clear and Convincing Evidence Standard of Proof in Physician Disciplinary Proceedings, 3 Ind. Health L. Rev. 107 (2006), recognizing that two-thirds of states require the lower preponderance of the evidence standard; Advisory Opinion to the Attorney General Re Public Protection From Repeated Medical Malpractice, 880 So.2d 667 (Fla. 2004), in which the court reviewed the proposed amendment. See also Kan. Stat. Ann. § 65–2836, allowing but not requiring disciplinary action when: "The licensee has an adverse judgment, award or settlement against the licensee resulting from a medical liability claim related to acts or conduct similar to acts or conduct which would constitute grounds for disciplinary action." Should discipline be mandatory in such a case?

2) Assume that your state's licensure statute provides only that disciplinary action may be taken when a physician has engaged in:

> Any conduct or practice which is or might be harmful or dangerous to the mental or physical health of a patient or the public; or incompetency, gross negligence or repeated negligence in the performance of the functions or duties of any profession licensed or regulated by this chapter. For the

purposes of this subdivision, "repeated negligence" means the failure, on more than one occasion, to use that degree of skill and learning ordinarily used under the same or similar circumstances by the member of the applicant's or licensee's profession.

Administrative agencies, such as state medical boards, have limited authority. One significant limitation is that an agency has only that authority delegated to it by the legislature in its enabling statute. Thus, any rulemaking by the agency must fall within its statutory authority. Does the medical board in this case have the authority to issue a rule or adopt a policy that it will sanction a doctor with final judgments of malpractice in three or more cases? A doctor with ten or more malpractice claims made?

Note: State Medical Boards and Telemedicine

The term telemedicine encompasses a wide range of activities—including online physician consultations with specialists, review of imaging by offsite radiologists, and continuing contact with a physician's patients through e-mail. These activities have generated volumes examining liability issues, the jurisdiction of dozens of regulatory bodies, credentialing, contract, and intellectual property issues, among other legal questions. See generally Symposium, E–Health: Perspective and Promise, 46 St. Louis U.L.J. 1 (2002); Archie A. Alexander, American Diagnostic Radiology Moves Offshore: Is this Field Riding the "Internet Wave" into a Regulatory Abyss?, 20 J. L. & Health 199 (2007). For a discussion of the broader reaches of telemedicine, see Nicolas P. Terry, Cyber–Malpractice: Legal Exposure for Cybermedicine, 25 Am. J. L. & Med. 327 (1999), part of a symposium issue.

Telemedicine is oblivious to state boundaries. Medical licensure, however, is controlled by each state individually; and physicians, with few exceptions, must hold a license in each state in which they practice. If the only contact between patient and doctor is via the Internet, has the doctor gone to the "out-of-state" patient or has the patient "come" to the doctor? Many states have adopted legislation specifically to regulate the practice of telemedicine. The state of Indiana, for example, permits physicians outside of Indiana to provide consultation services to Indiana physicians without any regulatory permit but otherwise requires an Indiana medical license for any physician who is "[p]roviding diagnostic or treatment services to a person in Indiana when [those services] are transmitted through electronic communications; and are on a regular, routine and non-episodic basis...." Ind. Code Ann. § 25–22.5–1–1.1(a)(4). Most states that have amended their licensure statutes have followed a similar form although some states do not include the exception for consultation. Ohio requires that physicians, licensed in another state, prescribing medication or treatment for Ohio residents over the Internet hold a certificate for the "practice of telemedicine" issued by the medical board. Ohio Rev. Code Ann. § 4731.296

States are particularly concerned about Internet prescribing for controlled substances. A California statute enacted in 2000 provides for civil penalties of $25,000 per occurrence for prescribing over the Internet without a good faith physical exam. Cal. Bus. & Prof. Code § 2242.1. In an early action under that statute, the Medical Board of California fined six out-of-state doctors for issuing just under 2,000 prescriptions to California residents over the Internet. The prescriptions were primarily for drugs to treat sexual dysfunction, hair loss, and obesity. Laura Mahoney, Medical Board Fines Six Doctors $48 Million for Internet Prescriptions, 12 Health L. Rep. 223 (2003). See also, North Dakota High–Volume Web Drug Prescriber Properly Disciplined for Lack of Care, 14 Health L. Rep. 184

(2005). For an argument advocating aggressive enforcement against online pharmacies, see Sara E. Zeman, Regulation of Online Pharmacies: A Case for Cooperative Federalism, 10 Annals Health L. 105 (2001). For a more cautious approach aimed at preserving benefits to patients, see David B. Brushwood, Responsive Regulation of Internet Pharmacy Practice, 10 Annals Health L. 75 (2001). See also, Jeremy W. Hochberg, Nailing Jell–O to a Wall: Regulating Internet Pharmacies, 37 J. Health L. 445 (2004); John D. Blum, Internet Medicine and the Evolving Legal Status of the Physician–Patient Relationship, 24 J. Leg. Med. 413 (2003); Nicolas P. Terry, Prescriptions sans Frontières (Or How I Stopped Worrying About Viagra on the Web But Grew Concerned about the Future of Healthcare Delivery), 4 Yale J. Health Pol'y L. & Ethics 183 (2004).

II.   COMPLEMENTARY AND ALTERNATIVE MEDICINE (CAM)

CAM is a group of diverse medical and health care systems, practices, and products that are not presently considered to be part of conventional medicine as practiced by holders of M.D. or D.O. degrees and by their allied health practitioners. ... The list of what is considered to be CAM changes continually, as those therapies that are proven to be safe and effective become adopted into conventional health care and as new approaches to health care emerge.

CAM practices [fall] into four domains: Whole medical systems [including] homeopathy, naturopathy, Chinese medicine, and ayurveda ...; Mind-body medicine [including] meditation, prayer, mental healing, and therapies that use ... art, music, or dance ...; Biologically based practices [that] use substances found in nature, such as herbs, foods, and vitamins ...; Energy medicine [including] biofield therapies [such as] qi gong, reiki, and therapeutic touch ... and bioelectromagnetic-based therapies [such as] pulsed fields, magnetic fields, or alternating-current or direct-current fields.

"What is CAM?" National Institutes of Health, National Center for Complementary and Alternative Medicine (NCCAM), available at http://nccam.nih.gov/health/whatiscam/

This definition of CAM represents a "medicalized" definition of alternative approaches to health care as it implies that approaches to health care that are not currently accepted by conventional medicine are so because they are not yet scientifically validated. This is, then, a controversial definition. It provides a workable definition for our task, however, as it captures the fluid sense of what is conventional and what is alternative as well as the vastness of what might be considered complementary and alternative "medicine." This medically oriented definition also captures the current legal framework for CAM, although that framework appears to be changing quickly.

The interest in alternative and complementary medicine, whether new and innovative or traditional but no longer mainstream, has increased dramatically. Some estimates place the spending on CAM at over $25 billion dollars annually. Notably, the utilization of alternative or complementary health services is increasing at higher rates among younger age groups: 30% of persons born before 1945 report using CAM, while 70% of those born between 1965 and 1979 report using these services. John Lunstroth, Voluntary Self–Regulation of Complementary and Alternative Medicine Practitioners, 70 Alb. L. Rev. 209 (2006), which provides an excellent treatise on health care licensure generally. The literature on the regulation of CAM is quite rich. See, e.g., Michael S. Goldstein, The Persistence and Resurgence of Medical Pluralism, 29 J. Health Pol. Pol'y & L. 925 (2004); Andrew M. Knoll, The Reawakening of Complementary and Alternative Medicine at the Turn of the Twenty–First Century: Filling the Void in Conventional Biomedicine, 20 J. Contemp. Health L. & Pol'y 329 (2004); Symposium, Complementary and Alternative Medicine: Here to Stay, But on What Terms?, 31 J. L. Med. & Ethics 183 (2003); Kathleen M. Boozang, Western Medicine Opens the Door to Alternative Medicine, 24 Am. J. L. & Med. 185 (1998); Michael H. Cohen, Complementary and Alternative Medicine: Legal Boundaries and Regulatory Perspectives (1998); The Role of Complementary and Alternative Medicine: Accommodating Pluralism (Daniel Callahan ed., 2002).

State professional licensure systems become involved in CAM in two ways. First, licensed doctors (or nurses, dentists, and so on) may utilize CAM therapies, integrating them within conventional medicine. This will attract the attention of the licensure board if the practice violates licensure standards for acceptable or appropriate treatment. See *McDonagh*, below. In addition, licensure boards may take action against CAM practitioners for violating the state's prohibition of the practice of medicine without a license. This second question is addressed in Section III of this Chapter.

STATE BOARD OF REGISTRATION FOR THE HEALING ARTS v. McDONAGH

123 S.W.3d 146 (Mo. 2003).

LAURA DENVIR STITH, JUDGE.

* * *

I.   FACTUAL AND PROCEDURAL BACKGROUND

The Board licensed Dr. McDonagh, D.O., as an osteopathic physician and surgeon in 1961. Soon after becoming licensed, he began employing alternative medical treatments in his family practice, including EDTA [ethylene diamine tetra-acetic acid] chelation therapy to treat atherosclerosis and other diseases. He also became certified by the American Board of Chelation Therapy, and has conducted research and written extensively on the use of this therapy.

A.   *Regulation of Chelation Therapy by the Board.*

Chelation therapy has been approved by the federal Food and Drug Administration (FDA) only as a means for the removal of heavy metals from the body. However, non-FDA-approved, or "off-label," use of medications by physicians is not prohibited by the FDA and is generally accepted in the medical profession. [ ] Approximately 1,000 physicians in the United States engage in the off-label use of chelation therapy to treat atherosclerosis and other vascular conditions.[4] Of these 1,000 United States-based physicians, 750

---

4. This practice, which began to emerge in the 1950s, involves the intravenous adminis-

tration of a diluted solution containing EDTA, as well as various vitamins and minerals. Pro-

belong to the American College for Advancement in Medicine (ACAM), which has 1,000 members worldwide and which endorsed chelation therapy as a valid course of treatment for occlusive vascular and degenerative diseases associated with aging.[5] To that end, ACAM developed a protocol, followed by Dr. McDonagh, for using chelation therapy to treat such diseases.

In 1989, the Board made an in-depth study of the efficacy of chelation therapy, but did not thereafter adopt any rules, regulations, or position papers on the use of this therapy. Then, in 1992 and 1994, two controlled studies were published that suggested that chelation therapy was ineffective in treating vascular disease. Dr. McDonagh disputes the validity of these studies. But, after the publication of the studies, the American Medical Association (AMA) adopted a position statement on chelation therapy, declaring that: "(1) [t]here is no scientific documentation that the use of chelation therapy is effective in the treatment of cardiovascular disease, atherosclerosis, rheumatoid arthritis, and cancer"; (2) chelation therapy proponents should conduct controlled studies and adhere to FDA research guidelines if they want the therapy to be accepted more broadly; and (3) "[t]he AMA believes that chelation therapy for atherosclerosis is an experimental process without proven efficacy." AMA, AMA Policy Compendium H–175 .994, H–175.997 (1994).

In spite of these developments, neither the FDA, the AMA, or the Board banned the use of chelation therapy to treat vascular disease, and Dr. McDonagh continued to prescribe and administer the therapy in his practice.

Effective October 30, 2001, the Board adopted a rule stating that chelation therapy was of no medical value but that it would not seek to discipline a physician for using it on a patient from whom appropriate informed consent is received:

(1) [T]he board declares the use of ethylinediaminetetracetic acid (EDTA) chelation on a patient is of no medical or osteopathic value except for those uses approved by the Food and Drug Administration (FDA) by federal regulation.

(2) The board shall not seek disciplinary action against a licensee based solely upon a non-approved use of EDTA chelation if the licensee has the patient sign the Informed Consent for EDTA Chelation Therapy form, included herein, before beginning the non-approved use of EDTA chelation on a patient. [CSR 150–2.165]

B. Complaints Against Dr. McDonagh.

In 1994, seven years prior to the adoption of CSR 150–2.165, and shortly after the two noted controlled studies, the Board filed a complaint against Dr. McDonagh arising out of two inquiries regarding his use of chelation therapy.

ponents contend EDTA "chelates"—or bonds—with substances that accumulate and block arteries, and, then, flushes these compounds from the body through the urine.

5. In 1999, the Federal Trade Commission and ACAM entered into a consent agreement under which ACAM agreed not to make any representations regarding EDTA chelation therapy's effectiveness as a treatment for ath-

erosclerosis. *In re Am. Coll. for Advancement in Med.*, No. C–3882 (Fed. Trade Comm'n June 22, 1999) *at* http:// www.ftc.gov/os/1999/07/ 9623147c3881acam.do.htm. *See also* American College for Advancement in Medicine, 64 Fed. Reg. 12,338 (Fed. Trade Comm'n Mar. 12, 1999) (extension of public comment period on consent agreement).

This complaint was later dismissed without prejudice. In 1996, the Board filed a thirteen-count complaint alleging cause to discipline Dr. McDonagh's medical license for violating section 334.100 by, among other things: endangering the health of patients through the inappropriate provision of chelation therapy; misrepresenting the efficacy of this therapy for atherosclerosis and other diseases; conducting unnecessary testing and treatment in some instances, and insufficient testing and treatment in others; and failing to maintain adequate medical records.

Dr. McDonagh denied that his treatments endangered his patients, denied using inappropriate testing or treatment, and denied inadequate record keeping. He also denied making misrepresentations to patients, noting that, prior to receiving chelation therapy, his patients signed a consent form explaining the possible benefits and side effects of the treatment (very similar to that later approved in 4 CSR 150–2.165), and stating that the treatment was not approved by the FDA, the AMA, or other recognized medical organizations for the treatment of vascular disease. In addition to chelation therapy, Dr. McDonagh encouraged patients to follow a diet and exercise plan, and did not discourage patients from seeing other physicians, including specialists.

The AHC held a hearing in November 1997. The Board introduced expert testimony that the use of chelation therapy to treat vascular disease is not generally accepted in the field of treatment of vascular disease and does not meet the standard of care for treatment of vascular disease. Dr. McDonagh offered expert testimony that supported his off-label use of chelation therapy to treat vascular disease. * * * The AHC ultimately * * * found no evidence of harm from chelation therapy, rejected all thirteen counts, and found no cause to discipline Dr. McDonagh's medical license.

The circuit court affirmed the AHC's decision. The Board appealed. * * *

* * *

The Board * * * argues that, [McDonagh's expert evidence] was insufficient to counter the Board's allegations in various counts, and through expert and other evidence, that Dr. McDonagh's use of chelation therapy constituted "repeated negligence" as that term is used in section 334.100.2(5). That section defines "repeated negligence" as "the failure, on more than one occasion, to use that degree of skill and learning ordinarily used under the same or similar circumstances by the member[s] of the applicant's or licensee's profession."

The Board submits that, in order to counter the Board's experts, Dr. McDonagh's experts needed to testify as to whether he used the degree of skill and learning ordinarily used by members of his profession. But, while his experts testified that his treatment of his patients met "the standard of care," they never identified that standard of care. The Board argues that the standard of care he met must be the standard of care generally accepted in the profession, and this means that Dr. McDonagh is negligent if he treats his patients in a way other than the treatment generally offered by doctors in the field. And, given Dr. McDonagh's experts' admission that mainstream doctors generally do not use chelation therapy to treat vascular disease, the Board suggests, Dr. McDonagh's experts cannot have used the correct standard of care in giving their opinion that his treatment met the required standard.

Dr. McDonagh admits that his experts did not state by what standard of care they were evaluating his treatment of his patients, but argues, * * * the standard is that used by doctors who apply chelation therapy. In effect, he argues that, because he used the protocol approved by ACAM, he could not be found to be negligent and necessarily met the requisite standard of care.

Neither party's argument is correct. * * * The relevant standard of care for discipline for repeated negligence is necessarily that set out in the statute addressing that conduct, section 334.100.2(5). * * * As the issue here is the treatment of persons with vascular disease, the appropriate standard of care *is that used by doctors treating persons with vascular disease.*

Application of this standard does not merely require a determination of what treatment is most popular. Were that the only determinant of skill and learning, any physician who used a medicine for off-label purposes, or who pursued unconventional courses of treatment, could be found to have engaged in repeated negligence and be subject to discipline. * * *

Rather the statute requires only what it says—that Dr. McDonagh use that degree of skill and learning used by members of the profession in similar circumstances. By analogy, one doctor may use medicine to treat heart problems while another might chose to perform a by-pass and a third to perform angioplasty, yet all three may be applying the requisite degree of skill and learning. That they came to differing conclusions by applying that skill and learning does not make one negligent and one non-negligent.

So too, here, if Dr. McDonagh's treatment, including his use of a diet and exercise regimen, and the lack of evidence of harm from his approach, demonstrates the application of the degree of skill and learning ordinarily used by members of his profession, then it is not a basis for discipline under the statute, even if other doctors would apply these facts to reach a different result.

Because, in concluding that Dr. McDonagh did not violate section 334.100.2(5), the AHC relied on Dr. McDonagh's experts' testimony and because this testimony failed to establish whether the experts were using the legal standard of care for "repeated negligence" set out in section 334.100.2(5), this Court must reverse and remand. The circuit court should remand to the AHC for reconsideration * * * in light of the standard of care contained in section 334.100.2(5).

* * *

Wolff, J., concurring in part and dissenting in part.

I write separately to offer ... gentle advice for the board on the future of this case against Dr. McDonagh.

* * *

The real question is: Is the healing arts board's use of section 334.100, which prescribes discipline for repeated acts of "negligence," an inappropriate use of the disciplinary process to impose the board's sense of orthodoxy?

Dr. McDonagh's use of chelation therapy to treat atherosclerosis and other vascular diseases may be unorthodox. None of the mainstream medical organizations endorse its use for vascular diseases. But, until 2001—after the acts the board complains of in this proceeding—there was no law or regulation regulating its use * * *

* * *

The administrative hearing commission heard evidence for eight days on the board's complaint against Dr. McDonagh for his use of chelation therapy and related matters. The commission, in its 70 pages of findings of fact and conclusions of law, found no cause for discipline.

Specifically responding to the board's position that the use of chelation therapy is cause for discipline, the commission concluded: "It is not an unnecessary, harmful or dangerous treatment." The commission characterized McDonagh's conduct as "giving patients a treatment that has provided benefit to many patients, harms no one, and is given with informed consent and the information that this treatment may not work with all patients." The commission further stated, "[T]he evidence shows that patients are being helped. We cannot state that an entire treatment method that provides benefits to patients without harming them constitutes incompetent, inappropriate, grossly negligent, or negligent treatment. Nor can we say that this treatment is misconduct, unprofessional, or a danger to the public."

The commission, based on the record, does acknowledge that chelation therapy involves risks, as of course do other treatments for vascular disease, such as coronary artery surgery. The risks of chelation therapy are disclosed, according to the commission, in the informed consent form that Dr. McDonagh has used with all his patients. * * *

There are scientific studies discussed in the commission's findings as to the efficacy of chelation therapy for vascular conditions. The mainstream organizations accept the conclusions of studies that found no value in treating vascular disease by chelation therapy. Dr. McDonagh and other like-minded physicians, including their American College for Advancement in Medicine, cite case reports and studies—arguably of less validity than the studies relied upon by the mainstream—that show benefits in such use of chelation therapy.

There is a provision of section 334.100 that would seem to cover unorthodox treatments that are of no value. Section 334.100.2(4)(f) provides for discipline where a licensee performs or prescribes "medical services which have been declared by board rule to be of no medical or osteopathic value." But the board did not have a rule against chelation therapy that would apply to Dr. McDonagh's acts, which occurred from 1978 to 1996. The board, long after the acts included in its complaint against Dr. McDonagh, promulgated a rule relating to chelation therapy. * * *

More to the point, when the board finally promulgated its rule that declares chelation therapy to be "of no medical or osteopathic value," the board's rule goes on to provide that the board "shall not seek disciplinary action against a licensee based solely upon a non-approved use of EDTA chelation if the licensee has the patient sign" the informed consent form that accompanies the regulation. [T]he consent form that Dr. McDonagh used for these patients—long before the consent form promulgated by the board—is very similar to the consent form accompanying the 2001 rule.

* * *

As to the board's claims heard in 1997 that are the subject of this appeal, it appears that the absence of a rule left the board to proceed against Dr. McDonagh under 334.100.2(5) for repeated acts of negligence. * * *

So is this off-label use of chelation therapy negligence? The real question—the answer to which is fatal to the board's position—is whether acts of negligence, as defined by this statute, can be cause for discipline if there is no showing that the physician's conduct "is or might be harmful or dangerous [meeting the statutory definition of negligence]." If there is no harm or danger, there is no cause for discipline under this section.

* * *

Physicians are afforded considerable leeway in the use of professional judgment to decide on appropriate treatments, especially when applying the negligence standard. * * * "Negligence" does not seem an appropriate concept where the physician has studied the problem and has made a treatment recommendation, even though that is not the prevailing view of the majority of the profession. The lack of general acceptance of a treatment does not necessarily constitute a breach of the standard of care. The use of negligence in licensing situations, in the absence of harm or danger, is particularly inappropriate.

One could argue that because chelation therapy is not accepted by mainstream medicine and is an off-label practice not approved by the FDA, it is therefore harmful and dangerous. If that were the board's position, the licensing statute would thwart advances in medical science. A dramatic example is the treatment of stomach ulcers, which were long thought to be caused by stress. In 1982, two Australians found the bacterium helicobacter pylori in the stomach linings of ulcer victims. Because helicobacter pylori is a bacterium, some physicians—a minority to be sure—began prescribing antibiotics to treat stomach ulcers as an infectious disease. The National Institutes of Health did not recognize antibiotic therapy until 1994; the FDA approved the first antibiotic for use in treating stomach ulcers in 1996; and the Centers for Disease Control began publicizing the treatment in 1997. Today's physicians accept as fact that most stomach ulcers are primarily caused by helicobacter pylori bacteria infection and not by stress. But, by the chronology of this discovery, if a physician in the late 1980s or early 1990s had treated ulcers with antibiotics, that treatment would have been "negligent" as the board in this case interprets that term because inappropriate use of antibiotics can be dangerous.

I do not mean to suggest that chelation therapy for vascular disease is of the same order as the use of antibiotics for treating stomach ulcers. In fact, I doubt it. But my point is that medicine is not readily regulated by a standard cookbook or set of rules. The board's position in publishing its 2001 rule on chelation therapy seems to recognize this point better than its position in this disciplinary action. If chelation therapy for vascular disease were dangerous, the board's rule that allows its use would be unconscionable.

* * *

The board conceded that there was no evidence of harm from chelation therapy. In the 35 years that he has used chelation therapy, Dr. McDonagh reports that the therapy has not resulted in infection, injury, or death for any of his patients. The commission repeatedly found that chelation therapy "harms no one" and provides "benefit to many patients."[7]

* * *

This case needs to be over. The board should end the case itself rather than suffer the indignity of further adverse commission and judicial rulings, to say nothing of the waste of public resources that such proceedings will entail.

Notes and Questions

1. Assume that you are on the Administrative Hearings Commission to which the Missouri Supreme Court remanded the *McDonagh* case. As you anticipated, the experts produced by the Board, none of whom practice chelation therapy, testify that it does not meet the standard of care and that no self-respecting M.D. or D.O. would use it, while McDonagh's experts testify that anecdotal evidence indicates that it benefits some patients with cardiovascular disease; that Dr. McDonagh meets the standard of care used by those who are willing to provide patients with chelation therapy; and that he uses ordinary medical tests to monitor his patients' progress with the therapy. Do you discipline McDonagh, or do you reject the Board's recommendation? Assume that among McDonagh's patients you find one who refused to undergo cardiac bypass surgery recommended by his cardiologist and who some months later died of a heart attack. What result now? Some are concerned that licensed health care professionals may defraud patients by misrepresenting the risks and benefits of the alternative treatment they prefer. How can the Board respond to that concern?

2. If a medical board is not in a position to test the safety and effectiveness of particular treatments, can it instead rely upon prevailing practice in the medical community? See, In re Guess, 327 N.C. 46, 393 S.E.2d 833 (1990). In this case, Dr. Guess practiced family medicine but regularly incorporated homeopathic medical treatments into his care of his patients. (Homeopathy differs from allopathy, which is the dominant medical approach in the U.S.; but it has a long history and is a recognized form of medicine in a few states. For a brief guide to homeopathy, see http://nccam.nih.gov/health/homeopathy/#q1) The North Carolina medical board charged Guess with unprofessional conduct under a statute that defined such conduct as "any departure from . . . the standards of acceptable and prevailing medical practice . . . irrespective of whether or not a patient is injured thereby." The North Carolina Supreme Court held that Guess violated the statute even though no patient was harmed and that it was within the state's police power to enact a law that prohibited certain conduct based on a judgment that there was some inherent risk in allowing physicians to depart from prevailing standards. Why the difference in result between *Guess* and *McDonagh*? If the North Carolina statute had been in effect in Missouri, would the Board's discipline of McDonagh have been upheld? Which of these two approaches to nonconforming treatment better serves the public interest—North Carolina's or Missouri's?

3. After the *Guess* decision, the North Carolina legislature amended the grounds for discipline to limit the section under which Dr. Guess was penalized:

> The Board shall not revoke the license of or deny a license to a person solely because of that person's practice of a therapy that is experimental, nontradi-

---

7. In contrast, according to the commission, cardiac bypass surgery—an approved therapy for severe arteriosclerosis—has an operative mortality rate of between two and 30 percent, depending on where you are in the United States, and mental impairment occurs in as many as 18 percent of cardiac bypass patients.

tional, or that departs from acceptable and prevailing medical practices unless, by competent evidence, the Board can establish that the treatment has a safety risk greater than the prevailing treatment or that the treatment is generally ineffective. N.C. Gen. Stat. 90–14(a)(6).

How would the North Carolina Board prove the alternative treatment is less safe than prevailing practice where there may be little evidence that the current practice is safe? See, e.g., E. Haavi Morreim, A Dose of Our Own Medicine: Alternative Medicine, Conventional Medicine, and the Standards of Science, 31 J. L. Med. & Ethics 222 (2003). A root problem in the meeting of CAM and allopathic medicine, and in the work of the NCCAM, is the argument that CAM is not amenable to scientific method in testing effectiveness. See discussion in Julie Stone & Joan Matthews, Complementary Medicine and the Law (1996), arguing that while some alternative or complementary practices have a technological base and are subject to the same type of verification as allopathic medicine, other practices are not amenable to such testing; and, therefore, conventional quality-control regulation is inadequate. Some states have enacted legislation to ensure that medical boards be informed about CAM. See, e.g., N.Y. Pub. Health § 230, requiring that the Board include CAM practitioners among its members.

4.   No matter what your conclusion on the merits of particular legislation, understand that these choices are allocated to the legislature. Courts generally do not reject the particular line-drawing that the legislature chooses. See, e.g., In re Guess, supra; Sherman v. Cryns, 203 Ill.2d 264, 271 Ill.Dec. 881, 786 N.E.2d 139, 151 (2003). See discussion of constitutional claims in note 8 after *Ruebke*, below.

5.   Judge Wolff in his concurring opinion notes that the Missouri Board has the statutory authority "for disciplining medical quackery—even where it causes no harm" because under the Missouri statute the Board can issue a rule declaring that a medical service has "no medical or osteopathic value" and then discipline doctors who provide that medical service. How would the court have ruled if the Board had issued a rule prohibiting the use of chelation therapy for particular purposes? For an interesting article on the challenges of identifying quackery, see Maxwell J. Mehlman, Quackery, 31 Am. J. L. & Med. 349 (2005).

6.   The Federation of State Medical Boards issued Model Guidelines for the Use of Complementary and Alternative Therapies in Medical Practices in 2002. http://www.fsmb.org. The Guidelines address CAM and mainstream medicine together and apply particular practice guidelines (including, medical evaluation and informed consent, for example) equally to both. Some states have issued general guidance that addresses both conventional medicine and CAM. The Kentucky Board, for example, issued the following statement:

> Physicians may incorporate non-validated treatments if the research results are very promising, if the physician believes that a particular patient may benefit, if the risk of harm is very low, and if the physician adheres to the conventions that govern the doctrine of informed consent for non-validated treatment. Available at http://www.state.ky.us/agencies/

How would Dr. McDonagh have fared under such a policy? Are these the appropriate standards for more conventional medical treatment decisions as well, including off-label prescribing?

7.   While licensed health care professionals are increasingly incorporating CAM into their standard medical and nursing practices, practitioners offering solely alternative health care services without conventional medical or nursing training or licensure are a very significant arm of the movement toward CAM. In fact, a dominant strain in the CAM movement would argue that only alternative providers can offer such services effectively and authentically. Some states license

practitioners of particular CAM therapies. See, e.g., Ariz. Rev. Stat. § 32–1521 and Alaska Stat. § 08.45.030 (licensing naturopaths); Nev. Rev. Stat. § 630A.155 (licensing homeopaths); Cal. Bus. & Prof. Code § 4935 (licensing acupuncturists). Although medical licensure does not require specific license for specific specialties, some states require that licensed physicians who practice certain forms of CAM hold a separate state license or registration to do so. This seems particularly common with acupuncture. See, for example, Haw. Rev. Stat. § 436–E. Should CAM be treated differently from the allopathic medical specialties by requiring separate licensure? See the Problem that begins the next section.

8.   Is marijuana a complementary medical approach for some conditions? See Institute of Medicine, Marijuana and Medicine (J. Joy, et al., eds., 1999), concluding that "cannabinoid drugs" have potential value for pain relief, control of nausea, and vomiting and appetite stimulation, especially for persons with wasting diseases, and generally for palliative care. Should a state medical board discipline physicians for discussing the medical effects of marijuana with their patients? Several states have legalized marijuana for medical uses although the federal DEA still enforces federal prohibitions. Andrew Boyd, Medical Marijuana and Personal Autonomy, 37 J. Marshall L. Rev. 1253 (2004). See discussion of federal-state controversy over marijuana for medical purposes in Section I, above.

III.   UNLICENSED PROVIDERS

The state medical board has the primary responsibility for enforcing the prohibition against the unauthorized practice of medicine by unlicensed providers. This prohibition is enforced by criminal sanctions against the unlicensed practitioner and license revocation against any physician who aids and abets the unlicensed practitioner. The state medical practice acts prohibit anyone but licensed physicians and other licensed health care professionals practicing within the bounds of their own licensure from practicing medicine. The board responsible for licensure and discipline for nursing has parallel authority to pursue unlicensed practitioners charged with engaging in the practice of nursing. The issue of the scope of practice of licensed health care professionals is taken up in Section IV of this chapter. In this section, we focus on the practitioner who does not have a license.

Problem: Making Room for Alternative Practitioners

Cal. Bus. & Prof. Code § 2052

[A]ny person who practices or attempts to practice, or who advertises or holds himself or herself out as practicing, any system or mode of treating the sick or afflicted in this state, or who diagnoses, treats, operates for, or prescribes for any ailment, blemish, deformity, disease, disfigurement, disorder, injury, or other physical or mental condition of any person . . . is guilty of a public offense, punishable by a fine not exceeding ten thousand dollars ($10,000), by imprisonment in the state prison, by imprisonment in a county jail not exceeding one year, or by both the fine and either imprisonment.

Cal. Bus. & Prof. Code § 2053.5

. . . [A] person who complies with the requirements of Section 2053.6 shall not be in violation of Section 2052 unless that person does any of the following:

(1) Conducts surgery or any other procedure on another person that punctures the skin or harmfully invades the body.

(2) Administers or prescribes X-ray radiation . . . .

(3) Prescribes or administers legend drugs or controlled substances . . . .

(4) Recommends the discontinuance of legend drugs or controlled substances prescribed by an appropriately licensed practitioner.

(5) Willfully diagnoses and treats a physical or mental condition of any person under circumstances or conditions that cause or create a risk of great bodily harm, serious physical or mental illness, or death.

(6) Sets fractures.

(7) Treats lacerations or abrasions through electrotherapy.

(8) Holds out, states, indicates, advertises, or implies to a client or prospective client that he or she is a physician, a surgeon, or a physician and surgeon.

Cal. Bus. & Prof. Code § 2053.6

(a) A person who provides services pursuant to Section 2053.5 . . . shall, prior to providing those services, do the following:

(1) Disclose to the client in a written statement using plain language the following information:

(A) That he or she is not a licensed physician.

(B) That the treatment is alternative or complementary to healing arts services licensed by the state.

(C) That the services to be provided are not licensed by the state.

(D) The nature of the services to be provided.

(E) The theory of treatment upon which the services are based.

(F) His or her educational, training, experience, and other qualifications regarding the services to be provided.

(G) . . . Obtain a written acknowledgement from the client stating that he or she has been provided with [this] information. . . .

Assume that your state is considering the same legislation. Would you amend specific provisions or recommend a different approach entirely? Would you prefer that the state establish a licensure system for alternative medicine providers? How would you define the services they would be allowed to provide? See Michael H. Cohen, Complementary and Alternative Medicine: Legal Boundaries and Regulatory Perspectives (1998), recommending licensure; John Lunstroth, Voluntary Self–Regulation of Complementary and Alternative Medicine Practitioners, 70 Alb. L. Rev. 209 (2006), arguing in favor of unlicensed practice.

As you read the following case, consider how the language of the California amendments may apply in a state that does not otherwise provide for lay midwifery.

STATE BOARD OF NURSING AND STATE BOARD OF HEALING ARTS v. RUEBKE

Supreme Court of Kansas, 1996.
259 Kan. 599, 913 P.2d 142.

LARSON, JUSTICE:

The State Board of Healing Arts (Healing Arts) and the State Board of Nursing (Nursing) appeal the trial court's denial of a temporary injunction by which the Boards had sought to stop E. Michelle Ruebke, a practicing lay midwife, from continuing her alleged practice of medicine and nursing.

* * *

FACTUAL BACKGROUND

* * *

The hearing on the temporary injunction revealed that Ruebke acts as a lay midwife comprehensively assisting pregnant women with prenatal care, delivery, and post-partum care. She is president of the Kansas Midwives Association and follows its promulgated standards, which include a risk screening assessment based upon family medical history; establishing prenatal care plans, including monthly visitations; examinations and assistance in birth; and post-partum care. She works with supervising physicians who are made aware of her mode of practice and who are available for consultation and perform many of the medical tests incident to pregnancy.

* * *

Dr. Debra L. Messamore, an obstetrician/gynecologist, testified she had reviewed the Kansas Midwives Association standards of care and opined those standards were similar to the assessments incident to her practice as an OB/GYN. Dr. Messamore concluded that in her judgment the prenatal assessments made by Ruebke were obstetrical diagnoses.

Dr. Messamore testified that the prescriptions Ruebke has women obtain from their physicians are used in obstetrics to produce uterine contractions. She further testified the Kansas Midwives Association standard of care relating to post-delivery conditions of the mother and baby involved obstetrical judgments. She reviewed the birth records of [one] birth and testified that obstetrical or medical judgments were reflected. [She admitted] that many procedures at issue could be performed by a nurse rather than a physician. * * * She also stated her opinion that so defined obstetrics as a branch of medicine or surgery.

Ginger Breedlove, a Kansas certified advanced registered nurse practitioner and nurse-midwife, testified on behalf of Nursing. She reviewed the records [of two births] and testified nursing functions were involved. She admitted she could not tell from the records who had engaged in certain practices and that taking notes, giving enemas, and administering oxygen is often done by people who are not nurses, although education, experience, and minimum competency are required.

* * * The court held that provisions of both acts were unconstitutionally vague, Ruebke's midwifery practices did not and were not intended to come within the healing arts act or the nursing act, and her activities fell within exceptions to the two acts even if the acts did apply and were constitutional.

The factual findings, highly summarized, were that Ruebke had not been shown to hold herself out as anything other than a lay midwife; has routinely used and consulted with supervising physicians; was not shown to administer any prescription drugs; was not shown to do any suturing or episiotomies, make cervical or vaginal lacerations, or diagnose blood type; and had engaged only in activities routinely and properly done by people who are not physicians.

REGULATORY HISTORY OF MIDWIFERY

One of the specific statutory provisions we deal with, K.S.A. 65–2802(a), defines the healing arts as follows:

> The healing arts include any system, treatment, operation, diagnosis, prescription, or practice for the ascertainment, cure, relief, palliation, adjustment, or correction of any human disease, ailment, deformity, or injury, and includes specifically but not by way of limitation the practice of medicine and surgery; the practice of osteopathic medicine and surgery; and the practice of chiropractic.

K.S.A. 65–2869 specifically provides that for the purpose of the healing arts act, the following persons shall be deemed to be engaged in the practice of medicine and surgery:

> (a) Persons who publicly profess to be physicians or surgeons, or publicly profess to assume the duties incident to the practice of medicine or surgery or any of their branches.

> (b) Persons who prescribe, recommend or furnish medicine or drugs, or perform any surgical operation of whatever nature by the use of any surgical instrument, procedure, equipment or mechanical device for the diagnosis, cure or relief of any wounds, fractures, bodily injury, infirmity, disease, physical or mental illness or psychological disorder, of human beings.

* * *

[M]idwifery belonged to women from Biblical times through the Middle Ages. However, subsequent to the Middle Ages, women healers were often barred from universities and precluded from obtaining medical training or degrees. With the rise of barber-surgeon guilds, women were banned from using surgical instruments.

When midwives immigrated to America, they occupied positions of great prestige. Some communities licensed midwives and others did not. This continued until the end of the 19th century. In the 19th and 20th centuries, medical practice became more standardized. Economically and socially well-placed doctors pressed for more restrictive licensing laws and for penalties against those who violated them. [One commentator] suggests that licensure was a market control device; midwives were depriving new obstetricians of the opportunity for training; and elimination of midwifery would allow the science of obstetrics to grow into a mature medical specialty.

There is a notable absence of anything in the history of Kansas healing arts regulation illustrating any attempt to specifically target midwives. In 1870, the Kansas Legislature adopted its first restriction on the practice of medicine. * * *

[T]here can be little doubt that in 1870 Kansas, particularly in rural areas, there were not enough educated physicians available to deliver all of the children born in the state. In fact, until 1910 approximately 50 percent of births in this country were midwife assisted. [ ]

* * *

Although obstetricians held themselves out as a medical specialty in the United States as early as 1868, midwives were not seen as engaged in the practice of obstetrics, nor was obstetrics universally viewed as being a branch of medicine. In 1901, North Carolina recognized obstetricians as engaged in the practice of medicine but women midwives, as a separate discipline, were exempted from the licensure act. [ ] * * *

Although many states in the early 1900s passed laws relating to midwifery, Kansas has never expressly addressed the legality of the practice. In 1915 [ ] this court implied that a woman with considerable midwife experience was qualified to testify as an expert witness in a malpractice case against an osteopath for allegedly negligently delivering the plaintiff's child.

* * *

The 1978 Kansas Legislature created a new classification of nurses, Advanced Registered Nurse Practitioner (ARNP). [ ] One classification of ARNP is certified nurse midwives. Although the regulations permitting the practice of certified nurse midwives might be argued to show additional legislative intent to prohibit the practice of lay midwives, this argument has been rejected elsewhere. [ ]

In 1978, Kansas Attorney General opinion No. 78–164 suggested that the practice of midwifery is a violation of the healing arts act. * * * Although potentially persuasive, such an opinion is not binding on us.

Most probably in response to the 1978 Attorney General opinion, a 1978 legislative interim committee undertook a study of a proposal to recognize and regulate the practice of lay midwifery. However, the committee reached no conclusion.

* * *

A 1986 review of the laws of every state found that lay midwifery was specifically statutorily permitted, subject to licensing or regulation, in 25 jurisdictions. Twelve states, including Kansas, had no legislation governing or prohibiting lay midwifery directly or by direct implication. Several states recognized both lay and nurse midwives. Some issued new licensing only for nurse midwives, while others regulated and recognized both, often as separate professions, subject to separate standards and restrictions. [ ]

* * *

In April 1993, the Board of Healing Arts released Policy Statement No. 93–02, in which the Board stated it reaffirmed its previous position of August 18, 1984, that

> [m]idwifery is the practice of medicine and surgery and any practice thereof by individuals not regulated by the Kansas State Board of Nursing or under the supervision of or by order of or referral from a

licensed medical or osteopathic doctor constitutes the unlicensed practice of medicine and surgery.

* * *

This historical background brings us to the question of whether the healing arts act is unconstitutionally vague. * * *

* * *

[A] statute "is vague and violates due process if it prohibits conduct in terms so vague that a person of common intelligence cannot understand what conduct is prohibited, and it fails to adequately guard against arbitrary and discriminatory enforcement." [ ] A statute which requires specific intent is more likely to withstand a vagueness challenge than one, like that here, which imposes strict liability. [ ]

* * *

We have held that the interpretation of a statute given by an administrative agency within its area of expertise is entitled to deference, although final construction of a statute always rests with courts. [ ] * * *

We do, of course, attempt wherever possible to construe a statute as constitutional [ ]. * * *

* * *

The definition of healing arts uses terms that have an ordinary, definite, and ascertainable meaning. The trial court's conclusion that "disease, ailment, deformity or injury" are not commonly used words with settled meanings cannot be justified.

* * *

* * * Although we hold the act not to be unconstitutionally vague, we also hold the definitional provisions do not cover midwifery. In their ordinary usage the terms in K.S.A. 65–2802(a) used to define healing arts clearly and unequivocally focus exclusively on pathologies (i.e., diseases) and abnormal human conditions (i.e., ailments, deformities, or injuries). Pregnancy and childbirth are neither pathologies nor abnormalities.

* * *

Healing Arts argues that the "practice of medicine" includes the practice of obstetrics. It reasons, in turn, that obstetrics includes the practices traditionally performed by midwives. From this, it concludes midwifery is the practice of medicine.

However, equating midwifery with obstetrics, and thus with the practice of medicine, ignores the historical reality, discussed above, that midwives and obstetricians coexisted for many years quite separately. From the time of our statehood, the relationship between obstetricians and midwives changed from that of harmonious coexistence, cooperation, and collaboration, to open market competition and hostility. [ ]

* * *

To even the most casual observer of the history of assistance to child-birth, it is clear that over the course of this century the medical profession has extended its reach so deeply into the area of birthing as to almost completely occupy the field. The introduction of medical advances to the childbirth process drew women to physicians to assist during the birth of their children. Yet, this widespread preference for physicians as birth attendants hardly mandates the conclusion that only physicians may assist with births.

* * * The fact that a person with medical training provides services in competition with someone with no medical degree does not transform the latter's practices into the practice of medicine.

* * *

Although we hold the practice of midwifery is not itself the practice of the healing arts under our statutory scheme, our conclusions should not be interpreted to mean that a midwife may engage in any activity whatsoever with regard to a pregnant woman merely by virtue of her pregnancy. * * *

* * * However, we need not decide the precise boundaries of what a midwife may do without engaging in the practice of the healing arts because, in the case before us, Ruebke was found to have worked under the supervision of physicians who were familiar with her practices and authorized her actions. Any of Ruebke's actions that were established at trial, which might otherwise have been the practice of the healing arts, were exempt from the healing arts act because she had worked under the supervision of such physicians.

K.S.A. 65–2872 exempts certain activities from the licensure require-ments of the healing arts act. In relevant part it provides:

The practice of the healing arts shall not be construed to include the following persons:

    (g) Persons whose professional services are performed under the supervi-sion or by order of or referral from a practitioner who is licensed under this act.

* * *

In light of the uncontested factual findings of the trial court, which were supported by competent evidence in the record, we agree with the trial court that the exception to the healing arts act recognized by K.S.A. 65–2872(g) applies to any of Ruebke's midwifery activities which might otherwise be considered the practice of the healing arts under K.S.A. 65–2802(a) and K.S.A. 65–2869.

* * *

As we have held, the legislature has never specifically acted with the intent to restrict or regulate the traditional practice of lay midwifery. Never-theless, Nursing argues such birth assistants must be licensed nurses before they may render aid to pregnant women. In oral argument, Nursing conceded much of its argument would be muted were we to hold, as we do above, that the practice of midwifery is not the practice of the healing arts and thus not part of a medical regimen.

* * *

The practice of nursing is defined [in the Kansas nurse practice act] by reference to the practitioner's substantial specialized knowledge in areas of the biological, physical, and behavioral sciences and educational preparation within the field of the healing arts. Ruebke claims no specialized scientific knowledge, but rather readily admits she has no formal education beyond high school. Her assistance is valued not because it is the application of a firm and rarified grasp of scientific theory, but because, like generations of midwives before, she has practical experience assisting in childbirth.

Moreover, "nursing" deals with "persons who are experiencing changes in the normal health processes." As these words are commonly understood, pregnancy and childbirth do not constitute changes in the normal health process, but the continuation of it.

* * * As we have held, the practice of lay midwifery has, throughout the history of the regulation of nursing, been separate and distinct from the practice of the healing arts, to which nursing is so closely joined. While we have no doubt of the legislature's power to place lay midwifery under the authority of the State Board of Nursing, the legislature has not done so.

We find no legislative intent manifested in the language of the nursing act clearly illustrating the purpose of including the historically separate practice of midwifery within the practice of nursing. [ ] Assistance in childbirth rendered by one whose practical experience with birthing provides comfort to the mother is not nursing under the nursing act, such that licensure is required.

Affirmed in part and reversed in part.

Notes and Questions

1. Although a wide variety of health care services and providers have been subject to prosecution for the unauthorized practice of medicine, the realm of assistance at childbirth has been a particularly contentious area. Doctors, nurses, nurse-midwives, physician assistants, and lay (or "traditional," "professional," or "direct-entry") midwives have all exerted a claim to participation in assisting in childbirth. *Ruebke* provides a short history of midwifery in Kansas. Many articles and books provide a more detailed history of the waxing and waning of lay or direct-entry midwifery as well as the emergence of nurse-midwifery. See, e.g., Stacey A. Tovino, American Midwifery Litigation and State Legislative Preferences for Physician–Controlled Childbirth, 11 Cardozo Women's L. J. 61 (2004), examining the intersection of legislation and judicial opinions against the background of class, race, and gender conflicts; Katherine Beckett & Bruce Hoffman, Challenging Medicine: Law, Resistance, and the Cultural Politics of Childbirth, 39 Law & Soc'y Rev. 125 (2005), providing a sociological analysis of the "alternative birth movement" and the sources of influence in legislatures and in litigation on behalf of lay midwifery.

2. Courts have adopted many approaches to analyzing whether services provided in assistance at childbirth constitute the unauthorized practice of medicine as defined in the relevant statutes. Some have examined individual actions that may be performed during childbirth. For example, in Leigh v. Board of Reg. in Nursing, 395 Mass. 670, 481 N.E.2d 1347 (1985), the court distinguished "ordinary assistance in the normal cases of childbirth" from that in which a lay midwife used "obstetrical instruments" and "printed prescriptions or formulas," and concluded that the former does not constitute the practice of medicine while

the latter does. In People v. Jihan, 127 Ill.2d 379, 130 Ill.Dec. 422, 537 N.E.2d 751 (1989), the court distinguished "assisting" at birth from "delivering" the child. Statutes authorizing childbirth services by traditional midwives also set boundaries on their practice and may exclude, for example, use of any surgical instrument or assisting childbirth "by artificial or mechanical means." See, e.g., Minn. Stat. Ann. § 147D.03. Does dividing childbirth assistance into discrete activities reflect health and safety concerns?

3. *Ruebke* illustrates that lay midwifery confronts the unauthorized practice prohibitions of both nursing and medicine. In Sherman v. Cryns, 203 Ill.2d 264, 271 Ill.Dec. 381, 786 N.E.2d 139 (2003), the court held that the state had successfully established a prima facie case against a lay midwife for practicing nursing without a license. In *Cryns*, the court relied largely on the prenatal care in finding that Cryns had violated the nursing statute. The court distinguished its case from *Ruebke* on the basis of the breadth of the definition of professional nursing in the Illinois statute. The language of the Illinois statute is quite similar to that of the statute in *Sermchief* in the next section. The Illinois statute specifically provided for licensure for certified nurse midwives but was silent on the question of lay midwifery. See also, Hunter v. State, 110 Md.App. 144, 676 A.2d 968 (Ct. Spec. App. 1996), concluding that the legislative history of certification of nurse midwives (similar to the Kansas provisions cited in *Ruebke*) required the conclusion that the statute permitted only registered nurses certified by the board as nurse midwives to provide midwifery services.

4. If a state authorizes a nurse to provide midwifery services, is there any need for lay midwives? In Leggett v. Tennessee Board of Nursing, 612 S.W.2d 476 (Tenn. Ct. App. 1980), the court considered a case in which a nurse violating the nursing board's prohibition against assistance at home births by nurse midwives claimed to be acting as a lay midwife instead. The court concluded that the exemption for lay midwifery in the medical practice act allowed the nurse to claim that she was acting as a lay midwife rather than as a nurse midwife. See also Lori B. Andrews, The Shadow Health Care System: Regulation of Alternative Health Care Providers, 32 Hous. L. Rev. 1273 (1996). Some states have enacted statutes specific to home births. See e.g., Alaska § 08.65.140; Mont. Code Ann. § 37–27–311 (both providing for mandatory informed consent). A major study of planned home births assisted by certified professional direct-entry midwives in North America (N = 5418) determined that these births produced a substantially lower risk of medical intervention (including C-sections and forceps deliveries) and the same intrapartum and neonatal mortality as low-risk hospital births in the U.S. Approximately 12% of women were transferred to a hospital during the course of labor. Kenneth Johnson & Betty–Anne Daviss, Outcomes of Planned Home Births with Certified Professional Midwives: Large Prospective Study in North America, 330 Brit. Med. J. 1416 (2005).

5. The court in *Ruebke* ultimately concludes that the midwife was operating within a common exception to the prohibition against the unauthorized practice of medicine by working under the supervision of a physician. That exception is not limitless. See Marion OB/GYN v. State Med. Bd., 137 Ohio App.3d 522, 739 N.E.2d 15 (Ct. App. 2000), in which the court held that delivering infants was beyond the scope of practice allowed a physician assistant although state law allowed licensed nurses to practice midwifery. See the discussion of physician assistants in Section IV, below.

6. Should the Kansas Supreme Court have analyzed research on the quality and safety of services provided by nurse midwives as compared to direct-entry or lay midwives? If it did so, would the court have been usurping the role of the

legislature or simply trying to interpret an ambiguous statute? The Kansas statute on certified nurse midwives describes substantial educational requirements for the provision of nurse midwife services. The court concluded, however, that formal education is unnecessary and that practical experience can be valued as highly. Given the opportunity to amend its statute, should the legislature provide for minimal educational requirements for persons assisting in childbirth? Should that education adopt an obstetrical model or a midwifery model for childbirth? Should it require certification as a nurse midwife? Susan Corcoran, To Become a Midwife: Reducing Legal Barriers to Entry into the Midwifery Profession, 80 Wash. U.L.Q. 649 (2002), proposing a single route for licensure for midwifery services, bifurcated into a lay track and a nursing track; Julie Harmon, Statutory Regulation of Midwives: A Study of California Law, 8 Wm. & Mary J. Women & L. 115 (2001). See also, Sara K. Hayden, The Business of Birth: Obstacles Facing Low–Income Women in Choosing Midwifery Care After the Licensed Midwifery Practice Act of 1993, 19 Berkeley Women's L. J. 257 (2004), arguing that California's recognition of lay midwifery with a requirement of direct physician supervision drastically reduces the availability of lay midwife services; Jason M. Storck, A State of Uncertainty: Ohio's Deficient Scheme of Midwifery Regulation in Historical and National Context, 8 Quinnipiac Health L. J. 89 (2004). The North American Registry of Midwives provides certification for direct-entry or professional midwives. www.narm.org. Several states have incorporated certification by NARM within their standards for recognition of lay midwives. See, e.g., Minn. § 47D.01; Utah Code 1953 § 58–77–302.

7.   Claims of a constitutional right to choice of provider of health care services consistently fail even when made in the context of the woman's right to privacy in reproductive decision making, the lack of empirical evidence of better outcomes with commonly used obstetrical technology, and the substantial history of conflict between medical and other approaches to childbirth. See, e.g., Lange–Kessler v. Department of Educ., 109 F.3d 137 (2d Cir.1997); Hunter v. State, 110 Md.App. 144, 676 A.2d 968 (Ct. Spec. App. 1996). See also Chris Hafner–Eaton & Laurie K. Pearce, Birth Choices, the Law, and Medicine: Balancing Individual Freedoms and Protection of the Public's Health, 19 J. Health Pol. Pol'y & L. 813 (1994); Lisa C. Ikemoto, The Code of Perfect Pregnancy: At the Intersection of the Ideology of Motherhood, the Practice of Defaulting to Science, and the Interventionist Mindset of Law, 53 Ohio St. L. J. 1205 (1992); Amy F. Cohen, The Midwifery Stalemate and Childbirth Choice: Recognizing Mothers-to-Be as the Best Late Pregnancy Decisionmakers, 80 Ind. L. J. 849 (2005). Nor do claims that the unauthorized practice prohibitions violate the First Amendment rights of practitioners succeed. See, e.g., People v. Rogers, 249 Mich.App. 77, 641 N.W.2d 595 (Ct. App. 2001) holding that non-M.D. practicing naturopathy was penalized for conduct, not speech.

8.   *Ruebke* is in the overwhelming majority in refusing to declare the medical practice or nursing practice act void for vagueness. See, e.g., Weyandt v. State, 35 S.W.3d 144 (Tex. Ct. App. 2000); Sherman v. Cryns, 203 Ill.2d 264, 271 Ill.Dec. 881, 786 N.E.2d 139 (2003). But see, Miller v. Medical Ass'n of Georgia, 262 Ga. 605, 423 S.E.2d 664 (Ga. 1992).

IV.   SCOPE OF PRACTICE REGULATION

Licensed nonphysician health care providers cannot legally practice medicine, but practices that fall within their own licensure (for example, as a nurse or a physician assistant) are not considered the practice of medicine. So, for example, a nurse who is providing services authorized under the nurse practice act would not be practicing medicine while an unlicensed practitioner providing the same services would be guilty of the unauthorized practice of medicine or nursing. If a nurse engages in practices that exceed those authorized in the nurse practice act, however, that nurse would be guilty of exceeding the authorized scope of practice of the profession of nursing as well as violating the prohibition against the unauthorized practice of medicine.

Scope of practice regulation focuses on boundary-setting between the professions and attempts to separate medicine from nursing from other health care disciplines. In doing so, it faces an inherent difficulty, as you saw in *Ruebke*. To the extent that scope of practice regulation depends on identifying discrete activities that "belong" to each profession, it applies a notion that reflects neither the overlapping competencies of health care professionals nor the nature of treatment for illness or injury.

Modern health care delivery regularly consists of multi-professional groups including nurse practitioners, doctors, physician assistants, and others. Regulatory systems have lagged a bit however. See, Barbara Safreit, Closing the Gap Between Can and May in Health–Care Providers' Scope of Practice: A Primer for Policymakers, 19 Yale J. on Reg. 301 (2002).

The AMA and several other groups have formed the Scope of Practice Partnership (SOPP) as an advocacy group to influence the regulation of non-physician health care providers, while a coalition of other health care professional associations, including the American Nurses Association, has formed the Coalition for Patients' Rights (CPR) to respond to the efforts of SOPP to limit their scope of practice. Scope of Practice: Allied Health Professionals Form Coalition to Oppose Efforts to Restrict Their Practice, 15 Health L. Rep. 711 (2006). On the role of professional associations in scope of practice legislation, see James W. Hilliard, State Practice Acts of Licensed Health Professions: Scope of Practice, 8 DePaul J. Health Care L. 237 (2004).

One compromise position that is often taken on the regulatory front in expanding the scope of practice of non-physician health care professionals is to require that they practice only under the supervision of a licensed physician. As you read *Sermchief* and materials that follow, consider what is gained and lost in adopting requirements that certified nurse-midwives or certified nurse anesthetists, for example, practice only under the direct supervision of a licensed physician. Consider also the alternative forms of physician-nurse collaboration that may be available. As you consider these issues for nursing and medicine, recall that similar conflicts arise between oral surgeons and dentists, between physical therapists and chiropractors, and the list goes on.

SERMCHIEF v. GONZALES

Supreme Court of Missouri, 1983.
660 S W.2d 683.

WELLIVER, JUDGE.

This is a petition for a declaratory judgment and injunction brought by two nurses and five physicians[6] employed by the East Missouri Action Agency (Agency) wherein the plaintiff-appellants ask the Court to declare that the

---

6. The physicians are joined for the reason that they are charged with aiding and abetting the unauthorized practice of medicine by the nurses.

practices of the Agency nurses are authorized under the nursing law of this state, § 335.016.8, RSMo 1978 and that such practices do not constitute the unauthorized practice of medicine under Chapter 334 relating to the Missouri State Board of Registration For the Healing Arts (Board). * * * The holding below was against appellants who make direct appeal to this Court alleging that the validity of the statutes is involved. [ ]. * * *

I

The facts are simple and for the most part undisputed. The Agency is a federally tax exempt Missouri not-for-profit corporation that maintains offices in Cape Girardeau (main office), Flat River, Ironton, and Fredericktown. The Agency provides medical services to the general public in fields of family planning, obstetrics and gynecology. The services are provided to an area that includes the counties of Bollinger, Cape Girardeau, Perry, St. Francis, Ste. Genevieve, Madison, Iron and Washington. Some thirty-five hundred persons utilized these services during the year prior to trial. The Agency is funded from federal grants, Medicaid reimbursements and patient fees. The programs are directed toward the lower income segment of the population. Similar programs exist both statewide and nationwide.

Appellant nurses Solari and Burgess are duly licensed professional nurses in Missouri pursuant to the provisions of Chapter 335 and are employed by the Agency. Both nurses have had post-graduate special training in the field of obstetrics and gynecology. Appellant physicians are also employees of the Agency and duly licensed to practice medicine (the healing arts) pursuant to Chapter 334. Respondents are the members and the executive secretary of the Missouri State Board of Registration for the Healing Arts (Board) * * *.

The services routinely provided by the nurses and complained of by the Board included, among others, the taking of history; breast and pelvic examinations; laboratory testing of Papanicolaou (PAP) smears, gonorrhea cultures, and blood serology; the providing of and giving of information about oral contraceptives, condoms, and intrauterine devices (IUD); the dispensing of certain designated medications; and counseling services and community education. If the nurses determined the possibility of a condition designated in the standing orders or protocols that would contraindicate the use of contraceptives until further examination and evaluation, they would refer the patients to one of the Agency physicians. No act by either nurse is alleged to have caused injury or damage to any person. All acts by the nurses were done pursuant to written standing orders and protocols signed by appellant physicians. The standing orders and protocols were directed to specifically named nurses and were not identical for all nurses.

The Board threatened to order the appellant nurses and physicians to show cause why the nurses should not be found guilty of the unauthorized practice of medicine and the physicians guilty of aiding and abetting such unauthorized practice. Appellants sought Court relief in this proceeding.

* * *

III

The statutes involved are:

It shall be unlawful for any person not now a registered physician within the meaning of the law to practice medicine or surgery in any of its departments, or to profess to cure and attempt to treat the sick and others afflicted with bodily or mental infirmities, or engage in the practice of midwifery in this state, except as herein provided.

Section 334.010.

This Chapter does not apply ... *to nurses licensed and lawfully practicing their profession within the provisions of chapter 335, RSMo;* ...

Section 334.155, RSMo Supp.1982 (emphasis added).

Definitions.—As used in sections 335.011 to 335.096, unless the context clearly requires otherwise, the following words and terms shall have the meanings indicated:

* * *

(8) "Professional nursing" is the performance for compensation of any act which requires substantial specialized education, judgment and skill based on knowledge and application of principles derived from the biological, physical, social and nursing sciences, including, but not limited to:

(a) Responsibility for the teaching of health care and the prevention of illness to the patient and his family; or

(b) Assessment, nursing diagnosis, nursing care, and counsel of persons who are ill, injured or experiencing alterations in normal health processes; or

(c) The administration of medications and treatments as prescribed by a person licensed in this state to prescribe such medications and treatments; or

(d) The coordination and assistance in the delivery of a plan of health care with all members of the health team; or

(e) The teaching and supervision of other persons in the performance of any of the foregoing.

Section 335.016.8(a)–(e).

At the time of enactment of the Nursing Practice Act of 1975, the following statutes were repealed:

2. A person practices professional nursing who for compensation or personal profit performs, *under the supervision and direction of a practitioner authorized to sign birth and death certificates,* any professional services requiring the application of principles of the biological, physical or social sciences and nursing skills in the care of the sick, in the prevention of disease or in the conservation of health.

Section 335.010.2, RSMo 1969 (emphasis added).

Nothing contained in this chapter shall be construed as conferring any authority on any person to practice medicine or osteopathy or to undertake the treatment or cure of disease.

Section 335.190, RSMo 1969.

The parties on both sides request that in construing these statutes we define and draw that thin and elusive line that separates the practice of medicine and the practice of professional nursing in modern day delivery of health services. A response to this invitation, in our opinion, would result in an avalanche of both medical and nursing malpractice suits alleging infringement of that line and would hinder rather than help with the delivery of health services to the general public. Our consideration will be limited to the narrow question of whether the acts of these nurses were permissible under § 335.016.8 or were prohibited by Chapter 334.

* * *

The legislature substantially revised the law affecting the nursing profession with enactment of the Nursing Practice Act of 1975. Perhaps the most significant feature of the Act was the redefinition of the term "professional nursing," which appears in § 335.016.8. Even a facile reading of that section reveals a manifest legislative desire to expand the scope of authorized nursing practices. Every witness at trial testified that the new definition of professional nursing is a broader definition than that in the former statute. A comparison with the prior definition vividly demonstrates this fact. Most apparent is the elimination of the requirement that a physician directly supervise nursing functions. Equally significant is the legislature's formulation of an open-ended definition of professional nursing. The earlier statute limited nursing practice to "services ... in the care of the sick, in the prevention of disease or in the conservation of health." § 335.010.2, RSMo 1969. The 1975 Act not only describes a much broader spectrum of nursing functions, it qualifies this description with the phrase "including, but not limited to." We believe this phrase evidences an intent to avoid statutory constraints on the evolution of new functions for nurses delivering health services. Under § 335.016.8, a nurse may be permitted to assume responsibilities heretofore not considered to be within the field of professional nursing so long as those responsibilities are consistent with her or his "specialized education, judgment and skill based on knowledge and application of principles derived from the biological, physical, social and nursing sciences." § 335.016.8.

The acts of the nurses herein clearly fall within this legislative standard. All acts were performed pursuant to standing orders and protocols approved by physicians. Physician prepared standing orders and protocols for nurses and other paramedical personnel were so well established and accepted at the time of the adoption of the statute that the legislature could not have been unaware of the use of such practices. We see nothing in the statute purporting to limit or restrict their continued use.

Respondents made no challenge of the nurses' level of training or the degree of their skill. They challenge only the legal right of the nurses to undertake these acts. We believe the acts of the nurses are precisely the types of acts the legislature contemplated when it granted nurses the right to make assessments and nursing diagnoses. There can be no question that a nurse undertakes only a nursing diagnosis, as opposed to a medical diagnosis, when she or he finds or fails to find symptoms described by physicians in standing orders and protocols for the purpose of administering courses of treatment prescribed by the physician in such orders and protocols.

The Court believes that it is significant that while at least forty states have modernized and expanded their nursing practice laws during the past fifteen years neither counsel nor the Court have discovered any case challenging nurses' authority to act as the nurses herein acted.

* * * The hallmark of the professional is knowing the limits of one's professional knowledge. The nurse, either upon reaching the limit of her or his knowledge or upon reaching the limits prescribed for the nurse by the physician's standing orders and protocols, should refer the patient to the physician. There is no evidence that the assessments and diagnoses made by the nurses in this case exceeded such limits.

* * *

Having found that the nurses' acts were authorized by § 335.016.8, it follows that such acts do not constitute the unlawful practice of medicine for the reason that § 334.155 makes the provisions of Chapter 334 inapplicable "to nurses licensed and lawfully practicing their profession within the provisions of Chapter 335 RSMo."

This cause is reversed and remanded with instructions to enter judgment consistent with this opinion.

Notes and Questions

1. The nurse practice act in *Sermchief* contains an open-ended definition of the practice of nursing. Who has the authority to define the authorized practice of nursing under this type of definition? If the board of nursing had issued regulations embracing the plaintiffs' practice within the authorized practice of nursing, under what standard would the court review such regulations if challenged? Would the regulation of the board of nursing prevent the board of medicine from proceeding against the nurses? See e.g., North Carolina Med. Soc'y [and Med. Bd.] v. North Carolina Bd. of Nursing, 169 N.C.App. 1, 610 S.E.2d 722 (Ct. App. 2005), considering whether medical board's statements on nurse anesthetist practice in physician office setting violated earlier consent decree; Oklahoma Bd. of Med. Lic. & Supervision v. Oklahoma Bd. of Exam'rs in Optometry, 893 P.2d 498 (Okla. 1995), allowing medical board to challenge regulations of optometry board; Washington State Nurses Ass'n v. Board of Med. Exam'rs, 93 Wash.2d 117, 605 P.2d 1269 (1980), challenging medical board rules expanding practice for physician assistants. In most such disputes, the key legal question is whether the board's rule is consistent with the state statute governing the specific practice or is otherwise arbitrary. See, e.g., Hoffman v. State Med. Bd. of Ohio, 113 Ohio St.3d 376, 865 N.E.2d 1259 (2007), holding that board's rule that anesthesiologist assistants could not perform epidurals and spinal anesthetic procedures was inconsistent with the reasonable interpretation of the statute's provision that the anesthesiologist assistant "assists" the physician.

2. Why did the *Sermchief* plaintiffs seek a declaratory judgment action if they had not been charged with violating the statute? See Lori B. Andrews, The Shadow Health Care System: Regulation of Alternative Health Care Providers, 32 Hous. L. Rev. 1273 (1996), on this point and for a comprehensive analysis of the legal issues relating to nonphysician providers.

3. Authority to prescribe medication has been a major issue in debates over the appropriate scope of practice of nurses and physician assistants as well as other nonphysician providers. Why would this be such a key issue? See e.g., Mary

Beck, Improving America's Health Care: Authorizing Independent Prescriptive Privileges for Advanced Practice Nurses, 29 U.S.F. L. Rev. 951 (1995); Phyllis Coleman & Ronald A. Shellow, Extending Physician's Standard of Care to Non–Physician Prescribers: The Rx for Protecting Patients, 35 Idaho L. Rev. 37 (1998). For a very good delineation of current legal boundaries, including prescribing, and the practice of nurses, PAs, and CAM practitioners, see Joy L. Delman, The Use and Misuse of Physician Extenders, 24 J. Legal Med. 249 (2003). Most states now authorize nurses to prescribe medications, at least under a doctor's supervision. Other health professions also seek prescribing authority. See, e.g., James E. Long, Power to Prescribe: The Debate over Prescription Privileges for Psychologists and the Legal Issues Implicated, 29 L. & Psychol. Rev. 243 (2005).

4. Physician assistants and nurses have assumed different professional identities. Physician assistants are educated in a medical model of care and view themselves as practicing medicine through physician delegation of tasks and under the supervision of physicians. In nursing, nurse practitioners or advanced practice nurses (including nurse midwives, nurse anesthetists, and other specialist nurse practitioners) view themselves as operating from a nursing model of health care and acting as independent practitioners who collaborate with physicians. The relationship described in *Sermchief* illustrates a collaborative practice. Currently, organized medicine asserts that both physician assistants and nurse practitioners must be supervised by physicians, a position accepted by the American Academy of Physician Assistants, but rejected by the American Nurses Association.

What is at issue in the controversy over whether the nurse practitioner is required to practice under a doctor's supervision or in collaboration with a doctor or even more independently? Will it have an impact on the location of the nurse's practice? On control of the practice? On nurses' ability to charge insurers directly for services provided?

Some advanced practice nursing statutes require that the nurse practitioner practice under the supervision of a physician. See e.g., Cal. Bus. & Prof. Code § 2746.5(b) (certificate authorizes nurse-midwife to practice nurse-midwifery "under the supervision of a licensed physician and surgeon who has current practice or training in obstetrics"); Cal. Bus. & Prof. Code § 2836.1(d), requiring physician supervision for the furnishing of drugs or devices by nurse practitioner. Others recognize advanced practice nursing in collaboration with licensed physicians. See e.g., Mo. Ann. Stat. § 334.104, enacted after *Sermchief*, authorizing collaborative practice arrangements in the form of written agreements, protocols or standing orders, but describing the prescriptive authority of the nurse practitioner as delegated. Some describe the advanced nursing practice without reference to the participation of a supervisory or collaborative physician. See e.g., Md. Code Ann., Health Occ. § 8–601 (recognizing nurse midwives).

5. Physician assistants first practiced under general delegation exceptions included in medical practice acts. Delegation exceptions in medical practice acts tend to be quite broad, as you saw in *Ruebke*. States vary in the standards and methods they use to assure that delegation to physician assistants is appropriate and supervision is adequate. Some states take an individualized approach and require the physician assistant or supervising physician to submit particular details about the specific position for review by an agency. See e.g., Md. Code Ann., Health Occ. § 15–302. Some limit the number of physician assistants a doctor may supervise. See e.g., Ohio Rev. Code Ann. § 4730.21. Other states simply define "supervision," with great variations. See e.g., Mo. Ann. Stat. § 334.735(10), defining supervision as "control exercised over a physician assistant working within the same facility as the supervising physician sixty-six

percent of the time a physician assistant provides patient care, except a physician assistant may make follow-up patient examinations in hospitals, nursing homes, patient homes, and correctional facilities, each such examination being reviewed, approved and signed by the supervising physician." Some provide specific requirements for prescribing authority. See e.g., Cal. Bus. & Prof. Code § 3502.1.

6. Should the professional boards consider reductions in the cost of health care in defining the scope of practice of non-physician health professionals? See Barbara J. Safriet, Health Care Dollars and Regulatory Sense: The Role of Advanced Practice Nursing, 9 Yale J. or. Reg. 417 (1992), including reviews of the literature on comparative quality. See also Jerry Cromwell, Barriers to Achieving a Cost–Effective Workforce Mix: Lessons from Anesthesiology, 24 J. Health Pol,. Pol'y & L. 1331 (1999).

7. Public health responses to epidemics and other catastrophic health episodes have highlighted the need to suspend scope of practice barriers in responding to such a crisis. See, e.g., James G. Hodge, et al., Scope of Practice for Public Health Professionals and Volunteers, 33 J. L. Med. & Ethics 53 (2005).

8. Negligence and malpractice litigation forms the greatest volume of litigation involving scope of practice. See, e.g., Johannesen v. Salem Hosp., 336 Or. 211, 82 P.3d 139 (2003), reviewing application of statute that allowed punitive damages in malpractice cases where nurse exceeded scope of practice; and Rockefeller v. Kaiser Found. Health Plan, 251 Ga.App. 699, 554 S.E.2d 623 (Ct. App. 2001), holding that prescribing by physician assistant was beyond the PA's scope of practice and constituted per se negligence. See also Linda M. Atkinson, Who's Really in Charge?, Trial, May, 2007.

Problem: Physicians, Physician Assistants, and Nurses

Drs. Allison Jones and Emily Johnson have a practice in Jerrold, which is located in south St. Louis County. Both Drs. Jones and Johnson are board-certified internists with a rather broad family practice. They would like to expand their practice to Jackson County, a primarily rural area about seventy miles south of Jerrold. They are especially interested in Tesson, a town of approximately 6,000 that is centrally located among the four or five small towns in the area. They are interested in Tesson because it has a small community hospital and is located close to the interstate highway. They also believe the town is underserved by physicians. There is no pediatrician in Tesson, although there is one thirty miles away. The town has one internist. It has no obstetricians, although Joan Mayo, a certified nurse midwife, has an office in a small town about eighteen miles distant from Tesson.

Ms. Mayo has been providing childbirth, family planning and other women's health services. She has an agreement with an obstetrician in Jerrold through which protocols and standing orders for her practice were established and are maintained. She can consult with this OB by phone at any time, and they make it a practice to meet once a month to discuss Ms. Mayo's patients. Ms. Mayo refers patients who require special services to this OB or to the internist in Tesson. Ms. Mayo has clinical privileges for childbirth services at the community hospital, though her patients must be admitted by the internist. She also has assisted at a few home births, though it is not her custom to do so.

Drs. Jones and Johnson would like to open an office in Tesson and employ a physician assistant and a pediatric nurse practitioner to staff the office full-time. Either Dr. Jones or Dr. Johnson would have office hours at that office once a week. They are also interested in establishing an affiliation with Ms. Mayo because they see room for growth in that area. They hope to serve the needs of Tesson by establishing active obstetrical and pediatric practices.

They have a physician assistant in their office in Jerrold. The PA is not certified, but they have been impressed with her handling of the "routine" patients that come to the office with minor injuries such as cuts and sprains and illnesses such as chicken pox and strep throat. In most cases, the assistant examines the patient, decides on a course of treatment and prescribes medication using pre-signed prescription slips. In more difficult cases, the physician assistant asks for advice from one of the physicians. There is high patient satisfaction with her work. The doctors would like her to provide services in their Tesson office as well.

For their Tesson office, they would like to find a physician assistant with extensive experience in trauma so that the assistant could care for the high incidence of farming and hunting injuries expected in that area. This PA, then, would complement the doctors' own skills as the doctors have had little experience with such injuries.

Drs. Jones and Johnson have come to you for advice concerning their plans. They have many questions, including whether their plans are consistent with the laws regulating practice in Allstate. Please specify how they might comply with the law while maintaining a "low cost" practice. If for some reason the Board decides to take action against them, what is the likelihood of the physicians' success in challenging the Board's action?

If you were counsel to Ms. Mayo, would you advise her to affiliate with Drs. Jones and Johnson? What advantages and disadvantages might such an affiliation bring? Is her current practice authorized within the Allstate statutes?

In solving this problem, assume that Allstate's:

1) relevant caselaw is identical to *Sermchief* and *Ruebke*;

2) medical practice act includes a delegation exception identical to the Kansas statute quoted in *Ruebke*;

3) has a nurse practice act that provides for a definition of nursing identical to the Missouri statute in *Sermchief*; and

4) has only the following additional statutory provisions:

Allstate Stat. § 2746.5.

The practice of nurse-midwifery constitutes the furthering or undertaking by any certified person, under the supervision of a licensed physician and surgeon who has current practice or training in obstetrics, to assist a woman in childbirth so long as progress meets criteria accepted as normal. All complications shall be referred to a physician immediately. The practice of nurse-midwifery does not include the assisting of childbirth by any artificial, forcible, or mechanical means. As used in this article, "supervision" shall not be construed to require the physical presence of the supervising physician. A nurse-midwife is not authorized to practice medicine and surgery by the provisions of this chapter.

Allstate Stat. § 147A.18

(a) A supervising physician may delegate to a physician assistant who is registered with the board, certified by the National Commission on Certification of Physician Assistants, and who is under the supervising physician's supervision, the authority to prescribe, dispense, and administer legend drugs, medical devices, and controlled substances subject to the requirements in this section.

(b)The delegation must be appropriate to the physician assistant's practice and within the scope of the physician assistant's training. Supervising physicians shall retrospectively review, on a daily basis, the prescribing, dispensing, and administering of legend and controlled drugs and medical devices by physician assistants. During each daily review, the supervising physician shall document by signature and date that the prescriptive, administering, and dispensing practice of the physician assistant has been reviewed.

Problem: Retail Clinics

A national pharmacy chain wants to open health clinics in several of their stores in your state. These health clinics would be staffed by nurse practitioners or physician assistants and would handle non-emergency cases with referral relationships to hospitals and cooperative physicians in the area. The development of these retail clinics is generating some controversy, including conflict between your medical board and your board of nursing both represented by you as the state's Attorney General. Some states have engaged in negotiated rulemaking over such conflicts, and you have decided to give it a try. This would involve gathering stakeholders to engage in assisting the boards in developing rules or regulations applicable to the clinics. Who has a stake in regulatory standards applicable to the scope of practice of nursing or physician assistants in this setting such that they would be involved in the negotiation process? What positions do you expect to be taken by the stakeholders you have identified? Where does the public interest lie?

Chapter 3

QUALITY CONTROL REGULATION OF HEALTH CARE INSTITUTIONS

INTRODUCTION

Patient safety and well-being are directly dependent on the quality of health care institutions as much as on the quality of the individual patient's doctor or nurse or therapist. The range of institutional factors that can pose a danger to patients extends from building design, maintenance, and sanitation through health information technology and management; from fiscal soundness through the selection, training, and monitoring of the individuals directly providing care; from staffing levels through food service. The patient safety movement (discussed in Chapter 1), in fact, focuses on the quality of systems within health care organizations rather than on the behaviors of individual caregivers standing alone.

A variety of public and private efforts influence the quality of health care facilities. For many consumer goods and services, the market plays a significant role in setting an acceptable level of quality. State and federal governments are making efforts to strengthen the influence of the market over the quality of health care facilities. Most of these efforts have focused on collecting and posting quality data to allow consumers to select among facilities and to encourage facilities to take action to improve their performance on reportable factors. Significant barriers to the working of the market, such as a persistent lack of relevant, timely, and accurate information on quality measures; inability to evaluate available information; and decision making processes that place the choice of facility in the hands of someone other than the patient, still diminish the impact of consumer choice in health care.

In the face of market failure, state and federal governments often use a "command-and-control" system of licensure or certification for many key health care organizations through which the government sets standards, monitors for compliance, and imposes sanctions for violations. The debate over whether the market or direct governmental regulation of performance is most effective in improving the quality of health care institutions has raged for decades. See, for example, Timothy S. Jost, Our Broken Health Care System and How to Fix It: An Essay On Health Law and Policy, 41 Wake Forest L. Rev. 537 (2006); Symposium, Who Pays? Who Benefits? Distributional Issues in Health Care, 69 Law & Contemp. Probs. 1 (2006), examining, *inter alia*, the net of costs and benefits of regulation in health care.

State and federal governments are not the only players in the quality arena, of course. Private nonprofit organizations, for example, offer a voluntary accreditation process through which facilities can measure their compliance with standards accepted by their own segment of the industry. Facilities themselves also engage in internal quality assurance and quality improvement efforts, as a result of governmental mandate, accreditation standards, or risk of liability. In addition, private tort and related litigation raises the cost of poor quality in health care facilities. Finally, professionals working in health care facilities have ethical and legal obligations of their own to assure the quality of the organizations in which they care for patients.

These public and private mechanisms do not work the same across the wide variety of health care organizations and facilities that offer services to patients. The strength of external and internal quality efforts, including command-and-control regulation; market enhancement; private accreditation; intraorganizational quality initiatives; litigation; and ethical norms, varies across segments of the health care industry. Many institutional factors influence the strength of the market or the deterrent effect of litigation risks or the power of private accreditation organizations. The question of the appropriate mix of quality control mechanisms does not produce a one-size-fits-all answer.

I. NEW HEALTH CARE SERVICE CONFIGURATIONS

A state agency may regulate only within its statutory authority. If there is no legislative authorization for the regulation of a specific organizational form of health care delivery, the agency may not reach that entity. A major challenge for quality control regulation in health care is the rapidly changing structure of health care organizations as they respond to incentives in payment systems and disincentives in regulatory requirements. To illustrate the range of health care institutions regulated in a typical state, consider the Illinois Public Health and Safety Code, which includes specific regulatory requirements for the following institutional health care providers, as defined by the statute:

> Hospitals: any institution ... devoted primarily to the maintenance and operation of facilities for the diagnosis and treatment or care of ... persons admitted for overnight stay or longer in order to obtain medical ... care of illness, disease, injury, infirmity, or deformity. 210 ILCS 85/3.

> Long-term care facility: a private home, institution ... or any other place, ... which provides ... personal care, sheltered care or nursing for 3 or more persons ... not includ[ing] ... a hospital. 210 ILCS 45/1–113.

> Home health agency: a public agency or private organization that provides skilled nursing services [in a patient's home] and at least one other home health service. 210 ILCS 5E/2.04.

> Full Hospice: a coordinated program of home and inpatient care providing ... palliative and supportive medical, health and other services to terminally ill patients and their families. 210 ILCS 60/3.

Ambulatory surgical treatment center: any institution [or place located within an institution, subject to some restrictions] ... devoted primarily to the maintenance and operation of facilities for the performance of surgical procedures. 210 ILCS 5/3.

What health care organizations are missing from this list? Are there freestanding emergicenters, assisted living centers, rehabilitation institutes, birthing centers, mobile mammogram services, infusion centers, chemical dependency care units, sub-acute facilities, or other health care facilities in your area? Are these organizations covered by the provisions of the Illinois statute? If a "hospital" provides services in a person's home after discharge, is it required to get a license as a "home health agency?"

MAUCERI v. CHASSIN

Supreme Court, Albany County, New York, 1993.
156 Misc.2d 802, 594 N.Y.S.2d 605.

* * *

Since 1979, the plaintiff has operated a business out of her home providing patients and their families with the names of home health aides. It is up to the patient or the family to contact the home health aide and work out the specific pay scale, hours, and duties. The plaintiff receives compensation directly from the patient or the patient's family at a flat rate of 80 cents per hour for each hour the home health aide works for the client. Plaintiff does not conduct any investigation as to the qualifications of the aides, nor does she create a care plan for the patient, or maintain medical records. During 1990, the Department of Health received a complaint that the plaintiff was referring home health aides without being licensed as a home care services agency. Plaintiff took the position that the services that she rendered were not encompassed by the statutory definition of home care services agency. The defendants disagree.

* * *

If the plaintiff, and other small businesses such as hers, are forced to comply with all of the requirements of article 36 of the public health law, and the regulations thereunder, the cost of home health aides to the general public will undoubtedly increase. That is because the overhead expense of the recordkeeping and supervisory duties the plaintiff and others performing similar functions will be required to perform must be passed along in the price she charges. In a time of rising health care costs, that hardly seems a worthy goal of state government. Moreover, to those adherents of free enterprise still operating within this state it is no doubt abhorrent that a patient or his or her family cannot hire an agent to assist in employing a home health aide without that agent being subject to the requirement of having a license from the department of health. Be that as it may, the construction given to a statute by the agency charged with implementing it should be upheld if not irrational [ ]. Subdivision 2 of section 3602 of the public health law provides as follows:

"2. 'Home care services agency' means an organization primarily engaged in arranging and/or providing directly or through contract arrangement one or more of the following: Nursing services, home health aide services, and other therapeutic and related services which may include, but shall not be limited to, physical, speech and occupational therapy, nutritional services, medical social services, personal care services, homemaker services, and housekeeper or chore services, which may be of a preventive, therapeutic, rehabilitative, health guidance, and/or supportive nature to persons at home".

Clearly, the plaintiff's business is an organization engaged in arranging for home health aide services. The fact that the plaintiff does not provide or supervise those services does not mean that she is not arranging for them when she provides her clients with a list of home health aides. Since the defendants' interpretation of the statute is not irrational, it will be upheld. That being the case, plaintiff will be enjoined from operating her home health care referral service until such time she has been licensed under article 36.
* * *

Notes and Questions

1. If a family simply hired a person to provide home care services, would that person require a license as a "home care agency?" Had plaintiff made any warranties about her own services? Why would families choose to hire individuals outside of a professional agency? Karen Donelan, et al., Challenged to Care: Informal Caregivers in a Changing Health System, 21 Health Affairs 222 (2002).

2. What might explain the absence of legislation regulating a particular health care organization or service? Noticeably absent from the list of facilities requiring a license in Illinois, for example, are doctors' offices. Why is that? Why would Illinois define home health agency as it does rather than more broadly?

Problem: To Regulate or Not to Regulate? That is the Question

There is great demand for living arrangements that include supportive services for elderly persons who cannot live entirely on their own but do not require the more institutionalized environment of nursing homes or assisted living. As the market responds to that demand, new configurations of housing and services are developing. In some states, a model has emerged where the building may be owned by an independent, unlicensed person or organization and units are rented to residents. Additional services, such as home health care; physical therapy; and monitoring of self administration of medication, are provided by contract with licensed providers. These operations are described as "housing with services establishments" or "multiunit assisted housing with services," or similar terms. See AARP, Assisted Living in Unlicensed Housing: The Regulatory Experience of Four States (2007). See also, The Assisted Living Reform Act of 2004, N.Y. Pub. Health § 4650 which reaches a range of housing-services arrangements.

Would the relevant state agency in Illinois be able to impose any obligations on the residential provider in these arrangements under the excerpts above? Should your state consider legislation requiring licensure or certification of the residential provider? What particular risks are you concerned about, if any? If you support some degree of intervention, would you focus solely on requiring certain information to be provided to consumers considering these options, or would you impose specific obligations on the residential provider such as special safety standards due to the age and dependency of the residents or procedural requirements for termination of services and evictions? Are you concerned about raising the costs of this housing option?

II. REGULATORY SYSTEMS

The materials in this chapter focus primarily on long-term care, a critically important and growing segment of our nation's health care sector. Nursing homes are subject to a high degree of public quality control regulation by both federal and state governments, especially as compared to hospitals, home health agencies, and other health care organizations. Enforcement of nursing home standards over the past three decades has created a revealing case study of the challenges of public quality control regulation. The contrast between nursing homes and hospitals also provides a framework for understanding the factors that determine under what circumstances particular forms of quality control efforts, e.g., market enhancing efforts as compared to licensure, are likely to be more or less effective.

A. DIFFERENCES BETWEEN HOSPITALS AND NURSING HOMES

Hospitals and nursing homes are quite distinctive organizations even though they both provide medical and nursing care for patients/residents. They differ in their patient population; their scope of services; the composition of their staffing; and other internal organizational characteristics. They are also subject to different external pressures.

Differences in Patient Population and Scope of Services

Part of what makes nursing homes unique in the health care system is their responsibility for the complete and total environment of their residents typically over a very long time. Their involvement with the daily life of residents usually includes assistance in bathing, dressing, toileting, and eating. The majority of residents of a nursing home typically have resided in the facility for more than a year, but the average length of stay for persons entering nursing homes is only a few months. Only 11 in 1000 persons 65–74 years of age reside in nursing homes compared to 46 out of 1000 persons 75–84 and 192 out of 1000 persons 85 years of age or older. E. Kramarow et al., Health and Aging Chartbook. Health, United States (1999).

Nursing home residents typically bear multiple serious, chronic, and intractable medical conditions. Unlike hospital patients, nursing home residents are chronically rather than acutely ill. With the increasing utilization of home care and assisted living, however, the average nursing home patient is much sicker than those of the 1980s. Their physical frailty often requires rigorous and sophisticated care. Younger people who are severely disabled or mentally ill also reside in nursing homes; and regulations addressing their needs are attracting more enforcement effort as well.

The choice of nursing home is unlike the choice of other consumer goods or even the selection of a doctor or a hospital. The selection of a nursing home is typically made under duress, often upon discharge from an unexpected hospitalization; with uncertainty as to the individual's prognosis which influences, for example, whether the admission will be a short-stay rehabilitation admission or a longer term admission; and by an individual other than the patient/resident themselves with resultant persuasion or coercion even when the patient/resident is competent. See, e.g., Deborah Stone, Shopping for

Long–Term Care, 23 Health Affairs 191 (2004). The ability of a resident to transfer from a facility providing unsatisfactory services is limited as well due to the physical and mental frailty of the resident. Furthermore, once serious considerations (such as level of care, proximity to family due to potential lengthy stay, and the nursing home's acceptance of Medicaid payments upon admission or once personal funds are exhausted) are accounted for, the remaining choice can be quite slim.

Differences in Organizational Structure

While hospitals developed in the United States as charitable institutions often under the direction of religious organizations, nursing homes developed originally as "mom-and-pop" enterprises, in which individuals boarded elderly persons in private homes. After the advent of Medicare and Medicaid, nursing homes attracted substantial activity from investors and were viewed primarily as real estate investments. Even today, most nursing homes are for-profit, while most hospitals are not-for-profit. National for-profit chains own a significant segment of the nursing home industry. In contrast to studies of the hospital industry, studies of nursing homes consistently find that nonprofit facilities offer higher quality care. M.P. Hilmer, Nursing Home Profit Status and Quality of Care: Is There Any Evidence of an Association?, 62 Med. Care Res. Rev. 139 (2005), reviewing studies published in 1990–2002. See also Charles Duhigg, At Many Homes, More Profit and Less Nursing, N.Y.Times 11 (Sept. 23, 2007), reporting on citations against investor-owned facilities.

Physicians are still largely absent from nursing homes, and professional nurses act primarily as administrators rather than direct care providers. Thus, the peer review oversight processes that are well-entrenched in hospitals are relatively new or absent in nursing homes. Further, hospitals have long subjected themselves to accreditation by the Joint Commission (formerly the Joint Commission on Accreditation of Healthcare Organizations, or JCA-HO), while private accreditation of nursing homes is not as well established or influential. See discussion in Section IV, below.

In contrast to the typical hospital market, the demand for nursing home care exceeds available beds although demand may be ebbing somewhat in the face of more alternatives, such as assisted living facilities. Certificate of need programs in the majority of states restrict the number of nursing homes in a particular area on the theory that more beds will raise health care costs. David C. Grabowski, Medicaid Reimbursement and the Quality of Nursing Home Care, 20 J. Health Econ. 549 (2001). Low supply and excess demand, however, have been associated with lower quality perhaps because of weak competition or because enforcement efforts are constrained by the lack of alternatives for continuing care of the residents. John V. Jacobi, Competition Law's Role in Health Care Quality, 11 Ann. Health L. 45 (2002); John A. Nyman, Prospective and "Cost–Plus" Medicaid Reimbursement, Excess Medicaid Demand, and the Quality of Nursing Home Care, 4 J. Health Econ. 237 (1985).

The Medicaid program paid for nearly half of nursing home care in the U.S. in 2002, while about 15% is paid for by Medicare, leaving approximately 36% paid out-of-pocket by residents or their families, a miniscule portion of which may be covered by long-term-care insurance. Cathy Cowan, et al.,

National Health Expenditures 2002, 25 Health Care Fin. Rev. 143 (2004). Because nursing home care consumes the bulk of the Medicaid dollar and Medicaid is the largest spending item in state budgets, Medicaid payment levels for nursing homes are contentious. Research on whether increases in payment levels improve the quality of nursing home care, however, has produced mixed results. See, e.g., David C. Grabowski, et al., Medicaid Payment and Risk–Adjusted Nursing Home Quality Measures, 23 Health Affairs 243 (2004), concluding that higher payment levels were associated with lower incidence of pressure sores and use of restraints but not with improvements in pain management; GAO, Nursing Homes: Quality of Care More Related to Staffing than Spending (2002).

Differences in the Impact of Private Litigation over Quality

Hospitals are subject to frequent and substantial lawsuits for injuries to patients. In contrast, the characteristics of the nursing home population generally limit their ability to bring suit themselves for harms suffered as a result of poor care or abuse. Causation may be difficult to prove. Physical injuries in very frail elderly persons may be caused either by ordinary touching or by poor care or abuse. Mental impairment makes many nursing home residents poor witnesses. Limited remaining life spans and disabilities minimize legally recognizable damages. They do not suffer lost wages, and medical costs for treatment of injuries generally will be covered by Medicaid or Medicare. See, e.g., Marshall Kapp, Malpractice Liability in Long–Term Care: A Changing Environment, 24 Creighton L. Rev 1235 (1991); J. Thomas Rhodes III & Juliette Castillo, Proving Damages in Nursing Home Cases, 36 Trial 41 (2000).

The incidence and success of private lawsuits against these facilities have increased significantly in some regions of the country, however, particularly in Florida and Texas. Some cases have produced particularly large verdicts, but these are rare. In Muccianti v. Willow Creek Care Center, 108 Cal.App.4th 13, 133 Cal.Rptr.2d 1 (Ct. App. 2003), for example, the court specifically recognized that such litigation performs a public function regarding the quality of nursing home care. In *Muccianti*, the court rejected a post-verdict settlement in which the parties agreed to the payment of $1 million instead of the $5 million awarded by the jury. In rejecting the settlement, the court stated that "the public trust clearly could be undermined where a nursing facility has findings of negligence and willful misconduct expunged from the public record," and that "a court-ordered vacation of the judgment could well be interpreted as a judicial nullification of the jury's findings." See also, Stogsdill v. Healthmark Partners, 377 F.3d 827 (8th Cir. 2004), applying constitutional limits to reduce $5 million punitive damages award to $2 million.

Although some of the awards against nursing homes have been spectacular, they may give a mistaken impression of liability risks for nursing homes. See review of data in Michael L. Rustad, Heart of Stone: What Is Revealed About the Attitude of Compassionate Conservatives Toward Nursing Home Practices, Tort Reform, and Noneconomic Damages, 35 New Mex. L. Rev. 337(2005). Even in states where private litigation has grown, the litigation is concentrated in just a few facilities. See, Toby S. Edelman, An Advocate's Response to Professor Sage, 9 J. Health Care L. & Pol'y 291 (2006), noting studies in Florida and the District of Columbia (where two facilities accounted for over half of the cases filed over an eight-year period and ten of D.C.'s 19 nursing homes had never had a suit filed against them). Increased frequency of litigation against nursing homes has raised concerns that such litigation might divert resources for care. Jennifer L. Troyer & Herbert G. Thompson, The Impact of Litigation on Nursing Home Quality, 29 J. Health Pol., Pol'y & L. 11 (2004); David Stevenson & David Studdert, The Rise of Nursing Home Litigation: Findings From a National Survey of Attorneys, 22 Health Affairs 219 (March/April 2003). Litigation successes in pursuing private remedies for negligence and abuse could make the risk of liability a new potent influence in improving the quality of care in nursing homes. Even with increased rates in some states, however, the risk of private litigation against nursing homes pales in comparison to that experienced by hospitals.

While many states enacted legislation some years ago to encourage nursing home patients to pursue private remedies as a means of enforcing regulatory standards, many states have since amended these statutes to make such litigation less viable by limiting damages and attorneys' fees or subjecting such claims to limitations included in general tort reform legislative packages. See discussion in Ellen J. Scott, Punitive Damages in Lawsuits Against Nursing Homes, 23 J. Legal Med. 115 (2002). In an unusual provision in Florida, a plaintiff receiving an award of punitive damages is required to pay half to the Quality of Long–Term Care Facility Improvement Trust Fund. F.S.A. § 400.0238. Finally, nursing homes now frequently include binding arbitration clauses in admission agreements that preclude the award of punitive or exemplary damages to injured residents. While most courts have enforced these clauses unless the resident or legally authorized representative did not sign the agreement, a few decisions have concluded that particular clauses violated public policy by abrogating statutory remedies for nursing home residents. Florida appellate courts have disagreed on this question, for example. See, Fletcher v. Huntington Place Ltd. Partnership, 952 So.2d 1225 (Fla. App. 5th Dist. 2007) and Bland v. Health Care and Retirement Corp., 927 So.2d 252 (Fla. App. 2d Dist. 2006).

Notes and Questions

1. Prepare a report card on the relative strengths and weaknesses of the various internal and external forces that influence the quality or the accountability of nursing homes as compared to hospitals. Grade each force according to its comparative strength. For general discussion, see Marshall Kapp, Quality of Care and Quality of Life in Nursing Facilities: What's Regulation Got To Do With It? 31 McGeorge L.Rev. 707 (2000); Jennifer Brady, Long–Term Care Under Fire: A Case for Rational Enforcement, 18 J. Contemp Health L. & Pol'y 1 (2001); Alexander D. Eremia, When Self–Regulation, Market Forces, and Private Legal Actions Fail: Appropriate Government Regulation and Oversight is Necessary to Ensure Minimum Standards of Quality in Long–Term Health Care, 11 Annals Health L. 93 (2002).

2. Over the past several years, federal and state governments have increased mandates for the collection and disclosure of data concerning the performance of health care facilities, including both hospitals and nursing homes. The theory of these efforts is that they will create incentives for quality improvement by enhancing market choices by consumers (or proxy decision makers such as doctors and discharge planners) and by better informing facilities themselves of their

comparative performance. See discussion in Chapter 1. Does the theory apply equally well to hospitals and to nursing homes? If not, are such programs worth doing anyway in terms of cost and prioritization of governmental resources for quality control? David G. Stevenson, Is a Public Reporting Approach Appropriate for Nursing Home Care?, 31 J. Health Pol. Pol'y & L. 773 (2006), reporting on impact of reporting/disclosure mandates on hospitals and comparing that with nursing homes; Dana Mukamel & William Spector, Quality Report Cards and Nursing Home Quality, 43 The Gerontologist 558 (2003). The Centers for Medicare & Medicaid Services (CMS) debuted a national public Internet-based database on nursing homes in 1998. In 2002, CMS implemented the Nursing Home Quality Initiative, a national effort aimed at improving care by sharing data with the public on quality in ten functional areas already provided to CMS by the facilities. The data is available at http://www.medicare.gov/NHCompare/home.asp. One of the key issues in report cards and other mandated report systems is the selection of the information that will be collected and posted. The GAO issued a report the day after the national rollout of the data in Nursing Home Compare saying that it was premature and that CMS had not done an effective evaluation of the usefulness of the pilot program it had conducted. GAO: Nursing Homes, Public Reporting of Quality Indicators Has Merit, but National Implementation is Premature, GAO 03–187 (2002). Consumers Union warns that persons searching for a nursing home should ignore the federal web site (in favor of the Nursing Home Quality Monitor database that CU produces, available at http://www.con sumerreports.org/cro/health-fitness/nursing-home-guide/nursing-home-quality-monitor/0608–nursing-home-quality-monitor.htm), because the federal site provides only vague generalities about deficiencies. Consumer Reports (Sept. 2006). If you had to respond to the GAO or Consumers Union, how would you design a study to test the effectiveness of this initiative?

3.   As you read the following materials, remember these institutional differences and consider what demands they make on governmental quality control programs. How will standards differ as between nursing home regulation and hospital regulation? How might the survey or inspection process differ? Would the tenor of the regulatory effort be the same or would one be more enforcement oriented while another might rely on a more collegial learning approach?

B.   NURSING HOMES: LICENSURE AND MEDICARE/MEDICAID

Only nursing homes who wish to receive payment for services to Medicare or Medicaid beneficiaries must meet federal standards in order to be certified to enter into a provider agreement with those programs. Medicare and Medicaid standards apply to every resident in the facility, however, and not only to beneficiaries of those programs. If a nursing facility chooses not to participate in Medicare or Medicaid, it will be subject only to state licensure requirements. Realistically, however, most nursing homes cannot survive without Medicare payments, even though Medicare pays only a small portion of the nation's expenditures on institutional long-term care and offers very limited nursing home benefits.

The federal and state nursing home quality-control programs have engaged in a mutually influential relationship for decades. Until the late 1980s, the federal government largely deferred to the state licensure systems to monitor quality for Medicare and Medicaid. With federal nursing home reform in 1987 (the Nursing Home Reform Act in the Omnibus Budget Reconciliation Act of 1987), however, the federal government established standards and methods for the inspection and sanctions process to be used to enforce

Medicare and Medicaid requirements, although it continued to rely on the states for on-site inspections. The new federal standards borrowed from a few states that had pioneered initiatives such as intermediate sanctions and, in turn, influenced other states to follow. For more on the federal-state relationship, see *Smith*, below.

The history of nursing homes in the U.S. is characterized by a pattern of scandals, periodic waves of media coverage, and episodes of intense federal and state response. Nursing home abuses and quality failures are once again front-page news and the subject of government reports. See e.g., GAO, Continued Attention is Needed to Improve the Quality of Care in Small but Significant Share of Homes, GAO–07–794T (May 2007), reporting that serious and dangerous conditions persist in almost 20% of facilities and enforcement efforts suffer from data management problems in tracking violators, delays in imposing sanctions, inconsistencies in inspections and reports of violations, and inability to hire competent inspectors. See also GAO, Efforts to Strengthen Federal Enforcement Have Not Deterred Some Homes from Repeatedly Harming Residents, GAO 07–241 (Mar. 2006). These reports recognize that the number of nursing homes cited for deficiencies decreased between 1999–2005 but associate that decrease with less effective inspection and enforcement systems rather than improvements in quality. Consumers Union, in a study funded by the Commonwealth Fund, concluded that poor care is widespread and persistent. At the same time, the HHS reported that quality of care in nursing homes has improved. Nursing Home Quality Improves, HHS Says in Announcing Expanded Initiative, 14 Health L. Rep. 34 (2005). See also Marshall B. Kapp, Improving the Quality of Nursing Homes, 26 J. Leg. Med. 1 (2005).

CMS has taken a number of steps to supplement federal-state enforcement of Medicaid/Medicare standards. In addition to making data on nursing homes available to the public (as discussed earlier), CMS has contracted with private Quality Improvement Organizations (QIOs)to provide consulting services to a particular subset of nursing homes that want to undertake internal efforts to improve quality. The GAO has reported that it is difficult to assess the impact of the QIO initiative because of the unreliability of the CMS's quality measurement data. GAO, Federal Actions Needed to Improve Targeting and Evaluation Assistance by Quality Improvement Organizations, GAO–07–373 (May 2007).

CMS is also considering revising payment systems to create more incentives for providing higher quality care. An Institute of Medicine study of pay-for-performance, however, recommended that implementation be delayed in the case of skilled nursing facilities as a group because of concerns over inadequate measures and data applicable to the short-stay, rehabilitative nursing home services paid for by Medicare, Institute of Medicine, Rewarding Provider Performance: Aligning Incentives in Medicare (2007). See also Jennifer L. Hilliard, The Nursing Home Quality Initiative. 26 J. Leg. Med. 41 (2005).

For a detailed analysis of the history of nursing home regulation as well as current controversies, see David A. Bohm, Striving for Quality Care in America's Nursing Homes: Tracing the History of Nursing Homes and the Effect of Recent Federal Government Initiatives to Ensure Quality Care in the Nursing Home Setting, 4 DePaul J. Health Care L. 317 (2001); Jennifer Brady, Long–Term Care Under Fire: A Case for Rational Enforcement, 18 J. Contemp. Health L. & Pol'y. 1 (2001); Symposium, The Crisis in Long Term Care, 4 J. Health Care L. & Pol'y 308 (2001). For a provocative comparative study of nursing home regulation, see John Braithwaite, et al., Regulating Aged Care: Ritualism and the New Pyramid (2007).

C. THE REGULATORY PROCESS

The regulatory process—whether licensure or Medicare/Medicaid certification–involves three functions: standard setting; inspection (known as "survey" in nursing home regulation); and sanctions.

1. *Standard Setting*

IN RE THE ESTATE OF MICHAEL PATRICK SMITH v. HECKLER

United States Court of Appeals, Tenth Circuit, 1984.
747 F.2d 583.

McKay, Circuit Judge:

Plaintiffs, seeking relief under 42 U.S.C.A. § 1983, brought this class action on behalf of Medicaid recipients residing in nursing homes in Colorado. They alleged that the Secretary of Health and Human Services (Secretary) has a statutory duty under Title XIX of the Social Security Act, 42 U.S.C.A. §§ 1396–1396n (1982), commonly known as the Medicaid Act, to develop and implement a system of nursing home review and enforcement designed to ensure that Medicaid recipients residing in Medicaid-certified nursing homes actually receive the optimal medical and psychosocial care that they are entitled to under the Act. The plaintiffs contended that the enforcement system developed by the Secretary is "facility-oriented," not "patient-oriented" and thereby fails to meet the statutory mandate. The district court found that although a patient care or "patient-oriented" management system is feasible, the Secretary does not have a duty to introduce and require the use of such a system. [ ]

The primary issue on appeal is whether the trial court erred in finding that the Secretary does not have a statutory duty to develop and implement a system of nursing home review and enforcement, which focuses on and ensures high quality patient care. * * *

Background

The factual background of this complex lawsuit is fully discussed in the district court's opinion. [ ] Briefly, plaintiffs instituted the lawsuit in an effort to improve the deplorable conditions at many nursing homes. They presented evidence of the lack of adequate medical care and of the widespread knowledge that care is inadequate. Indeed, the district court concluded that care and life in some nursing homes is so bad that the homes "could be characterized as orphanages for the aged." [ ]

* * *

THE MEDICAID ACT

An understanding of the Medicaid Act (the Act) is essential to understand plaintiffs' contentions. The purpose of the Act is to enable the federal government to assist states in providing medical assistance to "aged, blind or disabled individuals, whose income and resources are insufficient to meet the costs of necessary medical services, and ... rehabilitation and other services to help such ... individuals to attain or retain capabilities for independence or self care." 42 U.S.C.A. § 1396 (1982). To receive funding, a state must submit to the Secretary and have approved by the Secretary, a plan for medical assistance, which meets the requirements of 42 U.S.C.A. § 1396a(a).

* * * A state seeking plan approval must establish or designate a single state agency to administer or supervise administration of the state plan, 42 U.S.C.A. § 1396a(a)(5), and must provide reports and information as the Secretary may require. *Id.* § 1396a(a)(6). Further, the state agency is responsible for establishing and maintaining health standards for institutions where the recipients of the medical assistance under the plan receive care or services. *Id.* § 1396a(a)(9)(A). The plan must include descriptions of the standards and methods the state will use to assure that medical or remedial care services provided to the recipients "are of high quality." *Id.* § 1396a(a)(22)(D).

The state plan must also provide "for a regular program of medical review ... of each patient's need for skilled nursing facility care ..., a written plan of care, and, where applicable, a plan of rehabilitation prior to admission to a skilled nursing facility...." *Id.* § 1396a(a)(26)(A). Further, the plan must provide for periodic inspections by medical review teams of:

> (i) the care being provided in such nursing facilities ... to persons receiving assistance under the State plan; (ii) with respect to each of the patients receiving such care, the adequacy of the services available in particular nursing facilities ... to meet the current health needs and promote the maximum physical well-being of patients receiving care in such facilities ...; (iii) the necessity and desirability of continued placement of such patients in such nursing facilities ...; and (iv) the feasibility of meeting their health care needs through alternative institutional or noninstitutional services. *Id.* § 1396a(a)(26)(B).

The state plan must provide that any skilled nursing facility receiving payment comply with 42 U.S.C.A. § 1395x(j), which defines "skilled nursing facility" and sets out standards for approval under a state plan. *Id.* § 1396a(a)(28). The key requirement for purposes of this lawsuit is that a skilled nursing facility must meet "such other conditions relating to the health and safety of individuals who are furnished services in such institution or relating to the physical facilities thereof as the Secretary may find necessary...." *Id.* § 1395x(j)(15).

The state plan must provide for the appropriate state agency to establish a plan, consistent with regulations prescribed by the Secretary, for professional health personnel to review the appropriateness and quality of care and services furnished to Medicaid recipients. *Id.* § 1396a(a)(33)(A). The appropriate state agency must determine on an ongoing basis whether participating institutions meet the requirements for continued participation in the Medicaid program. *Id.* § 1396a(a)(33)(B). While the state has the initial responsibility for determining whether institutions are meeting the conditions of participation, section 1396a(a)(33)(B) gives the Secretary the authority to "look behind" the state's determination of facility compliance, and make an independent and binding determination of whether institutions meet the requirements for participation in the state Medicaid plan. Thus, the state is responsible for conducting the review of facilities to determine whether they comply with the state plan. In conducting the review, however, the states must use federal standards, forms, methods, and procedures. 42 C.F.R. § 431.610(f)(1) (1983). * * *

IMPLEMENTING REGULATIONS

Congress gave the Secretary a general mandate to promulgate rules and regulations necessary to the efficient administration of the functions with which the Secretary is charged by the Act. 42 U.S.C.A. § 1302 (1982). Pursuant to this mandate the Secretary has promulgated standards for the care to be provided by skilled nursing facilities and intermediate care facilities. See 42 C.F.R. § 442.200–.516 (1983). * * *

The Secretary has established a procedure for determining whether state plans comply with the standards set out in the regulations. This enforcement mechanism is known as the "survey/certification" inspection system. Under this system, the states conduct reviews of nursing homes pursuant to 42 U.S.C.A. § 1396a(a)(33). The Secretary then determines, on the basis of the survey results, whether the nursing home surveyed is eligible for certification and, thus, eligible for Medicaid funds. The states must use federal standards, forms, methods, and procedures in conducting the survey. 42 C.F.R. § 431.610(f)(1). At issue in this case is the form SSA–1569, [ ], which the Secretary requires the states to use to show that the nursing homes participating in Medicaid under an approved state plan meet the conditions of participation contained in the Act and the regulations. Plaintiffs contend that the form is "facility-oriented," in that it focuses on the theoretical capability of the facility to provide high quality care, rather than "patient-oriented," which would focus on the care actually provided. The district court found, with abundant support in the record, that the "facility-oriented" characterization is appropriate and that the Secretary has repeatedly admitted that the form is "facility-oriented." [ ]

THE PLAINTIFFS' CLAIMS
* * *

The plaintiffs do not challenge the substantive medical standards, or "conditions of participation," which have been adopted by the Secretary and which states must satisfy to have their plans approved. See 42 C.F.R. § 405.1101–.1137. Rather, plaintiffs challenge the enforcement mechanism the Secretary has established. The plaintiffs contend that the federal forms, form SSA–1569 in particular, which states are required to use, evaluate only the physical facilities and theoretical capability to render quality care. The surveys assess the care provided almost totally on the basis of the records, documentation, and written policies of the facility being reviewed. [ ] Further, out of the 541 questions contained in the Secretary's form SSA–1569 which must be answered by state survey and certification inspection teams, only 30 are "even marginally related to patient care or might require any patient observation. ..." [ ] Plaintiffs contend that the enforcement mechanism's focus on the facility, rather than on the care actually provided in the facility, results only in "paper compliance" with the substantive standards of the Act. Thus, plaintiffs contend, the Secretary has violated her statutory duty to assure that federal Medicaid monies are paid only to facilities, which meet the substantive standards of the Act—facilities which actually provide high quality medical, rehabilitative, and psychosocial care to resident Medicaid recipients.

THE DISTRICT COURT'S HOLDING

After hearing the evidence, the district court found the type of patient care management system advocated by plaintiffs clearly feasible and characterized the current enforcement system as "facility-oriented." [ ] However, the court concluded that the failure to implement and require the use of a "patient-oriented" system is not a violation of the Secretary's statutory duty. [ ] The essence of the district court's holding was that the State of Colorado, not the federal government, is responsible for developing and enforcing standards which would assure high quality care in nursing homes and, thus, the State of Colorado, not the federal government, should have been the defendant in this case. [ ]

* * *

THE SECRETARY'S DUTY

After carefully reviewing the statutory scheme of the Medicaid Act, the legislative history, and the district court's opinion, we conclude that the district court improperly defined the Secretary's duty under the statute. The federal government has more than a passive role in handing out money to the states. The district court erred in finding that the burden of enforcing the substantive provisions of the Medicaid Act is on the states. The Secretary of Health and Human Services has a duty to establish a system to adequately inform herself as to whether the facilities receiving federal money are satisfying the requirements of the Act, including providing high quality patient care. This duty to be adequately informed is not only a duty to be informed at the time a facility is originally certified, but is a duty of continued supervision.

Nothing in the Medicaid Act indicates that Congress intended the physical facilities to be the end product. Rather, the purpose of the Act is to provide medical assistance and rehabilitative services. 42 U.S.C.A. § 1396. The Act repeatedly focuses on the care to be provided, with facilities being only part of that care. For example, the Act provides that health standards are to be developed and maintained, *id*. § 1396a(a)(9)(A), and that states must inform the Secretary what methods they will use to assure high quality care. *Id*. § 1396a(a)(22). In addition to the "adequacy of the services available," the periodic inspections must address 'the care being provided" in nursing facilities. *Id*. § 1396a(a)(26)(B). State plans must provide review of the "appropriateness and quality of care and services furnished," *id*. § 1396a(a)(33)(A), and do so on an ongoing basis. *Id*. § 1396a(a)(33)(B).

While the district court correctly noted that it is the state, which develops specific standards and actually conducts the inspection, there is nothing in the Act to indicate that the state function relieves the Secretary of all responsibility to ensure that the purposes of the Act are being accomplished. The Secretary, not the states, determines which facilities are eligible for federal funds. [ ] While participation in the program is voluntary, states who choose to participate must comply with federal statutory requirements. [ ] The inspections may be conducted by the states, but the Secretary approves or disapproves the state's plan for review. Further, the inspections must be made with federal forms, procedures, and methods.

It would be anomalous to hold that the Secretary has a duty to determine whether a state plan meets the standards of the Act while holding that the Secretary can certify facilities without informing herself as to whether the facilities actually perform the functions required by the state plan. The Secretary has a duty to ensure more than paper compliance. The federal responsibility is particularly evident in the "look behind" provision. 42 U.S.C.A. § 1396a(a)(33)(B) (1982). We do not read the Secretary's "look behind" authority as being "nothing more than permitted authority . . . "as the district court found. Rather, we find that the purpose of that section is to assure that compliance is not merely facial, but substantive.

* * *

By enacting section 1302 Congress gave the Secretary authority to promulgate regulations to achieve the functions with which she is charged. The "look-behind" provision and its legislative history clearly show that Congress intended the Secretary to be responsible for assuring that federal Medicaid money is given only to those institutions that actually comply with Medicaid requirements. The Act's requirements include providing high quality medical care and rehabilitative services. In fact, the quality of the care provided to the aged is the focus of the Act. Being charged with this function, we must conclude that a failure to promulgate regulations that allow the Secretary to remain informed, on a continuing basis, as to whether facilities receiving federal money are meeting the requirements of the Act, is an abdication of the Secretary's duty. While the Medicaid Act is admittedly very complex and the Secretary has "exceptionally broad authority to prescribe standards for applying certain sections of the Act" [ ] the Secretary's authority cannot be interpreted so as to hold that that authority is merely permissive authority. The Secretary must insure that states comply with the congressional mandate to provide high quality medical care and rehabilitative services.

* * * Having determined that the purpose and the focus of the Act is to provide high quality medical care, we conclude that by promulgating a facility-oriented enforcement system the Secretary has failed to follow that focus and such failure is arbitrary and capricious. [ ]

Reversed and Remanded.

Notes and Questions

1. What explains the opposition of the federal government to patient-oriented standards in the *Smith* litigation? Should an administrative agency, as a matter of principle, simply resist all judicial mandates in standard setting? Do the courts have the expertise necessary for setting quality standards? After the *Smith* litigation, Congress commissioned the Institute of Medicine to conduct a study of nursing home regulation. See, Improving the Quality of Care in Nursing Homes (1986). The report significantly influenced the subsequent federal Nursing Home

Reform Act, commonly referenced as OBRA 1987, which represented a comprehensive change in standards, surveillance methods, and enforcement and still provides the core of federal regulation of nursing homes.

2. Did the plaintiffs in *Smith* contest the standards as enacted in the statute? As promulgated in regulations? Would a challenge to the statute itself likely be successful? On what basis would plaintiffs be able to challenge the regulations? Why would the survey forms themselves be of interest to attorneys representing facilities or residents? For similar litigation, see Rolland v. Patrick, 483 F.Supp.2d 107 (D. Mass. 2007), in which advocates challenged the state's standards for measuring mandated treatment for mentally retarded and developmentally disabled individuals in nursing homes.

3. As you read in Chapter 1, quality standards can be divided into three categories, depending on what the standard measures: structure, process, and outcome standards. The plaintiffs in *Smith* were concerned that federal standards at the time measured only the facility's "theoretical capability to render quality care." Structure and process standards tend to focus on capacity to provide care, as described in the next Problem; and outcome standards tend to measure quality by examining the condition of the patients/residents themselves. The CMS Nursing Home Quality Initiative (NHQI) identifies quality measurements (QMs) for nursing homes, using data collected in the Minimum Data Set (an instrument established in OBRA 1987 to require each facility to collect and report standardized data on each resident). For long-stay residents, the quality measurements are the percentage of residents with infections, pain, pressure sores (with residents allocated into low-risk and high-risk groups), physical restraints, and loss of ability in basic daily tasks. Data on these quality measures are posted on the Nursing Home Compare web site and may eventually be used for incentive-based payment programs. If you were an administrator of a nursing home and wanted to improve your performance on these outcome measures, you might increase or reorganize staff effort or other resources. Outcome measures at times create perverse incentives, however. For example, the measure of assistance in basic daily tasks excludes from the count patients who are terminally ill but does not exclude patients who have Alzheimer's disease or have suffered a stroke for whom natural progression may be increasing losses in self-care. Thus, the outcomes standards in the NHQI may encourage facilities to avoid admitting particular types of residents. Jennifer L. Hilliard, The Nursing Home Quality Initiative, 26 J. Legal. Med. 41 (2005); Katherine Berg, et al., Identification and Evaluation of Existing Nursing Home Quality Indicators, 23 Health Care Fin. Rev. 19 (2002); Steven Clauser & Arlene Bierman, Significance of Functional Status Data for Payment and Quality, 24 Health Care Fin. Rev. 1 (2003).

4. If the statute specifies certain structural or process standards (e.g., requiring that a nursing home be administered by a licensed nursing home administrator or requiring minimum staffing ratios or staff training), could a facility contest enforcement of those standards for lack of empirical evidence of an impact on quality? In Beverly California Corporation v. Shalala, 78 F.3d 403 (8th Cir.1996), the ALJ reviewing termination of the facility's Medicaid certification determined that termination was inappropriate because the government had not proved that any resident had suffered actual harm as a result of the deficiencies. The Appeals Council overturned the ALJ's decision and affirmed the Secretary's sanction stating that "deficiencies which substantially limit a facility's capacity to render adequate care or which adversely affect the health and safety of residents constitute noncompliance.... [A] strong potential for adverse effect on resident health and safety will constitute noncompliance as will an actual adverse effect or

'actual harm'.'' The District Court and the Eighth Circuit affirmed the Appeals Council decision.

5. When the Secretary finally issued final regulations to implement a new survey system as ordered by the court in *Smith,* she refused to include the survey instrument itself in the regulations: ''[T]he new forms and instructions are not set forth in these regulations, and any future changes will be implemented through general instructions, without further changes in these regulations. This allows flexibility to revise and improve the survey process as experience is gained.'' 51 Fed.Reg. 21550 (June 13, 1986). What else does this allow the agency to do? The federal district court rejected the final rules because they did not include the survey instruments or instructions and held the Secretary in contempt of court. Smith v. Bowen, 675 F.Supp. 586 (D.Colo. 1987). What was the judge's concern?

6. OBRA '87 appears to have had a positive effect on several practices. For example, the use of physical restraints declined by 50%; inappropriate use of antipsychotic drugs declined at least 25%; the incidence of dehydration was reduced by 50%; the use of indwelling catheters by nearly 30%; and hospitalizations by 25%. Bruce C. Vladeck, The Past, Present and Future of Nursing Home Quality, 275 JAMA 425 (1996), reviewing the literature. But see, Catherine Hawes, et al., The OBRA–87 Nursing Home Regulations and Implementation of the Resident Assessment Instrument: Effects on Process Quality, 45 J. Am. Geriatrics Soc'y 977 (1997), discussing the difficulty of proving that changes in practices and outcomes were caused by the new regulations. Marshall Kapp, in an article that is quite skeptical about research indicating that the standards of OBRA 1987 have had a significant positive effect, notes that government studies of the quality of nursing home care reveal persistent problems in the quality of care and the effectiveness of the regulatory system. Marshall B. Kapp, Quality of Care and Quality of Life in Nursing Facilities: What's Regulation Got To Do With It? 31 McGeorge L. Rev. 707 (2000).

7. The court's opinion in *Smith* describes the allocation of authority in the federal-state Medicaid quality control program. Exactly which functions are allocated to the state and which to the federal government? Is the federal-state effort duplicative and inefficient? Should Congress consider requiring that nursing facilities receiving Medicaid or Medicare dollars merely be licensed by the state? What is the justification for the federal role in this situation? See, e.g., OIG, Nursing Home Complaint Investigations (OEI–01–04–00340) (July 2006), reporting that CMS fails to monitor states' investigation of complaints and that the states are not in compliance with federal standards. For further discussion of federal-state relations, see Senator Charles Grassley, The Resurrection of Nursing Home Reform: A Historical Account of the Recent Revival of the Quality of Care Standards for Long–Term Care Facilities Established in the Omnibus Reconciliation Act of 1987, 7 Elder L.J. 267 (1999); William Gromley & Christine Boccuti, HCFA and the States: Politics and Intergovernmental Leverage, 26 J. Health Pol. Pol'y and L. 557 (2001).

8. Federal standards aimed at reducing the use of physical and chemical restraints represented not only a regulatory change but a fundamental shift in the foundation of a customary practice. Prior to the mid 1980s, physically restraining a nursing home resident was viewed as protective of the patient in that it prevented falls. It was also believed that a nursing home would be liable for injuries due to falls if it did not restrain patients. Research in the field changed that view. See, for example, Julie A. Braun & Elizabeth A. Capezuti, The Legal and Medical Aspects of Physical Restraints and Bed Siderails and Their Relationship to Falls and Fall–Related Injuries in Nursing Homes, 4 DePaul J. of Health

Care Law 1 (2000); Evan Meyers, Physical Restraints in Nursing Homes: An Analysis of Quality of Care and Legal Liability, 10 Elder L.J. 217 (2002); Sandra H. Johnson, The Fear of Liability and the Use of Restraints in Nursing Homes, 18 Law, Med. & Health Care 263 (1990). See also 71 Fed. Reg. 71378–01 (Dec. 8, 2006), promulgating final rule for extersion of restrictions on use of restraints in hospitals and describing justification for the rule. The Department of Justice Civil Rights Division has approached the inappropriate use of physical and chemical restraints as a violation of the civil rights of residents of public nursing homes under the Civil Rights of Institutional Persons Act. 42 U.S.C. § 1997. See DOJ report at http://www.usdoj.gov/crt/split/cripa.htm. You will work with the nursing home restraints standards in the Problem "Residents' Rights" below.

Problem: Setting Standards for Staffing

Staff-to-resident and nurse-to-resident ratio is a structural standard that is receiving increasing support as a key indicator of quality in nursing homes and hospitals. See, e.g., GAO, Nursing Homes: Quality of Care More Related to Staffing than Spending (2002). An ICM report recommended increased nurse staffing levels in nursing homes and hospitals as essential to reducing hazards to patient care. Donald M. Steinwachs, Keeping Patients Safe: Transforming the Work Environment of Nurses (2003). The federal government and the states are responding to the evidence underlying these recommendations. See, Theresamarie Mantese, et al., Nurse Staffing, Legislative Alternatives and Health Care Policy, 9 DePaul J. Health Care L. 1171 (2006). A few states have established mandatory staffing ratios. See, e.g., Del. Code Ann. Tit. 16, § 1162; Cal. Health & Safety Code § 1276.5. (See discussion of nurse labor union activity in the passage and implementation of the California statute in Chapter 9.)

CMS requires that nursing homes receiving Medicaid or Medicare post their daily resident count and their nurse (including RNs, LPNs, and CNAs) staffing numbers for each shift in a public place at the facility. 70 Fed. Reg. 62065 (Oct. 28, 2005). CMS also includes staffing data on its Nursing Home Compare web site.

Assume that you are an attorney working for CMS or the state licensing agency or for the American Health Care Association (representing for-profit nursing homes) or for an advocacy group representing nursing home residents. The staffing issue has landed on your desk. Should CMS require more than posting and increase the required nurse staffing levels for nursing homes? If it does so, should it increase Medicare and Medicaid payments to reflect increased costs? What data would you want to consider in responding to this question? (See, e.g., CMS, Health Care Industry Market Update–Nursing Facilities (2002); Med-PAC, March 2007 Report to Congress, Medicare Payment Policy, Nursing Homes available at www.medpac.gov/documents/Mar07_EntireReport.pdf.) Should the federal government raise the staffing levels for the Medicare program but not Medicaid? Are facilities with inadequate staffing violating existing standards of care, and can private litigation respond effectively? Should the federal or state government establish a financial incentive program to reward facilities that reduce turnover or increase the professional level or numbers of staff?

Problem: Residents' Rights

Assume that you are the attorney for Pine Acres Nursing Home, located in an older section of the city. The administrator has approached you regarding problems with certain patients. One patient, Francis Scott, aged 88, has been a resident of the facility for a few months. Scott's mental and physical condition has been deteriorating slowly for several years and much more rapidly in the past six months. His family placed him in the nursing home because they wanted him to be safe. They were concerned because he had often left his apartment and become totally lost on the way back. Mr. Scott's family always promptly pays the monthly fee. Scott is angry about the placement, tends to be rude and insists on walking through the hallways and around the fenced-in grounds of the facility on his own. He has always been an early riser and likes to take his shower at the crack of dawn. He refuses to be assisted in showering by a nurses' aide. In addition, his friends from the neighborhood like to visit. They like to play pinochle when they come, and they usually bring a six-pack.

Another patient, Emma Kaitz, has fallen twice, apparently while trying to get out of bed. The staff is very concerned that she will be hurt. The physician who is medical director of the facility will write an order for restraints "as needed" for any resident upon the request of the director of nursing. Mrs. Kaitz's daughter is willing to try whatever the doctor advises. The staff have begun using "soft restraints" (cloth straps on her wrists) tied to the bedrails, but Mrs. Kaitz becomes agitated and cries. She says she feels like a dog when they tie her up. Other times they just use the bedrails alone. When she becomes agitated, she is given a sedative to help her relax, but it also tends to make her appear confused. To avoid the agitation as much as possible during the day, they have been able to position her wheelchair so that she can't get out by herself. She stops trying after a while and becomes so relaxed she nods off.

The administrator wants to know what he can do. What would you advise this administrator? Can he restrict the visiting hours for Mr. Scott? Can he require Mr. Scott to be assisted in the shower? Can Mr. Scott be transferred or discharged? Is the facility providing quality care for Mrs. Kaitz? How should an inspector treat Mr. Scott's and Mrs. Kaitz's complaints? What does your nursing home client expect of you here? What role should you play in regard to quality of care standards?

The text that follows includes excerpts from the Residents' Rights section of the Medicaid statute; the regulation on the use of physical restraints; and the interpretive guidelines on physical restraints provided to surveyors for the inspection of Medicaid facilities.

42 U.S.C.A. § 1396r

(b)(1) QUALITY OF LIFE.—

(A) IN GENERAL.—A nursing facility must care for its residents in such a manner and in such an environment as will promote maintenance or enhancement of the quality of life of each resident.

* * *

(c) REQUIREMENTS RELATING TO RESIDENTS' RIGHTS—

(1) GENERAL RIGHTS.—

(A) SPECIFIED RIGHTS.—A nursing facility must protect and promote the rights of each resident, including each of the following rights:

(i) FREE CHOICE.—The right to choose a personal attending physician, to be fully informed in advance about care and treatment that may affect the resident's well-being, and (except with respect to a resident adjudged incompetent) to participate in planning care and treatment or changes in care and treatment.

(ii) FREE FROM RESTRAINTS.—The right to be free from physical or mental abuse, corporal punishment, involuntary seclusion, and any physical or chemical restraints imposed for purposes of discipline or convenience and not required to treat the resident's medical symptoms. Restraints may only be imposed—

(I) to ensure the physical safety of the resident or other residents, and

(II) only upon the written order of a physician that specifies the duration and circumstances under which the restraints are to be used (except in emergency circumstances specified by the Secretary until such an order could reasonably be obtained).

(iii) PRIVACY.—The right to privacy with regard to accommodations, medical treatment, written and telephonic communications, visits, and meetings of family and of resident groups. [Does not require private rooms.]

(v) ACCOMMODATION OF NEEDS.—The right—

(I) to reside and receive services with reasonable accommodations of individual needs and preferences, except where the health or safety of the individual or other residents would be endangered, and

(II) to receive notice before the room or roommate of the resident in the facility is changed.

(viii) PARTICIPATION IN OTHER ACTIVITIES.—The right of the resident to participate in social, religious, and community activities that do not interfere with the rights of other residents in the facility.

* * *

(D) USE OF PSYCHOPHARMACOLOGIC DRUGS.

Psychopharmacologic drugs may be administered only on the orders of a physician and only as part of a plan (included in the written plan of care ...) designed to eliminate or modify the symptoms for which the drugs are prescribed and only if, at least annually an independent, external consultant reviews the appropriateness of the drug plan of each resident receiving such drugs.

(2) TRANSFER AND DISCHARGE RIGHTS.—

(A) IN GENERAL.—A nursing facility must permit each resident to remain in the facility and must not transfer or discharge the resident from the facility unless—

(i) the transfer or discharge is necessary to meet the resident's welfare and the resident's welfare cannot be met in the facility;

(ii) the transfer or discharge is appropriate because the resident's health has improved sufficiently so the resident no longer needs the services provided by the facility;

(iii) the safety of individuals in the facility is endangered;

(iv) the health of individuals in the facility would otherwise be endangered;

(v) the resident has failed, after reasonable and appropriate notice, to pay ... for a stay at the facility; or

(vi) the facility ceases to operate.

* * *

(B) PRE–TRANSFER AND PRE–DISCHARGE NOTICE.—

(i) IN GENERAL.—Before effecting a transfer or discharge of a resident, a nursing facility must—

(I) notify the resident (and, if known, an immediate family member of the resident or legal representative) of the transfer or discharge and the reasons therefore,

(II) record the reasons in the resident's clinical record * * * and

(III) include in the notice the items described in clause (iii). [concerning appeal of transfer]

(ii) TIMING OF NOTICE.—The notice under clause (i)(I) must be made at least 30 days in advance of the resident's transfer or discharge except—

(I) in a case described in clause (iii) or (iv) of subparagraph (A);

(II) in a case described in clause (ii) of subparagraph (A), where the resident's health improves sufficiently to allow a more immediate transfer or discharge;

(III) in a case described in clause (i) of subparagraph (A), where a more immediate transfer or discharge is necessitated by the resident's urgent medical needs; or

(IV) in a case where a resident has not resided in the facility for 30 days.

In the case of such exceptions, notice must be given as many days before the date of the transfer or discharge as is practicable. [The statute also requires the state to establish a hearing process for transfers and discharges contested by the resident or surrogate.]

(3) ACCESS AND VISITATION RIGHTS.—A nursing facility must—

(A) permit immediate access to any resident by any representative of the Secretary, by any representative of the State, by an ombudsman . . . , or by the resident's individual physician;

(B) permit immediate access to a resident, subject to the resident's right to deny or withdraw consent at any time, by immediate family or other relatives of the resident;

(C) permit immediate access to a resident, subject to reasonable restrictions and the resident's right to deny or withdraw consent at any time, by others who are visiting with the consent of the resident;

(D) permit reasonable access to a resident by any entity or individual that provides health, social, legal, or other services to the resident, subject to the resident's right to deny or withdraw consent at any time; and

(E) permit representatives of the State ombudsman . . . , with the permission of the resident (or the resident's legal representative) and consistent with State law, to examine a resident's clinical records.

(4) EQUAL ACCESS TO QUALITY CARE.—

A nursing facility must establish and maintain identical policies and practices regarding transfer, discharge and the provision of services . . . for all individuals regardless of source of payment.

42 C.F.R. § 483.13(a)

Restraints. The resident has the right to be free from any physical or chemical restraints imposed for purposes of discipline or convenience, and not required to treat the resident's medical symptoms.

GUIDANCE TO SURVEYORS: § 483.13(a)

Medicare State Operations Manual, Appendix PP—Guidance to Surveyors—Long Term Care Facilities (Sept. 7, 2000), available at http://cms.hhs.gov/manuals/pm_trans/R20SOM.pdf.

Convenience is defined as any action taken by the facility to control a resident's behavior or manage a resident's behavior with a lesser amount of effort by the facility and not in the resident's best interest.

Restraints may not be used for staff convenience. However, if the resident needs emergency care, restraints may be used for brief periods to permit medical treatment to proceed unless the facility has a notice indicating that the resident has previously made a valid refusal of the treatment in question. If a resident's unanticipated violent or aggressive behavior places him/her or others in imminent danger, the resident does not have the right to refuse the use of restraints. In this situation, the use of restraints is a measure of last resort to protect the safety of the resident or others and must not extend beyond the immediate episode.

Physical Restraints are defined as any manual method or physical or mechanical device, material, or equipment attached or adjacent to the resident's body that the individual cannot remove easily which restricts freedom of movement or normal access to one's body.

"Physical restraints" include, but are not limited to, leg restraints, arm restraints, hand mitts, soft ties or vests, lap cushions, and lap trays the resident cannot remove easily. Also included as restraints are facility practices that meet the definition of a restraint, such as:

Using side rails that keep a resident from voluntarily getting out of bed;

Tucking in or using velcro to hold a sheet, fabric, or clothing tightly so that a resident's movement is restricted;

Using devices in conjunction with a chair, such as trays, tables, bars or belts, that the resident cannot remove easily, that prevent the resident from rising;

Placing a resident in a chair that prevents a resident from rising; and

Placing a chair or bed so close to a wall that the wall prevents the resident from rising out of the chair or voluntarily getting out of bed.

* * *

The same device may have the effect of restraining one individual but not another, depending on the individual resident's condition and circumstances.

For example, partial rails may assist one resident to enter and exit the bed independently while acting as a restraint for another ...

* * *

The resident's subjective symptoms may not be used as the sole basis for using a restraint. Before a resident is restrained, the facility must determine the presence of a specific medical symptom that would require the use of restraints, and how the use of restraints would treat the medical symptom, protect the resident's safety, and assist the resident in attaining or maintaining his or her highest practicable level of physical and psychosocial well-being....

While there must be a physician's order reflecting the presence of a medical symptom, [CMS] will hold the facility ultimately accountable for the appropriateness of that determination. The physician's order alone is not sufficient to warrant the use of the restraint....

In order for the resident to be fully informed, the facility must explain, in the context of the individual resident's condition and circumstances, the potential risks and benefits of all options under consideration including using a restraint, not using a restraint, and alternatives to restraint use.... In addition, the facility must also explain the potential negative outcomes of restraint use which include, but are not limited to, declines in the resident's physical functioning (e.g., ability to ambulate) and muscle condition, contractures, increased incidence of infections and development of pressure sores/ulcers, delirium, agitation, and incontinence. Moreover, restraint use may constitute an accident hazard.... Finally, residents who are restrained may face a loss of autonomy, dignity and self respect, and may show symptoms of withdrawal, depression, or reduced social contact....

In the case of a resident who is incapable of making a decision, the legal surrogate or representative may exercise this right based on the same information that would have been provided to the resident. [ ] However, the legal surrogate or representative cannot give permission to use restraints for the sake of discipline or staff convenience or when the restraint is not necessary to treat the resident's medical symptoms....

* * *

2.   *Survey and Inspection*

An effective quality-control regulatory system requires an effective inspection process that, with an acceptable degree of accuracy, detects and documents violations of standards. Providers tend to believe that inspectors are overly aggressive; resident advocates, that they are too lax. Several studies have concluded that state and federal surveys seriously understate deficiencies, failing to cite for deficiencies or categorizing cited deficiencies as less serious than they are. See, e.g., GAO, Nursing Home Quality: Prevalence of Serious Problems, While Declining, Reinforces Importance of Enhanced Oversight, GAO–03–561 (July 2003), also noting that state inspections are "predictable in their timing, allowing homes to conceal problems;" GAO, Continued Attention is Needed to Improve Quality of Care in Small but Significant Share of Homes, GAO–07–794T (May 2007).

Surveyors may have difficulty with patient-focused and outcome-oriented survey techniques. In particular, researchers have reported that surveyors hesitate to cite facilities because they may be uncomfortable with the sophisticated level of assessment required for a citation on an outcome standard and may instead opt to cite the facility for less serious but more easily documented violations. Michael J. Stoil, Surveyors Stymied by Survey Criteria, Researchers Find, 43 Nursing Homes 58 (1994); Kathy J. Vaca, et al., Review of Nursing Home Regulation, 7 MedSurg Nursing 165 (June 1998). What might steer surveyors toward "documentable" citations and away from problems on which there might be more room for disagreement?

Studies have consistently concluded that there is wide variation among the states in terms of the number of citations. See, e.g., GAO–07–794T, supra. Does this variation reflect the quality of facilities or of inspection processes? What role should the courts play in the question of surveyor discretion or inconsistency? Should the survey standards be more rigid?

Facilities that attack the survey process itself, as applied to the facility in a particular instance, are unlikely to succeed. In EPI Corp. v. Chater, 91 F.3d 143 (6th Cir. 1996), the court rejected claims that the survey team failed to follow appropriate procedures holding that the survey team had substantially complied with survey procedures; and that the plaintiff facility did not suffer substantial prejudice to its interests by the surveyors' failure to complete a particular form in advance of the exit conference. See also, Beverly California Corp. v. Shalala, 78 F.3d 403 (8th Cir. 1996). But see, Southern Health Facilities v. Somani, 1995 WL 765161 (Ohio Ct. App. 1995), reversing dismissal of facility's claim that the survey did not comply with federal and state rules in failing to conduct an exit conference.

What relationship should the surveyor establish with the facility? Is the surveyor a consultant or advisor? Should the surveyor offer suggestions for improvement? Should the surveyor commend the facility on noted improvements or other indicators of quality identified during the inspection? For a critique of the enforcement-oriented survey process, see John Braithwaite, et al., Regulating Aged Care: Ritualism and The New Pyramid (2007); John Braithwaite, The Nursing Home Industry, 18 Crime & Justice 11 (1993); Mary Kathleen Robbins, Nursing Home Reform: Objective Regulation or Subjective Decisions?, 11 Thomas Cooley L. Rev. 185 (1994). (Recall the earlier discussion of the consultative role of private contractor Quality Improvement Organizations (QIOs)).

3. Sanctions

FAIRFAX NURSING HOME, INC. v. U.S. DEP'T OF HEALTH & HUMAN SERVICES

United States Court of Appeals for the Seventh Circuit, 2002.
300 F.3d 835, cert. den., 537 U.S. 1111, 123 S.Ct. 901, 154 L.Ed.2d 784 (2003).

RIPPLE, CIRCUIT JUDGE.

* * * Fairfax was assessed a civil monetary penalty ("CMP") by the Center for Medicare and Medicaid Services ("CMS") because of its failure to comply substantially with Medicare regulations governing the care of respirator-dependent nursing home residents. Fairfax appealed to the Department

Appeals Board of the Department of Health and Human Services ("HHS"); after a hearing before an Administrative Law Judge, both the ALJ and the Appellate Division affirmed the CMP. * * * Fairfax appeals that decision to this court. * * *

I

Background

Fairfax is a skilled nursing facility ("SNF"), [ ] participating in Medicare and Medicaid (collectively "Medicare") as a provider. Regulation of SNFs is committed to the Center for Medicare and Medicare Services, formerly known as the Health Care Financing Administration ("HCFA"), and to state agencies with whom the Secretary of Health and Human Services has contracted. [ ] The primary method of regulation is by unannounced surveys of SNFs, conducted in this case by surveyors of the Illinois Department of Public Health ("IDPH"). [ ] These surveys are conducted at least once every 15 months. [ ] If the state survey finds violations of Medicare regulations, the state may recommend penalties to CMS. The civil monetary penalty imposed here was based on an IDPH recommendation.

On December 20, 1996, R10, a ventilator-dependent resident at Fairfax, suffered respiratory distress and required emergency care.[1] Respiratory therapists administered oxygen directly to R10, and one therapist turned off R10's ventilator because the alarm was sounding. Once R10 was stabilized, the therapists left, but neglected to turn the ventilator back on. As a result, R10 died. Prompted by this incident, Fairfax began to develop a policy for the care of ventilator-dependent residents. That policy was completed in February 1997 and was implemented in early March of that year. * * *

On March 2, 1997, R126 was observed to have a low oxygen saturation level, an elevated pulse and temperature, and to be breathing rapidly. These signs indicated that the resident was having respiratory difficulties. R126's physician was called; he ordered a chest x-ray and gave several other instructions. However, contrary to Fairfax's policy, R126's medical chart did not reflect whether these orders were carried out. R126 died shortly thereafter.

On March 5, 1997, R127 was found with low oxygen saturation and mottled extremities. Fairfax staff failed to make a complete assessment, took no vital signs, made no follow-up assessments and did not notify a physician. On March 7, R127 was found cyanotic and required five minutes of ambu-bagging. Nurses charted four follow-up notes, but only observed R127's color and oxygen saturation and took no other vital signs. Also on March 7, during the 7 a.m. to 3 p.m. shift, three episodes of respiratory distress were noted, each of which required ambu-bagging. No physician was called. On March 10, R127's skin was observed turning blue, but there was no record of treatment for respiratory distress and no vital signs or assessments were charted. On March 21, R127 had another episode, this time with mottled legs, shaking and a dangerously low oxygen saturation. The physician was present; R127 was ambu-bagged and administered Valium. There was no complete assessment and no follow-up. On March 25, R127 was found to have a severe infection and died on March 27.

---

1. All residents are denoted by number to respect their privacy.

On March 23, 1997, R83 was found nonresponsive with low oxygen saturation, low blood pressure, an elevated pulse rate and a low respiratory rate. R83 was ambu-bagged, and the treating physician was called. The first noted follow-up was an hour later and 2–1/2 hours passed before R83 was monitored again.

On April 2, 1997, a state surveyor observed a Fairfax employee fail to use sterile procedures while performing tracheostomy care on R6 and R11. * * *

* * *

After a survey on April 8, 1997, IDPH surveyors determined that Fairfax's actions and omissions posed "immediate jeopardy" to the health and safety of its residents. Specifically, Fairfax had violated 42 C.F.R. § 483.25(k), which pertains in part to the special care of ventilator-dependent residents. CMS concurred and notified Fairfax by a letter dated May 7, 1997, that CMS was imposing a CMP of $3,050 per day for a 105–day period, from December 20, 1996, through April 3, 1997, during which Fairfax was not in substantial compliance with HHS regulations governing the care of ventilator-dependent residents. * * *

* * * The ALJ found that all but one of the surveyors' reported violations constituted a risk to patients at the immediate jeopardy level. The ALJ emphasized the repeated monitoring failures and the threat those failures posed to the residents. The ALJ found that "there is not only a prima facie case of noncompliance here, but the preponderance of the evidence is that Petitioner was not complying substantially" with the regulations governing the proper care of vent-dependent residents. Finally, the ALJ found that the amount of the CMP was reasonable.

* * *

We first address Fairfax's argument that the ALJ employed the incorrect legal standard. The regulations set up two basic categories of conduct for which CMPs may be imposed. [ ] The upper range, permitting CMPs of $3,050 per day to $10,000 per day, is reserved for deficiencies that constitute immediate jeopardy to a resident or, under some circumstances, repeated deficiencies. [ ] By contrast, the lower range of CMPs, which begin at $50 per day and run to $3,000 per day, is reserved for "deficiencies that do not constitute immediate jeopardy, but either caused actual harm or have the potential for causing more than minimal harm." [ ] "Immediate jeopardy" is defined as "a situation in which the provider's noncompliance with one or more requirements of participation has caused, or is likely to cause, serious injury, harm, impairment, or death to a resident." [ ]

Fairfax emphasizes the ALJ's use of the term "potential" to describe the probability of harm in several of the ALJ's findings. It submits that the ALJ's use of this terminology establishes that the deficiencies in question were deserving of "lower range" penalties. We take each in turn.

[T]he ALJ found that "Petitioner was woefully inadequate in the treatment and care of R126.... Such conduct caused or was likely to cause serious injury, harm, impairment or death to the resident." The ALJ found that "[t]he record presents a picture of a lackadaisical staff, rather than a staff aggressively treating a pneumonia that was further aggravating the resident's already compromised health." The ALJ clearly was aware of the proper standard for immediate jeopardy and applied it correctly.

* * * The ALJ found that [the] monitoring failure [of R127] "had the potential for serious injury, harm, impairment, or death to the resident and constitutes immediate jeopardy." * * * Again, the ALJ's discussion of this finding demonstrates that he was well aware of the proper standard and applied it correctly. The ALJ devoted four pages of his opinion to discussing the treatment of R127, and addressed the specific risks posed to the resident by Fairfax's failure to monitor R127 after several respiratory episodes in close succession. He closes his analysis with a finding that the failures of the staff to assess properly and monitor the patient, as well as the failure to call the treating physician, "exposed the resident to risk of serious injury, harm, impairment, or death."

* * *

* * * The ALJ's conclusion with respect to R83 makes manifestly clear that there was no misunderstanding of the applicable standard: "That R83 survived Petitioner's incompetent care and treatment does not excuse the fact that he was placed at risk of serious injury, harm, impairment, or death." * * * In similar language, the ALJ concluded that patients R6 and R11 were "placed at serious risk of injury, harm, impairment or death" from the "deficient tracheostomy" care that they received.

[A] fair reading of the ALJ's opinion also makes clear that he focused not simply on the situation of each individual patient, but also on the entire state of readiness in the facility during the time in question. Fairly read, his "bottom line" is that a respiratory patient in Fairfax during the time in question was in continuous jeopardy of serious injury or death because of the systemic incapacity of the facility to render the necessary care to sustain life and avoid serious injury. The record is replete with references to the danger of infection to vent-dependent residents living in nursing homes.

* * *

We also believe that the HHS' decision is supported by substantial evidence. The state surveyors documented numerous instances of Fairfax's failure to care adequately for its respirator-dependent residents. The common thread running through most of these omissions is Fairfax's repeated lack of follow-up and monitoring after a resident experienced respiratory distress. * * * The record firmly supports HHS' determination that a state of immediate jeopardy to resident health existed at Fairfax from December 20, 1996, until April 3, 1997.

Notes and Questions

1. The development of intermediate sanctions was a major effort among the states in the late 1970s and 1980s, and was adopted by the federal government in OBRA 1987. In Vencor Nursing Ctrs. v. Shalala, 63 F. Supp.2d 1 (D.D.C. 1999), the court described the rationale for intermediate sanctions:

> In enacting the enforcement provisions to the Medicare and Medicaid Acts, Congress expressly wished to expand the panoply of remedies available to HHS. [ ]. Committee reports noted with concern the "yo-yo" phenomenon in which noncomplying facilities temporarily correct their deficiencies before an

on-site survey and then quickly lapse into noncompliance until the next review. [ ]. Presumably, the new version of the statute ameliorates this problem by giving HHS a set of intermediate sanctions to choose from rather than the extreme choices of termination or no sanction. There is no indication in the legislative history that Congress wished to limit HHS's ability to terminate a persistently noncompliant facility. [ ]. In fact, the recurring theme emerging from the legislative history is that the new provisions would grant HHS remedial powers in addition to those already available. [ ].

2. Should CMS have terminated Fairfax's certification and provider agreement? Was the less severe sanction more appropriate? Will the care of the remaining residents be compromised because of the fine? The fine was a daily fine, so on what basis does the court conclude that Fairfax was noncompliant during the entire period? See Sea Island Comprehensive Healthcare Corp. v. U.S. Dept. of Health & Human Services, 79 Fed. Appx. 563 (4th Cir. 2003).

3. An OIG report on CMS's implementation of mandatory statutory sanctions found that the agency failed to terminate the provider agreement in 30 out of 55 cases in which the facility remained out of compliance (on those specific citations) past the six-month deadline for reaching compliance or had an unabated condition that presented immediate jeopardy to the health and safety of the residents for more than 23 days. Nursing Home Enforcement: Application of Mandatory Remedies, OEI–06–03–00410 (May 2006). CMS also failed to deny payment for new admissions to 28% of the over 700 facilities that remained out of compliance for over 3 months after citation, as required by statute. CMS reported to the OIG that it did not intend to make any changes to its policies or practices:

> While the law requires that mandatory actions occur at specified times and under specific circumstances, it also contemplates that sanctions will be used to motivate improvements and lasting corrections. Where these expectations may be in conflict, we seek to resolve the conflict with the solution that best protects the well-being of the resident. Nursing Homes that Merit Punishment Not Terminated, Federal Review Finds, 15 Health L. Rep. 628 (2006).

Is this statement persuasive? Could a nursing home residents' advocacy group bring a *Smith v. Heckler* action against CMS for violation of the federal statute? See, California Advocates for Nursing Home Reform v. California Dept. of Health Services, 2006 WL 2829865 (Cal. Super. 2006), granting writ of mandamus on claim that Department failed to investigate complaints filed with the Department against nursing homes. See also Ineffective Enforcement Process Thwarts Efforts to Ban Poor Performers, Paper Finds, 13 Health L. Rep. 1237 (2004).

4. Among the reported judicial opinions reviewing sanctions under Medicare/Medicaid, it appears that the most frequently litigated questions are the determination of "immediate jeopardy,' as in *Fairfax*, and the appropriateness of the sanction chosen. In *Vencor, supra*, in which the facility contested termination of the provider agreement as inconsistent with the statute, the court describes the rationale for the deferential scope of review over the choice of sanctions:

> Broad deference is particularly warranted where the regulation "concerns a complex and highly technical regulatory program," like Medicare, "in which the identification and classification of relevant criteria necessarily require significant expertise and entail the exercise of judgment grounded in policy concerns."

What are the policy concerns in the choice of sanctions?

5. If a facility is cited for but then corrects a deficiency, should it still be penalized for that violation? What arguments would support an emphasis on correction rather than punishment? What would argue against? One study con-

cluded that the nursing home regulatory system relies extensively on correction and voluntary compliance rather than punishment even though the emphasis in OBRA was to use penalties as a deterrent. Still, the study concludes that the emphasis on surveillance in the U.S. system has led to more regimentation and inflexibility in U.S. nursing homes than in other countries with different systems, implying that quality of care and quality of life suffer. John Braithwaite, The Nursing Home Industry, 18 Crime & Justice 11 (1993). See also, Richard L. Peck, Does Europe Have the Answers?, 49 Nursing Homes 54 (June 2000). The OIG report, *supra* in Note 3, noted that 23 of the 30 facilities that exceeded the statutory timeline for correction actually came into compliance 17 days after the statutory deadline. Would this prove that CMS's choice to forego termination was the right decision after all? The GAO also reported patterns of merely temporary compliance and repetitive violations while noting that the number of sanctions decreased significantly from 2000–2005. GAO, Nursing Homes: Efforts to Strengthen Federal Enforcement Have Not Deterred Some Homes from Repeatedly Harming Residents, GAO–07–241 (Mar. 2006).

6. State and federal health care fraud agencies have stepped up their actions against nursing homes. These agencies prosecute on the basis that deficiencies in the quality of care amount to fraud against the government because the facilities failed to deliver what the government paid for. See discussion of Medicare and Medicaid fraud and abuse in Chapter 11. In 2003, for example, two nursing homes in New York agreed to pay $3 million to settle, without an admission of guilt, charges that they operated with inadequate staff. The facilities also agreed to establish a corporate compliance program; to submit monthly staffing reports to the attorney general; and to cooperate with an independent consultant to monitor compliance. A nursing home chain pled guilty to criminal charges and paid $1 million for understaffing and falsifying staff records. The suits were brought by the New York Medicaid Fraud Control Unit. Two Facilities Will Pay New York State $3 Million to Settle Staffing Allegations, 12 Health L. Rep. 1597 (2003). For discussion, see Michael Clark, Whether the False Claims Act Is A Proper Tool for the Government to Use for Improving the Quality of Care in Long–Term Care Facilities, 15 Health Lawyer 12 (2002); Seymour Moskowitz, Golden Age in the Golden State: Contemporary Legal Developments in Elder Abuse and Neglect, 36 Loy. L. A. L. Rev. 589 (2003). Should Congress require that the multimillion dollar recoveries in the false claims litigation be allocated to CMS specifically for the improvement of its nursing home quality enforcement efforts? See Joan H. Krause, A Patient–Centered Approach to Health Care Fraud Recovery, 96 J. Crim. L. & Criminology 579 (2006), proposing a change in the current treatment of fraud recoveries.

7. Should nursing home administrators, owners, or medical directors face criminal charges in particularly egregious cases? See, Jennifer Phan, The Graying of America: Protecting Nursing Home Residents By Allowing Regulatory and Criminal Statutes to Establish Standards of Care in Private Negligence Actions, 2 Houston J. Health L. & Pol'y 297 (2002); Victoria Vron, Using RICO to Fight Understaffing in Nursing Homes, 71 Geo. Wash. L. Rev. 1025 (2003).

8. In *Fairfax*, the nursing home challenged the imposition of a sanction by the federal Medicare agency. If the agency had found the facility to be out of compliance, but had not levied a sanction or had rescinded a sanction, the nursing home does not have the right to a hearing on the finding of noncompliance. See discussion of *Shalala v. Ill. Council on Long Term Care* in Chapter 8. See also Ruqalijah A. Yearby, A Right to No Meaningful Review under the Due Process

Clause: The Aftermath of Judicial Deference to the Federal Administrative Agencies, 16 Health Matrix 773 (2006).

Problem: Restful Manor

Restful Manor is a skilled nursing facility licensed by the state and operating in its largest city. It has 117 residents, all of whom are elderly. Only twenty percent of the residents are ambulatory. Until eighteen months ago, the home had a good record of compliance with state nursing home standards. The facility has begun to have problems with compliance, although it still consistently has corrected violations or has submitted an acceptable plan of correction. The facility has also experienced some financial difficulties recently.

The most recent inspection of the facility took place four months ago. At that time, the facility was out of compliance with several standards relating to quality of meals, cleanliness of the kitchen, and maintenance of patients' medical records. The facility also had some staffing problems. Other problems included the lack of a qualified dietitian and a high, though borderline acceptable, rate of errors in the administration of medications by the nurses. As a result of this inspection report, the facility was required to submit a written plan of correction in which it agreed to remedy the violations. The next on-site inspection was scheduled to take place within six to eight weeks to check on progress in correcting the violations.

Prior to that inspection, however, an investigative news team from a local television station visited the facility with a hidden camera. The news team posed as potential out-of-town buyers interested in the facility. The visit revealed several patients who were soiled and unattended and several others who were restrained in wheelchairs. A recorded conversation with the Director of Nursing indicated that there was one nurses' aide for every ten patients, which the D.O.N. thought was probably "not enough to do a good job for some of these patients." When asked about these incidents, the owner attributed these "temporary" problems to financial constraints and to his inability to hire a good administrator who was willing to work within a reasonable budget.

The news team showed portions of the videotape on the nightly news. Three days later it followed up with a report that one of the ambulatory, mentally-impaired patients at the facility had wandered out of the building. A passerby had found the patient walking aimlessly along the main thoroughfare near the facility and called the police. The state agency felt pressured to respond. It conducted an unannounced inspection two days after the latest news report. The surveyor conducting this inspection cited the facility for violations of several regulations including the following:

1. Each resident should receive adequate skin care that supports his or her health and well-being and avoids decubitus ulcers (bed sores). (The surveyor found that the facility was not turning or positioning bed-bound patients in the manner that is advised for avoidance of ulcers. The facility also lacked supportive supplies, such as certain kinds of pads, ordinarily used to reduce the incidence of ulcers. At the time of the inspection, however, only two patients had minor incipient pressure sores. The surveyor believes, but could not confirm, that another patient had been transferred to the hospital eight months ago for serious bedsores.)

2. The facility must assure that a resident who did not present mental or psychosocial adjustment difficulties at admission does not display patterns of decreased social interaction or increased withdrawal, angry or depressive behaviors, unless the residents' clinical condition demonstrates that

such a pattern was unavoidable. (The surveyor identifies several residents who report boredom, lethargy, loss of appetite and feelings of uselessness and who complain of a lack of interesting things to do. Their medical records do not indicate any clinical diagnosis that would explain their psychosocial states.)

3. The facility shall provide a nursing staff that is appropriately trained and adequate in number to care for the residents of the facility. (The surveyor wrote in his report that the facility provided one nurses' aide for every ten patients and that this was "inadequate in light of the dependency of the residents.")

4. The facility shall employ a certified dietitian. (The surveyor noted that "the facility currently does not employ a certified dietitian, but in the exit conference the owner reported that he has been trying to hire one for the last three months.")

5. The nurses of the facility shall administer ordered medications safely and adequately. An error rate in excess of 5% in the administration of medication is unacceptable and shall constitute a violation of this standard. (The surveyor reported an error rate of 5% in one sample medications pass and an error rate of 4.9% in another.)

Even though the facility is currently in violation of several standards, families of Restful Manor's patients have rallied to the facility's support. They believe the care is good despite the problems cited. The Department disagrees.

The Department of Health expects litigation as a result of any enforcement action it takes in this case. It has come to the office of the state's Attorney General for advice. The Director of the Department wants to be aggressive in this case in part because the poor condition of the facility has become public knowledge. She believes that the agency's effectiveness has been challenged and that the facility is seriously deficient and heading for more problems.

Several students should serve as the assistant A.G. who has been assigned to this case. Please advise the Department on the course of action they should follow in this instance. Other students should serve in the role of attorneys representing the facility. Please identify any defenses available to the facility, your strategy and the course the dispute is likely to take. The state statute (an edited version of the federal statute) is excerpted below.

Having worked through these provisions, what recommendations for change would you make to the legislature, both as to enforcement mechanisms and as to the standards?

488.404.　Factors to be considered in selecting remedies

(b) To determine the seriousness of the deficiency, the State must consider at least the following factors:

(1) Whether a facility's deficiencies constitute—

(i) No actual harm with a potential for minimal harm; (ii) No actual harm with a potential for more than minimal harm, but not immediate jeopardy; (iii) Actual harm that is not immediate jeopardy; or (iv) Immediate jeopardy to resident health or safety.

(2) Whether the deficiencies—

(i) Are isolated; (ii) Constitute a pattern; or (iii) Are widespread.

(c) Following the initial assessment, the State may consider other factors, which may include, but are not limited to the following:

(1) The relationship of the one deficiency to other deficiencies resulting in noncompliance.

(2) The facility's prior history of noncompliance in general and specifically with reference to the cited deficiencies.

488.408. Selection of remedies

(a) In this section, remedies are grouped into categories and applied to deficiencies according to how serious the noncompliance is.

(c) (1) Category 1 remedies include the following:

(i) Directed plan of correction.

(ii) State monitoring.

(iii) Directed in-service training.

(2) The State must apply one or more of the remedies in Category 1 when there—

(i) Are isolated deficiencies that constitute no actual harm with a potential for more than minimal harm but not immediate jeopardy; or (ii) Is a pattern of deficiencies that constitutes no actual harm with a potential for more than minimal harm but not immediate jeopardy.

(3) Except when the facility is in substantial compliance, the State may apply one or more of the remedies in Category 1 to any deficiency.

(d) (1) Category 2 remedies include the following

(i) Denial of payment for new admissions.

(iii) Civil money penalties of $50–$3,000 per day.

(iv) Civil money penalty of $1,000–$10,000 per instance of noncompliance.

(2) The State must apply one or more of the remedies in Category 2 when there are—

(i) Widespread deficiencies that constitute no actual harm with a potential for more than minimal harm but not immediate jeopardy; or (ii) One or more deficiencies that constitute actual harm that is not immediate jeopardy.

(3) The State may apply one or more of the remedies in Category 2 to any deficiency except when—

(i) The facility is in substantial compliance; or (ii) The State imposes a civil money penalty for a deficiency that constitutes immediate jeopardy, the penalty must be in the upper range of penalty amounts.

(e) (1) Category 3 remedies include the following:

(i) Temporary management.

(ii) Immediate licensure revocation.

(iii) Civil money penalties of $50–$3,000 per day.

(iv) Civil money penalty of $1,000–$10,000 per instance of noncompliance

(2) When there are one or more deficiencies that constitute immediate jeopardy to resident health or safety—

(i) The State must do one or both of the following;

(A) Impose temporary management; or

(B) Revoke the facility license;

(ii) The State may impose a civil money penalty of $3,050–$10,000 per day or $1,000–$10,000 per instance of noncompliance, in addition to imposing temporary management.

(3) When there are widespread deficiencies that constitute actual harm that is not immediate jeopardy, the State may impose temporary management, in addition to Category 2 remedies.

488.410.   Action when there is immediate jeopardy

(a) If there is immediate jeopardy to resident health or safety, the State must either revoke the facility license within 23 calendar days of the last date of the survey or appoint a temporary manager to remove the immediate jeopardy . . .

(b) The State may also impose other remedies, as appropriate.

(d) The State must provide for the safe and orderly transfer of residents when the facility is terminated.

488.412.   Action when there is no immediate jeopardy

(a) If a facility's deficiencies do not pose immediate jeopardy to residents' health or safety, and the facility is not in substantial compliance, the State may revoke the facility's license agreement or may allow the facility to continue to participate for no longer than 6 months from the last day of the survey if—

(1) The State survey agency finds that it is more appropriate to impose alternative remedies than to terminate the facility's provider agreement;

(2) The facility has submitted an approved plan and timetable for corrective action.

488.415.   Temporary management

(a) Temporary management means the temporary appointment by the State of a substitute facility manager or administrator with authority to hire, terminate or reassign staff, obligate facility funds, alter facility procedures, and manage the facility to correct deficiencies identified in the facility's operation.

III.   PRIVATE ACCREDITATION OF HEALTH CARE FACILITIES

Private accreditation is a nongovernmental, voluntary activity typically conducted by not-for-profit associations. The Joint Commission (formerly the Joint Commission on Accreditation of Healthcare Organizations or JCAHO), which offers accreditation programs for hospitals, nursing homes, home health, and other facilities, and the National Committee on Quality Assurance

(NCQA), which accredits managed care plans and other providers, are two of the leading organizations in the accreditation of health care entities. You can review the scope of their activities and new developments through their websites at www.jointcommission.org and www.ncqa.org.

As a voluntary process, accreditation may be viewed as a private communicative device, providing the accredited health care entity merely with a seal of approval—a method for communicating in shorthand that it meets standards established by an external organization. See, Clark C. Havighurst, Foreword: The Place of Private Accrediting Among the Instruments of Government, 57 L. & Contemp. Probs. 1 (1994). In practice, however, there is a much closer marriage between some private accreditation programs and government regulation of health care facilities. This is especially true of the Joint Commission hospital accreditation program as virtually all U.S. hospitals with more than 25 beds are accredited by the Joint Commission. The Joint Commission's hospital accreditation program is the largest and most influential of its accreditation programs. In a survey identifying the most powerful influences on hospitals' adoption of patient safety initiatives, for example, hospital administrators reported that the Joint Commission was the key factor and that their patient safety programs were linked specifically to its patient safety standards and goals. Kelly J. Devers, et al., What is Driving Hospitals' Patient–Safety Efforts?, 23 Health Affairs 103 (2004).

Both state and federal governments rely to a great extent on accreditation in their hospital licensure and Medicare/Medicaid hospital certification programs. Most states have incorporated the Commission's accreditation standards, some explicitly, into their hospital licensure standards. Some have accepted accreditation in lieu of a state license. See e.g., Tex. Health & Safety Code § 222.024. Under the Medicare statute, Joint Commission accredited hospitals are "deemed" to have met requirements for Medicare certification. 42 U.S.C. §§ 1395x(e), 1395bb. Although the Secretary retains a look-behind authority, the Joint Commission substitutes for the routine surveillance process.

Originally, the acceptance of accreditation by the Medicare program was designed to entice an adequate number of hospitals to participate in the then-new Medicare program. That original rationale has dissipated as hospitals have become much more dependent on Medicare payments. At the same time, the federal government's reliance on private accreditation as a substitute for routine government surveillance has expanded considerably beyond the original hospital setting and now extends to clinical laboratories and home health care, among others.

What might explain this extensive reliance on private organizations for public regulation? Some argue that private accreditation more effectively encourages voluntary compliance and avoids some of the prosecutorial environment of a government-conducted inspection program. Furthermore, and perhaps more pragmatically, deemed status allows the government to shift the cost of the inspection process because accredited facilities pay for the costs of accreditation, including the site visit.

In 1981, The Reagan Administration proposed extending deemed status to nursing homes accredited by the Joint Commission. This proposal was opposed vigorously by consumer advocates and was withdrawn with the effect that deemed status for Medicare certification still does not extend to nursing homes. Should nursing homes be treated differently, and arguably more restrictively, than other Medicare providers on the question of deemed status?

How does the private accreditation process compare to public regulation? Private accreditation programs traditionally have engaged in practices that encourage voluntary subscription to the accreditation program. For example, accreditation programs often perform only announced site visits and keep negative evaluations confidential, at least until the accreditation itself is reduced or not renewed. Standards established by accreditation programs, which are often dominated by professionals in the industry rather than consumer groups, may differ from those set by a process that arguably fosters broader public participation. With the Joint Commission, in particular, governance and policymaking are dominated by physician organization members such as the AMA.

The Joint Commission accreditation survey is explicitly consultative in nature. For example in regard to its survey of home health agencies, the Joint Commission states that "[a]n important characteristic of the Joint Commission survey process is on-site education and consultation conducted . . . throughout the survey as surveyors offer suggestions for approaches and strategies that may help your organization better meet the intent of the standards and . . . improve performance." The Joint Commission also offers a subsidiary consulting service, "Joint Commission Resources," to help health care organizations meet accreditation standards (http://www.jcrinc.com/); and this has raised some concerns. See Members of Congress Question "Conflict" in JCAHO's For–Profit Consulting Subsidiary, 15 Health L. Rep. 631 (2006).

In recognizing deemed status for a particular accreditation program, the federal government typically requires that the program meet particular standards. For example, the recognition of deemed status for home health agencies includes the following requirements: release of survey reports to HHS routinely and to the public upon request; reporting of evidence of fraud and abuse; harmonization of Joint Commission standards with Medicare conditions of participation; and implementation of unannounced surveys utilizing federal methodology. CMS retains the right to inspect any facility certified through deemed status and will do validation and complaint surveys to monitor Joint Commission performance. 58 Fed. Reg. 35007 (June 30, 1993). Has the department adequately preserved its interests and authority? The GAO concluded that CMS lacks adequate information to monitor Joint Commission performance in hospital accreditation and lacks legal authority to take effective action if problems are detected. GAO, CMS lacks Adequate Authority to Adequately Oversee Patient Safety in Hospitals, GAO–04–850 (July 2004). This study noted that "JCAHO's pre–2004 hospital accreditation process did not identify most of the hospitals found by state survey agencies in CMS' annual validation survey sample to have deficiencies in Medicare requirements." Joint Commission accreditation surveys had failed to identify 69% of Medicare deficiencies and 78% of the hospitals with deficiencies. The Joint Commission had been subjecting only a sample of 5% of its accredited organizations to unannounced surveys. In June, 2006, the American Nurses Association filed suit against HHS seeking a declaratory judgment that HHS' Delegation of Authority to the Joint Commission was unlawful in that Joint Commission standards regarding staffing are not equivalent to those required by the Medicare program and an order that HHS establish an effective system for determining that Joint Commission and HHS Medicare standards are equivalent. Nurses Association Lawsuit Latest Salvo in Campaign to Tackle Staffing Problems, 15 Health L. Rep. 1366 (2006).

The Joint Commission began performing its inspections on an unannounced basis in Spring, 2006. In addition, the Joint Commission has adopted several initiatives to focus its standards toward continuous quality improvement and toward medical error monitoring and patient safety as described in Chapter 1. The "Sentinel Event" initiative, for example, encourages facilities to report errors and root cause analyses for the benefit of systemic change in areas such as wrong-site surgery and medication errors. Its "Shared Visions—New Pathways" initiative focuses on on-going compliance and self-assessment.

For a history of the Joint Commission and a broad review of legal issues related to private accreditation, see Timothy S. Jost, The Joint Commission on Accreditation of Hospitals: Private Regulation of Health Care and the Public Interest, 24 B.C.L.Rev. 835 (1983). For a discussion of the relation between private accreditation and public regulation, see Jody Freeman, The Private Role in Public Governance, 75 N.Y.U. L.Rev. 543 (2000); Symposium on Private Accreditation in the Regulatory State, 57 Law and Contemp. Prob.1 (1994); Gillian Metzger, Privatization as Delegation, 103 Col. L. Rev. 1367 (2003), discussing claims of state action in relation to accreditation. More recently, scholars have begun to view private efforts, such as accreditation, and public regulatory efforts as a "new governance" framework for achieving a variety of goals in health care, including the goal of quality vigilance. See, e.g., Rand E. Rosenblatt, The Four Ages of Health Law, 14 Health Matrix 155 (2004); Louise G. Trubek, New Governance and Soft Law in Health Care Reform, 3 Ind. Health L. Rev. 139 (2006).

Chapter 4

HEALTH CARE COST AND ACCESS: THE POLICY CONTEXT

I. THE PROBLEM

Millions of Americans are just a pink slip away from losing their health insurance, and one serious illness away from losing all of their savings. Millions more are locked into the jobs they have now just because they or someone in their family had once been sick and they have what is called a pre-existing condition. And on any given day, over 37 million Americans—most of them working people and their little children—have no health insurance at all. And in spite of all this, our medical bills are growing at over twice the rate of inflation, and the United States spends over a third more of its income on health care than any other nation on earth. And the gap is growing, causing many of our companies in global competition severe disadvantage.

President Clinton, Address to Congress on Health Care, September 22, 1993.

Much has changed in the years since then-President Clinton proposed his Health Security Act, but the problems he identified still are very much with us. On the one hand, the problem of access to health care has gotten worse—at least ten million more persons are uninsured today than in 1993. This is true even though Medicaid coverage expanded dramatically during the intervening decade and a half and the State Children's Health Insurance Program, created in 1997, now covers over six million American children. Health care costs also continue to climb, not as sharply as they did following the turn of the millennium, but more rapidly than they did in the years immediately following Clinton's initiative. Finally, other problems have achieved new prominence since the Clinton plan was rejected in 1994, such as the financial hardships suffered by households with high deductible and low coverage insurance policies and the ever-growing loss of retiree health benefits.

This chapter presents the policy context for the chapters that follow. It first describes the problems that many Americans experience obtaining access to health insurance and health care. Second, it considers the issue of cost: How big a problem is health care cost inflation? What causes it? The chapter then turns to a discussion of proposals for health care reform. This section begins by presenting proposals for public and private solutions to the problem of access. Second it analyzes market and regulatory solutions to the cost problem. With respect to both of these issues it also looks at the experience of other nations.

A. THE PROBLEM OF ACCESS

Between 2005 and 2006, the last year for which data are available as of this writing, the number of Americans not covered by health insurance grew from 44.8 to 47 million. An estimated 15.8 percent of the population lacked health insurance in 2006, up from 15.3 percent in 2005. Much larger numbers of Americans lacked health insurance at some point over longer periods of time.

Who are the uninsured? Most are adults under the age of 65, living in families with incomes of over $25,000 a year and with at least one full-time worker. The ethnic group with the largest number of uninsured members is white, non-Hispanic. Those most at risk of being uninsured, however, are male adults between the ages of 18 and 24; racial and ethnic minorities (particularly Hispanics from Mexico or Central and South America); non-citizens; members of families with only part-time workers or no workers; workers employed in low-paying jobs; individuals in families with incomes below 200 percent of the federal poverty level; and children being cared for by persons other than their own parents. Coverage also differs significantly among the various states, with the proportion of the entire population of a state not covered by insurance ranging from 24.1 percent in Texas to 8.5 percent in Minnesota in 2006. See, Carmen DeNavas–Walt, Bernadette D. Proctor, & Jessica Smith, U.S, Census Bureau, Income, Poverty, and Insurance Coverage in the United States, 2006 (2007).

Why are these persons uninsured? Most are uninsured because they lack employment-related insurance and are also ineligible for Medicaid because they do not fit into a covered category, such as the elderly or children, or earn too much, or are undocumented aliens. Although virtually all employers with 200 or more employees offer health insurance, only about 59 percent of employers with 199 or fewer employees do (down from 68 percent in 2000). Moreover, many employees who work for employers who insure their full-time employees are not eligible for coverage, either because they work part-time or are temporary or seasonal employees (e.g. in agriculture or construction). Only 24 percent of firms offering health care coverage extend it to part-time workers, and only 2 percent to temporary employees. A growing number of "1099 workers" also do not have employment-related insurance because they are formally independent contractors rather than employees. See Kaiser Family Foundation/Health Research and Educational Trust, Employer Health Benefits, 2007 Annual Survey (2007).

At least as important as employer offer rates, however, may be employee acceptance rates. Only 65 percent of employees of employers who offer insurance are insured through their own employer (although many who are not insured through their own employer are insured through a spouse's employer). Employees currently pay $3281 per year for family coverage, 28 percent of the premiums. Employees of small or low-wage firms tend to face higher premium costs for health insurance than employees of large or high-wage firms, and an increasing number of employees have been declining coverage rather than paying this cost. Indeed, 74 percent of uninsured adults report that they do not have health insurance because it costs too much, only 3 percent report as their most important reason for not having health insurance that they do not think they need it.

Many Americans believe that the uninsured can get medical care when they need it from physicians and hospitals. An overwhelming and steadily growing body of evidence, however, shows a direct correlation between lack of insurance, lack of health care, and poor health. The long-term uninsured are more likely than the insured to fail to get necessary medical care for serious conditions, forego filling prescriptions or getting recommended tests, experience hospitalization for avoidable conditions like pneumonia or uncontrolled diabetes, and be diagnosed for cancer at later stages when treatment is less likely to succeed. They are less likely than the insured to have a regular doctor or to receive cancer screening, cardiovascular risk-reduction assistance, or diabetes care. The uninsured also suffer financially. More than half of adults who have been uninsured at any time in the preceding year report medical debt problems, and 40 percent of those currently uninsured with medical debt problems report that those problems are interfering with their ability to pay for basic necessities. Half have used up all their savings, 11 percent have taken out a mortgage or loan to pay for medical debt, and almost a quarter have taken on credit card medical debt. See Sara Collins, et al. Gaps in Health Insurance: An All–American Problem. http://www.commonwealth fund.org/usr_doc/Collins_gapshltins_920.pdf?section=4039 (2006). The long-term uninsured face a 25 percent greater likelihood of premature death than do insured Americans, and uninsured Americans with breast or colorectal cancer are 30 to 50 percent more likely to die prematurely. An estimated 22,000 Americans die every year because they are uninsured (over seven times the number who died in the September 11 attacks).

The Institute of Medicine has published a series of six books comprehensively documenting the problems caused by uninsurance in America. See http://www.iom.edu/CMS/3809/4660/12313.aspx. The Census Bureau keeps regular track of the rate of uninsurance. Their most recent report as of this writing is found at http://www.census.gov/Press–Release/www/releases/ar chives/income_wealth/010583.html (Aug. 28, 2007). The Kasier Family Foundation and Health Research and Educational Trust issue an annual report on the state of employee health benefits, found at the Kaiser website, www.kff. org. Finally, the Kaiser Commission on Medicaid and the Uninsured provides a steady flow of information at http://www.kff.org/uninsured/index.cfm. A patchwork of laws that provide very limited protection for those without health insurance are discussed in the next chapter.

Not only the uninsured, but also insured Americans experience financial problems because of health care needs. Many Americans are "underinsured," with inadequate coverage and high cost-sharing obligations. In a recent survey, three-fifths of Americans reporting health-care related financial problems were insured. Many insured Americans also forego medical care that they need but cannot afford or have credit card debt or home equity loans because of medical expenses. Almost half of all bankruptcies have some medical cause. See Collins, Gaps in Health Insurance, *supra*; Cathy Schoen, et al., Insured But Not Protected: How Many Americans are Underinsured, Health Affairs Web. Excl., June 15, 2005, and Elizabeth Warren & Melissa Jacoby. "Beyond Hospital Misbehavior: An Alternative Account of Medical–

Related Financial Distress," 100 Northwestern Law Review 535 (2006). As insurance deductibles, coinsurance, and copayments steadily increase, it is likely that even more insured Americans will suffer financial distress.

Problem: Getting Covered

Do you have health insurance? If not, why not? If you are uninsured, how much would it cost you to purchase insurance? If you were involved in a serious accident on your way home today, who would pay for your medical care? If you are insured, how much does your insurance cost? Do you pay for this cost yourself directly, do you pay indirectly, or does someone else bear the cost? Does the cost of your insurance reflect accurately your preferences for medical care as compared to other goods and services? How much is the deductible that you much pay before your insurance begins to cover your health care costs? Are you also obligated to pay coinsurance or copayments if you use services? Do you think your coverage is adequate for your need for medical care? Is your insurance coverage excessive? Why did you buy this particular policy? Did you get what you thought you bought?

Visit the benefits department of your university or check their website. Do they offer insurance to all employees? To full-time permanent employees only? Is there a waiting period before they become eligible? Do employees pay a premium for individual coverage? For family coverage? How much?

Now consider how the choices available under your University's plan might be viewed by:

- A 53 year-old single janitor, earning just over minimum wage, who has asthma.

- A 38 year-old administrative assistant earning $40,000 a year, who is a single mother with two children, no child support. She has credit card debt and is paying off the mortgage on her home, leaving only $500 in disposable income a month.

- A 24 year-old graduate assistant, who is a tri-athlete. She earns $20,000 a year and has no assets but wants to buy a car. She has never been seriously ill.

- A 60 year-old professor, thinking seriously about taking early retirement in a year or two and heading for Florida. He needs a plan with coverage in Florida.

- A 50 year-old professor who has heart problems and wants access to the best specialists he can find, regardless of cost.

B.   THE PROBLEM OF COST

1.   Recent Developments in Health Care Cost Inflation

By any measure, Americans spend a great deal on health care. In 2006, the most recent year for which data are available, we spent $2.1 trillion dollars on health care, 16 percent of the gross national product, $7,026 for every man, woman, and child. We spend more on health care than on anything else. In 2004, Americans spent $1,677 billion on personal medical care compared to $1,221 billion on housing, $1,222 billion on food and tobacco, and $979 billion on transportation. We also spend more than anyone else. In 2004, the United States spent 15.3 percent of its GDP, $6,102 per capita, on health care. By contrast, the United Kingdom spent 8.3 percent of its GDP, $2,546 per capita, and Canada 9.9 percent of its GDP, $3,165 per capita, on health care.

Health care cost growth has been fairly steady in recent years at rates higher than those experienced in the mid–1990s, lower than those of a half-decade ago. United States national health expenditures grew by 6.7 percent in 2006, down from growth rates of 8 to 9 percent in the early 2000s, but still greater than general inflation.

Continuing growth in health care costs has two particularly disturbing consequences. First, the steady increase in premiums for employment-related insurance is driving employers to pass an ever-increasing share of the cost of health insurance on to employees, either by requiring them to bear an increasing share of the premium through increased cost-sharing or through cut-backs in benefits. In 2007, the average cost of employment-related family coverage was $12,106. Between 2006 and 2007, the cost of health insurance increased 6.1 percent. Between 2001 and 2004, health insurance premiums had increased at rates exceeding 10 percent a year. Between 2000 and 2007, the average employee contribution for family health insurance increased from $135 to $273. During the same period, employee cost sharing in the form of deductibles, coinsurance, and copayments increased dramatically. The net effect of these cost increases is that employers are less willing to offer insurance coverage, and employees less willing to accept it when it is offered. Thus increasing costs lead directly to increasing numbers of the uninsured.

Second, public expenditures are growing dramatically, contributing to a sense that public programs are in crisis. Direct government health care programs spent $713.4 billion in 2002, accounting for forty-six percent of health care expenditures. If one adds to the cost of direct government programs, however, the cost of public employee's health benefits and of public tax subsidies that encourage the purchase of private insurance, the government in fact pays for nearly 60 percent of national health care expenditures. See Steffie Woolhandler and David U. Himmelstein, Paying for National Health Insurance—And Not Getting It, 21 Health Aff., July/Aug. 2002 at 88. After a period in the late 1990s and early 2000s when public health care expenditures grew rather slowly, they are growing again rapidly as we reach the end of the first decade of the twenty-first century. Because this expenditure growth has been coupled with generous tax cuts at both the federal and state level, and with sharply-increased expenditures on national security, there is a sense that the public household is badly out of balance, and therefore that public programs are in crisis and are unsustainable.

Each year Health Affairs publishes in its January/February issue the report of the National Health Statistics Group of the Office of the Actuary of the Center for Medicare and Medicaid Services on national health expenditures for the year preceding the previous year (i.e. the January/February 2008 issue covers 2006). Later in the year it publishes OECD comparative data comparing health care expenditures in the United States to those of other countries. Public health expenditure data is also available at the Center for Medicare and Medicaid Services (CMS) website. These are among the most convenient sources for tracking health care costs.

2. *A Primer on Health Economics*

America's ongoing health care reform debate, which promises to be back on the agenda at least for the 2008 election, is based in large part on the premises that we spend too much on health care and that our expenditures on health care are growing too rapidly. But do we spend too much? How would we know it if we did?

The fact that we spend more proportionately on health care than other developed nations is not necessarily a bad thing. Other nations spend more proportionately on food or housing than we do, but this does not mean that they spend too much. In the excerpt above, President Clinton asserted that the high cost of employer-financed health insurance raises the prices of American products, decreasing their competitiveness in international markets. Economists generally agree, however, that in the long run increases in health insurance premiums are reflected in lower wages, not higher prices, and that in any event adjustments in international financial markets compensate for higher prices by diminishing the value of the dollar. In fact, between 1970 and 1991, the years in which the United States experienced the greatest growth of health care costs, real wages and salaries per employee grew only .4 percent, while employer health expenditures per employee grew 234.1 percent. But if workers prefer to take their compensation in health benefits rather than take-home pay, is there a problem? See Mark V. Pauly, Should we be Worried About High Real Medical Spending Growth in the United States? Health Aff. Web Excl., (Jan. 8, 2003).

Indeed, while health care is expensive, it is also valuable, and becoming more valuable all the time. In recent decades, we have seen dramatic improvements in our ability to alleviate cardiovascular problems, save low weight babies, treat mental illness, and replace worn out joints, lengthening our lives and improving their quality. Arguably, the value of our advances in health care has outweighed the cost of those advances. David Cutler, Your Money or Your Life (2004).

It is nonetheless widely believed that the market for health care is distorted, and that the amount we spend on health care is not the amount we would freely choose to spend in a true competitive market. More particularly, it is argued that the allocation of compensation just described is not that which would have been chosen by employees in a non-distorted market. The excerpt that follows offers a classic explanation of the problem.

CONGRESSIONAL BUDGET OFFICE, ECONOMIC IMPLICATIONS OF RISING HEALTH CARE COSTS

(1992).

In most circumstances, the free market provides an efficient mechanism for allocating resources in the economy. To achieve such efficiencies, however, free markets must operate under certain conditions. They work best when the consumer has good information about the characteristics of products and their prices—information that is most easily obtained if products are well defined and standardized and if prices can be readily ascertained without excessive search. In addition, market efficiency requires that a large number of sellers compete with each other over prices that reflect true resource costs. With a large number of sellers, no single vendor has the power to control prices, and price competition among sellers lowers prices to the point that they reflect the marginal costs of production.

The market for health care, however, does not meet many of these conditions. * * *

Consumers lack key information about the quality and price of medical services. Their ignorance about quality has two dimensions. First, most consumers do not have the expertise they need to evaluate the qualifications of their health care providers. Second, when consumers need medical care, they may not have information (independent of what they are told by a provider) about the full range of alternative treatments and the prospective outcomes of these alternatives.

Consumers also lack rudimentary information about the prices of the medical care they buy and have difficulty assessing what that price information means. Price information, such as that concerning physicians' charges, in many cases is not available to patients in advance of treatment. In some instances, the patient can call a doctor and obtain quotes for different services, but prices of physicians' services are not advertised and it may be embarrassing to ask. Sometimes even the doctor does not know the full costs of treatment, especially if it requires hospitalization or drugs. Although a patient can acquire some price information with repeated visits to a doctor, many reasons for seeing a doctor do not occur again.

Even if the price information is available, it can be hard to interpret. If a doctor charges a low price, he or she could be offering a bargain—or inferior—service. Without information on quality, price information has no meaning. * * *

Because consumers delegate a considerable amount of decision-making authority to their physicians, medical practitioners act both as agents for consumers and suppliers of medical services. With such power, physicians are in the position of being able to create a demand for their own services.

Such a delegation of authority occurs in other markets as well. For instance, when consumers take their cars in for repair, they usually have to rely heavily on the advice of their mechanics, who (like physicians) are put in the powerful position of giving advice that can determine demand. But there is an upper limit on how much it is worth to fix a car. By contrast, when they are sick, few people limit what they are willing to pay to be made well, in part because they do not expect to pay for all of it themselves. This gives physicians extraordinary power.

Physicians' training and professional standards strongly predispose them to use their power to give the best possible medical care without regard to cost. To many physicians, it is unethical to do otherwise. * * * Moreover, because physicians can earn higher incomes by providing more care, their financial self-interest may also contribute to excessive spending.

Efficient use of medical resources requires consumers and providers to weigh the costs and benefits of alternative medical treatments. Unfortunately, this is very difficult. Obviously, patients have little knowledge upon which to judge the benefits of a new technology. But even physicians cannot always be fully informed about all the new treatments and technologies, especially given the rapid pace of complex medical advances. More important, good statistical information concerning the effectiveness of many treatments—even many common treatments—is simply not available.

The lack of good information on the outcomes of many medical treatments has created an environment in which the doctors' preferences for particular procedures—rather than science—appear to determine how they are used, a situation that leads to significant variations in the patterns and costs of medical care around the country. * * *

* * *

For markets to allocate resources efficiently, sellers must actively compete. In a competitive environment, individual vendors have no control over the price of what they sell or over the number of competitors. Also, more efficient suppliers can offer lower prices than those who fail to control their costs.

Although there are obviously many providers in the health care sector, they do not always compete effectively on price. Of course, the medical market is diverse, and active competition can be found in some subsectors of that market. But too often, competition among medical care providers for consumers (and for the services of other providers) is directed toward the nonprice aspects of medical care. * * * This type of competition, however, can tend to increase costs. Moreover, once a new technology is introduced, it tends to be used regardless of cost.

The lack of price competition in the medical market reflects many factors. The presence of third-party payers dulls the incentives for consumers to pay much attention to costs at the point of service. The tax subsidy for employment-based insurance * * * also reduces some of the pressures on workers to pay attention to the costs of insurance. Difficulties in assessing information about the quality of doctors weaken the already weak incentives for consumers to seek out the lowest-cost providers. And last, many consumers have long-standing relationships with their physicians and may be reluctant to switch doctors to save money.

* * *

Moreover, consumers are legally or effectively prohibited from making many medical decisions. Although there is a vast market for over-the-counter drugs and home remedies, most advanced drugs are sold only by prescription. In many cases, a sick person can obtain treatment only if it is prescribed by a physician, who may be highly trained but perhaps more expensive than the patient can afford. Gaining access to health services—other than those supervised by the physician, or what the druggist is willing to offer—is generally difficult.

Limited entry and control over demand are the key elements that allow a provider to earn more than necessary to attract talented, well-trained people into the profession. Economists use the term "rents" to describe a situation in which the returns to labor or capital are above the returns needed to attract the appropriate supply of resources to an activity.

It seems likely that physicians earn rents in their profession, for two reasons. First, the number of qualified applicants for medical school is far greater than the number of student slots available, so the entry limits probably matter. Second, studies of the financial returns from education and training suggest that the private returns on an investment in medical school compare favorably with the returns on investments in general and exceed the returns in most other occupations.

In addition, physicians in the United States earn about five and one-half times the average annual compensation of other wage earners. The gap is smaller in other countries. * * *

* * *

The bulk of medical care is purchased through third-party payers. These payers include not only private insurance companies but federal, state, and local governments.

As new and more elaborate methods of treatment are developed, the cost of an episode of illness can become extremely high. In addition, an individual's need for major medical care occurs largely by chance and is difficult to predict. Most types of illnesses are statistically predictable, however, for groups of individuals. Health insurance enables consumers to take advantage of this group predictability by pooling their risks for serious accidents or diseases.

Insurance, however, imposes its own costs. Insurance means that the effective price that the patient faces at the time of treatment is much lower than the actual cost of treatment. Sick individuals and their doctors have every incentive to buy expensive treatments and tests as long as they do any good at all, because the patient does not bear much of the cost. * * *

* * *

The market for medical care is also different from other markets because of the large role played by government. In particular, the government subsidizes health care, which allows some consumers greater access to medical care than they would otherwise have. Although these programs provide essential— and in some cases life-saving—medical care to millions of people, the programs also dull the price signals from the health care markets, encouraging overuse of services. The major subsidies are provided in three ways: Medicare, Medicaid, and tax expenditures.

* * *

Although there is strong justification for government involvement in health care, this involvement may cause markets to work less well in conventional terms of efficiency. When the government subsidizes the purchase or becomes the insurer, the budget constraints on consumers of health care are relaxed and, as a result, lose some effectiveness in controlling less-valued spending. Likewise, federal budget constraints for health care do not operate with the same force as they do in the private sector or in much of the rest of the public-sector budget. * * *

* * *

Notes and Questions

1. This excerpt was written over a decade and a half ago, when our health care system looked quite different than it does today. Did the decisive movement

to managed care in the American health care system in the 1990s and the rise of consumer-driven health care in the recent past (described later in this chapter and in Chapter 9) alter or eliminate the problems described above? What role has competition among managed care organizations played in bringing down costs? Although managed care seemed to succeed at constraining cost increases in the mid–1990s, costs increased again dramatically in the early 2000s. What caused this resurgence and will the consumer-driven movement subdue it? What new problems are created by the changed incentives found in managed care or consumer-driven health care? Think about these questions as you work through the remaining sections of this chapter, and through Chapters 5, 6, 7, and 8 below. Also recall our discussion of issues of quality and justice in health care in Chapter 1.

2. The classic exploration of the peculiar economics of health care was Kenneth Arrow's, Uncertainty and the Welfare Economics of Medical Care, 53 Am. Econ. Rev. 941 (1963). An excellent retrospective on this article, comprehensively exploring and updating the issues it raised, was published in the Journal of Health Politics, Policy and Law in October of 2001 edited by Peter Hammer, Deborah Haas–Wilson, and William Sage.

3. Most economists have placed particular emphasis on the role of tax subsidies for health insurance in driving health care cost increases. Payments for employee-related health insurance are taxable neither to employers nor employees. Federal income and state tax subsidies for health benefits are estimated to have exceeded $200 billion in 2006, making this expenditure program our largest federal health care program after Medicare and Medicaid. Because before-tax dollars are more valuable than after-tax dollars, it is believed that workers might prefer to take compensation in the form of health benefits even though they might have preferred to take compensation in cash absent the tax subsidy. This in turn leads to higher health care expenditures because once employees are insured, health care is either free or costs much less than it would have cost without insurance. Because these tax subsidies are offered through exclusions rather than credits, moreover, they are highly inequitable: the per worker tax subsidy in "high income" establishments where more than half of the workers earn $23.07 per hour or more was $2,525 in 2006, while the average subsidy in "low-wage" establishments where half the workers earn $10.43 or less was $637. See Thomas Selden and Bradley Gray, Tax Subsidies for Employment–Related Health Insurance Estimates for 2006, 25 Health Affairs 1568, 1573–74 (2006).

Are there any arguments in favor of the tax exclusion and deduction, however? Is it not possible that the tax exclusion has served us relatively well in creating a system where the vast majority of working age Americans are covered by private insurance? See David Hyman and Mark A. Hall, Two Cheers for Employment–Based Insurance, 2 Yale J. Health Pol'y, L., & Ethics 27 (2001); Jonathan Gruber & Larry Levitt, Tax Subsidies for Health Insurance: Costs and Benefits, 19 Health Aff., Jan./Feb. 2000, at 72. Is it not also possible that employees might opt for health benefits even without tax subsidies? Many Medicare recipients, for example, buy Medigap policies, even though these policies are purchased with after-tax dollars. Is it possible that we should build our health care system on the aspiration of providing access to health care for all Americans rather than on the fear that insured persons will abuse their coverage? See Malcolm Gladwell, The Moral Hazard Myth, The New Yorker, Aug. 29, 2005.

3. *Factors That Explain High American Health Care Costs*

While understanding the economic mechanisms that drive health care cost growth might help us to understand better the high cost of health care, it might also be helpful to consider the factors that contribute to cost growth, and in particular the respects in which the American health care system differs from those of countries where costs are much lower. A number of factors have been nominated as major factors in causing high health care costs in the United States and major drivers of health care increases. We will consider these in turn:

- National Wealth. One reason why health care costs so much more here than elsewhere is the fact that we are a very wealthy country. Health care seems to be a "luxury" good in the sense that wealthier countries spend a higher proportion of their gross domestic product (GDP) on health care than do poorer countries. The relationship between GDP and percent of GDP spent on health care is nearly linear, indeed about 90 percent of variation in spending among nations can be explained by this one factor alone. But when American expenditures are graphed against those of other nations the United States is a clear outlier. Indeed in 2001 the United States spent 43 percent more for health care than would have been predicted given its national wealth. See Uwe Reinhardt, Peter S. Hussey, and Gerard F. Anderson, U.S. Healthcare Spending in an International Context, 23 Health Aff. 10, 12 (2004).

- Population aging. The population of the United States is steadily aging, and older people, particularly those over 80, require a great deal of health care. This change explains, however, only a small proportion of the general growth in health care costs, perhaps 7 percent over the past thirty years. Aging of the population does have a greater impact on public programs, where eligibility is often age-related. As people reach the age of 65 they become eligible for Medicare (and for Medicaid if they are financially needy). Additionally, if they retire, they cease contributing to the Medicare trust fund and reduce payments of the taxes that support Medicaid. The growth in the "very old" segment of the population also disproportionately affects public programs, which bear most of the cost of the very expensive long-term care consumed by this population. As Medicaid is the primary source of payment for nursing home care in the United States, demographic shifts have hit Medicaid particularly hard. Though the elderly make up only 9 percent of the Medicaid population, they account for 27 percent of the program's costs. Nevertheless, the United States has one of the youngest populations of any developed nation, and all other countries have been able to keep their health care expenditures well below ours despite their older populations. See Joseph White, (How) is Aging a Health Policy Problem? 4 Yale J. Health Pol'y, L. and Ethics 47 (2004)

- Waste, fraud and abuse. There is a widespread belief among the general public that waste, fraud, and abuse are major factors contributing to health care costs. It is convenient to believe this, for if it were true, health care costs could be controlled painlessly without limiting "necessary" care. Fraud and abuse probably account for more than a trivial share of health care costs—aggressive enforcement of the fraud and abuse laws appears to have played a role in decreasing Medicare costs in the late 1990s. But combating fraud and abuse also imposes costs—both the direct costs of law enforcement and the indirect costs of more intrusive oversight of physician and patient behavior. "Waste" is more difficult to define and police than fraud and abuse. The practice of medicine remains far from an exact science, and tests and procedures that some regard as wasteful others regard as necessary. There is considerable evidence, however, of dramatic differences across geographic areas on the use of health care services, which suggest that health care resources are being "wasted" in some areas. In particular, Jack Wennberg, who has conducted research on health care variations for a generation, has identified dramatic variations in what he terms "supply sensitive" services, services that tend to be provided in greater volume where the capacity to provide them is greater. Patients with non-surgical medical conditions, for example, are more likely to be hospitalized in regions with more hospital beds, while Medicare enrollees are seen by cardiologists much more often in areas with more cardiologists. Most disconcerting is the finding of this body of research that some measures of quality, including mortality rates, may be in fact worse in regions where supply-sensitive service use is higher. Excess spending is doing harm, not good. See John E. Wennberg, Elliot S. Fisher, Jonathan S. Skinner, Geography and the Debate over Medicare Reform, Health Aff. Web Excl. (Feb. 13, 2002); Elliott S. Fisher, et al., The Implications of Regional Variations in Medicare Spending. Part 2: Health Outcomes and Satisfaction With Care, 138 Annals of Int. Med. 288, 291–92 (2003).

- Market structure. It has long been believed that competition has been limited by entry requirements such as licensure and certificate of need requirements. More recently, the market for certain health care services—including health insurance, hospital care, and specialty physician services—has become highly concentrated in many geographic areas. Market concentration can facilitate collusive attempts to raise prices and dampen competition. Some believe that "pushback" from increasingly powerful hospitals and physician groups had much to do with the declining effectiveness of managed care in holding down prices in the late 1990s and early 2000s. See Federal Trade Commission and Department of Justice, Improving Health Care: A Dose of Competition (2004); William B. Vogt and Robert Town, How Has Hospital Consolidation Affected the Price and Quality of Hospital Care? (2006) http://www.rwjf.org/publications/synthesis/reports_and_briefs/issue9.html; and Chapter 12.

- Administrative costs. We pay more proportionately for administrative costs than any other nation in the world, $1059 per person in 1999, compared to $307 per person in Canada. Steffie Woolhandler, Terry Campbell and David Himmelstein, Costs of Health Care Administration in the United States and Canada, 349 New Eng. J. Med. 768 (2003). Private insurance systems simply cost more to administer than public systems because private systems carry with them costs for marketing, underwriting, monitoring, and billing that do not exist in public systems. While Medicare spends 2 cents on the dollar on administrative costs, private health insurance companies spend up to 25 cents on the dollar in small group markets and 5.5 cents on the dollar in large-group markets for administrative costs. A doctor in the United States must contend with the particular billing forms and practices of dozens of insurance companies and managed care plans, while in most other countries, and in public programs in the United States, there is only one form and one payer to deal with. Any health care system costs something to administer, and as long as we remain committed to a private insurance-based system of health care finance we must expect relatively high administrative costs. On the other hand, many believe that private markets bring with them efficiencies that outweigh their higher administrative costs, and thus, in the end, cost less.

- Malpractice. Though malpractice continues to be a major source of irritation to medical professionals, it is not a major contributor to medical costs. The direct costs of malpractice premiums account for less than 1 percent of health care costs, though these costs tend to be borne disproportionately by physicians in particular specialties and geographic areas. Defensive medicine arguably is of greater concern, but the extent to which it contributes to health care costs has not been reliably measured. See GAO, Medical Malpractice: Implications of Rising Premiums on Access to Health Care, GAO–03–836 (2003). See discussion in Chapter 1.

- The Changing Nature of Disease. There is evidence that Medicare expenditures have grown most rapidly in recent years for beneficiaries who do not have serious diseases or functional limitations, but rather metabolic disorders, such as high blood pressure or high cholesterol, that are not in themselves symptomatic diseases. In a number of recent articles, Kenneth Thorpe and associates have contended that a major factor in the increase of Medicare expenditures is the rise in obesity among the elderly. In general, health care costs are higher for persons with chronic diseases, but these costs are to some extent self-limiting. People with chronic diseases tend to die earlier, and thus, although their medical care costs more per year, they live fewer years. On the other hand, healthy people live longer, and although their medical care costs less per year, their expenses are spread over more years. In the end, moreover, all of us die, and dying is usually expensive. Healthy people are not necessarily that much less expensive than those with chronic diseases. It appears, however, however, that obese people, who often suffer from diabetes and hypertension or other conditions, not only need high cost medical care on an ongoing basis, but also tend to live as long, probably even longer, than persons of normal weight. They are thus, over a lifetime, very expensive to care for. The proportion of Americans who are obese has been growing rapidly in recent years, and this may account for a considerable share of recent increases in health care costs. See Kenneth E. Thorpe and David H. Howard, The Rise in Spending Among Medicare Beneficiaries: The Role of Chronic Disease Prevalence and Changes in Treatment Intensity, Health Aff. Web Excl., Aug. 22, 2006, w380; Kenneth E. Thorpe, et al., The Impact of Obesity on Rising Medical Spending, Health Aff. Web. Excl., W4–480, Oct. 20, 2004; Darius N. Lakdawalla, Dana P. Goldman, and Baoping Shang, The Health and Cost Consequences of Obesity Among the Future Elderly, Health Aff. Web Excl., W–5–R–30, Sept. 26, 2005.

- Treating "hopeless cases." Some have argued that we spend far too much in the United States prolonging the life of patients who are near death through heroic interventions. In fact, studies show that we spend relatively little on truly hopeless cases. Ezekiel Emanuel & Linda Emanuel, The Economics of Dying: The Illusion of Cost Savings at the End of Life, 330 New Eng. J. Med. 540 (1994). The problem is that it is often not clear at the outset when treatment is futile, and that a great deal is spent on persons who are expected to live but die, or expected to die but live. It should not be surprising that most health care is consumed by those who are the sickest, and even those who are clearly dying require at least comfort care. Widespread use of advanced directives could contribute to cost control, but probably not significantly. Disease management programs, which deal with high-cost chronic diseases, might do more. See Steven M. Lieberman, et al., Reducing the Growth of Medicare Spending: Geographic Versus Patient–Based Strategies, Health Affairs Web Exclusive. http://content.healthaffairs.org/cgi/reprint/hlthaff.w3.603v1.pdf (Dec. 10, 2003).

• Higher prices. A striking feature of the American health care system is that even though we spend more on health care than any other nation, we consume no more health care than do many other nations if some measures of utilization are considered and less than most other nations if other measures are. The average American sees a doctor 5.8 times a year, compared to 6.4 for the average Canadian or 5.4 for the average Englishman. The average American spends .7 days per year in a hospital, compared to 1.9 days for the average German and .9 for the average Englishman. On the other hand, we pay dramatically more per unit of health care consumed and, in many instances, per health care worker, than do most other nations. (We also, incidentally, pay more for drugs than do the citizens of many other nations, even for the same drugs). See, Gerard F. Anderson, et al., It's the Prices, Stupid: Why the United States is so Different from Other Countries, 22 Health Aff., May/June 2003 at 89.

> This observation has two ramifications. First, it implies that the true "cost" of medical care in the United States, in terms of productive resources allocated to health care that could be allocated elsewhere, is relatively low. Mark Pauly, U S. Health Care Costs: The Untold True Story, Health Affairs, Fall 1993 at 100. We just pay more for the resources we use for health care. Second, it means that we could, at least in theory, cut health care costs without diminishing the volume of health care we receive if we could pay less to those who provide health care. Uwe Reinhardt, Resource Allocation in Health Care: The Allocation of Lifestyles to Providers, 65 Milbank Q. 153 (1987). Arguably, if we could put in place mechanisms to counter market failures that cause us to pay excessive prices for health care, we could reach the lower "true" market resource price.

> This second observation is particularly important, because it explains one of the ways in which managed care can contribute to cost control. Managed care companies pay high salaries to their executives and employ a host of workers who monitor and administer health care rather than providing health care services. The administrative costs of managed care organizations are far higher than the costs of Medicare or of the public health insurance programs of other coun-

tries. See Kip Sullivan, On the "Efficiency" of Managed Care Plans, 19 Health Aff., July/Aug. 2000, 139. On the other hand, managed care plans not only control the utilization of health care, but also demand much deeper discounts from health care professionals or providers than do other insurance plans, public or private. Physician annual income growth slowed dramatically in the mid–1990s as managed care grew, and has not yet returned to earlier growth rates. To the extent that the costs of administering managed care firms are less than the savings they achieve in driving down the use and costs of health care labor, managed care has resulted in health care savings.

● Technology. Most health economists believe that the primary reason why health care costs so much in the United States, and indeed, why the cost of health care is increasing so rapidly, is because of the widespread and rapid adoption of health care technology. Mark Pauly, a leading health economist, states:

> The growth rate of spending on new medical care technology is so large that any effective effort to slow it appreciably would soon swamp any alternative program to improve efficiency, say, by reducing geographic variation in spending or spending on overuse of tried-and-true medical services. Taking out the effect of economy wide inflation (at 2 percent), more than half of the 6.8 percent per capita real health spending growth in 2002 is accounted for explicitly by technology (here called "utilization" and defined to include the "quality and mix of services"). Moreover, some of the second-largest component, medical price increases, almost surely includes some changes in the nature of the product.

> Mark Pauly, Competition and New Technology, 24(6) Health Affairs 1523, 1424 (2004). See also Timothy Stoltzfus Jost, The American Difference in Health Care Costs: Is There a Problem? Is Medical Necessity the Solution? 43 St. Louis U. L. J. 1 (1999).

See, further exploring these issues, Sherry Glied, Chronic Condition: Why Health Reform Fails (1997): 93–101. Anderson, et al., It's the Prices Stupid, *supra*; Victor Fuchs, No Pain, No Gain, Perspectives on Cost Containment, 269 JAMA 631 (1993); Jerry L. Mashaw & Theodore R. Marmor, Conceptualizing, Estimating, and Reforming Fraud, Waste, and Abuse in Healthcare Spending, 11 Yale J. Reg. 456 (1994) and Joseph P. Newhouse, An Iconoclastic View of Health Care Cost Containment, Health Affairs, Supp. 1993 at 152.

How much value do you place on health care? Do you think that we as a society spend too much, too little, about the right amount on health care? Do you think that you as an individual spend too much, too little, or the right amount? Would you be willing to tolerate diminished access to expensive, high technology, diagnostic or treatment equipment to save health care costs? Would you be willing to travel further or wait longer to gain access to such equipment? Would your answer be the same if you were desperately ill? Should public programs such as Medicare consider the cost of technologies in deciding whether or not to pay for them? What would be the consequences of compelling the reduction of the income of health care professionals? What would be the consequences of forcing drug companies to accept lower prices?

Should cost considerations play a role in deciding when to terminate care for dying persons?

II. APPROACHES TO EXPANDING ACCESS AND CONTROLLING COSTS

Approaches to expanding access to and controlling the cost of health care can be basically divided between those that rely on direct public action and those that rely more on private initiatives and markets. All nations, including the United States, have adopted a mixed strategy for addressing cost control issues. All have public programs for providing health insurance or health care to a portion of their population. Even in the United States, the bastion of private enterprise, almost half of health care expenditures are borne by the government (more if one adds tax expenditures and the cost of insurance for government employees), even though government programs cover less than one third of the population. All nations also have private insurance markets. Even in England, whose National Health Service is the quintessential example of socialized medicine, about one ninth of the population has private insurance.

This section will begin by considering the options available for expanding access to health care, describing first the range of options for providing publicly financed health care, then examining options offering tax subsidies for private health insurance, which are more likely to succeed politically in the United States. Next we will examine options for controlling health care costs, looking first at regulatory options, then at market-based options.

A. OPTIONS FOR EXPANDING ACCESS TO CARE

1. Public Health Insurance

While all developed nations have private health insurance markets, the United States is very unusual in the extent to which it relies on private finance of health care, and unique in that it fails to provide some form of public coverage for all those who cannot afford private insurance. The models of health care finance followed by European nations (as well as other developed nations) are described in the excerpt that follows:

TIMOTHY STOLTZFUS JOST, WHY CAN'T WE DO WHAT THEY DO? NATIONAL HEALTH REFORM ABROAD

Journal of Law, Medicine and Ethics, vol. 32, pp. 432–35 (2004).

* * *

All other developed nations of the world [other than the United States], including developed countries in Western Europe, Asia, North and South America, and on the Pacific Rim, provide health care for all or most of their residents. Although private health insurance products are available for purchase on a voluntary basis in virtually every country, no other developed country relies on private insurance as does the United State to provide primary coverage for its population. All developed nations have recognized that voluntary private insurance cannot cover everyone, (as it does not in the U.S.) and have developed some form of public health insurance.

Two primary models can be found in the world: social insurance and national health insurance. Each term refers to a specific approach to the task of financing and organizing a nation's system for providing personal health care. The first, and older, model is social insurance, often called the Bismarck model after the German leader who established the first social health insurance system. The second, more recent, is the national health insurance model, often called the Beveridge model after Lord Beveridge who proposed this approach for the U.K. during World War II.

Chancellor Bismarck established the German social insurance system in 1883 in an attempt to turn back the tide of socialism that he feared would engulf Germany. Under the German system as it has developed, most citizens have an obligation to secure health insurance coverage, which in turn is paid for, usually by a deduction from earnings, on the basis of the insured's income rather than the insured's risk status or family size, in order to ensure affordability. In Germany the conceptual foundation of health insurance lies in a belief that members of a society have obligations to each other, a concept referred to as "solidarity," rather than in the belief that individuals are responsible only for themselves. This insurance obligation is effectuated through a system that collects the necessary revenues needed to sustain health care. Employers and employees each contribute a percentage of wages to social insurance funds; in turn, these funds provide health insurance for employees and their families. Most persons in Germany whose income falls below a certain level (46,350 Euros in 2004) must participate in this social health insurance program. Persons with incomes above this level are not required to participate, and many buy private insurance instead. However, about 60 percent of all of these upper income persons in fact participate in the public system because family coverage costs extra in the private system but not in the public, private insurance rates are risk-adjusted while social insurance rates are not, and persons who opt out of the social insurance system may not in most instances ever return.

Social insurance funds in Germany are not administered by the government, but rather by non-profit organizations, which are accountable to their members (and their members' employers). There are many of these funds, some tied to a particular employer, others occupation based, and still others locally-based. * * * All social insurance funds operate within a framework of laws, and all cover essentially the same services and charge similar (though not identical) premiums. In order to ensure the stability of the health funds— and thus the effectuation of a truly nationwide system—health plans that have younger and less costly members must transfer money through a risk-equalization scheme to the plans that have older and more expensive patients, but the plans also compete with each other for members and thus have some incentive to keep their premiums down.

Health insurers have traditionally paid hospitals on the basis of negotiated budgets, though Germany is moving toward payment on a diagnosis related group (DRG) basis. Physicians and dentists in Germany who furnish health care to plan members are organized into corporate bodies that resemble unions. In other words, while physicians and dentists are private businessmen, they negotiate with the health insurers collectively, much like an independent practice association would do in the U.S. In recent years these corporate entities have negotiated with social insurers for a fixed budget, which they have allocated among their members on a fee-for-service basis.

* * *

For each component of the health care sector (physician services, hospitals, pharmaceuticals, etc.) and in each region, budgets in Germany are established globally within a framework of "premium stability." This framework limits the rate of increase in social insurance premiums to the rate of increase in inflation generally and tends to ensure that practice style and practice choices evolve within a fundamental environment of overall health care spending control. * * *

The social insurance model created in Germany has been adopted in much of the world. Other central European countries, including Austria, Switzerland, France, Belgium, and the Netherlands have social insurance systems, as do many South American and Asian countries for at least part of their workforce. Many of the emerging democracies of Eastern Europe have also embraced the social insurance model. Part A of the U.S. Medicare program in most respects resembles a social insurance system. Though these systems vary in many important respects, in each one health insurance is financed primarily by payroll taxes or wage-based premiums, and services are purchased from independent health care providers who often are in private practice.

If the social insurance model was adopted by conservative governments to suppress the growth of socialism in the late nineteenth and early twentieth century, the national health insurance model emerged from the triumph of socialism in Europe after World War II. The United Kingdom had adopted a limited social insurance system in 1911, but many people were excluded from it, and the U.K. emerged from WWII determined to provide health care as a right to its entire population. Access to health care would no longer depend on belonging to a social insurance plan (which was usually, in some sense, employment-related), but rather would be free at point-of-service to all residents. Thus, universal coverage was created independent of the economic or employment status of any individual.

The English NHS is financed through general revenue taxation. These funds are administered by local units called primary care trusts. These units purchase services from NHS hospital trusts, which are currently public corporations, as well as from general practitioners, who are private businessmen. These services are then provided to the general public, in most instances without cost, although co-payments are imposed for some things like drugs, and a few services—like most dental care—are provided mainly in the private sector.

The U.K., like many European countries, has a strong gatekeeper system. Every Briton has a general practitioner (GP), and a patient's first contact with the health care system is almost always with the GP. GPs still make house calls in the U.K., and the level of satisfaction with primary care in the U.K. is very high. Specialist services, including surgery, are only provided through hospitals and upon referral from a GP.

Many nations have adopted the national health insurance model of public health insurance in the past half century, although, again, in each nation the model looks somewhat different. Canada, Australia, the Scandinavian countries, Spain, Portugal, Italy, and some Latin American and Asian countries have national health insurance systems. Other countries, particularly less developed countries, provide services through public hospitals and clinics without necessarily developing a full and comprehensive national system of health care finance that would be essential to make such a network of services accessible to all persons. Our own Medicaid program, as well as our veterans', military, and Indian health services, resemble the "national health insurance" model in that all use general revenue funds to pay for health services, but they are different in that their coverage is limited to certain narrowly delineated populations, which may even, as with Medicaid, vary from state to state.

* * *

Countries that have national health insurance programs cover all of their citizens and long-term residents, although in most countries individuals can choose to carry private insurance and obtain services privately. Some countries with social insurance funds, such as France or Austria, cover their entire populations as well. Others, however, such as Germany, only require people whose income falls below a certain level to be part of the social insurance program. Although people with higher incomes can choose to be uninsured, few make this choice. * * *

A number of countries apply means tests for determining coverage for certain services or for determining the applicability or level of cost-sharing. The Irish health care system is partially means tested: only low income holders of medical cards (about a third of the population) have free access to general practitioner services, and higher income people without medical cards must pay a co-payment for hospital and pharmacy services under some circumstances. In the U.K. where long-term nursing home care is primarily regarded as a social service, nursing homes are publicly funded only for those who do not have the means to pay privately. Pharmaceutical coverage in the U.K. is also means tested to the extent that the system waives required co-payments for low-income persons, although the government also waives co-payment for children, the elderly, and persons with certain chronic conditions. No developed nation other than the U.S., however, makes access to public health insurance depend totally on economic "medical dependency" (Medicaid), or on age and disability status (Medicare). And no other developed country has nearly as high a proportion of its population uninsured.

Social insurance and national health insurance programs vary somewhat in the benefits they offer. The Canadian health insurance program, for example, only requires the provinces to cover hospital, physician, and surgical dental services, though most provinces also cover pharmaceutical costs for at least some of their residents. Coverage in Australia is limited to hospital, physician, and pharmaceutical care. Most countries do not cover nursing home care or cover it as a social service rather than a health care service. In some countries some benefits that are nominally covered are in fact not generally available because of high cost sharing obligations, limited coverage, or lack of provider participation.

Though public finance of health care services is quite common in other countries, public provision of health care services is less universal. In most public insurance countries, many health care services are furnished by private entities and health professionals in private practice. Only in a few countries, for example, does the government directly employ primary care physicians or dentists. Pharmaceuticals and medical devices are generally produced by private manufacturers and sold through private pharmacies or medical equipment suppliers. In most national health insurance countries public hospitals are dominant, but in some countries private nonprofit or private hospitals also exist. Private hospitals are even more common in social insurance countries.

* * *

Notes and Questions

1. The possibility of a publicly financed health care system (often called a "single-payer" system, though this term does not accurately describe social insurance systems), has been debated in the United States for decades. It has always, however, faced strong opposition from some sectors of the health care industry (in the 40s, 50s and 60s from physicians, now primarily from insurers), and has rarely enjoyed broad political support. Even when some form of national health reform seemed possible in the early 1990s, the single-payer alternative received little attention. The political institutions and ideological bent of the United States are quite different from that of Canada and most European countries, and were, in particular, very different in the post-World War II era when many of these nations adopted public health insurance systems. See Theodore Marmor, The Politics of Medicare (2d ed. 2000); Carolyn Hughes Tuohy, Accidental Logics (1999); Timothy Jost, Why Can't We Do What They Do? Journal of Law, Med. & Ethics (2004).

What explains the political aversion of most Americans to a national health system? Why has the rest of the world not followed our example? What benefits does our privately financed system offer? What problems does it cause? See Timothy S. Jost, Disentitlement? The Threats Facing our Public Health–Care Programs and a Rights–Based Response (2003).

2. Although it has long been known that the United States has the most expensive health care system in the world and yet lags in providing access to health care, less has been known until recently about the comparative quality of our health care system. In recent years, however, the Commonwealth fund has conducted a series of surveys of patients and providers in six countries (the U.S., Canada, New Zealand, Australia, the United Kingdom, and Germany.) A recent summary of these data demonstrate that the United States ranks first among these countries in providing preventive services, but ranks last or second to last on every other measure. The United States, for example, ranked relatively poorly in providing chronic care, in avoiding medical errors, in coordinating care, and in "patient-centeredness." One particular area in which the United States lags behind public systems is in the adoption of health information technology. Karen Davis, et al., Mirror, Mirror on the Wall: An International Update on Comparative Performance of American Health Care, http://www.commonwealthfund.org/ publications/publications_show.htm?doc_id=482678 (2007).

3. One of the best sources of information on the health care systems of European countries is the website of the European Observatory on Healthcare Systems, http://www.euro.who.int/observatory/toppage, which has country profiles on most European countries. See also, for further information on legal issues

affecting access to health care in other nations, Timothy Stoltzfus Jost, Readings in Comparative Health Law and Bioethics (2d. ed., 2007).

4.   In addition to our big health care financing programs—Medicare, Medicaid, and SCHIP—the state and federal governments play an important, and often unrecognized role, in direct funding or provision of health care services through "safety-net" providers. In 2004, 940 federally qualified health centers and 1100 public hospitals provided services to millions of Americans, most of them poor and many of them uninsured. These safety net providers, like their patients, have in recent years endured a precarious financial existence, but, along with hundreds of private charitable clinics, play a vital role in serving Americans who otherwise lack access to health care. See Catherine Hoffman and Susan Starr Sered, Threadbare: Holes in America's Safety Net, http://www.kff.org/uninsured/upload/ Threadbare–Holes-in-America-s-Health–Care–Safety–Net-report.pdf   (2005); Institute of Medicine, America's Health Care Safety Net: Intact but Endangered (Marion Lewin and Stuart Altman, eds., 2000).

5.   An alternative approach to government involvement in the financing of health care that has received some attention in recent years is reinsurance. As noted earlier, most of the cost of health care in any particular year is incurred by a small percentage of the population that needs very costly health care. One of the primary reasons why health insurance for individuals and small groups is so costly is because insurers need to cover the risk of ending up with high cost claims. Government reinsurance of costly claims, therefore, can lower the risk for insurers and the cost of small group and nongroup insurance, making it more affordable. It could also allow the government to play a role in improving the management of high cost diseases. Finally, government reinsurance of high cost cases might be more politically acceptable than direct public funding of health care. See John Jacobi, The Present and Future of Government–Funded Reinsurance, 51 St. Louis U.L.J. 369 (2007); John Jacobi, Government Reinsurance Programs and Consumer–Driven Care, 53 Buff. L. Rev. 537 (2005); Katherine Swartz, Reinsuring Health: Why More Middle–Class People are Uninsured and What Government Can Do (2006). A number of states have for some time sponsored voluntary or mandatory reinsurance pools in the small group market which have allocated risk among private insurers. Since 2001, the Healthy New York program has provided government reinsurance for lower-income households in the small group and individual market, which currently covers 90 percent of the cost of individual cases with expenses of $5000 to $75,000 per year. The program had 130,000 enrollees as of January 2007, and is credited with bringing about a significant drop in the number of uninsured in New York.

2.   *Approaches to Encouraging the Purchase of Private Insurance*

a.   *Tax Credits*

If publicly-financed approaches to insuring the uninsured are not politically feasible at this time, proposals based on providing tax incentives for the purchase of private insurance might be. A broad range of analysts and interest groups, centered on the right but in fact spanning much of the political spectrum, have proposed that we build on our current system of tax subsidies for health insurance by offering tax credits to uninsured persons to purchase health insurance.

Many advocates of tax credits further propose that credits replace our current tax exclusions and deductions for employee health benefits, which, as noted above, benefit wealthier persons more than poorer, and arguably lead to inefficient levels of insurance coverage. Proposals to abolish one of the most widely used tax subsidies offered by the federal government, however, and to replace it with a subsidy much less valuable to many taxpayers (particularly wealthy taxpayers) are unlikely to be politically popular. Proposals to use tax credits for expanding the purchase of private insurance by those currently uninsured, however, enjoy broad political favor. How effective would this strategy be?

First, for tax credits to be of any value they would have to be fully refundable. In other words, the credits would have to be available to taxpayers whether or not tax liability was sufficient to cover the credits. Because many of those Americans currently uninsured do not have tax liabilities approaching the level of subsidy proposed, (e.g., $1000 for an individual, up to $3000 for a family proposed by the Bush administration in 2005) a standard nonrefundable tax credit (i.e. one that is simply subtracted from taxes due), would be of little help. Administering a refundable tax credit, however, is complex administratively, as a program must be established to review applications, set payment levels, and mail out checks. It is particularly important that tax credits be refundable in advance, as a credit is of little value to an uninsured person if it arrives months after the cost of a policy is incurred. On the other hand, projecting future income initially, and reconciling projected income with actual income at the end of the year leads to further bureaucratic complexities. These difficulties can be addressed by basing tax credit on the income of the previous year, but this solution will not help people who lose their job or otherwise face a sudden change in economic circumstances.

A bigger problem with tax credit proposals is that to really make a difference, tax credits need to be set at a high enough level that they actually make the purchase of health insurance viable. In 2007, the average annual premium for employer-provided health insurance, according to one survey, was $4,479 for single coverage, $12,106 for family coverage. Individual non-group insurance usually costs less, but nongroup policies generally have much thinner coverage and higher cost-sharing because the premiums have to cover higher underwriting, marketing, and administrative costs than those of group policies. Moreover, individual policies cost much more for older persons and persons with serious health problems. Nongroup policies that would be affordable at rates anywhere close to the tax credit rates generally proposed would leave those who purchase them exposed to significant health care costs, which would still, in combination with the premiums charged by the insurers, represent a very heavy burden on low-income individuals.

In fact, tax credits are likely to be of most use to those who are already purchasing individual policies. The availability of such credits will also, moreover, undoubtedly tempt many employers now offering insurance coverage as an employee benefit to drop it, urging their employees instead to avail themselves of the tax credit and purchase their own policies. Any such program is likely to have a substantial "crowd out" effect, therefore. One simulation of the implementation of the Bush administration's proposed refundable tax credits (worth up to $1000 for singles and $3000 for families) estimated that 3.12 million uninsured would take up the credit, but that it would cause employers to drop coverage for 3.4 million individuals, 1.3 million of whom would become uninsured, leaving a net gain of 1.8 million insured, at a cost to the federal government of $2.23 for every $1.00 of insurance value gained. See Leonard E. Berman and Jonathan Gruber, Tax Credits for Health Insurance, http://www.urban.org/UploadedPDF/311189_IssuesOptions_11.pdf (2005).

Tax credit proposals could be made more feasible by detaching them from the inefficient individual insurance market and targeting them at particular groups of the uninsured. An alternative that has attracted bipartisan attention is the use of tax credits to purchase group insurance, either through employers or through public programs for targeted populations, such as the unemployed. The first step in this direction was taken by Congress in the Trade Adjustment Assistance Reform Act of 2002, which provided a 65 percent subsidy to allow workers who lost their employment because of increased imports or trade-related business relocations to purchase certain types of health insurance. Although the TAARA tax credit can be used by affected workers to pay for individual insurance policies that they already have at the time of job loss, it can also be used to pay for COBRA continuation coverage (see Chapter 7 below), employment-related group coverage through the affected individual's spouse's employer; or, under certain circumstances, for state insurance programs such as state high-risk pools, state employee insurance programs, or arrangements entered into between states and insurers. Participation in the program has been disappointing, in part because the worker's share of the premium is often unaffordable (costing between 21 and 25 percent of the worker's monthly unemployment check), and in part because the complexity of the program has deterred enrollment. See Statement of Sigurd R. Nilsen, Trade Adjustment Assistance: Changes Needed to Improve States' Ability to Provide Benefits and Services to Trade–Affected Workers (GAO–070995T, 2007).

In his 2007 State of the Union Address, President Bush changed course, proposing a tax deduction (of $15,000 for families, $7500 for individuals) for households with health insurance rather than a tax credit. This deduction would replace the current health insurance deduction, and thus limit the amount currently deductible to this amount. http://www.whitehouse.gov/state oftheunion/2007/initiatives/healthcare.html. The deduction approach, of course, is of even less help than tax credits to those who do not otherwise pay taxes, and the proposal was not taken seriously by the Democrat-controlled Congress.

Whatever their faults, tax credits remain the most politically viable approach to expanding health care access to the uninsured. As of this writing, most of the 2008 presidential candidates have included a tax credit or deduction proposal in their health care plans.

Why do tax credit proposals enjoy such popularity? What benefits do they offer to the uninsured? What benefits do they offer to the insurance industry? Why might they prove more attractive to some employers than the current system of deductions? Will they prove to be more attractive to currently-insured employees? If we are to use tax credits to subsidize the purchase of insurance, should they be used to subsidize individual or group insurance policies?

b. *Mandates*

Another strategy governments can pursue to extend private insurance coverage for health care is to simply mandate the purchase of health insurance. The idea of an insurance mandate is not new. Many states have long required drivers to purchase automobile liability insurance and employers to purchase workers' compensation insurance. The Netherlands and Switzerland have achieved universal coverage by requiring their residents to purchase health insurance cover. A mandate requiring all who were not otherwise covered to purchase private insurance might achieve universal coverage while still preserving private health care finance markets.

Mandates could be imposed either on employers or on individuals. The United States has long depended on employment-related group health insurance as its primary strategy for covering the general population. Most employers provide health insurance as an employment benefit, and a mandate could extend insurance to populations currently not covered (such as part-time or temporary employees) and to employers who do not currently provide insurance. This strategy was attempted in a limited way by Maryland. As will be explored further in Chapter 7, however, the preemption provisions of the Employee Retirement Income Security Act of 1974 (ERISA) block the states from mandating employer coverage. That leaves states with mandates imposed on individuals.

Individual insurance mandates cannot in themselves provide universal coverage. Lower-income households cannot afford health insurance, and will need public subsidies, provided either directly or through tax credits. A sixth of uninsured Americans, however, come from households earning $75,000 or more per year, and these households should pay their own way and not be dependent on safety-net providers. If the government can organize the small group and non-group market to reduce the risk to insurers and standardize insurance products, insurance can be made affordable to these households.

In 2006 Massachusetts enacted a law mandating individual insurance coverage. The mandate was supplemented by an expanded Medicaid program, public subsidies for lower income households, and a program to organize the nongroup market. It is described in the excerpt that follows:

CHRISTIE HAGER, THE MASSACHUSETTS HEALTH CARE PLAN

Health reform legislation enacted in Massachusetts in April of 2006 (Chapter 58 of the Acts of 2006) combines a new program of public insurance subsidies for low-income individuals, Medicaid expansions and increased SCHIP eligibility for children, and private insurance market reforms, with a requirement for all adults to obtain health insurance if they can afford it, and several new ways for employers to contribute to the health of their workers. Built on the principle of "shared responsibility," the law necessarily requires individuals, employers, and government all to take steps designed to bring Massachusetts to nearly universal coverage over the course of a three-year implementation period, much of it under rules imposed by a renewed Medicaid Waiver.

A strong track record of success under the state's Section 1115 Medicaid Waiver, robust state-based survey data on the uninsured and employer-sponsored insurance, as well as consumer-oriented private insurance market regulation provided the foundation for a legislative package that tailored public benefits and subsidies and private market reforms to target the various segments of the approximately 550,000 residents who were uninsured in 2005.

Medicaid expansions included the restoration of previously cut benefits, including adult dental and vision services. Children's eligibility in the state's Medicaid program, MassHealth, was raised to 300% from 200%. And, $3 million dollars in funding was appropriated for comprehensive, community-based outreach and enrollment efforts to ensure that all those eligible for public insurance would be identified and successfully enrolled. The Act provides for long-overdue increases in reimbursement for Medicaid providers, in the amount of $540 million over three years, much of which is contingent on meeting new "pay for performance" requirements.

The quasi-public Commonwealth Health Insurance Connector Authority ["Connector"] was created as a central distribution mechanism for new insurance products: the Commonwealth Care Health Insurance Program for individuals up to 300% of FPL, in which individuals below 150% now pay no deductibles or co-pays; and the Commonwealth Choice program, in which new, affordable insurance policies are offered to individuals whose income is too high for eligibility in either MassHealth or Commonwealth Care.

Changes in the state's $1.3 billion-dollar Uncompensated Care Pool were instituted to redirect monies to public subsidies in the Commonwealth Care program, and to revise reimbursement methodologies in the successor Health Safety Net Fund.

Private health insurance market reforms included extended dependent coverage until the earlier of age 26 or two years past loss of dependent status, new Young Adult Products for 19–26–year–olds. Merging the small-and non-group markets was estimated to realize reductions of approximately 15% for current non-group rates.

An individual mandate for adults aged 18 and over requires those individuals to purchase insurance only if it is affordable to them. The affordability contingency requires the Connector to establish a schedule of affordability each year, under which income guidelines determine who will be subject to financial penalties for not obtaining insurance. Penalties, imposed on state income tax filers, consist in the first year of implementation of the loss of one's personal exemption (approx. $219) and in the second year and beyond, 50% of the equivalent of the premium of the least expensive policy affordable during each month of uninsurance.

Several provisions address employer responsibility for the health of their workers. These include requirement on employers with 11 or more full-time equivalent workers to make a "fair and reasonable" contribution to the health insurance premiums of their workers or pay an annual fee of $295 per worker, and to offer a Section 125 plan or be subject to assessment for a portion of their workers' Health Safety Net Fund-provided services in the state's hospitals and community health centers.

A new Health Care Quality and Cost Council is created, to establish the priority of improved quality and cost-containment in the health care delivery system, and several measures aimed at improving public health and eliminating racial and ethnic health disparities are contained within Chapter 58 as well.

See, Symposium, The Massachusetts Health Plan, 55 Kansas Law Review 1091ff (2007).

B.   COST CONTROL

1.   *Cost Control Regulation*

Both regulatory and market-based strategies are also possible for addressing the problem of cost control. In most developed nations, costs are controlled through public program budgets. In countries like the United Kingdom, where most funds come from a single source, budgeting is a relatively straightforward process—funds are allocated by the central government to the NHS, which distributes them to the various local primary care trusts according to an allocation formula. These local purchasers in turn use the funds for purchasing health care. Health care costs are, quite simply, whatever the government decides to spend on health care in a given year, supplemented by a modest amount of private funds spent on private care. In countries like Germany, social insurance programs are administered by a number of quasi-private insurance funds which must negotiate budgets with corporately organized providers. The government only sets general guidelines for budgets, which are in turn worked out on a decentralized basis. Control over cost, of course, is less possible in this type of system. Controlling costs is also more difficult in federal systems like Canada where both the federal and provincial governments provide funds for health care. Nevertheless, countries with public systems have generally been able to limit costs with considerable success.

Cost control through budgets, however, imposes its own costs. Countries that place relatively severe limits on cost, like the United Kingdom, tend to develop shortages and waiting lists. Access to the latest technology and to elective procedures like hip replacements, that are not life-saving but increase comfort and functioning, may be limited. Countries with more generous budgets face fewer rationing constraints, indeed rationing is rare in social insurance based systems. Waiting times are not related only to cost-constraints, but are also related to bottlenecks in health care resource availability as well as to the method by which services are reimbursed (fee-for-service payments contribute to shorter wait times). See Luigi Siciliani and Jeremy. Hurst, Explaining Waiting Time Variations for Elective Surgery Across OECD Countries. (OECD, 2003), available at http://www.oecd.org/dataoecd/31/10/17256025.pdf.

Within the United States public budgets have rarely been tried. Our Medicare and Medicaid programs are not budget limited. They are rather entitlement programs, under which providers are entitled to payment for all covered goods and services provided to eligible beneficiaries. Cost control efforts in Medicare and Medicaid have focused rather on limiting the prices paid for goods and services, or on the use of managed care, but have rarely tried to limit the volume of services received directly. These themes are explored further below in Chapter 8. Because, however, it is difficult to imagine the United States adopting anything resembling a single payer system in the foreseeable future, little time needs to be spent here debating the merits or demerits of budgets as a means of controlling health care costs in the United States. See, Timothy Jost, Disentitlement (2003), exploring these themes further.

The United States has also attempted other regulatory interventions to control private health care costs. Historically, our most significant cost control program was the health planning, certificate of need program, which was established at the federal level in 1974 and abolished in 1986, but which still continues in many states. State health planning programs attempt to project need for various health services through a state health plan, and then require health care providers (particularly hospitals and nursing homes) to demonstrate compliance with this plan in order to obtain a "certificate of need" prior to adding new beds or making major expenditures for technology. These programs were based on the theory that controlling supply would control demand, but they have only a limited effect on costs and have been abandoned by many states. They continue to be used in a number of states, however, to control capital investment in health care. Health planning is discussed further in Chapter 10. The other major state regulatory program for controlling costs was hospital rate setting, which was attempted by a number of states in the 1970s and 1980s. At this point rate setting has been abandoned everywhere but in Maryland. There is little enthusiasm currently among health policy analysts or health economists for using traditional public-utility type regulation for cost control.

2. *Managed Competition*

If the problem of health care costs is ultimately attributable to market failure, then the market for health care services must be reformed to make it work. Potential markets exist, however, both at the level of health care delivery and of health care finance. Therefore, market reforms can alternatively attempt to create functioning markets for health care services or for health insurance. The point of health service purchase strategy is commonly referred to as the "consumer-driven" or "consumer-directed" approach. Alternatively, "managed competition" strategies, which create competition at the point of insurance purchase, would control costs by enhancing competition among health insurers and managed care plans for individual consumers. In fact, health care costs were substantially controlled in the 1990s by managed care plans operating in largely unmanaged markets (though this control faded in the 2000s), thus the alternative of simple managed care must also be considered.

Managed competition, the approach which formed the basis of the Clinton Plan in the 1990s and of the Medicare + Choice and Medicare Advantage programs (see Chapter 8), attempts to organize the market for health care finance to make health insurers, managed care plans, and integrated delivery systems (usually designated collectively as "health plans") compete with each other for beneficiary enrollment. Under managed competition proposals, consumers are often organized into purchasing alliances to give them market power in dealing with health plans. Under such proposals, health plans are usually required to sell a uniform product or a manageable number of standardized products to permit price and quality comparisons. Explicit risk selection is a real danger under managed competition, as plans could easily compete with each other for the best risks rather than by offering the best deals. Risk selection, therefore, is often outlawed and open-enrollment and community or modified community rating is required. (See Chapter 6 below for an exploration of these concepts.) Alternatively, payments to health plans may also be standardized based on risk (risk adjusted) so that health plans do not face incentives to try to select insureds based on risk.

The hope of managed competition is that health plans will compete for the business of health insurance consumers, who will be provided with comparative quality and price information to facilitate intelligent selection of health plans. Health plans, forced to keep their costs low through market competition, will in turn bargain with providers for low prices and high quality. In short, an organized market for health insurance will correct the market failures discussed earlier. See Alain C. Enthoven, Connecting Consumer Choice to the Healthcare System 39 J. Health L. 289 (2006); Alain C. Enthoven, Competition in Health Care: It Takes Systems to Pursue Quality and Efficiency, Health Aff. Web. Excl. Sept. 7, 2005, W5–420.

The strategy of managed competition was originated by Alain Enthoven, a Stanford economist. See Alain Enthoven, Health Plan (1980). It was developed by the Jackson Hole group, consisting of Enthoven, Paul Ellwood, and others. See Alain C. Enthoven, The History and Principles of Managed Competition, Health Affairs, Supp. 1993 at 24. It formed the basis, not only for the Clinton plan, but also for health reform legislation adopted in a number of states, including Florida, Minnesota, and Washington, in the early 1990s. A form of managed competition is currently found in the Massachusetts "Commonwealth Connector" program described above. Managed competition has long been represented by the Federal Employees Health Benefits Program, the California Public Employees Retirement System (CalPERS), and the Medicare Advantage program.

Established and proposed structures for facilitating managed competition vary considerably. Proposals usually require the creation of some sort of purchasing organization to organize a market within which health plans compete for the business of organization members. The market could include all insureds in a geographic area, all insureds except for employees of firms large enough to exercise substantial power in the market themselves, or only insureds who are not employed or are employed by firms small enough to be at a substantial disadvantage in purchasing insurance. In the Medicare Advantage program, all beneficiaries effectively become members of a market supervised by the Center for Medicare and Medicaid Services. In the FEHBP, all federal employees become part of a purchasing alliance supervised by the Office of Personnel Management. To be effective, the organized market must be large enough to achieve administrative economies of scale and for the purchasing organization to possess significant power in bargaining with health plans. As more insureds are permitted to opt out of the market, both of these strengths are compromised.

Existing examples of managed competition have enjoyed some success with holding down costs. Getting a comprehensive national system of managed competition underway, however, would be a daunting task. A particular problem would be assuring the development of enough health plans to compete in each relevant market, particularly in rural markets. The Medicare

Advantage program has addressed this problem by offering heavy subsidies for rural plans and private fee-for-service plans, but this defeats the goal of cost control. Control over risk selection by the plans would also likely be a major problem. If plans were allowed to compete for the most healthy and least costly insureds, they would have little reason to compete with respect to price. It is questionable, however, whether the technology exists currently to adjust payments made to health plans adequately for risk and thus to avoid risk selection. Managed competition also would do little to control administrative costs; indeed, it might simply add another layer of administration.

The most prevalent variant of managed competition found today is not in formal purchasing alliances, but rather at the employer level. The vast majority of large employers (and many smaller employers) offer their employees a choice among health care plans, usually requiring greater employee contributions where employees choose more expensive plans that offer greater choice of provider or other additional benefits. Many of these employers attempt to provide their employees information with which to make an informed choice, including sometimes quality information. The employee then chooses among the options, weighing cost, provider choice, and other factors. This form of managed competition has reportedly proved successful for some employers in holding down premium costs.

Several legal scholars have suggested an alternative approach to using health financing entities for controlling health care costs. Clark Havighurst, long an advocate of market-strategies, contends that health plan contracts could be written to accurately articulate and enforce consumer preferences for levels of coverage, and thus for health care cost. See Clark Havighurst, Health Care Choices (1995). Contracts could, for example, reference practice guidelines or limit liability for practitioners who adopted economical approaches to delivering care, and thus limit health care cost to the level preferred by the purchaser. Mark Hall has similarly suggested that health insurance contracts be written to limit costs. See Mark A. Hall, Making Medical Spending Decisions (1997). This model could supplement, or perhaps serve as an alternative to, managed competition.

3. *Managed Care*

Although managed competition did not in fact catch on during the 1990s as a widely applied strategy for reducing health care costs, managed care did. While managed competition involves reorganizing markets to force competition among health plans, managed care refers to the cost-control functions of health plans themselves.

There is considerable support for the argument that managed care plans were effective in controlling health care costs in the United States in the 1990s. Managed care grew rapidly during the 1990s, and remains the dominant approach to financing health care in the United States at the beginning of the 21st century. It is clear that health care cost increases slowed dramatically during the mid–1990s, and that they took off again at the beginning of the 2000s as managed care controls weakened in response to a provider, consumer, media, and legislative backlash. See Jon Gabel, et al., Health Benefits in 2003: Premiums Reach Thirteen–Year High as Employers Adopt New Forms of Cost Sharing, 22 Health Aff., Sept./Oct. 2003 at 117. There is evidence that managed care organizations were able to reduce the utilization of health care services and to negotiate significant discounts with providers, both of which held down the cost of medical care. There is, further, some evidence that higher market penetration by HMOs, the most restrictive form of managed care, can lead to moderation of cost growth through the entire market. Laurence C. Baker, et al., HMO Market Penetration and the Costs of Employer–Sponsored Health Plans, 19 Health Aff., Sept./Oct. 2000 at 121. As health care costs have risen in the past half-decade, some employers have turned back to more restrictive forms of managed care in hopes of stemming the tide.

Some argue, however, that the role of managed care in decreasing increases in health care costs has been oversold. The administrative costs of managed care are higher than those of traditional health insurance, and there is far less evidence for a causal relationship between the growth of managed care and the reduction of health care cost increases in the 1990s than is commonly assumed. See Kip Sullivan, On the "Efficiency" of Managed Care Plans, 19 Health Aff., July/August 2000 at 139. It is also possible that managed care led to a one time reduction in costs, but is not capable of stemming the long term trend of continual cost increases.

Accepting the general belief that managed care has proved an effective cost control strategy, it bears noting that the growth in managed care was driven primarily by large purchasers, employers, unions, multi-employer associations, and government programs—sophisticated purchasers that could drive a hard bargain with managed care plans. See William S. Custer, et al., Why We Should Keep the Employment–Based Health Insurance System, 18 Health Aff., Nov./Dec. 1999 at 115; Robert Kuttner, Employer–Sponsored Health Care, 340 New. Eng. J. Med. 248 (1999). Managed care growth has not primarily been driven by government policy, except in public programs, primarily Medicaid. It was also not directly driven by consumer behavior, if consumers are defined as the individuals and families who ultimately consume health care services. Consumers, indeed, are widely perceived as having resisted the excesses of managed care, contributing to the growth of less restrictive preferred provider or point-of-service plans at the expense of the more restrictive, but less costly, health maintenance organizations during the late 1990s. It may be, therefore, that market-based strategies for decreasing health care costs should focus on purchasers rather than consumers.

4. Consumer Choice in Purchasing Health Care Services: The Health Savings Account

The other point where competition might control costs is at the point of purchase of health care products and services. In general, more politically conservative or libertarian reformers have proposed the creation of markets at the point of purchase by encouraging cost-sharing and health savings accounts, primarily through changes in the tax code. Proponents of this "consumer-driven" strategy believe that the primary factor driving health care cost inflation is insurance, which shields individuals from the consequences of their own health care purchasing decisions. The collective consequence of this irresponsible individual conduct is spiraling health care inflation. The fact that employer payments for insurance premiums are not subject to income tax exacerbates this problem by encouraging individuals to purchase more insurance coverage than they would if it were not tax-subsidized.

Without insurance, consumer-driven analysts argue, excessive health care costs would not be a problem. Each individual would decide whether to spend money for a hip replacement or a new car when confronted with the choice. In the real world, however, insurance exists and is widely purchased by those who can afford it or expected as an employee benefit. Moreover, because medical expenses may in many situations outstrip the resources of all but the most wealthy, some form of insurance, private or public, is probably necessary if consumers are to have access to necessary health care services and providers are to be paid.

Advocates of the consumer-driven approach recognize the need for health insurance to cover catastrophic events, but would encourage high levels of cost-sharing (deductibles, coinsurance, and copayments) so that, to the extent possible, consumers would make trade-off choices at the point of purchase of services. Cost-sharing both encourages consumers to avoid unnecessary care and to shop for the least expensive providers when care is necessary. Some advocates of this approach would tax employee health benefits to force health insurance to compete with other consumer goods on a level playing field, although it is generally recognized that the abolition of a very popular tax subsidy would be politically impossible. Alternatively, they favor tax subsidies for health savings accounts, a form of individual self-insurance. This approach has been advocated by free market advocacy groups such as the National Center for Policy Analysis, the Cato and Galen Institutes, and the Heritage Foundation and American Enterprise Institute. See Michael F. Cannon and Michael D. Tanner, Healthy Competition: What's Holding Back Health Care and How to Free It (2005); John C. Goodman, Gerald L. Musgrave, and Devon M. Herrick, Lives at Risk (2004); John Goodman & Gerald Musgrave, Patient Power: Solving America's Health Care Crisis (1992).

Haavi Morreim has been an articulate proponent of the consumer-driven position in the legal literature:

E. HAAVI MORREIM, REDEFINING QUALITY BY REASSIGNING RESPONSIBILITY

20 Am. J.L. & Med., 79, 99 (1994).

Broad choices among health care plans are important, but probably insufficient by themselves. If patients' sole economic involvement is to select one plan over another, even with year-end monetary savings to reward a wise choice, many patients will bring to these plans the same entitlement mentality that currently prompts people to game the system or to demand virtually limitless care on the ground that paying their premium endows them with a right to receive whatever they think they need. On a narrower level, then, patients arguably need to experience directly some economic consequences of their decisions. * * *

In one proposal a high deductible, such as $3000, might be matched by a tax exempt Medical Savings Account (MSA) from which to pay routine medical bills, with supplementary catastrophic insurance to address costs exceeding this amount. The MSA funds might be initially raised by the patient, the employer, the government, or even the insurer. Since the patient would pay directly for all the ordinary costs of care, he would have serious reason to inquire whether a proposed intervention is really necessary, and how else his medical needs might be met most efficiently. At the same time, he never lacks the money to pay for care. The MSA fund is ready and waiting, and for the relatively few patients who exceed it, the catastrophic policy takes over. Further, directly paying for care in this way could save enormous administrative costs by bypassing the need to file myriad small claims with insurers. A debit card, presented at the time of service, would obviate the need to bill the patient or insurer. Any money left in the fund from year to year becomes a cushion against potential future illness and could be used for the higher health care costs usually incurred after retirement, or could even be rolled over into that person's retirement fund.

See also, E. Haavi Morreim, Diverse and Perverse Incentives of Managed Care: Bringing Patients Into Alignment, 1 Widener Law Symposium J. 89 (1996).

The question of whether this policy should be adopted at the federal level has been debated since the mid–1990s. In 1996, the Health Insurance Portability and Accountability Act established partial tax subsidies for deposits into and distributions from "medical savings accounts" for a limited number of self-employed persons and employees of small employers for a limited period of time, ultimately extended through 2003. A similar experiment was established for Medicare beneficiaries under the Medicare + Choice program by the 1997 Balanced Budget Act. In fact, very few people took advantage of the HIPAA program and no plans stepped forward to offer MSAs to Medicare recipients under the 1997 Balanced Budget Act. See GAO, Medical Savings Accounts: Results from Surveys of Insurers (GAO/HEHS–99–34, 1998).

In 2003, however, the Medicare Modernization Act renamed MSAs "health savings accounts" (HSAs) and stripped most of the limits of the HIPAA MSA program. 26 U.S.C.A. § 223. Under the MMA, favored tax treatment is extended to deposits made into HSAs (trust accounts administered by banks or insurance companies for covering qualified medical expenses) that are accompanied by insurance policies ("high-deductible health plans" or HDHPs that have at least $1100 deductibles for individual coverage and $2200 deductibles for family coverage (indexed amounts for 2007). Out-of-pocket expenses must be limited under the insurance plans to $5500 for individual coverage and $11,000 for family coverage (for 2007). The maximum tax deduction allowed for contributions into an HSA by an HSA owner or the HSA owner's employer is $2850 for an individual account and $5650 for a family account in 2007. Persons who participate in HSAs who (or whose spouses) are over 55 can deduct larger sums specified in the statute. HSA policies may cover preventive care without regard to the deductible otherwise in place. Distributions from an HSA account are not subject to taxation if they are used for medical expenses, but are subject to regular taxes plus a 10 percent excise tax if they are withdrawn for other purposes (except on the event of the participant dying or becoming disabled or becoming eligible for Medicare at age 65).

The HSA has been joined by another new health savings device, the health reimbursement arrangement, or HRA. The HRA was created not by a statute but rather by the Internal Revenue Service, which in, 2002 determined that existing legislation authorized the offer of tax subsidies for employer contributions to health savings vehicles funded by employers alone. Rev. Rul. 2002–41. The HRA has proved attractive to employers because the accounts can be held as notional accounts and thus need not be funded until the account is in fact drawn on, and because the funds in them also need not go with the employee if he or she leaves employment.

HSAs remain controversial. Debates continue, for example, as to whether HSAs coupled with high deductible health plans (HDHPs) will favor the healthy and wealthy at the expense of the poor and those with chronic medical conditions; whether consumer-driven health care (CDHC) will result in decreased health care expenditures, in increased expenditures if HSA holders spend more money on products and services that qualify for tax subsidies but are not ordinarily covered by insurance, or perhaps no significant change if the most expensive medical conditions, which result in most health care costs, are not affected by cost sharing; and whether consumers have sufficient information to make wise choices in health care or will merely find CDHC very confusing. Extensive research conducted by the Rand Corporation in the early 1980s demonstrated that requiring consumers to bear part of the costs of medical care (usually referred to as cost-sharing) in fact lowers health care expenditures. See Willard G. Manning, et al., Health Insurance and the Demand for Medical Care: Evidence from a Randomized Experiment, 77 Am. Econ. Rev. 251 (1987). But neither that study nor other less ambitious studies since that show elasticity of demand for health care have proven that cost-sharing can reduce total system-wide health care expenditures, let alone tell us how HSAs will otherwise affect health care.

The use of HSAs and HRAs has expanded rapidly since 2003, and at least 4.5 million Americans were enrolled in CDHC plans as of 2007. Our experience with these accounts is beginning to suggest some answers to the questions posed above, although many questions are still open. First, there is considerable evidence that CDHC plans tend to be chosen by wealthier persons but it is not clear that they are disproportionately chosen by healthier enrollees. In fact, many enrollees are simply members of group health plans whose employer has chosen a HDHP and offered no alternate choices to employees. Second, premiums are clearly lower for HDHPs than for conventional plans, although coverage is of course thinner. Some employers share premium savings with employees by contributing to the employees HSA, but many do not. About two thirds of employers make no contribution to the HSAs of employees with single coverage, and about half make no contribution to the HSAs of employees with family coverage. One in five HSA holders contributes nothing to an HSA. Some HSA enrollees are accumulating funds in their accounts from year to year but many are exhausting their accounts each year. Third, some studies report that CDHC members are using doctors and emergency rooms less often, are switching to generic drugs, are searching for information on providers, are carefully following treatment regimens for chronic conditions, are taking necessary medications, and are not forgoing preventive care. Other studies, however, find that CDHC plan members, and particularly those with lower incomes, are foregoing or delaying necessary medical care and skipping doses or not filling prescriptions of necessary medications. Many CDHC plans are making more comparative cost and some comparative quality information available to their members, but this information is often incomplete and primitive and often not used well. Finally, and most importantly, a two tier market seems to be developing for consumer-driven products, with poorer households receiving little in tax benefits and increasingly relying on credit card debt and even home equity loans to finance health care and facing severe financial difficulties when they encounter high cost medical problems. See Timothy Stoltzfus Jost, Health Care at Risk: A Critique of the Consumer–Driven Movement 119–49 (2007) Melinda Beeuwkes Buntin, et al., Consumer–Directed Health Care: Early Evidence About Effects on Cost and Quality, Health Aff. web excl. Oct. 24, 2006, at 516; w519; Paul Fronstin & Sara R. Collins, The 2nd Annual EBRI/Commonwealth Fund Consumerism in Health Care Survey, 2006 (2006).

Consumer-driven health care recasts the relationship between the professional and patient into a merchant-consumer relationship raising a host of issues as to medical negligence, assumption of risk, and informed consent. It also raises a number of state regulatory issues examined in Chapter 5. The law review literature on consumer-driven health care is large and growing, including Marshall Kapp, Patient Autonomy in the Age of Consumer–Driven Health Care: Informed Consent and Informed Choice, 28 J. Legal ed.(2007); W. Eugene Basanta, Consumer–Driven Health Care: Legal and Policy Implications, 29 J. Legal Med. 1 (2007); Arnold J. Rosoff, Consumer–Driven Health Care: Questions, Cautions, and an Inconvenient Truth, 28 J. Legal Med. 11 (2007); Michele Melden, Guarding Against the High Risk of High Deductible Health Plans: A Proposal for Regulatory Protections, 18 Loy. Consumer L. Rev. 403 (2006); David Pratt, Healthy, Wealthy, and Dead: Health Savings Accounts, 19 St. Thomas L. Rev. 7 (2006); Amy Monahan, The Promise and Peril of Ownership Society Health Policy, 80 Tul. L. Rev. 777 (2006); Richard L. Kaplan, Who's Afraid of Personal Responsibility? Health Savings Accounts and the Future of American Health Care, 36 McGeorge L. Rev. 535 (2005); John V. Jacobi, Consumer–Directed Health Care and the Chronically Ill, 38 U. Mich. J. L. Ref. 531 (2005); and Wendy K. Mariner, Can Consumer–Choice Plans Satisfy Patients, 69 Brook. L. Rev. 485 (2004). See also, exploring more closely the implications of consumer-driven health care for the legal relationships of patients and health care professionals and providers, Mark A. Hall and Carl E. Schneider, Courts, Contracts, and the New Medical Marketplace, 106 Mich. L. Rev. 643 (2008); Peter D. Jacobson and Michael R. Tunick, Consumer–Directed Health Care and the Courts: Let The Buyer (And Seller) Beware, 26(3) Health Aff., May/June 2007 at 704; Mark A. Hall, Paying for What You Get and Getting What You Pay For: Legal Responses to Consumer–Driven Health Care, 69 Law & Contemp. Probs. 159 (2006); and E. Haavi Morreim, High–Deductible Health Plans: New Twists on Old Challenges from Tort and Contract, 59 Vand. L. Rev. 1207 (2006).

Problem: Consumer–Driven Health Care

Would you enroll (or have you enrolled) in a CDHC plan (an HDHP coupled with an HSA or HRA)? How would its value to you compare with your current insurance plan? How would a CDHC plan affect your health care purchasing decisions? How might it simplify, or complicate, your life? What information would you need to make responsible decisions? Would you spend more money than you do now on products and services (such as some over-the-counter drugs or alternative therapies) that are not usually covered by insurance but may be tax deductible if paid for through an HSA? Would you use more or less preventive care? Would you see your personal physician more or less often? Would you use the emergency room more or less often? If you had an accidental head injury (bicycling, for example), and the emergency room physician recommended a CT scan, how would the fact that you have a $3000 deductible health plan affect your decisions?

Now consider each of the people in the *Getting Covered* problem above, the 53 year-old single janitor, the 38 year-old administrative assistant, the 24 year-old graduate assistant, and the 60 and 50 year-old professors. Assume that the university, their employer, offers a consumer-driven HDHP/HSA option with a deductible of $1500 for individual coverage and $3000 for family coverage, and with 15 percent coinsurance for further services up to out-of-pocket maximums conforming to the federal requirements. (The university's standard PPO plan has copayments that vary from $20 per visit to a primary care physician to $50 per visit to an emergency room). The consumer-driven product offers cost and quality ratings for local hospitals, and some price information for routine procedures performed by local medical groups. The consumer-driven plan costs the employee $300 a year less for individual coverage or $700 a year less for family coverage than the standard PPO plan, and the university contributes $400 a year for individuals, $700 a year for families, to the employee's HSA. Which of the employees identified in the problem would you advise to sign up for a consumer-driven plan if it were offered by their university to employees? Which would benefit most from the tax subsidy, and which not at all? Which would be most capable of putting money aside in an HSA, and which might not be able to? Which would likely face higher out-of-pocket expenses with an HSA, and which might be able to accumulate savings in their HSA? Which would be most capable of using the consumer information provided by the plan?

Problem: Health Reform

Imagine that you have been asked by a president, who was elected as a centrist (pick the party you prefer), with a vague but emphatic promise to bring down the number of uninsured while holding down health care cost inflation. You have the confidence of the President, who is distracted by many other issues. The public is generally supportive of health care reform, but is unclear on what it wants, generally suspicious of government, and opposed to major new public expenditures. Your party dominates Congress, though Congress is not necessarily responsive to presidential leadership. There is the possibility, however, of getting a reform package through, particularly if it promises to control the costs of public programs. You are asked to consider alternatively plans based on an individual mandate; tax credits for lower income families (up to 300 percent of the poverty level); high deductible health plans coupled with HSAs; a Medicare-for-all single payer system; or some mix of these options. Design a system, following these steps:

1) Clarify the values that you think should drive and govern the health care reform effort. Which is more important if trade-offs must be made—equity or efficiency? Is universal coverage essential? How quickly must it be achieved? Is it important that markets be preserved? What level of government intervention in markets is tolerable?

2) Identify the key interest groups and what their goals will be with respect to the reform package. Obvious interest groups include health care providers (doctors, hospitals, nursing facilities, pharmaceutical companies, etc.), insurers,

managed care companies, big businesses, small businesses, the states, the elderly, pro-life groups, and persons with particular diseases. Can you think of others? What divisions might occur within these groups: primary care physicians versus specialists; academic medical centers versus community hospitals; large employers versus small employers; large insurers, Blue Cross/Blue Shield plans, small insurers, and managed care plans against each other; the old versus the young, etc.? What alliances do you see forming to support or oppose various approaches? What will be the wedge issues weakening these alliances?

3) Now design a reform program that is consistent with the values that you believe are important and politically feasible, given the interest groups that you believe will be active in the debate. Consider:

a) How will you pay for the program? Will you use social insurance contributions, the income tax, mandated premium payments, some other form of tax? How will you get this part of the program through Congress?

b) What benefits should be offered by the program? Should long-term care be included? If so, should both nursing facility and home health care be covered? To what extent should mental health and substance abuse benefits be mandated? Should abortions be covered, and to what extent? What limits, if any, should be placed on coverage of "futile" care? Should utilization review be required, forbidden, or regulated? Should coverage be limited to traditional medicine, or should nurse practitioners, chiropractors, massage therapists, acupuncturists, and/or reflexologists be covered? What about eyeglasses and dental care? Should all persons get the same benefits? What organizing principle or principles govern your choices among these alternatives?

c) Who should administer and/or regulate the program? What should be the respective roles of government and private insurers or providers? What should be the respective roles of the federal and state governments? If you support a large role for the states, what effect will this have on large businesses that operate throughout the country? Should regulatory responsibilities be borne by government or private accreditation bodies?

d) Design a strategy for getting your program through Congress and implemented. Alternatively, should you tell the president that health care reform should not be the task of the federal government, but that the states should rather be allowed to experiment with different approaches to health care reform?

4) After you complete this exercise as an individual, attempt as a class to reach a consensus on each of the issues you have considered as an individual.

5) Review your response to this problem after you have completed the next chapters dealing with current programs for private and public health care financing.

Chapter 5

ACCESS TO HEALTH CARE: THE OBLIGATION TO PROVIDE CARE

INTRODUCTION

This chapter sets out the legal obligations of doctors and hospitals to treat patients needing medical care. Among the cases you will read in this chapter are cases in which patients were refused medical treatment apparently because they couldn't pay; because of their race; or because of their particular medical condition.

Ability to Pay

It is tempting to confine concerns over ability to pay for medical care to the segment of the U.S. population that is uninsured. That narrow approach misses a good portion of the problem, however.

In 2005, 43.6 million Americans (43.3 million under the age of 65) were uninsured: 9.3% of children and 19.8% of adults in the United States, percentages that were slightly increased over those of 2004 and significantly higher than those of a decade earlier. An additional 54.5 million individuals lacked health insurance for at least a part of that year; however, approximately three-fourths of those without insurance at the time of the survey (30.5 million individuals under the age of 65) had been uninsured for more than a year. CDC, Health Insurance Coverage: Early Release of Estimates from the National Health Interview Survey, 2006, available at, www.cdc.gov/nchs/data/nhis/earlyrelease/insur200706.pdf. See Hanns Kuttner & Matthew Rutledge, Higher Income and Uninsured: Common or Rare?, 26 Health Affairs 1745 (2007), for discussion of income levels of uninsured individuals.

Even those who carry some form of health insurance may find themselves unable to pay for necessary care. Private health insurance plans frequently incorporate caps on coverage or high deductibles or co-pays that may exclude individuals or families from necessary health care. See discussion of "consumer-driven" health care which relies on greater financial risk for health care expenses for insured individuals in Chapter 4.

Recent empirical work on the distribution of medical debt among individuals filing for bankruptcy gives a picture of the nature of the financial burdens of medical care and loss of income due to illness or disability. These studies indicate that inadequate funds to pay for the costs of illness reach families far above the poverty level. In fact, study participants with private health insurance faced higher out-of-pocket costs for health care on average ($13,460) than those that were uninsured when they or a family member became ill ($10,893). Furthermore, one-third of bankruptcy filers with significant medical debt had health insurance at the onset of illness but lost coverage at some point during their illness. While a generation ago only hospitalization was considered a catastrophic medical expense, nearly 60% of bankruptcy filers with medical debt identified non-hospital costs as their biggest single medical expense, including 21% identifying prescription drugs and 20%, doctor bills. Melissa B. Jacoby & Elizabeth Warren, 100 Nw. U. L. Rev. 535 (2006). See also Melissa B. Jacoby, et al., Rethinking the Debates Over Health Care Financing: Evidence From the Bankruptcy Courts, 76 N.Y.U.L.Rev. 375 (2001), concluding that "[n]early half of all bankruptcies involved a medical problem, and certain groups—particularly women heads of households and the elderly—were even more likely to report a health-related bankruptcy ... and about eighty percent [of filers] had some form of medical insurance." See also Symposium, From Risk to Ruin: Shifting the Cost of Health Care to Consumers, 51 St. Louis U. L.J. 293 (2007).

Publicly funded health insurance programs in the U.S. are quite selective. Only persons over the age of 65 (with some few interesting additions) qualify for Medicare; and only low-income individuals who fit into particular demographic groups (e.g., children, women with children, persons in nursing homes) qualify for Medicaid. See Chapter 8. In addition, particularly for individuals relying on Medicaid, access to medical care may be severely limited by the small number of physicians accepting payment from the program.

As you study the legal obligations of health care providers in this chapter, consider to what extent they reach patients who cannot pay for services. Should such obligations be broadened, or would this simply make health care providers bear social obligations that should be borne by society as a whole or responsibilities that lie with the individual patient? See discussion of distributive justice in Chapter 1.

Race-based Disparities in Treatment

From the post-Civil War era through the mid–1960s, nearly the entire hospital industry was openly racially segregated. See David Barton Smith, Healthcare's Hidden Civil Rights Legacy, 48 St. Louis U. L.J. 37 (2003) and Section IIC of this chapter. Of course, continuing residential patterns originally established as a matter of *de jure* segregation in housing produce continuing *de facto* segregation in health care facilities. David Barton Smith, et al., Separate and Unequal: Racial Segregation and Disparities in Quality Across U.S. Nursing Homes, 26 Health Affairs 1448 (2007), documenting that "blacks were significantly more likely to be served by [nursing homes] in the bottom quartile of many structural and performance measures of quality" just as blacks were more likely to be cared for in hospitals with higher mortality rates and lower technology. The story of persistent racial disparities in access to quality health care is not captured entirely in the story of formal segregation, however.

Generations of studies have reported that African–Americans, for example, experience unequal health care, whether measured in terms of access to health care services or disparities in outcomes or health status. See, e.g., Institute of Medicine (IOM), Unequal Treatment: Confronting Racial and Ethnic Disparities in Health Care (Brian D. Smedley, et al., eds., 2002); David R. Williams, Race, Health, and Health Care, 48 St. Louis U.L.J. 13(2003); Sidney D. Watson, Health Law Symposium Foreword, 48 St. Louis U.L.J. 1 (2003); Agency for Healthcare Research and Quality, National Health Care Disparities Report 2006, available at http://www.ahrq.gov/qual/nhdr06/nhdr 06.htm, finding that that African Americans received poorer quality of care on approximately three-fourths of the quality indicators studied as compared to Whites and better care on 9% of the indicators, with similar disparities for Hispanics, while poor people received lower quality care on 71% of the indicators.

One of the most influential early studies of health disparities documented that physicians' recommendations for cardiac catheterization depended entirely on the race and gender of the patient. In this study, doctors made treatment recommendations based on videotaped interviews of patients who all used the same script and presented the same symptoms but differed in race and gender. Kevin A. Schulman, et al., The Effect of Race and Sex on Physicians' Recommendations for Cardiac Catheterization, 340 NEJM 618 (1999). This and other studies expanded the focus on racial health disparities to include the quality of health care and clinical decisions. Louise G. Trubek & Maya Das, Achieving Equality: Healthcare Governance in Transition, 7 DePaul J. Health Care L. 245 (2004). The 2002 IOM study, supra, confirmed the clinical studies in finding serious "racial or ethnic differences in the quality of healthcare that are not due to access-related factors or clinical needs, preferences and appropriateness of intervention." See also, Symposium, Disentangling Fact from Fiction: The Realities of Unequal Health Care Treatment, 9 DePaul J. Health Care L. 667 (2005); Symposium, Inequities in Health Care, 29 Am. J. L. Med. 151 (2003); Symposium, Current Racial and Ethnic Disparities in Health, 1 Yale J. Health Pol'y, L. & Ethics 1 (2001); Rene Bowser, Racial Profiling in Health Care: An Institutional Analysis of Medical Treatment Disparities, 7 Mich. J. Race & L. 79 (2001); Gwendolyn Majette, Access to Health Care: What a Difference Shades of Color Make, 12 Annals Health L. 121 (2003); Lisa C. Ikemoto, In the Shadow of Race: Women of Color in Health Disparities Policy, 39 U.C. Davis L. Rev. 1023 (2006).

The development of genetic medicine has sharpened the question of whether biological differences explain some disparity in health status. Racial categories are not the equivalent of genetic categories, even though long traditions in the U.S. associate biological determinism with race. Ichiro Kawachi, et al., Health Disparities By Race and Class: Why Both Matter, 24 Health Affairs 343 (2005); Sharona Hoffman, "Racially–Tailored" Medicine Unravelled, 55 Am. U. L. Rev. 395 (2005). Furthermore, biological differences can't explain why African–Americans do not receive some medical interventions that are considered standard of care for other populations or why African–Americans are more likely to receive care in lower quality health care facilities.

Nor does socioeconomic status explain the extent of racial health disparities in the U.S. Although receiving identical coverage under Medicare, for example, significant differences in the utilization of the most common surgical procedures (including hip replacement and coronary surgeries) between black and white Medicare beneficiaries persisted. David Barton Smith, The Racial Integration of Health Facilities, 18 J. Health Pol., Pol'y & L. 851 (1993). While most empirical studies of race-based access problems are designed to exclude the impact of socioeconomic status, some argue that focusing solely on race without accounting for the interaction between race and class misses a critical part of the key for improving health status and health care access. See, e.g., Vernellia R. Randall, Racist Health Care: Reforming an Unjust Health Care System to Meet the Needs of African–Americans, 3 Health Matrix 127 (1993). See also, Camille A. Nelson, Considering Tortious Racism, 9 DePaul J. Health Care L. 905 (2005), arguing that the experience of racism increases susceptibility to certain medical conditions that seriously impact health status. The IOM report, *supra*, observed that separating race and socioeconomic status in analyzing health disparities "risks presenting an incomplete picture of the complex interrelationship between racial and ethnic minority status, socioeconomic differences and discrimination .... [and] remains an artificial exercise."

As you read the materials that follow, ask how, or whether, the legal framework of obligations on the part of providers can contribute to improving health care access by race.

Access Barriers by Medical Condition

Payment systems often distinguish among their enrollees or beneficiaries by virtue of their medical condition For example, the exclusion or severe restriction of mental health services by most private insurance plans results in inadequate access to treatment for such conditions. See, e.g., Ensuring Quality and Access in Mental Health Services, 25 Health Affairs 680 (2006). The impact can be more subtle as well: the underreimbursement of geriatricians, for example, is associated with reduced interest in the specialty and resulting negative health and cost impacts on the older population. Some persons with relatively rare medical conditions, so-called "orphan diseases," may face access problems that are generated primarily by a lack of public or private investment in interventions that could be useful.

Furthermore, some treatable medical conditions are stigmatized. Physicians hesitate to take on patients with chronic pain, for example, in part because the management of chronic pain can be a time-consuming process and require skill sets that the doctor may not have. In addition, however, physicians refuse chronic pain patients because of fear that prescribing necessary medications to effectively treat the pain will attract investigation and penalties from legal authorities. See discussion in Chapter 2. Chronic pain patients are also subject to stereotypes of addiction and malingering. There is substantial evidence that denial of adequate treatment for pain intersects directly with race and gender as well. Vence Bonham, Race, Ethnicity, and The Disparities in Pain Treatment: Striving to Understand the Causes and Solutions to the Disparities in Pain Treatment, 29 J. L. Med & Ethics 52 (2001); Diane E. Hoffmann & Anita J. Tarzian, The Girl Who Cried Pain: A Bias Against Women in the Treatment of Pain, 29 J. L. Med. & Ethics 13 (2001).

Although a good number of medical conditions are associated with social stigma, perhaps the classic presentation is the case of HIV/AIDS. Two of the cases you will study in this chapter involve patients with HIV/AIDS, a patient population that has encountered very significant barriers to treatment produced, only in part, by fears over the transmissibility of the disease. See, for example, Scott Burris, Dental Discrimination Against the HIV–Infected: Empirical Data, Law and Public Policy, 13 Yale J. on Reg. 1 (1996); Linda C. Fentiman, AIDS as a Chronic Illness: A Cautionary Tale for the End of the Twentieth Century, 61 Alb. L. Rev. 989 (1998), part of a Symposium on Health Care Policy: What Lessons Have We Learned from the AIDS Pandemic?

Two federal statutes (the Americans with Disabilities Act and the Rehabilitation Act) provide the major vehicle for claims of discrimination in care based on medical condition. As you read these materials, consider whether these statutes are adequate.

I. COMMON LAW APPROACHES

The traditional legal principle governing the physician-patient relationship is that it is a voluntary and personal relationship which the physician may choose to enter or not. Legal obligations on the part of providers to furnish care operate as exceptions to this general rule. Most of the expansion of duties to provide care has been legislative. Only very limited legal obligations have emerged from common law doctrines, as you will see in the first set of cases below.

RICKS v. BUDGE

Supreme Court of Utah, 1937.
91 Utah 307, 64 P.2d 208.

EPHRAIM HANSON, JUSTICE.

This is an action for malpractice against the defendants who are physicians and surgeons at Logan, Utah, and are copartners doing business under the name and style of the "Budge Clinic." * * * [P]laintiff alleges that he was suffering from an infected right hand and was in immediate need of medical and surgical care and treatment, and there was danger of his dying unless he received such treatment; that defendants for the purpose of treating plaintiff sent him to the Budge Memorial Hospital [BMH] at Logan, Utah; that while at the hospital and while he was in need of medical and surgical treatment, defendants refused to treat or care for plaintiff and abandoned his case. * * *

* * *

[T]he evidence shows that when plaintiff left the hospital on March 15th, Dr. [S.M.] Budge advised him to continue the same treatment that had been given him at the hospital, and that if the finger showed any signs of getting worse at any time, plaintiff was to return at once to Dr. Budge for further treatment; that on the morning of March 17th, plaintiff telephoned Dr. Budge, and explained the condition of his hand; that he was told by the doctor to come to his office, and in pursuance of the doctor's request, plaintiff reported to the doctor's office at 2 p.m. of that day. Dr. Budge again examined the hand, and told plaintiff the hand was worse; he called in Dr. D.C. Budge, another of the defendants, who examined the hand, scraped it some, and indicated thereon where the hand should be opened. Dr. S.M. Budge said to plaintiff: "You have got to go back to the hospital." * * * Within a short time after the arrival of plaintiff, Dr. S.M Budge arrived at the hospital. Plaintiff testified: "He [meaning Dr. S.M. Budge] came into my room and said, 'You are owing us. I am not going to touch you until that account is taken care of.'" (The account referred to was according to plaintiff, of some years' standing and did not relate to any charge for services being then rendered.) Plaintiff testified that he did not know what to say to the doctor, but that he finally asked the doctor if he was going to take care of him, and the doctor replied: "No, I am not going to take care of you. I would not take you to the operating table and operate on you and keep you here thirty days, and then there is another $30.00 at the office, until your account is taken care of." Plaintiff replied: "If that is the idea, if you will furnish me a little help, I will try to move."

[A]fter being dressed, he left [BMH] to seek other treatment. At that time it was raining. He walked to the Cache Valley Hospital [CVH], a few blocks away, and there met Dr. Randall, who examined the hand. Dr. Randall testified that when the plaintiff arrived at [CVH], the hand was swollen with considerable fluid oozing from it; that the lower two-thirds of the forearm was red and swollen from the infection which extended up in the arm, and that there was some fluid also oozing from the back of the hand, and that plaintiff required immediate surgical attention; that immediately after the arrival of plaintiff at the hospital he made an incision through the fingers and through the palm of the hand along the tendons that led from the palm, followed those tendons as far as there was any bulging, opened it up thoroughly all the way to the base of the hand, and put drain tubes in. * * * About two weeks after the plaintiff entered [CVH], it became necessary to amputate the middle finger and remove about an inch of the metacarpal bone.

* * *

Defendants contend: (1) That there was no contract of employment between plaintiff and defendants and that defendants in the absence of a valid contract were not obligated to proceed with any treatment; and (2) that if there was such a contract, there was no evidence that the refusal of Dr. S.M. Budge to operate or take care of plaintiff resulted in any damage to plaintiff.

* * *

Under this evidence, it cannot be said that the relation of physician and patient did not exist on March 17th. It had not been terminated after its commencement on March 11th. When the plaintiff left the hospital on March 15th, he understood that he was to report to Dr. S.M. Budge if the occasion required and was so requested by the doctor. Plaintiff's return to the doctor's office was on the advice of the doctor. While at the doctor's office, both Dr. S.M. Budge and Dr. D.C. Budge examined plaintiff's hand and they ordered that he go at once to the hospital for further medical attention. That plaintiff was told by the doctor to come to the doctor's office and was there examined by him and directed to go to the hospital for further treatment would create the relationship of physician and patient. That the relationship existed at the time the plaintiff was sent to the hospital on March 17th cannot be seriously questioned.

We believe the law is well settled that a physician or surgeon, upon undertaking an operation or other case, is under the duty, in the absence of an agreement limiting the service, of continuing his attention, after the first operation or first treatment, so long as the case requires attention. The obligation of continuing attention can be terminated only by the cessation of the necessity which gave rise to the relationship, or by the discharge of the physician by the patient, or by the withdrawal from the case by the physician after giving the patient reasonable notice so as to enable the patient to secure other medical attention. A physician has the right to withdraw from a case, but if the case is such as to still require further medical or surgical attention, he must, before withdrawing from the case, give the patient sufficient notice so the patient can procure other medical attention if he desires.[ ]

* * *

We cannot say as a matter of law that plaintiff suffered no damages by reason of the refusal of Dr. S.M. Budge to further treat him. The evidence shows that from the time plaintiff left the office of the defendants up until the time that he arrived at [CVH] his hand continued to swell; that it was very painful; that when he left [BMH] he was in such condition that he did not know whether he was going to live or die. That both his mental and physical suffering must have been most acute cannot be questioned. While the law cannot measure with exactness such suffering and cannot determine with absolute certainty what damages, if any, plaintiff may be entitled to, still those are questions which a jury under proper instructions from the court must determine.

* * *

FOLLAND, JUSTICE (concurring in part, dissenting in part).

* * *

* * * The theory of plaintiff as evidenced in his complaint is that there was no continued relationship from the first employment but that a new relationship was entered into. He visited the clinic on March 17th; the Doctors Budge examined his hand and told him an immediate operation was necessary and for him to go to the hospital. I do not think a new contract was entered into at that time. There was no consideration for any implied promise that Dr. Budge or the Budge Clinic would assume the responsibility of another operation and the costs and expenses incident thereto. As soon as Dr. Budge reached the hospital he opened negotiations with the plaintiff which might have resulted in a contract, but before any contract arrangement was made the plaintiff decided to leave the hospital and seek attention elsewhere. As soon as he could dress himself he walked away. There is conflict in the evidence as to the conversation. Plaintiff testified in effect that Dr. Budge asked for something to be done about an old account. The doctor's testimony in effect was that he asked that some arrangement be made to take care of the doctor's bill and expenses for the ensuing operation and treatment at the hospital. The result, however, was negative. No arrangement was made. The plaintiff made no attempt whatsoever to suggest to the doctor any way by which either the old account might be taken care of or the expenses of the ensuing operation provided for. * * * Dr. Budge had a right to refuse to incur the obligation and responsibility incident to one or more operations and the treatment and attention which would be necessary. If it be assumed that the contract relationship of physician and patient existed prior to this conversation, either as resulting from the first employment or that there was an implied contract entered into at the clinic, yet Dr. Budge had the right with proper notice to discontinue the relationship. While plaintiff's condition was acute and needed immediate attention, he received such immediate attention at [CVH]. There was only a delay of an hour or two, and part of that delay is accounted for by reason of the fact that the doctor at [CVH] would not operate until some paper, which plaintiff says he did not read, was signed. Plaintiff said he could not sign it but that it was signed by his brother before the operation was performed. We are justified in believing that by means of this written obligation, provision was made for the expenses and fees about to be incurred. I am satisfied from my reading of the record that no injury or damage resulted from the delay occasioned by plaintiff leaving the Budge Hospital and going to [CVH]. He was not in such desperate condition but that he was able to walk the three or four blocks between the two hospitals. * * *

CHILDS v. WEIS

Court of Civil Appeals of Texas, 1969.
440 S.W.2d 104.

WILLIAMS, J.

On or about November 27, 1966 Daisy Childs, wife of J.C. Childs, a resident of Dallas County, was approximately seven months pregnant. On that date she was visiting in Lone Oak, Texas, and about two o'clock A.M. she presented herself to the Greenville Hospital emergency room. At that time she stated she was bleeding and had labor pains. She was examined by a nurse who identified herself as H. Beckham. According to Mrs. Childs, Nurse Beckham stated that she would call the doctor. She said the nurse returned and stated "that the Dr. said that I would have to go to my doctor in Dallas. I stated to Beckham that I'm not going to make it to Dallas. Beckham replied that yes, I would make it. She stated that I was just starting into labor and that I would make it. The weather was cold that night. About an hour after leaving the Greenville Hospital Authority I had the baby while in a car on the way to medical facilities in Sulphur Springs. The baby lived about 12 hours."

[Dr. Weis] said that he had never examined or treated Daisy Childs and in fact had never seen or spoken to either Daisy Childs or her husband, J.C. Childs, at any time in his life. He further stated that he had never at any time agreed or consented to the examination or treatment of either Daisy Childs or her husband. He said that on a day in November 1966 he recalled a telephone call received by him from a nurse in the emergency room at the Greenville Surgical Hospital; that the nurse told him that there was a negro girl in the emergency room having a "bloody show" and some "labor pains." He said the nurse advised him that this woman had been visiting in Lone Oak, and that her OB doctor lived in Garland, Texas, and that she also resided in Garland. The doctor said, "I told the nurse over the telephone to have the girl call her doctor in Garland and see what he wanted her to do. I knew nothing more about this incident until I was served with the citation and a copy of the petition in this lawsuit.''

* * *

Since it is unquestionably the law that the relationship of physician and patient is dependent upon contract, either express or implied, a physician is not to be held liable for arbitrarily refusing to respond to a call of a person even urgently in need of medical or surgical assistance provided that the relation of physician and patient does not exist at the time the call is made or at the time the person presents himself for treatment.

* * *

Applying these principles of law to the factual situation here presented we find an entire absence of evidence of a contract, either express or implied, which would create the relationship of patient and physician as between Dr. Weis and Mrs. Childs. Dr. Weis, under these circumstances, was under no duty whatsoever to examine or treat Mrs. Childs. When advised by telephone that the lady was in the emergency room he did what seems to be a reasonable thing and inquired as to the identity of her doctor who had been treating her. Upon being told that the doctor was in Garland he stated that the patient should call the doctor and find out what should be done. This action on the part of Dr. Weis seems to be not only reasonable but within the bounds of professional ethics.

We cannot agree with appellant that Dr. Weis' statement to the nurse over the telephone amounted to an acceptance of the case and affirmative instructions which she was bound to follow. Rather than give instructions which could be construed to be in the nature of treatment, Dr. Weis told the nurse to have the woman call her physician in Garland and secure instructions from him.

The affidavit of Mrs. Childs would indicate that Nurse Beckham may not have relayed the exact words of Dr. Weis to Mrs. Childs. Instead, it would seem that Nurse Beckham told Mrs. Childs that the doctor said that she would "have to go" to her doctor in Dallas. Assuming this statement was made by Nurse Beckham, and further assuming that it contained the meaning as placed upon it by appellant, yet it is undisputed that such words were uttered by Nurse Beckham, and not by Dr. Weis. * * *

[The court affirmed summary judgment in favor of the defendant.]

WILLIAMS v. U.S.

United States Court of Appeals, Fourth Circuit.
242 F.3d 169 (2001).

NIEMEYER, CIRCUIT JUDGE:

* * *

The revised amended complaint in this case alleges that in October 1997, Berlie White, while at a restaurant in Cherokee, North Carolina, became short of breath, developing "various signs of respiratory distress." Asserting that he was suffering from a medical emergency, White presented himself at about 7:00 p.m. to the emergency room of the nearby Cherokee Indian Hospital

[CIH], an Indian hospital operated on the Cherokee Reservation by the United States Public Health Service. Federal employees operating the hospital refused to treat White or to refill his oxygen tank because he was not Indian. [The hospital was funded under the federal Indian Health Care Improvement Act which prohibits the hospital from treating non-Indians, with the exception of emergency medical treatment which the hospital is permitted but not required to provide to non-Indians.] They referred him to the Swain County Hospital [SCH] * * *, approximately 10 miles away. When White arrived at [SCH], he was in extreme respiratory distress, and he died the next day. The complaint alleges that White's death was caused by CIH's "refusal to provide any treatment or assistance" and "the delay of his access to medical care."

The United States filed a motion to dismiss. * * * The district court agreed, dismissing the action. In doing so, it held that * * * North Carolina has no law creating a duty in favor of a private person to provide medical treatment or to recover for a discriminatory refusal to provide medical treatment. [The plaintiff, representing White's estate, brought several claims under federal law, all of which also were dismissed.]

* * *

The North Carolina Supreme Court has held that a physician has no duty to render services to every person seeking them. See Childers v. Frye, 201 N.C. 42, 158 S.E. 744 (1931). The *Childers* court based its decision on a contract theory, concluding that a physician's decision of whether to treat a person amounts to a decision of whether to enter into a contractual relationship. In the case of an unconscious patient, where a traditional contract relationship could not be formed, the court explained that liability would then be established only if "the physician actually accepted an injured person as a patient and undertook to treat him." Holding that the common law does not limit a medical provider's discretion to turn away potential patients, the court found it unobjectionable that the doctor had refused to treat the patient because he mistakenly believed the patient was drunk.

Despite the holding in *Childers,* Williams advances four theories as to why a healthcare provider in North Carolina has a duty not to discriminate in the provision of emergency medical care. First, [plaintiff] argues that N.C.G.S. § 58–65–85, which prohibits nonprofit hospitals from discriminating on the basis of race, color, and national origin, would provide her with a cause of action against a private hospital. This provision, however, is part of North Carolina's Insurance Code and applies only to nonprofit hospitals seeking reimbursement from the North Carolina Department of Insurance. Moreover, the statute does not apply to every private hospital. Most importantly, we have been unable to find any North Carolina case that interprets this statute to give rise to a private cause of action.

Second, [plaintiff] directs us to N.C.G.S. § 131A–8, a statute pertaining to hospitals receiving state financing, which states, "All health care facilities shall be operated to serve and benefit the public and there shall be no discrimination against any person based on race, creed, color or national origin." Again, this statute does not provide a private enforcement mechanism. Arguably, the North Carolina Medical Care Commission is authorized to enforce this nondiscrimination rule under § 131A–4(B) (allowing the Commission to sue and be sued). While § 131A–15 permits "[a]ny holder of bonds or notes issued under the provisions of this Chapter" to bring suit to enforce his contractual rights under the bond, this provision does not authorize a private enforcement action against a hospital that has discriminated in violation of § 131A–8.

Third, [plaintiff] relies on the Patients' Bill of Rights, § 3C.4103, a state agency rule promulgated pursuant to the Hospital Licensure Act, N.C.G.S. § 131E–75. Again, however, the legislature provided for enforcement of this Act only by the North Carolina Department of Health and Human Services.

Finally, [plaintiff], relying on a Georgia case, asserts a common law duty based on her theory that a hospital emergency room is a "public utility." See Williams v. Hosp. Auth., 119 Ga.App. 626, 168 S.E.2d 336, 337 (1969) ("To say that a public institution which has assumed this duty and held itself out as giving such aid can arbitrarily refuse to give emergency treatment to a member of the public who presents himself with 'a broken arm and in a state of traumatic injury, suffering mental and physical pain visible and obvious to the hospital employees' is repugnant to our entire system of government"). In *Williams*, however, the court "express[ed] no opinion on the [existence of a] duty of a *private* hospital in Georgia." Id. (emphasis added). * * *

The scope of duties imposed by positive law is necessarily narrower than the reach of moral command, and this case presents a tragic circumstance, if the allegations of the complaint are true, that could have been avoided by simple obedience to a moral command. That individuals at [CIH] would deny Berlie White the most meager of medical assistance—that of refilling his oxygen tank when it had run out—at a time of extreme need is incomprehensible, particularly when these individuals were not prohibited by law from providing White with this assistance. If they did deny White this minimal care, the burden of their moral failure will surely remain with them.

AFFIRMED.

Notes and Questions

1. Why did the doctor refuse to treat Mr. Ricks? Ms. Childs? Should the courts distinguish among such cases on the basis of the reason for the refusal? If the court were willing to make a distinction, how would you go about proving the basis for the refusal in each of these cases?

2. Could you devise a claim for the plaintiff in *Williams* under the principle enunciated in *Ricks*? See, for example, New Biloxi Hospital, Inc. v. Frazier, 245 Miss. 185, 146 So.2d 882 (Miss. 1962), in which the court held a hospital liable for the death of a patient who remained untreated in the emergency room for over two hours and died twenty-five minutes after transfer to a Veterans Administration hospital. The court based its holding on the hospital's breach of the duty to exercise reasonable care once treatment had been "undertaken." The court described the scene in detail:

> Sam Frazier was a 42 year old Negro man, who had lost his left eye and his left arm, just below the elbow, during World War II. He and his wife had two young children.... [Mr. Frazier was brought to the ED after being shot.] The blast made two large holes in the upper arm and tore away the brachial artery.... Ambulance attendants carried him into the emergency room, where one of the Hospital's nurses just looked at him and walked away. He was bleeding profusely at that time. There was blood all over the ambulance

cot, and while waiting in the hospital, blood was streaming from his arm to the floor, forming a puddle with a diameter of 24–30 inches. After about twenty minutes, another Hospital nurse came, looked at Frazier and walked away.... Neither [the nurse] nor the doctor made any effort to stop the bleeding in any way. [The nurse] continued to come in and out of the emergency room on occasion, but simply looked at Frazier. He asked to see his little boy, and for water. His bleeding continued.... This summary of the evidence reflects that Frazier was permitted to bleed to death....

See also Wilmington Gen. Hospital v. Manlove, 174 A.2d 135 (Del. 1961), holding that a hospital must provide emergency care to a person who relies on the presence of an emergency room in coming to the hospital. Do the varying theories of these cases make a difference in litigating a duty to provide care? The scope of that duty? See Karen Rothenberg, Who Cares? The Evolution of the Legal Duty to Provide Emergency Care, 26 Hous.L.Rev. 21 (1989); Thomas Gionis, et al., The Intentional Tort of Patient Dumping: A New State Cause of Action to Address the Shortcomings of the Federal Emergency Medical Treatment and Active Labor Act, 52 Am. U.L. Rev. 173 (2002).

3. The court may find that a doctor has a duty to treat a particular patient based on a contractual commitment to a third party. See, for example, Hiser v. Randolph, 126 Ariz. 608, 617 P.2d 774 (1980), holding that the physician had an obligation to treat the patient in the hospital under his on-call contract with the hospital. In *Hiser*, there was some evidence that the physician refused to treat the patient because she was the wife of an attorney, although the doctor claimed it was because he was not qualified to treat her condition. See also, Miller v. Martig, 754 N.E.2d 41 (Ind. Ct. App. 2001); Millard v. Corrado, 14 S.W.3d 42 (Mo. Ct. App. 1999). But see, Seeber v. Ebeling, 36 Kan.App.2d 501, 141 P.3d 1180 (2006), holding no claim available against on-call specialist who refused to come to the hospital due to fatigue. See also, discussion of on-call physicians in Section IIA, below. Physician contracts with managed care plans usually require physicians to treat any subscriber to the plan. How might such a contract apply to discrimination claims? Under *Ricks* or *Childs,* may the doctor be liable to the patient for nontreatment if a current patient's health care plan has refused authorization for the proposed treatment? See discussion of managed care liability in Chapter 6.

4. *Williams* considers state law governing not-for-profit organizations. Federal tax-exempt status requires, arguably, that hospitals provide some level of charity care. See Chapter 10.

5. The health care provider may not have a duty to continue to treat a particular patient for a variety of reasons, including: 1) termination by mutual consent; 2) explicit dismissal by the patient; 3) services required by the patient that are outside the provider's competence and training; 4) services outside the scope of the original agreement, where the provider has limited the contract to a type of procedure, to an office visit, or to consultation only; 5) failure of the patient to cooperate with care. The "lack of cooperation" cases require actions by the patient that suggest an implied unilateral termination of the relationship on the part of the patient; for example, when the patient refuses to comply with the prescribed course of treatment or fails to return for further treatment. See, e.g., Payton v. Weaver, 131 Cal.App.3d 38, 182 Cal.Rptr. 225 (1982). All of these defenses are very fact-sensitive.

Problem: Cheryl Hanachek

Cheryl Hanachek, a resident of Boston, discovered she was pregnant during an "action" called by the city's obstetricians in protest against increasing malpractice insurance premiums for physician childbirth services. Ms. Hanachek first called Dr. Cunetto, who had been her obstetrician for the birth of her first child two years earlier. Dr. Cunetto's receptionist informed Ms. Hanachek that Dr. Cunetto was not able to take any new patients because her practice was "full." In fact, Dr. Cunetto had limited her practice due to her patient load.

About two weeks later, Ms. Hanachek called Dr. Simms, who had been recommended by her friends. Dr. Simms' receptionist told Ms. Hanachek that Dr. Simms was not taking any new patients as his malpractice premiums were so high that he was even considering discontinuing his obstetrical practice. Ms. Hanachek reported to the receptionist that she was having infrequent minor cramping, and the receptionist told her that this was "nothing to worry about at this stage." Later that night Ms. Hanachek was admitted to the hospital on an emergency basis. Ms. Hanachek was in shock from blood loss due to a ruptured ectopic pregnancy. As a result of the rupture and other complications, Ms. Hanachek underwent a hysterectomy.

She has brought suit against Dr. Cunetto and Dr. Simms. If you were representing Ms. Hanachek, how would you proceed in arguing and proving your case?

Assume now that Dr. Cunetto actually was limiting her practice on terms other than sheer volume and that she was establishing a "concierge" practice. In concierge or "boutique" medical practices, physicians limit their practice to a small number of patients who are willing to pay initial and monthly fees for increased access and other more personalized services. Sometimes these practices do not accept insurance payment for physician services. While Ms. Hanachek has insurance, assume that she could not afford to or chose not to pay the additional fees. Should the state consider restricting or prohibiting such arrangements because of the effect they may have on access to care? See Sandra J. Carnahan, Law, Medicine, and Wealth: Does Concierge Medicine Promote Health Care Choice, or Is It a Barrier to Access?, 17 Stan. L. & Pol'y Rev. 121 (2006); Frank Pasquale, The Three Faces of Retainer Care: Crafting a Tailored Regulatory Response, 7 Yale J. Health Pol'y, L. & Ethics 39 (2007).

Problem: Ethics and Law: Never the Twain Shall Meet?

The American Medical Association has adopted the following ethical principles, among others, concerning a physician's ethical duty to provide treatment to patients:

A physician shall, in the provision of appropriate patient care, except in emergencies, be free to choose whom to serve, with whom to associate, and the environment in which to provide medical care. AMA Code of Ethics.

Each physician has an obligation to share in providing care to the indigent. The measure of what constitutes an appropriate contribution may vary with circumstances such as community characteristics, geographic location, the nature of the physician's practice and specialty, and other conditions. . . . Caring for the poor should be a regular part of the physician's practice schedule. . . . Physicians are meeting their obligation, and are encouraged to continue to do so, in a number of ways such as seeing indigent patients in their offices at no cost or at reduced cost, serving at freestanding or hospital clinics that treat the poor, and participating in government programs that provide health care to the poor. . . . E–9.065 issued in 1994, AMA Council on Ethical and Judicial Affairs.

Disparities in medical care based on immutable characteristics such as race must be avoided.... Physicians should examine their own practices to ensure that racial prejudice does not affect clinical judgment in medical care. E–9.121 issued in 1992, AMA Council on Ethical and Judicial Affairs.

Assume that you represent a plaintiff: How might these ethical principles be used in a tort claim against a physician who refused to treat a particular patient or provided substandard care? Are they legally enforceable?

Now assume that you are a member of the state's medical licensure board: Would you recommend that the state adopt these standards, or perhaps some of them, as grounds for disciplinary action? See, for example, New York's medical licensure statute which provides that "[r]efusing to provide professional service to a person because of such person's race, creed, color, or national origin" constitutes grounds for discipline. N.Y.Educ. Law § 6509(6). This may be the only state statute of its kind, although a few states have incorporated prohibitions against racial discrimination in the disciplinary statutes governing other types of health care professionals, including emergency medical technicians (S.C. Code Ann. § 44–61–80(f)(7); Tenn. Code Ann. § 68–140–511(a)(1)(E)(12)) and nursing home administrators (Fla. Stat. Ann. § 468.1755), for example. Is there any reason to treat doctors differently from these other regulated professions?

If you would support incorporating these norms within the licensure statute, would you also support creating a private right of action on the part of patients so that they can sue for violations? The regulations promulgated under the hospital licensure statute of North Carolina at issue in *Williams*, for example, provide that:

> [t]he patient has the right to expect emergency procedures to be implemented without unnecessary delay [and] the right to medical and nursing services without discrimination based upon race, color, religion, sex, sexual preference, national origin, or source of payment. 10A N.C.Admin. Code tit. 13B.3302(f) & (m).

The regulations also provide that hospitals must establish internal procedures for investigating complaints of violations and that the state hospital licensing authority will investigate violations. 10A N.C.Admin. Code 13B.3303. *Williams* held that there was no private right of action under these regulations, but see Thompson v. Sun City Community Hospital, Inc., 141 Ariz. 597, 688 P.2d 605 (1984), where the court relied on state hospital regulations and standards of the Joint Commission to find a duty enforceable through private litigation. See also Vernellia R. Randall, Eliminating Racial Discrimination in Health Care: A Call for State Health Care Anti–Discrimination Law, 10 DePaul J. Health Care L. 1 (2006).

II. STATUTORY EXCEPTIONS TO THE COMMON LAW

A. EMTALA

The federal Emergency Medical Treatment and Labor Act. 42 U.S.C.A. § 1395dd (EMTALA) was enacted in response to "patient dumping," a practice in which patients are transferred from one hospital's emergency room to another's for other than therapeutic reasons. An influential study reported that transfers from private hospitals to public hospitals in Chicago increased from 1295 in 1980 to 6769 in 1983, with 24% of patients being unstable at time of transfer. Lack of insurance was the reason given for 87% of the transfers. The cost to the public hospital was $3.35 million, of which $2.81

million would not be reimbursed by insurance, Medicaid, or Medicare. Robert L. Schiff, et al., Transfers to a Public Hospital, 314 NEJM 552 (1986), one of several studies documenting such transfers. Such studies challenged the effectiveness of state law relating to emergency care and stimulated the passage of EMTALA.

EMTALA applies *only* to hospitals that accept payment from Medicare *and* operate an emergency department; however, EMTALA applies to all patients of such a hospital and not just to Medicare beneficiaries. EMTALA does not require a hospital to offer emergency room services, although some state statutes do and federal tax law strongly encourages tax-exempt hospitals to do so. As of 2007, CMS began requiring that all hospitals participating in Medicare, including those without dedicated emergency departments, be capable of providing initial treatment in emergency situations as well as arrange for referral or transfer to more comprehensive facilities as a matter of compliance with the Medicare Conditions of Participation (COPs) for hospitals. This policy targets specialty hospitals in response to cases in which such hospitals relied on 911 to provide emergency services to their patients at significant risk to their health. The application of COPs to such cases, however, does not create a private right of action for injured patients. CMS Clarifies Emergency Services Conditions of Participation for Most Medicare Facilities, 16 Health L. Rep. 565 (2007).

EMTALA specifically empowers patients to bring civil suits for damages against participating hospitals, 42 U.S.C.A. § 1395dd(d)(2)(A) but does not provide a private right of action against a treating physician. The Office of the Inspector General (OIG) of HHS enforces EMTALA against both hospitals and physicians. EMTALA litigation has burgeoned, while government enforcement has been less active. Administrative enforcement actions under EMTALA are few; monetary penalties are small; exclusion from Medicare is very rare; and there are regional differences in the number of complaints of EMTALA violations as well as the number of investigations and citations. Correction of violations rather than sanctions has been the primary goal of enforcement. GAO, Emergency Care: EMTALA Implementation and Enforcement Issues, GAO 01_747 (June 2001). HHS reported collecting $80,000 in fines from October 2006 through March 2007, approximately 20% of the amount collected in the same time frame the previous year. http://oig.hhs.gov/publications/docs/semiannual/2007/Semiannualfirsthalf07.pdf.

EMERGENCY MEDICAL TREATMENT AND LABOR ACT

42 U.S.C. § 1395dd.

(a) Medical screening requirement. In the case of a hospital that has a hospital emergency department, if any individual ... comes to the emergency department and a request is made on the individual's behalf for examination or treatment for a medical condition, the hospital must provide for an appropriate medical screening examination within the capability of the hospital's emergency department, including ancillary services routinely available to the emergency department, to determine whether or not an emergency medical condition ... exists.

(b) Necessary stabilizing treatment for emergency medical conditions and labor.

(1) In general. If any individual . . . comes to a hospital and the hospital determines that the individual has an emergency medical condition, the hospital must provide either—

(A) within the staff and facilities available at the hospital, for such further medical examination and such treatment as may be required to stabilize the medical condition, or

(B) for transfer of the individual to another medical facility in accordance with subsection (c).

(c) Restricting transfers until individual stabilized.

(1) Rule. If an individual at a hospital has an emergency medical condition which has not been stabilized . . ., the hospital may not transfer the individual unless—

(A) (i) the individual (or a legally responsible person acting on the individual's behalf) after being informed of the hospital's obligations under this section and of the risk of transfer, in writing requests transfer to another medical facility,

(ii) a physician . . . has signed a certification that[,] based upon the information available at the time of transfer, the medical benefits reasonably expected from the provision of appropriate medical treatment at another medical facility outweigh the increased risks to the individual and, in the case of labor, to the unborn child from effecting the transfer, or

(iii) [if no physician is available, another qualified person has signed the certificate] and

(B) the transfer is an appropriate transfer . . . to that facility. . . .

(2) Appropriate transfer. An appropriate transfer to a medical facility is a transfer—

(A) in which the transferring hospital provides the medical treatment within its capacity which minimizes the risks to the individual's health and, in the case of a woman in labor, the health of the unborn child;

(B) in which the receiving facility—

(i) has available space and qualified personnel for the treatment of the individual, and

(ii) has agreed to accept transfer of the individual and to provide appropriate medical treatment;

(C) in which the transferring hospital sends to the receiving facility all medical records . . . related to the emergency condition for which the individual has presented, available at the time of the transfer . . .; [and]

(D) in which the transfer is effected through qualified personnel and transportation equipment. . . .

(d) Enforcement.

(1) Civil monetary penalties.

(A) A participating hospital that negligently violates a requirement of this section is subject to a civil money penalty of not more than $50,000 for each such violation. . . .

(B) [A]ny physician who is responsible for the examination, treatment, or transfer of an individual in a participating hospital ... and who negligently violates a requirement of this section ... is subject to a civil money penalty of not more than $50,000 for each such violation and, if the violation is gross and flagrant or is repeated, to exclusion from participation in [Medicare and Medicaid]. . . .

(2) Civil enforcement.

(A) Personal harm. Any individual who suffers personal harm as a direct result of a participating hospital's violation of a requirement of this section may, in a civil action against the participating hospital, obtain those damages available for personal injury under the law of the State in which the hospital is located, and such equitable relief as is appropriate.

(B) Financial loss to other medical facility. Any medical facility that suffers a financial loss as a direct result of a participating hospital's violation of a requirement of this section may, in a civil action against the participating hospital, obtain those damages available for financial loss, under the law of the State in which the hospital is located, and such equitable relief as is appropriate. . . .

(e) Definitions. In this section:

(1) The term "emergency medical condition" means—

(A) a medical condition manifesting itself by acute symptoms of sufficient severity (including severe pain) such that the absence of immediate medical attention could reasonably be expected to result in—

(i) placing the health of the individual (or, with respect to a pregnant woman, the health of the woman or her unborn child) in serious jeopardy,

(ii) serious impairment to bodily functions, or

(iii) serious dysfunction of any bodily organ or part; or

(B) with respect to a pregnant woman who is having contractions—

(i) that there is inadequate time to effect a safe transfer to another hospital before delivery, or

(ii) that transfer may pose a threat to the health or safety of the woman or the unborn child. . . .

* * *

(3) (A) The term "to stabilize" means ... to provide such medical treatment of the condition as may be necessary to assure, within reasonable medical probability, that no material deterioration of the condition is likely to result from or occur during the transfer of the individual from a facility. . . .

(B) The term "stabilized" means ... that no material deterioration of the condition is likely, within reasonable medical probability, to result from or occur during the transfer of the individual from a facility, or, with respect to an emergency medical condition described in paragraph (1)(B), that the woman has delivered (including the placenta). . . .

(h) No delay in examination or treatment. A participating hospital may not delay provision of an appropriate medical screening examination required under subsection (a) ... or further medical examination and treatment required under subsection (b) ... in order to inquire about the individual's method of payment or insurance status.

BABER v. HOSPITAL CORPORATION OF AMERICA

United States Court of Appeals, Fourth Circuit, 1992.
977 F.2d 872.

WILLIAMS, CIRCUIT JUDGE:

Barry Baber, Administrator of the Estate of Brenda Baber, instituted this suit against Dr. Richard Kline, Dr. Joseph Whelan, Raleigh General Hospital (RGH), Beckley Appalachian Regional Hospital (BARH), and the parent corporations of both hospitals. Mr. Baber alleged that the Defendants violated the Emergency Medical Treatment and Active Labor Act (EMTALA)[ ]. The Defendants moved to dismiss the EMTALA claim under Rule 12(b)(6) of the Federal Rules of Civil Procedure. Because the parties submitted affidavits and depositions, the district court treated the motion as one for summary judgment. See Fed.R.Civ.P. 12(b).

* * *

Mr. Baber's complaint charged the various defendants with violating EMTALA in several ways. Specifically, Mr. Baber contends that Dr. Kline, RGH, and its parent corporation violated EMTALA by:

(a) failing to provide his sister with an "appropriate medical screening examination;"

(b) failing to stabilize his sister's "emergency medical condition;" and

(c) transferring his sister to BARH without first providing stabilizing treatment.

* * *

After reviewing the parties' submissions, the district court granted summary judgment for the Defendants. * * * Finding no error, we affirm.

* * *

* * * Brenda Baber, accompanied by her brother, Barry, sought treatment at RGH's emergency department at 10:40 p.m. on August 5, 1987. When she entered the hospital, Ms. Baber was nauseated, agitated, and thought she might be pregnant. She was also tremulous and did not appear to have orderly thought patterns. She had stopped taking her anti-psychosis medications, * * * and had been drinking heavily. Dr. Kline, the attending physician, described her behavior and condition in the RGH Encounter Record as follows: Patient refuses to remain on stretcher and cannot be restrained verbally despite repeated requests by staff and by me. Brother has not assisted either verbally or physically in keeping patient from pacing throughout the Emergency Room. Restraints would place patient and staff at risk by increasing her agitation.

In response to Ms. Baber's initial complaints, Dr. Kline examined her central nervous system, lungs, cardiovascular system, and abdomen. He also ordered several laboratory tests, including a pregnancy test.

While awaiting the results of her laboratory tests, Ms. Baber began pacing about the emergency department. In an effort to calm Ms. Baber, Dr. Kline gave her [several medications]. The medication did not immediately control her agitation. Mr. Baber described his sister as becoming restless, "worse and more disoriented after she was given the medication," and wandering around the emergency department.

While roaming in the emergency department around midnight, Ms. Baber * * * convulsed and fell, striking her head upon a table and lacerating her scalp. [S]he quickly regained consciousness and emergency department personnel carried her by stretcher to the suturing room, [where] Dr. Kline examined her again. He obtained a blood gas study, which did not reveal any oxygen deprivation or acidosis. Ms. Baber was verbal and could move her head, eyes, and limbs without discomfort. * * * Dr. Kline closed the one-inch laceration with a couple of sutures. Although she became calmer and drowsy after the wound was sutured, Ms. Baber was easily arousable and easily disturbed. Ms. Baber experienced some anxiety, disorientation, restlessness, and some speech problems, which Dr. Kline concluded were caused by her preexisting psychiatric problems of psychosis with paranoia and alcohol withdrawal.

Dr. Kline discussed Ms. Baber's condition with Dr. Whelan, the psychiatrist who had treated Ms. Baber for two years. * * * Dr. Whelan concluded that Ms. Baber's hyperactive and uncontrollable behavior during her evening at RGH was compatible with her behavior during a relapse of her serious psychotic and chronic mental illness. Both Dr. Whelan and Dr. Kline were concerned about the seizure she had while at RGH's emergency department because it was the first one she had experienced. * * * They also agreed Ms. Baber needed further treatment * * * and decided to transfer her to the psychiatric unit at BARH because RGH did not have a psychiatric ward, and both doctors believed it would be beneficial for her to be treated in a familiar setting. The decision to transfer Ms. Baber was further supported by the doctors' belief that any tests to diagnose the cause of her initial seizure, such as a computerized tomography scan (CT scan), could be performed at BARH once her psychiatric condition was under control. The transfer to BARH was discussed with Mr. Baber who neither expressly consented nor objected. His only request was that his sister be x-rayed because of the blow to her head when she fell.

* * *

Because Dr. Kline did not conclude Ms. Baber had a serious head injury, he believed that she could be transferred safely to BARH where she would be under the observation of the BARH psychiatric staff personnel. At 1:35 a.m. on August 6, Ms. Baber was admitted directly to the psychiatric department of BARH upon Dr. Whelan's orders. She was not processed through BARH's emergency department. Although Ms. Baber was restrained and regularly checked every fifteen minutes by the nursing staff while at BARH, no physician gave her an extensive neurological examination upon her arrival. Mr. Baber unsuccessfully repeated his request for an x-ray.

At the 3:45 a.m. check, the nurse found Ms. Baber having a grand mal seizure. At Dr. Whelan's direction, the psychiatric unit staff transported her to BARH's emergency department. Upon arrival in the emergency department, her pupils were unresponsive, and hospital personnel began CPR. The emergency department physician ordered a CT scan, which was performed around 6:30 a.m. The CT report revealed a fractured skull and a right subdural hematoma. BARH personnel immediately transferred Ms. Baber back to RGH because that hospital had a neurosurgeon on staff, and BARH did not have the facility or staff to treat serious neurological problems. When RGH received Ms. Baber for treatment around 7 a.m., she was comatose. She died later that day, apparently as a result of an intracerebrovascular rupture.

The district court granted summary judgment for Dr. Kline and Dr. Whelan because it found that EMTALA does not give patients a private cause of action against their doctors. We review this finding de novo because the interpretation of a statute is a question of law.[ ] Because we hold EMTALA does not permit private suits for damages against the attending physicians, we affirm the district court's grant of summary judgment for Dr. Whelan and Dr. Kline.

* * *

Mr. Baber * * * alleges that RGH, acting through its agent, Dr. Kline, violated several provisions of EMTALA. These allegations can be summarized into two general complaints: (1) RGH failed to provide an appropriate medical screening to discover that Ms. Baber had an emergency medical condition as required by 42 U.S.C.A. § 1395dd(a); and (2) RGH transferred Ms. Baber before her emergency medical condition had been stabilized, and the appropriate paperwork was not completed to transfer a non-stable patient as required by 42 U.S.C.A. § 1395dd(b) & (c). Because we find that RGH did not violate any of these EMTALA provisions, we affirm the district court's grant of summary judgment to RGH.

Mr. Baber first claims that RGH failed to provide his sister with an "appropriate medical screening". He makes two arguments. First, he contends that a medical screening is only "appropriate" if it satisfies a national standard of care. In other words, Mr. Baber urges that we construe EMTALA as a national medical malpractice statute, albeit limited to whether the medical screening was appropriate to identify an emergency medical condition. We conclude instead that EMTALA only requires hospitals to apply their standard screening procedure for identification of an emergency medical condition uniformly to all patients and that Mr. Baber has failed to proffer sufficient evidence showing that RGH did not do so. Second, Mr. Baber contends that EMTALA requires hospitals to provide some medical screening. We agree, but conclude that he has failed to show no screening was provided to his sister.

* * *

While [the Act] requires a hospital's emergency department to provide an "appropriate medical screening examination," it does not define that term other than to state its purpose is to identify an "emergency medical condition."

* * *

[T]he goal of "an appropriate medical screening examination" is to determine whether a patient with acute or severe symptoms has a life threatening or serious medical condition. The plain language of the statute requires a hospital to develop a screening procedure[6] designed to identify such critical conditions that exist in symptomatic patients and to apply that screening procedure uniformly to all patients with similar complaints.

[W]hile EMTALA requires a hospital emergency department to apply its standard screening examination uniformly, it does not guarantee that the emergency personnel will correctly diagnose a patient's condition as a result of this screening.[7] The statutory language clearly indicates that EMTALA does not impose on hospitals a national standard of care in screening patients. The screening requirement only requires a hospital to provide a screening examination that is "appropriate" and "within the capability of the hospital's emergency department," including "routinely available" ancillary services. 42 U.S.C.A. § 1395dd(a). This section establishes a standard, which will of necessity be individualized for each hospital, since hospital emergency departments have varying capabilities. Had Congress intended to require hospitals to provide a screening examination which comported with generally-accepted medical standards, it could have clearly specified a national standard. Nor do we believe Congress intended to create a negligence standard based on each hospital's capability. * * * EMTALA is no substitute for state law medical malpractice actions.

* * *

The Sixth Circuit has also held that an appropriate medical screening means "a screening that the hospital would have offered to any paying patient" or at least "not known by the provider to be insufficient or below their own standards."

* * *

Applying our interpretation of section (a) of EMTALA, we must next determine whether there is any genuine issue of material fact regarding whether RGH gave Ms. Baber a medical screening examination that differed from its standard screening procedure. Because Mr. Baber has offered no evidence of disparate treatment, we find that the district court did not err in granting summary judgment.

* * *

6. While a hospital emergency room may develop one general procedure for screening all patients, it may also tailor its screening procedure to the patient's complaints or exhibited symptoms. For example, it may have one screening procedure for a patient with a heart attack and another for women in labor. Under our interpretation of EMTALA, such varying screening procedures would not pose liability under EMTALA as long as all patients complaining of the same problem or exhibiting the same symptoms receive identical screening procedures. We also recognize that the hospital's screening procedure is not limited to personal observation and assessment but may include available ancillary services through departments such as radiology and laboratory.

7. Some commentators have criticized defining "appropriate" in terms of the hospital's medical screening standard because hospitals could theoretically avoid liability by providing very cursory and substandard screenings to all patients, which might enable the doctor to ignore a medical condition. See, e.g., Karen I. Treiger, Note, Preventing Patient Dumping: Sharpening COBRA's Fangs, 61 N.Y.U.L.Rev. 1186 (1986). Even though we do not believe it is likely that a hospital would endanger all of its patients by establishing such a cursory standard, theoretically it is possible. Our holding, however, does not foreclose the possibility that a future court faced with such a situation may decide that the hospital's standard was so low that it amounted to no "appropriate medical screening." We do not decide that question in this case because Ms. Baber's screening was not so substandard as to amount to no screening at all.

Mr. Baber does not allege that RGH's emergency department personnel treated Ms. Baber differently from its other patients. Instead, he merely claims Dr. Kline did not do enough accurately to diagnose her condition or treat her injury.[ ] The critical element of an EMTALA cause of action is not the adequacy of the screening examination but whether the screening examination that was performed deviated from the hospital's evaluation procedures that would have been performed on any patient in a similar condition.

* * *

Dr. Kline testified that he performed a medical screening on Ms. Baber in accordance with standard procedures for examining patients with head injuries. He explained that generally, a patient is not scheduled for advanced tests such as a CT scan or x-rays unless the patient's signs and symptoms so warrant. While Ms. Baber did exhibit some of the signs and symptoms of patients who have severe head injuries, in Dr. Kline's medical judgment these signs were the result of her pre-existing psychiatric condition, not the result of her fall. He, therefore, determined that Ms. Baber's head injury was not serious and did not indicate the need at that time for a CT scan or x-rays. In his medical judgment, Ms. Baber's condition would be monitored adequately by the usual nursing checks performed every fifteen minutes by the psychiatric unit staff at BARH. Although Dr Kline's assessment and judgment may have been erroneous and not within acceptable standards of medical care in West Virginia, he did perform a screening examination that was not so substandard as to amount to no examination. No testimony indicated that his procedure deviated from that which RGH would have provided to any other patient in Ms. Baber's condition.

* * *

The essence of Mr. Baber's argument is that the extent of the examination and treatment his sister received while at RGH was deficient. While Mr. Baber's testimony might be sufficient to survive a summary judgment motion in a medical malpractice case, it is clearly insufficient to survive a motion for summary judgment in an EMTALA case because at no point does Mr. Baber present any evidence that RGH deviated from its standard screening procedure in evaluating Ms. Baber's head injury. Therefore, the district court properly granted RGH summary judgment on the medical screening issue.

Mr. Baber also asserts that RGH inappropriately transferred his sister to BARH. EMTALA's transfer requirements do not apply unless the hospital actually determines that the patient suffers from an emergency medical condition. Accordingly, to recover for violations of EMTALA's transfer provisions, the plaintiff must present evidence that (1) the patient had an emergency medical condition; (2) the hospital actually knew of that condition; (3) the patient was not stabilized before being transferred; and (4) prior to transfer of an unstable patient, the transferring hospital did not obtain the proper consent or follow the appropriate certification and transfer procedures.

* * *

Mr. Baber argues that requiring a plaintiff to prove the hospital had actual knowledge of the patient's emergency medical condition would allow hospitals to circumvent the purpose of EMTALA by simply requiring their personnel to state in all hospital records that the patient did not suffer from an emergency medical condition. Because of this concern, Mr. Baber urges us to adopt a standard that would impose liability upon a hospital if it failed to provide stabilizing treatment prior to a transfer when the hospital knew or should have known that the patient suffered from an emergency medical condition.

The statute itself implicitly rejects this proposed standard. Section 1395dd(b)(1) states the stabilization requirement exists if "any individual ... comes to a hospital and the hospital determines that the individual has an emergency medical condition." Thus, the plain language of the statute dictates a standard requiring actual knowledge of the emergency medical condition by the hospital staff.

Mr. Baber failed to present any evidence that RGH had actual knowledge that Ms. Baber suffered from an emergency medical condition. Dr. Kline stated in his affidavit that Ms. Baber's condition was stable prior to transfer and that he did not believe she was suffering from an emergency medical condition. While Mr. Baber testified that he believed his sister suffered from an emergency medical condition at transfer, he did not present any evidence beyond his own belief that she actually had an emergency medical condition or that anyone at RGH knew that she suffered from an emergency medical condition. In addition, we note that Mr. Baber's testimony is not competent to prove his sister actually had an emergency medical condition since he is not qualified to diagnose a serious internal brain injury.

* * * [W]e hold that the district court correctly granted RGH summary judgment on Mr. Baber's claim that it transferred Ms. Baber in violation of EMTALA.

* * *

Therefore, the district court's judgment is affirmed.

Notes and Questions

1. Under what authority does the federal government require hospitals to provide emergency medical screening and treatment to people who are not covered by Medicare? Is this an appropriate use of that authority? Why does Congress not provide Medicare or other funds specifically to reimburse hospitals for EMTALA care? Why did Congress link EMTALA to participation in Medicare rather than Medicaid?

2. How far, if at all, should legal obligations of uncompensated care extend? Where did the costs now borne by the hospitals fall before the enactment of EMTALA? See, e.g., Peter J. Hammer, Medical Code Blue or Blue Light Special: Where Is the Market for Indigent Care?, 6 J. L. Soc'y 82 (2005), arguing that cross-subsidies from Medicare and private insurance traditionally allowed hospitals and doctors to provide "the types of assistance that most people would agree is something that society should provide" in the absence of a political will to make direct support possible. Should this be so? Congress has provided some funding to hospitals for providing EMTALA-required services to persons living in the United States illegally. The funding requires that the hospitals document that a patient is in the country illegally and provide that information to the federal government. Health care professionals are concerned that the documentation and reporting process discourages patients from seeking necessary care. Susan Carhart, Hospi-

tals Wait to See if New ER Funds for Undocumented Aliens Justify Costs, Risk, 14 Health L. Rep. 1443 (2005).

3. Hospital emergency departments are severely strained, but EMTALA is not the culprit. In fact, emergency department overcrowding is attributable to a number of factors that do not relate to uncompensated care; and the rate of increase in patient volume in the ED predates EMTALA. Laura D. Hermer, The Scapegoat: EMTALA and Emergency Department Overcrowding, 14 J. L & Pol'y 695 (2006), arguing that EMTALA's unfunded mandate makes the poor and uninsured scapegoats for increased emergency department overcrowding. See also, Institute of Medicine, The Future of Emergency Care in the United States Health System–Report Brief (June 2006), summarizing three reports issued by the IOM and reporting that ED overcrowding relates to changes in the hospital industry and to patterns of care for insured as well as uninsured patients. As to the hospital industry, hospital closures (often a result of increased competitive pressures; consolidation in the industry; and closure of public hospitals) resulted in fewer emergency departments at the same time as the number of patient visits increased by 20,000,000 annually. In the same vein, hospitals reduced the number of inpatient beds in order to reduce costs; and this has resulted in longer waits for admission from the ED causing patients to occupy the ED unnecessarily. Staffing issues relating to nurse shortages mean that even existing in-patient beds may be unstaffed and unavailable. The lack of medical specialists willing to be on call for ED service also results in longer occupancy per patient in the ED. Finally, the IOM reports that insured patients actually are seeking non-emergent care more frequently in the ED for several reasons, including the practice of referring insured patients to the ED when care is needed outside of regular office hours or when tests or procedures cannot be done in the office. See also Sara Rosenbaum, et al., EMTALA and Hospital "Community Engagement": The Search for a Rational Policy, 53 Buff. L. Rev. 499 (2005), reporting on effective management intervention to coordinate patient movement from ED to inpatient care in reducing overcrowding and ambulance diversion. Despite the data on ED patterns, there is still a strong perception that EMTALA is the cause of ED overcrowding. See, e.g., James Cohen, EMTALA, Is the Cure Worse Than the Disease? 21 J. of Emergency Med. 439 (2001), calling for a "major overhaul" including "an appropriate financing mechanism, a better understanding of ED operations, and the elimination of the punitive attitude toward well-trained staff who routinely treat patients rejected by the rest of the health care system."

4. The Sixth Circuit, in considering EMTALA, declared the word "appropriate" to be "one of the most wonderful weasel words in the dictionary, and a great aid to the resolution of disputed issues in the drafting of legislation." Cleland v. Bronson Health Care Group, 917 F.2d 266 (6th Cir. 1990). Why would Congress choose to leave a critical term undefined? *Baber* is typical of the majority of cases interpreting this term. How does the standard differ from that which would be used in a medical malpractice case? In contrast to the standard the courts have applied to the adequacy of medical screening, the standard generally applied to the question of whether the patient was discharged or transferred in an unstable condition is an objective professional standard. How should plaintiff structure discovery to meet these two standards? What would be the role for expert testimony, if any? May the plaintiff simply choose to pursue an "unstable transfer or discharge" claim instead of an "inappropriate screening" claim?

5. The great majority, of EMTALA claims are resolved through summary judgment, possibly reflecting judicial concerns that the Act is too broad. What is at stake for plaintiffs and defendants when federal courts resolve most EMTALA

screening claims on summary judgment rather than submitting the case to the jury? Consider whether summary judgment is appropriate:

It was for the jury, not the district court or this court, to determine the relative credibility of the parties and what occurred in the emergency room that day. We should not assume that the doctor did not hear Summers or forgot about his complaints. Nor should we assume that it was the physician's medical judgment that prompted his failure to give Summers a chest x-ray. It is possible that the doctor heard Summers' complaints and, for no legitimate reason, failed to do anything about them. That alternative would establish the essentials of an EMTALA cause of action. Dissenting opinion (Judge Heaney), Summers v. Baptist Med. Ctr. Arkadelphia, 91 F.3d 1132 (8th Cir. 1995)

6. The Supreme Court has held that proof of improper motive is not required for a violation of the EMTALA requirement that the patient be *stabilized*. Roberts v. Galen of Va., Inc., 525 U.S. 249, 119 S.Ct. 685, 142 L.Ed.2d 648 (1999). The Court expressed no opinion as to whether proof of improper motive is essential for a claim of failure to provide an appropriate screening. Is it possible to distinguish the two provisions at issue? How are they different? See Stringfellow v. Oakwood Hosp. & Med. Ctr., 409 F.Supp.2d 866 (E.D. Mich. 2005), dismissing EMTALA claim where plaintiff failed to allege improper motive for inadequate screening. The Circuits, except for the Sixth Circuit in *Cleland*, supra, have almost uniformly held that EMTALA reaches beyond economically motivated decisions and that proof of motive is not required for either a screening or a stabilization claim. Could proof of improper motive be useful to the plaintiff in distinguishing negligent misdiagnosis from an EMTALA claim? How might such proof assist plaintiff in making his or her case? How would you go about proving motive once the physician and hospital claim medical judgment as the basis for discharge or transfer?

7. In 2003, HHS promulgated final regulations detailing the circumstances that determine whether a patient has "come to" the hospital's emergency room and triggered the EMTALA obligation. 42 C.F.R. § 489.24(b). This question arises primarily when a person presents himself to a unit of the hospital (e.g., the admissions desk or a satellite facility or a separate but on-campus unit, such as a doctors' office building) or when a person carried by an ambulance, especially a hospital-owned ambulance, is taken to another, more distant hospital. In a rather notorious case, a hospital emergency department refused to aid a teenager who had been shot and lay dying 35 feet from the ER doors. Kristine M. Meece, The Future of Emergency Department Liability after the Ravenswood Hospital Incident: Redefining the Duty to Treat?, 3 DePaul J. Health Care L. 101 (1999). After this case, HHS established the "250 yard rule" requiring hospitals to satisfy EMTALA obligations if patients got that close to the hospital; but the 2003 final regulations may have reduced the zone covered by EMTALA. See, Rosenbaum, et al., supra. But see, William M. McDonnell, Will EMTALA Changes Leave Emergency Patients Dying on the Hospital Doorstep?, 38 J. Health L. 77 (2005).

8. For many years, courts dealt with the question of whether the EMTALA obligation continues once an emergency room patient has been admitted to the hospital for care. See, e.g., Bryant v. Adventist Health System/West, 289 F.3d 1162 (9th Cir. 2002), holding that the EMTALA stabilization requirement ends with admission for inpatient care unless the "admission was a ruse to avoid EMTALA's requirements;" Morgan v. North Miss. Med. Ctr., Inc., 458 F.Supp.2d 1341 (S.D. Ala. 2006), granting summary judgment to hospital where patient died hours after being discharged from inpatient care as plaintiff failed to prove a bad faith hospital admission; Thornton v. Southwest Detroit Hosp., 895 F.2d 1131 (6th Cir. 1990), holding no EMTALA claim where patient was later discharged to home

despite the documented need for post-stroke therapy which patient's insurance would not cover. HHS finally promulgated regulations in 2003 concerning the application of EMTALA to such situations. See the Problem below.

9.   The issue of the impact of hospital admission on EMTALA obligations and the question of when the patient has "come to" the emergency department intersect in the care of seriously ill newborns. See Preston v. Meriter Hospial, Inc., 284 Wis.2d 264, 700 N.W.2d 158 (2005), holding that plaintiff stated a claim for violation of EMTALA screening obligation for failure to attempt resuscitation of a premature infant born at the hospital's birthing center, with the dissent arguing that the EMTALA screening requirement does not apply to inpatients who experience emergent conditions; Lima–Rivera v UHS of Puerto Rico, Inc., 476 F.Supp.2d 92 (D.P.R. 2007), holding that EMTALA stabilization duty applies to infants born at the hospital and formally admitted to the hospital and declining to follow the 2003 regulation that dissolves the EMTALA obligations upon good faith admission. See also, CMS, Guidance on the Interaction of the Born–Alive Infants Protection Act and EMTALA, § 5410.0, State Operations Manual, stating that infants born in the hospital, but outside the emergency department may meet the requirements of having come to the emergency department but that a newborn admitted to the hospital in good faith would no longer be covered by EMTALA, although other Medicare Conditions of Participation would apply. An individual patient does not have a private cause of action for violation of COPs although the COP may be evidence of standard of care for a state malpractice or negligence claim.

10.   Emergency treatment in the ED may be provided by the emergency doctor or nurse, but it often will require the services of an on-call specialist as well. The hospital generally doesn't employ on-call specialists, but may contract with individual physicians to provide on-call services or may try to require on-call coverage by physicians with admitting privileges. The division of labor inherent in the ED/on-call relationship can be contentious and raise EMTALA risks. Consider Cherukuri v. Shalala, 175 F.3d 446 (6th Cir. 1999):

> Dr. Cherukuri determined by 4:00 A.M. that it would be best to operate on both [accident victims] to stop the internal bleeding.... But he was unable to do so for the next three hours because Dr. Thambi, the anesthesiologist on call, advised strongly against operating and did not come to the hospital. [H]e advised Dr. Cherukuri that the patients should be immediately transferred.... He advised repeatedly and adamantly that administering anesthesia for the abdominal surgery was too risky because they had no equipment to monitor its effect on the pressure in the brain.

> Dr. Cherukuri testified that over the next two hours [he and a nurse] requested Dr. Thambi by phone several times to come to the hospital but he maintained that anesthesia was out of the question and did not come. They tried to locate other anesthesiologists during this period but were unsuccessful.

* * *

> While recognizing that Dr. Thambi had made his position very clear that he did not intend to provide anesthesiology because it might kill the brain injured patients, the ALJ concluded that EMTALA required the surgeon to force Dr. Thambi to perform by expressly ordering him to administer anesthesia. The ALJ states ... that the law "necessarily required" Dr. Cherukuri to stop the bleeding for the patients to be considered "stabilized" under the statute and that this required Dr. Cherukuri to force Dr. Thambi against his

will to administer anesthesia. Nothing in EMTALA demands such a confrontation, and for good reasons.

EMTALA obligations in relation to on-call doctors are now addressed by regulations but remain an intractable problem for hospitals. See the Problem below. See also Lawrence Bluestone, Straddling the Line of Medical Malpractice: Why There Should Be a Private Cause of Action Against Physicians via EMTALA, 28 Cardozo L. Rev. 2829 (2007).

Problem: Mrs. Miller

On May 21, Mrs. Nancy Miller, who was eight months pregnant, called her obstetrician, Dr. Jennifer Gibson, at 2:00 a.m. because she was experiencing severe pain which appeared to her to be labor contractions. Dr. Gibson advised Mrs. Miller to go to the emergency department of the local hospital and promised to meet her there shortly. Mrs. Miller was admitted to the emergency department of General Hospital at 2:30 a.m., and Dr. Gibson joined her there at 3:14 a.m. After examining Mrs. Miller, Dr. Gibson concluded that Mrs. Miller had begun labor and that, despite the fact that the pregnancy had not reached full-term, the labor should be continued to delivery. At that time, Dr. Gibson asked that the on-call anesthesiologist, Dr. Martig, see Mrs. Miller to discuss anesthesia during the delivery. At the same time, the procedure to admit Mrs. Miller to the hospital's maternity floor was begun. The nurse informed Mrs. Miller that there would be a short wait because there was no space available at that point.

Dr. Martig saw Mrs. Miller at 4:00 a.m. When asked, Dr. Martig informed Mrs. Miller that he was not qualified to and would not be able to perform an epidural (a spinal nerve-block anesthesia, often used in childbirth). Instead, he gave her Demerol and left the emergency department.

At 4:30 a.m., Mrs. Miller was admitted to the labor and delivery floor. At 4:45 a.m., the obstetrical nurse observed fetal distress and called Dr. Gibson. At 4:50 a.m., Dr. Gibson concluded that Mrs. Miller had a prolapsed umbilical cord and ordered an emergency caesarean section. The OB nurse paged Dr. Martig, but he could not be located. (Dr. Martig later stated that his pager had malfunctioned.) Because Dr. Martig could not be located, Dr. Gibson and a resident performed the C-section without an anesthetic and delivered the child healthy and alive. (These facts are based on Miller v. Martig, 754 N.E.2d 41 (Ind. Ct. App. 2001).)

Assume that Mrs. Miller has brought suit against the hospital and Dr. Martig. What federal and state claims might Mrs. Miller make? Assume that Dr. Martig has filed a motion for summary judgment on all claims. What result? In your discussion of this case, include consideration of the following regulations issued by HHS under EMTALA in September 2003:

42 C.F.R. § 489.24

(d)(2) . . . Application [of screening, stabilization and transfer obligations] to inpatients

(i) If a hospital has screened an individual . . . and found the individual to have an emergency medical condition, and admits that individual as an inpatient in good faith in order to stabilize the emergency medical condition, the hospital has satisfied its special responsibilities under this section with respect to that individual.

(ii) This section is not applicable to an inpatient who was admitted for elective (nonemergency) diagnosis or treatment.

[The language of section (i) was altered from that used in the proposed regulations. The earlier language had provided: "If a hospital admits an individual with an unstable emergency medical condition for stabilizing treatment, as an inpatient, and stabilizes that individual's emergency medical condition, the period of stability would be required to be documented by relevant clinical data in the individual's medical record, before the hospital has satisfied its special responsibilities under this section with respect to that individual...." 67 Fed.Reg. 314045–01, 31496]

(j) Availability of on-call physicians.

(1) Each hospital must maintain an on-call list of physicians on its medical staff in a manner that best meets the needs of the hospital's patients who are receiving services required under this section in accordance with the resources available to the hospital, including the availability of on-call physicians.

(2) The hospital must have written policies and procedures in place—

(i) To respond to situations in which a particular specialty is not available or the on-call physician cannot respond because of circumstances beyond the physician's control....

[The proposed regulations had not included the limiting phrase: "in accordance with the resources available to the hospital."]

B. THE AMERICANS WITH DISABILITIES ACT AND SECTION 504 OF THE REHABILITATION ACT

The Americans with Disabilities Act (ADA) prohibits discrimination against persons who have or are considered to have a "disability" as defined in the statute. You may have encountered the ADA elsewhere in this casebook. Title I of the Act (42 U.S.C. § 12111), applies to employment; Title II (42 U.S.C. § 12131), applies to state and local government services; Title III (42 U.S.C. § 12181), applies to public accommodations; Title IV (42 U.S.C. § 12201) includes miscellaneous provisions, including important provisions regarding insurance. See, e.g., Chapter 2 (application to professional licensure); Chapter 7 (Medicaid); and Chapter 9 (employment).

The ADA extends an earlier federal statute (Section 504 of the Rehabilitation Act of 1973 (29 U.S.C. § 749)) which also prohibits discrimination against the disabled. The ADA and § 504 are quite similar in most respects, and courts have used cases under the Rehabilitation Act to assist in interpreting the later ADA. The Rehabilitation Act, however, is limited to programs and services receiving federal funding while the ADA applies to private programs and services as well, including hospitals and physician practices.

Patients may bring claims against health care providers directly under both the ADA and the Rehabilitation Act. The federal government has enforcement authority as well.

BRAGDON v. ABBOTT

Supreme Court of the United States, 1998.
524 U.S. 624, 118 S.Ct. 2196, 141 L.Ed.2d 540.

KENNEDY, J., delivered the opinion of the Court, in which STEVENS, SOUTER, GINSBERG, and BREYER, JJ., joined. STEVENS, J., filed a concurring opinion.

REHNQUIST, C.J., filed an opinion concurring in the judgment in part and dissenting in part, in which SCALIA and THOMAS, JJ., joined, and in Part II of which O'CONNOR, J., joined. O'CONNOR, J., filed an opinion concurring in the judgment in part and dissenting in part.

. . . We granted certiorari to review * * * whether the Court of Appeals, in affirming a grant of summary judgment, cited sufficient material in the record to determine, as a matter of law, that respondent's infection with HIV posed no direct threat to the health and safety of her treating dentist.

I

Respondent Sidney Abbott has been infected with HIV since 1986. When the incidents we recite occurred, her infection had not manifested its most serious symptoms. On September 16, 1994, she went to the office of petitioner Randon Bragdon in Bangor, Maine, for a dental appointment. She disclosed her HIV infection on the patient registration form. Petitioner completed a dental examination, discovered a cavity, and informed respondent of his policy against filling cavities of HIV-infected patients. He offered to perform the work at a hospital with no added fee for his services, though respondent would be responsible for the cost of using the hospital's facilities. Respondent declined.

* * *

* * * Notwithstanding the protection given respondent by the ADA's definition of disability, petitioner could have refused to treat her if her infectious condition "posed a direct threat to the health or safety of others."[ ] The ADA defines a direct threat to be "a significant risk to the health or safety of others that cannot be eliminated by a modification of policies, practices, procedures, or by the provision of auxiliary aids or services."[ ] * * *

The ADA's direct threat provision stems from the recognition in School Bd. of Nassau Cty. v. Arline[ ] of the importance of prohibiting discrimination against individuals with disabilities while protecting others from significant health and safety risks, resulting, for instance, from a contagious disease. In *Arline,* the Court reconciled these objectives by construing the Rehabilitation Act not to require the hiring of a person who posed "a significant risk of communicating an infectious disease to others."[ ] * * * [The ADA's] direct threat provision codifies *Arline.* Because few, if any, activities in life are risk free, *Arline* and the ADA do not ask whether a risk exists, but whether it is significant.[ ]

The existence, or nonexistence, of a significant risk must be determined from the standpoint of the person who refuses the treatment or accommodation, and the risk assessment must be based on medical or other objective evidence.[ ] As a health care professional, petitioner had the duty to assess the risk of infection based on the objective, scientific information available to him and others in his profession. His belief that a significant risk existed, even if maintained in good faith, would not relieve him from liability. To use the words of the question presented, petitioner receives no special deference simply because he is a health care professional. It is true that *Arline* reserved "the question whether courts should also defer to the reasonable medical judgments of private physicians on which an employer has relied."[ ] At most, this statement reserved the possibilty that employers could consult with individual physicians as objective third-party experts. It did not suggest that an individual physician's state of mind could excuse discrimination without regard to the objective reasonableness of his actions.

* * * In assessing the reasonableness of petitioner's actions, the views of public health authorities, such as the U.S. Public Health Service, CDC, and the National Institutes of Health, are of special weight and authority.[ ] The views of these organizations are not conclusive, however. A health care professional who disagrees with the prevailing medical consensus may refute it by citing a credible scientific basis for deviating from the accepted norm.[ ]

[An] illustration of a correct application of the objective standard is the Court of Appeals' refusal to give weight to the petitioner's offer to treat respondent in a hospital.[ ] Petitioner testified that he believed hospitals had safety measures, such as air filtration, ultraviolet lights, and respirators, which would reduce the risk of HIV transmission.[ ] Petitioner made no showing, however, that any area hospital had these safeguards or even that he had hospital privileges.[ ] His expert also admitted the lack of any scientific basis for the conclusion that these measures would lower the risk of transmission.[ ] Petitioner failed to present any objective, medical evidence showing that treating respondent in a hospital would be safer or more efficient in preventing HIV transmission than treatment in a well-equipped dental office.

We are concerned, however, that the Court of Appeals might have placed mistaken reliance upon two other sources. In ruling no triable issue of fact existed on this point, the Court of Appeals relied on the CDC Dentistry Guidelines and the 1991 American Dental Association Policy on HIV.[ ] This evidence is not definitive. * * * [T]he CDC Guidelines recommended certain universal precautions which, in CDC's view, "should reduce the risk of disease transmission in the dental environment."[ ] The Court of Appeals determined that, "[w]hile the guidelines do not state explicitly that no further risk-reduction measures are desirable or that routine dental care for HIV-positive individuals is safe, those two conclusions seem to be implicit in the guidelines' detailed delineation of procedures for office treatment of HIV-positive patients."[ ] In our view, the Guidelines do not necessarily contain implicit assumptions conclusive of the point to be decided. The Guidelines set out CDC's recommendation that the universal precautions are the best way to combat the risk of HIV transmission. They do not assess the level of risk.

Nor can we be certain, on this record, whether the 1991 American Dental Association Policy on HIV carries the weight the Court of Appeals attributed to it. The Policy does provide some evidence of the medical community's objective assessment of the risks posed by treating people infected with HIV in dental offices. It indicates:

"Current scientific and epidemiologic evidence indicates that there is little risk of transmission of infectious diseases through dental treatment if recommended infection control procedures are routinely followed. Patients with HIV infection may be safely treated in private dental offices when appropriate infection control procedures are employed. Such infection control procedures provide protection both for patients and dental personnel."[ ]

We note, however, that the Association is a professional organization, which, although a respected source of information on the dental profession, is not a public health authority. It is not clear the extent to which the Policy was based on the Association's assessment of dentists' ethical and professional duties in addition to its scientific assessment of the risk to which the ADA refers. Efforts to clarify dentists' ethical obligations and to encourage dentists to treat patients with HIV infection with compassion may be commendable, but the question under the statute is one of statistical likelihood, not professional responsibility. Without more information on the manner in which the American Dental Association formulated this Policy, we are unable to determine the Policy's value in evaluating whether petitioner's assessment of the risks was reasonable as a matter of law.

* * *

We acknowledge the presence of other evidence in the record before the Court of Appeals which, subject to further arguments and examination, might support affirmance of the trial court's ruling. For instance, the record contains substantial testimony from numerous health experts indicating that it is safe to treat patients infected with HIV in dental offices.[ ] We are unable to determine the import of this evidence, however. The record does not disclose whether the expert testimony submitted by respondent turned on evidence available in September 1994.[ ]

There are reasons to doubt whether petitioner advanced evidence sufficient to raise a triable issue of fact on the significance of the risk. Petitioner relied on two principal points: First, he asserted that the use of high-speed drills and surface cooling with water created a risk of airborne HIV transmission. The study on which petitioner relied was inconclusive, however, determining only that "further work is required to determine whether such a risk exists."[ ] Petitioner's expert witness conceded, moreover, that no evidence suggested the spray could transmit HIV. His opinion on airborne risk was based on the absence of contrary evidence, not on positive data. Scientific evidence and expert testimony must have a traceable, analytical basis in objective fact before it may be considered on summary judgment.[ ]

[P]etitioner argues that, as of September 1994, CDC had identified seven dental workers with possible occupational transmission of HIV.[ ] These dental workers were exposed to HIV in the course of their employment, but CDC could not determine whether HIV infection had resulted.[ ] It is now known that CDC could not ascertain whether the seven dental workers contracted the disease because they did not present themselves for HIV testing at an appropriate time after their initial exposure.[ ] It is not clear on this record, however, whether this information was available to petitioner in September 1994. If not, the seven cases might have provided some, albeit not necessarily sufficient, support for petitioner's position. Standing alone, we doubt it would meet the objective, scientific basis for finding a significant risk to the petitioner.

* * *

We conclude the proper course is to give the Court of Appeals the opportunity to determine whether our analysis of some of the studies cited by the parties would change its conclusion that petitioner presented neither objective evidence nor a triable issue of fact on the question of risk.

JUSTICE STEVENS, with whom JUSTICE BREYER joins, concurring.

... I do not believe petitioner has sustained his burden of adducing evidence sufficient to raise a triable issue of fact on the significance of the risk posed by treating respondent in his office. ... I join the opinion even though I would prefer an outright affirmance.[ ]

CHIEF JUSTICE REHNQUIST, with whom JUSTICE SCALIA and JUSTICE THOMAS join, and with whom JUSTICE O'CONNOR joins as to Part II, concurring in the judgment in part and dissenting in part.

* * *

II

I agree with the Court that "the existence, or nonexistence, of a significant risk must be determined from the standpoint of the person who refuses the treatment or accommodation," as of the time that the decision refusing treatment is made.[ ] I disagree with the Court, however, that "in assessing the reasonableness of petitioner's actions, the views of public health authorities ... are of special weight and authority."[ ] Those views are, of course, entitled to a presumption of validity when the actions of those authorities themselves are challenged in court, and even in disputes between private parties where Congress has committed that dispute to adjudication by a public health authority. But in litigation between private parties originating in the federal courts, I am aware of no provision of law or judicial practice that would require or permit courts to give some scientific views more credence than others simply because they have been endorsed by a politically appointed public health authority (such as the Surgeon General). In litigation of this latter sort, which is what we face here, the credentials of the scientists employed by the public health authority, and the soundness of their studies, must stand on their own. The Court cites no authority for its limitation upon the courts' truth-finding function, except the statement in School Bd. of Nassau Cty. v. Arline,[ ] that in making findings regarding the risk of contagion under the Rehabilitation Act, "courts normally should defer to the reasonable medical judgments of public health officials." But there is appended to that dictum the following footnote, which makes it very clear that the Court was urging respect for *medical* judgment, and not necessarily respect for "official" medical judgment over "private" medical judgment: "This case does not present, and we do not address, the question whether courts should also defer to the reasonable medical judgments of private physicians on which an employer has relied."[ ]

Applying these principles here, it is clear to me that petitioner has presented more than enough evidence to avoid summary judgment on the "direct threat" question. ... Given the "severity of the risk" involved here, i.e., near certain death, and the fact that no public health authority had outlined a protocol for *eliminating* this risk in the context of routine dental treatment, it seems likely that petitioner can establish that it was objectively reasonable for him to conclude that treating respondent in his office posed a "direct threat" to his safety.

* * *

JUSTICE O'CONNOR, concurring in the judgment in part and dissenting in part.

* * *

I join in Part II of The Chief Justice's opinion concurring in the judgment in part and dissenting in part, which concludes that the Court of Appeals failed to properly determine whether respondent's condition posed a direct threat. Accordingly, I agree that a remand is necessary on that issue.

Notes and Questions

1. On remand, the Ninth Circuit upheld the District Court's grant of summary judgment in favor of the plaintiff:

> The [American Dental] Association formulates scientific and ethical policies by separate procedures, drawing on different member groups and different staff complements. The Association's Council on Scientific Affairs, comprised of 17 dentists (most of whom hold advanced dentistry degrees), together with a staff of over 20 professional experts and consultants, drafted the Policy at issue here. By contrast, ethical policies are drafted by the Council on Ethics, a wholly separate body. Although the Association's House of Delegates must approve policies drafted by either council, we think that the origins of the Policy satisfy any doubts regarding its scientific foundation.

> For these reasons, we are confident that we appropriately relied on the Guidelines and the Policy.... Thus, we again conclude, after due reevaluation, that Ms. Abbott served a properly documented motion for summary judgment.

> We next reconsider whether Dr. Bragdon offered sufficient proof of direct threat to create a genuine issue of material fact and thus avoid the entry of summary judgment.... The Supreme Court suggested that one such piece of evidence—the seven cases that the CDC considered "possible" HIV patient-to-dental worker transmissions—should be reexamined. Since an objective standard pertains here, the existence of the list of seven "possible" cases does not create a genuine issue of material fact as to direct threat.... Each piece of evidence to which [defendant directs] us is still "too speculative or too tangential (or, in some instances, both) to create a genuine issue of material fact."

Abbott v. Bragdon, 163 F.3d 87 (1st Cir. 1998), cert. denied, 526 U.S. 1131, 119 S.Ct. 1805, 143 L.Ed.2d 1009 (1999).

2. Fear of transmission has been a significant though not the sole reason for rejection of patients with HIV by health care providers. As of December 2001, there have been 57 documented cases of transmission from patients to health care workers. http://www.cdc.gov/hiv/resources/factsheets/hcwprev.htm. The CDC recommends that precautions against transmission of infectious diseases (including hepatitis) generally be taken and that, for HIV in particular, certain post-exposure treatment protocols be followed to prevent seroconversion in the health care worker who is exposed to the virus. The risk of transmission of disease from needlestick is 0.3% for HIV; 1.8% for hepatitis C; and 6 to 30% for hepatitis B. For further discussion of risks of transmission from patient to health care worker and health care worker to patient, see Chapter 12.

3. In 2006, the CDC significantly altered its policy on routine screening for HIV. Under the new policy, routine voluntary HIV screening is to be "a normal part of medical practice" for all adults unless the prevalence of HIV infection is "documented" to be less than .1% in a particular provider's patient population. In addition, informed consent, beyond a general consent to medical treatment, is not required. Instead, the health care professional need only notify the patient that an HIV test will be performed unless the patient declines. Finally, the CDC asserts that counseling should not be linked to HIV testing. CDC, Revised Recommendations for HIV Testing of Adults, Adolescents, and Pregnant Women in Health–Care Settings, Sept. 22, 2006; available at http://www.cdc.gov/mmwr/preview/mmwrhtml/rr5514a1.htm. The aim of the CDC policy is to prevent AIDS transmission in the general public. The new policy raises issues concerning access to treatment for those testing positive; confidentiality of results; whether routinization of testing will lead to a practice of testing without notice; and discrimination against persons with HIV. The new screening recommendations may be barred by state law, but the CDC intends to encourage states to revise their statutes. See generally Sarah Schalman–Bergen, CDC's Call for Routine HIV Testing Raises Implementation Concerns, 35 J. L. Med. & Ethics 223 (2007); Lawrence Gostin, HIV Screening in Health Care Settings, 296 JAMA 2023 (2006). The CDC justifies its new recommendations in part upon the success of treatment for HIV/AIDS. Is access to available treatments critical to this justification?

4. *Bragdon* was eagerly awaited to resolve the question of whether asymptomatic HIV constituted a disability under the ADA. By a 5 to 4 majority the Court concluded that asymptomatic HIV qualifies as a "disability" under the ADA because, as required by the statute, it substantially limits a major life activity (of reproduction because of the risk of infection during intercourse and the risk of infection to the child). Justices Rehnquist, Scalia, and Thomas wrote a dissenting opinion arguing that reproduction is not the sort of major life activity anticipated by the Act; and further, that the assessment of limitation on reproduction must be individualized and requires the plaintiff to prove that she or he would have had a child absent the HIV. Justice O'Connor agreed with both points in a separate opinion. Subsequent to *Bragdon*, the Fifth Circuit affirmed a district court ruling that a plaintiff with asymptomatic HIV was not disabled because the record showed that his wife had undergone a surgical sterilization procedure prior to his infection with HIV. Blanks v. Southwestern Bell Communications, 310 F.3d 398 (5th Cir. 2002). But see Birch v. Jennco 2, 2006 WL 1049477 (W.D.Wis. 2006).

HOWE v. HULL
U.S. District Court, Northern District, Ohio (1994).
874 F.Supp. 779.

JOHN W. POTTER, SENIOR DISTRICT JUDGE.

* * *

Plaintiff brought suit in the current action alleging that on April 17, 1992, defendants refused to provide Charon medical treatment because he was infected with HIV. Plaintiff claims that defendants' actions violate the Americans with Disabilities Act (ADA) [and] the Federal Rehabilitation Act of 1973 (FRA). * * * The defendants vehemently dispute these claims and allegations and have moved for summary judgment on all of plaintiff's claims.

* * *

On April 17, 1992, Charon and plaintiff Howe were travelling through Ohio, on their way to vacation in Wisconsin. Charon was HIV positive. That morning Charon took a floxin tablet for the first time. Floxin is a prescription antibiotic drug. Within two hours of taking the drug, Charon began experiencing fever, headache, nausea, joint pain, and redness of the skin.

Due to Charon's condition, Charon and plaintiff checked into a motel and, after consulting with Charon's treating physician in Maine, sought medical care at the emergency room of Fremont Memorial Hospital. Charon was examined by the emergency room physician on duty, Dr. Mark Reardon. There is some dispute over what Dr. Reardon's initial diagnosis of Charon's condition was.

Dr. Reardon testified that Charon suffered from a severe drug reaction, and that it was his diagnosis that this reaction was probably Toxic Epidermal Necrolysis (TEN).[2] This diagnosis was also recorded in Charon's medical records. Dr. Reardon also testified regarding Charon's condition that "possibly it was an early stage of toxic epidermal necrolysis, although I had never seen one." Dr. Reardon had no prior experience with TEN, other than what he had read in medical school.

Plaintiff's medical expert Calabrese, however, testified that, after reviewing the medical records and Reardon's deposition, while Charon did appear to be suffering from a severe allergic drug reaction, Calabrese "did not believe that [TEN] was the likely or even probable diagnosis. * * *"

Prior to Charon's eventual transfer to the Medical College of Ohio, Dr. Reardon called Dr. Lynn at MCO and asked Lynn if he would accept the transfer of Charon. Dr. Lynn testified that at no time did Dr. Reardon mention that plaintiff had been diagnosed with the extremely rare and deadly TEN. Dr. Reardon also did not inform the ambulance emergency medical technicians that plaintiff was suffering from TEN.

Dr. Reardon determined that Charon "definitely needed to be admitted" to Memorial Hospital. Since Charon was from out of town, procedure required that Charon be admitted to the on-call physician, Dr. Hull. Dr. Reardon spoke with Dr. Hull on the telephone and informed Dr. Hull that he wanted to admit Charon, who was HIV-positive and suffering from a non-AIDS related severe drug reaction.

While Dr. Reardon and Dr. Hull discussed Charon's situation, the primary area of their discussion appears to have been whether Charon's condition had advanced from HIV to full-blown AIDS. Dr. Hull inquired neither into Charon's physical condition nor vital signs, nor did he ask Dr. Reardon about the possibility of TEN. During this conversation, it is undisputed that Dr. Hull told Dr. Reardon that "if you get an AIDS patient in the hospital, you will never get him out," and directed that plaintiff be sent to the "AIDS program" at MCO. When Dr. Hull arrived at the hospital after Dr. Reardon's shift but prior to Charon's transfer, he did not attempt to examine or meet with Charon.

* * *

2. TEN is a very serious, very rare, and often lethal skin condition that causes an indi- vidual's skin to slough off the body.

Charon was transferred to the Medical College of Ohio some time after 8:45 P.M. on April 17. After his conversation with Dr. Hull and prior to the transfer, Dr. Reardon told Charon and plaintiff that "I'm sure you've dealt with this before...." Howe asked, "What's that, discrimination?" Dr. Reardon replied, "You have to understand, this is a small community, and the admitting doctor does not feel comfortable admitting [Charon]."

* * *

Charon was admitted and treated at the Medical College of Ohio (MCO). Despite the TEN diagnosis, Charon was not diagnosed by MCO personnel as having TEN and, in fact, was never examined by a dermatologist. After several days, Charon recovered from the allergic drug reaction and was released from MCO.

* * *

Before examining the merits of defendants' contentions, the Court must look at and compare the applicable parameters of the ADA and FRA. There are three basic criteria plaintiff must meet in order to establish a prima facie case of discrimination under the ADA:

a) the plaintiff has a disability;

b) the defendants discriminated against the plaintiff; and

c) the discrimination was based on the disability.

42 U.S.C. § 12182(a); 42 U.S.C. § 12182(b). The discrimination can take the form of the denial of the opportunity to receive medical treatment, segregation unnecessary for the provision of effective medical treatment, unnecessary screening or eligibility requirements for treatment, or provision of unequal medical benefits based upon the disability. 42 U.S.C. § 12182(b)(1)(A)(i), § 12182(b)(1)(A)(iii), § 12182(b)(2)(A)(i), § 12182(b)(1)(A)(ii). A defendant can avoid liability by establishing that it was unable to provide the medical care that a patient required. 28 C.F.R. § 36.302(b)(1).

Similarly, to establish a prima facie case under the FRA the plaintiff must show

a) the plaintiff has a disability;

b) plaintiff was otherwise qualified to participate in the program;

c) defendants discriminated against plaintiff solely on the basis of the disability; and

d) the program received federal funding.

29 U.S.C. § 794(a).

[A] reasonable jury could conclude that the TEN diagnosis was a pretext and that Charon was denied treatment solely because of his disability. Further, there is no evidence to support the conclusion that Memorial Hospital was unable to treat a severe allergic drug reaction. In fact, the evidence indicates that Dr. Reardon initially planned to admit Charon for treatment. Therefore, Charon was "otherwise qualified" for treatment within the meaning of the FRA. * * *

The FRA states that "no otherwise qualified individual with a disability ... shall, solely by reason of his or her disability ... be subjected to discrimination. . . ." 29 U.S.C. § 794(a). The equivalent portion of the ADA reads "No individual shall be discriminated against on the basis of disability. . . ." 42 U.S.C. § 12182(a). It is abundantly clear that the exclusion of the "solely by reason of . . . disability" language was a purposeful act by Congress and not a drafting error or oversight:

> The Committee recognizes that the phrasing of [42 U.S.C. § 12182(a)] differs from section 504 by virtue of the fact that the phrase "solely by reason of his or her handicap" has been deleted. The deletion of this phrase is supported by the experience of the executive agencies charged with implementing section 504. The regulations issued by most executive agencies use the exact language set out in [42 U.S.C. § 12182(a)] in lieu of the language included in the section 504 statute. H.R.Rept. 101–485(II), 101st Cong., 2d Sess., 85 (1990).

The inquiry under the ADA, then, is whether the defendant, despite the articulated reasons for the transfer, improperly considered Charon's HIV status. More explicitly, was Charon transferred for the treatment of a non-AIDS related drug reaction because defendant unjustifiably did not wish to care for an HIV-positive patient? Viewing the evidence in the light most favorable to the plaintiff, the Court finds plaintiff has presented sufficient evidence to preclude a grant of summary judgment on these claims. Defendant Memorial Hospital's motion for summary judgment on the plaintiff's ADA and FRA claims will be denied.

Notes and Questions

1. Although persons with HIV/AIDS require very specialized treatment, most also need the same medical services as other generally healthy individuals and as other chronically or intermittently disabled persons. The AMA Code of Ethics provides that "a physician may not ethically refuse to treat a patient whose condition is within the physician's current realm of competence solely because the patient is seropositive for HIV." Code of Ethics, E–9.131 HIV–Infected Patients and Physicians (1992). What is the significance of the AMA's use of the word "solely?" Does the AMA's statement address the risk of transmission in medical situations? Does it intend to address unsupported fears of transmission? Does it reach homophobia? Racism? Again, should the reason for refusing the patient make a difference? Many state legislatures have amended their medical practice acts to provide that discrimination against persons with HIV is grounds for disciplinary action, and usually this is the only antidiscrimination provision in the medical practice act. See e.g., Wis. Stat. § 252.14.

2. It may be difficult in a particular case to prove the reason for the refusal of treatment. In Lesley v. Hee Man Chie, 250 F.3d 47 (1st Cir. 2001), the District Court adopted the following standard:

> The case requires us to determine how far courts should defer to a doctor's judgment as to the best course of treatment for a disabled patient in the context of discriminatory denial of treatment claims. We hold that the doctor's judgment is to be given deference absent a showing by the plaintiff that the judgment lacked any reasonable medical basis.

How would you go about proving or defending against a claim that the medical judgment defense is a subterfuge? Haavi Morreim offers the following as indicators of discriminatory decisions to withhold treatment: where the medical judgment is based on "inaccurate facts" resulting from presumptions or prejudices against persons with the patient's medical condition; where the reasoning under-lying the treatment decision is "irrational" as, for example, where a surgeon would decide not to perform surgery only because of the high risk of mortality even though the surgery would provide the patient's only hope of survival; or where the decision is based on "inappropriate values" such as a conclusion that certain persons are by race or gender inherently inferior. E. Haavi Morreim, Futilitarianism, Exoticare, and Coerced Altruism: The ADA Meets Its Limits, 25 Seton Hall L. Rev. 833 (1995). See also Mary A. Crossley, Of Diagnoses and Discrimination: Discriminatory Nontreatment of Infants with HIV Infection, 93 Colum. L. Rev. 1581 (1993). For an overview of the psychological variables surrounding a physician's refusal to treat, see Dana Richter, Not in My Office: Medical Professionals and Their Refusal to Treat HIV/AIDS Patients, 23 L. & Psych. Rev. 179 (1999). How does *Bragdon* deal with the question of medical judgment in its consideration of the direct threat issue?

Dr. Chie had been Ms. Lesley's OB/GYN for thirteen years when he discover-ed her HIV-positive status after testing as part of prenatal care. Lesley's pregnan-cy was high-risk before the diagnosis of HIV due to several factors. After making the diagnosis, Chie consulted with Lesley's psychiatrist and numerous community resources on the treatment of HIV and transmission reduction to the child and contacted the hospital and attempted to order a supply of AZT to administer during labor and delivery. Chie then recommended to Lesley that she obtain treatment at a nearby hospital that participated in NIH studies of treatment for HIV-positive women and infants and arranged for her enrollment in that protocol.

3.   The *Howe* case also included a claim under EMTALA. The court held that the plaintiff succeeded in presenting issues of material fact concerning whether or not he was stabilized prior to transfer.

C. TITLE VI

U.S. hospitals and other health care facilities were segregated by law well into the late 1960s and by custom for some time thereafter. White-only hospitals refused admission to African–American citizens, and those white-dominated hospitals that did admit African–Americans segregated them to separate units. Even publicly owned hospitals and hospitals funded by the federal government were segregated by race.

The post-World War II Hill–Burton program invested millions of federal tax dollars in the construction of hospitals across the country. The Hill–Burton legislation specifically institutionalized federally funded racial discrim-ination as it allowed federally funded hospitals to exclude African–Americans if other facilities were available. The segregated facilities available were hardly equal either by definition or in fact. For example, the ward for African Americans in the community hospital in Wilmington, North Carolina, held only 25 beds and two toilets in a building separated from the main building so that surgery patients had to be transported across an open yard and neither of the two hospitals (one public and one private) in Broward County, Florida, admitted patients from the more than 30,000 African Americans residing in the county. Segregation certainly trumped ability to pay. In 1950s Chicago, African American union members with generous health insurance plans were steered almost entirely to Cook County Hospital despite the presence of nearer facilities. See David Barton Smith, Health Care Divided: Race and Healing A Nation (1999). Not until 1962, did a federal Court of Appeals declare the "separate but equal" provision of the Hill–Burton Act unconstitutional. Simkins v. Moses H. Cone Mem'l Hosp., 323 F.2d 969 (4th Cir. 1963), cert. denied, 376 U.S. 938 (1964). That decision provided an impetus for civil rights legislation and came just as Medicare and Medicaid legislation was being considered by Congress.

Title VI of the Civil Rights Act of 1964 (42 U.S.C.A. § 2000d *et seq.*) prohibits discrimination on the basis of race, color, or national origin by any program receiving federal financial assistance. With the advent of Medicare and Medicaid, enforcement of the nondiscrimination requirement of Title VI would have reached into most parts of the health care system from hospitals to physician offices to nursing homes. For some hospitals, Title VI may have provided cover for them to integrate in the face of opposition from some members of the public, their medical staffs, or their boards. See David Barton Smith, supra.

The implementation of Title VI, however, proved to be quite limited. First, the precursor of HHS declared that Title VI did not apply to physicians who received payment under Part B of Medicare, interpreting that program as a "contract of insurance" rather than payment of public funds. Second, hospitals could remain segregated *de facto* even while assuring the federal government that they did not discriminate if the physicians with admitting privileges refused to admit African Americans and if doctors who would admit more broadly were excluded from privileges. The Department originally threatened such hospitals, but then retreated. See David Barton Smith, Healthcare's Hidden Civil Rights Legacy, 48 St. Louis U. L.J. 37 (2003). See also Rene Bowser, Medical Civil Rights: The Exclusion of Physicians of Color from Managed Care: Business or Bias?, 4 Hastings Race Poverty L.J. 1 (2006).

Finally, the U.S. Supreme Court decided a landmark case in 2001 restricting the ability of individuals to sue under Title VI. In Alexander v. Sandoval, 532 U.S. 275, 121 S.Ct. 1511, 149 L.Ed.2d 517 (2001), the Court held that only intentional discrimination is actionable through private suit under Title VI. The 5–4 majority held that only the federal government has the power to pursue a remedy for disparate impact claims.

Prior to *Sandoval*, the most successful of Title VI private litigation efforts challenged Tennessee's Medicaid plan. Linton v. Commissioner of Health and Environment, 779 F.Supp. 925 (M.D. Tenn. 1990), aff'd, 65 F.3d 508 (6th Cir. 1995), cert. denied, 517 U.S. 1155, 116 S.Ct. 1542, 134 L.Ed.2d 646 (1996), illustrates the impact of financing programs and institutional organization upon access to health care. Plaintiffs in *Linton* challenged state law that allowed nursing homes to limit the number of beds that would be certified for Medicaid and to decertify individual beds (i.e., accepting private pay and excluding Medicaid beneficiaries) rather than foregoing Medicaid payments entirely. The trial court in *Linton* concluded:

> [T]he limited bed certification policy . . . leads to disruption of care and displacement of Medicaid patients after they have been admitted to a nursing home. Such displacement often occurs when a patient exhausts his or her financial resources and attempts transition from private pay to Medicaid. In this situation, a patient who already occupies a bed in a nursing home is told that his or her bed is no longer available to the patient because he or she is dependent upon Medicaid. . . .

... The Court is persuaded by the depositions, affidavits and exhibits concerning the severe impact of the limited bed certification policy. Finally, the Court is mindful of the Medicaid eligibility rules which allow eligibility for relatively more affluent patients already residing in nursing homes than those seeking initial admission. This phenomenon combined with the limited bed certification policy often renders the poorest and most medically needy Medicaid applicants unable to obtain the proper nursing home care ...

... Because of the higher incidence of poverty in the black population, and the concomitant increased dependence on Medicaid, a policy limiting the amount of nursing home beds available to Medicaid patients will disproportionately affect blacks.

Indeed, while blacks comprise 39.4 percent of the Medicaid population, they account for only 15.4 percent of those Medicaid patients who have been able to gain access to Medicaid-covered nursing home services. In addition, testimony indicates that the health status of blacks is generally poorer than that of whites, and their need for nursing home services is correspondingly greater. Finally, such discrimination has caused a "dual system" of long term care for the frail elderly: a statewide system of licensed nursing homes, 70 percent funded by the Medicaid program, serves whites; while blacks are relegated to substandard boarding homes which receive no Medicaid subsidies....

How would *Sandoval* impact the *Linton* litigation or the following claims: institutional decisions such as the decision to move from urban to suburban locations; to require pre-admission deposits or admission only by a physician with staff privileges; to place childbirth services at a suburban rather than urban hospital within an integrated delivery system; to acquire physician practices only in high income areas; or to limit the home-care agency's services to a particular geographic area? If a nursing home requires the resident or family to prove that they have resources adequate to support one or two years of care upon admission in order to be eligible for a Medicaid bed in the facility when it is needed later, is that nursing home acting in a racially discriminatory way if its Medicaid patient population is, in fact, 95% white in an area where the population is 40% minorities? What difference does *Sandoval* make to a plaintiff challenging the facility's decision? On Title VI and the problem of hospital closures in minority communities, see Brietta R. Clark, Hospital Flight From Minority Communities: How Our Existing Civil Rights Framework Fosters Racial Inequality in Healthcare, 9 DePaul J. Health Care L. 1023 (2005). On continuing segregation in nursing homes, see David Barton Smith, et al., Separate and Unequal: Racial Segregation and Disparities in Quality Across U.S. Nursing Homes, 26 Health Affairs 1448 (2007) (reporting that such segregation is most pronounced in the Midwest).

For more on the issues raised by Title VI and *Sandoval*, see Sara Rosenbaum & Joel Teitelbaum, Civil Rights Enforcement in the Modern Healthcare System: Reinvigorating the Role of the Federal Government in the Aftermath of Alexander v. Sandoval, 3 Yale J. Health Pol'y, L. & Ethics 215 (2003), in which the authors review enforcement of Title VI through private litigation and agency enforcement (which they find to be particularly lax after *Sandoval*) and propose that Congress mandate that HHS institute agency-wide initiatives to incorporate anti-discrimination standards within all federal health care funding programs. A leading expert and litigator in Title VI cases proposes new civil rights legislation to address discrimination in health care. Sidney D. Watson, Race, Ethnicity and Quality of Care: Inequalities and Incentives, 27 Am.J.L. & Med. 203 (2001) and Reforming Civil Rights with Systems Reform: Health Care Disparities, Translation Services, and Safe Harbors, 9 Race & Ethnic Anc. L. J. 13 (2003). Title VI has been enforced by the federal government, even after *Sandoval*, as it applies to requiring interpreters for patients with limited English proficiency. Lisa Ikemoto, Racial Disparities in Health Care and Cultural Competency, 48 St. Louis U. L. J. 75 (2003); Leighton Ku & Glenn Flores, Pay Now or Pay Later: Providing Interpreter Services in Health Care, 24 Health Affairs 435 (2005), discussing absence of payment for interpreters.

Legal strategies for pursuing unequal treatment as a violation of law are following different paths at this point. For example, Dayna Matthew argues that the False Claims Act can provide a cause of action for inadequate care and allow private claimants to pursue damages. A New Strategy to Combat Racial Inequality in American Health Care Delivery, 9 DePaul J. Health Care L. 793 (2005). For the use of the False Claims Act in quality of care cases, see Chapters 3 and 11. See also, Sidney D. Watson, Equity Measures and Systems Reform as Tools for Reducing Racial and Ethnic Disparities in Health Care, The Commonwealth Fund (August 2005); Mary Crossley, Infected Judgment: Legal Responses to Physician Bias, 48 Vill. L. Rev. 195 (2003); Kevin Outterson, Tragedy and Remedy: Reparations for Disparities in Black Health, 9 DePaul J. Health Care L. 735 (2005).

Problem: Emmaus House

You are a volunteer attorney for a nonprofit organization that provides services to the homeless through a community center called Emmaus House. You and several other attorneys come to Emmaus House to offer legal services a couple of hours each week as part of a program organized by the local bar association. While you are there, the director of the center comes rushing into the cubicle where you are conducting interviews and tells you there is an emergency.

Mr. Jack Larkin, a homeless man who comes frequently to the center, is complaining of chest pains and shortness of breath. He has had these episodes before and, in fact, went to the public hospital very early this morning because of them. The doctor at the public hospital examined Mr. Larkin and concluded that he was not having a heart attack but rather was suffering from influenza. You and the director get Mr. Larkin into your car and take him to the nearest hospital which happens to be Eastbrook Memorial, a private hospital. Mr. Larkin is guided to a cubicle where the emergency room physician examines him. The doctor then tells you that they are going to transfer Mr. Larkin to the public hospital, twenty minutes away. What do you do?

Assume that Mr. Larkin is admitted to the public hospital but dies within the week. If you brought suit against Eastbrook, what would you have to prove? How would you structure discovery? Do you have a claim against the doctor?

Problem: What Kind of Care?

Elaine Osborne lives in Springfield. Ms. Osborne works in a minimum-wage job that provides no health insurance. As a woman with no dependent children, she would not qualify for Medicaid even if she met the income standards for eligibility. There is no public hospital in her city.

Ms. Osborne attended a free public health fair, and an evaluation by a volunteer medical student revealed a site suspicious for melanoma (cancer) on her face and some swelling of her lymph nodes. The student recommended that Ms. Osborne have a dermatologist do a biopsy as a follow up to the screening. Ms. Osborne went to the emergency department of each of the three local hospitals but was told that she was not in need of emergency care. Does Ms. Osborne have a claim against the hospitals or the medical student or the public health fair? She also called several doctors' offices but was told that they required insurance or payment in advance.

Eight months later, Ms. Osborne went to Westhaven Hospital complaining of pain and shortness of breath. She was admitted to Westhaven because it was suspected that she had had a heart attack. The emergency physicians eventually concluded, however, that her pain and shortness of breath were due to the spread of the cancer. Ms. Osborne was discharged from the hospital with a prescription for pain medication. Does she have a claim against Westhaven or the emergency physicians?

In your own community, where could Ms. Osborne go for treatment of the cancer? If Ms. Osborne had breast cancer rather than melanoma, she would probably qualify for Medicaid coverage for treatment of the cancer under the Breast and Cervical Cancer Prevention and Treatment Act of 2000, PL 106–354, which allowed states to add this particular group to their Medicaid programs. What, if anything, justifies the preferential status of breast/cervical cancer as compared to other medical conditions?

Chapter 6

PRIVATE HEALTH INSURANCE AND MANAGED CARE: STATE REGU-LATION AND LIABILITY

I. INSURANCE AND MANAGED CARE: SOME BASIC CONCEPTS

A. THE CONCEPT OF MANAGED CARE

The United States is unique among modern industrialized nations in the extent to which it relies on private payment for health care services. In 2006 Americans paid $256.5 billion out-of-pocket to health care providers for health care services, twelve percent of the $2,105.5 billion national health expenditures in that year. Private health insurance, amounting to $723.4 billion, covered thirty-four percent of personal health care costs. The federal and state governments paid $970.3 billion, most of the rest, or forty-six percent of the total. The government, however, finances primarily health care for the elderly and disabled, and for lower-income pregnant women and children. Most working age Americans rely on private health insurance to cover the cost of their health care. Today, of course, private health insurance is usually provided through some form of managed care.

Until the early 1990s, it was possible, and indeed sensible, to make a distinction between insurance (meaning indemnity or service benefit insurance) and managed care as different approaches to financing health care. In fact, state regulatory programs continue even now to treat traditional commercial insurance, Blue Cross and Blue Shield plans, and some forms of managed care organizations differently. But, in general, health insurance has become managed care, and it no longer makes sense to consider them as distinct approaches to health care finance, although it continues to be useful to distinguish between the insurance and care management function of managed care.

Health insurance in the United States is of quite recent origin. It did not become truly widespread until the Great Depression of the 1930s. Some employers and unions offered employee medical care programs earlier, often through their own contracted physicians or clinics. Nevertheless, prior to the 1930s, health insurance was very unusual. Most Americans paid for health care services out of pocket. During the Depression, however, hospitals reacted to their extreme financial distress by forming hospital-sponsored health plans to ensure a more consistent flow of revenues, and these plans became the Blue Cross plans. These plans were called "service benefit" plans because they paid hospitals for services directly, based on payment rates that were negotiated with participating hospitals. They charged the same "community-rated" premium to the whole community. The states created special incorporation statutes and regulatory programs for Blue Cross plans, and often exempted them from state taxes as well. In the late 1930s and 1940s, doctors followed on the accomplishment of the Blue Cross plans by creating their own Blue Shield plans, which operated in much the same way.

Observing the success of Blue Cross and Blue Shield plans, commercial insurers began to offer health insurance themselves, providing "indemnity coverage." Commercial insurers, unlike the Blue Cross and Blue Shield plans, did not pay providers directly, but rather indemnified their insureds for services, first for hospital expenses, and later for surgery and medical services. Commercial insurers were often able to pick off less expensive groups by offering lower premiums based on the lower expected costs of these groups, i.e. by using "experience rating."

Originally, most employment-related group insurance plans were paid for through a payroll check-off system, under which employers simply took the premiums out of the employee's wages. After World War II, however, unions focused collective bargaining negotiations on getting employers to pick up the cost of health care. Provisions of the 1954 Internal Revenue Code that permitted employers to claim health insurance premiums as business expenses, while not taxing the premiums to employees as income, encouraged the rapid spread of health insurance as an employee benefit and commercial insurers encouraged employers to fund health insurance by offering employers "rebates" of a portion of the premiums they paid. The Employee Retirement Income Security Act of 1974 (ERISA) further encouraged employment-based insurance by freeing employers who self-insured from state insurance regulation. By the 1970s and 1980s the vast majority of Americans had health insurance through their jobs. See Timothy Stoltzfus Jost, Health Care at Risk, 42–69 (2007).

Throughout the second half of the twentieth century there were always prepaid health plans, such as the Kaiser Permanente group in California, the Group Health Association of Washington, D.C., and the Health Insurance Plan of Greater New York. Prepaid medical practice was vigorously opposed by organized medicine, however. Indeed, the AMA was convicted of criminal antitrust violations in 1942 for its efforts to suppress it. AMA v. United States, 130 F.2d 233 (D.C.Cir.1942), affirmed, 317 U.S. 519, 63 S.Ct. 326, 87 L.Ed. 434 (1943). In the 1970s, Paul Ellwood renamed prepaid health care "Health Maintenance Organizations," and federal legislation to encourage the growth of HMOs was adopted in 1973.

It was not federal incentives, however, but double-digit percentage increases in health insurance premiums in the late 1980s and early 1990s that led to the triumph of "managed care," a term that emerged to describe HMOs and other forms of health insurance that attempted not just to pay for, but also to control the price, utilization, and sometimes even quality of, health care services. Most of the surviving Blue Cross and Blue Shield plans (and indeed most state Medicaid programs and, to a lesser extent, Medicare) now predominantly offer managed care products. Private health care finance in the United States has become managed care. But what exactly is "managed care"?

JACOB S. HACKER AND THEODORE R. MARMOR, HOW NOT TO THINK ABOUT "MANAGED CARE"

32 U. Mich. J. L. Ref. 661 (1999).

* * * The very term "managed care"—much like that ubiquitous reform phrase of the early 1990s, "managed competition"—is a confused assemblage of sloganeering, aspirational rhetoric, and business school jargon that sadly reflects the general state of discourse about American medical institutions. Because "managed care" is an incoherent subject, most claims about it will suffer from incoherence as well. * * *

* * *

The expression "managed care" came into widespread use only in the past decade. * * * The term "managed care" does not appear once in Paul Starr's exhaustive 1982 history of American medical care, The Social Transformation of American Medicine, nor can it be found in other books on American health policy written before the early 1980s. * * *

From the beginning, "managed care" was a category with a strong ideological edge, employed to imply competence, concern, and, above all, control over a dangerously unfettered health insurance structure. "Managed care," * * * was an alternative "to the unbridled fee-for-service non-system" that sent "blank checks to hospitals, doctors, dentists, etc." and led to "referrals of dubious necessity" and "unmanaged and uncoordinated care . . . of poor or dubious quality." As these words indicate, managed care was portrayed less as a means to control patient behavior than as a way to bring doctors and hospitals in line with perceived economic realities. Moreover, managed care promised not only cost-control but also coordination and cooperation, not only better management but also better care. By imposing managerial authority on an anarchic "non-system," managed care would simultaneously restrain costs and rationalize an allegedly archaic structure of medical care finance and delivery.

What exactly constitutes "managed care," however, has never been made clear, even by its strongest proponents. To some, the crucial distinguishing feature is a shift in financing from indemnity-style fee-for-service, in which the insurer is little more than a bill-payer, to capitated payment, in which medical providers are paid a fixed amount to treat an individual patient regardless of the volume of services delivered. However, there is nothing intrinsic in fee-for-service payment that requires open-ended reimbursement or passive insurance behavior. Conversely, many, if not most, health insurance plans labeled "managed care" do not rely primarily on capitation. To other proponents, the distinctive characteristic is the creation of administrative protocols for reviewing and sometimes denying care demanded by patients or medical professionals. Such micro-level managerial controls are likewise not universal among so-called managed care health plans. In fact, such controls may be obviated by particular payment methods, like capitation or regulated fee-for-service reimbursement, that create more diffuse constraints on medical practice. Finally, to some, what distinguishes managed care is its reliance on "integrated" networks of health professionals from which patients are required to obtain care. Yet some self-styled managed care plans have no such networks, and what is called a network by many plans is little more than a list of providers willing to accept discounted fee-for-service payments—hardly the dense coordination and integration that industry insiders routinely celebrate.

Perhaps the most defensible interpretation of "managed care" is that it represents a fusion of two functions that once were regarded as largely separate: the financing of medical care and the delivery of medical services. This interpretation, at least, provides a reasonably accurate description of the most familiar organizational entity that marched under the managed care banner until the late 1980s: the health maintenance organization (HMO), a successor to the pre-paid group practice plans that began in the 1930s. Today, however, that is no longer the case. In 1997, * * * between eighty and ninety-eight percent of today's private health insurers appear to fall into the broad category of managed care. "Managed care" therefore does not offer any guidance as to how to distinguish among the vast majority of contemporary health plans.

The standard response to this problem has been to subdivide the managed care universe into a collage of competing acronyms, most coined by industry executives and marketers: HMOs, Preferred Provider Organizations (PPOs), and Exclusive Provider Organizations (EPOs). This is the approach taken by Jonathan Weiner and Gregory de Lissovoy in their frequently cited 1993 article, Razing a Tower of Babel: A Taxonomy for Managed Care and Health Insurance Plans. [18 J. Health Pol. Pol'y & L. 75 (1993).]

* * *

The central problem with Weiner and de Lissovoy's taxonomy—and, indeed, with most contemporary commentary about health insurance—is the tendency to confuse reimbursement methods, managerial techniques, and organizational forms. For example, fee-for-service, a payment method, is regularly contrasted with "managed care," presumably an organizational form. * * *

The practice of conflating organization, technique, and incentives leads to unnecessary confusion. It means that when we contrast health plans we are often comparing them across incommensurable dimensions. * * * By conflating distinct characteristics, we also are tempted to presume necessary relationships between particular features of health plans (such as their payment method) and specific outcomes that are claimed to follow from these features (such as the degree of integration of medical finance and delivery). Finally, the desire to describe an assortment of disparate plan features with a few broad labels encourages a wild goose chase of efforts to come up with black-and-white standards for identifying plan types. * * *

* * *

In understanding the structure of health insurance, the crucial relationship is between those who deliver medical care and those who pay for it. Even a passive indemnity insurer stands between the patient and the medical provider as a financial intermediary and an underwriter of risk. Today, with risk shifting from insurers to employers, and with financial intermediaries playing more of an administrative role than in the past, the trilateral relationship is more complex. Nonetheless, it still remains the locus of the insurance contract. To characterize this trilateral relationship, we focus on three of its essential features: first, the degree of risk-sharing between providers and the primary bearer of risk (whether an insurer or a self-insured employer); second, the degree to which administrative oversight constrains clinical decisions; and, third, the degree to which enrollees in a plan are required to receive their care from a specified roster of providers. * * *

* * * Our argument is that health plans differ across at least [these] three principal dimensions * * *. Each dimension crucially affects the trilateral connections among provider, patient, and plan. We also wish to emphasize that there is no simple relationship between plan label and the placement of a plan along these axes. Staff-model HMOs may seem like the quintessence of "managed care," yet because they place financial constraints at the group level they do not necessarily concentrate as much risk on physicians as do other network-based health plans, nor do they necessarily entail as much clinical regulation at the micro-level. Microregulation may go hand in hand with restrictions on patient choice of provider, but it also may not. Indeed, management of individual clinical decisions and the creation of broad incentives for conservative practice patterns may very well be alternative mechanisms for lowering the cost of medical care. Finally, as recent developments in the health insurance market suggest, greater risk-sharing can co-exist with almost any set of arrangements. It does not require a closed network, much less strict utilization review. * * *

Notice, too, that [we make] no mention of those popular buzzwords "integration" and "coordination." Movement toward a closed network, toward greater utilization control, or toward increased risk-sharing can create the conditions under which integration or coordination may occur. They do not imply, however, that such integrative activities actually take place. Getting the right care to the right patient at the right time is a managerial accomplishment, not a product of labels.

Finally, the conventional fee-for-service versus capitation dichotomy does not remain a useful means of distinguishing among different health plans. Instead, the crucial issue is what incentives medical providers actually face. The particular mix of payment methods that create those incentives is less important and will undoubtedly change as health plans experiment with new reimbursement modalities in the future.

* * *

Note

Following the lead of Hacker and Marmor, we will not primarily examine the regulation of managed care in terms of traditional distinctions among various types of managed care organizations, but rather focus on how the states regulate the various techniques described above for managing care: networks, utilization controls, and provider incentives. Because the abbreviations Hacker and Marmor disparage are used so ubiquitously in the health law and policy literature, and because many states base their regulatory schemes on these concepts, however, we offer definitions of them here.

● Health Maintenance Organizations (HMOs) usually limit their members to an exclusive network of providers permitting their members to go to non-network providers only in extraordinary circumstances, like medical emergencies. They have also historically emphasized preventive care, and usually use incentives such as capitation payments to direct the behavior of their professionals and providers. Some HMOs provide care through their own employees or the employees of affiliated foundations (staff model HMOs), while others contract with independent networks of providers to deliver care.

● Point-of-service plans (POSs) resemble HMOs, but allow their members to obtain services outside the network with additional cost-sharing (deductibles, coinsurance, or copayments), and often subject to gatekeeper controls.

● Preferred Provider Organizations (PPOs) are organized systems of health care providers who agree to provide services on a discounted basis to subscribers. PPO subscribers are not limited to preferred, in-plan, providers, but face financial disincentives, such as deductibles or larger copayment or coinsurance obligations, if they elect non-preferred providers. PPOs usually pay their providers on a fee-for-service basis, and often use utilization review controls for certain kinds of services, like hospital admissions.

● Finally, provider-sponsored-organizations (PSOs), also called, in their various guises, integrated delivery systems (IDSs), physician-hospital organizations (PHOs), and provider-sponsored networks (PSNs), are networks organized by providers that contract directly with employers or other purchasers of health benefits to provide their own services on a capitated basis.

Before we proceed to discuss how managed care entities are regulated, however, we must first learn a bit about health insurance regulation.

B. THE CONCEPT OF INSURANCE

Even though managed care has become pervasive in the United States, it continues to make analytic sense to consider separately the insurance and the health care management functions of private health care financing. Insurance involves by definition the transfer of risk from the insured (also called the beneficiary, recipient, member, or enrollee) to a financing entity (the insurer, managed care organization, or self-insured benefits plan). It is invariably the case in health care that a small proportion of all insureds account for a very high proportion of health care costs. According to one commonly-cited source, ten percent of the population account for nearly seventy percent of health care costs in any given year, two percent for thirty-eight percent of costs. Marc L. Berk and Alan C. Monheit, the Concentration of Health Care Expenditures Revisited, 20 Health Aff., March/April 2001 at 9, 12 (although there is some evidence that the concentration of health care expenditures may be moderating a little as inpatient hospital care becomes less common and management of conditions with medication more common.) Health insurance essentially involves transferring risk from those insureds, who account for most of health care costs, to low-risk insureds, who pay most of the premiums, through the medium of the insurer.

Insurers deal with risk by pooling the risks of large numbers of insureds. The insurer, however, must be prudent about the risk it assumes from these insureds, and assure that it has the resources to cover the risk. When judging a particular applicant, the insurer must first assess the risk presented by an applicant, then determine whether or not to take that risk on (a process called "underwriting"), and finally set an appropriate premium.

When financing is provided through employment-related group insurance, of course, part of the premium is paid by the employer and the underwriting is of the group as a whole. When an employer self-insures its employee benefits plan, no premium exchanges hands (except insofar as the employee pays part of the cost of the plan the employer purchases stop-loss reinsurance) and there is no underwriting, except insofar as a person's health status might affect an employer's willingness to take on the person as an employee, or when the employer purchases stop-loss reinsurance.

Although managed care plans typically include an insurance function, managed care plans have not always been regarded as insurers. Managed care entities that themselves provide care, such as the classic staff-model HMO or the more recent provider-based integrated delivery system (or provider-sponsored organization), have sometimes been regarded as sellers of services on a prepaid basis (a bit like appliance service agreements) rather than insurers. But managed care organizations in fact do assume, and spread, risk, a fact finally settled by by the Supreme Court in Rush Prudential HMO, Inc. v. Moran, 536 U.S. 355, 366–370, 122 S.Ct. 2151, 153 L.Ed.2d 375 (2002), and are often, although not always, regulated much like insurers.

There are a number of concepts that must be mastered to understand health insurance and health insurance law. The excerpt that follows discusses these:

CONGRESSIONAL RESEARCH SERVICE, INSURING THE UNINSURED: OPTIONS AND ANALYSIS

(House Comm. on Education & Labor, Comm. Print, 1988).

II. PRINCIPLES OF HEALTH INSURANCE

* * *

For insurance to operate, there has to be a way to predict the likelihood or probability that a loss will occur as a result of a specific outcome. Such predictions in insurance are based upon probability theory and the law of large numbers. According to probability theory, "while some events appear to be a matter of chance, they actually occur with regularity over a large number of trials."[ ] By examining patterns of behavior over a large number of trials, it is therefore possible for the insurer to infer the likelihood of such behaviors in the future.

* * * Applied to insurance, probability allows the insurer to make predictions on the basis of historical data. In so doing, the insurer " . . . implicitly says, 'if things continue to happen in the future as they happened in the past, and if our estimate of what has happened in the past is accurate, this is what we may expect.' "[ ]

Losses seldom occur exactly as expected, so insurance companies have to make predictions about the extent to which actual experience might deviate from predicted results. For a small group of insured units, there is a high probability that losses will be much greater or smaller than was predicted. For a very large group, the range of probable error diminishes, especially if the insured group is similar in composition to the group upon which the prediction is based. Thus, to predict the probability of a loss, insurers seek to aggregate persons who are at a similar risk for that loss. * * *

In theory all probabilities of loss can be insured. Insurance could cover any risk for a price. As the probability of loss increases, however, the premium will increase to the point at which it approaches the actual potential pay-out.

To keep premiums competitive, there are in practice some risks that insurers will not accept. In general, insurable risks must meet the following criteria:

- There has to be uncertainty that the loss will occur, and that the loss must be beyond the control of the insured. Insurers will not sell hospital insurance to a person who is on his way to a hospital, nor fire insurance to someone holding a lit match. * * *

- The loss produced by the risk must be measurable. The insurer has to be able to determine that a loss has occurred and that it has a specific dollar value.

- There must be a sufficiently large number of similar insured units to make the losses predictable. * * *

- Generally, the loss must be significant, but there should be a low probability that a very high loss will occur. * * *

* * *

III. RATEMAKING

Ratemaking is the "process of predicting future losses and future expenses and allocating those costs among the various classes of insureds." The outcome of the ratemaking process is a "premium" or price of policy. The premium is made up of expected claims against the insurer and the insurer's "administrative expenses." The term "administrative expenses" is used to mean any expense that the insurance company charges that is not for claims (including reserves for potential claims). * * * In the case of employer group coverage, a third part of the premium is set aside in a reserve held against unexpected claims. This reserve is often refundable to the employer if claims do not exceed expectations.

In the textbook descriptions of ratemaking for health insurance, insurers predict losses on the basis of predicted claims costs. This prediction involves an assessment of the likely morbidity (calculated in terms of the number of times the event insured against occurs) and severity (the average magnitude of each loss) of the policyholder or group of policyholders. * * *

* * *

There are different approaches to determining rates. In health insurance, the most frequently used approaches are "experience rating" and "community rating."

Under experience rating, the past experience of the group to be insured is used to determine the premium. For employer groups, experience rating would take into account the company's own history of claims and other expenses. * * *

* * *

The advantage of experience rating is that it adjusts the cost of insurance for a specific group in a manner more commensurate with the expected cost of that particular group than is possible through the exclusive use of manual rates. In addition, the increasingly competitive environment among insurers demands that each one "make every effort to retain groups with favorable experience. Unless an insurer can provide coverage to such groups at a reasonable cost, it runs the risk of losing such policyholders to another insurer which more closely reflects the expected costs of their programs in its rates."[ ]

Under community rating, premium rates are based on the allocation of total costs to all the individuals or groups to be insured, without regard to the past experience of any particular subgroup. * * * Community or class rating has the advantage of allowing an insurer to apply a single rate or set of rates to a large number of people, thus simplifying the process of determining premiums.

* * *

IV. ADVERSE AND FAVORABLE SELECTION

If everyone in the society purchased health insurance, and if everyone opted for an identical health insurance plan, then insurance companies could adhere strictly to the models of prediction and rate-setting described above. However, everyone does not buy insurance, nor do all the purchasers of insurance choose identical benefits. People who expect to need health services are more likely than others to purchase insurance, and are also likely to seek coverage for the specific services they expect to need. * * *

Insurers use the term "adverse selection" to describe this phenomenon. Adverse selection is defined by the health insurance industry as the "tendency of persons with poorer than average health expectations to apply for, or continue, insurance to a greater extent than do persons with average or better health expectations."[ ]

* * *

Adjusting premiums for adverse selection results in further adverse selection. As the price of insurance goes up, healthier people are less likely to want to purchase insurance. Each upward rate adjustment will leave a smaller and sicker group of potential purchasers. If there were only a single insurance company, it would serve a steadily shrinking market paying steadily increasing premiums. However, because multiple insurance companies are operating in the market, each company may strive to enroll the lower cost individuals or groups, leaving the higher cost cases for its competitors. In this market, adverse selection consists (from the insurer's point of view) of drawing the least desirable cases from within the pool of insurance purchasers. "Favorable" selection occurs if the insurer successfully enrolls lower risk clients than its competitors.

It is thus necessary to distinguish between the more traditional use of "adverse selection," as a term to describe the differences between people who do and do not buy insurance, and the sense in which the term is often used today, to describe the differences among purchasers choosing various insurers or types of coverage. This second type of adverse selection can occur within an insured group, if the individuals in that group are permitted to select from among different insurance options.

Insurers are still concerned about the more traditional type of adverse selection. They use underwriting rules, to exclude or limit the worst risks. Some insurers may also attempt to limit adverse selection by careful selection of where they market and to whom they sell a policy. For example, a company offering a Medicare supplement (Medigap) plan might be more likely to advertise its plan in senior citizen recreation centers, where the patrons tend to be relatively young and healthy, than in nursing homes, where the residents are probably older and have chronic health conditions. Thus, from the perspective of the individual or group applying for insurance, the insurer's attempts to avoid adverse selection may result in lack of availability of coverage, denial of coverage, incomplete coverage or above-average premiums.

* * *

Notes and Questions

1. Adverse selection is one of the two major problems with which insurers must contend. The other is moral hazard. Moral hazard is the tendency of insured persons to use excessively products and services for which they are insured. Absent significant cost-sharing, insurance greatly reduces the price of insured products and services as experienced by consumers, thus increasing consumer demand. Many purchasing decisions in health care, moreover, are made by professionals (the decision to prescribe a drug or to admit to a hospital), and these professionals are even less sensitive to cost. Fully-insured consumers have little incentive to shop around for products and services to get lower prices. Although insurers attempt to use managed care tools to assure that health care in fact is "medically necessary," insurers still have to pay for many products and services that their insureds receive that are in fact of little value.

Advocates of consumer-driven health care contend that moral hazard is the central problem of our health care system. Their beliefs about moral hazard, and their prescriptions for addressing it, are discussed further in Chapter 4.

2. The reading asserts that the purpose of insurance is to spread risk from individuals to all members of a group. This suggests a vision of distributive justice that distributes risk broadly. Indeed, social insurance, based on the principle of social solidarity, distributes risk among the broadest possible group, the entire citizenry. But insurance can also be based on an alternative vision of justice, that of actuarial fairness under which every individual pays for insurance based on his own risks. Which principle best explains the market for health insurance, as it exists in the United States today?

DEBORAH STONE, THE STRUGGLE FOR THE SOUL OF HEALTH INSURANCE

18 J. Health Pol. Pol'y & L. 287, 289–290 (1993).

Mutual aid among a group of people who see themselves as sharing common interests is the essence of community; a willingness to help each other is the glue that holds people together as a society, whether at the level of a simple peasant community, an urban ghetto, or a modern welfare state.
* * *

* * *

While in most societies sickness is widely accepted as a condition that should trigger mutual aid, the American polity has had a weak and wavering commitment to that principle. The politics of health insurance can only be understood as a struggle over the meaning of sickness and whether it should be a condition that automatically generates mutual assistance. However, this is more than a cultural conflict or a fight over meanings. The private insurance industry, the first line of defense in the U.S. system of mutual aid for sickness, is organized around a principle profoundly antithetical to the idea of mutual aid, and indeed, the growth and survival of the industry depends on its ability to finance health care by charging the sick and to convince the public that "each person should pay for his own risk."

The central argument of this essay is this: Actuarial fairness—each person paying for his own risk—is more than an idea about distributive justice. It is a method of organizing mutual aid by fragmenting communities into ever-smaller, more homogeneous groups and a method that leads ultimately to the destruction of mutual aid. This fragmentation must be accomplished by fostering in people a sense of their differences, rather than their commonalities, and their responsibility for themselves only, rather than their interdependence. Moreover, insurance necessarily operates on the logic of actuarial fairness when it, in turn, is organized as a competitive market.

Having now introduced the basic concepts of insurance and managed care, we will proceed to examine relevant state law, first considering the liability of insurers and managed care organizations under state contract and tort law, and then looking at state programs that regulate health insurers and managed care organizations.

II. CONTRACT LIABILITY OF PRIVATE INSURERS AND MANAGED CARE ORGANIZATIONS

Insurance companies and insurance contracts have historically been governed primarily by state law, and states continue to have primary responsibility for regulating managed care. In the first instance, insurance and managed care contracts are governed by contract law, and the failure of an insurer or managed care plan to perform to the expectations of the insured may result in contract litigation in state court. Our discussion begins, therefore, with an examination of state insurance contract law.

LUBEZNIK v. HEALTHCHICAGO, INC.

Appellate Court of Illinois, 1994.
268 Ill.App.3d 953, 206 Ill.Dec. 9, 644 N.E.2d 777.

JUSTICE JOHNSON delivered the opinion of the court:

Plaintiff, Bonnie Lubeznik, filed this action in the Circuit Court of Cook County seeking a permanent injunction requiring defendant, HealthChicago, Inc., to pre-certify her for certain medical treatment. Following a hearing, the trial court granted the injunction. Defendant appeals, contending the trial court improperly (1) determined that the requested treatment was a covered benefit under plaintiff's insurance policy; * * *, and (4) granted the injunction

We affirm.

The record reveals that in November 1988 plaintiff was diagnosed with Stage III ovarian cancer. At the time of her diagnosis, the cancer had spread through plaintiff's abdomen and liver and she had a 20 percent survival rate over the next five years. * * *

In June 1991, plaintiff was referred to Dr. Patrick Stiff, the director of the bone marrow treatment program at Loyola University Medical Center (hereinafter Loyola). Dr. Stiff sought to determine the prospect of treating plaintiff with high dose chemotherapy with autologous bone marrow transplant (hereinafter HDCT/ABMT). HDCT/ABMT is a procedure where bone marrow stem cells are removed from the patient's body and frozen in storage until after the patient has been treated with high dose chemotherapy. Following chemotherapy, which destroys the cancer, the marrow previously extracted is reinfused to proliferate and replace marrow destroyed by the chemotherapy. HDCT/ABMT had been a state of the art treatment for leukemia and Hodgkin's disease for many years. It began to be used in the late 1980's for women who were in the late stages of breast cancer.

* * *

On October 28, 1991, Dr. Stiff contacted defendant requesting that it pre-certify plaintiff for the HDCT/ABMT, i.e., agree in advance to pay for the treatment. Plaintiff's insurance policy required her to get pre-certified before receiving elective treatment, procedures and therapies. Dr. Wayne Mathy, defendant's medical director, received Dr. Stiff's pre-certification request and telephoned him shortly thereafter. During his conversation with Dr. Stiff, Dr. Mathy stated that the ABMT/HDCT was not a covered benefit under plaintiff's insurance policy because the treatment was considered experimental.

On October 31, 1991, plaintiff filed a two-count complaint against defendant * * *. In count one, plaintiff sought a mandatory injunction against defendant to pre-certify her for the HDCT/ABMT. * * *

Following a hearing, the trial court denied defendant's motion to dismiss and defendant filed its answer instanter. Thereafter, a hearing on the complaint was held at which Dr. Stiff testified that the HDCT/ABMT was an effective treatment for plaintiff given that all conventional treatment for her had been exhausted. He stated that he had performed 21 HDCT/ABMT procedures on patients with Stage III ovarian cancer and as a result, 75 percent of those patients were in complete remission.

During further testimony, Dr. Stiff opined that the HDCT/ABMT was not experimental and presented documents and literature in support of his testimony. * * *

Dr. Mathy testified at the hearing that his responsibilities as defendant's medical director included determining whether a requested medical treatment is covered under an insurance policy issued by defendant. He stated that after he received plaintiff's request for pre-certification, a member of defendant's benefit analysis staff contacted the National Institutes of Health, the National

Cancer Institute, and Medicare seeking an assessment as to whether the requested treatment was experimental. According to Dr. Mathy, defendant determined that the HDCT/ABMT was experimental based on information received from those medical assessment bodies. * * *

During cross-examination, Dr. Mathy testified that he first learned on October 29, 1991, that Dr. Stiff was contemplating treating plaintiff with HDCT/ABMT. Dr. Mathy admitted that immediately upon learning of the proposed treatment, he decided that the HDCT/ABMT was experimental and that plaintiff's pre-certification request should be denied. Dr. Mathy stated that he did not consult with the National Institutes of Health or the National Cancer Institute before making the decision to deny plaintiff's request.

At the conclusion of the testimony, the parties presented final arguments to the trial court. Subsequently, the trial court issued an injunction against defendant ruling that the ABMT/HDCT is neither an experimental therapy for ovarian cancer, * * *. Defendant then filed this appeal.

Defendant initially argues that the trial court erroneously determined that the HDCT/ABMT procedure is a covered benefit under plaintiff's insurance policy. Defendant claims it supported its determination that the procedure is experimental with similar conclusions by appropriate medical technology boards as required by plaintiff's insurance contract. Plaintiff's insurance policy provides that "[e]xperimental medical, surgical, or other procedures as determined by the [Insurance] Plan in conjunction with appropriate medical technology assessment bodies," are excluded from coverage. Defendant contends that the trial court improperly disregarded the terms of the insurance contract, which, defendant argues, were clear and unambiguous.

At the outset, we note that coverage provisions in an insurance contract are to be liberally construed in favor of the insured to provide the broadest possible coverage.[ ] In determining whether a certain provision in an insurance contract is applicable, a trial court must first determine whether the specific provision is ambiguous.[ ] A provision which is clear or unambiguous, i.e., fairly admits but of one interpretation, must be applied as written.[ ] However, where a provision is ambiguous, its language must be construed in favor of the insured.[ ]

Moreover, where an insurer seeks to deny insurance coverage based on an exclusionary clause contained in an insurance policy, the clause must be clear and free from doubt.[ ] This is so because all doubts with respect to coverage are resolved in favor of the insured. * * *

After carefully reviewing the evidence, we cannot agree with defendant that the trial court improperly determined the HDCT/ABMT to be a covered benefit under plaintiff's insurance policy. First, we disagree with defendant that the exclusionary language was clear and unambiguous. We note that the plaintiff's insurance policy does not define the phrase "appropriate medical technology boards." The plain language of the policy does not indicate who will determine whether a certain medical board is appropriate. Further, the policy fails to outline any standards for determining how a medical board is deemed appropriate. Thus, the phrase, without more, gives rise to a genuine uncertainty about which medical boards are considered appropriate and how and by whom the determination is made.

Second, [the court concluded that the defendant's determination was not justified by a state statute on organ transplantation coverage].

Third, we must note that even if the exclusionary language did apply, defendant failed to follow the terms of the insurance policy. Plaintiff's insurance policy excludes from coverage medical and surgical procedures that are considered experimental by defendant "in conjunction with appropriate technology assessment bodies." At the hearing, Dr. Mathy testified that upon learning of plaintiff's pre-certification request, he had already determined that the HDCT/ABMT was experimental prior to receiving or reviewing any information from the medical assessment boards. Given our careful review of the evidence, including defendant's admitted disregard for the terms of the insurance policy, we hold that the trial court did not err in ruling that the requested treatment was a covered benefit under the policy.

* * *

Lastly, defendant claims that the trial court improperly granted the mandatory injunction because plaintiff failed to meet the requirements for an injunction to issue. An injunction may be granted only after the plaintiff establishes that (1) a lawful right exists; (2) irreparable injury will result if the injunction is not granted; and (3) his or her remedy at law is inadequate.[ ] * * *

* * *

At the hearing, Dr. Stiff testified that given the steady development of plaintiff's disease, it was imperative to begin the HDCT/ABMT treatment as quickly as possible. He opined that delaying the HDCT/ABMT any further might have rendered plaintiff ineligible for such treatment due to further development of the disease. Based on our understanding of Dr. Stiff's testimony, we do not believe, as defendant now posits, that plaintiff was not eligible for the treatment.

Moreover, Dr. Stiff further testified that the HDCT/ABMT was an effective treatment for plaintiff and offered her a "very high chance of a complete disappearance of her disease." In addition, when asked during direct examination to give a prognosis of plaintiff's condition, Dr. Stiff gave the following response:

> "[Plaintiff] has a fatal illness with a zero percent to one percent chance of being alive at five years, let alone alive and disease free."

Given the evidence presented at the hearing, including Dr. Stiff's testimony, we do not agree with defendant that plaintiff failed to show she would suffer irreparable harm without the treatment.[ ] Therefore, we hold that the trial court did not abuse its discretion in granting the requested injunctive relief.

* * *

Notes and Questions

1. Courts have traditionally viewed insurance contracts as adhesion contracts and interpreted them under the doctrine of *contra proferentem*. This has made it difficult for insurance companies to control their exposure to risk through

general clauses that refuse payment for care that is not "medically necessary" or that is "experimental." Usually when such clauses are litigated, as in the principal case, the treating physician testifies that care is standard and is urgently necessary, while the insurer's medical director testifies that the care is experimental or unnecessary. What conflicts of interest does each face? Whom should the court believe? Are there more appropriate ways of resolving these disputes? What are the ramifications of these disputes for the cost of medical care?

2. Litigation challenging the refusal of insurance companies to cover ABMT provides a fascinating case study of the use of the courts to determine access to health care services, which is described in detail in Peter D. Jacobson and Stefanie A. Doebler, "We Were All Sold a Bill of Goods:" Litigating the Science of Breast Cancer Treatment, 52 Wayne L. Rev. 43 (2006). Nearly one hundred cases were litigated from the late 1980s to the early 2000s by women with breast cancer seeking coverage of ABMT. Many insurers refused to cover the procedure, claiming that it was experimental. In most litigated cases, as in *Lubeznik*, the plaintiff's treating physician testified for the plaintiff, claiming that the procedure was not only standard treatment, but also necessary to save the plaintiff's life. The insurer's medical director (often supported by other expert witnesses), on the other hand, usually testified that the procedure was still experimental, and thus excluded by the language of the policy. Occasionally the insurer was also able to introduce into evidence a consent form signed by the insured acknowledging that the procedure was experimental. Plaintiffs won about half of these cases, with the other half going for the insurers. In 1993 a California jury awarded $89 million in damages against an insurer that had refused to cover ABMT, including $77 million of punitive damages. Fox v. HealthNet (No. 219692 [Cal. Super. Ct. Riverside Cty. December 28, 1993]). After that point, the focus of litigation and settlement negotiations turned from whether insurers had improperly denied the treatment to whether they had done so in bad faith, although defendants still continued to win cases. (Was the denial in *Lubeznik* in bad faith?) Coverage of the procedure also became much more common. In the year 2000, clinical trials of ABMT were finally published, demonstrating that in fact HDC/ABMT was not effective for treating breast cancer. By that time, however, 30,000 women had received ABMT at a cost of $3 billion. What can we learn from this about the nature of the development of medical knowledge? What can we learn about the nature of medical litigation? See also E. Haavi Morreim, From the Clinics to the Courts: The Role Evidence Should Play in Litigating Medical Care, 26 J. Health Pol., Pol'y & L. 409, 411–13 (2001); Karen Antman, *et al.*, High Dose Chemotherapy for Breast Cancer, 282 JAMA 1701 (1999).

3. Another interesting empirical study of coverage disputes is described in Mark Hall, *et al.*, Judicial Protection of Managed Care Consumers: An Empirical Study of Insurance Coverage Disputes, 26 Seton Hall L. Rev. 1055 (1996). Professor Hall found that patients win coverage disputes over half of the time, and that the specificity of the language with which the insurer attempts to exclude coverage does not significantly affect its likelihood of winning. The issue of how medical necessity should be defined and who should determine it has become an important and controversial issue in managed care reform proposals. See Sara Rosenbaum, David M. Frankford, Brad More & Phyllis Borzi, Who Should Determine When Health Care is Medically Necessary? 340 JAMA 229 (1999) and the discussion of Utilization Controls in Section V below. See also, regarding experimental treatment exclusions, J. Gregory Lahr, What is the Method to Their "Madness?" Experimental Treatment Exclusions in Health Insurance Policies, 13 J. Contemp. Health L. & Pol'y 613 (1997).

III. TORT LIABILITY OF MANAGED CARE

Insurance and managed care coverage disputes present not only contract interpretation issues, but also issues of tort law.

A. VICARIOUS LIABILITY

Health maintenance organizations (HMOs) and Independent Practice Associations (IPAs) in theory face the same vicarious and corporate liability questions as hospitals, since they provide services through physicians, whether the physicians are salaried employees or independent contractors. These medical services can injure patients/subscribers, leading to a malpractice suit for such injuries.

Vicarious liability theories provided the first wave of successful litigation against managed care organizations.

PETROVICH v. SHARE HEALTH PLAN OF ILLINOIS, INC.

Supreme Court of Illinois, 1999.
188 Ill.2d 17, 241 Ill.Dec. 627, 719 N.E.2d 756.

JUSTICE BILANDIC delivered the opinion of the court:

The plaintiff brought this medical malpractice action against a physician and others for their alleged negligence in failing to diagnose her oral cancer in a timely manner. The plaintiff also named her health maintenance organization (HMO) as a defendant. The central issue here is whether the plaintiff's HMO may be held vicariously liable for the negligence of its independent-contractor physicians under agency law. The plaintiff contends that the HMO is vicariously liable under both the doctrines of apparent authority and implied authority.

* * *

FACTS

In 1989, plaintiff's employer, the Chicago Federation of Musicians, provided health care coverage to all of its employees by selecting Share and enrolling its employees therein. Share is an HMO and pays only for medical care that is obtained within its network of physicians. In order to qualify for benefits, a Share member must select from the network a primary care physician who will provide that member's overall care and authorize referrals when necessary. Share gives its members a list of participating physicians from which to choose. Share has about 500 primary care physicians covering Share's service area, which includes the counties of Cook, Du Page, Lake, McHenry and Will. Plaintiff selected Dr. Marie Kowalski from Share's list, and began seeing Dr. Kowalski as her primary care physician in August of 1989. Dr. Kowalski was employed at a satellite facility of Illinois Masonic Medical Center (Illinois Masonic), which had a contract with Share to provide medical services to Share members.

In September of 1990, plaintiff saw Dr. Kowalski because she was experiencing persistent pain in the right sides of her mouth, tongue, throat and face. Plaintiff also complained of a foul mucus in her mouth. Dr. Kowalski referred plaintiff to two other physicians who had contracts with Share: Dr. Slavick, a neurologist, and Dr. Friedman, an ear, nose and throat specialist.

Plaintiff informed Dr. Friedman of her pain. Dr. Friedman observed redness or marked erythema alongside plaintiff's gums on the right side of her mouth. He recommended that plaintiff have a magnetic resonance imaging (MRI) test or a computed tomography (CT) scan performed on the base of her skull. According to plaintiff's testimony at her evidence deposition, Dr. Kowalski informed her that Share would not allow new tests as recommended by Dr. Friedman. Plaintiff did not consult with Share about the test refusals because she was not aware of Share's grievance procedure. Dr. Kowalski gave Dr. Friedman a copy of an old MRI test result at that time. The record offers no further information about this old MRI test.

Nonetheless, Dr. Kowalski later ordered an updated MRI of plaintiff's brain, which was performed on October 31, 1990. Inconsistent with Dr. Friedman's directions, however, this MRI failed to image the right base of the tongue area where redness existed. Plaintiff and Dr. Kowalski discussed the results of this MRI test on November 19, 1990, during a follow-up visit. Plaintiff testified that Dr. Kowalski told her that the MRI revealed no abnormality.

Plaintiff's pain persisted. In April or May of 1991, Dr. Kowalski again referred plaintiff to Dr. Friedman. This was plaintiff's third visit to Dr. Friedman. Dr. Friedman examined plaintiff and observed that plaintiff's tongue was tender. Also, plaintiff reported that she had a foul odor in her mouth and was experiencing discomfort. On June 7, 1991, Dr. Friedman performed multiple biopsies on the right side of the base of plaintiff's tongue and surrounding tissues. The biopsy results revealed squamous cell carcinoma, a cancer, in the base of plaintiff's tongue and the surrounding tissues of the pharynx. Later that month, Dr. Friedman operated on plaintiff to remove the cancer. He removed part of the base of plaintiff's tongue, and portions of her palate, pharynx and jaw bone. After the surgery, plaintiff underwent radiation treatments and rehabilitation.

Plaintiff subsequently brought this medical malpractice action against Share, Dr. Kowalski and others. Dr. Friedman was not named a party defendant. Plaintiff's complaint, though, alleges that both Drs. Kowalski and Friedman were negligent in failing to diagnose plaintiff's cancer in a timely manner, and that Share is vicariously liable for their negligence under agency principles. Share filed a motion for summary judgment, arguing that it cannot be held liable for the negligence of Dr. Kowalski or Friedman because they were acting as independent contractors in their treatment of plaintiff, not as Share's agents. Plaintiff countered that Share is not entitled to summary judgment because Drs. Kowalski and Friedman were Share's agents. The parties submitted various depositions, affidavits and exhibits in support of their respective positions.

Share is a for-profit corporation. At all relevant times, Share was organized as an "independent practice association-model" HMO under the Illinois Health Maintenance Organization Act (Ill.Rev.Stat.1991, ch. 111 ½, par. 1401 et seq.). This means that Share is a financing entity that arranges and pays for health care by contracting with independent medical groups and practitioners. [ ] Share does not employ physicians directly, nor does it own, operate, maintain or supervise the offices where medical care is provided to its members. Rather, Share contracts with independent medical groups and physicians that have the facilities, equipment and professional skills necessary to render medical care. Physicians desiring to join Share's network are required to complete an application procedure and meet with Share's approval.

Share utilizes a method of compensation called "capitation" to pay its medical groups. Share also maintains a "quality assurance program." Share's capitation method of compensation and "quality assurance program" are more fully described later in this opinion.

Share provides a member handbook to each of its members, including plaintiff. The handbook states to its members that Share will provide "all your healthcare needs" and "comprehensive high quality services." The handbook also states that the primary care physician is "your health care manager" and "makes the decisions" about the member's care. The handbook further states that Share is a "good partner in sickness and in health." Unlike the master agreements and benefits contract discussed below, the member handbook which plaintiff received does not contain any provision that identifies Share physicians as independent contractors or nonemployees of Share. Rather, the handbook describes the physicians as "your Share physician," "Share physicians" and "our staff." Furthermore, Share refers to the physicians' offices as "Your Share physician's office" and states: "All of the Share staff and Medical Offices look forward to serving you * * *."

Plaintiff confirmed that she received the member handbook. Plaintiff did not read the handbook in its entirety, but read portions of it as she needed the information. She relied on the information contained in the handbook while Drs. Kowalski and Friedman treated her.

The record also contains a "Health Care Services Master Agreement," entered into by Share and Illinois Masonic. Dr. Kowalski is a signatory of this agreement. The agreement states, "It is understood and agreed that [Illinois Masonic] and [primary care physicians] are independent contractors and not employees or agents of SHARE." A separate agreement between Share and Dr. Friedman contains similar language. Plaintiff did not receive these agreements.

Share's primary care physicians, under their agreements with Share, are required to approve patients' medical requests and make referrals to specialists. These physicians use Share's standard referral forms to indicate their approval of the referral. Dr. Kowalski testified at an evidence deposition that she did not feel constrained by Share in making medical decisions regarding her patients, including whether to order tests or make referrals to specialists.

Another document in the record is Share's benefits contract. The benefits contract contains a subscriber certificate. The subscriber certificate sets forth a member's rights and obligations with respect to Share. Additionally, the subscriber certificate states that Share's physicians are independent contractors and that "SHARE Plan Providers and Enrolling Groups are not agents or employees of SHARE nor is SHARE or any employee of SHARE an agent or employee of SHARE Plan Providers or Enrolling Groups." The certificate elaborates: "The relationship between a SHARE Plan Provider and any Member is that of provider and patient. The SHARE Plan Physician is solely responsible for the medical services provided to any Member. The SHARE Plan Hospital is solely responsible for the Hospital services provided to any Member.''

Plaintiff testified that she did not recall receiving the subscriber certificate. In response, Share stated that Share customarily provides members with this information. Share does not claim to know whether Share actually provided plaintiff with this information. Plaintiff acknowledged that she received a "whole stack" of information from Share upon her enrollment.

Plaintiff was not aware of the type of relationship that her physicians had with Share. At the time she received treatment, plaintiff believed that her physicians were employees of Share.

In the circuit court, Share argued that it was entitled to summary judgment because the independent-contractor provision in the benefits contract established, as a matter of law, that Drs. Kowalski and Friedman were not acting as Share's agents in their treatment of plaintiff. The circuit court agreed and entered summary judgment for Share.

The appellate court reversed, holding that a genuine issue of material fact is presented as to whether plaintiff's treating physicians are Share's apparent agents. 296 Ill.App.3d 849, 231 Ill.Dec. 364, 696 N.E.2d 356. The appellate court stated that a number of factors support plaintiff's apparent agency claim, including plaintiff's testimony, Share's member handbook, Share's quality assessment program and Share's capitation method of compensation. The appellate court therefore remanded the cause for trial. The appellate court did not address the theory of implied authority.

ANALYSIS

This appeal comes before us amidst great changes to the relationships among physicians, patients and those entities paying for medical care. Traditionally, physicians treated patients on demand, while insurers merely paid the physicians their fee for the services provided. Today, managed care organizations (MCOs) have stepped into the insurer's shoes, and often attempt to reduce the price and quantity of health care services provided to patients through a system of health care cost containment. MCOs may, for example, use prearranged fee structures for compensating physicians. MCOs may also use utilization-review procedures, which are procedures designed to determine whether the use and volume of particular health care services are appropriate. MCOs have developed in response to rapid increases in health care costs.

HMOs, i.e., health maintenance organizations, are a type of MCO. HMOs are subject to both state and federal laws. [ ] Under Illinois law, an HMO is defined as "any organization formed under the laws of this or another state to provide or arrange for one or more health care plans under a system which causes any part of the risk of health care delivery to be borne by the organization or its providers." Ill.Rev.Stat.1991, ch. 111 ½, par. 1402(9), now 215 ILCS 125/1–2(9) (West 1998). Because HMOs may differ in their structures and the cost-containment practices that they employ, a court must discern the nature of the organization before it, where relevant to the issues. As earlier noted, Share is organized as an independent practice association (IPA)-model HMO. IPA-model HMOs are financing entities that arrange and pay for health care by contracting with independent medical groups and practitioners. [ ]

This court has never addressed a question of whether an HMO may be held liable for medical malpractice. Share asserts that holding HMOs liable for medical malpractice will cause health care costs to increase and make health care inaccessible to large numbers of people. Share suggests that, with this consideration in mind, this court should impose only narrow, or limited, forms of liability on HMOs. We disagree with Share that the cost-containment role of HMOs entitles them to special consideration. The principle that organizations are accountable for their tortious actions and those of their agents is fundamental to our justice system. There is no exception to this principle for HMOs. Moreover, HMO accountability is essential to counterbalance the HMO goal of cost-containment. To the extent that HMOs are profit-making entities, accountability is also needed to counterbalance the inherent drive to achieve a large and ever-increasing profit margin. Market forces alone "are insufficient to cure the deleterious [e]ffects of managed care on the health care industry." Herdrich v. Pegram, 154 F.3d 362, 374–75 (7th Cir. 1998), cert. granted, 527 U.S. 1068, 120 S.Ct. 10, 144 L.Ed.2d 841 (1999). Courts, therefore, should not be hesitant to apply well-settled legal theories of liability to HMOs where the facts so warrant and where justice so requires.

Indeed, the national trend of courts is to hold HMOs accountable for medical malpractice under a variety of legal theories, including vicarious liability on the basis of apparent authority, vicarious liability on the basis of respondeat superior, direct corporate negligence, breach of contract and breach of warranty. [ ] * * * Share concedes that HMOs may be held liable for medical malpractice under these five theories.

This appeal concerns whether Share may be held vicariously liable under agency law for the negligence of its independent-contractor physicians. We must determine whether Share was properly awarded summary judgment on the ground that Drs. Kowalski and Friedman were not acting as Share's agents in their treatment of plaintiff. Plaintiff argues that Share is not entitled to summary judgment on this record. Plaintiff asserts that genuine issues of material fact exist as to whether Drs. Kowalski and Friedman were acting within Share's apparent authority, implied authority or both.

* * *

As a general rule, no vicarious liability exists for the actions of independent contractors. Vicarious liability may nevertheless be imposed for the actions of independent contractors where an agency relationship is established under either the doctrine of apparent authority [ ] or the doctrine of implied authority [ ].

I. APPARENT AUTHORITY

Apparent authority, also known as ostensible authority, has been a part of Illinois jurisprudence for more than 140 years. [ ] Under the doctrine, a principal will be bound not only by the authority that it actually gives to another, but also by the authority that it appears to give. [ ]. The doctrine functions like an estoppel. [ ]. Where the principal creates the appearance of authority, a court will not hear the principal's denials of agency to the prejudice of an innocent third party, who has been led to reasonably rely upon the agency and is harmed as a result.[ ]

* * *

We now hold that the apparent authority doctrine may also be used to impose vicarious liability on HMOs. * * * [ ]

To establish apparent authority against an HMO for physician malpractice, the patient must prove (1) that the HMO held itself out as the provider of health care, without informing the patient that the care is given by independent contractors, and (2) that the patient justifiably relied upon the conduct of the HMO by looking to the HMO to provide health care services, rather than to a specific physician. Apparent agency is a question of fact. [ ]

A. Holding Out

The element of "holding out" means that the HMO, or its agent, acted in a manner that would lead a reasonable person to conclude that the physician who was alleged to be negligent was an agent or employee of the HMO. [ ] Where the acts of the agent create the appearance of authority, a plaintiff must also prove that the HMO had knowledge of and acquiesced in those acts. [ ] The holding-out element does not require the HMO to make an express representation that the physician alleged to be negligent is its agent or employee. Rather, this element is met where the HMO holds itself out as the provider of health care without informing the patient that the care is given by independent contractors. [ ] Vicarious liability under the apparent authority doctrine will not attach, however, if the patient knew or should have known that the physician providing treatment is an independent contractor. [ ]

Here, Share contends that the independent-contractor provisions in the two master agreements and the benefits contract conclusively establish, as a matter of law, that Share did not hold out Drs. Kowalski and Friedman to be Share's agents. Although all three of these contracts clearly express that the physicians are independent contractors and not agents of Share, we disagree with Share's contention for the reasons explained below.

First, the two master agreements at issue are private contractual agreements between Share and Illinois Masonic, with Dr. Kowalski as a signatory, and between Share and Dr. Friedman. The record contains no indication that plaintiff knew or should have known of these private contractual agreements between Share and its physicians. Gilbert expressly rejected the notion that such private contractual agreements can control a claim of apparent agency. [ ] * * * We hold that this same rationale applies to private contractual agreements between physicians and an HMO. [ ] Because there is no dispute that the master agreements at bar were unknown to plaintiff, they cannot be used to defeat her apparent agency claim.

Share also relies on the benefits contract. Plaintiff was not a party or a signatory to this contract. The benefits contract contains a subscriber certificate, which states that Share physicians are independent contractors. Share claims that this language alone conclusively overcomes plaintiff's apparent agency claim. We do not agree.

Whether a person has notice of a physician's status as an independent contractor, or is put on notice by the circumstances, is a question of fact. [ ] In this case, plaintiff testified at her evidence deposition that she did not recall receiving the subscriber certificate. Share responded only that it customarily provides members with this information. Share has never claimed to know whether Share actually provided plaintiff with this information. Thus, a question of fact exists as to whether Share gave this information to plaintiff. If this information was not provided to plaintiff, it cannot be used to defeat her apparent agency claim.

* * *

Evidence in the record supports plaintiff's contentions that Share held itself out to its members as the provider of health care, and that plaintiff was not aware that her physicians were independent contractors. Notably, plaintiff stated that, at the time that she received treatment, plaintiff believed that Drs. Kowalski and Friedman were Share employees. Plaintiff was not aware of the type of relationship that her physicians had with Share.

Moreover, Share's member handbook contains evidence that Share held itself out to plaintiff as the provider of her health care. The handbook stated to Share members that Share will provide "all your healthcare needs" and "comprehensive high quality services." The handbook did not contain any provision that identified Share physicians as independent contractors or nonemployees of Share. Instead, the handbook referred to the physicians as "your Share physician," "Share physicians" and "our staff." Share also referred to the physicians' offices as "Your Share physician's office." The record shows that Share provided this handbook to each of its enrolled members, including plaintiff. Representations made in the handbook are thus directly attributable to Share and were intended by Share to be communicated to its members.

* * *

We hold that the above testimony by plaintiff and Share's member handbook support the conclusion that Share held itself out to plaintiff as the provider of her health care, without informing her that the care was actually provided by independent contractors. Therefore, a triable issue of fact exists as to the holding-out element. We need not resolve whether any other evidence in the record also supports plaintiff's claim. Our task here is to review whether Share is entitled to summary judgment on this element. We hold that Share is not.

B. Justifiable Reliance

A plaintiff must also prove the element of "justifiable reliance" to establish apparent authority against an HMO for physician malpractice. This means that the plaintiff acted in reliance upon the conduct of the HMO or its agent, consistent with ordinary care and prudence. [ ]

The element of justifiable reliance is met where the plaintiff relies upon the HMO to provide health care services, and does not rely upon a specific physician. This element is not met if the plaintiff selects his or her own personal physician and merely looks to the HMO as a conduit through which the plaintiff receives medical care. [ ]

Concerning the element of justifiable reliance in the hospital context, Gilbert explained that the critical distinction is whether the plaintiff sought care from the hospital itself or from a personal physician. * * *

This rationale applies even more forcefully in the context of an HMO that restricts its members to the HMO's chosen physicians. Accordingly, unless a person seeks care from a personal physician, that person is seeking care from the HMO itself. A person who seeks care from the HMO itself accepts that care in reliance upon the HMO's holding itself out as the provider of care.

Share maintains that plaintiff cannot establish the justifiable reliance element because she did not select Share. * * *

* * * We reject Share's argument. It is true that, where a person selects the HMO and does not rely upon a specific physician, then that person is relying upon the HMO to provide health care. This principle, derived directly from Gilbert, is set forth above. Equally true, however, is that where a person has no choice but to enroll with a single HMO and does not rely upon a specific physician, then that person is likewise relying upon the HMO to provide health care.

In the present case, the record discloses that plaintiff did not select Share. Plaintiff's employer selected Share for her. Plaintiff had no choice of health plans whatsoever. Once Share became plaintiff's health plan, Share required plaintiff to obtain her primary medical care from one of its primary care physicians. If plaintiff did not do so, Share did not cover plaintiff's medical costs. In accordance with Share's requirement, plaintiff selected Dr. Kowalski from a list of physicians that Share provided to her. Plaintiff had no prior relationship with Dr. Kowalski. As to Dr. Kowalski's selection of Dr. Friedman for plaintiff, Share required Dr. Kowalski to make referrals only to physicians approved by Share. Plaintiff had no prior relationship with Dr. Friedman. We hold that these facts are sufficient to raise the reasonable inference that plaintiff relied upon Share to provide her health care services.

Were we to conclude that plaintiff was not relying upon Share for health care, we would be denying the true nature of the relationship among plaintiff, her HMO and the physicians. Share, like many HMOs, contracted with plaintiff's employer to become plaintiff's sole provider of health care, to the exclusion of all other providers. Share then restricted plaintiff to its chosen physicians. Under these facts, plaintiff's reliance on Share as the provider of her health care is shown not only to be compelling, but literally compelled. Plaintiff's reliance upon Share was inherent in Share's method of operation.

* * *

In conclusion, as set forth above, plaintiff has presented sufficient evidence to support justifiable reliance, as well as a holding out by Share. Share, therefore, is not entitled to summary judgment against plaintiff's claim of apparent authority.

* * *

II. IMPLIED AUTHORITY

Implied authority is actual authority, circumstantially proved. [ ] One context in which implied authority arises is where the facts and circumstances show that the defendant exerted sufficient control over the alleged agent so as to negate that person's status as an independent contractor, at least with respect to third parties. [ ] The cardinal consideration for determining the existence of implied authority is whether the alleged agent retains the right to control the manner of doing the work. [ ] Where a person's status as an independent contractor is negated, liability may result under the doctrine of respondeat superior.

Plaintiff contends that the facts and circumstances of this case show that Share exerted sufficient control over Drs. Kowalski and Friedman so as to negate their status as independent contractors. Share responds that the act of providing medical care is peculiarly within a physician's domain because it requires the exercise of independent medical judgment. Share thus maintains that, because it cannot control a physician's exercise of medical judgment, it cannot be subject to vicarious liability under the doctrine of implied authority.

* * *

We now address whether the implied authority doctrine may be used against HMOs to negate a physician's status as an independent contractor. Our appellate court in Raglin suggested that it can. [ ] Case law from other jurisdictions lends support to this view as well. [ ]

* * *

We do not find the above decisions rendered in the hospital context to be dispositive of whether an HMO may exert such control over its physicians so as to negate their status as independent contractors. We can readily discern that the relationships between physicians and HMOs are often much different than the traditional relationships between physicians and hospitals. * * *

Physicians, of course, should not allow the exercise of their medical judgment to be corrupted or controlled. Physicians have professional ethical, moral and legal obligations to provide appropriate medical care to their patients. These obligations on physicians, however, will not act to relieve an HMO of its own legal responsibilities. Where an HMO effectively controls a physician's exercise of medical judgment, and that judgment is exercised negligently, the HMO cannot be allowed to claim that the physician is solely responsible for the harm that results. In such a circumstance, both the physician and the HMO are liable for the harm that results. We therefore hold that the implied authority doctrine may be used against an HMO to negate a physician's status as an independent contractor. An implied agency exists where the facts and circumstances show that an HMO exerted such sufficient control over a participating physician so as to negate that physician's status as an independent contractor, at least with respect to third parties. [ ] No precise formula exists for deciding when a person's status as an independent contractor is negated. Rather, the determination of whether a person is an agent or an independent contractor rests upon the facts and circumstances of each case. [ ] As noted, the cardinal consideration is whether that person retains the right to control the manner of doing the work. [ ] * * *

With these established principles in mind, we turn to the present case. Plaintiff contends that her physicians' status as independent contractors should be negated. Plaintiff asserts that Share actively interfered with her physicians' medical decisionmaking by designing and executing its capitation method of compensation and "quality assurance" programs. Plaintiff also points to Share's referral system as evidence of control.

Plaintiff submits that Share's capitation method of compensating its medical groups is a form of control because it financially punishes physicians for ordering certain medical treatment. The record discloses that Share utilizes a method of compensation called "capitation."[ ]. Under capitation, Share prepays contracting medical groups a fixed amount of money for each member who enrolls with that group. In exchange, the medical groups agree to render health care to their enrolled Share members in accordance with the Share plan. Each medical group contracting with Share has its own capitation account. Deducted from that capitation account are the costs of any services provided by the primary care physician, the costs of medical procedures and tests, and the fees of all consulting physicians. The medical group then retains the surplus left in the capitation account. The costs for hospitalizations and other services are charged against a separate account. Reinsurance is provided for the capitation account and the separate account for certain high cost claims. Share pays Illinois Masonic in accordance with its capitation method of compensation. Dr. Kowalski testified that Illinois Masonic pays her the same salary every month. Plaintiff maintains that a reasonable inference to be drawn from Share's capitation method of compensation is that Share provides financial disincentives to its primary care physicians in order to discourage them from ordering the medical care that they deem appropriate. Plaintiff argues that this is an example of Share's influence and control over the medical judgment of its physicians.

Share counters that its capitation method of compensation cannot be used as evidence of control here because Dr. Kowalski is paid the same salary every month. We disagree with Share that this fact makes Share's capitation system irrelevant to our inquiry. Whether control was actually exercised is not dispositive in this context. Rather, the right to control the alleged agent is the proper query, even where that right is not exercised. [ ]

[The court rejects Share's "quality assurance program" as evidence of control, since it is done primarily to comply with state regulations of the Department of Public Health. The court however allows as evidence of control chart review by Share; control over referral to specialists; and use of primary care physicians as gatekeepers].

We conclude that plaintiff has presented adequate evidence to entitle her to a trial on the issue of implied authority. All the facts and circumstances before us, if proven at trial, raise the reasonable inference that Share exerted such sufficient control over Drs. Kowalski and Friedman so as to negate their status as independent contractors. As discussed above, plaintiff presents relevant evidence of Share's capitation method of compensation, Share's "quality assurance review," Share's referral system and Share's requirement that its primary care physicians act as gatekeepers for Share. These facts support plaintiff's argument that Share subjected its physicians to control over the manner in which they did their work. The facts surrounding treatment also support plaintiff's argument. According to plaintiff's evidence, Dr. Kowalski referred plaintiff to Dr. Friedman. Dr. Friedman evaluated plaintiff and recommended that plaintiff have either an MRI test or a CT scan performed on the base of her skull. Dr. Friedman, however, did not order the test that he recommended for plaintiff. Rather, he reported this information back to Dr. Kowalski in her role as plaintiff's primary care physician. Dr. Kowalski initially sent Dr. Friedman a copy of an old MRI test. Dr. Kowalski later ordered that an updated MRI be taken. In doing so, she directed that the MRI be taken of plaintiff's "brain." Hence, that MRI failed to image the base of plaintiff's skull as recommended by Dr. Friedman. Dr. Kowalski then reviewed the MRI test results herself and informed plaintiff that the results revealed no abnormality. From all the above facts and circumstances, a trier of fact could reasonably infer that Share promulgated such a system of control over its physicians that Share effectively negated the exercise of their independent medical judgment, to plaintiff's detriment.

We note that Dr. Kowalski testified at an evidence deposition that she did not feel constrained by Share in making medical decisions regarding her patients, including whether to order tests or make referrals to specialists. This testimony is not controlling at the summary judgment stage. The trier of fact is entitled to weigh all the conflicting evidence above against Dr. Kowalski's testimony.

In conclusion, plaintiff has presented adequate evidence to support a finding that Share exerted such sufficient control over its participating physicians so as to negate their status as independent contractors. Share, therefore, is not entitled to summary judgment against plaintiff's claim of implied authority.

* * *

CONCLUSION

An HMO may be held vicariously liable for the negligence of its independent-contractor physicians under both the doctrines of apparent authority and implied authority. Plaintiff here is entitled to a trial on both doctrines. The circuit court therefore erred in awarding summary judgment to Share. The appellate court's judgment, which reversed the circuit court's judgment and remanded the cause to the circuit court for further proceedings, is affirmed.

Affirmed.

PAGARIGAN v. AETNA U.S. HEALTHCARE OF CALIFORNIA, INC.

California Court of Appeal, 2005.
2005 WL 2742807.

In this case we consider the liability of an HMO which contracts out its health care responsibilities to various providers when one or more of those providers denies medically necessary services or commits malpractice in the delivery of those services. We conclude the HMO owes a duty to avoid contracting with deficient providers or negotiating contract terms which require or unduly encourage denials of service or below-standard performance by its providers. While appellants' complaint in its present form even with the amendments it tendered fails to adequately state a cause of action based on this theory, we find facts alleged which imply they may be able to do so if offered the chance. Accordingly, we allow appellants one more opportunity to file good faith amendments as to two of the nine proposed causes of action involving Aetna. * * *.

FACTS AND PROCEEDINGS BELOW

Appellants (and plaintiffs) are the children of an elderly woman, Johnnie Pagarigan (decedent) who died at a nursing home, allegedly as a result of elder abuse and malpractice. The respondents are the HMO which the decedent had joined and its parent corporation (collectively Aetna). Aetna, in turn, had contracted with a management organization, Greater Valley Management Services Organization, which contracted with medical groups Greater Valley Medical Group and Greater Valley Physician Association (collectively "Greater Valley") which contracted with Magnolia Gardens nursing home (owned and operated by Libby Care Center, Inc. and Longwood Management Corp.) and a physician, Dr. Buttleman, to care for decedent.

After their mother's death, and learning of what they saw as serious deficiencies in the care provided her by the physician and the nursing home, appellants sued all layers of this complex arrangement-including the HMO at the top, Aetna. They asserted ten causes of action as successors-in-interest to their mother (negligence, willful misconduct, elder abuse, constructive fraud, and fraud) and one for wrongful death. (This appeal, however, only involves the HMO and the trial court's action sustaining a demurrer and dismissing the complaint as to the HMO and its parent company.)

According to the allegations of this complaint, decedent was already on Medicare in 1995 when she enrolled in an Aetna HMO, Aetna Health Care of California, Inc., and remained a member of that HMO until her death in June 2000. In February of 2000, decedent suffered a debilitating stroke. As a member of the HMO, she was assigned to Magnolia Gardens and under the supervision of Dr. Buttleman. Allegedly, the deficient care she received at Magnolia Gardens caused her condition to deteriorate rapidly. In quick order she became malnourished and dehydrated, developed a huge pressure sore on her lower back and a severe infection and abscess at the site of the gastric tube insertion, and eventually her abdomen became protuberant and discolored.

Despite the critical nature of her condition, Dr. Buttleman delayed months before transferring decedent to an acute care hospital. By that time, it was too late for the hospital to cure her condition and she was sent home to die. In their brief but not in their complaint, appellants allege Aetna as well as Greater Valley requested the delay for economic reasons. As long as decedent remained at Magnolia Gardens the state's MediCal program reimbursed it for her medical care. But if and when she moved to an acute care hospital Aetna and its contracting parties would be financially responsible.

* * *

DISCUSSION

Before discussing the nine counts of the complaint implicating Aetna, we set the scene by providing some necessary background information about the health care industry and the specie of Health Maintenance Organization involved in this case. The core issue here is when, if ever, an HMO that contracts out its coverage decisions as well as its medical care responsibilities to health care providers like physician groups or to intermediary health management firms, or both, can be held liable when those contracting parties deny service or commit malpractice in the delivery of those services.

I BACKGROUND ON HMOS AND THEIR USE OF CAPITATION-BASED CONTRACTS TO ARRANGE FOR THE PROVISION OF HEALTH CARE TO THEIR MEMBERS THROUGH HEALTH CARE PROFESSIONALS AND INTERMEDIARIES

At the beginning, health insurance plans—and later Medicare and Medicaid funded plans—were primarily organized on a pure fee-for-service reimbursement basis. A pure fee-for-service health insurance plan employs no doctors and owns no hospitals. It merely pays the bills doctors and hospitals submit for the services they provide to patients from the insured population. Consequently, the insurer normally is not liable for malpractice the doctors whose bills they pay may commit. Moreover, only to the extent the health insurance company makes coverage decisions and refuses to pay for certain services a patient may require and a doctor or hospital stands ready to supply, may it be held liable if a court decides that denial was improper and caused injury or death to one of the plan's insureds.

In contrast, the classic form of HMO, such as the original Kaiser Permanente plan, employs its own doctors and operates its own hospitals. Thus, these HMOs are liable both for any improper denials of coverage and for any malpractice their patients experience.

Aetna calls its plan an HMO, but it is far from the classic model. Rather, in common with a classic fee-for-service health insurer, Aetna's plan employs no doctors and owns no hospitals. Consequently, it purports to avoid liability for any malpractice its insureds may suffer.

The shift in decision-making responsibility and financial risk is accomplished through what the industry calls a "capitation" arrangement. Aetna agrees to pay the management firm or provider a specified amount per year for each person its "HMO" has admitted into its "HMO" plan and then assigns to that firm or provider. The management firm or provider receives the same amount for a particular person whether that insured is so healthy he or she never incurs a single health-related expense the entire year as it receives for one who instead experiences a serious disease requiring hospitalization and a series of operations entailing hundreds of thousands of dollars in medical expenses over the year. Furthermore, if some patient's only chance for recovery is some expensive but experimental or otherwise problematical treatment, in theory at least it is not Aetna but the management firm or provider who must decide whether to offer-and pay for-that treatment. It also is that management firm or provider Aetna expects to bear the consequences should an insured or the insured's survivors successfully sue because the denial of some extraordinary or even ordinary treatment caused the insured serious injury or death.

In 2001, the California Supreme Court determined many of the claims appellants plead in this case avoid federal preemption under the Medicare laws. In that opinion, *McCall v. PacifiCare*, our high court, however, expressly reserved the question whether these claims state valid causes of action. "This case does not call upon us to determine the sufficiency of any of the McCalls' allegations to state a cause of action under California law, and we express no opinion on whether the claims ultimately will be proven." True, there is some ambiguity whether the Supreme Court meant to question the viability of the theories of liability embodied in the claims it discussed in *McCall* or merely the adequacy of the words used in the complaint to invoke those theories. Nonetheless, we assume it is both when addressing appellants' attempt to state those same theories in their complaint.

II.   STANDARD OF REVIEW

[The Court's discussion is omitted.]

III.   APPELLANTS' PRESENT ALLEGATIONS FAIL TO STATE A VALID NEGLIGENCE CAUSE OF ACTION OR WRONGFUL DEATH CAUSE OF ACTION, ALTHOUGH IT IS POSSIBLE APPELLANTS COULD SUBMIT AMENDMENTS WHICH WOULD CURE THE DEFECTS IN THEIR PLEADINGS AS TO THESE CAUSES OF ACTION

In their first cause of action the Pagarigans essentially allege Aetna's negligent conduct caused decedent's injuries and ultimate death. Aetna responded and the trial court ruled Aetna owed no duties to decedent which it breached. Whatever happened to decedent at Magnolia Gardens nursing home was the responsibility of the nursing home staff and the supervising physician (Dr. Buttleman). Vicarious liability may extend to the owners and operators of the nursing home, but not to Aetna which was just the insurance company that paid the nursing home and physician to take care of decedent.

As their primary theory of liability, the Pagarigans focus on Aetna's role as a health management organization. They urge as such Aetna has "non-delegable" duties toward its enrollees for the quality of the care they receive from the health care providers Aetna contracts to provide that care. The Pagarigans find these "non-delegable" duties in the language of certain statutes. While we conclude Aetna is not directly responsible for its contractees' breaches of duties they owe the plan's enrollees, we also conclude Aetna owes its own duties to those enrollees. These include a duty of due care when choosing the providers who will supply health services to enrollees. They also include a duty to avoid executing contracts with those providers containing terms, especially low levels of capitation payments, which foreseeably require or unduly encourage below-standard care.

We find the above duties inherent in the common law and to require no statutory basis. But we also note the Legislature enacted Section 3428(a) which became effective shortly after Mrs. Pagarigan's treatment at Magnolia Gardens and confirmed the existence of such duties.

In other provisions, 3428 appears to exempt health insurance plans, such as Aetna, from liability for acts of malpractice committed by health care providers it contracts to care for its enrollees. "This section does not create any new or additional liability on the part of a health care service plan or managed care entity for harm caused that is attributable to the medical negligence of a treating physician or other treating health care provider."

But 3428(a) imposes a statutory duty on Aetna and like plans comparable to the common law duty this court finds to have existed before the Legislature acted—a duty of due care when arranging health care services for its enrollees. "A health care service plan or managed care entity . . . shall have a duty of ordinary care to arrange for the provision of medically necessary health care service to its subscribers and enrollees ... and shall be liable for any and all harm legally caused by its failure to exercise that ordinary care ..."

Such a duty of due care is not satisfied by contracting with just any old providers or on any terms whatsoever. To select a provider or to allow the selection of a provider the plan knows or should know is deficient or prone to malpractice is to violate that duty. Moreover, this breach of the plan's own specific duty toward its enrollees also constitutes a contributing cause when an enrollee suffers injury or death due to malpractice attributable in part to the plan's careless selection of the deficient provider organization.

A plan likewise breaches this duty when "arranging" services for its enrollees if it negotiates contract terms with a provider—or allows the negotiation of contract terms with such provider—that foreseeably enhance the likelihood the provider will offer below-standard services that will injure or kill a substantial number of the plan's enrollees. Although other terms may have this result, the most critical term is the level of the "capitation" payment. The plan breaches its duty of ordinary care in arranging services for its enrollees if the plan negotiates a per capita payment so low the plan knows or should know it will require the provider to furnish substandard services and/or deny medically necessary services in order to survive. And, once again this breach of the plan's own duty to its enrollees qualifies as a contributing cause of any injury or death an enrollee suffers at the hands of a provider attributable at least in part to the plan's serious underpayment to the provider for the services it is expected to supply.

Throughout their complaint, the Pagarigans repeat a refrain—Aetna creates economic incentives for providers to deny medically necessary services or to supply below-standard services. Aetna responds with its own refrain. What the Pagarigans are complaining about is the "capitation" system, which the Legislature has expressly endorsed. Thus, the Pagarigans cannot predicate a cause of action on economic incentives this legislatively-approved system may generate.

It is true economic analysis and anecdotal data both tell us a "capitation" system creates incentives to underinvest in health care services just as a "fee for service" approach creates incentives to overinvest. A provider maximizes profits by furnishing fewer services (and thus spending less) per capita if compensated on a "capitation" basis, but maximizes profits by furnishing more services (and billing more) per capita when compensated on a "fee for service" basis.

For this reason, the Pagarigans repetitive allegations charging Aetna's providers had "conflicts of interest" in the sense of economic incentives to deny services, fail to make outside referrals, and the like, are not inaccurate. But Aetna also is correct in pointing out these incentives are inherent in the "capitation" compensation system both the federal and state governments have approved. Thus, as a general proposition, the ordinary incentives and "conflicts of interest" inherent in a "capitation" approach to health care financing cannot supply the foundation for a negligence cause of action against an HMO like Aetna.

But this does not mean Aetna cannot be held liable for breaches of due care in the way it carries out this "capitation" system. If the way it "arranges for the provision of medically necessary health care service to" enrollees generates economic incentives to deny services or furnish low quality care which are substantially stronger than those inherent in the "capitation" system, Aetna or any other HMO can be liable for this negligent conduct. Thus, for example, as discussed earlier, an HMO violates its duty of due care if it negotiates a "capitation" rate with a given provider which it knows or should know is so low the provider will have an undue economic incentive to deny medically necessary services or to deliver below-standard care. Likewise, as discussed above, an HMO can be liable where it chooses to arrange for the provision of services through a provider it knows or should know is seriously understaffed, poorly administered or otherwise likely to deny medically necessary services or deliver below-standard levels of care.[28]

The Pagarigans' complaint contains fragments of allegations which together approach, but do not quite state a valid cause of action claiming Aetna indeed violated its duty of due care in arranging medically necessary health care services by selecting—or allowing selection of—at least one deficient provider, Magnolia Gardens nursing home. In paragraph 15, it is alleged Aetna and Greater Valley contracted with the owners and operators of Magnolia Gardens "to provide long term care services to enrollees ... [in order to] satisfy Aetna's own obligation under a written agreement with Decedent and with Medicare, by which it had agreed to provide such long term care services to Decedent." In paragraph 25, the Pagarigans then allege, decedent "developed a very severe pressure sore ... because the [Magnolia Gardens] skilled nursing facility ... was *improperly administered* and their care operations were *inadequately funded.* Because of said *maladministration and inadequate funding,* there was insufficient staff to provide the care which Decedent required.... And when Decedent needed careful supervision of her 'G–Tube' and a prompt and proper response to the development of an infection, such care was not provided because such care was not available from an *undertrained and understaffed* nursing service." (Italics added.)

Missing from the above set of allegations, however, is an essential element—that Aetna *knew or should have known* Magnolia Gardens was improperly administered and inadequately funded and inadequately staffed. Nor is it alleged Aetna had itself negotiated—or knew or should have known the capitation rate negotiated with Magnolia Gardens by an intermediary management company—was so low it meant Magnolia Gardens would be inadequately funded and staffed to care for Aetna insured patients. Nor is it alleged Aetna knew or should have known Magnolia Gardens had become inadequately funded and staffed to properly care for Aetna insured patients after entering into the contract to provide services to those patients.

It is one thing when an HMO negotiates a contract with a reasonably capable provider and at a reasonable capitation level and then sees that provider make an erroneous decision, deliberate or negligent, to deny some

---

28. These duties and potential breaches of duty are akin to the "institutional negligence" cause of action the Illinois Supreme Court approved as a basis for holding an HMO liable for its provider's negligence in Jones v. Chicago HMO of Illinois [ ]. In that case the HMO breached its duty to arrange adequate care by allowing the assignment of too many patients to a small group of physicians. This closely resembles the action of contracting with or allowing patient assignments to an understaffed and underfunded medical provider such as a nursing home

medically necessary service, or commit malpractice in delivering that service. That is not a violation of the HMO's own duty of due care in arranging the provision of services to its enrollees. But it is quite another thing when an HMO chooses to contract with a provider that is "improperly administered" with an "undertrained and understaffed" nursing corps or at a capitation level which supplies the provider "inadequate funding" to give the HMO's enrollees proper care.

We have no idea whether the Pagarigans in good faith will be able to allege—to say nothing of proving—Aetna knew or should have known it was choosing a "maladministered, understaffed, and undertrained" provider—or indeed if Magnolia Gardens skilled nursing facility fits that characterization. Nor is it clear they will be able to honestly allege and later demonstrate Aetna knew or should have known the capitation rate negotiated with Magnolia Gardens left the latter so underfunded the nursing home was destined to deny needed care and/or deliver inadequate care—or whether the capitation rate indeed was that low. But we are convinced appellants should be afforded the opportunity to determine whether they can file such amendments in good faith.

In their eleventh and final cause of action, the Pagarigans reallege many of the earlier allegations in the complaint, including the facts discussed above which bear on Aetna's own duties and negligence. The count then simply alleges: "As a result of the wrongful conduct of the Defendants [including Aetna] as alleged, Decedent died." This death, in turn, caused the Pagarigans to be "deprived of the care, comfort, society and love of the Decedent...." For the same reasons we concluded the Pagarigans should be offered another opportunity to state a valid negligence action against Aetna, we find they should be afforded the same opportunity to plead a valid wrongful death action against this HMO.

[The court's discussion of causes of action for elder abuse and negligent infliction of emotional distress, sections IV and V, are omitted.]

VI.   APPELLANTS HAVE FAILED TO STATE A VALID CONSTRUCTIVE FRAUD CAUSE OF ACTION FOR AETNA'S ALLEGED FAILURE TO DISCLOSE TO DECEDENT AND OTHER ENROLLEES ITS CONTRACTS WITH PROVIDERS WERE BASED ON A "CAPITATION" PAYMENT SYSTEM

In their sixth cause of action, the Pagarigans allege defendants including Aetna were liable for constructive fraud because at the time they were making treatment decisions while decedent was at Magnolia Gardens they failed to disclose Aetna's financial arrangements with its provider organizations were based on a capitation basis. This capitation arrangement, the Pagarigans allege, created conflicts of interest Aetna (and the other defendants) were required to disclose to the Pagarigans.

Aetna responds it had no duty to disclose because a constructive fraud claim depends on the existence of a fiduciary relationship between Aetna and its enrollees. Because no fiduciary relationship exists between an insurer and its insured, Aetna further argues, it is not liable on a constructive fraud cause of action, even if it did fail to disclose it was paying its providers on a capitation basis.

We have some question whether an insurance company which chooses to operate an entity it labels a "health maintenance organization," as opposed to an insurance plan, can deny it has a fiduciary relationship with those who choose to become members of that health maintenance organization. We also have some question whether, assuming no fiduciary relationship, such an HMO at least owes a duty to reveal its financial relationships with entities providing health care to its members—especially when those arrangements affect the economic incentives influencing the behavior of those providers.

Nonetheless, we have no reason to inquire further into these concerns at this point, because the Pagarigans do not allege a failure to disclose at the time it would be reasonable to require Aetna to do so. Instead they object to the failure to disclose these financial arrangements only "at the time [the Magnolia Gardens owner and operator], Greater Valley and Buttleman considered treatment options, recommended treatment, and during the time they provided care and treatment to the Decedent." The Pagarigans did not allege Aetna failed to disclose its "capitation" arrangements earlier, especially in the various documents it provided decedent and other enrollees in its HMO when they were deciding to enroll. Accordingly, despite appellants' "last chance" amendments, we find the present allegations fall short of stating a viable cause of action against Aetna for constructive fraud.

[The court's discussion of the causes of action for fraudulent concealment and a Randi violation, section VII and VIII, are omitted.]

IX. FALSE REPRESENTATIONS IN AN HMO'S MARKETING MATERIALS CAN BE ACTIONABLE, BUT APPELLANTS' ALLEGATIONS ARE NOT SUFFICIENTLY SPECIFIC OR OF A NATURE TO STATE A VALID CAUSE OF ACTION UNDER THAT THEORY OF LIABILITY

In their ninth cause of action, again focused only on Aetna (and Does 1–5) the Pagarigans allege "fraud" based on misrepresentations and false promises the HMO allegedly included in its "marketing materials" aimed at prospective enrollees. The complaint describes the alleged misrepresentations and promises in the most general of terms, e.g., the care would include all benefits Medicare covers, would comply with state law, and the like. It then alleges "[s]aid representations and promises were, when made, false." And the motive? For economic reasons. Aetna, allegedly "had no intention of providing such care . . . if the cost . . . was higher than [that consistent with the] goals for the financial performance of AETNA's business operation . . . even if . . . reasonably . . . necessary for . . . good medical practice and even if . . . required under the law."The complaint then alleges the purpose of the fraud was "tricking and inducing" decedent and others to enroll as members of the Aetna HMO. Finally, it alleges decedent enrolled because she relied on the fraudulent marketing materials.

We find the trial court reached the correct result, sustaining a demurrer to this cause of action, but apparently for the wrong reason. The court appeared to rule it would be impossible to found a fraud claim on misrepresentations made in "marketing materials" issued by an HMO or other health provider. It found such representations are inherently merely generalized expressions of opinion and "puffery" on which no one is entitled to rely. In so ruling, the court appeared to rely heavily on Pulvers v. Kaiser Foundation Health Plan, Inc. In that case involving an HMO's marketing materials,

Division Four held representations the plan "would provide 'high standards' of medical service" represent "generalized puffing" not amounting to a warranty of high quality service.

While we have no quarrel with that portion of the *Pulvers* opinion, we find it is a limited observation about certain types of representations commonly found in advertising, including HMO marketing materials. We do not read it to rule out the possibility of other misrepresentations an HMO's marketing materials might contain which would be actionable. Imagine, for instance, Aetna's marketing materials claimed this HMO employed its own physicians and owned its own hospitals and nursing homes—or would lead an average reader to gain that impression. Or perhaps those materials asserted Aetna's HMO provided certain specified services which it did not. Or what if the materials advised prospective enrollees Aetna did not pay its contracting providers on a capitation basis. Could such brazen lies be excused as "mere puffery"? Obviously not.

Indeed Medicare enrollees, like decedent, have been allowed to sue an HMO for misrepresentations in the plan's marketing materials. For example, in *Solorzano v. Superior Court,* Division One issued a writ overturning a judgment on the pleadings and allowing a lawsuit by Medicare recipients against an HMO for fraudulent representations in its marketing materials. The suit sought compensatory and punitive damages as well as injunctive relief.

The problem here for the Pagarigans is not the viability of their theory, but the manner of its execution. As is true of their other fraud-type counts, their present allegations lack both specificity and substance.

Ordinarily, plaintiffs must specifically plead the time, place and content of every misrepresentation they allege. The Pagarigans seek to excuse the lack of specificity because the marketing materials were part of a large scale advertising program and thus "the defendant must necessarily possess full information concerning the facts ... ' Certainly, in such situations plaintiffs should not be required to identify each of the scores or hundreds or thousands of brochures, advertisements, broadcasts and the like they allege contain misrepresentations. But this does not mean they need not be specific about the *content* of the statements those plaintiffs deem to constitute fraud. Here, the Pagarigans describe the statements in only the most general of terms-far short of the specificity required in fraud actions.

The alleged misrepresentations also lack substance. They are not statements of fact but only vague promises. Indeed they are too vague and modest even to qualify as true "puffery"—instead merely claiming the HMO will adhere to California law, will provide what Medicare requires, and something more, etc. But although they fall short of "puffery" they clearly are akin to the sort of statements the *Pulvers* court found not to be actionable.

Notably, in these counts as amended, the Pagarigans never tender factual allegations supporting an inference Aetna's marketing materials even imply the Aetna HMO is a traditional HMO which employs or otherwise controls the physicians, hospitals, nursing homes, and other providers who will be supplying the enrollees' health care. As a result, they are in no position to claim the marketing materials create an "apparent agency" (or "ostensible agency") cause of action, as has been recognized in Illinois, Pennsylvania and other states.[29] Nor do those allegations, at present, even imply the materials suggest the Aetna HMO does not pay its providers on a capitation basis, or state anything else that is both material and false.

* * *

The judgment is reversed and the cause remanded to the trial court with instructions to sustain the demurrer with leave to amend as to the first and eleventh causes of action in the Pagarigans' complaint and to sustain the demurrer without leave to amend as to the remaining counts against Aetna, and for further proceedings consistent with this opinion. Each side to bear its own costs on appeal.

Notes and Questions

1. Does a subscriber to an IPA-style managed care organization look to it for care rather than solely to the individual physicians? In an IPA, there is no central office, staffed by salaried physicians; the subscriber instead goes to the individual offices of the primary care physicians or the specialists. What justifies extending ostensible agency doctrine to this arrangement?

Managed care advertising often holds out the plan in words such as "total care program", as "an entire health care system". A reliance by the subscriber on the managed care organization for their choice of physicians, and any holding out by the MCO as a provider, is sufficient. See McClellan v. Health Maintenance Organization of Pennsylvania, 413 Pa.Super. 128, 604 A.2d 1053 (1992) (ostensible agency based on advertisements by HMO claiming that it carefully screened in primary care physicians).

In *Petrovich*, the court allowed both an apparent authority claim and an implied authority claim. Implied authority required a court to find sufficient elements of plan control over a physician to reject the independent contractor defense. The court found that utilization review, limits on referrals to specialists and hospitals, and other financial constraints were sufficient to create implied authority.

2. IPA-model HMOs that become "the institution", that "hold out" the independent contractor as an employee, and also restrict provider selection are vulnerable to ostensible agency arguments. Where the HMO exercises substantial control over the independent physicians by controlling the patients they must see and by paying on a per capita basis, an agency relationship has been found. See Dunn v. Praiss, 256 N.J.Super. 180, 606 A.2d 862 (App.Div.1992); Boyd v. Albert Einstein Medical Center, 377 Pa.Super. 609, 547 A.2d 1229 (1988).

3. The court in Decker v. Saini, 14 Employee Benefits Cas. 1556, 1991 WL 277590 (Mich.Cir.Ct.1991) observed that the application of vicarious liability has a powerful incentive effect on MCOs to select better physicians:

29. In Petrovitch v. Share Health Plan of Illinois [ ], the Illinois Supreme Court issued a unanimous opinion holding an HMO which contracted with independent medical groups and practitioners to supply health care and paid them on a "capitation" basis was nonetheless liable for malpractice by those medical groups and practitioners. The reason? The written materials the HMO supplied its members created an agency relationship under the "apparent authority doctrine." Those materials "stated SHARE [the HMO] will provide 'all your healthcare needs' and 'comprehensive high quality services.'.... [The materials] referred to the physicians as 'your Share physician,' 'Share physicians' and 'our staff.' Share also referred to the physicians' offices as 'your Share physician's office.' "[ ]

As a matter of public policy, the Court notes that imposing vicarious liability on HMOs for the malpractice of their member physicians would strongly encourage them to select physicians with the best credentials. Otherwise, HMO's would have no such incentive and might be driven by economics to retain physicians with the least desirable credentials, for the lower prices.

4. Some courts have pushed the boundaries even further, using agency principles to reach consulting physicians chosen by physicians employed by the HMO. In Schleier v. Kaiser Foundation Health Plan, 876 F.2d 174 (D.C.Cir.1989), a staff model HMO was held vicariously liable for physician malpractice, not of its employee-physician, but of an independent consulting physician. The court found four grounds for holding the HMO vicariously liable: (1) the consultant physician had been engaged by an HMO-employed physician, (2) the HMO had the right to discharge the consultant, (3) services provided by the consultant were part of the regular business of the HMO, and (4) the HMO had some ability to control the consultant's behavior, since he answered to an HMO doctor, the plaintiff's primary care physician. This judicial willingness to impose respondeat superior liability for the negligence of a consulting, non-employee physician clearly applies to the IPA model HMOs and even PPOs.

5. The development of complex cost and quality controls, which strengthen the supervisory role of the MCO, together with use of the capitation method of physician compensation, has led courts to hold the IPA model HMO-physician relationship to respondeat superior liability. Even a plan-sponsored network risks exposure to ostensible agency arguments if a court can find that the plan sponsor has created an expectation on the part of patients that the plan will provide high-quality providers of care. If the plan restricts a member's choice of providers, as will be likely in most situations, the network providers look like "agents" of the sponsor. The alternative—disclaimers in a PPO directory or other subscriber material as to quality of care, reminders to patients that they are responsible for choosing their physicians—may provide a legal shield against ostensible agency arguments. Such disclaimers are, however, not very reassuring when marketing to subscribers of a network plan. Capitation has begun to fade as a tool of managed care in the face of physician resistance and subscriber anxiety. Use of fee-based service claims that doctors must submit for each procedure is becoming more common. See Leigh Page, Capitation At The Crossroads, 44 AMA News 17 (March 5, 2001).

6. A breach of contract suit can be brought against an MCO on the theory of a "contract" to provide quality health care. In Williams v. HealthAmerica, 41 Ohio App.3d 245, 535 N.E.2d 717 (1987), a subscriber sued an IPA model HMO, and her primary care physician, for injuries resulting from a delay in referring her to a specialist. The theory was that the physician and HMO failed to deliver quality health benefits as promised, i.e. the right to be referred to a specialist. The court upheld the breach of contract action against the primary care physician but recast the action against the HMO as a tort claim for breach of the duty to handle the plaintiff's claim in good faith.

MCO contracts and literature may also contain provisions to the effect that "quality" health care will be provided or that the organization will promote or enhance subscriber health. The *Share* literature contained such language (see fn. 29 in Pagarigan). Where such assurances are made in master contracts of HMO-physician agreements, subscribers may be able to bring a contract action under a third party beneficiary theory. In *Williams*, for example, the court suggested that the subscriber could be a third-party beneficiary of the HMO-physician contract that required the physician to "promote of the rights of enrollees as patients."

A claim for breach of an express contract or an implied contract may also be argued based on representations by an HMO as to quality of care. This would seem to overlap with a malpractice claim to the extent it is based on a contract to provide "adequate and qualified medical care in accordance with the generally accepted standards of the community". Natale v. Meia, 1998 WL 236089 (Sup.Ct. Conn., 1998)(defendant's motion to strike denied). Express promises, if proven, can give rise to a separate claim.

Health care providers are not held to guarantee a cure, based on general language. "Mere puffery", as the courts view it, is not the same as a warranty of a good result, and will not create a claim. Pulvers v. Kaiser Foundation Health Plan, Inc., 99 Cal.App.3d 560, 160 Cal.Rptr. 392 (1979)(breach of warranty claim rejected on grounds that a warranty of a good result was just "generalized puffing.") However, an assurance of high quality care in marketing materials and brochures might be treated by a court or jury as a promise that standards of quality will be met, leading to warranty liability.

MCOs also typically market themselves by describing the quality of the providers on the panel. An assertion of quality furnishes courts another reason to impose on the organization the duty to investigate the competency of participating physicians. Such assertions might even be viewed as a warranty that all panel members maintain a certain minimum competence.

7.   Common law fraud or state consumer fraud statutes are another possible source of recovery. Representations in contracts and marketing brochures, or omissions of material information from these documents, inducing the patient to subscribe to the MCO or submit to a certain medical treatment, might be actionable. These theories are more demanding, however, often requiring proof of intentional misrepresentation and justifiable reliance.

Common law bad faith claims may be brought against non-ERISA managed care plans. Courts have held that a staff model HMO acts as an insurer when it refers a subscriber to an out-of-network provider, under the contract, and then denies reimbursement for that out-of-network care without reasonable grounds. This kind of non-medical, coverage-related decision is subject to a bad faith analysis. McEvoy v. Group Health Cooperative of Eau Claire, 213 Wis.2d 507, 570 N.W.2d 397 (1997) (allowing bad faith action against a non-ERISA HMO for a coverage denial). The managed care organization is liable for any damages from the breach, including damages. Such actions are not intended to be duplicative of malpractice actions. They require a showing "by clear, satisfactory, and convincing evidence that an HMO acted improperly, and that financial considerations were given unreasonable weight in the decision maker's cost-benefit analysis." Id. at 405. The court in McEvoy noted that HMO subscribers are "in an inferior position for enforcing their contractual health care rights" Id. at 403. Such actions are likely to be rare in light of the higher burden of proof required and ERISA preemption, but the question of what "unreasonable weight" means in considering the financial effects of treatment opens the door to more litigation. Pilot Life Insurance Co. v. Dedeaux, 481 U.S. 41, 107 S.Ct. 1549, 95 L.Ed.2d 39 (1987) held that actions such as bad faith sufficiently "relate to" employee benefits plans to fall within ERISA preemption.

B. DIRECT INSTITUTIONAL LIABILITY: CORPORATE NEGLIGENCE

SHANNON v. McNULTY

Superior Court of Pennsylvania, 1998.
718 A.2d 828.

ORIE MELVIN, JUDGE:

Mario L. Shannon and his wife, Sheena Evans Shannon, in their own right and as co-administrators of the Estate of Evan Jon Shannon, appeal from an order entered in the Court of Common Pleas of Allegheny County denying their motion to remove a compulsory nonsuit. This appeal concerns the Shannons' claims of vicarious and corporate liability against HealthAmerica stemming from the premature delivery and subsequent death of their son. We reverse the order refusing to remove the compulsory nonsuit and remand for trial.

This medical malpractice action arises from the pre-natal care provided by appellees, Larry P. McNulty, M.D. and HealthAmerica, to Mrs. Shannon. The Shannons claimed Dr. McNulty was negligent for failing to timely diagnose and treat signs of pre-term labor, and HealthAmerica was vicariously liable for the negligence of its nursing staff in failing to respond to Mrs. Shannon's complaints by timely referring her to an appropriate physician or hospital for diagnosis and treatment of her pre-term labor. The Shannons also alleged HealthAmerica was corporately liable for its negligent supervision of Dr. McNulty's care and its lack of appropriate procedures and protocols when dispensing telephonic medical advice to subscribers.

[The trial court granted HealthAmerica's motion for compulsory nonsuit, and the Shannons appealed.]

* * *

[Thompson v. Nason Hospital, 527 Pa. 330, 591 A.2d 703 (Pa.1991), set out four corporate negligence duties:

> (1) Use of "reasonable care in the maintenance of safe and adequate facilities and equipment;"
>
> (2) Selection and retention of competent physicians;
>
> (3) Oversight of "all persons who practice medicine within its walls as to patient care;" and
>
> (4) Formulation, adoption and enforcement of "adequate rules and policies to ensure quality care for patients," including upholding "the proper standard of care owed its patient." Id. at 708.]

* * *

The evidence introduced by the Shannons may be summarized in relevant part as follows. Mrs. Shannon testified during the trial of this case that she was a subscriber of the HealthAmerica HMO when this child was conceived. It was Mrs. Shannon's first pregnancy. When she advised HealthAmerica she was pregnant in June 1992, they gave her a list of six doctors from which she could select an OB/GYN. She chose Dr. McNulty from the list. [ ] Her HealthAmerica membership card instructed her to contact either her physician or HealthAmerica in the event she had any medical questions or emergent medical conditions. The card contained the HealthAmerica emergency phone number, which was manned by registered nurses. [ ] She testified it was confusing trying to figure out when to call Dr. McNulty and when to call HealthAmerica because she was receiving treatment from both for various medical conditions related to her pregnancy, including asthma and reflux.[ ]

She saw Dr. McNulty monthly but also called the HealthAmerica phone line a number of times for advice and to schedule appointments with their in-house doctors. [ ] She called Dr. McNulty on October 2, 1992 with complaints of abdominal pain. The doctor saw her on October 5, 1992 and examined her for five minutes. He told Mrs. Shannon her abdominal pain was the result of a fibroid uterus, he prescribed rest and took her off of work for one week. He did no testing to confirm his diagnosis and did not advise her of the symptoms of pre-term labor. [ ]

She next called Dr. McNulty's office twice on October 7 and again on October 8 and October 9, 1992, because her abdominal pain was continuing, she had back pain, was constipated and she could not sleep. She asked Dr. McNulty during the October 8th call if she could be in pre-term labor because her symptoms were similar to those described in a reference book she had on labor. [ ] She told Dr. McNulty her pains were irregular and about ten minutes apart, but she had never been in labor so she did not know what it felt like. He told her he had just checked her on October 5th, and she was not in labor.[ ] The October 9th call was at least her fourth call to Dr. McNulty about her abdominal pain, and she testified that Dr. McNulty was becoming impatient with her. [ ]

On October 10th, she called HealthAmerica's emergency phone line and told them about her severe irregular abdominal pain, back pain, that her pain was worse at night, that she thought she may be in pre-term labor, and about her prior calls to Dr. McNulty. The triage nurse advised her to call Dr. McNulty again. [ ] Mrs. Shannon did not immediately call Dr. McNulty because she did not feel there was anything new she could tell him to get him to pay attention to her condition. She called the HealthAmerica triage line again on October 11, 1992, said her symptoms were getting worse and Dr. McNulty was not responding. The triage nurse again advised her to call Dr. McNulty. [ ] Mrs. Shannon called Dr. McNulty and told him about her worsening symptoms, her legs beginning to go numb, and she thought that she was in pre-term labor. He was again short with her and angry and insisted that she was not in pre-term labor.[ ]

On October 12, 1992, she again called the HealthAmerica phone service and told the nurse about her symptoms, severe back pain and back spasms, legs going numb, more regular abdominal pain, and Dr. McNulty was not responding to her complaints. One of HealthAmerica's in-house orthopedic physicians spoke with her on the phone and directed her to go to West Penn Hospital to get her back examined. [ ] She followed the doctor's advice and drove an hour from her house to West Penn, passing three hospitals on the way. At West Penn she was processed as having a back complaint because those were HealthAmerica's instructions, but she was taken to the obstetrics wing as a formality because she was over five (5) months pregnant. She delivered a one and one-half pound baby that night. He survived only two days and then died due to his severe prematurity. [ ]

The Shannons' expert, Stanley M. Warner, M.D., testified he had experience in a setting where patients would call triage nurses. Dr. Warner opined that HealthAmerica, through its triage nurses, deviated from the standard of care following the phone calls to the triage line on October 10, 11 and 12, 1992, by not immediately referring Mrs. Shannon to a physician or hospital for a cervical exam and fetal stress test. As with Dr. McNulty, these precautions would have led to her labor being detected and increased the baby's chance of survival. [ ] Dr. Warner further testified on cross examination that Mrs. Shannon turned to HealthAmerica's triage nurses for medical advice on these three occasions when she communicated her symptoms. She did not receive appropriate advice, and further, if HealthAmerica's triage nurses intended for the referrals back to Dr. McNulty to be their solution, they had a duty to follow up Mrs. Shannon's calls by calling Dr. McNulty to insure Mrs. Shannon was actually receiving the proper care from him.[ ]

CORPORATE LIABILITY

[The court concludes that the third duty of *Thompson*, the duty to oversee all those who deliver care, is applicable.] * * *

Similarly, in the present case Dr. Warner, on direct examination, offered the following opinion when asked whether or not HealthAmerica deviated from the standard of care:

> I believe they did deviate from the standard of care. I believe on each occasion of the calls on October 10th, 11th, and October 12th, that Mrs. Shannon should have been referred to the hospital, and the hospital notified that this woman was probably in preterm labor and needed to be handled immediately. They did have the alternative of calling for a physician, if they wanted to, for him to agree with it, but basically she needed to be evaluated in a placd [sic] where there was a fetal monitor and somebody to do a pelvic examination to see what was happening with her.

[ ]. When asked whether this deviation increased the risk of harm Dr. Warner stated that "it did increase the risk of harm to the baby, and definitely decreased the chance of [the baby] being born healthy." Id., at 147.

Dr. Warner further testified, in response to a series of hypothetical questions, that severe abdominal pain should have led the triage nurse either to call the doctor so he could instruct the patient to get to the hospital, or tell the patient to get to the hospital as soon as possible, and on each of the three days that Shannon called Health America, the standard of care dictated that she be sent to hospital to determine if she was in preterm labor.]

Viewing the evidence in the light most favorable to the Shannons as the non-moving party, our examination of the instant record leads us to the conclusion that the Shannons presented sufficient evidence to establish a prima facie case of corporate liability pursuant to the third duty set forth in Thompson, *supra*. However, due to the different entities involved, this determination does not end our inquiry. The Welsh case involved a suit against a hospital and thus Thompson was clearly applicable. Instantly, HealthAmerica, noting this Court's decision not to extend corporate liability under the facts in McClellan v. Health Maintenance Organization of Pennsylvania, 413 Pa.Super. 128, 604 A.2d 1053 (Pa.Super.1992), argues that the Thompson duties are inapplicable to a health maintenance organization. We disagree.

In adopting the doctrine of corporate liability the Thompson court recognized "the corporate hospital's role in the total health care of its patients." Thompson, at 708. Likewise, we recognize the central role played by HMOs in the total health care of its subscribers. A great deal of today's healthcare is channeled through HMOs with the subscribers being given little or no say so in the stewardship of their care. Specifically, while these providers do not practice medicine, they do involve themselves daily in decisions affecting their subscriber's medical care. These decisions may, among others, limit the length of hospital stays, restrict the use of specialists, prohibit or limit post hospital care, restrict access to therapy, or prevent rendering of emergency room care. While all of these efforts are for the laudatory purpose of containing health care costs, when decisions are made to limit a subscriber's access to treatment, that decision must pass the test of medical reasonableness. To hold otherwise would be to deny the true effect of the provider's actions, namely, dictating and directing the subscriber's medical care.

Where the HMO is providing health care services rather than merely providing money to pay for services their conduct should be subject to scrutiny. We see no reason why the duties applicable to hospitals should not be equally applied to an HMO when that HMO is performing the same or similar functions as a hospital. When a benefits provider, be it an insurer or a managed care organization, interjects itself into the rendering of medical decisions affecting a subscriber's care it must do so in a medically reasonable manner. Here, HealthAmerica provided a phone service for emergent care staffed by triage nurses. Hence, it was under a duty to oversee that the dispensing of advice by those nurses would be performed in a medically reasonable manner. Accordingly, we now make explicit that which was implicit in McClellan and find that HMOs may, under the right circumstances, be held corporately liable for a breach of any of the Thompson duties which causes harm to its subscribers.

[The court also held that HealthAmerica was vicariously liable for the negligent rendering of services by its triage nurses, under Section 323 of the Restatement (Second) of Torts.]

Notes and Questions

1. Consider the underlying failures of the system in *Shannon*. The treating physician was impatient and inattentive to warning signs, but it was the triage nurses staffing the phone lines who failed to properly direct Shannon to a physician or hospital. How should the system have been designed to avoid such an error? What would you suggest to avoid a repetition of this kind of disaster?

2. *Poor Plan Design.* Many of the ERISA preemption cases involve claims of negligent design of the managed care plan, including telephone call-in services staffed by nurses, as in *Shannon*. Other claims of negligent design and administration of the delivery of health care services have been allowed. See McDonald v. Damian, 56 F.Supp.2d 574 (E.D.Pa.1999) (claim for inadequacies in the delivery of medical services). The court in *Pappas v. Asbel* noted that contractual benefits

provided in "such a dilatory fashion that the patient was injured are intertwined with the provision of safe care," and would give rise to a negligent administration claim. 555 Pa. 342, 724 A.2d 889, 893 (1998). In *Pappas*, the issue was a delay in transporting the plaintiff to a specialty trauma unit for care. The delay was arguably caused by the utilization review process of the managed care organization, which did not allow transport to the best hospital unit in the area for spinal injuries. *Pappas* involves a delay induced by a plan determination as to out-of-network care and a benefits question as to which hospitals were available to U.S. Healthcare providers.

3. *Negligent Selection of Providers.* The managed care organization, like the hospital, has been held to owe its subscribers a duty to properly select its panel members. In Harrell v Total Health Care, Inc., 1989 WL 153066 (Mo.App.1989), affirmed, 781 S.W.2d 58 (Mo.1989), the court stated that an IPA model HMO owed a duty to its participants to investigate the competence of its panel members and to exclude physicians who posed a 'foreseeable risk of harm." This logic also applies to PPOs, which control entry of physicians to the provider panel. While the merits of this claim were not reached, the case suggests that courts are willing to impose upon managed care organizations the duty to determine the competency of the providers on its panel.

The logic of a direct duty imposed on MCOs to properly select providers is even stronger for an MCO than for a hospital. In the hospital setting, the patient usually has selected the physician. He is then admitted to the hospital because his physician has admitting privileges at that hospital. By contrast, in a managed care program the patient has chosen the particular program, but not the physicians who are provided. The patient must use the physicians on the panel. The patient thus explicitly relies on the MCO for its selection of health care providers. The MCO's obligations for the patient's total care are more comprehensive than in the hospital setting. A plan sponsor that establishes provider networks and channels patients to those networks is likely to be liable for negligent selection. If, however, a plan sponsor uses a PPO sponsor as an intermediary to set up PPO networks, the chance of liability is less likely, although a court may still find a duty to properly select and monitor the sponsor.

A duty of proper selection will expose a managed care organization to liability both for failing to properly screen its physicians' competence, and also for failing to evaluate physicians for other problems. If the MCO selects a panel physician or dentist who has evidenced incompetence in her practice, it may risk liability. This is comparable to negligently granting staff privileges to an impaired physician with alcohol or other substance abuse problems, or one with sexual pathologies that might affect patients. See McClellan v. Health Maintenance Organization of Pennsylvania, 413 Pa.Super. 128, 604 A.2d 1053 (1992), where the court allowed a suit against HMO to proceed for negligence in selecting, retaining and evaluating primary care physician, misrepresenting the screening process for selecting its primary care physicians, and breach of contract.

4. *Failures to supervise and control staff.* Hospitals are required to supervise the medical care given to patients by staff physicians; to detect physician incompetence; and to take steps to correct problems upon learning of information raising concerns of patient risk. A hospital should also properly restrict the clinical privileges of staff physicians who are incompetent to handle certain procedures, or detect concealment by a staff doctor of medical errors.

Managed care organizations are likely to face similar duties to supervise. MCO liability for negligent control of its panel physicians derives from the same common law duty that underlies the negligent selection basis of liability as well as federal and state quality assurance regulations. As courts continue to characterize MCOs as health care providers, suits are likely to increase. Only PPOs with their reduced level of physician control might have an argument that liability should not be imposed for negligent supervision. However, statutes in some states require PPOs to implement quality assurance programs and others contemplate the use of such programs by PPOs. Iowa Code Ann. § 514.21; Ky. Rev. Stat. § 211.461; La. Stat. Ann.—Rev.Stat. § 22:2021; Me. Rev. Stat. Ann. tit. 24 § 2342 & tit. 24–A § 2771. The existence of such systems, with the PPOs having the right to remove a participating physician from the panel based on information generated by the quality assurance mechanism, imposes a duty to supervise. Managed care is likely to be forced to undertake both a duty to select with care and a duty to engage in continuous supervision.

5.   Managed care organizations are motivated by goals of both quality and efficiency—the objective of cost sensitive health care. The style of practice in MCOs is different from fee-for-service practice, assuming a more conservative, less intensive level of intervention, specialist use, and hospitalization. Some courts have recognized that managed care plans should give providers leeway to practice a more conservative, cost-effective style. See, e.g., Harrell v. Total Health Care, Inc., 781 S.W.2d 58, 61 (Mo.1989)("People are concerned both about the cost and the unpredictability of medical expenses. A plan such as Total offered would allow a person to fix the cost of physicians' services.").

C.   PHYSICIAN INCENTIVE SYSTEMS

BRANNAN v. NORTHWEST PERMANENTE, P.C.

United States District Court, W.D. Washington, 2006.
2006 WL 2794881.

INTRODUCTION

Plaintiffs move to compel production of certain documents regarding Mike G. Lin, M.D., Mrs. Brannan's primary care physician. Plaintiffs argue that Dr. Lin failed to order an evaluation of Mrs. Brannan's cardiovascular condition and possible heart pathology. Plaintiffs contend that HMOs, like Kaiser Permanente, frequently have an incentive system in place discouraging staff physicians from making referrals and ordering diagnostic tests. Plaintiffs argue that their attempt at Dr. Lin's deposition to determine whether his employment contract contained such an incentive provision was appropriate and the Court should order the production to Plaintiffs of Dr. Mike G. Lin's employment compensation contract with Kaiser for 2001–2002 as well as any other documents that pertain to bonuses and how such bonuses were to be calculated because the documents are not privileged and are highly relevant to this matter.

Defendants respond that Dr. Lin's deposition focused on the reasons why he did not refer Mrs. Brannan to a cardiologist for evaluation and testing. At the deposition, Dr. Lin responded to questions about any bonus that he did not know how his bonus is determined, and the question of a bonus was irrelevant to his determination of whether to make a referral for tests on a particular patient and the decision was determined on the basis of what the patient required. Defendants argue inquiry into Dr. Lin's financial matters should be precluded as it amounts to annoyance or embarrassment under Fed.R.Civ.P. 26 and also that such inquiry is not likely to lead to discoverable information. Defendants argue that motive is not relevant in a medical malpractice claim, Rogers v. Meridian Park Hospital,[ ], where the fundamental issue is whether the defendant breached the standard of care and caused injury to the plaintiff, regardless of what the defendant's state of mine was. Defendants cite authorities form other jurisdictions for this principle as well:[ ].

Defendants also argue that this motion is an attempt to bring up the now dismissed managed care or health plan liability claims within the scope of ERISA and that this motion to compe. was filed on September 1, 2006, outside the discovery deadline of August 14, 2006.

DISCUSSION AND CONCLUSION

Defendants' arguments are well taken, and Plaintiffs' motion to compel production of Dr. Mike G. Lin's employment compensation contract with Kaiser for 2001–2002 as well as any other documents that pertain to bonuses and how such bonuses were to be calculated must be denied. Determination of whether Dr. Lin breached the standard of care will not be aided by reviewing his employment contract. As the Court in *Rogers* stated in excluding an "error-of-judgment" instruction: "Medical malpractice cases are nothing more than negligence actions against medical professionals. The fundamental issue in these cases, as in all negligence cases, is whether the defendant breached the standard of care and caused injury to the plaintiff." *Rogers, id.* at 619. In another medical malpractice case, the Court addressed an instruction that introduced the element of good faith: 'The introduction of that concept allows the jury to consider the motivations of the defendants. Such consideration has no place in an action for ordinary negligence."[ ] An Illinois court referred to *Ellis* on the introduction of motive into consideration of medical malpractice claims. The Court set forth the specific duty, breach, and causation elements and disallowed evidence of a physician's financial incentives in a medical malpractice case as irrelevant: "We are not required to probe into defendants' motive in a medical malpractice claim. Motive is not an element of this cause of action. The question is did [the doctor] deviate from the standard of care? The reason or motive, if any exists, is of no consequence."[ ] Finally, the court in Pulvers v. Kaiser Foundation Health Plan, [ ] stated:

> The use of "incentive" plans is not only recommended by professional organizations as a means of reducing unnecessarily high medical costs, but that they are specifically required by Section 1301 of the Health Maintenance Organization Act of 1973 [ ]. We can see in the plan no suggestion that individual doctors act negligently or that they refrain from recommending whatever diagnostic procedures or treatments the acceptable standards of their profession require.

The foregoing authorities are persuasive that Dr. Lin's employment compensation contract with Kaiser for 2001–2002, as well as any other documents that pertain to bonuses and how such bonuses were to be calculated, are irrelevant, and Plaintiffs' motion to compel their production must be denied.

Notes and Questions

1. Most managed care programs have three relevant features from a liability perspective. First, such programs select a restricted group of health care professionals who provide services to the program's participants. Second, such programs accept a fixed payment per subscriber, in exchange for provision of necessary care. This pressures managed care organizations to search for ways to minimize costs. Third, following from number two, managed care organizations use a variety of strategies to ensure cost effective care. Altering physician incentives is central to managed care, since physicians influence seventy percent of total health spending, while receiving only about twenty percent of each health care dollar. Such plans use utilization review techniques, incentives systems, and gatekeepers to control costs. Managed care organizations create a new set of relationships between payers, subscribers and providers. These new relationships create new liability risks. The subscriber typically pays a fee to the MCO rather than the provider, relinquishing control over treatment and choice of treating physician. The payor in turn shifts some of its financial risk to its approved providers, who must also accept certain controls over their practice.

2. The argument that physician judgment might be "corrupted" by cost-conserving payment systems in managed care systems has been litigated over the years without much success. In an early case, Bush v. Dake, File No. 86–25767 NM–2, Saginaw Ctry. Circuit Court, Michigan, 1989, the court allowed the case to proceed beyond summary judgment on the issue of the effect of an HMO payment system. The issue was whether Dr. Dake failed to timely diagnose and treat the plaintiff's uterine cancer, because of the incentive effects of how he was paid. He failed to make a referral to a specialist when the plaintiff's bleeding persisted. A pap smear would have detected the cancer at an earlier stage.

> GHS set aside a certain amount of money each year for a "referral pool" and a "hospital/ancillary pool" for the Network physicians. The money in these pools would be depleted with each referral to a specialist or hospitalization of a patient during the year. At the end of the year, any money left over in these pools would be divided between GHS and the individual physicians in Network. The result was that the fewer referrals a doctor made and the fewer hospitalizations he ordered for his patients, the more money he made.

The court held that such a payment system was a jury issue in the case. Bush v. Dake, an unpublished opinion, is one of the early cases raising the issue of the effect of HMO incentives on the medical care received by beneficiaries. While on appeal it was settled.

See also, Sweede v. Cigna Healthplan of Delaware, Inc., 1989 WL 12608 (Del.Super.1989) (claim that doctor withheld necessary care because of financial incentives rejected on facts of case) and Teti v. U.S. Healthcare, Inc., 1989 WL 143274 (E.D.Pa.1989) (RICO claim against HMO for failing to disclose physician incentives to withhold medical care dismissed). What explains the paucity of such cases, which are greatly outnumbered by articles in the popular and trade press noting their potential? Is it the difficulty of proving what motivates physician decisionmaking? How would you establish that a particular HMO payment structure motivated physicians to forego needed care for their patients? What other countervailing pressures operate on physicians?

3. Every medical decision is also a spending decision. Since physicians as agents for patients control a large percentage of the health care dollar, should we trust them to have unfettered freedom to spend the money of others and use others's resources? The record of health care cost inflation suggests that unfet-

tered physician discretion is not desirable. Managed care organizations are institutional structures developed as a response to health care inflation, to better manage the cost of health care by reducing utilization of hospitalization, specialists and testing. See E. Haavi Morreim, Playing Doctor: Corporate Medical Practice and Medical Malpractice, 32 U.Mich.J.L.Ref. 939, 972–73 (1999).

The incentives that HMOs create for providers to under-utilize health care for their patients raise the possibility that these incentives will "corrupt" the medical judgment of a physician. The fear with managed care—and its goal of reducing expenditures by its physicians—is that some patients will be undertreated and suffer injury as a result. Bush v. Dake is a early example of these concerns. These concerns have led managed care plans to offer less restrictive plan operation and to ease constraints on providers. As managed care does less "managing", the promise of a tort theory that is based on distortion of provider incentives is distinctly reduced. For a description of some of these market changes, see Debra A. Draper, Robert E. Hurley, Cara S. Lesser, and Bradley C. Strunk, The Changing Face of Managed Care, 21 Health Affairs 11 (2002).

4. The Supreme Court addressed the role of managed care design and incentives in Pegram v. Herdrich, infra at Chapter 7. In *Pegram*, the treating plan physician refused to order an ultrasound at a local hospital, instead making her wait eight additional days for an ultrasound to be performed at a Carle facility more than 50 miles away. Herdrich's appendix ruptured, causing peritonitis.

The U.S. Supreme Court rejected the reasoning of the Seventh Circuit. With regard to the incentive structure of managed care organizations, Justice Souter, writing for the Court, stated:

> Like other risk-bearing organizations, HMOs take steps to control costs. At the least, HMOs, like traditional insurers, will in some fashion make coverage determinations, scrutinizing requested services against the contractual provisions to make sure that a request for care falls within the scope of covered circumstances (pregnancy, for example), or that a given treatment falls within the scope of the care promised (surgery, for instance). They customarily issue general guidelines for their physicians about appropriate levels of care. See id., at 568–57C. And they commonly require utilization review (in which specific treatment decisions are reviewed by a decisionmaker other than the treating physician) and approval in advance (precertification) for many types of care, keyed to standards of medical necessity or the reasonableness of the proposed treatment. [ ] These cost-controlling measures are commonly complemented by specific financial incentives to physicians, rewarding them for decreasing utilization of health-care services, and penalizing them for what may be found to be excessive treatment [ ]. Hence, in an HMO system, a physician's financial interest lies in providing less care, not more. The check on this influence (like that on the converse, fee-for-service incentive) is the professional obligation to provide covered services with a reasonable degree of skill and judgment in the patient's interest. [ ]

> The adequacy of professional obligation to counter financial self-interest has been challenged no matter what the form of medical organization. HMOs became popular because fee-for-service physicians were thought to be providing unnecessary or useless services; today, many doctors and other observers argue that HMOs often ignore the individual needs of a patient in order to improve the HMOs' bottom lines. See, e.g., 154 F.3d, at 375–378 (citing various critics of HMOs). In this case, for instance, one could argue that Pegram's decision to wait before getting an ultrasound for Herdrich, and her insistence that the ultrasound be done at a distant facility owned by Carle,

reflected an interest in limiting the HMO's expenses, which blinded her to the need for immediate diagnosis and treatment.

The Court thus acknowledged a national health care policy to use managed care to constrain the rapid health care cost inflation so evidence by the 1970s.

Little evidence exists that HMO incentives have a detrimental effect on patient care. The argument about incentives assumes that physicians' sensitivity to financial incentives is so fine-tuned that they will vary the intensity of care they give to each patient. The alternative possibility is that professional norms, risk of malpractice suits, and the daily pressures of practice will be more powerful forces on physician behavior. This would mean that a physician will treat all patients in light of his sense of best practice as adopted to a particular locality. The evidence has not yet resolved this question of physician response to incentives. Some form of incentive for cost-conservation in health care is desirable, and the ongoing debate is over the extent to which payment incentives can strike the right balance. While incentives may create conflicts of interest, they also give physicians flexibility in their clinical decision-making. The alternative—administrative rules and review mechanisms for denying benefits—is both more inefficient and arguably more constraining of physician decision-making. This debate—incentives versus rules—is an ongoing one. Plaintiffs have nonetheless argued that payment systems can cause a reduction in the quality of care delivered by physicians in managed care organizations, an argument that *Pegram* finally rejected. Robert H. Miller and Harold S. Left, Does Managed Care Lead to Better or Worse Quality of Care? 16 Health Affairs 7, 18 (1997); David Orentlicher, Paying Physicians More to Do Less: Financial Incentives to Limit Care, 30 U.Rich.L.Rev. 155 (1996); Uwe E. Reinhardt, The Economist's Model of Physician Behavior, 281 J.A.M.A. 462, 464 (1999); Lawrence C. Baker, Association of Managed Care Market Share and Health Expenditures for Fee–For–Service Medicare Patients, 281 J.A.M.A. 432 (1999). See William M. Sage, Physicians As Advocates, 35 Houston L.Rev. 1529, 1620 (1999) (" . . . the use of financial incentives in managed care preserves professional autonomy and improves efficiency even if it compromises advocacy at the margin.")

The debate over the use of physician incentives to promote cost sensitive practice has abated, largely because managed care companies have decided, in the face of class action litigation and bad publicity, to restrict their use of some incentives. Aetna has announced that it will end the use of financial incentives to physicians that might have the effect of restricting member access to care. Aetna will limit the use of capitated fees, as well as the use of medical guidelines created by actuarial firms and used by some insurers to restrict reimbursement for care. See Milo Geyelin and Barbara Martinez, Aetna Weighs a Managed–Care Overhaul, Wall St. J. A3–10 (January 17, 2001).

Problem: The Overworked HMO Physician

Sara Dawson's three-month-old daughter Shawna was ill. Dawson called Dr. Jones' office, as she had been instructed to do by Sunrise HMO. Dawson related Shawna's symptoms, specifically that she was sick, was constipated, was crying a lot and felt very warm. An assistant advised Dawson to give Shawna some castor oil. When Dawson insisted on speaking with Dr. Jones, the assistant stated that Dr. Jones was not available but would return her call. Dr. Jones returned Dawson' call late that evening. After Dawson described the same symptoms to Dr. Jones, he also advised Dawson to give castor oil to Shawna.

The next day Dawson took Shawna to a hospital emergency room because her condition had not improved. Sunrise HMO authorized Shawna's admission. Shawna was diagnosed with bacterial meningitis, secondary to bilateral otitis media, an ear infection. As a result of the meningitis, Shawna is permanently disabled. If a three-month-old infant is warm, irritable and constipated, the standard of care requires a physician to schedule an immediate appointment to see the infant or, alternatively, to instruct the parent to obtain immediate medical care for the infant through another physician.

Dr. Jones was a solo practitioner. He divided his time equally between his offices in Homewood and Sunrise Heights. Dr. Jones was under contract with Sunrise HMO, a for-profit HMO, for both sites. In addition, Dr. Jones was under contract with 20 other HMOs, and he maintained his own private practice of non-HMO patients. Dr. Jones estimated that he was designated the primary care physician of 3,000 Sunrise HMO members and 1,500 members of other HMOs. In contrast to Dr. Jones's estimate, Sunrise HMO's own "Provider Capitation Summary Reports" listed Dr. Jones as being the primary care provider of 4,527 Sunrise HMO patients. Federal guidelines specified that a primary care physician in an HMO should be assigned no more than 3,500 patient, a number that could be expanded depending on the number of physicians in the office and the number of hours of operation. Dr. Jones had a parttime physician and four nurses working for him in his offices.

Sunrise HMO's "Member Handbook" told members in need of medical care to "Call your Sunrise HMO doctor first when you experience an emergency or begin to feel sick." Sunrise HMO gave its contract physicians a "Provider Manual." The manual contains certain provisions with which the providers are expected to comply. The manual contains a section entitled, "The Appointment System/Afterhours Care," which states that all HMO sites are statutorily required to maintain an appointment system for their patients.

Dr. Jones related that his office worked on an appointment system and had its own written procedures and forms for handling patient calls and appointments. When a patient called and Dr. Jones was not in the office, written forms were used by his staff or his answering service to relay the information to him. If Dr. Jones was in the office, he would decide over the phone what further care was needed.

Patients were provided services on a prepaid capitation basis. The Agreement between Sunrise and its subscribers specified that Sunrise HMO "shall provide or arrange to have provided all covered services to all Beneficiaries under this Agreement." Sunrise HMO "shall provide all Beneficiaries with medical care consistent with prevailing community standards." Another article stated that, although Sunrise HMO may furnish the services required by the agreement by means of subcontractors, Sunrise HMO 'shall remain responsible for the performance of the subcontractors."

The agreement stated that Sunrise HMO "shall encourage members to be seen by appointment, except in emergencies." The agreement also stated that "[m]embers with more serious or urgent problems not deemed emergencies shall be triaged and provided same day service, if necessary," and that "emergency treatment shall be available on an immediate basis, seven days a week, 24–hours a day." Finally, the agreement directed that Sunrise HMO "shall have an established policy that scheduled patients shall not routinely wait for more than one hour to be seen by a provider and no more than six appointments shall be made for each primary care physician per hour."

What approach will you take against Sunrise in your suit on behalf of Shawna?

Problem: Wanting the "Best"

Cheryl Faber, twenty years old and newly married, joined a managed care organization, Freedom Plus [the Plan], one of several choices offered by her employer, Primerica Bank. Cheryl had examined the literature for the various plan choices during her open enrollment period. She chose the Plan because its literature talked of a "high quality" program, with the "best doctors" in the area, and "no cost-cutting where subscriber health is concerned".

The Plan sets aside a certain amount of money each year for a "referral pool" and a "hospital/ancillary pool" for Plan physicians. The money in these pools is depleted with each referral to a specialist or hospitalization of a patient during the year. At the end of the year, any money left over in these pools is divided between the Plan and the individual physicians.

Cheryl went to her primary care physician in the Plan, Dr. Hanks, for her initial physical examination. Dr. Hanks found small lumps in her breasts, which he noted in the patient record as fibroid tumors. He talked briefly with Cheryl about the lumps, but stated that she shouldn't worry.

A year later Cheryl came back for another checkup. Dr. Hanks had left the Plan. It turned out Dr. Hanks had been the defendant in several malpractice suits filed against him in the five years he had worked for another HMO and he was terminated by that HMO. The Plan could have discovered this by accessing the National Practitioners Data Bank, or by calling up the previous employer.

Cheryl was then examined by another primary care physician, Dr. Wick. Dr. Wick was concerned about the lumps, and she prepared a referral to an oncologist, Dr. Scanem, who had recently joined the panel of specialists affiliated with the Plan. Cheryl went to Dr. Scanem, who ordered a biopsy and confirmed that the lumps were malignant Stage III cancer. Stage III cancers have about a 10% five year survival rate, Stage II a 40% five year survival, and Stage I almost 100% survival with prompt treatment.

Dr. Scanem recommended a treatment regime for Cheryl that included limited radical mastectomy and chemotherapy. He planned to use a new drug for breast cancers that had recently become available through a research protocol in which he was participating. This drug appeared to offer a slightly higher cure rate with young patients such as Cheryl with advanced breast cancer.

The Plan approved Dr. Scanem's recommendations, with the exception of the new drug. The Plan rejected his proposal for use of this drug, stating that it only reimbursed for chemotherapy using the standard drugs used generally by oncologists. The new drug was extremely expensive, and would have increased the cost of Cheryl's chemotherapy by about 200%. Dr. Scanem was angry about the refusal by the Plan to reimburse Cheryl's treatment in full, and told her so. He told her that there was nothing he could do about it, and so he said he would use the standard approach that most oncologists used. Cheryl was a very nervous patient, terrified of her cancer. Dr. Scanem was worried about upsetting her too much, given the other stresses created by the surgery and the side-effects from chemotherapy. She asked him what her chances were, and he said only that she had "a reasonable shot at beating it, with luck and prayer." He did not tell her anything more about the prognosis, nor did she ask.

Cheryl underwent the radical mastectomy and chemotherapy. Optimistic about her chances, Cheryl proceeded to get pregnant. She and her husband also bought a new house, assuming that she would recover and her salary would continue.

Cheryl's cancer proved to be too far advanced to respond to treatment. She died six months after the chemotherapy regime finished. Her fetus could not be saved, in spite of efforts by Plan obstetricians to do so. Her husband lost their new house since he could no longer afford the mortgage payments.

What advice will you give Mr. Faber about the merits of litigation against the Plan?

IV. REGULATION OF PRIVATE HEALTH INSURANCE UNDER STATE LAW

A. TRADITIONAL INSURANCE REGULATION

Historically, the states bore primary responsibility for regulating private health care finance, a role confirmed by Congress in the McCarran–Ferguson Act of 1945. 15 U.S.C.A. §§ 1011–1015. In the next chapter we will consider the effect that the Employee Retirement Income Security Act of 1974 (ERISA) has had on state regulation. Although ERISA places some limits on the ability of the states to regulate employee benefit plans, the states still remain primarily responsible for regulating insurers who insure employee benefits plans as well as all health insurance plans not governed by ERISA, such as individual health insurance plans, group insurance plans covering church employees or employees of state and local government, no-fault auto insurance, uninsured motorist policies, and workers' compensation.

All states tax the premiums of commercial insurers and most tax Blue Cross/Blue Shield plan premiums (though some at a lower rate than commercial plans). States oversee the financial solvency of insurers by imposing minimal requirements for financial reserves and for allowable investments, and through requiring annual statements and conducting periodic examinations of insurers (usually on a triennial basis). Why might insurer insolvencies be of greater concern to government than bankruptcies in other sectors of the economy?

In most states, insurers must file policy forms with the state insurance regulatory agency. Some states allow a form to be used once it has been filed with the insurance agency (if it is not disapproved), while others require explicit approval of a policy form before it can be used. States also regulate insurance marketing and claims practices, including coordination of benefits where an insured is covered by more than one policy. (This is often the case in today's society with two-income and blended families.) State insurance commissions investigate consumer complaints and place insolvent companies into receivership. The National Association of Insurance Commissioners (NAIC) has issued model codes and regulations on many of these subjects, the wide adoption of which has brought about some uniformity among the states. See www.naic.org.

How do these traditional concerns of insurance regulation change in a managed care environment? Should health maintenance organizations be subject to the same solvency and reserve requirements as commercial insurers? Should provider-sponsored integrated delivery systems also be required to meet solvency and reserve requirements? Should independent practice associations, physician groups, and other provider entities that assume "downstream" risk from HMOs be subject to solvency requirements, or is it sufficient that the HMO agrees to assume the risk of solvency of such groups? (In the late 1990s hundreds of risk-bearing groups covering millions of patients became insolvent, see Brant S. Mittler and Andre Hampton, The Princess and the Pea: The Assurance of Voluntary Compliance Between the Texas Attorney General and Aetna's Texas HMOs and its Impact on Financial Risk Shifting by Managed Care, 83 F.U.L.Rev. 553 (2003)). Are marketing and claims practices more or less of a concern under managed care?

B. ATTEMPTS TO INCREASE ACCESS TO INSURANCE THROUGH REGULATION

States have not historically regulated the rates of commercial health insurers. Because the market for health insurance has been relatively competitive and because most insurance is sold to employers or large groups that have some bargaining power and expertise, rate regulation was not generally thought necessary. Rates and rate information are commonly filed with the insurance commissioner, and some states permit the commissioner to disapprove these filings if benefits do not bear a reasonable relationship to premiums charged. But most states have historically not set health insurance rates as such and have rarely intervened in insurer rate-setting processes. States have also not traditionally regulated underwriting practices, other than to attempt to assure that rates were not obviously discriminatory (e.g. treating different racial groups differently). Regulation of nonprofit Blue Cross and Blue Shield rates and underwriting, however, has been much more common because of a belief that the Blues have had a greater obligation to make their services readily available to the public at a fair rate in exchange for the favorable tax and regulatory treatment they have historically received. As many Blue plans have become for profit, this distinction has faded.

In recent years, however, states have increasingly regulated underwriting practices and premium rate-setting in an effort to assure equity of access to insurance. As was noted in Chapter 4, the number of uninsured in America has grown through most of the past decade, and at this writing over 47 million Americans are uninsured. Most of the uninsured are either employed or the dependents of employed persons. A major reason why so many employed persons are uninsured is that persons who are either self-employed or employed by small employers are far less likely to be insured, or even to have insurance available through their place of employment, than are employees of large businesses. Only about 45 percent of employers with fewer than 10 employees offer health insurance benefits, while nearly all employers with more than 200 do for their full-time employees. This is in part due to the fact that individual and small group insurance tends to be much more expensive than insurance covering large groups. This in turn is true because administrative, marketing, and underwriting costs are much higher for individual and small group coverage, and because insurers have to cover themselves against the greater risk of adverse selection inherent in insuring individuals and small groups. Although the growth in the number of the uninsured in recent years is attributable to increases in the number of employees declining insurance offered by their employers (usually because of high premium costs), as well as increases in the number of part-time or temporary workers not covered by employment-related insurance, the fact that small employers disproportionately do not offer their employees insurance is a key cause of lack of insurance in the United States.

For purposes of regulation, states usually distinguish between large groups, small groups, and individuals. While the boundaries vary from state to state (and can sometimes be manipulated by insurers), small groups are usually defined as groups with between 2 and 50 members, large groups with more than 50 members. The underwriting of insurance for large group plans is unregulated in most states. Most states, on the other hand, do regulate underwriting practices with respect to individuals. Every state has, moreover, adopted small group reforms during the past decade, which usually go further in limiting insurer discretion than reforms in individual insurance markets. These reforms were encouraged by the 1996 federal Health Insurance Portability and Accountability Act (HIPAA), which mandated the enactment of certain small group and individual reforms discussed in detail in the next chapter. Many of the reforms required by HIPAA, however, were already in place in numerous states before it went into effect, while many states have also adopted reforms going beyond HIPAA, thus HIPAA may have added little to state regulation in many states. Why might access to affordable insurance be less of a problem for large groups? Why might states be more willing to pass laws protecting small groups than individuals? What protections do small groups need?

COLONIAL LIFE INSURANCE COMPANY OF AMERICA v. CURIALE

Supreme Court, Appellate Division, Third Department, 1994.
205 A.D.2d 58, 617 N.Y.S.2d 377.

PETERS, JUSTICE.

* * *

Petitioner is a commercial insurance company which issues small group health insurance policies in this State. Petitioner challenged two regulations promulgated by respondent Superintendent of Insurance to implement chapter 501 of the Laws of 1992. Chapter 501 requires a commercial insurer doing business in this State to employ "community rating" and to offer "open enrollment"[2] for any insurance policies issued in this State. The underpinning of the new law was to spread the risk among more people and provide greater rate stability. The Superintendent was directed to promulgate regulations designed to protect insurers writing policies from claim fluctuations and "unexpected significant shifts in the number of persons insured"[ ]. Pursuant thereto, the Superintendent promulgated 11 NYCRR parts 360 and 361 which implemented what he deemed a statutory directive that insurers be required to share the risk of high-cost claims by establishing a pool system which compares the risk of insurers in seven regions of the State[ ]. After these comparisons were made, insurers with worse than average demographic

---

2. Open enrollment requires that any individual or small group applying for health insurance coverage must be accepted for any coverage offered by the insurer[ ].

factors would get money from regional pooling funds, while insurers with better than average factors would pay money into these pooling funds.

Petitioner commenced this proceeding seeking to have 11 NYCRR part 361 and two provisions of 11 NYCRR part 360 invalidated. Supreme Court [The trial court in New York] dismissed the petition to the extent that it challenged 11 NYCRR part 361, but granted the petition with respect to 11 NYCRR part 360. The parties have cross-appealed from the adverse portions of the court's judgment.

* * *

Petitioner contends that the pool system established by 11 NYCRR part 361 violates the intent of chapter 501 since the Legislature did not intend that (1) contributions to the system be mandatory, (2) contributions be based on existing policies, and (3) Empire Blue Cross and Blue Shield (hereinafter Empire) participate. * * *

The Superintendent established the pool system pursuant to Insurance Law § 3233 which provided that "the superintendent shall promulgate regulations to assure an orderly implementation and ongoing operation of the open enrollment and community rating required by [Insurance Law §§ 3231 and 4317] * * *. The regulations shall apply to all insurers and health maintenance organizations subject to community rating" (Insurance Law § 3233[a]). Based upon such language, there exists a clear expression by the Legislature that regulations shall be promulgated to further open enrollment which "shall include reinsurance or a pooling process involving insurer contributions to, or receipts from, a fund"[ ] and that those regulations "shall apply to all insurers and health maintenance organizations subject to community rating"[ ]. * * *

[The Court next held that the regulations were not improperly retroactive, and that Empire Blue Cross was properly included in the scheme].

Finally, petitioner contends that 11 NYCRR part 361 imposes an unconstitutional tax, gives State money to private organizations and takes property without just compensation. Our review indicates that the Legislature intended pool payments be mandatory and that those payments consist of the amounts necessary to permit sharing or equalization of the risk of high cost claims[ ]. Having chosen to require such payments, the Legislature could therefore delegate the responsibility to the Superintendent to collect such amounts[ ] We find that such pool contributions are a valid exercise of the Legislature's power to regulate[ ] and as the enactment intended to regulate rather than generate revenue it is not a tax[ ].

* * * We further agree with Supreme Court that there has not been an unconstitutional taking of what petitioner contends is its low-risk value of its book of business. We find, as did Supreme Court, that petitioner cannot support its contention that it has a constitutionally protected interest in maintaining a healthier than average risk pool[ ].

Supreme Court invalidated 11 NYCRR 360.4(c) and 360.3(a)(1)(ii), holding that they exceeded the scope of the authority delegated to the Superintendent by chapter 501. The Superintendent promulgated 11 NYCRR 360.4(c) in response to his understanding of the statutory directive contained in Insurance Law § 3231(b), which [regulation] reads as follows:

Nothing herein shall prohibit the use of premium rate structures to establish different premium rates for individuals as opposed to family units or separate community rates for individuals as opposed to small groups. Individual proprietors and groups of two must be classified in the individual or small group rating category by the insurer.

Supreme Court held that this requirement exceeded the Superintendent's authority, determining that Insurance Law § 3231(b) applied only to the rating of policies and "does not provide authority for requiring insurers of small groups to extend coverage to individual proprietors and groups of two". Should the Superintendent's regulation be permitted to stand, [the trial court] reasoned, and we agree, that the definition of "small group" contained in Insurance Law § 3231(a) would be impermissibly expanded to now require small group insurers to cover individual proprietors and/or groups of two contrary to the clear and unambiguous language in the statute.[ ] * * *

As to 11 NYCRR 360.3(a)(1)(ii), we find that Supreme Court's findings should not be disturbed. Under Insurance Law § 4235(c)(1), if less than 50 percent of employees in a group do not agree to participate in a plan, the insurer does not have to offer coverage to the group. The Superintendent, however, promulgated 11 NYCRR part 360.3(a)(1)(ii) which provides as follows

[F]or purposes of determining said participation requirements, insurers must include as participating all eligible employees or members of the group covered under all the alternative health maintenance organization plans made available by the group.

Supreme Court properly invalidated the regulation since chapter 501 did not amend or change the minimum participation requirements set forth in Insurance Law § 4235(c)(1) and the Superintendent therefore exceeded his authority by redefining the calculation of participation levels[ ].

* * *

Notes and Questions

1. What is the purpose of laws requiring community rating and open enrollment? Why do these requirements in turn result in the need to create a pool to share risk among insurers? Why would commercial insurers object to including Blue Cross in this pool? Why are individual insureds not included in the small group pooling requirements? Why are insurers permitted to exclude from coverage groups in which fewer than 50 percent of the group members elect to be insured?

2. All states currently require insurers that sell in small group markets to offer coverage and guarantee renewal to any small group that requests it, regardless of the health status or claims experience of the group's members. Thirty-eight states had guaranteed issue and forty-three guaranteed renewal requirements before HIPAA, but HIPAA made these requirements universal. HIPAA also requires restrictions on preexisting conditions clauses (clauses that exclude coverage for conditions that existed prior to the inception of the insurance contract). Forty-five states had restricted preexisting conditions clauses for small group policies before HIPAA. A number of states continue to go beyond HIPAA in limiting preexisting conditions clauses, moreover, including three states that outlaw them altogether.

Although HIPAA does not address the level of insurance premiums, many states do. As of the end of 2006, 37 states limited the variation in premiums insurers charge to small groups, only allowing insurers to vary premiums because of claims experience, health status, or duration of coverage of the group within a specified range. Insurance rating limitations, for example, may allow the highest premiums charged by an insurer to be twice as high as the lowest premiums charged. Twelve states went further, requiring a form of community rating by prohibiting rating based on experience, health status, or duration of coverage. New York, the most restrictive of the states, even limited variance of premiums based on age. Seven states also had established mandatory reinsurance pools and 19 voluntary reinsurance pools, assuring that small group plans that end up carrying high risk groups can spread some of their risks to other insurers with more favorable risk experience. See Blue Cross Blue Shield Association, State Legislative Health Care and Insurance Issues: 2006 Survey of Plans (2007). What would you expect to be the effect of these laws?

3.   Most of the states have also attempted to reform the individual insurance market. The most common individual market reform is guaranteed renewal, required by HIPAA but adopted by twenty-one states before HIPAA. As of the end of 2006, thirty one states had adopted restrictions on preexisting conditions limitations covering persons beyond those who must be covered under HIPAA. Among other individual market reforms adopted by the states are 1) community rating requirements (8 states); 2) rating bands (i.e. requiring that the highest premiums charged not be more than a specified percentage higher than the lowest premiums charged) or other restrictions on rates (10 states); 3) provision for voluntary or mandatory participation in reinsurance pools (8 states); and 4) preexisting conditions limitations (31 states).

4.   One issue that has seen a great deal of state legislative action in recent years has been insurance underwriting based on genetic information. All but a handful of states have adopted laws prohibiting insurers from establishing eligibility rules that take into account genetic information or from using genetic information for risk selection or classification. About half the states also prohibit insurers from requiring genetic tests or information. In most states these requirements apply to both the group and individual market, but in some states they apply only to one or the other.

5.   As a general rule, small groups get better insurance rates than individuals, and large groups better than small groups. One approach to making insurance more affordable, therefore, has been to promote "association health plans," (AHPs) which allow individuals or small business to band together to purchase insurance or to self-insure, thus limiting marketing, underwriting, and administrative costs. Legislation has been introduced into Congress each year in the recent past that would additionally permit association plans to be sold across state lines, regulated by the federal government or by a single state, and otherwise freeing these AHPs from state law underwriting requirements and coverage mandates. This legislation has received strong support from small businesses and insurers, who believe that it would reduce the cost of insurance. It has been opposed by consumer advocates, state insurance commissioners and Blue Cross and Blue Shield plans. Opponents claim that AHPs plans would attract lower risk insureds and thus destabilize state insurance markets. In particular, freeing AHPs from some state mandates, like required coverage of mental health or substance abuse treatment, would allow AHPs to attract less costly favorable risks, leaving other insurers with more costly groups and individuals. See, exploring these

issues, Mila Kofman, *et al.*, Association Health Plans: What's All the Fuss About? 25(6) Health Affairs 1591, 1598 (2006) Mila Kofman, Association Health Plans: Loss of State Oversight Means Regulatory Vacuum and More Fraud (Georgetown Health Policy Institute 2005); Mark A. Hall, Elliot K. Wicks and Janice S. Lawlor, Health Marts, HIPCs, MEWAs, and AHPs: A Guide for the Perplexed, 20 Health Aff. (1), 142–53 (2001). See, discussing specifically one recent attempt to free nongroup health insurance from state regulation, Elizabeth A. Pendo, The Health Care Choice Act: The Individual Insurance Market and the Politics of "Choice," 29 W. New. Eng. L. Rev. 473 (2007).

6. Another focus of regulatory concern in recent years has been "post claims underwriting." The issue here is insurance companies accepting applications for insurance and then, often after collecting premiums for some time, canceling coverage after the insured files a substantial claim, asserting that the insured misrepresented health status on the original application. The California Department of Managed Health Care in March, 2007, fined California Blue Cross $1 million for this practice, which violates the Knox–Keene Health Care Service Plan Act. The Department alleged that Blue Cross had not shown that the applicants had wilfully misrepresented their health status, and that the plans had failed to conduct an adequate pre-enrollment medical history investigation, or to conform to their own underwriting policies. See BNA Health Law Reporter, Mar. 29, 2007, 392. See also Hailey v. California Physicians' Service, 2007 WL 1986107 (Cal.Ct. App. June 7, 2007) finding that the post-claims underwriting practices of Blue Shield of California violated the Knox–Keene Act. Blue Cross of California also recently sent letters to the doctors of members enclosing a copy of the members' health plan applications and asking the doctors to disclose any pre-existing conditions not noted on the applications. Many doctors strenuously objected. Lisa Girion, Doctors Balk at Request for Data, Los Angeles Times, Feb. 12, 2008. What are the hazards to consumers posed by post-claims underwriting? How would insurers argue that this is a legitimate practice?

7. In the end, regulatory approaches seem to have done little toward making insurance available in small group and individual markets, although the reforms have certainly helped some individuals and firms that might otherwise not have been able to secure insurance. In part, their limited effect seems to be due to the endless creativity of insurers in evading regulation and limiting their risk. By manipulating coverage imposing cost-sharing obligations, and marketing selectively, as well as by creating "association" plans or using other devices that allow small group or individual plans to masquerade as large group plans, insurers can still often control the risk to which they are exposed, allowing them to remain prosperous, but on the other hand, to continue to exclude high-risk individuals.

On the other hand, the disastrous effects of these reforms that many in the health insurance industry had predicted have also not materialized. Insurers have generally remained in business even in states that have adopted rigorous reforms, and markets have remained competitive, though individual reforms have had a more damaging effect on markets than small group reforms have had. To a considerable degree, however, the effects that small group reforms might have had on insurers or insureds have been masked by a dramatic growth of managed care in small group markets, which has held down increases in premiums that reforms might otherwise have caused.

Mark Hall has written an excellent series of articles on health insurance reforms as part of a project funded by the Robert Wood Johnson Foundation, including The Competitive Impact of Small Group Health Insurance Reforms, 32 Mich J.L.Ref. 685 (1999); The Competitive Impact of Small Group Health Insurance Reform Laws, 37 Inquiry 376 (2001); The Geography of Health Insurance Regulation 19 Health Aff., March/Apr.2000 at 173; and two contributions to a symposium on the individual health insurance market, in volume 25 of the Journal of Health Politics, Policy and Law. Other useful sources include Alan C. Monheit & Joel C. Cantor, eds., State Health Insurance Market Reform (Routledge: New York, 2004) 113, 116; Beth Fuchs, Expanding the Individual Health Insurance Market: Lessons from the State Health Insurance Reforms of the 1990s, Robert Wood Johnson Synthesis Project, 2004; Gail A. Jensen and Michael A. Morrisey, Small Group Reforms and Insurance Provision by Small Firms, 1989–1995, 36 Inquiry 176 (1999); and John Gabel, *et al.*, Health Benefits of Small Employers in 1998 (1999). For a comparative perspective, see Timothy S. Jost, Private or Public Approaches to Insuring the Uninsured: Lessons from International Experience with Private Insurance, 76 N.Y.U. L. Rev. 419 (2001).

Problem: Expanding Insurance Coverage

You are a state legislator and the chair of the legislative health and welfare committee. You have run on a platform calling for increased regulation to address the problem of the uninsured, which is quite serious in your state. You would like to make insurance coverage more attractive to small businesses, which often do not offer insurance to their employees in your state, and to self-employed individuals. What regulatory strategies will you consider? Are there non-regulatory strategies you might consider as well, such as tax credits or penalties or mandates? Whom will you invite to testify at hearings you will hold on this subject? What do you expect them to say at the hearings? Review the discussion of the Massachusetts plan in Chapter 4. Also reconsider this problem after you study the discussion of ERISA preemption of state reform efforts in Chapter 7.

V. STATE REGULATION OF MANAGED CARE

A. INTRODUCTION

Managed Care Organizations (MCOs) differ from traditional health insurers, of course, insofar as they manage care. As Marmor and Hacker note above, they do this through restricting members to the use of particular providers, reviewing the utilization of services, and creating incentives for limiting the cost of care. Some MCOs also attempt to oversee the quality of care their members receive. Though managed care was generally welcomed at first as offering the potential both to restrain costs and to improve quality, beginning in the late 1990s a decided "backlash" against managed care gathered steam. See Alice A. Noble and Troyen A. Brennan, The Stages of Managed Care Regulation: Developing Better Rules, in John E. Billi and Gail B. Agrawal, The Challenge of Regulating Managed Care, 29 (2001). There was a general perception—encouraged by the media—that managed care controls had become excessive, threatening access to care. Almost every state has adopted some form of legislation, nearly 1000 statutes in all, during the last half of the 1990s. While many of these statutes address fairly narrow problems, a number of states have adopted comprehensive legislation addressing a variety of problems. The following law, adopted in 2000 by Massachusetts, addresses most of the issues with which such legislation has been concerned.

MASSACHUSETTS GENERAL LAWS ANNOTATED: AN ACT RELATIVE TO MANAGED CARE PRACTICES IN THE INSURANCE INDUSTRY

* * *

Chapter 111, Section 217. (a) There is hereby established within the department [of public health] an office of patient protection. The office shall:

(2) establish a site on the internet and through other communication media in order to make managed care information collected by the office readily accessible to consumers. Said internet site shall, at a minimum, include (i) the health plan report card developed [by the state], (ii) a chart, prepared by the office, comparing the information obtained on premium revenue expended for health care services as provided pursuant to * * *, and (iii) [HEDIS data, see below];

(3) assist consumers with questions or concerns relating to managed care, including but not limited to exercising the grievance and appeals rights * * *;

* * *

(c) Each entity that compiles the health plan employer data and information set, [HEDIS] so-called, for the National Committee on Quality Assurance, or collects other information deemed by the entity as similar or equivalent thereto, shall * * * concurrently submit to the office of patient protection a copy thereof excluding, at the entity's option, proprietary financial data.

* * *

Chapter 176G: Section 5. (a) As used in this section, the following words shall have the following meanings:

* * *

"Emergency medical condition", a medical condition, whether physical or mental, manifesting itself by symptoms of sufficient severity, including severe pain, that the absence of prompt medical attention could reasonably be expected by a prudent layperson who possesses an average knowledge of health and medicine, to result in placing the health of a member or another person in serious jeopardy, serious impairment to body function, or serious dysfunction of any body organ or part, or, with respect to a pregnant woman, as further defined in [EMTALA, see Chapter 5].

"Stabilization for discharge", an emergency medical condition shall be deemed to be stabilized for purposes of discharging a member, * * *, when the attending physician has determined that, within reasonable clinical confidence, the member has reached the point where further care, including diagnostic work-up or treatment, or both, could be reasonably performed on an outpatient basis or a later scheduled inpatient basis if the member is given a reasonable plan for appropriate follow-up care and discharge instructions, * * *. Stabilization for discharge does not require final resolution of the emergency medical condition.

* * *

(b) A health maintenance organization shall cover emergency services provided to members for emergency medical conditions. After the member has been stabilized for discharge or transfer, the health maintenance organization or its designee may require a hospital emergency department to contact * * * the health maintenance organization * * * for authorization of post-stabilization services to be provided. * * * Such authorization shall be deemed granted if the health maintenance organization or its designee has not responded to said call within 30 minutes. Notwithstanding the foregoing provision, in the event the attending physician and * * * on-call physician do not agree on what constitutes appropriate medical treatment, the opinion of the attending physician shall prevail and such treatment shall be considered appropriate treatment for an emergency medical condition provided that such treatment is consistent with generally accepted principles of professional medical practice and a covered benefit under the member's evidence of coverage. * * *

* * *

(e) * * * No member shall in any way be discouraged from using the local pre-hospital emergency medical service system, the 911 telephone number, or the local equivalent, or be denied coverage for medical and transportation expenses incurred as a result of an emergency medical condition.

* * *

Chapter 176O: Health Insurance Consumer Protections.

Section 1. As used in this chapter, the following words shall have the following meanings:—

"Adverse determination", a determination, based upon a review of information provided by a carrier or its designated utilization review organization, to deny, reduce, modify, or terminate an admission, continued inpatient stay, or the availability of any other health care services, * * *.

* * *

"Grievance", any oral or written complaint submitted to the carrier which has been initiated by an insured, or on behalf of an insured with the consent of the insured, concerning any aspect or action of the carrier relative to the insured, including, but not limited to, review of adverse determinations regarding scope of coverage, denial of services, quality of care and administrative operations, * * *.

* * *

"Incentive plan", any compensation arrangement between a carrier and licensed health care professional or licensed health care provider group or organization that employs or utilizes services of one or more licensed health care professionals that may directly or indirectly have the effect of reducing or limiting services furnished to insureds of the organization.

* * *

"Medical necessity" or "medically necessary", health care services that are consistent with generally accepted principles of professional medical practice.

* * *

Section 4. A carrier * * * shall not refuse to contract with or compensate for covered services an otherwise eligible health care provider solely because such provider has in good faith communicated with or advocated on behalf of one or more of his prospective, current or former patients regarding the provisions, terms or requirements of the carrier's health benefit plans as they relate to the needs of such provider's patients, or communicated with one or more of his prospective, current or former patients with respect to the method by which such provider is compensated by the carrier for services provided to the patient. Nothing in this section shall be construed to preclude a * * * carrier from requiring a health * * * provider to hold confidential specific compensation terms.

Section 5. No contract between a carrier * * * and a health * * * care provider for the provision of services to insureds may require the health care provider to indemnify the carrier for any expenses and liabilities, including, without limitation, judgments, settlements, attorneys' fees, court costs and any associated charges, incurred in connection with any claim or action brought against the carrier based on the carrier's management decisions, utilization review provisions or other policies, guidelines or actions.

Section 6. (a) A carrier shall issue and deliver to at least one adult insured in each household residing in the commonwealth, upon enrollment, an evidence of coverage and any amendments thereto. Said evidence of coverage shall contain a clear, concise and complete statement of:

(1) the health care services and any other benefits which the insured is entitled to on a nondiscriminatory basis;

* * *

(3) the limitations on the scope of health care services and any other benefits to be provided, including an explanation of any deductible or copayment feature and all restrictions relating to preexisting condition exclusions;

(4) the locations where, and the manner in which, health care services and other benefits may be obtained;

(5) the criteria by which an insured may be disenrolled or denied enrollment and the involuntary disenrollment rate among insureds of the carrier;

(6) a description of the carrier's method for resolving insured complaints, including a description of the formal internal grievance process * * * and the external grievance process * * * for appealing decisions pursuant to said grievances, as required by this chapter;

* * *

(8) a summary description of the procedure, if any, for out-of-network referrals and any additional charge for utilizing out-of-network providers;

(9) a summary description of the utilization review procedures and quality assurance programs used by the carrier, including the toll-free telephone number to be established by the carrier that enables consumers to determine the status or outcome of utilization review decisions;

(10) a statement detailing what translator and interpretation services are available to assist insureds * * *;

(11) a list of prescription drugs excluded from any restricted formulary available to insureds under the health benefit plan * * *;

(12) a summary description of the procedures followed by the carrier in making decisions about the experimental or investigational nature of individual drugs, medical devices or treatments in clinical trials;

(13) a statement on how to obtain the report regarding grievances from the office of patient protection * * *;

(14) the toll-free telephone number, facsimile number, and internet site for the office of patient protection in the department of public health * * *;

* * *

Section 7. (a) A carrier shall provide to at least one adult insured in each household upon enrollment, and to a prospective insured upon request, the following information:

(1) a list of health care providers in the carrier's network, organized by specialty and by location and summarizing for each such provider the method used to compensate or reimburse such provider; provided, however, that nothing in this clause shall be construed to require disclosure of the specific details of any financial arrangements between a carrier and a provider * * *;

(2) a statement that physician profiling information, so-called, may be available from the board of registration in medicine;

(3) a summary description of the process by which clinical guidelines and utilization review criteria are developed;

(4) the voluntary and involuntary disenrollment rate among insureds of the carrier;

* * *

(b) A carrier shall provide all of the information required under section 6 and subsection (a) of this section to the office of patient protection in the department of public health and, in addition, shall provide to said office the following information:

(1) a list of sources of independently published information assessing insured satisfaction and evaluating the quality of health care services offered by the carrier;

(2) the percentage of physicians who voluntarily and involuntarily terminated participation contracts with the carrier during the previous calendar year * * * and the three most common reasons for voluntary and involuntary physician disenrollment;

(3) the percentage of premium revenue expended by the carrier for health care services provided to insureds for the most recent year for which information is available; and

(4) a report detailing, for the previous calendar year, the total number of: (i) filed grievances, grievances that were approved internally, grievances that were denied internally, and grievances that were withdrawn before resolution; and (ii) external appeals pursued after exhausting the internal grievance process and the resolution of all such external appeals. The report shall identify for each such category, to the extent such information is available,

the demographics of such insureds, which shall include, but need not be limited to, race, gender and age.

* * *

Section 10. (a) No contract between a carrier, * * * and a licensed health * * * care provider group shall contain any incentive plan that includes a specific payment made to a health * * * care professional as an inducement to reduce, delay or limit specific, necessary services covered by the * * * contract. Health * * * care professionals shall not profit from provision of covered services that are not necessary and appropriate. Carriers * * * shall not profit from denial or withholding of covered services that are necessary and appropriate. Nothing in this section shall prohibit contracts that contain incentive plans that involve general payments such as capitation payments or shared risk agreements that are made with respect to health * * * care providers or which are made with respect to groups of insureds if such contracts, which impose risk on such health * * * care providers for the costs of care, services and equipment provided or authorized by another * * * provider, comply with subsection (b).

(b) In order that patient care decisions are based on need and not on financial incentives, no carrier * * * shall enter into a new contract, revise the risk arrangements in an existing contract or, after July 1, 2001, revise the fee schedule in an existing contract with a health * * * care provider which imposes financial risk on such provider for the costs of care, services or equipment provided or authorized by another provider unless such contract includes specific provisions with respect to the following: (1) stop loss protection, (2) minimum patient population size for the provider group, and (3) identification of the health * * * care services for which the provider is at risk.

(c) A carrier or utilization review organization shall conduct an annual survey of insureds to assess satisfaction with access to specialist services, ancillary services, hospitalization services, durable medical equipment and other covered services. Said survey shall compare the actual satisfaction of insureds with projected measures of their satisfaction. Carriers that utilize incentive plans shall establish mechanisms for monitoring the satisfaction, quality of care and actual utilization compared with projected utilization of health care services of insureds.

* * *

Section 12. (a) Utilization review conducted by a carrier or a utilization review organization shall be conducted pursuant to a written plan, under the supervision of a physician and staffed by appropriately trained and qualified personnel, * * *.

A carrier or utilization review organization shall * * * conduct all utilization review activities pursuant to [written] criteria. The criteria shall be, to the maximum extent feasible, scientifically derived and evidence-based, and developed with the input of participating physicians, consistent with the development of medical necessity criteria * * *.

Adverse determinations rendered by a program of utilization review, or other denials of requests for health services, shall be made by a person licensed in the appropriate specialty related to such health service and, where applicable, by a provider in the same licensure category as the ordering provider.

(b) A carrier or utilization review organization shall make an initial determination regarding a proposed admission, procedure or service that requires such a determination within two working days of obtaining all necessary information. * * * In the case of a determination to approve an admission, procedure or service, the carrier or utilization review organization shall notify the provider rendering the service by telephone within 24 hours. * * * In the case of an adverse determination, the carrier or utilization review organization shall notify the provider rendering the service by telephone within 24 hours, * * *.

(c) A carrier or utilization review organization shall make a concurrent review determination within one working day of obtaining all necessary information. * * * The service shall be continued without liability to the insured until the insured has been notified of the determination.

(d) The written notification of an adverse determination shall include a substantive clinical justification therefor that is consistent with generally accepted principles of professional medical practice, and shall, at a minimum: (1) identify the specific information upon which the adverse determination was based; (2) discuss the insured's presenting symptoms or condition, diagnosis and treatment interventions and the specific reasons such medical evidence fails to meet the relevant medical review criteria; (3) specify any alternative treatment option offered by the carrier, if any; and (4) reference and include applicable clinical practice guidelines and review criteria.

(e) A carrier or utilization review organization shall give a provider treating an insured an opportunity to seek reconsideration of an adverse determination from a clinical peer reviewer in any case involving an initial determination or a concurrent review determination. Said reconsideration process shall occur within one working day of the receipt of the request and shall be conducted between the provider rendering the service and the clinical peer reviewer * * *. If the adverse determination is not reversed by the reconsideration process, the insured, or the provider on behalf of the insured, may pursue the grievance process * * *. The reconsideration process allowed herein shall not be a prerequisite to the formal internal grievance process or an expedited appeal required by section 13.

Section 13. (a) A carrier or utilization review organization shall maintain a formal internal grievance process that provides for adequate consideration and timely resolution of grievances, which shall include but not be limited to: * * * (2) the provision of a clear, concise and complete description of the carrier's formal internal grievance process and the procedures for obtaining external review * * *; (3) the carrier's toll-free telephone number for assisting insureds in resolving such grievances and the consumer assistance toll-free telephone number maintained by the office of patient protection; (4) a written acknowledgment of the receipt of a grievance within 15 days and a written resolution of each grievance within 30 days from receipt thereof; and (5) a procedure to accept grievances by telephone, in person, by mail, or by electronic means, * * *.

(b) The formal internal grievance process maintained by a carrier or utilization review organization shall provide for an expedited resolution of a grievance concerning a carrier's coverage or provision of immediate and urgently needed services. Said expedited resolution policy shall include, but not be limited to:

(i) a resolution before an insured's discharge from a hospital if the grievance is submitted by an insured who is an inpatient in a hospital;

(ii) provisions for the automatic reversal of decisions denying coverage for services * * *, pending the outcome of the appeals process, within 48 hours, * * *, of receipt of certification by said physician that, in the [treating] physician's opinion, the service * * * at issue in a grievance or appeal is medically necessary, that a denial of coverage for such services * * * would create a substantial risk of serious harm to the patient, and that the risk of that harm is so immediate that the provision of such services * * * should not await the outcome of the normal appeal or grievance process * * *;

(iii) a resolution within five days from the receipt of such grievance if submitted by an insured with a terminal illness.

* * *

(c) A grievance not properly acted on by the carrier within the time limits required by this section shall be deemed resolved in favor of the insured.

Section 14. (a) An insured who remains aggrieved by an adverse determination and has exhausted all remedies available from the formal internal grievance process * * *, may seek further review of the grievance by a review panel established by the office of patient protection * * *. The insured shall pay the first $25 of the cost of the review to said office which may waive the fee in cases of extreme financial hardship. The commonwealth shall assess the carrier for the remainder of the cost of the review * * *. The office of patient protection shall contract with at least three unrelated and objective review agencies * * *, and refer grievances to one of the review agencies on a random selection basis. The review agencies shall develop review panels appropriate for the given grievance which shall include qualified clinical decision-makers experienced in the determination of medical necessity, utilization management protocols and grievance resolution, and shall not have any financial relationship with the carrier making the initial determination. The standard for review of a grievance by such a panel shall be the determination of whether the requested treatment or service is medically necessary, as defined herein, and a covered benefit under the policy or contract. * * * The panel shall send final written disposition of the grievance, and the reasons therefor, to the insured and the carrier within 60 days of receipt of the request for review, * * *.

(b) If a grievance is filed concerning the termination of ongoing coverage or treatment, the disputed coverage or treatment shall remain in effect through completion of the formal internal grievance process. An insured may apply to the external review panel to seek continued provision of health care services which are the subject of the grievance during the course of said external review upon a showing of substantial harm to the insured's health absent such continuation, or other good cause as determined by the panel.

(c) The decision of the review panel shall be binding. The superior court shall have jurisdiction to enforce the decision of the review panel.

* * *

(e) The grievance procedures authorized by this section shall be in addition to any other procedures that may be available to any insured pursuant to contract or law, and failure to pursue, exhaust or engage in the procedures described in this subsection shall not preclude the use of any other remedy provided by any contract or law.

* * *

Section 15. (a) A carrier that allows or requires the designation of a primary care physician shall notify an insured at least 30 days before the disenrollment of such insured's primary care physician and shall permit such insured to continue to be covered for health services, consistent with the terms of the evidence of coverage, by such primary care physician for at least 30 days after said physician is disenrolled, other than disenrollment for quality-related reasons or for fraud. * * *

(b) A carrier shall allow any female insured who is in her second or third trimester of pregnancy and whose provider in connection with her pregnancy is involuntarily disenrolled, * * * to continue treatment with said provider, consistent with the terms of the evidence of coverage, for the period up to and including the insured's first postpartum visit.

(c) A carrier shall allow any insured who is terminally ill and whose provider in connection with said illness is involuntarily disenrolled, * * *, consistent with the terms of the evidence of coverage, until the insured's death.

(d) A carrier shall provide coverage for health services for up to 30 days from the effective date of coverage to a new insured by a physician who is not a participating provider in the carrier's network if: (1) the insured's employer only offers the insured a choice of carriers in which said physician is not a participating provider, and (2) said physician is providing the insured with an ongoing course of treatment or is the insured's primary care physician. * * *

* * *

(f) A carrier that requires an insured to designate a primary care physician shall allow such a primary care physician to authorize a standing referral for specialty health care provided by a health care provider participating in such carrier's network when (1) the primary care physician determines that such referrals are appropriate, (2) the provider of specialty health care agrees to a treatment plan for the insured and provides the primary care physician with all necessary clinical and administrative information on a regular basis, and (3) the health care services to be provided are consistent with the terms of the evidence of coverage. * * *

(g) No carrier shall require an insured to obtain a referral or prior authorization from a primary care physician for the following specialty care provided by an obstetrician, gynecologist, certified nurse-midwife or family practitioner participating in such carrier's health care provider network: (1) annual preventive gynecologic health examinations, including any subsequent obstetric or gynecological services determined by such obstetrician, gynecologist, certified nurse-midwife or family practitioner to be medically necessary as a result of such examination; (2) maternity care; and (3) medically necessary evaluations and resultant health care services for acute or emergency gynecological conditions. * * *

(h) A carrier shall provide coverage of pediatric specialty care, including mental health care, by persons with recognized expertise in specialty pediatrics to insureds requiring such services.

(i) A carrier * * * shall provide health * * * care providers applying to be participating providers who are denied such status with a written reason or reasons for denial of such application.

(j) No carrier shall make a contract with a health care provider which includes a provision permitting termination without cause. A carrier shall provide a written statement to a provider of the reason or reasons for such provider's involuntary disenrollment.

(k) A carrier * * * shall provide insureds, upon request, interpreter and translation services related to administrative procedures.

Section 16. (a) The physician treating an insured, shall, consistent with generally accepted principles of professional medical practice and in consultation with the insured, make all clinical decisions regarding medical treatment to be provided to the insured, including the provision of durable medical equipment and hospital lengths of stay. Nothing in this section shall be construed as altering, affecting or modifying either the obligations of any third party or the terms and conditions of any agreement or contract between either the treating physician or the insured and any third party.

(b) A carrier shall be required to pay for health care services ordered by a treating physician if (1) the services are a covered benefit under the insured's health benefit plan; and (2) the services are medically necessary. A carrier may develop guidelines to be used in applying the standard of medical necessity, as defined herein. Any such medical necessity guidelines utilized by a carrier in making coverage determinations shall be: (i) developed with input from practicing physicians in the carrier's or utilization review organization's service area; (ii) developed in accordance with the standards adopted by national accreditation organizations; (iii) updated at least biennially or more often as new treatments, applications and technologies are adopted as generally accepted professional medical practice; and (iv) evidence-based, if practicable. In applying such guidelines, a carrier shall consider the individual health care needs of the insured.

* * *

Notes and Questions

What information about health plans must be provided under this legislation to consumers? Is this information that will be useful to consumers? How might they use it? What information is provided only to the regulator and not to consumers? Why? What information does the statute permit plans to conceal from consumers? Why does it permit this? Are the emergency access provisions (which also extend, under separate provisions, to commercial insurers, Blue Cross and Blue Shield plans, and preferred provider organizations) adequate to assure that members will be covered for true emergency care? Who might benefit from these provisions other than plan members? What is the concern that motivated the statute's prohibition against "gag clauses"(ch. 176O, § 4)? What exactly do the statute's limitations on incentives prohibit? Does this provide sufficient protection for consumers? Do the restrictions go too far? How many layers of internal and external review does this statute provide? Are all of these mechanisms necessary? Useful? Are the statute's time limits reasonable? How does the statute use the term "grievance"? What limitations does the statute impose on termination of provider contracts? What effect might these limitations have on health plans? How much discretion does this statute give physicians to decide what care is medically necessary? How much control does it give to MCOs (carriers)? What explains the choice of specialists to which members are given direct access? How great an impact will these requirements have on primary care gatekeeper plans? What protections does this statute afford providers? Might these protections also be of use to consumers? How much will this legislation cost health plans? Who will pay for these costs? How will these costs affect access to care?

Problems: Advising Under State Managed Care Law

Resolve the following problems under the Massachusetts statute reproduced above:

1) Sam Rogers has been feeling severe pain on the left side of his chest for the past two hours. It is Saturday, and his primary care physician is not available. He is reluctant to go to the emergency department at the local hospital, however, because he knows that emergency care is very expensive, and he has heard that managed care organizations sometimes refuse to pay for emergency department care when they later determine that it was not necessary. He does not know the exact terms of his own policy (and can't find it), but knows that the arrangement he is under is very restrictive. What should Sam do?

2) Mary Gomez found out several months ago that she has cancer. She discovered the cancer fairly late, and it is quite advanced. Through her own research on the web, however, she has learned of a new form of treatment that is still in clinical trials. She has found a specialist in her health plan that is willing to attempt the procedure. He is concerned, however, as to whether Mary's health plan will cover it. Under what circumstances can Mary's plan refuse to cover the procedure? She needs the procedure very quickly if she is to have it at all, so she also wants to know how quickly the plan must make a decision on her request? What avenues are open to Mary to appeal the decision if her plan denies coverage? To whom can she turn for help, if she needs it? Would your answer be different if she needed a prescription drug not covered by her health plans drug formulary instead of a medical procedure?

3) The Omega Health Plan has entered into a contract with the Springdale Medical Group to provide primary care services to its members. Under the terms of the arrangement, Springdale receives a fixed payment every month for each patient and is fully responsible for its own services and for any specialist services or medical tests that its doctors order for patients insured by Omega. Omega provides stop-loss coverage if specialist or test procedures for any member of Omega exceed $100,000 a year. Is this arrangement legal? Dr. Johnson, a physician affiliated with Springdale, is very unhappy with this arrangement, and has sent his patients who are insured with Omega a letter informing them of the arrangement and asking that they complain to Omega about it. Can Omega terminate Dr. Johnson's credentials as a plan provider?

4) Cindy Sparks has just changed jobs and become insured with the Red Sickle health plan. She is in her sixth month of pregnancy and is in treatment with Dr. Samuels. Dr. Samuels is not a network provider under Red Sickle. Can she remain in treatment with Dr. Samuels throughout the delivery? If she changes obstetricians, and her new obstetrician is subsequently terminated from plan participation, can she remain with him through the delivery?

5) Sue Shank has just begun working for a new employer. Her employer offers her a choice of four different HMOs. She would like to learn as much as she can about each of them before she chooses among them. What information is she entitled to under the law? How would she get access to it?

The Hacker and Marmor excerpt at the beginning of this chapter identified strategies through which MCOs managed care. The sections that follow examine each of these strategies and the forms of managed care legislation that address each of them. The best source for keeping up with managed care legislation is the National Conference of State Legislature's website (www.ncsl.org) and the Blue Cross and Blue Shield Association's annual State Legislative Health Care and Insurance Issues, Survey of Plans, from which many of the statistics below have been drawn.

B.   STATE LAW REGULATING MCO NETWORKS

Virtually all MCOs either limit their members to a particular network of providers or impose disincentives to discourage their members from "going out of network." As noted earlier, the type of limitations on access to providers imposed by an MCO has historically been seen as a defining characteristic of some forms of MCO, separating PPOs from HMOs from POSs.

Why might MCOs want to limit their members to particular providers? Of course, if the providers have agreed to deliver services to MCO members at a discount the answer is obvious, but more is at stake than this. MCOs are also interested in limiting participating professionals and providers to those who share their vision of cost and utilization control. They may additionally want to limit participating professionals and providers to those who offer high quality care, or at least to exclude providers who present clear quality problems. Finally, MCOs also often try to control access to specialists through gatekeeper arrangements to assure that the problems that can be handled more cheaply by primary care physicians are not passed on to specialists, in effect creating separate networks of primary care and specialist physicians.

The earliest response of the states to network limitations was to enact "free choice of provider" laws, which limited the ability of MCOs/insurers to build provider networks. Free choice laws prohibit MCOs from restricting their members to particular providers or, more often, limit the size of the cost-sharing obligations that MCOs can impose on their members who go out of plan. About 23 states currently have free choice of provider laws, though most antedate the mid–90s, and the vast majority apply only to pharmacies.

Another regulatory response to networks has been "any willing provider" (AWP) laws, which require MCO/insurers to accept into their network any provider who is willing to accept the terms offered by the MCO. Although the Supreme Court recently affirmed the ability of states to impose AWP laws on ERISA plans in Kentucky Association of Health Plans, Inc. v. Miller, 538 U.S. 329, 123 S.Ct. 1471, 155 L.Ed.2d 468 (2003), few have been adopted in recent years, and most of the laws on the books date from the mid–1990s or earlier. About 23 states have AWP statutes, though in most states these apply only to pharmacies.

More recent legislative efforts to limit the ability of MCOs to restrict access of their members to providers have been more modest in their reach. Some laws focus on network adequacy, requiring MCOs to maintain an acceptable ratio of providers to enrollees. Other states require MCOs to allow members to go out of network if network coverage is inadequate. Other states simply require plans to disclose their provider selection criteria.

Most recent legislation also focuses on narrower access issues, such as those found in section 15 of the Massachusetts law. A number of states have adopted laws guaranteeing MCO members access to particular specialists, such as gynecologists or pediatricians. Forty-two states currently require MCOs to allow women direct access to obstetrical and gynecological providers. Many states also require plans to allow specialists to serve as primary care providers, especially when a patient with a chronic condition is under the regular care of a specialist. A number of states require MCOs to offer "standing referrals" of persons with chronic conditions to specialists in lieu of requiring continual re-referrals from primary care physicians.

Also common are "continuity of care" requirements, which assure plan members continuing access to a particular health care provider for a period of time after the plan terminates the provider. Some continuity of care statutes permit new members to continue to see their previous, non-network, provider for a period of time if the patient has a serious condition or is pregnant. Thirty states now have continuity of care provisions, with transitional care periods lasting from 30 to 120 days.

Finally, a number of states have adopted laws that protect network providers. Almost forty states, for example, have adopted "prompt payment" laws that require insurers to pay "clean" provider claims (claims that are complete and not disputed) within periods ranging from 15 to 60 days. A smaller number of states require notices of disputed claims within similar periods. A number of states impose interest or fines for claims that are not paid promptly. A number of states have been quite aggressive in enforcing these laws. At least twelve states have adopted "due process" requirements, limiting the ability of MCOs to terminate providers from their networks or to deny providers access to their networks without permitting some form of appeal. Other statutes go further, prohibiting "without cause" terminations. MCO plan terminations of providers are discussed in Chapter 9 below.

C. UTILIZATION CONTROLS

Utilization review (UR) seems to be the approach to managing care that most irritates consumers and providers. UR refers to case-by-case evaluations conducted by insurers, purchasers, or UR contractors to determine the necessity and appropriateness (and sometimes the quality) of medical care. It is based on the knowledge that there are wide variations in the use of many medical services, and the belief that considered review of medical care by payers can eliminate wasteful and unnecessary care.

UR can take several forms. The oldest form is retrospective review, under which an insurer denies payment for care already provided, normally by judging it to be medically unnecessary, experimental, or cosmetic. Retrospective review is of limited value for containing costs since the cost of the care has already been incurred by the time the review takes place.

Contemporary UR programs stress prior or concurrent review and high-cost case management. Prior and concurrent review techniques include preadmission review (before elective hospital admissions); admission review (within 24 to 72 hours of emergency or urgent admissions); continued stay review (to assess length of stay and sometimes accompanied by discharge planning); preprocedure or preservice review (to review specific proposed procedures); and voluntary or mandatory second-opinions. High-cost case management addresses the small number (one to seven percent) of very expensive cases that account for most benefit plan costs. Case managers create individualized treatment plans for high-cost beneficiaries. Compliance with the plan is usually voluntary, but may be rewarded by the plan paying for services not otherwise covered by the insurer (such as home health or nursing home care), but less costly than covered alternatives. Disease management programs are similar but are designed to assure appropriate care for particular chronic or recurring medical conditions and often focus on self-care, prevention, and appropriate use of pharmaceuticals.

UR seems to reduce inpatient hospital use and costs. One of the best studies found that it reduced hospital admissions by 12.3 percent, inpatient days by 8 percent, and hospital expenditures by 11.9 percent. In particular, it reduced patient days by 34 percent and hospital expenditures by 30 percent for groups that had previously had high admission rates. Paul Feldstein, *et al.*, Private Cost Containment, 318 New Eng.J.Med. 1310 (1988). It is less clear that UR reduces total health care costs, however, since it often moves care from inpatient to outpatient settings, increasing outpatient costs as it reduces inpatient costs. Moreover, UR is most effective in the short run and has less effect on long-term cost increases. See, on UR generally, Institute of Medicine, Controlling Costs and Changing Patient Care?: The Role of Utilization Management (1989).

At the margins, utilization control blends into other care management strategies. Many MCOs have, for example, retreated from individual case review, instead keeping track of the practice patterns of particular physicians and using the information to decide which physicians to decertify from plan participation. Primary care gatekeeper systems, on the other hand, delegate UR decisions to primary care physicians, but motivate them to control utilization through the use of financial incentives.

UR decisions are basically coverage determinations—UR denies payment for experimental and medically unnecessary care because such care is not covered under the plan contract. UR decisions are also, however, medical treatment determinations, because in most instances they determine whether or not the insured will receive medical treatment. UR determinations can thus raise issues of medical practice regulation. Is the utilization review entity or its employees engaged in the unauthorized practice of medicine when it makes coverage decisions? Is a physician reviewer retained by a utilization review entity engaged in unauthorized practice of medicine if she reviews a case in a state in which she is not licensed? Might the acts of a utilization review entity violate a state's corporate practice of medicine statute or doctrine? Compare Murphy v. Board of Medical Examiners, 190 Ariz. 441, 949 P.2d 530 (Ct.App.1997) (utilization review physician practicing medicine); with Morris v. District of Columbia Board of Medicine, 701 A.2d 364 (D.C. 1997) (Blue Cross medical director not practicing medicine in particular UR situation). Thirty-two states have adopted statutes or regulations requiring that HMO medical directors meet specific requirements, usually to be a licensed physician in the state where they do reviews. See also, E. Haavi Morreim, Playing Doctor: Corporate Medical Practice and Medical Malpractice, 32 Mich. J. L. Ref. 939 (1999); J. Scott Andresen, Is Utilization Review the Practice of Medicine: Implications for Managed Care Administrators, 19 J. Legal Med. 431 (1998); John Blum, An Analysis of Legal Liability in Health Care Utilization Review and Case Management, 26 Hous.L.Rev. 191 (1989). Do these provisions protect patients or doctors?

UR has, as was noted above, become perhaps the most unpopular approach to managing care. While plans in fact infrequently deny coverage, coverage denial can have disastrous consequences for insureds. Also, the hassle involved in fulfilling UR requirements (the interminably busy fax, the voicemail messages that are never returned, the endless arguing with reviewers) undoubtedly deters physicians from offering or ordering services that would otherwise have been given.

A variety of regulatory strategies have been adopted for addressing utilization review issues. Every state has now adopted a law requiring MCOs to offer their members internal consumer grievance and appeal procedures (a requirement also imposed by ERISA for employee health benefit plans, see Chapter 7). These statutes often establish time frames for the appeals (again requiring expedited hearings for emergencies), specify who must decide the appeal (specifying, for example, the professional credentials of the decision maker, or requiring a decision maker not involved in the initial decision), and provide the format for the final decision (in writing, giving reasons, etc.).

Forty-four states also require external or independent reviews. Review statutes generally specify who may make the decision, usually an independent reviewer appointed or approved by the regulatory authority. Statutes again commonly provide time limits for proceedings. Most states provide that the external review decision is binding on the MCO, the remainder either explicitly state that it is non-binding or do not address the issue. See, on the resolution of grievances, appeals, and other disputes in managed care, Nan D. Hunter, Managed Process, Due Care: Structures of Accountability in Health Care, 6 Yale J. Health Pol'y, L. & Ethics 93 (2006); Carole Roan Gresenz and David M. Studdert, External Review of Coverage Denials by Managed Care Organizations in California, 2(3) Journal Empirical Legal Studies 449 (2005); Eleanor Kinney, Protecting American Health Care Consumers (2002); Gerard F. Anderson and Mark A. Hall, The Management of Conflict Over Health Insurance Coverage, in M. Gregg Bloche, ed., The Privatization of Health Care Reform (2003).

A key issue in UR decisions is the definition of medical necessity. About half of the states have adopted statutory definitions of medical necessity, though in some states the definition applies only to particular insurers (Medicaid, HMOs) or particular areas of care (mental health, long term care, inpatient care). A number of these statutes also require some level of deference to the decision of the treating physician on medical necessity issues.

With respect to some forms of care, state statutes have simply preempted coverage decisions by imposing mandates. Providers and consumer groups have for decades lobbied successfully for state insurance "mandates" that require insurance companies to provide certain benefits (mammography, mental health and substance abuse treatment); cover the services of certain providers (chiropractors, podiatrists); or cover certain insureds or dependents (newborn infants, laid-off employees). In recent years, however, state statutes mandating particular benefits have also often limited the reach of utilization controls.

Among the most common examples of this are emergency care mandates, which have been adopted in all but three states. (See chapter 176G, sec. 5, of the Massachusetts statute and Chapter 5 above discussing emergency care). A study of the effects of these laws found that many insurers were already applying a prudent layperson standard before these laws were adopted, and that the laws do not seem to have led to a significant increase in costs, although many MCOs reacted by raising copayments for emergency care. Mark A. Hall. The Impact and Enforcement of Prudent Layperson Laws, 43 Annals of Emergency Medicine 558 (2004).

Other statutes address length of stay issues, requiring at least 48 hours of hospitalization coverage for vaginal or 96 hours for Cesarean deliveries (the famous "drive through delivery" statutes of the mid–1990s) or hospitalization coverage for mastectomies. Still other statutes prohibit plans from denying access to particular benefits, such as off-formulary drugs (usually specifically for cancer or life-threatening diseases) or clinical trials. Popular benefit mandates in recent years include requirements of coverage for mental health care, cancer screenings, contraceptives, infertility treatment, osteoporosis prevention, newborn hearing treatments, and reconstructive surgery following mastectomy.

Finally, fourteen states have adopted laws providing for liability suits against plans for failure to exercise ordinary care in the provision of medical care. To the extent that UR decisions are in fact decisions with respect to plan provision of medical care, they would seem to be covered by these liability statutes. Though these statutes are not enforceable against ERISA plans (see Chapter 10), they do apply to non-ERISA insurers.

D. PROVIDER INCENTIVES

The third strategy that MCOs have used to manage care is financial incentives for professionals and providers. The earliest form was capitation. Under capitation the provider gets paid a fixed fee for providing care for the MCO beneficiary for a fixed period of time. If the services the beneficiary receives cost more than this payment, the provider loses money; if the services cost less, the provider makes money. In other words, the provider becomes the true insurer—i.e. risk bearer—with respect to the patient.

A provider (e.g., a primary care physician) may be capitated for his, her, or its own services, but can also be paid on a capitated basis for other services the patient may need, such as specialist services, laboratory tests, hospitalization, or even drugs. Some of these services, however, cost far more than primary care services, and putting a single primary care physician, or even physician group, at risk for these services might in many instances impose unreasonable risks.

Instead, MCOs usually put the primary care provider only partially at risk. This is done through the use of bonuses or withholds. A pool is established either from money withheld from payments made directly to the physician (a withhold) or from funds provided in addition to regular payments (a bonus). Specified expenses—for specialists or hospitalization, for example— are paid out of this pool. Any money left over at the end of an accounting period (e.g., a year), is paid over to the physician. In addition, the physician may or may not be fully capitated for his or her own services.

Alternatively, the MCO can capitate physicians and hospitals separately, putting the hospital at risk for its expenses and physicians at risk for theirs. An HMO receives a premium, for example, and after subtracting its administrative costs and premiums, gives part to a hospital and part to a physician group, which may provide multispecialty services or might provide primary care and be at risk for paying specialists on a fee-for-service basis.

While incentives are an effective way to hold down costs, they can also result in underservice if the responses they elicit from providers are excessive. It is more difficult to regulate incentives, however, than it is to regulate network or utilization controls because it is more difficult to identify discrete unacceptable practices or to address these practices through enforcement procedures.

Thirty states in fact currently have statutes purporting to ban the use of financial incentives, usually prohibiting incentives that "deny, reduce, limit or delay medically necessary care." The statutes, however, usually go on, as does section 10 of the Massachusetts statute, to say that they are not intended to prohibit MCOs from using capitation payments or other risk-sharing arrangements. As MCOs would generally insist that their incentives are intended to deter unnecessary, rather than necessary care, these statutes have little effect on MCO incentive programs. More useful are statutes or regulations that more explicitly limit excessive incentives, restricting, for example, the proportion of a provider's income that can be put at risk or the size of the pool of patients or providers over which the risk is spread, or requiring stop-loss insurance.

A rather different regulatory approach is simply to require disclosure of financial incentives. Not surprisingly, there are problems with this approach as well. First, the vast majority of insured Americans receive their health coverage through their place of employment, and half of all employees are offered a choice of only one (33%) or two (17%) plans. Even employees offered a choice of two or more plans, of course, may not have much of a choice among incentive plan structures. Second, it is not at all clear how most plan members can use information about incentive plans structures, i.e. whether their understanding of health care finance and delivery is sophisticated enough to evaluate incentive structures. Finally, requiring disclosure imposes costs both on regulators, who need to devise a meaningful form of disclosure and police compliance, and on MCOs, which need to compile and disseminate the information.

Even if requiring plan disclosure to allow consumer choice is problematic, there may be other reasons for requiring disclosure. In a thoughtful article, William Sage identifies three other reasons why we might want to require MCOs and providers to disclose information. First, disclosure increases the likelihood that providers and MCOs will act as honest agents for their patients and members, while it facilitates the ability of patients and members to monitor fiduciary loyalty. Second, requiring collection and disclosure of particular kinds of performance-related information might increase incentives to direct practice in certain directions deemed to be socially important. Requiring disclosure of immunization rates, for example, may promote immunization programs. Finally, disclosure of more information might facilitate public deliberation and provider and MCO accountability. William M. Sage, Regulating Through Information: Disclosure Laws and American Health Care, 99 Columb. L. Rev. 1701 (1999). See also Tracy E. Miller & William M. Sage, Disclosing Physician Financial Incentives, 281 JAMA 1424 (1999).

E.   QUALITY REGULATION

The final issue addressed by state managed care statutes is the quality of care provided by MCOs. One of the aspirations of managed care has always been to manage care to improve quality. The term "health maintenance organization" evidences a commitment to maintaining health, not simply to providing medical services, and MCO marketing materials often talk about coordination or integration of care.

In a sense, most of the statutory provisions discussed so far at least touch on quality issues. Assuring better access to care and accuracy in plan or provider decision making, for example, presumably improves the care received by the plan member. Quality of care is addressed more directly, however, by statutes or regulations requiring MCOs to have quality assurance or improvement programs or to take quality of care into consideration in provider credentialing. Other statutes require or encourage MCOs to seek accreditation in the hope that accreditation agencies will provide quality oversight. Finally, a number of statutes require disclosure of quality-related information through the use of report cards or other forms of disclosure. See Barry R. Furrow, Regulating the Managed Care Revolution: Private Accreditation and a New System Ethos, 43 Vill. L. Rev. 361 (1998).

Problem: Regulating Managed Care

You are the legal staff for the Health Committee of a state that adopted a managed care regulation statute identical to the Massachusetts statute. You are now considering repealing parts of the statute. Examine the statute again. Which of these provisions in the statute address provider networks? Whom do these provisions primarily benefit? What effect do these provisions have on the cost of coverage? To the extent that they increase costs, what effect might this have on access? Which of the provisions in the Massachusetts statute above address UR issues? Which of these provisions is likely to be most strongly supported by plan members? Which are most likely in fact to be of use to them? Which provisions also benefit providers? Which providers benefit from these provisions? Which provisions are likely to be opposed most strongly by managed care trade associations? Which of the requirements in the Massachusetts statute address plan incentive structures? How enforceable are these limitations? How useful are they to plan members? Which provisions, if any, address quality of care, and are they likely to be effective? Considering only the interest of the public, which provisions will you recommend keeping and which repealing?

VI. PERSPECTIVES ON MANAGED CARE REGULATION AND INSURANCE COVERAGE MANDATES

The topic of managed care regulation has unleashed an avalanche of academic commentary, sharply divided along lines that have come to typify health policy debate. On the one hand are those who distrust the ability of health care markets to protect consumer's interests absent government intervention and, on the other, those who trust markets and have little faith in government. An article by George Annas, a long-time champion of patient's rights, for example, exemplifies the position of those who favor protective legislation:

GEORGE J. ANNAS, A NATIONAL BILL OF PATIENTS' RIGHTS
338 New Eng. J. Med. 695, 696 (1998).

The key to understanding patients' rights in managed care is to understand managed care's attempt to transform the patient into a consumer. Persons can be considered consumers of health plans if they can choose a plan on the basis of cost, coverage, and quality. But the choice of a health plan is usually made by employers, and even when it is not, the choice is necessarily much more often based on cost than on coverage or quality. Nor is being a consumer of a health plan the same as being a consumer of health care. In virtually all settings, patients (not consumers) seek the help of physicians when they are sick and vulnerable because of illness or disability. * * * Sick people, who are in no position to bargain and who know little about medicine, must be able to trust their physicians to be on their side in dealing with pain, suffering, disease, or disability.

Attempts to transform the physician-patient relationship into a business transaction fundamentally threaten not just physicians as professionals but people as patients. This threat is real, frightening, and intolerable, which is why the new patients' rights movement aims not simply to preserve the physician-patient relationship in general but also to eliminate the financial conflicts of interest in managed care that are most threatening to the relationship. Thus, the new patients' rights movement seeks to shift power * * * from managed-care companies, insurance companies, and health care facilities to patients and their physicians.

———————

See also, contending that a consumer model does not adequately protect patient's rights, Wendy K. Mariner, Standards of Care and Standard Form Contracts: Distinguishing Patient Rights and Consumer Rights, 15 J. Contemp. Health L. & Pol'y 1 (1998).

Holding down the other end of the spectrum, David Hyman has written a series of articles trashing the patient bill of rights movement:

DAVID HYMAN, REGULATING MANAGED CARE: WHAT'S WRONG WITH A PATIENT BILL OF RIGHTS

73 S. Cal. L. Rev. 221 (2000).

Set aside for just a moment what everyone "knows" about the perils of managed care and the need for a patient bill of rights. Set aside as well the inconvenient fact that customer surveys show a high degree of satisfaction among managed care participants, and extensive research indicates that the quality of care is as good (or better) in managed care plans than in fee-for-service health care. Instead, consider the case for regulation from an empirical perspective. If the absence of regulation is a bad thing, one would expect the frequency of complaints and avoidable bad outcomes to be higher (and the quality of care that is rendered to be lower) in managed care plans that are subject to fewer regulations. [Because of ERISA (see next chapter)] * * *, some forms of health insurance are heavily regulated, others are subject to only modest regulation, and others effectively fall into a regulatory "free-fire" zone. If there is any evidence suggesting that complaints and avoidable bad outcomes are less frequent in plans which are more aggressively regulated, I am unaware of it. Similarly, if there is any evidence suggesting that the quality of care is better in plans which are aggressively regulated, I am unaware of it. One would have thought such evidence would be readily available (and widely trumpeted by advocates of consumer protection) if the problems with managed care are as severe as the anecdotes suggest. In the absence of empirical evidence regarding such matters, the case for a patient bill of rights is based on fear (of markets) and faith (in anecdote-driven regulation), but not on fact.

Despite its popular appeal, a patient bill of rights is a deeply flawed strategy for addressing the inadequacies of managed care. The kinds of rights which are likely to result from the legislative process (and have emerged to date) are likely to make things worse, rather than better, whether one considers cost, quality, or access. The backlash against managed care may have been sold to the public as a response to concerns about quality, but the legislation that has emerged has more to do with "provider lobbying, gut instincts, negative anecdotes, and popular appeal" than with quality. Indeed, the unfortunate reality is that quality has long been used as a stalking horse by providers wishing to disguise less public spirited objectives. * * *

Worse still, to the extent the patient bill of rights strategy is based on the sanctity of physician discretion, it makes it much more difficult to address the real quality-based problems with American medicine, which, in fact, are attributable to the unconstrained discretion previously accorded physicians. Legislators have ignored this basic point; the patient bills of rights that have been offered demonstrate a distinct preference for safeguarding physician decisionmaking from MCO interference. However, if physicians are such good agents for patients with regard to medical spending decisions, why is there such significant geographic variation in the delivery of health care services? Why did hospital lengths-of-stay decline so precipitously after Medicare abandoned cost-based per-diem reimbursement, and moved to prospective payment based on discharge diagnosis? * * * Why did the Institute of Medicine recommend a systems-based approach to improving health care quality?

* * *

It is understandable that managed care horror stories trigger outrage and a demand for additional regulations. However, any given rule or standard for making coverage and treatment decisions will necessarily have imperfections. So long as we have created the appropriate institutional arrangements—and there certainly remains much to do with regard to that goal—leaving well enough alone with regard to the specifics of the resulting coverage is likely to be sufficient unto the day. Such a strategy lacks the moral certainty of stringing up a few managed care desperados in black hats, but it will do more to improve the status quo than any ten patient bills of rights.

Notes and Questions

Insurers, business organizations, and market advocacy organizations have long decried insurance mandates, including managed care regulation, as special interest legislation that protects providers rather than consumers. Christopher Conover, in a paper published by the libertarian Cato Institute, asserts that insurance regulation costs $99.3 billion a year, while providing $84.9 billion in benefits. Christopher Conover, Health Care Regulation: A $169 Billion Hidden Tax, Cato Policy Analysis, 2004. See also criticizing managed care regulation, Robert F. Rich and Christopher T. Erb, The Two Faces of Managed Care Regulation & Policymaking, 16 Stan. L. & Pol'y Rev. 233 (2005).

Some scholars, however, contend that market failures necessitate some forms of insurance regulation. Russell Korobkin, for example—relying on mathematical game theory and empirical evidence that consumers have cognitive limitations that render their decisions only "boundedly rational"—argues that government regulation of managed care, even including coverage mandates, might be justifiable in some instances. Russell Korobkin, The Efficiency of Managed Care "Patient Protection" Laws: Incomplete Contracts, Bounded Rationality, and Market Failure, 85 Cornell L. Rev. 1 (1999). Marc Rodwin argues for particular reforms to empower consumers in their dealings with MCOs, through supporting consumer advocacy and requiring external review. See Marc A. Rodwin, Backlash as Prelude to Managing Managed Care, 24 J. Health Pol., Pol'y & L. 1115 (1999).

On the basis of extensive surveys of provider and patient advocates, health plan managers, regulators, and industry observers, Mark Hall has concluded that laws regulating managed care have not been primarily adopted to serve provider interests and in fact have not had much of an economic effect on providers. Instead the laws seem to have emerged from an alignment of interests between providers, consumer advocates, and lawmakers. Mark Hall, Managed Care Patient Protection or Provider Protection? A Qualitative Assessment, 117 American Journal of Medicine 932 (2004). In a separate article describing the findings of the same research, Hall concludes that managed care regulations have had less of an impact than market forces on the changing nature of managed care. Mark Hall, The Death of Managed Care: A Regulatory Autopsy, 30 J. Health Pol., Pol'y & Law 427 (2005). This point is also made in M. Gregg Bloche, One Step Ahead of the Law: Market Pressures and the Evolution of Managed Care, in M. Gregg

Bloche, ed., The Privatization of Health Care Reform: Legal and Regulatory Perspectives (2003).

In a recent symposium in Law and Contemporary Problems, Clark Havighurst and Barak Richman focus on the equity effects of insurance regulation, contending that the costs of insurance regulation and mandates (and, indeed, of health care regulation generally) are borne disproportionately by lower-income workers. Starting with the generally accepted proposition that the cost of employment-related health insurance is borne by employees (through reduction in wages) rather than by employers, they contend that in fact this cost is imposed disproportionately on the lower income employees of firms, since both higher and lower income employees have their wages reduced to the same extent to pay for insurance and the higher income employees tend to use more and higher cost medical services. Lower-income employees are forced to purchase expensive, comprehensive insurance, which is demanded by higher-income workers and sometimes required by state mandates, as well as to use licensed physicians who must conform to standards of care adopted in response to the demands of higher income patients. Absent government regulation, lower income workers could use cheaper unlicensed physicians, sign away their rights to sue for malpractice, and purchase bare-bones insurance policies that would better suit their tastes and pocket books. In the same issue, economist Mark Pauly responds that the distribution of insurance costs among higher and lower income employees is an issue on which we lack empirical proof, but that it is likely that lower income employees bear less of the cost than higher income employees since lower income employees are likely to value health insurance less proportionate to higher wages. Jonathan Oberlander in the same issue contends that markets will never meet the health care needs of lower-income Americans and that if we really care about low income employees, we should support public health insurance. See Who Pays? Who Benefits? Distributional Issues in Health Care, 69 Law and Contemp. Probs. 1–282 (2006).

This symposium is useful for refocusing our attention on the central problem of American health policy, the problem of those Americans who are excluded from managed care—and from all other form of health insurance—our 44 million uninsured. See, David M. Frankford, Regulating Managed Care: Pulling Tails to Wag the Dog, 24 J. Health Pol, Pol'y & L. 1191 (1999); Deborah Stone, Managed Care and the Second Great Transformation, 24 J. Health Pol, Pol'y & L. 1213 (1999). Surely their access problems are much more persistent than are the problems of those who struggle with the irrationalities of MCOs.

Few states have adopted new managed care regulation since the year 2000, perhaps because most had already adopted comprehensive laws, perhaps because some states began to worry that they had already gone too far, but more likely because managed care in the 2000s has been much less restrictive than it was in the 1990s largely because of market forces. The predominant form of MCO in the 2000s has been PPOs with broad and inclusive provider networks and few constraints on utilization. Analysts have proclaimed, and some mourned, the death of managed care. See Symposium, The Managed Care Backlash, 24 J.Health Pol. Pol'y & L. 873 (1999); Thomas Greaney, From Hero to Goat: Managed Care in the 1990s, 47 St. Louis. L. J. 217 (2003); Clark C. Havighurst, How the Health Care Revolution Fell Short, 65 Law & Contemp. Probs. 55 (2002); Clark C. Havighurst, The Backlash Against Managed Health Care: Hard Politics Make Bad Policy, 34 Ind. L. Rev. 395 (2001); David Orentlicher, The Rise and Fall of Managed Care: A Predictable "Tragic Choices" Phenomenon, 47 St. Louis U. L.J.

411 (2003). Some even began to seek its slayer. Peter D. Jacobson, Who Killed Managed Care? A Policy Whodunit, 47 St. Louis U.L.J. 365 (2003).

VII. WHAT FOLLOWS MANAGED CARE? CONSUMER–DIRECTED HEALTH CARE

If managed care is not the force it once was, what comes next? Many commentators have claimed that it will be consumer-driven health care. CDHC, and the philosophy behind it, were introduced in Chapter 4. As broadly defined, CDHC could include a number of different approaches to health care organization and finance. It certainly includes the availability of more and better information on health care providers for consumers. It could include tiered networks, where insureds choose among a menu of coverage options, and receive access to different networks of providers based on the health plan they choose (paying more for access to the academic medical center, less for access to the community hospital). But most discussions of CDHC focus on health savings accounts (HSAs) coupled with high deductible health plans (HDHPs). The 2003 Medicare Modernization Act expanded federal tax subsidies for HSAs, making subsidies available to anyone who purchases a high-deductible health plan. The MMA, however, leaves consumer-driven health care largely unregulated, prescribing only minimum and maximum deductibles and maximum out-of-pocket limits for HDHPs and limiting tax-free expenditures from HSAs (prior to age 65) to "qualified medical expenses." As we have seen, the states have traditionally regulated health insurance and extensively regulated managed care. Do they have a role in regulating consumer-driven health care?

TIMOTHY S. JOST AND MARK A. HALL, THE ROLE OF STATE REGULATION IN CONSUMER– DRIVEN HEALTH CARE

31 American Journal of Law and Medicine 395 (2005).

[This article analyzes the findings of a survey of stakeholders examining state regulation of high deductible health plans(HDHPS) and health savings accounts (HSAs) in the spring of 2005].

Most public discussion of state regulatory issues affecting HSAs and HDHPs to date has centered around three issues, * * *. The first of these is * * * the problem of state mandates that bar high deductibles for particular services. * * * HSAs only qualify for tax subsidies under the [Medicare Modernization Act] if they are coupled with HDHPs that have minimum deductibles of at least $1000 for individuals, $2000 for families. [These amounts have subsequently been adjusted upwards for inflation]. * * *

At the time the MMA was adopted, a number of states mandated coverage of specific * * * health services * * * either without a deductible or with a low deductible. * * *

Most states quickly [repealed these laws]. * * * The states' responses were remarkably rapid and widespread. Without any specific federal requirement or threatened penalty, most were willing to set aside the particular public health or provider protection considerations that caused them to enact various benefits mandates in order to facilitate the federally-led consumer-driven market initiative.

* * *

[Discussion of the other two issues, whether an HMO can offer a HDHP and state tax subsidies for HSAs, is omitted.]

* * * As the states gain more experience with HSAs and HDHPs, they may well encounter a range of additional regulatory issues. Early recognition of these issues is important because it enables states to deal with them responsibly rather than waiting for a crisis to provoke precipitous or over-reactive action. Experiences from managed care regulation in the 1990s reveal that case-specific or crisis-driven regulation is often neither efficient nor effective.

First, how the health savings accounts are administered may raise several state regulatory issues. * * *

Under the MMA, HSAs may be administered by banks, insurance companies or "another person who demonstrates to the satisfaction of the Secretary [of the Treasury] that the manner in which such person will administer the trust will be consistent with the requirements of this section." * * * Most states, however, do not appear to have a regulatory mechanism that oversees insurers offering financial services. None of our interview sources could point to any actual regulatory requirements or consequences for insurers that administer their own HSAs, other than that the funds must be maintained in a separate account and must not be commingled with insurer funds that are at risk. If these funds are kept separate from the insurer's other funds, then they are not subject to, and do not effect, the insurer's solvency and reserve requirements.

The financial institutions, other than insurers, that the MMA authorizes to administer HSAs are familiar types of heavily regulated financial entities. Consumers who choose insurers to administer their HSAs will likely assume there is some similar oversight of financial services from insurers. The first time HSA holders (or providers who expect to be paid by HSAs) encounter major problems in getting an insurance administrator to honor checks or debit card transactions questions will undoubtedly surface about state regulatory oversight. Why did insurance regulators allow the problem to arise? Will state insurance guaranty funds cover the obligations of insolvent insurers under their HSAs, or only under their HDHPs? Do unfair claims practice laws cover HSA claims? We found little evidence in our interviews that insurers or insurance regulators were considering these issues.

A second issue HSAs raise is how state statutes and regulations that regulate managed care will apply to HSA transactions. * * *

All of the HDHP insurers with whom we spoke make their negotiated network discounts available to HSA holders. This is a great advantage to HSA owners, as it gives them the benefit of the considerable market power that insurers command for extracting discounts from providers. Insurers also use their standard claims processing systems, including medical necessity review, to determine when the policy deductible (and, ultimately, the out-of-pocket maximum) has been met for any particular subscriber. In general, only insured expenses can be counted against a deductible. If a subscriber with a

$3,000 deductible receives an outpatient surgery costing $2,500, insurers are unlikely to credit the cost of the surgery fully against the deductible without determining whether the surgery was a covered expense, whether $2,500 was a reasonable charge, and whether the subscriber received pre-approval for the surgery if required under the policy. In short, even while spending their own money from HSAs, subscribers will be subject to some managed care controls to the extent that they attempt to claim these expenses against their insurance deductibles. * * *

This raises a host of questions, however. If an insurer refuses to credit the cost of the surgery fully against the deductible because it was not medically necessary, can the HSA holder appeal the decision under the state's claims review laws? If a network provider is treating an HSA holder and that provider's contract with the HDHP is terminated, must the provider continue to offer the HSA holder the HDHP negotiated discount for the period of time that a state's continuity of care statute requires the HDHP to cover services? Do state any-willing-provider statutes apply to HDHP networks for HSA-covered services as well as for HDHP funded services once the deductible is met? * * *

The answer to these questions in general is yes. Virtually all regulators and insurers we talked to assumed this to be the case, but this assumption has not yet been challenged or tested, as it might be if, for instance, a particular provider insisted it was not bound by the restraints in its managed care contract for services paid directly by patients through their HSAs. Even if the current understanding holds, it means that HDHPs will face no less of a restrictive regulatory environment than do conventional managed care plans. * * *

The interplay between the HSA and HDHP does not just raise questions as to how state managed care regulations apply; it also presents the very real potential for consumer misunderstanding and confusion. To understand clearly how MMA HSAs work when coupled with HDHPs, consumers first need to realize that HSAs are savings accounts, not insurance. * * * Next, consumers must appreciate that HSAs can pay for a broader range of qualified medical services than those covered by the HDHP. It is easy to imagine some consumers exhausting their HSAs on miscellaneous expenses that do not count toward the deductible at all and then facing the rude surprise of "catastrophic" medical expenses once a serious accident or illness strikes and learning that insurance coverage is still a long way off. * * * Added to this consumer burden are the already confusing distinctions between billed versus allowable charges, and in-network versus out-of-network providers, which bedevil all but the most expert readers of insurers' "explanation of benefits" forms. All of this is to say that HSA/HDHPs raise significant issues for consumer education and dispute resolution, and that these issues will likely reach the attention of state insurance regulators.

* * *

[Another] traditional focus of state insurance regulation has been improving access to health insurance for the uninsured by controlling insurer underwriting and rating practices primarily in the small group market, but also in the individual market in some states. * * *

A number of commentators have expressed a concern that HDHPs might further fragment insurers' risk pools by attracting mainly low-risk subscribers, leaving high-risk subscribers in separate risk pools with ever-increasing premiums for conventional insurance. HSAs and HDHPs are thought to be more attractive to low-risk subscribers because they are less likely to exhaust their high deductibles and therefore more likely to build up substantial savings in their accounts. Also, high-risk people are less likely in general to make any change in their health insurance, so at least initially any new type of policy, whatever kind it is, will tend to attract people who are healthier than average. HSA/HDHP advocates, on the other hand, argue that the flexibility available to HSA holders will be attractive to the chronically ill, as will be the absolute caps the MMA imposes on out-of-pocket expenses and lower premiums. * * *

* * *

Most of the regulators we interviewed felt that risk segmentation was not a pressing problem and that the rating issue just identified had not proven to be problematic. * * *

One reason this issue may not have emerged as a regulatory problem is that the major insurers may not be attempting to take advantage of any favorable risk selection. Several insurer representatives we spoke to said that PPO products are rated as a single risk pool in each market, adjusting only for deductible levels and other benefit differences, rather than pricing HSA plans as an entirely separate risk pool from other offerings. * * *

Another reason regulators may have refrained from scrutinizing rating practices for HDHPs is the growing disillusionment with traditional approaches to expanding access to coverage, which we detected in several quarters. Regulators seemed very sensitized to the "zero-sum" logic that, for every high risk subscriber whose rates are lowered by regulation, several lower risk subscribers must pay higher rates, which at the margin may deter some of them from purchasing any insurance. * * * Therefore, regulators appear willing to try approaches such as HSA/HDHPs that might make insurance dramatically more affordable for average purchasers. * * *

* * *

Overall, the states' initial response to the MMA has been quite remarkable. Most states have responded affirmatively to the latest federal legislation, despite its lack of explicit compulsion, by removing any regulatory barriers to qualified HDHPs. * * *

Perhaps the experience with managed care regulation has caused most states to lose their taste for insurance regulation; or perhaps the receptive regulatory response is explained by the newness of the HSA/HDHP product and thus the lack of experience with problems it might cause. Whatever the explanation, the new approach to federalism in insurance regulation evidenced by the MMA appears to have been very successful. At least for the moment, the lure of tax incentives has been sufficient to launch HSA/HDHPs successfully in most states without the need for either direct preemption of state law or the imposition of direct federal regulation of insurance, thus avoiding all of the friction and controversies that have accompanied these strategies under ERISA or HIPAA. * * *

* * *

———————

Notes and Questions

1. Consumer-driven health plans, which include both HSA-based HDHPs and HDHPs paired with health reimbursement accounts (HRAs), are introduced in Chapter 4. CDHC presents fascinating legal issues involving the physician-patient relationship. What cost information, for example, must a physician offer a patient who is paying for care out of her own health savings account to assure that the patient can give informed consent to a proposed treatment? If a physician recommends a particular procedure (or drug), and the patient declines it as too expensive, might the physician be liable for ensuing injury, or can the physician claim assumption of risk or comparative negligence, or even lack of proximate cause. Does a physician or hospital have any obligation to provide necessary treatment that a patient refuses to pay for? Must a physician or hospital contract with a patient beforehand for the patient to cover the cost of a procedure, or can the physician recover a reasonable charge? See Timothy S. Jost, Health Care at Risk: A Critique of the Consumer Driven Movement, 150–65 (2007); Mark A. Hall and Carl E. Schneider, Patients as Consumers: Courts, Contracts, and the New Medical Marketplace, 106 Mich. L. Rev. 643 (2008); Haavi Morreim, High–Deductible Health Plans: New Twists on Old Challenges from Tort to Contract. Vanderbilt Law Review (2006), and Chapter 4 supra.

2. See also, on the federal requirements for HSAs, David Pratt, Health and Wealthy and Dead: Health Savings Accounts, 19 St. Thomas L. Rev. 7 (2006); Richard L. Kaplan, Who's Afraid of Personal Responsibility? Health Savings Accounts and the Future of American Health Care, 36 McGeorge L. Rev. 534 (2005). See, discussing state regulation, Michele Melden, Guarding Against the High Risk of High Deductible Health Plans: A Proposal for Regulatory Protections, 18 Loy. Consumer L. Rev. 403 (2006). See generally, discussing the legal and policy issues raised by CDHC, Timothy S. Jost, Health Care at Risk: A Critique of the Consumer–Driven Movement (2007); The Promise and Peril of Ownership Society Health Care Policy, 80 Tul. L. Rev. 777 (2006); John Jacobi, After Managed Care: Gray Boxes, Tiers and Consumerism, 47 St. Louis U. L.J. 397 (2003).

Problems: Consumer–Driven Health Care

1. Return to problem 1 in the *Problems: Advising Under State Managed Care Law* at the end of section V.A. above. Assume that Sam Rogers has a high deductible health plan with a $5000 deductible and 20 percent coinsurance requirement until an out-of-pocket maximum of $10,000 has been reached. He is not sure how much of his deductible he has met for this year, but has already exhausted the $300 his employer has deposited in his HSA. Assume further that his household income is $20,000 a year. How will this state of affairs affect the likelihood of him going to the emergency department to check out his chest pains? Is this a good or bad thing?

2. Consider the facts of problem 2 above. Assume that Mary Gomez also has a $5000 deductible policy. She has only met $500 of the deductible but has $3000

in her HSA. Her health plan provides that only services that would be covered under the terms of the health plan count toward the deductible and that "experimental" treatment is not covered under the plan. How would Mary Gomez determine whether the proposed cancer treatment would count against her deductible? Does she have any route of appeal if she asks her plan and says no? Can she pay for the treatment out of her HSA?

3. Review problem 4 above. Assume that Cindy Sparks was insured with a $3000 deductible, $5000 out-of-pocket maximum, health plan under her old job and is similarly insured under her new plan. Assume that she had a health reimbursement account with her old job that had a $5000 balance. The rules established by her previous employer provide that all funds left in an HRA upon resignation from the firm are forfeited. Does she have any recourse? Assume instead that she has $5000 in an HSA and the funds continue to be available. What advantages does this give Ms. Sparks over the situation she would be in with a traditional health plan? Assume that Doctor Samuels is not a network provider under her new employer's plan, or that he is, and is terminated by the plan before her delivery is due. Do either of these facts affect her situation in any way?

Chapter 7

REGULATION OF INSURANCE AND MANAGED CARE: THE FEDERAL ROLE

I. INTRODUCTION

Although regulation of health insurance has traditionally been the responsibility of the states, federal law has in recent years taken a more significant role. The most important federal statute affecting health insurance is the Employee Retirement Income Security Act of 1974, ERISA, which has already been alluded to several times in previous chapters. ERISA's primary role throughout the 1980s and 1990s was deregulatory, as its preemptive provisions repeatedly blocked state common law actions against health plans as well as state attempts at plan regulation. The Supreme Court seemed to relax its interpretation of ERISA preemption in the late 1990s, however, giving the states somewhat more flexibility for regulating insured health plans, although it has recently become clear that there are limits to this flexibility. Finally, ERISA itself provides employee health plan beneficiaries with a positive right to sue to recover denied benefits, while also imposing fiduciary obligations on plan fiduciaries. ERISA regulations also afford procedural rights to plan beneficiaries.

ERISA is not the only federal statute to affect health plans. The Americans with Disabilities Act places at least minimal constraints on the ability of employers and insurers to discriminate against the disabled in the provision of health insurance. The Health Insurance Portability and Accountability Act of 1996 (which amended ERISA, as well as other federal statutes) limits the use of preexisting condition clauses while prohibiting intragroup discrimination in coverage and rates. It also offers certain protections in the small group and individual insurance markets. The Consolidated Omnibus Budget Reconciliation Act of 1985 provides some protection for some who lose employee coverage. Finally, Congress has adopted in the past few years a handful of coverage mandates. Each of these federal initiatives will be considered in this chapter.

II. THE EMPLOYEE RETIREMENT INCOME SECURITY ACT OF 1974 (ERISA)

A. ERISA PREEMPTION OF STATE HEALTH INSURANCE REGULATION

As noted in the introduction, the main effect of ERISA in recent decades has been deregulatory as ERISA has been interpreted as preempting a broad range of state laws. Section 514 of ERISA (codified as 29 U.S.C.A. § 1144) expressly preempts state regulatory statutes and common law claims that "relate to" employee benefit plans. Section 502 of ERISA (codified as 29 U.S.C.A. § 1132), has been interpreted by the Supreme Court as providing for exclusive federal court jurisdiction over and an exclusive federal cause of action for cases that could be brought as ERISA claims. Section 514, however, also explicitly exempts state regulation of insurance from preemption, while also prohibiting state regulation of self-insured plans. The text of these provisions follows:

29 U.S.C.A. § 1132 (Section 502)

A civil action may be brought—

(1) by a participant or beneficiary—

* * *

(B) to recover benefits due to him under the terms of his plan, to enforce his rights under the terms of the plan, or to clarify his rights to future benefits under the terms of the plan;

(2) by the Secretary, or by a participant, beneficiary or fiduciary for appropriate relief under section 1109 of this title [which imposes on plan fiduciaries the obligation to "make good" to a plan any losses resulting from a breach of fiduciary duties, and authorizes "other equitable or remedial relief" for breaches of fiduciary obligations];

(3) by a participant, beneficiary, or fiduciary (A) to enjoin any act or practice which violates any provision of this subchapter or the terms of the plan, or (B) to obtain other appropriate equitable relief (i) to redress such violations or (ii) to enforce any provisions of this subchapter or the terms of the plan;

* * *

29 U.S.C.A. § 1144 (Section 514)

(a) Except as provided in subsection (b) of this section, the provisions of this subchapter and subchapter III of this chapter shall supersede any and all State laws insofar as they may now or hereafter relate to any employee benefit plan * * *

(b) Construction and application

* * *

(2)(A) Except as provided in subparagraph (B), nothing in this subchapter shall be construed to exempt or relieve any person from any law of any State which regulates insurance, banking, or securities.

(B) Neither an employee benefit plan * * * nor any trust established under such a plan, shall be deemed to be an insurance company * * * or to be engaged in the business of insurance or banking for purposes of any law of any State purporting to regulate insurance companies, insurance contracts, banks, trust companies, or investment companies.

The task of sorting out ERISA's complex preemption scheme has resulted in a tremendous volume of litigation, including, to date, over twenty Supreme Court decisions and hundreds of state and federal lower court decisions. In this subsection we will examine the effect of Section 502 and 514 preemption on state regulatory laws. In this context we will also consider the effect of Section 514's "savings clause," (§ 514(b)(2)(A)), which saves from preemption state laws "which regulate insurance," as well as § 514's "deemer" clause (§ 514(b)(2)(B)), which exempts self-insured ERISA plans from state insurance regulation. In the second subsection, we look at the effects of ERISA preemption on state health care reform efforts. In the fourth and final subsection of this section, we will consider the effect of ERISA preemption on state common law tort causes of action against managed care plans and insurers. In the third subsection of this chapter, among these preemption discussions, we will review *Pegram v. Herdrich*, a recent Supreme Court case examining the interrelationship between ERISA fiduciary claims and state tort claims against managed care plans, which lays the groundwork for an understanding of ERISA preemption of state tort claims.

We begin with one of the most recent Supreme Court cases, which set out the basic framework of ERISA preemption and debates the policies that ground it.

RUSH PRUDENTIAL HMO, INC. v. DEBRA C. MORAN, ET AL.

Supreme Court of the United States.
536 U.S. 355, 122 S.Ct. 2151, 153 L.Ed.2d 375 (2002).

JUSTICE SOUTER delivered the opinion of the Court.

* * *

Petitioner, Rush Prudential HMO, Inc., is a health maintenance organization (HMO) that contracts to provide medical services for employee welfare benefit plans covered by ERISA. Respondent Debra Moran is a beneficiary under one such plan, sponsored by her husband's employer. Rush's "Certificate of Group Coverage," issued to employees who participate in employer-sponsored plans, promises that Rush will provide them with "medically necessary" services. The terms of the certificate give Rush the "broadest possible discretion" to determine whether a medical service claimed by a beneficiary is covered under the certificate. * * *

As the certificate explains, Rush contracts with physicians "to arrange for or provide services and supplies for medical care and treatment" of covered persons. Each covered person selects a primary care physician from those under contract to Rush, while Rush will pay for medical services by an unaffiliated physician only if the services have been "authorized" both by the primary care physician and Rush's medical director.[ ]

In 1996, when Moran began to have pain and numbness in her right shoulder, Dr. Arthur LaMarre, her primary care physician, unsuccessfully administered "conservative" treatments such as physiotherapy. In October 1997, Dr. LaMarre recommended that Rush approve surgery by an unaffiliated specialist, Dr. Julia Terzis, who had developed an unconventional treatment for Moran's condition. Although Dr. LaMarre said that Moran would be "best served" by that procedure, Rush denied the request and, after Moran's internal appeals, affirmed the denial on the ground that the procedure was not "medically necessary."[ ] Rush instead proposed that Moran undergo standard surgery, performed by a physician affiliated with Rush.

In January 1998, Moran made a written demand for an independent medical review of her claim, as guaranteed by § 4–10 of Illinois's HMO Act,[ ] which provides:

> Each Health Maintenance Organization shall provide a mechanism for the timely review by a physician * * * who is unaffiliated with the Health Maintenance Organization, jointly selected by the patient ..., primary care physician and the Health Maintenance Organization in the event of a dispute between the primary care physician and the Health Maintenance Organization regarding the medical necessity of a covered service proposed by a primary care physician. In the event that the reviewing physician determines the covered service to be medically necessary, the Health Maintenance Organization shall provide the covered service. * * *

* * *

When Rush failed to provide the independent review, Moran sued in an Illinois state court to compel compliance with the state Act. Rush removed the suit to Federal District Court, arguing that the cause of action was "completely preempted" under ERISA.[ ]

While the suit was pending, Moran had surgery by Dr. Terzis at her own expense and submitted a $94,841.27 reimbursement claim to Rush. Rush treated the claim as a renewed request for benefits and began a new inquiry to determine coverage. The three doctors consulted by Rush said the surgery had been medically unnecessary.

Meanwhile, the federal court remanded the case back to state court on Moran's motion, concluding that because Moran's request for independent review under § 4–10 would not require interpretation of the terms of an ERISA plan, the claim was not "completely preempted" so as to permit removal * * * The state court enforced the state statute and ordered Rush to submit to review by an independent physician. * * * [The reviewer] decided that Dr. Terzis's treatment had been medically necessary, based on the definition of medical necessity in Rush's Certificate of Group Coverage, as well as his own medical judgment. Rush's medical director, however, refused to concede that the surgery had been medically necessary, and denied Moran's claim in January 1999.

Moran amended her complaint in state court to seek reimbursement for the surgery as "medically necessary" under Illinois's HMO Act, and Rush again removed to federal court, arguing that Moran's amended complaint stated a claim for ERISA benefits and was thus completely preempted by ERISA's civil enforcement provisions, 29 U.S.C. § 1132(a) [§ 502], * * * The District Court treated Moran's claim as a suit under ERISA, and denied the claim on the ground that ERISA preempted Illinois's independent review statute.

The Court of Appeals for the Seventh Circuit reversed. * * *

* * *

To "safeguar[d] ... the establishment, operation, and administration" of employee benefit plans, ERISA sets "minimum standards ... assuring the equitable character of such plans and their financial soundness,"[ ] and contains an express preemption provision that ERISA "shall supersede any and all State laws insofar as they may now or hereafter relate to any employee benefit plan...." § 1144(a)[§ 514(a)]. A saving clause then reclaims a substantial amount of ground with its provision that "nothing in this subchapter shall be construed to exempt or relieve any person from any law of any State which regulates insurance, banking, or securities." § 1144(b)(2)(A) [§ 514(b)(2)(A)]. The "unhelpful" drafting of these antiphonal clauses * * * occupies a substantial share of this Court's time. In trying to extrapolate congressional intent in a case like this, when congressional language seems simultaneously to preempt everything and hardly anything, we "have no choice" but to temper the assumption that " 'the ordinary meaning ... accurately expresses the legislative purpose,' "[ ] with the qualification " 'that the historic police powers of the States were not [meant] to be superseded by the Federal Act unless that was the clear and manifest purpose of Congress.' "[ ]

It is beyond serious dispute that under existing precedent § 4–10 of the Illinois HMO Act "relates to" employee benefit plans within the meaning of § 1144(a). * * * As a law that "relates to" ERISA plans under § 1144(a), § 4–10 is saved from preemption only if it also "regulates insurance" under § 1144(b)(2)(A). * * *

[The Court then proceeded to apply the savings clause analysis method that it had developed in earlier cases, concluding that the Illinois external review law was saved from preemption. As this analysis was superceded by the Court's decision in *Kentucky Association of Health Plans v. Miller*, described below, the discussion is omitted here. Ed.]

* * *

Given that § 4–10 regulates insurance, ERISA's mandate that "nothing in this subchapter shall be construed to exempt or relieve any person from any law of any State which regulates insurance," 29 U.S.C. § 1144(b)(2)(A), ostensibly forecloses preemption. [ ] Rush, however, does not give up. It argues for preemption anyway, emphasizing that the question is ultimately one of congressional intent, which sometimes is so clear that it overrides a statutory provision designed to save state law from being preempted. * * *

In ERISA law, we have recognized one example of this sort of overpowering federal policy in the civil enforcement provisions, 29 U.S.C. § 1132(a), ** * In *Massachusetts Mut. Life Ins. Co. v. Russell*,[ ] we said those provisions amounted to an "interlocking, interrelated, and interdependent remedial scheme,"[ ] which *Pilot Life* described as "represent[ing] a careful balancing of the need for prompt and fair claims settlement procedures against the public interest in encouraging the formation of employee benefit plans"[ ]. So, we have held, the civil enforcement provisions are of such extraordinarily preemptive power that they override even the "well-pleaded complaint" rule for establishing the conditions under which a cause of action may be removed to a federal forum. *Metropolitan Life Ins. Co. v. Taylor*[ ].

Although we have yet to encounter a forced choice between the congressional policies of exclusively federal remedies and the "reservation of the business of insurance to the States,'[ ] we have anticipated such a conflict, with the state insurance regulation losing out if it allows plan participants "to obtain remedies ... that Congress rejected in ERISA."

In *Pilot Life*, an ERISA plan participant who had been denied benefits sued in a state court on state tort and contract claims. He sought not merely damages for breach of contract, but also damages for emotional distress and punitive damages, both of which we had held unavailable under relevant ERISA provisions.[ ] We not only rejected the notion that these common-law contract claims "regulat[ed] insurance,"[ ] but went on to say that, regardless, Congress intended a "federal common law of rights and obligations" to develop under ERISA,[ ] without embellishment by independent state remedies.

Rush says that the day has come to turn dictum into holding by declaring that the state insurance regulation, § 4–10, is preempted for creating just the kind of "alternative remedy" we disparaged in *Pilot Life*. As Rush sees it, the independent review procedure is a form of binding arbitration that allows an ERISA beneficiary to submit claims to a new decisionmaker to examine Rush's determination *de novo*, supplanting judicial review under the "arbitrary and capricious" standard ordinarily applied when discretionary plan interpretations are challenged[ ]. * * *

We think, however, that Rush overstates the rule expressed in *Pilot Life*. * * *

* * *

[T]his case addresses a state regulatory scheme that provides no new cause of action under state law and authorizes no new form of ultimate relief. While independent review under § 4–10 may well settle the fate of a benefit claim under a particular contract, the state statute does not enlarge the claim beyond the benefits available in any action brought under § 1132(a). And although the reviewer's determination would presumably replace that of the HMO as to what is "medically necessary" under this contract, the relief ultimately available would still be what ERISA authorizes in a suit for benefits under § 1132(a). * * *

Rush still argues for going beyond *Pilot Life*, making the preemption issue here one of degree, whether the state procedural imposition interferes unreasonably with Congress's intention to provide a uniform federal regime of "rights and obligations" under ERISA. However, "[s]uch disuniformities ... are the inevitable result of the congressional decision to 'save' local insurance regulation."[ ][11] Although we have recognized a limited exception from the saving clause for alternative causes of action and alternative remedies in the sense described above, we have never indicated that there might be additional justifications for qualifying the clause's application. * * *

To be sure, a State might provide for a type of "review" that would so resemble an adjudication as to fall within *Pilot Life's* categorical bar. Rush, and the dissent,[ ] contend that § 4–10 fills that bill by imposing an alternative scheme of arbitral adjudication at odds with the manifest congressional purpose to confine adjudication of disputes to the courts. * * *

In the classic sense, arbitration occurs when "parties in dispute choose a judge to render a final and binding decision on the merits of the controversy and on the basis of proofs presented by the parties."[ ] Arbitrators typically hold hearings at which parties may submit evidence and conduct cross-examinations.[ ]

Section 4–10 does resemble an arbitration provision, then, to the extent that the independent reviewer considers disputes about the meaning of the HMO contract and receives "evidence" in the form of medical records, statements from physicians, and the like. But this is as far as the resemblance to arbitration goes, for the other features of review under § 4–10 give the proceeding a different character, one not at all at odds with the policy behind § 1132(a). The Act does not give the independent reviewer a free-ranging power to construe contract terms, but instead, confines review to a single term: the phrase "medical necessity," used to define the services covered under the contract.[ ] This limitation, in turn, implicates a feature of HMO benefit determinations that we described in *Pegram v. Herdrich,*[ ] We explained that when an HMO guarantees medically necessary care, determinations of coverage "cannot be untangled from physicians' judgments about reasonable medical treatment."[ ] This is just how the Illinois Act operates; the independent examiner must be a physician with credentials similar to those of the primary care physician,[ ] and is expected to exercise independent medical judgment in deciding what medical necessity requires. * * *

Once this process is set in motion, it does not resemble either contract interpretation or evidentiary litigation before a neutral arbiter, as much as it looks like a practice (having nothing to do with arbitration) of obtaining another medical opinion. * * *

The practice of obtaining a second opinion, however, is far removed from any notion of an enforcement scheme, and once § 4–10 is seen as something akin to a mandate for second-opinion practice in order to ensure sound

---

11. Thus, we do not believe that the mere fact that state independent review laws are likely to entail different procedures will impose burdens on plan administration that would threaten the object of 29 U.S.C. § 1132(a); it is the HMO contracting with a plan, and not the plan itself, that will be subject to these regulations, and every HMO will have to establish procedures for conforming with the local laws, regardless of what this Court may think ERISA forbids. This means that there will be no special burden of compliance upon an ERISA plan beyond what the HMO has already provided for. And although the added compliance cost to the HMO may ultimately be passed on to the ERISA plan, we have said that such "indirect economic effect[s],"[ ] are not enough to preempt state regulation even outside of the insurance context. We recognize, of course, that a State might enact an independent review requirement with procedures so elaborate, and burdens so onerous, that they might undermine § 1132(a). No such system is before us.

medical judgments, the preemption argument that arbitration under § 4–10 supplants judicial enforcement runs out of steam.

Next, Rush argues that § 4–10 clashes with a substantive rule intended to be preserved by the system of uniform enforcement, stressing a feature of judicial review highly prized by benefit plans: a deferential standard for reviewing benefit denials. Whereas *Firestone Tire & Rubber Co. v. Bruch,*[ ] recognized that an ERISA plan could be designed to grant "discretion" to a plan fiduciary, deserving deference from a court reviewing a discretionary judgment, § 4–10 provides that when a plan purchases medical services and insurance from an HMO, benefit denials are subject to apparently *de novo* review. If a plan should continue to balk at providing a service the reviewer has found medically necessary, the reviewer's determination could carry great weight in a subsequent suit for benefits under § 1132(a), depriving the plan of the judicial deference a fiduciary's medical judgment might have obtained if judicial review of the plan's decision had been immediate.[15]

Again, however, the significance of § 4–10 is not wholly captured by Rush's argument, which requires some perspective for evaluation. First, in determining whether state procedural requirements deprive plan administrators of any right to a uniform standard of review, it is worth recalling that ERISA itself provides nothing about the standard. It simply requires plans to afford a beneficiary some mechanism for internal review of a benefit denial, * * *.

Not only is there no ERISA provision directly providing a lenient standard for judicial review of benefit denials, but there is no requirement necessarily entailing such an effect even indirectly. When this Court dealt with the review standards on which the statute was silent, we held that a general or default rule of *de novo* review could be replaced by deferential review if the ERISA plan itself provided that the plan's benefit determinations were matters of high or unfettered discretion[ ]. Nothing in ERISA, however, requires that these kinds of decisions be so "discretionary" in the first place; whether they are is simply a matter of plan design or the drafting of an HMO contract. In this respect, then, § 4–10 prohibits designing an insurance contract so as to accord unfettered discretion to the insurer to interpret the contract's terms. As such, it does not implicate ERISA's enforcement scheme at all, and is no different from the types of substantive state regulation of insurance contracts we have in the past permitted to survive preemption, such as mandated-benefit statutes and statutes prohibiting the denial of claims solely on the ground of untimeliness.[ ] * * *

* * *

15. An issue implicated by this case but requiring no resolution is the degree to which a plan provision for unfettered discretion in benefit determinations guarantees truly deferential review. In *Firestone Tire* itself, we noted that review for abuse of discretion would home in on any conflict of interest on the plan fiduciary's part, if a conflict was plausibly raised. That last observation was underscored only two Terms ago in *Pegram v. Herdrich,*[ ] when we again noted the potential for conflict when an HMO makes decisions about appropriate treatment[ ]. It is a fair question just how deferential the review can be when the judicial eye is peeled for conflict of interest. Moreover, as we explained in *Pegram,* "it is at least questionable whether Congress would have had mixed eligibility decisions in mind when it provided that decisions administering a plan were fiduciary in nature."[ ] Our decision today does not require us to resolve these questions.

In deciding what to make of these facts and conclusions, it helps to go back to where we started and recall the ways States regulate insurance in looking out for the welfare of their citizens. Illinois has chosen to regulate insurance as one way to regulate the practice of medicine, which we have previously held to be permissible under ERISA[ ]. While the statute designed to do this undeniably eliminates whatever may have remained of a plan sponsor's option to minimize scrutiny of benefit denials, this effect of eliminating an insurer's autonomy to guarantee terms congenial to its own interests is the stuff of garden variety insurance regulation through the imposition of standard policy terms. * * * And any lingering doubt about the reasonableness of § 4–10 in affecting the application of § 1132(a) may be put to rest by recalling that regulating insurance tied to what is medically necessary is probably inseparable from enforcing the quintessentially state-law standards of reasonable medical care. See *Pegram v. Herdrich* [ ]. To the extent that benefits litigation in some federal courts may have to account for the effects of § 4–10, it would be an exaggeration to hold that the objectives of § 1132(a) are undermined. The savings clause is entitled to prevail here, and we affirm the judgment.

JUSTICE THOMAS, with whom THE CHIEF JUSTICE, JUSTICE SCALIA, and JUSTICE KENNEDY join, dissenting.

This Court has repeatedly recognized that ERISA's civil enforcement provision, § 502 of the Employee Retirement Income Security Act of 1974 (ERISA), 29 U.S.C. § 1132, provides the exclusive vehicle for actions asserting a claim for benefits under health plans governed by ERISA, and therefore that state laws that create additional remedies are pre-empted.[ ] Such exclusivity of remedies is necessary to further Congress' interest in establishing a uniform federal law of employee benefits so that employers are encouraged to provide benefits to their employees.[ ]

* * * Therefore, as the Court concedes,[ ] even a state law that "regulates insurance" may be pre-empted if it supplements the remedies provided by ERISA, despite ERISA's saving clause,[ ]. Today, however, the Court takes the unprecedented step of allowing respondent Debra Moran to short circuit ERISA's remedial scheme by allowing her claim for benefits to be determined in the first instance through an arbitral-like procedure provided under Illinois law, and by a decisionmaker other than a court.[ ] * * *

From the facts of this case one can readily understand why Moran sought recourse under § 4–10. * * *

In the course of its review, petitioner informed Moran that "there is no prevailing opinion within the appropriate specialty of the United States medical profession that the procedure proposed [by Moran] is safe and effective for its intended use and that the omission of the procedure would adversely affect [her] medical condition."[ ] Petitioner did agree to cover the standard treatment for Moran's ailment,[ ] concluding that peer-reviewed literature "demonstrates that [the standard surgery] is effective therapy in the treatment of [Moran's condition]."[ ]

Moran, however, was not satisfied with this option. * * * She invoked § 4–10 of the Illinois HMO Act, which requires HMOs to provide a mechanism for review by an independent physician when the patient's primary care physician and HMO disagree about the medical necessity of a treatment proposed by the primary care physician. * * *

Dr. A. Lee Dellon, an unaffiliated physician who served as the independent medical reviewer, concluded that the surgery for which petitioner denied coverage "was appropriate," that it was "the same type of surgery" he would have done, and that Moran "had all of the indications and therefore the medical necessity to carry out" the nonstandard surgery. * * * Under § 4–10, Dr. Dellon's determination conclusively established Moran's right to benefits under Illinois law.

* * *

Section 514(a)'s broad language provides that ERISA "shall supersede any and all State laws insofar as they ... relate to any employee benefit plan," except as provided in § 514(b). 29 U.S.C. § 1144(a). This language demonstrates "Congress's intent to establish the regulation of employee welfare benefit plans 'as exclusively a federal concern.' "[ ] It was intended to "ensure that plans and plan sponsors would be subject to a uniform body of benefits law" so as to "minimize the administrative and financial burden of complying with conflicting directives among States or between States and the Federal Government" and to prevent "the potential for conflict in substantive law ... requiring the tailoring of plans and employer conduct to the peculiarities of the law of each jurisdiction."[ ]

* * * [T]he Court until today had consistently held that state laws that seek to supplant or add to the exclusive remedies in § 502(a) of ERISA, 29 U.S.C. § 1132(a), are pre-empted because they conflict with Congress' objective that rights under ERISA plans are to be enforced under a uniform national system.[ ] The Court has explained that § 502(a) creates an "interlocking, interrelated, and interdependent remedial scheme," and that a beneficiary who claims that he was wrongfully denied benefits has "a panoply of remedial devices" at his disposal. * * *

* * *

Section 4–10 cannot be characterized as anything other than an alternative state-law remedy or vehicle for seeking benefits. In the first place, § 4–10 comes into play only if the HMO and the claimant dispute the claimant's entitlement to benefits; the purpose of the review is to determine whether a claimant is entitled to benefits. * * *

There is no question that arbitration constitutes an alternative remedy to litigation.[ ] Consequently, although a contractual agreement to arbitrate— which does not constitute a "State law" relating to "any employee benefit plan"—is outside § 514(a) of ERISA's pre-emptive scope, States may not circumvent ERISA preemption by mandating an alternative arbitral-like remedy as a plan term enforceable through an ERISA action.

To be sure, the majority is correct that § 4–10 does not mirror all procedural and evidentiary aspects of "common arbitration."[ ] But as a binding decision on the merits of the controversy the § 4–10 review resembles nothing so closely as arbitration. * * *

* * *

[I]t is troubling that the Court views the review under § 4–10 as nothing more than a practice "of obtaining a second [medical] opinion." * * * [W]hile a second medical opinion is nothing more than that—an opinion—a determination under § 4–10 is a conclusive determination with respect to the award of benefits. * * *

Section 4–10 constitutes an arbitral-like state remedy through which plan members may seek to resolve conclusively a disputed right to benefits. Some 40 other States have similar laws, though these vary as to applicability, procedures, standards, deadlines, and consequences of independent review. * * *

For the reasons noted by the Court, independent review provisions may sound very appealing. Efforts to expand the variety of remedies available to aggrieved beneficiaries beyond those set forth in ERISA are obviously designed to increase the chances that patients will be able to receive treatments they desire, and most of us are naturally sympathetic to those suffering from illness who seek further options. Nevertheless, the Court would do well to remember that no employer is required to provide any health benefit plan under ERISA and that the entire advent of managed care, and the genesis of HMOs, stemmed from spiraling health costs. To the extent that independent review provisions such as § 4–10 make it more likely that HMOs will have to subsidize beneficiaries' treatments of choice, they undermine the ability of HMOs to control costs, which, in turn, undermines the ability of employers to provide health care coverage for employees.

As a consequence, independent review provisions could create a disincentive to the formation of employee health benefit plans, a problem that Congress addressed by making ERISA's remedial scheme exclusive and uniform. While it may well be the case that the advantages of allowing States to implement independent review requirements as a supplement to the remedies currently provided under ERISA outweigh this drawback, this is a judgment that, pursuant to ERISA, must be made by Congress. I respectfully dissent.

Notes and Questions

1. ERISA only governs employee benefit plans, i.e. benefit plans established and maintained by employers to provide benefits to their employees. It does not reach health insurance purchased by individuals as individuals (including self-employed individuals) or health benefits not provided through employment-related group plans, such as uninsured motorist insurance policies or workers' compensation. Certain church and government-sponsored plans are also not covered. See Macro v. Independent Health Ass'n, Inc., 180 F. Supp.2d 427 (W.D.N.Y.2001). Finally, ERISA does not regulate group insurance offered by insurers to the employees of particular businesses without employer contributions or administrative involvement. See 29 C.F.R. § 2510.3–1(j); Taggart Corp. v. Life & Health Benefits Admin., Inc., 617 F.2d 1208 (5th Cir.1980), cert. denied, 450 U.S. 1030, 101 S.Ct. 1739, 68 L.Ed.2d 225 (1981). Nevertheless, ERISA does govern the vast majority of private health insurance provided in America, which is provided through employment-related group plans.

2. Part of the confusion inherent in ERISA preemption decisions is attributable to the fact that there are three distinct forms of ERISA preemption. One of these is express preemption based on § 514(a) (29 U.S.C. § 1144(a)). Section 514(a), reproduced above, provides that ERISA "supersedes" any state law that

"relates to" an employee benefits plan. Express 514(a) preemption, however, is subject to the "savings" clause, and thus does not reach state insurance regulation.

Just because a law is saved from 514(a) preemption, however, does not mean that it is not preempted, as the controversy in *Rush* illustrates. ERISA preemption can also be based on § 502(a) of ERISA (29 U.S.C. § 1132(a)) which provides for federal court jurisdiction over specified types of claims against ERISA plans. The Supreme Court has long held that ERISA plans may remove into federal court claims that were brought in state courts but that could have been brought under § 502(a) in federal court. Removal is permitted under the "complete preemption" exception to the well-pleaded complaint rule. The well-pleaded complaint rule normally limits removal of cases from state into federal court on the basis of federal question jurisdiction (under 28 U.S.C.A. § 1331) to cases in which federal claims are explicitly raised in the plaintiff's complaint. However, under the "complete preemption" exception to this rule (sometimes called "superpreemption") federal jurisdiction is permitted when Congress has so completely preempted an area of law that any claim within it is brought under federal law, and thus is removable to federal court. "Complete preemption" is, in reality, not a preemption doctrine, but rather a rule of federal jurisdiction.

Third, Section 502(a) also plays another role in ERISA jurisprudence, ousting state claims and remedies that would take the place of § 502 claims. The federal courts have interpreted this section to indicate a Congressional intent to preempt comprehensively the "field" of judicial oversight of employee benefits plans. Thus state tort, contract, and even statutory claims that could have been brought as claims for benefits or for breach of fiduciary duty under § 502(a) have been held to be preempted by § 502(a). As *Moran* demonstrates, § 502(a) preemption, like § 514(a) explicit preemption, is not comprehensive. In particular, ERISA does not necessarily preempt state court malpractice cases brought against managed care plans that provide as well as pay for health care, as we will see in subsection D. Also claims brought by persons who are not proper plaintiffs under § 502(a) or against persons who are not ERISA fiduciaries evade ERISA § 502(a) preemption. *Moran* also holds that external review procedures imposed by the states prior to the onset of litigation also may be exempt from § 502 preemption.

Section 502(a) and § 514(a) preemption are not, however, coextensive. Just because a lawsuit invokes a law that might be preempted as relating to an employee benefits claim does not mean that the claim could be brought under § 502(a), and is thus subject to "complete preemption." Not infrequently federal courts remand cases that could not have been brought as § 502(a) claims to state court for resolution of § 514(a) preemption issues. As we see below in *Aetna Health Insurance v. Davila*, moreover, laws that are saved from preemption by an exception to § 514(a), may still be preempted as inconsistent with § 502(a) field preemption.

3. Early cases interpreting § 514(a) read it very broadly. The Supreme Court's first consideration of § 514(a), Shaw v. Delta Air Lines, Inc., 463 U.S. 85, 103 S.Ct. 2890, 77 L.Ed.2d 490 (1983), adopted a very literal and liberal reading of "relates to" as including any provisions having a "connection with or reference to" a benefits plan. The Court rejected narrower readings of ERISA preemption that would have limited its reach to state laws that explicitly attempted to regulate ERISA plans or that dealt with subjects explicitly addressed by ERISA. For over a decade following *Shaw*, the Court applied the § 514(a) tests developed in *Shaw* expansively in a variety of contexts, almost always finding preemption when it found an ERISA plan to exist. The Court repeatedly expressed allegiance

to the opinion that ERISA § 514(a) preemption had a "broad scope" (Metropolitan Life v. Massachusetts, 471 U.S. 724, 739, 105 S.Ct. 2380, 85 L.Ed.2d 728 (1985)), and "an expansive sweep" (Pilot Life Ins. Co. v. Dedeaux, 481 U.S. 41, 47, 107 S.Ct. 1549, 95 L.Ed.2d 39 (1987)), and that it was "conspicuous for its breadth," (FMC Corp. v. Holliday, 498 U.S. 52, 58, 111 S.Ct. 403, 112 L.Ed.2d 356 (1990)).

Attending to these Supreme Court pronouncements, lower courts in the 1980s and 1990s held a wide range of state regulatory programs and common law claims that arguably "related to" the administration of an ERISA plan or imposed costs upon plans to be preempted. As the *Fiedler* case below demonstrates, the "connection with or reference to" test continues to sweep broadly. The Supreme Court finally recognized the limits of ERISA preemption, however, in New York State Conference of Blue Cross and Blue Shield Plans v. Travelers Ins. Co., 514 U.S. 645, 115 S.Ct. 1671, 131 L.Ed.2d 695 (1995). *Travelers* held that a New York law that required hospitals to charge different rates to insured, HMO, and self-insured plans was not preempted by § 514(a). Retreating from earlier expansive readings of ERISA preemption, the Court reaffirmed the principle applied in other areas of the law that Congress is generally presumed not to intend to preempt state law. 514 U.S. at 654. The Court proceeded to note that in cases involving traditional areas of state regulation, such as health care, congressional intent to preempt state law should not be presumed unless it was "clear and manifest." Id. at 655. Recognizing that the term "relate to" was not self-limiting, the Court turned for assistance in defining the term to the purpose of ERISA, which it defined as freeing benefit plans from conflicting state and local regulation. Id. at 656–57. Preemption was intended, the Court held, to affect state laws that operated directly on the structure or administration of ERISA plans, id. at 657–58, not laws that only indirectly raised the cost of various benefit options, id. at 658–64. Accordingly, the Court held that the challenged rate-setting law was not "related to" an ERISA plan, and thus not preempted.

The Court's post-*Travelers* preemption cases suggest that the Court in fact turned a corner in *Travelers*. It has rejected ERISA preemption in the majority of these cases, though it had almost never done so before *Travelers*. Post-*Travelers* lower court cases on the whole continued to apply ERISA preemption broadly, generally finding that state programs aimed at regulating insurance and managed care "relate to" ERISA plan. Some, however, have limited ERISA preemption. See, for example, Louisiana Health Service & Indemnity Co. v. Rapides Healthcare System, 461 F.3d 529 (5th Cir.2006), holding that a Louisiana statute that required insurance companies to honor all assignments of benefits by patients to hospitals did not have an impermissible connection with ERISA. See, reviewing comprehensively federal and state court cases applying ERISA to managed care regulation, Robert F. Rich, Christopher T. Erb, and Louis J. Gale, Judicial Interpretation of Managed Care Policy, 13 Elder L.J. 85 (2005).

4. As *Moran* notes, a state law that is otherwise preempted under § 514(a) is saved from preemption if it regulates insurance under the "savings clause" found in § 514(b)(2)(A) (29 U.S.C.A. § 1144(b)(2)(A)). In its early cases interpreting this clause, the Court read it conservatively, applying both a "common sense" test as well as the three part test developed in antitrust cases applying the McCarran–Ferguson Act for determining whether a law regulated "the business of insurance" to determine whether the savings clause applied. Metropolitan Life Ins. Co. v. Massachusetts, 471 U.S. 724, 740–44, 105 S.Ct. 2380, 85 L.Ed.2d 728 (1985), Pilot Life Ins. Co. v. Dedeaux, 481 U.S. 41, 107 S.Ct. 1549, 95 L.Ed.2d 39 (1987).

In Kentucky Association of Health Plans v. Miller, 538 U.S. 329, 123 S.Ct. 1471, 155 L.Ed.2d 468 (2003) the court abandoned its earlier precedents and crafted a new approach to interpreting the savings clause. This case involved the claim of an association of managed care plans that Kentucky's "any willing provider" law was preempted by ERISA. The Sixth Circuit had held that the regulatory provision was saved from preemption under ERISA's savings clause. In a brief and unanimous opinion written by Justice Scalia (who had dissented in *Moran*), the Court held that the law was saved from preemption, abandoning its previous savings clause jurisprudence. The Court acknowledged that use of the McCarran–Ferguson test had "misdirected attention, failed to provide clear guidance to lower federal courts, and * * * added little to relevant analysis." The Court also admitted that the McCarran–Ferguson tests had been developed for different purposes and interpreted different statutory language.

The Court concluded:

> Today we make a clean break from the McCarran–Ferguson factors and hold that for a state law to be deemed a 'law ... which regulates insurance' under § 1144(b)(2)(A), it must satisfy two requirements. First, the state law must be specifically directed toward entities engaged in insurance.[ ] Second, * * * the state law must substantially affect the risk pooling arrangement between the insurer and the insured. Kentucky's law satisfies each of these requirements. 123 S.Ct. at 1479.

Earlier in the opinion it had interpreted the "risk pooling" requirement as follows:

> We have never held that state laws must alter or control the actual terms of insurance policies to be deemed 'laws ... which regulat[e] insurance' under § 1144(b)(2)(A); it suffices that they substantially affect the risk pooling arrangement between insurer and insured. By expanding the number of providers from whom an insured may receive health services, AWP laws alter the scope of permissible bargains between insurers and insureds * * *. No longer may Kentucky insureds seek insurance from a closed network of health-care providers in exchange for a lower premium. The AWP prohibition substantially affects the type of risk pooling arrangements that insurers may offer. 123 S.Ct. at 1477–78.

Kentucky Association significantly clarifies, and expands, the coverage of ERISA's savings clause. Virtually any state law that requires insurers to provide particular benefits would seem to be covered. See Matthew O. Gatewood, The New Map: The Supreme Court's New Guide to Curing Thirty Years of Confusion in ERISA Savings Clause Analysis, 62 Wash. & Lee U. L. Rev. 643 (2005). What effect is this green light to state regulation of managed care and health insurance likely to have on the willingness of employers to offer health insurance plans to their workers? Might Justice Thomas' prediction on this matter prove true? See Haavi Morreim, ERISA Takes a Drubbing: Rush Prudential and Its Implications for Health Care, 38 Tort Trial and Ins. Practice J. 933 (2003). Ironically, this expansion of state regulatory authority comes at a time when many states have lost interest in more aggressive regulation of managed care.

5. As *Moran* acknowledges, even a statute saved from § 514(a) preemption by the savings clause may nevertheless, under *Pilot Life*, be preempted by § 502(a) if it provides a state remedy that takes the place of § 502(a). Aetna Health Inc. v. Davila, 542 U.S. 200, 124 S.Ct. 2488, 159 L.Ed.2d 312 (2004), reproduced below, applied this exception, holding that the Texas Health Care Liability Act, which allowed lawsuits against managed care companies for failing to exercise ordinary care in making coverage decisions, was preempted. Section 502 preemption is not limited to tort cases, but also extends to state statutes that

provide private actions for civil penalties to the extent that these cases could have been brought under § 502. See, for example, Prudential Insurance Co. v. National Park Medical Center, Inc., 413 F.3d 897 (8th Cir.2005), holding that the provisions of the Arkansas Patient Protection Act allowing private suits for injunctive relief, damages of at least $1,000, and attorney's fees were preempted by ERISA § 502 to the extent that they could have been brought under § 502. Thus an action to recover payment denied by a plan for the services of a provider who should have been qualified for payment under a state's "any willing provider" law would be preempted. In Hawaii Management Alliance Assoc. v. Insurance Comm'r, 106 Hawai'i 21, 100 P.3d 952 (2004), the Hawaiian Supreme Court held that Hawai'i's external review statute was preempted by ERISA because it provided a remedy alternative to § 502. Would any of the provisions of the Massachusetts managed care regulation statute in Chapter 6 be preempted under § 502?

6.   ERISA's § 514(b)(2)(A) savings clause is subject to its own exception, the § 514(b)(2)(B) "deemer" clause. This subsection, reproduced above, provides that "neither an employee benefit * * * nor any trust established under such a plan, shall be deemed to be an insurance company or other insurer, * * * or to be engaged in the business of insurance * * * for purposes of any law of any State purporting to regulate insurance companies, [or] insurance contracts, * * *." 29 U.S.C.A. § 1144(b)(2)(B). In FMC Corporation v. Holliday, 498 U.S. 52, 111 S.Ct. 403, 112 L.Ed.2d 356 (1990), the Supreme Court interpreted this clause broadly to exempt self-funded ERISA plans entirely from state regulation and state law claims. None of the provisions of the Massachusetts managed care regulation statute in Chapter 9, for example, would apply to self-insured ERISA plans.

The deemer clause offers a significant incentive for employers to become self-insured, as a self-insured plan can totally escape state regulation, and in particular, benefit mandates. Self-insurance, however, also has disadvantages—it imposes upon the employer the burden of administering the plan as well as open-ended liability for employee benefit claims made under the plan. To avoid these problems, self-insured employers often contract with third-party administrators to administer claims and with stop-loss insurers to limit their claims exposure. The courts have overwhelmingly held that employer plans remain self-insured even though they are reinsured through stop-loss plans, and have prohibited state regulation of stop-loss coverage for self-insured plans. See, e.g., Bill Gray Enterprises, Inc. Employee Health and Welfare Plan v. Gourley, 248 F.3d 206 (3rd Cir.2001) and Lincoln Mutual Casualty v. Lectron Products, Inc. 970 F.2d 206 (6th Cir.1992). Third-party administrators that administer self-insured plans are also protected from state insurance regulation. NGS American, Inc. v. Barnes, 805 F.Supp. 462, 473 (W.D.Texas 1992). Thus an employer who is willing to bear some risk can escape state regulation under the "deemer" clause, even though most of the risk of insuring the plan is borne by a stop-loss insurer and the burden of administering the plan is assumed by a third-party administrator. Can the states, however, impede this means of escape from state insurance regulation by prohibiting stop-loss insurers from selling policies that cover losses below a certain level, or requiring a specified level of self-insured coverage before a stop loss policy kicks in? See, arguing that such regulation is permitted under the savings clause, Russell Korobkin, The Battle Over Self–Insured Health Plans, or "One Good Loophole Deserves Another," 5 Yale J. Health Pol'y, L. & Ethics 89 (2005).

7.   One issue that arose occasionally in pre-*Moran* savings clause litigation is whether health maintenance organizations are in the business of insurance and thus subject to state regulation. Early cases tended to say no, often on very

formalistic grounds, see, e.g., O'Reilly v. Ceuleers, 912 F.2d 1383 (11th Cir.1990). *Moran* seems to have settled this issue once and for all. The defendant, Rush, argued that an HMO was a health care provider rather than an insurer, and thus regulations affecting it would not be protected by the savings clause. The Court responded:

> The answer to Rush is, of course, that an HMO is both: it provides health care, and it does so as an insurer. Nothing in the saving clause requires an either-or choice between health care and insurance in deciding a preemption question. and as long as providing insurance fairly accounts for the application of state law, the saving clause may apply. * * *

> The defining feature of an HMO is receipt of a fixed fee for each patient enrolled under the terms of a contract to provide specified health care if needed. *Pegram v. Herdrich,*[ ]. "The HMO thus assumes the financial risk of providing the benefits promised: if a participant never gets sick, the HMO keeps the money regardless, and if a participant becomes expensively ill, the HMO is responsible for the treatment...." *Id.,* * * *. 536 U.S. at 367.

9.   Among the most litigated ERISA issues in the past decade has been the effect ERISA has on the rights of health plans to recover amounts they paid for health care when a beneficiary subsequently recovers a tort judgment for the injuries that necessitated the care. These cases are either brought by a plan trying to recover from the beneficiary or by a beneficiary trying to block recovery by the plan or to get money back that a plan has already obtained by exercising its rights of subrogation. Some cases involve state statutes limiting a plan's right of subrogation. The Supreme Court has decided two recent cases involving the rights of plans to recover benefits under ERISA, Sereboff v. Mid Atlantic Medical Services, Inc., 547 U.S. 356, 126 S.Ct. 1869, 164 L.Ed.2d 612 (2006) and Great–West Life & Annuity Ins. Co. v. Knudson, 534 U.S. 204, 122 S.Ct. 708, 151 L.Ed.2d 635 (2002). These decisions interpret provisions of ERISA authorizing equitable relief and turn on arcane interpretations of the historical distinction between law and equity. They are beyond the scope of this chapter.

Problem: ERISA Preemption of State Managed Care Regulation

Two years ago, as part of a comprehensive managed care reform statute, your state adopted three new regulatory provisions. The first provides that all health insurance plans in your state, including all employee benefits plans that cover physician and hospital services, must cover all care that is "medically necessary." It defines "medically necessary" to include any care recommended by a plan member's treating physician that is recognized as "standard" by at least a "respectable minority" of physicians. The second provision establishes a state external review program to which any insured or plan member can appeal the decision of an insurer or benefit plan refusing coverage of a service as not "medically necessary" if internal plan remedies have been exhausted. A third statute provides a cause of action under state law that allows any plan member or insured who has been denied payment for services by a plan after those services have been decided by an external review entity to be medically necessary to sue the plan in state court for injunctive relief, and also for any consequential damages attributable to the plan's service denial.

An association of insurers and an association of self-insured ERISA plans have both sued in federal court asking that the court declare that all three provisions are preempted by and unenforceable under ERISA. At the same time, Joseph Ditka, who has health benefits through his employer covered by Health Star, Inc., a managed care organization has sued the plan for damages he alleges that he suffered when Health Star refused to cover a procedure that his doctor recommended last year and that the state's external review program determined to be medically necessary. Who wins each claim, and why?

B. ERISA PREEMPTION AND STATE HEALTH CARE REFORM

Although *Moran* and *Miller* seemed to beat back the threat that ERISA had posed to state managed care regulation, ERISA preemption has recently reemerged on another front as a significant barrier to state health care reform. ERISA has long limited the ability of states to reform health care. A quarter of a century ago, Hawaii's mandate that employers provide health insurance to their employees was struck down as impermissibly interfering in the terms of employee benefit plans in violation of ERISA, Standard Oil Co. of California v. Agsalud, 633 F.2d 760 (CA9 1980), summarily aff'd, 454 U.S. 801, 102 S.Ct. 79, 70 L.Ed.2d 75 (1981). In 1983, Congress amended ERISA to exempt from preemption certain provisions of the Hawaii Act in place before the enactment of ERISA, but no other state has been afforded such an exemption. Recent attempts by other states to expand insurance coverage have tried to evade ERISA preemption, but the first ERISA challenge brought against such a statute was completely successful.

RETAIL INDUSTRY LEADERS ASSOCIATION v. FIEDLER

United States Court of Appeals, Fourth Circuit, 2007.
475 F.3d 180.

NIEMEYER, CIRCUIT JUDGE:

On January 12, 2006, the Maryland General Assembly enacted the Fair Share Health Care Fund Act, which requires employers with 10,000 or more Maryland employees to spend at least 8% of their total payrolls on employees' health insurance costs or pay the amount their spending falls short to the State of Maryland. Resulting from a nationwide campaign to force Wal–Mart Stores, Inc., to increase health insurance benefits for its 16,000 Maryland employees, the Act's minimum spending provision was crafted to cover just Wal–Mart. The Retail Industry Leaders Association, of which Wal–Mart is a member, brought suit against James D. Fielder, Jr., the Maryland Secretary of Labor, Licensing, and Regulation, to declare that the Act is preempted by the Employee Retirement Income Security Act of 1974 ("ERISA") and to enjoin the Act's enforcement. * * *

Because Maryland's Fair Share Health Care Fund Act effectively requires employers in Maryland covered by the Act to restructure their employee health insurance plans, it conflicts with ERISA's goal of permitting uniform nationwide administration of these plans. We conclude therefore that the Maryland Act is preempted by ERISA and accordingly affirm.

I

Before enactment of the Fair Share Health Care Fund Act ("Fair Share Act"), [ ] the Maryland General Assembly heard extensive testimony about the rising costs of the Maryland Medical Assistance Program (Medicaid and children's health programs). * * * The General Assembly also perceived that Wal–Mart Stores, Inc., a particularly large employer, provided its employees with a substandard level of healthcare benefits, forcing many Wal–Mart employees to depend on state-subsidized healthcare programs. Indeed, the

Maryland Department of Legislative Services * * * prepared an analytical report of the proposed Fair Share Act for the General Assembly, that discussed only Wal–Mart's employee benefits practices. * * *

* * *

Some states claim many Wal–Mart employees end up on public health programs such as Medicaid. A survey by Georgia officials found that more than 10,000 children of Wal–Mart employees were enrolled in the state's children's health insurance program (CHIP) at a cost of nearly $10 million annually. Similarly, a North Carolina hospital found that 31% of 1,900 patients who said they were Wal–Mart employees were enrolled in Medicaid, and an additional 16% were uninsured.

* * *

According to the [New York] Times, Wal–Mart said that its employees are mostly insured, citing internal surveys showing that 90% of workers have health coverage, often through Medicare or family members' policies. Wal–Mart officials say the company provides health coverage to about 537,000, or 45% of its total workforce. As a matter of comparison, Costco Wholesale provides health insurance to 96% of eligible employees.

In response, the General Assembly enacted the Fair Share Act in January 2006, to become effective January 1, 2007. The Act applies to employers that have at least 10,000 employees in Maryland, * * * and imposes spending and reporting requirements on such employers. The core provision provides:

> An employer that is not organized as a nonprofit organization and does not spend up to 8% of the total wages paid to employees in the State on health insurance costs shall pay to the Secretary an amount equal to the difference between what the employer spends for health insurance costs and an amount equal to 8% of the total wages paid to employees in the State.

[ ] An employer that fails to make the required payment is subject to a civil penalty of $250,000.[ ]

The Act also requires a covered employer to submit an annual report on January 1 of each year to the Secretary, in which the employer must disclose: (1) how many employees it had for the prior year, (2) its "health insurance costs," and (3) the percentage of compensation it spent on "health insurance costs" for the "year immediately preceding the previous calendar year." * * *

Any payments collected * * * may be used only to support the Maryland Medical Assistance Program, which consists of Maryland's Medicaid and children's health programs.[ ]

The record discloses that only four employers have at least 10,000 employees in Maryland: * * * The parties agree that only Wal–Mart, who employs approximately 16,000 in Maryland, is currently subject to the Act's minimum spending requirements. Wal–Mart representatives testified that it spends about 7 to 8% of its total payroll on healthcare, falling short of the Act's 8% threshold.

The legislative record also makes clear that legislators and affected parties assumed that the Fair Share Act would force Wal–Mart to increase its spending on healthcare benefits rather than to pay monies to the State. * * *

* * *

III
* * *

A

ERISA establishes comprehensive federal regulation of employers' provision of benefits to their employees. It does not mandate that employers provide specific employee benefits but leaves them free, "for any reason at any time, to adopt, modify, or terminate welfare plans." * * *

* * *

The primary objective of ERISA was to "provide a uniform regulatory regime over employee benefit plans."[ ] To accomplish this objective, § 514(a) of ERISA broadly preempts "any and all State laws insofar as they may now or hereafter *relate to* any employee benefit plan" covered by ERISA.[ ] This preemption provision aims "to minimize the administrative and financial burden of complying with conflicting directives among States or between States and the Federal Government" and to reduce "the tailoring of plans and employer conduct to the peculiarities of the law of each jurisdiction."[ ]

The language of ERISA's preemption provision—covering all laws that "relate to" an ERISA plan—is "clearly expansive."[ ] The Supreme Court has focused judicial analysis by explaining that a state law "relates to" an ERISA plan "if it has a *connection with* or *reference to* such a plan."[ ] But even these terms, "taken to extend to the furthest stretch of [their] indeterminacy," would have preemption "never run its course."[ ] Accordingly, we do not rely on "uncritical literalism" but attempt to ascertain whether Congress would have expected the Fair Share Act to be preempted.[ ] To make this determination, we look "to the objectives of the ERISA statute" as well as "to the nature of the effect of the state law on ERISA plans,"[ ].

* * * States continue to enjoy wide latitude to regulate healthcare *providers*.[ ] And ERISA explicitly saves state regulations of *insurance companies* from preemption.[ ] But unlike laws that regulate healthcare providers and insurance companies, "state laws that mandate[ ] employee benefit structures or their administration" are preempted by ERISA.[ ]

* * *

In line with *Shaw,* [v. Delta Air Lines, Inc., 463 U.S. 85 (1983)] courts have readily and routinely found preemption of state laws that act directly upon an employee benefit plan or effectively require it to establish a particular ERISA-governed benefit.[ ] Likewise, *Shaw* dictates that ERISA preempt state laws that directly regulate employers' contributions to or structuring of their plans.[ ]

A state law that directly regulates the structuring or administration of an ERISA plan is not saved by inclusion of a means for opting out of its requirements. * * * Additionally, a proliferation of laws like Washington's would have undermined ERISA's objective of sparing plan administrators the task of monitoring the laws of all 50 States and modifying their plan documents accordingly.[ ]

In sum, a state law has an impermissible "connection with" an ERISA plan if it directly regulates or effectively mandates some element of the structure or administration of employers' ERISA plans. On the other hand, a state law that creates only indirect economic incentives that affect but do not bind the choices of employers or their ERISA plans is generally not preempted.[ ] In deciding which of these principles is applicable, we assess the effect of a state law on the ability of ERISA plans to be administered uniformly nationwide.[ ] A state law is preempted also if it contains a "reference to" an ERISA plan, the alternative characterization referred to in *Shaw* for finding that it "relates to" an ERISA plan.[ ] The district court did not reach this issue because it found that preemption through the Fair Share Act's "connection with" ERISA plans. * * *

* * * At its heart, the Fair Share Act requires every employer of 10,000 or more Maryland employees to pay to the State an amount that equals the difference between what the employer spends on "health insurance costs" * * * and 8% of its payroll. * * *

In effect, the only rational choice employers have under the Fair Share Act is to structure their ERISA healthcare benefit plans so as to meet the minimum spending threshold. * * * Because the Fair Share Act effectively mandates that employers structure their employee healthcare plans to provide a certain level of benefits, the Act has an obvious "connection with" employee benefit plans and so is preempted by ERISA.

* * *

While the Secretary argues that the Fair Share Act is designed to collect funds for medical care under the Maryland Medical Assistance Program, the core provision of the Act aims at requiring covered employers to provide medical benefits to employees. The effect of this provision will force employers to structure their recordkeeping and healthcare benefit spending to comply with the Fair Share Act. Functioning in that manner, the Act would disrupt employers' uniform administration of employee benefit plans on a nationwide basis. * * *

This problem would not likely be confined to Maryland. As a result of similar efforts elsewhere to pressure Wal–Mart to increase its healthcare spending, other States and local governments have adopted or are considering healthcare spending mandates that would clash with the Fair Share Act. * * * If permitted to stand, these laws would force Wal–Mart to tailor its healthcare benefit plans to each specific State, and even to specific cities and counties. * * *

* * *

The Secretary argues that the Act is not mandatory and therefore does not, for preemption purposes, have a "connection with" employee benefit plans because it gives employers two options to avoid increasing benefits to employees. An employer can, under the Fair Share Act, (1) increase healthcare spending on employees in ways that do not qualify as ERISA plans; or (2) refuse to increase benefits to employees and pay the State the amount by which the employer's spending falls short of 8%. Because employers have these choices, the Secretary argues, the Fair Share Act does not preclude Wal–Mart from continuing its uniform administration of ERISA plans nationwide. He maintains that the Fair Share Act is more akin to the laws upheld in *Travelers,* 514 U.S. at 658–59, 115 S.Ct. 1671, and *Dillingham,* 519 U.S. at 319, 117 S.Ct. 832, which merely created economic incentives that affected employers' choices while not effectively dictating their choice. This argument fails for several reasons.

First, the laws involved in *Travelers* and *Dillingham* are inapposite because they dealt with regulations that only *indirectly* regulated ERISA plans. * * *

* * *

In contrast to *Travelers* and *Dillingham,* the Fair Share Act *directly* regulates employers' structuring of their employee health benefit plans. * * *

Second, the choices given in the Fair Share Act, on which the Secretary relies to argue that the Act is not a mandate on employers, are not meaningful alternatives by which an employer can increase its healthcare spending to comply with the Fair Share Act without affecting its ERISA plans. * * *

In addition to on-site medical clinics, employers could, under the Fair Share Act, contribute to employees' Health Savings Accounts as a means of non-ERISA healthcare spending. Under federal tax law, eligible individuals may establish and make pretax contributions to a Health Savings Account and then use those monies to pay or reimburse medical expenses.[ ] Employers' contributions to employees' Health Savings Accounts qualify as healthcare spending for purposes of the Fair Share Act.[ ] This option of contributing to Health Savings Accounts, however, is available under only limited conditions, which undermine the impact of this option. For example, only if an individual is covered under a high deductible health plan and no other more comprehensive health plan is he eligible to establish a Health Savings Account. * * * In addition, for an employer's contribution to a Health Savings Account to be exempt from ERISA, the Health Savings Account must be established voluntarily by the employee. *See* U.S. Dep't of Labor, Employee Benefits Sec. Admin., Field Assistance Bulletin 2004–1. This would likely shrink further the potential for Health Savings Accounts contributions as many employees would not undertake to establish Health Savings Accounts.

* * * The undeniable fact is that the vast majority of any employer's healthcare spending occurs through ERISA plans. Thus, the primary subjects of the Fair Share Act are ERISA plans, and any attempt to comply with the Act would have direct effects on the employer's ERISA plans. * * *

Perhaps recognizing the insufficiency of a non-ERISA healthcare spending option, the Secretary relies most heavily on its argument that the Fair Share Act gives employers the choice of paying the State rather than altering their healthcare spending. * * * The Secretary contends that, in certain circumstances, it would be rational for an employer to choose to do so. * * * [I]ndeed, identifying the narrow conditions under which the Act would not force an employer to increase its spending on healthcare plans only reinforces the conclusion that the overwhelming effect of the Act is to mandate spending increases. This conclusion is further supported by the fact that Wal–Mart representatives averred that Wal–Mart would in fact increase healthcare spending rather than pay the State. *AFFIRMED.*

MICHAEL, CIRCUIT JUDGE, dissenting:

* * *

I respectfully dissent on the issue of ERISA preemption because the Act does not force a covered employer to make a choice that impacts an employee benefit plan. An employer can comply with the Act either by paying assessments into the special fund or by increasing spending on employee health insurance. The Act expresses no preference for one method of Medicaid support or the other. As a result, the Act is not preempted by ERISA.

* * *

Notes and Questions

1. What routes are open to a state that wants to engage employers in an attempt to expand insurance coverage? Clearly a direct mandate requiring employers to offer specified coverage to their employees is out of the question. On the other hand, state initiatives that offer tax credits to employers to expand coverage, create voluntary purchasing pools to enhance the purchasing power of small businesses, use Medicaid or State Children's Health Insurance Program funds to subsidize employment-based insurance for low-income workers, or require insurers to offer low cost insurance policies to small businesses should not be affected by ERISA because they do not impose any requirements on employers or on ERISA plans The provisions of the Massachusetts plan that penalize employers who do not allow their employees to purchase health insurance with after-tax money through a § 125 cafeteria plan (which excludes from income taxation money that employees spend on health care) might survive an ERISA challenge, since § 125 plans are not technically benefit plans (because employers do not contribute to them) and thus should not be governed by ERISA. State tax-financed universal insurance programs funded through a payroll tax should also survive an ERISA challenge, although they would arguably affect the likelihood of employers offering employee-benefit health plans. Finally, universal coverage systems based solely on an individual mandate should not implicate ERISA, because, again, they impose no obligations on employers.

The big question, however, is what, if anything, can be done to make a "pay-or-play" system pass ERISA muster after *Fiedler*. Several municipalities, including New York and San Francisco, have adopted pay-or-play ordinances. San Francisco's "pay-or-play" ordinance was struck down in 2007 under ERISA preemption. Golden Gate Restaurant Ass'n v. City and County of San Francisco, 535 F.Supp.2d 968 (N.D.Cal.2007). As of this writing, the district court's judgment has been stayed by the Ninth Circuit Court of Appeals pending appeal. The Massachusetts "fair-share" assessment and "premiums" that Vermont imposes on employers to cover their uninsured workers would also seem vulnerable because they do impose obligations on employers. But the penalty imposed on Massachusetts employers who do not comply, $295 per employee, per year, is much smaller than that imposed by the Maryland law and will not compel employers to comply with the law who choose not to. Pay-or-play laws that are not focused on a particular employer, do not refer to ERISA plans, do not impose penalties substantial enough to force an employer to provide benefits, and do not require the employer to establish any particular kind of benefit plan may pass muster, but will almost certainly be challenged, and, if other courts follow the Fourth Circuit, may be difficult to defend. State laws that impose significant record-keeping obligations on employers will also face ERISA challenges, even if they do not require employer financial contributions, because they essentially require an employer to spend money for administrative costs. See, discussing these issues, Edward A. Zelinsky, The New Massachusetts Health Law: Preemption and Experimentation, 49 Wm. & Mary L. Rev. 229 (2007); Amy Monahan, Pay or Play Laws, ERISA Preemption, and Potential Lessons from Massachusetts, 55 Kansas Law Review 1203 (2007); Patricia A. Butler, ERISA Implications for State Health Care Access Initiatives: Impact of the Maryland "Fair Share Act" Court Decision, National Academy for State Health Policy (2006); and Patricia A. Butler, ERISA Update: Federal Court of Appeals Agrees ERISA Preempts Maryland's "Fair Share Act," National Academy for State Health Policy, 2007.

2. Does the fact that ERISA is a federal law that preempts state attempts to regulate employee benefit plans mean that federal legislation will be necessary to expand health care coverage to the uninsured? Or is the nation better off with a "laboratory of the states" approach to expanding health care coverage, even if the states have a quite limited range of approaches to expanding health care coverage, the most realistic of which are also very costly? Should Congress amend ERISA to allow states to adopt "pay-or-play" laws? What effects would this have on the national uniformity of employer obligations that seems to be an important value in ERISA jurisprudence?

C. THE RELATIONSHIP BETWEEN FEDERAL ERISA FIDUCIARY LAW AND STATE TORT CLAIMS AGAINST MANAGED CARE PLANS

As will be seen in the next subsection, one of the most frequently litigated ERISA preemption issues involves its effect on state tort claims against managed care organizations. This issue might have been less important, however, if adequate relief had been made available under ERISA to deal with the perceived abuses of managed care. One possible route for raising claims against managed care organizations could have been through ERISA's fiduciary obligation provisions. In 2000, however, the Supreme Court slammed the door shut on this approach.

PEGRAM v. HERDRICH

Supreme Court of the United States, 2000.
530 U.S. 211, 120 S.Ct. 2143, 147 L.Ed.2d 164.

JUSTICE SOUTER delivered the opinion of the Court.

The question in this case is whether treatment decisions made by a health maintenance organization, acting through its physician employees, are fiduciary acts within the meaning of the Employee Retirement Income Security Act of 1974 (ERISA)[ ]. We hold that they are not.

Petitioners, Carle Clinic Association, P. C., Health Alliance Medical Plans, Inc., and Carle Health Insurance Management Co., Inc. (collectively Carle) function as a health maintenance organization (HMO) organized for profit. Its owners are physicians providing prepaid medical services to participants whose employers contract with Carle to provide such coverage. Respondent, Cynthia Herdrich, was covered by Carle through her husband's employer, State Farm Insurance Company.

The events in question began when a Carle physician, petitioner Lori Pegram, examined Herdrich, who was experiencing pain in the midline area of her groin. Six days later, Dr. Pegram discovered a six by eight centimeter inflamed mass in Herdrich's abdomen. Despite the noticeable inflammation, Dr. Pegram did not order an ultrasound diagnostic procedure at a local hospital, but decided that Herdrich would have to wait eight more days for an ultrasound, to be performed at a facility staffed by Carle more than 50 miles away. Before the eight days were over, Herdrich's appendix ruptured, causing peritonitis.[ ]

Herdrich sued Pegram and Carle in state court for medical malpractice, and she later added two counts charging state-law fraud. Carle and Pegram responded that ERISA preempted the new counts, and removed the case to federal court, where they then sought summary judgment on the state-law fraud counts. The District Court granted their motion as to the second fraud count but granted Herdrich leave to amend the one remaining. This she did by alleging that provision of medical services under the terms of the Carle HMO organization, rewarding its physician owners for limiting medical care, entailed an inherent or anticipatory breach of an ERISA fiduciary duty, since these terms created an incentive to make decisions in the physicians' self-interest, rather than the exclusive interests of plan participants.

Herdrich sought relief under 29 U.S.C. § 1109(a), which provides that

"[a]ny person who is a fiduciary with respect to a plan who breaches any of the responsibilities, obligations, or duties imposed upon fiduciaries by this subchapter shall be personally liable to make good to such plan any losses to the plan resulting from each such breach, and to restore to such plan any profits of such fiduciary which have been made through use of assets of the plan by the fiduciary, and shall be subject to such other equitable or remedial relief as the court may deem appropriate, including removal of such fiduciary."

When Carle moved to dismiss the ERISA count for failure to state a claim upon which relief could be granted, the District Court granted the motion, accepting the Magistrate Judge's determination that Carle was not "involved [in these events] as" an ERISA fiduciary.[ ] The original malpractice counts were then tried to a jury, and Herdrich prevailed on both, receiving $35,000 in compensation for her injury.[ ] She then appealed the dismissal of the ERISA claim to the Court of Appeals for the Seventh Circuit, which reversed. The court held that Carle was acting as a fiduciary when its physicians made the challenged decisions and that Herdrich's allegations were sufficient to state a claim:

"Our decision does not stand for the proposition that the existence of incentives automatically gives rise to a breach of fiduciary duty. Rather, we hold that incentives can rise to the level of a breach where, as pleaded here, the fiduciary trust between plan participants and plan fiduciaries no longer exists (i.e. where physicians delay providing necessary treatment to, or withhold administering proper care to, plan beneficiaries for the sole purpose of increasing their bonuses)."[ ]

We granted certiorari[ ] and now reverse the Court of Appeals.

* * *

Traditionally, medical care in the United States has been provided on a "fee-for-service" basis. * * * In a fee-for-service system, a physician's financial incentive is to provide more care, not less, so long as payment is forthcoming. The check on this incentive is a physician's obligation to exercise reasonable medical skill and judgment in the patient's interest.

Beginning in the late 1960's, insurers and others developed new models for health-care delivery, including HMOs.[ ] The defining feature of an HMO is receipt of a fixed fee for each patient enrolled under the terms of a contract to provide specified health care if needed. The HMO thus assumes the financial risk of providing the benefits promised: if a participant never gets sick, the HMO keeps the money regardless, and if a participant becomes expensively ill, the HMO is responsible for the treatment agreed upon even if its cost exceeds the participant's premiums.

Like other risk-bearing organizations, HMOs take steps to control costs. At the least, HMOs, like traditional insurers, will in some fashion make coverage determinations, scrutinizing requested services against the contractual provisions to make sure that a request for care falls within the scope of covered circumstances (pregnancy, for example), or that a given treatment falls within the scope of the care promised (surgery, for instance). They customarily issue general guidelines for their physicians about appropriate levels of care.[ ] And they commonly require utilization review (in which specific treatment decisions are reviewed by a decisionmaker other than the treating physician) and approval in advance (precertification) for many types of care, keyed to standards of medical necessity or the reasonableness of the proposed treatment.[ ] These cost-controlling measures are commonly complemented by specific financial incentives to physicians, rewarding them for decreasing utilization of health-care services, and penalizing them for what may be found to be excessive treatment.[ ] Hence, in an HMO system, a physician's financial interest lies in providing less care, not more. The check on this influence (like that on the converse, fee-for-service incentive) is the professional obligation to provide covered services with a reasonable degree of skill and judgment in the patient's interest.[ ]

The adequacy of professional obligation to counter financial self-interest has been challenged no matter what the form of medical organization. HMOs became popular because fee-for-service physicians were thought to be providing unnecessary or useless services; today, many doctors and other observers argue that HMOs often ignore the individual needs of a patient in order to improve the HMOs' bottom lines.[ ] In this case, for instance, one could argue that Pegram's decision to wait before getting an ultrasound for Herdrich, and her insistence that the ultrasound be done at a distant facility owned by Carle, reflected an interest in limiting the HMO's expenses, which blinded her to the need for immediate diagnosis and treatment.

Herdrich focuses on the Carle scheme's provision for a "year-end distribution,"[ ] to the HMO's physician owners. She argues that this particular incentive device of annually paying physician owners the profit resulting from their own decisions rationing care can distinguish Carle's organization from HMOs generally, so that reviewing Carle's decisions under a fiduciary standard as pleaded in Herdrich's complaint would not open the door to like claims about other HMO structures. While the Court of Appeals agreed, we think otherwise, under the law as now written.

Although it is true that the relationship between sparing medical treatment and physician reward is not a subtle one under the Carle scheme, no HMO organization could survive without some incentive connecting physician reward with treatment rationing. The essence of an HMO is that salaries and profits are limited by the HMO's fixed membership fees.[ ] This is not to suggest that the Carle provisions are as socially desirable as some other HMO organizational schemes; they may not be.[ ] But whatever the HMO, there must be rationing and inducement to ration.

Since inducement to ration care goes to the very point of any HMO scheme, and rationing necessarily raises some risks while reducing others (ruptured appendixes are more likely; unnecessary appendectomies are less so), any legal principle purporting to draw a line between good and bad HMOs would embody, in effect, a judgment about socially acceptable medical risk. A valid conclusion of this sort would, however, necessarily turn on facts to which courts would probably not have ready access: correlations between malpractice rates and various HMO models, similar correlations involving fee-for-service models, and so on. And, of course, assuming such material could be obtained by courts in litigation like this, any standard defining the unacceptably risky HMO structure (and consequent vulnerability to claims like Herdrich's) would depend on a judgment about the appropriate level of expenditure for health care in light of the associated malpractice risk. But such complicated fact finding and such a debatable social judgment are not wisely required of courts * * *.[ ]

We think, then, that courts are not in a position to derive a sound legal principle to differentiate an HMO like Carle from other HMOs. For that reason, we proceed on the assumption that the decisions listed in Herdrich's complaint cannot be subject to a claim that they violate fiduciary standards unless all such decisions by all HMOs acting through their owner or employee physicians are to be judged by the same standards and subject to the same claims.

We turn now from the structure of HMOs to the requirements of ERISA. A fiduciary within the meaning of ERISA must be someone acting in the capacity of manager, administrator, or financial adviser to a "plan," see 29 U.S.C. §§ 1002(21)(A)(i)–(iii), and Herdich's ERISA count accordingly charged Carle with a breach of fiduciary duty in discharging its obligations under State Farm's medical plan.[ ] ERISA's definition of an employee welfare benefit plan is ultimately circular: "any plan, fund, or program ... to the extent that such plan, fund, or program was established ... for the purpose of providing ... through the purchase of insurance or otherwise ... medical, surgical, or hospital care or benefits." § 1002(1)(A). One is thus left to the common understanding of the word "plan" as referring to a scheme decided upon in advance.[ ] Here the scheme comprises a set of rules that define the rights of a beneficiary and provide for their enforcement. Rules governing collection of premiums, definition of benefits, submission of claims, and resolution of disagreements over entitlement to services are the sorts of provisions that constitute a plan.[ ] Thus, when employers contract with an HMO to provide benefits to employees subject to ERISA, the provisions of documents that set up the HMO are not, as such, an ERISA plan, but the agreement between an HMO and an employer who pays the premiums may, as here, provide elements of a plan by setting out rules under which beneficiaries will be entitled to care.

As just noted, fiduciary obligations can apply to managing, advising, and administering an ERISA plan, the fiduciary function addressed by Herdrich's ERISA count being the exercise of "discretionary authority or discretionary responsibility in the administration of [an ERISA] plan," 29 U.S.C. § 1002(21)(A)(iii). And as we have already suggested, although Carle is not an ERISA fiduciary merely because it administers or exercises discretionary authority over its own HMO business, it may still be a fiduciary if it administers the plan.

In general terms, fiduciary responsibility under ERISA is simply stated. The statute provides that fiduciaries shall discharge their duties with respect to a plan "solely in the interest of the participants and beneficiaries," § 1104(a)(1), that is, "for the exclusive purpose of (i) providing benefits to participants and their beneficiaries; and (ii) defraying reasonable expenses of administering the plan," § 1104(a)(1)(A). These responsibilities imposed by ERISA have the familiar ring of their source in the common law of trusts.[ ] Thus, the common law (understood as including what were once the distinct rules of equity) charges fiduciaries with a duty of loyalty to guarantee beneficiaries' interests: "The most fundamental duty owed by the trustee to the beneficiaries of the trust is the duty of loyalty. . . . It is the duty of a trustee to administer the trust solely in the interest of the beneficiaries."[ ] ("Perhaps the most fundamental duty of a trustee is that he must display throughout the administration of the trust complete loyalty to the interests of the beneficiary and must exclude all selfish interest and all consideration of the interests of third persons")[ ].

Beyond the threshold statement of responsibility, however, the analogy between ERISA fiduciary and common law trustee becomes problematic. This is so because the trustee at common law characteristically wears only his fiduciary hat when he takes action to affect a beneficiary, whereas the trustee under ERISA may wear different hats.

Speaking of the traditional trustee, Professor Scott's treatise admonishes that the trustee "is not permitted to place himself in a position where it would be for his own benefit to violate his duty to the beneficiaries." [ ] Under ERISA, however, a fiduciary may have financial interests adverse to beneficiaries. Employers, for example, can be ERISA fiduciaries and still take actions to the disadvantage of employee beneficiaries, when they act as employers (e.g., firing a beneficiary for reasons unrelated to the ERISA plan), or even as plan sponsors (e.g., modifying the terms of a plan as allowed by ERISA to provide less generous benefits). * * *

ERISA does require, however, that the fiduciary with two hats wear only one at a time, and wear the fiduciary hat when making fiduciary decisions.[ ] Thus, the statute * * * defines an administrator, for example, as a fiduciary only "to the extent" that he acts in such a capacity in relation to a plan. 29 U.S.C. § 1002(21)(A). In every case charging breach of ERISA fiduciary duty, then, the threshold question is not whether the actions of some person employed to provide services under a plan adversely affected a plan beneficiary's interest, but whether that person was acting as a fiduciary (that is, was performing a fiduciary function) when taking the action subject to complaint.

The allegations of Herdrich's ERISA count that identify the claimed fiduciary breach are difficult to understand. In this count, Herdrich does not point to a particular act by any Carle physician owner as a breach. She does not complain about Pegram's actions, and at oral argument her counsel confirmed that the ERISA count could have been brought, and would have been no different, if Herdrich had never had a sick day in her life.[ ]

What she does claim is that Carle, acting through its physician owners, breached its duty to act solely in the interest of beneficiaries by making decisions affecting medical treatment while influenced by the terms of the Carle HMO scheme, under which the physician owners ultimately profit from their own choices to minimize the medical services provided. * * *[ ]

The specific payout detail of the plan was, of course, a feature that the employer as plan sponsor was free to adopt without breach of any fiduciary duty under ERISA, since an employer's decisions about the content of a plan are not themselves fiduciary acts.[ ][Likewise it is clear that there was no violation of ERISA when the incorporators of the Carle HMO provided for the year-end payout. The HMO is not the ERISA plan, and the incorporation of the HMO preceded its contract with the State Farm plan.[ ]

The nub of the claim, then, is that when State Farm contracted with Carle, Carle became a fiduciary under the plan, acting through its physicians. At once, Carle as fiduciary administrator was subject to such influence from the year-end payout provision that its fiduciary capacity was necessarily compromised, and its readiness to act amounted to anticipatory breach of fiduciary obligation.

The pleadings must also be parsed very carefully to understand what acts by physician owners acting on Carle's behalf are alleged to be fiduciary in nature.[8] It will help to keep two sorts of arguably administrative acts in mind. Cf. Dukes v. U.S. Healthcare, Inc., 57 F.3d 350, 361 (C.A.3 1995) (discussing dual medical/administrative roles of HMOs). What we will call pure "eligibility decisions" turn on the plan's coverage of a particular condition or medical procedure for its treatment. "Treatment decisions," by contrast, are choices about how to go about diagnosing and treating a patient's condition: given a patient's constellation of symptoms, what is the appropriate medical response?

These decisions are often practically inextricable from one another, as amici on both sides agree.[ ] This is so not merely because, under a scheme like Carle's, treatment and eligibility decisions are made by the same person,

---

7. It does not follow that those who administer a particular plan design may not have difficulty in following fiduciary standards if the design is awkward enough. A plan might lawfully provide for a bonus for administrators who denied benefits to every 10th beneficiary but it would be difficult for an administrator who received the bonus to defend against the claim that he had not been solely attentive to the beneficiaries' interests in carrying out his administrative duties. The important point is that Herdrich is not suing the employer, State Farm, and her claim cannot be analyzed as if she were.

8. * * * Although we are not presented with the issue here, it could be argued that Carle is a fiduciary insofar as it has discretionary authority to administer the plan, and so it is obligated to disclose characteristics of the plan and of those who provide services to the plan, if that information affects beneficiaries' material interests.[ ] * * *

the treating physician. It is so because a great many and possibly most coverage questions are not simple yes-or-no questions, like whether appendicitis is a covered condition (when there is no dispute that a patient has appendicitis), or whether acupuncture is a covered procedure for pain relief (when the claim of pain is unchallenged). The more common coverage question is a when-and-how question. Although coverage for many conditions will be clear and various treatment options will be indisputably compensable, physicians still must decide what to do in particular cases. The issue may be, say, whether one treatment option is so superior to another under the circumstances, and needed so promptly, that a decision to proceed with it would meet the medical necessity requirement that conditions the HMO's obligation to provide or pay for that particular procedure at that time in that case. The Government in its brief alludes to a similar example when it discusses an HMO's refusal to pay for emergency care on the ground that the situation giving rise to the need for care was not an emergency,[ ][9] In practical terms, these eligibility decisions cannot be untangled from physicians' judgments about reasonable medical treatment, and in the case before us, Dr. Pegram's decision was one of that sort. She decided (wrongly, as it turned out) that Herdrich's condition did not warrant immediate action; the consequence of that medical determination was that Carle would not cover immediate care, whereas it would have done so if Dr. Pegram had made the proper diagnosis and judgment to treat. The eligibility decision and the treatment decision were inextricably mixed, as they are in countless medical administrative decisions every day.

The kinds of decisions mentioned in Herdrich's ERISA count and claimed to be fiduciary in character are just such mixed eligibility and treatment decisions: physicians' conclusions about when to use diagnostic tests; about seeking consultations and making referrals to physicians and facilities other than Carle's; about proper standards of care, the experimental character of a proposed course of treatment, the reasonableness of a certain treatment, and the emergency character of a medical condition.

We do not read the ERISA count, however, as alleging fiduciary breach with reference to a different variety of administrative decisions, those we have called pure eligibility determinations, such as whether a plan covers an undisputed case of appendicitis. Nor do we read it as claiming breach by reference to discrete administrative decisions separate from medical judgments; say, rejecting a claim for no other reason than the HMO's financial condition. * * *

Based on our understanding of the matters just discussed, we think Congress did not intend Carle or any other HMO to be treated as a fiduciary to the extent that it makes mixed eligibility decisions acting through its physicians. We begin with doubt that Congress would ever have thought of a mixed eligibility decision as fiduciary in nature. At common law, fiduciary duties characteristically attach to decisions about managing assets and distributing property to beneficiaries. * * *

9. ERISA makes separate provision for suits to receive particular benefits. See 29 U.S.C. § 1132(a)(1)(B). We have no occasion to discuss the standards governing such a claim by a patient who, as in the example in text, was denied reimbursement for emergency care. Nor have we reason to discuss the interaction of such a claim with state-law causes of action[ ].

Mixed eligibility decisions by an HMO acting through its physicians have, however, only a limited resemblance to the usual business of traditional trustees. To be sure, the physicians (like regular trustees) draw on resources held for others and make decisions to distribute them in accordance with entitlements expressed in a written instrument (embodying the terms of an ERISA plan). * * * [But p]rivate trustees do not make treatment judgments, whereas treatment judgments are what physicians reaching mixed decisions do make, by definition. Indeed, the physicians through whom HMOs act make just the sorts of decisions made by licensed medical practitioners millions of times every day, in every possible medical setting: * * *. The settings bear no more resemblance to trust departments than a decision to operate turns on the factors controlling the amount of a quarterly income distribution. Thus, it is at least questionable whether Congress would have had mixed eligibility decisions in mind when it provided that decisions administering a plan were fiduciary in nature. Indeed, when Congress took up the subject of fiduciary responsibility under ERISA, it concentrated on fiduciaries' financial decisions, * * *.

Our doubt that Congress intended the category of fiduciary administrative functions to encompass the mixed determinations at issue here hardens into conviction when we consider the consequences that would follow from Herdrich's contrary view.

First, we need to ask how this fiduciary standard would affect HMOs if it applied as Herdrich claims it should be applied, not directed against any particular mixed decision that injured a patient, but against HMOs that make mixed decisions in the course of providing medical care for profit. Recovery would be warranted simply upon showing that the profit incentive to ration care would generally affect mixed decisions, in derogation of the fiduciary standard to act solely in the interest of the patient without possibility of conflict. Although Herdrich is vague about the mechanics of relief, the one point that seems clear is that she seeks the return of profit from the pockets of the Carle HMO's owners, with the money to be given to the plan for the benefit of the participants. See 29 U.S.C. § 1109(a) (return of all profits is an appropriate ERISA remedy). Since the provision for profit is what makes the HMO a proprietary organization, her remedy in effect would be nothing less than elimination of the for-profit HMO. Her remedy might entail even more than that, although we are in no position to tell whether and to what extent nonprofit HMO schemes would ultimately survive the recognition of Herdrich's theory. It is enough to recognize that the Judiciary has no warrant to precipitate the upheaval that would follow a refusal to dismiss Herdrich's ERISA claim. The fact is that for over 27 years the Congress of the United States has promoted the formation of HMO practices. The Health Maintenance Organization Act of 1973,[ ] allowed the formation of HMOs that assume financial risks for the provision of health care services, and Congress has amended the Act several times, most recently in 1996.[ ] * * *

The Court of Appeals did not purport to entertain quite the broadside attack that Herdrich's ERISA claim thus entails,[ ] and the second possible consequence of applying the fiduciary standard that requires our attention would flow from the difficulty of extending it to particular mixed decisions that on Herdrich's theory are fiduciary in nature.

The fiduciary is, of course, obliged to act exclusively in the interest of the beneficiary, but this translates into no rule readily applicable to HMO decisions or those of any other variety of medical practice. While the incentive of the HMO physician is to give treatment sparingly, imposing a fiduciary obligation upon him would not lead to a simple default rule, say, that whenever it is reasonably possible to disagree about treatment options, the physician should treat aggressively. After all, HMOs came into being because some groups of physicians consistently provided more aggressive treatment than others in similar circumstances, with results not perceived as justified by the marginal expense and risk associated with intervention; excessive surgery is not in the patient's best interest, whether provided by fee-for-service surgeons or HMO surgeons subject to a default rule urging them to operate. Nor would it be possible to translate fiduciary duty into a standard that would allow recovery from an HMO whenever a mixed decision influenced by the HMO's financial incentive resulted in a bad outcome for the patient. It would be so easy to allege, and to find, an economic influence when sparing care did not lead to a well patient, that any such standard in practice would allow a factfinder to convert an HMO into a guarantor of recovery.

These difficulties may have led the Court of Appeals to try to confine the fiduciary breach to cases where "the sole purpose" of delaying or withholding treatment was to increase the physician's financial reward,[ ]. But this attempt to confine mixed decision claims to their most egregious examples entails erroneous corruption of fiduciary obligation and would simply lead to further difficulties that we think fatal. While a mixed decision made solely to benefit the HMO or its physician would violate a fiduciary duty, the fiduciary standard condemns far more than that, in its requirement of "an eye single" toward beneficiaries' interests[ ]. But whether under the Court of Appeals's rule or a straight standard of undivided loyalty, the defense of any HMO would be that its physician did not act out of financial interest but for good medical reasons, the plausibility of which would require reference to standards of reasonable and customary medical practice in like circumstances. That, of course, is the traditional standard of the common law.[ ] Thus, for all practical purposes, every claim of fiduciary breach by an HMO physician making a mixed decision would boil down to a malpractice claim, * * *.

What would be the value to the plan participant of having this kind of ERISA fiduciary action? It would simply apply the law already available in state courts and federal diversity actions today, and the formulaic addition of an allegation of financial incentive would do nothing but bring the same claim into a federal court under federal-question jurisdiction. It is true that in States that do not allow malpractice actions against HMOs the fiduciary claim would offer a plaintiff a further defendant to be sued for direct liability, and in some cases the HMO might have a deeper pocket than the physician. But we have seen enough to know that ERISA was not enacted out of concern that physicians were too poor to be sued, or in order to federalize malpractice litigation in the name of fiduciary duty for any other reason. It is difficult, in fact, to find any advantage to participants across the board, except that allowing them to bring malpractice actions in the guise of federal fiduciary breach claims against HMOs would make them eligible for awards of attorney's fees if they won. * * *

The mischief of Herdrich's position would, indeed, go further than mere replication of state malpractice actions with HMO defendants. For not only would an HMO be liable as a fiduciary in the first instance for its own breach of fiduciary duty committed through the acts of its physician employee, but the physician employee would also be subject to liability as a fiduciary on the same basic analysis that would charge the HMO. The physician who made the mixed administrative decision would be exercising authority in the way described by ERISA and would therefore be deemed to be a fiduciary.[ ] Hence the physician, too, would be subject to suit in federal court applying an ERISA standard of reasonable medical skill. This result, in turn, would raise a puzzling issue of preemption. On its face, federal fiduciary law applying a malpractice standard would seem to be a prescription for preemption of state malpractice law, since the new ERISA cause of action would cover the subject of a state-law malpractice claim.[ ] To be sure, New York State Conference of Blue Cross & Blue Shield Plans v. Travelers Ins. Co., 514 U.S. 645, 654–655, 115 S.Ct. 1671, 131 L.Ed.2d 695 (1995), throws some cold water on the preemption theory; there, we held that, in the field of health care, a subject of traditional state regulation, there is no ERISA preemption without clear manifestation of congressional purpose. But in that case the convergence of state and federal law was not so clear as in the situation we are positing; the state-law standard had not been subsumed by the standard to be applied under ERISA. We could struggle with this problem, but first it is well to ask, again, what would be gained by opening the federal courthouse doors for a fiduciary malpractice claim, save for possibly random fortuities such as more favorable scheduling, or the ancillary opportunity to seek attorney's fees. And again, we know that Congress had no such haphazard boons in prospect when it defined the ERISA fiduciary, nor such a risk to the efficiency of federal courts as a new fiduciary-malpractice jurisdiction would pose in welcoming such unheard-of fiduciary litigation.

We hold that mixed eligibility decisions by HMO physicians are not fiduciary decisions under ERISA. Herdrich's ERISA count fails to state an ERISA claim, and the judgment of the Court of Appeals is reversed.

Notes and Questions

1. A number of thoughtful academics had hoped that the Supreme Court would use *Pegram* as a platform for articulating a law of fiduciary obligations based on ERISA that would supplement, and perhaps replace in part, the law of tort and contract for administering disputes between managed care organizations and their members. See, e.g., Peter D. Jacobson and Michael T. Cahill, Applying Fiduciary Responsibilities in the Managed Care Context, 26 Am. J.L. & Med. 155 (2000). In fact the Supreme Court seems to have comprehensively rejected this possibility in *Pegram*, and most of the commentary on the case was quite critical. See E. Haavi Morreim, Another ERISA Twist: The Mysterious Case of *Pegram* and the Missing Fiduciary, 63 U.Pitt.L.Rev. 235 (2002); Michael T. Cahill and Peter D. Jacobson, *Pegram*'s Regress: A Missed Chance for Sensible Judicial Review of Managed Care Decisions, 27 Am.J.L. & Med. 421 (2001). Other commentators, however, pointed out that *Pegram* does not totally close the door on fiduciary claims. Footnote seven, for example, leaves the door cracked slightly for claims raising breach of fiduciary duty in plan design, while footnote eight leaves open the possibility of nondisclosure claims, and the discussion of types of claims seems to acknowledge that ERISA plan administrators act as fiduciaries in

making eligibility decisions. Peter J. Hammer, *Pegram v. Herdrich*: Of Peritonitis, Preemption, and the Elusive Goal of Managed Care Accountability, 26 J. Health Pol., Pol'y & L. 767 (2001) and Arnold J. Rosoff, Breach of Fiduciary Duty Lawsuits Against MCOs: What's Left After *Pegram v. Herdrich*, 22 J. Legal Med. 55 (2001). Still others have contended that *Pegram* opened the door to state law fiduciary claims. See Thomas R. McLean & Edward P. Richards, Managed Care Liability for Breach of Fiduciary Duty after *Pegram v. Herdrich*: The End of ERISA Preemption for State Law Liability for Medical Care Decision Making, 53 Fla. L. Rev. 1 (2001). See also Peter Jacobson, Strangers in the Night: Law and Medicine in the Managed Care Era (2002), examining the idea of fiduciary obligation as a principle for governing the relationship between managed care organizations and their members.

2.   One of the underlying puzzles of *Pegram* is the question of remedy. The law was clear at the time *Pegram* was brought that breach of the fiduciary obligations imposed by ERISA could only result in recoveries for the benefit of the plan, not for individual participants. Ms. Herdrich herself did not stand to benefit individually from her lawsuit. Massachusetts Mut. Life Ins. Co. v. Russell, 473 U.S. 134, 105 S.Ct. 3085, 87 L.Ed.2d 96 (1985). In LaRue v. DeWolff, Boberg & Associates, Inc., __ U.S. __, 128 S.Ct. 1020, 169 L.Ed.2d 847 (2008), the Supreme Court held that a member of a defined contribution pension plan could sue under ERISA for individual relief for a breach of fiduciary duty affecting his individual account. If employee health benefits move from a defined benefit to a defined contribution model (for example, though increased use of health reimbursement accounts), claims for individual relief for breach of ERISA fiduciary duties might become more common.

3.   In other contexts, cases continue to be brought claiming that ERISA plan administrators have breached their fiduciary obligations. Occasionally such cases succeed, or at least survive motions to dismiss or for summary judgment. See, e.g., Bannistor v. Ullman, 287 F.3d 394 (5th Cir.2002) (suit against officers and parent corporation of bankrupt employer for failing to have forwarded employees' premiums to insurer prior to bankruptcy); Vescom Corp. v. American Heartland Health Admin., Inc., 251 F.Supp. 2d 950 (D.Me.2003) (suit by self-insured employer against reinsurer for breach of fiduciary obligations in management of funds). Most, however, fail, either because the court holds that the plan administrator has no fiduciary obligation under ERISA (see, e.g., Alves v. Harvard Pilgrim Health Care, Inc.), 204 F.Supp.2d 198 (D.Mass.2002), aff'd, 316 F.3d 290 (1st Cir.2003) (no fiduciary breach for health plan to charge flat copayment amount in excess of cost of prescription drugs) or because a claim for equitable relief for breach of fiduciary duty under § 502(a)(3) is not available if a plan beneficiary can instead sue under § 502(a)(1). See, e.g., Lefler v. United Healthcare of Utah, 72 Fed. Appx. 818 (10th Cir.2003).

4.   Among other obligations imposed on ERISA administrators are duties to disclose information to ERISA plan beneficiaries. The most important of these is the obligation to provide plan beneficiaries with a "summary plan description" that includes specific information about the rights and obligations of plan beneficiaries and which "shall be written in a manner calculated to be understood by the average plan participant, and shall be sufficiently accurate and comprehensive to reasonably apprise such participants and beneficiaries of their rights and obligations under the plan." 29 U.S.C. § 1022. In a number of cases, beneficiaries have sued ERISA managed care organizations for failing to disclose in addition information about the financial incentive structure of the plan. Plaintiffs in these cases have argued that the financial incentive structures of plans encourage

physicians to deny care to beneficiaries and that beneficiaries should be informed of these incentives. This is the argument alluded to by footnote eight of Pegram.

One of the few cases that has been receptive to such claims is Shea v. Esensten, 107 F.3d 625 (8th Cir.1997). Mr. Shea's physician failed to give him a referral to a cardiologist in spite of warning signs of a cardiac condition. Mr. Shea's widow contended that, had her husband's ERISA benefits plan disclosed that his doctor could earn a bonus for treating less, he would have sought out his own cardiologist. The Seventh Circuit found that a financial incentive system aimed at influencing a physician's referral patterns is "a material piece of information," Id. at 628, and that a subscriber has a right to know that his physician's judgment could be "colored" by such incentives. The court rested its conclusion on the obligation of an ERISA fiduciary to speak out if it "knows that silence might be harmful." The court held that information about a plan's financial incentives must be disclosed when they might lead a treating physician to deny necessary referrals for conditions covered by the plan.

Most courts that have heard such claims, however, have rejected them, at least in the absence of facts suggesting that the lack of disclosure actually made a difference in a beneficiary's health or treatment options. In Horvath v. Keystone Health Plan East, Inc., 333 F.3d 450 (3d Cir.2003), for example, the third Circuit affirmed a district court decision holding that the plaintiff "failed to create any issues of material fact with respect to her claim because (1) she failed to request the information Keystone offered to make available regarding its methods of physician compensation,[ ] (2) there was no set of circumstances pursuant to which Keystone should have known that such information was necessary to prevent Horvath from making a harmful decision regarding her healthcare coverage,[ ] and (3) she failed to explain how the information at issue was material in light of the fact that her employer offers no other options for healthcare coverage[ ]." 333 F.3d at 463. See also, Ehlmann v. Kaiser Found. Health Plan of Tex., 198 F.3d 552 (5th Cir.), cert. dismissed, 530 U.S. 1291, 121 S.Ct. 12, 147 L.Ed.2d 1036 (2000).

For excellent discussions of the general issue of disclosure of compensation arrangements, see Tracy E. Miller and William M. Sage, Disclosing Physician Financial Incentives, 281 JAMA 1424 (1999); William M. Sage, Physicians as Advocates, 35 Houston L.Rev. 1529 (1999); Kim Johnston, Patient Advocates or Patient Adversaries? Using Fiduciary Law to Compel Disclosure of Managed Care Financial Incentives, 35 San Diego L.Rev. 951 (1998); Bethany J. Spielman, Managed Care Regulation and the Physician–Advocate, 47 Drake L.Rev. 713 (1999).

5. Should ERISA plans be considered to be fiduciaries with respect to their beneficiaries, or should they rather be considered to be arms-length contractors? If plan administrators are considered to be fiduciaries, should fiduciary obligations only extend to management of trust funds, or should they also extend to provision of medical treatment? Should employment-related plans have obligations beyond those imposed on non-group insurance plans? Should employers have fiduciary obligations to their employees in the selection of health insurers, benefit plans, and benefits, and how should these obligations be reconciled with obligations to shareholders/owners?

D. ERISA PREEMPTION OF STATE TORT LITIGATION

Courts have struggled to determine the nature and extent of ERISA preemption in medical malpractice cases. Managed care plans as defendants are subject to the same theories of liability as hospitals—vicarious liability, corporate negligence, ordinary negligence. Vicarious liability has been allowed by most courts that have considered the question. The Supreme Court however has severely limited the reach of state tort actions against ERISA-qualified health plans.

AETNA HEALTH INC. v. DAVILA

Supreme Court of the United States, 2004.
542 U.S. 200, 124 S.Ct. 2488, 159 L.Ed.2d 312.

JUSTICE THOMAS delivered the opinion of the Court.

In these consolidated cases, two individuals sued their respective health maintenance organizations (HMOs) for alleged failures to exercise ordinary care in the handling of coverage decisions, in violation of a duty imposed by the Texas Health Care Liability Act (THCLA)[ ]. We granted certiorari to decide whether the individuals' causes of action are completely pre-empted by the "interlocking, interrelated, and interdependent remedial scheme,"[ ] found at § 502(a) of the Employee Retirement Income Security Act of 1974 (ERISA)[ ]. We hold that the causes of action are completely pre-empted and hence removable from state to federal court. The Court of Appeals, having reached a contrary conclusion, is reversed.

I

A

Respondent Juan Davila is a participant, and respondent Ruby Calad is a beneficiary, in ERISA-regulated employee benefit plans. Their respective plan sponsors had entered into agreements with petitioners, Aetna Health Inc. and CIGNA HealthCare of Texas, Inc., to administer the plans. Under Davila's plan, for instance, Aetna reviews requests for coverage and pays providers, such as doctors, hospitals, and nursing homes, which perform covered services for members; under Calad's plan sponsor's agreement, CIGNA is responsible for plan benefits and coverage decisions.

Respondents both suffered injuries allegedly arising from Aetna's and CIGNA's decisions not to provide coverage for certain treatment and services recommended by respondents' treating physicians. Davila's treating physician prescribed Vioxx to remedy Davila's arthritis pain, but Aetna refused to pay for it. Davila did not appeal or contest this decision, nor did he purchase Vioxx with his own resources and seek reimbursement. Instead, Davila began taking Naprosyn, from which he allegedly suffered a severe reaction that required extensive treatment and hospitalization. Calad underwent surgery, and although her treating physician recommended an extended hospital stay, a CIGNA discharge nurse determined that Calad did not meet the plan's criteria for a continued hospital stay. CIGNA consequently denied coverage for the extended hospital stay. Calad experienced postsurgery complications forcing her to return to the hospital. She alleges that these complications would not have occurred had CIGNA approved coverage for a longer hospital stay.

Respondents brought separate suits in Texas state court against petitioners. Invoking THCLA § 88.002(a), respondents argued that petitioners' refusal to cover the requested services violated their "duty to exercise ordinary care when making health care treatment decisions," and that these refusals "proximately caused" their injuries. Ibid. Petitioners removed the cases to Federal District Courts, arguing that respondents' causes of action fit within the scope of, and were therefore completely pre-empted by, ERISA § 502(a). The respective District Courts agreed, and declined to remand the cases to state court. Because respondents refused to amend their complaints to bring explicit ERISA claims, the District Courts dismissed the complaints with prejudice.

B

Both Davila and Calad appealed the refusals to remand to state court. The United States Court of Appeals for the Fifth Circuit consolidated their cases with several others raising similar issues. The Court of Appeals recognized that state causes of action that "duplicat[e] or fal[l] within the scope of an ERISA § 502(a) remedy" are completely pre-empted and hence removable to federal court.[ ]. After examining the causes of action available under § 502(a), the Court of Appeals determined that respondents' claims could possibly fall under only two: § 502(a)(1)(B), which provides a cause of action for the recovery of wrongfully denied benefits, and § 502(a)(2), which allows suit against a plan fiduciary for breaches of fiduciary duty to the plan.

Analyzing § 502(a)(2) first, the Court of Appeals concluded that, under *Pegram v. Herdrich,*[ ], the decisions for which petitioners were being sued were "mixed eligibility and treatment decisions" and hence were not fiduciary in nature.[1] The Court of Appeals next determined that respondents' claims did not fall within § 502(a)(1)(B)'s scope. It found significant that respondents "assert tort claims," while § 502(a)(1)(B) "creates a cause of action for breach of contract,"[ ], and also that respondents "are not seeking reimbursement for benefits denied them," but rather request "tort damages" arising from "an external, statutorily imposed duty of 'ordinary care,'"[ ]. From *Rush Prudential HMO, Inc. v. Moran,*[ ], the Court of Appeals derived the principle that complete pre-emption is limited to situations in which "States ... duplicate the causes of action listed in ERISA § 502(a)," and concluded that "[b]ecause the THCLA does not provide an action for collecting benefits," it fell outside the scope of § 502(a)(1)(B). 307 F.3d, at 310–311.

II

A

Under the removal statute, "any civil action brought in a State court of which the district courts of the United States have original jurisdiction, may be removed by the defendant" to federal court.[ ] One category of cases of which district courts have original jurisdiction is "[f]ederal question" cases: cases "arising under the Constitution, laws, or treaties of the United States." § 1331. We face in these cases the issue whether respondents' causes of action arise under federal law.

---

1. In this Court, petitioners do not claim or argue that respondents' causes of action fall under ERISA § 502(a)(2). Because petitioners do not argue this point, and since we can resolve these cases entirely by reference to ERISA § 502(a)(1)(B), we do not address ERISA § 502(a)(2).

Ordinarily, determining whether a particular case arises under federal law turns on the " 'well-pleaded complaint' "rule.[ ] The Court has explained that

"whether a case is one arising under the Constitution or a law or treaty of the United States, in the sense of the jurisdictional statute[,] ... must be determined from what necessarily appears in the plaintiff's statement of his own claim in the bill or declaration, unaided by anything alleged in anticipation of avoidance of defenses which it is thought the defendant may interpose."[ ].

In particular, the existence of a federal defense normally does not create statutory "arising under" jurisdiction,[ ], and "a defendant may not [generally] remove a case to federal court unless the *plaintiff's* complaint establishes that the case 'arises under' federal law,"[ ]. There is an exception, however, to the well-pleaded complaint rule. "[W]hen a federal statute wholly displaces the state-law cause of action through complete pre-emption," the state claim can be removed.[ ] This is so because "[w]hen the federal statute completely pre-empts the state-law cause of action, a claim which comes within the scope of that cause of action, even if pleaded in terms of state law, is in reality based on federal law."[ ] ERISA is one of these statutes.

B

Congress enacted ERISA to "protect ... the interests of participants in employee benefit plans and their beneficiaries" by setting out substantive regulatory requirements for employee benefit plans and to "provid[e] for appropriate remedies, sanctions, and ready access to the Federal courts."[ ]. The purpose of ERISA is to provide a uniform regulatory regime over employee benefit plans. To this end, ERISA includes expansive pre-emption provisions, see ERISA § 514,[ ], which are intended to ensure that employee benefit plan regulation would be "exclusively a federal concern."[ ]

ERISA's "comprehensive legislative scheme" includes "an integrated system of procedures for enforcement."[ ] This integrated enforcement mechanism, ERISA § 502(a),[ ] is a distinctive feature of ERISA, and essential to accomplish Congress' purpose of creating a comprehensive statute for the regulation of employee benefit plans. As the Court said in *Pilot Life Ins. Co. v. Dedeaux,*[ ]:

"[T]he detailed provisions of § 502(a) set forth a comprehensive civil enforcement scheme that represents a careful balancing of the need for prompt and fair claims settlement procedures against the public interest in encouraging the formation of employee benefit plans. The policy choices reflected in the inclusion of certain remedies and the exclusion of others under the federal scheme would be completely undermined if ERISA-plan participants and beneficiaries were free to obtain remedies under state law that Congress rejected in ERISA. 'The six carefully integrated civil enforcement provisions found in § 502(a) of the statute as finally enacted ... provide strong evidence that Congress did *not* intend to authorize other remedies that it simply forgot to incorporate expressly.' "[ ]

Therefore, any state-law cause of action that duplicates, supplements, or supplants the ERISA civil enforcement remedy conflicts with the clear congressional intent to make the ERISA remedy exclusive and is therefore pre-empted.[ ]

The pre-emptive force of ERISA § 502(a) is still stronger. In *Metropolitan Life Ins. Co. v. Taylor,*[ ] the Court determined that the similarity of the language used in the Labor Management Relations Act, 1947 (LMRA), and ERISA, combined with the "clear intention" of Congress "to make § 502(a)(1)(B) suits brought by participants or beneficiaries federal questions for the purposes of federal court jurisdiction in like manner as § 301 of the LMRA," established that ERISA § 502(a)(1)(B)'s pre-emptive force mirrored the pre-emptive force of LMRA § 301. Since LMRA § 301 converts state causes of action into federal ones for purposes of determining the propriety of removal,[ ] so too does ERISA § 502(a)(1)(B). Thus, the ERISA civil enforcement mechanism is one of those provisions with such "extraordinary pre-emptive power" that it "converts an ordinary state common law complaint into one stating a federal claim for purposes of the well-pleaded complaint rule."[ ] Hence, "causes of action within the scope of the civil enforcement provisions of § 502(a) [are] removable to federal court."[ ]

III

A

ERISA § 502(a)(1)(B) provides:

"A civil action may be brought—(1) by a participant or beneficiary—. . . (B) to recover benefits due to him under the terms of his plan, to enforce his rights under the terms of the plan, or to clarify his rights to future benefits under the terms of the plan."[ ]

This provision is relatively straightforward. If a participant or beneficiary believes that benefits promised to him under the terms of the plan are not provided, he can bring suit seeking provision of those benefits. A participant or beneficiary can also bring suit generically to "enforce his rights" under the plan, or to clarify any of his rights to future benefits. Any dispute over the precise terms of the plan is resolved by a court under a *de novo* review standard, unless the terms of the plan "giv[e] the administrator or fiduciary discretionary authority to determine eligibility for benefits or to construe the terms of the plan."[ ]

It follows that if an individual brings suit complaining of a denial of coverage for medical care, where the individual is entitled to such coverage only because of the terms of an ERISA-regulated employee benefit plan, and where no legal duty (state or federal) independent of ERISA or the plan terms is violated, then the suit falls "within the scope of" ERISA § 502(a)(1)(B)[ ]. In other words, if an individual, at some point in time, could have brought his claim under ERISA § 502(a)(1)(B), and where there is no other independent legal duty that is implicated by a defendant's actions, then the individual's cause of action is completely pre-empted by ERISA § 502(a)(1)(B).

To determine whether respondents' causes of action fall "within the scope" of ERISA § 502(a)(1)(B), we must examine respondents' complaints, the statute on which their claims are based (the THCLA), and the various plan documents. Davila alleges that Aetna provides health coverage under his employer's health benefits plan.[ ]. Davila also alleges that after his primary care physician prescribed Vioxx, Aetna refused to pay for it.[ ]. The only action complained of was Aetna's refusal to approve payment for Davila's Vioxx prescription. Further, the only relationship Aetna had with Davila was its partial administration of Davila's employer's benefit plan.[ ].

Similarly, Calad alleges that she receives, as her husband's beneficiary under an ERISA-regulated benefit plan, health coverage from CIGNA.[ ]. She alleges that she was informed by CIGNA, upon admittance into a hospital for major surgery, that she would be authorized to stay for only one day.[ ] She also alleges that CIGNA, acting through a discharge nurse, refused to authorize more than a single day despite the advice and recommendation of her treating physician.[ ] Calad contests only CIGNA's decision to refuse coverage for her hospital stay.[ ] And, as in Davila's case, the only connection between Calad and CIGNA is CIGNA's administration of portions of Calad's ERISA-regulated benefit plan.[ ].

It is clear, then, that respondents complain only about denials of coverage promised under the terms of ERISA-regulated employee benefit plans. Upon the denial of benefits, respondents could have paid for the treatment themselves and then sought reimbursement through a § 502(a)(1)(B) action, or sought a preliminary injunction,[ ].

Respondents contend, however, that the complained-of actions violate legal duties that arise independently of ERISA or the terms of the employee benefit plans at issue in these cases. Both respondents brought suit specifically under the THCLA, alleging that petitioners "controlled, influenced, participated in and made decisions which affected the quality of the diagnosis, care, and treatment provided" in a manner that violated "the duty of ordinary care set forth in §§ 88.001 and 88.002."[ ] Respondents contend that this duty of ordinary care is an independent legal duty. They analogize to this Court's decisions interpreting LMRA § 301,[ ] with particular focus on *Caterpillar Inc. v. Williams,* (suit for breach of individual employment contract, even if defendant's action also constituted a breach of an entirely separate collective-bargaining agreement, not pre-empted by LMRA § 301). Because this duty of ordinary care arises independently of any duty imposed by ERISA or the plan terms, the argument goes, any civil action to enforce this duty is not within the scope of the ERISA civil enforcement mechanism.

The duties imposed by the THCLA in the context of these cases, however, do not arise independently of ERISA or the plan terms. The THCLA does impose a duty on managed care entities to "exercise ordinary care when making health care treatment decisions," and makes them liable for damages proximately caused by failures to abide by that duty.[ ] However, if a managed care entity correctly concluded that, under the terms of the relevant plan, a particular treatment was not covered, the managed care entity's denial of coverage would not be a proximate cause of any injuries arising from the denial. Rather, the failure of the plan itself to cover the requested treatment would be the proximate cause.[3] More significantly, the THCLA clearly states that "[t]he standards in Subsections (a) and (b) create no obligation on the

---

3. To take a clear example, if the terms of the health care plan specifically exclude from coverage the cost of an appendectomy, then any injuries caused by the refusal to cover the appendectomy are properly attributed to the terms of the plan itself, not the managed care entity that applied those terms.

part of the health insurance carrier, health maintenance organization, or other managed care entity to provide to an insured or enrollee treatment which is not covered by the health care plan of the entity."[ ] Hence, a managed care entity could not be subject to liability under the THCLA if it denied coverage for any treatment not covered by the health care plan that it was administering.

Thus, interpretation of the terms of respondents' benefit plans forms an essential part of their THCLA claim, and THCLA liability would exist here only because of petitioners' administration of ERISA-regulated benefit plans. Petitioners' potential liability under the THCLA in these cases, then, derives entirely from the particular rights and obligations established by the benefit plans. So, unlike the state-law claims in *Caterpillar, supra,* respondents' THCLA causes of action are not entirely independent of the federally regulated contract itself.[ ].

Hence, respondents bring suit only to rectify a wrongful denial of benefits promised under ERISA-regulated plans, and do not attempt to remedy any violation of a legal duty independent of ERISA. We hold that respondents' state causes of action fall "within the scope of" ERISA § 502(a)(1)(B),[ ] and are therefore completely pre-empted by ERISA § 502 and removable to federal district court.[4]

B

The Court of Appeals came to a contrary conclusion for several reasons, all of them erroneous. First, the Court of Appeals found significant that respondents "assert a tort claim for tort damages" rather than "a contract claim for contract damages," and that respondents "are not seeking reimbursement for benefits denied them."[ ] But, distinguishing between pre-empted and non-pre-empted claims based on the particular label affixed to them would "elevate form over substance and allow parties to evade" the pre-emptive scope of ERISA simply "by relabeling their contract claims as claims for tortious breach of contract." * * *[ ]. Nor can the mere fact that the state cause of action attempts to authorize remedies beyond those authorized by ERISA § 502(a) put the cause of action outside the scope of the ERISA civil enforcement mechanism. In *Pilot Life, Metropolitan Life,* and *Ingersoll-Rand,* the plaintiffs all brought state claims that were labeled either tort or tort-like.[ ] And, the plaintiffs in these three cases all sought remedies beyond those authorized under ERISA.[ ] And, in all these cases, the plaintiffs' claims were pre-empted. The limited remedies available under ERISA are an inherent part of the "careful balancing" between ensuring fair and prompt enforcement of rights under a plan and the encouragement of the creation of such plans.[ ].

Second, the Court of Appeals believed that "the wording of [respondents'] plans is immaterial" to their claims, as "they invoke an external, statutorily imposed duty of 'ordinary care.' "[ ] But as we have already discussed, the

---

4. Respondents also argue that ERISA § 502(a) completely pre-empts a state cause of action only if the cause of action would be pre-empted under ERISA § 514(a); respondents then argue that their causes of action do not fall under the terms of § 514(a). But a state cause of action that provides an alternative remedy to those provided by the ERISA civil enforcement mechanism conflicts with Congress' clear intent to make the ERISA mechanism exclusive.[ ].

wording of the plans is certainly material to their state causes of action, and the duty of "ordinary care" that the THCLA creates is not external to their rights under their respective plans.

Ultimately, the Court of Appeals rested its decision on one line from *Rush Prudential.* * * * Nowhere in *Rush Prudential* did we suggest that the preemptive force of ERISA § 502(a) is limited to the situation in which a state cause of action precisely duplicates a cause of action under ERISA § 502(a).

Nor would it be consistent with our precedent to conclude that only strictly duplicative state causes of action are pre-empted. Frequently, in order to receive exemplary damages on a state claim, a plaintiff must prove facts beyond the bare minimum necessary to establish entitlement to an award.[ ]. In order to recover for mental anguish, for instance, the plaintiffs in *Ingersoll-Rand* and *Metropolitan Life* would presumably have had to prove the existence of mental anguish; there is no such element in an ordinary suit brought under ERISA § 502(a)(1)(B).[ ] This did not save these state causes of action from pre-emption. Congress' intent to make the ERISA civil enforcement mechanism exclusive would be undermined if state causes of action that supplement the ERISA § 502(a) remedies were permitted, even if the elements of the state cause of action did not precisely duplicate the elements of an ERISA claim.

C

Respondents also argue—for the first time in their brief to this Court— that the THCLA is a law that regulates insurance, and hence that ERISA § 514(b)(2)(A) saves their causes of action from pre-emption (and thereby from complete pre-emption).[5] This argument is unavailing. The existence of a comprehensive remedial scheme can demonstrate an "overpowering federal policy" that determines the interpretation of a statutory provision designed to save state law from being pre-empted.[ ] ERISA's civil enforcement provision is one such example.[ ]

As this Court stated in *Pilot Life,* "our understanding of [§ 514(b)(2)(A)] must be informed by the legislative intent concerning the civil enforcement provisions provided by ERISA § 502(a).[ ]" The Court concluded that "[t]he policy choices reflected in the inclusion of certain remedies and the exclusion of others under the federal scheme would be completely undermined if ERISA-plan participants and beneficiaries were free to obtain remedies under state law that Congress rejected in ERISA."[ ] The Court then held, based on

> "the common-sense understanding of the saving clause, the McCarran–Ferguson Act factors defining the business of insurance, and, *most importantly,* the clear expression of congressional intent that ERISA's civil enforcement scheme be exclusive, . . . that [the plaintiff's] state law suit asserting improper processing of a claim for benefits under an ERISA-regulated plan is not saved by § 514(b)(2)(A)."[ ]

Pilot Life's reasoning applies here with full force. Allowing respondents to proceed with their state-law suits would "pose an obstacle to the purposes and objectives of Congress."[ ] As this Court has recognized in both *Rush*

---

5. ERISA § 514(b)(2)(A)[ ] reads, as relevant: "[N]othing in this subchapter shall be construed to exempt or relieve any person from any law of any State which regulates insurance, banking, or securities."

Prudential and *Pilot Life*, ERISA § 514(b)(2)(A) must be interpreted in light of the congressional intent to create an exclusive federal remedy in ERISA § 502(a). Under ordinary principles of conflict pre-emption, then, even a state law that can arguably be characterized as "regulating insurance" will be pre-empted if it provides a separate vehicle to assert a claim for benefits outside of, or in addition to, ERISA's remedial scheme.

IV

Respondents, their *amici*, and some Courts of Appeals have relied heavily upon *Pegram v. Herdrich*,[ ], in arguing that ERISA does not pre-empt or completely pre-empt state suits such as respondents'. They contend that *Pegram* makes it clear that causes of action such as respondents' do not "relate to [an] employee benefit plan " ERISA § 514(a),[ ] and hence are not pre-empted.[ ]

Pegram cannot be read so broadly. In *Pegram,* the plaintiff sued her physician-owned-and-operated HMO (which provided medical coverage through plaintiff's employer pursuant to an ERISA-regulated benefit plan) and her treating physician, both for medical malpractice and for a breach of an ERISA fiduciary duty.[ ] The plaintiff's treating physician was also the person charged with administering plaintiff's benefits; it was she who decided whether certain treatments were covered.[ ] We reasoned that the physician's "eligibility decision and the treatment decision were inextricably mixed."[ ] We concluded that "Congress did not intend [the defendant HMO] or any other HMO to be treated as a fiduciary to the extent that it makes mixed eligibility decisions acting through its physicians."[ ]

A benefit determination under ERISA, though, is generally a fiduciary act.[ ] "At common law, fiduciary duties characteristically attach to decisions about managing assets and distributing property to beneficiaries."[ ] Hence, a benefit determination is part and parcel of the ordinary fiduciary responsibilities connected to the administration of a plan.[ ] The fact that a benefits determination is infused with medical judgments does not alter this result.

Pegram itself recognized this principle. *Pegram,* in highlighting its conclusion that "mixed eligibility decisions" were not fiduciary in nature, contrasted the operation of "[t]raditional trustees administer[ing] a medical trust" and "physicians through whom HMOs act."[ ] A traditional medical trust is administered by "paying out money to buy medical care, whereas physicians making mixed eligibility decisions consume the money as well."[ ] And significantly, the Court stated that "[p]rivate trustees do not make treatment judgments."[ ] But a trustee managing a medical trust undoubtedly must make administrative decisions that require the exercise of medical judgment. Petitioners are not the employers of respondents' treating physicians and are therefore in a somewhat analogous position to that of a trustee for a traditional medical trust.

ERISA itself and its implementing regulations confirm this interpretation. ERISA defines a fiduciary as any person "to the extent ... he has any discretionary authority or discretionary responsibility in the administration of [an employee benefit] plan.[ ]. When administering employee benefit plans, HMOs must make discretionary decisions regarding eligibility for plan benefits, and, in this regard, must be treated as plan fiduciaries.[ ]" Also, ERISA

§ 503, which specifies minimum requirements for a plan's claim procedure, requires plans to "afford a reasonable opportunity to any participant whose claim for benefits has been denied for a full and fair review by the appropriate named fiduciary of the decision denying the claim."[ ] This strongly suggests that the ultimate decisionmaker in a plan regarding an award of benefits must be a fiduciary and must be acting as a fiduciary when determining a participant's or beneficiary's claim. The relevant regulations also establish extensive requirements to ensure full and fair review of benefit denials.[ ] These regulations, on their face, apply equally to health benefit plans and other plans, and do not draw distinctions between medical and nonmedical benefits determinations. Indeed, the regulations strongly imply that benefits determinations involving medical judgments are, just as much as any other benefits determinations, actions by plan fiduciaries.[ ] Classifying any entity with discretionary authority over benefits determinations as anything but a plan fiduciary would thus conflict with ERISA's statutory and regulatory scheme.

Since administrators making benefits determinations, even determinations based extensively on medical judgments, are ordinarily acting as plan fiduciaries, it was essential to *Pegram*'s conclusion that the decisions challenged there were truly "mixed eligibility and treatment decisions,"[ ], i.e., medical necessity decisions made by the plaintiff's treating physician *qua* treating physician and *qua* benefits administrator. Put another way, the reasoning of *Pegram* "only make[s] sense where the underlying negligence also plausibly constitutes medical maltreatment by a party who can be deemed to be a treating physician or such a physician's employer."[ ] Here, however, petitioners are neither respondents' treating physicians nor the employers of respondents' treating physicians. Petitioners' coverage decisions, then, are pure eligibility decisions, and *Pegram* is not implicated.

V

We hold that respondents' causes of action, brought to remedy only the denial of benefits under ERISA-regulated benefit plans, fall within the scope of, and are completely pre-empted by, ERISA § 502(a)(1)(B), and thus removable to federal district court. The judgment of the Court of Appeals is reversed, and the cases are remanded for further proceedings consistent with this opinion.[7]

It is so ordered.

[See Justice Ginsburg and Breyer's concurrence in Note 4 following *Doe*, *infra*.]

Notes and Questions

1. What state law claims are left to plaintiff plan subscribers after *Davila*? Consider some of the language of *Davila*:

7. The United States, as *amicus,* suggests that some individuals in respondents' positions could possibly receive some form of "make-whole" relief under ERISA § 502(a)(3).[ ] However, after their respective District Courts denied their motions for remand, respondents had the opportunity to amend their complaints to bring expressly a claim under ERISA § 502(a). Respondents declined to do so; the District Courts therefore dismissed their complaints with prejudice.[ ] Respondents have thus chosen not to pursue any ERISA claim, including any claim arising under ERISA § 502(a)(3). The scope of this provision, then, is not before us, and we do not address it.

"... [A]ny state-law cause of action that duplicates, supplements, or supplants the ERISA civil enforcement remedy conflicts with the clear congressional intent to make the ERISA remedy exclusive and is therefore preempted.

"It is clear, then, that respondents complain only about denials of coverage promised under the terms of ERISA-regulated employee benefit plans. Upon the denial of benefits, respondents could have paid for the treatment themselves and then sought reimbursement through a § 502(a)(1)(B) action, or sought a preliminary injunction."

"Hence, respondents bring suit only to rectify a wrongful denial of benefits promised under ERISA-regulated plans, and do not attempt to remedy any violation of a legal duty independent of ERISA."

"'Congress' intent to make the ERISA civil enforcement mechanism exclusive would be undermined if state causes of action that supplement the ERISA § 502(a) remedies were permitted, even if the elements of the state cause of action did not precisely duplicate the elements of an ERISA claim."

"* * * [T]he reasoning of *Pegram* 'only make[s] sense where the underlying negligence also plausibly constitutes medical maltreatment by a party who can be deemed to be a treating physician or such a physician's employer.'[ ]. Here, however, petitioners are neither respondents' treating physicians nor the employers of respondents' treating physicians. Petitioners' coverage decisions, then, are pure eligibility decisions, and *Pegram* is not implicated."

Commentators have noted how restrictive *Davila* is. First, it allows tort actions for direct or vicarious liability only for physician owned and operated managed care plans. And these are a dying breed. The typical health plan today is an insurance vehicle that imposes coverage constraints on providers in its network, and would not be subject to tort liability. As Jost observes, "... [t]his will create yet another incentive for employers and managed care plans to move away from tighter staff model HMOs to preferred provider organizations (PPOs) and looser HMO or point-of-service (POS) arrangements." Second, *Davila* leaves a "regulatory vacuum" in which consumer have no remedies if they are injured as the result of health care provided through health plans. Third, *Davila* sharpens the framework for ERISA limits on plans, allowing internal and external claims review, with possible federal judicial review of coverage denials under 502. Fourth, *Davila* states that ERISA plan administrators are fiduciaries as to coverage decisions. *Pegram* however noted that such administrators may have mixed allegiances, balancing health plan financial and other interests. Fifth, the court dangles the possibility that broader damages might be allowed under ERISA itself.

See Timothy S. Jost, The Supreme Court Limits Lawsuits Against Managed Care Organizations, Health Affairs Web Exclusive 4–417 (11 August 2004). See also Theodore W. Ruger, The Supreme Court Federalizes Managed Care Liability, 32 J.L. Med. & Ethics 528, 529 (2004) (criticizing the current ERISA enforcement scheme as crabbed and penurious, failing to serve remedial goals of either tort or contract.). For a full discussion of litigation leading up to *Davila*, see generally Margaret Cyr–Provost, Aetna v. Davila: From Patient–Centered Care to Plan–Centered Care, A Signpost or the End of the Road? 6 Hous. J. Health L. & Pol'y 171 (2005); M.Gregg Bloche and David Studdert, A Quiet Revolution: Law as an Agent of Health System Change, 23 Health Affairs 2942 (2004). See also Peter Jacobson, Strangers in the Night (New York: Oxford, 2002).

2. What litigation theories remain after *Davila* and *Pegram*? Could a state legislature pass a statute subjecting all managed care plans to liability for negligent treatment decisions of their physicians? Would section 514 of ERISA

preempt such a statute? Would it be a law regulating insurance, thereby saved from preemption? Or are all such escape holes plugged?

What about negligent plan design, either based on the incentives for paying physicians, or some other flaw in the design of the system? What about negligent selection of providers, the heart of most corporate negligence claims against hospitals?

a. *Negligent Plan Design.* Consider Smelik v. Mann Texas Dist. Ct. (224th Jud. Dist., Bexar Co. No. 03–CI–06936 (2006)), where a Texas jury awarded $7.4 million in actual damages to the family of an HMO participant who died from complications of acute renal failure. The jury found Humana liable for 35 percent of the $7.4 million in actual damages for negligence, but found no evidence that Humana committed fraud. The jury also determined that Humana's behavior was consistent with gross negligence, and the company stipulated to $1.6 million in punitive damages pursuant to an out-of-court agreement. Humana was found to be responsible for a total of $4.2 million.

Smelik is an attempt to escape from *Davila*'s restrictions, since the plaintiff argued that Humana was liable for "mismanaged managed care", or negligence in the coordination of medical care, rather than for a denial of medical care, as in *Davila*. Plaintiffs convinced the jury that Humana failed to follow its own utilization management policies, failing to refer Smelik to a kidney specialist or to its disease management program. Plaintiffs also established that Humana negligently approved payment for a combination of drugs considered dangerous for patients with kidney problems.

b. *Vicarious liability for physician negligence.* In Badal v. Hinsdale Memorial Hospital, 2007 WL 1424205 (N.D.Ill.2007), plaintiff's injured ankle was misdiagnosed by a plan physician as only a "sprain", and he suffered serious injury. The court analyzed ERISA preemption arguments, in light of *Davila*. The court noted that the plaintiff's claims under *Davila* were brought under THCLA, the Texas Health Care Liability Act, and its duties do not arise independently of ERISA or the plan terms. *Davila* was about wrongful denial of benefits. In *Badal,* by contrast, the plaintiff alleged that "[w]hile committing the above acts and omissions, Dr. Lofthouse failed to apply, use or exercise the standard of care ordinarily exercised by reasonably well qualified or competent medical doctors." . . . The court noted that the plaintiff was not complaining of the wrongful denial of benefits, quoting the plaintiff: "Plaintiff is asking for damages for the injuries caused, and does not give one iota if it was covered under the plan, or whether it should in the future be covered under some plan[ ]. In short, whether or not it was a violation of ERISA is of no concern to plaintiff."

c. *Negligent Misrepresentation.* In McMurtry v. Wiseman, 445 F. Supp.2d 756 (2006) the U.S. District Court for the Western District of Kentucky held that negligent misrepresentations by an insurance broker that induced the plaintiff to buy disability insurance coverage were not ERISA preempted. The plaintiff claimed that the agent Botts' duty was independent of any duty related to ERISA, and that he, like any insurance agent, had a duty not to negligently misrepresent the terms of the policy and/or fraudulently induce the Plaintiff to purchase the coverage. The court quoted with approval the language of Morstein v. National Ins. Services, Inc., 93 F.3d 715, 723 (11th Cir.1996) "[a]llowing preemption of a fraud claim against an individual insurance agent will not serve Congress's purpose for ERISA. As we have discussed, Congress enacted ERISA to protect the interests of employees and other beneficiaries of employee benefit plans. To immunize insurance agents from personal liability for fraudulent misrepresentation regarding ERISA plans would not promote this objective."

The court held that the plaintiff's claims for "fraud and negligent misrepresentation did not arise directly from the plan, but rather from Botts' inducement to have the Plaintiff join the plan. The legal duty not to misrepresent the plan did not arise from the plan itself, but from an independent source of law; state tort law within Tennessee."

d. *Administrative/Clerical Errors.* In Duchesne–Baker v. Extendicare Health Services, Inc., 2004 WL 2414070 (E.D. La. Oct. 28, 2004), the district court concludes that while Aetna was a defendant in both this action and in *Davila* and each case was removed to federal court, there was no other similarity between these two cases. The court noted that *Davila* fell within the scope of ERISA Section 502(a)(1)(B) because an essential part of the plaintiffs' state law claim in *Davila* required an examination and interpretation of the relevant plan documents. By contrast, the allegation in *Duchesne-Baker* was that the insurance coverage was wrongly terminated due to a clerical error and Aetna failed to exercise due care to correct this error. Thus, the court concluded that, because the allegation did not involve improper processing of a benefit claim and did not otherwise seek enforcement of the plaintiff's rights under the plan or to clarify future right under the plan, the claim in Duchesne–Baker was distinguishable from Davila and, therefore, required remand back to the state court.

3.   ERISA was interpreted by the federal courts in the first wave of litigation as totally preempting common law tort claims. See, e.g., Ricci v. Gooberman, 840 F.Supp. 316 (D.N.J.1993); It appeared from this caselaw that any managed care plan that was ERISA-qualified would receive virtually complete tort immunity.

The federal courts began to split, however, as to the limits of such preemption. The result was a litigation explosion against managed care as theories were imported from hospital liability caselaw, fiduciary law, and contract law to use against managed care organizations. Prihoda v. Shpritz, 914 F.Supp. 113 (D.Md. 1996) (ERISA does not preempt an action against physicians and an HMO for physicians' failure to diagnose a cancerous tumor, allowing a vicarious liability action to proceed). See also Independence HMO, Inc. v. Smith, 733 F.Supp. 983 (E.D.Pa.1990) (ERISA does not preempt medical malpractice-type claims brought against HMOs under a vicarious liability theory); Elsesser v. Hospital of the Philadelphia College of Osteopathic Medicine, 802 F.Supp. 1286 (E.D.Pa.1992) (same for a claim against an HMO for the HMO's negligence in selecting, retaining, and evaluating plaintiff's primary-care physician); Kearney v. U.S. Healthcare, Inc., 859 F.Supp. 182 (E.D.Pa.1994) (ERISA preempts plaintiff's direct negligence claim, but not its vicarious liability claim). See generally Barry Furrow, Managed Care Organizations and Patient Injury: Rethinking Liability, 31 Ga. L. Rev. 419 (1997)

Dukes v. U.S. Healthcare, Inc., 57 F.3d 350 (3d Cir.1995) was the watershed case that opened up a major crack in ERISA preemption of common law tort claims. In *Dukes*, the Third Circuit found that Congress intended in passing ERISA to insure that promised benefits would be available to plan participants, and that section 502 was "intended to provide each individual participant with a remedy in the event that promises made by the plan were not kept." The court was unwilling, however, to stretch the remedies of 502 to "control the quality of the benefits received by plan participants." The court concluded that "... [q]uality control of benefits, such as the health care benefits provided here, is a field traditionally occupied by state regulation and we interpret the silence of

Congress as reflecting an intent that it remain such." The court developed the distinction between benefits to care under a plan and a right to good quality care, holding that " * * * patients enjoy the right to be free from medical malpractice regardless of whether or not their medical care is provided through an ERISA plan." Quality of care could be so poor that it is essentially a denial of benefits. Or the plan could describe a benefit in terms that are quality-based, such as a commitment that all x-rays will be analyzed by radiologists with a certain level of training. But absent either of these extremes, poor medical care—malpractice—is not a benefits issue under ERISA.

Theories of liability based on the organizational structure of health plans were used by most courts to determine what is preempted and what allowed under ERISA. While some meaningful functional distinctions can be made, the courts were not been consistent, and liability was often variable, depending on the court's attitude toward managed care. See Peter J. Hammer, Pegram v. Herdrich: On Peritonitis, Preemption, and the Elusive Goal of Managed Care Accountability, 26 J. Health Pol. Pol'y & L. 767, 768 n.2 (2001). The federal courts were often hostile to managed care plans, and struggled mightily to work around ERISA preemption and allow a common law tort action to go forward.

For an excellent overview of the interaction of ERISA preemption and MCO malpractice liability, see generally Gail B. Agrawal and Mark A. Hall, What If You Could Sue Your HMO? Managed Care Liability Beyond the ERISA Shield, 47 St. Louis U. L.J. 235 (2003). See also Wendy K. Mariner, Slouching Toward Managed Care Liability: Reflections on Doctrinal Boundaries, Paradigm Shifts, and Incremental Reform, 29 J.L. Med. & Ethics 253 (2001) (favoring enhanced liability); David Orentlicher, The Rise and Fall of Managed Care: A Predictable "Tragic Choices" Phenomenon, 47 St. Louis U. L.J. 411 (2003) (analyzing managed care as a device for concealing and avoiding tragic choices in a public forum).

E. BENEFICIARY REMEDIES PROVIDED BY ERISA

ERISA takes away, but ERISA also gives. ERISA obligates employee benefit plans to fulfill their commitments to their beneficiaries, and provides a federal cause of action under § 502 when they fail to do so. But the vision of health insurance that undergirds ERISA is very different from that which undergirds state insurance regulation.

State insurance regulation has generally been driven by a concern for access rights: e.g., the right of employees to have continued access to insurance coverage when they lose their jobs; the right of insureds to obtain mental health or mammography screening coverage; the right of chiropractors to have their services paid for by insurance; the right of "any willing provider" to participate in a PPO or pharmacy benefits plan; the right of small businesses to purchase insurance at affordable rates; the right of beneficiaries to insure compliance with the insurance contract; and the right of beneficiaries to fair procedure. This body of state law looks to public utility regulation, and, more recently, civil rights laws, for its models.

The categories of law that define ERISA, on the other hand, are trust law and classical contract law. ERISA does not compel employers to provide health insurance and prohibits the states from imposing such a requirement. If, however, employers choose voluntarily (or under collective bargaining agreements) to establish health benefit plans, any contributions made by employers (or employees) to such plans are held in trust for all of the participants (employee plan members) and beneficiaries (dependents and others covered under a participant's policy) of the plan and must be paid out according to the contract that defines its terms. If the plan fiduciary or administrator wrongfully withholds benefits, a participant or beneficiary is entitled to sue in federal or state court. If a fiduciary or administrator exercises properly delegated discretion to withhold benefits that are not expressly granted or denied by the plan, however, the court must defer to the judgment of the administrator or fiduciary. When the fiduciary or administrator wrongfully withholds benefits, moreover, no matter how egregious its conduct in doing so, the court will merely order the plan to pay the beneficiary the amount due. ERISA does not as interpreted by the Supreme Court, authorize tort relief or punitive damages.

While the limited rights that beneficiaries enjoy under ERISA trouble courts and commentators, they are consistent with ERISA's underlying theory. State insurance laws—be they the common law of *contra proferentem* or statutory mandates enacted by the legislature—focus on the absolute claim of a beneficiary whose life or health is in jeopardy to the assets held by the insurer: your money or my life. They also honor the political claims of providers who demand their turn at the insurance trough. The health insurance pot is, apparently, infinitely elastic and must be expanded to fulfill the demands of many claimants, each of whom, considered individually, makes a compelling case.

ERISA, by contrast, sees a zero sum game. The pot is only so big, and when it is empty it is empty. To fudge the rules in favor of one beneficiary may result in the plan not being able to honor the legitimate claims of other beneficiaries. If one claimant who has been treated egregiously by the plan is permitted to recover extracontractual damages from its administrator, these damages will ultimately come out of the pockets of the other beneficiaries, who have themselves done nothing wrong. In a world of scarce resources, not everyone can be taken care of. But the administrator, nevertheless, is also a fiduciary, and there are some limits to its discretion.

DOE v. GROUP HOSPITALIZATION & MEDICAL SERVICES

United States Court of Appeals, Fourth Circuit, 1993.
3 F.3d 80.

NIEMEYER, CIRCUIT JUDGE:

John Doe, a 59–year–old law partner of Firm Doe in Washington, D.C., was diagnosed in late 1991 with multiple myeloma, a rare and typically fatal form of blood cancer. His physician, Dr. Kenneth C. Anderson of the Dana–Farber Cancer Institute, affiliated with Harvard Medical School, prescribed a treatment that involved an initial course of chemotherapy to reduce the percentage of tumor cells. Provided Doe responded to the therapy and achieved a "minimal disease status,' Dr. Anderson recommended that Doe then undergo high-dose chemotherapy and radiation therapy combined with an autologous bone marrow transplant. * * * The cost of the entire treatment was estimated at $100,000. Dr. Anderson stated that the prescribed treatment "offers this gentleman his only chance of long-term survival."

John Doe and Firm Doe sought health insurance benefits for the prescribed treatment from Group Hospitalization and Medical Services, Inc., doing business as Blue Cross and Blue Shield of the National Capital Area (Blue Cross). Blue Cross insured and administered Firm Doe's employee welfare benefit plan pursuant to a group insurance contract entered into effective January 1, 1989. Relying on language in the contract that excludes benefits for bone marrow transplants undergone in treating multiple myeloma, as well as for "related" services and supplies, Blue Cross denied benefits. John Doe and Firm Doe promptly filed suit against Blue Cross under § 502 of the Employee Retirement Insurance Security Act (ERISA), 29 U.S.C. § 1132, claiming that Blue Cross denied benefits based solely upon improperly adopted amendments to the group insurance contract and that, in any event, the contract's language as amended did not exclude coverage for the treatment. On cross-motions for summary judgment, the district court entered judgment for Blue Cross, holding that "Blue Cross may properly deny coverage to John Doe and his physicians based on the Group Contract and amendments thereto." This appeal followed.

* * *

The group insurance contract to which we must look to resolve the issues in this case was purportedly amended by a letter sent to Firm Doe dated November 30, 1990. The amendment is important because it supplied the language on which Blue Cross relied to deny coverage and gave Blue Cross discretion in deciding eligibility and contract interpretation issues.

* * *

In December 1991 John Doe was evaluated and diagnosed with multiple myeloma * * *. By letter dated January 30, 1992, John Doe's physician, Dr. Anderson, prescribed a treatment of chemotherapy and radiation that included an autologous bone marrow transplant. On March 30, 1992, Dr. Gregory K. Morris, vice president and medical director of Blue Cross, wrote Dr. Anderson denying the request for coverage of the proposed treatment. Specifically referring to the language of the November 30, 1990, amendment that excludes from coverage treatment of myeloma by means of bone marrow transplant and services and supplies related thereto, Dr. Morris stated that Blue Cross will be "unable to provide benefits for Mr. [Doe]." * * **

The November 30 letter was a form letter apparently sent to all administrators of Blue Cross group insurance contracts. It opens by stating that its purpose is to "inform you of updates" to the group contract. It then addresses changes to no less than eight separate aspects of coverage in four single-spaced pages, including one headed "Organ Transplants" that includes the language in question. * * *

John Doe and Firm Doe contend that the amendment was ineffective for two reasons: It was not adopted in accordance with the contract's specified

---

* After denying coverage and rejecting John Doe's appeal, Blue Cross amended the group insurance contract on May 28, 1992, effective August 1, 1992, to confirm its interpretation of the contract and to exclude the treatment for which John Doe had requested precertification. Because ERISA requires that specific reasons for denial of a claim be given, see 29 U.S.C. § 1133, our review in this case is limited to only those reasons which Blue Cross gave for denying coverage.[ ] However, any attempt by Blue Cross to rely on a post-precertification pre-therapy amendment to deny benefits to John Doe, which would be inappropriate to anticipate now, might raise serious questions concerning Blue Cross' duties, both as a fiduciary and under the insurance contract with Firm Doe, and its good faith.

time periods for making amendments, and, even if it was timely, the language of the amendment misled the contract holder, Firm Doe, and its employees about the nature of the changes.

[The court found that the amendment was effective because Blue Cross had provided 30 days notice of the change in accordance with the contract. Ed.]

In connection with their second point, John Doe and Firm Doe argue that while the language contained in the section headed "Organ Transplants" purports to "clarify" the types of transplants covered ("In order to *clarify* which types of transplants are covered, a list of the covered procedures [is] being added to your Contract as follows" (emphasis added)), coverage was in fact narrowed by the amendment because before the amendment transplants were simply not addressed and were therefore presumptively covered so long as they were not excluded under some other provision. They argue, therefore, that Blue Cross failed to disclose the intended effect of the limitation for organ transplants, downplaying the significance of the letter. * * * In short, they maintain that Blue Cross failed to put Firm Doe on notice of an amendment. From our review of the letter and the parties' conduct in response to it, we find this argument unpersuasive.

Health care benefits provided in an employee benefit plan are not vested benefits; the employer may modify or withdraw these benefits at any time, provided the changes are made in compliance with ERISA and the terms of the plan. * * * Firm Doe established its benefit plan through a contract with Blue Cross, and as part of this contract, Firm Doe accepted the provision that "benefits, provisions, terms, or conditions" could be changed by Blue Cross upon timely written notice. We believe that the November 30 letter provided sufficient notice that benefits under the contract were being changed. It states at the outset that the letter is an "update" of the terms of the contract. The body of the letter refers to specific coverages, outlining the changes in the language for each. * * *

Evidence was also presented that Firm Doe in fact relied on the changes made by the November 30 letter in connection with other coverages and it continued to pay premiums under the contract without objection. Moreover, the amendment was circulated well before John Doe evidenced any symptoms of or was diagnosed with cancer. More than 15 months after the amendment was sent, Blue Cross relied on its language in reviewing the coverage, and we believe that it was correct in doing so.

John Doe and Firm Doe contend that even the amended language of their group insurance contract with Blue Cross does not provide a basis for the insurance company's decision to deny John Doe benefits. Before turning to the validly amended contract to review this decision, we must address the appropriate standard of review to apply.

Court actions challenging the denial of benefits under 29 U.S.C. § 1132(a)(1)(B) are subject to the standard of review announced in Firestone Tire and Rubber Co. v. Bruch, 489 U.S. 101, 109 S.Ct. 948, 103 L.Ed.2d 80 (1989). The Court observed there, deriving guidance from principles of trust law, that in reviewing actions of a fiduciary who has been given discretionary powers to determine eligibility for benefits and to construe the language of an ERISA plan deference must be shown, and the fiduciary's actions will be reviewed only for abuse.[ ] If discretionary authority is not provided, denials of claims are to be reviewed de novo.[ ] Thus, where a fiduciary with authorized discretion construes a disputed or doubtful term, we will not disturb the interpretation if it is reasonable, even if we come to a different conclusion independently.[ ] In Firestone, however, the Supreme Court went on to recognize that a conflict of interest could lower the level of deference to be applied to a discretionary decision by a fiduciary:

> Of course, if a benefit plan gives discretion to an administrator or fiduciary who is operating under a conflict of interest, that conflict must be weighed as a "facto[r] in determining whether there is an abuse of discretion."[ ]

Under the group insurance contract with Firm Doe, the employer, Blue Cross both insures and administers the payment of health care benefits for Firm Doe's employee welfare benefit plan. In its role as plan administrator, Blue Cross clearly exercises discretionary authority or discretionary control with respect to the management of the plan and therefore qualifies as a fiduciary under ERISA. 29 U.S.C. § 1002(21)(A). Only if Blue Cross has also been given discretionary authority with regard to decisions about eligibility for benefits and construction of the plan, however, will those decisions be entitled to deferential review.[ ]

Blue Cross asserts that it has been given discretionary authority to review claims, determine eligibility, and construe contract terms and that our review of its decision to deny Doe benefits is therefore only for abuse of discretion. We agree that the express terms of the group insurance contract give Blue Cross discretion to the extent it claims. The terms were stated in the November 30, 1990, letter of amendment as follows:

> [Blue Cross] shall have the full power and discretionary authority to control and manage the operation and administration of the Contract, subject only to the Participant's rights of review and appeal under the Contract. [Blue Cross] shall have all powers necessary to accomplish these purposes in accordance with the terms of the contract including, but not limited to:
>
> a.   Determining all questions relating to Employee and Family Member eligibility and coverage;
>
> b.   Determining the benefits and amounts payable therefor to any Participant or provider of health care services;
>
> c.   Establishing and administering a claims review and appeal process; and
>
> d.   Interpreting, applying, and administering the provisions of the Contract.

John Doe and Firm Doe contend, however, that in denying benefits to John Doe, Blue Cross operated under a conflict of interest, and that therefore no deference to its discretion is warranted. They note that ERISA imposes on fiduciaries a duty of loyalty to act "with respect to a plan solely in the interest of the participants and beneficiaries and for the exclusive purpose of providing benefits ... and defraying reasonable expenses." 29 U.S.C. § 1104(a)(1)(A)[ ]. Blue Cross apparently is compensated by a fixed premium, and when it pays a claim it funds the payment from the premiums collected. No evidence has been presented to suggest it has a mechanism to collect from the employer retrospectively for unexpected liabilities. It therefore bears the financial risk for claims made beyond the actuarial norm. John Doe and Firm Doe point out that "each time [Blue Cross] approves a payment of benefits, the money comes out of its own pocket" and argue that Blue Cross' fiduciary role as decisionmaker in approving benefits under the plan therefore "lies in perpetual conflict with its profitmaking role as a business."[ ] They urge that, because of this conflict, when we review Blue Cross' decision to deny Doe benefits, no deference to its judgment is due. * * *

We were first presented with the question of what effect a fiduciary's conflict of interest might have in De Nobel [v. Vitro Corp., 885 F.2d 1180 (4th Cir.1989)]. There, the employee-claimants, who were beneficiaries of an employee retirement plan, contended that decisions of the administrators of the plan were not entitled to deferential review because the administrators operated under a conflict of interest arising from their dual role as plan administrators and employees of the sponsoring company. The beneficiaries argued that decisions by the administrator favorable to the employer would save the plan "substantial sums."[ ] In deciding the case, however, we never reached the effect that a conflict of interest might have on the applicable standard of review because we concluded that no substantial conflict existed when the plan was fully funded and any savings would inure to the direct benefit of the plan, and therefore to the benefit of all beneficiaries and participants. * * *

In this case, Blue Cross insured the plan in exchange for the payment of a fixed premium, presumably based on actuarial data. Undoubtedly, its profit from the insurance contract depends on whether the claims allowed exceed the assumed risks. To the extent that Blue Cross has discretion to avoid paying claims, it thereby promotes the potential for its own profit. That type of conflict flows inherently from the nature of the relationship entered into by the parties and is common where employers contract with insurance companies to provide and administer health care benefits to employees through group insurance contracts. * * *

* * *

Because of the presence of a substantial conflict of interest, we therefore must alter our standard of review. We hold that when a fiduciary exercises discretion in interpreting a disputed term of the contract where one interpretation will further the financial interests of the fiduciary, we will not act as deferentially as would otherwise be appropriate. Rather, we will review the merits of the interpretation to determine whether it is consistent with an exercise of discretion by a fiduciary acting free of the interests that conflict with those of the beneficiaries. In short, the fiduciary decision will be entitled to some deference, but this deference will be lessened to the degree necessary to neutralize any untoward influence resulting from the conflict.[ ] With that lessened degree of deference to Blue Cross' discretionary interpretation of the group insurance contract, we turn to review Blue Cross' decision to deny benefits.

[The court then described the high dose chemotherapy, autologous bone marrow transplantation procedure. Ed.]

* * *

Without consideration of a potential bone marrow transplant, treatment of blood cancer by chemotherapy and radiation is accordingly clearly covered by the contract.

* * *

* * * [T]he contract as amended November 30, 1990, provides that an autologous bone marrow transplant for multiple myeloma and "services or supplies for or related to" the transplant are excluded from the plan's coverage.

Blue Cross argues that the language excluding "services or supplies for or related to" the autologous bone marrow transplant reaches to exclude high-dose chemotherapy and radiation treatments because without the autologous bone marrow transplant, the high-dose chemotherapy could not be performed. * * * We believe that such an argument misdirects the analysis required for determining the scope of coverage and fails to accommodate harmoniously all provisions of the contract.

The bone marrow transplant, while necessary to avoid a disastrous side effect, is not the procedure designed to treat the cancer. The first question to be asked, therefore, is whether the cancer treating procedure is covered by the contract, and, as already noted, we have found it is. While Blue Cross is well within its rights to exclude from coverage the ancillary bone marrow transplant procedure, the exclusion should not, in the absence of clear language, be construed to withdraw coverage explicitly granted elsewhere in the contract.

* * *

We additionally note that in determining whether a decision has been made solely for the benefit of the participants, we may take account of the principle that in making a reasonable decision, ambiguity which remains in the scope of the "related to" language must be construed against the drafting party, particularly when, as here, the contract is a form provided by the insurer rather than one negotiated between the parties.[ ]

Because Blue Cross' discretionary interpretation to the contrary is not entitled to the deference we might otherwise accord, * * * we will construe the contract for the benefit of its beneficiaries and enforce the coverage provided by Part 3 of the group insurance contract and not otherwise explicitly excluded.

* * *

AFFIRMED IN PART, REVERSED IN PART, AND REMANDED FOR FURTHER PROCEEDINGS.

Notes and Questions

1. Section 502(a) of ERISA, reproduced at the beginning of this chapter, permits a plan participant or beneficiary to sue to "recover benefits due to him under the terms of the plan * * *" in federal or state court. 29 U.S.C.A. § 1132(a)(1). Although on its face this provision permits a suit against a plan for benefits denied, the courts have treated it instead as authorizing a review of the decision of the ERISA plan, i.e. the ERISA administrator is treated as an independent decisionmaker whose decision is subject to judicial review, much like an administrative agency, rather than as a defendant who has allegedly breached

a contract. See Semien v. Life Insurance Co. of North America, 436 F.3d 805, 814 (7th Cir.2006); Jay Conison, Suits for Benefits Under ERISA, 54 U. Pitt. L. Rev. 1 (1992).

As the principal case notes, Firestone Tire & Rubber Co. v. Bruch, 489 U.S. 101, 109 S.Ct. 948, 103 L.Ed.2d 80 (1989), held that the courts should apply de novo review in reviewing ERISA plan decisions. In doing so the Court rejected the "arbitrary and capricious" standard of review generally applied in earlier lower federal court ERISA review cases. The Court went on to observe, however, that arbitrary and capricious review, rather than de novo review, would apply if "the benefit plan gives the administrator or fiduciary discretionary authority to determine eligibility for benefits or to construe the terms of the plan." 489 U.S. at 115, 109 S.Ct. at 957.

In doing so, the Court created an exception that swallowed the rule, since post-*Firestone* plans are almost always drafted to give the plan administrator discretionary authority. The language found in the *Doe* policy is typical. Even where de novo review is available, moreover, some appellate courts have cabined it by limiting judicial review to consideration of the evidence considered by the plan administrator, Perry v. Simplicity Engineering, 900 F.2d 963 (6th Cir.1990); or by retaining deferential review for factual determinations of plan administrators and limiting de novo review to plan interpretations. Pierre v. Connecticut General Life Ins. Co., 932 F.2d 1552 (5th Cir.1991).

2. Although *Firestone* authorized arbitrary and capricious review where a plan fiduciary is granted decision-making discretion, it also observed that if "an administrator or fiduciary * * * is operating under a conflict of interest, that conflict must be weighed as a 'facto[r] in determining whether there is an abuse of discretion.' " 489 U.S. at 114. The various circuits are divided in their approaches to determining whether an administrator faces a conflict of interest in making the benefit determination, and what effect a conflict should have on the level of review if a conflict is found. See Kathryn J. Kennedy, Judicial Standard of Review in ERISA Benefit Claim Cases, 50 Am.U.L.Rev. 1083 (2001); Judith C. Brostron, The Conflict of Interest Standard in ERISA Cases: Can it be Avoided in the Denial of High Dose Chemotherapy Treatment for Breast Cancer?, 3 DePaul J. Health Care L. 1 (1999); Haavi Morreim, Benefits Decisions in ERISA Plans: Diminishing Deference to Fiduciaries and an Emerging Problem for Provider-Sponsored Organizations, 65 Tenn. L. Rev. 511 (1998).

At one end of the spectrum, the First, Second, and Seventh circuits have held that the "structural conflict of interest" that arises when an insurer both reviews and pays claims is rarely a problem because health plans must satisfy their customers in competitive markets. The denial of any one claim by a benefit plan, they contend, has a negligible effect on the profit margins of a plan, but routine denial of claims will give a plan a bad reputation and make it less competitive. See Denmark v. Liberty Life Assurance Company of Boston, 481 F.3d 16 (1st Cir. 2007); Pari–Fasano v. ITT Hartford Life & Accident Ins. Co., 230 F.3d 415, 418 (1st Cir.2000); Mers v. Marriott International Group Accidental Death & Dismemberment Plan, 144 F.3d 1014 (7th Cir.1998); Sullivan v. LTV Aerospace & Def. Co., 82 F.3d 1251, 1255–56 (2d Cir.1996). One Seventh Circuit decision opined that there is no reason to fear that insurance companies will be any more partial in making benefit decisions than federal judges in deciding income tax cases. Perlman v. Swiss Bank Corp. Comp. Disability Protection Plan, 195 F.3d 975, 981 (7th Cir.1999).

At the other end of the spectrum, some courts hold that if the plaintiff demonstrates that the fiduciary is operating under a substantial conflict of interest, the fiduciary's decision is afforded little deference, and should be subjected to de novo review. See Armstrong v. Aetna Life Ins. Co., 128 F.3d 1263, 1265 (8th Cir.1997). Some courts hold that the plaintiff must show a conflict of interest or procedural irregularity, but that the burden then shifts to the plan administrator to show that its decisions was reasonable. Hollingshead v. Blue Cross & Blue Shield of Oklahoma, 216 Fed.Appx. 797 (10th Cir.2007). The Eleventh Circuit has worked out an even more elaborate review process to address conflicts of interest. First, it reviews a plan administrator's decision de novo. If the decision is "wrong," it then determines whether the administrator was vested with discretion. If not, the process is at an end, but if the decision was discretionary, the court then applies the "arbitrary and capricious" standard. If the decision is reasonable, the court then determines whether there is a conflict of interest, and if so applies a "heightened arbitrary and capricious" standard. Helms v. General Dynamics Corp., 222 Fed.Appx. 821 (11th Cir. 2007).

In the middle, most circuits do not see conflicts of interest as changing the standard of review, but rather as a factor to take into account in deciding whether a decision is arbitrary and capricious or not. See Fay v. Oxford Health Plan, 287 F.3d 96, 108 (2d Cir.2002); Friedrich v. Intel Corp., 181 F.3d 1105 (9th Cir.1999); ; Hunter v. Federal Express Corp., 169 Fed. Appx. 697, 701 (3d Cir.2006). For example, the failure of a plan to consult independent reviewers in processing a claim, Woo v. Deluxe Corp., 144 F.3d 1157 (8th Cir.1998), or to follow internal plan procedures, Friedrich v. Intel Corp., 181 F.3d 1105 (9th Cir.1999), could be evidence of improper decision-making. On the other hand, decisions made through the use of independent consultants or by salaried employees who do not face direct incentives to approve or deny claims, or through the application of fair procedures, will generally be accepted. See Hendrix v. Standard Ins. Co., 182 F.3d 925 (9th Cir.1999). Most courts articulate this as a "sliding scale" approach, using an arbitrary and capricious review standard, but exercising greater scrutiny where a greater conflict is found. See Vega v. National Life Ins. Services, Inc., 188 F.3d 287, 289 (5th Cir.1999); Wolberg v. AT & T Broadband Pension Plan, 123 Fed. Appx. 840, 843–46 (10th Cir.2005). Of course, in some cases, courts can avoid the whole problem by simply holding that under any standard the plan's decision should be either accepted or rejected. See, e.g., Mario v. P & C Food Markets, Inc., 313 F.3d 758 (2d Cir.2002). As this book went to press, the Supreme Court decided MetLife v. Glenn, ___ U.S. ___, 128 S.ct. 2343 (2008) partially resolving the questions left open by *Firestone*. The Court decided that 1) insurers administering ERISA plans and self-insured plan administrators indeed have a conflict of interest, 2) their decisions are still entitled to a deferential rather than de novo review, but 3) the conflict must be taken into account as a factor in reviewing a plan determination. The Court suggested that an important consideration in determining the weight to give these factors is the procedures that an administrator had in place to keep the conflict from biasing plan decisions. A vigorous dissent by Scalia and Thomas contended that a conflict was relevant only if the claimant could prove that it resulted in a biased plan determination.

3.   What deference, if any, should federal courts afford plan administrators in reviewing ERISA benefit decisions? Should plan drafters be permitted to evade de novo review simply by drafting plan documents to give discretion to plan administrators? Do the interests of plan administrators inevitably conflict with the interests of plan participants and beneficiaries? Does the degree of conflict vary depending on whether the administrator is a self-insured employer, a third-party administrator for a self-insured employer, a risk-bearing insurer, a trust affiliated

with a labor union, or a multiple employer trust that administers health benefits for a number of small employers? Do non-profit Blue Cross plans, like the one in *Doe,* lack the conflict of interest that affects for-profit plans? See Pitman v. Blue Cross and Blue Shield of Oklahoma, 217 F.3d 1291, 1296 (10th Cir.2000) (no). Does the market for insurance in fact correct the conflict-of-interest problem? Could a state regulating insurers under the savings clause prohibit insured plans from giving plan administrators discretion to make coverage determinations? A number of states have adopted statutes or regulations to do so. See NAIC Model Act #42, Discetionary Clause Prohibition Act, and Donald T. Bogan, ERISA: State Regulation of Insured Plans After *Davila*, 38 J. Marshall L. Rev. 693 (2005). Should courts be permitted to consider evidence not presented initially to plan administrators when they review plan decisions, or should they be limited to reviewing the plan administrator's decision on the record? Most courts limit review to the administrative record. See Taft v. Equitable Life Ass. Soc'y, 9 F.3d 1469, 1472 (9th Cir.1993). Might concern on the part of federal courts about being swamped by insurance claims affect the eagerness of the courts to review these claims? Should it?

4.   Whether or not extracontractual damages can ever be available under ERISA is a question that has provoked considerable controversy. The answer seems to be no, though a good argument can be made that this is not the result Congress intended. George Flint, ERISA: Extracontractual Damages Mandated for Benefit Claims Actions, 36 Ariz. L. Rev. 611 (1994); Note, Available Remedies Under ERISA Section 502(a), 45 Ala. L. Rev. 631 (1994). In Massachusetts Mutual Life Insurance Co. v. Russell, 473 U.S. 134, 105 S.Ct. 3085, 87 L.Ed.2d 96 (1985), the Supreme Court held that ERISA does not authorize recovery of extracontractual damages by plan participants for breach of fiduciary duty. In Mertens v. Hewitt Associates, 508 U.S. 248, 113 S.Ct. 2063, 124 L.Ed.2d 161 (1993), the Court read provisions of ERISA permitting plan participants and beneficiaries "to obtain other appropriate equitable relief to redress such violations ..." (29 U.S.C.A. § 1132(a)(3)) to not authorize damage actions, as damages are not equitable in nature.

The effect of these cases is that an ERISA participant or beneficiary denied benefits can only recover the value of the claim itself and cannot recover damages caused by the claim denial. Punitive damages are also unavailable against plan administrators and fiduciaries under even the most egregious circumstances. What effect might the lack of this relief have on ERISA fiduciaries and administrators? To what extent might the fact that ERISA permits courts to award attorneys' fees in some cases ameliorate this effect? 29 U.S.C.A. § 1132(g). Would state tort cases against ERISA plan managed care organizations be necessary if more comprehensive remedies were available under ERISA? See, arguing that many of the problems that the courts have encountered in dealing with state claims against ERISA plans could have been avoided had the Court interpreted ERISA's remedial provisions to include broader remedies, John.H. Langbein, What ERISA Means by "Equitable": The Supreme Court's Trail of Error in Russell, Mertens and Great-West, 103 Columbia Law Review 1317 (2003).

Some members of the Court seem to be open to reconsidering this jurisprudence. In *Davila*, the Supreme Court's most recent foray into ERISA claims jurisprudence, Justice Ginsberg, joined by Justice Breyer, suggested in concurrence that the Court should revisit the question:

The Court today holds that the claims respondents asserted under Texas law are totally preempted by § 502(a) of [ ] ERISA [ ]. That decision is consistent with our governing case law on ERISA's preemptive scope. I therefore join the

Court's opinion. But, with greater enthusiasm, as indicated by my dissenting opinion in Great–West Life & Annuity Ins. Co. v. Knudson,[ ], I also join "the rising judicial chorus urging that Congress and [this] Court revisit what is an unjust and increasingly tangled ERISA regime." DiFelice v. Aetna U.S. Healthcare, 346 F.3d 442, 453 (C.A.3 2003) (Becker, J., concurring).

Because the Court has coupled an encompassing interpretation of ERISA's preemptive force with a cramped construction of the "equitable relief" allowable under § 502(a)(3), a "regulatory vacuum" exists: "[V]irtually all state law remedies are preempted but very few federal substitutes are provided."[ ]

A series of the Court's decisions has yielded a host of situations in which persons adversely affected by ERISA-proscribed wrongdoing cannot gain make-whole relief. First, in Massachusetts Mut. Life Ins. Co. v. Russell,[ ], the Court stated, in dicta: "[T]here is a stark absence—in [ERISA] itself and in its legislative history—of any reference to an intention to authorize the recovery of extracontractual damages" for consequential injuries.[ ] Then, in Mertens v. Hewitt Associates,[ ], the Court held that § 502(a)(3)'s term "equitable relief" ... refer[s] to those categories of relief that were typically available in equity (such as injunction, mandamus, and restitution, but not compensatory damages).[ ] Most recently, in Great–West, the Court ruled that, as "§ 502(a)(3), by its terms, only allows for equitable relief," the provision excludes "the imposition of personal liability ... for a contractual obligation to pay money."[ ]

As the array of lower court cases and opinions documents,[ ] fresh consideration of the availability of consequential damages under § 502(a)(3) is plainly in order.[ ]

The Government notes a potential amelioration. Recognizing that "this Court has construed Section 502(a)(3) not to authorize an award of money damages against a non-fiduciary," the Government suggests that the Act, as currently written and interpreted, may "allo[w] at least some forms of 'make-whole' relief against a breaching fiduciary in light of the general availability of such relief in equity at the time of the divided bench." Brief for United States as Amicus Curiae[ ]. * * * "Congress ... intended ERISA to replicate the core principles of trust remedy law, including the make-whole standard of relief."[ ] I anticipate that Congress, or this Court, will one day so confirm.

Seven other justices, of course, were silent on this question, although remedies under ERISA were not at issue in the case. To date, attempts to obtain monetary relief in ERISA actions through traditional equitable remedies such as restitution or surcharge have failed. See Knieriem v. Group Health Plan, Inc. 434 F.3d 1058 (8th Cir.2006).

5.   While ERISA preempts state common law, federal courts have, with some hesitancy, developed federal common law (such as the law of unconscionability) or applied traditional equity principles in ERISA cases to protect ERISA participants or beneficiaries. See Jayne Zanglein, Closing the Gap: Safeguarding Participants' Rights by Expanding the Federal Common Law of ERISA, 72 Wash. U.L Q. 671 (1994); William Carr & Robert Liebross, Wrongs Without Rights: The Need for A Strong Federal Common Law of ERISA, 4 Stanford L & Pol'y Rev. 221 (1993). Under what circumstances might federal common law or equitable doctrine apply? See Kane v. Aetna Life Insurance, 893 F.2d 1283 (11th Cir.1990) (court can apply equitable estoppel to interpret but not to change the terms of an ERISA plan); Nash v. Trustees of Boston Univ., 946 F.2d 960 (1st Cir.1991) (fraud in the inducement can be raised as an affirmative defense in ERISA case); but see

Watkins v. Westinghouse Hanford Co., 12 F.3d 1517 (9th Cir.1993) (equitable doctrines may not be relied on to provide remedies not available under ERISA).

Should the federal courts adopt state insurance common law in interpreting ERISA policies, or do different considerations govern in ERISA cases? In particular, should courts apply the contract interpretation principle of *contra proferentem* (applied in *HealthChicago*) in an ERISA case? Several appellate courts have held that *contra proferentem* is not appropriate in cases where the plan administrator is granted discretion to interpret the plan. Kimber v. Thiokol Corp., 196 F.3d 1092 (10th Cir.1999); Morton v. Smith, 91 F.3d 867 (7th Cir.1996), while others have held that it is appropriate when reviewing plan interpretation decisions when the court is applying de novo review, Fay v. Oxford Health Plan, 287 F.3d 96, 104 (2nd Cir.2002). Yet other courts have recognized another general principal of insurance law–that ambiguous plan terms must be construed to accord with the reasonable expectations of the insured. Bynum v. Cigna Healthcare of N.C., Inc., 287 F.3d 305, 313–14 (4th Cir.2002).

6.   One aspect of ERISA jurisprudence highlighted by the principal case is that, although the courts often act as though they were applying contract law in interpreting and enforcing ERISA plan provisions, ERISA plans are based on very unusual contracts. First, the insurance contract itself is between the employer and insurer, and the beneficiary rarely knows fully, or even has immediate access to, its terms. Second, the employer-insurer agreement tends to evolve over time, yet the beneficiary may be bound by terms that were far from clear at the time the claim was made. See, e.g., Mizzell v. Paul Revere Ins. Co., 278 F.Supp.2d 1146 (D.C Cal.2003), in which the court deferred to the discretion of the insurer even though the provision granting discretion to the insurer was not finalized until after the claim was submitted. Despite this, courts seem usually to have little trouble binding beneficiaries by the terms of ERISA contracts.

7.   ERISA does not by its terms permit providers to sue plans to collect payments due them for providing services to beneficiaries. Courts have generally rejected the argument that providers are "beneficiaries" under ERISA plans. Pritt v. Blue Cross & Blue Shield of West Virginia, Inc., 699 F.Supp. 81 (S.D.W.Va. 1988). Providers have been more successful in asserting their rights as assignees of participants or beneficiaries, City of Hope Nat. Med. Ctr. v. HealthPlus, Inc., 156 F.3d 223 (1st Cir.1998); Hermann Hosp. v. MEBA Med. & Benefits Plan, 845 F.2d 1286 (5th Cir.1988), though a few courts have held that assignees have no standing to sue as they are not mentioned as protected parties within the statute. Other courts have upheld anti-assignment clauses in plan contracts.

Courts have split on whether providers can recover from insurers when the insurer leads the provider to believe that the insured or the service is covered, and then subsequently refuses payment and claims ERISA protection. Several courts have held that ERISA is intended to control relationships between employers and employees and should not preempt common law or statutory misrepresentation claims brought by providers. Transitional Hospitals Corp. v. Blue Cross & Blue Shield of Texas, Inc., 164 F.3d 952 (5th Cir.1999); Hospice of Metro Denver, Inc. v. Group Health Ins. of Okla., Inc., 944 F.2d 752 (10th Cir.1991). Other courts have held that misrepresentation claims are claims for benefits that are preempted by ERISA. Cromwell v. Equicor–Equitable HCA Corp., 944 F.2d 1272 (6th Cir.1991). Finally, several courts have allowed a provider to sue an ERISA plan on a contract or state statutory claim, stating that the claim was not preempted by ERISA because the provider had no standing to sue under ERISA. See Medical and Chirurgical Faculty v. Aetna U.S. Healthcare, Inc., 221 F.Supp.2d 618 (D.Md.2002), Foley v. Southwest Texas HMO, Inc., 226 F.Supp.2d 886 (E.D.Tex.

2002). See, generally, Scott C. Walton, Note, ERISA Preemption of Third–Party Provider Claims: A Coherent Misrepresentation of Coverage Exception, 88 Iowa L. Rev. 969 (2003).

8. ERISA requires health benefit plans to acknowledge and effectuate "qualified medical child support orders." These are state court orders that require a group health plan that covers dependents to extend group medical coverage to the children of a plan participant, even though the participant does not have legal custody of the children. 29 U.S.C.A. § 1169. Under this law, adopted in 1993, a plan participant can be required under court order to pay for family coverage to cover a dependent child not in the parent's custody, even though the parent might have otherwise chosen not to purchase coverage. Who benefits from this law, other than the children it protects?

Problem: ERISA Litigation

John Mendez is in the advanced stages of a condition that results in degeneration of his nervous system. His doctor believes that he would be helped by a new gene therapy. John receives coverage under his employer's self-insured employee benefits plan. The plan has denied coverage for the therapy, claiming that it is experimental. The terms of the plan give the administrator discretion to decide whether or not to cover experimental procedures, but the plan does not define "experimental." John's doctor claims that the procedure is still quite new, but has advanced beyond the experimental stage. What standard will a court apply in reviewing the administrator's decision if John sues under § 502? How does this standard differ from that which a court would have applied had John sued an insurer under an individual health insurance policy under standard state insurance contract law?

F. ADMINISTRATIVE CLAIMS AND APPEALS PROCEDURES UNDER ERISA

29 U.S.C.A. § 1133 (§ 503) provides:

In accordance with regulations of the Secretary, every employee benefit plan shall—

(1) provide adequate notice in writing to any participant or beneficiary whose claim for benefits under the plan has been denied, setting forth the specific reasons for such denial, written in a manner calculated to be understood by the participant, and

(2) afford a reasonable opportunity to any participant whose claim for benefits has been denied for a full and fair review by the appropriate named fiduciary of the decision denying the claim.

Rules implementing this statute are currently found at 29 C.F.R. § 2560.503–1.

The Rules require employee benefit plans to "establish and maintain reasonable procedures governing the filing of benefit claims, notification of benefit determinations, and appeal of adverse benefit determinations," and then provide that claims procedures will be considered reasonable only if they comply with specific requirements. Those provisions prohibit, for example, the requirement of the payment of a fee for the filing of an appeal or "the denial of a claim for failure to obtain a prior approval under circumstances that would make obtaining such prior approval impossible or where application of the prior approval process could seriously jeopardize the life or health of the claimant." The regulations prohibit plans from requiring a claimant to file more than two appeals prior to suing under § 502(a), though they do allow plans to interpose an additional opportunity for voluntary arbitration as long as the plan does not require it and any statutes of limitations are tolled while arbitration is pursued. The regulations preclude plans from imposing a requirement of arbitration which is binding and not reviewable under 502(a).

The regulations impose time limits for handling claims and appeals, including a maximum of seventy-two hours for processing "urgent care claims." Pre-service claims must be decided within fifteen days (thought the period can be extended by another fifteen days under certain circumstances) and post-service claims must be decided within thirty days (subject to one fifteen-day extension if necessary due to matters beyond the plan's control). A claim denial must explain the reason for the adverse decision, referencing the plan provision on which the denial is based. If the decision is based on a medical necessity or experimental treatment limitation, "either an explanation of the scientific or clinical judgment for the determination, applying the terms of the plan to the claimant's medical circumstances, or a statement that such explanation will be provided free of charge upon request" must be provided.

Group health plans must provide appeal procedures that "[p]rovide for a review that does not afford deference to the initial adverse benefit determination and that is conducted by an appropriate named fiduciary of the plan who is neither the individual who made the adverse benefit determination that is the subject of the appeal, nor the subordinate of such individual." The rules also provide time frames for appeals, seventy-two hours for urgent care claims, thirty days for pre-service claims (or fifteen days for each stage if two stage appeals are provided), and sixty days for post-service plans. The information that the plan must provide in an adverse appeal decision is similar to that which must be provided under an initial adverse decision.

The rules have their own provision for preemption of state law:

29 C.F.R. § 2560.503–1.

(k) Preemption of State law. (1) Nothing in this section shall be construed to supersede any provision of State law that regulates insurance, except to the extent that such law prevents the application of a requirement of this section.

(2)(i) For purposes of paragraph (k)(1) of this section, a State law regulating insurance shall not be considered to prevent the application of a requirement of this section merely because such State law establishes a review procedure to evaluate and resolve disputes involving adverse benefit determinations under group health plans so long as the review procedure is conducted by a person or entity other than the insurer, the plan, plan fiduciaries, the employer, or any employee or agent of any of the foregoing.

(ii) The State law [external review] procedures * * * [permitted under the regulations] are not part of the full and fair review required by section 503 of the Act. Claimants therefore need not exhaust such State law procedures prior to bringing suit under section 502(a) of the Act.

Finally, the rules also provide a sanction against plans that fail to follow them:

(*l*) In the case of the failure of a plan to establish or follow claims procedures consistent with the requirements of this section, a claimant shall be deemed to have exhausted the administrative remedies available under the plan and shall be entitled to pursue any available remedies under section 502(a) of the Act on the basis that the plan has failed to provide a reasonable claims procedure that would yield a decision on the merits of the claim.

Notes and Questions

1. As is discussed in the previous chapter, all states have adopted laws prescribing internal review procedures for health plans, and most require external reviews as well. Are these state law provisions enforceable under this regulation? In what respects does this regulation supplement state law for insured employee benefit plans? Return to the *Problems: Advising Under State Managed Care Law* in the previous chapter. How, if at all, do your resolutions of those problems change if the problem involves the same state law but an insured employee benefits plan? A self-insured plan?

2. Why does the regulation prohibit binding arbitration? Why does it limit plans to two stage appeals? The 1998 proposed regulations prohibited plan provisions that required claimants to submit claims to arbitration or to file more than one appeal. Can you see why these provisions proved quite controversial?

3. Though ERISA itself does not require a claimant to exhaust administrative remedies before pursuing judicial review, every circuit court of appeals has held that exhaustion is necessary. See, e.g. Amato v. Bernard, 618 F.2d 559, 566–68 (9th Cir.1980). Exhaustion is sometimes excused, however, where the claimant can establish futility or denial of meaningful access to plan remedies by a plan's failure to comply with ERISA requirements. See, e.g. Lee v. California Butchers' Pension Trust Fund, 154 F.3d 1075 (9th Cir.1998).

4. Whether or not a plan's violation of the ERISA procedural rules should result in de novo judicial review is an unsettled question. Some courts have held that violation of procedural requirements does not change the arbitrary and capricious standard of review that courts apply in ERISA cases where plans have discretion unless the violation results in substantive harm, Gatti v. Reliance Standard Life Ins. Co., 415 F.3d 978 (9th Cir.2005), but when procedural violations cause substantive harm, they may render a plan's decisions arbitrary and capricious, Blau v. Del Monte Corp. 748 F.2d 1348, 1353–54 (9th Cir.1984). A plan's failure to make a decision within time limits imposed by the regulations and plan might also be considered to be a plan's failure to exercise its discretion. Jebian v. Hewlett-Packard Co., 349 F.3d 1098 (9th Cir.2003); Gilbertson v. Allied Signal, Inc., 328 F.3d 625 (10th Cir.2003). It is an open question whether the new rules make de novo review mandatory when plans fail to comply with the time frames found in the rules, and a claimant is thus deemed to have exhausted remedies. Compare Goldman v. Hartford Life and Accident Ins. Co., 417 F.Supp.2d 788 (E.D.La.2006) (no) with Reeves v. Unum Life Ins. Co. of America, 376 F.Supp.2d 1285 (W.D.Okla.2005).

III.   FEDERAL INITIATIVES TO EXPAND PRIVATE INSURANCE COVERAGE: THE HEALTH INSURANCE PORTABILITY AND ACCOUNTABILITY ACT OF 1996, THE CONSOLIDATED OMNIBUS BUDGET RECONCILIATION ACT OF 1985, AND THE AMERICANS WITH DISABILITIES ACT

Although ERISA has done much to limit the rights that participants in employee benefit plans might otherwise have had under state law and ERISA's own remedial provisions do not completely fill the void left by preemption, federal law also provides privately-insured individuals some rights that they might not have had under state law. The most important of these are the rights to insurance portability and to freedom from discrimination on the basis of health status provided by the Health Insurance Portability and Accountability Act of 1996 (HIPAA); the continuation of coverage benefits available under the Consolidated Omnibus Budget Reconciliation Act of 1985, commonly called "COBRA coverage"; and the right to freedom from discrimination on the basis of disability found in the Americans with Disabilities Act (ADA). This section examines these federal rights.

A.   THE HEALTH INSURANCE PORTABILITY AND ACCOUNTABILITY ACT OF 1996 AND COBRA COVERAGE REQUIREMENTS

HIPAA began as an attempt to enact the least controversial elements of the much more ambitious Clinton health insurance reform proposals of 1993 and 1994. In the end it became a lengthy "Christmas tree" bill addressing a hodge-podge of topics. HIPAA included, for example, major changes in the fraud and abuse laws and tax subsidies for medical savings accounts, discussed elsewhere in this book. It also provided tax incentives intended to encourage the purchase of long term care insurance and the availability of accelerated death benefits for the terminally and chronically ill, and encouraged the creation of state insurance pools to benefit high-risk individuals. In the past few years, HIPAA has been identified predominantly with its privacy provisions, which have provided the statutory underpinnings for far-reaching regulations issued by the Department of Health and Human Services. HIPAA was named, however, after the provisions it included amending ERISA, the Public Health Services Act, and the Internal Revenue Code to increase the portability and accessibility of health insurance, which were initially seen as its most important provisions. HIPAA does this in several ways.

First, HIPAA limits the use of preexisting conditions requirements. Preexisting conditions clauses are commonly used by insurers to limit adverse selection—the tendency of persons who are already ill disproportionately to seek out insurance. HIPAA provides that group health insurers can only impose a preexisting condition exclusion if the exclusion relates to a physical or mental condition for which medical advice, diagnosis, care, or treatment was recommended or received within the six-month period ending on the enrollment date. 29 U.S.C.A. §§ 1181 a)(1), 300gg(a)(1). A preexisting condition exclusion may only last for a maximum period of twelve months (or eighteen months in the case of a person who enrolls in a plan later than the time the plan is initially available to that person, unless the delay was based on the fact that the enrollee was covered under COBRA continuation coverage or as a dependent of another covered person) 29 U.S.C.A. §§ 1181(a)(2), 300gg(a)(2), (f)(1). Moreover, the period during which any such preexisting condition exclusion can be imposed must be reduced by the aggregate of the periods of time that the beneficiary had previously been enrolled under another private or public health plan, (called "creditable coverage" under HIPAA) provided that it has not been more than sixty-three days since coverage under the other policy ended. In other words, if a person who has been insured under a group health plan at one job for twelve months or more moves directly into another job, covered under a different plan, without being uninsured for more than two months between jobs, the new plan cannot impose a preexisting condition exclusion. Preexisting condition clauses cannot be imposed on the basis of a genetic predisposition to a particular condition. They also cannot ordinarily be imposed with respect to newborns, adopted children, or pregnant women.

HIPAA's preexisting conditions limitation was one of its most popular provisions. Why had preexisting conditions clauses been relatively common in insurance policies? What are the distributional effects of preexisting conditions clauses? Why might they be less important to insurers (or employer-financed health plans) in situations where applicants are merely changing insurers (usually incident to a change of jobs) rather than applying for insurance for the first time? Why might insurers and employers prefer a longer preexisting condition exclusion where employees who have previously declined offered insurance change their minds and request it? Why should coverage of pregnancy or of newborn or adopted children be specially excluded from preexisting condition exclusions? Preexisting conditions clauses were, prior to HIPAA, believed to have resulted in "job-lock" because employees could not change employers without losing coverage for "preexisting conditions." See GAO, Employer–Based Health Insurance, High Costs, Wide Variation Threaten System (1992). Does HIPAA adequately address this issue?

HIPAA also imposes several other requirements on ERISA plans. First, it prohibits group health plans from discriminating against individuals in determining eligibility to enroll or in setting premiums on the basis of health status-related characteristics of the insured individual or a dependent of the insured individual, including health status, medical conditions (including both physical and mental illnesses), claims experience, receipt of health care, medical history, genetic information, evidence of insurability (including conditions arising out of acts of domestic violence), or disability. 29 U.S.C.A § 1182(a) & (b).

HIPAA also requires insurers that sell insurance in the individual market to make insurance available to all applicants with 18 months or more of creditable coverage who have lost that coverage and exhausted COBRA coverage (see below) and who have not had a gap of more than sixty-three days between the end of their insurance coverage and their application for extension coverage. Insurers cannot impose preexisting conditions clauses on such individuals, 42 US.C.A. §§ 300gg–41. Insurers do not need to comply with the individual insurance mandate, however, in a state that makes available alternative means of coverage to uninsured individuals. All but seven of the states have chosen to adopt such alternative mechanisms for extending coverage to individuals, thus the federal rules apply in only twelve states. Twenty-eight of the alternative states are using a high-risk pool to provide coverage. Even in the states following the federal rule, there has been evidence of widespread ignorance of HIPAA protections and some indication that HIPAA has been circumvented by insurers who refuse to pay brokers commissions for selling it, delay processing of applications to cause a break in coverage in excess of the sixty-three days permitted by the statute, or suspend issuance of individual policies during the HIPAA implementation period. Even complying insurers have charged very high rates for HIPAA policies, sometimes exceeding 200 percent of the rates charged for non-HIPAA policies. See U.S.General Accounting Office, Health Insurance Standards: New Federal Law Creates Challenges for Consumers, Insurers, Regulators, GAO/HEHS–98–67 (Feb. 1998); U.S. General Accounting Office, Private Health Insurance: Progress and Challenges in Implementing 1996 Federal Standards, GAO/HEHS–99–100 (1999). HIPAA also requires insurers selling insurance in the individual market to renew coverage at the option of the insured at the expiration of a policy, except under certain circumstances as where the insured has failed to pay premiums. 42 U.S.C. 300gg–42.

Finally, HIPAA also requires insurance companies that sell insurance in the small group market to guarantee availability and renewability to all employers who apply for small group coverage, and to all individuals employed by such employers who opt for coverage on a timely basis. 42 U.S.C.A. §§ 300gg–11, 300gg–12. The legislation does not, however, regulate the rates that insurers may charge employers.

The HIPAA requirement of guaranteed issue to individuals supplements the earlier requirements of COBRA. COBRA applies to private employers and state and local government entities that employ twenty or more employees on a typical business day and that sponsor a group health plan. 29 U.S.C.A. § 1161. COBRA protects "qualified beneficiaries" whose group insurance is terminated because of a "qualifying event." Qualified beneficiaries include covered employees (or, in some circumstances, formerly covered employees) and their spouses and dependent children who were plan beneficiaries on the day before the qualifying event. 29 U.S.C.A. § 1167(3). Qualifying events entitling the employee or spouses and dependent children of an employee to continuation coverage include loss of coverage due to the death of the covered employee; termination of the employee's employment or reduction in hours (not caused by the employee's "gross misconduct"); divorce or legal separation of the covered employee from the employee's spouse; eligibility of the employee for Medicare; or the cessation of dependent child status under the health plan. 29 U.S.C.A. § 1163. Filing of bankruptcy proceedings by an employer is a qualifying event with respect to a retired employee (and the employee's previously covered spouse, dependent child, or surviving spouse) if the employee retired before the elimination of coverage and, with respect to the employee's spouse, dependent child, or surviving spouse, where the employer substantially eliminates coverage within one year of the bankruptcy filing. 29 U.S.C.A. § 1163(6).

Qualified beneficiaries are entitled upon the occurrence of a qualifying event to purchase continuation coverage for up to eighteen months where the qualifying event is termination of work or reduction in hours, or for up to thirty-six months for most other qualifying events. 29 U.S.C.A. § 1162(2). The right to continuation coverage may terminate before the end of the coverage period if the employer ceases to provide group health insurance to any employee; the qualified beneficiary fails to make a timely payment of the plan premium; the qualified beneficiary becomes covered under another group health plan that does not exclude or limit coverage for a preexisting condition; or the qualified beneficiary becomes eligible for Medicare. 29 U.S.C.A. § 1162(2)(B), (C), (D).

COBRA offers some enrollees a significant advantage over the individual insurance guarantees of the HIPAA—beneficiaries need only pay a premium which may not exceed 102 percent of the total cost of the plan for similarly situated beneficiaries who continued to be covered. 29 U.S.C.A. §§ 1162(3), 1164. Where the employer is self-insured, the employer may either make a reasonable estimate of plan cost for similarly situated beneficiaries on an actuarial basis or base the premium on the costs of the preceding determination period adjusted for inflation. 29 U.S.C.A. § 1164(2). Who pays for COBRA coverage: employers, insurers, employees or health insurance consumers? Under what circumstances would a person eligible for COBRA coverage be well advised to decline it and rather seek coverage in the nongroup market? Final regulations implementing COBRA, promulgated in 2001, are found at 26 C.F.R. §§ 59.4980B1–B10.

Notes and Questions

1. Do the following situations involve preexisting condition exclusions subject to HIPAA's limitations? 1) The plan covers cosmetic surgery for accidental injuries, but only for those that occur while the beneficiary is covered by the plan. 2) The plan covers diabetes care without limitations, but imposes a $10,000 lifetime limit on expenditures if the beneficiary was diagnosed with diabetes before joining the plan. 3) Benefits under the plan for pregnancy are only available after a twelve month waiting period. See 26 C.F.R. § 54.9801–3.

2. Congress for the first time in 1996 adopted limited benefit coverage mandates, including a "drive through delivery" bill requiring health plans to offer at least forty-eight hours of hospital coverage for vaginal deliveries, ninety-six hours for C–Sections; and a mental health parity law forbidding health plans from placing lifetime or annual limits on mental health coverage less generous than those placed on medical or surgical benefits. As this book goes to press, Congress is debating the terms under which mental health parity legislation will be extended. In 1998 Congress adopted the Women's Health and Cancer Rights Act, imposing a third mandate requiring health plans that cover mastectomies to also cover breast reconstruction surgery.

Does the drive through delivery bill address a real or imagined problem? If you were a lobbyist representing health plans, how strenuously would you argue against it? What would be your arguments? What are the likely effects of the mental health parity bill? Why is Congress beginning to impose coverage requirements on health plans? Why were these particular coverage requirements chosen?

Problem: Advising under HIPAA and COBRA

Martha Phillips has recently lost her job at Naturalway.com, a short-lived attempt to sell dietary supplements on the web. She was only with the company for ten months, most of its brief existence. She was covered during the ten month period by Naturalway's group health plan. Martha is experienced with web-based sales, and thinks she will soon be again employed. She is quite concerned, however, because she has chronic diabetes and needs to have health insurance coverage. She asks:

1) Does any federal law give her the right to insurance coverage? If so, what would be the terms of the coverage?

2) If she is able to find employment with health insurance coverage, as she hopes, can she be subjected to a preexisting conditions clause that will exclude coverage for her diabetes?

3) If she is able to find employment with health insurance coverage, can she be charged higher rates than other employees because of her diabetes?

B. FEDERAL PROHIBITIONS AGAINST DISCRIMINATION ON THE BASIS OF DISABILITY

Among the most important provisions of the HIPAA are those protecting individuals insured under group policies from discrimination on the basis of health status in terms of health insurance availability or premiums. Persons with chronic or costly diseases, such has AIDS, have faced a particularly difficult time finding health insurance in the individual insurance market, and increasingly in the group insurance market as well. Much has been written on the problem of AIDS and health insurance. Among the many good articles are Michael T. Isbell, AIDS and Access to Care: Lessons for Health Care Reformers, 3 Cornell J. L. & Pub. Pol'y 7 (1993); Randall Bovbjerg, AIDS and Insurance: How Private Health Coverage Relates to HIV/AIDS Infection and to Public Programs, 77 Iowa L. Rev. 1561 (1992); Alan Widiss, To Insure or Not to Insure Persons Infected with the Virus that Causes AIDS, 77 Iowa L. Rev. 1617 (1992); Henry Greeley, AIDS and the American Health Care Financing System, 51 U.Pitt.L.Rev. 73, 96–97 (1989); and Daniel Fox, Financing Health Care for Persons with HIV Infection: Guidelines for State Action, 16 Am.J.L. & Med. 223 (1990).

Does HIPAA completely solve the problems faced by persons with AIDS who seek private insurance coverage for medical care? Consider the following quote from the conference committee report that accompanied the bill:

> It is the intent of the conferees that a plan cannot knowingly be designed to exclude individuals and their dependents on the basis of health status. However, generally applicable terms of the plan may have a disparate impact on individual enrollees. For example, a plan may exclude all coverage of a specific condition, or may include a lifetime cap on all benefits, or a lifetime cap on specific benefits. * * * [S]uch plan characteristics would be permitted as long as they are not directed at individual sick employees or dependents. 142 Cong. Rec. H9473, H9519.

Regulations implementing HIPAA promulgated in 2006 clarify that plans do not have to provide any particular benefits as long as the same benefits are available to all similarly situated individuals, and benefit limitations or cost-sharing obligations are not directed at any particular person based on any health factor. Plans may offer different benefit plan designs to different groups of participants or beneficiaries, but participant groups can only be treated differently on the basis of bona fide employment classifications consistent with the employer's general business practices. Thus full time employees may be offered different benefits than part time, or benefits may vary based on length of service or occupation. Plans may also limit coverage of injuries resulting from participation in dangerous activities (such as bungee jumping), but may not limit coverage for injuries that result from domestic violence or medical conditions (such as injuries resulting from a suicide attempt caused by depression). Finally, health plans may treat individuals with adverse health factors more favorably than others, for example, covering disabled children past the age of twenty-three, when other dependent children would lose coverage. 29 C.F.R. § 2590.702(a)(2), (b), (d) & (g).

Are other legal strategies available for defending persons with disabilities against limitations on access to insurance that are legal under the HIPAA? Are such access limitations defensible when imposed by insurance companies or self-insured employers? Are they necessary?

Prior to the adoption of the HIPAA, the clearest prohibition against discrimination on the basis of health status was found in the Americans with Disabilities Act, which forbids discrimination in the terms, conditions, and privileges of employment, in the use and enjoyment of public accommodations, and by public entities on the basis of disability. The EEOC has in fact obtained settlements in several ADA enforcement actions brought against employers who limited insurance benefits for persons with AIDS. See, discussing the ADA, Michael Zablocki, et al., Americans With Disabilities Act Update, 15 Whittier L. Rev. 177, 181–82 (1994); Note, The Future of Self–Funded Health Plans, 79 Iowa L.Rev. 413, 421–425 (1994); and Lawrence Gostin & Alan Widiss, What's Wrong With the ERISA Vacuum? 269 JAMA 2527 (1993).

When the ADA (42 U.S.C.A. §§ 12101–12113) was adopted in 1990, it was widely believed that the Act would limit the ability of employers and insurers to vary the terms and conditions of insurance coverage on the basis of medical condition. In fact, however, judicial interpretation of the ADA has resulted in it having a very limited impact on health care financing. The following case concerns a long-term disability rather than a health insurance policy, but the issues raised are identical to those at stake in the health insurance setting. As the notes following the case indicate, it is unusually sympathetic to the claimant.

WINSLOW v. IDS LIFE INSURANCE CO.

United States District Court, Minnesota, 1998.
29 F.Supp.2d 557.

DAVIS, DISTRICT JUDGE.

Susan M. Winslow filed this action for declaratory and injunctive relief and for damages under the Americans with Disabilities Act ("ADA"), 42 U.S.C. § 12101 et seq., and the Minnesota Human Rights Act ("MHRA"), Minn.Stat. § 363.01 et seq. when she applied for and was denied long-term disability insurance by IDS Life Insurance Co. due to her current history of treatment for a mental health condition. The matter is before the Court on Defendant's motion for summary judgment which, for the foregoing reasons, is denied in part and granted in part.

Background

On approximately October 27, 1994, Plaintiff Susan Winslow applied to IDS Life Insurance Co. for standard long-term disability insurance or, in the alternative, long-term disability insurance with a rider excluding coverage for periods of disability due to her mental health condition. Plaintiff indicated on her application that she had been treated for mental illness—dysthymia or mild depression—within the past year and was currently taking Zoloft, an anti-depressant. IDS refused both requests for insurance based on its policy of automatically denying long-term disability insurance to applicants who report having received treatment for a mental or nervous condition, regardless of seriousness, within the twelve months prior to application. The IDS policy allows such applicants to be reconsidered for long-term disability insurance after a year has passed since their last treatment for a mental or nervous condition. IDS asserts that its above-stated policy is based on industry-wide claims experience and actuarial data that indicates that the highest number of payments are made for depression-related claims. Plaintiff notes, however, that the IDS policy differs from that in the Paul Revere Underwriting Manual—a manual used by IDS in making other underwriting decisions— which does not require automatic rejection of applicants with current histories of mental or nervous conditions, such as Plaintiff's dysthymia, but instead provides for a long-term disability insurance policy with a longer exclusion period.[ ]

Plaintiff received notice of the denial of her long-term disability insurance application in November 1994 and requested reconsideration. In her request for reconsideration Plaintiff asserted to IDS that she had never been hospitalized or missed work due to her mental health condition and provided corroborative letters from two psychiatrists from whom she had received treatment, affirming that Plaintiff suffered only mild symptoms, which did not manifest themselves in work situations. * * * IDS received Plaintiff's additional documents, and after internal discussions, agreed that denial of Plaintiff's application was appropriate.

* * *

II.   DISABILITY UNDER THE ADA

In order to defeat summary judgment plaintiff Winslow must demonstrate that she is a person with a disability as defined by the ADA and therefore a plaintiff covered by the ADA. The ADA defines "disability" as "(A) a physical or mental impairment that substantially limits one or more of the major life activities of such individual; (B) a record of such an impairment; or (C) being regarded as having such an impairment." 42 U.S.C. § 12102(2)(A)–(C). Winslow does not argue that she meets criteria (A) or (B) of the ADA definition. Instead, Plaintiff asserts that IDS regarded her as disabled and treated her as having "a physical or mental impairment that substantially limits one or more of the major life activities," in this case, her future ability to work.[ ]

* * * Both the ADA and EEOC regulations establish that a plaintiff, such as Winslow, whose claim asserts only that she was regarded by a defendant as having a substantially limiting impairment, need not prove that she in fact suffered such impairment. * * *

Plaintiff claims that the "major life activity" that Defendant perceives as "substantially limited" by her dysthymia is her future ability to work. It is undisputed that work is a "major life activity," which if substantially limited or regarded as substantially limited by a significant impairment qualifies a person as disabled under the ADA.[ ] 29 C.F.R. § 1630.2(i).[ ]

This Court finds, as a matter of law, that when IDS denied Plaintiff Winslow's application for long-term disability insurance based on her depression and anxiety, diagnosed as dysthymia, IDS implicitly considered her to be "impaired" and likely unable to perform "either a class of jobs or a broad range of jobs in various classes" in the future. * * *

Defendant asserts that even if Plaintiff can show that IDS regarded her as likely to suffer a substantially limiting impairment in the future, she has failed to show that IDS regarded her as disabled at the time it denied her application for long-term disability insurance as required by the statutory language of the ADA, which contains no future tense. See 42 U.S.C. § 12102(2)(C) ("regarded as having such an impairment"). * * *

In Doukas v. Metropolitan Life Insurance Company, 1997 WL 833134 (D.N.H.), the court held that "the distinction between present and future limitations [in the ADA] is not dispositive."[ ] In Doukas, Plaintiff Susan Doukas applied for and was denied mortgage disability insurance by MetLife. MetLife based its denial on information in Doukas' application indicating that she had been diagnosed with and was being treated for bipolar disorder and was therefore likely to become totally disabled from work in the future. MetLife moved for summary judgment on the grounds that Doukas did not fall within the ADA definition of disabled because she was not regarded as currently disabled and incapable of working but rather as presenting a future risk of disability. The court denied MetLife's motion, finding that "the 'regarded as' definition of disability seeks to eradicate discrimination based on prejudice or irrational fear. Fear, almost by definition, refers not to actual present conditions, but to anticipated future consequences."[ ] Courts have noted that the perception of impairment is included by Congress within the definition of disabled to combat the effects of " 'archaic attitudes,' erroneous perceptions, and myths that work to the disadvantage of persons with or regarded as having disabilities." * * *

* * * This Court finds the reasoning set forth in Doukas persuasive and holds that the purpose of the ADA requires that ADA protection extend to cover perception of possible future disability.

III. *Applicability of the ADA to Insurance Policies*

Title III of the ADA provides:

> No individual shall be discriminated against on the basis of disability in the full and equal enjoyment of the goods, services, facilities, privileges, advantages, or accommodations of any place of public accommodation by any person who owns, leases (or leases to), or operates a place of public accommodation.

42 U.S.C. § 12182(a). Section 12181(7) provides an illustrative list of entities considered public accommodations for the purposes of Title III. See Parker v. Metropolitan Life Ins. Co., 121 F.3d 1006, 1010 (6th Cir.1997); Carparts Distribution Center, Inc. v. Automotive Wholesaler's Association of New England, Inc., 37 F.3d 12, 19 (1st Cir.1994). The issue before this Court is whether "public accommodations" are limited to actual physical structures

or whether Title III of the ADA prohibits more than physical impediments to public accommodations for the disabled.

This issue is one of first impression for the Eighth Circuit and has been decided only by the First and Sixth Circuits, which split on the matter, and a smattering of district courts, some of which have followed the First Circuit in Carparts and others of which have adopted the reasoning of the Sixth Circuit in Parker.

In Parker, the Sixth Circuit reviewed the regulations applicable to Title III of the ADA to interpret "places" of public accommodation and found that a "place," as defined by 28 C.F.R. § 36.104, is "a facility, operated by a private entity, whose operations affect commerce and fall within at least one of the twelve 'public accommodation' categories."[ ] A "facility," in turn, is defined by 28 C.F.R. § 36.104 as "all or any portion of buildings, structures, sites complexes, equipment, rolling stock or other conveyances, roads, walks, passageways, parking lots, or other real or personal property, including the site where the building, property, structure, or equipment is located." Parker, 121 F.3d at 1011. The court concluded that the plain meaning of the statutory language and the applicable regulations is that places of public accommodation are limited to physical places open to public access.[ ]

In Carparts, the First Circuit reached the opposite conclusion, determining that "public accommodations" are not limited to actual physical structures. Kotev v. First Colony Life Insurance Company, 927 F.Supp. 1316 (C.D Cal.1996) followed the Carparts holding and addressed the issue at greater length. Kotev noted that the limited interpretation of "public accommodation" adopted by the Parker court would contravene the broadly stated purpose of the ADA to "provide a clear and comprehensive national mandate for the elimination of discrimination against individuals with disabilities . . . and invoke the sweep of congressional authority . . . in order to address the major areas of discrimination faced day-to-day by people with disabilities."[ ]

"Disability" under the ADA includes both physical and mental impairments as well as those with records of or regarded as having such impairments. See 42 U.S.C. § 12102(2)(A)–(C). By restricting "public accommodations" to include only physical structures, the protection under the ADA for individuals with mental disabilities would be virtually negated, absent circumstances in which a physical structure denied access to the mentally impaired.[ ]

Especially relevant to the present case is ADA statutory language that would be rendered irrelevant if Title III were held to apply only to physical access to public accommodations:

> (i) the imposition or application of eligibility criteria that screen out * * * an individual with a disability * * * from fully and equally enjoying any goods, services, facilities, privileges, advantages, or accommodations, unless such criteria can be shown to be necessary . . .

> (ii) a failure to make reasonable modifications in policies, practices, or procedures, when such modifications are necessary to afford such goods, services, facilities, privileges, advantages, or accommodations to individuals with disabilities . . .

* * *

42 U.S.C. § 12182(b)(2)(A)(i)–(iii)[ ]. Also rendered superfluous by such a narrow interpretation would be the Title III provision for injunctive relief set forth in 42 U.S.C. § 12188(a)(2) that "shall also include requiring the . . . modification of policy."

Further supporting the conclusion reached by Kotev and a growing number of district courts (that ADA Title III applies to the provision of insurance policies) is the "Safe Harbor" provision of Title III, specifically addressing insurance. * * * The Safe Harbor provision states, in relevant part:

> Subchapters I through III of this chapter and Title IV of this Act shall not be construed to prohibit or restrict—

> (1) an insurer, hospital or medical service company, health maintenance organization, or any agent, or entity that administers benefit plans, or similar organizations from underwriting risks, classifying risks, or administering such risks that are based on or not inconsistent with State law;

> Paragraphs (1), (2), and (3) shall not be used as a subterfuge to evade the purposes of subchapter[s] I and III of this chapter. 42 U.S.C. § 12201(c).

Courts have concluded, and this Court agrees, that the Safe Harbor provision would be superfluous if "insurers could never be liable under Title III for conduct such as discriminatory denial of insurance coverage."[ ]

* * * The DOJ [in its legislative history of the ADA also] interprets Title III as prohibiting "differential treatment of individuals with disabilities in insurance offered by public accommodations unless the differences are justified."

* * *

Based on the legislative history, the DOJ interpretation of Title III of the ADA, and the reasoning adopted by a growing number of district courts, this Court finds that Title III of the ADA is applicable to insurance policies and not limited to access to actual physical structures.

A.   The McCarran–Ferguson Act

Defendant argues that the McCarran–Ferguson Act, 15 U.S.C. § 1012 et seq., precludes application of the ADA to insurance policies because Title III is not intended to regulate the business of private insurance carriers. The McCarran–Ferguson Act provides, in relevant part:

> No Act of Congress shall be construed to invalidate, impair or supersede any law enacted by any State for the purpose of regulating the business of insurance . . . unless such Act is specifically related to the business of insurance.

15 U.S.C. § 1012(b)[ ]. The McCarran–Ferguson Act bars the application of a federal statute if:

> (1) the statute does not specifically relate to the business of insurance; (2) a state statute has been enacted for the purpose of regulating

the business of insurance; and (3) the federal statute would invalidate, impair, or supersede the state statute.

* * *

This Court identifies two fundamental provisions of the ADA that specifically relate to the business of insurance. The Court finds that the "subterfuge" provision of the ADA, see *supra*, 42 U.S.C. § 12201(c), which prohibits the use of the Safe Harbor provision to evade the purpose of Title III of the ADA is a statutory provision specifically related to the business of insurance. * * * The Court also interprets the inclusion of an "insurance office" as an entity considered a public accommodation for the purposes of Title III of the ADA, see 42 U.S.C. § 12181(7)(F), as an explicit indication that the ADA is intended to specifically relate to the business of insurance.

* * *

The McCarran–Ferguson Act is a form of inverse preemption, so principles defining when state remedies conflict with ... federal law are pertinent in deciding when federal rules " 'invalidate, impair, or supersede' state rules."[ ] * * * "[D]uplication is not conflict '[however] and * * * as a general rule,' state and federal rules that are substantively identical but differ in penalty do not conflict with or displace each other," * * *. This court * * * holds that the McCarran–Ferguson Act does not "invalidate, impair, or supersede" the relevant Minnesota statutes and does not bar plaintiff's ADA claims.

IV. THE SAFE HARBOR PROVISION

As indicated above, the ADA provides a Safe Harbor provision for insurance providers under the ADA. See *supra*, 42 U.S.C. § 12201(c). Under the Safe Harbor provision, the risk underwriting engaged in by insurance companies must be based on or not inconsistent with state law.[ ] The subterfuge provision, see *supra* 42 U.S.C. § 12201(c), provides, however, that even if an insurer's practices are consistent with applicable state law, they can still violate the ADA if plaintiff demonstrates that the insurance policies are a subterfuge to evade the purpose of the ADA.[ ] Thus, the Court must perform a two-part analysis to determine whether the IDS policies in question violate the Safe Harbor provision of the ADA: (1) is the eligibility criteria employed by IDS based on and consistent with state law; and (2) is the eligibility criteria a subterfuge to evade the purposes of the ADA.

Minn. Stat. § 72A.20 provides in relevant part:

> Subd. 9. Making or permitting any unfair discrimination between individuals of the same class and of essentially the same hazard in the amount of premium, policy fees, or rates charged for any policy or contract of accident or health insurance or in the benefits payable thereunder, or in any terms or conditions of such contract, or in any other manner whatever, or in making or permitting the rejection of an individual's application for accident or health insurance coverage, as well as the determination of the rate class for such individual, on the basis of a disability, shall constitute an unfair method of competition and an unfair and deceptive act or practice, unless the claims experience and actuarial

projections and other data establish significant and substantial differences in class rates because of the disability.

Subd. 19. No life or health insurance company doing business in this state shall engage in any selection or underwriting process unless the insurance company establishes beforehand substantial data, actuarial projections, or claims experience which support the underwriting standards used by the insurance company. * * *

Minn.Stat. § 72A.20, subd. 9, 19.

IDS categorically denies long-term disability insurance to any applicant who has been treated for a mental health condition within the past year, allowing the applicant to be reconsidered after one year has passed since the last treatment. To comply with Minnesota law, IDS must justify such eligibility criteria with claims experience, actuarial projections, or other data to "establish significant and substantial differences in class rates because of the disability."[ ]

IDS asserts that it has presented such justification for its eligibility criteria and therefore does not violate state law. The Court acknowledges that IDS presents specific industry data based on claims experience and actuarial projections that show a dramatic increase in payments on long-term disability insurance claims due to mental health and nervous disorders. Plaintiff counters that while Defendant establishes that claims for disability due to mental or nervous conditions have increased since 1989, Defendant fails to demonstrate that individuals receiving treatment for mental or nervous conditions at or near the time of application for insurance are more likely to file claims under their long-term disability insurance. Furthermore, Plaintiff notes that the Paul Revere Underwriting Manual includes various impairments, such as dysthymia, and establishes procedures for processing applications from individuals with such impairments without recommending total denial of insurance for such applicants. * * * Thus, Plaintiff claims that a genuine issue of material fact exists as to whether IDS' long-term disability insurance eligibility criteria conforms to sound actuarial principles, claims experience, or substantial data as required by Minnesota state law. The Court agrees and denies summary judgment on the matter.

Defendant also asserts that it is entitled to Safe Harbor protection under Title III of the ADA because its eligibility criteria are not a subterfuge. See *supra*, 42 U.S.C. § 12201(c). * * * As this Court has determined that a genuine issue of material fact exists as to whether IDS eligibility criteria violates Minnesota law, the Court need not pass on the issue as to whether the criteria is a subterfuge of the ADA.

V.   DISABILITY-BASED DISTINCTION UNDER THE ADA

Plaintiff asserts that the IDS policy of denying long-term disability insurance to all applicants having received mental health treatment within the past year is founded on a disability-based distinction violative of the ADA. Courts have found that broad-based distinctions that distinguish between mental and physical health conditions do not qualify as illicit disability-based distinctions under the ADA because the ADA is only applicable to discrimination against disabled persons compared to non-disabled persons, not discrimination among the disabled.[ ] [EEOC Interim Enforcement Guidelines also permit broad-based distinctions between mental and physical conditions for health care benefits. Ed.]

The aforementioned cases and the EEOC Interim Guidance, however, address disability-based discrimination among the disabled that affects the quality and extent of coverage offered to one class of disabled as compared to another and do not address the categorical denial of access to insurance coverage to a class of disabled individuals. When courts have addressed the exclusion of a class of disabled from an insurance plan, they have found such exclusions violative of the ADA.[ ]

Legislative history of Title III of the ADA further supports the proposition that while disability-based distinctions in an insurance policy's terms are permissible under the ADA, a policy to deny insurance coverage categorically to mentally disabled is unacceptable. * * *

This Court finds that as Defendant's policy of denying long-term disability insurance to those treated for mental conditions within the past year denies said individuals access to insurance coverage, the policy is founded on a disability-based discrimination violative of the ADA.

VI. MINNESOTA HUMAN RIGHTS ACT

[The court also found that IDS denial violated the Minnesota Human Rights Act, which is similar to the ADA, but concluded that punitive damages were not available under that Act, because the defendant's conduct did not demonstrate "willful indifference" to the plaintiff's rights.]

Notes and Questions

Title I of the ADA prohibits discrimination "against a qualified individual with a disability because of the disability of such individual in regard to * * * [the] terms, conditions, and privileges of employment." 42 U.S.C.A. § 12112. Discrimination prohibited by the statute extends to "fringe benefits." 42 U.S.C.A. § 12112(b)(4); 29 C.F.R. § 1630.4(f). Title II similarly prohibits discrimination by public entities. 42 U.S.C.A. § 12132. Title III proscribes discrimination "on the basis of disability in the full and equal enjoyment of the goods, services, facilities, privileges, advantages, or accommodations of any place of public accommodation * * *." 42 U.S.C.A. § 12182. "Public accommodation" is specifically defined to include an "insurance office." 42 U.S.C.A. § 12181(7)(F). Finally, Title V of the Act contains a specific "safe harbor" providing that the ADA is not to be construed to restrict insurers, HMOs, employers, plans or administrators from "underwriting risks, classifying risks, or administering such risks that are based on or not inconsistent with State law," as long as the entity does not use this provision "as a subterfuge to evade the purposes" of the ADA. 42 U.S.C.A. § 12201(c).

The ADA would seem to prohibit insurers and employers administering benefit plans from imposing coverage terms and conditions that discriminate against persons with particular disabilities. Cases have been brought under the ADA, therefore, challenging policies that provided less coverage for treatment of mental illnesses than for treatment of physical conditions, Rogers v. Department of Health and Envtl. Control, 174 F.3d 431 (4th Cir.1999); Ford v. Schering–Plough Corp., 145 F.3d 601 (3d Cir.1998); Fletcher v. Tufts University, 367 F.Supp.2d 99 (D.Mass.2005); that capped coverage for AIDS but not for other conditions, Doe v. Mutual of Omaha Ins. Co., 179 F.3d 557 (7th Cir.1999); or that excluded coverage for particular services, like heart transplants, Lenox v. Health-wise of Kentucky, Ltd., 149 F.3d 453 (6th Cir.1998); or infertility, Krauel v. Iowa Methodist Medical Center, 95 F.3d 674 (8th Cir.1996).

Although some of these cases have succeeded, they have encountered increasingly serious obstacles. First, most courts have held that the ADA does not require employers or insurers to offer any particular form of coverage, but merely prohibits them from offering different terms and conditions of coverage to disabled persons than those offered to nondisabled persons. EEOC v. Staten Island Sav. Bank, 207 F.3d 144 (2nd Cir.2000); Weyer v. Twentieth Century Fox Film Corp., 198 F.3d 1104 (9th Cir.2000); Doe v. Mut. of Omaha Ins. Co., 179 F.3d 557 (7th Cir.1999); Ford v. Schering–Plough Corp., 145 F.3d 601 (3d Cir.1998). These courts hold that the ADA does not demand that all disabilities be treated similarly, but only that disabled persons not be disfavored in comparison to nondisabled persons. Providing different coverage for different conditions, more-over, is not even necessarily prohibited unless the condition itself is a disability or unless discrimination in coverage of a particular condition disproportionately affects disabled persons. By this reasoning, an employer or insurer who offers limited coverage for mental illness and unlimited coverage for physical conditions is in ADA compliance, as long as it offers the same terms and conditions of coverage to all of its employees, regardless of disability. Rogers v. Department of Health and Envtl. Control, 174 F.3d 431 (4th Cir.1999). With respect to the specific problem of differential coverage of mental and physical conditions, courts have relied further on the limited scope of the Mental Health Parity Act of 1997 (mentioned above) to support their position that Congress did not intend the ADA to bring about sweeping parity in treatment for all conditions. Lewis v. Kmart Corp., 180 F.3d 166 (4th Cir.1999); Parker v. Metro. Life Ins. Co., 121 F.3d 1006, 1017–18 (6th Cir.1997) (en banc). One court has held, interpreting the Supreme Court's opinion in Olmstead v. L.C., 527 U.S. 581, 119 S.Ct. 2176, 144 L.Ed.2d 540 (1999), that the ADA does prohibit differential treatment of mental disabilities, but that decision was vacated by the circuit en banc, Johnson v. K Mart Corp., 273 F.3d 1035 (11th Cir.2001), and its interpretation of *Olmstead* has been rejected by other courts. *Weyer, supra,* 198 F.3d at 1117–18. Two district courts, however, have followed *Johnson* in holding that treating mental conditions differently from physical conditions can violate the ADA. Fletcher v. Tufts Univ., 367 F.Supp.2d 99, 109–14 (D.Mass.2005); Iwata v. Intel Corp., 349 F.Supp.2d 135, 147–54 (D.Mass.2004).

Second, there is considerable debate as to when and whether the ADA applies to insurance policies. Though Title III clearly covers insurance offices, several courts have held that Title III only applies to physical places, i.e. the physical accessibility of insurance offices, and does not extend to the terms and conditions of the products the insurers offer independent of these places. Weyer v. Twentieth Century Fox Film Corp., 198 F.3d 1104 (9th Cir.2000); McNeil v. Time Ins., Co., 205 F.3d 179 (5th Cir.2000); Ford v. Schering–Plough Corp., 145 F.3d 601 (3d Cir.1998); Lenox v. Healthwise of Ky., Ltd., 149 F.3d 453 (6th Cir.1998); Parker v. Metro. Life Ins. Co., 121 F.3d 1006 (6th Cir.1997) (en banc). The EEOC Guide-lines and a number of other courts, on the other hand, have held that Title III might extend to the contents of insurance policies as well. Doe v. Mut. of Omaha Ins. Co. 179 F.3d 557, 558–59 (7th Cir.1999); Pallozzi v. Allstate Life Ins. Co., 198 F.3d 28 (2d Cir.1999); Carparts Distribution Ctr., Inc. v. Automotive Wholesaler's Ass'n of New England, 37 F.3d 12 (1st Cir.1994); Fletcher v. Tufts Univ., 367 F.Supp.2d 99, 114–115 (D.Mass.2005). See Jeffrey S. Manning, Are Insurance Companies Liable Under the Americans With Disabilities Act? 88 Cal.L.Rev. 607 (2000); Jill L. Schultz, Note: The Impact of Title III of the Americans with

Disabilities Act on Employer–Provided Insurance Plans: Is the Insurance Company Subject to Liability? 56 Wash. & Lee L. Rev 343 (1999). Of course, if insurance is offered through an employer, discrimination is prohibited under Title I even if the insurer's practices are not covered by Title III, although the employer, not the insurer, would be the proper defendant.

Third, several courts have read Title V's insurance "safe harbor" broadly to protect insurer practices that are not intentional stratagems to effectuate discrimination, following Supreme Court precedent in interpreting the term "subterfuge" in the ADEA in Public Employees Retirement System of Ohio v. Betts, 492 U.S. 158, 109 S.Ct. 2854, 106 L.Ed.2d 134 (1989). See Ford v. Schering–Plough Corp., 145 F.3d 601 (3d Cir.1998) and Krauel v. Iowa Methodist Med. Ctr., 95 F.3d 674, 678–9 (8th Cir.1996). Other courts, however, have required actuarial support for treating different conditions differently, particularly when the insurance practice is also suspect under state law. Morgenthal v. American Tel. and Tel. Co., 1999 WL 187055 (S.D.N.Y.1999); Chabner v. United of Omaha Life Ins. Co., 994 F.Supp. 1185 (N.D.Cal.1998).

Fourth, the McCarran–Ferguson Act, discussed earlier, is emerging as a brooding presence in ADA insurance litigation. Some courts are reluctant to find that Congress meant to turn over to the federal courts the job of regulating insurance underwriting practices, which has traditionally fallen to the states, in the absence of excruciatingly clear Congressional intent to accomplish this result—intent that is lacking in the ADA setting. Doe v. Mutual of Omaha Ins. Co., 179 F.3d 557 (7th Cir.1999). Other courts, like that in the principal case, reject this position. Pallozzi v. Allstate Life Ins. Co., 198 F.3d 28 (2d Cir.1999).

Finally, a number of courts have limited Title I ADA actions to current employees, contending that former employees, such as retirees, have no rights under the statute. See, e.g. EEOC v. CNA Ins. Cos., 96 F.3d 1039, 1045 (7th Cir.1996). But see, Castellano v. City of N.Y., 142 F.3d 58 (2d Cir.1998).

The ADA is far from dead as a means of challenging egregious insurance practices. The absolute refusal of an employer or insurer to provide health insurance on the basis of disability, for example, would violate the Act. Nevertheless, the Act is increasingly proving a disappointment for advocates who had hoped that it would lead to more equitable and rational insurance coverage.

C. OTHER ANTIDISCRIMINATION LAWS

A number of other federal laws prohibit discrimination in health insurance on other bases, though their impact is relatively modest. First, an employer covered by Title VII of the Civil Rights Act cannot treat medical costs associated with pregnancy or childbirth different than other medical costs covered by its health insurance plan. Title VII prohibits sex discrimination and the Pregnancy Discrimination Act of 1978 (PDA) defines sex discrimination to include treatment of pregnancy, childbirth, or related medical conditions differently from other medical conditions under fringe benefit programs. 42 U.S.C.A. § 2000e(k). Maternity-related medical conditions must, therefore, be treated the same as other medical conditions under group health insurance with respect to terms of reimbursement (including payment maximums); deductibles, copayments, coinsurance, and out-of-pocket maximums; preexisting condition limitations; extension of benefits following termination of employment; and limitations on freedom of choice. See 29 C.F.R. App. to Pt. 1604, Questions 25–29. The Eighth Circuit, however, has held that the

PDA does not require coverage of fertility services. Saks v. Franklin Covey Co., 316 F.3d 337 (2d Cir.2003); Krauel v. Iowa Methodist Med. Ctr., 95 F.3d 674 (8th Cir.1996). The Eighth Circuit has also recently rejected the position of the EEOC and held that neither the PDA nor Title VII require employee benefit plans to cover contraceptives. In re Union Pacific Railroad Employment Practices Litigation, 479 F.3d 936 (8th Cir.2007).

Second, the Age Discrimination in Employment Act (ADEA) 29 U.S.C.A. §§ 621–630, limits the ability of covered employers to discriminate among employees with respect to the provision of health insurance benefits. The Older Workers Benefit Protection Act of 1990 amended the ADEA to clarify that discrimination in the provision of benefits, including health insurance benefits is prohibited. 29 U.S.C.A. § 630(l). In 2000, the Third Circuit held that an employer who offers Medicare-eligible retirees inferior benefits to retirees who are not eligible for Medicare was in violation of the ADEA unless its practice was protected by a safe harbor in the Act, which permits employers offering bona fide benefit plans to offer older workers fewer benefits or to charge older workers more for benefits in voluntary contributory plans (as long as the proportion of total premium charged the employee does not change with age), if the distinctions are justified by cost data and the employer does not pay less than it does for benefit plans for younger workers. Erie County Retirees Assoc. v. County of Erie, 220 F.3d 193 (3d Cir.2000), applying 29 U.S.C.A. § 623(f)(2)(B)(1); 29 C.F.R. § 1625.10. In April of 2004 the EEOC issued a rule stating that employers could reduce or eliminate health benefits for Medicare-eligible beneficiaries without violating the ADEA. 68 Fed. Reg. 41542 (2003). The EEOC rule was upheld by American Ass'n of Retired Persons v. EEOC, 489 F.3d 558 (3d Cir. 2007).

Third, § 105 of the Internal Revenue Code limits the ability of self-insured employer health plans to discriminate in favor of highly-compensated individuals. 26 U.S.C.A. § 105(h), 26 C.F.R. §§ 1–105–1 through 1–105–11(c), while § 125 proscribes discrimination in favor of highly-compensated individuals by tax-subsidized cafeteria plans. 26 U.S.C.A. § 125(b) & (c).

Do any of these laws limit significantly the ability of insurers to discriminate against the unhealthy? See Mary Crossley, Discrimination Against the Unhealthy in Health Insurance, 54 U. Kan. L. Rev. 73 (2005).

Problem: Private Cost Containment

You are an attorney representing Amtech Inc., which employs about 1,500 employees. Since its founding in 1990, Amtech's business has grown rapidly and profits have been high. Amtech has traditionally offered generous salaries and an extensive benefits plan to attract the well-trained and educated employees it needs. During the last two years, however, growth and profits have flagged. Moreover, Amtech has recently been purchased on a highly-leveraged basis and must cut costs to service its high debt. Finally, last year the premiums of Amtech's group health plan, which it has always purchased from a commercial insurer, increased dramatically. The new management has decided, therefore, that action is necessary to control corporate costs generally and health care costs in particular.

The group health plan that Amtech has offered its employees since its inception was a traditional indemnity insurance plan. Individual coverage has been free to employees. Family coverage has been offered subject to payment of a small premium, which has risen slowly to its present level of about $100.00 a month. The health plan covered basic hospitalization on a first dollar basis. It paid hospitals directly on a reasonable charge basis. Physician services were covered on an indemnity basis, subject to a $250.00 deductible for family coverage and a ten percent coinsurance payment for which the employee was responsible. There was no maximum for plan benefits, nor was there a maximum out-of-pocket expenditure limit. Prescription drugs were also covered subject to twenty percent coinsurance. Claims were subject to utilization review, but rarely denied.

Amtech's benefits manager has devised the following plan for controlling benefit's costs: Amtech will offer its employees a triple option. Employees may opt for coverage through an HMO, a provider-sponsored PPO, or a conventional indemnity plan with utilization review. They must make their choice of plans within two months of the introduction of the new benefits scheme, and will only be able to change plans once a year during a one month open enrollment period.

Amtech will enter into a competitive bidding process with the five HMOs currently operating in the area, and will select the one that offers it the lowest price for coverage similar in breadth to the existing conventional plan. Employees who choose the HMO option will have to pay no more for coverage than they do currently, but will be strictly limited to the HMO for medical care and receive no payment for care provided outside of the HMO, even in emergencies.

Amtech will also offer to contract directly with Community Memorial, a large hospital located near Amtech's plant to provide care to its employees. Initial contacts with Community Memorial, which has recently experienced a sharp drop in occupancy, indicate that it is very interested in such a contract and would be willing to offer a substantial discount from its normal charges. Community Memorial will identify primary care physicians and specialists with privileges at Community Memorial to participate in the plan on a contract basis, and negotiate discounts with them. Primary care physicians will operate as "gatekeepers," i.e. access to specialists will only be available upon referral from one of the plan's primary care physicians.

The Community Memorial plan will provide for care with cost-sharing terms similar to those now in place under the current conventional plan. Plan enrollees can receive care out-of-plan (that is, they can choose care from a specialist or hospital not affiliated with the plan), but will be responsible for a $500 deductible and thirty percent coinsurance for out-of-plan care.

Third, Amtech will also continue to offer a plan identical to its current conventional contract, raising the deductible to $500 per individual and raising the coinsurance amount to twenty percent for physician's services and five percent for hospitalization. Amtech will offer this coverage on a self-funded basis, renegotiating its contract with the current insurer as an administrative services only contract. Amtech will purchase a $500,000 deductible reinsurance policy for coverage for which it is at risk.

Coverage for prescription drugs under all three options will be provided through a plan administered by a pharmacy benefits management company and subject to a ten dollar copayment for generic drugs and twenty dollar copayment for name brand. Only drugs on a formulary maintained by the pharmacy benefits manager will be covered. Mental health and substance abuse benefits will also be covered separately under all three plans through a managed behavioral care plan. Mental health and substance abuse benefits will be capped at $10,000 a year.

Amtech will contract with a utilization management firm to provide preadmission and length of stay review for hospitalization and preprocedure review for surgery under the PPO and conventional plans. Unapproved care will not be covered. The utilization management contract will establish performance goals, including denial of about five percent of claims per year, given estimates from the literature that the incidence of unnecessary care is much higher than this. All three plan contracts also provide that "experimental treatment" is not covered (the term is not defined) and that the plan administrator may deny payment for unnecessary care at its own discretion. Decisions of the plan administrator in either event are reviewable only through binding arbitration.

All plans will be subject to a preexisting conditions exclusion for new employees, or for existing employees who have not previously enrolled in a plan but do so for the first time. Under this exclusion, the plan will not cover any expenditures attributable to medical conditions for which the employee received treatment or for which treatment was recommended during the six month period preceding the employee's request for coverage. The exclusion will last for the first year of coverage.

Regardless of the employee's choice of plan, Amtech will only pay an employer contribution equal to that it must make for the HMO plan. (It will separately cover the mental health and pharmacy benefits without required employee contributions). Any additional premium costs required for coverage under the PPO or conventional plan have to be paid for by employees. Employees whose medical costs exceed 500 percent of the average medical expenditures incurred per employee in any particular year will have their premiums increased by 100 percent the following year.

Amtech asks you to review the proposal and identify any potential legal problems under federal law, or under the Massachusetts law found in the previous chapter. Comment on any potential problems you see with the plan and make suggestions as to how it could be improved.

Chapter 8

PUBLIC HEALTH CARE FINANCING PROGRAMS: MEDICARE AND MEDICAID

I. INTRODUCTION

Government provision or financing of health care has a long history in the United States. The first federal medical program was established in 1798 to provide care for sick seamen in the coastal trade. State hospitals for the mentally ill and local public hospitals were well established by the mid-nineteenth century.

Today, government at all levels finances a plethora of health care institutions and programs. In 2006, direct government health care financing programs accounted for $970.3 billion, 46 percent, of total national expenditures on personal health care. The federal government provides health care to millions of veterans in 1400 veterans' hospitals, clinics, and nursing facilities; 5.5 million members of the military and their dependents through the TRICARE program; 1.5 million Native Americans in over 600 facilities run by the Indian Health Service; disabled coal miners through the Black Lung program; and a variety of special groups through block grants to the states for maternal and child health, alcohol and drug abuse treatment, mental health, preventive health, and primary care. States provide health care both through traditional programs like state mental hospitals, state university hospitals, and workers' compensation, but also increasingly through a variety of newer programs intended to shore up the tattered safety net, including insurance pools for the high-risk uninsured, pharmaceutical benefit programs, and programs to provide health insurance for the poor uninsured. County and local governments operate local hospitals. Federal, state, and local governments provide comparatively generous health insurance programs for their own employees and less generous health care programs for their prisoners (the only Americans constitutionally entitled to government-funded health care). If one adds to the cost of direct government health care programs the cost of government employee health benefits and tax subsidies that support private health benefits, tax-financed health care spending in the United States amounts to sixty percent of total health care spending. See Steffie Woolhandler and David Himmelstein, Paying For National Health Insurance—And Not Getting It, Health Affairs, July/Aug. 2002, at 88, 91, 93.

By far the largest public health care programs, however, are the federal Medicare program and the state and federal Medicaid program, which respectively spent about $401.3 billion and $310.6 billion in 2006. This chapter focuses on these two programs, although it also briefly discusses the State Children's Health Insurance Program, established in 1997 to provide health insurance for poor children.

For the past decade, the health care reform debate at the federal level has focused primarily on the future of Medicare and Medicaid. There are several reasons why this debate has focused on these programs and why it has been so passionate and contentious. First, Medicare and Medicaid policy have been driven by federal budget policy. Together the two programs consume over 20 percent of the federal budget. Moreover, if one excludes from consideration the costs of defense, Social Security, and the national debt—all of which are more or less protected from budget cuts at this time—Medicare and Medicaid consume over forty percent of what remains of the federal budget. Medicaid is also one of the largest, and fastest growing, items in state budgets. Congress is very aware of the cost of these programs.

Second, growth in the Medicare program threatens not only to continue to claim a large slice of the federal budget, but also ultimately to overwhelm the financing mechanisms that currently support it. The Part A trust fund (which funds the hospital insurance part of Medicare and is in turn funded by payroll taxes) is currently projected to go into deficit status in 2019. Part B expenditures (which cover the services of physicians and other professionals, as well as other non-institutional care), three quarters of which are covered by federal general revenue funds, are growing even faster than Part A expenditures. The financing of the program is projected to become even more problematic as a huge group of baby-boomers becomes eligible for Medicare in the first half the 21st century. By 2030, Medicare will be responsible for the health care of twenty-two percent of the American population, compared to fourteen percent today. By 2050, moreover, there will be 2.2 workers for every Medicare beneficiary compared to today's 3.8 to one ratio.

Third, debates about how to reform the programs touch repeatedly upon issues that divide policy makers sharply along ideological lines. Can costs be most effectively controlled through regulatory or market strategies? Should Medicare remain available to all beneficiaries equally, or should it be means tested in some way? Should the financing of health care services for the poor be a federal or state responsibility? Should poor persons have an entitlement to health care coverage, or should states have discretion to limit access? Or should the states simply receive block grants from the federal government for health care?

Finally, Medicare and Medicaid together insure about a quarter of the American population, including one of the most politically active segments of the American populace (the elderly). They also affect immediately the fortunes of most health care providers, who are invariably contributors to political campaigns. Politicians are acutely aware, therefore, of the existence and the exigencies of these programs.

To understand the debates raging around these programs, we must first understand how the programs work. Anyone designing or seeking to understand a public health care financing program must consider several basic questions.

First, who receives the program's benefits? Are the targeted recipients characterized by economic need, a particular disease, advanced age, disability, residence in a particular geographic jurisdiction, employment in a certain industry, or status as an enrollee and contributor to a social insurance fund? From these questions others follow: Who in fact receives most of the program's benefits? Whom does the program leave out? Why are some groups included and others excluded? Also, should beneficiaries receive an entitlement or should coverage otherwise be subject to governmental discretion?

Second, what benefits will be provided? Should the program stress institutional services such as hospitalization or nursing home care or non-institutional alternatives such as home health care, or should it encourage preventive care? Should the program be limited to services commonly covered by private insurance like hospital and physician care, or should it also cover services such as dental care and eyeglasses that private insurance covers less often because their use is more predictable and middle class insureds can afford to pay for them out of pocket? These services may be inaccessible to the poor unless the program covers them. Should the program cover medically controversial services, such as care provided by chiropractors or midwives? Should a public program cover socially controversial services such as abortion or treatment for erectile dysfunction? Should it cover services that provide relatively small marginal benefits at a very high cost, such as some organ transplants or some last ditch cancer therapies? Finally, how can the benefits package be kept up to date? In particular, how should it evaluate new technologies as they become available?

Third, how should the program provide or pay for benefits? Should it pay private professionals and institutions to deliver the services, as do Medicare and Medicaid, or should it deliver services itself directly, as does the Veterans' Administration and community health centers? Should it purchase services through "vendor payments" based on cost or charge, as Medicare used to, or through an administered price system, as Medicare does now for most services, or on a capitated basis through managed care plans, as Medicare does through parts C and D and most state Medicaid plans do for many recipients? Alternatively, should beneficiaries simply be given vouchers and be expected to purchase their own insurance in the private market? Should public health insurance programs be defined-contribution or defined-benefit programs? Should recipients be expected to share in the costs through coinsurance or deductibles?

Who should play what role in administering the program? Should the program be run by the federal, state, or local government? Should policy be set by the legislature or by an administrative agency (or by the courts)? Should payments to providers be administered by the government or by private contractors? Should program beneficiaries (or providers) have rights enforceable in court, or should the government retain unreviewable discretion in running the program? If rights are recognized, should these rights be enforceable in state or federal court, or perhaps only through administrative proceedings?

How should the program be financed? Through payroll taxes, income taxes, consumption taxes, or premiums? By state or federal taxes? Should taxes be earmarked (hypothecated) for health care, or should a program be funded through general revenue funds? If premiums play a role, should they be means tested?

This chapter will explore each of these issues with respect first to the Medicare and then to the Medicaid and SCHIP programs.

As you consider these major questions, keep in mind several other themes. First, notice the fragmentation and disconnectedness of our public health care financing programs. Unlike some other nations, we do not have a single public system creating a safety net for all of society, but rather a patchwork of programs, creating a variety of safety nets, some higher and some lower, many fairly tattered, and none catching everyone. Whom do the safety nets miss? What problems does this fragmented system create? What opportunities does it offer?

Second, notice who, other than covered populations of patients, benefits from federal and state programs. Consider which providers benefit most from public programs. Note the role Medicare and Medicaid have played in financing medical education or in subsidizing rural hospitals and safety net providers, such as inner city hospitals. Consider how providers position their operations to maximize their benefits from public programs, and how the mix of health care services in this country reflects the policies of these programs.

II. MEDICARE

BELLEVUE HOSPITAL CENTER v. LEAVITT

United States Court of Appeals, Second Circuit, 2006.
443 F.3d 163.

KATZMANN, CIRCUIT JUDGE.

Seventy-six hospitals, plaintiffs-appellants here, challenge the Department of Health and Humans Services' ("HHS") implementation of a statutory requirement that the agency adjust hospitals' reimbursements for the costs of administering care to Medicare recipients to reflect "differences in hospital wage levels" across "geographic area[s]." 42 U.S.C. § 1395ww(d)(3)(E)(I).

For more than two decades, HHS has divided the nation into geographic areas for these purposes by adopting the Metropolitan Statistical Areas ("MSAs") formulated by the Office of Management and Budget ("OMB"). Most recently, in 2004, it adopted the version of the MSAs released by OMB in 2003. Compared with previous iterations, the New York City MSA was slightly expanded and now includes certain additional hospitals in northern New Jersey. Because the New Jersey hospitals' wages are somewhat lower, the average wage level in the MSA dropped, along with the wage adjustment for hospitals in that MSA. Plaintiffs allege they will receive $812 million less in reimbursements over the next ten years than they would have under their former wage adjustment.

* * *

The Medicare program, established by Title XVIII of the Social Security Act, 42 U.S.C. § 1395 et seq., pays for covered medical services provided to eligible aged and disabled persons. Of relevance to this case, it reimburses hospitals for the cost of serving Medicare beneficiaries. [ ]

From the inception of Medicare in 1965 until 1983, hospitals were reimbursed for their actual costs in treating beneficiaries, so long as those costs were reasonable. In 1983, Congress overhauled the reimbursement system, switching to what is known as the Inpatient Prospective Payment System ("IPPS"). [ ] Under the IPPS, hospitals are not reimbursed for their actual costs, but are instead paid fixed rates for providing specific categories of treatment, known as "diagnosis related groups," or "DRGs." [ ] Separate DRG rates are set for hospitals in urban and rural areas. [ ] The purpose of this switch was to "encourage health care providers to improve efficiency and reduce operating costs." [ ]

Of particular significance for this case, the Secretary [of Health and Human Services] must adjust DRG payment rates for the relative labor costs in each hospital's geographic area. Accordingly, the base DRG payment rate is divided into two portions: the labor-related costs, which get adjusted for these geographic differences, and the non-labor-related costs, which do not. While the relative proportions of these two cost sources formerly were "estimated by the Secretary from time to time." [ ] Congress has removed the Secretary's discretion and set the labor-cost proportion at sixty-two percent of the base DRG payment. * * * [T]he Secretary must, at least once annually, compute a wage factor for each hospital "reflecting" the relative wage level in that hospital's "geographic area," and then apply that factor to the sixty-two percent of the DRG base rate that is attributable to labor costs. These adjustments must be cost neutral, so that any increase in one hospital's wage factor must be offset by a decrease in another's.

From its initial implementation of this law in 1985 through the present, CMS has consistently grouped hospitals into geographic areas by adopting the Metropolitan Statistical Areas ("MSAs") developed by the Office of Management and Budget ("OMB") for use throughout the federal government. Since the beginning, CMS has acknowledged that MSAs, which were not designed for this specific purpose, are an imperfect proxy for labor markets, particularly with respect to hospitals in rural areas. It has promised to consider alternative methodologies that are based on "objective criteria that will provide more equitable labor market area definitions than the current MSA/non-MSA classifications." [ ]

* * * By 1995, CMS had rejected * * * other proposed modifications. It concluded that "there is no clear 'best' labor market area option" that would be obviously superior to the MSA system. [ ] Because the industry itself could reach "no consensus" (unsurprisingly, since any modification to a cost-neutral system means much of the industry loses money), and because CMS was less than captivated by any of the alternatives, it decided to simply stay with the MSA system.* * *

Although well aware of this controversy, Congress has never directed CMS to implement any methodology for dividing core [i.e. urban] from ring [i.e surrounding areas] or otherwise deviate in any fundamental way from the MSA system. Instead, Congress has enacted a series of exceptions by which hospitals particularly aggrieved by MSA cut-offs can get some relief by, for example, relocating into other MSAs or having dramatic changes to their wage factors phased in over a period of time.[ ]

On December 27, 2000, OMB announced various changes to its methodology for computing MSAs. * * *

On June 6, 2003, OMB published its revised list of MSAs, incorporating information from the 2000 Census and using its new methodology. * * * Most previously existing MSAs became smaller. However, the old New York City MSA, which already had included the outlying New York counties of Westchester, Putnam, and Rockland, was expanded to include the New Jersey counties of Bergen, Passaic, and Hudson. [ ] * * *

On May 18, 2004, CMS proposed to adopt OMB's new MSAs. [ ] On July 12, 2004, plaintiffs' trade association filed comments in opposition, arguing that hospitals in the New Jersey counties had much lower wages ("only" 117 percent of the national average) and should not be included in the New York City MSA, since their inclusion would trim plaintiffs' wage index from 136 percent of the national average to 133 percent, cutting into plaintiffs' reimbursements at a time when New York City hospitals were struggling financially for other reasons. * * *

On August 11, 2004, CMS adopted OMB's new MSAs for purposes of the hospital wage index. * * * CMS observed that commenters had proposed completely inconsistent alternatives, with some emphasizing "expanding existing MSAs" and others calling for "creating smaller units or at least distinguishing segments within larger MSAs." [ ] It added that, while many commenters had demonstrated that their proposals would better serve their "specific situations," it could not adopt any alternative without assessing "all of the effects that these proposed revisions might have." * * *

* * *

In 2000, Congress directed CMS to refine its survey of hospital wages in geographic areas by controlling for differences in hospitals' occupational mixes. [ ] Specifically, Congress instructed the Secretary of HHS to "provide for the collection of data every 3 years on occupational mix for employees of each [covered] hospital ... in the provision of inpatient hospital services, in order to construct an occupational mix adjustment in the hospital area wage index." As codified, CMS's instruction is to "measure the earnings and paid hours of employment by occupational category and [to] exclude data with respect to the wages and wage-related costs incurred in furnishing skilled nursing facility services." [ ] In uncodified language that is a subject of the instant controversy, Congress added: "By not later than September 30, 2003, for application beginning October 1, 2004, the Secretary shall first complete (A) the collection of data [on occupational mix]; and (B) the measurement [of earnings and paid hours of employment by occupational category]."

By the summer of 2001, CMS had promulgated a final rule as to how it would collect these data and expressed its intention to survey hospitals during the 2002 calendar year. [ ] Nonetheless, for reasons that are unclear, not until September 19, 2003 did CMS publish a final notice of intent to collect data. [ ]

In the final rule being challenged here, CMS stated that it lacked full confidence in its data for several reasons * * *. In light of its lack of confidence in its data, CMS decided to apply the occupational mix adjustment to only ten percent of the wage index for FY 2005, an action that was supported by a "majority of commenters." [ ] The following year, rather than conduct a new survey (an action which, it noted, the statute only compels it to take once every three years), CMS used largely the same data. * * * [B]ecause CMS had the same concerns about the robustness of its data, it continued to apply the occupational mix adjustment to only ten percent of the wage index. Id.

* * *

On November 1, 2004, plaintiffs filed this action in the Southern District of New York pursuant to the Administrative Procedure Act ("APA"), 5 U.S.C. § 701 et seq., as well as the judicial review provision of the Medicare Act, see 42 U.S.C. § 1395oo(f)(1), challenging CMS's adoption of the new MSAs and its decision to implement the occupational mix adjustment at only ten-percent effectiveness. * * *

* * *

At the outset, we describe the scope of our review. On appeal from a grant of summary judgment in a challenge to agency action under the APA, we review the administrative record and the district court's decision de novo. [ ]

With respect to each challenged action, we begin by reviewing the agency's construction of the statute at issue. We do so by applying the familiar two-step process of statutory interpretation set forth in Chevron U.S.A. Inc. v. Natural Resources Defense Council, Inc., 467 U.S. 837 (1984). Under Chevron, the first question is "whether Congress has directly spoken to the precise question at issue"; if so, our inquiry is at in end. [ ] If there is silence or ambiguity in the statute on the question, then the agency has discretion in its implementation, and we ask only if the construction it has given the statute is reasonable.[11]* * *[ ]

Assuming the agency's action was authorized by statute, we then ask whether it was "arbitrary, capricious, [or] an abuse of discretion," 5 U.S.C. § 706(2)(A), or "unsupported by substantial evidence," id. § 706(2)(E). Such a finding, which is required to overturn an agency action, can be made only where the agency "has relied on factors which Congress has not intended it to consider, entirely failed to consider an important aspect of the problem, offered an explanation for its decision that runs counter to the evidence before the agency, or is so implausible that it could not be ascribed to a difference in view or the product of agency expertise." [ ] Our task, then, is limited. We have no license to substitute our policy judgment for that of the agency, but only to overturn actions that are not authorized by statute or that are arbitrary or capricious. [ ]

We first review the defendant's use of OMB's MSAs. * * *

CMS's task is unambiguous: to calculate a factor that reflects geographic-area wage-level differences, and nothing else. We reject defendant's conten-

---

11. Defendant argues that even greater deference is required in all cases interpreting the Medicare statute, given the complex and highly technical nature of much of the statute- ry scheme. However, the discrete issue here is as readily reviewable as is any other administrative action.[ ]

tion that this provision, or any other in the Medicare Act, confers upon him the discretion to take into account all sorts of unrelated policy considerations, such as whether certain hospitals receive unwarranted advantages from other provisions of the Medicare reimbursement scheme.

At the same time, as plaintiffs conceded at argument, the statute leaves considerable ambiguity as to the term "geographic area," * * * . CMS's discretion in interpreting this ambiguous term is cabined by the need to fulfill two somewhat contradictory policies expressed by the text of the provision and the legislative history of the IPPS: (1) the geographic areas must be small enough to actually reflect differences in wage levels and, (2) each geographic area must include enough hospitals that their costs can be meaningfully averaged and individual hospitals do not get reimbursed for their own actual costs. In balancing these two considerations, the agency has considerable discretion. Moreover, even after determining the scale of each geographic area, lines must be drawn between areas that inevitably will be contested and may seem arbitrary; once again, the statute is silent as to how this process is to take place, leaving the agency with broad discretion.

There is no question that MSAs are, literally, "geographic areas," and thus their use complies with the language of the statute. Furthermore, their use comports with the two purposes set out above. Because MSAs are based on commuting patterns into and out of the central county, hospitals in each MSA presumably compete in the same labor market, and so it is likely that their wages bear at least rough similarity. On the other hand, each MSA provides a large enough pool of hospitals to allow cost averaging. We conclude that the use of MSAs to fill the gap left by the ambiguous term "geographic areas" is reasonable. In doing so, we express no opinion as to whether any alternative interpretation would have been "better," as we are not empowered to set aside a reasonable interpretation on that basis. [ ] * * *

Finally, we observe that CMS has now used MSAs to fill this statutory gap for more than two decades without any action from Congress suggesting disapproval. The fact that defendant has now adopted an MSA-based wage index multiple times certainly counsels deference to its decision to do so this time. * * *

Having concluded that the Medicare statute authorizes an MSA's use as a proxy for a "geographic area," we now ask whether this policy choice was arbitrary or capricious. Before undertaking this inquiry, we pause to note that an agency's burden of supplying a "reasoned analysis" justifying its policy is lower where, as here, an agency is continuing a long-standing policy compared to where the agency is suddenly changing that policy. * * *

* * *

Finally, we would think that, despite the plaintiffs' fears that the agency favors rural hospitals, the consistent use of MSAs has dampened any such favoritism. MSAs, after all, are constructed through an objective methodology, deliberately without reference to any political considerations, by a different agency that has no involvement in this rulemaking. [ ] All other things being equal, it is rational and permissible for an agency to adopt an already extant measure that uses objective criteria rather than assuming the task of creating its own measure in the face of a sharply divided regulated industry that has not proposed any clearly superior alternatives. [ ] Under these circumstances, the agency's continued use of MSAs was not arbitrary and capricious.

In an uncodified section of the 2000 Bill, Congress instructed the agency as follows: "By not later than September 30, 2003, for application beginning October 1, 2004, the Secretary shall first complete (A) the collection of data [on occupational mix]; and (B) the measurement [of earnings and paid hours of employment by occupational category]." [ ]

This provision requires interpretation as to what action was required of the agency on October 1, 2004. Indeed, by its literal terms, it does not command the Secretary to actually apply the adjustment on that date at all, but rather to complete various preparations to do so by September 30, 2003. However, defendant does not read the provision as imposing no obligation to apply the adjustment at all on October 1, 2004, but rather as imposing an obligation only to "begin" applying it, in whatever limited force the agency decides is appropriate. Plaintiffs, as well as the district court, construe the provision to require full implementation of the adjustment on October 1, 2004 under any and all circumstances. We cannot agree with either interpretation.

We think that the provision can only be fairly read to contemplate application in full on October 1, 2004. Congress need not explicitly tell an agency to implement a program "in full," any more than it need tell the agency to do the job "competently"; any reasonable reader trying to do justice to Congress's intent will infer that meaning. Nor is a call for application "beginning on" a date certain reasonably interpreted as a grant of discretion to the agency to apply the adjustment on that date at whatever limited strength the agency believes is appropriate. There is no ambiguity in the statute on this point, and so the defendant's interpretation does not receive deference under Chevron.

* * *

* * * Not only are the agency's actions violative of the statute, but they are arbitrary and capricious. CMS simply asserts that its data justify implementation at precisely ten percent effectiveness, with no explanation given as to why ten percent was chosen instead of, e.g., twenty percent or fifty percent. In addition, the agency has not accounted for its continuing failure to comply with Congress's unambiguous mandate that the agency complete the necessary data collection and measurement by September 30, 2003. Without any explanation, the agency did not even begin its data collection until September 19, 2003, although it appeared to be ready two years earlier. When the data it then gathered in rushed fashion predictably proved inadequate to permit full implementation on schedule, the agency simply stated its intent to do better the next time it believed it was required to collect data, three years later, and until then apparently intends to continue applying the adjustment at greatly limited effectiveness. Under these circumstances, it was arbitrary and capricious for the agency not to return to data gathering immediately, or at least explain why it is not doing so, rather than proceed as if it had successfully completed the initial data gathering.

* * *

Having easily concluded that the agency's actions were in violation of law, we move to the more difficult task of formulating a remedy. Obviously, at this late date the agency cannot be ordered into compliance with the schedule set by Congress. We therefore recognize at the outset that any remedy we devise is necessarily imperfect. However, we must endeavor, to the extent possible, to honor Congress's intent as well as the language of the statute.

The district court simply granted plaintiff its requested relief and ordered CMS to immediately apply the occupational mix adjustment in full based on the data it has already collected. While this approach holds some appeal, in that it would prevent any further agency delay, we think it is not what Congress would have wanted. * * * We think immediate application of the adjustment using such flawed data not only would result in irrational policy (and almost certainly damage some of the intended beneficiaries of this adjustment, through no fault of their own) but would contravene Congress's purpose in setting up this two-step schedule.

Accordingly, we instead order the agency to immediately return to the first step and collect data that are sufficiently robust to permit full application of the occupational mix adjustment. All data collection and measurement and any other preparations necessary for full application should be complete by September 30, 2006, at which time we instruct the agency to immediately apply the adjustment in full. * * * Although we cannot undo the past and remedy the agency's failure to comply with its statutory obligations through one full round of data collection, we can order the agency to follow the schedule originally anticipated by Congress from this date forward.

* * *

Notes and Questions

What does this case tell us about Medicare? What is the role of law in the administration of the program? What are the respective roles of the Center for Medicare and Medicaid Services (a division of the Department of Health and Human Services mysteriously referred to as CMS rather than CMMS), Congress, and the courts? What practical constraints does CMS face in making determinations such as this, i.e. what trade-offs are necessary? How much deference should the courts afford CMS in making these determinations, and does *Chevron* strike the right balance? What services are the plaintiff providers providing? How are they being paid for their services? What are they complaining about? What policy decisions does the method of payment under consideration represent? What is the stake of Medicare beneficiaries in this litigation? What is the interest of taxpayers? Think about these questions as you study the materials that follow.

A. ELIGIBILITY

Medicare covers nearly thirty-seven million elderly and 6.6 million disabled beneficiaries, one in seven Americans. Medicare eligibility is generally linked to that of the Social Security program, the other major social insurance program of the United States. Persons who are eligible for retirement benefits under Social Security are automatically eligible for Medicare upon reaching age 65. Spouses or former spouses who qualify for Social Security as dependents may also begin receiving Medicare at 65, as may former federal employees eligible for Civil Service Retirement and Railroad Retirement beneficiaries, 42 U.S.C.A. § 426(a).

Disabled persons who are eligible for Social Security or Railroad Retirement benefits may also receive Medicare, but only after they have been eligible for cash benefits for at least two years, 42 U.S.C.A. § 426(b). The number of disabled persons covered by Medicare is growing rapidly. Benefits are also available to persons who are eligible for Social Security, although not necessarily receiving it, and have end-stage renal (kidney) disease, who may receive Medicare benefits after a three-month waiting period, 42 U.S.C.A. § 426–1. About 350,000 Medicare beneficiaries are eligible for this reason.

Why is Medicare, a social insurance program, only available to the elderly and disabled? Why is it available to all members of these groups, regardless of their income or wealth? Is it a good idea to charge more for program benefits to those who have higher incomes, as does the Medicare Modernization Act which means-tests premiums for Part B? What effect does Medicare have on the workers who support it through their payroll taxes? What effect does it have on the children of Medicare recipients? What effect might it have on the children of Medicare recipients at the death of the recipient? The idea surfaces from time to time of extending Medicare to cover all of the uninsured. Why has this idea not been adopted?

Medicare has been generally successful in assuring broad and equitable access to health care for many who would probably otherwise be uninsured. Almost half of Medicare beneficiaries have incomes of 200 percent of the federal poverty level or less, and sixty percent of elderly Medicare beneficiaries receive at least half of their income from Social Security. When the program began only fifty-six percent of the elderly had hospital insurance and the poor and nonwhite elderly received substantially less medical care than did the wealthier or white elderly. While these disparities have been substantially reduced, problem still remain. In particular, there is a great deal of evidence that racial and ethnic minority Medicare beneficiaries have poorer health status than white beneficiaries, as well as evidence that they receive fewer common medical procedures. See Marian E. Gornick, Effects of Race and Income on Mortality and Use of Services Among Medicare Beneficiaries, 335 New Eng. J. Med. 791 (1996); A. Marshall McBean and Marian Gornick, Difference by Race of Procedures Performed in Hospitals for Medicare Beneficiaries, Health Care Fin. Rev., Summer 1994 at 77 (1994); Bruce C. Vladeck, Paul N. Van de Water, and June Eichner, eds., Strengthening Medicare's Role in Reducing Racial and Ethnic Health Disparities (2006), http://www.nasi.org/publications2763/publications_show.htm?doc_id=410031; Timothy Stoltzfus Jost, Racial and Ethnic Disparities in Medicare: What the Department of Health and Human Services and the Center for Medicare and Medicaid Services Can, and Should, Do, 1 DePaul J. Health Care L. 667 (2005).

B. BENEFITS

1. *Coverage*

The Medicare Hospital Insurance (HI) program, Part A, pays for hospital, nursing home, home health and hospice services. The Medicare Supplemental Medical Insurance (SMI) program, Part B, covers physicians' services and a variety of other items and services including outpatient hospital services, home health care, physical and occupational therapy, prosthetic devices, durable medical equipment, and ambulance services. Medicare covers only 90 days of hospital services in a single benefit period ("spell of illness"*). Each beneficiary also has an extra 60 "lifetime reserve" days of hospital coverage. A one time deductible, set at $1024 in 2008, must be paid each year before hospital coverage begins, and a daily copayment of $256 (in 2008) must be paid after the sixtieth day of hospital care, 42 U.S.C.A. § 1395e. Although the Medicare statute provides for coverage of up to 100 days of skilled nursing care, 42 U.S.C.A. § 1395d(a)(2), the nursing home benefit is intended to cover those recovering from an acute illness or injury and not to cover long term chronic care. Hospice benefits are provided on a limited basis, 42 U.S.C.A. § 1395d(a)(4). Physicians' services are provided subject to an annual deductible of $135 (for 2008) and a twenty percent coinsurance amount. In recent years, Medicare has added many preventive services, including prostate cancer screening; bone mass density measurement; diabetes self-management; mammography screening; glaucoma screening; pap smears; an initial physical examination; cardiovascular screening blood tests; diabetes screening tests; and hepatitis B, pneumococcal, and flu shots.

Leaving aside these preventive services, the Medicare benefits package still closely resembles the standard federal employee or Blue Cross/Blue Shield benefits package available in the mid–1960s when Medicare was established and is thus quite antiquated. It is very different, therefore, from standard benefit packages available today, which are likely to be managed care rather than fee-for-service based, have relatively low fixed-dollar copayments or percentage coinsurance requirements, have variable cost-sharing between in and out-of-plan providers, and have higher catastrophic coverage limits. Medicare's lack of out-of-pocket limits for beneficiary cost-sharing for Part B services and caps on the number of covered days of hospitalization are particularly problematic.

Medicare pays for about forty-nine percent of the health care received by the elderly in this country, while private sources (including both private insurance and out-of-pocket expenditures) pay for thirty percent, Medicaid for fifteen percent, and other sources for the rest. Many Medicare recipients purchase, or more commonly receive as a retirement benefit, Medicare Supplement (Medigap) insurance, which covers their cost-sharing obligations and some services not covered by Medicare. The average Medicare beneficiary spends nineteen percent of household income on medical expenses not covered by Medicare, but the average beneficiary below the poverty level pays thirty-five percent of household income for medical expenses. Medicare accounts for twenty-nine percent of the nation's expenditures for hospital care, twenty-one percent of physician expenditures, and thirty-eight percent of home health expenditures.

Beyond the broad political decisions of what categories of medical care Medicare will finance are the far more numerous decisions as to whether a particular item or service will be covered by Medicare at all or for a particular beneficiary. Decisions as to whether Medicare will finance new technologies are made at different levels.

---

* A spell of illness begins when a patient is hospitalized, and continues until the patient has been out of a hospital or nursing home for at least 60 days. 42 U.S.C.A. § 1345x(a). Thus, a chronically ill person could remain indefinitely in a single spell of illness.

A beneficiary in need of a noncovered item or service may request a national coverage determination (NCD). 42 U.S.C.A. § 1395ff(f)(4) & (5). CMS must act on the request within ninety days (although if CMS determines that the review will take longer than ninety days, it can simply say so and explain why). CMS also often reviews technologies in response to informal requests from technology manufacturers or from others. In making these decisions, CMS often consults with its Medicare Evidence Development Coverage Advisory Committee (MEDCAC), which consists of 120 health care experts. CMS also commissions extramural technology assessments to be used by the MEDCAC or by itself for evaluating technologies. The procedures followed by CMS in these decisions are described at 42 C.F.R. Part 426, and in Timothy S Jost, The Medicare Coverage Determination Process in the United States, in Timothy S. Jost, ed., Health Care Coverage Determinations: An International Comparative Study, 207 (2004). Technologies may also be evaluated by local Medicare contractors, which make local coverage determinations (LCDs), valid only in the area covered by the contractor. LCDs are far more common than NCDs, as NCDs tend to be limited to more controversial and expensive technologies. These contractors are usually private insurers (such as Blue Cross plans) that process claims for Medicare so that private entities are essentially deciding what products and services Medicare covers. Manufacturers often attempt to get a technology covered by a number of contractors through LCDs before attempting to get an NCD. See Susan Bartlett Foote, The Impact of the Medicare Modernization Act's Contractor Reform on Fee-for-Service Medicare, 1 St. Louis U. J. Health L. & Pol'y 63 (2007); Susan Bartlett Foote, Focus on Locus: Evolution of Medicare's Local Coverage Policy, 22 Health Aff., July/Aug. 2003, at 137.

Not surprisingly, since there is a great deal of money involved, the Medicare coverage process is highly politicized, and CMS comes under tremendous pressure from the drug and device industry, professional and disease groups (which are often funded in part by industry), and Congress when it denies or threatens to deny coverage for a new technology. Medicare has taken steps to focus the process more on effectiveness review, and thus perhaps to depoliticize it. Under a new guidance issued in July of 2006, Medicare has two tracks for using coverage determinations to review effectiveness. First, it approves some technologies on a "coverage with appropriateness determination" or CAD basis, where additional information will be required at the time of use of the technology to assure clinical appropriateness. Second, some technologies are approved only for use in clinical trials on the "coverage with study participation" track, to further determine effectiveness. Through these processes, coverage is being used to drive research, which in turn can support more accurate coverage determinations process.

A beneficiary adversely affected by an NCD may seek review by the Departmental Appeals Board (DAB), subject to judicial review. 42 U.S.C.A. § 1395ff(f)(1). LCDs may be appealed to administrative law judges, and then further to the DAB. 42 U.S.C. § 1395ff(f)(2). Mediation is also available for disputes involving LCDs. The only persons with standing to appeal a coverage determination are Medicare beneficiaries who need or have received the items or services that are the subject of the coverage determination. 42 C.F.R. § 426.110(1). Contrary to the normal practice in Medicare appeals generally, moreover, a beneficiary appealing a coverage determination may not assign his or her rights to appeal to a provider. 42 C.F.R. § 426.320(b). CMS, however, will give public notice of each complaint, and allow "interested parties" to submit written or brief oral statements as amici. 42 C.F.R. §§ 426.510(f), 426.513. In actual practice, most coverage appeals are sponsored by manufacturers or providers with a stake in the particular technology, but the appeal has to be brought in the name of a particular beneficiary, who will be the identified party of interest in the case.

CMS rules also circumscribe the relief that ALJs may grant in reviewing LCDs or the DAB in reviewing NCDs. The DAB, for example, may not order CMS to add language to an NCD, order CMS to pay a specific claim, set a time limit for CMS to establish a new or revised NCD, or address how CMS implements an NCD. All an ALJ or the DAB can do is hold the determination to be invalid, at which point CMS will ask its contractors to readjudicate the claim without consideration of the LCD or NCD, and to review future claims without using the NCD. 42 C.F.R. §§ 426.455, 426.460, 426.555, 426.560.

In spite of these complex procedures, many coverage decisions in individual cases are in fact made less formally by Medicare's contractors, and are reviewable primarily through the general Medicare appeals process described below. Ultimately, whether any particular service is provided to any particular Medicare beneficiary will depend on the decision of a private Medicare contractor interpreting federal policy as mediated by Medicare regulations, manuals and manual transmittals, regional office instructions, NCDs and LCDs, rumor, and innuendo. This process is attended by a fair bit of inconsistency.

Sizeable sectors of the health care industry have emerged or developed in particular ways largely because of the availability of Medicare coverage and payment policy. The home health care industry, for example, burgeoned and then withered in response to Medicare policy. In 1967, when Medicare began, there were 1,850 Medicare-certified home health agencies in the United States, by 1997 there were about 10,000. In the three years following 1981, when Medicare home health benefits were dramatically expanded, about 1,600 new home health agencies were certified. Wayne Callahan, Medicare Use of Home Health Services, 7 Health Care Financing Review Winter, 1985 at 89. Home health expenditures grew rapidly in the early 1990s from $3.7 billion in 1990 (3.2 percent of total Medicare expenditures) to $17.8 billion (nine percent) in 1997. This represented a growth rate of 25.2 percent per annum, compared to eight percent for the program generally. During the same period the number of Medicare home health users grew from 57 to 109 per 1,000 beneficiaries, and the average number of visits per user went from 36 to 73.

The 1997 Balanced Budget Act put the brakes on home health expenditures, imposing limits on payments for visits and a per beneficiary cap, and mandating the creation of a prospective payment system. Medicare home health spending dropped to about nine billion dollars in 2000, while the number of home health agencies dropped by about 3,000, the number of users per 1,000 beneficiaries to seventy, and the number of visits per user to 31.6. The post-BBA decline in use does not seem to have had an adverse effect on patient outcomes. See Christopher M. Murtaugh, Trends in Medicare Home Health Care Use: 1997–2001, 22 Health Affairs, Sept./Oct. 2003, at 146. In 2000, Medicare implemented a new payment system for home health, and through the early 2000s, home health spending consistently grew once again at double-digit levels, accounting for the most rapid spending growth of any health care service from 2003 to 2005.

What categories of services should Medicare cover? Should its coverage be identical to employment-related benefit packages, or should it vary in some respects? What items might be more, or less, important to its beneficiary population than to working-age Americans? Should Medicare cover nursing home care—a benefit of obvious interest to the elderly—to a greater extent? Should Medicare take cost into account in setting coverage policy for new technologies? If so, what role should cost play in coverage determinations? Though "added value" is among the criteria that CMS proposed in 2000 for evaluating technologies, Medicare claims not to consider cost explicitly. Is the public interest served by having private "contractors" make many coverage decisions with few opportunities for appeal?

2. Prescription Drugs

At the time Medicare was created in 1965, private insurance policies did not generally cover outpatient prescription drugs. Prescription drugs were still relatively affordable and were not as an important part of the management of medical problems as they are today. Not surprisingly, therefore, Medicare did not include a drug benefit. Medicare was expanded briefly to cover prescription drugs by the 1988 Medicare Catastrophic Coverage Act, but the legislation proved intensely unpopular with higher-income beneficiaries who were charged higher premiums. It was repealed in 1989 before it could even be implemented. By the late 1990s, however, sharply escalating drug costs brought a Medicare prescription drug benefit back to the top of the political agenda. Pressure built on Congress to do something.

The national political leadership that took on the challenge of providing a Medicare drug benefit in the early 2000s, however, was very different from that which led the country in 1965 when the Medicare program was established. Whereas the presidency and both houses of Congress were held by Democrats in 1965, the presidency and both houses of Congress were held by Republicans in 2003. Whereas the inspiration for the Medicare program in 1965 had been the Social Security program and social insurance programs like it in other developed countries, the conservative leadership of the Republican Congress in 2003 was enamored with market approaches to providing health care coverage. The 2003 Congress had benefitted heavily from political contributions from drug manufacturers and from insurance and managed care companies, and thus was oriented toward a solution that would help rather than harm these interests. Any drug legislation adopted by Congress, therefore, had to meet several requirements.

First, the program had to be a voluntary program that beneficiaries could choose to join or not to join, like Part B. To encourage voluntary membership, however, the program would have to appeal to beneficiaries who had relatively low drug costs as well as to those with higher costs. Second, it had to be administered by private "prescription drug plans," rather than directly by the government. In particular, administered prices set by the Medicare program, which have been used in other parts of the Medicare program to hold down costs, were not acceptable to the drug companies and not acceptable to congressional leadership. Third, the cost of the program could not exceed $400 billion over ten years. This meant that Medicare beneficiaries would have to continue to bear a considerable share of total Medicare drug costs through cost-sharing obligations and premiums. Finally, the legislation had to provide some relief for the poor from these cost-sharing obligations. Medicare would not continue to be a social insurance program available to all on equal terms, but would become partially means tested.

As negotiations continued through the fall of 2003 between the House and Senate, other decisions were made. Medicare rather than Medicaid would cover the drug costs of beneficiaries eligible for both programs and employers who continued to provide drug benefits for their retirees would receive subsidies for doing so. In November of 2003, Congress, after an all-night session and by the narrowest of margins, adopted a Medicare drug benefit, signed into law by President Bush as Public Law 108–173.

This legislation created a voluntary Prescription Drug Benefit Program, establishing a new Part D of Medicare, which went into effect on January 1, 2006. All Medicare beneficiaries are eligible for the program. Beneficiaries who enroll in Part D pay a premium, the amount of which is basically set at twenty-six percent of the cost of the benefits provided (as calculated using a complex formula). The premiums vary from plan to plan relative to each plan's bid amount, and are increased if the beneficiary receives supplemental benefits. Those who chose not to join the program initially (or when they later become eligible for Medicare or lose drug coverage from some other source) are penalized by having to pay higher premiums. The vast majority of the cost of the program is borne by government, which pays not only three quarters of the premium cost, but also most of the cost of catastrophic coverage (and heavily subsidizes Medicare Advantage plans).

Drug benefits are provided by private Prescription Drug Plans (PDPs), by Medicare Advantage Medicare managed care plans, and by employers who offer drug coverage to employed or retired beneficiaries. Medicare Advantage plans usually offer drug coverage at much lower premiums than free-standing PDPs. The U.S. is divided up into thirty-four PDP regions, and PDPs submit bids to cover these regions. Plans are paid their bid price, adjusted to reflect the risk profile of their members. Each beneficiary must have a choice of at least two PDPs or of one PDP and one Medicare Advantage plan.

Free-standing risk-bearing drug plans did not exist at the time the legislation was adopted. To encourage the creation of such plans and to lure them into the Medicare market, the legislation transferred much of the risk for providing drug benefits to the Medicare program. Even "full-risk" plans in fact only bear risk within "risk corridors." Medicare also provides "reinsurance" at a level of eighty percent to plans for allowable costs of enrollees whose costs exceed the out-of-pocket threshold, described below.

The benefits offered by PDPs vary from plan to plan. "Standard prescription drug coverage" under the legislation is defined largely in terms of cost-sharing obligations. For 2008, "standard" coverage includes a $275 deductible and a twenty-five percent enrollee coinsurance obligation for the next $2235 in drug costs. This relatively generous coverage at the low end is intended to attract relatively healthy beneficiaries to the program. Once total expenditures reach $2510, however, the beneficiary hits the "doughnut hole" and receives no further coverage from the program until he or she has spent $4050 out of pocket (or until total drug costs, including both the beneficiary's and the program's payments, reach $5976.25). At this "out-of-pocket threshold" amount, stop-loss coverage kicks in, and the beneficiary is thereafter responsible for only five percent of further costs (or for a copayment of $2.25 to $5.60 if this is higher).

Though this is "standard coverage," almost ninety percent of plans offer instead "actuarially equivalent" coverage, which in most cases do not have a deductible and have tiered copayments (which differ by whether the beneficiary purchases a generic, preferred multiple source, or other drug) instead of coinsurance. Plans also offer "supplemental prescription coverage" in terms of reduced cost-sharing or access to additional drugs. In any event, plans must pass on to the beneficiary the actual prices that they negotiate for drugs, including any discounts, concessions, rebates, or other remuneration, even in situations where no benefits are payable because of cost-sharing obligations.

The legislation provides a number of protections for PDP beneficiaries. PDP sponsors are required to permit the participation of any pharmacy that accepts a plan's terms and conditions, although PDPs may reduce cost-sharing obligations to encourage the use of in-network pharmacies. Plans must secure participation of enough pharmacies in their networks to meet "convenient access" requirements, and may not charge more for using community rather than mail-order pharmacies. PDPs may use formularies (lists of drugs covered by the plan), but a formulary must be based on scientific standards, and must include each therapeutic category and class of covered Part D drugs. Benefits may not be designed so as to discourage enrollment by particular categories of beneficiaries. PDPs must offer grievance and appeal procedures like those available in the Medicare Advantage program, including independent review. A beneficiary may gain access to drugs not included in the formulary or avoid increased cost-sharing for non-preferred drugs only if the prescribing physician determines that formulary or preferred drugs are not as effective for the beneficiary, cause adverse effects, or both. PDP sponsors must be licensed by their state or meet federal solvency requirements. See Geraldine Dallek, Consumer Protection Issues Raised by the Medicare Prescription Drug, Improvement, and Modernization Act of 2003, http //www.kff.org/medicare/upload/Consumer-Protection-Issues-Raised-by-the-Medicare-Prescription-Drug-Improvement-and-Modernization-Act-of-2003. pdf (2004); Vicki Gottlich, Beneficiary Challenges in Using the Medicare Part D Appeals Process to Obtain Medically Necessary Drugs http://www.kff.org/medicare/7557.cfm (2006); Vicki Gottlich, The Exceptions and Appeals Process: Issues and Concerns in Obtaining Coverage Under the Medicare Part D Prescription Drug Benefit, http://www.kff.org/medicare/7433.cfm (2005).

Because the high cost-sharing obligations imposed by the legislation would limit its value to low-income beneficiaries, the Act provides additional assistance for low-income beneficiaries. Persons who are eligible for Medicaid, or whose incomes fall below 135 percent of the poverty level and have resources in 2008 below $6,120 for an individual or $9,190 for a couple receive a subsidy that covers their premium, relieves them from any deductible, and limits their cost-sharing obligations up to the out-of-pocket threshold to $2.25 for generic or preferred multiple source drugs or $5.60 for other drugs. Dual eligibles (persons eligible for both Medicare and Medicaid) with incomes up to

100 percent of poverty level only have to pay $1.05 for generic or multiple source drugs and $3.10 for other drugs, and nursing home residents on Medicaid have no cost-sharing obligations. Persons with incomes between 135 percent and 150 percent of the poverty level and with up to $10,210 in resources for an individual or $20,410 for a couple benefit from a sliding scale premium subsidy, a $56 deductible, and cost-sharing up to the out-of-pocket threshold of $2.25 for generic or preferred multiple source drugs, and $5.60 for other drugs. As of 2007, about 3 to 4.7 million beneficiaries eligible for low income assistance were not receiving it.

The states are required to pay over to the Medicare program a "claw back" amount initially equal to ninety percent of what they would have spent to cover the dual eligibles under the Medicaid program. That amount will be reduced gradually to seventy-five percent after 2015. States may face marginally lower expenses than they would have faced had Medicaid continued to be responsible for these costs, but will have less control over spending.

What effect is this program likely to have on drug prices? PDPs negotiate with drug manufacturers over drug prices, but HHS is prohibited from interfering in these negotiations. Why did Congress choose this approach rather than an administrative price approach, as Medicare uses elsewhere? (The Democratic-controlled Congress elected in 2005 has sought to change this to permit government negotiations, as of this writing without success.) Who has more bargaining power, the federal government or prescription drug plans? Why might PDPs have considerable bargaining power, even though their market share is much less than that of the federal government? What can they do that the federal government cannot? Which approach is in the end more likely to lead to lower drug costs? What other effects might either approach have? What interest groups other than drug companies will benefit from the approach Congress initially chose? Who in particular among Medicare beneficiaries is most likely to benefit from this legislation; who will be least helped by it?

Early results of the prescription drug program were in many respects impressive, although the program remains controversial. Average premiums for 2006 were significantly below the levels initially estimated, and premiums remained low for 2007, although they rose in 2008, in some instances dramatically. Average premium rates are also deceptive, because they include the premiums of Medicare Advantage plans, which are heavily subsidized by Medicare and offer drug premiums much lower than stand-alone drug plans. In 2007, all states except Alaska had at least fifty plans available, and seventeen plans were available nationwide, although only two plans covered forty percent of beneficiaries nationally. By 2007, twenty-four million beneficiaries had Part D coverage, and almost ninety percent of beneficiaries, had some form of drug coverage, though four million beneficiaries remained without coverage. On the other hand, the costs of drugs used by seniors continued to increase significantly and the administrative costs of the program are very high.

See, describing the drug legislation, Richard L. Kaplan, The Medicare Drug Benefit: A Prescription for Confusion, 1 NAELA J. 165 (2005); Kaiser Family Foundation, Fact Sheet: The Prescription Drug Benefit (2008 and updated regularly); and other resources available at the Kaiser Family Foundation website, http://www.kff.org/medicare/rxdrugbenefit.cfm.

Problem: The Medicare Prescription Drug Benefit

Mary Belmont has just become eligible for Medicare and is trying to decide in which Medicare pharmacy benefit plan to enroll. Three options are available in her area. One PDP costs thirty dollars a month and offers the benefits of the standard benefit package, though its formulary does not cover two of the drugs she is currently using, and she would have to switch to drugs that the plan designates as therapeutically equivalent. The second PDP costs only twenty-five dollars a month, has no deductible, offers generic drug coverage in the donut hole and covers all of the drugs that she is currently using, but imposes an actuarially equivalent tiered copayment plan (i.e. it charges higher copays for brand name than generic drugs and even higher copays for non-preferred brand-name drugs) and would require her to pay fifty dollars each for a thirty day supply of two of her drugs. Her third option is a Medicare Advantage plan that covers drugs, and that also has a limited formulary, but that has a 200 dollar deductible for drugs and a tiered copayment formula with a maximum copayment of thirty-five dollars per prescription. To join the Medicare Advantage plan, however, she would have to leave her current primary care doctor, whom she has seen for ten years, because he is not part of the plan's network. The Medicare Advantage plan would only charge a twenty dollars a month premium for drug benefits. The first PDP plan also offers a supplementary drug plan at an additional thirty dollars a month that would reduce her cost-sharing obligations from twenty-five percent to twenty percent for the first $2,000 of coverage, and also cover certain over-the-counter drugs. Which plan should she choose? Should she be grateful for all of these choices?

C. PAYMENT FOR SERVICES

1. Introduction

The *Bellevue Hospital* case that began this section, like most litigated cases involving the Medicare program, concerned neither eligibility nor benefit coverage, but rather payment for services. Over Medicare's history, the program has relied primarily on three payment strategies: cost- or charge-based reimbursement, prospective payment, and managed competition. At the outset, it followed the then current practice of health insurers by paying institutions on the basis of their reported costs and professionals on the basis of their charges. This proved, not surprisingly, to be wildly inflationary, and over time Medicare increasingly imposed restrictions on cost- and charge-based payment. In the end Medicare abandoned cost- and charge-based payment in favor of administered payment systems, under which Medicare itself sets the price it will pay for services. It began by implementing prospective payment for hospitals in the early 1980s. The next major step toward prospective payment was the resource-based relative value scale for paying physicians, implemented in the early 1990s. Under the Balanced Budget Act of 1997 Medicare implemented prospective payment systems for home health, skilled nursing facilities, outpatient hospital care, and inpatient rehabilitation hospitals. Paying for almost one-third of the nation's hospital care and one-fifth of physician care, Medicare has been able to offer payment rates to many professionals and providers on a take-it-or-leave-it basis, and to hold rates to levels that are below those paid generally in the private market.

It has been less successful, however, at controlling the volume of services it pays for, leading to continuing increases in overall costs.

Between 1993 and 1997, Medicare experienced cost increases in excess of those experienced by the private insurance market (7.5 percent as compared to 3.5 percent). The private insurance market had by the mid–1990s turned to managed care, and conservative critics, who had always disliked Medicare's administered price approach, argued that this disparity proved that the use of administered prices is inferior to managed care as a strategy for controlling costs. Some went further, contending that Medicare should merely provide vouchers to its recipients, who could then purchase insurance in the private insurance and managed care market. The Republican Balanced Budget Act of 1995 would have turned Medicare into a voucher-based managed competition program, but it was vetoed by President Clinton. The more moderate Balanced Budget Act of 1997, created a new Medicare Part C, the Medicare + Choice managed care program, and attempted to woo rather than drive Medicare patients into managed care. After 1997, paradoxically, the tables turned and Medicare expenditures rose much less quickly than private insurance expenditures (1.2 percent growth for Medicare compared to 7.2 percent for private insurance between 1997 and 1998). By 2001, Medicare expenditures were growing at a rate of 7.8 percent per year, while private insurance premiums were increasing 10.5 percent But, despite this reality, calls for making Medicare function more like the private sector continued unabated, and the 2003 Medicare Modernization Act attempted again to expand Medicare managed care through the new Medicare Advantage program. By the mid–2000s, Medicare costs were growing faster than private insurance costs (although much of the growth was due to the expansion of Medicare coverage to prescription drugs), with the Medicare Advantage program costing significantly more than traditional Medicare.

The following subsections describe briefly two of the major administered price programs under Medicare, the diagnosis-related group prospective payment system for hospitals and the resource-based relative value scale for physicians. The final subsection examines the Medicare Advantage program.

It is important to have some understanding of how Medicare's administer-price payment systems work, not just because they provide a contrast to managed care alternatives, but also because they are used for dispensing tens of billions of dollars of Medicare payments and have a predictably significant effect on the behavior of health care providers. In particular, lawyers are often called upon to help health care providers structure themselves to maximize access to these Medicare payments.

2. *Medicare Prospective Payment Under Diagnosis–Related Groups*

Congress established the diagnosis-related group (DRG) prospective payment system for hospitals in 1982. A DRG is a means of categorizing patients to reflect relative intensity of use of services. DRG-based payment treats hospitals as coordinating services to produce particular products, such as the diagnosis and treatment of heart attacks, ulcers, or tumors. The DRG system groups patients primarily by principal (admitting) diagnoses, which, together with other factors, are used to categorize patients. The purpose of this analysis is to yield groups of hospital patients, each covered by a distinct DRG, that more or less require the same quantity of medical resources. Once DRGs were defined, Medicare arrayed DRGs by relative intensity of resource consumption, with average resource use defired as a single unit. Thus, for 2007, DRG 75, surgery, major chest procedures, is weighted at 3.0340 (or over three times the average admission cost); DRG 59, tonsillectomy and/or adenoidectomy only on a patient over 17 years of age, at .6831 (a little more than two-thirds average cost).

To determine a hospital's actual payment for caring for a Medicare patient, the relative DRG weight assigned to that patient is first multiplied by standardized amounts for labor, non-labor, and capital costs. The standardized amounts in theory represent the cost to an efficient hospital of an average case. For FY 2007, the standardized amounts for hospitals that complied with performance disclosure requirements was $3,400.13 for labor costs, $1,478.10 for non-labor costs, and $427.38 for capital costs. These amount are multiplied by the DRG weight (e.g. .6831 for tonsillectomy) to achieve the basic DRG reimbursement amount per case.

This basic amount, however, is only the starting point for determining PPS hospital reimbursement. The sum of the product of the DRG weight and standardized amounts (or rather the sum of the products of the total DRG weights of all Medicare cases treated in the hospital during the payment period and the standardized amounts) is adjusted in several respects to determine a hospital's actual PPS payment. Because labor costs vary greatly throughout the country, the labor-related portion of the PPS payment is adjusted by an area wage index factor. How hospitals should be categorized for this purpose was the issue in the *Bellevue Hospital* case. PPS payments are further adjusted to recognize the cost of extraordinarily expensive cases, or "outliers." PPS payments are also enhanced to compensate teaching hospitals for the indirect costs of operating educational programs. CMS has also recently adopted a system of "severity adjusted" DRGS which take more account of co-morbidities and complications. Finally, PPS payments are increased or otherwise adjusted to benefit special categories of hospitals, such as disproportionate share hospitals (which serve large numbers of low-income patients, who presumably cost more to treat) or sole-community hospitals (which serve communities distant from other hospitals, and are protected by federal policy). These adjustments can be very important for hospitals in particular situations. Whereas straight unadjusted PPS payment accounts for 91 percent of Medicare payment for non-teaching hospitals, major urban teaching hospitals receive about 32 percent of their PPS payments from disproportionate share and indirect medical education cost adjustments.

A few categories of hospital costs continue to be reimbursed on a cost basis. The direct costs of medical education programs are reimbursed on a pass-through cost basis, as are hospital bad debts related to uncollectible Medicare deductible and coinsurance amounts and a few other miscellaneous expenses.

Any evaluation of DRG–PPS must certainly be mixed. PPS succeeded at its principal goal, limiting the escalation of Medicare expenditures for inpatient care. PPS also resulted in (or at least was accompanied by) a massive shift of care within hospitals from inpatient to outpatient settings or to long-term care units, often located within or owned by the same hospitals that had previously provided inpatient care. A great deal of surgery that used to be done on an inpatient basis, such as cataract surgery, is now done outpatient. PPS payment also encouraged hospitals to find ways to align their interests with those of their doctors, who in the end are responsible for admitting and discharging patients and ordering the tests and procedures that increase hospital costs. This led to many of the restructuring strategies discussed in chapter 10 and questionable incentive schemes discussed in chapter 11. There is also considerable evidence that there has been "DRG creep" over the years, as hospitals have moved to coding cases as more complicated and thus earned higher payment. In its latest rule, CMS has included a 2.4 percent rate reduction as a "behavioral offset" to acknowledge the likelihood that hospitals will inflate coding of case severity as CMS moves to severity-adjusted DRGs.

One apparent effect of DRG reimbursement has been the rise of specialty hospitals. There have always been a few hospitals that specialized in specific conditions, but within the last decade there has been a dramatic upswing in the number of hospitals specializing in cardiac, orthopedic, surgical and women's care. These hospitals are predominantly located in states that do not have health planning programs, and tend to be for profit. Most are owned at least to some extent by the physicians who refer to them. They are less likely to have emergency departments, they treat fewer Medicaid patients, and they derive a smaller share of their revenues from inpatient hospital services than general hospitals. These hospitals also tend to treat patients who are less severely ill than general hospitals, and are on average more profitable than general hospitals. Why would the DRG reimbursement system encourage the growth of such hospitals? See General Accounting Office, Specialty Hospitals: Geographic Location, Services Provided and Financial Performance. GAO–04–167 (2003). Specialty hospitals are further discussed in chapters 10. For good summaries of the literature on the effects of PPS, see the annual Medicare Payment Advisory Commission's Report to Congress on Medicare Payment Policy, filed every March. Earlier sources critiquing PPS and describing its effects include David Frankford, The Medicare DRGs: Efficiency and Organizational Rationality, 10 Yale J. Reg. 273 (1993); David Frankford, The Complexity of Medicare's Hospital Reimbursement System: Paradoxes of Averaging, 78 Iowa L. Rev. 517 (1993).

Bellevue Hospital notwithstanding, PPS does not seem to be making much business for lawyers. Most of the important issues PPS raises are not justiciable. Issues raised by PPS are either political questions, such as the standardized amount update level for any particular year, or technical questions, such as how a particular DRG should be weighted or which DRG should be assigned by a hospital to a particular admission. Congress has made it clear that it does not want the courts getting involved in these determinations:

42 U.S.C.A. § 1395ww(d)(7)

There shall be no administrative or judicial review under Section 1395oo of this title or otherwise of

(A) the determination of the requirement, or the proportional amount of any adjustment effected pursuant to subsection (e)(1) of this section [providing for updates in the standardized amount] * * *, and

    (B) the establishment of diagnosis-related-groups, of the methodology for the classification of discharges within groups, and of the appropriate weighing of factors thereof * * *

Congress has established a tripartite dialogue among itself, CMS, and the Medicare Payment Advisory Commission (an independent advisory body established to advise Congress through the annual reports mentioned above and special reports), to determine these questions and has left no place for the courts. See Timothy Stoltzfus Jost, Governing Medicare, 51 Admin. L. Rev. 39 (1999); Eleanor Kinney, Making Hard Choices Under the Medicare Prospective Payment System: One Administrative Model for Allocating Resources under a Government Health Insurance Program, 19 Ind. L. Rev. 1151 (1986). Such Medicare provider payment litigation as continues under DRG–PPS consists primarily of fact-intensive disputes entailing particular providers, such as whether a hospital qualifies for special treatment under PPS as a disproportionate share hospital. See North Broward Hosp. Dist. v. Shalala, 172 F.3d 90 (D.C.Cir. 1999).

Insofar as PPS generates work for lawyers, it is primarily in the area of advising clients how to take advantage of PPS. Consider the following problem:

Problem: PPS

    You are the in-house counsel for a large urban hospital that has a high percentage of Medicare patients. In recent years your hospital has either lost money or barely broken even. At the request of the hospital's CEO, you are serving on a committee considering how to improve the financial situation of the hospital, focusing particularly on your situation with respect to Medicare.

    What strategies might be available for increasing your hospital's PPS revenues? Would changing your case-mix help? How might you achieve that? What opportunities might be available in terms of how discharges are coded? (Reconsider this question after you study Medicare fraud and abuse in chapter 14). What possibilities are available under Medicare prospective payment for increasing your Medicare payments that are not strictly tied to your case-mix? How does the teaching mission of your hospital affect your Medicare reimbursement? How might you go about increasing your Medicare reimbursement for non-inpatient services?

    Alternatively, how might you go about lowering the cost of treating Medicare patients? In particular, what strategies can you use to create incentives for your doctors to reduce costs? (See chapters 10 and 11 for further discussion of these strategies.) Will cost reductions be accompanied by Medicare payment reductions?

3. Medicare Payment of Physicians

Medicare Part B payment for most services (including physician services) was based initially, at least in theory, on reimbursement of actual charges (minus deductibles and coinsurance). A number of concerns, however, including the rapid rise in the cost of physician services, increasing "balance-billing" to beneficiaries, and inequities in payments among medical specialties, led to consensus that payment reform was needed. In 1989 a political consensus came together around a package of reforms that were enacted by the Omnibus Budget Reconciliation Act of 1989 and codified at 42 U.S.C.A. 1395w–4(a) to (j).

At the heart of the payment reform was the creation of a physician fee schedule. As with Part A prospective payment, fees are determined by multiplying a weighted value (in this case representing a medical procedure rather than a diagnosis) times a conversion factor, which is adjusted to consider geographic variations in cost. Relative value units (RVUs) are assigned to procedures based on the CMS Common Procedure Coding System (HCPCS) and AMA Common Procedural Terminology (CPT) codes. The Relative Value Scale consists of three components: a physician work component, a practice expense component, and a malpractice component. Thus, for example, for CPT 45378, "diagnostic colonoscopy" under the proposed rule for 2008, the work RVU is 3.69; the practice expense RVU is 6.35 if the procedure is done in a physician's office; and the malpractice RVU is .30.

The physician work component is based on estimates of the relative time and intensity of physician work involved in delivering specified services. With respect to major surgeries, physician work is defined globally to include pre-operative evaluation and consultation (inpatient or outpatient), beginning with the day before surgery, and post-operative care for a normal recovery from surgery for the ninety days following the surgery.

The practice expense component accounts for physician overhead, including rent and office expenses. The practice expense is based on resource use. Different practice expense RVUs are applied depending on whether the services are furnished in a facility (hospital, SNF or ASC) or in a physician's office. Malpractice expenses for particular services are separated out from other practice expenses, and are based on the malpractice expense resources required to furnish the service.

The RVUs are adjusted by a geographic practice cost index (GPCI) to recognize differences in cost in various parts of the country and then multiplied by a conversion factor to reach a final fee payment amount (of which Medicare pays eighty percent, the other twenty percent representing the beneficiary coinsurance obligation). While most practice expenses are fully adjusted for geographic variation, physician work is only adjusted for one quarter of the variation, which offers some incentive for physicians to work in rural areas. The RBRVS system also provides special bonuses for physicians working in health practitioner shortage areas and for physicians working in rural areas. Rates are also adjusted downward for physicians who are not participating providers (i.e., who do not accept assignment for the claims of all of their Medicare patients).

While the resource-based prices set by RBRVS addressed the problem of price inflation in physician payment, previous attempts to control prices through fee freezes had been defeated by providers simply increasing the volume of their services. To address this problem, the 1989 legislation established the Medicare Volume Performance Standard (MVPS), which represented Congress's attempt to create a global budget for physician expenditures. The volume performance adjustment in RBRVS failed to achieve its goal, and in the 1997 Balanced Budget Act Congress abandoned the MVPS in favor of a "sustainable growth rate," applicable to all specialties and based on growth in the real gross domestic product and increases in Medicare population and coverage. 42 U.S.C. § 1395w–4(f). Congress has repeatedly intervened, however, to provide physicians price increases above those indicated by this formula, assuring an increase in price even while the volume of services continues to increase.

Problem: Resource–Based Payment for Lawyers

It has recently become apparent to Congress that the high cost of legal services is having a substantial negative effect on the American economy and on our international competitive position. Congress also becomes concerned that there are gross and irrational disparities among the payments lawyers receive for legal services. Congress, therefore, proposes the adoption of a resource-based relative value schedule, limiting lawyers to the charges allowed by such a schedule (plus 15 percent where the client agrees). Adherence to the charges is enforced by criminal laws plus civil penalties ($5000 per infraction).

Legal services for representing corporations in corporate takeovers and tax and securities work and for representing individuals in estate planning, domestic relations, real estate transactions or criminal defense matters, will all be evaluated considering the (1) time, (2) mental effort and judgment, and (3) psychological stress involved in delivering each service.* Geographic variations in practice overhead will also be recognized in fee-setting, though historic geographical variations in payments for the work of lawyers will be recognized only to a very limited extent (i.e., a lawyer will be paid for his or her own work—as opposed to overhead—the same payment for similar work whether it is performed in Manhattan or in Peoria). No explicit recognition will be given in the fee schedule for experience, skill, or law school class standing of individual practitioners.

How might such a fee schedule affect access to legal services? The volume of legal services provided? The geographic and specialty distribution of lawyers? The quality of legal services? Innovation in developing new legal theories? Your plans after law school? How hard you study for the final in this class?

Where does the analogy between this problem and RBRVS break down? How, that is, does the market for physician services differ from the market for legal services?

4. Pay for Performance

Even though DRG–PPS and RBRVS moved Medicare payment toward rewarding efficiency in service delivery, they still basically pay simply for providing a service and do little to recognize the quality of the service provided. In recent years, however, Medicare has begun to move towards paying for the quality of services with "pay for performance" or P4P programs. Medicare has already implemented two programs for hospital payment that link payment to quality measures–the Hospital Quality Initiative in which hospitals are given a small payment for reporting their performance on 10 quality measures, and the Premier Hospital Quality Incentive Demonstration, under which almost 300 hospitals are competing for incentive payments based on their performance with respect to thirty-four quality measures.

---

* These factors plus technical skill and physical effort are all considered in setting the physician RBRVS, see William Hsaio, et al., Estimating Physicians' Work for a Resource–Based Relative–Value Scale, 319 New Eng. J. Med. 835 (1988). Unless the additional physical exertion on the golf course consumed in soliciting corporate clients is considered, this latter factor does not seem relevant to legal services.

Medicare has also begun to implement its first P4P project for physicians, the physician group practice demonstration project, in which ten large group practices will be able to earn performance-based payments by achieving quality and cost-saving goals. Two other physician P4P demonstration projects were authorized by the Medicare Modernization Act. Finally, CMS has announced that beginning in October, 2008 it will not pay hospitals for preventable errors.

On its face, P4P seems like a good idea. It hardly makes sense to reward nonperformance or poor performance. High quality care is something that Medicare should be prepared to pay for. Despite the obviousness of P4P, it has not been greeted universally with open arms. The main objections to P4P group into two general categories—technical or mechanical objections on the one hand, and philosophical or policy objections on the other.

An initial technical problem is what performance we want to pay for. This breaks down into a number of subsidiary questions. To begin, how many measures should be used? The answer to this seems to be enough to encourage a range of behavior, but not so many as to create an excessive burden on providers. Most programs seem to settle on one dozen to three dozen measures.

Not only is the number of indicators important, the specific indicators that are picked are obviously vital as well. First, and most important, they should be indicators that in fact correlate with high quality care across the board, if it is possible to identify such indicators. One of the most serious problems with P4P is that if it pays professionals and providers to do certain things, they will place a priority on doing those things, in all likelihood at the cost of doing other things. But the things for which providers are not paid (often because these things are difficult to measure) may in fact be the most important determinants of quality. On the other hand, providers can only be paid for performance that can be measured. This means that P4P programs must usually start with data that are already available, or can feasibly be assembled. The data most readily available are administrative data, such as claims data, which are already collected and reported. But these data were not collected to measure quality, but rather for other purposes, usually for payment. These data may overcount some activities but will almost certainly undercount others. The alternative is glean information for the particular purpose of quality reporting from medical records. But medical record abstraction is costly, in particular for the majority of providers who do not have electronic medical records.

Another question most often raised with respect to indicators is whether to look at structure, process, or outcome, using the typology established years ago by Avedis Donabedian. The advantages and disadvantages of each are discussed in Chapter One. Structure is easiest to measure but least predictive of quality. Process is usually more easily measured than outcome, but is only important if it leads to good outcomes. Before too much is paid for process performance, therefore, some certainty is needed that the processes being rewarded are in fact likely to result in the outcomes desired. Outcome measures, on the other hand, are often not feasible for use as quality indicators. Outcomes are often not fully known until long after a medical intervention takes place, and when they occur often are difficult to attribute to a particular medical intervention, particularly if the patient has been treated by a number of providers. Attributing success or failure in the treatment of patients with chronic diseases who are not receiving treatment from an integrated health care system is difficult, if not impossible. Moreover, humans are infinitely variable, and often respond in very different ways to the same interventions. It is not fair to hold providers accountable for results that they cannot influence or determine. It is tempting to rely on surrogate or intermediate outcomes when it is difficult to perceive and measure final outcomes, but these may not be sure markers of final outcomes.

Yet another consideration in measuring outcomes is sample size. If a provider treats only a few Medicare patients or only a few patients to which a particular indicator is relevant during a measurement period, the provider's outcomes may not establish any reliably measured pattern. Random variation may become the most important driver of outcome. Medical data privacy is another consideration that becomes particularly salient with small providers or sample sizes. Yet another problem for small providers may be lack of infrastructure to report necessary data. It is not accidental that Medicare's first P4P program for physicians involves large, technically sophisticated, group practices. Moving P4P to solo or small practices will be very challenging, both for Medicare and for the practices.

A final problem with using outcomes is that they only make sense if results are risk-adjusted. Obviously, outcomes are likely to be worse for patients who are in worse condition ab initio. The easiest way for a provider to achieve great outcomes, therefore, might be to avoid the sickest or most at risk patients. This might not be an entirely bad thing–there are probably many procedures being done today on patients who are not good candidates for them–but on the whole it is not a good idea to reward providers for avoiding high-risk patients.

Even more important, there is considerable evidence that severity of some medical conditions correlates with racial and ethnic or socio-economic status (SES). Providers may also fear, justifiably or otherwise, that some minorities or persons of lower SES may find it more difficult to comply with medical regimens. It is well established that racial and ethnic minorities already receive disproportionately less and worse care under Medicare, and it would be a great tragedy if our attempts to improve quality exasperated these disparities. See Lawrence P. Casalino and Arthur Elster, Will Pay-for-Performance And Quality Reporting Affect Health Care Disparities? Health Aff. Web Excl., April 10, 2007.

Once we determine what we want to measure and reward, we need to determine what benchmarks to use for measurement. One goal would be to shoot for six sigma quality, essentially perfection. For most services perfect outcomes are not a realistic expectation. Rather, realistic goals must be set for the best levels of achievement that can be hoped for. If levels are set too high, few will achieve them, and others may become discouraged and not even try. But if levels are set too low, all may achieve them, and the incentives may fail in their original purpose. P4P may end up rewarding mediocrity and simply adding cost to the system. Even benchmarks set relatively high may end up providing considerable rewards to already high-achieving providers who simply maintain the status quo.

Another major risk of paying for performance is that it is likely to have undesired effects on provider behavior. It is likely that the first result of paying for performance will be that it will improve reporting of whatever performance is paid for. Events that previously went unnoted will now be meticulously recorded and reported, because something now turns on them. This will be true not just for the actual indicators measured, but also for any other data that feeds into the P4P system, such as risk-adjustment factors. Of course, increased recording and reporting may be good thing, but it is far from costless and gathering and processing this additional information must be taken into account as one of the costs of P4P.

Not only will data be reported more frequently, however, it will also inevitably be manipulated. Of course, some reporting may be fraudulent, and once the false claims act and qui tam statute kick in and the HHS Office of Inspector General (OIG) and Department of Justice come down hard on a few violators, behavior may improve. Much reporting, however, will simply be creative rather than fraudulent, particularly once coding consultants get involved, and reporting will be difficult, and costly, to police. Not only is reporting subject to manipulation, however, so are patients. If performance is measured by, for example, length of time to discharge or to return to work, patients may be discharged or returned to work prematurely. Under a worst case scenario, infections or bed sores may not be noted, or perhaps even treated, if providers are rewarded for their absence.

These are some of the technical problems presented by P4P, but P4P also raises important policy, even philosophical questions, which must also be addressed. First, and most practically, P4P measures tend disproportionately to address underuse of services. Rewards are often directed, for example, at providing preventive services. As long as Medicare basically pays for services on a fee-for-service or per-admission basis, however, addressing underuse is going to result in increased costs for the entire system. A second cost consideration is that P4P may end up rewarding providers for behavior that does not in fact cause them to incur additional costs. Medicare may end up simply paying more for the same services it now gets (though hopefully of better quality). Better quality care may cost more, but it also may cost the same or even less. Given the limited funds available to Medicare, does it make sense to pay providers more if the increased funds simply go into additional profit?

Another fundamental issue that must be considered is the relationship between incentives and behavior. P4P is based on underlying rational choice assumptions that if Medicare can just get incentives right behavior will follow. The relationship between incentives and behavior is often, however, complex. An initial problem here is the incredibly complex nature of Medicare payment. DRG–PPS and RBRVS are trying to do a lot of things, from providing incentives for medical education, to serving rural areas, to recognizing the higher costs of institutions that provide services to the uninsured. Simply adding a small incremental payment for performance on top of the already large amounts Medicare is paying based on other considerations may not have much of an effect on performance. Of course, Medicare payment incentives must also be considered in the context of all of the other incentives providers face. The cost of compliance relative to its reward will be a key factor here. How much of a provider's practice is paid for by Medicare, as opposed to how much is paid for by other payers, could make an important difference. Noneconomic incentives affect behavior as well, and while these can be expected to reinforce P4P, this may not always be the case.

P4P explicitly highlights the problem of competency. If the standards Medicare comes up with for P4P are valid and realistic, but some providers are not reaching them, should Medicare beneficiaries be exposed to those providers? Why should Medicare continue to pay incompetent providers at all? Does it have an obligation to protect beneficiaries from them? Should tax dollars be used to purchase substandard care? Also, if providers who do not merit P4P disproportionately serve the poor or minorities, does Medicare have an obligation to get other providers to serve these populations?

There is also the problem of rewarding professionals to simply do what professionals ought to do. Should a doctor be paid significantly more for doing what the doctor would be doing anyway if the doctor were competent? Is payment, moreover, the most important motivation for professionals? And if so, should we focus on bonuses for good quality care or penalties for poor quality care (as in not paying for costs attributable to medical errors)? What should motivate health care professionals?

Indeed, one must wonder what P4P will do to the doctor-patient relationship. Many outcomes and processes depend on patient, and for that matter family, cooperation. What will happen to professional/patient relationship if a physician's payment depends on patient's behavior? Will doctors be discouraged from caring for noncompliant or difficult patient? But "compliance" is in one sense another way of describing patient preferences. Should a doctor be penalized if his or her patients strongly object to vaccinations? On the other hand, should patients also share in compensation if their behavior is key? Should we pay patients for having screening tests done or for receiving preventive services?

Moreover, paying hospitals for performance presumes that they are in turn capable of getting the professionals that practice within them to improve performance. What problems might hospitals face in creating incentives for those professionals? See William H. Thompson, Aligning Hospital and Physician Incentives in the Era of Pay-for-Performance, 3 Ind. Health L. Rev. 327 (2006).

Is P4P, after all, a good idea? See, arguing for P4P, Robert Berenson, Paying for Quality and Doing it Right, 60 Wash. & Lee L. Rev 1315 (2003), and taking a more negative view, Bruce Vladeck, If Paying for Quality is Such a Bad Idea, Why is Everyone for It? 60 Wash. & Lee L. Rev. 1345 (2003) and Michael Cannon, Pay for Performance: Is Medicare a Good Candidate? 7 Yale J. Health Pol'y, L. & Ethics 1 (2007). Finally, see, examining the theoretical basis of P4P, William M. Sage, Pay for Performance: Will it Work in Theory? 3 Ind. Health L. Rev. 305 (2006).

Problem: Pay for Performance

You are working for CMS and have been asked to design a pay-for-performance incentive program for Medicare. The system will redirect five percent of physician payments to reward high quality care. What measures of performance will you recommend, and how many of them? Will you focus on rewarding the absolute level of performance or improvement in performance from current levels?

How will you assure that your system does not penalize physicians who care for high-risk patients or racial and ethnic minority patients? How will you assure that the data on which payment is based is accurate? How will you reduce the payments that physicians would otherwise receive to make sure that the program does not increase Medicare expenditures?

5. *Medicare Managed Care*

Although Medicare began as a fee-for-service program, it has offered managed care options from the beginning. Managed care enrollment grew slowly at first, but growth was rapid in the mid–1990s: between 1995 and 1997 enrollment doubled from three to six million. Prior to the Balanced Budget Act of 1997, Medicare health maintenance organizations (HMOs) were paid ninety-five percent of the cost of Medicare fee-for-service costs in the same county (with crude risk adjustment). Because of biased selection (i.e. HMOs got healthier beneficiaries), HMOs did very well, particularly in counties with high fee-for-service costs. Because they were required to share their excess income with beneficiaries, Medicare managed care plans generally offered attractive benefit packages–in particular prescription drug coverage– which in turn led to rapid growth. The Balanced Budget Act of 1997 created the Medicare + Choice program, attempting to encourage continued growth in Medicare managed care, while at the same time dealing with some of the problems of the prior program. The hope was that Medicare + Choice would give beneficiaries a choice of health plans, benefits, and cost-sharing options, and that managed competition among health plans would hold down the cost of the Medicare program. The BBA changes, however, were a disaster for Medicare managed care, leading to a rapid decline in plan participation and enrollment. This, in turn, led to the Medicare Modernization Act, which dramatically increased payment for managed care plans, and, in turn, enrollment. The current state of the program is described in the excerpt that follows:

PATRICIA NEWMAN, MEDICARE ADVANTAGE: KEY ISSUES AND IMPLICATIONS FOR BENEFICIARIES, THE HENRY J. KAISER FAMILY FOUNDATION, JUNE 2007

* * *

Characteristics of Medicare Advantage Enrollees

The number of Medicare beneficiaries enrolling in Medicare Advantage plans is on the rise, yet the majority of Medicare beneficiaries continue to be covered under Medicare's traditional fee-for-service program. Today, 8.7 million beneficiaries—about 20 percent—are enrolled in a Medicare Advantage plan, up from 5.3 million in 2003, but there is wide variation in enrollment rates across states. Fewer than 10 percent of beneficiaries are enrolled in a Medicare Advantage plan in 19 states, while more than 30 percent of beneficiaries are in Medicare Advantage plans in 8 states.

Recent discussions have focused on whether Medicare Advantage plans serve a disproportionate share of people who are among the most vulnerable in Medicare, focusing on income, race/ethnicity, and rural location. Our analysis of the most recent data available from the Centers for Medicare and

Medicaid Services (CMS) in the 2005 Medicare Current Beneficiary Survey finds:

- *Income.* Medicare Advantage enrollees are neither disproportionately low-income nor high-income. Roughly the same share (50 percent) of beneficiaries in traditional Medicare and in Medicare Advantage plans lives on an income below $20,000. * * *

- *Race/Ethnicity.* Medicare Advantage enrollment rates are similar for white and African American beneficiaries. A larger share of Hispanic beneficiaries is enrolled in Medicare Advantage plans; half of all Hispanic Medicare Advantage enrollees live in California and Florida.

- *Rural Location.* Access to Medicare Advantage plans for beneficiaries living in rural areas has increased considerably in the past two years. In 2005, only 2 percent of all Medicare beneficiaries living in rural areas were enrolled in a Medicare Advantage plan. In 2006, the rate was up to 7 percent, according to MedPAC's more recent analysis of enrollment data.

- *Health Status.* Self-assessed health status is generally considered to be a relatively strong predictor of future medical needs and our analysis finds a smaller share of Medicare Advantage enrollees reporting that they are in fair or poor health than their counterparts in traditional Medicare. Medicare Advantage plans also enroll a smaller share of beneficiaries who are under age 65 and have permanent disabilities, as well as a smaller share of beneficiaries living in nursing homes and other institutional settings.

* * *

Benefits and Out-of-Pocket Costs

While Medicare Advantage enrollees are generally healthier than beneficiaries in traditional Medicare, a key concern for the 24 percent of Medicare Advantage enrollees who say their health status is fair or poor is likely to be the adequacy of their plan's coverage and out-of-pocket costs associated with their medical care.

Medicare Advantage plans generally provide benefits that are covered under the traditional Medicare program, but are permitted to vary cost-sharing and deductibles as long as the overall benefit package is equivalent in value to traditional Medicare. In addition, many plans provide additional benefits to their enrollees that are not covered under traditional Medicare. Current law requires plans to use 75% of "extra payments" (the difference between the plan's bid for services under parts A and B and the benchmark amount determined by CMS) to fund extra benefits, which are broadly defined and can include marketing and other administrative costs.

Beneficiaries may be attracted to Medicare Advantage plans by the promise of additional benefits and lower cost-sharing, but beneficiaries are not always better off financially in Medicare Advantage plans than in traditional Medicare. For any given beneficiary, out-of-pocket costs depend on many factors, including their individual medical needs and the particular plan they choose. On the one hand, many Medicare Advantage plans waive deductibles, reduce cost-sharing requirements, offer a stop-loss limit on catastrophic spending for services covered under Parts A and B and provide some additional benefits, including Part D drug coverage, and other benefits, such as vision and dental. On the other hand, many Medicare Advantage plans impose daily hospital copayments, daily copayments for home health visits, and daily copayments for the first several days in a skilled nursing facility that are not required under traditional Medicare.

Of course, extra benefits may result in lower out-of-pocket costs for some beneficiaries. Yet, even with extra benefits, enrollees could end up paying more in a Medicare Advantage plan than they would pay under traditional Medicare, which may seem counter-intuitive. Consider the following hypothetical case of an 80–year old widow, Mrs. Rollins, who broke her hip, was admitted to the hospital for eight days, transferred to a skilled nursing facility for 27 days, and then sent home where she received 47 home health visits to support her rehabilitation. For ease of illustration, this case example does not take into account the variety of other medical services and supplies she may need.

- If Mrs. Rollins were covered under traditional Medicare, she would pay $1,860 out-of-pocket in traditional Medicare, plus $1,122/year in Part B premiums for a total of $2,982. She would pay this amount regardless of where she lives because Part B premiums, deductibles and skilled nursing facility copayments are uniform throughout the country.

- If Mrs. Rollins lived In Oakland, California (zip code 94601) and chose to enroll in a Medicare Advantage plan, she would be able to choose from nearly two dozen Medicare Advantage plans in her area. Under five of the plans, she would pay less than she would under traditional Medicare for premiums, hospital and post-acute care (although none of these plans include a prescription drug benefit). But under the majority of plans offered in her area, she could pay substantially more out-of-pocket than she would under traditional Medicare for her medical needs in this scenario, with annual out-of-pocket costs, including premiums, ranging from $2,515 to $5,210.

- In Pensacola, Florida (zip code 32425), a more rural area, there are fewer Medicare Advantage plans available, but a similar picture emerges. Mrs. Rollins would pay less under four plans than she would under traditional Medicare, but under the remaining 12 plans, she would pay more, with total costs ranging from $2,515 to $6,062 across all plans offered in her area.

Mrs. Rollins could end up with lower out-of-pocket costs under a Medicare Advantage plan than she would under traditional Medicare. However, a big challenge for beneficiaries like Mrs. Rollins is predicting what services they are likely to need before they enroll in a plan. This is especially difficult given the wide variation in benefits which severely limits the ability of consumers to make apples-to-apples comparisons across plans.

A review of plans in Oakland and Pensacola raises a number of issues.

- Seniors with inpatient and post-acute needs could pay substantially more for their medical care under some Medicare Advantage plans than under traditional Medicare; this is true even in plans that have out-of-pocket spending limits as many Medicare Advantage plans do.

- For seniors with limited incomes, out-of-pocket costs may consume a significant share of income. If Mrs. Rollins' income is equal to the mean for Medicare beneficiaries, which is about $18,000, her average out-of-pocket costs for premiums, hospital and post-acute care could consume between 14 percent and 29 percent of her income in Oakland. Under traditional Medicare, she would pay 17 percent of her income in premiums and cost-sharing for these services.

- Some plans charge daily copayments for hospital stays that can add up to substantially more than the Medicare Part A deductible ($992).

* * *

- Annual supplemental premiums vary widely ($0 to $1,932 in Oakland) and can contribute significantly to annual costs. Some plans with supplemental premiums do not offer a prescription drug benefit.

- Most but not all Medicare Advantage plans offer prescription drug coverage; some plans with supplemental premiums do not offer prescription drug benefits; none of the plans offered in Oakland or Pensacola cover brand-name drugs in the Part D coverage gap, consistent with national data [].

Equity Concerns: Who Gets Extra Benefits and Who Pays?

Relatively generous payments allow Medicare Advantage plans to offer extra benefits to enrollees, as noted above. As a result, the current payment system essentially finances additional benefits for the one in five beneficiaries who are enrolled in Medicare Advantage plans, without providing similar coverage to the other four out of five beneficiaries enrolled in traditional Medicare. This un-level playing field has raised questions about the extent to which Medicare distributes extra benefits equitably across the Medicare population.

A second equity issue relates to financing; the current payment system translates into higher Part B premiums for beneficiaries to help support higher payments to Medicare Advantage plans. This is because Medicare Advantage plans cover benefits under Medicare Parts A and B, so the costs associated with Part B benefits provided by Medicare Advantage plans are financed by general revenues (paid by taxpayers) and by Part B premiums (paid by all beneficiaries, or by Medicaid which pays premiums on behalf of low-income beneficiaries who have Medicaid as a supplement to Medicare).

As a result, nearly 30 million beneficiaries in traditional Medicare pay higher monthly Part B premiums to help support the current payment system to Medicare Advantage plans, but of course do not receive the extra benefits that Medicare Advantage plans offer to their enrollees. The HHS Office of the Actuary recently reported that the current Medicare Advantage payment system has increased Part B premiums by an additional $2 per month. * * *

Further, the current payment system has the effect of cutting short by two years the solvency of the Part A trust fund, according to the HHS Office of the Actuary, potentially affecting coverage for current beneficiaries as well as younger adults who are approaching the age of Medicare eligibility.

* * *

Notes

Although traditional managed care has to date enjoyed limited success as an alternative to traditional fee-for-service managed care, might there be advantages in incorporating managed care strategies, such as the use of networks, utilization review, or financial incentives into the traditional Medicare program. What legal barriers might this strategy face? Could Medicare, for example, limit program participation to a limited number of high-quality, low-cost, providers? See Robert A. Berenson and Dean M. Harris, Using Managed Care Tools in Traditional Medicare—Should We? Could We? 65 L. & Contemp. Probs. 139 (2002).

Note: The Medicare Advantage Program

Samuel Johnson observed that remarriage evidences the triumph of hope over experience. The same can certainly be said of the Medicare Advantage program. Medicare Advantage (MA) is the name that Congress gave the Medicare + Choice program in the Medicare Prescription Drug, Improvement, and Modernization Act of 2003 to give that failed program a fresh start. Congress evidently learned its own lessons from the failure of the Medicare + Choice program, and tried to respond to them in this legislation. These are:

1. *Medicare managed care cannot compete with traditional fee-for-service Medicare on a level playing field.* Unless Congress is willing to pay Medicare managed care plans at rates subsstantially in excess of the cost of traditional Medicare, private managed care plans will not join and stick with the program. Congress had raised rates for Medicare + Choice plans in 1999 and again in 2000, but plans kept leaving the program. The 2003 legislation lavishes money on Medicare managed care plans. Medicare payments for MA plans are established under a complex procedure that combines bidding and benchmark formulas, keyed to fee-for-service payments. They are too complex to explain here. See Mark Merlis, Medicare Advantage Payment Policy (2007), http://www.nhpf.org/pdfs_bp/BP_MAPaymentPolicy_09-24-07.pdf. The formulas, however assure that MA plans are paid at least as much as Medicare would have paid under the traditional Medicare program for a particular beneficiary, and often far more.

Other aspects of the Medicare law further guarantee MA plans rates of payment significantly greater than the costs of traditional Medicare for caring for the same beneficiaries. First, traditional Medicare, as noted above, is required to make some payments that are not directly linked to the cost of caring for Medicare beneficiaries, such as payments for direct and indirect medical education costs and disproportionate share hospital payments, or special payments to rural providers. MA rates are reduced to exclude direct medical education costs, but otherwise are not modified to reflect payments made by traditional Medicare for non-Medicare purposes, even though MA plans do not have to cover these costs when they make payments to providers. Second, although payments to MA plans are supposed to be risk-adjusted to take into account the fact that Medicare managed care beneficiaries are usually younger, healthier, and less expensive than beneficiaries who stay with traditional Medicare, risk adjustment is far from an exact science. In fact, MA plans have received payments substantially in excess of the cost of traditional Medicare because they draw a healthier population. In 2005, every plan in the country was paid more than its enrollees would have cost in traditional Medicare (12.4 percent more on average), for a total of $5.2 billion, $922 per enrollee. Brian Biles, et al., The Cost of Privatization: Extra Payments to Medicare Advantage Plans–Updated and Revised (Commonwealth Fund Issue Brief, Nov. 2006). The Medicare Payment Advisory Committee estimated in 2007 that leveling the playing field so that MA plans were paid the same amount per beneficiary as traditional Medicare paid would save the program $54 billion over five years, $149.1 billion over ten years. See also, Robert A. Berenson & Melissa A. Goldstein, Will Medicare Wither on the Vine? How Congress Has Advantaged Medicare Advantage—And What's a Level Playing Field Anyway?, 1 St. Louis U. J. Health L. & Pol'y 5 (2007); GAO, Medicare Advantage: Increased Spending Relative to Medicare Fee-for-Service May Not Always Reduce Beneficiary Out-of-Pocket Costs, GAO-08-359 (Feb. 2008).

2. *Managed care plans will not serve large areas of the country unless they receive even greater incentives.* Prior to the MMA, Medicare managed care had never reached large parts of the country, particularly rural areas and areas where the low cost of traditional Medicare led to low Medicare managed care rates. The MMA, however, encouraged the creation of regional or national MA PPO plans to fill this gap, and offered them significant financial incentives.

Even more successful in reaching rural areas, however, have been "private fee-for-service" (PFFS) plans which were created by the 1997 Balanced Budget Act but were offered more favorable payment rates by the MMA, which essentially treats them as managed care plans. PFFS plans offer essentially the same benefits and free choice of provider as does traditional Medicare, but also may provide Part D drug benefits and catastrophic coverage. Medicare providers are not required to participate in PFFS plans, but if they accept PFFS beneficiaries, they cannot bill more than they would bill under traditional Medicare. Because PFFS plans offer essentially the same providers as traditional Medicare without managed care restrictions, and because they usually offer additional benefits to those offered by traditional Medicare, they have grown very quickly, 535 percent from December 2005 to February 2007. By early 2007, they covered 1.34 million beneficiaries, including many enrollees in rural areas. PFFS plans, however, were paid in 2006 119% of the local costs of traditional Medicare, making them far more profitable than other MA plans, even before adjusting for the fact that PFFS plans are probably attracting healthier beneficiaries. Unless one believes as a matter of faith that choice is in itself very valuable, it is hard to see what the added value was received for these extra payments. See Jonathan Blum, Ruth Brown, and Miryam Frieder, An Examination of Medicare Private Fee-for-Service Plans (Kaiser Family Foundation, March 2007).

3. *Medicare can be nudged towards managed competition, but not too quickly or overtly.* Under the scheme set out in the MMA, beginning in 2010, a "comparative cost adjustment" program will be implemented that for the following six years will expand direct competition between MA plans and traditional Medicare. The program will be implemented only in six sites where MA market penetration is at least twenty-five percent and at least two MA plans are available. In these areas, Part B premiums would be reduced or raised depending on whether traditional Medicare costs more or less than MA plans. Traditional Medicare will have to compete with a handicap, as it has to cover some costs MA plans do not. Traditional Medicare is likely also to be hindered in the competition by being burdened with more costly beneficiaries.

Direct competition between traditional Medicare and MA plans proved to be one of the most controversial provisions of the MMA. It should be noted, however, that Medicare managed care plans have always been in competition with traditional Medicare. The comparative adjustment project only raises the possibility that Medicare beneficiaries who stick with traditional Medicare may face increases in their Part B premiums, and not just the loss of additional benefits or lower premiums that they might gain by switching to MA plans. The real problem, however, is the terms of the competition, which unfairly burden traditional Medicare and favor MA plans.

Indeed, the most striking feature of the Medicare Advantage program is the irony that the legislation should have acknowledged so openly—indeed embraced—the fact that Medicare managed care, which has long been looked to by market advocates as the salvation of the Medicare program, simply costs more than traditional Medicare.

4. *If they receive high enough subsidies, Medicare private plans can offer beneficiaries generous coverage, and therefore become very popular with beneficiaries.* Some of the excess payments will be kept by MA plans to cover their high expenses and as profits. But some must also, under existing law, be returned to beneficiaries in the form of enriched benefits or lower premiums or cost-sharing. This has allowed MA plans to lure many beneficiaries away from traditional Medicare by offering generous benefits at low premiums. In particular, MA plans offer drug benefits at much lower premiums than stand-alone PDP plans. As of April, 2007, 8.5 million beneficiaries were enrolled in MA plans, up from 5.3 million in 2003. The question remains, of course, why not use the extra money that MA pays for MA plans to make additional benefits available or to lower premiums for all Medicare beneficiaries?

If managed care does not save money, of what use is it? An analysis of the Medicare + Choice program by a distinguished study panel acknowledged that the program has not saved money for Medicare, but also concluded that:

> Access to coordinated care plans has allowed some beneficiaries to reduce significantly the burden of paperwork and improve their financial security. In addition, coordinated care plans have improved diagnosis of illness and reduced disparities related to race and income for preventive services.

The Report also contended that managed care has the potential to save money for Medicare, though this potential has not yet been realized. See Kathleen M. King and Mark Schlesinger, eds., Final Report of the Study Panel on Medicare and Markets–The Role of Private Health Plans in Medicare: Lessons from the Past, Looking to the Future (2003), available at http://www.nasi.org/publications2763/publications_show.htm?doc_id=197700.

Another argument made vociferously during the 2007 debate on cutting MA funding was that MA plans favor minorities and low income beneficiaries. See America's Health Insurance Plans, Low Income and Minority Beneficiaries in Medicare Advantage Plans (February 2007); Adam Atherly and Kenneth Thorpe, Value of Medicare Advantage to Low–Income and Minority Beneficiaries (Blue Cross and Blue Shield Ass'n, 2005). Indeed, during the 2007 MA subsidy debate, the NAACP and League of United Latin American Citizens opposed cuts. In fact, the data show that very low income beneficiaries overwhelmingly are covered by Medicaid and traditional Medicare, high income beneficiaries tend to have retiree coverage or traditional Medicare supplemented by Medigap, but that beneficiaries with low to middle incomes tend disproportionately to sign up for Medicare Advantage. This group includes many minority beneficiaries, but on balance minorities are as likely to enroll in Medicare Advantage as whites (though much more likely to receive Medicaid). The larger question, of course, is whether the high costs paid for MA are justified by whatever advantages it offers to minority beneficiaries.

Are there any other arguments for Medicare managed care? Are there other explanations as to why it has proved so popular with lawmakers?

Note on Beneficiary Protections in Medicare Managed Care

Medicare beneficiaries receiving care from managed care organizations are potentially subject to all of the abuses discussed in Chapter 6 above, which may be potentially greater because of the greater needs and lesser capacities of some beneficiaries. MA organizations are, therefore, subject to a host of regulatory requirements. MA organizations are responsible for providing their members with detailed descriptions of plan provisions, including disclosure of any coverage limitations or regulations. 42 U.S.C.A. § 1395w–22(c). MA coordinated care plans must provide access to providers 24 hours a day, 7 days a week; ensure services are "culturally competent" and that hours of operation of providers are convenient and non-discriminatory; provide adequate and coordinated specialist treatment for persons with complex or serious medical conditions; and allow women enrollees direct access to women's health specialists. 42 U.S.C.A. § 1395w–22(d), 42 C.F.R. § 422.112. MA plans must have an ongoing quality assurance and performance improvement program. 42 U.S.C.A. § 1395w–22(e). They must have mechanisms in place to detect both under-and over-utilization. Most types of plans must make provision for independent quality review. Organizations accredited by approved national accreditation agencies can be deemed to meet quality requirements. 42 U.S.C.A. § 1395w–22(e)(4).

MA organizations may not discriminate against professionals on the basis of their licensure or certification, and must provide notice and hearing to physicians whose participation rights are terminated. 42 C.F.R. §§ 422.202, 205. MA Organizations may not interfere with provider advice to enrollees regarding care and treatment. 42 U.S.C.A. § 1395w–22(j)(3). Plans that fail substantially to provide medically necessary services where the failure adversely affects (or is substantially likely adversely to affect) health; impose unpermitted premiums; wrongly expel or refuse to reenroll a beneficiary; provide false information; interfere with practitioner's advice to enrollees; or commit other specified wrongful acts may be subject to civil money penalties of not more than $25,000. Plans that deny or discourage enrollment of persons on the basis of medical condition or provide false information to CMS are subject to fines of up to $100,000. 42 U.S.C.A. 1395w–27(g)(2). CMS may also impose civil penalties of $25,000 for deficiencies that directly affect or have a substantial likelihood of adversely affecting enrollees, plus $10,000 a week if the deficiency remains uncorrected. 42 U.S.C.A. § 1395w–27(g)(2).

One of the primary criticisms that the managed care industry leveled at the Medicare + Choice program was that it imposed excessive regulations. The 2003 legislation, however, left the previous law largely untouched. The most important change that it made was to clarify that MA plans are not subject to state laws except for licensing and solvency requirements.

Which of the regulations described above would you abolish? Why?

D. ADMINISTRATION AND APPEALS

As demonstrated by the *Bellevue Hospital* case, the major decisions about federal Medicare and Medicaid policy are ultimately made by the United States Congress, which is constantly tinkering with the program. Congressional decisions are in turn fleshed-out by the Center for Medicare and Medicaid Services (CMS) at the Department of Health and Human Services (HHS) and implemented by the private Medicare contractors that make individual claims determinations. Although some of the provisions of the

Medicare Act are overly detailed, it has often been in the interest of Congress to enact very general provisions and to leave the hard and politically dangerous work of hammering out the details of the program to HHS. In the early years of Medicare, HHS frequently deferred to the health care industry and attempted to make program decisions by consensus. Since the late 1970s, however, HHS has exercised its authority more aggressively, as is illustrated by the DRG hospital reimbursement and RBRVS physician payment programs discussed above. See Timothy Stoltzfus Jost, Governing Medicare, 51 Admin. L. Rev. 39 (1999); Lawrence Brown, Technocratic Corporatism and Administrative Reform in Medicare, 10 J. Health Pol. Pol'y and L. 579 (1985).

The courts have had only a minor role in making major policy decisions about Medicare, but have been active at the fringes, trying to correct some of the program's worst bureaucratic excesses. Their role has been circumscribed by the strict limits placed on judicial review by the Supreme Court's interpretation of the Social Security Act. 42 U.S.C.A. § 1395ii provides that 42 U.S.C.A. § 405(h) applies to the Medicare program. Section 405(h) provides, in part, that:

> No findings of fact or decision of the Secretary shall be reviewed by any person, tribunal, or governmental agency except as herein provided. No action against the United States, the Secretary, or any officer or employee thereof shall be brought under section 1331 or 1346 of title 28 to recover on any claim arising under this subchapter.

The Supreme Court's most recent interpretations of these statutes are discussed in the following case:

SHALALA v. ILLINOIS COUNCIL ON LONG TERM CARE, INC.

Supreme Court of the United States, 2000.
529 U.S. 1, 120 S.Ct. 1084, 146 L.Ed.2d 1.

JUSTICE BREYER.

The question before us is one of jurisdiction. An association of nursing homes sued, inter alios, the Secretary of Health and Human Services (HHS) * * * (hereinafter Secretary) in Federal District Court claiming that certain Medicare-related regulations violated various statutes and the Constitution. The association invoked the court's federal-question jurisdiction, 28 U.S.C. § 1331. The District Court dismissed the suit on the ground that it lacked jurisdiction. It believed that a set of special statutory provisions creates a separate, virtually exclusive, system of administrative and judicial review for denials of Medicare claims; and it held that one of those provisions explicitly barred a § 1331 suit. See 42 U.S.C. § 1395ii (incorporating to the Medicare Act 42 U.S.C. § 405(h), which provides that "[n]o action . . . to recover on any claim" arising under the Medicare laws shall be "brought under section 1331 . . . of title 28"). The Court of Appeals, however, reversed.

We conclude that the statutory provision at issue, § 405(h), as incorporated by § 1395ii, bars federal-question jurisdiction here. The association or its members must proceed instead through the special review channel that the Medicare statutes create.[ ]

* * * Medicare Act Part A provides payment to nursing homes which provide care to Medicare beneficiaries after a stay in hospital. To receive

payment, a home must enter into a provider agreement with the Secretary of HHS, and it must comply with numerous statutory and regulatory requirements. State and federal agencies enforce those requirements through inspections. Inspectors report violations, called "deficiencies." And "deficiencies" lead to the imposition of sanctions or "remedies."[ ]

The regulations at issue focus on the imposition of sanctions or remedies. [The sanctions imposed under these regulations are described in Chapter 3 above. Ed.] * * *

* * *

The association's complaint filed in Federal District Court attacked the regulations as unlawful in four basic ways. In its view: (1) certain terms, e.g., "substantial compliance" and "minimal harm," are unconstitutionally vague; (2) the regulations and manual, particularly as implemented, violate statutory requirements seeking enforcement consistency,[ ] and exceed the legislative mandate of the Medicare Act; (3) the regulations create administrative procedures inconsistent with the Federal Constitution's Due Process Clause; and (4) the manual and other agency publications create legislative rules that were not promulgated consistent with the Administrative Procedure Act's demands for "notice and comment" and a statement of "basis and purpose," 5 U.S.C. § 553.[ ]

* * *

The case before us began when the Illinois Council on Long Term Care, Inc. (Council), an association of about 200 Illinois nursing homes participating in the Medicare (or Medicaid) program, filed the complaint * * * in Federal District Court. * * * The District Court, as we have said, dismissed the complaint for lack of federal-question jurisdiction.[ ] In doing so, the court relied upon § 405(h) as interpreted by this Court in Weinberger v. Salfi, 422 U.S. 749, 95 S.Ct. 2457, 45 L.Ed.2d 522 (1975), and Heckler v. Ringer, 466 U.S. 602, 104 S.Ct. 2013, 80 L.Ed.2d 622 (1984).[ ]

The Court of Appeals reversed the dismissal.[ ] In its view, a later case, Bowen v. Michigan Academy of Family Physicians, 476 U.S. 667, 106 S.Ct. 2133, 90 L.Ed.2d 623 (1986), had significantly modified this Court's earlier case law. * * *

Section 405(h) purports to make exclusive the judicial review method set forth in § 405(g). Its second sentence says that "[n]o findings of fact or decision of the [Secretary] shall be reviewed by any person, tribunal, or governmental agency except as herein provided." § 405(h). Its third sentence, directly at issue here, says that "[n]o action against the United States, the [Secretary], or any officer or employee thereof shall be brought under section 1331 or 1346 of title 28 to recover on any claim arising under this subchapter."

The scope of the * * * language "to recover on any claim arising under" the Social Security (or, as incorporated through § 1395ii, the Medicare) Act is, if read alone, uncertain. Those words clearly apply in a typical Social Security or Medicare benefits case, where an individual seeks a monetary benefit from the agency (say a disability payment, or payment for some medical procedure), the agency denies the benefit and the individual challenges the lawfulness of that denial. The statute plainly bars § 1331 review in such a case, irrespective of whether the individual challenges the agency's denial on evidentiary, rule-related, statutory, constitutional, or other legal grounds. But does the statute's bar apply when one who might later seek money or some other benefit from (or contest the imposition of a penalty by) the agency challenges in advance (in a § 1331 action) the lawfulness of a policy, regulation, or statute that might later bar recovery of that benefit (or authorize the imposition of the penalty)? * * *

In answering the question, we temporarily put the case on which the Court of Appeals relied, Michigan Academy, *supra*, to the side. Were we not to take account of that case, § 405(h) as interpreted by the Court's earlier cases of Weinberger v. Salfi, *supra*, and Heckler v. Ringer, *supra*, would clearly bar this § 1331 lawsuit.

In Salfi, * * * [t]his Court held that § 405(h) barred § 1331 jurisdiction for all members of the class because "it is the Social Security Act which provides both the standing and the substantive basis for the presentation of th[e] constitutional contentions." * * *

* * *

In Ringer, four individuals brought a § 1331 action challenging the lawfulness (under statutes and the Constitution) of the agency's determination not to provide Medicare Part A reimbursement to those who had undergone a particular medical operation. The Court held that § 405(h) barred § 1331 jurisdiction over the action, even though the challenge was in part to the agency's procedures, the relief requested amounted simply to a declaration of invalidity (not an order requiring payment), and one plaintiff had as yet no valid claim for reimbursement because he had not even undergone the operation and would likely never do so unless a court set aside as unlawful the challenged agency "no reimbursement" determination. * * *

As so interpreted, the bar of § 405(h) reaches beyond ordinary administrative law principles of "ripeness" and "exhaustion of administrative remedies," [ ] doctrines that in any event normally require channeling a legal challenge through the agency. * * * Doctrines of "ripeness" and "exhaustion" contain exceptions, however, which exceptions permit early review when, for example, the legal question is "fit" for resolution and delay means hardship,[ ] or when exhaustion would prove "futile," [ ].

Insofar as § 405(h) prevents application of the "ripeness" and "exhaustion" exceptions, i.e., insofar as it demands the "channeling" of virtually all legal attacks through the agency, it assures the agency greater opportunity to apply, interpret, or revise policies, regulations, or statutes without possibly premature interference by different individual courts applying "ripeness" and "exhaustion" exceptions case by case. But this assurance comes at a price, namely, occasional individual, delay-related hardship. In the context of a massive, complex health and safety program such as Medicare, embodied in hundreds of pages of statutes and thousands of pages of often interrelated regulations, any of which may become the subject of a legal challenge in any of several different courts, paying this price may seem justified. In any event, such was the judgment of Congress as understood in Salfi and Ringer. [ ]

* * *

The Court of Appeals held that Michigan Academy modified the Court's earlier holdings by limiting the scope of "1395ii and therefore § 405(h)" to "amount determinations."[ ] But we do not agree. Michigan Academy involved a § 1331 suit challenging the lawfulness of HHS regulations that governed procedures used to calculate benefits under Medicare Part B—which Part provides voluntary supplementary medical insurance, e.g., for doctors' fees. [ ] The Medicare statute, as it then existed, provided for only limited review of Part B decisions. It allowed the equivalent of § 405(g) review for "eligibility" determinations.[ ] It required private insurance carriers (administering the Part B program) to provide a "fair hearing" for disputes about Part B "amount determinations."[ ] But that was all.

Michigan Academy first discussed the statute's total silence about review of "challenges mounted against the method by which . . . amounts are to be determined."[ ] It held that this silence meant that, although review was not available under § 405(g), the silence did not itself foreclose other forms of review, say review in a court action brought under § 1331.[ ]

The Court then asked whether § 405(h) barred 28 U.S.C. § 1331 review of challenges to methodology. Noting the Secretary's Salfi/Ringer-based argument that § 405(h) barred § 1331 review of all challenges arising under the Medicare Act and the respondents' counter-argument that § 405(h) barred challenges to "methods" only where § 405(g) review was available, [ ] the Court wrote:

> "Whichever may be the better reading of Salfi and Ringer, we need not pass on the meaning of § 405(h) in the abstract to resolve this case. Section 405(h) does not apply on its own terms to Part B of the Medicare program, but is instead incorporated mutatis mutandis by § 1395ii. The legislative history of both the statute establishing the Medicare program and the 1972 amendments thereto provides specific evidence of Congress' intent to foreclose review only of 'amount determinations'—i.e., those [matters] . . . remitted finally and exclusively to adjudication by private insurance carriers in a 'fair hearing.' By the same token, matters which Congress did not delegate to private carriers, such as challenges to the validity of the Secretary's instructions and regulations, are cognizable in courts of law." [ ]

The Court's words do not limit the scope of § 405(h) itself to instances where a plaintiff, invoking § 1331, seeks review of an "amount determination." Rather, the Court said that it would "not pass on the meaning of § 405(h) in the abstract."[ ] Instead it focused upon the Medicare Act's cross-referencing provision, § 1395ii, which makes § 405(h) applicable "to the same extent as" it is "applicable" to the Social Security Act.[ ] It interpreted that phrase as applying § 405(h) "mutatis mutandis," i.e., "[a]ll necessary changes having been made."[ ] And it applied § 1395ii with one important change of detail—a change produced by not applying § 405(h) where its application to a particular category of cases, such as Medicare Part B "methodology" challenges, would not lead to a channeling of review through the agency, but would mean no review at all. The Court added that a " 'serious constitutional question' . . . would arise if we construed § 1395ii to deny a judicial forum for constitutional claims arising under Part B."[ ]

More than that: Were the Court of Appeals correct in believing that Michigan Academy limited the scope of § 405(h) itself to "amount determinations," that case would have significantly affected not only Medicare Part B cases but cases arising under the Social Security Act and Medicare Part A as well. It accordingly would have overturned or dramatically limited this Court's earlier precedents, such as Salfi and Ringer, which involved, respectively, those programs. It would, moreover, have created a hardly justifiable distinction between "amount determinations" and many other similar HHS determinations.* * * This Court does not normally overturn, or so dramatically limit, earlier authority sub silentio. And we agree with those Circuits that have held the Court did not do so in this instance. [ ]

Justice THOMAS [in dissent] maintains that Michigan Academy "must have established," by way of a new interpretation of § 1395ii, the critical distinction between a dispute about an agency determination in a particular case and a more general dispute about, for example, the agency's authority to promulgate a set of regulations, i.e., the very distinction that this Court's earlier cases deny. * * *

* * *

* * * [I]t is more plausible to read Michigan Academy as holding that § 1395ii does not apply § 405(h) where application of § 405(h) would not simply channel review through the agency, but would mean no review at all. * * * This latter holding, as we have said, has the virtues of consistency with Michigan Academy's actual language; consistency with the holdings of earlier cases such as Ringer; and consistency with the distinction that this Court has often drawn between a total preclusion of review and postponement of review. * * * As we have said, * * * Congress may well have concluded that a universal obligation to present a legal claim first to HHS, though postponing review in some cases, would produce speedier, as well as better, review overall. And this Court crossed the relevant bridge long ago when it held that Congress, in both the Social Security Act and the Medicare Act, insisted upon an initial presentation of the matter to the agency. * * *

The Council argues that in any event it falls within the exception that Michigan Academy creates, for here as there, it can obtain no review at all unless it can obtain judicial review in a § 1331 action. In other words, the Council contends that application of § 1395ii's channeling provision to the portion of the Medicare statute and the Medicare regulations at issue in this case will amount to the "practical equivalent of a total denial of judicial review." [ ] The Council, however, has not convinced us that is so.

The Council says that the special review channel that the Medicare statutes create applies only where the Secretary terminates a home's provider agreement; it is not available in the more usual case involving imposition of a lesser remedy, say the transfer of patients, the withholding of payments, or the imposition of a civil monetary penalty.

* * *

The Secretary states in her brief that the relevant "determination" that entitles a "dissatisfied" home to review is any determination that a provider has failed to comply substantially with the statute, agreements, or regulations, whether termination or "some other remedy is imposed." * * * The statute's language, though not free of ambiguity, bears that interpretation. And we are aware of no convincing countervailing argument. We conclude that the Secretary's interpretation is legally permissible. See Chevron U.S.A. Inc. v. Natural Resources Defense Council, Inc., 467 U.S. 837, 843 (1984); [ ].

* * *

Proceeding through the agency * * * provides the agency the opportunity to reconsider its policies, interpretations, and regulations in light of those challenges. Nor need it waste time, for the agency can waive many of the procedural steps set forth in § 405(g),[ ] and a court can deem them waived in certain circumstances,[ ] even though the agency technically holds no "hearing" on the claim.[ ] At a minimum, however, the matter must be presented to the agency prior to review in a federal court. This the Council has not done.

* * *

For these reasons, this case cannot fit within Michigan Academy's exception. The bar of § 405(h) applies. The judgment of the Court of Appeals is Reversed.

Notes and Questions

1. *Illinois Council* was decided by a five to four vote, with Justices Stevens, Scalia, Thomas and Kennedy dissenting in three separate opinions. The dissenters would have expanded on *Michigan Academy* to allow federal question jurisdiction over cases involving "challenges to the validity of the Secretary's instructions and regulations" as opposed to individualized benefit determinations, which would still have to first be presented to HHS through administrative channels.

2. Although *Illinois Council* involved an attempt to challenge Medicare regulations pursuant to federal question jurisdiction, other earlier cases have rejected challenges under the Administrative Procedures Act, Califano v. Sanders, 430 U.S. 99, 97 S.Ct. 980, 51 L.Ed.2d 192 (1977); or in the Court of Claims, United States v. Erika, Inc., 456 U.S. 201, 102 S.Ct. 1650, 72 L.Ed.2d 12 (1982).

3. In the year that *Michigan Academy* was decided, Congress adopted 42 U.S.C.A. § 1395ff to permit judicial review of Part B decisions where the amount in controversy was $1,000 or more. Part B appeal procedures were further amended by the Omnibus Budget Reconciliation Act of 1987 to permit administrative law judges to certify legal issues to the federal district court when they determine, on motion of an appellant, that no factual issues exist in a case. The 2003 MMA created an additional new procedure under which a provider or beneficiary who is pursuing an appeal may petition a special review entity composed of up to three ALJs or Departmental Appeals Board (DAB) members, and assert that the appeal raises questions of law or regulation over which the DAB has no jurisdiction and that no material issues of fact are in dispute. This body must decide whether or not this is true within 60 days, and if it approves the petition (or fails to act within 60 days), the petitioner may go directly to court without exhausting administrative remedies. 42 U.S.C. § 1395ff(b)(2). The statute also provides for expedited review of provider terminations and the imposition of intermediate sanctions.

Though these provisions extended judicial review over Medicare cases, serious questions still remain as to whether judicial review is available for several classes of cases. There is still for example, no judicial review for Part A and B claims involving less than $1,000. Moreover, situations can also still arise, as in *Heckler v. Ringer*, where providers will not provide services that CMS refuses to cover, making it impossible for a recipient to file a claim and thus to begin to exhaust administrative remedies. This situation is partially addressed by a provision of the 2003 MMA, which created a new "prior determination process," which allows, depending on the circumstances, either a physician or beneficiary to request a determination as to whether Medicare covers certain physician services before those services are received. This determination would be subject to reconsideration, but not to further administrative or judicial review.

4. Not only do the courts defer to HHS procedurally by refusing to take jurisdiction over direct challenges to HHS regulations, they also defer substantively by generally upholding HHS's interpretation of the Medicare statutes and its own regulations (as we see in *Illinois Council*). This deference is stronger in the appellate courts than at the district court level, and has grown over time. The Supreme Court has ruled in favor of HHS in all five Medicare cases it has decided since 1990, and a recent study found that the courts of appeals and district courts in two one-year periods during the 1990s had ruled for HHS 88 percent and 70 percent of the time respectively. In particular, the courts have applied the *Chevron* rule of agency deference more faithfully with respect to Medicare than in other areas. See Jost, Governing Medicare, *supra*. Even as the Supreme Court has qualified the scope of *Chevron* deference in recent cases, courts continue to defer to CMS in its administration of the Medicare program, although deference does not always carry the day. See, e.g. Yale-New Haven Hosp. v. Leavitt, 470 F.3d 71 (2d Cir. 2006) (Medicare manual provision prohibiting reimbursement for investigational cardiac device not approved by the FDA found arbitrary and capricious.)

Should Medicare decisions and policies be immediately reviewable by the courts? Should the courts be able to review all Medicare claims, or just those involving more than a certain amount of money? Is it more important that providers or beneficiaries have access to the courts? (Justice Stevens in dissent in *Illinois Council* argued that the statute only precluded direct review of beneficiaries' claims to benefits, not claims of providers to reimbursement, 120 S.Ct. at 1102). Why might the courts defer to HHS in its interpretation of the statute? What might be the effect of such deference on beneficiaries? On providers? What problems do providers face if, like the plaintiffs in *Illinois Council*, they can only obtain review of a regulation by violating it and then facing enforcement actions by HHS. See Reqaiijah A. Yearby, A Right to No Meaningful Review Under the Due Process Clause: The Aftermath of Judicial Deference to the Federal Administrative Agencies, 16 Health Matrix 723 (2006); Virginia Burke, Violate, Incur Sanctions, and Exhaust: The Steep Price of Judicial Review Under *Illinois Council*, 36 J. Health L. 403 (2003).

5. A few cases have, post-*Illinois Council*, successfully evaded the requirements of 405(h) based on the case's "no review at all" exception. See, e.g. Furlong v. Shalala, 238 F.3d 227, 233 (2nd Cir. 2001); American Lithotripsy Soc'y v. Thompson, 215 F.Supp.2d 23, 30 (D.D.C. 2002).

Notes: Medicare Administrative Appeals

1. We have already discussed procedures that Medicare makes available for appealing national or local coverage determinations and managed care plan decisions. Most Medicare decisions, however, involve individual cases in which a Medicare contractor decides that care provided to a particular beneficiary in a particular instance is not covered. This Medicare appeals process was dramatically changed by sections 521 and 522 of the Medicare, Medicaid and State Children's

Health Insurance Program Benefits Improvement and Protection Act of 2000, or BIPA (which amended 42 U.S.C.A. § 1395ff). These provisions of BIPA established a uniform appeals process for Part A and Part B. This five-step appeal process begins with the initial contractor determination. A beneficiary aggrieved by such a decision must request a redetermination by the contractor within 120 days (42 U.S.C.A. § 1395ff(a)(3)). A beneficiary dissatisfied with this redetermination may then request a reconsideration (42 U.S.C.A. § 1395ff(b)(1)(A)). This reconsideration is handled by a new group of twelve "qualified independent contractors" (QICs), private entities with which Medicare contracts to make these decisions. (42 U.S.C.A. § 1395ff(b)(2) & (c)). A beneficiary who remains dissatisfied may appeal to an Administrative Law Judge (ALJ) if the claim involves $100 or more, then to the Medicare Appeals Council (MAC) of the Departmental Appeals Board (DAB), and finally, if the claim involves $1000 or more, to the federal district court (42 U.S.C.A. § 1395ff (b) & (d)).

BIPA imposes time limits at every step of the review process, thirty days at the contractor and QIC level, ninety days at the ALJ and MAC level. (42 U.S.C.A. §§ 1395ff(a)(3)(C)(ii); (c)(3)(C), (d)). (The 2003 MMA extended the deadlines to sixty days at the contractor and QIC level). BIPA also provides for expedited (seventy-two hour) reconsideration where a provider plans to discharge a patient or to terminate services where the failure to provide the services is likely to put the beneficiary's health at significant risk. 42 U.S.C.A. §§ 1395ff(b)(1)(F); (c)(3)(C)(iii). Finally, BIPA provides for de novo, rather than appellate review at the MAC level. 42 U.S.C.A. § 1395ff(d)(2)(B). See, Andrew B. Wachler and Abby Pendleton, The New Medicare Appeals Process, 3 Health Law. 8 (2005).

2. One of the key changes that BIPA makes in the previous law is that it specifies the consequences of the failure of DHHS and its contractors to meet appellate deadlines. The provisions dealing with ALJ and MAC decisions follow: 42 U.S.C. § 1395ff (d)

(3) Consequences of failure to meet deadlines

(A) Hearing by administrative law judge—In the case of a failure by an administrative law judge to render a decision by the end of the period described in paragraph (1) [90 days], the party requesting the hearing may request a review by the Departmental Appeals Board [of which the MAC is a part] of the Department of Health and Human Services, notwithstanding any requirements for a hearing for purposes of the party's right to such a review.

(B) Departmental Appeals Board review—In the case of a failure by the Departmental Appeals Board to render a decision by the end of the period described in paragraph (2), [90 days] the party requesting the hearing may seek judicial review, notwithstanding any requirements for a hearing for purposes of the party's right to such judicial review.

How should the courts treat appellants who have skipped appellate steps because of these provisions? If no record has been developed below because the case has moved up at each level for failure to meet time deadlines, what would be the basis of judicial review? (The statute also provides for automatic advancement to the next level for failure to meet deadlines at the redetermination level). Should the court remand for failure to exhaust administrative remedies? Should it try the case itself? What opportunities does the new system offer to appellants who detect that one level of the review process is friendlier than others? What temptations does it create for reviewers under great time pressure (as it takes less time to rule for the appellant than to justify a decision against the appellants). If the courts remand to DHHS for the development of a record, what happens next? How should Congress have dealt with speeding up appeals? See Eleanor D. Kinney,

Medicare Beneficiary Appeals Processes, in Eleanor D. Kinney, ed., Guide to Medicare Coverage Decision–Making and Appeals, 65 (2002). Interim rules to implement the BIPA appeals requirement were published at 70 Fed. Reg. 11420 (March 8, 2005).

3. The Medicare statute and regulations provide a variety of other procedures for administrative appeals and judicial review. Medicare eligibility determinations, for example, are made by the Social Security Administration and are subject to administrative review through SSA's three level reconsideration, administrative hearing, and Appeals Council procedures. A Part A provider dissatisfied with the amount of reimbursement may receive a hearing before a contractor hearing officer if the amount at issue is between $1,000 and $10,000. 42 C.F.R. § 405.1811. If the amount is $10,000 or more (or if smaller claims involving a common controversy can be aggregated in an amount of $50,000 or more), the provider can receive a hearing before the Medicare Provider Reimbursement Review Board (PRRB), 42 U.S.C.A. § 1395oo(a)(2), (b). If both the provider and Medicare contractor agree, these cases can be mediated. See Kathleen Scully–Hayes, Mediation and Medicare Part A Provider Appeals: A Useful Alternative, 5 J. Health Care L & Pol'y 356 (2002).

4. Medicare Advantage organizations must provide their beneficiaries with meaningful grievance resolution mechanisms. 42 U.S.C.A. § 1395w–22(f). They must explain their adverse coverage determinations in writing and must make initial determinations within thirty days for payment decisions, fourteen days for health care services requests, and seventy-two hours for requests for services where lack of the service could seriously jeopardize life or health. If a reconsideration is requested, it must be completed within thirty days if a health service is requested, and within seventy-two hours in emergencies. Coverage reconsideration may be appealed to an independent review organization under contract with CMS, and may ultimately be appealed to an administrative law judge if $100 or more is at stake, and to court if the amount in controversy is $1,000 or more. 42 U.S.C.A. § 1395w–22(g)(4) & (5).

In Grijalva v. Shalala, 152 F.3d 1115 (9th Cir.1998), certiorari granted and judgment vacated and case remanded, 526 U.S. 1096, 119 S.Ct. 1573, 143 L.Ed.2d 669 (1999), the Ninth Circuit held that notice and appeal provisions then in effect for Medicare managed care organizations violated the requirements of the Due Process Clause. The court held that the HMOs were making decisions for the Medicare program, and were thus "government actors" rather than private entities, and thus covered by the Constitution. The Supreme Court vacated and remanded the Ninth Circuit appeal for further consideration in light of the new managed care appeal procedures imposed by the BBA and implementing regulations. Significantly, however, the Court also required further consideration in light of its decision in American Manufacturers Mutual Insurance Co. v. Sullivan, 526 U.S. 40, 119 S.Ct. 977, 143 L.Ed.2d 130 (1999), which had held that the decisions of private insurers participating in a workers' compensation program were not state actors when they made medical necessity determinations, and thus not subject to the due process clause. The case was subsequently settled. Rules implementing the BBA and *Grijalva* were published at 68 Fed. Reg. 16652 (2003).

If the Supreme Court were ultimately to hold that Medicare managed care organizations are private actors not subject to constitutional constraints, the federal government would be effectively permitted to contract out its responsibilities under the Medicare program beyond constitutional control, although it would probably still have to provide some governmental means of review for managed care decisions. But is Medicare sufficiently different from state workers' compensation programs that the holding of *Sullivan* might not apply to managed care organizations to which Medicare contracts out its statutory responsibilities? See Healey v. Shalala, 2000 WL 303439 (D.Conn.2000) (*Sullivan* does not support the argument that home health agencies providing Medicare benefits are not state actors). See also, Jennifer E. Gladieux, Medicare + Choice Appeal Procedures: Reconciling Due Process Rights and Cost Containment, 25 Am.J.L. & Med. 61 (1999); Jody Freeman, The Private Role in Public Governance, 75 N.Y.U. Law Rev. 543 (2000).

Problem: Administrative Appeals

You represent Viola Trettner who has been denied payment by her Medicare contractor for home health services she has received because the contractor believes that home health care was not medically necessary. How does she appeal the decision? Can she sue Medicare for the denial? You also represent Joseph Spencer who has been denied coverage for a new diagnostic procedure ordered by his doctor because a local coverage determination has rejected coverage for the procedure. How might the appeal procedures in Mr. Spencer's case differ from those pursued in Ms. Trettner's case?

E. MEDICARE FUNDING

Medicare Part A, like traditional social insurance programs, is funded through payroll taxes, paid by both employers and employees. These payroll taxes are paid into a "trust fund" which is supposed to accumulate funds for future fund imbalances as the population ages, but since the trust fund is invested in federal savings bonds, the trust fund is effectively a mechanism for funding general federal government deficit spending. The 2008 Medicare Trust Fund Report projects that Trust Fund expenditures will exceed income after 2013, with the Trust Fund being exhausted by 2019. In future years, Medicare expenditures as a percentage of the federal budget and of the gross domestic product are also certain to climb as the cost of medical care continues to grow and the population continues to age. Moreover, funding Medicare Part A through a payroll tax will become less feasible, as the ratio of the population over 65 to that in the workforce continues to worsen, and as wages become a smaller part of the national income relative to other forms of income, such as rent, dividends, interest, or capital gains.

Coverage under Part B of the Medicare program is only available to those who enroll in the program and pay the Part B premium. The premium covers about one fourth of the costs of the Part B program, the remaining costs being covered by taxes. Until 2007, all Part B beneficiaries paid the same premium, regardless of income, although state Medicaid programs paid the premium for some low-income persons. Beginning in 2007, however, beneficiaries who earn more than $80,000 a year for an individual or $160,000 for a couple pay an increased premium equal to thirty-five percent of Part B costs. Wealthier beneficiaries pay higher premiums, which increase in a stepwise fashion to eighty percent of Part B costs for individuals whose incomes exceed $200,000 per year ($400,000 for a couple). Enrollment in Part C (the Medicare Advantage managed care program) and Part D (the Medicare drug program) is voluntary, and participants must pay premiums that cover part of the cost of those programs, the remaining costs being covered by tax funding.

Over time, the proportion of the Medicare program funded by general revenue funds (income and other taxes) continues to increase. Under the

Medicare Modernization Act, the Trustees must inform Congress if it appears that more than forty-five percent of Medicare expenditures are financed by general revenue funds within the succeeding seven years. When this happens in three successive years (which happened in 2008), the President must send to Congress legislation to address the situation, and Congress must consider it on an expedited basis. President Bush sent such a recommendation to Congress in February of 2008, mainly recommending cuts in provider payments and increased means-testing, but Congress was in no position to enact major changes to the Medicare program in an election year.

One possible solution to Medicare's increasing costs is to require beneficiaries to pay more, either through cost-sharing or premiums. A quarter of beneficiaries already spend thirty percent of their income on health care, however, while forty percent spend a fifth of their income or more. Many beneficiaries have little margin for further expenditures. See Patricia Newman, et al., How Much 'Skin in the Game' Do Medicare Beneficiaries Have? The Increasing Financial Burden of Health Care Spending, 1997—2003, 26 Health Aff. 1692 (2007). On Medicare funding generally, see Kaiser Family Foundation, Medicare Financing and Spending, http://www.kff.org/medicare/upload/7305–02.pdf (2007).

III. MEDICAID

LANKFORD v. SHERMAN

United States Court of Appeals, Eighth Circuit, June 22, 2006.
451 F.3d 496.

BENTON, CIRCUIT JUDGE.

Plaintiffs—disabled adult Medicaid recipients—seek a preliminary injunction prohibiting Missouri's Director of Social Services from enforcing a state regulation curtailing the provision of durable medical equipment ("DME") to most categorically-needy Medicaid recipients. [ ] Invoking 42 U.S.C. § 1983 and the Supremacy Clause, U.S. Const. Art. VI, cl. 2, they allege that the regulation violates Medicaid's comparability and reasonable-standards requirements. See 42 U.S.C. §§ 1396a(a)(10)(B), (a)(17). The district court denied a preliminary injunction, finding the regulation consistent with the Medicaid Act. Plaintiffs appeal.* * * [T]his court vacates the order of the district court, and remands for further proceedings.

Before the 2005 legislative session, Missouri provided DME as a standalone Medicaid benefit to all recipients. Under the DME program, plaintiffs received wheelchairs, wheelchair batteries and repairs, orthotics, orthopedic devices, parenteral nutrition, augmentative communication devices, hospital beds, bed rails, lifts, and other prosthetics. [ ] Citing budget constraints, the General Assembly passed a new statute eliminating the DME program as a covered Medicaid service, except for recipients who are blind, pregnant, or needy children, or for those who receive home health care services under the state plan. * * *

* * *

Plaintiffs, adult Medicaid recipients, have disabilities ranging from paralysis to cardiopulmonary disease. Before the new regulation, they received medically-prescribed DME from Medicaid. Under the new regulation, however, plaintiffs claim they are ineligible to receive DME items that are necessary for their medical care and independence (which they cannot afford).* * *

* * * Plaintiffs contend that Missouri may not provide additional DME benefits to blind recipients [unless Missouri provides those benefits to all adult recipients]. Plaintiffs assert violations of federal comparability and reasonable-standards requirements that the State treat Medicaid recipients equally and with reasonable, non-discriminatory standards. *See* 42 U.S.C. §§ 1396a(a)(10)(B), (a)(17). *See also* 42 C.F.R. § 440.230. * * *

In the district court, the State defended the DME regulation primarily by arguing that it had applied to the Centers for Medicare and Medicaid Services ("CMS") for a waiver of the federal comparability requirement, which would permit additional benefits for the blind. *See* 42 U.S.C. § 1396n(b). * * * The State also claimed that plaintiffs can still obtain necessary DME if they (1) qualify for home health care, or (2) seek an exception for non-covered DME items through the exceptions process. * * *

The district court denied a preliminary injunction. * * * Plaintiffs appeal.

* * *

The Medicaid Act is a federal aid program designed to help the states provide medical assistance to financially-needy individuals, with the assistance of federal funding. [ ] Participation is voluntary, but if a state decides to participate, it must comply with all federal statutory and regulatory requirements. [ ] To participate, a state submits a plan to the Secretary of the Department of Health and Human Services that meets the requirements of 42 U.S.C. § 1396a(a). [ ] Once the plan is approved, the federal government subsidizes the state's medical-assistance services. See 42 U.S.C. § 1396 [ ].

Participating states must furnish medical assistance to the "categorically needy," a group that includes financially-needy blind, aged, and disabled individuals, pregnant women, and children. See 42 U.S.C. § 1396a(a)(10)(A). A state may also choose to provide medical assistance to the "medically needy"—those who do not qualify under a federal program, but lack the resources to obtain adequate medical care. See id. § 1396(a)(10)(C); [ ] Missouri elects to provide medical assistance only to the categorically needy. [ ]

Once a state decides which groups will receive medical assistance under the plan, it then determines which services it will provide. See 42 U.S.C. § 1396d(a). To receive federal approval, the Medicaid Act mandates that a plan include only seven enumerated medical services. See id. §§ 1396a(a)(10), 1396d(a)(1)-(5), (17), (21) (including as mandatory: inpatient hospital, outpatient hospital, laboratory and x-ray, nursing facility, physician, nurse-midwife, and nurse-practitioner services).

A state may also elect to provide optional medical services, such as dental services, prosthetics, and prescription drugs. See id. §§ 1396(a)(10)(A), 1396(d)(a) (listing 27 categories of medical assistance, only seven of which are mandatory). Once the state offers an optional service, it must comply with all federal statutory and regulatory mandates. [ ]

DME is an optional service under the Medicaid Act, unless the recipient qualifies for home health care. See 42 U.S.C. § 1396a(a)(10)(D). * * *

* * *

A. COMPARABILITY

The new regulation eliminates coverage of most DME items for the categorically-needy who are aged or disabled. The regulation maintains full DME coverage for categorically-needy recipients who are blind. Plaintiffs claim this violates Medicaid's comparability requirement that states provide an equal "amount, duration, [and] scope" of medical assistance to all categorically-needy. See 42 U.S.C. § 1396a(a)(10)(B)(I); 42 C.F.R. §§ 440.240(a), (b)(1); [ ] As the comparability mandate prevents discrimination against or among the categorically needy, it applies equally to mandatory and optional medical services. [ ]

The district court found that the DME regulation complies with Medicaid's comparability requirement, primarily because Missouri had a comparability waiver pending with CMS. The record has significantly changed. CMS denied the waiver. The Director of Social Services and the Missouri Attorney General represent to this court that Missouri has now deleted the part of its state plan that calls for federal funding of additional services to the blind. As the current state plan provides an equal amount, duration, and scope of DME services to all categorically-needy recipients, and Missouri uses only state funding to provide additional DME services to the blind, the State contends that its program is consistent with the comparability requirement.

While a state plan must comply with all federal statutory and regulatory requirements, a state may give additional medical assistance under its own legislation, independent of federal reimbursement. [ ] As Missouri represents to this court that it does not accept federal assistance, and uses only state funds, to provide additional DME benefits to blind Medicaid recipients, this court finds that the DME regulation (as currently funded) does not violate the federal comparability requirement.

Plaintiffs next allege that the DME regulation violates Medicaid's requirement that the state create reasonable standards for determining the extent of medical assistance under the plan, which are consistent with Medicaid's objectives. 42 U.S.C. § 1396a(a)(17). [ ] While a state has considerable discretion to fashion medical assistance under its Medicaid plan, this discretion is constrained by the reasonable-standards requirement. [ ] Each service the state elects to provide "must be sufficient in amount, duration, and scope to reasonably achieve its purpose." 42 C.F.R. § 440.230(b). Additionally, a state "may not arbitrarily reduce the amount, duration, or scope of a required service ... solely because of the diagnosis, type of illness, or condition." Id. § 440.230(c).

While optional DME programs are not explicitly subject to these requirements, CMS * * * maintains that the reasonable-standards provisions apply to all forms of medical assistance, including a state's provision of DME. [ ] See also St. Mary's Hosp. of Rochester v. Leavitt, 416 F.3d 906, 914 (8th Cir.2005); Cmty. Health Ctr. v. Wilson–Coker, 311 F.3d 132, 138 (2d Cir.2002) (according "considerable deference" to CMS's interpretations due to the "complexity of the statute and the considerable expertise of the agency").

Plaintiffs argue that the limited DME services in the Missouri regulation are inconsistent with these mandatory reasonableness requirements, because they discriminate on the basis of diagnosis, do not provide a sufficient amount of DME services to meet Medicaid's objectives, and fail to establish a procedure for recipients to obtain non-covered DME items. Citing conflicts between the Missouri regulation and the federal reasonable-standards requirements, they also contend that the state regulation is preempted under the Supremacy Clause. * * *

* * *

The State asserts that there is no individualized federal right to reasonable Medicaid standards, enforceable under 42 U.S.C. § 1983. * * *

* * *

For legislation enacted pursuant to Congress's spending power, like the Medicaid Act, a state's non-compliance typically does not create a private right of action for individual plaintiffs, but rather an action by the federal government to terminate federal matching funds. See Pennhurst State Sch. & Hosp. v. Halderman, 451 U.S. 1, 28, 101 S.Ct. 1531, 67 L.Ed.2d 694 (1981). While the Supreme Court has rarely found enforceable rights in spending clause legislation, it has not foreclosed the possibility that individual plaintiffs may sue to enforce compliance with such legislation. See Wright v. City of Roanoke Redevelopment & Hous. Auth., 479 U.S. 418, 430, 107 S.Ct. 766, 93 L.Ed.2d 781 (1987) (Federal Housing Act supports a cause of action under section 1983); Wilder v. Va. Hosp. Ass'n, 496 U.S. 498, 510, 110 S.Ct. 2510, 110 L.Ed.2d 455 (1990) (Medicaid providers had an individual right to reasonable reimbursement rates under the now-repealed Boren Amendment). Still, the Court has since limited the circumstances where a private right of action is found under section 1983. See Suter v. Artist M., 503 U.S. 347, 363, 112 S.Ct. 1360, 118 L.Ed.2d 1 (1992) (no private right of action under the Adoption Assistance and Child Welfare Act, which requires states to make "reasonable efforts" to keep children out of foster homes); Blessing v. Freestone, 520 U.S. 329, 344–45, 117 S.Ct. 1353, 137 L.Ed.2d 569 (1997) (no private right of action under Title IV–D of the Social Security Act, which requires states to "substantially comply" with requirements designed to ensure timely payment of child support); Gonzaga, 536 U.S. at 290, 122 S.Ct. 2268 (no private right of action under the Family Educational Rights and Privacy Act, which prohibits federal funding of educational institutions that have a policy of releasing confidential records to unauthorized persons).

A three-part test determines whether Spending Clause legislation creates a right of action under 42 U.S.C. § 1983:(1) Congress intended the statutory provision to benefit the plaintiff; (2) the asserted right is not so "vague and amorphous" that its enforcement would strain judicial competence; and (3) the provision clearly imposes a mandatory obligation upon the states. Blessing, 520 U.S. at 340–41, 117 S.Ct. 1353. If the legislation meets this test, there is a presumption it is enforceable under section 1983. Id. at 341, 117 S.Ct. 1353. The presumption is rebutted if Congress explicitly or implicitly forecloses section 1983 enforcement. Id. (noting that implied foreclosure occurs if

Congress creates "a comprehensive enforcement scheme that is incompatible with individual enforcement"). The availability of administrative mechanisms alone, however, cannot defeat the plaintiff's ability to invoke section 1983, so long as the other requirements of the three-part test are met. See id. at 347, 117 S.Ct. 1353.

In Gonzaga University v. Doe, the Supreme Court clarified the first prong, holding that "anything short of an unambiguously conferred right" does not support an individual right of action under section 1983. Gonzaga, 536 U.S. at 283, 122 S.Ct. 2268. As section 1983 enforces "rights," as opposed to "benefits" or "interests," the statutory language must clearly evince an intent to individually benefit the plaintiff. Id. at 284, 122 S.Ct. 2268 ("where a statute does not include this sort of explicit 'right-or duty-creating language' we rarely impute to Congress an intent to create a private right of action"). Accordingly, the statute must focus on an individual entitlement to the asserted federal right, rather than on the aggregate practices or policies of a regulated entity, like the state. Id. at 287–88, 122 S.Ct. 2268.

Medicaid's reasonable-standards requirement provides that a state Medicaid plan must "include reasonable standards . . . for determining eligibility for and the extent of medical assistance under this plan." 42 U.S.C. § 1396a(a)(17). Like the Ninth Circuit—the only other circuit to address this issue—this court finds the statutory language insufficient to evince a congressional intent to create individually-enforceable federal rights. * * * First, the statute is not phrased in terms of the individuals it intends to benefit, as it lacks any reference to "individuals" or "persons." [ ] Rather than focusing on an individual entitlement to medical services, the reasonable-standards provision focuses on the aggregate practices of the states in establishing reasonable Medicaid services. [ ] This is insufficient to establish an individual right to reasonable standards under the first prong of the three-part test.

Even if the statute referenced the individuals benefitted, "the right it would create is too vague and amorphous for judicial enforcement." * * * The only guidance Congress provides in the reasonable-standards provision is that the state establish standards "consistent with [Medicaid] objectives"—an inadequate guidepost for judicial enforcement. [ ]* * *

Plaintiffs claim that the Missouri DME regulation is preempted by the Supremacy Clause, because it directly conflicts with Medicaid's reasonable-standards requirements. U.S. Const. Art. VI, cl. 2. The Supremacy Clause is not the direct source of any federal right, but "secures federal rights by according them priority whenever they come in conflict with state law." [ ] Preemption claims are analyzed under a different test than section 1983 claims, affording plaintiffs an alternative theory for relief when a state law conflicts with a federal statute or regulation.[ ]

Under the preemption doctrine, state laws that "interfere with, or are contrary to the laws of congress, made in pursuance of the constitution" are preempted. [ ] Where Congress has not expressly preempted or entirely displaced state regulation in a specific field, as with the Medicaid Act, "state law is preempted to the extent that it actually conflicts with federal law." [ ] An actual conflict arises where compliance with both state and federal law is a "physical impossibility," or where the state law " 'stands as an obstacle to the accomplishment and execution of the full purposes and objectives of Congress.' "[ ] While Medicaid is a system of cooperative federalism, the same analysis applies; once the state voluntarily accepts the conditions imposed by Congress, the Supremacy Clause obliges it to comply with federal requirements. [ ]

In this case, plaintiffs claim that Missouri's DME regulation conflicts with the federal regulations that implement Medicaid's reasonable-standards requirement. See 42 C.F.R. § 440.230(b). * * * As with their section 1983 claim, plaintiffs allege that the state regulation is unreasonable, because it does not provide a sufficient amount of DME services to meet Medicaid's basic objectives and fails to establish a procedure for recipients to obtain non-covered DME items. Importantly, these arguments differ from those involving claims of discrimination, as they do not facially attack the provision of additional DME services to the blind as compared to other adult Medicaid recipients. Rather, they allege that the limited list of DME items that the state provides to all Medicaid recipients—with the assistance of federal funding—is so limited that it fails Medicaid's objectives. The district court did not address these claims.

When a state receives federal matching funds, its medical assistance program must comply with all federal statutory and regulatory requirements.* * * Accordingly, the federally-funded DME program must comply with Medicaid's reasonable-standards requirement, and its implementing regulations.

Missouri's amended plan includes only three categories of "prosthetic devices" available to all adult Medicaid recipients: ostomy supplies, oxygen and respiratory equipment, and wheelchairs. The DME regulation says that adult Medicaid recipients are also entitled to diabetic supplies and equipment, but not artificial larynxes, CPAPs, BiPAPs, IPPB machines, humidification items, suction pumps, apnea monitors, wheelchair accessories, or scooters. [ ] Plaintiffs argue that these limitations make Missouri's amended Medicaid plan unreasonable in light of the purposes of Medicaid. See 42 U.S.C. §§ 1396, 1396a(a)(17); 42 C.F.R. § 440.230(b).

Plaintiffs contend that the limited DME items available to all adult Medicaid recipients are insufficient in amount and scope to reasonably achieve the purpose of the DME program. See 42 C.F.R. § 440.230(b). For example, the regulation covers wheelchairs, but excludes funding for the batteries, filters, accessories, repairs, and other types of replacement parts necessary to keep the equipment functioning. * * * Moreover, the regulation completely excludes items like augmentative communication devices, catheters, and par-enteral nutrition supplies. Given these limits, plaintiffs claim that the regulation does not meet Medicaid's goals of providing medically-necessary services, rehabilitation, or the capability of independence and self-care. See 42 U.S.C. § 1396.

While a state has discretion to determine the optional services in its Medicaid plan, a state's failure to provide Medicaid coverage for non-experimental, medically-necessary services within a covered Medicaid category is both per se unreasonable and inconsistent with the stated goals of Medicaid. [ ] Because Missouri has elected to cover DME as an optional Medicaid service, it cannot arbitrarily choose which DME items to reimburse under its Medicaid policy.

The State responds that pre-approved lists of DME are acceptable under Medicaid's reasonable-standards provisions. See 42 C.F.R. § 440.230(d) (allowing utilization controls as a means of administrative convenience). While a state may use a pre-approved list, CMS has directed that the state must include specific criteria for the extent of DME coverage under the plan, and a mechanism for recipients to request timely reimbursement for non-covered, medically-necessary items. [ ] According to CMS, a policy without a meaningful procedure for requesting non-covered items is inconsistent with the reasonable-standards requirement and the objectives of Medicaid. [ ] While these requirements are not explicit in the federal Medicaid regulations, CMS's interpretation is entitled to considerable deference. [ ]

The State contends that it meets these federal mandates, as all Medicaid recipients have two options for receiving non-covered DME items under the state Medicaid plan. First, recipients can qualify for home health care services, requiring necessary DME items to be provided. [ ] Second, recipients can seek reimbursement for non-covered items through the established exceptions process. * * *

Plaintiffs aver—although the state questions—that they do not qualify for home health care under Missouri's plan, because it is available only to individuals who both require skilled-nursing services and are confined to the home. * * *

* * *

Plaintiffs also assert that Missouri's exceptions process [which is very restrictive and does not cover items at issue] does not provide them with an adequate mechanism to obtain non-covered DME items. * * *

* * *

Because the DME regulation restricts available DME, and plaintiffs have no other procedure to obtain it, the regulation—on the present record—appears unreasonable under directives from both CMS and this court.[ ] Plaintiffs have established a likelihood of success on the merits of their preemption claim as it relates to Medicaid's reasonable-standards requirement.

* * * Accordingly, this court vacates the order of the district court, and remands for further proceedings * * *

Note

Medicare is a social insurance program whose benefits are available to the elderly and disabled without regard for their means. It is popular and enjoys broad-based support. The debate surrounding Medicare has focused on its enormous cost and on how the mechanisms used to pay for items and services under Medicare might be altered to lower that cost. There has been little discussion about cutting eligibility or benefits, or about devolving responsibility for Medicare from the federal to the state governments. Medicaid, on the other hand, is a welfare program for the poor. It was created almost as an afterthought during the Medicare debate in the 1960s and has always been controversial, always vulnerable. All aspects of the program, eligibility, benefits, payment mechanisms, federal and state responsibility for the program—even whether Medicaid should continue to exist at all as an entitlement program—have been hotly contested over the past decade. Despite this, Medicaid now covers millions of Americans and has grown into a more expensive program than Medicare.

This section will examine Medicaid as it has developed over nearly four decades and as it exists in the fall of 2007. When you read this book, Medicaid may have continued to evolve slowly and incrementally or it may have radically changed. It is indeed possible that it will no longer exist. The poor, however, will always be with us, and they will always need health care. Any governmental program intended to help them obtain health care will need to consider the issues of eligibility, benefits, payment structure, administration, and financing addressed in this section.

A. ELIGIBILITY

Problem: Medicaid Eligibility

Four generations of the Sawatsky family live together in two neighboring apartments. Stanislaus Sawatsky immigrated from Poland in the 1970s. He became a U.S. citizen ten years later and has worked for thirty years in construction. Work has been intermittent, however, and he has never been able to build up a nest egg. For the past year Stanislaus, now in his late 50s, has been unable to work because of his heart condition. He was recently awarded federal supplemental security assistance (SSI) because of his disability. His son, Peter, is married to Maria and lives next door to Stanislaus with his three children, aged 1, 5, and 7. Peter was recently laid off from his job in a trailer factory. Maria is currently pregnant and not employed outside the home. Finally, Stanislaus mother, Elzbieta, aged 83, has been living with Peter for a year now. She came to the U.S. from Poland last year on a tourist visa, and has not returned (even though the visa has expired). She fell yesterday and is in the hospital with a broken hip. No one in the family can afford to help pay her medical bills, and the hospital is saying she will need to be discharged to a nursing home. Who in this group, if anyone, is eligible for Medicaid? What sources of law would you consult to answer this question? What additional facts would you have to know to determine eligibility?

Medicaid eligibility is very complex. Medicaid is a state-administered program, and each state decides whom to cover and establishes its own eligibility requirements, although the discretion that the states have in determining eligibility is constrained by federal laws and regulations. Because Medicaid is a welfare program, eligibility is almost always related to economic need and virtually every Medicaid applicant must show that his or her income and resources fall below certain levels set by the states pursuant to broad federal guidelines.* Not every poor person is eligible for Medicaid, however. Rather Medicaid is intended to assist certain favored groups of the needy who are considered to be the "deserving"

---

* The only group eligible for Medicaid without regard to income or resources are women who have been screened through the Center for Disease Control and Prevention's early detection program and have been found to have breast or cervical cancer and who do not have private insurance or other health care coverage. This group was granted coverage by Breast and Cervical Cancer Prevention and Treatment Act of 2000, P.L. 106–354. This is an optional category, but most states now cover it.

poor, though in recent years utilitarian considerations such as providing prenatal care or care for infants to avoid more expensive conditions later have arguably become as important as moral judgments in determining who should receive Medicaid. See Sandra Tanenbaum, Medicaid Eligibility Policy in the 1980s: Medical Utilitarianism and the "Deserving" Poor, 20 J. Health Pol., Pol'y & L. 933 (1995). The CCH Medicare and Medicaid Guide (an excellent source of legal information respecting these programs) identifies over three dozen discrete categories of the poor that must be covered by state Medicaid programs under current federal law, and about two dozen groups that may, but need not, be covered, 4 Medicare & Medicaid Guide (CCH), ¶¶ 14,231—14,247, 14,251.

Who are the "deserving" poor? Historically they were the aged, blind, and permanently and totally disabled, who were either eligible for assistance under the Federal Supplemental Security Income Program (SSI) or, if a state elected the "209(b)" option, persons who would have been eligible for state assistance under the eligibility requirements in effect in 1972 for the former state Aid to the Aged, Blind and Disabled program. They were also dependent children and their caretaker relatives who were eligible for assistance under the former federal/state Aid to Families with Dependent Children (AFDC) Program. These groups were known as the "categorically needy" and states that participate in the Medicaid program have generally been required to cover these groups. The deserving poor also included the "optional categorically needy," a variety of groups that states may choose to cover, but who then must be provided the full scope of benefits offered the categorically needy. 42 C.F.R. § 435.201. Such groups include persons who would be eligible for Medicaid if institutionalized, but who are instead receiving services in the community. 42 C.F.R. § 436.217.

States have also long been permitted to cover a third group, the "medically needy" if they choose to do so. The medically needy are categorically-related (aged, disabled, blind, or families with dependent children) persons whose income exceeds the financial eligibility levels established by the states, but who incur regular medical expenses that, when deducted from their income, bring their net disposable income below the eligibility level for financial assistance. Thirty-five states plus the District of Columbia currently cover the medically needy. The medically needy are generally persons in need of expensive nursing home or hospital care. The medically needy program is effectively a catastrophic health insurance program for those who fall into the categories favored by the welfare system.

In recent years, the traditional categories of "worthy poor" have ceased to define Medicaid eligibility. Beginning with gradual Medicaid expansions in the mid–1980s, eligibility has become decoupled from welfare recipient status. This decoupling became complete for families with dependent children with the abolition of AFDC and creation of the Temporary Assistance for Needy Families (TANF) program by the Personal Responsibility and Work Opportunities Reconciliation Act (PRWORA) of 1996 (though for some groups Medicaid eligibility continues to be tied awkwardly to former AFDC eligibility).

Medicaid today covers primarily four groups. First, coverage of pregnant women has been extended: every state Medicaid program must cover all pregnant women in families with incomes of up to 133 percent of the poverty level, and states may cover pregnant women in families with incomes of up to 185 percent of poverty level. (The federal poverty level is $10,210 for an individual, $20,650 for a family of four for the year 2007.) States also have the flexibility to use "less restrictive" financial eligibility methodologies for pregnant women. Twenty-one states currently cover pregnant women with incomes of up to 200 percent of poverty or above, while sixteen more cover women with incomes of up to 185 percent of the level. This expansion is eminently pragmatic—expenditures on prenatal care are widely considered to be highly cost effective in avoiding future health care costs. In 2002, Medicaid paid for more than 1.6 million births, forty percent of the births in the United States, and in nine states paid for half or more of all births.

Second, Medicaid coverage has expanded to cover children. States must currently cover all children under age six with family incomes below 133 percent of the poverty level and children under age nineteen in families with incomes up to 100 percent of the poverty level. States have the option of offering more generous coverage. (States may also cover children at levels up to 200 percent of poverty or up to 150 percent of the state's Medicaid eligibility levels, whichever is higher, through the State Children's Health Insurance Program (SCHIP), described at the end of this chapter, which gives the states more flexibility and higher federal matching rates.) Several states now cover children in families with incomes at 200 percent of the poverty level or below, and three states up to 300 percent of the poverty level. States must also cover all children who would have been eligible for AFDC when that program was abolished in 1996 ("Section 1931 children") and, for a limited time, children whose parents are returning to work after leaving welfare ("Transitional Medical Assistance"). Medicaid covered twenty-eight million children in 2005, one quarter of the children in the United States, and many more are eligible for Medicaid but not covered, often because of bureaucratic barriers or poor outreach at the state level, but sometimes because they are covered as dependents on their parents employment-related policies. Almost half of Medicaid recipients (forty-nine percent in 2003) are children, but children are very cheap to cover, accounting for only eighteen percent of Medicaid expenditures. Medicaid also covers the parents of some of these children, but income eligibility levels for parents are set usually much lower, so that in many families the children are insured but not the parents.

Third, Medicaid has become a Medicare supplement policy for low-income elderly and disabled Medicare recipients, so-called "dual eligibles." Under amendments adopted in the late 1980s and early 1990s, Medicaid must today cover the Medicare premiums and cost-sharing obligations for "Qualified Medicare Beneficiaries," Medicare-eligible individuals whose income does not exceed 100 percent of the poverty level. It must also cover Medicare Part B premiums for "Specified Low–Income Medicare Beneficiaries," persons who would otherwise qualify as QMBs except that their income is between 100 percent and 120 percent of the federal poverty level. States also receive funds to cover all or part of the Part B premium for "qualifying individuals" above this level, but coverage is not an entitlement and is available on a first come, first served basis. Finally, Medicaid covers services for dual eligibles who are not covered by Medicare, of which nursing home care (a service only marginally covered by Medicare) is the most important. Dual eligibles tend to be in much worse health than other Medicaid recipients, and account for forty percent of Medicaid spending.

Fourth, Medicaid has become our most important program for providing medical care to disabled children and adults. Most are currently eligible because they are covered by the federal Supplemental Security Income (SSI) program. Many states provide home-and-community-based care services to disabled persons under federal Medicaid waiver programs, which under certain circumstances permit the use of more liberal eligibility standards than those that normally govern Medicaid eligibility. The 1997 Balanced Budget Act and the Ticket to Work and Work Incentives Improvement Act of 1999 also permit states to cover working disabled persons whose income would otherwise have rendered them ineligible for Medicaid, or who would otherwise have lost eligibility coverage due to "medical improvement." Finally, the 2006 Family Opportunity Act authorizes states to allow families with incomes up to 300 percent of the poverty level to purchase Medicaid coverage for disabled children. The disabled are a very expensive group of Medicaid enrollees. Though they constitute fourteen percent of enrollees, they account for forty-two percent of expenditures.

Although Medicaid must cover certain populations, many of the categories described above are optional. Overall, approximately twenty-nine percent of Medicaid beneficiaries fall into optional categories. These recipients, however, account for sixty percent of Medicaid spending, since they tend disproportionately to include the elderly and disabled.

Medicaid by no means covers all of America's poor. Approximately fourteen percent of low-income children remain uninsured, although it is estimated that three quarters of uninsured children are eligible for Medicaid or SCHIP. Single adults who are under sixty-five and not disabled are ineligible under federal law, as are couples who do not have children living with them, except in a handful of states that cover some of them through Medicaid waivers. Financial eligibility levels for parents are very low in many states, and only about eighteen percent of adults whose income is between 100 and 200 percent of the poverty level are covered by Medicaid. Coverage also still varies significantly from state to state, both because states differ in their financial eligibility levels (and methodologies for determining eligibility) and because states make more or less generous choices with respect to coverage of optional categories or participation in waiver programs. A number of states have used Medicaid waivers or state funds to dramatically expand coverage of the uninsured, including adults not otherwise covered by Medicaid. Others, however, have maintained very restrictive eligibility requirements and fail to cover many of their residents for whom they could legally receive federal matching funds.

Medicaid coverage is limited to U.S. citizens and qualified aliens (except in emergency situations). Until 2006, an applicant could attest citizenship under penalty of perjury. Under the 2006 Deficit Reduction Act, however, a Medicaid applicant needs to prove citizenship, using a U.S. passport, certificate of citizenship or of naturalization, a valid driver's license in states that require proof of citizenship to get a license, or a combination of two specified documents (such as a birth certificate and voter registration card). SSI and Medicare recipients, as well as foster children and children receiving adoption assistance are exempt from these requirements. States can also used computerized matches of their data sources to determine eligibility.

Assume that you represent a Hurricane Katrina victim who was born and raised in Louisiana, but lost all of her household belongings in the flooding, including all identity papers. Your client does not summer in Europe, and has never had a passport. How does your client prove eligibility? Assume that you represent a hospital that is caring for a newborn baby, just born to an undocumented alien in your hospital, in the United States. How do you establish Medicaid eligibility for the child? (CMS took the position in an interim final rule in 2006 that infants born to undocumented aliens in the U.S. would not automatically qualify for Medicaid, even though children born on U.S. soil are U.S. citizens. In March of 2007 CMS abandoned this position.)

The best source of information on Medicaid eligibility and coverage is the website of the Kaiser Commission on Medicaid and the Uninsured, http://www.kff.

org. One of the most comprehensive sources of information on Medicaid eligibility (and on all other Medicaid topics), is the Kaiser Commission's Medicaid Resource Book (2002). Another excellent general source on Medicaid law, including eligibility issues, is Jane Perkins and Sarah Somers, An Advocate's Guide to the Medicaid Program (National Health Law Program, 2001). For a thoughtful history of the politics of Medicaid eligibility decisions, see Colleen Grogan and Eric Patashnik, Between Welfare Medicine and Mainstream Entitlement: Medicaid at the Political Crossroads, 28 J. Health Pol., Pol'y & L. 821 (2002).

Note: The Policy Context of Medicaid Eligibility and "Medicaid Planning"

Determining who should be covered by welfare programs such as Medicaid poses intractable public policy problems. First, limiting Medicaid eligibility to individuals and families with very low incomes creates significant disincentive for poor persons to become employed. Part-time jobs and jobs that pay at or near minimum wage levels often do not come with health insurance. If a family has any significant medical needs, it can be worse off if its wage earners work at low paying jobs without health benefits than it would be with less income but Medicaid coverage. 42 U.S.C. § 1396r–6(a), which permits families of persons who lose Temporary Assistance to Needy Families eligibility because of increased income from employment to continue to receive Medicaid for up to twelve months thereafter, is a partial response to this problem. The 1999 Ticket to Work legislation for the disabled is an even more generous response.

The role of assets in determining eligibility is as important as the role of income. Sooner or later many persons who require long-term nursing facility care become impoverished, regardless of their financial status at the time they entered a nursing facility, as nursing homes cost on average over $75,000 a year. Medicaid eligibility requirements mandate that such persons "spend down" their assets until they reach Medicaid asset eligibility levels, and thereafter spend all of their income except a very small personal needs allowance on their medical care, with Medicaid paying the difference between the amount the recipient can pay and the allowed nursing facility reimbursement level. A temptation exists, therefore, for persons who anticipate the need for nursing home care to transfer their assets to their children or to others in order to establish premature Medicaid eligibility. They may also be tempted (or advised by lawyers who specialize in Medicaid planning) to put their assets into a trust so that they can continue to enjoy the benefit of the assets until such time as nursing home care is required and then become impecunious. Finally, if the institutionalized individual leaves behind a spouse in the community, it is necessary to provide for the needs of the community spouse at some decent level before directing the income of the institutionalized spouse toward the cost of care.

Beginning in 1980, Congress (encouraged by the states and the long term care insurance industry) adopted a series of laws attempting to deter asset transfers intended to create eligibility. In response, attorneys who specialize in Medicaid planning became increasingly creative in devising strategies for circumventing these restrictions. In a series of budget reconciliation acts, Congress fought back. Finally, in a fit of pique, Congress adopted in 1996 a provision stipulating that a person who "knowingly and willfully disposes of assets (including by any transfer in trust) in order for an individual to become eligible for medical assistance under [Medicaid], if disposing of the assets results in the imposition of a period of ineligibility for [Medicaid]" is guilty of a federal crime. Pub.L. 104–191, § 217. This "granny goes to jail" provision provoked a public outcry and the following year Congress revoked the rule, putting in its place a statute providing that a person who "knowingly and willfully counsels or assists an individual to dispose of assets" to become eligible for Medicaid could be fined $10,000 and imprisoned for a year. 42 U.S.C.A. § 1320a–7b(a)(6). Attorney General Reno refused to defend the constitutionality of this provision, and its enforcement was enjoined. New York State Bar Association v. Reno, 999 F.Supp. 710 (N.D.N.Y.1998). See Note, John M. Broderick, To Transfer or Not to Transfer: Congress Failed to Stiffen Penalties for Medicaid Estate Planning, But Should the Practice Continue? 6 Elder L. J. 257 (1999).

The current law, as amended in 2006, provides that anyone who transfers assets for less than their market value within sixty months before entering a nursing facility and applying for Medicaid, is ineligible for Medicaid for the number of months of nursing home care that the assets would have covered beginning with the date the applicant would otherwise have been eligible for Medicaid. There are special rules affecting annuities, life estates, loans, trusts, entry fees to continuing care communities, and other approaches to reducing assets. The law also allows states to deny Medicaid to persons who have over $500,000 in home equity (which can be extended to $750,000 at a state's option). There are special rules for hardship cases and for transfers to certain individuals (such as spouses), but the law makes voluntary impoverishment quite difficult. See 42 U.S.C.A. § 1396p. What is the rationale for exempting the value of a house? Does it make sense given the availability of reverse mortgages?

For all of the passion that Medicaid estate planning unleashes among lawmakers, it does not appear to be a major cause of expenditures to state Medicaid programs. A 2007 nationwide survey by the GAO found that ninety percent of the Medicaid nursing home applicants it surveyed had nonhousing assets of $30,000 or less, and that although ten percent of those surveyed had transferred assets for less than fair market value (with a median value of $15,152), only 0.5 percent of those surveyed experienced any delay in eligibility because of transfers. GAO, Medicaid: Long–Term Care: Few Transferred Assets Before Applying for Nursing Home Coverage; Impact of Deficit Reduction Act on Eligibility is Uncertain (2007). This is one of the few areas of Medicaid representation of interest to the private bar, however, and results in a steady trickle of articles in practitioner bar journals.

Significant public policy issues are also encountered if Medicaid eligibility is considered in the context of the potential support networks in which Medicaid recipients are found. Most poor persons have families, and those families may or may not themselves be impoverished. One of the pervasive tensions in welfare programs is the conflict between familial and social responsibility. Should adult children be responsible for the medical expenses of their indigent elderly parents? Is it fair for elderly persons to expect the taxpayers to finance their medical care through Medicaid rather than look to their children for help? On the other hand, is it fair to require children of indigent parents to contribute to their support, when our society does not otherwise expect adult children to support their parents? What effect would such a requirement have on parent-child relationships? Would it perpetuate a cycle of poverty? Might the cost of collecting from children exceed the funds collected? Should children be responsible for the cost of care of parents who did not support them when they were young or who abused them? See Norman Daniels, Just Health Care (1985); Daniel Callahan, What Kind of Life: The Limits of Medical Progress (1990); James Callahan, et al., Responsibility of Families for their Severely Disabled Adults, 1 Health Care Fin. Rev., Winter 1980 at 29; Norman Daniels, Family Responsibility Initiatives and Justice Between Age Groups, 13 Law, Medicine & Health Care 153 (1985). The Medicaid act expressly forbids holding adult children responsible for the care of their parents, 42 U.S.C.A. § 1396a(a)(17)(D). Many states, however, have "filial responsibility" laws on the books (which date back to the Elizabethan poor laws), which impose criminal penalties for failing to support parents but are rarely enforced.

Should parents bear the full burden of the very expensive care required by severely disabled children in nursing facilities? Institutionalized disabled children are currently eligible regardless of the wealth of their families because SSI eligibility rules do not attribute the income or resources of parents to a child who has been institutionalized for more than 30 days. States electing this "Katie Beckett" Medicaid option can also provide Medicaid coverage to noninstitutionalized disabled children who are being cared for in their homes, but who would be eligible for SSI if institutionalized. In states not electing this option, middle class parents may need to institutionalize their children to get Medicaid coverage.

Should the federal government mandate state coverage of particular groups? What explains the current law's choice of some groups for mandated eligibility, others for optional coverage? Which optional categories does your state cover? Would removal of a federal mandate in fact result in other groups being dropped from coverage? Which groups would most likely be dropped in your state? Why?

B. BENEFITS

Problem: Medicaid Benefits

Each member of the Sawatsky family needs medical services. Elzbieta is in the hospital and needs a hip replacement and a nursing home placement. Stanislaus needs to take regularly an expensive medication for his heart, and worries that he may need another bypass operation like the one he had last year. Peter badly needs some dental work. Maria, of course, needs prenatal care and will soon need maternity care. The teacher of the seven-year-old boy claims that he has attention deficit disorder, while the five year old needs glasses and the one year old has recurrent earaches. If the Sawatsky's are entitled to Medicaid, to what services are they entitled? What problems might they encounter in receiving covered services?

As is true with eligibility, the benefits provided by Medicaid programs vary from state to state. They will undoubtedly vary more under the provisions of the Deficit Reduction Act (DRA) adopted in 2006. This section describes the traditional law as well as DRA changes in that law.

The Medicaid statute identifies about three dozen categories of services that states may cover, but also permits under the final category coverage of "any other medical care, and any other type of remedial care recognized under State law, specified by the Secretary." 42 U.S.C.A. § 1396d(a)(28). At least one state has covered acupuncture under this category. Prior to 2006, states were required to provide the categorically needy with inpatient hospital services; outpatient hospital services and rural health clinic services; other laboratory and X-ray services; nursing facility services; rural health clinic (RHC) and federally-qualified health center (FQHC) services; early and periodic screening, diagnostic and treatment (EPSDT) services for children; family planning services and supplies; physicians' services; and nurse-midwife and other certified nurse practitioner services. 42 U.S.C.A. § 1396a(a)(10)(A).

States have had considerably more discretion in the benefits that they provide to the medically needy. There have been some limits to this discretion, however. States that elect to cover the medically needy must provide ambulatory services for children and prenatal and delivery services for pregnant women, 42 U.S.C.A. § 1396a(a)(10)(C)(iii)(II), and states that provide institutional services for any group must also cover ambulatory services, 42 U.S.C.A. § 1396a(a)(10)(C)(iii)(I). Moreover, if a state covers institutional care for the mentally ill or retarded, it must also provide them either the services it provides to the categorically needy or any seven services offered generally to Medicaid recipients, and if a state covers nursing facility services, it must also pay for home health services, 42 U.S.C.A. § 1396a(a)(10)(C)(iv). What policy considerations explain these requirements?

Some Medicaid services are aimed at specific population groups. The most prominent example of these is the EPSDT program, which requires not only that states provide screenings to diagnose physical or mental conditions in children, but also obligates states to provide treatment for identified conditions, whether or not the services required are otherwise included in its Medicaid plan. Much of the litigation challenging state Medicaid programs has involved the EPSTD program. See, e.g., Frew v. Hawkins, 540 U.S. 431, 124 S.Ct. 899, 157 L.Ed.2d 855 (2004); Oklahoma Chapter of the American Academy of Pediatrics v. Fogarty, 472 F.3d 1208 (10th Cir. 2007); Westside Mothers v. Olszewski, 454 F.3d 532 (6th Cir. 2006); Pediatric Specialty Care, Inc. v. Arkansas Department of Human Serv's, 293 F.3d 472 (8th Cir. 2002); Antrican v. Odom, 290 F.3d 178 (4th Cir. 2002). On the key role that EPSDT plays in child health, see, Sara Rosenbaum and Paul H. Wise, Crossing the Medicaid–Private Insurance Divide: The Case of EPSDT, 26 Health Aff.(2), 382 (2007). The Medicaid statute also requires coverage of certain categories of providers, such as nurse midwives and nurse practitioners.

Under the Medicaid law as it existed prior to 2006, a state's Medicaid plan was required to specify the "amount, duration, and scope" of each service that it provided for the categorically needy and each group of the medically needy. 42 C.F.R. § 440.230(a). Each service was required to be of sufficient amount, duration, and scope to achieve its purpose reasonably. 42 C.F.R. § 440.230(b). The Medicaid agency was not allowed to arbitrarily deny or reduce the amount, duration, or scope of a required service solely because of the diagnosis, type of illness, or condition. 42 C.F.R. § 440.230(c). States could refuse to cover specified optional categories of services (such as eyeglasses or dental care), but if they did cover a service, they could not simply decide to cover it for some medical diagnoses or conditions and not for others. Thus a state provision covering eyeglasses for individuals suffering from eye disease, but not for individuals with refractive error, was invalidated, White v. Beal, 555 F.2d 1146 (3d Cir.1977), as was a $50,000 cap on payment for hospital services which precluded coverage of $200,000 liver transplants, Montoya v. Johnston, 654 F.Supp. 511 (W.D.Tex.1987), and a state's refusal to cover sex reassignment surgery (which would fall within the general mandatory categories of hospital and physician services), Smith v. Rasmussen, 57 F.Supp.2d 736 (N.D.Iowa 1999). Although some courts have held that the benefits of a state Medicaid program are sufficient if they meet the needs of the Medicaid population of the state as a whole, Desario v. Thomas (139 F.3d 80, 95 (2d Cir. 1998) cert. granted, judgment vacated on other grds, sub nom. Slekis v. Thomas, 525 U.S. 1098, 119 S.Ct. 864, 142 L.Ed.2d 767 (1999); Charleston Mem. Hosp. v. Conrad, 693 F.2d 324 (4th Cir. 1982)) most circuits have held that Medicaid must fund all medically necessary services within a covered category (see *Lankford, supra*; Hern v. Beye, 57 F.3d 906, 911 (10th Cir. 1995); Dexter v. Kirschner, 984 F.2d 979, 983 (9th Cir. 1992)), which seems also to be the position of CMS (T.L. v. Colorado Dept. of Health Care Pol'y and Fin. 42 P.3d 63, 66 (2002)).

The Deficit Reduction Act (DRA) of 2005 (actually adopted in 2006), dramatically changed these requirement for some groups of Medicaid recipients, allowing state Medicaid plans to ignore statutory requirements regarding mandatory and optional service coverage, state-wideness, freedom of choice, and comparability with respect to these groups. A number of groups remain subject to the preexisting laws governing benefits, including pregnant women with incomes below 133 percent of the poverty level, blind and disabled recipients, dually-eligible Medicare beneficiaries, most institutionalized recipients, the medically needy, parents receiving Temporary Assistance to Needy Families (TANF), and children in foster care. As to others, including mostly children, working parents, and pregnant women with incomes above 133 percent of FPL, states may, instead of complying with the prior law, provide coverage through "benchmark" or "benchmark equivalent" plans. Benchmark plans include the standard Blue Cross/Blue Shield PPO option under the Federal Employees Health Benefit Plan, the HMO plan with the largest commercial enrollment in state, any generally-available state employees plan (regardless of whether anyone actually enrolls in it) or any plan approved by HHS. These options are much like those which the states may offer under the SCHIP program. The DRA is unclear as to whether states have to provide EPSDT coverage beyond that provided by benchmark plans, though CMS has interpreted the statute to say that they do.

As of the spring of 2007, the four states that have established benchmark plans have chosen HHS approved coverage plans, i.e. set up plans for which they have themselves defined limited benefits. West Virginia, for example, is implementing a program that denies mental health counseling and other services and limits prescription drugs for recipients who do not sign a pledge to "do my best to stay healthy," "attend health improvement programs as directed," have routine checkups and screenings, keep appointments, take medicines as prescribed and go to emergency rooms only for real emergencies. Health care providers are expected under the West Virginia program to inform Medicaid if their patients are not complying with the pledge. Is such a program likely to improve recipient health? Is it likely to save money? What ethical issues does it pose for providers? See Judith Solomon, West Virginia's Medicaid Changes Unlikely to Reduce State Costs or Improve Beneficiaries' Health, available at http://www.cbpp.org/5–31–06health. htm(2006). See generally, describing the DRA, Sara Rosenbaum, Medicaid at Forty: Revisiting Structure and Meaning in a Post–Deficit Reduction Era, 9 J. Health Care L. & Pol'y 5 (2006). Were your state to adopt a DRA option, how would it affect your answer to the problem at the beginning of this section?

Notes and Questions

1.   Who should make coverage decisions under the Medicaid program: the personal physicians of beneficiaries, low level state bureaucrats, national professional consensus groups, grass roots consensus panels? What should be the relationship between the federal and state governments in making coverage decisions? In particular, what role should the federal courts play?

2.   The additional flexibility provided the states by the DRA for benefit coverage merely supplements the flexibility already provided under § 1115 of the Social Security Act which authorizes demonstration projects. Since the beginning of the Medicaid program, the federal government has under this provision permitted the states to deviate from federal Medicaid requirements to conduct "demonstration" projects (42 U.S.C. § 1315). In fact, many § 1115 waiver programs have

not been true research projects, and indeed many have continued for years without effective review, in essence resulting in administrative waiver of statutory requirements. The DRA supplements § 1115 waiver authority, authorizing up to ten states to establish "health opportunity account" programs which provide high deductible plans coupled with health savings accounts for Medicaid recipients. But even prior to the DRA, CMS had authorized state programs that were very different from the traditional Medicaid model. Florida, for example, has received a § 1115 waiver to establish a "defined contribution" Medicaid program that pays flat, risk-adjusted amounts from which recipients can purchase private insurance. South Carolina has requested a waiver for a system of state-funded "personal health accounts" which beneficiaries may use to purchase private insurance or to purchase services directly from providers. What are the advantages and disadvantages of a defined contribution model for Medicaid? Health savings accounts were introduced in Chapter 4. What additional considerations beyond those raised in that discussion affect the use of such accounts for Medicaid recipients?

3. A striking feature of the benefit packages provided by Medicaid traditionally is its emphasis on institutional care. In 2006, fifty-eight percent of Medicaid personal health expenditure payments went to hospitals and nursing homes (compared to about forty-four percent of personal health care expenditures in the U.S. generally). Medicaid pays for forty-three percent of the nursing home care provided in the United States, over six times the amount paid for by private insurance (which is primarily long-term care insurance, since most health insurance policies do not cover nursing home care). Eighty-five percent of Medicaid spending on long-term care is "optional," much of it for home and community-based services. Medicaid also pays for much of the care provided by intermediate care facilities for the mentally disabled. Most of the residents of nursing facilities and ICF–MRs are very debilitated, physically and mentally. Many of these people would not have survived in other periods in history or in other cultures. Medicaid is, in a very real sense, the cost that we pay as a society for valuing the lives of these persons.

While all state Medicaid programs cover some optional services, like intermediate care facility services and pharmaceuticals, some states do not cover other optional services, such as podiatry, dental care, eyeglasses, or dentures. All in all, sixty-five percent of Medicaid expenditures go for optional services. But when economic conditions or federal cutbacks have resulted in state Medicaid cutbacks, optional services are often the first to go. During the financial crises of the early 2000s, a number of states reduced dental and vision services, for example. Others restructured or limited their prescription drug coverage, in some instances capping the number of prescriptions a recipient could fill in a month. What explains the choice of services states cover under Medicaid or drop in lean times? Does Medicaid cover the services that are most vital to health or that are most cost-effective? Are covered services those that poor persons or elderly persons would themselves choose to have covered if they were purchasing insurance? Why does Medicaid cover some services for which private insurance is not generally purchased, such as nursing home care or birth control? What role might provider associations, their lawyers and lobbyists play in determining benefit coverage? Might services currently available under Medicaid mirror those covered by health programs previously financed by the states with their own money before federal matching funds became available (many of the residents of ICF–MRs were formerly in state mental institutions)?

In considering these questions, it is important to realize that Medicaid, like Medicare, does not just purchase services for its beneficiaries, but also plays a vital role in supporting the nation's health care infrastructure. Medicaid disproportionate share payments (i.e. payments to hospitals that provide a disproportionate amount of care to Medicaid and uninsured patients and are therefore unable to rely on private-pay patients to cross-subsidize the burden of caring for these patients) constitute almost six percent of Medicaid expenditures (although this money does not necessarily end up with the hospitals themselves, as will be explained later). Medicaid pays for much of the obstetric and pediatric care delivered in the United States, and plays a vital role in supporting teaching hospitals. Medicaid and Medicare (which also covers medical education costs) are largely responsible, therefore, for there being a safety net in the United States even for those not eligible for Medicaid itself.

4.   Does the Constitution have any relevance to the question of whether certain items or services should be covered by public benefits programs? Harris v. McRae, 448 U.S. 297, 100 S.Ct. 2671, 65 L.Ed.2d 784 (1980) addressed the constitutionality of the Hyde Amendment, which limits Medicaid funding for abortions. In upholding the Hyde amendment against due process and equal protection challenges, Justice Stewart wrote for the court:

> * * * [R]egardless of whether the freedom of a woman to choose to terminate her pregnancy for health reasons lies at the core or the periphery of the due process liberty recognized in Roe v. Wade, 410 U.S. 113, 93 S.Ct. 705, 35 L.Ed.2d 147 (1973), it simply does not follow that a woman's freedom of choice carries with it a constitutional entitlement to the financial resources to avail herself of the full range of protected choices. * * * Although the liberty protected by the Due Process Clause affords protection against unwarranted government interference with freedom of choice in the context of certain personal decisions, it does not confer an entitlement to such funds as may be necessary to realize all the advantages of that freedom * * *

Harris v. McRae, 448 U.S. 297, 100 S.Ct. 2671, 65 L.Ed.2d 784 (1980).

Since *Harris v. McRae*, thirteen state supreme courts have recognized a state constitutional right to have state Medicaid programs pay for abortions as it does other medical procedures. See Right to Choose v. Byrne, 91 N.J. 287, 450 A.2d 925 (1982); Moe v. Secretary of Administration and Finance, 382 Mass. 629, 417 N.E.2d 387 (1981); Committee to Defer d Reproductive Rights v. Myers, 29 Cal.3d 252, 172 Cal.Rptr. 866, 625 P.2d 779 (1981), while four more states cover abortion voluntarily. In these states, the state pays 100 percent of these costs (as Missouri covered DME for the blind out of state funds in *Lankford*), because federal financial participation is not available for the costs of abortions except where necessary to save the mother's life or in cases of rape or incest.

5.   Various civil rights acts might also limit state discretion in determining what benefits to provide under the Medicaid program. In Olmstead v. L.C., 527 U.S. 581, 119 S.Ct. 2176, 144 L.Ed.2d 540 (1999), Justice Ginsburg, writing for a majority of the Court, concluded that, under Title II of the Americans with Disabilities Act of 1990 (ADA) and implementing regulations requiring public entities to administer "programs in the most integrated setting appropriate to the needs of qualified individuals with disabilities," 28 CFR § 35.130(d), the state of Georgia was obligated to care for persons with mental disabilities in community-based programs rather than state institutions when the state's treatment professionals had concluded that community placement was appropriate, the transfer from institutional care to a less restrictive setting was not opposed by the affected individual, and the placement could reasonably be accommodated, taking into account the resources available to the State and the needs of others with mental disabilities. The Court noted specifically that since 1981, the federal Medicaid

program had provided funding for state-run home and community-based care through a waiver program, and did not as a matter of policy favor institutional over community-based treatment.

Justice Ginsburg, joined by Justice O'Connor, Justice Souter, and Justice Breyer, concluded in Part III–B of the opinion that the State's responsibility to provide community-based treatment to qualified persons with disabilities was not unlimited. The State, they contended, should be allowed to show that immediate relief for the plaintiffs would be inequitable given the State's responsibility to care for a large and diverse population of persons with mental disabilities. The opinion further stated that the ADA did not obligate the state to eliminate institutions for the mentally disabled, which might be appropriate for some patients. The opinion approved a rationing approach to allocation of places in community-based facilities. Ginsburg stated that, if the State were to demonstrate that it had a comprehensive, effectively-working plan for placing qualified persons with mental disabilities in less restrictive settings, and a waiting list that moved at a reasonable pace not controlled by the State's endeavors to keep its institutions fully populated, persons at the top of the community-based treatment waiting list should not be displaced by individuals lower down simply because they had sued under the ADA. *Olmstead* has spawned a host of ADA Medicaid cases. See, e.g., ARC of Washington State Inc. v. Braddock, 427 F.3d 615 (9th Cir. 2005); Fisher v. Oklahoma Health Care Authority, 335 F.3d 1175 (10th Cir. 2003); Townsend v. Quasim, 328 F.3d 511 (9th Cir. 2003); Bruggeman v. Blagojevich, 324 F.3d 906 (7th Cir. 2003); Sara Rosenbaum, Joel Teitelbaum and Alexandra Stewart, Olmstead v. L.C.: Implications for Medicaid and Other Publicly Funded Health Services, 12 Health Matrix 93 (2002). See also, reviewing the litigation issues involved in attempting to expand the benefits of Home and Community Based services waiver programs, Margaret K. Feltz, Playing the Lottery: HCBS Lawsuits and Other Medicaid Litigation on Behalf of the Developmentally Disabled, 12 Health Matrix 181 (2002).

C. PAYMENT FOR SERVICES

1. *Fee-for-Service Medicaid*

The original vision of the Medicaid program was that it would provide mainstream care for its recipients. In line with this dream, the Medicaid statute guaranteed recipients free choice of participating providers. 42 U.S.C.A. § 1396a(a)(23). With respect to access to physician services, however, this goal has always been more a dream than a reality. Physicians also have freedom to choose whether or not to participate in Medicaid. Medicaid physician fee schedules have been largely driven by state budget constraints, and low Medicaid fees have discouraged physician participation in the program. One recent study found that, on average, Medicaid only pays physicians about sixty-nine percent of Medicare rates, which are themselves well below private rates, although Medicaid fees in fact increased significantly in the late 1990s and early 2000s. Stephen Zuckerman, et al., Changes in Medicaid Fees, 1998–2003: Implications for Physician Participation, Health Aff., Web. Excl. June 23, 2004. Low payment levels, along with paperwork and billing hassles and possibly the characteristics of Medicaid recipients, have contributed to low physician participation in Medicaid. In 2001, only sixty-two percent of physicians, and (only 54 percent of primary care physicians) were accepting most or all new Medicaid patients.

Fee-for-service Medicaid recipients have also received a very distinctive sort of physician care. One study of pediatricians who treated a high volume of Medicaid patients in New York City, for example, found that ninety-one percent had attended medical schools outside the United States, only forty-two percent were board certified (compared to eighty-nine percent statewide), and only 49 percent had hospital admitting privileges. Gerry Fairbrother, et al., New York City Physicians Serving High Volumes of Medicaid Children, 32 Inquiry 345 (Fall 1995). When physicians are not readily available, Medicaid recipients have often had to rely on hospital outpatient clinics and emergency rooms for primary care.

Hospitals and nursing homes are more limited in their ability to refuse Medicaid patients. Many hospitals are obligated to serve Medicaid patients because of their tax-exempt status or because of lingering obligations under the Hill–Burton program. Many nursing homes also are not able to count on enough private pay business to permit them to decline Medicaid participation.

Prior to 1997 federal law required that the states pay hospitals and nursing homes "reasonable" rates, and many lawsuits were brought by providers challenging low state rates. The 1997 Balanced Budget Act repealed these provisions, but did not end litigation over Medicaid rates. Federal Medicaid law also requires payment rates to be "consistent with efficiency, economy, and quality of care and * * * sufficient to enlist enough providers so that care and services are available under the plan at least to the extent that such care and services are available to the general population in the geographic area." 42 U.S.C.A. § 1396a(a)(30). Several courts have held that this statute gives providers enforceable rights, Minnesota HomeCare Ass'n, Inc. v. Gomez, 108 F.3d 917 (8th Cir.1997); Methodist Hospitals, Inc. v. Sullivan, 91 F.3d 1026 (7th Cir.1996); Arkansas Medical Soc'y v. Reynolds, 6 F.3d 519 (8th Cir.1993); Visiting Nurse Ass'n of N. Shore, Inc. v. Bullen, 93 F.3d 997 (1st Cir.1996). But more recent cases, postdating the repeal of the Boren Amendment have held that providers cannot sue to enforce this provision under § 1983. This seems to be part of a general trend, discussed below, toward limiting the enforceability of Medicaid requirements in federal court against the states. See Sanchez v. Johnson, 416 F.3d 1051 (9th Cir. 2005); Long Term Care Pharmacy Alliance v. Ferguson, 362 F.3d 50 (1st Cir.2004); Pennsylvania Pharmacists Ass'n v. Houstoun, 283 F.3d 531 (3d Cir.2002). See also Evergreen Presbyterian Ministries Inc. v. Hood, 235 F.3d 908 (5th Cir.2000) (beneficiaries have right to sue under equal access provision, but not providers). See Abigail Moncrieff, Payments to Medicaid Doctors: Interpreting the "Equal Access" Provision, 73 U. Chi. L. Rev. 673 (2006).

Problem: Representing Providers in Medicaid Litigation

You represent a hospital association in a state that has just cut Medicaid hospital payments by five percent to address a state budget crisis. Do you challenge the cut through litigation, or do you rather try lobbying or grass-roots organizing? Do you sue in federal or state court if you litigate? What evidence would you present if you litigate under § 1396a(a)(30) (and if the court lets your proceed under this section) arguing that the rates do not meet the standards set forth in that section? What arguments and evidence would you expect the state to present? Would your strategy be different if you represented a group of physicians and physician payments were at issue?

2. *Medicaid Cost Sharing*

As noted in Chapter 4, one strategy for controlling health care utilization and cost favored by conservative advocates is increased cost-sharing by consumers. Whatever merits this strategy may offer in the private sector, it has very limited possibilities in the Medicaid program because of the poverty of Medicaid recipients. Until 2006, the law permitted only very nominal cost-sharing for Medicaid recipients, and prohibited cost sharing altogether for children, pregnant women with respect to pregnancy-related services, terminally ill individuals in hospice, and institutionalized recipients. Perhaps most importantly, the law prohibited Medicaid providers from denying services to recipients who could not afford a copayment.

The 2006 Deficit Reduction Act dramatically changed this. The DRA allows cost-sharing of up to ten percent of service cost for recipients with income of 100 to 150 percent of the poverty level, and up to twenty percent of the service cost for recipients with incomes above 150 percent of the poverty level, capped at five percent of total income. The DRA also allows states to charge premiums for recipients with incomes above 150 percent of the poverty level. Cost-sharing is still prohibited for the recipients listed above, as well as for emergency and family planning services. Special rules apply to non-preferred drugs and to non-emergency use of emergency rooms (see also chapter eight on emergency room use). States may allow participating providers to refuse services to recipients who do not pay cost-sharing obligations. What reasons can be given for imposing additional cost-sharing obligations on recipients? Do the general arguments for consumer-cost sharing reviewed in Chapter 4 apply to Medicaid recipients? What effect might cost sharing have on access to services for recipients? See Bill J. Wright, et al., The Impact of Increased Cost Sharing on Medicaid Enrollees, 24 Health Aff. (4) 1106 (2005); Leighton Ku & Victoria Wachino, The Effect of Increased Cost–Sharing in Medicaid: A Summary of Research Findings, http://www.cbpp.org/5–31–05 health2.pdf (2005).

3. *Medicaid Managed Care*

Although the original vision of Medicaid was that recipients would have the same free choice of providers then enjoyed by the general population, Medicaid has in recent years, like private health insurance, moved dramatically in the direction of managed care. By 2006, 29.8 million Medicaid beneficiaries (sixty-five percent) were enrolled in managed care, compared to 2.7 million in 1991. In twenty-five states, over seventy percent of Medicaid recipients were enrolled in managed care, and in Tennessee and Missouri, 100 percent were enrolled.

This move to managed care has been driven by several factors. The most important, perhaps, has been the hope of saving money. Managed care seemed to have cut costs in the private sector, and it was hoped that it would work for Medicaid as well. Managed care advocates claimed that it might not only reduce the price of services, but that it would also reduce inappropriate use of expensive services like emergency room care. The move to managed care was also driven by the hope, however, that it would increase access by Medicaid recipients to providers and improve quality and coordination of care. A number of states, including Tennessee and Oregon, hoped further that savings from managed care might enable them to expand coverage to low income uninsured not otherwise eligible for Medicaid.

Attempts to move Medicaid recipients to managed care were thwarted for a time by federal requirements that guaranteed Medicaid recipients free choice of providers. In the late 1980s and 1990s, however, it became increasingly common for states to seek waivers under § 1915(b) of the Social Security Act (42 U.S.C.A. § 1396n(b)) which permitted CMS to waive the freedom of choice requirement, or under § 1115 (42 U.S.C.A. § 1315), which permits CMS to waive virtually all statutory requirements in the context of approved research and demonstration projects.

Arizona, which had previously refused to establish a Medicaid program, set up a statewide Medicaid managed care program under a § 1115 waiver in 1992. Arizona's program has matured over the years and has been regarded as one of the most successful Medicaid managed care programs. Tennessee launched its TennCare program under a § 1115 waiver in 1994, seeking both to control rapidly-growing Medicaid costs and to expand dramatically coverage to the uninsured. Tennessee's program got off to a rocky start, both because the program was implemented very quickly and because Tennessee had minimal experience with managed care before the program began. As the program has matured, it has enjoyed some success, but it has recently experienced difficulties and cutbacks See, analyzing the TennCare program and the legal issues raised by managed care in great depth, James F. Blumstein and Frank A. Sloan, Health Care Reform Through Medicaid Managed Care: Tennessee (TennCare) as a Case Study and a Paradigm, 53 Vand. L. Rev. 125 (2000). See, also reporting on the early TennCare experience, Sidney Watson, Medicaid Physician Participation: Patients, Poverty, and Physician Self–Interest, 21 Am. J. L. & Med. 191 (1995).

The 1997 Balanced Budget Act amended the Medicaid statute to permit states to require recipients to enroll with Medicaid Managed Care (MMC) organizations or a primary care case manager. 42 U.S.C. § 1396u–2. States are not permitted, however, to require dual-eligible Medicare beneficiaries, Native Americans, or special needs children to enroll in managed care plans without federal permission. States must generally permit recipients a choice of two or more MMC plans, but this requirement is loosened in rural areas. 42 U.S.C.A. § 1396u–2(a)(3). Medicaid recipients who do not exercise their choice may be assigned by the State through a default enrollment process, and states may establish enrollment priorities for plans that are oversubscribed. 42 U.S.C.A. § 1396u–2(a)(4)(c) & (D). Recipients may terminate (or change) enrollment in an MMC organization for cause at any time, but may only do so without cause during the ninety day period following enrollment and once a year thereafter. 42 U.S.C.A. § 1396u–2(a)(4)(A). MMC plans are not permitted to discriminate on the basis of health status or need for health service in enrollment, reenrollment, or disenrollment of recipients. 42 U.S.C.A. § 1396b(m)(2)(A)(v).

Medicaid managed care plans are subject to many of the same consumer rights afforded private managed care members under state law described in chapter 9. See 42 U.S.C.A. §§ 1396b(m)(2)(A)(vii); 1396u–2(b)(2),(3) & (4); 1396u–2(c)(1). States must have available "intermediate sanctions" for dealing with MMC organizations that violate program requirements. 42 U.S.C.A.

§§ 1396u–2(e). In a number of instances, recipients have brought class actions against states for operating managed care programs in violation of federal requirements. See Michelle M. Mello, Policing Medicaid and Medicare Managed Care: The Role of Courts and Administrative Agencies, 27 J. Health Pol, Pol'y & L. 465 (2002).

Medicaid managed care has, not surprisingly, a mixed record. In particular, it has created problems in some instances for safety net providers, including public hospitals, academic medical centers, and federally qualified health centers, which have traditionally been heavily dependent on Medicaid for support. Commercial Medicaid managed care plans can refuse to contract with some safety net providers and may pay others less than traditional Medicaid has paid. On the other hand, in some communities, managed care organizations built around safety net providers are proving to be the most reliable managed care partners for Medicaid programs. Despite early commercial managed care plan interest in Medicaid managed care, Medicaid managed care is often very different from their normal lines of business. Medicaid recipients are needy and often plagued by chronic and expensive problems. Medicaid pays parsimoniously, but imposes demanding program requirements. In particular, it requires services that many commercial plans do not cover and coverage of populations that live in places where commercial plans do not have providers. Providers that contract with commercial plans, moreover, are often not eager to have Medicaid recipients in their waiting rooms. Increasingly, commercial plans have abandoned Medicaid, leaving the market to safety net plans or niche commercial plans that specialize in the Medicaid market. See Debra A Draper, Robert E Hurley, and Ashley C. Short, Medicaid Managed Care: The Last Bastion of the HMO? 23(2) Health Aff. 155 (2004); Robert E. Hurley and Stephen A. Somers, Medicaid and Managed Care: A Lasting Relationship, 22(1) Health Aff. 101 (2003);Sidney D. Watson, Commercialization of Medicaid, 45 St.Louis U.L.J. 53 (2001).

The states have generally found it relatively easy to move Medicaid-covered children and their families to MMC. This population is relatively healthy and their care inexpensive and predictable. It has proved more difficult to provide managed care for the disabled and elderly, which account for the vast majority of Medicaid costs. Disabled and elderly populations are very different than the population that is normally covered by commercial managed care. They are more expensive to cover, and present managed care organizations with greater risks. Managed care plans are not accustomed to covering chronic health care services like nursing home care or home health care that are rarely needed by beneficiaries of employment-related plans. Some states "carve out" these services and contract with separate managed care plans (like behavioral health plans) to cover them; other states simply cover them directly though fee-for-service payments. See, e.g., Kaiser Commission on Medicaid and the Uninsured, Medicaid's Disabled Population and Managed Care (2001); Sara Rosenbaum and David Rousseau, Medicaid at Thirty–Five, 45 St. Louis U. L.J. 7 (2001); Mary Crossley, Medicaid Managed Care and Disability Discrimination Issues, 54 Tenn. L. Rev. 419 (1998); S.A. Somers, et al, The Coverage of Chronic Populations under Medicaid Managed Care: An Essay on Emerging Challenges, 65 Tenn. L. Rev. 649 (1998); Robert N., Swidler, Special Needs Plans: Adapting Medicaid Managed Care for Persons with Serious Mental Illness or HIV/AIDS, 61 Alb.L.Rev. 1113 (1998).

In the end, managed care has arguably proved more successful in Medicaid than in Medicare. In most states managed care has not saved Medicaid programs a great deal of money, but neither has it added to program cost. Several studies show that it has decreased dependence of Medicaid recipients on emergency rooms, but most studies show that access to care has otherwise been unaffected. In some states, however, money has been saved and access and quality improved. The bottom line seems to be that in most states Medicaid was such a poor program before managed care that improvement was not difficult and was sometimes achieved. See Robert Hurley and Stephen Zuckerman, Medicaid Managed Care: State Flexibility in Action (2002).

D. PROGRAM ADMINISTRATION AND FINANCING: FEDERAL/STATE RELATIONSHIPS

Perhaps the most contentious of all of the controversial issues surrounding the Medicaid program has been the nature of the relationship between the federal and state governments in setting policy and administering the program. This is the primary issue addressed by *Lankford*, with which we began this section. Particularly controversial has been the role of the federal courts in enforcing the rights that the program affords recipients and providers.

As of this writing in late 2007, Medicaid is still a federal entitlement program administered and partially funded by the states. It is an entitlement program in the sense that the federal Medicaid statute and regulations create at least some rights under federal law enforceable against the states. The federal government also contributes a share of the Medicaid program's cost, known as Federal Financial Participation or FFP, which currently ranges from fifty percent to seventy-six percent.

The Medicaid program is also in a very real sense a state program. As should be clear by now, state legislatures and Medicaid agencies have significant discretion in deciding what groups to cover, which benefits to provide, how much to pay for benefits, and how to provide benefits. Nevertheless, states often consider the federal role in the Medicaid program as intrusive and oppressive.

Medicaid state programs are subject to federal oversight at several levels. States must submit a Medicaid state plan to CMS demonstrating that their programs conform with the federal statutes and regulations. If a state Medicaid program ceases to be in substantial compliance with federal requirements, CMS may, after a hearing, terminate federal funding to the state. Because this remedy is so drastic, CMS has rarely convened a hearing and has never terminated a state program. Additional statutory provisions permit HHS to disallow reimbursement claimed by the state where the services covered by the state (such as elective abortions) are not eligible for reimbursement, 42 C.F.R. §§ 457.204, 457.212. These provisions are used more frequently, and occasionally result in litigation between the federal government and the states. For an excellent review of the range of administrative law issues involved in the governance of the Medicaid Program, see Eleanor Kinney, Rule and Policy Making for the Medicaid Program: A Challenge to Federalism, 51 Ohio St.L.J. 855 (1990).

Perhaps most objectionable to the states, however, is the fact that the courts have for a quarter century permitted both recipients and providers a federal cause of action under 42 U.S.C.A. § 1983 to sue for violations of rights guaranteed by the Medicaid statute. See, e.g., Wilder v. Virginia Hosp. Ass'n, 496 U.S. 498, 110 S.Ct. 2510, 110 L.Ed.2d 455 (1990); Doe v. Chiles, 136 F.3d 709 (11th Cir.1998). The courts have also held that Medicaid recipients and providers can obtain injunctive relief against the states to compel compliance with the Medicaid statute, even though the Eleventh Amendment bars damage actions against the states for past violations of the Act. Edelman v. Jordan, 415 U.S. 651, 94 S.Ct. 1347, 39 L.Ed.2d 662 (1974). (What, incidentally, might the Eleventh Amendment, which bars any retroactive relief, have to do with why the plaintiffs in *Lankford* were fighting for a preliminary injunction?)

The 2001 lower court decision in Westside Mothers v. Haveman, 133 F.Supp.2d 549 (E.D. Mich. 2001), sent shockwaves through the Medicaid advocacy community. It effectively held that Medicaid was no longer a federal entitlement (i.e. the rights of Medicaid recipients and, by extension, providers, were no longer enforceable in federal court under § 1983, and actions to enforce them prospectively were barred by the Eleventh Amendment). In 2002, the district court decision was reversed, in a Sixth Circuit opinion that thoroughly explores the legal nature of the Medicaid entitlement:

WESTSIDE MOTHERS v. HAVEMAN

United States Court of Appeals, Sixth Circuit, 2002.
289 F.3d 852.

MERRITT, Circuit Judge.

This suit filed under 42 U.S.C. § 1983 alleges that the state of Michigan has failed to provide services required by the Medicaid program. Plaintiffs, Westside Mothers, * * * allege that defendants James Haveman, director of the Michigan Department of Community Health,* * * did not provide the early and periodic screening, diagnosis, and treatment services mandated by the Medicaid Act and related laws.

* * *

At issue here is the federal requirement that participating states provide "early and periodic screening, diagnostic, and treatment services ... for individuals who are eligible under the plan and are under the age of 21." *Id.* § 1396d(a)(4)(B)[ ]. The required services include periodic physical examinations, immunizations, laboratory tests, health education, *see* 42 U.S.C. § 1396d(r)(1), eye examinations, eyeglasses, *see id.* § 1396d(r)(2), teeth maintenance, *see id.* § 1396d(r)(3), diagnosis and treatment of hearing disorders, and hearing aids, *see id.* § 1396d(r)(4).

In 1999, plaintiffs sued the named defendants under § 1983, which creates a cause of action against any person who under color of state law deprives an individual of "any right, privileges, or immunities secured by the Constitution and laws" of the United States. 42 U.S.C. § 1983. They alleged that the defendants had refused or failed to implement the Medicaid Act, its enabling regulations and its policy requirements, by (1) refusing to provide, and not requiring * * * HMOs [participating in the Medicaid program] to provide, the comprehensive examinations required by §§ 1396a(a)(43) and 1396d(r)(1) and 42 C.F.R. § 441.57; (2) not requiring participating HMOs to provide the necessary health care, diagnostic services, and treatment required by § 1396d(r)(5); (3) not effectively informing plaintiffs of the existence of the screening and treatment services, as required by § 1396a(a)(43); (4) failing to provide plaintiffs the transportation and scheduling help needed to take advantage of the screening and treatment services, as required by § 1396a(a)(43)(B) and 42 C.F.R. § 441.62; and (5) developing a Medicaid program which lacks the capacity to deliver to eligible children the care required by §§ 1396(a)(8), 1396a(a)(30)(A), and 1396u–2(b)(5).[ ]

Defendants moved to dismiss the plaintiffs and for dismissal of the suit. * * *

In March 2001 the district court granted defendants' motion to dismiss all remaining claims. *See Westside Mothers v. Haveman,* 133 F.Supp.2d 549, 553 (E.D.Mich.2001). In a detailed and far-reaching opinion, the district court held that Medicaid was only a contract between a state and the federal government, that spending-power programs such as Medicaid were not supreme law of the land, that the court lacked jurisdiction over the case because Michigan was the "real defendant and therefore possess[ed] sovereign immunity against suit," *id.,* that in this case *Ex parte Young* was unavailable to circumvent the state's sovereign immunity, and that even if it were available § 1983 does not create a cause of action available to plaintiffs to enforce the provisions in question.

This appeal followed. We reverse on all issues presented.

Analysis

A. Medicaid Contracts and the Spending Power

Much of the district court's decision rests on its initial determinations that the Medicaid program is only a contract between the state and federal government and that laws passed by Congress pursuant to its power under the Spending Clause are not "supreme law of the land." We address these in turn.

1. Whether Medicaid is only a contract.—The district court held that "the Medicaid program is a contract between Michigan and the Federal government." [ ] The program, it points out, is not mandatory; states choose whether to participate. [ ] If a state does choose to participate, Congress may then "condition receipt of federal moneys upon compliance by the recipient with federal statutory and administrative directives." [ ]

To characterize precisely the legal relationship formed between a state and the federal government when such a program is implemented, the district court turned to two Supreme Court opinions on related subjects. In *Pennhurst State School and Hosp. v. Halderman ("Pennhurst I"),* the Court described the Medicaid program as "much in the nature of a contract," and spoke of the " 'contract' "formed between the state and the federal government. [ ] * * *

Justice Scalia expanded on this contract analogy in his concurrence in *Blessing v. Freestone.* He maintained that the relationship was "in the nature of a contract" because:

The state promises to provide certain services to private individuals, in exchange for which the Federal government promises to give the State funds. In contract law, when such an arrangement is made (A promises to pay B money, in exchange for which B promises to provide services to C), the person who receives the benefit of the exchange of promises between two others C is called a third-party beneficiary.

520 U.S. 329, 349, 117 S.Ct. 1353, 137 L.Ed.2d 569 (1997) (Scalia, J., concurring).

Drawing on above language, the district judge then concluded that the "Medicaid program is a contract between Michigan and the Federal government," [ ] * * * The only significant difference between Medicaid and an ordinary contract, he asserted, is "the sovereign status of the parties," which limits the available remedies each can seek against the other. [ ]

Contrary to this narrow characterization, the Court in *Pennhurst I* makes clear that it is using the term "contract" metaphorically, to illuminate certain aspects of the relationship formed between a state and the federal government in a program such as Medicaid. It does not say that Medicaid is *only* a contract. It describes the program as "much in the nature of" a contract, and places the term "contract" in quotation marks when using it alone. [ ] It did not limit the remedies to common law contract remedies or suggested that normal federal question doctrines do not apply. * * *

Binding precedent has put the issue to rest. The Supreme Court has held that the conditions imposed by the federal government pursuant to statute upon states participating in Medicaid and similar programs are not merely contract provisions; they are federal laws. In Bennett v. Kentucky Department of Education, Kentucky argued that a federal-state grant agreement "should be viewed in the same manner as a bilateral contract." 470 U.S. 656, 669, 105 S.Ct. 1544, 84 L.Ed.2d 590 (1985). The Court rejected this approach, holding that, "[u]nlike normal contractual undertakings, federal grant programs originate in and remain governed by statutory provisions expressing the judgment of Congress concerning desirable public policy." * * *

2. Whether acts passed under the Spending Power are Supreme Law of the Land.—After holding that Medicaid is only a contract to pay money enacted under the spending power, the district court then held that programs enacted pursuant to the Constitution's spending power are not the "supreme law of the land" and do not give rise to remedies invoked for the violation of federal statutes.[ ] Relying on its determination that Medicaid and similar programs are "contracts consensually entered into by the States with the Federal Government . . . ," the district court then reasons that they are "not statutory enactments by which States must automatically submit to federal prerogatives." [ ]. There are two ways to understand this passage. One is that the district court is merely following the logic of its previous finding, and holding that federal-state programs are not supreme law because they are only contracts. We have already rejected the line of reasoning that begins with the assumption that Medicaid is only a contract.

The district court may also be claiming that acts passed under the spending power are not supreme law because the spending power only gives Congress the power to set up these programs, not to force states to participate in them.* * * *South Dakota* [v. Dole] upholds the power of Congress to place conditions on a state's receipt of federal funds. 483 U.S. at 211–12, 107 S.Ct. 2793. *Pennhurst I* holds that if Congress wishes to impose obligations on states that choose to participate in volitional spending power programs, it must make the obligations explicit. 451 U.S. at 25, 101 S.Ct. 1531.

* * *

The district court acknowledges that "the Supreme Court has in the past held that federal-state cooperative programs enacted under the Spending Power fall within the ambit of the Supremacy Clause." [ ] It then states that in "recent years ... the Supreme Court has conducted a more searching analysis of the nature and extent of the Supremacy Clause," suggesting erroneously that its departure from precedent is dictated by recent Supreme Court jurisprudence. [ ] * * * The well-established principle that acts passed under Congress's spending power are supreme law has not been abandoned in recent decisions.

* * *

B.   Whether the Suit is Barred Under Sovereign Immunity

The district court next held that the plaintiffs' suit is foreclosed by doctrines of sovereign immunity because Michigan is the "real party at interest" in the suit and plaintiffs cannot invoke any of the exceptions to sovereign immunity that would allow their suit. [ ]

As explained by the Supreme Court in many cases, sovereign immunity, though partially codified in the Eleventh Amendment, is a basic feature of our federal system. [ ] * * *

Under the doctrine developed in *Ex parte Young* and its progeny, a suit that claims that a state official's actions violate the constitution or federal law is not deemed a suit against the state, and so barred by sovereign immunity, so long as the state official is the named defendant and the relief sought is only equitable and prospective. [ ]

Of course, *Ex parte Young* is a ' fiction" to the extent it sharply distinguishes between a state and an officer acting on behalf of the state, but it is a necessary fiction, required to maintain the balance of power between state and federal governments. "The availability of prospective relief of the sort awarded in *Ex parte Young* gives life to the Supremacy Clause."[ ] * * * On its surface this case fits squarely within *Ex parte Young*. Plaintiffs allege an ongoing violation of federal law, the Medicaid Act, and seek prospective equitable relief, an injunction ordering the named state officials henceforth to comply with the law.

The district court nonetheless held that *Ex parte Young* was inapplicable for four separate reasons. Two can be quickly dismissed. First, it held that plaintiffs could not invoke *Ex parte Young* because that doctrine can only be invoked to enforce federal laws that are supreme law of the land. [ ] Since we held above that spending clause enactments are supreme law of the land, they may be the basis for an *Ex parte Young* action. Second, the district court held *Ex parte Young* is unavailable because under this doctrine a court lacks "authority to compel state officers performing discretionary functions." [ ] This correctly states the holding in *Young,* but misunderstands what it means by "discretion." "An injunction to prevent [a state official] from doing that which he has no legal right to do is not an interference with the discretion of an officer." *Ex parte Young,* 209 U.S. at 159, 28 S.Ct. 441. Since the plaintiffs here claim that the defendants are acting unlawfully in refusing to implement mandatory elements of Medicaid's screening and treatment program, they seek only to prevent the defendants from doing "what [they] have no legal right to do," and their suit is permitted under *Ex parte Young.*

Third, the district court asserts that *Ex parte Young* is unavailable because the state "is the real party in interest when its officers act within their lawful authority." [ ] It has two reasons for finding Michigan the real party in interest. Its first reason follows from its finding that Medicaid is a contract. If Medicaid were only a contract, then this would be a suit seeking to compel a state to specific performance of a contract. Such suits are barred under a nineteenth century Supreme Court case, *In re Ayers,* 123 U.S. 443, 8 S.Ct. 164, 31 L.Ed. 216 (1887), which held that a "claim for injunctive relief against state officials under the Contracts Clause is barred by state sovereign immunity because the state [is] the real party at interest." [ ] We have already held that Medicaid is not merely a contract, but a federal statute. This suit seeks only to compel state officials to follow federal law, and thus is not barred by *Ayers.*

The district court also says erroneously that Michigan is the real party in interest because "[t]here is no personal, unlawful behavior attributed" to the defendants that plaintiffs seek to enjoin [ ]. In their initial complaint, plaintiffs make clear that they are suing the named defendants because of "their failure to provide children in Michigan ... with essential medical, dental, and mental health services *as required by federal law.*" [ ]

Finally, the district court refused to allow plaintiffs to proceed under *Young* because of the Supreme Court's holding in *Seminole Tribe* that "[w]here Congress has prescribed a detailed remedial scheme for the enforcement against a State of a statutorily created right, a court should hesitate before casting aside those limitations and permitting an action against a state officer based upon *Ex parte Young.*" [ ] The Medicaid Act allows the Secretary of Health and Human Services to reduce or cut off funding to states that do not comply with the program's requirements.[ ] This one provision, the district court held, was a detailed remedial scheme sufficient to make *Ex parte Young* unavailable. [ ]

We disagree. In *Seminole Tribe,* the Supreme Court found *Ex parte Young* was unavailable because Congress had established a *"carefully crafted and intricate* remedial scheme.... for the enforcement of a *particular* federal right." [ ] The scheme here, in contrast, simply allows the Secretary to reduce or cut off funds if a state's program does not meet federal requirements. *See* 42 U.S.C. § 1396c. This is not a detailed "remedial" scheme sufficient to show Congress's intent to preempt an action under *Ex parte Young.* [ ]

Plaintiffs seek only prospective injunctive relief from a federal court against state officials for those officials' alleged violations of federal law, and they may proceed under *Ex parte Young.*

C. Whether There is a Private Right of Action Under § 1983

Section 1983 imposes liability on anyone who under color of state law deprives a person of "rights, privileges, or immunities" secured by the laws or the constitution of the United States. 42 U.S.C. § 1983. The Supreme Court and this court have held that in some circumstances a provision of the Medicaid scheme can create a right privately enforceable against state officers through § 1983. *See Wilder* [ ].

In *Blessing,* the Supreme Court set down the framework for evaluating a claim that a statute creates a right privately enforceable against state officers through § 1983. [ ] A statute will be found to create an enforceable right if, after a particularized inquiry, the court concludes (1) the statutory section was intended to benefit the putative plaintiff, (2) it sets a binding obligation on a government unit, rather than merely expressing a congressional preference, and (3) the interests the plaintiff asserts are not so " 'vague and amorphous' that [their] enforcement would strain judicial competence." [ ] If these conditions are met, we presume the statute creates an enforceable right unless Congress has explicitly or implicitly foreclosed this.[ ] The district court erred when it did not apply this test to evaluate plaintiffs' claims.

We now apply this test. First, the provisions were clearly intended to benefit the putative plaintiffs, children who are eligible for the screening and treatment services. [ ] We have found no federal appellate cases to the contrary. Second, the provisions set a binding obligation on Michigan. They are couched in mandatory rather than precatory language, stating that Medicaid services *"shall* be furnished" to eligible children, 42 U.S.C. § 1396a(a)(8) (emphasis added), and that the screening and treatment provisions *"must* be provided," *id.* § 1396a(a)(10)(A). Third, the provisions are not so vague and amorphous as to defeat judicial enforcement, as the statute and regulations carefully detail the specific services to be provided. *See* 42 U.S.C. § 1396d®. Finally, Congress did not explicitly foreclose recourse to § 1983 in this instance, nor has it established any remedial scheme sufficiently comprehensive to supplant § 1983. [ ]

Plaintiffs have a cause of action under § 1983 for alleged noncompliance with the screening and treatment provisions of the Medicaid Act.

* * *

Notes

1.   The debate over the nature of the Medicaid entitlement has focused since *Westside Mothers* on the enforceability of Medicaid rights under 42 U.S.C. § 1983, particularly after the Supreme Court again tightened the screws on § 1983 claims in Gonzaga University v. Doe, 536 U.S. 273, 122 S.Ct. 2268, 153 L.Ed.2d 309 (2002). This issue is discussed in *Lankford* at the beginning of this section. In recent cases, the courts have been examining the Medicaid statute section by section, holding that some provisions offer enforceable rights to recipients (or perhaps to providers), while other sections are only statements of policy and do not create rights enforceable under § 1983. Even if provisions of the Medicaid statute are not enforceable as federal laws under § 1983, however, they may be enforceable under the Supremacy Clause. *Lankford* is one of the few appellate cases to discuss this issue, although the Supreme Court has allowed suits to be brought against the states under the Supremacy Clause in Medicaid litigation without expressly addressing the issues See PhRMA v. Walsh, 538 U.S. 644, 123 S.Ct. 1855, 155 L.Ed.2d 889 (2003). What difference does it make for the nature of the Medicaid program whether or not a federal cause of action is available against the states? See, discussing these issues, Jane Perkins, Using Section 1983 to Enforce Federal Laws, Clearinghouse Review, March/April 2005 at 720; Lauren K.

Saunders, Preemption as an Alternative to Section 1983, Clearinghouse Review, March/April 2005 at 704; Timothy Stoltzfus Jost, The Tenuous Nature of the Medicaid Entitlement, Health Affairs, Jan./Feb. 2003, at 145. Note that attorneys' fees are available under 42 U.S.C. § 1988 in 1983 actions.

2. Federal Medicaid obligations are often enforced against the states through consent decrees. These often result in further litigation. In Frew v. Hawkins, 540 U.S. 431, 124 S.Ct. 899, 157 L.Ed.2d 855 (2004), the state of Texas had entered into a lengthy consent decree to settle litigation challenging the state's operation of the EPSDT program. The state later resisted enforcement of the decree, arguing successfully to the Fifth Circuit that "the Eleventh Amendment prevented enforcement of the decree unless the violation of the consent decree was also a statutory violation of the Medicaid Act that imposed a clear and binding obligation on the state." Frazar v. Gilbert, 300 F.3d 530, 543 (5th Cir.2002). The Supreme Court reversed unanimously. The Court held that "[t]he decree is a federal court order that springs from a federal dispute and furthers the objectives of federal law." 124 S.Ct. at 904. This order, the Court held, was agreed to by state officials, and under *Ex Parte Young,* was enforceable against them. "Federal courts," the Court stated, "are not reduced to approving consent decrees and hoping for compliance. Once entered, a consent decree may be enforced." 124 S.Ct. at 905. The Court did, however, acknowledge the importance of state sovereignty, and suggested that the state request modification of the decree if there was a change of fact or law justifying amendment. It also suggested that the federal courts should give the states "latitude and substantial discretion" in meeting their federal obligations. 124 S.Ct. at 906.

3. While the states complain about federal oversight, the states have also proved quite adept at manipulating the program to serve their own ends. It has always been true that states that spend more on Medicaid can attract more federal matching funds and that federal funds flow disproportionately to a few states with generous programs. Over the past decade and a half, however, states have become even more creative in extracting federal financial participation (FFP).

One early means to this end was the use of provider donations or provider-specific taxes. The idea behind these exactions was that money could be taken from providers, passed through the Medicaid program where it would be matched by FFP, and paid back to the providers to enhance their payments, without any additional state money entering the system. This practice was accompanied by expanded state definitions of disproportionate share hospitals (DSH), which permitted the states to target reimbursement at certain hospitals from which it had extracted funds, or to public hospitals and nursing homes. In some states, DSH payments were in turn extracted by the state from public providers though intergovernmental transfers (IGTs), in some instances to be used for purposes unrelated to the Medicaid program. By 1995, thirty-four states were using provider taxes and donations, and DSH payments constituted eight percent of state Medicaid spending. DSH payments were one of the most significant factors causing growth in the Medicaid program in the late 1990s, and still constitute almost six percent of Medicaid costs. Legislation adopted by Congress in 1991 to curb these abuses was only partially successful.

In the late 1990s, the states adopted yet another revenue-maximizing practice, taking advantage of the fact that federal upper payment limits (UPLs) for hospitals were set on an aggregate basis for all hospitals. States stinted non-public hospitals so as to channel payments to public hospitals that significantly exceeded the cost of services, which were then channeled back to the states through IGTs. For example, a state with a fifty percent federal match could pay $6 million to a public hospital (including $3 million in state funds, $3 million in federal), then extract $4 million from the hospital through an IGT, leaving the hospital with $2 million and itself with $1 million, without spending any state money. Some states have also submitted excessive claims to the Medicaid program for school health services, thus using the Medicaid program as a means for financing their schools. State "creative financing" not only costs the federal government money, it also distorts the nature of the public debate about Medicaid by making the program appear to cost the states far more than it actually does. On the other hand, the states contend that DSH payments and IGTs are necessary to fund safety net facilities and programs. CMS has proposed a rule that would eliminate the use of IGTs but its implementation was blocked for a year by legislation adopted in 2007. An excellent description of these practices is found in the Kaiser Commission on Medicaid and the Uninsured's Medicaid Resource Book (2002), at 105–115.

IV. THE STATE CHILDREN'S HEALTH INSURANCE PROGRAM (SCHIP)

Though one of the primary functions of Medicaid in recent years has been to provide health insurance for children, many children have remained uninsured. Even after Medicaid eligibility expansions in the late 1980s and early 1990s, over 10 million children many of them in low-income families, were still without health insurance. In response to this continuing problem, Congress created, as part of the 1997 BBA, the State Children's Health Insurance Program (SCHIP), title XXI of the Social Security Act. 42 U.S.C.A. §§ 1397aa–1397jj.

The SCHIP program, however, was created in a very different political climate than that which saw the birth of the Medicaid program. (It was, therefore, not created as an entitlement for recipients, but rather as a grant-in-aid program to the states, established for ten years and affording the states considerable flexibility in program administration within broad federal guidelines.) As this book goes to the publisher, late in 2007, Congress has twice passed legislation extending and expanding the SCHIP program, and President Bush has twice vetoed that legislation. This section reports on the program as it exists under continuing resolution early in 2008.

SCHIP enrollment grew rapidly through 2002 but has grown more slowly since. As of June of 2007, the program covered 4.4 million persons, although over the course of a year about 6 million children are at some point covered. See. Genevieve Kenney and Justin Yee, SCHIP At A Crossroads: Experiences to Date and Challenges Ahead, 26 Health Aff. (2) 356 (2007); Lisa Dubay, et al., Medicaid at the Ten–Year Anniversary of SCIP: Looking Band and Moving Forward, 26 Health Aff. (2) 370 (2007).

States that wish to participate in the SCHIP program may use SCHIP funds either to expand Medicaid coverage for children or to establish a new SCHIP program to cover children who are neither eligible for Medicaid nor covered by private health insurance, or use a combination of these approaches. As of 2007, 18 states had separate SCHIP programs, 11 states plus the District of Columbia had expanded Medicaid, and 21 states used a combined approach. Although SCHIP is intended to provide health insurance for children, a number of states have obtained § 1115 waiver authority to use it to cover adults as well. Through waivers, eight states (as of 2007) were using SCHIP to cover parents, four to cover childless adults, and 11 to cover pregnant women (by considering fetuses to be unborn children). The 2006 DRA prohibits new waivers for covering childless adults.

SCHIP programs are supposed to target children in families with incomes of at or below 200 percent of the federal poverty level or 150 percent of the state's Medicaid income level, whichever is greater. 42 U.S.C.A. §§ 1397bb(b)(1); 1397jj(b), (c)(4). States may set eligibility standards that take into account geographic location, age, income and resources, residency, disability status, access to other health coverage, and duration of eligibility. They cannot discriminate on the basis of diagnosis or exclude children on the basis of preexisting condition.

SCHIP explicitly does not create an entitlement for any particular child to receive coverage. 42 U.S.C.A. § 1396bb(b)(4). Children who are eligible for Medicaid coverage, however, must be enrolled under Medicaid, and SCHIP coverage is not to substitute for coverage under group health plans. States are also not supposed to cover children with higher family incomes unless children from poorer families are covered, nor may they cover children in state institutions or children eligible for insurance as dependents of state employees. States may subsidize premiums for employment-related insurance to use this route for expanding coverage. States are to establish outreach programs to identify children eligible for SCHIP coverage or other public programs, including Medicaid.

States that choose to establish separately-administered SCHIP programs must provide health care benefit packages equivalent to coverage provided by one of several benchmark benefit plans; or that include certain basic services and have an aggregate actuarial value equal to a benchmark plan, or that are approved by HHS. 42 U.S.C.A. § 1397cc(a)–(c). Benefit coverage is in general less comprehensive than that offered by Medicaid.

States may impose cost-sharing obligations on SCHIP beneficiaries, including premiums and copayments, subject to statutory limits. About half the states require either premium payments or copayments for services, in part to reduce program costs, but also to make the program look less like a welfare program and to discourage "crowd out" (i.e., families dropping employment-related insurance for SCHIP coverage). Though cost-sharing might achieve these results, it also discourages participation and increases administrative complexity. See Mary Jo O'Brien, et al., State Experiences with Cost–Sharing Mechanisms in Children's Health Insurance Expansions (Commonwealth Fund, 2000). Further, although early studies seemed to show high levels of crowd-out, the most recent research demonstrates that a very small proportion of SCHIP enrollees—fewer than ten percent—in fact had affordable private coverage that they gave up in favor of SCHIP. Anna Sommers, et al., Substitution of SCHIP for Private Coverage: Results from a 2002 Evaluation in Ten States, 26 Health Aff. 529 (2007).

States that participate in SCHIP must match federal funds in accordance with a formula that provides more generous federal participation than is afforded under Medicaid. This invites gaming on the part of the states to move children from Medicaid to SCHIP, even though this is prohibited under the statute. Federal funds are allotted according to a formula that takes into account the number of low income children in the states and geographic variations in health care costs.

In summary, SCHIP is a remarkably different program than Medicaid, evidencing a very different philosophy of federal responsibility for health care financing. SCHIP affords maximum flexibility to the states in the apparent hope that they will generously and responsibly provide for poor children if given an incentive to do so. On the other hand, it provides minimal protection to beneficiaries, who are wholly dependent on state generosity and responsibility.

What explains the differences between the SCHIP program and Medicaid? Why was a separate program created instead of Medicaid expanded? Why was Medicaid coverage of indigent children continued when SCHIP was created? What barriers does SCHIP erect to participation that are not present with Medicaid? Why might SCHIP reach some children who whose families might refuse Medicaid coverage? An excellent analysis of the SCHIP program is found in Sara Rosenbaum, et al., Public Health Insurance Design for Children The Evolution from Medicaid to SCHIP, 1 J. Health & Biomedical L. 1 (2004).

Problem: Health Care Coverage for the Poor

Imagine that you are a member of the staff of a recently elected member of the House of Representatives who is very concerned about reforming the Medicaid program. You are working for this congresswoman because her ideological commitments mirror your own. She asks you to review the current Medicaid program and to come up with a proposal that would substantially improve the current program. Consider your response to her request in light of the following questions:

Whom should the program cover? What financial eligibility requirements should be imposed? What provisions should be made for family responsibility for individuals? Spousal impoverishment? Should eligibility be defined in terms of some definition of the worthy poor? How would you decide who is worthy and who is not?

What benefits should be afforded by the program? Should specific services be mandated, such as hearing aids, nurse midwife services, physical therapy, hospice? What mix of preventive, acute, and long-term care benefits should be covered? How should providers be paid? What role should managed care organizations play in providing care?

What should be the respective roles of the federal and state governments in administering the plan? What should be the respective roles of the legislative, executive, and judicial branches? Should recipients have any federally defined rights? Should providers have any rights? Should these rights be enforceable in federal or state court?

What interest groups do you expect to be most supportive of or opposed to your proposal? Would you expect that the members of any of these groups might be major contributors to your congresswoman? Do the members of these groups represent voting blocks important to your congresswoman?

Chapter 9

PROFESSIONAL RELATIONSHIPS IN HEALTH CARE ENTERPRISES

INTRODUCTION

Access to hospital facilities is essential to the practice of most physicians and many other health care professionals; however, a relationship with one or more hospitals is no longer the only affiliation required for successful medical practice. Increasingly, the professional's relationships with third-party payers, especially with managed care organizations, and with primary care, specialist, or diversified group practices are also critical.

Along with a shift in important practice affiliations has come a change in the relative power of physicians and the health care organization. In the context of the customary staff privileges system, with which this chapter begins, physicians exercised considerable control over the conditions under which they practiced; the resources that the hospital would provide them; the selection of other physicians permitted to practice in the hospital; and the oversight exercised over physician decisionmaking. Doctors generally no longer have this degree of control over their relationships with hospitals.

Changes in the financing of health care, particularly the emergence of managed care and other cost containment measures, have allowed organizations to exert more control over physician decisionmaking. In addition, the emerging data banks maintained by health care organizations as a result of electronic medical records are stimulating significant expectations, and perhaps capacity, for such organizations to monitor outcomes and other aspects of the intra-organization practices of individual physicians.

These changes have increased insecurity for physicians—from termination of hospital contracts, layoffs from employment with physician partnerships and group practices, and "deselection" from managed care provider panels. At the same time, doctors have integrated the entrepreneurial lessons of the new payment and delivery forms and are sometimes direct competitors of the hospitals in which they practice.

In most instances, the law governing professional relationships has borrowed from very familiar legal tools to structure professional relationships that respond to the health care environment of the twenty-first century. This chapter examines how different legal relationships—whether staff privileges, contract, or employment—can be used to allocate power, control, and financial risk in the health care system.

I. STAFF PRIVILEGES AND HOSPITAL–PHYSICIAN CONTRACTS

A physician or other health care professional may treat patients in a particular hospital only if the practitioner has "privileges" at that hospital. The hospital does not pay a fee or salary to a health care professional who only holds privileges and who has no other relationship (such as employment, a contract for services, or a joint business venture) with the hospital.

Hospital privileges include several distinct parts. Privileges may include admitting privileges for the authority to admit patients to the hospital and clinical privileges for the authority to use hospital facilities to treat patients, among other subsets of authority. The scope of an individual provider's clinical privileges must be delineated specifically by the hospital. A provider who is awarded privileges by the hospital is usually also a member of the hospital's medical staff and so is said to hold staff privileges.

The hospital medical staff historically has functioned as a relatively independent association within the hospital organization, operating within the hospital's by-laws but under its own medical staff by-laws as well. The medical staff as an entity traditionally has held substantial authority over the hospital's internal quality assurance system including the credentialing process through which physicians receive and maintain privileges. Only the hospital's governing board has legal authority to grant, deny, limit, or revoke privileges; but it is the hospital's medical staff that generally controls the credentialing process to that ultimate point.

There is, then, an inherent tension built into the common organizational structure of a hospital. This tension periodically erupts into spectacular conflicts that press on the unresolved ambiguity in this tripartite structure where authority is divided among the administration, the board of directors or trustees, and the medical staff. John D. Blum, Feng Shui and the Restructuring of the Hospital Corporation: A Call for Change in the Face of the Medical Error Epidemic, 14 Health Matrix 5 (2004), questioning the continuing viability of this "wobbly three-legged stool" structure.

The medical staff structure has allowed substantial physician control over access to hospital privileges for the purpose of assuring the quality of patient care through the staff's medical expertise and devotion to professional values. Most observers of the exercise of this control conclude that its purpose is not always fulfilled, however. Doctors sometimes have used access to privileges to achieve an advantage over competing physicians rather than solely for the benefit of the quality of care provided to patients.

When hospitals depended entirely on doctors for a stream of patients and when the hospital's interests and doctors' interests coalesced around the principle that more is better (i.e., longer stays, more tests, more interventions, more staff, and more equipment), hospitals were more likely to allow their medical staffs great latitude in the governance of privileges. Even so, the hospital's potential liability to injured patients for neglect in the credentialing process as well as the potential for antitrust liability for anticompetitive restriction of privileges provided significant disincentives for wholesale deference to the medical staff. See Chapters 6 and 15 for a discussion of these areas.

More recent developments have pushed hospitals toward even greater administrative control of physician decisionmaking in general and staff privileges in particular. Greater emphasis on outcomes and patient safety raises the stakes for hospitals in regard to physician behavior, and greater consumer access to online information about physicians and hospitals raises the risk that such information will be used in litigation against the hospital. Cost containment mechanisms that place hospitals at financial risk for length of stay and utilization of resources per patient—decisions traditionally directed by the patient's doctor—also prodded hospitals to exert more control over physician practices. Because the positive and negative financial consequences of physician practices are experienced by the hospital, many facilities explicitly consider the financial impact of a doctor's treatment patterns in their privileges decisions. As physicians have more frequently become direct rivals of the hospitals in which they practice, some hospitals are taking this competition into account in their credentialing as well.

The staff privileges system has changed in several ways that reflect these pressures, as you will see in this chapter. For example, hospitals have shifted their relationships with physicians in some practice areas toward contract or employment relationships and away from the more independent traditional staff privileges relationships. Contracts for medical services are especially prevalent among the hospital-based practice areas such as radiology, anesthesiology, pathology, and emergency medicine as well as in some particular functions including hospitalists who oversee or manage the in-hospital care of patients admitted to the hospital by private physicians. Hospitals and physicians in the 1980s frequently entered into mutually beneficial enterprises which involved the exchange of services, joint ownership of resources, and other financial and business relationships. These relationships, including the acquisition of physician practices by hospitals or other practice groups, typically use the structures discussed in this chapter as building blocks. In the late 1990s, however, a trend toward "disintegration" was clearly observable. In the past few years, competition between doctors and hospitals has escalated, with much controversy surrounding the ownership of "specialty hospitals," which compete with general hospitals for the most lucrative patient services, by physicians on the general hospital's own medical staff.

Generalizations about the relative power of hospitals and physicians are likely to be inaccurate in any particular circumstance. Each geographic market is different—including the extent of managed care coverage; the supply of physicians; and the degree of integration among facilities or among physicians. Each hospital is different in terms of its own relationships with managed care plans; its own dependence on physicians as the direct source of patients; and its own competitive position in the market for hospital and related services.

The Joint Commission has stated that:

The purpose of the credentialing ... process is to assure that the practitioners ... meet—at all times—the basic requirements set by the hospital for the performance of specific tasks. These processes should also identify potentially suboptimal practitioners who might require timely support to improve their performance or whose performance is at such variance with accepted practice that their privileges must be restricted. In the most extreme circumstances, the ... processes should have the capability of isolating those practitioners whose performance fundamentally threatens patient safety and who must therefore be removed from the medical staff. Discussion Brief, April 30, 2007.

As you review the materials in this section, consider whether this statement standing alone captures the interests and goals of the credentialing process and whether the legal framework supports or undermines these goals.

SOKOL v. AKRON GENERAL MEDICAL CENTER

United States Court of Appeals for the Sixth Circuit, 1999.
173 F.3d 1026.

NORRIS, CIRCUIT JUDGE.

Plaintiff is a cardiac surgeon on staff at Akron General. The Medical Council at Akron General received information in the mid–1990's indicating that plaintiff's patients had an excessively high mortality rate. Concerned about plaintiff's performance of coronary artery bypass surgery ("CABG"), the Medical Council created the CABG Surgery Quality Task Force in 1994 to conduct a review of the entire cardiac surgery program at Akron General. The Task Force hired Michael Pine, M.D., a former practicing cardiologist who performs statistical risk assessments for evaluating the performance of hospitals. At a presentation in 1994 attended by plaintiff, Dr. Pine identified plaintiff as having a mortality rate of 12.09%, a "high risk-adjusted rate." Risk adjustment analyzes the likelihood that a particular patient or group of patients will die, as compared to another patient or group of patients. Dr. Pine stated in a summary of his findings that the predicted mortality rate for plaintiff's CABG patients was 3.65%, and plaintiff's "high mortality rate was of great concern and warrants immediate action."

James Hodsden, M.D., Chief of Staff at Akron General, requested that the Medical Council consider plaintiff for possible corrective action. Pursuant to the Medical Staff Bylaws, the Medical Council forwarded the complaint to the chairman of plaintiff's department, who appointed an Ad Hoc Investigatory Committee to review plaintiff's CABG surgery performance. The Medical Staff Bylaws require the Investigatory Committee to interview the staff member being reviewed and provide the Medical Council with a record of the interview and a report. The Investigatory Committee met with plaintiff three times. At the first meeting, the Investigatory Committee identified the issues before it to include addressing questions raised by plaintiff about the Pine study and determining the cause of plaintiff's excessive mortality rate. At the second meeting, the Investigatory Committee examined the mortality rate of plaintiff's patients using the Society of Thoracic Surgeons ("STS") methodology. Under STS methodology, the Investigatory Committee, like Dr. Pine, determined that plaintiff's CABG risk-adjusted mortality rate was roughly three times higher than the predicted mortality rate. The Investigatory Committee discussed the results of this analysis with plaintiff at the meeting.

At the third meeting, the Investigatory Committee reviewed with plaintiff various records of his twenty-six CABG patients who died either during or around the time of surgery. The Investigatory Committee determined that one factor leading to the deaths of these patients was poor case selection, meaning plaintiff did not adequately screen out those patients for whom CABG surgery was too risky. The Investigatory Committee also found that the excessive number of deaths may have been due to insufficient myocardial protection, which led to heart attacks.

The Investigatory Committee ultimately reported to the Medical Council that plaintiff's mortality rate was excessively high and that the two principal causes for this high mortality rate were poor case selection and "improper myocardial protection." The Investigatory Committee recommended that all cases referred to plaintiff for CABG surgery undergo a separate evaluation by another cardiologist who could cancel surgery felt to be too risky. It also recommended that plaintiff not be permitted to do emergency surgery or serve on "cathlab standby" and that there be an ongoing review of his CABG patients by a committee reporting to the Medical Council. Finally, it recommended that a standardized myocardial protection protocol be developed, and that all cardiac surgeons should be required to comply with the protocol.

Plaintiff appeared before the Medical Council on November 21, 1996, and the Medical Council voted to implement the recommendations. Under the Akron General Medical Staff Bylaws, when the Medical Council makes a decision adverse to the clinical privileges of a staff member, the staff member must be given notice of the decision of the Medical Council, and the notice shall specify "what action was taken or proposed to be taken and the reasons for it." This notice allows the staff member to prepare for a hearing to review the Medical Council's decision. . . .

Plaintiff and representatives from the Medical Council appeared before an Ad Hoc Hearing Committee on March 27, 1997. Plaintiff was represented by legal counsel, submitted exhibits, and testified on his own behalf. Dr. Gardner, a member of the Investigatory Committee, testified that although the Pine study and the STS methodology tended to underestimate the actual risk in some of plaintiff's cases, the Investigatory Committee concluded that the STS risk stratification tended to corroborate the Pine analysis. When asked about the Medical Council's determination that plaintiff engaged in poor case selection, Dr. Gardner had difficulty identifying specific cases that should not have had CABG surgery, yet he stated that "in the aggregate" there was poor case selection.

The Hearing Committee recommended that the Medical Council restore all plaintiff's CABG privileges. The Medical Council rejected the recommendation of the Hearing Committee and reaffirmed its original decision. In accordance with the Bylaws, plaintiff appealed the Medical Council's determination to the Executive Committee of the Board of Trustees of Akron General. This Committee affirmed the Medical Council's decision. Plaintiff then asked the district court for injunctive relief against Akron General.

* * *

Under Ohio law, private hospitals are accorded broad discretion in determining who will enjoy medical staff privileges at their facilities, and courts should not interfere with this discretion "unless the hospital has acted in an arbitrary, capricious or unreasonable manner or, in other words, has abused its discretion." [ ] However, hospitals must provide "procedural due process ... in adopting and applying" "reasonable, nondiscriminatory criteria for the privilege of practicing" surgery in the hospital. [ ]

A. INSUFFICIENT NOTICE

This appeal requires us to examine the extent of the procedural protections afforded plaintiff under Ohio law. In addition to an appeals process, "[f]air procedure requires meaningful notice of adverse actions and the grounds or reasons for such actions" when a hospital makes an adverse decision regarding medical staff privileges. [ ] Akron General's Medical Staff Bylaws require that notice of an adverse decision by the Medical Council state "what action was taken or proposed to be taken and the reasons for it" and thus do not contractually provide for a quality of notice exceeding that required by Ohio law.

The President of Akron General sent plaintiff a letter notifying him of the Medical Council's initial decision. The letter refers plaintiff to the minutes of the Medical Council's meeting which set out the reasons for the Council's decision. These minutes, provided to plaintiff, indicate that the findings and recommendations of the Investigatory Committee were presented. The Investigatory Committee found that "[t]he number and percentage of deaths in Dr. Sokol's population was excessively high compared to the published national statistics and other local surgeons." Two reasons for this high percentage were offered—poor case selection and problems with protecting against myocardial infarctions. * * *

According to the magistrate judge, the notice provided plaintiff was insufficient because [it failed] to provide Dr. Sokol with specific cases where he engaged in poor case selection and where he failed to provide appropriate myocardial protection.

The sort of notice demanded by the magistrate judge was not required by the circumstances of this case. Had Akron General restricted plaintiff's rights because the Medical Council determined that he had poor case selection or provided insufficient protections against myocardial infarctions, then perhaps specific patient charts should have been indicated, along with specific problems with each of those charts. However, Akron General had a more fundamental concern with plaintiff's performance: too many of his patients, in the aggregate, were dying, even after accounting for risk adjustment. Poor case selection and problems in preventing myocardial infarction were just two reasons suggested by the Investigatory Committee for the high mortality rate.

Plaintiff takes issue with the Pine study and the STS algorithm, claiming that they do not present an accurate picture of his performance as a surgeon because he is the "surgeon of last resort." In other words, so many of his patients die because so many of his patients are already at death's door. Perhaps plaintiff is correct about that. However, it is not for us to decide whether he has been inaccurately judged by the Investigatory Committee and the Medical Council. Instead, we are to determine whether plaintiff had sufficient notice of the charges against him to adequately present a defense before the Hearing Committee. He knew that the Medical Council's decision was based upon the results of the Pine study and the STS analysis, knew the identity of his patients and which ones had died, and had access to the autopsy reports and medical records of these patients. * * * Manifestly, he had notice and materials sufficient to demonstrate to the Hearing Committee's satisfaction that limiting his privileges was inappropriate.

It was well within Akron General's broad discretion to base its decision upon a statistical overview of a surgeon's cases. We are in no position to say that one sort of evidence of a surgeon's performance—a statistical overview—is medically or scientifically less accurate than another sort of evidence—the case-by-case study plaintiff suggests we require of Akron General.

B. ARBITRARY DECISION

The magistrate judge also ruled that the Medical Council's decision was arbitrary. She reasoned that because Akron General did not have a fixed mortality rate by which to judge its surgeons before it limited plaintiff's privileges, it was arbitrary to take action against him based upon his mortality rate. We cannot agree. Surely, if plaintiff's mortality rate were 100%, the Medical Council would not be arbitrary in limiting his medical staff privileges, despite not having an established mortality rate. The magistrate judge's reasoning would prevent the Medical Council from instituting corrective action unless there were a preexisting standard by which to judge its staff. It is true that surgeons must be judged by "nondiscriminatory criteria." [ ]. However, in this context, that means, for example, that if it came to the attention of the Medical Council that another surgeon had a mortality rate as high as plaintiff's, the latter surgeon's medical privileges would be similarly limited. * * *

On appeal, plaintiff argues that the Medical Council's decision was so wrong that it was arbitrary, capricious, or unreasonable. He points to evidence tending to show that the Medical Council's case against him was assailable. Indeed, the Hearing Committee recommended that plaintiff's full privileges be restored. But as the Ohio Supreme Court has recognized, "[t]he board of trustees of a private hospital has broad discretion in determining who shall be permitted to have staff privileges." [ ] The board of trustees will not have abused its discretion so long as its decision is supported by any evidence. Here, the Medical Council had both the Pine Study and the STS analysis. While it is conceivable that these are inaccurate measurements of plaintiff's performance, they are evidence that the hospital was entitled to rely upon, and accordingly, we are unable to say that Akron General abused its discretion in limiting plaintiff's privileges.

MERRITT, CIRCUIT JUDGE, dissenting.

* * *

The heart surgeon has been treated unfairly by his hospital. The Hearing Committee was the only group composed of experts independent of the hospital administration. * * * The Committee completely exonerated Dr. Sokol. No one has cited a single operation or a single instance in which Dr. Sokol has made a mistake, not one.

* * *

Notes and Questions

1.   Are the public's interests well-served by statutory or common law requirements of minimum procedures for actions against a doctor's staff privileges, or do these efforts create an obstacle to the removal of incompetent physicians? The court in *Sokol* examines the fairness of the procedures used by the hospital. The basis for this requirement of fair process is not the constitutional doctrine of due process which is applicable to public hospitals (see, e.g., Patel v. Midland Mem. Hosp. & Med. Ctr., 298 F.3d 333 (5th Cir. 2007)); rather, it is the common law doctrine of "fundamental fairness" applied to private associations. The requirements of fundamental fairness have been established on a case-by-case basis, and so its minimum requirements are not always clear. See the discussion in *Potvin* in the next section. Some states impose additional procedural requirements by statute. See e.g., N.Y. Public Health Law § 2801–b, which requires that the hospital provide a written statement of reasons and provides for review by the state's Public Health Council of any denial or diminution of privileges. The Health Care Quality Improvement Act, 42 U.S.C. § 11101, discussed below, also establishes minimum procedures for hospitals that desire HCQIA immunity.

2.   In *Sokol*, the court, applying Ohio law, limits its scope of review over the merits of the hospital's decision, testing only whether the hospital's decision was arbitrary. A few other states also allow limited judicial review of the merits of staff privileges decisions. For example, California allows courts to review privileges decisions under a substantial evidence standard. Gill v. Mercy Hosp., 199 Cal. App.3d 889, 245 Cal.Rptr. 304 (1988). (*Cf.* Sadler v. Dimensions Healthcare Corp., 378 Md. 509, 836 A.2d 655 (2003), holding that substantial evidence review is inappropriate.) Would a substantial evidence standard change the result in *Sokol*?

3.   In contrast to *Sokol*, the law in most states does not allow the courts to review the merits of privileges decisions at all. Instead, most states restrict judicial review to the question of whether the hospital followed its own by-laws; and for most of these states, the question is limited to compliance with the by-laws' procedural requirements only. See, e.g., Goldberg v. Rush Univ. Med. Ctr., 371 Ill.App.3d 597, 309 Ill.Dec. 197, 863 N.E.2d 829 (2007); Samuel v. Herrick Mem. Hosp., 201 F.3d 830 (6th Cir. 2000). What policy and practical considerations support broader and narrower judicial review? Why is the staff privileges system generally considered protective of physicians if judicial review is so limited in the majority of states? Do the procedures described in *Sokol* provide any insight here?

4.   The hospital relied on outcomes data for its actions regarding Dr. Sokol's privileges. Greater capacity for aggregating and analyzing patient data should mean that such actions will be increasing. Barry R. Furrow, Data Mining and Substandard Medical Practice: The Difference Between Privacy, Secrets and Hidden Defects, 51 Vill. L. Rev. 803 (2006), arguing that a hospital that fails to use available data effectively in peer review is negligent in credentialing. See also, Unnamed Physician v. Board of Trustees of St. Agnes Med. Ctr., 93 Cal.App.4th 607, 113 Cal.Rptr.2d 309 (2001); Lo v. Provena Covenant Med. Ctr., 342 Ill.App.3d 975, 277 Ill.Dec. 521, 796 N.E.2d 607 (2003). See also Katherine Van Tassel, Hospital Peer Review Standards and Due Process: Moving From Tort Doctrine Toward Contract Principles Based on Clinical Practice Guidelines, 36 Seton Hall L. Rev. 1179 (2006), expressing concern about the quality of outcomes data.

5.   The Joint Commission (formerly JCAHO) has had the most significant influence on credentialing procedures through its hospital accreditation standards. The Commission identified improvements in the staff privileges process as a

special focus of accreditation in 2004 and it began implementing new criteria in 2007. These new criteria emphasize three central expectations: that privileging and re-privileging assess physician performance against several competencies including patient care, medical/clinical knowledge, interpersonal and communication skills, and professionalism, among others; that there be continuous evaluation of practitioners rather than annual or biennial reviews alone; and that a separate standardized process be established to flag practitioners when there are competency concerns, including a process for newly credentialed physicians. Joint Commission Discussion Brief, April 30, 2007. These standards are likely to accelerate the use of data such as that relied upon in *Sokol*.

6. Hospitals are increasingly willing to take action against the privileges of physicians who engage in disruptive behavior. These actions face two threshold issues. First, can a hospital limit the privileges of a physician on the basis of behavior if the medical staff by-laws make no specific provision for this? (See the discussion of medical staff-hospital authority in the notes following *Mahan*, below.) Second, do such actions meet the requirements of the HCQIA, discussed below, which provide that only actions concerned with the quality of health care receive immunity? See, e.g., Gordon v. Lewistown Hosp., 423 F.3d 184 (3d Cir. 2005), holding that the hospital had immunity for actions based on disruptive conduct. See also, Poirier v. Our Lady of Bellefonte Hosp., 2006 WL 358241 (Ky. Ct. App. 2006), holding that by-laws provision requiring doctors to "use a generally recognized professional level of quality" would reach a doctor engaging in a "recurring pattern of unacceptable and unprofessional behavior." In one of the few cases denying the hospital summary judgment on the question of HCQIA immunity, a court held that the physician's dismissal was based on "his apparently good faith reporting of perceived improper hospital conduct to appropriate outside agencies" including "reports and letters to outside doctors and regulatory agencies, complaining about the care and procedures the hospital employed in its child psychiatric practice, scheduling of doctors, and in-patient insurance policies." Clark v. Columbia/HCA Information Services, Inc., 117 Nev. 468, 25 P.3d 215 (2001). See Zachary L. Erwin, Analyzing the Disruptive Physician: How State and Federal Courts Should Handle Whistleblower Cases Brought by Disruptive Physicians, 44 Duquesne L. Rev. 275 (2006) and Sections II, IIIA, and IIIB2 of this chapter.

7. Hospitals can reduce the risk of litigation over credentialing decisions considerably by including clauses in their physician contracts or medical staff by-laws in which physicians waive their right to sue over adverse actions. See, e.g., Sadler v. Dimensions Healthcare Corp., 378 Md. 509, 836 A.2d 655 (2003), suggesting that hospitals pursue this option. See also, the discussion of "clean sweep" clauses in the notes following *Mateo-Woodburn*, below.

Note: Immunity for Privileges Decisions

What interests argue in favor of allowing doctors subjected to the financial, reputational, and emotional impact of adverse credentialing decisions access to the courts to pursue injunctive relief or damages against the hospital? What interests argue in favor of blocking or greatly restricting the ability of such doctors to subject hospitals to lengthy, expensive, and acrimonious litigation over their peer review decisions? Both federal and state legislatures have taken a shot at sheltering the peer review process from litigation costs while trying to assure that the process is fair to doctors depending on staff privileges.

The federal Health Care Quality Improvement Act (HCQIA), 42 U.S.C. § 11101, affords hospitals complying with its requirements immunity from damages actions, except for civil rights claims. (See Section IV, below.) The HCQIA strikes the balance of interests in credentialing by providing immunity to hospitals (and other entities) only if their credentialing decisions meet substantive and procedural statutory standards. Several states have also enacted local variations on the HCQIA, as the Act does not override or preempt state laws which provide "incentives, immunities, or protection for those engaged in a professional review action that is in addition or greater than that provided" in the federal statute. 42 U.S.C. § 11115. See, e.g., Tex. Occ. Code Ann. § 160.010(a).

The HCQIA creates a presumption that the credentialing decision ("professional review action") complies with the standards of the Act. To rebut this presumption, the plaintiff must prove by a preponderance of the evidence that the health care entity did not act reasonably. Under the Act, the plaintiff must prove that the hospital: (1) did not act in the reasonable belief that the action was in furtherance of quality health care; (2) did not make a reasonable effort to obtain the facts of the matter; (3) did not afford the physician adequate notice and hearing procedures and such other procedures required by fairness under the circumstances; or (4) did not act in the reasonable belief that the action was warranted by the facts known after such reasonable effort to determine the facts and after meeting the Act's procedural requirements. For a case that clearly lays out the plaintiff's burden, see Van v. Anderson, 199 F.Supp.2d 550 (N.D. Tex. 2002).

In testing the "four reasonables," courts use an objective standard of reasonableness. Neither the ultimate accuracy of the hospital's conclusions nor direct evidence of improper motive or bad faith is considered relevant to the objective reasonableness of the hospital's actions. See Austin v. McNamara, 979 F.2d 728 (9th Cir. 1992), first establishing the objective standard so that immunity would be decided at an early stage of litigation. The courts have been supportive of adverse credentialing decisions, ordinarily resolving cases through summary judgment in favor of the hospital. In fact, physicians only rarely succeed in overturning the rebuttable presumption of immunity. One notable exception is Poliner v. Texas Health Systems, 2003 WL 22255677 (N.D. Tex.), which the court allowed to proceed to a jury trial with a resultant verdict of $366 million, later reduced by the court to $22,550,001.

Even with the courts' deferential interpretation of the HCQIA, however, the hospital that makes an adverse credentialing decision must engage in litigation testing whether the hospital complied with the Act. The likelihood that the litigation will be terminated with summary judgment is quite a significant advantage for the hospital, of course, but it doesn't completely remove the costs of litigation on the hospital's side. Unlike a motion to dismiss the claim, summary judgment requires significant discovery. Resolving HCQIA immunity claims on a motion to dismiss, however, is inappropriate as the Act requires some inquiry into the reasonableness of the hospital's actions in light of the facts of the particular case. See, e.g., Hilton v. Children's Hosp. San Diego, 107 Fed. Appx. 731 (9th Cir. 2004), reversing trial court's dismissal of physician's claims.

The HCQIA provides that physicians who bring frivolous or bad faith suits challenging credentialing decisions may be ordered to pay defendant's attorney's fees and costs. See Joshi v. St. Luke's Episcopal Presbyterian Hosp., 142 S.W.3d 862 (Mo. Ct. App. 2004), affirming denial of attorney's fees to hospital defendant. But see, Laurino v. Syringa Gen'l Hosp., 2005 WL 1847173 (D. Idaho 2005); Sithian v. Staten Island Univ. Hosp., 189 Misc.2d 410, 734 N.Y.S.2d 812 (Sup.Ct. 2001), aff'd sub nom. Sithian v. Spence, 300 A.D.2d 387, 750 N.Y.S.2d 783 (App.Div. 2002), each awarding fees.

The HCQIA also established the National Practitioner Data Bank (NPDB). In order to earn the immunity available under the Act, hospitals must report certain adverse credentialing decisions to the NPDB and must check Data Bank records on the individual physician when considering an application for privileges and every two years for physicians who hold privileges at the hospital. The HCQIA provides hospitals limited immunity for their reports to the Data Bank, with the physician bearing the burden of proving that the hospital did not enjoy immunity. See discussion of the NPDB in Chapter 2.

The hospital's obligation to report to the NPDB extends to situations where the physician has resigned once an investigation into quality of care issues has begun but before an adverse action has been taken. This has created a small window where a physician may resign prior to the beginning of an "investigation." Some argue that this allows hospitals too great an opportunity to bypass reporting while enjoying immunity for activities that precede a final action. In any case, it is not entirely clear when the opportunity to resign without report has passed. See, e.g., Wheeler v. Methodist Hosp., 95 S.W.3d 628 (Tex. Ct. App.2002); Ulrich v. City and County of San Francisco, 308 F.3d 968 (9th Cir. 2002); and Hooper v. Columbus Reg'l Healthcare System, 956 So.2d 1135 (Ala. 2006).

MATEO–WOODBURN v. FRESNO COMMUNITY HOSPITAL

Court of Appeal, Fifth District, 1990.
221 Cal.App.3d 1169, 270 Cal.Rptr. 894.

BROWN, J.

* * *

Prior to August 1, 1985, and as early as 1970, the FCH department of anesthesiology operated as an open staff. The department was composed of anesthesiologists who were independently competing entrepreneurs with medical staff privileges in anesthesiology. Collectively, the anesthesiologists were responsible for scheduling themselves for the coverage of regularly scheduled, urgent and emergency surgeries.

[E]ach anesthesiologist was rotated, on a daily basis, through a first-pick, second-pick, etc., sequence whereby each anesthesiologist chose a particular operating room for that particular date. Usually no work was available for one or more anesthesiologists at the end of the rotation schedule. Once an anesthesiologist rotated through first-pick, he or she went to the end of the line. In scheduling themselves, the anesthesiologists established a system that permitted each anesthesiologist on a rotating basis to have the "pick" of the cases. This usually resulted in the "first-pick" physician taking what appeared to be the most lucrative cases available for that day.

The rotation system encouraged many inherent and chronic vices. For example, even though members of the department varied in their individual abilities, interests, skills, qualifications and experience, often "first-picks" were more consistent with economic advantage than with the individual abilities of the physician exercising his or her "first-pick" option. At times, anesthesiologists refused to provide care for government subsidized patients, allegedly due to economic motivations.

The department chairman had the authority to suggest to fellow physicians that they only take cases for which they were well qualified. However, the chairman was powerless to override the rotation system in order to enforce these recommendations.

Under the open-staff rotation system, anesthesiologists rotated into an "on call" position and handled emergencies arising during off hours. This led to situations where the "on-call" anesthesiologist was not qualified to handle a particular emergency and no formal mechanism was in place to ensure that alternative qualified anesthesiologists would become promptly available when needed. * * *

* * *

These chronic defects in the system led to delays in scheduling urgent cases because the first call anesthesiologists in charge of such scheduling at times refused to speak to each other. Often, anesthesiologists, without informing the nursing staff, left the hospital or made rounds while one or more of their patients were in post-anesthesia recovery. This situation caused delays as the nurses searched for the missing anesthesiologist.

The trial court found these conditions resulted in breaches of professional efficiency, severely affected the morale of the department and support staff, and impaired the safety and health of the patients. As a result of these conditions, the medical staff (not the board of trustees) initiated action resulting ultimately in the change from an "open" to a "closed" system. We recite the highlights of the processes through which this change took place.

* * *

[Mr.] Helzer, President and Chief Executive Officer of FCH, established an "Anesthesia Task Force" to study the proposed closure. In a subsequent memo to Helzer, dated April 6, 1984, the task force indicated it had considered four alternative methods of dealing with problems in the department of anesthesiology: (1) continuation of the status quo, i.e., independent practitioners with elected department chairman, (2) competitive groups of anesthesiologists with an elected department chairman, (3) an appointed director of anesthesia with independent practitioners and (4) an appointed director with subcontracted anesthesiologists, i.e., a closed staff.

The memo noted that under the third alternative—a director with independent practitioners—the director would have no power to determine who would work in the department of anesthesiology. "Any restriction or disciplinary action recommended by the director would need to go through the usual hospital staff procedure, which can be protracted." It was also noted in the memo that a director with subcontracted practitioners "would have the ability to direct their activities without following usual hospital staff procedures." The committee recommended a director with subcontracted practitioners.

[The board accepted the committee's recommendation and formed a search committee to recruit a director for the department.]

* * *

Mateo–Woodburn was offered the position of interim director on June 13, 1984, which position she accepted. Mateo–Woodburn was interviewed for the position of director on September 25, 1984. Hass was interviewed for the position on March 7, 1985.

At a special meeting of the board of trustees held on April 10, 1985, the anesthesia search committee recommended to the board that Hass be hired as director of the department of anesthesiology, and the recommendation was accepted by the board.

At the same April 10 meeting, the board authorized its executive committee to close the department of anesthesiology. On the same day, the executive committee met and ordered the department closed.

* * *

An agreement between FCH and the Hass corporation was entered into on June 7, 1985. On June 18, 1985, Helzer sent a letter to all members of the department of anesthesiology which states in relevant part:

* * *

"The Board of Trustees has now entered into an agreement with William H. Hass, M.D., a professional corporation, to provide anesthesiology services for all hospital patients effective July 1, 1985. The corporation will operate the Department of Anesthesia under the direction of a Medical Director who will schedule and assign all medical personnel. The corporation has appointed Dr. Hass as Medical Director, and the hospital has concurred with the appointment. The agreement grants to the corporation the exclusive right to provide anesthesia services to all hospital patients at all times."

"To provide the services called for by the agreement, it is contemplated that the Hass Corporation will enter into contractual arrangements with individual physician associates who must obtain Medical Staff membership and privileges as required by the staff bylaws. The negotiations with such associates are presently ongoing, and the hospital does not participate in them."

"Effective August 1, 1985, if you have not entered into an approved contractual agreement, with the Hass Corporation, you will not be permitted to engage in direct patient anesthesia care in this hospital. However, at your option, you may retain your staff membership and may render professional evaluation and assessment of a patient's medical condition at the express request of the attending physician."

The contract between the Hass corporation and FCH provided that the corporation was the exclusive provider of clinical anesthesiology services at the hospital; the corporation was required to provide an adequate number of qualified physicians for this purpose; physicians were to meet specific qualifications of licensure, medical staff membership and clinical privileges at FCH, and to have obtained at least board eligibility in anesthesiology; and the hospital had the right to review and approve the form of any contract between the corporation and any physician-associate prior to its execution.

Subject to the terms of the master contract between the Hass corporation and FCH, the corporation had the authority to select physicians with whom it would contract on terms chosen by the corporation subject to the approval of FCH. The contract offered to the anesthesiologists, among many other details, required that a contracting physician be a member of the hospital staff and be board certified or board eligible. The Hass corporation was contractually responsible for all scheduling, billing and collections. Under the contract, the corporation was to pay the contracting physician in accordance with a standard fee arrangement. The contracting physician was required to limit his or her professional practice to FCH except as otherwise approved by the FCH board of trustees.

[The contract also provided:] " ... Provider shall not be entitled to any of the hearing rights provided in the Medical Staff Bylaws of the Hospital and Provider hereby waives any such hearing rights that Provider may have. However, the termination of this Agreement shall not affect Provider's Medical Staff membership or clinical privileges at the Hospital other than the privilege to provide anesthesiology services at the Hospital."

Seven of the thirteen anesthesiologists on rotation during July 1985 signed the contract. Of the six plaintiffs in this case, five refused to sign the contract offered to them. The sixth plaintiff, Dr. Woodburn, was not offered a contract but testified that he would not have signed it, had one been offered.

* * *

Some of the reasons given for refusal to sign the contract were: (1) the contract required the plaintiffs to give up their vested and fundamental rights to practice at FCH; (2) the 60–day termination clause contained no provisions for due process review; (3) the contract failed to specify amounts to be taken out of pooled income for administrative costs; (4) the contract required plaintiffs to change medical malpractice carriers; (5) the contract required plaintiffs to obtain permission to practice any place other than FCH; (6) the contract imposed an unreasonable control over plaintiffs' financial and professional lives; (7) the contract failed to provide tenure of employment. The Hass corporation refused to negotiate any of the terms of the contract with plaintiffs.

* * *

* * * Numerous cases recognize that the governing body of a hospital, private or public, may make a rational policy decision or adopt a rule of general application to the effect that a department under its jurisdiction shall be operated by the hospital itself through a contractual arrangement with one or more doctors to the exclusion of all other members of the medical staff except those who may be hired by the contracting doctor or doctors. * * *

* * *

[The position] of a staff doctor in an adjudicatory one-on-one setting, wherein the doctor's professional or ethical qualifications for staff privileges is in question, take[s] on a different quality and character when considered in light of a rational, justified policy decision by a hospital to reorganize the method of delivery of certain medical services, even though the structural change results in the exclusion of certain doctors from the operating rooms. If the justification is sufficient, the doctor's vested rights must give way to public and patient interest in improving the quality of medical services.

It is also noted, where a doctor loses or does not attain staff privileges because of professional inadequacy or misconduct, the professional reputation of that doctor is at stake. In that circumstance, his or her ability to become a member of the staff at other hospitals is severely impaired. On the other hand, a doctor's elimination by reason of a departmental reorganization and his failure to sign a contract does not reflect upon the doctor's professional qualifications and should not affect his opportunities to obtain other employment. The trial court correctly found the decision to close the department of anesthesiology and contract with Hass did not reflect upon the character, competency or qualifications of any particular anesthesiologist.

* * *

[I]f the hospital's policy decision to make the change is lawful, and we hold it is, then the terms of the contracts offered to the doctors was part of the administrative decision and will not be interfered with by this court unless those terms bear no rational relationship to the objects to be accomplished, i.e., if they are substantially irrational or they illegally discriminate among the various doctors.

Given the conditions existing under the open rotation method of delivering anesthesia services, including among others the lack of control of scheduling and the absence of proper discipline, we cannot say the terms of the contract were irrational, unreasonable or failed to bear a proper relationship to the object of correcting those conditions. Considered in this light, the terms are not arbitrary, capricious or irrational.

* * *

As to the contract provision which required waiver of hearing rights set forth in the staff bylaws, * * * those rights do not exist under the circumstances of a quasi-legislative reorganization of a department by the board of trustees. This quasi-legislative situation is to be distinguished from a quasi-judicial proceeding against an individual doctor grounded on unethical or unprofessional conduct or incompetency. Accordingly, the waiver did not further detract from or diminish plaintiffs' rights.

* * *

Plaintiffs contend the department of anesthesiology could not be reorganized without amending the bylaws of the medical staff in accordance with the procedure for amendment set forth therein. Closely allied to this argument is the assertion the hospital unlawfully delegated to Hass the medical staff's authority to make staff appointments.

* * * The hospital's action did not change the manner or procedure by which the medical staff passes upon the qualifications, competency or skills of particular doctors in accordance with medical staff bylaws. * * * In fact, plaintiffs remain members of the staff and the contract requires contracting anesthesiologists to be members of the staff. Moreover, it is clear the medical staff does not appoint medical staff members—it makes recommendations to the board of trustees who then makes the final medical staff membership decision. Hass was never given authority to appoint physicians to medical staff and never did so. Hass was merely hired to provide anesthesiology services to the hospital. His decision to contract with various anesthesiologists in order to provide those services was irrelevant to medical staff appointments except that all persons contracting with Hass were required to qualify as members of the medical staff.

We conclude the trial court's determination that the defendants' "actions were proper under the circumstance and that plaintiffs' Medical Staff privileges were not unlawfully terminated, modified or curtailed" is fully supported by the evidence and is legally correct.

Notes and Questions

1. *Mateo-Woodburn* considers two issues related to exclusive contracting. In addition to resolving the question of the procedural rights of the physician who held privileges prior to the institution of the exclusive contract, it reviews the termination provision in the exclusive contract itself. What contractual provision is made for termination of the contract and termination of staff privileges between Hass, P.C., and the anesthesiologists at Fresno Community Hospital? Would a contract clause that provides that termination of the contract will result automatically in termination of staff privileges without benefit of the by-laws' procedures (known as a "clean sweep" clause) be enforceable? See, for example, Madsen v. Audrain Health Care, 297 F.3d 694 (8th Cir. 2002) which, like most cases, upholds clean sweep agreements. Do the policy concerns underlying the procedural protections for credentialing decisions dissipate where there is a contract? Contracts such as those in *Mateo-Woodburn* allocate power and control differently than does the traditional staff privileges relationship. Which situation is more compatible with a goal of cost containment? With a goal of quality?

2. "Economic credentialing," at least as defined by the AMA, occurs when a hospital makes privileges decisions based on financial factors unrelated to quality. Traditionally, any local physician who presented credentials that sufficiently attested to their competency would be granted hospital privileges, unless the hospital operated as a "closed staff" hospital (such as a teaching hospital that required faculty status) or the credentialing process was corrupted by the medical staff's own economic interests. Economic credentialing signaled a major sea change in the relationship between doctors and hospitals. James W. Marks & Jayme R. Matchinski, Conflicts Credentialing: Hospitals and the Use of Financial Considerations to Make Medical Staffing Decisions, 31 Wm. Mitchell L. Rev. 1009 (2005). Of course, a single factor, such as overutilization of medical interventions, may relate both to cost and to quality. If cost control is a legitimate concern for hospitals, payers, and patients, one might argue that hospital efforts to monitor physician practices is beneficial; of course, others would be concerned that such controls threaten patients with inadequate diagnostic or medical care. For an excellent analysis, see John D. Blum, Beyond the ByLaws: Hospital–Physician Relationships, Economics, and Conflicting Agendas, 53 Buff. L. Rev. 459 (2005). Conflicts over economic credentialing have intensified as hospitals have used their credentialing process to exclude physicians who have business interests, such as ambulatory surgical centers or specialty hospitals, that compete directly with those of the hospital itself. See, *Mahan*, below.

3. Exclusive contracting, as in *Mateo-Woodburn*, has sometimes been viewed as a form of economic credentialing as the hospital seeks the best deal in its contracting with physician groups and can exert more control over the group's practice patterns. As you saw in that case, however, exclusive contracting can have a quality justification, for example in assuring adequate coverage of particular services. Even when hospitals have justified a contracting decision entirely on the basis of financial benefit, however, courts have accepted that reason standing alone as a legitimate ground for structuring the medical staff. See e.g., St. Mary's Hosp. of Athens, Inc. v. Radiology Prof'l Corp., 205 Ga.App. 121, 421 S.E.2d 731 (1992). But see, Ray v. St. John's Health Care Corp., 582 N.E.2d 464 (Ind. Ct. App.1991).

4. Courts often separate "staff privileges" from the privilege to admit and treat patients with the result that hospitals are not required to use procedures required for revocation of staff privileges when they have revoked or limited only the clinical privileges held by the physician. See, e.g., Plummer v. Community Gen'l Hosp. of Thomasville, Inc., 155 N.C.App. 574, 573 S.E.2d 596 (2002), holding that the hospital did not revoke privileges from a physician whose exclusive contract for anesthesiology had been terminated even though the hospital's entering an exclusive contract with another entity foreclosed plaintiff from practicing anesthesiology at the hospital. See also, Garibaldi v. Applebaum, 194 Ill.2d 438, 252 Ill.Dec. 29, 742 N.E.2d 279 (2000).

5. In *Mateo-Woodburn* there was no implication of any performance or quality problems in any single physician's practice. If there had been, would the doctors have been entitled to a hearing? In Major v. Memorial Hosps. Assn., 71 Cal.App.4th 1380, 84 Cal.Rptr.2d 510 (1999), the court considered a case in which a hospital entered into an exclusive contract for anesthesiology after repeated scheduling problems, altercations among the doctors, and quality problems attributed specifically to the plaintiff doctors. The plaintiffs claimed that they were entitled to a hearing under *Mateo-Woodburn* because the revocation of their privileges required by the closing of the anesthesiology staff reflected on their personal character and competency and so required the by-laws' procedures. The court rejected this argument.

6. The court in *Mateo-Woodburn* issued its opinion more than ten years ago, and it now represents the majority view of cases considering a hospital's authority to restructure its medical staff without recourse to the hearings provisions of the medical staff by-laws. See, for example, Tenet Health Ltd. v. Zamora, 13 S.W.3d 464 (Tex.App.2000); Van Valkenburg v. Paracelsus Healthcare Corp., 606 N.W.2d 908 (N.D.2000). But see, Volcjak v. Washington County Hosp. Assn., 124 Md.App. 481, 723 A.2d 463 (1999). Some hospitals in contracting situations employ a version of their fair hearing procedures as a way of processing their contracting decision. See, e.g., Radiation Therapy Oncology, P.C. v. Providence Hosp., 906 So.2d 904 (Ala. 2005), affirming summary judgment in favor of hospital that transferred its hospital-based radiation oncology process to an office-based practice related to the hospital. In the unusual case in which a hospital is considered a public hospital or a "quasi-public" hospital, however, it may be restricted in its ability to close its medical staff through exclusive contracting as the hospital's status may require an open staff or may implicate due process concerns. See, e.g., Kessel v. Monongalia County Gen'l Hosp., 215 W.Va. 609, 600 S.E.2d 321 (2004).

7. Many states have enacted legislation relevant to economic credentialing, some restrictive and some permissive. See Beverly Cohen, An Examination of the Right of Hospitals to Engage in Economic Credentialing, 77 Temp. L. Rev. 705 (2004).

MAHAN v. AVERA ST. LUKE'S

Supreme Court of South Dakota, 2001.
621 N.W.2d 150.

GILBERTSON, JUSTICE.

Orthopedic Surgery Specialists (OSS), a South Dakota corporation, and its individual physicians, commenced this action against Avera St. Lukes (ASL) alleging breach of contract. The trial court granted OSS' motion for summary judgment and entered a mandatory permanent injunction against ASL. ASL then filed this appeal. We reverse.

FACTS AND PROCEDURE

ASL is a private, nonprofit, general acute care hospital located in Aberdeen, South Dakota, organized under the nonprofit corporation laws of South Dakota. [Ed. Note: OSS opened a freestanding orthopedic surgery center, unrelated to the hospital, shortly before the hospital's decisions at issue in this case.]

ASL is part of Avera Health, a regional health care system sponsored by the Sisters of the Presentation of the Blessed Virgin Mary of Aberdeen, South Dakota. Since 1901, the Presentation Sisters have been fulfilling their mission statement "to respond to God's calling for a healing ministry ... by providing quality health services" to the Aberdeen community. ASL has expanded its mission beyond the Aberdeen community to become the only full-service hospital within a 90–mile radius of Aberdeen.

* * *

In mid-1996, ASL's neurosurgeon left Aberdeen. After his departure, the Board passed a resolution to recruit two neurosurgeons or two spine-trained orthopedic surgeons to fill the void. During the recruitment process, ASL learned that most neurosurgeon applicants would not be interested in coming to Aberdeen if there was already an orthopedic spine surgeon practicing in the area. This was due to the small size of the community and the probable need for the neurosurgeon to supplement his or her practice by performing back and spine surgeries. Back and spine surgeries are also performed by orthopedic spine surgeons and the applicants were doubtful whether Aberdeen could support the practice of both a neurosurgeon and an orthopedic spine surgeon.

ASL was successful in recruiting a neurosurgeon who arrived in December, 1996. Around this time, ASL learned that OSS, a group of Aberdeen orthopedic surgeons, had decided to build a day surgery center that would directly compete with ASL. During the first seven months that OSS' surgery center was open, ASL suffered a 1000 hour loss of operating room usage. In response to the loss of operating room income, ASL's Board passed two motions on June 26, 1997. The first motion closed ASL's medical staff with respect to physicians requesting privileges for three spinal procedures: (1) spinal fusions, (2) closed fractures of the spine and (3) laminectomies. The second motion closed ASL's medical staff to applicants for orthopedic surgery privileges except for two general orthopedic surgeons being recruited by ASL. The effect of "closing" the staff was to preclude any new physicians from applying for privileges to use hospital facilities for the named procedures. The Board's decision did not affect those physicians that had already been granted hospital privileges, including the physician-members of OSS. In making its decision, the Board specifically determined that the staff closures were in the best interests of the Aberdeen community and the surrounding area.

In the summer of 1998, OSS recruited Dr. Mahan (Mahan), a spine-fellowship trained orthopedic surgeon engaged in the practice of orthopedic surgery. While OSS was recruiting Mahan, one of the OSS physicians advised Mahan that the staff at ASL had been closed to orthopedic surgery privileges. Despite this warning, Mahan began practicing with OSS. On at least two occasions, Mahan officially requested an application for staff privileges with ASL. These requests were denied due to the Board's decision on July 26, 1997.

In September of 1998, Mahan and OSS (Plaintiffs) commenced this action against ASL, challenging the Board's decision to close the staff. Plaintiffs claimed that the action was a breach of the medical/dental staff bylaws (Staff Bylaws) and sought a writ of mandamus and permanent injunction ordering ASL to consider Mahan's application for hospital privileges. Both parties submitted cross motions for summary judgment. After a hearing, the circuit court determined that ASL had breached the Staff Bylaws by closing the staff. In making its decision, the circuit court relied exclusively on the Staff Bylaws. The circuit court determined that the Board had delegated a significant amount of its power and authority concerning staff privileges to the medical staff. The circuit court reasoned that because of this delegation, the Board no longer had the power to initiate actions that affected the privileges of the medical staff. The circuit court concluded the Board had breached its contract with the medical staff when it closed the staff to the named procedures without first consulting the staff. Plaintiffs' request for a permanent injunction was granted, requiring ASL to consider Mahan's application for privileges. ASL appeals raising the following issues:

1. Whether the individual OSS physicians have standing to challenge the Board's decision.

2. Whether the Board's decision breached its contract with the Staff.

ANALYSIS

1. Whether the individual OSS physicians have standing to challenge the Board's decision.

It is well settled in South Dakota that "a hospital's bylaws constitute a binding contract between the hospital and the hospital staff members." [ ] It is also well settled that when such bylaws are approved and accepted by the governing board they become an enforceable contract between the hospital and its physicians. [ ]

* * *

In regard to whether the OSS staff doctors suffered an injury, the circuit court found:

"It is undisputed that the Board's decision resulted in an economic benefit for ASL and an economic hardship for these doctors in their private medical practice, OSS. It is also undisputed that the OSS staff doctors, through their medical corporation OSS, spent time and money to recruit Mahan, only to end up with him unable to perform certain procedures because of his inability to obtain staff privileges at ASL. As a result, the OSS staff doctors have had to support Mahan while being unable to build their practice or increase their patient base as expected. Clearly [the OSS] [d]octors ... have standing."

The circuit court properly found that the OSS staff doctors have standing to bring a cause of action for breach of contract.

2. Whether the Board's decision breached its contract with the Staff.

* * *

Pursuant to its authority, the Board of ASL has delegated certain powers associated with the appointment and review of medical personnel to its medical staff. These designated powers are manifested in the Staff Bylaws. Plaintiffs now claim that the Staff Bylaws trump the decision-making ability of the Board as to all decisions relating in any way to, or incidentally affecting, medical personnel issues. We do not agree.

The circuit court failed to give sufficient weight to the fact that the Staff Bylaws are derived from the Corporate Bylaws. Under Article XIV, section 14(u) of the Corporate Bylaws, any powers supposedly granted under the Staff Bylaws must originate from, and be authorized by, the Board pursuant to the Corporate Bylaws. Their legal relationship is similar to that between statutes and a constitution. They are not separate and equal sovereigns. * * *

Therefore, the medical staff has no authority over any corporate decisions unless specifically granted that power in the Corporate Bylaws or under the laws of the State of South Dakota. Plaintiffs have not alluded to any powers that arise under the statutory or common-law of South Dakota.

* * *

Under section 14(u), all that is designated to the medical staff is the responsibility to make recommendations to the Board regarding the professional competence of staff members and applicants. Article XVI, section 1(a) directs the Board to organize the staff under medical-dental bylaws, which must be approved by the Board before they become effective. Finally, article XVI, section 2(a) commands the Board to "assign to the medical-dental staff reasonable authority for ensuring appropriate professional care to the hospital's patients."

Clearly, under these explicit powers, the Board has the authority to make business decisions without first consulting the medical staff. Nowhere in the Corporate Bylaws is the staff explicitly authorized to make business decisions on behalf of the corporation. Plaintiffs instead rely on the Staff Bylaws as their source of authority to assume the Board's power. Yet, even within the Staff Bylaws, there is no explicit provision granting the medical staff control over personnel issues. Instead, the circuit court found that the actions of the Board violated "the spirit of the bylaws taken as a whole." Such reliance on the "spirit of the [Staff] bylaws" turns the corporate structure of ASL upside down, granting control over day to day hospital administration to a medical staff that is not legally accountable for the hospital's decisions, has no obligation to further the mission of the Presentation Sisters, and has unknown experience in running a hospital or meeting the medical needs of the community. * * *

When the Board made its decision to close the medical staff to the three procedures on June 26, 1997, it was acting within the powers granted it in the Corporate Bylaws. When making these decisions, the Board specifically determined that the staff closures were in the Aberdeen community's best interests, and were necessary to insure 24-hour neurosurgical coverage for the Aberdeen area. By preserving the profitable neurosurgical services at ASL, the Board also insured that other unprofitable services would continue to be offered in the Aberdeen area. When, as here, it is clear from the Corporate Bylaws that the Board has the authority to manage the corporation, that authority "would necessarily include decisions on how to operate individual departments in order to best serve the corporation's purposes.... The cost of such care and promotion of community health is vitally important to the community and a legitimate concern for the board." ASL cannot continue to offer unprofitable, yet essential services including the maternity ward, emergency room, pediatrics and critical care units, without the offsetting financial benefit of more profitable areas such as neurosurgery. The Board responded to the effect the OSS hospital would have on the economic viability of ASL's hospital and the health care needs of the entire Aberdeen community. These actions were within the power of the Board. It surely has the power to attempt to insure ASL's economic survival. As such, the courts should not interfere in the internal politics and decision making of a private, nonprofit hospital corporation when those decisions are made pursuant to its Corporate Bylaws.

* * *

* * * [M]erely because a decision of the Board affects the staff does not give the staff authority to overrule a valid business decision made by the Board. Allowing the staff this amount of administrative authority would effectively cripple the governing Board of ASL. ASL would cease to function in its current corporate form if its staff were given such power.

In its decision, the circuit court attempted to distinguish between this present situation and the situation wherein a hospital enters into an exclusive contract. We find this attempt to be unpersuasive. * * * Such exclusive contracts are common practice for most hospitals today, and have been almost universally found valid and enforceable, even if not explicitly provided for in corporate bylaws. [ ] * * *.

* * * There is no logical reason why ASL could close certain areas of its facility to all but a few physicians (via an exclusive contract), yet not be allowed to close its facilities to any new orthopedic surgeons performing certain, named procedures. In a sense, ASL has entered into an implied exclusive contract with all current orthopedic spine surgeons. The same implicit authority that allows the Board to enter into exclusive contracts allows it to close ASL's staff as was done here.

* * *

The Board's decision to close the hospital's facility for certain, named procedures was a reasonable administrative decision. It had determined that the closures were necessary to insure the continued viability of the hospital. The Board must be allowed to make such reasonable, independent decisions if it is to continue to provide comprehensive medical services to the Aberdeen community. * * * Therefore, any allegations that ASL breached its implied duty of good faith must fail. * * *[8]

* * *

8. How can a doctor who is a part owner of the for-profit OSS be expected to fulfill his or her duties towards his or her co-owners and in the same instance fulfill the duties towards the principal, ASL, who is a not-for-profit hospital? This does not imply ill-will on the part of the doctor, it simply faces fundamental medical issues such as at which institution does the doctor place his or her patients, OSS or ASL? We have often stated that an agent cannot

Because the actions of ASL's Board were permissible under the Corporate Bylaws and done in good faith, there has been no breach of the contract between the Board and the staff. Therefore, the circuit court's judgment is reversed.

Notes and Questions

1.   "Conflicts credentialing," so called because of the apparent conflict of interest of a physician who is both a member of a hospital's medical staff and the owner of an entity that competes directly with the hospital, has escalated the controversy over economic credentialing. Although ambulatory surgery centers raise similar issues, specialty hospitals have been a lightening rod for conflicts between doctors and hospitals. The specialty hospital typically treats only a defined set of cases, such as neurosurgery or orthopedic surgery, which are profitable. Hospitals claim that specialty hospitals cherry pick the profitable procedures and patients, leaving the general hospital to satisfy all of the remaining needs, including meeting the community's needs for emergency care and charity care, without the ability to cross-subsidize. They also charge that the physician-entrepreneurs rely on the general hospital as a place to provide services to their less profitable cases. Payers are concerned about the self-referral aspect of physicians receiving payment as the owner of the facility to which they refer. Proponents of specialty hospitals argue that patients gain in lower cost, more efficient, and more reliably scheduled services and that the specialty focus increases quality in terms of repetition and innovation. See, e.g., Beverly Cohen, An Examination of the Right of Hospitals to Engage in Economic Credentialing, 77 Temp. L. Rev. 705 (2004); John K. Iglehart, The Emergence of Physician–Owned Specialty Hospitals, 352 NEJM 78 (2005). Studies of the impact and performance of specialty hospitals are quite mixed. See, GAO, Specialty Hospitals: Geographic Location, Services Provided, and Financial Performance, GAO–04–167 (Oct. 2003); MedPAC, Physician-owned Specialty Hospitals (Mar. 2005); Lawrence P. Casalino, et al., Focused Factories? Physician–Owned Specialty Facilities, 22 Health Affairs 56 (2003). For a complete discussion of the legal status of specialty hospitals including additional cases of conflicts credentialing, see Mike J. Wyatt, Leveling the Healing Field: Specialty Hospital Legal Reform as a Cure for an Ailing Health Care System, 46 Washburn L.J. 547 (2007); Anne S. Kimbol, The Debate Over Specialty Hospitals: How Physician–Hospital Relationships Have Reached a New Fault Line Over These "Focused Factories," 38 J. Health L. 633 (2005). See further discussion of the organization of these hospitals in Chapter 10; fraud and abuse issues in Chapter 11; and antitrust implications in Chapter 12.

2.   If the majority of courts have accepted hospitals' exclusive contracting for financial gain and credentialing that considers the financial impact of physicians' practice patterns, should the courts accept conflicts credentialing? Are the justifications the same? If doctors holding staff privileges decided to use the hospital's credentialing process to deny privileges to physicians who compete with them as opposed to the hospital generally, would the *Mahan* court be likely to uphold the denial of privileges in such a case? Is there anything that would distinguish that situation, which is generally viewed as impermissible (see the discussion of the HCQIA, above, and antitrust law in Chapter 12), from the conflicts clause at issue in *Mahan*? If hospitals are concerned about doctors taking unfair advantage of information gained as members of their medical staff or influencing the medical staff's decisions in a fashion that advantaged their competing enterprise, could the conflicts clause be more closely written to simply exclude such doctors from leadership positions in the hospital? David Argue, An Economic Model of Competi-

serve two masters. This rule applies to medical
professionals as well.

tion Between General Hospitals and Physician-owned Specialty Facilities, 20 Antitrust Health Care Chronicle 1 (2006); Elizabeth Weeks, The New Economic Credentialing: Protecting Hospitals from Competition by Medical Staff Members, 36 J. Health L. 247 (2003). In contrast to *Mahan*, the Arkansas Supreme Court affirmed a preliminary injunction against the exclusion of competing doctor-owners holding, in part, that the doctors were likely to succeed in their claims that the hospital intended that the exclusion of the doctor-owners interfere with their relationships with their patients and that the hospital's action violated the state deceptive trade practices statute (as an "unconscionable" act) thus making the principle of nonreview of privileges decisions in state law inapplicable. Baptist Health v. Murphy, 365 Ark. 115, 226 S.W.3d 800 (2006).

3. Several states have enacted legislation that prohibits hospitals from excluding physicians who simply hold clinical privileges and treat patients at multiple hospitals, as many physicians in urban areas do; but these statutes do not necessarily cover ownership of competing hospitals. See, Cohen, *supra*. Should states enact legislation prohibiting conflicts credentialing as well? Jennifer Wagner, Mahan v. Avera St. Luke's: Has the South Dakota Supreme Court Set a Precedent Allowing Non–Profit Hospitals the Right to Eliminate Competitors?, 49 S.D. L. Rev. 573 (2004). Does the one hospital in a one-hospital town have a stronger or weaker case supporting credentialing standards aimed at undermining a new specialty hospital? The court in *Mahan* introduces the hospital with a description of the religious order that operates the hospital and its religious mission. Do you think this influenced the court? Should it?

4. The imposition of conflicts prohibitions usually raises the ire of the hospital's medical staff and can spawn an acrimonious battle over whether the hospital has the authority to add a conflicts standard to the credentialing process without the agreement of the medical staff as an entity. These battles illustrate just how "wobbly" the three-legged stool can be. The most notorious of these disputes involved Community Memorial Hospital of San Buenaventura, California. The medical staff voted unanimously to reject the hospital board's establishment of a conflict of interest policy as a unilateral amendment to the medical staff by-laws and elected as their president a physician who was an investor in an organization competing directly with the hospital. The hospital refused to accept the medical staff's elected president because the appointment would violate the hospital's new conflicts policy which barred physicians with conflicts from holding leadership positions in which they could have access to competitive information. The medical staff sued; and after receiving a favorable ruling from the trial court, entered into a settlement with the hospital in which the medical staff agreed to have a conflicts policy but one defined and enforced by the medical staff itself. Hospital, Doctors Settle Bitter Dispute Over Independence, Responsibility of Medical Staff, 13 Health L. Rep. 1253 (2004). The *Mahan* court viewed the medical staff as subordinate to the hospital. In contrast, the Buenaventura battle produced legislation that recognizes the medical staff as an independent entity to some extent. See the Problem below. See James W. Marks & Jayme R. Matchinski, Conflicts Credentialing: Hospitals and the Use of Financial Considerations to Make Medical Staffing Decisions, 31 Wm. Mitchell L. Rev. 1009 (2005), discussing this case in detail. See also John D. Blum, Beyond the Bylaws: Hospital–Physician Relationships, Economics, and Conflicting Agendas, 53 Buff. L. Rev. 459 (2005); Thomas L. Greaney, New Governance Norms and Quality of Care in Nonprofit Hospitals, 14 Annals Health L. 421 (2005).

Problem: Dr. Bennett and Onyx General Hospital

Onyx General Hospital (OGH) is a 300–bed hospital in Metropolis, a major city with six other hospitals. Several health insurance plans and major employers have negotiated substantial discounts with Metropolis hospitals for hospital services provided to their insureds or to their employees. The hospitals have actually been quite interested in such negotiations because the insurers and employers asking for the discounts control the choice of hospital for thousands of insured individuals in Metropolis. What the hospital might lose in the "discount," it hopes it will gain in having a relatively stable stream of patients.

OGH has been constrained in its negotiations for a number of reasons, however. For example, it has exclusive contracts for physician services in anesthesiology and radiology that are comparatively costly. The contracts are near the end of their terms, and OGH wants to renegotiate the terms of the contracts or replace the current physician groups with others more compatible with a cost-conscious and outcomes-oriented style of practice. The anesthesiology group, Physicians' Practice Group (PPG), has been responsive to the needs of the hospital relating to coverage and quality of anesthesia services; but a new group, General Anesthesiology Services (GAS), has approached OGH with much more favorable terms. Although the surgeons have been very happy with PPG, OGH believes that they will become equally satisfied with GAS. OGH has agreed to enter into an exclusive contract with GAS and has given PPG notice that their exclusive contract will not be renewed. The OGH–PPG contract provides for termination of the contract without cause.

Two of the three PPG anesthesiologists have already joined GAS, though at lower salaries than they enjoyed with PPG. GAS has refused to consider hiring Dr. Bennett, however. Dr. Bennett is considered somewhat difficult. He does not work well with the nurse anesthetists, and sometimes has conflicts with the surgeons. He has had two malpractice suits filed against him in the last few years; but both were dropped by the plaintiffs, one after the payment of a settlement and one without any payment. Other than these problems, his work has been of good quality, although he often tells patients that they should "just get tough" when they complain of post-operative pain.

Dr. Bennett's contract with PPG provides that PPG may terminate him "without cause with 60 days' notice," but is silent on the question of his privileges at OGH. The PPG contract with OGH states that the contract is exclusive and "only physician members of PPG may provide anesthesiology services at OGH." The original letter from OGH awarding Dr. Bennett staff privileges, including clinical privileges in anesthesiology, states: "Because you will be providing services at OGH under an exclusive contract, your clinical privileges will be automatically terminated upon termination of that contract." Each of the subsequent renewal letters contained the same statement. The medical staff was quite concerned a few years ago about automatic termination of privileges of physician administrators dismissed from their administrative positions and amended its bylaws to provide: "A physician member of the medical staff providing services to the hospital under contract will retain privileges even if that contract is terminated." The Board of Directors never approved this amendment and has essentially ignored it.

What should OGH do? Should it simply terminate Bennett's privileges without procedural review and for no cause? Or, should it follow the procedures in the by-laws? Should OGH proceed against Dr. Bennett on the basis of the quality of his work? If the medical staff by-laws provide that the hospital may revoke privileges of "any physician whose inability to work well with others jeopardizes patient care," would you recommend that they proceed under that clause? Are there any other alternatives? How might a court handle the case under each of these alternatives should Bennett sue? How would you redraft the termination provisions of these contracts for use with GAS?

OGH is facing another problem as well. Several of their surgeons are developing and will be co-owners of SportsMed, Inc., a 30–bed specialty hospital limited to diagnostic imaging, orthopedic surgery, and post-operative physical therapy. Originally, OGH had approached the SportsMed developers with a proposal that it enter into a joint venture with the hospital. During those discussions, OGH let it be known that it may decide not to grant privileges to doctors recruited by SportsMed or to renew privileges for SportsMed doctors who already had privileges at OGH. SportsMed declined the offer, and OGH has since informed its medical staff that privileges at OGH would not be granted or renewed for doctors who practiced at SportsMed. Finally, it has informed both GAS and PPG that it will immediately terminate their exclusive contract at OGH if they provide services to SportsMed.

At this point, the surgeons on the medical staff at OGH are up in arms, and the state medical association has succeeded in having the following bill introduced in your state legislature, based on Cal. Bus. & Prof. Code § 2282.5:

An Act to Protect Hospital Patients

(a) The medical staff's right of self-governance shall include, but not be limited to, all of the following:

(1) Establishing, in medical staff by-laws, rules, or regulations, criteria and standards for medical staff membership and privileges, and enforcing those criteria and standards.

(2) The ability to retain and be represented by independent legal counsel at the expense of the medical staff.

(3) Initiating, developing, and adopting medical staff by-laws, rules, and regulations, and amendments thereto, subject to the approval of the hospital governing board, which approval shall not be unreasonably withheld.

(b) With respect to any dispute arising under this section, the medical staff and the hospital governing board shall meet and confer in good faith to resolve the dispute. Whenever any person or entity has engaged in or is about to engage in any acts or practices that hinder, restrict, or otherwise obstruct the ability of the medical staff to exercise its rights, obligations, or responsibilities under this section, the superior court of any county, on application of the medical staff, and after determining that reasonable efforts, including reasonable administrative remedies provided in the medical staff by-laws, rules, or regulations, have failed to resolve the dispute, may issue an injunction, writ of mandate, or other appropriate order.

At this point, OGH has called you for legal advice. What do you tell them? If the bill passes, would that change your advice?

II. MANAGED CARE CONTRACTS

POTVIN v. METROPOLITAN LIFE INS. CO.

California Supreme Court, 2000.
22 Cal.4th 1060, 95 Cal.Rptr.2d 496, 997 P.2d 1153.

KENNARD, J.

* * *

On September 10, 1990, Metropolitan Life Insurance (MetLife) entered into an agreement with Dr. Louis E. Potvin, an obstetrician and gynecologist, to include him as one of 16,000 participants on two of its preferred provider lists. Potvin had practiced medicine for more than 35 years; he was a past president of the Orange County Medical Association; and he held full staff privileges at Mission Regional Hospital, where he had served as Chairman of the Obstetrics and Gynecology Department for nine years. Under the contract, Potvin was to provide medical services to MetLife's insureds in return for agreed-upon payment by MetLife. The agreement created no employment or agency relationship, and it allowed Potvin to also "contract with other preferred provider organizations, health maintenance organizations or other participating provider arrangements." It provided for termination by either party "at any time, with or without cause, by giving thirty (30) days prior written notice to the other party."

On July 22, 1992, MetLife notified Potvin in writing that effective August 31, 1992, it was terminating his preferred provider status. Potvin asked for clarification; MetLife replied that the termination, which the parties here also refer to as "delistment," was consistent with the contract, which allowed termination "without cause." When Potvin insisted on a further explanation, MetLife reiterated its right to terminate without cause. MetLife then stated that even though it did not have to give a reason, Potvin's "delistment from the provider network was related to the fact that [he] did not meet [MetLife's] current selection and retention standard for malpractice history." At the time, MetLife would not include or retain on its preferred provider lists any physician who had more than two malpractice lawsuits, or who had paid an aggregate sum of $50,000 in judgment or settlement of such actions. Potvin's patients had sued him for malpractice on four separate occasions, all predating his 1990 agreement with MetLife. In three of these actions, the plaintiffs had abandoned their claims, while the fourth case had settled for $713,000.

After MetLife failed to respond to Potvin's request for a hearing, Potvin filed this lawsuit. * * * Potvin alleged that MetLife's termination of his preferred provider status devastated his practice, reducing it to "a small fraction" of his former patients. He asserted that he was required to reveal his termination to other insurers and managed care entities, which then removed him from their preferred provider lists, and that he suffered rejection by "physician groups ... dependent upon credentialing by MetLife" and by current MetLife preferred provider physicians, who ceased referring patients to him.

The trial court granted MetLife's motion for summary judgment. * * *

The Court of Appeal reversed. It disagreed with the trial court that Potvin's complaint failed to allege a claim for violation of the common law right to fair procedure. It also held that, before removing Potvin from its preferred provider lists, MetLife should have given him notice of the grounds for its action and a reasonable opportunity to be heard. With respect to Potvin's assertion that the removal violated [the California statute] setting forth procedures for physician peer review, the Court of Appeal agreed with the trial court that those provisions did not apply to the preferred provider contract involved here.

* * * We affirm the Court of Appeal's reversal of the trial court's grant of summary judgment for MetLife, but we disagree with the Court of Appeal that MetLife necessarily must comply with the common law doctrine of fair procedure before removing physicians from its preferred provider lists. In this case, that issue needs to be resolved by further proceedings in the trial court under the standards set forth below.

* * *

Plaintiff here points out that when an insurance company with fiduciary obligations to its insureds maintains a list of preferred provider physicians to render medical services to the insureds, a significant public interest is affected. One practical effect of the health care revolution, which has made quality care more widely available and affordable through health maintenance organizations and other managed care entities, is that patients are less free to choose their own doctors for they must obtain medical services from providers approved by their health plan. The Managed Care Health Improvement Task Force stressed in its 1997 report to the California Legislature that the provision of health care "has a special moral status and therefore a particular public interest." [ ] But an even greater public interest is at stake when those medical services are provided through the unique tripartite relationship among an insurance company, its insureds, and the physicians who participate in the preferred provider network. * * *

Our conclusion that the relationship between insurers and their preferred provider physicians significantly affects the public interest does not necessarily mean that every insurer wishing to remove a doctor from one of its preferred provider lists must comply with the common law right to fair procedure. The obligation to do so arises only when the insurer possesses power so substantial that the removal significantly impairs the ability of an ordinary, competent physician to practice medicine or a medical specialty in a particular geographic area, thereby affecting an important, substantial economic interest.[2]

* * *

Here, plaintiff's amici curiae, the American Medical Association and the California Medical Association, assert in their joint brief that "the managed care organizations operating in California hold substantial economic power

2. Our decision here does not apply to employer-employee contractual relations. Rather, it applies only to an insurer's decision to remove individual physicians from its preferred providers lists. We express no view on whether the factors giving rise to the common law right of fair procedure would be present when an insurer, acting to limit its service in a geographic area or medical field, reduces the total number of physicians on its preferred provider lists.

over physicians and their patients." They also contend that "the control exercised by managed care organizations makes access to provider panels a 'practical prerequisite' to any effective practice as a health care provider." * * * If participation in managed care arrangements is a practical necessity for physicians generally and if only a handful of health care entities have a virtual monopoly on managed care, removing individual physicians from preferred provider networks controlled by these entities could significantly impair those physicians' practice of medicine.

Potvin alleged that among the adverse effects of removal from MetLife's preferred provider lists were rejection by "physician groups which were dependent upon credentialing by MetLife" and devastation of his practice, which was reduced to "a small fraction" of his former patients. Proof of these allegations might establish that, in terminating a physician's preferred provider status, MetLife wields power so substantial as to significantly impair an ordinary, competent physician's ability to practice medicine or a medical specialty in a particular geographic area, thereby affecting an important, substantial economic interest.

* * *

Our holding does not prevent an insurer subject to obligations of common law fair procedure from exercising its sound business judgment when establishing standards for removal of physicians from its preferred provider lists. We simply hold that, under principles recognized by the common law of this state for over a century, such removal must be "both substantively rational and procedurally fair."

* * *

MetLife contends that even if removal of a physician from its preferred provider lists is subject to the common law right to fair procedure, here Potvin waived that right by agreeing that MetLife could terminate the provider arrangement without cause. Potvin responds that the public policy considerations supporting the common law right to fair procedure render the "without cause" clause in the MetLife preferred provider agreement unenforceable. * * * California courts are loathe to enforce contract provisions offensive to public policy. [ ] We therefore agree with Potvin that the "without cause" termination clause is unenforceable to the extent it purports to limit an otherwise existing right to fair procedure under the common law.

The judgment of the Court of Appeal is affirmed.

GEORGE, C.J., MOSK, J., and WERDEGAR, J., concur.

Dissenting Opinion by BROWN, J.

* * * With its decision today, the majority, in effect, declares that it is the public policy of this state that physicians are entitled to a minimum income and, therefore, if removal of a physician from an insurer's preferred provider list would reduce the physician's income below that guaranteed minimum, the physician is entitled to a hearing and to the judicial review that would inevitably follow upon an adverse decision. * * *

* * *

* * * According to Dr. Potvin, the average physician who practices his specialty, obstetrics/gynecology, has been sued for malpractice 2.3 times. MetLife wishes to restrict its preferred provider lists to physicians with a slightly better than average malpractice history, to those who have not been sued more than twice. Potvin, by contrast, has been sued 4 times—nearly twice the average. Now the majority's public policy antennae may be more sensitive than mine, but I suspect the jury is still out on the question of whether an insurer should be able to control its costs by restricting its preferred provider lists to physicians with slightly better than average malpractice histories. That, surely, is a business judgment, and if the insurer makes the wrong judgment by depriving itself of doctors that patients insist upon, then the market will punish the insurer and force it to retreat from the impracticable standard.

* * *

Moreover, despite the majority's effort to cloak it in the public interest, this case has never been about Dr. Potvin's ability to practice medicine. It has been about money. * * * As far as we can tell from this record, during the three and a half years that passed between his initial correspondence with MetLife and the filing of his motion for summary adjudication, Potvin's ability to practice medicine and his medical specialty was unaffected. He just wasn't making as much money at it.

* * *

BAXTER, J., and CHIN, J., concur.

Notes and Questions

1.   Is Dr. Potvin entitled to a hearing prior to being delisted by MetLife? If he is entitled to a hearing, the Court indicates that he is also entitled to have MetLife's decision reviewed on the basis of whether it is "rational." How would each of the following fare under a standard that considers "rationality" or "good faith:" de-capitation for a Caesarean section rate in excess of the norm for plan physicians or in excess of the plan's target rate; disenrollment for specialist referrals or hospital stays in excess of the average of all plan physicians; termination for disclosure of the plan's physician financial incentive systems to patients or to a competing plan?

2.   Is *Potvin* consistent with *Mateo-Woodburn*, also a California case, in its treatment of no-cause termination clauses? Should the decisions be consistent? The California Court of Appeals, in an unpublished decision, declined to extend *Potvin* in Siegel v. CHW West Bay, 2002 WL 31599012 (Cal. Ct. App. 2002). The Court held that even if *Potvin* were extended to hospitals, the facts did not meet the *Potvin* requirement that the decisionmaker hold economic power substantial enough to impair the physician's ability to practice. See also, Edson v. Valleycare Health System, 21 Fed.Appx. 721 (9th Cir. 2001).

3.   The HCQIA applies to adverse decisions against physicians by HMOs and health plans that have a formal review process that meets the requirements of the Act. See, for example, Singh v. Blue Cross/Blue Shield of Massachusetts, Inc., 308 F.3d 25 (1st Cir. 2002). Would you advise a managed care plan or a medical group practice to adopt formal procedures like those used in hospitals to gain HCQIA immunity? What would they gain or lose?

4. *Potvin* was an eagerly awaited decision (taking nearly three years for the court to issue its decision), but its actual impact on caselaw nationally has been minimal. Several state courts have addressed the issues in *Potvin* with varying results. See, for example, Mayer v. Pierce County Med. Bureau, 80 Wash.App. 416, 909 P.2d 1323 (1995), holding that a no-cause termination clause was enforceable; Grossman v. Columbine Med. Group, 12 P.3d 269 (Colo. Ct. App. 1999, as modified Jan. 14, 2000), holding that a state statute established public policy supporting no-cause terminations; Harper v. Healthsource New Hampshire, 140 N.H. 770, 674 A.2d 962 (1996), prohibiting bad faith use of no-cause termination clause.

5. Many states enacted legislation in the early 1990s in response to physician claims that MCOs threatened to terminate them if they advocated on behalf of their patients or if they told patients about the financial controls and incentives imposed by the MCO. See Virginia Gray, et al., The Political Management of Managed Care: Explaining Variations in State Health Maintenance Organization Regulations, 32 J. Health Pol. Pol'y & L. 457 (2007), analyzing sources of influence that explain variations among the states; Mitesh S. Patel, et al., The Impact of the Adoption of Gag Laws on Trust in the Patient–Physician Relationship, 32 J. Health Pol Pol'y & L. 819 (2007), presenting empirical data. See also, Robert F. Rich & Christopher T. Erb, The Two Faces of Managed Care Regulation & Policymaking, 16 Stan. L. & Pol'y Rev. 233 (2005), identifying conflicts in federal and state policies regarding managed care. Massachusetts enacted one of the more comprehensive legislative packages, establishing a Bureau of Managed Care within the Division of Insurance. Health Insurance Consumer Protections. M.G.L.A. ch. 1760 § 1. See also, Colo.Stat. § 10-16-705, providing that no-cause terminations simply require 60 days' notice, but that physicians cannot be delisted for reporting quality concerns to federal or state agencies, for disclosing financial incentives to patients or for giving patients "standing referrals" to specialists. See also Cal. Bus. & Prof. Code § 2056, providing that a physician may not be terminated or penalized when he or she:

> advocate[s] for medically appropriate health care [meaning] to appeal a payor's decision to deny payment for a service pursuant to the reasonable grievance or appeal procedure established by a ... payer, or to protest a decision, policy, or practice that the physician, consistent with that degree of learning and skill ordinarily possessed by reputable physicians practicing according to the applicable legal standard of care, reasonably believes impairs the physician's ability to provide medically appropriate health care ....

Does this statute adequately protect physicians and patients? Would it have saved Dr. Potvin? Does it inappropriately gut managed care? See discussion of state regulation of managed care in Chapter 6. Eusterman v. Northwest Permanente, P.C., 204 Or.App. 224, 129 P.3d 213 (2006), holding that a similar statute was inadequate to support wrongful discharge claim for physician.

III. LABOR AND EMPLOYMENT

A. EMPLOYMENT–AT–WILL

Doctors, nurses, administrators, and in-house counsel working without an employment contract or under a contract that does not provide for a specific term of employment are subject to the doctrine of employment-at-will. Employees working under a collective bargaining agreement or under a contract with express provisions concerning length of employment or termination for just cause alone are not employees-at-will.

The common law at-will doctrine varies widely among the states, but generally provides that the employment relationship can be terminated without cause at the will of either the employer or the employee. The at-will doctrine allows a few exceptions, which in most states are relatively narrow.

The majority of nurses have long practiced as at-will employees. In contrast, doctors traditionally have practiced as owners of their own practices and have had the further protection of the staff privileges system for their economically necessary relationship with a hospital. Increasingly, however, doctors have become employees (often at-will employees) of group practices, HMOs, or hospitals. Some courts have borrowed from at-will doctrine in deciding cases of physician termination or delisting from health plans.

WRIGHT v. SHRINERS HOSPITAL FOR CRIPPLED CHILDREN

Supreme Court of Massachusetts, 1992.
412 Mass. 469, 589 N.E.2d 1241.

O'CONNOR, JUSTICE.

In this case, which is here on direct appellate review, we consider the sufficiency of the evidence to warrant a jury's verdict of $100,000 in favor of the plaintiff, Anita Wright against her employer, the defendant Shriners Hospital for Crippled Children (Shriners Hospital), on Wright's claim that Shriners Hospital wrongfully terminated her at-will employment in violation of public policy. * * * We hold that the evidence was insufficient to warrant [the] verdict and that the trial judge should have allowed the defendants' motion for judgment notwithstanding the verdict. * * *

We summarize the evidence in the light most favorable to the plaintiff. [ ] Shriners Hospital hired Wright, a registered nurse, in 1976. Subsequently, she became assistant director of nursing, and she held that position until she was discharged in late February of 1987. At all times, she was an employee at will. Wright received excellent evaluations throughout her employment, including an evaluation in December, 1986, two months before her discharge. In June, 1986, a former assistant head nurse wrote a letter to the director of clinical affairs for the Shriners national headquarters detailing her concerns about the medical staff and administration at Shriners Hospital. Shriners Hospital is a separate corporation, but it is one of many Shriners facilities that are affiliated with the national headquarters. As a result of the letter, the national headquarters notified the defendant hospital administrator, Russo, that a survey team would visit Shriners Hospital in November, 1986. Russo was visibly upset. He spoke to the director of nursing about the letter and asked her: "Are you behind this? Is Anita Wright behind this?" The director of nursing denied that she was responsible for the letter. She did not address the question whether Wright was "behind" the letter.

The survey team visited the hospital in November and interviewed Wright and other employees. Wright told the survey team that there were communication problems between the medical and nursing staffs. She detailed problems with the assistant chief of staff and gave specific examples of patient care problems. The survey team reported Wright's comments to the assistant chief of staff.

Two members of the survey team prepared reports. In his report issued on December 22, 1986, Dr. Newton C. McCollough, director of medical affairs for the national organization, wrote: "The relationships between nursing administration, hospital administration, and chief of staff are much less than satisfactory, and significant friction exists both as regard nursing/administration relationships and nursing/medical staff relationships. Communication and problem solving efforts in this relationship are poor to nonexistent." A report issued on January 5, 1987, by Jack D. Hoard, executive administrator for the national Shriners organization, also documented the problematic relationship between the nursing and medical staff. Both reports recommended a follow-up site survey to determine the impact of this conflict on patient care. McCollough's report stated that during her interview, Wright had made severe criticisms of the medical staff and had expressed concern over a lack of consistent procedures and standards for patient care. Hoard's report stated that Wright discussed the breakdown in communication between the nursing staff and the attending medical staff, which she said was leading to deteriorating morale among nurses.

* * *

Upon reading the survey team's reports, Russo again became upset and told the director of nursing that it was the nursing department's fault that the team was making another visit. The survey team returned on February 18 and 19, 1987, specifically to review the problems between the medical and nursing staffs. On February 26, after consulting with the chairman and several officers of the board of governors of Shriners Hospital and with national corporate counsel, Russo ordered that Wright's employment be terminated for "patient care issues that had arisen as a result of the surveys."

Wright contends, and the defendants dispute, that the jury would have been warranted in finding that Shriners Hospital fired her from her employment at will in retaliation for her having criticized the hospital, specifically in regard to the quality of care rendered to patients, to the Shriners national headquarters survey team. Wright further asserts that such a retaliatory firing violates public policy and is therefore actionable. We hold that a termination of Wright's employment at will in reprisal for her critical remarks to the survey team would not have violated public policy. * * *

We begin with the general rule that "[e]mployment at will is terminable by either the employee or the employer without notice, for almost any reason or for no reason at all." [ ] We have recognized exceptions to that general rule, however, when employment is terminated contrary to a well-defined public policy. Thus, "[r]edress is available for employees who are terminated for asserting a legally guaranteed right (e.g., filing workers' compensation claim), for doing what the law requires (e.g., serving on a jury), or for refusing to do that which the law forbids (e.g., committing perjury)." [ ] * * *

The trial judge's view of the law was that public policy was violated if Shriners Hospital fired Wright in reprisal for her having criticized the hospital in interviews with the survey team. As is clear from his instructions to the jury, the judge's view was based in part on "the duty of doctors and nurses, found in their own code of ethics, to report on substantial patient care issues." We would hesitate to declare that the ethical code of a private professional organization can be a source of recognized public policy. * * *

It is also clear from his instructions that the judge's view was based in part on "various state laws of the commonwealth, requiring reports on patient abuse." The judge did not identify the State laws he had in mind. General Laws c. 119, § 51A (1990 ed.), requires nurses and others to make a report to the Department of Social Services concerning any child under eighteen years of age who they have reason to believe is suffering from physical or sexual abuse or neglect. Similarly, G.L. c. 19A, § 15(a) (1990 ed.), requires nurses and others who have reasonable cause to believe that an elderly person is suffering from abuse to report it to the Department of Elder Affairs. Subsection (d) of that provision provides that no employer or supervisor may discharge an employee for filing a report. Finally, G.L. c. 111, § 72G (1990 ed.), requires nurses and others to report to the Department of Public Health (department) when they have reason to believe that any patient or resident of a facility licensed by the department is being abused, mistreated, or neglected and provides a remedy of treble damages, costs, and attorney's fees for any employee who is discharged in retaliation for having made such a report. None of these statutes applies to Wright's situation, however, and we are unaware of any statute that does. Also, we are unaware of any statute that clearly expresses a legislative policy to encourage nurses to make the type of internal report involved in this case. In fact, Wright testified that she did not consider the patient care that caused her concern to be abuse, neglect, or mistreatment warranting a report to the department, nor did she feel that there was an issue of physician incompetence warranting a report to the board of registration in medicine as required by G.L. c. 112, § 5F (1990 ed.).

Wright urges us to recognize a regulation promulgated by the Board of Registration in Nursing as a source of public policy sufficient to create an exception to the general rule regarding termination of at-will employment. Title 244 Code Mass.Regs. § 3.02(3)(f) (1986) describes the responsibilities and functions of a registered nurse, including the responsibility to "collaborate, communicate and cooperate as appropriate with other health care providers to ensure quality and continuity of care." Even if that regulation called for Wright to report perceived problems or inadequacies to the survey team, a doubtful proposition, we have never held that a regulation governing a particular profession is a source of well-defined public policy sufficient to modify the general at-will employment rule, and we decline to do so now. Furthermore, as we have noted above, Wright's report was an internal matter, and "[i]nternal matters," we have previously said, "could not be the basis of a public policy exception to the at-will rule."

* * *

We reverse the judgments for the plaintiff and remand to the Superior Court for the entry of judgments for the defendants.

LIACOS, CHIEF JUSTICE (dissenting).

I disagree with the court's conclusion that a hospital employer violates no public policy when it fires an employee for alerting supervisors to matters detracting from good patient care. The court has construed far too narrowly the public policy exception to the doctrine of employment at will. Moreover, in demanding a statutory basis for public policy, the court has relinquished to the Legislature its role in shaping the common law. I dissent.

* * *

Given the public interest in good patient care, it must be the public policy of the Commonwealth to protect, if not encourage, hospital employees who perceive and report detriments to patient care. Only when problems are identified can they be adequately addressed; an employee's failure to report perceived detriments to patient care may allow the problems to persist. A hospital employer therefore violates public policy when it fires an employee for trying to improve the quality of patient care. That an employer may deter other employees from reporting problems (for fear of losing their jobs) inhibits the provision of good patient care and offends the public interest.

* * * The plaintiff was not terminated for contributing to the hospital's problems, nor for refusing to accept her supervisor's method of addressing the problems; she was fired for reporting the problems to appropriate accreditation authorities. Such a termination offends the public interest and is actionable. I dissent.

Notes and Questions

1. *Wright* represents the majority view concerning the scope of the public policy exception to employment-at-will. Most courts employ a narrow concept of public policy and exclude, for example professional codes of conduct as a legitimate basis for an exception to at-will employment. For example, in Warthen v. Toms River Community Mem. Hosp., 199 N.J.Super. 18, 488 A.2d 229 (1985), the court rejected the nurse's claim of wrongful discharge under the public policy exception where a nurse refused to dialyze a patient who had twice suffered heart attacks and severe internal hemorrhaging during dialysis. Warthen based her legal claim on a provision of the American Nurses Association Code for Nurses allowing nurses to refuse to provide treatment that was contrary to the nurse's personal beliefs so long as the patient would not be abandoned. The court held as a matter of law that the Code did not state public policy, but rather was beneficial only to the nursing profession and the individual nurse. See also, Jaynes v. Centura Health Corp. 148 P.3d 241 (Colo. Ct. App. 2006), rejecting the ANA code as a basis for the public policy exception. In the unusual case of risk to a specific patient, at least one court in a state with a narrow public policy exception allowed a wrongful discharge claim to survive. Kirk v. Mercy Hosp. Tri–County, 851 S.W.2d 617 (Mo.App.1993). In *Kirk*, the nurse had asked her supervisor repeatedly about a patient admitted with life-threatening toxic shock syndrome for whom no antibiotics had been ordered. The nurse alleged that she had been told to document the situation and "stay out of it." The patient died, and the nurse suggested to the family that they obtain the patient's medical record. See also, LoPresti v. Rutland Reg. Health Services, 177 Vt. 316, 865 A.2d 1102 (2004), reversing summary judgment against physician claiming that his termination was a result of his refusal to refer patients to substandard physician co-employees; Deerman v. Beverly California Corp., 135 N.C.App 1, 518 S.E.2d 804 (1999), holding that a nurse would have a claim of wrongful discharge if she could prove she was terminated because she advised a patient's family to replace the patient's doctor.

2. The nurse in *Warthen*, above, claimed her refusal to treat the patient was a matter of conscience. While the employment-at-will doctrine does not admit a general conscience claim, state and federal legislation may protect health care professionals, including at-will employees, in refusing to participate in otherwise

lawful treatment that they object to as a matter of conscience, whether on religious or moral bases. These statutes tend to be quite specific: for example, most such statutes apply only to particular interventions, including abortion or end-of-life care. These statutes balance a number of competing interests and moral claims, including the autonomy and well-being of the patient; the autonomy of the health care professional; and the objectives of the health care organization, among others. See Rebecca Dresser, Professionals, Conformity, and Conscience, 35 Hastings Ctr. Rep. 6 (2005); Edmund Pellegrino, The Physician's Conscience, Conscience Clauses, and Religious Belief: A Catholic Perspective, 30 Fordham U. Urban L. J. 221 (2002); Mark Wicclair, Conscientious Objection in Medicine, 14 Bioethics 205 (2000); Martha Swartz, "Conscience Clauses" or "Unconscionable Clauses": Personal Beliefs versus Professional Responsibilities, 6 Yale J. Health Pol'y L. & Ethics 269 (2006).

3. Nurse Wright claimed that she was discharged for reporting concerns about quality of care. Absent a specific whistleblower statute, courts apply their state's ordinary exceptions to employment-at-will in such cases. See, e.g., Scott v. Missouri Valley Physicians, P.C., 460 F.3d 968 (8th Cir. 2006), holding that physician employee could not claim wrongful discharge under the public policy exception as he did not report his concerns about violation of federal anti-kickback laws to anyone outside of his employer physician group, which the court viewed as reporting only to the "purported wrongdoer"; Goodman v. Wesley Med. Ctr., 276 Kan. 586, 78 P.3d 817 (2003), holding that public policy exception did not extend to discharge of nurse who gave information on patients and on understaffing to a plaintiff's attorney. But see, Yonker v. Centers for Long Term Care of Gardner, 2006 WL 516851 (D. Kan. 2006), denying employer's motion to dismiss employee's claim that termination violated public policy exception when employee reported possible Medicaid fraud to state agency. Should doctors and nurses working under at-will arrangements receive broader legal protection than other employees for complaints and actions concerning quality of patient care or illegal financial arrangements? See Colorado statute providing for protection for health care workers specifically. C.R.S.A. § 8–2–123.

4. The federal government and many states have whistleblower statutes that protect employees who report wrongdoing to government agencies in specific circumstances. These statutes typically are drafted narrowly and have been interpreted by the courts quite strictly. See e.g., United States ex rel. Howard v. Life Care Ctrs. of America, 2005 WL 2674939 (E.D. Tenn. 2005); Hays v. Beverly Enterprises, 766 F.Supp. 350 (W.D.Pa.1991); Minnesota Assn. of Nurse Anesthetists v. Unity Hosp., 59 F.3d 80 (8th Cir. 1995). As detailed in *Wright*, some state abuse reporting statutes may provide some protection to reporters. Several states also have statutes that provide limited protection for health care professionals in advocating for patients. See California's statute in the notes following *Potvin*, above. Health care professionals working in public hospitals may also have some limited protection under the First Amendment for their opposition to hospital policies. See, e.g., Ulrich v. City and County of San Francisco, 308 F.3d 968 (9th Cir. 2002). In addition, professionals who are within the protection of the National Labor Relations Act may be protected from some adverse employment actions, as described in Section B, below. See also Section I, above, concerning disruptive physicians.

5. Most states accept a theory of "implied contract" to take a relationship out of the at-will category. Personnel manuals may be a source of an implied contract, but employers can avoid this effect by inserting an unambiguous and prominently displayed disclaimer stating that the manual does not constitute a

contract and that employees are terminable at will. While courts may view medical staff by-laws as contractual for other purposes, by-laws have not been accepted as implied contracts in the context of at-will employment. See, e.g., Hrehorovich v. Harbor Hosp. Ctr., 93 Md.App. 772, 614 A.2d 1021 (1992).

6. For a very informative treatise on employment-at-will case law and relevant statutes, see Frank J. Cavico & Nancy M. Cavico, Employment-at-Will, Public Policy, and the Nursing Profession, 8 Quinnipiac Health J. 161 (2005). You can exercise your understanding of employment-at-will by working the Problem "Changing Things" which appears at the end of Section B, below.

B. NATIONAL LABOR RELATIONS ACT

The beginning of the 21st century has seen a surge in unionization in the health care field, including unionization of doctors and nurses. In fact, a group of health law experts included labor law in its "Top Ten for 2007," noting that "[u]nion campaigns and initiatives will make labor and employment a big issue as workers seek to expose inequities and alleged quality of care deficiencies." 16 Health L. Rep. 5 (2007).

Union organizing among nurses has provided a platform for advocacy on staffing issues in hospitals and nursing homes. See, e.g., SEIU Contract with Allegheny Hospital Provides Specific Nurse-to-Patient Ratios, 15 Health L. Rep. 1110 (2006). California nurse unions were instrumental in the passage and implementation of legislation establishing minimum nursing staff ratios for particular hospital services. California Governor Drops Appeal in Fight Over Hospital Staffing Ratios, 14 Health L. Rep. 1489 (2005). Staffing ratios are associated closely with quality of care, as discussed in Chapter 3. See GAO, Nursing Homes: Quality of Care More Related to Staffing than Spending (2002); Donald M. Steinwachs, Keeping Patients Safe: Transforming the Work Environment of Nurses, Institute of Medicine (2003), recommending increased nurse staffing levels in nursing homes and hospitals as essential to reducing hazards to patient care. Advocacy on staffing by the nurse unions is self-interested as well. Does that matter? Of course, nurse unions also focus on compensation. See also discussion of antitrust claims against hospitals for collusion in setting nurse wages in Chapter 12.

Doctors also have engaged in collective action, especially in connection with managed care relationships. In 1999, the American Medical Association created a union to represent doctors. Physicians for Responsible Negotiation, the AMA union, currently represents doctors at several sites. Doctors also have joined together for "strikes" and "white-coat days" in state legislatures focusing on managed care and, more recently, on malpractice reform.

The health care professions traditionally resisted unionization stridently as an indicator of a lack of professionalism. What explains the turnaround? Are the factors that have changed the profession's view of unions the same for nurses as for doctors? See, generally, Marion Crain, The Transformation of the Professional Workforce, 79 Chi.-Kent L. Rev. 543 (2004).

In contrast to the doctrine of at-will employment discussed in the previous section, the National Labor Relations Act offers significant protections to workers who fall within its coverage. The material below focuses on two issues that present particular challenges in the health care setting: the determination of whether an employee is a supervisor, as supervisors are not protected by the Act; and the prohibition against retaliation by the employer against employees who engage in concerted activities.

1. *Supervisor?*

OAKWOOD HEALTHCARE, INC.

348 NLRB No. 37 (2006).

I. FACTS

The Employer has approximately 181 staff RNs who provide direct care to patients in 10 patient care units at Oakwood Heritage Hospital, an acute care hospital with 257 licensed beds.... The RNs report to the on-site nursing manager, clinical managers, clinical supervisors, and assistant clinical managers-all stipulated supervisors.... RNs may direct less-skilled employees to perform tasks such as feeding, bathing, and walking patients. RNs may also direct employees to perform tests that are ordered by doctors for their patients.

Many RNs at the hospital serve as charge nurses. Charge nurses are responsible for overseeing their patient care units, and they assign other RNs, licensed practical nurses (LPNs), nursing assistants, technicians, and paramedics to patients on their shifts. Charge nurses also monitor the patients in the unit, meet with doctors and the patients' family members, and follow up on unusual incidents. Charge nurses may also take on their own patient load, but those who do assume patient loads will sometimes, but not always, take less than a full complement of patients. When serving as charge nurses, RNs receive an additional $1.50 per hour.

Twelve RNs at the hospital serve permanently as charge nurses on every shift they work, while other RNs take turns rotating into the charge nurse position. In the patient care units of the hospital employing permanent charge nurses, other RNs may serve as charge nurses on the permanent charge nurses' days off or during their vacations. Depending on the patient care unit and the work shift, the rotation of the charge nurse position may be worked out by the RNs among themselves, or it may be set by higher-level managers. The frequency and regularity with which a particular RN will serve as a "rotating" charge nurse depends on several factors (i.e., the size of the patient care unit in which the RN works, the number of other RNs who serve as rotating charge nurses in that unit, and whether the unit has any permanent charge nurses). However, some RNs do not serve as either rotating or permanent charge nurses at the hospital. Most individuals who fit in this category are either new employees at the hospital or those who work in the operating room or pain clinic units. There are also a handful of RNs at the hospital who choose not to serve as charge nurses.

[The union argued that all the charge nurses should be included in the bargaining unit, and the employer argued that all the charge nurses should be excluded.]

II. LEGAL PRINCIPLES

A. Introduction

* * *

Section 2(11) [of the NLRA] defines "supervisor" as

> any individual having the authority, in the interest of the employer, to hire, transfer, suspend, lay off, recall, promote, discharge, assign, reward, or discipline other employees, or responsibly to direct them, or to adjust their grievances, or effectively to recommend such action, if in connection with the foregoing the exercise of such authority is not of a merely routine or clerical nature, but requires the use of independent judgment.

Pursuant to this definition, individuals are statutory supervisors if (1) they hold the authority to engage in any 1 of the 12 supervisory functions (e.g., "assign" and "responsibly to direct") listed in Section 2(11); (2) their "exercise of such authority is not of a merely routine or clerical nature, but requires the use of independent judgment;" and (3) their authority is held "in the interest of the employer." ... The burden to prove supervisory authority is on the party asserting it.

* * *

Whether an individual possesses a 2(11) supervisory function has not always been readily discernible by either the Board or reviewing courts. Indeed, in applying Section 2(11), the Supreme Court has recognized that "[p]hrases [used by Congress] such as 'independent judgment' and 'responsibly to direct' are ambiguous."

As a general principle, the Board has exercised caution "not to construe supervisory status too broadly because the employee who is deemed a supervisor is denied rights which the Act is intended to protect." [ ] However, in applying that principle, the Board has occasionally reached too far. Indeed, on two occasions involving the healthcare industry, the industry at issue in this case, the Supreme Court rejected the Board's overly narrow construction of Section 2(11) as "inconsistent with the Act." Accordingly, although we seek to ensure that the protections of the Act are not unduly circumscribed, we also must be mindful of the legislative and judicial constraints that guide our application and interpretation of the statute....

* * *

B.   Assign and Responsibly to Direct

* * *

1.   Assign

[W]e construe the term "assign" to refer to the act of designating an employee to a place (such as a location, department, or wing), appointing an employee to a time (such as a shift or overtime period), or giving significant overall duties, i.e., tasks, to an employee.... In the health care setting, the term "assign" encompasses the charge nurses' responsibility to assign nurses and aides to particular patients....

[C]hoosing the order in which the employee will perform discrete tasks within those assignments (e.g., restocking toasters before coffeemakers) would not be indicative of exercising the authority to "assign." To illustrate our point in the health care setting, if a charge nurse designates an LPN to be the person who will regularly administer medications to a patient or a group of patients, the giving of that overall duty to the LPN is an assignment. On the other hand, the charge nurse's ordering an LPN to immediately give a sedative to a particular patient does not constitute an assignment....

* * *

Our dissenting colleagues would interpret "assign" to apply to a determination of an employee's (1) position, i.e., his or her job classification, (2) designated work site, i.e., facility or departmental unit, or (3) work hours, i.e., shift. While that interpretation overlaps in part with ours, it does not adequately differentiate between the other related supervisory functions of Section 2(11). For example, instead of interpreting "assign" to include, as we do, assigning overall tasks, the dissent would require that the assignment be to an overall job classification....

[T]he dissent also criticizes our interpretation of "assign" on the ground that it "threatens to sweep almost all staff nurses outside of the Act's protection." [W]e decline to start with an objective—for example, keeping all staff nurses within the Act's protection—and fashioning definitions from there to meet that targeted objective. We have given "assign" the meaning we believe Congress intended. We are not swayed to abandon that interpretation by predictions of the results it will entail....

2. Responsibly to Direct

We agree with the circuit courts that have considered the issue and find that for direction to be "responsible," the person directing and performing the oversight of the employee must be accountable for the performance of the task by the other, such that some adverse consequence may befall the one providing the oversight if the tasks performed by the employee are not performed properly....

Thus, to establish accountability for purposes of responsible direction, it must be shown that the employer delegated to the putative supervisor the authority to direct the work and the authority to take corrective action, if necessary. It also must be shown that there is a prospect of adverse consequences for the putative supervisor if he/she does not take these steps.

* * *

C. Independent Judgment

* * *

[Previously, the Board has taken the position that] even if the Section 2(11) function is exercised with a substantial degree of discretion, there was no independent judgment if the judgment was of a particular kind, namely, "ordinary professional or technical judgment in directing less-skilled employees to deliver services." [In reviewing the Board's position, the Supreme Court] held that it is the degree of discretion involved in making the decision, not the kind of discretion exercised-whether professional, technical, or otherwise-that determines the existence of "independent judgment" under Section 2(11)....

* * *

... Thus, for example, a registered nurse who makes the "professional judgment" that a catheter needs to be changed may be performing a supervisory function when he/she responsibly directs a nursing assistant in the performance of that work. Whether the registered nurse is a 2(11) supervisor will depend on whether his or her responsible direction is performed with the degree of discretion required to reflect independent judgment.

To ascertain the contours of "independent judgment," we turn first to the ordinary meaning of the term. "Independent" means "not subject to control by others." [ ] "Judgment" means "the action of judging; the mental or intellectual process of forming an opinion or evaluation by discerning and comparing." [ ] Thus, as a starting point, to exercise "independent judgment" an individual must at minimum act, or effectively recommend action, free of the control of others and form an opinion or evaluation by discerning and comparing data. . . .

[A]ctions form a spectrum between the extremes of completely free actions and completely controlled ones, and the degree of independence necessary to constitute a judgment as "independent" under the Act lies somewhere in between these extremes. [T]here are, at one end of the spectrum, situations where there are detailed instructions for the actor to follow. At the other end, there are other situations where the actor is wholly free from constraints. In determining the meaning of the term "independent judgment" under Section 2(11), the Board must assess the degree of discretion exercised by the putative supervisor.

[W]e find that a judgment is not independent if it is dictated or controlled by detailed instructions, whether set forth in company policies or rules, the verbal instructions of a higher authority, or in the provisions of a collective-bargaining agreement. Thus, for example, a decision to staff a shift with a certain number of nurses would not involve independent judgment if it is determined by a fixed nurse-to-patient ratio. Similarly, if a collective-bargaining agreement required that only seniority be followed in making an assignment, that act of assignment would not be supervisory.

On the other hand, the mere existence of company policies does not eliminate independent judgment from decision-making if the policies allow for discretionary choices. . . . [I]f the registered nurse weighs the individualized condition and needs of a patient against the skills or special training of available nursing personnel, the nurse's assignment involves the exercise of independent judgment. . . .

. . . Section 2(11) contrasts "independent judgment" with actions that are "of a merely routine or clerical nature." . . . The authority to effect an assignment, for example, must be independent, it must involve a judgment, and the judgment must involve a degree of discretion that rises above the "routine or clerical." [ ] If there is only one obvious and self-evident choice (for example, assigning the one available nurse fluent in American Sign Language (ASL) to a patient dependent upon ASL for communicating), or if the assignment is made solely on the basis of equalizing workloads, then the assignment is routine or clerical in nature and does not implicate independent judgment, even if it is made free of the control of others and involves forming an opinion or evaluation by discerning and comparing data. By contrast, if the hospital has a policy that details how a charge nurse should respond in an emergency, but the charge nurse has the discretion to determine when an emergency exists or the authority to deviate from that policy based on the charge nurse's assessment of the particular circumstances, those deviations, if material, would involve the exercise of independent judgment.

The dissent portends that our analysis in assessing supervisory status under Section 2(11) may exclude "most professionals" from coverage under the Act. We disagree.... For example, in the case of assignment and direction, even if the charge nurse makes the professional judgment that a particular patient requires a certain degree of monitoring, the charge nurse is not a supervisor unless and until he or she assigns an employee to that patient or responsibly directs that employee in carrying out the monitoring at issue. Thus, a charge nurse is not automatically a "supervisor" because of his or her exercise of professional, technical, or experienced judgment as a professional employee. And it is equally true that his or her professional status does not prevent the charge nurse from having statutory supervisory status if he or she exercises independent judgment in assigning employees work or responsibly directing them in their work....

D. Persons Who Are Supervisors Part of the Time

Where an individual is engaged a part of the time as a supervisor and the rest of the time as a unit employee, the legal standard for a supervisory determination is whether the individual spends a regular and substantial portion of his/her work time performing supervisory functions. Under the Board's standard, "regular" means according to a pattern or schedule, as opposed to sporadic substitution. The Board has not adopted a strict numerical definition of substantiality and has found supervisory status where the individuals have served in a supervisory role for at least 10–15 percent of their total work time. We find no reason to depart from this established precedent.

III. THE CASE AT BAR

* * *

... [T]he Employer has failed to establish that its charge nurses possess the authority to "responsibly to direct" employees within the meaning of Section 2(11). However, we also find that the Employer has adduced evidence sufficient to establish that certain of its permanent charge nurses are supervisors based on their delegated authority to assign employees using independent judgment. Finally, we find that the Employer has failed to establish that its rotating charge nurses, as opposed to the 12 permanent charge nurses we find to be supervisors, spend a regular and substantial portion of their work time performing supervisory functions. Consequently, we exclude only the 12 permanent charge nurses from the unit.

A. Responsible Direction

The Employer alleges that its charge nurses responsibly direct nursing staff by directing them to perform certain tasks. As part of their duties, the charge nurses are responsible for checking the crash cart, taking an inventory of narcotics, and providing statistical information to Heritage's administrative staff for their shifts. The charge nurses may undertake these tasks themselves or delegate them to another staff member working that shift. The delegation of these charge-nurse specific tasks is the sole basis for the Employer's claim that the charge nurses responsibly direct the nursing staff.

... The Employer has not demonstrated that the charge nurses meet this accountability standard. The record reveals no evidence that the charge nurses must take corrective action if other staff members fail to adequately check the crash cart, take the narcotics inventory, or provide the statistical information to management. There is no indication that the charge nurses are subject to discipline or lower evaluations if other staff members fail to adequately perform these charge nurse-specific tasks....

B. Assignment

... At the beginning of each shift, and as new patients are admitted thereafter, the charge nurses for each patient care unit (except the emergency room) assign the staff working the unit to the patients that they will care for over the duration of the shift.

In the emergency room, the process of assigning work operates differently.... The charge nurses do not assign nursing personnel to patients in this department. Rather, the charge nurses assign employees to geographic areas within the emergency room. In making these assignments, the charge nurses do not take into account employee skill or the nature or severity of the patient's condition. After these initial assignments, the employees then rotate geographical locations within the emergency room among themselves on a periodic basis.

The charge nurses' assignment of patients to other staff and assignment of nurses to specific geographic locations within the emergency room fall within our definition of "assign" for purposes of Section 2(11). In patient care units other than the emergency room, the actions of the charge nurses involve assigning nurses to patients in rooms and "giving significant overall tasks to an employee." The charge nurses in the emergency room designate employees to a particular place. The charge nurses' assignments determine what will be the required work for an employee during the shift, thereby having a material effect on the employee's terms and conditions of employment....

Having found that the charge nurses hold the authority to engage in one of the supervisory functions of Section 2(11), our next step is to determine whether the charge nurses exercise independent judgment in making these assignments.

C. Independent Judgment

... In addition to the charge nurse, there are two to six RNs on each shift, depending on the time of day and the unit, and many of the units also have licensed practical nurses or other licensed staff working each shift. In the health care context, choosing among the available staff frequently requires a meaningful exercise of discretion. Matching a nurse with a patient may have life and death consequences. Nurses are professionals, not widgets, and may possess different levels of training and specialized skills. Similarly, patients are not identical and may require highly particularized care....

* * *

The Employer provided evidence that the charge nurses at the hospital relied upon their assessments of the patients' conditions and needs, the nursing personnel's ability, and other factors they deemed relevant depending on their unit. Witnesses repeatedly testified that the charge nurses' assignments are based on "informed judgments" about the patients and staff. For example, there was testimony that charge nurses take other nurses' individual expertise into account, such as assigning a nurse who is particularly proficient in administering dialysis to a kidney patient. In addition, other testimony shows that in making patient care assignments, the charge nurses look to whether the available staff has particular skill or training in dealing with certain kinds of patients, such as chemotherapy, orthopedic, or pediatric patients, There was further testimony that the charge nurse tries to assign the same patients to the same staff if possible, to ensure continuity of care and familiarity with particular patient needs.

* * *

The Employer also has a written policy for assigning nursing personnel to deliver care to patients.... While this statement guides the charge nurses' decision-making process, it is not so detailed as to eliminate a significant discretionary component involved in matching nursing personnel to patients. First, the policy statement does not prescribe a formulary approach that must be followed by the charge nurses. Rather, the policy identifies factors that permit individual input or evaluation based on a given charge nurse's perspective of the situation....

... The record shows that the charge nurse role in the emergency room unit is structured in such a way as not to necessitate the exercise of independent judgment.... Most significantly, the emergency room charge nurses do not take into account patient acuity or nursing skill in making patient care assignments. Whereas the record contains evidence of situations in other units in which the charge nurses must assess individual professional or personal attributes of the nursing staff, there is no similar evidence for the charge nurses in the emergency room unit. Instead, the charge nurses in the emergency room assign the nursing staff to geographic areas of the emergency room. Furthermore, a charge nurse in the emergency room testified without contradiction that the staff nurses rotated assignments, without input from the charge nurse. This evidence does not show discretion to choose between meaningful choices on the part of the charge nurses in the emergency room.

[The Board finds that Oakwood's full-time charge nurses, except for those in the ER, are supervisors.]

D. "Rotating" Charge Nurses

* * *

... The Employer offered only superficial evidence as to the regularity with which [the] nonpermanent or "rotating" charge nurses serve in the charge nurse role. The record reveals that none of the units involved have an established pattern or predictable schedule for when and how often RNs take turns in working as charge nurses. In those units where the RNs decide among themselves who will serve as charge nurses, the record does not demonstrate any pattern for these selections. In those units where the managers are in charge of making assignments, the managers likewise do not use any particular system or order for assigning charge nurses.

* * *

Conclusion

In interpreting the statutory terms "assign," "responsibly to direct," and "independent judgment" as set forth in this decision, we have endeavored to provide clear and broadly applicable guidance for the Board's regulated community. Our dissenting colleagues predict that our definitions will "create a new class of workers" who are excluded from the Act but do not exercise "genuine prerogatives of management." We anticipate no such sea change in the law, and will continue to assess each case on its individual merits. In deciding this case, moreover, we intentionally eschewed a results-oriented approach; rather, we analyzed the terms of the Act and derived definitions that, in our view, best reflect the meanings intended by Congress in passing Section 2(11) and would best serve to effectuate the underlying purposes of the Act. If our adherence to the text of and intent behind the Act should lead to consequences that some would deem undesirable, the effective remedy lies with the Congress.

* * *

Notes and Questions

1. The Board's decision in *Oakwood* is a significant departure from the position held previously by the Board, a position that interpreted Section 2(11) much more narrowly and brought a wider range of health care professionals within the scope of the NLRA. In the years leading up to *Oakwood*, the Board and the federal trial and appellate courts were engaged in a long battle with the Supreme Court over the appropriate definition of supervisor. The Court in a 5–4 majority, in NLRB v. Health Care & Retirement Corp. of America, 511 U.S. 571, 114 S.Ct. 1778, 128 L.Ed.2d 586 (1994), rejected the Board's categorical exclusion of patient care from acts taken "in the interest of the employer." After *Health Care & Retirement Corp.*, the federal circuit courts of appeals were in serious conflict over the application of the Court's decision; and the NLRB continued to take a narrow view of the definition of supervisor in the health care setting. In 2001 the Supreme Court revisited the issue of supervisory status in NLRB v. Kentucky River Community Care, 532 U.S. 706, 121 S.Ct. 1861, 149 L.Ed.2d 939 (2001). In that case, the Court, in another 5–4 decision, rejected the Board's interpretation of "independent judgment" as excluding "ordinary professional and technical judgment in directing less skilled employees to deliver services." After *Kentucky River*, the Board took the unusual step of issuing an open invitation to parties and *amici* asking for assistance in interpreting *Kentucky River* in application to three cases pending before the Board, including *Oakwood*. The Board reviewed the responses in deciding *Oakwood*. For a history of the conflict over supervisory status in health care, see Michael W. Hawkings & Shawn P. Burton, Oakwood Healthcare: How Textualism Saved the Supervisory Exemption, 9 U. Pa. J. Lab. & Emp. L. 1 (2006).

2. The purpose of the exclusion of supervisors from the protections of the NLRA is to assure that supervisory employees are not in conflict between representing management and participating with other employees in collective action. A passionate dissenting opinion in *Oakwood* notes, however, that the

Board's decision "create[s] a new class of workers . . . : workers who have neither the genuine prerogatives of management, nor the statutory rights of ordinary employees." Should Congress amend the definition of supervisor as it applies in health care workplaces? Congressional Roundup, 16 Health L. Rep. 390 (2007). Some argue that a narrow definition of supervisor is critical to the viability of the labor movement as a broad definition, especially in the construction and health care industries, sweeps large categories of workers outside of the protections of the NLRA.

3.   *Oakwood* was one of two cases issued on the same day in which the Board applied its new interpretation of supervisory status to a health care work place. In *Golden Crest*, 348 NLRB 39, the Board concluded that a nursing home's charge nurses, usually RNs but sometimes LPNs, were not supervisors. The employer had argued that the charge nurses responsibly directed the work of certified nurse assistants. While the Board agreed that the charge nurses directed the work of the CNAs, it concluded that they were not accountable for that supervision and, hence, were not supervisors:

> We find that the Employer established that its charge nurses have the authority to direct the CNAs. The record shows that charge nurses oversee the CNAs' job performance and act to correct the CNAs when they are not providing adequate care. For instance, a charge nurse will correct a CNA if she perceives that the CNA is not using proper procedures in giving a resident a bath. The record also establishes that charge nurses will direct the CNAs to perform certain tasks when the charge nurse determines that such tasks are necessary. For instance, the charge nurses will direct CNAs to clip residents' toenails and fingernails, to empty catheters, or to change an incontinent resident. We find that this evidence is sufficient to establish that the charge nurses "direct" the CNAs within the meaning of the definition set forth in *Oakwood Healthcare.*

> The next question, then, is whether the Employer has established that the charge nurses are accountable for their actions in directing the CNAs. We find that the Employer has not met this burden. The Employer has not presented any evidence that any charge nurse has experienced any material consequences to her terms and conditions of employment, either positive or negative, as a result of her performance in directing CNAs. Nor has the Employer presented any evidence that a charge nurse was ever informed that any such material consequences might result from her performance in directing CNAs. . . .

> The Employer's evidence that its charge nurses are accountable for their performance in directing CNAs consists of evaluation forms used by the Employer to assess the performance of its charge nurses. On these forms, which are contained in the record, the charge nurses were rated for their performance on the factor, "Directs CNAs to ensure quality of care." . . .

> There is no evidence, however, that any action, either positive or negative, has been or might be taken as a result of the charge nurses' evaluation on this factor. The Employer does not award merit increases or any other type of bonus. In fact, DON Kepler testified that the only effect of a positive evaluation is that the employee gets to keep working at the facility. Further, the Employer did not introduce any evidence that any adverse action might be taken against a charge nurse as a result of a "Needs Improvement" evaluation on the "Directs CNAs" performance factor (or any other performance factor, for that matter), nor did the Employer ever inform the charge nurses that any adverse action might result from a negative rating on the "Directs CNAs" performance factor.

. . . Accountability under *Oakwood Healthcare* requires only a *prospect* of consequences. But there must be a more-than-merely-paper showing that such a prospect exists. That is, where accountability is predicated on employee evaluations, there must be evidence that a putative supervisor's rating for direction of subordinates may have, either by itself or in combination with other performance factors, an effect on that person's terms and conditions of employment.

4. The Board in *Oakwood* and *Golden Crest* eliminated categorical exclusions for health care professionals from the reach of the definition of supervisor. Instead, the Board now engages in a fact-intensive inquiry to decide whether nurses are supervisors in individual cases. Is there a more efficient way to resolve this question? Some unions have removed the interpretation of supervisory status for nurse-employees from the NLRB (and the Supreme Court) by entering into agreements with individual employers that specify that the employer's charge nurses are not supervisors. UAW Members OK Pact at Toledo Hospital That Protects Charge Nurses' Union Rights, 15 Health L. Rep. 1319 (2006); NLRB Upholds Decision, Sets New Vote by Registered Nurses at Hospital in Arizona, 16 Health L. Rep. 198 (2007). In light of *Oakwood* and *Golden Crest*, why would a hospital employer agree that it "will not seek, through unit clarifications, arbitration, or similar proceedings, to exclude leaders, charge persons, or persons in similar classifications from the bargaining unit?"

5. Doctors seek recognition as a formal union in part because it provides an exemption from the application of antitrust restrictions on concerted action. See discussion in Chapter 12. In order for an individual worker to be covered by the NLRA, however, he or she must work as an employee, and not as an independent contractor. The NLRA relies on the traditional common law distinction between independent contractors and employees, and thus focuses on the degree of control exercised over the work of the physician. See, e.g., AmeriHealth and United Food and Commercial Workers Union, 329 NLRB No. 76 (1999), considering whether a managed care organization exercised such a degree of control over the practices of contracting physicians that those physicians could be considered employees of the MCO and, therefore, covered by the Act. After discussing in significant detail the MCO's control over the doctor's right to accept or refuse patients, obligations regarding office facilities, equipment, accessibility, safety practices, and record keeping as well as standards for the number of patients seen per hour, maximum wait times, and annual performance reviews, the Board concluded that the doctors were independent contractors. The NLRB has certified physician unions in HMOs that employ rather than contract with doctors as well as in hospitals with physician employees. Where physicians are employed by hospitals, the NLRA will have an impact on staff privileges decisions. See, e.g., Scheiner v. N.Y.C. Health and Hospitals Corp., 1999 WL 771383 (S.D.N.Y.).

Problem: Supervisors or Not?

After its decisions in *Oakwood* and *Golden Crest*, the Board remanded 54 cases to its administrative law judges for reconsideration. NLRB, General Counsel Memorandum, OM–07–04 (Oct. 11, 2006). An ALJ deciding one of the remanded cases stated:

> Particularly in the nursing home context, where RNs and LPNs typically work in conjunction with nurses' aides, it is hard to imagine a situation in which competent counsel, after reading these opinions, would be unable to establish that any RN or LPN in a nursing home had the ability to responsibly direct the aides working with them. Loyalhanna Health Care Associates, 2007 WL 1160052 (NLRB Div. of Judges) (2007).

Assuming that you were "competent counsel," what would you advise Golden Crest and Oakwood to do to assure that all of its RNs and LPNs would be categorized as supervisors? What would your clients gain if they succeeded?

2. *Concerted Activities*

NEW YORK UNIVERSITY MED. CTR. AND ASSN. OF STAFF PSYCHIATRISTS, BELLEVUE PSYCHIATRIC HOSP.

324 N.L.R.B. No. 139 (1997).

[T]he evidence shows that the Association [of Staff Psychiatrists is a labor organization under the Act even though it is not a union because it] has an already defined unit, that of staff psychiatrists at Bellevue Psychiatric Hospital, was formed in 1973 for the purpose of dealing with the Respondent regarding such matters as salaries, working hours and conditions, and grievances of its members, has elected officials (executive board) by elections held every 2 years, has dues paying membership, holds membership meetings, and has actually dealt with the Respondent, mainly through the director of psychiatry, Dr. Manual Trujillo, concerning issues such as wages (equalizing or improving the salary structure of the psychiatrists at Bellevue), the hours and working conditions of the psychiatrists, and grievances. * * *

* * *

The complaint alleges in substance, that the Respondent violated Section 8(a)(1) of the Act by threatening employees with cutbacks, layoffs, and other consequences if they continued to protest a change in employee work hours, and violated Section 8(a)(1) and (3) of the Act by discharging Drs. John Graham, Ebrahim Kermani, Martin Geller, Jerome Steiner, Stanley Portnow, and Meave Mahon [all members of the executive committee of the Association] because they engaged in protected concerted activities.

* * *

Under an affiliated contract with HHC, the Respondent provides psychiatrists and other health care professionals to Bellevue Hospital Center for the purpose of delivering medical and psychiatrist patient care and services. * * * HHC is a quasi public corporation responsible for operating the municipal hospital system of New York City, including Bellevue Hospital. * * *

* * *

For a number of years, HHC had expressed dissatisfaction with a practice under which certain psychiatrists employed by the Respondent at Bellevue Hospital worked from 9 a.m. to 3 p.m. HHC maintained that * * * the affiliation contract required physicians to provide at least 40 hours of service per week, inclusive of unpaid meal hours. By memorandum dated September 30, 1994, HHC Executive Director Pam Brier advised Dr. Trujillo that because of an extremely serious fiscal situation, "Effective November 1, 1994, all full-time staff must fulfill the obligation explicitly delineated in the affiliate contract to work at least 35 hours per week. As we've discussed, there really can be no exception to this policy regardless of any informal agreements."

On September 30, 1994, the Respondent conducted the first of several staff meetings to discuss the "9 to 3" issue. About 30–40 psychiatrists attended, including association executive board members Drs. Graham, Kermani, Mahon, Geller, and Portnow, among others. Dr. Trujillo announced that because of budget problems there would no longer be any "9 to 3" hours, that everybody had to increase productivity and work 9 a.m. to 4:30 p.m. or take a decrease in salary, as the only solution. Dr. Maeve Mahon testified that she suggested that clinical work be assigned to [the physician] administrators. Dr. Mahon related that it was chiefly the members of the executive board [of the Association], particularly Drs. Graham and Kermani, who spoke out against the Respondent's announced changes in working hours. * * *

* * *

Dr. Mahon also testified that she attended another meeting in which Dr. Trujillo mentioned that the "9–3" psychiatrists were going to have to work more hours, and she asked why [the physician administrators] couldn't "come downstairs from their offices and do some clinical care?" Dr. Mahon testified that she perceived animosity from Dr. Trujillo at every meeting she attended as an elected member of the Association. Dr. Trujillo appeared angry, difficult, and stated that the Association wasn't a union or labor group and represented no one.

Dr. Portnow's testimony which substantially supported that of Dr. Mahon as to what occurred at these meetings testified that after [a] meeting had ended, and while he was waiting for an elevator, Dr. Trujillo told him that "Dr. Mahon's behavior was disgraceful, disloyal, undesirable and that it would lead to trouble for the attendings." Portnow also recalled that within the same day or the next Dr. Trujillo said to him that "the Association would be punished" for its position on the "9 to 3" issue; that it was a political issue and that "we should have taken the offer of renegotiating our time to eight-tenths time."

* * *

[I]n the fall of 1994 HHC notified the Respondent that the mental health portion of the affiliation contract budget at Bellevue had to be reduced by approximately $2 million. According to the testimony of several of the Respondent's witnesses they "tried to protect the psychiatrists working at Bellevue" by arguing against the reduction and offering an alternate proposal. After prolonged negotiations, however, HHC insisted on the budget cut and determined it could only be achieved by a reduction in the staff of 10 psychiatrists.

* * * Dr. Trujillo and his senior administrators implemented plans to reorganize the psychiatric department. * * * [T]hey first determined that the reduction should be made in the in-patient rather than the out-patient units. They then decided that a unit would have to be closed and other medical units combined or reorganized. Because the new system would require the implementation of a treatment plan to rapidly stabilize and dispose of patients, the Respondent began to review the productivity and performance, especially the management and leadership skills of psychiatrists and of the unit chiefs, to determine which would be most effective in the new structure and "enable the department to fulfill its mission with ten less psychiatrists."

[Six members of the executive committee of the Association were among the ten psychiatrists terminated in the reorganization.]

* * *

[T]he evidence clearly establishes that the Association and its member psychiatrists engaged in a series of concerted actions in protest against the Respondent's announced changes in their working hours and that the Respondent was aware of such activities.

* * *

* * * Dr. Trujillo [admitted] that he often told [a group of psychiatrists] that if they did not do something "constructive" to deal with the 9 a.m. to 3 p.m. issue, there would be further budgetary problems, that the problem would just get worse and effect everybody. Dr. Trujillo admitted that he may have [said] . . . that "it was not a good idea, in a budgeting shortness to have an open issue like the 9:00 to 3:00. It makes you very visible for the chopping block."

The record is replete with evidence of statements of animus by Dr. Trujillo toward the Association and the Association's executive board and would lend credence to the view that Dr. Trujillo would not hesitate to tell the Association that it would be "punished" for opposing a change in the 9 a.m. to 3 p.m. work schedules. The Respondent's contentions that Dr. Trujillo was simply trying to warn the psychiatrists that a failure to resolve the 9 a.m. to 3 p.m. issue would cause more budgeting problems and possibly layoffs is irrelevant. However, given Dr. Trujillo's demonstrated history of animus toward the Association and its officers, no reasonable person would have believed that Dr. Trujillo's pronouncements were anything but a threat. This remains true even if one credits Dr. Trujillo's statement that a failure to resolve the 9 to 3 issue makes the psychiatrists "very visible for the chopping block." * * *

* * *

* * * I am persuaded that * * * a motivating factor in the discharge of the six alleged discriminatees was their protected concerted activities based on the abundant evidence of animus toward the Association and its various executive board members on the part of the Respondent, their open opposition to the change in the 9 to 3 work schedule and other activities on behalf of the psychiatrists and the Respondent's knowledge thereof, the unlawful implicit threats of cutbacks, layoffs and other consequences if they continued to protest such change, and the timing of the discharges relative to their protected activity. Accordingly, the burden shifts to the Respondent to establish that it would have terminated [members of the Association] even in the absence of their protected concerted activities. [ ] The Respondent asserts that the layoff of the six alleged discriminatees was not in violation of Section 8(a)(1) and (3) of the Act because it was motivated by a reduction in budget mandated by the Health and Hospital Corporation of New York City and based on the Respondent's judgment concerning the best personnel to operate the reorganized department and not by their activity on behalf of the Association.

I do not agree.

* * *

Notes and Questions

1. The NLRA provides that "Employees shall have the right to self-organization, to form, join, or assist labor organizations, to bargain collectively through representatives of their own choosing, and to engage in other concerted activities for the purpose of collective bargaining or other mutual aid or protection." 29 U.S.C. § 157. The Act's protection for employees engaged in "concerted activities" does not require that the employees belong to a formal union. While the Association of Staff Psychiatrists was a statutory labor organization, even though it had not been "certified" as a union by the NLRB, even this level of organization is not required in order for an employee to be engaged in concerted action protected by the NLRA. For example, in NLRB v. Main Street Terrace Care Ctr., 218 F.3d 531 (6th Cir. 2000), the court held that a dietary aide who had helped other employees review their paychecks and report errors and who had made a statement about needing a union at the facility had engaged in concerted action and that her discharge was in retaliation for that activity. See also Misericordia Hosp. Med. Ctr. v. NLRB, 623 F.2d 808 (2d Cir. 1980), holding that a nurse engaged in concerted activity when she participated in preparing a report critical of the hospital.

2. The Board rejected NYU's defense because of statements made by the administrator. Once those statements were made, was there anything the University could have done to reduce the risk of an adverse decision by the Board, other than retaining the six psychiatrists? See, e.g., Hospital Cristo Redentor v. NLRB, 488 F.3d 513 (1st Cir. 2007), noting that if there is a showing that "union animus was *a* motivating factor in the adverse employment action, the employer must prove, as an affirmative defense, that it would have taken the same action even in the absence of the employee's protected activity." The concerns identified by NYU about the terminated doctors revolved around their "leadership skills." What kind of evidence should NYU produce to meet the standard? Does aggressive opposition to reductions in itself cause concern about the doctors' potential to lead the reduced departments?

3. A doctor or nurse who is vocal in her opposition to the organization's policies can be viewed as prophetic or disruptive or both, especially if she engages others in her activities. Such situations can strain relationships among employees; however, the NLRA protects those activities, at least to a point. But see, St. Luke's Episcopal–Presbyterian Hosps. v. NLRB, 268 F.3d 575 (8th Cir. 2001). The Board, consistent with long-standing decisions, had held that the reaction of coworkers was irrelevant in evaluating the employer's action. The court disagreed and found that the discharge was appropriate, stating:

> Patient lives are at stake in hospital surgeries.... Common sense teaches that patient care is directly affected by the ability of a team of physicians and nurses to work together in the confines of an operating room; that a hospital must not risk staffing the operating room with doctors and nurses who cannot work effectively together; and that surgeons cannot be expected to tolerate operating room staff who seem to be more interested in publicizing flaws in the process than in helping protect the patient.

Does this view reach only the operating room or beyond? Does it depend on how the employee voiced his concerns? Won't conflict usually cause tension? See also discussion of disruptive physicians and staff privileges in Section I; "gag clauses" in managed care contracting in Section II; and employment-at-will in Section IIIA of this chapter.

Problem: Changing Things

St. Margaret's Hospital has undertaken an initiative, called "Take Charge!", which is intended to increase volume, decrease costs, and improve quality. As part of this initiative, St. Margaret's has decided to enter into exclusive contracts for anesthesiology and radiology. The physicians who currently provide services in each of these departments hold staff privileges and are not paid a salary by the hospital, although the hospital provides all of their equipment, supplies, and nursing and technical staff. The hospital does the billing for services the doctors provide in the hospital, but the charges are payable directly to the doctors.

The departments hold regular medical staff meetings each quarter to review events at the hospital, to discuss concerns about nurse staffing and equipment, and to air any problems that might be developing. The medical staff in the departments elect their own chairperson to handle these meetings. The chair has no administrative appointment with the hospital itself. At a meeting last spring, the medical staff in the department of radiology decided to send a joint letter to hospital administration opposing the move to exclusive contracting. Dr. Ellen Stitch and Dr. Robert Morales agreed to draft the letter and to meet with administration to discuss the physicians' concerns. They did so. Although reports of the meeting vary, the hospital CEO apparently said that he thought Dr. Stitch and Dr. Morales should focus on more constructive responses to the situation. Later, when the hospital announced that it was seeking a physician group to provide exclusive radiology services, Dr. Stitch and Dr. Morales bid for the contract. St. Margaret's granted the contract to another group. Physicians who did not have a contract with that group, including Doctors Stitch and Morales, were told that they could retain privileges, but could not provide radiology services unless by specific request of a treating physician.

Also, as part of Take Charge!, St. Margaret's changed its nurse staffing in surgery to require nurses to work on a "prn" or as needed basis. If no surgeries are scheduled, the nurses are assigned to other units or are released for the day without pay. Nurse Georgia Jones was particularly vocal in her concern over this change. She was concerned that nurses would be sent to work in units where they were not qualified and that emergency surgeries would not be adequately covered. Nurse Jones felt a particular accountability for the nurses as she was the head nurse in the intensive care unit. As head nurse, she monitored the performance of the nurses in that unit and dealt with conflicts as they arose. She didn't have authority to hire or discipline the nurses who worked in her unit, but the Director of Nursing and the Personnel Office usually followed her suggestions.

Roberta Farr, the Director of Nursing, met privately with Nurse Jones, and Jones communicated the concerns over staffing. Ms. Farr subtly indicated that she shared Nurse Jones' concerns but said that the system should be tried first. The DON's comments quickly circulated along the hospital's grapevine. Ms. Farr demoted Nurse Jones who then went to the local newspaper to tell the story. One week later, the hospital discharged Ms. Farr.

Are Doctors Stitch and Morales and Nurses Jones and Farr covered by the NLRA? If they are included within the coverage of the Act, have they engaged in concerted activities of "mutual aid?" Would any of these individuals have a claim under other principles you studied in this Chapter? For wrongful discharge under employment-at-will? Under common law governing exclusive contracting?

IV. DISCRIMINATION LAW

Discrimination cases arise in the health care setting as they do in any workplace. For most issues, the health care workplace does not present unique issues for the application of state and federal law protecting individuals against employment discrimination on account of age (the Age Discrimination in Employment Act, 29 U.S.C. § 621), disability (the Americans with Disabilities Act, 42 U.S.C. § 12101, and the Rehabilitation Act, 29 U.S.C. § 701), gender, national origin, religion, or race (Title VII of the Civil Rights Act cf 1964, 42 U.S.C. § 2000e).

In the area of disability discrimination, however, the issue of risk to patients has been a special concern. As described in the principle case below, an employee claiming under one of the federal disability statutes must prove that he or she can perform the essential functions of the job either with or without accommodation for his or her disability. If the employee poses a "direct threat" to the employee's or others' health and safety, which cannot be eliminated through a reasonable accommodation, the employee is not qualified for the job and has no claim. In dealing with communicable diseases, the cases under the federal disability statutes require a number of inquiries. Has the employer made a reasonable accommodation, for example, in the form of job assignment, adjustment of duties, or provision of protective equipment, that would allow the disabled employee to perform the job safely? Or, is the job assignment or adjustment made by the employer itself discriminatory in excluding the employee from work he or she is capable of doing? As you will see, these inquiries inevitably require an assessment of risks particular to the employee and the employment setting. In assessing risks that are greater than absolute zero, the court must decide what level of risk is acceptable.

ESTATE OF MAURO v. BORGESS MEDICAL CENTER

United States Court of Appeals for the Sixth Circuit, 1998.
137 F.3d 398.

GIBSON, CIRCUIT JUDGE.

William C. Mauro brought an action against his former employer, Borgess Medical Center, alleging violations of the Americans with Disabilities Act, 42 U.S.C. §§ 12101–12213 (1994), and the Rehabilitation Act, 29 U.S.C. §§ 701– 796 (1994). The district court granted Borgess's motion for summary judgment, determining that Mauro, who was infected with human immunodeficiency virus, or HIV, the virus that causes AIDS, was a direct threat to the health and safety of others that could not be eliminated by reasonable accommodation and thus concluded that Borgess took no illegal action in removing Mauro from his position as surgical technician. [ ]. Mauro appeals, arguing that as a surgical technician at Borgess he did not pose a direct threat to the health and safety of others and that therefore the district court erred in granting summary judgment to Borgess. We affirm.

Borgess employed Mauro from May 1990 through August 24, 1992 as an operating room technician. In June of 1992, an undisclosed source telephoned Robert Lambert, Vice President of Human Resources for Borgess Medical Center and Borgess Health Alliance, and informed Lambert that Mauro had "full blown" AIDS. Because of Borgess's concern that Mauro might expose a patient to HIV, Georgiann Ellis, Vice President of Surgical, Orthopedic and Clinical Services at Borgess, and Sharon Hickman, Mauro's supervisor and Operating Room Department Director, created a new full-time position of case cart/instrument coordinator, a position that eliminated all risks of transmission of the HIV virus. In July of 1992, Borgess officials offered Mauro this position, which he refused.

After Mauro's refusal of the case cart/instrument coordinator position, Borgess created a task force to determine whether an HIV-positive employee could safely perform the job responsibilities of a surgical technician. Lambert and Ellis informed Mauro by a letter dated August 10, 1992, that the task force had determined that a job requiring an HIV-infected worker to place his or her hands into a patient's body cavity in the presence of sharp instrumentation represented a direct threat to patient care and safety. Because the task force had concluded that an essential function of a surgical technician was to enter a patient's wound during surgery, the task force concluded that Mauro could no longer serve as a surgical technician. Lambert and Ellis concluded by offering Mauro two choices: to accept the case cart/instrument coordinator position, or be laid off. Mauro did not respond by the deadline stated in the letter, and Borgess laid him off effective August 24, 1992. Mauro filed this suit in January 1994.

* * *

Mauro's first claim alleges that Borgess discriminated against him in violation of section 504 of the Rehabilitation Act, which provides that no otherwise qualified individual with handicaps shall, solely by reason of his or her handicap, be excluded from participation in, or be denied benefits of any program receiving federal financial assistance. Through the passage of the Rehabilitation Act, Congress intended to protect disabled individuals "from deprivations based on prejudice, stereotypes, or unfounded fear, while giving appropriate weight to such legitimate concerns ... as avoiding exposing others to significant health and safety risks." School Board of Nassau County v. Arline, 480 U.S. 273, 107 S.Ct. 1123, 94 L.Ed.2d 307 (1987). Arline specifically noted:

> Few aspects of a handicap give rise to the same level of public fear and misapprehension as contagiousness.... The Act is carefully structured to replace such reflexive reactions to actual or perceived handicaps with actions based on reasoned and medically sound judgments.... The fact that some persons who have contagious diseases may pose a serious health threat to others under certain circumstances does not justify excluding from the coverage of the Act all persons with actual or perceived contagious diseases. Such exclusion would mean that those accused of being contagious would never have the opportunity to have their condition evaluated in light of medical evidence.... Rather, they would be vulnerable to discrimination on the basis of mythology—precisely the type of injury Congress sought to prevent.

In order to recover under the Rehabilitation Act, a plaintiff must establish that he or she is "otherwise qualified" to do the job within the meaning of the Act. An "otherwise qualified" person is one who can perform the "essential functions" of the job at issue. [ ] In a situation regarding the employment of a person with a contagious disease, the inquiry should also include a determination of whether the individual poses "a significant risk of communicating the disease to others in the workplace." [ ]

Mauro's second claim alleges that Borgess discriminated against him in violation of the Americans with Disabilities Act, which provides that no qualified individual with a disability shall, by reason of such disability, be excluded from participation in or denied the benefits of the services of public entities.

To prevail under his Americans with Disabilities Act claim, Mauro must show that he is "otherwise qualified" for the job at issue. [ ] A person is "otherwise qualified" if he or she can perform the essential functions of the job in question. [ ] A disabled individual, however, is not "qualified" for a specific employment position if he or she poses a "direct threat" to the health or safety of others which cannot be eliminated by a reasonable accommodation. [ ]

The "direct threat" standard applied in the Americans with Disabilities Act is based on the same standard as "significant risk" applied by the Rehabilitation Act. [ ]. Our analysis under both Acts thus merges into one question: Did Mauro's activities as a surgical technician at Borgess pose a direct threat or significant risk to the health or safety of others?

Arline laid down four factors to consider in this analysis: (a) the nature of the risk (how the disease is transmitted), (b) the duration of the risk (how long is the carrier infectious), (c) the severity of the risk (what is the potential harm to third parties) and (d) the probabilities the disease will be transmitted and will cause varying degrees of harm. [ ]

To show that one is "otherwise qualified", neither Act requires the elimination of all risk posed by a person with a contagious disease. In Arline the Supreme Court determined that a person with an infectious disease "who poses a significant risk of communicating an infectious disease to others in the workplace," is not otherwise qualified to perform his or her job. [ ] If the risk is not significant, however, the person is qualified to perform the job. The EEOC guidelines provide further insight:

An employer, however, is not permitted to deny an employment opportunity to an individual with a disability merely because of a slightly increased risk. The risk can only be considered when it poses a significant risk, i.e. high probability, of substantial harm; a speculative or remote risk is insufficient. [ ]

* * * Thus, our analysis in the instant case must not consider the possibility of HIV transmission, but rather focus on the probability of transmission weighed with the other three factors of the Arline test.

The parties agree that the first three factors of the Arline test: the nature, duration, and severity of the risk, all indicate that Mauro posed a significant risk to others. Mauro argues, however, that because the probability of transmission, the fourth factor of Arline, was so slight, it overwhelmed the first three factors and created a genuine issue of material fact.

In determining whether Mauro posed a significant risk or a direct threat in the performance of the essential functions of his job as a surgical technician, Arline, instructs that courts should defer to the "reasonable medical judgments of public health officials." [ ] The Centers for Disease Control is such a body of public health officials. [ ] The Centers for Disease Control has released a report discussing its recommendations regarding HIV-positive health care workers. [ ]

The Report states that the risk of transmission of HIV from an infected health care worker to a patient is very small, and therefore recommends allowing most HIV-positive health care workers to continue performing most surgical procedures, provided that the workers follow safety precautions outlined in the Report. [ ] The Report, however, differentiates a limited category of invasive procedures, which it labels exposure-prone procedures, from general invasive procedures. [ ] General invasive procedures cover a wide range of procedures from insertion of an intravenous line to most types of surgery. [ ] Exposure-prone procedures, however, involve those that pose a greater risk of percutaneous (skin-piercing) injury. Though the Centers for Disease Control did not specifically identify which types of procedures were to be labeled exposure-prone, it supplies a general definition: "Characteristics of exposure-prone procedures include digital palpation of a needle tip in a body cavity or the simultaneous presence of the [health care worker's] fingers and a needle or other sharp instrument or object in a poorly visualized or highly confined anatomic site." [ ] The Report advises that individual health care institutions take measures to identify which procedures performed in their hospital should be labeled exposure-prone and recommends that HIV-infected health care workers should not perform exposure-prone procedures unless they have sought counsel from an expert review panel and have been advised under what circumstances they may continue to perform these procedures. The Report further recommends that those health care workers who engage in exposure-prone procedures notify prospective patients of their condition.

We must defer to the medical judgment expressed in the Report of the Centers for Disease Control in evaluating the district court's ruling on whether Mauro posed a direct threat in the essential functions of his job.

Mauro stated in his deposition that during surgery his work did not include assisting in surgery, but instead handing instruments to the surgeon and helping the surgeon with whatever else he or she needed. During surgery, Mauro would at times hold a retractor with one hand in the wound area, and pass instruments as needed with his other hand. When asked if he would be actually inside a wound holding a retractor, Mauro answered "Me personally, no." But when questioned further about his hands in the wound area, he stated: "Usually if I have my hands near the wound, it would be to like, on an abdominal incision, to kind of put your finger in and hold—kind of pull down on the muscle tissue and that—where the two met in like a V shape at the bottom and the top, and pull that back. But it happened very, very rarely because they had retractors to do that." The purpose of this action was to give the surgeon more room and more visibility.

The continued questioning led to a distinction between the wound and the body cavity. Mauro was asked if he ever had his hands in a body cavity, described as being past the wound area, and Mauro stated that he personally never had his hand in a body cavity because the small size of the surgical incision prevented too many hands from being placed inside the body cavity.

* * *

Mauro explained that during his training, discussion had occurred indicating that nicks and cuts were always a possibility for a surgical technician. In fact, the record included two incident reports involving Mauro. One report indicated that Mauro had sliced his right index finger while removing a knife blade from a handle on June 25, 1991, and another report indicated that he had scratched his hand with the sharp end of a dirty needle while threading it on June 8, 1990.

* * *

Sharon Hickman, a registered nurse, was the interim director of operating rooms at Borgess in June and July of 1992. While serving as interim director Hickman supervised the surgical technicians at Borgess, including Mauro. In her affidavit Hickman described a meeting of the Ad Hoc HIV Task Force for the hospital on July 23, 1992 and the statements she made at that meeting. Hickman stated that she told the task force that the duties of a surgical technician include preparing and maintaining the equipment used during surgery, but that, on an infrequent basis, the Surgical Technician is required to assist in the performance of surgery by holding back body tissue, with the use of either retractors or the Technician's hands, to assist the surgeon in visualizing the operative site. The Surgical Technician also may assist the surgeon with suturing and other duties related to the performance of the operation.

She also advised the task force that, although the need for a surgical technician's assistance in the performance of a surgical procedure arises infrequently, it is not possible to restructure the job to eliminate the surgical technician from performing such functions because this need arises on an emergency basis and cannot be planned in advance. In some cases, particularly on off-shifts, Hickman stated that the surgical technician is required to assist at the surgery because a registered nurse or surgical assistant is not available. In other surgical proceedings a nurse or surgical assistant may be present, but due to the complexity or other unexpected requirements of the procedure, another pair of hands may be needed in the operative site, and the surgical technician is then required to assist. Most often, the surgical technician is required to assist in the operative site because more hands are needed to visualize the surgical area.

* * *

We conclude that the district court did not err in determining that Mauro's continued employment as a surgical technician posed a direct threat to the health and safety of others.

* * *

BOGGS, CIRCUIT JUDGE, dissenting.

The concept of "significant risk" that emerges from the [statutes] directly mandates that patients be exposed to, and employers be required to expose their patients to, some amount of risk that is deemed "insignificant" to some determining body. As with other questions of fact and degree in a civil case, a district judge may find that the relevant risk is so small as to be insignificant as a matter of law; so large as to be significant as a matter of law (in each case because no reasonable person could differ with the court's judgment, even though the contrary is staunchly asserted by the opposing attorneys); or, somewhere in between, so that reasonable minds could differ on the degree of risk, and so a jury must be permitted to determine the question.

* * *

Mauro poses some risk. It is not ontologically impossible for him to transmit a disease of very great lethality. However, the chance that he will do so to any given patient is "small." Whether we call the risk "extremely small," "vanishingly small," "negligible," or whatever, assessing the risk remains a judgment that must be made by considering both the actual probability of harm and the degree of the consequences, just as the Supreme Court instructed us.

That is what the District Court did not do, and that is why I would reverse its decision and remand for reconsideration under the correct standard—a full assessment of both the risk and the consequence. * * * [T]he exact nature of Mauro's duties [is] a matter of considerable dispute, especially when the record is read, as we must read it, in a light most favorable to him. Whether the procedures he may perform cross the line from the merely "invasive" to the actionable "exposure-prone" is a genuine and material issue, on which reasonable minds can differ.

* * *

The CDC "has estimated that the risk to a single patient from an HIV-positive surgeon ranges from .0024% (1 in 42,000) to .00024% (1 in 417,000)." [ ] This estimate, of course, is for surgeons, who by the very nature of their work enter surgical wounds with sharp instruments during virtually every procedure they perform. Common sense—and, of course, the court's obligation to interpret the evidence in the light most favorable to the nonmovant— requires us to suppose, in the absence of contrary information, that the activities of a surgical technician such as Mauro who touched only the margin of the wound, and that only very rarely, would pose an even smaller risk. So may the resulting coefficients of risk—numbers somewhat smaller than .0024% to .00024%—still be deemed "significant?"

* * * To assess whether Mauro posed a significant risk, the decision-maker should know more about any particular hazards (physical or moral) that might have affected the likelihood that this individual would transmit HIV to others. If surgeons whom the surgical technician assisted were to testify, for instance, that the assistant had a record of impeccable reliability, technical skills, and professionalism, and that they themselves were not concerned about risks they incurred by performing surgery with him, then a fact-finder could easily conclude that an employee with a contagious blood-borne disease did not pose a significant risk. On the other hand, if the testimony showed that the employee's co-workers found him to be inattentive, careless, and physically clumsy, then the jury might well conclude that, however small the theoretical risk of transmission, it would not be a safe bet for this particular person to continue working in surgery, and that he was not, therefore, "otherwise qualified."

It is perhaps to this end that the court notes that "the record included two incident reports involving Mauro [one of which] indicated that Mauro had sliced his right index finger while removing a knife blade from a handle on

June 25, 1991, and another [of which] indicated that he had scratched his hand with the sharp end of a dirty needle while threading it on June 8, 1990." However, there is absolutely no indication in the record, other than Nurse Hickman's wholly vague assertion that one of these incidents "might have resulted in patient exposure," that either of these events occurred during surgery, in proximity to a patient or another worker, or threatened anyone other than Mauro in any way. * * * One can imagine many other important facts that could be developed at trial and influence a jury's conclusions—for instance, the employees' viral load (and therefore his degree of contagiousness) at the time of his termination, and whether the person reliably took prescribed antiviral medications, and the effectiveness thereof.

* * *

The court apparently has concluded, though without an explicit statement, that Mauro sometimes participated, or might be expected to participate, in "exposure-prone" procedures. This conclusion seems to flow from the belief that any time a health-care worker enters or touches the surgical wound with his fingers or hands, then it is an "exposure-prone" procedure. The court appears to have misunderstood the Guidelines, which clearly contemplate that in the ordinary case, "surgical entry into tissues, cavities, or organs or repair of major traumatic injuries" should be regarded only as "invasive" procedures, not "exposure-prone" ones.

* * *

Notes and Questions

1.   Risk assessment is a critical function in the ADA's direct-threat defense. For discussion of who bears the burden of proof, see Sarah R. Christie, AIDS, Employment, and the Direct Threat Defense: The Burden of Proof and the Circuit Court Split, 76 Fordham L. Rev. 235 (2007). What resources would you use in assessing the risk presented? Manju Gupta, Occupational Risk: The Outrageous Reaction to HIV Positive Public Safety and Health Care Employees in the Workplace, 19 J. L. & Health 39 (2004–2005); Sidney D. Watson, Eliminating Fear Through Comparative Risk: Docs, AIDS and the Anti–Discrimination Ideal, 40 Buffalo L. Rev. 739 (1992); Mary Anne Bobinski, Risk and Rationality: The Centers for Disease Control and the Regulation of HIV–Infected Workers, 36 St. Louis U.L.J. 213 (1991). See also *Bragdon v. Abbott*, in Chapter 5, in which the Supreme Court considered how risk should be assessed in the case of a dentist refusing to care for an HIV-positive patient.

2.   *Mauro* is typical of cases that have considered claims by health care workers performing surgical functions. See e.g., Doe v. University of Maryland Med. System Corp., 50 F.3d 1261 (4th Cir. 1995). In decisions involving nonsurgical health care jobs, the courts have often rejected claims of unacceptable risk, viewing those risks as speculative or hypothetical. In Doe v. Attorney General, 62 F.3d 1424 (9th Cir. 1995), for example, the appellate court held that an HIV-infected physician performing medical exams was "otherwise qualified" as defined under § 504 of the Rehabilitation Act.

3.   As of 2003, the CDC reported 57 documented cases of occupational transmission of the virus to health care workers. Of these, twenty-six workers developed AIDS. There were an additional 139 HIV-positive health care workers who reported no risk factors for HIV and who reported workplace exposure to the

virus but who tested negative after the exposure. Worker Health Chartbook 2004. NIOSH Publication No. 2004–146. Surveillance indicates that the route of exposure makes a difference in whether the individual will become infected with the virus. The risk after needlestick or cut exposure to HIV-infected blood is 0.3% (99.7% of those who are exposed in that way do not become infected) and exposure of the mouth, eyes, or nose to HIV-infected blood is 0.1%. Post-exposure prophylactic treatment does bring its own health risks, and so it is not recommended for the lowest-risk exposures (as defined by route of exposure and HIV status of patient). See, CDC, Updated U.S. Public Health Service Guidelines for the Management of Occupational Exposures to HIV and Recommendations for Postexposure Prophylaxis, MMWR, September 30, 2005. In contrast, the risk of transmission of hepatitis C from needlestick is 1.8%. CDC, Exposure to Blood (2003). Because needlesticks present the greatest risk of transmission for HIV and other bloodborne pathogens, there are several regulatory efforts to set prevention standards, including efforts to engineer safety devices to avoid needlesticks.

There have been only six patients infected with HIV, and these are all reported from a single dentist before 1990. Studies conducted on 22,000 patients treated by 63 HIV-positive health care providers found no evidence of transmission from the providers. Are Patients in a Health Care Setting at Risk of Getting HIV?, available at www.cdc.gov/hiv/pubs/faq/faq29.htm.

4. The most common bloodborne infection in the U.S. is hepatitis C, and it is estimated that 3.9 million people in the U.S. have been infected. Of persons infected with hepatitis C, 70% will develop chronic liver disease with a death rate of approximately 3%. The virus is responsible for forty percent of all chronic liver disease which is the tenth leading cause of death in adults. It is most commonly transmitted by people who do not feel ill and, therefore, do not know that they are infected. The CDC has not made recommendations restricting the duties of health care workers infected with hepatitis C, and health care workers are only tested after they are exposed to blood or body fluids of patients. CDC, Recommendations for Prevention and Control of Hepatitis C Virus Infection and HCV–Related Chronic Disease, MMWR 1998. See also, Viral Hepatitis Transmission in Ambulatory Health Care Settings (Dec. 2006), http://www.cdc.gov/ncidod/diseases/hepatitis/spotlights/ambulatory.htm, reporting on transmission of the virus to patients in ambulatory care and recommending standard prevention efforts for bloodborne pathogens.

5. Health care workers with a wide variety of disabilities have brought claims under § 504 and the ADA. These cases can raise similar issues of accommodation and patient risk as do the HIV cases. For an overview, see Laura F. Rothstein, Health Care Professionals With Mental and Physical Impairments: Developments in Disability Discrimination Law, 41 St. Louis U.L.J. 973 (1997).

6. To make a claim under the ADA, an individual must prove that he or she has a disability as defined in the Act. The Supreme Court has developed a very narrow interpretation of the term. See, e.g., Sutton v. United Air Lines, 527 U.S. 471, 119 S.Ct. 2139, 144 L.Ed.2d 450 (1999), holding that a person with a "correctable" vision impairment is not disabled under the Act. See discussion of HIV as a disability in Chapter 5.

7. The ADA, Title VII, and the ADEA each relate to employment; however, these statutes do not use that term in its commonly understood sense. If the plaintiff can prove that he or she is dependent upon the defendant for opportunities to practice, the plaintiff generally will meet the requirement of an employment relationship. Health care professionals whose only relationship with a

hospital is traditional staff privileges usually do not meet the statutory standard for employment. See e.g., Shah v. Deaconess Hosp., 355 F.3d 496 (6th Cir. 2004). In Clackamas Gastronenterology Associates v. Wells, 538 U.S. 440, 123 S.Ct. 1673, 155 L.Ed.2d 615 (2003), the Supreme Court reversed a Ninth Circuit holding that physicians who are director-shareholders in a professional corporation are employees within the definition of the ADA, and remanded for examination of whether the plaintiff was an owner/manager with authority to hire and fire, assign tasks, supervise performance, and decide how profit and loss are distributed. But see, Hetz v. Aurora Med. Ctr. of Manitowoc County, 2007 WL 1753428 (E.D. Wis.), holding that the non-employee physician plaintiff could state a claim under Title II of the ADA governing public accommodations.

Chapter 10

THE STRUCTURE OF THE HEALTH CARE ENTERPRISE

I. INTRODUCTION

In 1978, Waldo, a 35 year old graphic artist, visited his family physician, Doctor Goodscalpel, complaining of gas, bloating and irregularity. Doctor Goodscalpel, a solo practitioner, took a brief history and ordered blood tests, urinalysis and various chemistry tests, all of which were performed at Llama Labs. Llama Labs was an outpatient facility organized as a corporation, the shares of which were owned by Dr. Goodscalpel and two other physicians. On a subsequent office visit several weeks later, Dr. Goodscalpel performed a rigid sigmoidoscopy and ordered x-rays for an upper GI which were done at the Midstate Hospital. Midstate was a small community hospital from which Dr. Goodscalpel leased his office and at which he maintained staff privileges.

The results of these tests led Dr. Goodscalpel to recommend that Waldo consult a specialist, Dr. Jones, a gastroenterologist, who was a member of Practice Group, a professional corporation located in an adjacent town. Dr. Jones admitted Waldo as an inpatient and performed a colonoscopy at Mt. St. Hilda Hospital, a not-for-profit teaching hospital controlled by the Order of Caramel Fellowship, a religious denomination that operates 20 hospitals nationwide. Unfortunately, during this procedure Waldo suffered a perforated colon and required additional surgery which was performed by Dr. Smith, whom Waldo met the night before the surgery and Dr. Mack, a resident studying at Mt. St. Hilda.

The bill for these services ran four pages and included over 150 separate services, items and supplies. Waldo's not-for-profit health insurance company, Red Flag, paid each provider separately for their services, although Waldo was responsible for nominal co-payments and in some cases, for the "balance billing" where the billed charges of the provider exceeded Red Flag's "maximum allowable charges."

Waldo's encounter with the health care system brought him into contact with a number of different kinds of health care providers doing business in a variety of organizational structures. Arrangements of this kind were not unusual a few years ago and persist even today in many communities. What kinds of problems and inefficiencies do you see arising from this "system" of delivery of services? What are its advantages? As a "consumer" of health services, was Waldo well-served in this episode? For example, how were choices made and on what basis?

This chapter will explore the legal issues posed by many of these business and institutional arrangements. It will also analyze the trend toward integration that has created many new organizational structures designed to unite the various providers of care. These new arrangements, it will be seen, are still in their formative stages and entail a host of legal issues for the modern health law practitioner.

II. FORMS OF BUSINESS ENTERPRISES AND THEIR LEGAL CONSEQUENCES

Like other businesspersons, health care providers may choose among a variety of organizational forms for conducting their businesses. Lawyers advising clients in the health care industry are increasingly called upon to devise arrangements that satisfy a number of distinct (and sometimes conflicting) objectives. These include: complying with various legal constraints; promoting the client's business or strategic goals; allocating risk and power among the parties in accordance with their desires; minimizing tax liabilities; and numerous others. Usually there is no single "correct" choice of business form and the process is best described as more of an art than a science. Plainly, effective counseling in this area requires a firm grasp of the numerous legal and strategic issues that will be involved.

A. CHOICE OF ENTITY

The following section briefly reviews the alternative legal entities and their principal advantages and disadvantages. For the most part, state law governs the principal legal relationships among participants in these organizational forms. In many important respects, legal relationships may be altered by carefully drafted agreements or by modifications of the statutory norm through the organizational documents.

For–Profit Corporations. This form of business organization offers the important advantages of limited liability for its owners (shareholders), centralized management through a board of directors and its officers, continuity of existence, and easy transferability of ownership. Of great practical importance is the capacity of the for-profit corporation form to raise capital for business enterprises. A significant downside is the possibility of double taxation, as both the entity and its shareholders may be taxed on the same income. (One method of avoiding double taxation is choosing the S Corporation form; however, this option is in practice limited to small corporations because of requirements that it have 35 or fewer shareholders, ownership only by individuals and not business entities, and that it offer only one class of stock.)

Control of the corporation is shared by its shareholders, board of directors and officers. Shareholders elect the board and have voting rights on certain matters such as amending the articles of incorporation or bylaws, selling a major portion of corporate assets or merging with another business. However, shareholders have no control over routine business decisions. These powers are vested in the board of directors, which may delegate substantial authority to the corporate officers. The power to control the corporation flows from the power to elect the board of directors. Voting shares in "plain vanilla" corporate structures are distributed according to the shareholders' contributions of capital, property or services. However, it is possible to allocate control by a variety of devices, such as issuance of debt, preferred or other stock with limited voting rights, classified shares, and other means.

In large, publicly traded corporations, it is common for the board to perform at most an advisory or counseling role: in practice, the officers run the corporation. Members of the board of directors and officers are bound by common law and statutory fiduciary duties to exercise care and avoid self-dealing when overseeing the business affairs of the corporation. Publicly traded corporations, i.e. those whose shares are exchanged on national securities or over-the-counter exchanges, offer the ability to raise large amounts of capital more easily than other forms. However, state and federal securities laws may impose substantial costs on corporations that are not exempt from regulation.

Not-for-profit Corporations. Not-for-profit corporations do not have owners who share in the entity's profits. However, this form may have members who elect the board of directors and reserve certain powers such as amending the entity's articles of incorporation or bylaws. The defining characteristic of not-for-profit corporations is the so-called "nondistribution constraint." That is, although these entities may earn substantial profits (or "surpluses," as they are euphemistically called), those funds must be devoted to the entities' charitable, religious or other public purposes. Moreover, to avoid taxation, it must comply with the requirements for exemption under section 501 (c)(3) of the Internal Revenue Code. Although unable to sell stock, not-for-profits may obtain tax-exempt financing as a source of capital.

Professional Corporations. All states permit professionals to conduct business under the corporate form. For the most part these statutes adopt the same legal rules that apply to other business corporations. However, several important differences typically exist. First, shareholders are not shielded from personal liability for their own acts of professional negligence or for the acts of others working under their direct supervision. However, the statutes typically provide limited liability for the negligence of other professionals and for the corporation's liabilities for nonprofessional activities. Second, most statutes stipulate that only licensed professionals may be shareholders of professional corporations and that the board of directors must be comprised entirely or by a majority of professionals.

Partnerships. General partnerships are associations of two or more persons who act as co-owners of a business. Important features include unlimited personal liability of all partners for partnership debts and the ability of all partners to participate in the management of the partnership and to bind the partnership. A significant advantage of this business form is the absence of double taxation: While each partner is liable for his or her share of partnership income, the partnership is not taxed on its business income. A second attractive feature is the informal means by which business can be conducted.

Limited Partnerships. Limited partnerships differ from general partnerships in that the former include limited partners who enjoy limited liability similar to that of corporate shareholders. The limited partner is restricted in the extent to which he may participate in the management and control of the business. Limited partnerships must have at least one general partner who bears the same unlimited liability as a partner in a general partnership and who assumes responsibility for management of the business. Hence the limited partnership affords many of the corporate advantages of raising capital through passive investment. However, limited partnership interests are also treated as securities and are subject to regulation under federal and state securities laws.

Limited Liability Companies and Limited Liability Partnerships. All states have adopted statutes authorizing limited liability companies and limited liability partnerships. These business forms combine some of the most attractive features of partnerships and corporations: limited liability for all owners; pass-through tax treatment free transferability of ownership; and centralized management. The statutes generally place no ceiling on the permissible number of owners, permit different classes of ownership, and allow for ownership by entities such as corporations.

Questions

What are the advantages and disadvantages of each business form for two small-town family practitioners joining together to form a medical group? For a big city hospital establishing a jointly-owned MRI facility with its specialists? What factors would be relevant in making your recommendation? What information would you need to elicit from each client?

B. GOVERNANCE AND FIDUCIARY DUTIES IN BUSINESS ASSOCIATIONS

The governance of corporations is shared by three groups: shareholders (or members in the case of some not-for-profits), the board of directors, and officers. In practice, particularly in large corporations, the officers have almost complete control over the business affairs of the corporation. This separation of ownership and control in the for-profit corporate setting may give rise to the exploitation of shareholders. It also poses problems in not-for-profit corporations as boards may not faithfully or diligently pursue the entity's charitable purposes. To deal with this problem, the common law imposes fiduciary duties on those who govern the corporation, essentially obligating directors and officers to act in its best interests.

STERN v. LUCY WEBB HAYES NATIONAL TRAINING SCHOOL FOR DEACONESSES AND MISSIONARIES

United States District Court, District of Columbia, 1974.
381 F.Supp. 1003.

GESELL, DISTRICT JUDGE.

This is a class action which was tried to the Court without a jury. Plaintiffs were certified as a class under Rule 23(b)(2) of the Federal Rules of Civil Procedure and represent patients of Sibley Memorial Hospital, a District of Columbia non-profit charitable corporation organized under D.C.Code s 29–1001 et seq. They challenge various aspects of the Hospital's fiscal management. The amended complaint named as defendants nine members of the Hospital's Board of Trustees, six financial institutions, and the Hospital itself. Four trustees and one financial institution were dropped by plaintiffs prior to trial, and the Court dismissed the complaint as to the remaining financial institutions at the close of plaintiffs' case.

* * *

The two principal contentions in the complaint are that the defendant trustees conspired to enrich themselves and certain financial institutions with which they were affiliated by favoring those institutions in financial dealings with the Hospital, and that they breached their fiduciary duties of care and loyalty in the management of Sibley's funds. The defendant financial institutions are said to have joined in the alleged conspiracy and to have knowingly benefited from the alleged breaches of duty. The Hospital is named as a nominal defendant for the purpose of facilitating relief.

I. CORPORATE HISTORY

The Lucy Webb Hayes National Training School for Deaconesses and Missionaries was established in 1891 by the Methodist Women's Home Missionary Society for the purpose, in part, of providing health care services to the poor of the Washington area. The School was incorporated under the laws of the District of Columbia as a charitable, benevolent and educational institution by instrument dated August 8, 1894. During the following year, the School built the Sibley Memorial Hospital on North Capitol Street to facilitate its charitable work. Over the years, operation of the Hospital has become the School's principal concern, so that the two institutions have been referred to synonymously by all parties and will be so treated in this Opinion.

* * *

Under the ... by-laws, the Board was to consist of from 25 to 35 trustees, who were to meet at least twice each year. Between such meetings, an Executive Committee was to represent the Board, and was authorized, inter alia, to open checking and savings accounts, approve the Hospital budget, renew mortgages, and enter into contracts. A Finance Committee was created to review the budget and to report regularly on the amount of cash available for investment. Management of those investments was to be supervised by an Investment Committee, which was to work closely with the Finance Committee in such matters.

In fact, management of the Hospital from the early 1950's until 1968 was handled almost exclusively by two trustee officers: Dr. Orem, the Hospital Administrator, and Mr. Ernst, the Treasurer. Unlike most of their fellow trustees, to whom membership on the Sibley Board was a charitable service incidental to their principal vocations, Orem and Ernst were continuously involved on almost a daily basis in the affairs of Sibley. They dominated the Board and its Executive Committee, which routinely accepted their recommendations and ratified their actions. Even more significantly, neither the Finance Committee nor the Investment Committee ever met or conducted business from the date of their creation until 1971, three years after the death of Dr. Orem. As a result, budgetary and investment decisions during this period, like most other management decisions affecting the Hospital's finances, were handled by Orem and Ernst, receiving only cursory supervision from the Executive Committee and the full Board.

Dr. Orem's death on April 5, 1968, obliged some of the other trustees to play a more active role in running the Hospital. The Executive Committee, and particularly defendant Stacy Reed (as Chairman of the Board, President of the Hospital, and ex officio member of the Executive Committee), became more deeply involved in the day-to-day management of the Hospital while efforts were made to find a new Administrator. The man who was eventually selected for that office, Dr. Jarvis, had little managerial experience and his performance was not entirely satisfactory. Mr. Ernst still made most of the financial and investment decisions for Sibley, but his actions and failures to act came slowly under increasing scrutiny by several of the other trustees, particularly after a series of disagreements between Ernst and the Hospital Comptroller which led to the discharge of the latter early in 1971.

Prompted by these difficulties, Mr. Reed decided to activate the Finance and Investment Committee in the Fall of 1971. However, as Chairman of the Finance Committee and member of the Investment Committee as well as Treasurer, Mr. Ernst continued to exercise dominant control over investment decisions and, on several occasions, discouraged and flatly refused to respond to inquiries by other trustees into such matters. It has only been since the death of Mr. Ernst on October 30, 1972, that the other trustees appear to have assumed an identifiable supervisory role over investment policy and Hospital fiscal management in general.

Against this background, the basic claims will be examined.

II. CONSPIRACY

Plaintiffs first contend that the five defendant trustees and the five defendant financial institutions were involved in a conspiracy to enrich themselves at the expense of the Hospital. They point to the fact that each named trustee held positions of responsibility with one or more of the defendant institutions as evidence that the trustees had both motive and opportunity to carry out such a conspiracy.

* * *

Plaintiffs further contend that the defendants accomplished the alleged conspiracy by arranging to have Sibley maintain unnecessarily large amounts of money on deposit with the defendant banks and savings and loan associations, drawing inadequate or no interest. [T]he Hospital in fact maintained much of its liquid assets in savings and checking accounts rather than in Treasury bonds or investment securities, at least until the investment review instituted by Mr. Reed late in 1971. In that year, for example, more than one-third of the nearly four million dollars available for investment was deposited in checking accounts, as compared to only about $135,000 in securities and $311,000 in Treasury bills.

* * *

It is also undisputed that most of these funds were deposited in the defendant financial institutions. A single checking account, drawing no interest whatever and maintained alternately at Riggs National Bank and Security

National Bank, usually contained more than $250,000 and on one occasion grew to nearly $1,000,000.

Defendants were able to offer no adequate justification for this utilization of the Hospital's liquid assets. By the same token, however, plaintiffs failed to establish that it was [the] result of a conscious direction on the part of the named defendants.

* * *

[The court concluded that plaintiffs failed to establish a conspiracy between the trustees and the financial institutions or among the members of each group.]

III. BREACH OF DUTY

Plaintiffs' second contention is that, even if the facts do not establish a conspiracy, they do reveal serious breaches of duty on the part of the defendant trustees and the knowing acceptance of benefits from those breaches by the defendant banks and savings and loan associations.

A. The Trustees

Basically, the trustees are charged with mismanagement, nonmanagement and self-dealing. * * * [T]he modern trend is to apply corporate rather than trust principles in determining the liability of the directors of charitable corporations, because their functions are virtually indistinguishable from those of their "pure" corporate counterparts.

1. Mismanagement

Both trustees and corporate directors are liable for losses occasioned by their negligent mismanagement of investments. However, the degree of care required appears to differ in many jurisdictions. A trustee is uniformly held to a high standard of care and will be held liable for simple negligence, while a director must often have committed "gross negligence" or otherwise be guilty of more than mere mistakes of judgment.

This distinction may amount to little more than a recognition of the fact that corporate directors have many areas of responsibility, while the traditional trustee is often charged only with the management of the trust funds and can therefore be expected to devote more time and expertise to that task. Since the board members of most large charitable corporations fall within the corporate rather than the trust model, being charged with the operation of ongoing businesses, it has been said that they should only be held to the less stringent corporate standard of care. Beard v. Achenbach Mem. Hosp. Ass'n, 170 F.2d 859, 862 (10th Cir.1948). More specifically, directors of charitable corporations are required to exercise ordinary and reasonable care in the performance of their duties, exhibiting honesty and good faith. Beard v. Achenbach Mem. Hosp. Ass'n, *supra*, at 862.

2. Nonmanagement

Plaintiffs allege that the individual defendants failed to supervise the management of Hospital investments or even to attend meetings of the committees charged with such supervision. Trustees are particularly vulnerable to such a charge, because they not only have an affirmative duty to "maximize the trust income by prudent investment," Blankenship v. Boyle, 329 F.Supp. 1089, 1096 (D.D.C. 1971), but they may not delegate that duty, even to a committee of their fellow trustees. Restatement (Second) of Trusts § 171, at 375 (1959). A corporate director, on the other hand, may delegate his investment responsibility to fellow directors, corporate officers, or even outsiders, but he must continue to exercise general supervision over the activities of his delegates. Once again, the rule for charitable corporations is closer to the traditional corporate rule: directors should at least be permitted to delegate investment decisions to a committee of board members, so long as all directors assume the responsibility for supervising such committees by periodically scrutinizing their work.

Total abdication of the supervisory role, however, is improper even under traditional corporate principles. A director who fails to acquire the information necessary to supervise investment policy or consistently fails even to attend the meetings at which such policies are considered has violated his fiduciary duty to the corporation. While a director is, of course, permitted to rely upon the expertise of those to whom he has delegated investment responsibility, such reliance is a tool for interpreting the delegate's reports, not an excuse for dispensing with or ignoring such reports. A director whose failure to supervise permits negligent mismanagement by others to go unchecked has committed an independent wrong against the corporation; he is not merely an accessory under an attenuated theory of respondent [sic] superior or constructive notice.

3. *Self-dealing*

Under District of Columbia Law, neither trustees nor corporate directors are absolutely barred from placing funds under their control into a bank having an interlocking directorship with their own institution. In both cases, however, such transactions will be subjected to the closest scrutiny to determine whether or not the duty of loyalty has been violated. A deliberate conspiracy among trustees or Board members to enrich the interlocking bank at the expense of the trust or corporation would, for example, constitute such a breach and render the conspirators liable for any losses. In the absence of clear evidence of wrongdoing, however, the courts appear to have used different standards to determine whether or not relief is appropriate, depending again on the legal relationship involved. Trustees may be found guilty of a breach of trust even for mere negligence in the maintenance of accounts in banks with which they are associated, while corporate directors are generally only required to show "entire fairness" to the corporation and "full disclosure" of the potential conflict of interest to the Board.

Most courts apply the less stringent corporate rule to charitable corporations in this area as well. It is, however, occasionally added that a director should not only disclose his interlocking responsibilities but also refrain from voting on or otherwise influencing a corporate decision to transact business with a company in which he has a significant interest or control.

Although defendants have argued against the imposition of even these limitations on self-dealing by the Sibley trustees, the Hospital Board recently adopted a new by-law, based upon guidelines issued by the American Hospital Association, which essentially imposes the modified corporate rule. * * *

* * *

Having surveyed the authorities as outlined above and weighed the briefs, arguments and evidence submitted by counsel, the Court holds that a director or so-called trustee of a charitable hospital organized under the Non–Profit Corporation Act of the District of Columbia [ ] is in default of his fiduciary duty to manage the fiscal and investment affairs of the hospital if it has been shown by a preponderance of the evidence that:

(1) while assigned to a particular committee of the Board having general financial or investment responsibility under the by-laws of the corporation, he has failed to use due diligence in supervising the actions of those officers, employees or outside experts to whom the responsibility for making day-to-day financial or investment decisions has been delegated; or

(2) he knowingly permitted the hospital to enter into a business transaction with himself or with any corporation, partnership or association in which he then had a substantial interest or held a position as trustee, director, general manager or principal officer without having previously informed the persons charged with approving that transaction of his interest or position and of any significant reasons, unknown to or not fully appreciated by such persons, why the transaction might not be in the best interests of the hospital; or

(3) except as required by the preceding paragraph, he actively participated in or voted in favor of a decision by the Board or any committee or subcommittee thereof to transact business with himself or with any corporation, partnership or association in which he then had a substantial interest or held a position as trustee, director, general manager or principal officer; or

(4) he otherwise failed to perform his duties honestly, in good faith, and with a reasonable amount of diligence and care.

Applying these standards to the facts in the record, the Court finds that each of the defendant trustees has breached his fiduciary duty to supervise the management of Sibley's investments. All except Mr. Jones were duly and repeatedly elected to the Investment Committee without ever bothering to object when no meetings were called for more than ten years. Mr. Jones was a member of the equally inactive Finance Committee, the failure of which to report on the existence of investable funds was cited by several other defendants as a reason for not convening the Investment Committee. In addition, Reed, Jones and Smith were, for varying periods of time, also members of the Executive Committee, which was charged with acquiring at least enough information to vote intelligently on the opening of new bank accounts. By their own testimony, it is clear that they failed to do so. And all of the individual defendants ignored the investment sections of the yearly audits which were made available to them as members of the Board. In short, these men have in the past failed to exercise even the most cursory supervision over the handling of Hospital funds and failed to establish and carry out a defined policy.

The record is unclear on the degree to which full disclosure preceded the frequent self-dealing which occurred during the period under consideration. It is reasonable to assume that the Board was generally aware of the various bank affiliations of the defendant trustees, but there is no indication that these conflicting interests were brought home to the relevant committees when they voted to approve particular transactions. Similarly, while plaintiffs have shown no active misrepresentation on defendants' part, they have established instances in which an interested trustee failed to alert the responsible officials to better terms known to be available elsewhere.

It is clear that all of the defendant trustees have, at one time or another, affirmatively approved self-dealing transactions. Most of these incidents were of relatively minor significance.

* * *

That the Hospital has suffered no measurable injury from many of these transactions—including the mortgage and the investment contract—and that the excessive deposits which were the real source of harm were caused primarily by the uniform failure to supervise rather than the occasional self-dealing vote are both facts that the Court must take into account in fashioning relief, but they do not alter the principle that the trustee of a charitable hospital should always avoid active participation in a transaction in which he or a corporation with which he is associated has a significant interest.

* * *

IV. RELIEF
* * *

[The Court ordered by injunction (1) that the appropriate committees and officers of the Hospital present to the full Board a written policy statement governing investments and the use of idle cash in the Hospital's bank accounts and other funds, (2) the establishment of a procedure for the periodic reexamination of existing investments and other financial arrangements to insure compliance with Board policies, and (3) that each trustee fully disclose his affiliation with financial institutions doing business with the Hospital. Declining to remove defendant trustees from the Board or to impose personal liability on directors, Judge Gesell offered the following guidance.]

The management of a non-profit charitable hospital imposes a severe obligation upon its trustees. A hospital such as Sibley is not closely regulated by any public authority, it has no responsibility to file financial reports, and its Board is self-perpetuating. The interests of its patients are funneled primarily through large group insurers who pay the patients' bills, and the patients lack meaningful participation in the Hospital's affairs. It is obvious that, in due course, new trustees must come to the Board of this Hospital, some of whom will be affiliated with banks, savings and loan associations and other financial institutions. The tendency of representatives of such institutions is often to seek business in return for advice and assistance rendered as trustees. It must be made absolutely clear that Board membership carries no right to preferential treatment in the placement or handling of the Hospital's investments and business accounts. The Hospital would be well advised to restrict membership on its Board to the representatives of financial institutions which have no substantial business relationship with the Hospital. The best way to avoid potential conflicts of interest and to be assured of objective advice is to avoid the possibility of such conflicts at the time new trustees are selected.

As an additional safeguard, the Court will require that each newly-elected trustee read this Opinion and the attached Order. [The Court also required public disclosure of all business dealings between the hospital and any financial institution with which any officer or trustee of the hospital is affiliated and that the hospital make summaries of all such dealings available on request to all patients.]

IN RE CAREMARK INTERNATIONAL INC. DERIVATIVE LITIGATION

Court of Chancery of Delaware, 1996.
698 A.2d 959.

ALLEN, CHANCELLOR.

Pending is a motion ... to approve as fair and reasonable a proposed settlement of a consolidated derivative action on behalf of Caremark International, Inc. ("Caremark"). The suit involves claims that the members of Caremark's board of directors (the "Board") breached their fiduciary duty of care to Caremark in connection with alleged violations by Caremark employees of federal and state laws and regulations applicable to health care providers. As a result of the alleged violations, Caremark was subject to an extensive four year investigation by the United States Department of Health and Human Services and the Department of Justice. In 1994 Caremark was charged in an indictment with multiple felonies. It thereafter entered into a number of agreements with the Department of Justice and others. Those agreements included a plea agreement in which Caremark pleaded guilty to a single felony of mail fraud and agreed to pay civil and criminal fines. Subsequently, Caremark agreed to make reimbursements to various private and public parties. In all, the payments that Caremark has been required to make total approximately $250 million.

This suit was filed in 1994, purporting to seek on behalf of the company recovery of these losses from the individual defendants who constitute the board of directors of Caremark. The parties now propose that it be settled.

* * *

The ultimate issue then is whether the proposed settlement appears to be fair to the corporation and its absent shareholders.

* * *

Legally, evaluation of the central claim made entails consideration of the legal standard governing a board of directors' obligation to supervise or monitor corporate performance. For the reasons set forth below I conclude, in light of the discovery record, that there is a very low probability that it would be determined that the directors of Caremark breached any duty to appropriately monitor and supervise the enterprise. Indeed the record tends to show an active consideration by Caremark management and its Board of the Caremark structures and programs that ultimately led to the company's indictment and to the large financial losses incurred in the settlement of those claims. It does not tend to show knowing or intentional violation of law. Neither the fact that the Board, although advised by lawyers and accountants, did not accurately predict the severe consequences to the company that would ultimately follow from the deployment by the company of the strategies and practices that ultimately led to this liability, nor the scale of the liability, gives rise to an inference of breach of any duty imposed by corporation law upon the directors of Caremark.

[As part of its patient care business, which accounted for the majority of its revenues, Caremark provided alternative site health care services, including infusion therapy, growth hormone therapy, HIV/AIDS-related treatments and hemophilia therapy. Caremark's managed care services included prescription drug programs and the operation of multi-specialty group practices and it employed over 7,000 employees in ninety branch operations. It had a decentralized management structure but began to centralize operations in 1991 to increase supervision over branch operations. Caremark had taken a number of steps to assure compliance with the antikickback provisions of the Medicare fraud and abuse law discussed in Chapter 11. As early as 1989, Caremark's predecessor issued an internal "Guide to Contractual Relationships" ("Guide"), which was reviewed and updated, annually, to govern its employees in entering into contracts with physicians and hospitals. Caremark claimed there was uncertainty concerning the interpretation of federal antikickback laws because of the scarcity of court decisions and the "limited guidance" afforded by HHS "safe harbor" regulations. After the federal government had commenced its investigation, Caremark announced that it would no longer pay management fees to physicians for services to Medicare and Medicaid patients and required its regional officers to approve each contractual relationship it entered into with a physician. Caremark also established an internal audit plan designed to assure compliance with its business and ethics policies. Although a report by Price Waterhouse, its outside auditor, concluded that there were no material weaknesses in Caremark's control structure, the Board's ethics committee adopted a new internal audit charter, and took various other steps throughout to assure compliance with its policies.

In August and September, 1994, two federal grand juries indicted Caremark and individuals for violations of the anti-kickback laws, charging among other things that Caremark had made payments to a physician under "the guise of research grants ... and consulting agreements" so he would prescribe Protropin, a Caremark-manufactured drug. Plaintiff shareholders filed this derivative suit claiming Caremark directors breached their duty of care by failing adequately to supervise Caremark employees or institute corrective measures thereby exposing the company to liability. In September, 1994, Caremark publicly announced that as of January 1, 1995, it would terminate all remaining financial relationships with physicians in its home infusion, hemophilia, and growth hormone lines of business.]

B. DIRECTORS' DUTIES TO MONITOR CORPORATE OPERATIONS

The complaint charges the director defendants with breach of their duty of attention or care in connection with the on-going operation of the corporation's business. The claim is that the directors allowed a situation to develop and continue which exposed the corporation to enormous legal liability and that in so doing they violated a duty to be active monitors of corporate performance. The complaint thus does not charge either director self-dealing or the more difficult loyalty-type problems arising from cases of suspect director motivation, such as entrenchment or sale of control contexts. The theory here advanced is possibly the most difficult theory in corporation law upon which a plaintiff might hope to win a judgment. * * *

1. Potential liability for directorial decisions: Director liability for a breach of the duty to exercise appropriate attention may, in theory, arise in two distinct contexts. First, such liability may be said to follow from a board decision that results in a loss because that decision was ill advised or "negligent". Second, liability to the corporation for a loss may be said to arise from an unconsidered failure of the board to act in circumstances in which due attention would, arguably, have prevented the loss. The first class of cases will typically be subject to review under the director-protective business judgment rule, assuming the decision made was the product of a process that was either deliberately considered in good faith or was otherwise rational. What should be understood, but may not widely be understood by courts or commentators who are not often required to face such questions, is that compliance with a director's duty of care can never appropriately be judicially determined by reference to the content of the board decision that leads to a corporate loss, apart from consideration of the good faith or rationality of the process employed. That is, whether a judge or jury considering the matter after the fact, believes a decision substantively wrong, or degrees of wrong extending through "stupid" to "egregious" or "irrational", provides no ground for director liability, so long as the court determines that the process employed was either rational or employed in a good faith effort to advance corporate interests. To employ a different rule—one that permitted an "objective" evaluation of the decision—would expose directors to substantive second guessing by ill-equipped judges or juries, which would, in the long-run, be injurious to investor interests.[1] Thus, the business judgment rule is process oriented and informed by a deep respect for all good faith board decisions.

2. Liability for failure to monitor: The second class of cases in which director liability for inattention is theoretically possible entail circumstances in which a loss eventuates not from a decision but, from unconsidered inaction. Most of the decisions that a corporation, acting through its human agents, makes are, of course, not the subject of director attention. Legally, the board itself will be required only to authorize the most significant corporate acts or transactions: mergers, changes in capital structure, fundamental changes in business, appointment and compensation of the CEO, etc. As the facts of this case graphically demonstrate, ordinary business decisions that are made by officers and employees deeper in the interior of the organization can,

---

1. The vocabulary of negligence while often employed, is not well-suited to judicial review of board attentiveness, especially if one attempts to look to the substance of the decision as any evidence of possible "negligence." * * * It is doubtful that we want business men and women to be encouraged to make decisions as hypothetical persons of ordinary judgment and prudence might. The corporate form gets its utility in large part from its ability to allow diversified investors to accept greater investment risk. If those in charge of the corporation are to be adjudged personally liable for losses on the basis of a substantive judgment based upon what persons of ordinary or average judgment and average risk assessment talent regard as "prudent," "sensible" or even "rational", such persons will have a strong incentive at the margin to authorize less risky investment projects.

however, vitally affect the welfare of the corporation and its ability to achieve its various strategic and financial goals.

Modernly this question has been given special importance by an increasing tendency, especially under federal law, to employ the criminal law to assure corporate compliance with external legal requirements, including environmental, financial, employee and product safety as well as assorted other health and safety regulations. In 1991, pursuant to the Sentencing Reform Act of 1984, the United States Sentencing Commission adopted Organizational Sentencing Guidelines which impact importantly on the prospective effect these criminal sanctions might have on business corporations. The Guidelines set forth a uniform sentencing structure for organizations to be sentenced for violation of federal criminal statutes and provide for penalties that equal or often massively exceed those previously imposed on corporations. The Guidelines offer powerful incentives for corporations today to have in place compliance programs to detect violations of law, promptly to report violations to appropriate public officials when discovered, and to take prompt, voluntary remedial efforts.

* * *

[I]t would, in my opinion, be a mistake to conclude that our Supreme Court's [prior statements regarding directors' duty to monitor] means that corporate boards may satisfy their obligation to be reasonably informed concerning the corporation, without assuring themselves that information and reporting systems exist in the organization that are reasonably designed to provide to senior management and to the board itself timely, accurate information sufficient to allow management and the board, each within its scope, to reach informed judgments concerning both the corporation's compliance with law and its business performance.

Obviously the level of detail that is appropriate for such an information system is a question of business judgment. And obviously too, no rationally designed information and reporting system will remove the possibility that the corporation will violate laws or regulations, or that senior officers or directors may nevertheless sometimes be misled or otherwise fail reasonably to detect acts material to the corporation's compliance with the law. But it is important that the board exercise a good faith judgment that the corporation's information and reporting system is in concept and design adequate to assure the board that appropriate information will come to its attention in a timely manner as a matter of ordinary operations, so that it may satisfy its responsibility.

Thus, I am of the view that a director's obligation includes a duty to attempt in good faith to assure that a corporate information and reporting system, which the board concludes is adequate, exists, and that failure to do so under some circumstances may, in theory at least, render a director liable for losses caused by non-compliance with applicable legal standards.

* * *

[The Court went on to find that the Caremark directors had not breached their duty of care because, first, there was no evidence they knew of the violations of the law and they reasonably relied on expert reports that their company's practices, although "contestable," were lawful. Second, applying a test of whether there was a "sustained or systematic failure ... to exercise reasonable oversight," it found no actionable failure to monitor. The court concluded that the corporate oversight systems described above constituted a "good faith effort to be informed of relevant facts."]

Notes and Questions

1. Section 8.30 of The Revised Model Nonprofit Corporation Act adopts the corporate standard for the members of the board ("trustees") of not-for-profits, as do many state statutes. What arguments support a stricter standard for not-for-profit corporations? For one case applying a trust standard, see Lynch v. John M. Redfield Foundation, 9 Cal.App.3d 293, 88 Cal.Rptr. 86 (1970). See generally Daniel L. Kurtz, Board Liability: Guide for Nonprofit Directors 22 (1988). Might a shifting standard of care apply, depending on the nature of the decision and how important that decision is to the organization's core functions or the community benefits it was designed to supply? See James J. Fishman & Stephen Schwarz, Nonprofit Organizations, 225–6 (2d. ed. 2000); 1 Furrow, et al., Health Law § 5–15—5–16 (2d ed. 2000). See also discussion of IRC § 501(c)(3) requirements *infra* this chapter. Thoughtful discussions of the issue of fiduciary duties in nonprofit charities can be found in American Law Institute, Principles of the Law of Nonprofit Organizations, Tentative Draft No. 1 (March 19, 2007) and James Fishman, Improving Charitable Accountability, 62 Md. L. Rev. 218 (2003).

2. In the case of for-profit corporations, the business judgment rule has come to pose an almost impermeable shield protecting directors and officers charged with breaches of the duty of care in connection with business decisions that prove to be unwise or imprudent. As long as the director has made a business judgment that is informed, in good faith and free of conflicts of interest, that judgment will not be subject to attack, even if the decision would not meet the simple negligence standard applicable to the "ordinarily prudent person." See Charles Hansen, The ALI Corporate Governance Project: Of the Duty of Care and the Business Judgment Rule, 41 Bus. Law. 1237 (1986). Should the business judgment rule apply with equal force to not-for-profit corporations? See Beard v. Achenbach Mem. Hosp. Association, 170 F.2d 859, 862 (10th Cir.1948) (business judgment rationale used to uphold hospital's payment of questionable retroactive "incentive bonuses"). Does the absence of shareholders or a public market for the stock make a difference? Are directors of not-for-profit boards more or less likely to be vigilant and savvy businesspersons than their for-profit counterparts? As Evelyn Brody has noted, because of the "pervasive challenge" posed by the "financially generous supporter who has little interest in participating in governance," many recommend adopting structural arrangements such as "strong executive committees and advisory boards." ALI Principles of the Law of Nonprofit Organizations, Reporter's memorandum at xxxv. See also 1 Furrow et al., Health Law § 5–15a (2d ed. 2000); Michael Peregrine, Revisiting the Duty of Care of the Nonprofit Director, 36 J. Health L. 183 (2003). For the view that the decision in the Sibley Hospital case typified the tendency of courts to be more receptive to duty of care complaints where the transaction is tainted by duty-of-loyalty implications, see Evelyn Brody, The Limits of Charity Fiduciary Law, 57 Md. L. Rev. 1400, 1442 (1998) ("One wonders whether Judge Gesell would have found any duty-of-care breach—or, more important, even granted standing to the plaintiff patients—had the funds been deposited at banks where the hospitals' directors were not also directors."). On the fiduciary duties of boards in health care institutions generally, see Naomi Ono, Boards of Directors Under Fire: An Examination of Nonprofit Board Duties in the Health Care Environment, 7 Annals Health L. 107 (1998); Peggy Sasso, Comment, Searching for Trust in the

Not–For–Profit Boardroom: Looking Beyond the Duty of Obedience to Ensure Acccuntability, 50 UCLA L.Rev. 1485 (2003); Denise Ping Lee, Note, The Business Judgment Rule: Should it Protect Nonprofit Directors? 103 Colum. L.Rev. 925 (2003).

Does the standard established by the Chancellor in approving the settlement of the Caremark litigation give directors and senior officers of large, far-flung corporate enterprises sufficient incentives to ensure that their employees comply with the law? What factors mitigate against imposing a simple negligence standard with regard to the duty to monitor? Are the interests of the Caremark shareholders advanced by this holding? What role, if any, should the public interest in compliance with the anti-kickback laws play?

3. *Executive Compensation in Nonprofit Healthcare Organizations.* Consider also the increasingly controversial issue of executive compensation for nonprofit managers. Should the business judgment rule protect directors who pay little attention to the details of sometimes extravagant compensation packages they award to top executives? In the for-profit sector, the rule has shielded boards that have been extremely lax in their oversight of executive pay, although an emerging "good faith" requirement may give courts some additional elbowroom to review egregious abuses in this area. See In re Walt Disney Co. Derivative Litigation, 906 A.2d 27 (Del. Supr. 2006); Sarah H. Duggin & Stephan M. Goldman, Restoring Trust in Corporate Directors: The Disney Standard and the "New" Good Faith, 56 Am. U. L. Rev. 211 (2006).

> A GAO survey of the 65 largest nonprofit hospital systems found that most hospitals had in place an executive compensation committee or entire board with the primary responsibility of approving executives' compensation packages and a conflict of interest policy and processes that reviewed comparable market data of total compensation and benefits. However, almost 40% had no written criteria for the selection of compensation committee members and did not require that compensation consultants be free of conflicts of interest; furthermore, 16% allowed the CEO or other top executives to be a voting member of an Executive Compensation body. Kimberly Brooks, et al., General Accountability Office, Survey of Nonprofit Health Systems Executive Compensation Policies (June 2006), www.gao.gov/new.items/d06907r.pdf., George Anning, et al., AHLA Corporate Governance Task Force, Corporate Governance Implications of Nonprofit Executive Compensation (June 2007). Should the executive compensation practices of nonprofit hospitals be held to a different standard than for profit entities? For that matter, should executives be paid less than their counterparts in the private sector? If your answer is yes to these questions, is scrutiny of approval practices of boards using fiduciary duties an efficient way of assuring the best results? Note that we will revisit this issue later in the chapter in the discussion of federal tax policies. In addition, some commentators and courts also recognize a "duty of obedience" which obligates directors to see to it that nonprofit corporations comply with legal obligations and adhere at all times to their corporate purposes or mission. This duty is discussed in the following section of this chapter.

4. The duty of loyalty applies to a variety of transactions in which directors or officers acting in their corporate capacity serve their own interests at the expense of those of the corporation. Self-dealing, taking of corporate opportunities, and acting in competition with the corporation may violate this duty. See, e.g. Gilbert v. McLeod Infirmary, 219 S.C. 174, 64 S.E.2d 524 (1951) (sale of property by hospital to trustees void where board members participated in the approval of the transaction and the hospital did not seek other buyers); Delaware Open MRI

Radiology Associates v. Kessler, 898 A.2d 290 (Del. Ch. 2006) (directors representing majority shareholders of radiology group voting to "squeeze out" minority's ownership via merger constitutes conflict of interest and subjects transaction to judicial review of fairness of procedure and of buyout price). However, directors owe fiduciary duties only to their corporations, not to individual shareholders. Hence a professional corporation's termination of the contract of a physician shareholder-employee will not implicate the duty of loyalty. Berman v. Physical Medicine Associates, 225 F.3d 429 (4th Cir. 2000). State attorneys general have frequently advanced claims based on breaches of the duty of loyalty in cases involving conflicts of interest such as a hospital entering into an emergency room contract with a physician group owned by the chairman of its board; loans from a hospital to a physician serving on the board; and the hiring of architectural firms and employment agencies in which trustees have an interest. See Michael W. Peregrine, The Nonprofit Board's Duty of Loyalty in an "Integrated" World, 29 J. Health L. 211 (1996).

Most state statutes governing nonprofit and for-profit corporations make it relatively easy to resolve such conflicts of interest. (Can you explain the policy underlying this?) For example, most allow a majority of disinterested directors, shareholders or members in the case of not-for-profit corporations to validate in advance interested transactions provided there is full disclosure of all material facts about the transaction, and the approving directors reasonably believe the transaction is fair to the corporation. See, e.g., Revised Model Business Corp. Act. §§ 8.60 et seq.; Revised Model Nonprofit Corporations Act (RMNCA) § 8.30. Cf. ALI Tentative Draft §§ 310 & 330 (describing board member's general obligation under duty of loyalty to "act in a manner that he or she reasonably believes to be in the best interests of the charity, in light of its stated purposes" but subject to obligation "to handle appropriately" conflicts of interests e.g., by seeking approvals of disinterested members of the board). Conflicting interests involving not-for-profit corporations may also be resolved if the transaction was "fair" at the time it was entered into (i.e. it "carries the earmarks of an arms-length transaction"). RMNCA § 8.30(a), § 8.30 cmt. 2(a). Otherwise they may be approved before or after the transaction by the state attorney general, § 8.30(b)(2)(i), or a court of proper jurisdiction § 8.30(b)(2)(ii).

The obligation of fiduciaries to make full disclosures in self-dealing transactions is illustrated by Boston Children's Heart Foundation, Inc. v. Nadal–Ginard, 73 F.3d 429 (1st Cir.1996). The case involved the activities of a physician, Dr. Nadal–Ginard, who was president and a member of the board of Boston Children's Heart Foundation ("BCHF"), a non-profit corporation established to conduct the clinical and research activities of the cardiology department at Boston Children's Hospital. The defendant was also chairman of the cardiology department at the hospital and a member of the faculty of Harvard Medical School. Conflicting interest problems arose in connection with Dr. Nadal–Ginard's activities on behalf of the Howard Hughes Medical Institute ("Institute"), which provided him substantial compensation for directing the activities of the Institute's Laboratory of Cellular and Molecular Cardiology at Boston Children's Hospital. In his capacity as president of BCHF, Dr. Nadal–Ginard was empowered to set his own salary and determine other compensation-related matters. In so doing, however, Dr. Nadal–Ginard failed to disclose to the BCHF board that BCHF was paying him for much of the same work for which he was receiving substantial compensation from the Institute. The First Circuit concluded that Dr. Nadal–Girard's actions setting his own compensation at BCHF constituted self-dealing and required full disclosure of all material information regarding his salary and compensation determinations. Despite the fact that the BCHF by-laws granted Dr.

Nadal–Ginard exclusive authority to set his own salary, the Court found that he had not acted in good faith in failing to make full disclosures, specifically in failing to inform the BCHF board of his compensation from the Institute. 73 F.3d at 434. It further held the information regarding his compensation arrangements with the Institute was material because, had BCHF been armed with the information, it may have concluded that he was over-compensated. In so holding, the First Circuit rejected the defendant's claim that no breach occurred because the salary was fair and reasonable, as the failure to act in good faith was sufficient to establish the breach regardless of the reasonableness of the salary. Id. For an analysis of the implications of fiduciary duties and other legal obligations for physicians serving on hospital boards, see Michael Peregrine, Structuring Physician Membership on the Hospital Governing Board, 31 J. Health L. 133 (1998).

5. *Sarbanes Oxley for Nonprofits?* Enacted in 2002 in response to multiple corporate financial scandals such as Enron, the federal Sarbanes–Oxley law is one of the most important securities laws adopted in the United States since the Great Depression. Sarbanes–Oxley Act of 2002, Pub. L. No. 107–204, 116 Stat. 745 (codified in sections of 11, 15, 18, 28 and 29 U.S.C.). Although corporate governance has historically been the province of state law, many provisions of Sarbanes–Oxley impose highly specific requirements on publicly traded corporations, such as mandating they have an audit committee comprised of independent directors (and that at least one member of that committee be a financial expert); requiring that the corporation's president and treasurer attest to the accuracy of financial information and the soundness of the methodology used to generate that information; prohibiting personal loans to directors; prohibiting public accounting firm that performing audit services from providing consulting services; and requiring or encouraging disclosures of various kinds.

Importantly, while Sarbanes–Oxley for the most part does not apply to nonprofit corporations, a number of states have adopted or are considering adopting statutes that would apply similar requirements upon nonprofits. See Kansas Stat. Ann. § 17–1763(b)(15) (Supp. 2005) (requiring that larger nonprofits' audit and annual financial statement be signed by two officers); Cal. Corp. Gov't Code § 12586(e)(2) (West 2005) (large nonprofits must establish audit committee with independent members); Maine Nonprofit Corporation Act, 13–B M.R.S.A § 715 (requiring that nonprofits keep records of accounts and minutes of proceedings available for inspection by any officer, director, or voting member of the nonprofit corporation). See Lumen N. Mulligan, What's Good for the Goose is Not Good for the Gander: Sarbanes–Oxley–Style Nonprofit Reforms, 105 Mich. L. Rev. 1981 (2007). What factors militate in favor or against applying such rules to nonprofit hospitals and other health care institutions such as insurers or clinics? Are disclosure-based reforms likely to have a positive influence on how nonprofits are managed? Might there be risks in "corporatizing" the way nonprofits are run and how directors perceive their ethical obligations? See Nicole Gilkeson, For–Profit Scandal in the Non–Profit World: Should States force Sarbanes–Oxley Provisions onto Nonprofit Corporations?, 95 Geo. L.J. 831 (questioning the normative bases for SOX-style reforms on nonprofits); Dana Brakman Reiser, Enron.org: Why Sarbanes–Oxley Will not Ensure Comprehensive Nonprofit Accountability, 38 U.C. Davis L. Rev. 205; Jane Heath, Who's Minding the Nonprofit Store: Does Sarbanes–Oxley Have Anything to Offer Nonprofits?, 38 U.S.F. L. Rev. 781; Glen T. Troyer et al., Governance Issues for Nonprofit Healthcare Organizations and the Implications of the Sarbanes–Oxley Act, 1 Ind. Health L. Rev. 175; Wendy K. Szymanski, An Allegory of Good (and Bad)

Governance: Applying the Sarbanes–Oxley Act to Nonprofit Organizations., 2003 Utah L. Rev. 1303. See also Henry B. Hansmann, Reforming Nonprofit Corporation Law, 129 U. Pa. L. Rev. 497 (1981) (arguing for strict prohibition for self dealing by directors of "commercial" nonprofits such as hospitals).

Many nonprofit hospitals have voluntarily adopted some of the Sarbanes reforms. This trend may have been accelerated by the endorsement of certain elements of Sarbanes–Oxley by the major bond rating agencies. Finding a relationship between corporate accountability and credit worthiness, these entities consider adoption of certain "best practices" in their evaluations of the credit profile of nonprofit institutions. See e.g. Fitch Ratings, Special Report (Aug. 9, 2005); Michael W. Peregrine & James R. Schwartz, Key Nonprofit Corporate Law developments in 2005, 15 No.4 Health L. Rep. 116 (BNA) (2006) (rating agencies' emphasis on Sarbanes–Oxley compliance based on both support for basic principles of law and belief that regulatory bodies will compel adoption in the future). Others weighing in include The Panel on the Non Profit Sector, see Principles for Good Governance and Ethical Practice—A Guide for Charities and Foundations, and the IRS, which has set forth its own list of recommended practices and taken other actions affecting corporate governance in nonprofit organizations, see *infra*.

6.   *Charitable Trust Law.* States almost uniformly apply nonprofit corporate fiduciary standards to evaluate the actions of nonprofit corporate boards and find that they should not be treated as trusts for donations or other property they hold. See Revised Model Nonprofit Corporation Act, Comment to 2.02 (drafters' intent that nonprofit statute not be treated as charitable trust); Health Midwest v. Kline, 2003 WL 328845 (Kan. Dist. Ct. 2003) (applying corporate standard in conversion transaction). Nevertheless, charitable trust law may in some cases govern the responsibilities of boards of charitable corporations. For example, gifts to a nonprofit corporation for a specific purpose or with an express declaration of intent may create a charitable trust and establish stricter fiduciary duties associated with trust law. See, e.g. St. Joseph's Hospital v. Bennett, 281 N.Y. 115, 22 N.E.2d 305 (1939). Less clear however are circumstances in which a constructive or implied trust may exist. See discussion of Banner Health System litigation and other conversion cases in the following section. Some commentators accuse attorney generals of attempting to import stricter trust fiduciary standards to cases involving the conduct of directors of nonprofit corporations. See Peregrine and Schwartz, *supra*.

7.   State Attorneys General around the country have been active in challenging decisions of board members and officers of nonprofit health care organizations under various legal theories including breaches of fiduciary duties. See, e.g., Nathan Littauer Hospital Ass'n v. Spitzer, 287 A.D.2d 202, 734 N.Y.S.2d 671 (App. Div. 2001) (challenge to affiliation between two hospitals involving substantial changes to corporate purposes; restatement of purposes and required compliance with Religious Directives for Catholic Health Care Facilities do not constitute change of magnitude sufficient to require judicial review under New York law). These cases arise in a variety of contexts including change of control transactions, allegations of self-dealing and waste of charitable assets by insiders, and bankruptcies. In many of these cases the attorney general must balance her responsibility to protect the public interest in the operation of public charities against the need to give managers the flexibility they need to operate efficiently in the market. See Michael W. Peregrine & James R. Schwartz, The Application of Nonprofit Corporation Law to Health Care Organizations (2002). The following cases illustrate the twin responsibilities of state attorneys general.

AHERF. Before Enron, there was AHERF. The collapse of the Allegheny Health, Education, and Research Foundation (AHERF) was the nation's largest failure of a nonprofit health care corporation. Under the dominant leadership of its Chief Executive Officer, Sherif Abdelhak, AHERF grew rapidly, borrowed heavily, and collapsed precipitously. The many causes for AHERF's failure include poor business strategy, misleading and perhaps fraudulent accounting practices and financing arrangements, over-expansion, and unwise physician acquisitions. But the over-arching problem was the structure and performance of its governance system. The complex AHERF organization was governed by a parent board consisting of no less than thirty-five members. Ten other boards, having little overlapping membership, governed fifty-five corporations; each board was generally unaware of what other parts of the system were doing. Directors were chosen and dominated by Mr. Abdelhak and board meetings were, according to one analysis, "scripted affairs, intentionally staged to limit oversight and participation by board members ... Members received one thousand page briefing books and had little time to read them." See Lawton R. Burns et al., The Fall of the House of AHERF: The Allegheny Bankruptcy, 19 Health Affs. 7 (Jan/Feb 2000). Although the AHERF boards consisted of top-notch executives, all were extremely busy and unable to perform a broad oversight responsibility over the organization. In addition, the bylaws permitted many key decisions to be made by Mr. Abdelhak. Id. Over sixty lawsuits were filed, most alleging breaches of the duty of care and duty of loyalty by directors. A global settlement of almost all of the civil lawsuits ended with recovery by the Pennsylvania Attorney General of up to $35 million for losses to charitable endowment funds (the Attorney General had claimed restricted endowment funds had been diverted to system operation in violation of charitable trust law as well as other violations of state law). Criminal prosecutions also resulted in confinement for Mr. Abdelhak. See Editorial, AHERF Whimper, Pittsburgh Post–Gazette, Sept. 8, 2002, available at: www.post-gazette.com/forum/20020908edsharif0908p1.asp; Anatomy of a Bankruptcy (six part series published Jan. 17–Jan. 24, 1999) collected at www.post-gazette/com/aherf. The Attorney General's prosecution and its resulting recovery (which was funded primarily from director and officer insurance) stressed the role of nonprofit directors to safeguard assets and their responsibilities for effective oversight.

Allina and HealthPartners. Investigations by the Attorney General of Minnesota of two large nonprofit entities, Allina Health System (a large IDS that also operated an insurance plan, Medica) and HealthPartners (a large health insurer) revealed patterns of what he termed "lavish" and "wasteful" expenditures, conflicts of interest, lax oversight and other abuses. Pursuant to a Memorandum of Understanding, Allina agreed to spin off Medica with a new board selected by the Attorney General and adopt policies regarding expense reimbursement, executive compensation and other matters. Finding questionable expenditures for travel, consulting and compensation by HealthPartners and concluding that its board "did little to exercise independent judgment concerning the lavish activities of management," the Attorney General petitioned a court to appoint two new members to its board. The court declined to add new board members but agreed to appoint one of the individuals selected by the Attorney General as a special administrator with powers to make recommendations and report suspected abuses. Does the power of the Attorney General in these cases to personally select members of the board of nonprofit organizations blur the line between public and private institutions?

Problem: The Catch–22 of Divided Loyalty

As a result of changes in federal reimbursement policies and antikickback laws and because of persistently high maintenance costs, Corsica Medical Group,

LLC (CMG) has concluded that it is impractical for it to continue to own the lithotripter it uses in its outpatient clinic. As part of negotiations with Pianosa Community Hospital regarding a joint venture to operate outpatient facilities, CMG has offered to sell its lithotripter to the hospital. Dr. Daneka is a member of CMG and also serves on the board of directors of Pianosa Community Hospital. What advice would you give to CMG regarding its proposed transaction? What information should the Pianosa Community Hospital board review before making its decision?

C. CONVERSIONS, ASSET SALES, AND MERGERS OF NOT–FOR–PROFIT CORPORATIONS

Over the past decade, a large number of not-for-profit health insurance companies, HMOs and hospitals have chosen to convert to for-profit status or to merge with, be acquired by, or joint venture with for-profit entities. Most Blue Cross organizations have undertaken steps to do so, and hundreds of hospitals have been acquired by or entered into some form of joint venture with proprietary entities. James J. Fishman, Checkpoints on the Conversion Highway: Some Trouble Spots in the Conversion of Nonprofit Health Care Organizations to For-profit Status, 23 J. Corp. L. 701 (1998).

In the typical conversion, the assets of the not-for-profit organization are sold to a for-profit entity (often controlled by management of the not-for-profit). The proceeds must be distributed to organizations eligible under § 501(c)(3) of the Internal Revenue Code or pursuant to applicable state law. Once the assets are distributed, the not-for-profit entity dissolves. Often the for-profit entity later makes a public sale of its stock, which may occur at a substantial premium over the price paid by the investors. See John D. Colombo, A Proposal for An Exit Tax on Nonprofit Conversion Transactions, 23 J. Corp. L. 779 (1998) (estimating actual value of assets of California's HealthNet HMO to be approximately 500% higher than originally estimated and describing funding of charitable foundations on conversion of PacifiCare Health Systems at less than 1% of actual value of the enterprise). In a number of HMO conversions, insiders grossly undervalued the value of their corporations by persuading regulators to undervalue goodwill or the HMO's trademark or to ignore competing bids for the entity. For a detailed account of the numerous instances of undervaluation in such conversions and the successful efforts of Consumers Union to have hundreds of millions of dollars turned over to independent foundations, see Eleanor Hamburger et al., The Pot of Gold: Monitoring Health Care Conversions Can Yield Billions of Dollars for Health Care, 29 Clearinghouse Rev. 473 (1995).

The following case, involving the proposed sale of assets by a not-for-profit corporation illustrates the interplay of fiduciary responsibilities on statutory standards that govern board decisions of this kind.

MANHATTAN EYE, EAR AND THROAT HOSPITAL v. SPITZER

Supreme Court, New York County, New York, 1999.
186 Misc.2d 126, 715 N.Y.S.2d 575.

FINDINGS OF FACT

A. Manhattan Eye, Ear and Throat Hospital

Established in 1869, originally located on East 34th Street, and then on East 41st Street, MEETH relocated to its present East 64th Street location in

1906, where it ultimately erected three buildings: the Old Hospital Building, the New Hospital Building and the Annex. At this location, it presently operates a highly sophisticated research and teaching (until it terminated its residency program on June 30, 1999), world-renowned, acute care specialty hospital, providing outpatient and inpatient medical services in three specialized areas: ophthalmology, otolaryngology, and plastic surgery. In February 1995, MEETH opened an Outpatient Extension Center in Harlem (the "Harlem Center"), which, unlike the 64th Street facilities, does not provide in patient care. Instead, it currently functions similarly to the outpatient clinic at 64th Street, and refers patients to 64th Street, for subspecialty clinics and surgery.

According to its Certificate of Incorporation, MEETH's corporate purposes are:

> to establish, provide, conduct, operate and maintain a hospital in the City, County and State of New York for the general treatment of persons suffering from acute short-term illnesses; performing general plastic surgery; treating persons suffering from diseases of the eye, ear, nose or throat; and maintaining a school for post graduate instruction in the treatment of such illnesses, performing such surgery, and the treatment of such diseases, and conducting associated and basic research.

By all accounts, MEETH has outstandingly realized these corporate purposes.

* * *

[Changes in financing including reductions in Medicare and Medicaid revenues and the growth of managed care had impacted MEETH adversely. In 1993–1998 MEETH took various actions to cope with the changed landscape.] Then in 1999 MEETH's Board of Directors abruptly decided to sell the 64th Street facility to MSKCC (Memorial Sloan Kettering Cancer Center) and Downtown (Downtown Group/Colony Capital); to terminate its residency programs; to close the Hospital; to transform the Harlem Center and the planned Brooklyn Center from extension centers to free standing Diagnostic and Treatment ("D & T") Centers; and to eventually add further D & T centers in the South Bronx. Following these decisions, MEETH entered into a nonbinding "Memorandum of Understanding" for a sponsorship agreement with New York Presbyterian Hospital ("NYPH"), under which NYPH would become MEETH's sole corporate member. Implementation of these plans necessitated the sale of the 64th Street facility, i.e., substantially all of the assets of MEETH, and led to this litigation.

* * *

C. Decision to Monetize MEETH's Assets and to Sell the Hospital

[MEETH received an offer by MSKCC to buy its real estate—an offer which a report prepared for MEETH stated "came out of the blue in the middle of January of 1999." A committee was formed to review the offer and address concerns expressed by the medical staff about MEETH's future. The committee retained Shattuck Hammond Partners ("Shattuck Hammond"), an investment banking firm specializing in the healthcare industry, to advise it. MEETH agreed to pay Shattuck Hammond a retainer as well as a "Transaction Fee" of one percent (1%) of the "Aggregate Transaction Value" of the sale price. Shattuck Hammond concluded that MEETH's business as a hospital had no ongoing economic value, which the court found to be in conflict with the opinion of others such as the Chairman of Continuum Health Partners, Inc. (Continuum), who considered MEETH's name to have "great value," and the view of the Chief Operating Officer of Lenox Hill Hospital that MEETH had "marquis value" as "one of the top hospitals in the country." After receiving a report appraising the value of its real estate between $46–55 million, the board voted in late February to sell the hospital's real estate for a price as near as possible to $45 million. MEETH in the past had received expressions of interest from the New York Eye and Ear Infirmary and Continuum that would have maintained MEETH as an acute care specialty hospital. On March 11, 1999, MEETH entered into a thirty day binding agreement with another suitor, Mt. Sinai Hospital, for a sale price of $46,000,000 pursuant to which Mt. Sinai would continue to maintain MEETH's mission as an acute care specialty teaching hospital. However, the agreement between MEETH and Mt. Sinai lapsed, and at its April 15, 1999 meeting, Shattuck Hammond informed the Board that both MSKCC and Mt. Sinai had "backed away from their initial proposals and have indicated an interest only at a price substantially below the $46 million minimum amount . . . in the appraisal."]

* * *

[Two weeks later,] the MEETH Board voted to sell the hospital, at a price in excess of $40,000,000. There was no explanation for this decision to sell the real estate for *less* than its appraised value of $46 to $55 million. At this meeting, authorization to seek regulatory approvals was again provided. Moreover, the Board now realized that its sale and closure plan, leading to free standing D & T centers, would require an amendment to the Hospital's Certificate of Incorporation, and a proposed amendment was authorized, although never submitted.

Now, two months after the Board initially had voted to sell its real estate, the minutes for the first time identify . . . that the Board had decided that "the Hospital was going back to its original mission of serving the poor in underserved areas, and redirecting its charitable assets to accomplish this goal." Other than the Shattuck Hammond report, which discusses the Hospital's "original" mission, there is no written record concerning this momentous decision. There had been no study concerning this so-called return to the "original mission" and no proposal or recommendation on the subject was provided to the Board for its review and deliberation. Notably, there was no management plan or recommendation discussing the need to return to this "original" mission, nor do prior Board minutes report any discussion held on the subject.

By the May 5, 1999 Board meeting, four separate proposals had been received, including a $41,000,000 bid from Downtown and MSKCC (and two proposals from real estate developers). According to this offer, MSKCC would open a breast cancer facility in the New Hospital Building, and the remaining real estate, to be purchased by Downtown, would be used as a building site for an apartment building. Mt. Sinai submitted two alternative proposals: (1) a $27,500,000 offer for the real estate, with the hospital closed; and (2) an offer to acquire the Hospital and its operations for "a very substantially reduced price." . . .

The Board took no further steps to seek a bidder, which would save MEETH's long-established mission. . . . The Board then approved a sale to Downtown and MSKCC. . . . The May 5th minutes record that after the decision to sell was approved, "[t]he Board *then* discussed the issue of closing the Hospital. The Board noted that *no* actual decision had been made to close the Hospital." (Emphasis added.) Previously, on April 29, 1999, the Board had terminated the residency program and authorized the President to prepare for possible hospital closure. However, even as of May 5th, as the minutes show, the Board did not seem to believe that it was actually closing the Hospital. One has to wonder exactly what the Board thought it was doing. Then, without a record of further discussion or Board authorization following this May 5th meeting, MEETH submitted a closure plan to the DOH [NY State Department of Health] on June 14, 1999. . . . As of July 26th, the Board had neither received nor commissioned any study with regard to the Board's planned use of the sales proceeds to establish D & T centers, the necessity for such centers, or the viability of such centers. . . . Nonetheless, without such seemingly basic information, the decision to sell and close was made.

MEETH began to act, i.e., it terminated the residency program, upon the assumption that it would receive DOH approvals for closure and establishment of the D & T centers [and took other] steps to effectuate closure and receive regulatory approval for its plan, to enter into a contract for sale, and then to seek court approval under section 511 [Ed: Section 511 of the New York Not-for-Profit Law, governing sales of substantially all the assets of a corporation, is discussed in the opinion]. This would have had the effect of presenting the court with what would have been essentially a fait accompli. To put it another way, if everything went as hoped for, MEETH would have been able to present the section 511 petition pertaining to an *already* closed hospital, with DOH approval for the D & T centers, and it would have asked the court to find "that the purposes of the corporation . . . will be promoted." This would have effectively neutralized, or substantially compromised, any meaningful judicial role in the section 511 process. Indeed, under the scenario envisaged by MEETH, denial of the petition would have been a pyrrhic victory for its opponents: the hospital would already be closed; under such circumstances, a court order could hardly have restored MEETH.

The Court goes on to describe in detail MEETH's negotiations with two alternative purchasers. Continuum proposed to combine MEETH with another entity and thereby continue its mission as a hospital and continue operations of the Harlem Center while abandoning the plans to establish DET Centers. Shattuck Hammond rejected the proposal stating that the board had "decided to sell the real estate." Lenox Hill also promised it would make certain investments in MEETH, with the latter becoming a subsidiary of Lenox, and continuing operation of the hospital in the New Hospital Building on East 64th Street. Although Lenox had been asked by MEETH's advisors to provide further information about its offer, the court found that MEETH summarily filed a petition for approval of the sale to MSKCC.]

F. MEETH's Plan

MEETH's plan is to sell a part of its real estate to MSKCC, one of the world's outstanding cancer treatment and research centers. MSKCC plans to convert the New Hospital Building to expand its breast cancer center. Undeniably, this would be an extremely worthwhile use. However, the issue under section 511 is not the buyer's planned use of the real estate, however worthy that use may be, but whether seller's use of the sale proceeds will promote its own corporate purposes. [ ]The remaining real estate will be sold to Downtown, a real estate developer, which intends to erect an apartment building on the site.... Upon completion of the transaction, and following the hoped-for DOH approval, MEETH will close its existing specialty hospital [and] will then convert the existing Harlem Center, and the already approved thoughnot-yet built Brooklyn center to the proposed D & T centers ...

* * *

Conclusions of Law

At issue is whether, as required under section 511(d) of the Not-for-Profit Corporation Law, MEETH has shown "to the satisfaction of the court," both that the "consideration and the terms of the transaction are fair and reasonable"[2] and that "the purposes of the corporation ... will be promoted" by the sale of all or substantially all of the hospital's assets to Downtown and MSKCC. The few reported decisions dealing with this section have held that whether "the consideration and the terms of the transaction are fair and reasonable to the corporation" is to be evaluated at the time that the contract to sell is entered into. ... On the other hand, the cases hold that whether "the purposes of the corporation ... will be promoted" is to be evaluated "in light of conditions prevailing at the time the issue is presented to the court." ... Given my Findings of Fact, I conclude that MEETH has not satisfied either prong of section 511. Therefore I deny MEETH's petition to approve the proposed sale.

* * *

The Not-for-Profit Corporation Law addresses this lack of accountability by requiring court approval of fundamental changes in the life of a Type B charitable corporation, such as a disposition of all or substantially all assets, since there are no shareholders whose approval can be sought. The Attorney General is made a statutory party to such petitions, and his "active participation" is presumed. (See V. Bjorkland, [et al., New York Nonprofit Law and Practice] § 82[a], p. 238). This is to ensure that the interests of the ultimate beneficiaries of the corporation, the public, are adequately represented and protected from improvident transactions. ... It is pursuant to this mandate that this court is called upon to review the sale of substantially all of MEETH's assets to MSKCC and Downtown.

A charitable Board is essentially a caretaker of the not-for-profit corporation and its assets. As caretaker, the Board "ha[s] the fiduciary obligation to act on behalf of the corporation ... and advance its interests" [ ]in "good faith and with that degree of diligence, care and skill which ordinarily prudent

2. This requirement was added in 1972 (L.1972, c. 961 § 6). Prior to this amendment, judicial decisions had required "fair market value."

men would exercise under similar circumstances in like positions." (NPCL § 717[a]). This formulation of the Board's duty of care is an "expansion" of the comparable section of the Business Corporation Law which does not contain the words "care" and "skill." ...

It is axiomatic that the Board of Directors is charged with the duty to ensure that the mission of the charitable corporation is carried out. This duty has been referred to as the "duty of obedience." It requires the director of a not-for-profit corporation to "be faithful to the purposes and goals of the organization," since "[u]nlike business corporations, whose ultimate objective is to make money, nonprofit corporations are defined by their specific objectives: perpetuation of particular activities are central to the raison d'être of the organization." (Bjorkland, *op. cit.*, § 114[a], at p. 414). [T]he duty of obedience, perforce, must inform the question of whether a proposed transaction to sell all or substantially all of a charity's assets promotes the purposes of the charitable corporation when analyzed under section 511.

In recent years, across the United States, there have been a series of conversions of nonprofit hospitals into for-profit hospitals that, although certainly different from this petition, nevertheless resemble, in certain basics, MEETH's proposal. It has also resulted in some twenty states enacting or considering legislation regulating such conversions. [ ]

* * *

[T]he conversion analogy is analytically useful because, absent the for-profit component, which of course is absent in a Section 511 petition, a conversion is conceptually similar to MEETH's petition, inasmuch as in both there is a charitable organization which alleges that it is incapable of continuing its primary mission of operating a hospital, seeks approval of the sale of all its assets, and plans to apply the sale proceeds towards a newly revised mission. As is relevant to the analysis, for example, legislation in one state requires that the attorney general examine the transaction to determine "(2) Whether the nonprofit hospital exercised due diligence in deciding to sell, selecting the purchaser, and negotiating the terms and conditions of the sale; (3) Whether the procedures used by the seller in making its decision, including whether appropriate expert assistance was used (were fair); (4) Whether conflict of interest was disclosed, including, but not limited to, conflicts of interest [of] board members ... and experts retained by the seller[;] [and] (5) Whether the seller will receive reasonably fair value for its assets." [ ] [As summarized by the Attorney General and] in essence agreed to by MEETH's counsel, "Elementary principles of corporate and fiduciary law require the Board, after it has decided to sell the hospital, to entertain all responsible proposals, not to favor any bidder over another in the process, and to treat all bidders and potential bidders identically and fairly."

I turn now to the first prong of section 511, which requires that "the consideration and terms of the transaction are fair and reasonable to the corporation." Because the sale of the real estate, as proposed, is inextricably interwoven with the closure of MEETH as it exists today, I believe that the transaction as a whole must be examined, not just the "fair market value" of the real estate. This transaction is [not] a simple transaction which dealt only with the question of the value of a building being sold by the Church; there was no larger transaction involved. There do not appear to be reported decisions of more complex transactions, such as here, where implementing its decision to sell its real estate assets to MSKCC and Downtown would require the closing of MEETH and a fundamental change to its corporate purposes. The Board accepted Shattuck Hammond's conclusion that "the business [of MEETH] had no value," which I have found to be incorrect. Clearly MEETH, as a functioning acute care, specialty hospital, had value: major medical entities were willing to operate it and keep it open and guarantee the expenditure of substantial sums to do so. Thus, while it may be that the real estate was fairly valued, this is not enough. The transaction did not take into account MEETH's full value, and the NYPH proposal to establish a MEETH pavilion or building, with "plaques and/or signage," does not correct this since it does not necessarily contemplate preserving the business of MEETH, and therefore preserving the total assets of MEETH. Moreover, as I have also found, evidence at the hearing established that MEETH's name itself had significant value. Again under the terms of the proposed transaction, this value is not evaluated nor is it clear that it will be preserved. The Board disregarded these components of value when it decided to "monetize" its assets and sell the real estate. This is a fundamental flaw which leaves me unsatisfied that the terms and conditions of the proposed transaction are "fair and reasonable."

Under the second prong of section 511, which requires that "the purposes of the corporation . . . will be promoted" (N–PCL § 511[d]), MEETH's petition fares no better. Unfortunately, there is lacking judicial precedent concerning a proposal of this magnitude.[3] While MEETH has argued that the proposal to abandon the acute care, teaching and research hospital component of its mission and to pursue the D & T centers does not require an amendment, this argument is belied by the Board's own action on April 29th, authorizing submission of an Amendment to its Certificate of Incorporation (although never submitted) expressly providing for the D & T centers. This is behavioral evidence that the Board knew that it was proposing a fundamental change in the corporation's mission, which indeed it was doing. For generations MEETH's mission, as stated in its Certificate of Incorporation, was understood to be the operation of an acute care, specialty teaching and research hospital dedicated to "plastic surgery" and to the treatment of "persons suffering from diseases of the eye, ear, nose or throat." While it is certainly correct that the definition of "hospital" contained in section 2801(1) of the Public Health Law includes a diagnostic and treatment center, as MEETH now argues, it is sophistry to contend that this means that MEETH is not seeking a new and fundamentally different purpose, in light of the overwhelming evidence which demonstrates this is exactly what it is doing. The conclusion is inescapable that the proposed use of the assets involves a new and fundamentally different corporate purpose.

* * *

3. There are reported decisions dealing with somewhat complicated sales. (E.g. Agudist Council of Greater New York v. Imperial Sales Co., 158 A.D.2d 683, 551 N.Y.S.2d 955 [2d Dept., 1990] [sale disapproved where services provided to senior citizens will be disrupted] and Church of God, 76 A.D.2d 712, 431 N.Y.S.2d 834). Such decisions generally deal with the impact of the sale of the assets on the existing mission, and do not involve a concomitant proposal to change or reprioritize the existing mission.

While it may be appropriate, in certain cases, to solve financial difficulties by eliminating the organization's mission by selling its assets and then undertaking a new mission, the passage properly focuses attention upon the duty of obedience, which mandates that a Board, in the first instance, seek to preserve its original mission. Embarkation upon a course of conduct, which turns it away from the charity's central and well-understood mission, should be a carefully chosen option of last resort. Otherwise, a Board facing difficult financial straits might find sale of its assets, and "reprioritization" of its mission, to be an attractive option, rather than taking all reasonable efforts to preserve the mission which has been the object of its stewardship.

As has been documented in the Findings of Fact, the record is clear that this case is not a situation where the Board first made a reasoned and studied determination that there was a lack of need for MEETH as a hospital, or that the financial difficulties made it impossible to ensure the survival of MEETH. Rather, the credible evidence is that MEETH's decision to sell was impelled by MSKCC's offer, which caused the Board to recognize the value of the underlying real estate; then its realization that it could "monetize" this asset drove subsequent events.

The MSKCC offer initially drove the decision to retain a strategic advisor, Shattuck Hammond, which had a direct and substantial interest in a sale of the real estate, i.e., the 1% transaction fee. This arrangement, regardless of whether it was traditional in investment banking, as Mr. Hammond testified, resulted in a situation where the Board put its reliance upon a strategic advisor which had an actual interest in the recommendations of its strategic study. It is not necessary for me to conclude that this conflict of interest compromised the result; the fee arrangement certainly gives the appearance that the integrity of the process was flawed and that the Board had not obtained the assistance of a truly independent expert. Moreover, there does not appear to have been full disclosure to the Board of the potential for a conflict of interest in the expert. The evidence showed that two Board members were unaware of the percentage fee, which was a part of Shattuck Hammond's retention. Additionally, there was no discussion or deliberation by the Board over the fact that its strategic advisor had a direct, and perhaps disabling, financial interest in the outcome of the strategic option it was recommending. Nor was there a decision by the Board to retain and rely upon Shattuck Hammond, notwithstanding this issue. The issue simply was never raised. As a result, it cannot be concluded with confidence that the Board received wholly disinterested advice. This becomes more troubling in view of the manner in which Shattuck Hammond dealt with bidders such as Continuum and Lenox Hill, which were not interested in purchasing the real estate, by providing misleading information concerning their offers, often omitting crucial details, and by asserting that the only realistic option was the sale of the real estate.

It is also clear that the MSKCC offer, which drove the decision to "monetize" the assets, drove the subsequent decisions to create a new or "reprioritized" mission, to prematurely terminate the residency programs, to seek approval to close the hospital, and virtually every other decision made by the Board, as I have detailed above.

This decision to "monetize" drove the need to change the corporate purposes, and these new or reprioritized purposes then became the basis for the argument that "purposes of the corporation ... will be promoted." A careful evaluation of whether there was a basis for changing the corporate purposes should have determined the need to sell, not vice versa. The total absence of any study beforehand, concerning the D & T centers, and the retention of healthcare experts, only after submission of the proposal to the DOH, and only to prepare a business plan "for fulfillment" or in "support" of the D & T proposal, not to independently evaluate the plan's feasibility, buttresses the conclusion that the sale drove the change in purpose. Indeed, the report submitted by Dr. Cicero and Mr. Kachmarick states that "[t]he following business plan describes how MEETH will achieve [its] goal, in keeping with its expanded mission statement." To argue that MEETH was returning to its original purposes without an iota of evidence that it made this fundamental determination prior to the decision to sell and close, cannot obscure the fact that this decision, of necessity, eliminated MEETH's historic mission, its historic raison d'être.

Moreover, the record also demonstrates that the Board failed to properly consider the various alternatives submitted which would have preserved MEETH's mission. The Board had concluded that these alternatives were the equivalent of "giving the keys away," and summarily rejected them.[4] However, the Board has no independent vitality. It appears that the Board confused preservation of the Hospital with preservation of the Board, when the appropriate calculus should be what is good for the Hospital is good for the Board.

In sum, it is evident that this petition fails to meet the two pronged test of section 511. The terms of the transaction are not fair and reasonable to the corporation, inasmuch as no consideration was given to the value of MEETH as a going concern; rather, this value was disregarded. Moreover, evaluating the transaction at the time of the petition, it is clear that there has not been a showing that the sale will promote the purposes of the corporation. To the contrary, MEETH decided to sell, and then evolved its new or "reprioritized mission." There has been no reasoned determination that MEETH cannot continue to operate an acute care, specialty research and teaching hospital, as other medical institutions are proposing to do, and are willing to invest substantial sums to accomplish. MEETH instead chose to sell its real estate, to seek DOH approval to close its hospital, and then apply for judicial imprimatur of this plan. I conclude that this sales transaction should be disapproved.

Notes and Questions

1. The MEETH board retained a prominent, highly regarded investment-banking firm to advise it and help conduct negotiations. Why did the actions of the board in reliance on this firm not fall under the protections of the Business

---

4. See Bjorklund, *op. cit.,* § 8–2[c], at p. 246, n. 58, discussing when a charitable "business" is being transferred, and in exchange the acquirer is assuming all liabilities and guaranteeing continuation of the seller services and noting that the "value (i.e., total assets trans-ferred) may be much greater than the consideration (i.e., liabilities assumed)." Neither Continuum nor Lenox Hill was proposing this scenario, as was suggested by the "keys" metaphor.

Judgment Rule? What factors shape the directors' responsibilities when a financially troubled hospital is put up for sale? See Peregrine & Schwartz, *supra* ("*MEETH* should constitute a warning to directors/trustees of the importance of carefully considering the duty of obedience to purpose in the decision making process, particularly when considering a change in the corporation's principle charitable purpose.") Note, however, that the fiduciary duties of corporate directors may shift when an entity is approaching bankruptcy. In such circumstances, the board may owe fiduciary duties to creditors of the corporation that may, in some circumstances, trump their obligations to the corporation itself. See Michael W. Peregrine et al., The Fiduciary Duties of Health Care Directors in the "Zone of Insolvency." 35 J. Health L. 227 (2002).

2. *The Duty of Obedience and "Mission Primacy."* New York and some other jurisdictions characterize the special obligations facing directors of not-for-profit organizations as a distinct fiduciary obligation. This duty, which is similar to the duty of trustees to administer trusts in a manner faithful to the wishes of the creator of the trust, obligates directors to adhere to the dictates of the corporation's "mission" or other statement of charitable or public interest purpose. Any substantial deviation from such purpose may subject directors to personal liability. See Michael W. Peregrine, Charitable Trust Laws and the Evolving Nature of the Nonprofit Hospital Corporation, 30 J. Health L. 11 (1997). Courts generally allow directors considerable leeway in interpreting broadly stated corporate purposes (which are usually found in the corporation's charter or bylaws). However, directors must follow clearly stated charitable objectives even if other alternatives exist that are more profitable, efficient, or needed by the community. A board desiring to alter its corporate purposes must amend its articles and, in most states, give notice to the attorney general; failure to do so would constitute a breach of their fiduciary duty of obedience. Attorney General v. Hahnemann Hospital, 397 Mass. 820, 494 N.E.2d 1011 (1986).

Even when the duty of obedience is explicitly recognized, does it help solve the central problem that directors of nonprofits face, i.e. how to balance "mission and margin"? One proposal would establish a principle of "mission primacy" to guide directors and courts in situations in which business interests and charitable purposes conflict:

> As a general guiding principle, we suggest that "mission primacy" should be recognized as a central objective of the nonprofit enterprise with the corollary that directors enjoy presumptive deference in defining and, within limits, amending that mission. This focus would incorporate mission-centered values into interpretations of the traditional fiduciary duties of care and loyalty [while] preserving managerial discretion to balance the various constituents of the nonprofit firm including donors, consumers and the community.... [M]ission primacy would allow legitimate mission-centered factors to override corporate fiduciary standards in some cases while imposing a more exacting standard of care and loyalty where mission issues predominate.

Thomas L. Greaney & Kathleen Boozang, Mission, Margin and Trust in the Nonprofit Health Care Enterprise, 5 Yale J. Health Pol., L. & Ethics 1 (2005). Would recognition of mission primacy help clarify the analysis in MEETH? Would it help directors resolve issues posed by competing offers to buy a charitable hospital from two buyers, one for-profit and one not-for-profit, where the latter was offering more money? Would it affect the standard to be applied to lavish expenditures on perks for directors or executive compensation? See Peter Jacobson, Health Law 2005: An Agenda, 33 J.L.Med. & Ethics 725 (2005) (agreeing that mission primacy would provide a stronger doctrinal rationale for result in MEETH, but suggesting amendment to "place charitable mission in a paramount position, requiring compelling evidence to permit any deviation form the mission''). See also, Jill R. Horowitz, Why We Need the Independent Sector: The Behavior, Law and Ethics of Not–For–Profit Hospitals, 50 UCLA L. Rev. 1345, 1401 (2003) (proposing ''duty of integrity'' which would allow nonprofits to market profitable services in order to subsidize money-losing services and charity care); Robert A. Katz, Let Charitable Directors Direct: Why Trust Law Should Not Curb Board Discretion Over a Charitable Corporation's Mission and Unrestricted Assets, 80 Chi.-Kent L. Rev. 689, 701 (2005) (MEETH represents ''the most robust version of the duty of obedience effectively requir[ing] a board to advance the corporate mission for as long as that is possible (within reason))''.

3. *Charitable Trust Issues on Conversions.* California law, although not completely clear on this point, appears to require that property donated to a corporation, though held absolutely by the corporation, must be held in trust for the purposes set forth in its articles of incorporation. A leading case, perhaps unique to California, is Queen of Angels Hospital v. Younger, 66 Cal.App.3d 359, 136 Cal.Rptr. 36 (1977), in which a not-for-profit corporation sponsored by the Franciscan Sisters leased a hospital it had operated for 44 years to a proprietary organization, with the intention of using the proceeds to operate medical clinics providing free medical care in the community. The court found that the corporation's articles of incorporation, which described Queen of Angels as a ''hospital,'' and its history of functioning as a hospital established that its assets were held in trust for the purposes of operating a hospital. See also Daniel W. Coyne & Kathleen Russell Kas, The Not–For–Profit Hospital as a Charitable Trust: To Whom does Its Value Belong?, 24 J. Health & Hosp. L. 48 (1991). If the parties convince the court that maintaining the original purpose has become ''impossible, impractical or illegal,'' the equitable doctrine of *cy pres* may be available to clear the way for the alternative use of the assets. Where the court so finds, *cy pres* principles mandate that the trustees dedicate the charitable assets to a purpose that resembles the original intent of the settlor as closely as possible. See Evelyn Brody, The Limits of Charity Fiduciary Law, 57 Md. L. Rev. 1400 (1998); M. Gregg Bloche, Corporate Takeovers of Teaching Hospitals, 65 S. Cal. L. Rev. 1035, 1143–46 (1992).

In several states, attorneys general have relied upon the charitable trust doctrine or other features of their state's not-for-profit laws to challenge conversions and joint ventures. For example, Banner Health System, an Arizona not-for-profit corporation, sold its numerous health care facilities in various states and planned to use the proceeds of those sales to support its operations in other states. The Attorneys General of several states, including North Dakota, South Dakota and New Mexico, objected to the removal of assets from the communities in their states, based on charitable trust principles. They contented that donations received by local facilities were intended to be used only by that facility and not for the system's general purposes and that benefits conferred from exemption from local taxes should be returned to the community. Banner's position had been that it should be able to reinvest the proceeds from the sale of its North and South Dakota health care facilities in other areas where they are needed to further Banner's nonprofit health care mission. Banner also contended that the states' attempts to apply charitable trust law placed an unreasonable burden on its ability to fulfill its obligation to deliver high quality and affordable health care. Central to the Attorneys Generals' claim was the question of whether charitable trust law applies to corporations receiving the donations and benefits from the community that are not expressly limited to local use. The South Dakota Supreme Court has ruled that where no express trust is created by the gifts to the nonprofit organization, it is possible that an implied trust might be found based on principles of unjust enrichment or a breach of fiduciary duties by the corporation.

Banner Health System v. Long, 663 N.W.2d 242 (S.D. 2003). However, a North Dakota district court declined to find a constructive trust because the state had failed to demonstrate that Banner had a "confidential or fiduciary relationship." (Shortly after that decision the State Attorney General settled its case with Banner agreeing to pay $1 million to be devoted to charitable health care uses). See Banner Settlement, available at www.ag.state.nd.us/newsreleases/2003/12 15 03.pdf. See Patrick Coffee et al., The "Charitable Trust Controversy Confronting Banner Health and other Nonprofit Health Care Systems," 16 Health Lawyer 1 (2003). Complicating the matter, however, is the fact that there is considerable variation among the states as to whether they view nonprofit assets as subject to charitable trust principles. Some states appear automatically to so treat hospitals' assets, see e.g. N.H. Rev. Stat. Ann. § 7:10b (1997), while others take the view that their nonprofit corporation act of the state removes application of charitable trust principles except in instances of express restrictions. Thus, in the context of contested conversions, several courts have refused to apply charitable trust standards in reviewing the actions of directors of nonprofit corporations. See, e.g., Health Midwest v. Kline, 2003 WL 328845 (D. Kan. 2003).

4.   A further complication raised by the MEETH case is the overlapping and often uncoordinated regulatory schemes that a corporation faces in change of ownership transactions. State law regulating hospital licensure may come into conflict with or pose strategic conundrums when considered in light of corporate fiduciary obligations under nonprofit law. For example, MEETH took steps to begin closing the hospital before the attorney general could seek an injunction based on state nonprofit law. Without coordination between the DOH regulatory process and the attorney general's oversight, a green light from DOH could destroy the charitable asset even though the criteria under the New York nonprofit law might not be met. Scott Himes, The Collision of Healthcare and Corporate Law in a Hospital Closure Case, 34 J. Health L. 335 (2001).

5.   Conversions by not-for-profit insurers have focused considerable attention on the fiduciary duties of not-for-profit directors, the application of the charitable trust doctrine, and other legal issues surrounding this type of sale. The following conversion transactions illustrate divergent approaches under common law fiduciary and statutory standards.

Health Midwest. The acquisition of Health Midwest by HCA, Inc., for $1.125 billion, the largest nonprofit acquisition in the history of the country, renewed the ancient border war between the states of Missouri and Kansas. With Health Midwest operating facilities and having corporate entities in both states, the Attorneys General of Kansas and Missouri both laid claim to a share of the charitable assets created by the conversion of the Health Midwest health care properties to for-profit status. A settlement with the Attorney General of Missouri resulted in an arrangement providing for division of the assets and control of the resulting foundation highly favorable to the state of Missouri. See Memorandum of Understanding between Attorney General of Missouri and Health Midwest, www.ago.state.mo.us/lawsuits2003/012203healthmidwest.pdf. The state of Kansas sued in state court to challenge the transaction, alleging, inter alia, that the compensation packages received by directors of Health Midwest constituted self-dealing, that the approval of the transaction on the terms provided were not an exercise of sound business judgment, and that the transaction should be reviewed under principles of charitable trust law instead of the corporate law standard. The Kansas court held that the corporate law standard applied to transactions by nonprofit organizations involving changes of control and found no breaches of fiduciary duties by the board of Health Midwest. Health Midwest v. Kline, 2003

WL 328845 (D. Kan. 2003) (applying the business judgment rule and concluding that the board conducted a fair and reasonable examination of competing offers and that its conclusions were within the realm of discretion afforded by the rule). However, the court also concluded that the boards of certain subsidiary entities had not satisfied the business judgment rule standard in deciding to merge into a Missouri foundation with "little Kansas participation in governance and nebulous spending commitments to the citizens of Kansas" because they had not exercised their obligation to advance charitable goals and protect corporate assets pursuant to fiduciary duty and ultra vires principles. Id.

CareFirst. In 2003, the Maryland Insurance Administration (MIA) rejected the application of CareFirst BlueCross BlueShield to convert and be acquired by for-profit WellPoint Health Networks, Inc. In a report exceeding 350 pages, the Maryland Insurance Commissioner concluded that the proposed transaction did not satisfy the public interest standard set forth in the state's conversion statute. Subsequently, the Maryland legislature enacted legislation barring any attempts at future sales for five years, requiring removal of board members and creating a committee that would nominate ten new members to the 21–member board of directors and a new oversight body to monitor CareFirst's performance. Status. Kathy Lundy Springuel, Maryland Senate Votes to Maintain CareFirst's Nonprofit Status, Ban Sale for Five Years, 12 No. 14 Health L. Rep. 517 (BNA) (2003). In response the national association for Blues plans immediately filed a lawsuit in Illinois federal district court to prevent CareFirst from continuing to use the Blue Cross and Blue Shield trademark and names. After further litigation, a consent judgment was entered allowing CareFirst to retain its affiliation with Blue Cross and Blue. Kathy Lundy Springuel, Judicial Accord Ends CareFirst Dispute, Retains Carrier's Blues Plan Affiliation, 12 No. 24 Health L. Rep. 924 (BNA) (2003).

6. *Valuation Issues.* On the complex and controversial issues surrounding valuation of not-for-profit HMOs, see Theresa McMahon, Fair *Value*? The Conversion of Nonprofit HMOs, 30 U.S.F.L. Rev. 355 (1996); Stephen J. Weiser, Sale of a Tax Exempt Hospital to a For–Profit Corporation: Federal Tax Issues, 25 J. Health & Hosp. L. 129 (1992); see also Robert Kuttner, Columbia/HCA and the Resurgence of the For Profit Hospital Business (Pt. 1), 335 New Eng. J. Med. 362 (1996) (describing the difficulty in ascertaining whether purchase price will establish a foundation adequate to perpetuate a hospital's historic commitment to community services); Kenneth Thorpe, et al., Hospital Conversions, Margins, And The Provision Of Uncompensated Care, 19 Health Affs. 187 (Nov./Dec. 2000)(empirical study showing that uncompensated care declines after hospitals convert from not-for-profit to for profit form). The Attorney General of Tennessee intervened in a sale of a nonprofit hospital to a for-profit chain where it found the nonprofit hospital's board had failed to adequately inform itself about the value of the hospital when it voted to enter into a letter of intent. Burson v. Nashville Memorial Hospital Inc., No. 94–744–1 (Tenn. Ch. Ct. 1994) (consent decree mandating creation of new charitable trust and establishing conflict of interest rules for directors of the new foundation).

7. *State Statutes Regulating Conversions.* A majority of states have enacted statutes governing the process and setting standards for regulatory approvals of conversions of not-for-profit entities. E.g., Cal. Corp. Code §§ 5913–5919 (West 1999); Colo. Rev. Stat. § 10–16–324 (1998); 1997 Conn. Acts 188 (Reg. Sess.); 1998 Conn. Acts. 36 (Reg. Sess.); D.C. Code Ann. §§ 32–551 to 32–560 (1998); Neb. Rev. Stat. §§ 71–20,102 to 71–20,114 (1998). See generally 1 Furrow et al., Health Law (2d ed. 2000) § 5–22; Kevin F. Donahue, Crossroads in Hospital Conversions: A

Survey of Nonprofit Hospital Conversion Legislation, 8 Annals Health L. 39 (1999). Most place a variety of procedural requirements upon converting entities, such as mandating prior notification of conversion transactions and requiring information concerning the details of the transaction be provided to the reviewing authority and, in some cases, to the public. Some go further, specifying substantive standards that must be considered by the reviewer. To the extent that the statutes lack such specificity, traditional concepts of fiduciary duties, charitable trust law and nonprofit corporation law presumably apply to the regulators' review. For alternative approaches, see John D. Colombo, A Proposal for An Exit Tax on Nonprofit Conversion Transactions, 23 J. Corp. L. 779 (1998) (proposing an "exit tax" which would require nonprofit entities to surrender the value of appreciation of the economic assets of the entity where the converted enterprise has not needed the tax exemption to operate or where partnership principles would so dictate); Nat'l Ass'n of Attorneys General, Model Act for Nonprofit Healthcare Conversions. See also, Donahue, *supra*; Mark Krause, Comment, "First, Do No Harm": An Analysis of the Nonprofit Hospital Sale Acts, 45 UCLA L. Rev. 503 (1997).

Note on Certificate of Need Regulation

Many states require that local facilities obtain a certificate of need (CON) prior to undertaking construction or renovation of facilities, purchasing major equipment, or offering new health services. Operating under the mandates of state statutory schemes, health planning agencies require that health care facilities demonstrate the "need" for such improvements or purchases and meet other financial and regulatory requirements CON regulation is often criticized for inhibiting competition and innovation by requiring that providers satisfy regulatory requirements that are often vague, subjective, and conflicting. Moreover, the process of demonstrating need, financial feasibility, and quality of service may entail lengthy and costly administrative proceedings. At the same time CON laws provide the states one of the few mechanisms by which they can control the supply and location of health care resources.

State CON regulation was spawned by the 1974 National Health Planning and Resources Development Act, 42 U.S.C. §§ 300k–300t, Pub. L. No. 93–641 (1974) which conditioned eligibility for a variety of healthcare funding programs on adoption of state plans for allocating healthcare resources and CON laws to help implement those plans. As originally conceived, adoption of CON laws and CON proceedings would reduce healthcare costs by reducing wasteful duplication of facilities while also improving access by rationalizing the allocation of service providers. Although 49 states eventually adopted CON laws, the repeal of NHPRD in 1987 prompted many states to alter or eliminate their certificate of need statutes. As a result, today there is a wide array of statutory schemes. States vary considerably in the kinds of facilities subject to CON regulation (e.g., hospitals, skilled nursing facilities, intermediate care facilities, and ambulatory surgical facilities), the capital thresholds at which the law applies, and the standards used to determine need.

Most commentary is highly critical of CON regulation, arguing that it posed obstacles to efficient reorganization of healthcare markets, invited obstructionist behavior and was incompatible with the evolution of competitive health care markets. See e.g., Patrick J. McGinley, Beyond Health Care Reform: Reconsidering Certificate of Need Laws in a "Managed Competition" System, 23 Fla., St. U. L. Rev. 141, 137–68 (1995) ("Certificate of need laws shelter health care providers from the price-cutting demands of health care alliances.") Lauretta H. Wolfson, State Regulation of Health Facility Planning: The Economic Theory and Political

Realities of Certificate of Need, 4 DePaul J. Health Care L. 261, 310 (1997). ("The process of obtaining a CON has become an enterprise in itself, becoming so lucrative that it attracts many politicians and former politicians who successfully use their influence to weight the process for those who employ their services.") Other studies question whether CON achieved its purposes of lowering costs and allocating services more equitably. See e.g., Morrissey and Shafeldt, J. Reg. Econ. 187 (1991).

Another difficulty with CON statutes lies in their drafting. In many cases, the approach is to set forth a "laundry list" of numerous factors, many of which are vague and thus invite subjective determinations. For example, West Virginia's statute contains twenty-two criteria for assessing need; a twenty-third allows the regulators to utilize any additional criteria it sees fit in determining need. For an excellent analysis see Randall Bovjberg, Problems and Prospects for Health Planning: The Importance of Incentives, Standards and Procedures in Certificate of Need, 1978 Utah L. Rev. 83. Cases involving CON disputes raise a variety of issues, e.g., the tension between quantitative standards based on need for additional beds or sophisticated equipment and qualitative standards. See e.g., Department of Health and Rehabilitative Services v. Johnson and Johnson House Health Care, 447 So.2d 361 (Fla. Ct. App. 1984); the existence of anticompetitive conspiracies to deny a CON, see e.g., Hospital Building Co. v. Trustees of Rex Hosp., 791 F.2d 288 (4th Cir. 1986).

As noted, CON laws were widely regarded as out of step with the development of competitive health care markets. Can you make a case for maintaining or strengthening CON laws as part of a health care reform plan? We will revisit the role of CON regulation in several contexts such as its effect on the development of specialty hospitals and its importance in planning joint ventures and integrated systems.

Note on Limited Liability for Investors

An important objective for many investors is limited liability, i.e., the guarantee that they will not be personally liable for the acts or debts of the business except to the extent of their investment. Limited liability is a key characteristic of corporations, limited partnerships, limited liability companies and limited liability partnerships. Although it is not a common occurrence, courts have been willing to disregard the corporate form, or "pierce the corporate veil," and hold shareholders personally liable in certain circumstances. The jurisprudence on piercing is somewhat incoherent, with courts remarkably prone to rely on labels or characterizations of relationships (like "alter ego," "instrumentality" or "sham") or mechanically recite piercing factors (such as the failure to follow corporate formalities, the absence of adequate capitalization, or the commingling of personal and corporate assets) without explaining why it is appropriate to upset the parties' expectation of limited liability. Although piercing is rarely allowed, egregious facts, coupled with severe undercapitalization bordering on fraud, may occasionally justify disregard of the corporate entity. See, e.g., Autrey v. 22 Texas Services Inc., 79 F.Supp.2d 735 (S.D. Tex. 2000) (triable issues found in wrongful death action against severely undercapitalized corporation that owned forty nine nursing homes).

In cases involving hospital systems with multiple corporate entities, courts are usually reluctant to pierce the corporate veil even where the parent exercises extensive control over the subsidiary and its name is prominently displayed in the advertising, signs and literature of the subsidiary hospital. See, e.g., Humana, Inc. v. Kissun, 221 Ga.App. 64, 471 S.E.2d 514 (1996); see also, Ritter v. BJC Barnes

Jewish Christian Health Systems, 987 S.W.2d 377 (Mo. Ct. App. 1999) (refusing to hold parent entity liable on agency, veil-piercing, vicarious liability or apparent authority theories despite extensive control over subsidiary hospital's operations). However, where regulatory evasion is possible, piercing might be available. In United States v. Pisani, 646 F.2d 83 (3d Cir. 1981), the government sought to recover Medicare overpayments made to a corporation owned by a single physician/shareholder. The Third Circuit pierced the corporate veil, holding the physician personally liable despite the absence of fraud. Although some of the traditional factors militating in favor of disregard of the corporate entity were also present, the court stressed the clear legislative purpose embodied in the Medicare law that providers may only be reimbursed for the reasonable costs of their services. This purpose would be easily circumvented if providers could freely submit inflated cost reports, pocket the money through distributions or repayment of loans from a corporation and avoid personal liability. In other cases, courts have pierced the corporate veil despite the absence of any traditional factors where failure to do so would allow providers to avoid the strong statutory objective of preventing abuse of the Medicare and Medicaid program. United States v. Normandy House Nursing Home, Inc., 428 F.Supp. 421 (D. Mass. 1977); see also United States v. Arrow Medical Equip. Co., 1990 WL 210601 (E.D. Pa. 1990). On the other hand multiple corporate entities can effectively shield business operations from regulatory sanctions. See Joseph E. Casson & Julia McMillen, Protecting Nursing Home Companies: Limiting Liability Through Corporate Restructuring, 36 J. Health L. 577 (2003) (multi-corporate form enables nursing home chains to limit licensure revocation and Medicare sanctions to individual entities). See also, Charles Duhigg, Inquiries at Investor–Owned Nursing Homes, N.Y. Times (Oct. 24 2007) (Investigative report by the New York Times charging that private equity firms that have acquired thousands of nursing homes had shielded themselves from regulatory oversight and liability actions by employing complicated corporate structures has prompted Congressional investigations).

Many professional corporations statutes provide for: (1) limited liability for shareholders as to the ordinary business obligations of the corporation (e.g., business debts, negligence unassociated with professional services, bankruptcy); (2) unlimited liability as to the shareholder's own professional negligence and the negligence of those under her direct supervision and control; and (3) limited liability (or capped joint and several liability) for the negligent acts of other shareholders or other employees not under their supervision or control. See, e.g., Kan. Stat. Ann. § 17–2715 (Supp. 1994 ; 1995 Me. Legis. Serv. H. P. 231 (West). What policies justify these differences? Are they still valid in an era of greater integration among practitioners operating in business entities? What arrangements might you advise for a professional corporation that anticipates purchasing expensive assets like an MRI or valuable interests in real estate? Are there arrangements that might also help allocate capital expenditures in a multi-specialty practice where not every physician will be using the MRI?

Problem: Hope Springs Eternal

Hope Springs Eternal Health System, a not-for-profit hospital system headquartered in Hope Springs, Kansas operates three acute care hospitals in Kansas and one in New Budapest, Missouri. Two of its four hospitals (one in Kansas and one in Missouri) have lost money over the last two years and both are operating as a drain on the System's overall finances. One of the hospitals losing money, Western Missouri Hope (WMH), located in rural New Budapest, is the only hospital in its small town and its emergency room there operates at a large loss. The articles of incorporation, drafted upon WMH's formation during the Great

Depression, describe as its purpose "to operate a hospital and other facilities to best serve the health needs of the deserving in New Budapest."

WMH enjoys strong community support and receives substantial local donations, and volunteer services have kept it afloat for many years. The System's CEO is concerned about newspaper reports that Milo Minderbender, president and chairman of the board of WMH, has attended several expensive seminars in Las Vegas and San Francisco to learn from national experts about correcting the problems of distressed hospitals. The local newspaper in New Budapest has also gathered data showing that Minderbender's salary ranks in the top 1% of all hospital executives running comparable rural hospitals. Further, the paper has discovered that despite the considerable poverty in New Budapest, WMH Hospital provides less charity care than any other Missouri hospital located in similar economically deprived communities.

Without telling the System Board, the System's CEO hired a consultant to make recommendations regarding the future of WMH. The consultant's study confirmed the dire financial status of WMH, but explored only the option of closing the hospital. The consultant has made several recommendations which the CEO wants to put before the Board at its next meeting. She would like your advice on the legal risks associated with each proposal.

- Close the hospital in New Budapest and form a limited liability company with a group of local physicians to own and operate an ambulatory surgery center, leasing the old hospital facility to this joint venture. The hospital system will own 51% of the joint venture. According to the consultant, the venture should be sufficiently profitable to offset the losses of the other System hospital losing money and contribute to the capital needs of its other hospitals.

- Stop accepting patients who are insured by MissouriCares, a State-run insurance program for the working poor. MissouriCares, which is not affiliated with Medicaid or SCHIP, sets its reimbursement rates for hospitals at levels lower than Medicaid and fails to cover WMH's costs of service to its beneficiaries. The consultant believes this move might shake up state policy makers and get them to reconsider their rate structure for both Medicaid and MissouriCares.

- Award a large consulting contract to Dr. Homer Green, a senior board member of WMH who has just sold his medical practice in New Budapest. It is hoped that his strong professional and personal contacts in the medical community will be instrumental in obtaining the joint venture agreement with the physicians and facilitating the transition from operating a hospital to partnering with physicians to run an ambulatory surgery center.

D. PROFESSIONALISM AND THE CORPORATE PRACTICE OF MEDICINE DOCTRINE

BERLIN v. SARAH BUSH LINCOLN HEALTH CENTER

Supreme Court of Illinois, 1997.
179 Ill.2d 1, 227 Ill.Dec. 769, 688 N.E.2d 106.

JUSTICE NICKELS delivered the opinion of the court:

Plaintiff, Richard Berlin, Jr., M.D., filed a complaint for declaratory judgment and a motion for summary judgment seeking to have a restrictive covenant contained in an employment agreement with defendant, Sara [sic] Bush Lincoln Health Center (the Health Center), declared unenforceable. The circuit court of Coles County, finding the entire employment agreement unenforceable, granted summary judgment in favor of Dr. Berlin. The circuit court reasoned that the Health Center, as a nonprofit corporation employing a physician, was practicing medicine in violation of the prohibition on the corporate practice of medicine. A divided appellate court affirmed, and this court granted the Health Center's petition for leave to appeal.

The central issue involved in this appeal is whether the "corporate practice doctrine" prohibits corporations, which are licensed hospitals from employing physicians to provide medical services. We find the doctrine inapplicable to licensed hospitals and accordingly reverse.

BACKGROUND

The facts are not in dispute. The Health Center is a nonprofit corporation duly licensed under the Hospital Licensing Act to operate a hospital. In December 1992, Dr. Berlin and the Health Center entered into a written agreement whereby the Health Center employed Dr. Berlin to practice medicine for the hospital for five years. The agreement provided that Dr. Berlin could terminate the employment relationship for any reason prior to the end of the five-year term by furnishing the Health Center with 180 days advance written notice of such termination. The agreement also contained a restrictive covenant, which prohibited Dr. Berlin from competing with the hospital by providing health services within a 50–mile radius of the Health Center for two years after the end of the employment agreement.

On February 4, 1994, Dr. Berlin informed the Health Center by letter that he was resigning effective February 7, 1994, and accepting employment with the Carle Clinic Association. After his resignation, Dr. Berlin immediately began working at a Carle Clinic facility located approximately one mile from the Health Center. Shortly thereafter, the Health Center sought a preliminary injunction to prohibit Dr. Berlin from practicing at the Carle Clinic based on the restrictive covenant contained in the aforesaid employment agreement.

* * *

HOSPITAL EMPLOYMENT OF PHYSICIANS

The Health Center and its supporting amici curiae contend that no judicial determination exists which prohibits hospitals from employing physicians. In support of this contention, the Health Center argues that this court has acknowledged the legitimacy of such employment practices in past decisions. See, e.g., Gilbert v. Sycamore Municipal Hospital, 156 Ill.2d 511, 190 Ill.Dec. 758, 622 N.E.2d 788 (1993); Darling v. Charleston Community Memorial Hospital, 33 Ill.2d 326, 211 N.E.2d 253 (1965). In the alternative, the Health Center contends that if a judicial prohibition on hospital employment of physicians does exist, it should be overruled. In support of this contention, the Health Center argues that the public policies behind such a prohibition are inapplicable to licensed hospitals, particularly nonprofit hospitals.

The Health Center also contends that there is no statutory prohibition on the corporate employment of physicians. The Health Center notes that no statute has ever expressly stated that physicians cannot be employed by corporations. To the contrary, the Health Center argues that other legislative actions recognize that hospitals can indeed employ physicians.

Dr. Berlin and supporting amici curiae contend that this court, in People ex rel. Kerner v. United Medical Service, Inc. adopted the corporate practice of medicine doctrine, which prohibits corporations from employing physicians. Dr. Berlin concludes that the Health Center, as a nonprofit corporation, is prohibited by the Kerner rule from entering into employment agreements with physicians.

Dr. Berlin also disputes the Health Center's contention that public policy supports creating an exception to the Kerner rule for hospitals. He argues that, because no legislative enactment subsequent to the Kerner case expressly grants hospitals the authority to employ physicians, the legislature has ratified the corporate practice of medicine doctrine as the public policy of Illinois. At this point, a review of the corporate practice of medicine doctrine is appropriate.

Corporate Practice of Medicine Doctrine

The corporate practice of medicine doctrine prohibits corporations from providing professional medical services. Although a few states have codified the doctrine, the prohibition is primarily inferred from state medical licensure acts, which regulate the profession of medicine and forbid its practice by unlicensed individuals. See A. Rosoff, The Business of Medicine: Problems with the Corporate Practice Doctrine, 17 Cumb. L. Rev. 485, 490 (1987). The rationale behind the doctrine is that a corporation cannot be licensed to practice medicine because only a human being can sustain the education, training, and character screening, which are prerequisites to receiving a professional license. Since a corporation cannot receive a medical license, it follows that a corporation cannot legally practice the profession.

The rationale of the doctrine concludes that the employment of physicians by corporations is illegal because the acts of the physicians are attributable to the corporate employer, which cannot obtain a medical license. The prohibition on the corporate employment of physicians is invariably supported by several public policy arguments, which espouse the dangers of lay control over professional judgment, the division of the physician's loyalty between his patient and his profitmaking employer, and the commercialization of the profession.

Application of Doctrine in Illinois

This court first encountered the corporate practice doctrine in Dr. Allison, Dentist, Inc. v. Allison, 360 Ill. 638, 196 N.E. 799 (1935). In Allison, the plaintiff corporation owned and operated a dental practice. When defendant, a dentist formerly employed by plaintiff, opened a dental office across the street from plaintiff's location, plaintiff brought an action to enforce a restrictive covenant contained in defendant's employment contract. Defendant's motion to dismiss the action was granted on the grounds that plaintiff was practicing dentistry in violation of the Dental Practice Act. In affirming the judgment of the lower court, this court stated:

"To practice a profession requires something more than the financial ability to hire competent persons to do the actual work. It can be done only by a duly qualified human being, and to qualify something more than mere knowledge or skill is essential. The qualifications include personal characteristics, such as honesty, guided by an upright conscience and a sense of loyalty to clients or patients, even to the extent of sacrificing pecuniary profit, if necessary. These requirements are spoken of generically as that good moral character which is a pre-requisite to the licensing of any professional man. No corporation can qualify." [The Court next discussed cases finding the corporate practice doctrine barred corporations from operating dental clinics employing dentists and prevented a medical clinic providing medical services through licensed physicians.]

* * *

Prior to the instant action, apparently no Illinois court has applied the corporate practice of medicine rule set out in People ex rel. Kerner v. United Medical Service, Inc., or specifically addressed the issue of whether licensed hospitals are prohibited from employing physicians. We therefore look to other jurisdictions with reference to the application of the corporate practice of medicine doctrine to hospitals.

APPLICABILITY OF DOCTRINE TO HOSPITALS IN OTHER JURISDICTIONS

Although the corporate practice of medicine doctrine has long been recognized by a number of jurisdictions, the important role hospitals serve in the health care field has also been increasingly recognized. Accordingly, numerous jurisdictions have recognized either judicial or statutory exceptions to the corporate practice of medicine doctrine which allow hospitals to employ physicians and other health care professionals. See, e.g., Cal. Bus. & Prof. Code § 2400 (West 1990) (exception for charitable hospitals).... A review of this authority reveals that there are primarily three approaches utilized in determining that the corporate practice of medicine doctrine is inapplicable to hospitals.

First, some states refused to adopt the corporate practice of medicine doctrine altogether when initially interpreting their respective medical practice act. These states generally determined that a hospital corporation that employs a physician is not practicing medicine, but rather is merely making medical treatment available. See, e.g., State ex rel. Sager v. Lewin, 128 Mo. App. 149, 155, 106 S.W. 581, 583 (1907) ("[H]ospitals are maintained by private corporations, incorporated for the purpose of furnishing medical and surgical treatment to the sick and wounded. These corporations do not practice medicine but they receive patients and employ physicians and surgeons to give them treatment")....

Under the second approach, the courts of some jurisdictions determined that the corporate practice doctrine is inapplicable to nonprofit hospitals and health associations. These courts reasoned that the public policy arguments supporting the corporate practice doctrine do not apply to physicians employed by charitable institutions. See, e.g., Group Health Ass'n v. Moor, 24 F.Supp. 445, 446 (D.D.C. 1938) (actions of nonprofit association which contracts with licensed physicians to provide medical treatment to its members in no way commercializes medicine and is not the practice of medicine), aff'd, 107 F.2d 239 (D.C.Cir.1939)....

In the third approach, the courts of several states have determined that the corporate practice doctrine is not applicable to hospitals, which employ physicians because hospitals are authorized by other laws to provide medical treatment to patients. . . .

We find the rationale of the latter two approaches persuasive. We decline to apply the corporate practice of medicine doctrine to licensed hospitals. The instant cause is distinguishable from Kerner, Allison, and Winberry. None of those cases specifically involved the employment of physicians by a hospital. More important, none of those cases involved a corporation licensed to provide health care services to the general public.

The corporate practice of medicine doctrine set forth in Kerner was not an interpretation of the plain language of the Medical Practice Act. The Medical Practice Act contains no express prohibition on the corporate employment of physicians.[5] Rather, the corporate practice of medicine doctrine was inferred from the general policies behind the Medical Practice Act. Such a prohibition is entirely appropriate to a general corporation possessing no licensed authority to offer medical services to the public, such as the appellant in Kerner. However, when a corporation has been sanctioned by the laws of this state to operate a hospital, such a prohibition is inapplicable.

The legislative enactments pertaining to hospitals provide ample support for this conclusion. For example, the Hospital Licensing Act defines "hospital" as:

"any institution, place, building, or agency, public or private, whether organized for profit or not, devoted primarily to the maintenance and operation of facilities for the diagnosis and treatment or care of * * * persons admitted for overnight stay or longer in order to obtain medical, including obstetric, psychiatric and nursing, care of illness, disease, injury, infirmity, or deformity." (Emphasis added.) 210 ILCS 85/3 (West Supp.1995).

[The Court cites other statutes that require hospitals to furnish services.]

The foregoing statutes clearly authorize, and at times mandate, licensed hospital corporations to provide medical services. We believe that the authority to employ duly-licensed physicians for that purpose is reasonably implied from these legislative enactments. We further see no justification for distinguishing between nonprofit and for-profit hospitals in this regard. The authorities and duties of licensed hospitals are conferred equally upon both entities.

In addition, we find the public policy concerns, which support the corporate practice doctrine inapplicable to a licensed hospital in the modern health care industry. The concern for lay control over professional judgment is alleviated in a licensed hospital, where generally a separate professional medical staff is responsible for the quality of medical services rendered in the facility.[6]

---

5. In contrast, the Dental Practice Act, applied by this court in [the dental clinic and Allison cases], expressly prohibited a corporation from furnishing dentists and owning and operating a dental office.

6. Moreover, in the instant case, the employment agreement expressly provided that the Health Center had no control or direction over Dr. Berlin's medical judgment and practice, other than that control exercised by the

Furthermore, we believe that extensive changes in the health care industry since the time of the Kerner decision, including the emergence of corporate health maintenance organizations, have greatly altered the concern over the commercialization of health care. In addition, such concerns are relieved when a licensed hospital is the physician's employer. Hospitals have an independent duty to provide for the patient's health and welfare. [Citations to Darling and other cases omitted].

We find particularly appropriate the statement of the Kansas Supreme Court that "[i]t would be incongruous to conclude that the legislature intended a hospital to accomplish what it is licensed to do without utilizing physicians as independent contractors or employees. * * * To conclude that a hospital must do so without employing physicians is not only illogical but ignores reality." St. Francis Regional Med. Center v. Weiss, 254 Kan. 728, 745, 869 P.2d 606, 618 (1994). Accordingly, we conclude that a duly-licensed hospital possesses legislative authority to practice medicine by means of its staff of licensed physicians and is excepted from the operation of the corporate practice of medicine doctrine.

Consequently, the employment agreement between the Health Center and Dr. Berlin is not unenforceable merely because the Health Center is a corporate entity.

* * *

Notes and Questions

1. Consider the following rationale for the corporate practice of medicine doctrine offered by the Illinois Supreme Court:

> [T]he practice of a profession is subject to licensing and regulation and is not subject to commercialization or exploitation. To practice a profession ... requires something more than the financial ability to hire competent persons to do the actual work. It can be done only by a duly qualified human being, and to qualify something more than mere knowledge or skill is essential ... No corporation can qualify.

People v. United Medical Service, 362 Ill. 442, 200 N.E. 157, 163 (1936). Can you articulate the specific concerns that underlie the court's statement? Are the sources of the doctrine statutory or do they emanate from general public policy principles? If the latter, what are those principles and are they still valid today? For a decidedly negative assessment of the doctrine, see Mark A. Hall, Institutional Control of Physician Behavior: Legal Barriers to Health Care Cost Containment, 137 U. Pa. L. Rev. 431, 509–518 (1988)("puzzling doctrine ... clouded with confused reasoning and ... founded on an astounding series of logical fallacies"). See also Arnold J. Rosoff, The Business of Medicine: Problems with the Corporate Practice Doctrine, 17 Cumb. L. Rev. 485 (1986–87).

2. Does the corporate practice of medicine doctrine apply to nonphysicians and complementary and alternative medicine? The answer depends on whether the services in question implicate the policy concerns underlying the doctrine. If one construes the doctrine to apply to "healing" professions, it might reach many forms of CAM. However, courts, attorneys general and legislatures have tended to require that the healing practice in question must involve significant training and

---

professional medical staff. Dr. Berlin has never contended that the Health Center's lay management attempted to control his practice of medicine.

education, and that the practitioner exercise independent professional judgment. Thus, because massage therapy requires no training or licensure under Minnesota law, the Minnesota Supreme Court found the corporate practice doctrine inapplicable. Isles Wellness, Inc. v. Progressive Northern Insurance, 703 N.W.2d 513 (Minn. 2005). Likewise, because physical therapy services required an order of referral from a physician or certain other licensed practitioners, and in some cases periodic review of the treatment provided by the physical therapist, the court concluded that "the public policy concerns regarding a conflict of interest between the health care provider and the lay person or entity are lessened" and again declined to apply the CPM doctrine. Id. at 523. However, the court went on to find that the doctrine did apply to the practice of chiropractic because that profession requires extensive training and is provided without supervision by other professionals, whereas physical therapists direct patients under the order of referral or periodic review of other specified health care providers. Id. at 524. Does this mean that all contracts entered into by the corporation violating the CPM doctrine are automatically void? After remand and appeal, the Minnesota Supreme Court said "no." Noting that the corporation did not knowingly violate the law by practicing chiropractic under lay ownership and "the lack of clarity regarding the applicability of the corporate practice of medicine doctrine to chiropractors before this court's decision," the court declined to void the contracts entered into with insurance companies by the corporation. Isles Wellness, Inc. v. Progressive Northern Insurance, 725 N.W.2d 90, 95 (Minn. 2006).

3. The question of whether the holding in *Berlin* should be extended to other nonprofit health care organizations was addressed by the Illinois Supreme Court in Carter–Shields v. Alton Health Institute, 201 Ill.2d 441, 268 Ill.Dec. 25, 777 N.E.2d 948 (2002). The case involved a physician seeking to avoid application of a non-competition agreement she had signed with the Alton Health Institute, Inc. (AHI). AHI was a nonprofit corporation fifty-percent owned by St. Anthony's Health Systems, also a nonprofit corporation. Although not licensed as a hospital, St. Anthony's controlled two licensed hospitals in the area. The remaining fifty percent of AHI was owned by a partnership composed primarily of physician groups. The Court strongly reaffirmed the corporate practice of medicine doctrine, stating "the exercise of control or influence over the medical decision making of a physician by a lay, unlicensed corporation results in a division of the physician's loyalty between the often divergent interests of the corporation and the patient." Id. at 957. It declined to extend its holding in *Berlin*, characterizing that decision as "carving out a narrow exception for an entity, such as a hospital, that must meet certain professional criteria established by the legislature." Id. Although AHI was a charitable nonprofit health care organization, it lacked a legislatively-determined role and was not subject to comparable regulatory oversight. The court also refused to view federal Medicare regulations governing kickbacks and conflicts of interests as sufficient to invoke the *Berlin* exception.

4. As noted above, commentators have been highly critical of the corporate practice of medicine doctrine. Can it be argued that the doctrine can help rectify the problems associated with risk sharing and managed care? Does it help restore the fiduciary ties between patient and physician that have been eroded by managed care? For an affirmative answer, see Andre Hampton, Resurrection of the Prohibition on the Corporate Practice of Medicine: Teaching Old Dogma New Tricks, 66 U. Cin. L. Rev. 489 (1998).

5. Early on, concerns about "corporate medical practice" focused on corporations contracting with physicians to provide medical care for their employees for a fixed salary or corporations that marketed physicians' services to the public. The

AMA considered the corporate practice of medicine the "commercialization" of medicine, and believed that it would increase physician workload, decrease the quality of patient care, and would introduce lay control over the practice of medicine that would interfere with the physician-patient relationship. The AMA promulgated ethical guidelines that restricted or prohibited the corporate practice of medicine. The prohibition against corporate medical practice was enforced by the courts, using statutory prohibitions against the practice of medicine by unlicensed individuals. See Jeffrey F. Chase–Lubitz, The Corporate Practice of Medicine Doctrine: An Anachronism in the Modern Health Care Industry, 40 Vand. L. Rev. 445 (1987). What does it matter that a doctor is employed by a partnership of doctors or a professional corporation rather than by a lay person or business entity controlled by non-physicians? Should the state eliminate corporate practice prohibitions and pursue quality concerns directly through quality-control regulation or malpractice litigation?

6.   In states recognizing the corporate practice of medicine doctrine, what is the relationship between that doctrine's prohibitions and other statutes permitting physicians to organize their practice under a professional corporation form? In Pediatric Neurosurgery v. Russell, 44 P.3d 1063 (Colo. 2002), the Supreme Court of Colorado held that the state's professional corporation statute did not abolish the corporate practice of medicine doctrine but carved out an exception allowing corporations to practice medicine while prohibiting them from doing anything that violates medical standards of conduct. The court went on to conclude that principles of respondeat superior would apply and a professional corporation could be held vicariously liable for the torts of its employee doctors acting in the course of their employment.

7.   Although (by one estimate) as many as 37 states have statutory or common law prohibitions on the corporate practice of medicine and only 13 states either reject the doctrine or have no authority establishing it, in many states relevant precedent is quite old and in some cases widely ignored. See Adam M. Freiman, Comment, The Abandonment of the Antiquated Corporate Practice of Medicine Doctrine: Injecting a Dose of Efficiency into the Modern Health Care Environment, 47 Emory L.J. 697, 712–13 (1998). How should an attorney counsel a client as to the legal risks and propriety of undertaking actions that violate old precedent, which is likely to be overturned if ever challenged? See Norman P. Jeddeloh, Physician Contract Audits: A Hospital Management Tool, 21 J. Health & Hosp. L. 105 (1988) ("Obviously, in modern practice the rule against physician employment is honored mainly in the breach. That does not mean that these traditional prohibitions cannot again serve as a basis for hospital liability. ... Therefore, it is usually best, whenever possible, to establish true independent contractor arrangements or retain physicians through a separate corporation.") For an insightful analysis of the dangers of ignoring this latent doctrine, see Rosoff, *supra*.

III.   INTEGRATION AND NEW ORGANIZATIONAL STRUCTURES

WHERE'S WALDO—PART II

The year is 1996 and Waldo, now 53 years old, visits Dr. Goodscalpel for a routine check-up. Doctor Goodscalpel, who has joined a 10–doctor partnership called Medical Associates, recommends a PSA screening test. He sends Waldo down the hall to MedServices, an outpatient for-profit corporation owned by a subsidiary of the Llama Hilda Foundation. Llama Hilda is a not-for-profit corporation that now controls Mt. St. Hilda Hospital and numerous other entities providing health and administrative services. Unfortunately, the lab tests come back positive and Dr. Goodscalpel refers Waldo to a surgeon, Dr. Mack, who has joined Doctors Inc., a large (50 doctor) multi-specialist group organized as a professional corporation. Doctors Inc. and Medical Associates both are co-owners, along with Mt. St. Hilda Hospital, of a physician-hospital organization (PHO), an entity that negotiates contracts with insurance companies and supplies billing and other services to the medical groups.

After receiving prior approval from the PHO utilization manager, Dr. Mack sends Waldo to the Radiology Center for an MRI. The Radiology Center, an outpatient facility on Mt. St. Hilda's campus, is a joint venture organized as a corporation. Fifty percent of its stock is owned by Llama Hilda Foundation, and the other 50 percent is owned by a partnership comprised of 5 radiologists. After getting the MRI report back from the consulting radiologists, Dr. Mack recommends surgery to be performed at Mt. St. Hilda.

Waldo has joined BlueStaff's new managed care plan, CarePlan, which provides coverage only if he visits participating providers. Although Waldo had wanted Dr. Immel, an internationally known anesthesiologist who teaches at a local medical school, to assist in the operation, Dr. Immel was not a CarePlan participating provider and did not have staff privileges at Mt. St. Hilda hospital. Instead, Mt. St. Hilda has an exclusive contract with GasAssociates, a professional group organized as a limited liability company controlled by its anesthesiologist-owners. The anesthesia was furnished by a CRNA under the supervision of an anesthesiologist.

Most of the providers furnishing services to Waldo were paid on a prepaid capitated basis. Waldo was responsible for a small co-payment on certain services.

Comparing Waldo's recent episode of care to his experience in 1978 (set forth at the beginning of this chapter), what changes have occurred in terms of provider coordination and control of their activities? How do the organizational structures to which the physicians and hospitals belong accommodate the changed environment? How have the economic incentives facing the providers changed? Is Waldo, the "consumer," better off under managed care?

A. THE STRUCTURE OF THE MODERN HEALTH CARE ENTERPRISE

Organizational arrangements for the delivery of health services have undergone dramatic changes over the last forty years. As depicted in the Where's Waldo I episode, for many years health care services were delivered primarily by doctors working in solo practice or as members of small groups usually practicing the same specialty, and by non-profit hospitals operating independently or as part of relatively simple systems that shared a few administrative or operational services. This began to change with the advent of managed care in the 1980's as hospitals adopted more complex organizational structures and entered into joint ventures and alliances with other hospitals and with their physicians. Prompted by developments in health care financing and the possibility of health care reform, physicians, hospitals and other providers began to reorganize their business enterprises and contractual relationships. In particular, they developed so-called "integrated delivery systems" via physician practice acquisitions and mergers, and establishing physician hospital organizations, joint ventures and other organizations that enhanced inter-provider linkages in order to meet the demands of capitated payments and the requirements of managed care. With the "backlash" against managed care at the end of the 1990's and increasing concerns about patient safety and quality of care, a new era began and organizational structures began to change once again. Physicians and hospitals "disintegrated," with many organizations disbanding and hospitals selling back to physicians' their practices Looser networks of physicians and alliances became more prominent, while administrators focused on means of improving the flow of information both internally and to consumers. See Cara S. Lesser et al., The End of an Era: What Became of the "Managed Care Revolution?" 38 Health Serv. Research 337 (2003).

The health care organizations discussed in this section are business entities (e.g., corporations, LLCs, partnerships or contractual joint ventures) that link providers "horizontally" and "vertically" or on both levels. That is, physicians may combine horizontally with other physicians to form group practices, IPAs, PPOs, or other networks. Likewise, hospitals may merge or establish joint ventures and alliances with other hospitals. Hospitals and physicians have also integrated vertically by creating various kinds of integrated delivery systems, which bring together complementary provider services at several levels Some of these organizations only loosely link hospitals and physicians and are primarily devices to facilitate joint contracting with payers. Other forms of vertical integration more fully bind hospitals and physicians by having them share both financial risk and control. In these forms, physicians and hospitals may co-own and co-manage services or enterprises; the hospital may undertake administrative or management services for physicians; the hospital may purchase the physician practices, with the physicians becoming employees of or independent contractors for the organization; or the physicians may control the enterprise with hospitals assuming a contracting relationship. Vertical integration may also include the insurance component, as provider systems may integrate into insurance or insurers may integrate into delivery through HMOs or joint ventures with providers. The following excerpt from the Physician Payment Review Commission [predecessor to Medicare Payment Advisory Commission, MEDPAC,] describes many of the organizational models, and how they enhance integration.

PHYSICIAN PAYMENT REVIEW COMMISSION, ANNUAL REPORT TO CONGRESS

(1995).

* * *

INTEGRATING ORGANIZATIONS

Defining the new integrating organizations is not an easy task. Health care organizations are in flux as markets move toward more intensive management of care. A definition that describes the typical organization today might be obsolete two years from now as the typical style of practice changes.

Consequently there are no agreed-upon standard definitions, and these definitions should be taken as approximate only.

* * *

Independent Practice Association

The independent practice association (IPA) is typically a physician-organized entity that contracts with payers on behalf of its member physicians. The typical IPA negotiates contracts with insurers and pays physicians on a fee-for-service basis with a withhold. Physicians may maintain significant business outside the IPA, join multiple IPAs, retain ownership of their own practices, and typically continue in their traditional style of practice. Physicians usually invest a modest fee (a few thousand dollars) to join the IPA. IPAs may also undertake a variety of additional roles, including utilization review, and practice management functions such as billing and group purchasing, resulting in greater centralization and standardization of medical practice.

* * *

Physician–Hospital Organization

The physician-hospital organization [PHO] contracts with payers on behalf of the hospital and its affiliated physicians. The organization is responsible for negotiating health plan contracts, and in some cases, conducting utilization review, credentialing, and quality assurance. The PHO may centralize some aspects of administrative services or encourage use of shared facilities for coordination of clinical care.

The typical PHO is a hospital-sponsored organization that centers around a single hospital and its medical staff. PHOs may also form as joint ventures between hospitals and existing physician organizations such as a large multispecialty medical group or an IPA. PHOs are further divided into open PHOs, which are open to all members of the hospital's staff, and closed PHOs, where the PHO chooses some physicians and excludes others.

As with the IPA, the typical PHO accounts for only a modest share of the physician's (or the hospital's) business. Physicians retain their own practices, and their relationship to payers other than those with whom the PHO negotiates is unchanged. As with IPAs, the PHO can move toward greater centralized control over practice management and medical practice.

* * *

Group Practice

A medical group practice is defined as "the provision of health care services by three or more physicians who are formally organized as a legal entity in which business and clinical facilities, records, and personnel are shared. Income from medical services provided by the group are treated as receipts of the group and are distributed according to some prearranged plan."

The group practice is a well-established form of organization and one of the few organizational types for which good data are available. In 1991, physicians were split almost equally among three practice settings: group practice, solo or two-physician practice, or other patient care such as hospital-based practice.

* * *

Group Practice Without Walls

A group practice without walls (GPWW) refers to physicians in physically independent facilities who form a single legal entity to centralize the business aspects of their organization. In the typical case, the GPWW is organized by a strong, centralized clinic that adds individual physicians or small groups in satellite offices. In some cases, the GPWW is financially identical to a traditional group practice: It owns the assets of the individual practices and physicians share ownership of the GPWW, making it a unified business organization for the decentralized delivery of care. In other cases, physicians retain ownership of their own practices but enter into agreements for administrative and marketing functions. The GPWW may itself own certain ancillary services such as laboratory services.

Management Services Organization

The management services organization provides administrative and practice management services to physicians. An MSO may typically be owned by a hospital, hospitals, or investors. Large group practices may also establish MSOs as a way of capitalizing on their organizational skill by selling management services to otherwise unorganized physician groups.

MSOs can provide a very wide variety of services. Smaller and not-for-profit MSOs may limit operations to selling to physicians various administrative support services, such as billing, group purchasing, and various aspects of office administration. In other cases, hospital-owned MSOs are the vehicle through which hospitals purchase physician practices outright, leaving the physician either as an employee of the hospital or as an independent contractor with the physical assets of the practice owned by the hospital. Large, for-profit MSOs typically purchase the assets of physician practices outright, install office managers and other personnel, hire the physician through a professional services contract, and negotiate contracts with managed-care plans, all in exchange for a share of gross receipts typically based on the physicians' current practice expenses.

* * *

Hospital–Owned Medical Practice

In addition to the purchase of a medical practice through an MSO, hospitals can directly purchase medical practices, typically as part of their outpatient department.

* * *

Integrated Delivery System

Finally, a number of functionally similar organizations are built around hospitals and physicians linked in exclusive arrangements. In these integrated delivery systems (IDSs), a hospital or hospitals and large multispecialty group practices form an organization for the delivery of care, with all physician revenues coming through the organization.[7] These include foundation model, staff model, and equity model IDSs.

The main difference among these organizations is in the legal formalities of who works for whom and in the professional autonomy of the affiliated physicians. In a typical foundation model system, the hospital establishes a not-for-profit foundation that purchases the assets of an existing physician group, signing an exclusive professional services contract with the physician corporation. Payers pay the foundation, which then pays the physicians' professional corporation.[8] In a staff model system, physicians work directly for the system without the intervening not-for-profit foundation and professional corporation. In an equity model system, physicians own a part of the system and share significantly in its financial success or failure.

Notes

1. *Integration: Objectives.* The integrating organizations described above bring together in various combinations physicians, hospitals and other providers that had previously operated independently. In counseling in this area, it is obviously critical to have a firm understanding of the different objectives of the various parties. For example, physicians typically are looking for a structure that will assist them in the contracting process by providing capital, information systems, administrative support, patient referrals and access to a competitively strong network. At the same time, physicians want some assurance that their incomes will not erode and that they will have a substantial voice in the governance of the new organization. Hospitals are eager to assure themselves of an adequate flow of patients to fill their beds and outpatient facilities and a cadre of physicians committed to their organization. At the same time, hospitals are reluctant to give up control of the organizational structure of the enterprise (after all, they usually supply the lion's share of the financial investment), although shared control is sometimes attempted.

2. *Organizational Structures for Physician Integration.* Physicians face a choice of a number of structural and contractual organizations in which to conduct their practices. The most complete form of organization is the formation of a Fully Integrated Medical Group (FIMGs), which usually take the form of professional corporations or unincorporated entities such as LLCs and typically entails considerable operational integration. A tightly integrated FIMG, for example, might entail: centralized governance that controls all aspects of the group's business; formal quality control and utilization management programs; FIMG responsibility for entering into managed care contracts; and income allocation systems that rely on achievement of the group rather than individual performance. These groups may be formed among members of a single specialty or kind of practice (single specialty groups) or among practitioners of multiple specialties (multi-specialty groups). Less complete integration is available through several kinds of physician organizations. Partially Integrated Medical Groups (PIMGs) or Group Practices Without Walls (GPWWs) entail physicians operating as a single legal entity (e.g. a professional corporation) with common management, staff and administrative services. However, physicians in PIMGs may maintain their prac-

---

7. While some researchers would call these integrated delivery systems a form of PHO, most reserve the term PHO for those organizations where only a small fraction of the physicians' revenues come through the organization.

8. The presence of the foundation model system is due in part to state laws prohibiting the corporate practice of medicine, and the need for arms-length financial agreements between for-profit and not-for-profit entities.

tice locations and employment relationships with certain staff; they also retain autonomy in many respects, such as participation in managed care contracts and purchasing and other business decisions. Costs and profits are frequently allocated on an individualized or "cost center" basis.

Finally, physicians may join entities which are essentially contracting entities that enable them to offer a single network to payers, with perhaps some integration through common utilization controls. The Preferred Provider Organization, for example, which is typically a joint venture, usually entails contractual agreements to deliver care to a defined group of patients at discounted fee-for-service rates and to submit to certain controls on utilization or membership restrictions based on quality and utilization criteria. Similarly, physicians may join Independent Practice Associations (IPAs), which also involve only limited operational integration of physician practices through billing services and utilization review. Although IPA members sometimes agree to accept distributions of capitated revenues, which create incentives to alter practice styles, neither IPAs nor PPOs typically have controls over physician behavior and the percentage of each physician's revenues from the IPA is often not sufficient to cause significant changes in the way he or she provides care.

3. *Organizational Structures for Physician–Hospital Integration.* As described by the Physician Payment Review Commission above, physicians and hospitals desiring to achieve some degree of integration can choose from several organizational models: e.g., the MSO, the PHO or the staff, equity or foundation model (fully integrated) IDS. The PHO is in most respects the least structurally integrated and least complex form. Its primary purpose is to negotiate and administer managed care contracts for its providers, and may even do so on a capitated basis; in which case the PHO is regarded as a provider of care. However, PHOs typically provide fewer services for physician practices than do the other forms and do not significantly alter the clinical practice patterns of providers. MSOs also provide contracting services as well as many of the "back-room" functions necessary to operate physician offices, including billing, claims processing, ancillary services and many of the credentialing and utilization control services needed for contracting. In the more comprehensive form, MSOs may acquire physician practices outright or supply "turnkey" operations by purchasing and leasing equipment and office space and hiring staff for physicians. Finally, fully integrated systems, including the foundation model IDS, are entities that bring together ownership of an organization that supplies all types of health services and coordinates case management and the flow of information. This may be done through foundations or clinics that acquire physician practices or through "equity models" that enable physicians to acquire an ownership interest in the system.

4.   Through most of the 1990's, integration between hospitals and physicians grew rapidly, with most large hospital systems developing PHOs and acquiring physician practices. Many health industry experts confidently predicted that the new integrating organizations such as PHOs and MSOs were really transitional vehicles that would serve to "acclimate" hospitals and physicians to the new environment created by managed care. By this account, after becoming accustomed to cooperating with each other, most providers would ultimately wind up in more fully integrated organizations that entail employment relationships and asset purchases. However, predictions of an inevitable progression toward integration proved erroneous. Mark Pauly and Lawton Burns described it as follows:

> During the 1990's many hospitals pursued twin strategies of vertical and horizontal integration. Each type of integration assumed multiple forms.

Vertical combination included acquisition of primary care physicians, strategic alliances with physicians in [PHOs and MSOs, and the development of HMOs]. Horizontal combinations included the formation of Multi-hospital systems mergers, and strategic alliances with neighboring hospitals to form local networks ...

While the form of integration varied across hospitals and markets, their economic performance, after a decade of experience, was genuinely uniform: Nothing worked.

Lawton R. Burns & Mark V. Pauly, Integrated Delivery Networks: A Detour on the Road to Integrated Health Care? 21 Health Aff. 128 (July/Aug. 2002). Some large for-profit health systems that aggressively acquired or networked with physicians were spectacularly unsuccessful and several publicly traded physician practice management companies, once the darlings of Wall Street, also went into bankruptcy. The picture was no brighter in the nonprofit sector. Acquisitions of physician practices have imposed a monumental drain on the budgets of nonprofit hospitals; 80 percent of all physician practices acquired by hospitals lost money, by some estimates at a rate of nearly $50,000–100,000 per year per physician. Finally, countless large IPAs and group practices have been forced to disband for financial reasons. For accounts and analyses of these developments, see James Robinson, The Future of Managed Care, 18 Health Aff. 7 (March/April 1999); Thomas Bodenheimer, The American Health Care System—Physicians and the Changing Medical Marketplace, 340 New Eng. J. Med. (Feb. 18, 1999).

What explains these seismic shifts in organizational structures? Examining both the *ex ante* justifications for integration and the performance of various systems in recent years, Burns and Pauly conclude that the integration phenomenon was built on faulty premises such as the inevitable spread of capitation payment and the ability of hospitals to "partner" with physicians and achieve economic savings, and that most participants ignored obstacles to realizing significant economies of scale and developing an appropriate regulatory infrastructure. Burns & Pauly, *supra*.

B.   THE NEW LANDSCAPE FOR HEATHCARE ORGANIZATIONS

WHERE'S WALDO—PART III

It is the year 2008 and Waldo, now 62 years old, has developed diabetes and high blood pressure, both of which are treated with expensive drugs and require regular exams and tests. Responding to complaints from employees about the HMO options previously offered, Waldo's employer has decided to switch to consumer directed health care and now offers only two plans. CarePlan is a PPO with an annual deductible of $1,000, maximum out of pocket liability of $5,000, and tiered co-pays for doctors, hospitals and outpatient care and tests. The tier in which each participating physician is placed determines the insured's co-pay responsibility. CarePlan sets tiers according to various performance criteria and the terms of its contract with the provider, such as utilization history and quality indicators. Waldo's primary care physician and endocrinologist are Tier One Doctors for Care Plan (co-pay of 10%) and his cardiologist is a Tier 4 doctor (co-pay of 40%). Alternatively, Waldo may choose HealthSaver, a health savings account plan which features a tax-preferred health savings account and catastrophic coverage under a PPO plan. This plan has a large deductible ($2000) and allows him to put both his monthly contribution and his employer's contribution into a Health Savings

Account. Waldo hopes to retire when he reaches the age of 68. Unfortunately, after the passage of the Medicare Prescription Drug Improvement and Modernization Act of 2003, his employer dropped health coverage for retirees. In addition, CarePlan does not participate in Medicare Advantage. Waldo is concerned about both insurance coverage and maintaining his relationships with his long time internist, Dr. Goodscalpel, his endocrinologist, Dr. Douce, and his cardiologist, Dr. Coeur–Casse. Using what you've learned in this chapter and chapters 6, 7, and 8, what advice would you give to Waldo to help him evaluate his options?

1. Health Financing and Physician Practice Arrangements

The choice of organizational structures by physicians is highly responsive to changes in health care financing. Payment systems create financial incentives that affect how physicians organize their business relationships and how they interact with other providers in delivering care. The ways in which the new payment landscape have influenced physicians are discussed below.

Fee for Service Payment. As managed care payment grew, physicians began to join larger physician groups. This trend has continued but not to the degree or in the manner once predicted. Although the proportion of physicians in solo and two-physician practices has decreased significantly in recent years (from 40.7 percent in 1996–97 to 32.5 percent in 2004–05), physicians are not moving to multispecialty practices. The proportion of physicians in multispecialty practices decreased from 30.9 percent to 27.5 percent between 1998 and 2005, while the proportion of single specialty practices has grown considerably. Allison Liebhaber & Joy M. Grossman, Physicians Moving to Mid–Sized, Single Specialty Practice, Center for Studying Health System Change, Tracking Report No. 18 (August, 2007), http://www.hschange.org/CONTENT/941/. Is the trend toward practice in single specialty groups a good thing? What legal and policy issues are raised by these developments? Some studies suggest that large, multispecialty practices, which combine primary care physicians and a range of specialists in the same practice, offer the organizational structure with the greatest potential to provide consistently high-quality care. Francis J. Crosson, The Delivery System Matters, 24 No. 6 Health Affairs 1543 (November/December 2005). See also Lawrence Casalino et al., Benefits of and Barriers to Large Group Medical Practice in the United States, 163 Archives Internal Med. 1958 (September 2003).

Consider also the following analysis:

Most of the growth so far has been in mid-sized practices, which, although better equipped than solo and two-physician practices, do not yet approach the capabilities envisioned by quality improvement leaders. Moreover, increased consolidation in single-specialty practices raises the potential in some markets that certain specialties can drive up prices in negotiation with health plans. Some market observers are concerned that if physicians are aggregating into larger practices to provide profitable procedures and ancillary services, the greater ability of physicians to legally self-refer patients under exceptions to self-referral laws could lead to overuse of certain services, further driving up costs of care. At the same time, some benefits to society may be lost from the movement out of smaller practices and away from practice ownership. For example, [some] research shows that physicians in smaller practices with an ownership stake are substantially more likely to provide charity care than physicians in larger practices or non-owners.

Center for Studying Health System Change, *supra.*

Notice how the shift away from capitation and risk sharing financing influences physicians' choice of practice arrangements. While capitation encouraged the formation of multi-specialty groups and integrated delivery systems to facilitate cost-benefit trade offs among providers and services, fee-for-service reimbursement creates very different incentives. Under this form of payment, physicians have incentives to provide the most profitable procedures and ancillary services, with procedure- and service-intensive specialties benefiting more than other specialists and primary care physicians. Physicians in such specialties found they could form large single-specialty practices that could aggregate capital to invest in equipment and facilities to provide their services without having to redistribute income to primary care physicians—as is traditionally the case in multispecialty groups. See Center for Studying Health System Change, Tracking Report 18 *supra.* Furthermore, the decline in the use of gatekeepers and restrictions on referral have also helped fuel the movement toward single specialty practice and away from multi-specialty practice. Can you see why that may be the case? What role should antitrust policy play in monitoring these developments?

Pay for Performance. Pay for performance (P4P) initiatives by private health plans have also had an effect on the structure of delivery arrangements. Although most health plans have instituted some form of P4P, or have plans under development, their scope varies widely. Some P4P initiatives involve focused pilot programs targeting particular diseases, such as diabetes or mellitus, while others involve comprehensive efforts directed at the broader measures of performance of primary care physicians, specialists, and hospitals. In addition, "performance" may be gauged by a variety of criteria, e.g., provision of specified treatments, conformance to practice protocols, health outcomes, adoption of technology and information systems, and patient satisfaction. See also discussion of P4P under Medicare *supra* Chapter 8.

Designing and implementing P4P arrangements may be problematic in some cases. While payers and employers may want performance measures closely tied to outcomes, providers argue that they should be held to account only for those outcomes they are in a position to influence through changes in their medical practice. In markets in which physicians practice in small unintegrated practices and make referrals to independent specialists and facilities, it may not be possible to target individual physicians for the outcomes they are responsible for. See Michael F. Cannon, Pay–For–Performance: Is Medicare a Good Candidate?, 7 Yale J. Health Pol'y L. & Ethics 1 (2007). Likewise hospitals may not be fully accountable for outcomes where they can exercise little control over the choices made by the physicians who practice in their facilities. In addition, both physicians and hospitals argue they should not be held accountable for outcomes resulting from patients' choices stemming from their health insurance benefit design. For example, a patient might decline to seek preventive or follow up care because of large out-of-pocket costs in her plan. On the other side of the equation, in markets where there are dominant hospitals or specialty groups, it may be difficult to secure cooperation from providers, as they have little economic incentive to cooperate with plans hoping to institute performance based reimbursement. Thus while P4P might seem to create incentives pushing providers toward adopting more integrated structures, many factors may undermine the opportunity for P4P arrangements to get started. See Sally Trude et al., Health Plan Pay–For–Performance Strategies, 12 Am. J. Managed Care 537 (2006).

Consumer-Directed Health Care

As discussed in Chapter 6, the movement toward consumer directed health care (CDHC) has altered many of the contracting arrangements facing providers. It is true of course that CDHC has much in common with managed care Both models rely on markets and competition among providers to produce the optimal mix of quality and cost. Further, both assume that providers will respond to competition by creating organizational arrangements that optimize cost and quality controls and promote innovation. At the same time, however, the two models differ fundamentally with respect to who should make choices and what kind of infrastructure is needed to promote efficient outcomes. As a general matter, rather than rely on intermediary organizations such as integrated health plans, group practices, or employers to assist in comparing cost and quality of providers, CDHC vests consumers— aided by enhanced information-supplying tools—with responsibility to make choices that serve their particular needs and drive providers to offers care at a low cost and high quality. See Regina Herzlinger, Market Driven Health Care: Who Wins, Who Loses in the Transformation of America's Largest Service Industry (1997); Michael Porter, Redefining Competition in Health Care, 82 Harv. Bus. Rev. 64 (2004). For a comprehensive critique of CDHC, see Timothy Stoltzfus Jost, Health Care at Risk: A Critique of the Consumer– Driven Movement (2007). The difference between these paradigms has important implications for the structure of provider organizations. Rather than viewing large physician and hospital organizations as efficient and aiding patients by coordinating care, CDHC proponents views them as bureaucratic and emphasize the benefits of smaller physician practices, single specialty hospitals and illness-focused delivery systems. See James C. Robinson, Managed Consumerism in Health Care, 24 No. 6 Health Aff. 1478, 1480 (Nov./Dec. 2005). Physicians and hospitals may also change their practices radically to accommodate patients who are willing to pay a set fee for extensive service offerings, especially preventive care; assured and prompt access and greater amenities. See Frank Pasquale, The Three Faces of Retainer Care: Crafting a Tailored Regulatory Response, 7 Yale J. Health Pol'y, L. & Ethics 39 (2007), Sandra Carnahan, Concierge Medicine: Legal and Ethical Issues, 35 J. L. Med & Ethics 211 (2007).

2. *The Specialty Hospital Phenomenon*

An important recent development in health care organization has been the emergence of physician-owned "specialty hospitals." These facilities (also referred to as "carve-out" or "boutique" hospitals) are hospitals that only provide care for certain conditions or perform only specified procedures. See United States General Accounting Office ("GAO") Specialty Hospitals: Geographic Location, Services Provided, and Financial Performance, GAO–04–167 (Washington D.C.: Oct. 2003). Most physician specialty hospitals are owned by the specialty physicians who practice in them or by for-profit specialty chains.

Typically these hospitals concentrate their service in one of several profitable areas of medicine or illness such as heart care, surgery and orthopedics. A number of factors have contributed to the rapid growth of these facilities: generous reimbursement rates for certain hospital and facility-based services, such as cardiology; stagnant physician incomes for specialist physicians practicing in these fields; the declining effectiveness of certificate of need laws in limiting development of new facilities; and increased convenience for patients and doctors able to obtain care in different geographic location than older community hospitals. For physicians owning or investing in such hospitals, these hospitals are dreams come true. They can exercise greater control over the quality and conditions of practice in the facility; and with increased specialization and familiarity with staff, outcomes may improve and medical error can be reduced. Further, physician investors in specialty hospitals share in the facility fee paid by insurers for their services, thus enhancing their incomes considerably. With patients usually willing to "follow their doctor," the financial risk of the doctors' investment is often minimal.

For hospitals, the picture is rather less rosy. Community hospitals argue that specialty hospitals threaten their viability and do not compete on a level playing field. Not only are the most profitable services pulled out of the general purpose hospital, but it is left with EMTALA obligations and must bear regulatory costs that the specialty hospital does not. See Doctor Owned Specialty Hospitals Spur Investor Interest, Capital Hill Worries, 12 Health L. Rep. (BNA), April 17, 2003, at 623 (cardiac and orthopedic services carved out of general hospitals earn profit margins of 20 to 30 percent making the investment in such facilities lucrative to investors, while losing such services can be drastic for a hospital's bottom line); Boom in Specialty Hospitals Signals Payment Discrepancies, 57 Health Care Fin. Mgmt. 20 (2003) (cardiology services alone can account for 25% or hospital stays and 35% or more of community hospital revenues). In addition, there is the risk that specialty hospitals will "cherry pick" healthier patients, either because their doctors are admitting their costlier, sicker patients to the community hospital or because the staff privileging process will segment the market. See United States General Accounting Office, Specialty Hospitals: Information on National Market Share, Physician Ownership, and Patients Served, GAO–03–683R (Washington D.C.: April 2003) (specialty hospitals treated a lower percentage of severely ill patients than did general community hospitals). But see Allan Dobson, Randy Haught & Namarata Sen, Specialty Heart Hospital: A Comparative Study, 1 Am Heart Hosp. J. 21, 21 (2003) (specialty hospital sponsored study showing that specialty heart hospitals have a higher-case mix severity than patients at general community hospitals). See also, Newt Gingrich, A Health Threat We're Not Treating: Don't Let Doctors Rig the Market for Specialty Hospitals, Wash Post (Nov. 12, 2005) at A25 ("It's just human nature for [doctors with financial interest in hospitals] to increase their own income by the simple act of giving the specialty hospital . . . all the easy and inexpensive cases while sending very risky and expensive cases to the larger community hospital").

The physician-owned specialty hospital phenomenon has produced a torrent of studies and a number of legislative and regulatory responses. As part of the Medicare Modernization Act of 2003, Pub. L. No. 108–173, § 507 (2003). Congress imposed an eighteen month moratorium on physician referrals to cardiac, orthopedic or surgical specialty hospitals in which the physician had an ownership or investment interest, and requiring studies by HHS and MedPAC of the issue. CMS effectively extended the moratorium into 2006 through administrative actions suspending processing of Medicare enrollment applications submitted by specialty hospitals and Congress extended the suspension in the Deficit Reduction Act of 2005. A complex and sometimes contentious dialogue involving Congress, CMS, and MedPAC produced a number of studies and recommendations as to future courses of action in this area. Particularly influential have been reports mandated by Congress, MedPAC and CMS. See MedPAC, Report to the Congress: Physician–Owned Specialty Hospitals (March 2005); Michael Leavitt, Study of Physician Owned Specialty Hospitals (May, 2005), http://www.cms.hhs.gov/MLNProducts/Down loads/RTC–StudyoFPhysOwnedSpecHosp.pdf. The MedPAC report found that specialty hospitals tended to treat more profitable patients, captured most of their patients from community hospitals, and earned returns far in excess of the average margin of community hospitals in their market though they showed no appreciable improvements in efficiency. However MedPAC also found no evidence that specialty hospitals had a significant impact on the financial performance of community hospitals with which they competed. MedPac Report *supra*. The CMS report, which focused on six markets, found that specialty hospitals received Medicare referrals primarily from physician owners, that the care received at cardiac specialty hospitals was good or better than that received at competitor hospitals, and that community hospitals treated more severely ill patients. See also, Jeffrey Stensland & Ariel Winter, Do Physician–Owned Hospitals Increase Utilization 25 No.1 Health Aff. 119 (Jan./Feb. 2006) (markets with specialty hospitals have small increase in number of cardiac surgeries, but no increase in treating healthier patients). The Federal Trade Commission has weighed in on the competitive implications of physician-owned specialty hospitals and ambulatory surgical centers, observing that they may provide a needed source of competition in many markets and serve to "enhance quality of care, lower prices and improve access." The FTC emphasized the need for other reforms such as eliminating certificate of need regulation and refining payment rates to avoid cross subsidization among services as the preferred means of eliminating artificial incentives for these facilities. Prepared Statement of the Federal Trade Commission before the Senate Subcommittee on Federal Financial Mangement, Government Information and International Security (May 24, 2005) available at www.ftc.gove/os/2005/05/052405newentryintohopsitalcomp.pdf. Finally, because specialty hospitals lack the capability to deal with complications and emergency conditions, legislators have also raised concerns about patient safety. See Grassley Baucus Ask Specialty Hospitals About Patient Safety After 911 Calls (Press release, Aug. 2007) http://grassley.senate.gov/public (Senators reacting to an investigative report that specialty hospital made 911 calls to transfer 150 patients to community hospitals for emergency care).

The reason these arrangements are allowed in the first place, and not treated as illegal "self referral" arrangements under the federal Stark law, is that there is an exception for "whole hospital" joint ventures. (See Chapter 11 *infra*). Critics of physician owned specialty hospitals have introduced legislation to remove this exception and thereby effectively ban those entities from receiving referrals from their investor physicians. Since specialty hospitals have developed predominantly in those states lacking certificate of need laws (60% of all such hospitals are located in four states, Texas, Kansas, Oklahoma and South Dakota), some believe stronger state legislation is warranted. Some states have attempted to outlaw physician ownership of hospitals in which they practice, or mandate that specialty hospitals provide emergency services. See, e.g., S.B. 828, Gen. Assem., Reg. Sess. (Cal. 2003) available at www. leginfo.ca.gov/pub/bill/sen/sb_0801–0850/sb_828_bill_20030626_amended_asm. pdf; S.B. 1341, 145th Gen Assem., 2d. Reg. Sess. (Az. 2002). Those who believe specialty hospitals provide a potentially valuable source of competition and innovation support efforts to remove financial incentives in DRG and other payment systems that reward physicians for self referrals and harm community hospitals. CMS appears to have taken the position that its recently-adopted refinements to the prospective payment system together with requiring disclosure of hospital ownership information to patients will solve the problem. United States Department of Health and Human Services, Final Report to Congress and Strategic and Implementing Plan Required under Section 5006 of the Deficit Reduction Act of 2005, (August 2006), http:// www.cms.hhs.gov/PhysicianSelfReferral/06a_DRA_Reports.asp See also, Physician–Owned Specialty Hospitals: Profits Before Patients?: Hearing Before the Sen. Finance Comm., 109th Cong. 15 (2006) (statement of Mark McClellan, Administrator, Centers for Medicare and Medicaid Services) (stating that CMS has "proposed the most important reforms in the Diagnosis–Related Group payment system for hospitals since this system was created more than 20 years ago").

Problem: Making Policy Choices Under Uncertainty

You have just been designated by the new director of CMS to take a fresh look at the specialty hospital issue. How would you go about deciding what to do about physician-owned specialty hospitals? What would you define as the key policy issues? What empirical or other proof would you need to make a determination about whether to take action? What steps, legislative and regulatory, might be on the table and what are their risks and benefits?

Review Problem: Organizing All Saints Health Care

All Saints Health Care Enterprise, a not-for-profit religiously affiliated corporation, operates two hospitals, St. Timothy's and St. Patrick's, in River City. River City and the surrounding metropolitan area are served by 20 acute care hospitals and 3000 physicians. Like most markets, managed care has begun to make serious inroads in River City. As a result of the growth of managed care contracting, employers and insurers are insisting that hospitals and physicians assume financial risk through capitation or other means. A notable byproduct of these changes has been a sharp increase in the demand for primary care physicians and a surplus of specialists.

Two rivals have begun to form integrated systems. Madison Hospital, a large teaching hospital, has recently acquired five other hospitals and has developed a PHO, signing up as co-owners some 300 physicians who have staff privileges at these hospitals. Jefferson Medical Enterprises, a for-profit entity, owns three hospitals in the market and has formed an IPA-style HMO.

St. Timothy's Hospital, located in downtown River City, has 250 physicians with staff privileges, including 150 family practitioners and a large proportion of specialists practicing obstetrics and pediatric health specialties. A core group of 100 doctors, mostly in solo practice, concentrate their admissions at St. Timothy's. A relatively large proportion of these physicians are over 45 years old and many of the older doctors are amenable to selling their practices. Most of the remaining doctors, however, are fiercely independent and highly suspicious of managed care contract proposals being offered by insurance companies. There is a widespread consensus that St. Timothy's needs to recruit additional doctors to maintain its viability.

St. Patrick's, located in an affluent suburb adjacent to River City, has a much heavier proportion of specialists on its staff and offers a wide range of sophisticated services. Five group practices, including two large multispecialty groups, supply a large percentage of St. Patrick's inpatient and outpatient business.

Assuming you represent All Saints, what model or models of integrating organizations would you recommend that it consider forming? What form of business organization should each adopt and how should control be allocated between the hospital and physicians? What governance arrangements would you recommend to avoid conflicts and deadlocks in the future?

What advice would you give if you represented one of the multispecialty physician groups practicing at St. Patrick's? Suppose some of the independent All Saints physicians not currently in a group practice wanted to organize some form of entity before affiliating with the All Saints system. Explain the advantages and disadvantages of the organizational forms they might adopt.

IV. TAX–EXEMPT HEALTH CARE ORGANIZATIONS

INTRODUCTION

A. CHARITABLE PURPOSES: HOSPITALS

UTAH COUNTY v. INTERMOUNTAIN HEALTH CARE, INC.

Supreme Court of Utah, 1985.
709 P.2d 265.

DURHAM, JUSTICE:

Utah County seeks review of a decision of the Utah State Tax Commission reversing a ruling of the Utah County Board of Equalization. The Tax Commission exempted Utah Valley Hospital, owned and operated by Intermountain Health Care (IHC), and American Fork Hospital, leased and operated by IHC, from *ad valorem* property taxes. At issue is whether such a tax exemption is constitutionally permissible. We hold that, on the facts in this record, it is not, and we reverse.

IHC is a nonprofit corporation that owns and operates or leases and operates twenty-one hospitals throughout the intermountain area, including Utah Valley Hospital and American Fork Hospital. IHC also owns other subsidiaries, including at least one for-profit entity. It is supervised by a board of trustees who serve without pay. It has no stock, and no dividends or pecuniary profits are paid to its trustees or incorporators. Upon dissolution of the corporation, no part of its assets can inure to the benefit of any private person.

* * *

* * * These [tax] exemptions confer an indirect subsidy and are usually justified as the *quid pro quo* for charitable entities undertaking functions and services that the state would otherwise be required to perform. A concurrent rationale, used by some courts, is the assertion that the exemptions are granted not only because charitable entities relieve government of a burden, but also because their activities enhance beneficial community values or goals. Under this theory, the benefits received by the community are believed to offset the revenue lost by reason of the exemption.

* * *

An entity may be granted a charitable tax exemption for its property under the Utah Constitution only if it meets the definition of a "charity" or if its property is used exclusively for "charitable" purposes. Essential to this definition is the element of gift to the community.

* * * A gift to the community can be identified either by a substantial imbalance in the exchange between the charity and the recipient of its services or in the lessening of a government burden through the charity's operation.

* * *

Given the complexities of institutional organization, financing, and impact on modern community life, there are a number of factors which must be weighed in determining whether a particular institution is in fact using its property "exclusively for * * * charitable purposes." Utah Const. art. XIII, § 2 (1895, amended 1982). These factors are: (1) whether the stated purpose of the entity is to provide a significant service to others without immediate expectation of material reward; (2) whether the entity is supported, and to what extent, by donations and gifts; (3) whether the recipients of the "charity" are required to pay for the assistance received, in whole or in part; (4) whether the income received from all sources (gifts, donations, and payment from recipients) produces a "profit" to the entity in the sense that the income exceeds operating and long-term maintenance expenses; (5) whether the beneficiaries of the "charity" are restricted or unrestricted and, if restricted, whether the restriction bears a reasonable relationship to the entity's charitable objectives; and (6) whether dividends or some other form of financial benefit, or assets upon dissolution, are available to private interests, and whether the entity is organized and operated so that any commercial activities are subordinate or incidental to charitable ones. * * *

Because the "care of the sick" has traditionally been an activity regarded as charitable in American law, and because the dissenting opinions rely upon decisions from other jurisdictions that in turn incorporate unexamined assumptions about the fundamental nature of hospital-based medical care, we deem it important to scrutinize the contemporary social and economic context of such care. We are convinced that traditional assumptions bear little relationship to the economics of the medical-industrial complex of the 1980's. Nonprofit hospitals were traditionally treated as tax-exempt charitable institutions because, until late in the 19th century, they were true charities providing custodial care for those who were both sick and poor. The hospitals' income was derived largely or entirely from voluntary charitable donations, not government subsidies, taxes, or patient fees.[9] The function and status of hospitals began to change in the late 19th century; the transformation was substantially completed by the 1920's. "From charities, dependent on voluntary gifts, [hospitals] developed into market institutions financed increasingly out of payments from patients." The transformation was multidimensional: hospitals were redefined from social welfare to medical treatment institutions; their charitable foundation was replaced by a business basis; and their orientation shifted to "professionals and their patients," away from "patrons and the poor."

* * *

Also of considerable significance to our review is the increasing irrelevance of the distinction between nonprofit and for-profit hospitals for purposes of discovering the element of charity in their operations. The literature indicates that two models, described below, appear to describe a large number of nonprofit hospitals as they function today.

(1) The "physicians' cooperative" model describes nonprofit hospitals that operate primarily for the benefit of the participating physicians. Physicians, pursuant to this model, enjoy power and high income through their direct or indirect control over the nonprofit hospitals to which they bring their patients. * * * A minor variation of the above theory is the argument that many nonprofit hospitals operate as "shelters" within which physicians operate profitable businesses, such as laboratories. [ ]

(2) The "polycorporate enterprise" model describes the increasing number of nonprofit hospital chains. Here, power is largely in the hands of administrators, not physicians. Through the creation of holding companies, nonprofit hospitals have grown into large groups of medical enterprises, containing both for-profit and nonprofit corporate entities. Nonprofit corporations can own for-profit corporations without losing their federal nonprofit tax status as long as the profits of the for-profit corporations are used to further the nonprofit purposes of the parent organization.

* * *

* * * Dramatic advances in medical knowledge and technology have resulted in an equally dramatic rise in the cost of medical services. At the same time, elaborate and comprehensive organizations of third-party payers have evolved. Most recently, perhaps as a further evolutionary response to the unceasing rise in the cost of medical services, the provision of such services has become a highly competitive business.

* * *

9. Paul Starr, *The Social Transformation of American Medicine* at 150 (1982). "Voluntary' hospitals, like public hospitals (which evolved from almshouses for the dependent poor), performed a "welfare" function rather than a medical or curing function: the poor were housed in large wards, largely cared for themselves, and often were not expected to recover. *See id.* at 145, 149, 160. Early voluntary hospitals had paternalistic, communal social structures in which patients entered at the sufferance of their benefactors, "had the moral status of children," and received more moralistic and religious help than medical treatment. *Id.* at 149, 158. * * *

[Ed. note: The opinion relies on Starr's book extensively. Further citations have been omitted.]

The stated purpose of IHC regarding the operation of both hospitals clearly meets at least part of the first criterion we have articulated for determining the existence of a charitable use. Its articles of incorporation identify as "corporate purposes," among other things, the provision of "care and treatment of the sick, afflicted, infirm, aged or injured within and/or without the State of Utah." The same section prevents any "part of the net earnings of this Corporation" to inure to the private benefit of any individual. Furthermore, under another section, the assets of the corporation upon dissolution likewise may not be distributed to benefit any private interest.

The second factor we examine is whether the hospitals are supported, and to what extent, by donations and gifts. * * * [W]e have examined the testimony and exhibits in evidence on this question. The latter demonstrate that current operating expenses for both hospitals are covered almost entirely by revenue from patient charges. * * * The evidence was that both hospitals charge rates for their services comparable to rates being charged by other similar entities, and no showing was made that the donations identified resulted in charges to patients below prevailing market rates.

* * *

One of the most significant of the factors to be considered in review of a claimed exemption is the third we identified: whether the recipients of the services of an entity are required to pay for that assistance, in whole or in part. The Tax Commission in this case found as follows:

> The policy of [IHC's hospitals] is to collect hospital charges from patients whenever it is reasonable and possible to do so; however, no person in need of medical attention is denied care solely on the basis of a lack of funds.

The record also shows that neither of the hospitals in this case demonstrated any substantial imbalance between the value of the services it provides and the payments it receives apart from any gifts, donations, or endowments. The record shows that the vast majority of the services provided by these two hospitals are paid for by government programs, private insurance companies, or the individuals receiving care.

* * *

Between 1978 and 1980, the value of the services given away as charity by these two hospitals constituted less than one percent of their gross revenues. Furthermore, the record also shows that such free service as did exist was deliberately not advertised out of fear of a "deluge of people" trying to take advantage of it. Instead, every effort was made to recover payment for services rendered. * * *

The defendants argue that the great expense of modern hospital care and the universal availability of insurance and government health care subsidies make the idea of a hospital solely supported by philanthropy an anachronism. We believe this argument itself exposes the weakness in the defendants' position. It is precisely because such a vast system of third-party payers has developed to meet the expense of modern hospital care that the historical distinction between for-profit and nonprofit hospitals has eroded. * * *

The fourth question we consider is whether the income received from all sources by these IHC hospitals is in excess of their operating and maintenance expenses. Because the vast majority of their services are paid for, the nonprofit hospitals in this case accumulate capital as do their profit-seeking counterparts.

* * *

A large portion of the profits of most for-profit entities is used for capital improvements and new, updated equipment, and the defendant hospitals here similarly expend their revenues in excess of operational expenses. There can be no doubt, in reviewing the references in the record by members of IHC's administrative staff, that the IHC system, as well as the two hospitals in question, has consistently generated sufficient funds in excess of operating costs to contribute to rapid and extensive growth, building, competitive employee and professional salaries and benefits, and a very sophisticated management structure. While it is true that no financial benefits or profits are available to private interests in the form of stockholder distributions or ownership advantages, the user *entity* in this case clearly generates substantial "profits" in the sense of income that exceeds expenses.

* * *

On the question of benefits to private interests, certainly it appears that no individuals who are employed by or administer the defendants receive any distribution of assets or income, and some, such as IHC's board of trustees members, volunteer their services. We have noted, however, that IHC owns a for-profit entity, as well as nonprofit subsidiaries, and there is in addition the consideration that numerous forms of private commercial enterprise, such as pharmacies, laboratories, and contracts for medical services, are conducted as a necessary part of the defendants' hospital operations. The burden being on the taxpayer to demonstrate eligibility for the exemption, the inadequacies in the record on these questions cannot be remedied by speculation in the defendants' favor. * * *

Neither can we find on this record that the burdens of government are substantially lessened as a result of the defendants' provision of services. The record indicates that Utah County budgets approximately $50,000 annually for the payment of hospital care for indigents. Furthermore, the evidence described two instances within a three-month period where, after a Utah County official had declined to authorize payment for a person in the emergency room, Utah Valley Hospital refused to admit the injured person on the basis of that person's inability to pay. The county official was told in these instances to either authorize payment or to "come and get" the person. Such behavior on the hospital's part is inconsistent with its argument that it functions to relieve government of a burden. Likewise, as we have pointed out, there has been no showing that the tax exemption is a significant factor in permitting these defendants to operate, thereby arguably relieving government of the burden of establishing its own medical care providers. In fact, government is already carrying a substantial share of the operating expenses of defendants, in the form of third-party payments pursuant to "entitlement" programs such as Medicare and Medicaid.

* * *

We reverse the Tax Commission's grant of an *ad valorem* property tax exemption to defendants as being unconstitutional.

* * *

STEWART, JUSTICE (dissenting):

* * *

III.   DEFINITION OF CHARITY
* * *

The legal concept of charity does not require, as the majority apparently requires, that a hospital incur a deficit to qualify as a charitable institution. Charitable hospitals need not be self-liquidating.

* * *

It is true that the hospitals in this case receive substantial revenues from third-party payors and patients, but there is not a shred of evidence in this record, much less a finding by the Tax Commission, that one cent of the revenues is used for any purpose other than furthering the charitable purposes of providing hospital services to the sick and infirm. On the contrary, the Tax Commission's findings affirmatively establish that no person has profited from the revenues produced at either Utah Valley or American Fork Hospitals other than patients. Under time-honored legal principles, both hospitals qualify as charitable institutions.

IV.   UTAH VALLEY HOSPITAL'S AND AMERICAN FORK HOSPITAL'S GIFTS TO THE COMMUNITY
* * *

A.   *Direct Patient Subsidies*
* * *

During the years 1978–80, Utah Valley Hospital rendered wholly free services to indigents in the amount of $200,000, and in each of those years the amount increased substantially over the preceding year. During the same period, the hospital subsidized services rendered to Medicare, Medicaid, and worker's compensation patients in the amount of $3,174,024. The corresponding figures for American Fork Hospital were $39,906 in indigent care and $421,306 for subsidization of Medicare, Medicaid, and worker's compensation benefits.

However, the value of the charity extended to indigents is in fact greater than the amounts stated. The cost of the charity extended to patients who are first identified as charity patients *after* admission rather than *at* admission is charged to the "bad debts" account, along with traditional uncollectible accounts or bad debts, instead of being charged to charity.

* * *

In sum, the *direct* cost of patient charity given away by Utah Valley Hospital for the period in question is in excess of $3,374,024, but less than $4,942,779 (which includes bad debts). The *direct* cost of the charity given away by American Fork Hospital is in excess of $461,212, but less than $639,024 (which includes bad debts). * * * Unlike for-profit hospitals, Utah Valley and American Fork have a policy against turning away indigent patients. Therefore, that portion of the hospitals' bad debts which is attributable to indigency is bona fide charity since the charges would have been initially made to the charity account had the patient's indigency been discovered at admission. Those charges are not just ordinary business bad debts experienced by all commercial enterprises, as the majority would have it.

* * *

B. Capital Subsidies and Gifts

The most glaring lapse in the majority opinion, in my view, is its flat-out refusal to recognize that there would be no Utah Valley Hospital—at all—if it had not been given lock, stock, and barrel to IHC by the Church of Jesus Christ of Latter–Day Saints, which initially built the hospital. American Fork Hospital apparently was initially erected by taxpayers' money. At the City's request, IHC took over the operation of the hospital as a lessee of American Fork City to relieve the City of a governmental burden. It follows that all patients at both hospitals, whether indigent, part-paying, or fully paying patients, are direct beneficiaries of large monetary investments in land, buildings, and medical equipment. * * *

In addition to the "gift to the community" of the actual physical facilities, each and every patient benefits from the fact that IHC is a nonprofit corporation whose hospitals make no profit on the value of the assets dedicated to hospital care. The majority's effort to portray IHC hospitals as if they were operated as for-profit entities has no substance in the record whatsoever. A for-profit hospital, unlike a nonprofit hospital, must necessarily price its services to make a profit on its investment if it is to stay in business. The surplus that Utah Valley and American Fork budget for is not by any means the equivalent of profit, as the majority wrongly suggests. * * *

Furthermore, the majority inaccurately asserts that Utah Valley charges rates comparable to other similar entities. The evidence is to the contrary. Utah Valley Hospital, with its 385 beds and expensive, sophisticated acute care equipment, charges rates comparable to the rates charged by Payson Hospital, a small for-profit hospital that renders inexpensive types of services. * * * In addition, there are no "prevailing market rates" for tertiary care hospitals, if by that term the majority means prevailing rates of competitive for-profit hospitals. There is no for-profit tertiary care hospital in the entire state of Utah; all tertiary care hospitals are non-profit institutions. In fact, there is no other tertiary care hospital, whether nonprofit or for-profit, in the immense, sparsely populated area served by the Utah Valley Hospital, which extends from Utah County to the Nevada–Arizona border. Indeed, the facts strongly suggest that a for-profit tertiary care hospital could not survive in the geographical market area served by Utah Valley. * * *

V. TAX EXEMPT STATUS OF NON-PROFIT HOSPITALS UNDER THE MAJORITY OPINION

The record also demonstrates that the primary care hospital and the tertiary care hospital involved in this case relieve a significant governmental burden, one of the two alternative tests for determining whether a nonprofit hospital qualifies to be treated as a charitable institution. * * * In the wide-open spaces of the West, where small communities are widely separated, the profit motive has not been sufficient to provide the needed impetus for the building of community hospitals (except in rare instances). Nor has it resulted in the construction of tertiary care hospitals in the more populous parts of the state.

The majority's argument is that no government burden is relieved by providing hospital service to those who can pay for it on a for-profit basis. The argument misses the mark for two reasons. First, the alternatives are not for-profit or nonprofit hospitals. The alternatives are nonprofit hospital care or no hospital care at all, at least within the relevant geographical markets. Second, the charitable status of a hospital does not turn on whether it provides care for patients who can pay. The basic policy is not to tax the sick and infirm irrespective of ability to pay. A county provides many services to rich and poor alike without charging the rich for those services. Parks and playgrounds are but examples. Providing medical services may not be mandatory for counties or cities, but if they do, they most certainly promote the public health, safety, morals, and welfare in a most fundamental way. Surely cities and counties would, as a practical matter, be compelled to provide hospital services if the nonprofit hospitals in this state did not exist.

* * *

VI. DIFFERENCES BETWEEN FOR-PROFIT AND NONPROFIT HOSPITALS

* * *

[A] for-profit hospital's investment decisions as to what markets or communities to enter and what kinds of equipment to invest in are made from a basically different motive than a nonprofit hospital's. The decisions of a for-profit hospital corporation must be based upon careful calculations as to the rate of return that may be expected on invested capital. If the rate of return is not sufficient, the investment is not made. Whether the surplus is reinvested in part or paid out to investors in dividends in whole or in part, the investor receives personal monetary benefit either in the increased value of his stock or in dividends.

Nonprofit hospitals must, of course, be concerned with generating sufficient revenue to maintain themselves, but they are not concerned with earning a return on their investment for the benefit of stockholders. Their purposes are altruistic. Any surplus must be used in a manner that aggrandizes no one, such as for the lowering of rates, the acquisition of new equipment, or the improvement of facilities.

* * *

IHC's Board of Trustees considers itself a trustee of the health care facilities for the public. "[W]e see ourselves as owned by the community since the corporation owns itself and in effect the church gave the hospitals to the communities, and we're entrusted with the running of the hospitals. We see them as in effect owned by the communities."

* * *

Notes and Questions

1. The Intermountain Health Care opinion provides a useful history of the nonprofit hospital in America. How have changing practices, technologies, and payment systems affected those institutions? How do those factors influence the obligation to provide charity care? Should charity care be provided this way or through direct governmental expenditures? Critics of exemption point to the lack of oversight and control that occurs when care is financed publicly through foregone revenue, and that benefits awarded through the tax system are not subject to budgetary discipline as they are not reported as budget outlays. See Harry G. Gourevitch, Congressional Research Service, Tax Aspects of Health Care Reform: The Tax Treatment of Health Care Providers, 94 Tax Notes Today 94–90 (May 16, 1994).

2. A series of articles in the Wall Street Journal in 2003 inaugurated an intense debate about the charitable behavior of hospitals, leading federal and state tax officials to closely examine the practices of tax exempt hospitals, including unfair billing and collection practices, excessive executive compensation and participation in for profit ventures. See Lucette Lagnado, Full Price: A Young Woman, an Appendectomy, and a $19,000 Debt, Wall St. J. (Mar. 17, 2003); Nancy M. Kane, Tax–Exempt Hospitals: What is Their Charitable Responsibility and How Should it Be Defined and Reported? 51 St. Louis U. L.J. 459 (2007). Many states have also begun to look at whether the law should delineate more precisely the community benefits expected of hospitals that enjoy exemption from state taxes. While several states have had in place for many years legislation aimed at reducing the disparity between the amount of benefit provided by tax exempt hospitals and the amount of foregone state and local taxes, new reform proposals are proliferating. See, Peyton M. Sturges, Review of Community Benefit Standard Exposes Concerns About Other Approaches, 15 No. 38 Health L. Rep. 1093 (BNA) (Sept. 2006). See also, Jill R. Horwitz, Does Nonprofit Ownership Matter?, 24 Yale J. on Reg. 139 (Winter 2007). Some states have adopted a "process" approach, requiring tax exempt hospitals to adopt a mission statement, undertake community needs assessments, engage with their communities in planning, and report the amount of community benefit provided. Laws in other states require nonprofit hospitals to account for and report their community benefits. For example, California established a presumption that hospitals earning less than a ten percent surplus or making an appropriate showing concerning their use of profits are entitled to the welfare property tax exemption. Cal. Rev. & Tax'n Code § 214 (a)(1). See also Ind. Code Ann. § 16–21–6–6 et seq. (1997)(reporting and assessment requirements); N.Y. Public Health Law § 2803–1 (same).

A few states have adopted a more "prescriptive" approach, requiring hospitals to make specified minimum expenditures on community benefits. See, e.g. Pa. Cons. Stat. Ann. Sec. 371–85 (setting forth five statutory standards including providing uncompensated goods or services equal to at least 5% of costs or maintaining an open admissions policy and providing uncompensated goods or services equal to at least 75% of net operating income but not less than 3% of total operating expenses; also allowing payments in lieu of taxes). For an analysis of Pennsylvania's actions regarding community benefits, see T.J. Sullivan and Karen McAfee, To Shiver or Not to Shiver, 28 Exempt Organization Tax Review 471 (June 2000). The Attorney General of Illinois proposed, and subsequently withdrew, legislation that would have required each tax exempt hospital in the state to furnish charity care to any uninsured resident earning less than 150 percent of the poverty level and to furnish aggregate charity care in an amount equal to eight percent of its total operating costs; "charity care" was defined as the marginal cost of providing care and bad debt losses did not count. See Lawmakers Shelve Plan to Quantify Charity Care for Tax–Exempt Hospitals, 15 No. 13 Health L. Rep. 373 (BNA) (March 30, 2006). What arguments do you think were levied against this proposal?

3. State taxing authorities have also been increasingly willing to seek revocation of exempt status for failure to meet statutory standards of charitable conduct and purpose. In a decision that generated considerable alarm among nonprofits, the Illinois Department of Revenue revoked the property tax exemption of Provena Covenant Medical Center. Michael Bologna & Peyton M. Sturges, Illinois Department of Revenue Director Says Provena Covenant Hospital Taxable, 15 No. 39 Health L. Rep. 1129 (BNA) (2006). The decision stressed that the total charges that Provena had waived from patients unable to pay represented less than 1% of its revenues, based on the costs of those services; had "outsourced" the provision of many services such as pharmacy, clinical labs and MRI/CT services to for-profit entities; had used flat discount rates to gauge payment due from individuals in low income rather than assessing their ability to pay the amount otherwise due; and had referred patients with unpaid balances to collection agencies, a practice the decision characterized as "lacking in the warmth and spontaneity indicative of a charitable impulse." Id. at 1131. An Illinois Circuit Court issued a bench ruling summarily reversing the Department's decision and restoring Provena's property tax exemption. The hospital had argued that reliance on quantitative factors was unprecedented and inconsistent with state law. Do the other factors mentioned by the court provide convincing evidence that the hospital property was not used exclusively (defined to mean "primarily") for charitable purposes? See also City of Washington v. Board of Assessment, 550 Pa. 175, 704 A.2d 120 (1997) (applying five-part test governing hospitals' purposes and sufficiency of efforts to serve charitable ends). In contrast to *Intermountain* and the Pennsylvania actions, see Callaway Community Hospital Association v. Craighead, 759 S.W.2d 253 (Mo. Ct. App. 1988) (granting state tax exemption for a hospital that transferred indigent patients and viewing transfers as within individual physicians' and not hospital's control); see also Rideout Hospital Foundation, Inc. v. County of Yuba, 8 Cal.App.4th 214, 10 Cal.Rptr.2d 141 (1992) (upholding tax exemption to hospital with surplus revenue in excess of 10%).

4. Whether the amount of charity care provided by tax-exempt hospitals justifies the benefit of the tax exemption is hotly disputed. Studies comparing the value of tax exemptions for hospitals to the amount of charity care (measured in terms of costs, not charges) find that most hospitals could not justify their exemption on the basis of charity care alone. See Cong. Budget Office, Nonprofit Hospitals and the Provision of Community Benefits (Dec. 2006) http://www.cbo. gov/ftpdocs/76xx/doc7695/12–06–Nonprofit.pdf; David Walker, Nonprofit, For–Profit, and Government Hospitals: Uncompensated Care and Other Community Benefits, U.S. Government Accountability Office (2006) http://www.gao.gov/new. items/d05743t.pdf (little difference in uncompensated care burden shouldered by nonprofit and investor owned hospitals; government hospitals provide much greater proportion than either); cf. Michael Morrissey, et al., Do Nonprofit Hospitals Pay Their Way?, 15 Health Aff. 132 (1996) (hospitals failing to provide uncompensated care in excess of tax subsidy constitute only a small subset of all hospitals in California). Benchmarking the appropriate level of community benefits as the sum of those benefits provided by for profit hospitals plus the profits earned by those hospitals, another economic study concludes that nonprofit hospitals as a group are either underproviding community benefits or providing benefits that cannot be measured. Sean Nicholson et al., Measuring Community

Benefits Provided by For–Profit and Nonprofit Hospitals, 19 Health Affairs 168 (2000). See also Uwe E. Reinhardt, The Economics of For–Profit and Not–For–Profit Hospitals, 19 Health Affairs 178 (Nov./Dec. 2000).

What problems does *Intermountain Health Care* raise in relation to defining, evaluating and measuring charity care? For example, what should count as charity care? See David Burda, Stop Playing Politics With Charity, Mod. Healthcare (June 5, 2006) at 20 (describing disagreement between the Catholic Hospital Association and American Hospital Association about whether bad debt expenses and Medicare shortfalls should be considered community benefits); see generally, M. Gregg Bloche, Health Policy Below the Waterline: Medical Care and the Charitable Exemption, 80 Minn. L. Rev. 299 (1995). Are there other "community benefits" besides charity care that should be taken into account? Consider for example the empirical research conducted by Professor Jill Horwitz which shows that nonprofit hospitals are more likely than for-profits to offer unprofitable services needed by poor and uninsured patients though less so than government-controlled hospitals. Jill R. Horwitz, Why We Need the Independent Sector: The Behavior, Law and Ethics of Not–For–Profit Hospitals, 50 UCLA L. Rev. 1345 (2003). Making Profits and Providing Care: Comparing Nonprofit, For–Profit and Government Hospitals, 24 Health Aff. 790 (May/June 2005). See also Jack Needleman, The Role of Nonprofits in Health Care, 26 J. Health Pol., Pol'y & L. 1113 (2002) (noting that nonprofits may have stronger "commitment to place" and be more likely to engage in "trustworthy behavior"); Mark Schlesinger & Bradford H. Gray, How Nonprofits Matter in American Medicine and What to Do About It, 25 No. 4 Health Aff. 287 (June 20, 2006) (finding nonprofits less aggressive in marking up prices, less likely to make misleading claims and acting as "incubators of innovation"). Mark A. Hall and John D. Colombo offer another rationale: subsidization is appropriate for those organizations capable of attracting a substantial level of donative support in the face of market imperfections. The Charitable Status of Nonprofit Hospitals: Toward a Donative Theory of Tax Exemption, 66 Wash. L. Rev. 307 (1991). What implications does this research have for legislative proposals regarding the obligations of exempt hospitals? For attorneys general reviewing conversions of nonprofit hospitals?

5. In over seventy lawsuits filed against hundreds of hospitals, renowned plaintiffs' attorney Richard Scruggs charged that hospitals' failure to provide "mutually affordable medical care" violates a host of laws, including federal and state tax exemption standards, the Emergency Medical Treatment and Active Labor Act (EMTALA), charitable trust law, state consumer protection law, and implied contractual obligations to uninsured patients not to bill more than a fair and reasonable charge. The relief requested in these cases includes injunctions requiring hospitals to change their billing and collection practices, and imposing a constructive trust on hospitals savings from tax exempt status, profits, and assets, so as to assure the availability of affordable medical care. Courts have dismissed almost all of these claims on standing and substantive grounds. See e.g. Sabeta v. Baptist Hosp. of Miami, Inc., 410 F.Supp.2d 1224 (S.D. Fla. 2005) (holding that the hospital did not enter into an express or implied "charitable trust" to provide mutually affordable medical care to its uninsured patients by virtue of federal tax exempt status and that patients did not have an implied private right of action under Internal Revenue Code based on the hospital's federal tax exempt status). Despite their lack of success in court, these cases seem to have focused the attention of regulators, legislatures, and the public on the quantity of charity care provided nonprofit hospitals and their billing and collection practices.

Federal Tax Exemption: Charitable Purpose under Section 501(c)(3)

Exemption from federal taxation plays a more prominent role in the affairs of tax exempt hospitals than does state tax exemption. This is not necessarily because more money is at stake—the loss of state and local property tax exemptions may be more costly to a nonprofit hospital that has small or no earnings subject to income taxation—but because federal tax law reaches into many aspects of hospitals operations, including governance, relationships with other providers, and charity care policies. Of course Federal tax exempt status carries with it significant benefits. Besides exemption from liability for corporate income tax, it permits the organization to enjoy exemption from federal unemployment taxes, preferred postal rates and various other benefits respecting pensions and special treatment under various regulatory laws. Second, only donations to charitable organizations exempt under 501(c)(3) are deductible to donors under IRC Section 170. Third, only charitable organizations can issue tax exempt bonds, an important source of financing for nonprofit hospitals. IRC § 145. Finally, state property, sales and other tax exemptions (which as a matter of practical economics may be far more important than federal income exemption to many hospitals) often—but not always—follow federal standards.

Section 501(c)(3) of the Internal Revenue Code exempts from federal income tax entities "organized and operated exclusively for religious, charitable, scientific, testing for public safety, literary, or educational purposes, or to foster ... amateur sports competition ... or for the prevention of cruelty to animals." An organization must meet three important requirements to qualify for tax exempt status:

(1) no part of its net earnings may inure to the benefit of any private shareholder or individual;

(2) no substantial part of its activities may consist of certain activities aimed at influencing legislation; and

(3) it may not participate or intervene in any political campaign on behalf of any candidate for public office.

26 U.S.C.A. § 501(c)(3). Is there an internal logic to these requirements? Does the view that foregoing taxes on charitable and other organizations amounts to a "subsidy" help explain these provisions?

To qualify for § 501(c)(3) status, a health care facility must meet both an "organizational test," which requires that the hospital's constitutive documents, such as the corporate articles of incorporation, limit its activities to exempt purposes, and an "operational test," which requires that the hospital be operated primarily for exempt purposes, including "charitable," "educational," or "religious" purposes. Most hospitals must qualify as charities as healthcare is not specifically listed among exempt purposes. The definition of charitable purposes under the Code has been quite controversial, with the Internal Revenue Service attempting to adjust the definition to meet changes in the modern health care sector while the statute remained unchanged. Unfortunately, the federal tax authorities have not been clear or consistent in explaining when the provision of health care services are charitable. As a practical matter, few hospitals have failed to satisfy the flexible—some say overly flexible—standard that has evolved. However, as you read subsequent sections in this chapter, notice that the IRS and courts have, especially in recent years, been far less lenient with other kinds of health care entities.

The confused trail of the exemption standard for hospitals begins with a 1956 Revenue Ruling that required a tax-exempt hospital to be operated "to the extent of its financial ability for those not able to pay for the services rendered." Rev. Ruling 56–185. In 1958, the Tax Court upheld the denial of exempt status for a hospital that devoted between 2% and 5% of its revenue to care for the indigent (Lorain Avenue Clinic v. Commissioner 31 T.C. 141). Thus one can identify in the early history of IRS analysis of the issue a direct link between exempt status and the provision of a specified quantum of free care for the poor. A pivotal turning point, however, occurred in 1969 when an IRS Revenue Ruling adopted a "community benefit" standard, under which the provision of charity care was no longer the sine qua non for charitable status as long as the hospital "promot[ed] health for the general benefit of the community." The Ruling went on to suggest that the existence of a community board, an open emergency room treating indigent patients free of charge, an open medical staff and treatment of government-insured patients would provide adequate evidence the entity was serving charitable purposes. The Service illustrated its position by describing a hospital that operated an emergency room that was open to all regardless of ability to pay and whose care for the indigent was not otherwise described, which it stated met the Revenue Ruling's standards for exemption. This remarkable shift was not the product of an informed analysis of the benefits of nonprofit health care, nor did it involve legislative action. Instead it appears it was the result of the erroneous assumption of IRS staff attorneys that the recently-enacted Medicaid statute would obviate the need for charity care and that a new justification was therefore needed to preserve the dominant nonprofit hospital sector. See generally, Daniel M. Fox & Daniel C. Schaffer, Tax Administration as Health Policy: Hospitals, The Internal Revenue Service and the Courts, 16 J. Health Pol., Pol'y & L. 251 (1991)(describing political and legal issues involved in Rev. Ruling 69–545). The link to the provision of charity care under federal law was further diluted by a 1983 Revenue Ruling, in which a hospital that did not even operate an emergency room and usually referred indigent patients to another hospital was described as qualifying for tax-exempt status. The illustrative hospital did not operate an ER because the state health planning agency had concluded that the emergency room was not needed in the area, as other nearby hospitals had adequate emergency services. Rev. Rul. 83–157. Thus, for almost forty years federal tax exempt status has not been tied to the provision of charity care, or for that matter to doing anything terribly differently than for profit hospitals. For academic criticism of the standard and a thoughtful proposal to shift the IRS's focus to the question of whether an exempt hospital increases access to health services, see John D. Colombo, The Role of Access in Charitable Tax Exemption, 82 Washington U. L.Q. 343 (2004).

The intensifying scrutiny of nonprofit hospitals described earlier in this chapter appears to have awoken politicians and the IRS to the shortcomings of the community benefit standard. The Senate Finance Committee and House Ways and Means Committee have been particularly active, holding hearings on the issue in 2006 and pressing the IRS and GAO to survey and report on the provision of charity care by tax exempt hospitals. Charitable Care and Community Benefits at Nonprofit Hospitals: Hearing Before the Comm. on Finance, 109th Cong. (2006) (statement of Charles Grassley, Chairman). See also Nonprofit Hospitals and the Provision of Community Benefits, *supra* (study of five states finding that nonprofit hospitals as a group provide more charity care than for-profits; the amount of uncompensated care varied widely; and nonprofits provided care to fewer Medicaid-covered patients as a percentage of their overall patient population); IRS Interim Report (July 19, 2007) (finding wide variation in the definitions used by exempt entities to report charity care to the IRS) available at www.irs.gov/pub/irs-tege/eo_interim_hospital_report_072007.pdf. As this book was going to press, the minority staff of the Senate Finance Committee released a discussion draft of policy recommendations which proposed that hospitals must attain a minimum five percent charity care (measured by Medicare or Medicaid reimbursement rates or other actual rates and not including bad debt) and meet certain other requirements in order to retain 501(c)(3) status. Senate Finance Committee Minority Staff, Tax–Exempt Hospitals: Discussion Draft (July, 2007) www.senate.gov/?finance/press/Gpress2007/prg07/19/07a. The staff's wide ranging proposals also included placing restrictions on conversions, imposing requirements on joint ventures between nonprofit and for-profit hospitals, limiting charges billed to the uninsured, and curtailing unfair billing and collection practices.

Perhaps the most important outcome thus far of this flurry of activity has been the issuance by the IRS of a redesigned Form 990—the annual information return that most exempt hospitals file annually. Modeled to some extend on SEC disclosure forms, the new Form 990 would work revolutionary change in to the reporting requirements for nonprofit entities. Of particular relevance to the issues discussed in this chapter, the form creates a new Schedule H which requires each exempt organization to submit a Community Benefit Report that includes cost based data for community benefits including charity care and Medicaid, a description of its charity care policy, a statement of how it assess community needs and detailed information about billing and debt collection practices. Discussion Draft, www.irs.gov/charities/index.html. See Gerald M. Griffith et al., IRS Mandates Heightened Transparency in Redesigned Form 990, 11 Health Law. News 8 (Aug. 2007).

What factors might have prompted policymakers' rather sudden interest in the standard for tax exempt status applicable to hospitals? While it is impossible to predict whether legislation will be passed or IRS will amend the standard on its own, what would you recommend? Is the move toward greater disclosure and transparency enough? Are there pitfalls in attempting to define, quantify and prescribe the obligations of charitable institutions? In answering these questions, return to the underlying issue of why the law prefers (and subsidizes) a nonprofit sector. See Bloche, *supra*; Gabriel O. Aitsebaomo, The Nonprofit Hospital: A Call for New National Guidance Requiring Minimum Annual Charity Care to Qualify for Federal Tax Exemption, 26 Campbell L. Rev. 75 (2004); Jack E. Karns, Justifying the Nonprofit Hospital Tax Exemption in a Competitive Market Environment, 13 Widener L.J. 383 (2004).

Problem: St. Andrew's Medical Center

St. Andrew's Medical Center is a 750–bed not-for-profit hospital in a metropolitan area. It offers residency programs in internal medicine, obstetrics, surgery and several other areas. St. Andrew's is facing an uncertain financial future, and its Board of Directors is concerned about serious cutbacks in federal funds for graduate medical education, further reductions in health care reimbursement and its own inability to raise enough capital for modernization through retained earnings and donations. The Board is hesitant to increase the facility's substantial debt to make capital improvements in its 40–year–old physical plant. It also finds that it provides a significant amount of charity care each year in part because of its self-identified institutional mission and in part because it is one of only three hospitals in the area. The other two hospitals are a for-profit, 250–bed hospital operated by Americare, Inc., which is an investor-owned multi-facility system, and a municipal hospital, which regularly operates at 98% capacity and is often unable to receive transfers from St. Andrew's.

St. Andrew's has been approached by Health Care Enterprises (HCE), a for-profit corporation that owns eighty-five hospitals in thirty states and is interested in acquiring St. Andrew's. HCE has made an initial offer of $100 million for St. Andrew's, which would include the acquisition of all assets of St. Andrew's, including the name itself. The Board is very interested in the offer but is concerned that the provision of charity care continue at St. Andrew's and that HCE conform with the mission of St. Andrew's as a religiously affiliated hospital. For the Board, this latter concern relates, in part, to their interest in having St. Andrew's not offer abortion or assisted suicide services and in assuring an adequate pastoral care program.

HCE has suggested to St. Andrew's that St. Andrew's place $75 million (the amount of purchase money remaining after St. Andrew's pays off outstanding debts) into an endowment for a new St. Andrew's Foundation. The income from this endowment would then be paid to HCE for charity care and the medical education program at St. Andrew's. HCE has also suggested that it is itself also willing to provide "appropriate" charity care and adhere to the "traditional mission of St. Andrew's." HCE has suggested that it would agree to a buy-back provision in the sales agreement through which St. Andrew's could repurchase the hospital at a price to be agreed upon at the time of purchase should HCE fail to perform on either item.

The community is generally quite upset about the proposal. Many have charged that St. Andrew's is abandoning the community and that HCE is simply seeking to build a reputation by owning a teaching hospital and to "corner the market" by eliminating the only not-for-profit hospital in the metropolitan area. The Board has not attempted to solicit other offers. However, one of its members had a casual conversation with the Chair and CEO of St. Olaf's Hospital, another nonprofit charitable hospital, who indicated that it would be interested in buying St. Andrew's but could pay no more than $80 million.

The Board meeting to decide whether St. Andrew's will be sold to HCE is tomorrow morning. You are a member of the Board. What will you recommend? If the transfer is approved, how would you draft the agreement between St. Andrew's and HCE? For example, how would you draft a contract with enforceable standards for conformance with the religious mission? For "appropriate charity care"? How should the buy-back provision be structured? Will the hospital still be called "St. Andrew's"?

For excellent analyses of issues relating to religious affiliation see, Kathleen M. Boozang, Deciding The Fate of Religious Hospitals in The Emerging Health Care Market, 31 Hous. L. Rev. 1429 (1995); Lawrence E. Singer & Elizabeth Johnson Lantz, The Coming Millennium: Enduring Issues Confronting Catholic Health Care, 8 Annals Health L. 299 (1999).

As discussed earlier, conversions and sales of not-for-profit, tax-exempt entities to for-profit providers have been quite controversial. The Internal Revenue Service's authority in these situations is limited and the rules have not been interpreted to restrict conversions as long an entity remains properly organized as a nonprofit entity and continues to pursue an exempt purpose. However, the Internal Revenue Service has the authority to prevent private inurement, which may help ensure an adequate purchase price. See Section E *infra* and Anclote Psychiatric Ctr., Inc. v. Commissioner, T.C. Memo 1998–273, aff'd 190 F.3d 541 (11th Cir. 1999). With the enactment of intermediate sanctions authority, discussed *infra*, the IRS now has greater flexibility and capacity to monitor conflicts of interest; however, it still lacks legal authority to require advanced approval except for joint ventures between for-profit and nonprofit organizations. Consequently, regulation of conversions has been governed principally by state common law and statutes. See generally, IRS Should Oversee Sales of Nonprofit Hospitals, Organization Asserts, 95 Tax Notes Today 111–46 (June 8, 1995).

B. CHARITABLE PURPOSES: HEALTH MAINTENANCE ORGANIZATIONS

Health maintenance organizations typically deliver both office-based primary care and hospital-based acute care to their subscribers who prepay a premium to the HMO to cover needed services regardless of the amount or cost of medical services actually used. In this way, HMOs combine the functions of insurance and health care delivery. In their provision of office-based primary care, HMOs resemble doctors' medical practices, which traditionally have not been organized on a not-for-profit basis and have not received tax exemption.

The structure through which the HMO provides its physician services has been an important factor in whether it will qualify for § 501(c)(3) tax exempt status. As described earlier in this chapter, HMOs organize their provision of services in a variety of ways. Staff model HMOs employ physicians and operate primary care offices. Group model HMOs contract with physician partnerships or corporations to provide services to subscribers usually on a risk or a capitation basis. Typically, the group model HMO operates in a site owned or leased by the HMO. In the IPA model HMO, an independent practice association acts as agent for its physician members in negotiating and contracting with the HMO for medical services to be provided by its physician members in their own offices. Network HMOs typically contract with a number of physician group practices and other providers. Some HMOs use several of these methods.

IHC HEALTH PLANS, INC. v. COMMISSIONER OF INTERNAL REVENUE

United States Court of Appeals, Tenth Circuit, 2003.
325 F.3d 1188.

Before TACHA, CHIEF CIRCUIT JUDGE, HOLLOWAY, and EBEL, CIRCUIT JUDGES.

TACHA, CHIEF CIRCUIT JUDGE.

I. BACKGROUND

IHC Health Plans, Inc. ("Health Plans"), on its own behalf and as successor in interest to IHC Care, Inc. ("Care") and IHC Group, Inc. ("Group") (collectively "petitioners"), appeals the Tax Court's decision denying petitioners' request for tax exemption under 26 U.S.C. § 501(c)(3). The sole issue presented in this appeal is whether petitioners qualify for tax-exempt status under 26 U.S.C. § 501(c)(3) as organizations operated exclusively for charitable purposes.

A. *The IHC Integrated Delivery System*

[Intermountain Health Care Inc. ("IHC") formed IHC Health Services ("Health Services") in 1982 as a Utah nonprofit corporation to operate twenty-two hospitals located in Utah and Idaho, employing approximately 300 primary care physicians and 100 specialist physicians in its Physician Division and separately employing approximately 120 physicians in its Hospital Division.] Between 1997 and 1999, Health Services provided nearly $1.2 billion in health care services, without reimbursement to patients covered by Medicare, Medicaid, and other governmental programs. During the same period, Health Services furnished more than $91 million in free health-care services to indigent patients.

The Commissioner has recognized Health Services as a tax-exempt organization under section 501(c)(3).

* * *

3. *Health Plans, Care, and Group*

In order to further integrate its provision of health-care services, IHC formed Health Plans, Care, and Group to operate as health maintenance organizations ("HMOs") within the IHC Integrated Delivery System....

* * *

E. *The Commissioner's Decision*

In 1999, the Commissioner concluded that neither Health Plans, Care, nor Group operated exclusively for exempt purposes under section 501(c)(3). ... Accordingly, the Commissioner revoked Health Plans' tax-exempt status, retroactive to January 1, 1987, and denied exemptions to Care and Group.

Health Plans, Care, and Group brought suit in the United States Tax Court, seeking a declaratory judgment reversing the Commissioner's adverse determinations. On September 25, 2001, the Tax Court affirmed the Commissioner's conclusions in three separate opinions. [ ]¹¹ This appeal followed.

II. Discussion

A. *Standard of Review*

... The appropriate legal standard for determining whether an organization operates for a "charitable" purpose is a legal question, which we review de novo. Whether an organization in fact operates exclusively for a charitable purpose, however, is a question of fact, which we review for clear error. [ ]. As the taxpayer claiming entitlement to exemption, petitioners bear the burden of proof.

B. *Overview of Applicable Law*

... In this case, the sole question we must consider is whether Health Plans, Care, and Group operated exclusively for exempt purposes within the meaning of section 501(c)(3).

C. *Whether Health Plans, Care, and Group Operated for a Charitable Purpose*

This inquiry requires us to address two basic questions. First, we must consider whether the purpose proffered by petitioners qualifies as a "charitable" purpose under section 501(c)(3). "The term 'charitable' is used in section 501(c)(3) in its generally accepted legal sense and is ... not to be construed as limited by the separate enumeration in section 501(c)(3)." 26 C.F.R. § 1.501(c)(3)–1(d)(2). An organization will not be considered charitable, how-

---

11. The Tax Court did not consider the Commissioner's alternative conclusion under   26 U.S.C. § 501(m)(1).

ever, "unless it serves a *public rather than a private interest.*" 26 C.F.R. § 1.501(c)(3)–1(d)(1)(ii) (emphasis added).[12]

Second, we must determine whether petitioners in fact operated *primarily* for this purpose. [ ] Under the "operational test" set forth in the IRS regulations, "[a]n organization will be regarded as 'operated exclusively' for one or more exempt purposes only if it engages primarily in activities which accomplish one or more of such exempt purposes specified in section 501(c)(3). An organization will not be so regarded if more than an insubstantial part of its activities is not in furtherance of an exempt purpose."[13] 26 C.F.R. § 1.501(c)(3)–1(c)(1).

In this case, the Tax Court concluded that "the promotion of health for the benefit of the community is a charitable purpose," [ ] but found that neither Health Plans, Care, nor Group operated primarily to benefit the community. [ ] For the reasons set forth below, we agree.

1. *The promotion of health as a charitable purpose*

In defining "charitable," our analysis must focus on whether petitioners' activities conferred a *public* benefit.[ ] The public-benefit requirement highlights the *quid pro quo* nature of tax exemptions: the public is willing to relieve an organization from the burden of taxation in exchange for the public benefit it provides. [ ] As the Supreme Court has recognized, "[c]haritable exemptions are justified on the basis that the exempt entity confers a *public benefit*—a benefit which the society or the community may not itself choose or be able to provide, or which supplements and advances the work of public institutions already supported by tax revenues." *Bob Jones Univ. v. United States,* 461 U.S. 574, 591, 103 S.Ct. 2017, 76 L.Ed.2d 157 (1983) (emphasis added).

* * *

[The Court reviews the IRS and judicial interpretations of the community benefit standard]. Thus, under the IRS's interpretation of section 501(c)(3), in the context of health-care providers, we must determine whether the taxpayer operates *primarily for the benefit of the community.*[14] And while the concept of "community benefit" is somewhat amorphous, we agree with the IRS, the Tax Court, and the Third Circuit that it provides a workable standard for determining tax exemption under section 501(c)(3).

b. Defining "community benefit"

In giving form to the community-benefit standard, we stress that "not every activity that promotes health supports tax exemption under § 501(c)(3).

---

12. Although we are not bound by IRS regulations or revenue rulings, we do accord them deference. [ ]

13. The Supreme Court construed a similar provision under the Social Security Act in *Better Business Bureau v. United States,* concluding that "a single non-[exempt] purpose, if substantial in nature, will destroy the exemption regardless of the number or importance of truly [exempt] purposes." 326 U.S. 279, 283, 66 S.Ct. 112, 90 L.Ed. 67 (1945).

14. [C]ourt decisions have highlighted several factors relevant under the "community benefit" analysis. These factors include:

(1) size of the class eligible to benefit; (2) free or below-cost products or services; (3) treatment of persons participating in governmental programs such as Medicare or Medicaid; (4) use of surplus funds for research or educational programs; and (5) composition of the board of trustees.[ ] Douglas M. Mancino, *Income Tax Exemption of the Contemporary Nonprofit Hospital,* 32 ST. LOUIS U. L.J. 1015, 1037–70 (1988).

For example, selling prescription pharmaceuticals certainly promotes health, but pharmacies cannot qualify for … exemption under § 501(c)(3) on that basis alone." [ ] In other words, engaging in an activity that promotes health, *standing alone,* offers an insufficient indicium of an organization's purpose. Numerous for-profit enterprises offer products or services that promote health.

Similarly, the IRS rulings in 69–545 and 83–157 demonstrate that an organization cannot satisfy the community-benefit requirement based solely on the fact that it offers health-care services to all in the community[15] in exchange for a fee.[16] Although providing health-care products or services to all in the community is necessary under those rulings, it is insufficient, standing alone, to qualify for tax exemption under section 501(c)(3). Rather, the organization must provide some additional "plus."

This plus is perhaps best characterized as "a benefit which the society or the community may not itself choose or be able to provide, or which supplements and advances the work of public institutions already supported by tax revenues." [ ] Concerning the former, the IRS rulings provide a number of examples: providing free or below-cost services, *see* Rev. Rul. 56–185; maintaining an emergency room open to all, regardless of ability to pay, *see* Rev. Rul. 69–545; and devoting surpluses to research, education, and medical training, *see* Rev. Rul. 83–157. These services fall under the general umbrella of "positive externalities" or "public goods."[17] Concerning the latter, the primary way in which health-care providers advance government-funded endeavors is the servicing of the Medicaid and Medicare populations.

c. Quantifying "community benefit"

Difficulties will inevitably arise in quantifying the required community benefit. The governing statutory language, however, provides some guidance. Under section 501(c)(3), an organization is not entitled to tax exemption unless it operates for a charitable *purpose.* Thus, the existence of some incidental community benefit is insufficient. Rather, the magnitude of the community benefit conferred must be sufficient to give rise to a strong inference that the organization operates *primarily for the purpose of benefitting the community.* [ ]

Thus, our inquiry turns "not [on] the nature of the activity, but [on] the *purpose* accomplished thereby." Of course, because of the inherent difficulty

---

15. We recognize that certain health-care entities provide specialized services, which are not required by "all" in the community, and we do not mean to foreclose the possibility that such entities may qualify as "charitable" under section 501(c)(3). As the IRS recognized in Rev. Rul. 83–157:

Certain specialized hospitals, such as eye hospitals and cancer hospitals, offer medical care limited to special conditions unlikely to necessitate emergency care and do not, as a practical matter, maintain emergency rooms. These organizations may also qualify under section 501(c)(3) if there are present similar, significant factors that demonstrate that the hospitals operate exclusively to benefit the community.

16. At least where the fee is above cost. We express no opinion on whether an enterprise that sold health-promoting products or services entirely at or below cost would qualify for tax exemption under 501(c)(3).

17. Under the Treasury Department's view, for-profit enterprises are unlikely to provide such services since " 'market prices … do not reflect the benefit [these services] confer on the community as a whole.' "[ ] Thus, the provision of such "public goods"—at least when conducted on a sufficiently large scale—arguably supports an inference that the enterprise is responding to some inducement that is not market-based. *Cf. id.*

in determining a corporate entity's subjective purpose, we necessarily rely on objective indicia in conducting our analysis. [ ]In determining an organization's purpose, we primarily consider the manner in which the entity carries on its activities. [ ]

d.   The resulting test

In summary, under section 501(c)(3), a health-care provider must make its services available to all in the community *plus* provide additional community or public benefits. The benefit must either further the function of government-funded institutions or provide a service that would not likely be provided within the community but for the subsidy. Further, the additional public benefit conferred must be sufficient to give rise to a strong inference that the public benefit is the *primary purpose* for which the organization operates. In conducting this inquiry, we consider the totality of the circumstances. With these principles in mind, we proceed to review the Tax Court's decision in the present case.

* * *

3.   *The Tax Court correctly concluded that petitioners do not operate primarily to promote health for the benefit of the community.*

Petitioners ... argue that the Tax Court erred in concluding that petitioners did not operate primarily for the benefit of the community. We disagree.

a.   Nature of the product or service and the character of the transaction

In this case, we deal with organizations that do not provide health-care services directly. Rather, petitioners furnish group insurance entitling enrollees to services of participating hospitals and physicians. Petitioners determine premiums using two methods: (1) an adjusted community rating for individuals and small employers; and (2) past-claims experience for large employers. Thus, [ ] petitioners "sell [ ] insurance coverage ... extend[ing] benefits in return for a premium based generally on the risk assumed." [ ] In other words, petitioners primarily perform a "risk-bearing function." In *Church of the Brethren,* as in the instant case, the commercial nature of this activity inspired doubt as to the entity's charitable purpose. 759 F.2d at 795; *cf. Federation Pharmacy Servs., Inc. v. C.I.R.,* 72 T.C. 687, 691–92, 1979 WL 3712 (1979), *aff'd* 625 F.2d 804 (8th Cir.1980) (noting that selling pharmaceuticals is "an activity that is normally carried on by a commercial profit making enterprise[ ]"). Where, as here, "[i]t is difficult to distinguish the plaintiff corporation from a mutual insurance company," we must carefully scrutinize the organization's operation.[18]

b.   Free or below-cost products or services

The fact that an activity is normally undertaken by commercial for-profit entities does not necessarily preclude tax exemption, particularly where the

18. We are primarily concerned with this characteristic as it bears on our determination of petitioners' purpose. However, we also note that petitioners not only resemble commercial insurance providers, petitioners in fact compete with commercial insurance providers. Thus, "granting a tax exemption to [petitioners] would necessarily disadvantage other for-profit [entities] with which [petitioners] compete[ ]."

entity offers its services at or below-cost. [ ]. But petitioners provide virtually no free or below-cost health-care services.[ ] All enrollees must pay a premium in order to receive benefits.[19] As the Eighth Circuit has recognized, "[a]n organization which does not extend some of its benefits to individuals financially unable to make the required payments [generally] reflects a commercial activity rather than a charitable one." *Federation Pharmacy Servs., Inc. v. C.I.R.*, 625 F.2d 804, 807 (8th Cir.1980). Further, the fact that petitioners in no way subsidize dues for those who cannot afford subscribership distinguishes this case from the HMOs in *Sound Health Ass'n v. C.I.R.*, 71 T.C. 158, 1978 WL 3393 (1979), and *Geisinger I*, 985 F.2d at 1219.

We acknowledge, as did the Tax Court, that petitioners' "adjusted community rating system[ ] likely allowed its enrollees to obtain medical care at a lower cost than might otherwise have been available." [ ] Again, however, selling services at a discount tells us little about the petitioners' *purpose*. "Many profit making organizations sell at a discount." [ ] In considering price as it relates to an organization's purpose, there is a qualitative difference between selling at a discount and selling below cost.[20]

In sum, petitioners sole activity is arranging for health-care services in exchange for a fee. To elevate the attendant health benefit over the character of the transaction would pervert Congress' intent in providing for charitable tax exemptions under section 501(c)(3). Contrary to petitioners' insinuation, the Tax Court did not accord dispositive weight to the absence of free care. Neither do we. Rather, it is yet another factor that belies petitioners' professions of a charitable purpose.[21]

The court also found that nothing in the record indicates that petitioners conducted research or offered free educational programs to the public, noting that petitioners' "Core Wellness Program" was offered exclusively to enrollees.]

d.   The class eligible to benefit

(1) Health Plans

As the Tax Court noted, "[Health Plans] offered its [coverage] to a broad cross-section of the community including individuals, the employees of both large and small employers, and individuals eligible for Medicaid benefits." In fact, in 1999, Health Plans' enrollees represented twenty percent of Utah's total population and fifty percent of Utah residents eligible for Medicaid benefits.[22]

19. Petitioners note that Care and Group offered "risk" and "cost" Medicare health plans, and contend that Care and Group went forward with these plans "with the full knowledge that those plans might lose money." Care and Group discontinued these plans, however, based on concerns of "financial feasibility."

20. Further, as the Tax Court noted, "the benefit associated with these cost savings is more appropriately characterized as a benefit to petitioner[s]' enrollees as opposed to the community at large."

21. As the Eighth Circuit has noted, "a 'charitable' hospital may impose charges or fees for services rendered, and indeed its charity record may be comparatively low depending upon all the facts ... but a serious question is raised where its charitable operation is virtually inconsequential." *Federation Pharmacy*, 625 F.2d at 807 (8th Cir.1980) (quoting *Sonora Cmty. Hosp. v. C.I.R.*, 46 T.C. 519, 526, 1966 WL 1319 (1966)) (internal quotation marks omitted).

22. We acknowledge that Health Plans' service to Utah's Medicaid community provides some community benefit. The relevant inquiry, however, is not "whether [petitioner] benefited the community at all ... [but] whether it

Nevertheless, even though almost all Utahans were potentially eligible to enroll for Health Plans coverage, the self-imposed requirement of membership tells us something about Health Plans' operation. As the Third Circuit noted in *Geisinger I:*

> The community benefited is, in fact, limited to those who belong to [the HMO] since the requirement of subscribership remains a condition precedent to any service. Absent any additional indicia of a charitable purpose, this self-imposed precondition suggests that [the HMO] is primarily benefitting itself (and, perhaps, secondarily benefiting the community) by promoting subscribership throughout the areas it serves.

985 F.2d at 1219. Further, while the absence of a large class of potential beneficiaries may preclude tax-exempt status, its presence standing alone provides little insight into the organization's purpose. Offering products and services to a broad segment of the population is as consistent with self promotion and profit maximization as it is with any "charitable" purpose.

(2) Care and Group

Neither Care nor Group offered their health plans to the general public. Rather, both Care and Group limited their enrollment to employees of large employers (employers with 100 or more employees). Thus, as the Tax Court found, "[Care and Group] operate[d] in a manner that substantially limit[ed] [the] universe of potential enrollees." [ ] Based on this finding, the Tax Court correctly concluded that neither Care nor Group promoted health for the benefit of the community.

e.   Community board of trustees

Finally, we consider petitioners' board composition. Prior to 1996, Health Plans' bylaws provided that "[a] plurality of Board members shall represent the buyer-employer community and an approximately equal number of physicians and hospitals representatives shall be appointed." As the IRS noted, Health Plans' pre–1996 bylaws skewed control towards subscribers, rather than the community at large. In 1996, however, Health Plans amended its bylaws to require that a majority of board members be disinterested and broadly representative of the community.

It makes little difference whether we consider petitioners' board prior to 1996 or following the amendments. Even if we were to conclude petitioners' board broadly represents the community, the dearth of any actual community benefit in this case rebuts any inference we might otherwise draw.

4.   *Conclusion*

For the above reasons, we agree with the Tax Court's conclusion that petitioners, standing alone, do not qualify for tax exemption under section 501(c)(3).

* * *

primarily benefited the community, as an entity must in order to qualify for tax-exempt status." [ ]

[The Court next discussed the integral part doctrine, which follows in the next section of this casebook]

Notes and Questions

1. What factors short of operating a free emergency service will enable an HMO to obtain 501(c)(3) status? Why is charging a discounted premium to some subscribers regarded as insufficient? Does the IHC "plus" standard mean that the provision of health services is not a sufficient community benefit to carry the day? See also Geisinger Health Plan v. Commissioner, 985 F.2d 1210 (3d Cir. 1993) ("Geisinger I") (applying health plans and similar analysis of qualitative factors and also finding that providing subsidy to only 35 people constituted quantitatively an insufficient community benefit).

2. How do the requirements for § 501(c)(3) status for HMOs compare to those the IRS applies for hospitals? Should subsidized memberships, which satisfy an unmet need for primary care, be considered the equivalent of charity care? Should the provision of primary care in medically underserved areas be counted favorably as a charitable purpose? Or, does the fact that the subsidized or free enrollees become "members" of the HMO simply make it definitionally impossible for the subsidization to be counted as a "community" benefit?

3. What factors might influence whether other entities such as nursing homes, clinics and physician practice organizations can obtain exempt status? See Rev. Rul. 72–124 which states that 501(c)(3) exemption is conditioned on relieving financial distress by providing care and housing on a gratuitous or below cost basis and meets the "three primary needs of aged persons...for housing, ... health care ... and financial security." With regard to the need for financial security, it stated "the organization must be committed to an established policy, whether in writing or in actual practice, of maintaining in residence any persons who become unable to pay their regular charges." It can readily be seen that most physician practice associations, including physician corporations, provide private benefit and lack charitable purpose to qualify for exemption, although some may qualify based on their relationship to research and teaching hospitals or as an integral part of an integrated delivery system as discussed in the following case. See Kenneth L. Levine, Obtaining 501(c)(3) Status for Professional Medical Corporations 2 DePaul J. Health Care L. 231 (1998). In other instances, such as operation of a pharmacy, the business is regarded as "inherently commercial" and not eligible for exempt status. See Federation Pharmacy Services, Inc. v. Commissioner, 625 F.2d 804 (8th Cir. 1980).

4. A final hurdle for HMOs seeking exempt status is Section 501(m)(1) of the Internal Revenue Code which provides that an organization described in § 501(c)(3) or § 501(c)(4) shall be exempt "only if no substantial part of its activities consists of providing commercial-type insurance." Although the legislative history indicates that this provision was intended to bar continued § 501(c)(4) exemption for Blue Cross/Blue Shield organizations, which had enjoyed such status for many years, the IRS has applied the provision to deny exempt status to HMOs whose activities resemble those of commercial insurers. See H.R. Rep. No. 99–426, at 662–66 (1986). In a technical advice memorandum, the IRS revoked the § 501(c)(3) status of a health maintenance organization, finding that it essentially provided insurance under § 501(m)(1). The notice indicated the IRS will withdraw from its exempt organization manual prior it planned to withdraw its HMO guidelines pertaining to 501(m), suspend consideration of applications for exempt status under 501(c)4, and not apply Section 501(m) to revoke the tax-exempt status of an HMO. The change was in part a response to the Supreme Court's

decision in Rush Prudential HMO, Inc. v. Moran, 536 U.S. 355, finding that HMO contracting with physicians was properly subject to regulation as an insurer under state law. See Chapter 7. In addition, the experience with the subsection has been that because of the diversity of delivery and physician compensation models, it is often difficult to make a determination as to whether an HMO is "commercial type insurance."

Is a categorical exemption for HMOs appropriate? Bear in mind the differences between various models of HMO structures discussed in Chapter 6. See IRS Request for Comment on Tax Treatment of HMOs Draws Varying Reaction from Tax Attorneys, 12 Health L. Rep. (BNA), Sept. 18, 2003, at 1447. Competing priorities delayed the Internal Revenue Service's deadline for revising regulations to apply Internal Revenue Code Section 501(m) to health maintenance organizations. The IRS sought comments, it said in a field memorandum that it would withdraw from the Internal Revenue Manual the HMO section of the exempt organizations guideline handbook pertaining to Section 501(m). IRS Official Predicts Continued Delay in HMO Tax Rules, Says Suspension Possible, 13 No.43 Health L. Rep. 1552 (BNA) (2004).

C. CHARITABLE PURPOSES: INTEGRATED DELIVERY SYSTEMS

As discussed earlier in this chapter, integrated delivery systems like IHC and Geisinger combine physician, hospital and other provider services with management and support services and HMOs. The structures chosen for integration will have implications for the tax status of individual organizations within the system and of the integrated system itself. As illustrated in the case and notes that follow, courts have struggled to devise a test as to whether the HMO warrants exemption based on its relationship to the system.

* * *

IHC HEALTH PLANS, INC. v. COMMISSIONER OF INTERNAL REVENUE

United States Court of Appeals, Tenth Circuit, 2003.
325 F.3d 1188.

Tacha, Chief Circuit Judge.

* * *

D. *Whether Petitioners Qualify for Tax–Exempt Status as an "Integral Part" of Health Services.*

Petitioners contend that even if they do not qualify for tax exemption standing alone, they qualify based on the fact that their activities are an "integral part" of Health Services, essential to Health Services in accomplishing its tax-exempt purpose. We disagree.

In general, "separately incorporated entities must qualify for tax exemption on their own merits." [ ] Several circuits, however, have recognized a so-called "exception" to this general rule, commonly called the integral-part doctrine. [ ] ("[The] 'integral part doctrine' ... may best be described as an exception to the general rule that entitlement to exemption is derived solely from an entity's own characteristics."); [ ] Under the integral-part doctrine, where an organization's sole activity is an "integral part" of an exempt affiliate's activities, the organization may derive its exemption from that of its affiliate . . .

To the extent the integral-part doctrine rests on a derivative theory of exemption, it runs contrary to two fundamental tenets of tax law: (1) the "doctrine of corporate entity," under which a corporation is a separate and distinct taxable entity, and (2) the canon of statutory interpretation requiring strict construction of exemptions from taxation.[23] . . . IHC separately incorporated Health Services Health Plans, Care, and Group. "It cannot now escape the tax consequences of that choice, no matter how bona fide its motives or longstanding its arrangements." [ ] Further, we reject petitioners' contention that the integral-part doctrine constitutes a "less rigorous" road to tax exemption. The rigor of the charitable-purpose requirement remains constant, regardless of the theory upon which the taxpayer bases its entitlement to tax exemption under section 501(c)(3).

Nevertheless, to the extent the integral-part doctrine recognizes that we should consider the totality of the circumstances in determining an organization's purpose, the doctrine is in accord with our section 501(c)(3) jurisprudence. One of the myriad factors we may consider in determining an organization's purpose is whether an essential nexus exists between an organization seeking tax exemption and a tax-exempt affiliate. The example cited in the Treasury Regulations aptly illustrates the point: "a subsidiary organization which is operated for the sole purpose of furnishing electric power used by its parent organization, a tax-exempt educational organization, in carrying on its educational activities. "[24] 26 C.F.R. § 1.502–1(b). In other words, as we interpret the integral-part doctrine, it simply recognizes that "[t]he performance of a particular activity that is not inherently charitable may nonetheless further a charitable purpose.' Rev. Rul. 69–572, 1969 WL 19169. "The overall result in any given case is dependent on *why* and *how* that activity is actually being conducted." *Id.* (emphasis added).

Using the example cited in Treasury Regulation 1.502–1(b), if we were to consider the nature of the subsidiary's activity in isolation—furnishing electricity—we would have no indication that the subsidiary serves an exempt purpose. On the other hand, when we look at the totality of the circumstances, it becomes clear that the subsidiary's activity furthers the exempt purpose of education: the product provided is essential; the subsidiary furnishes its product solely to the tax-exempt affiliate; [ ] and the tax-exempt parent exercises control over the subsidiary. These facts, considered in conjunction with the exempt purpose for which the tax-exempt parent operates, support a strong inference that the subsidiary operates for the same exempt purpose as does the parent.

In this case, we need not decide whether petitioners provide a service necessary to Health Services in conducting its exempt activities. The required nexus between the activities of petitioners and Health Services is lacking. As the Tax Court noted, "petitioner[s]' enrollees received approximately 20

---

23. As the Third Circuit noted in *Geisinger II*, the "integral-part doctrine" is not codified. 30 F.3d at 499. Although it finds support in 26 C.F.R. § 1.502–1(b), it must ultimately be justified under section 501(c)(3) and its charitable-purpose requirement.

24. We need not decide whether such an organization operates for an exempt purpose per se. We merely note that these facts would suggest that the subsidiary operates for an exempt purpose.

percent of their physician services from physicians employed by or contracting with Health Services, while petitioner contracted for the remaining 80 percent of such physician services directly with independent physicians." *Health Plans,* 82 T.C.M. at 606. Thus, unlike the subsidiary furnishing electricity in Treasury Regulation § 1.502–1(b), petitioners do not function solely to further Health Services' performance of its exempt activities. Rather, a substantial portion (eighty percent) [ ] of petitioners' enrollees received physician services from "physicians with no direct link to [Health Services]."[25] *Health Plans,* 82 T.C.M. at 606. Thus, our consideration of petitioners' "connectedness" to Health Services in no way detracts from our earlier conclusion that petitioners do not qualify for a charitable tax exemption under section 501(c)(3).

Notes and Questions

1. In "Geisinger II," the HMO discussed in the notes in the previous section also contended that it would warrant exemption if it were merged into the clinic or other part of the large Geisinger integrated system. The Third Circuit developed the "boost" test, which asks whether the HMO's "relationship to its parent somehow enhances the subsidiary's own exempt character to the point that, when the boost provided by the parent is added to the contribution made by the subsidiary itself, the subsidiary would be entitled to 501(c)(3) status." Geisinger Health Plan v. Commissioner, 30 F.3d 494 (3d Cir. 1994). The Court noted that GHP, the HMO subsidiary, failed to satisfy this test:

> As our examination of the manner in which GHP interacts with other entities in the System makes clear, its association with those entities does nothing to increase the portion of the community for which GHP promotes health—it serves no more people as a part of the System than it would serve otherwise. It may contribute to the System by providing more patients than the System might otherwise have served, thus arguably allowing the System to promote health among a broader segment of the community than could be served without it, but its provision of patients to the System does not enhance its own promotion of health; the patients it provides—its subscribers—are the same patients it serves without its association with the System. To the extent it promotes health among non-GHP-subscriber patients of the System, it does so only because GHP subscribers' payments to the System help finance the provision of health care to others. An entity's mere financing of the exempt purposes of a related organization does not constitute furtherance of that organization's purpose so as to justify exemption....

> Id. at 499.

See Douglas M. Mancino, Tax Exemption Issues Facing Managed Care Organizations, in American Health Lawyers, Tax Issues for Healthcare Organizations (2000)(characterizing the "boost" test as "incomprehensible" and stating that it "cannot be distilled from prior decisions or Treasury regulations.") Does the IHC opinion's "essential nexus" test add any clarity to the integral part issue? Why does the provision of services by independent physicians detract from the "con-

---

25. We recognize that when we consider petitioners standing alone, drawing a distinction between a "staff-model HMO" (as in *Sound Health*) and a "contract HMO" (as in *Geisinger* and here) may not make sense. Colombo, *supra*, at 245. "[T]he 'community benefits' attributable to a particular [HMO] are the same whether treatment is performed by em-

ployee physicians or independent contractors pursuant to a service agreement." *Id.* at 245–46. Under the integral-part doctrine, however, the distinction is highly relevant, since we seek to determine whether an essential nexus exists between petitioners' operations and those of Health Services, the tax-exempt affiliate.

nectedness" to the integrated delivery system so as to bar application of the integral part doctrine?

Summarizing the impact of the IHC opinion's charitable purpose and integral part analyses on 501(c)(3) for HMOs, one commentator has stated, "If other circuits follow [IHC], it pretty much sounds the death knell for 501(c)(3) status for any HMO unless it's a staff model HMO, primarily a Medicaid plan, or a captive group model where all the participating physicians are employed by a related health system." Federal Appeals Court Upholds IRS Decision Denying Nonprofit Status to Three IHC HMOs, 12 Health L. Rep., (BNA), Apr. 17, 2003, at 626. Recall however HMOs may still obtain the somewhat less desirable exempt status under 501(c)(4), though the degree of community benefit under that provision remains uncertain. Id.

2. Both the Third and Tenth Circuit opinions state that the mere fact that an entity produces dollars that the exempt organization may then use for exempt purposes is not sufficient justification for tax exemption. This is a well-accepted principle and applies to all exempt organizations. For example, should a tax-exempt law school happen to own a pasta company, the fact that the pasta company's profits are devoted entirely to the law school's exempt activities does not of itself qualify the pasta company for tax-exempt status. See discussion of unrelated business income in section on joint ventures, below.

3. *Integrated Delivery Systems.* At the same time that it was opposing Geisinger's exempt status, the Service began issuing a number of favorable rulings to integrated delivery systems. See, e.g., Friendly Hills Healthcare Network Exemption Ruling, 93 Tax Notes Today 31–8 (Feb. 9, 1993); Facey Medical Foundation Exemption Ruling, 93 Tax Notes Today 83–116 (Apr. 15, 1993); Northwestern Healthcare Network Exemption Ruling, 93 Tax Notes Today 187–169 (Sept. 9, 1993); Rockford Memorial Health Services Corporation Exemption Ruling, 1994 WL 510148 (April 4, 1994); Private Letter Ruling 9636026 (Sept. 6, 1996); Private Letter Ruling 9635029 (Aug. 30, 1996). Although the IRS originally seemed to require that physicians represent no more than 20 percent of an exempt IDS's board, it subsequently adopted a flexible policy, stating that a board with a disinterested majority of board members that adopted a conflict of interest policy and routinely monitored compliance with the entity's charitable mission would satisfy its requirements. Model Conflicts of Interest Policy, 1997 CPE Text reprinted in 97 Tax Notes Today 198–30; see also Marlis L. Carson, IRS Eases Stance on Physician Board Representation, 96 Tax Notes Today 132–1 (July 8, 1996).

For a view questioning the community benefits provided by some IDSs, which involved large transfers of wealth to physicians (whose practices were acquired) and doubting whether new community benefits were being afforded, see Congressional Research Service, Tax Aspects of Health Care Reform: The Tax Treatment of Health Care Providers, April 25, 1994. Is increased efficiency sufficient justification for extending exempt status to an IDS? Improved competitive capacity? Since Friendly Hills, the Service has granted exempt status to many IDSs organized in a variety of ways.

4. Physician–hospital organizations (PHOs), described in detail earlier in this chapter, are often used as structures to more closely bind hospitals and physicians. PHOs generally negotiate health plan contracts to cover both physician and hospital services. Some also take on utilization review, credentialing and quality management activities, and some may foster shared administrative services. Many of the functions of the typical PHO will be provided within a fully

integrated tax-exempt IDS. Outside of a fully integrated system, however, PHOs standing alone face difficult issues in gaining tax-exempt status (including issues relating to control by physicians and charitable purpose) and typically do not qualify as tax-exempt. Because most PHOs do not themselves provide care and merely negotiate contracts on behalf of providers, it is difficult to make a case that a charitable purpose is served; even more difficult is compliance with the requirement that no more than incidental private benefits are provided. See Thomas K. Hyatt and Bruce R. Hopkins, The Law of Tax Exempt Health–Care Organizations § 23.2(b) (2001); Charles Kaiser and T.J. Sullivan, IRS Exempt Organizations CPE Technical Instruction Program Textbook: Part II, Chapter P: Integrated Delivery Systems. However, at least one PHO has run the gauntlet, although its approval may be attributable to its base in an academic medical center and other unique factors. See Hyatt & Hopkins, *supra*, § 23.2(b). Of course, a tax-exempt entity may establish or participate in a for-profit PHO if the tax-exempt entity abides by the restrictions of its tax-exempt status.

D. JOINT VENTURES BETWEEN TAX–EXEMPT AND FOR–PROFIT ORGANIZATIONS

Tax-exempt organizations may engage in business activities jointly with for-profit organizations; may own for-profit organizations; and may themselves directly engage in non-tax-exempt activities. An exempt organization's participation in a joint venture with a for-profit entity will not affect its tax exempt status provided the purpose of its involvement in the ventures is in furtherance of its exempt purpose. Section 501(c)(3) requires that the exempt entity be organized and operated "exclusively" for exempt purposes, but the Internal Revenue Code regulations interpret that standard as requiring that exempt organizations engage "primarily in activities that accomplish one or more ... exempt purposes" and further state that the exempt organization violates this standard if "more than an insubstantial" amount of its activities are not in furtherance of exempt purposes. 26 C.F.R. § 1.501(c)(3)–1(c)(1). Thus, § 501(c)(3) organizations may engage in trade or business unrelated to their exempt purposes, though income from such unrelated business is taxable and not tax-exempt.

GENERAL COUNSEL MEMORANDUM
39862.
(Dec. 2, 1991).

[The Service reviews a physician-hospital agreement in which the hospital sold its future net income from certain departments to entities that were owned by physicians who admitted and treated patients at the hospital. For example, obstetricians who treated patients at the hospital could invest in the hospital's OB department with the return on investment being a proportionate share of the net income of that department. Thus, the physician practicing in the department would experience financial gain or loss depending on the department's financial performance.]

The [net income stream] joint venture arrangements ... are just one variety of an increasingly common type of competitive behavior engaged in by hospitals in response to significant changes in their operating environment. Many medical and surgical procedures once requiring inpatient care, still the exclusive province of hospitals, now are performed on an outpatient basis, where every private physician is a potential competitor. The marked shift in governmental policy from regulatory cost controls to competition has fundamentally changed the way all hospitals, for-profit and not, do business.

A driving force behind the new hospital operating environment was the federal Medicare Program's 1983 shift from cost-based reimbursement for covered inpatient hospital services to fixed, per-case, prospective payments. This change to a diagnosis-related prospective payment system ("PPS") dramatically altered hospital financial incentives. PPS severed the link between longer hospital stays with more services provided each patient and higher reimbursement. It substituted strong incentives to control the costs of each individual inpatient's care while attracting a greater number of admissions. Medicare policies are highly influential; the program accounts for nearly 40% of the average hospital's revenues.

The need to increase admission volume was accompanied by a perceived need to influence physician treatment decisions which, by and large, were unaffected by the change to PPS. Hospitals realized that, in addition to attracting more patients, they needed to control utilization of ancillary hospital services, discharge Medicare beneficiaries as quickly as is medically appropriate, and operate more efficiently. Traditionally, physicians treating their private patients at a hospital had enjoyed nearly complete independence of professional judgement. Since they are paid separately by Medicare and other third party payers on the basis of billed charges, they still have an incentive to render more services to each patient over a longer period in order to enhance their own earnings. Once hospital and physician economic incentives diverged, hospitals began seeking ways to stimulate loyalty among members of their medical staffs and to encourage or reward physician behaviors deemed desirable.

* * *

.. Here, there appears to be little accomplished that directly furthers the hospitals' charitable purposes of promoting health. No expansion of health care resources results; no new provider is created. No improvement in treatment modalities or reduction in cost is foreseeable. We have to look very carefully for any reason why a hospital would want to engage in this sort of arrangement.

* * *

Assuming, arguendo, that [a hospital engaged in the transaction because it had] a pressing need for an advance of cash, we could examine this type of transaction strictly as a financing mechanism ... [W]e do not believe it would be proper under most circumstances for a charitable organization to borrow funds under an agreement, even with an outside commercial lender, where the organization would pay as interest a stated percentage of its earnings.... In any event, we do not believe these transactions were undertaken to raise needed cash.

Whether admitted or not, we believe the hospitals engaged in these ventures largely as a means to retain and reward members of their medical staffs; to attract their admissions and referrals; and to pre-empt the physicians from investing in or creating a competing provider [of outpatient services].

* * *

... In our view, there are a fixed number of individuals in a community legitimately needing hospital services at any one time. Paying doctors to steer patients to one particular hospital merely to improve its efficiency seems distant from a mission of providing needed care. We question whether the Service should ever recognize enhancing a hospital's market share vis-a-vis other providers, in and of itself, as furthering a charitable purpose. In many cases, doing so might hamper another charitable hospital's ability to promote the health of the same community.

* * *

Notes and Questions

1. Evaluate the economic incentives created by the proposed arrangement. How would a physician gain by making such an investment? Why would a hospital sell a share of its income? Isn't the potential improvement in the hospital's competitive position in the community or enhancement of its efficiency a community benefit? Compare these arrangements to "gainsharing" arrangements discussed in the next chapter which allow staff physicians to share in the savings arising from process improvement initiatives or other cost-effective methods which are attributable in part to the physician's efforts. What distinguishes gainsharing arrangements from the sale of revenue stream at issue in GCM 39862? See Stacey L. Murphy & Edward J. Buchholz, Internal Revenue Service Approval of Two Gainsharing Programs—The Rulings and Their Implications, 32 J. Health L. 381 (1999).

2. Unrelated trade or business is that which an exempt organization regularly carries on "the conduct of which is not substantially related (aside from the need of such organization for income or funds or the use it makes of the profits derived)" to its exempt purpose and is taxable as "unrelated business taxable income" (UBTI). 26 CFR § 1.513–1(a). Services that contribute to patient recovery and convenience are "related" to the exempt purposes of the health care organization and income from these activities is not taxable. Generally, services provided to non-hospital patients are taxable unless they fall within certain narrow exceptions relating to (1) whether the services to non-patients are otherwise available in the community or (2) whether the services to non-patients contribute to the achievement of other exempt purposes, such as medical education. Thus sales of pharmaceuticals to individuals who are not hospital patients are taxable, with limited exceptions made for situations in which there are no local alternatives. See Hi–Plains Hosp. v. U.S., 670 F.2d 528 (5th Cir. 1982). See also Private Letter Ruling 8125007 (undated), in which the Service decided that sophisticated lab services, not otherwise available and provided by an exempt hospital to industry for employee examinations, did not produce UBTI. The PLR concluded, however, that the provision of ordinary lab services performed for non-hospital patients of private physicians may do so. This may lead to rather confusing results. A hospital's revenues from providing MRI services to patients of another hospital or to outpatients served by its staff physicians might well be UBTI, though the revenues from the same services to admitted patients would not. Likewise income from management or administrative services sold by a tax-exempt hospital to physicians in private practices could certainly be considered UBTI. If the hospital purchased the physician practices, would the provision of

these services to the hospital-owned practices produce taxable income? On the issue of gift shops, parking facilities and cafeterias on hospital campuses, the law carves out an exception to taxable income by excluding business "carried on by the organization primarily for the convenience of its .. members, patients or employees." I.R.C. § 513(a) (2006).

3. In evaluating the permissibility of joint ventures between for-profit and exempt entities, the IRS has long used a two-prong "close scrutiny" test. That test requires (1) that the exempt organization's participation in the venture serves a charitable purpose and (2) that the structure of the venture permits the exempt organization to act exclusively in furtherance of its charitable purpose and whether the arrangement impermissibly benefits for profit persons. See Housing Pioneers, Inc. v. Commissioner, T.C. Memo 1993–120 (March 29, 1993), 65 T.C.M. 2191, aff'd 49 F.3d 1395 (9th Cir. 1995), amended, 58 F.3d 401 (9th Cir. 1995). Consider how the following Revenue Ruling and cases alter that test.

REVENUE RULING 98–15

1998–12 I.R.B. 6.

[In this Revenue Ruling, the IRS provides the following examples to illustrate whether an organization that operates an acute care hospital constitutes an organization whose principal purpose is providing charitable hospital care when it forms a limited liability company (LLC) with a for-profit corporation and then contributes its hospital and all of its related operating assets to the LLC, which then operates the hospital.]

Situation 1

A is a nonprofit corporation that owns and operates an acute care hospital. A has been recognized as exempt from federal income tax ... as an organization described in § 501(c)(3).... B is a for-profit corporation that owns and operates a number of hospitals.

A concludes that it could better serve its community if it obtained additional funding. B is interested in providing financing for A's hospital, provided it earns a reasonable rate of return. A and B form a limited liability company, C. A contributes all of its operating assets, including its hospital to C. B also contributes assets to C. In return, A and B receive ownership interests in C proportional and equal in value to their respective contributions.

C's Articles of Organization and Operating Agreement ("governing documents") provide that C is to be managed by a governing board consisting of three individuals chosen by A and two individuals chosen by B. A intends to appoint community leaders who have experience with hospital matters, but who are not on the hospital staff and do not otherwise engage in business transactions with the hospital.

The governing documents further provide that they may only be amended with the approval of both owners and that a majority of three board members must approve certain major decisions relating to C's operation including decisions relating to any of the following topics:

A. C's annual capital and operating budgets;

B. Distributions of C's earnings;

C. Selection of key executives;

D.   Acquisition or disposition of health care facilities;

E.   Contracts in excess of $x per year;

F.   Changes to the types of services offered by the hospital; and

G.   Renewal or termination of management agreements.

The governing documents require that C operate any hospital it owns in a manner that furthers charitable purposes by promoting health for a broad cross section of its community. The governing documents explicitly provide that the duty of the members of the governing board to operate C in a manner that furthers charitable purposes by promoting health for a broad cross section of the community overrides any duty they may have to operate C for the financial benefit of its owners. Accordingly, in the event of a conflict between operation in accordance with the community benefit standard and any duty to maximize profits, the members of the governing board are to satisfy the community benefit standard without regard to the consequences for maximizing profitability.

The governing documents further provide that all returns of capital and distributions of earnings made to owners of C shall be proportional to their ownership interests in C. The terms of the governing documents are legal, binding, and enforceable under applicable state law.

C enters into a management agreement with a management company that is unrelated to A or B to provide day-to-day management services to C. The management agreement is for a five-year period, and the agreement is renewable for additional five-year periods by mutual consent. The management company will be paid a management fee for its services based on C's gross revenues. The terms and conditions of the management agreement, including the fee structure and the contract term, are reasonable and comparable to what other management firms receive for similar services at similarly situated hospitals. C may terminate the agreement for cause.

None of the officers, directors, or key employees of A who were involved in making the decision to form C were promised employment or any other inducement by C or B and their related entities if the transaction were approved. None of A's officers, directors, or key employees have any interest, including any interest through attribution determined in accordance with the principles of § 318, in B or any of its related entities.

Pursuant to § 301.7701–3(b) of the Procedure and Administrative Regulations, C will be treated as a partnership for federal income tax purposes.

A intends to use any distributions it receives from C to fund grants to support activities that promote the health of A's community and to help the indigent obtain health care. Substantially all of A's grantmaking will be funded by distributions from C. A's projected grantmaking program and its participation as an owner of C will constitute A's only activities.

Situation 2

D is a nonprofit corporation that owns and operates an acute care hospital. D has been recognized as exempt from federal income tax ... as an organization described in § 501(c)(3).... E is a for-profit hospital corporation that owns and operates a number of hospitals and provides management services to several hospitals that it does not own.

D concludes that it could better serve its community if it obtained additional funding. E is interested in providing financing for D's hospital, provided it earns a reasonable rate of return. D and E form a limited liability company, F. D contributes all of its operating assets, including its hospital to F. E also contributes assets to F. In return, D and E receive ownership interests proportional and equal in value to their respective contributions.

F's Articles of Organization and Operating Agreement ("governing documents") provide that F is to be managed by a governing board consisting of three individuals chosen by D and three individuals chosen by E. D intends to appoint community leaders who have experience with hospital matters, but who are not on the hospital staff and do not otherwise engage in business transactions with the hospital.

The governing documents further provide that they may only be amended with the approval of both owners and that a majority of board members must approve certain major decisions relating to F's operation, including decisions relating to any of the following topics:

A. F's annual capital and operating budgets;

B. Distributions of F's earnings over a required minimum level of distributions set forth in the Operating Agreement;

C. Unusually large contracts; and

D. Selection of key executives.

F's governing documents provide that F's purpose is to construct, develop, own, manage, operate, and take other action in connection with operating the health care facilities it owns and engage in other health care-related activities. The governing documents further provide that all returns of capital and distributions of earnings made to owners of F shall be proportional to their ownership interests in F.

F enters into a management agreement with a wholly-owned subsidiary of E to provide day-to-day management services to F. The management agreement is for a five-year period, and the agreement is renewable for additional five-year periods at the discretion of E's subsidiary. F may terminate the agreement only for cause. E's subsidiary will be paid a management fee for its services based on gross revenues. The terms and conditions of the management agreement, including the fee structure and the contract term other than the renewal terms, are reasonable and comparable to what other management firms receive for similar services at similarly situated hospitals.

As part of the agreement to form F, D agrees to approve the selection of two individuals to serve as F's chief executive officer and chief financial officer. These individuals have previously worked for E in hospital management and have business expertise. They will work with the management company to oversee F's day-to-day management. Their compensation is comparable to what comparable executives are paid at similarly situated hospitals.

Pursuant to § 301.7701–3(b). F will be treated as a partnership for federal income tax purposes.

D intends to use any distributions it receives from F to fund grants to support activities that promote the health of D's community and to help the indigent obtain health care. Substantially all of D's grantmaking will be funded by distributions from F. D's projected grantmaking program and its participation as an owner of F will constitute D's only activities.

ANALYSIS

A § 501(c)(3) organization may form and participate in a partnership, including an LLC treated as a partnership for federal income tax purposes, and meet the operational test if participation in the partnership furthers a charitable purpose, and the partnership arrangement permits the exempt organization to act exclusively in furtherance of its exempt purpose and only incidentally for the benefit of the for-profit partners. Similarly, a § 501(c)(3) organization may enter into a management contract with a private party giving that party authority to conduct activities on behalf of the organization and direct the use of the organization's assets provided that the organization retains ultimate authority over the assets and activities being managed and the terms and conditions of the contract are reasonable, including reasonable compensation and a reasonable term. However, if a private party is allowed to control or use the non-profit organization's activities or assets for the benefit of the private party, and the benefit is not incidental to the accomplishment of exempt purposes, the organization will fail to be organized and operated exclusively for exempt purposes.

Situation 1

After A and B form C, and A contributes all of its operating assets to C, A's activities will consist of the health care services it provides through C and any grantmaking activities it can conduct using income distributed to C. A will receive an interest in C equal in value to the assets it contributes to C, and A's and B's returns from C will be proportional to their respective investments in C. The governing documents of C commit C to providing health care services for the benefit of the community as a whole and to give charitable purposes priority over maximizing profits for C's owners. Furthermore, through A's appointment of members of the community familiar with the hospital to C's board, the board's structure, which gives A's appointees voting control, and the specifically enumerated powers of the board over changes in activities, disposition of assets, and renewal of the management agreement. A can ensure that the assets it owns through C and the activities it conducts through C are used primarily to further exempt purposes. Thus, A can ensure that the benefit to B and other private parties, like the management company, will be incidental to the accomplishment of charitable purposes. Additionally, the terms and conditions of the management contract, including the terms for renewal and termination are reasonable. Finally, A's grants are intended to support education and research and give resources to help provide health care to the indigent. All of these facts and circumstances establish that, when A participates in forming C and contributes all of its operating assets to C, and C operates in accordance with its governing documents, A will be furthering charitable purposes and continue to be operated exclusively for exempt purposes.

* * *

Situation 2

When D and E form F, and D contributes its assets to F, D will be engaged in activities that consist of the health care services it provides through F and any grantmaking activities it can conduct using income distributed by F. However, unlike A, D will not be engaging primarily in activities that further an exempt purpose.... In the absence of a binding obligation in F's governing documents for F to serve charitable purposes or otherwise provide its services to the community as a whole, F will be able to deny care to segments of the community, such as the indigent. Because D will share control of F with E, D will not be able to initiate programs within F to serve new health needs within the community without the agreement of at least one governing board member appointed by E. As a business enterprise, E will not necessarily give priority to the health needs of the community over the consequences for F's profits. The primary source of information for board members appointed by D will be the chief executives, who have a prior relationship with E and the management company, which is a subsidiary of E. The management company itself will have broad discretion over F's activities and assets that may not always be under the board's supervision. For example, the management company is permitted to enter into all but "unusually large" contracts without board approval. The management company may also unilaterally renew the management agreement. Based on all these facts and circumstances, D cannot establish that the activities it conducts through F further exempt purposes. "[I]n order for an organization to qualify for exemption under § 501(c)(3) the organization must 'establish' that it is neither organized nor operated for the 'benefit of private interests.' "[ ] Consequently, the benefit to E resulting from the activities D conducts through F will not be incidental to the furtherance of an exempt purpose. Thus, D will fail the operational test when it forms F, contributes its operating assets to F, and then serves as an owner to F.

Notes and Questions

1. Some recommended changes for the hospital in Situation 2 to retain its § 501(c)(3) status include shortening the management term to five years, requiring a 24–hour emergency room at one or more of the LLC hospitals, and adopting a list of reserved powers similar to those in Situation 1. See Gerald M. Griffith, Revenue Ruling 98–15: Dimming the Future of All Nonprofit Joint Ventures?, 31 J. Health L. 71, 88 (1998). How do these relate to the criteria for tax exemption discussed earlier? What other changes would you recommend? Why?

2. Although eagerly awaited, the guidance offered by Revenue Ruling 98–15 has met with criticism for what it does not address. See Robert C. Louthian, III, IRS Provides Whole Hospital Joint Venture Guidance in Revenue Ruling 98–15, 7 Health L. Rep., Mar. 19, 1998, at 477. Many feel that the ruling's "polar opposite" situations do not help to clarify the many gray areas experienced in joint ventures. What situations would still be left unanswered by the ruling?

REDLANDS SURGICAL SERVICES v. COMMISSIONER OF INTERNAL REVENUE

United States Tax Court, 1999.
113 T.C. 47, aff'd per curiam 242 F.3d 904 (2001).

THORNTON, J.

[Petitioner Redlands Surgical Services is a nonprofit member corporation whose sole member is RHS Corp. (RHS), a nonprofit public benefit corporation that is also parent of tax-exempt Redlands Community Hospital. Surgical Care Affiliates Inc. (SCA), a for-profit, publicly held corporation that owns and manages 40 ambulatory surgical centers, owns two for-profit subsidiaries: Redlands–Centers and Redlands Management.

Petitioner entered into two partnerships relevant to this proceeding: (1) the Redlands Ambulatory Surgery Center Partnership (the General Partnership) with Redlands Centers as co-partner; and (2) the Inland Surgery Center Limited Partnership (Inland or the Operating Partnership) of which the General Partnership is the general partner and 32 physicians from Redlands Hospital's medical staff are limited partners. The Operating Partnership owned the Surgery Center, an ambulatory surgical center located two blocks away from Redlands Hospital. The IRS denied Petitioner's Application for Recognition of Exemption stating, "Basically all you have done is invest in a for-profit entity, Inland, and transfer the profits from this investment to your parent."]

OPINION

I.   The Parties' Positions

Respondent contends that petitioner is not operated exclusively for charitable purposes because it operates for the benefit of private parties and fails to benefit a broad cross-section of the community. In support of its position, respondent contends that the partnership agreements and related management contract are structured to give for-profit interests control over the Surgery Center. Respondent contends that both before and after the General Partnership acquired an ownership interest in it, the Surgery Center was a successful profit-making business that never held itself out as a charity and never operated as a charitable health-care provider.

Petitioner argues that it meets the operational test under section 501(c)(3) because its activities with regard to the Surgery Center further its purpose of promoting health for the benefit of the Redlands community, by providing access to an ambulatory surgery center for all members of the community based upon medical need rather than ability to pay, and by integrating the outpatient services of Redlands Hospital and the Surgery Center. Petitioner argues that its dealings with the for-profit partners have been at arm's length, and that its influence over the activities of the Surgery Center has been sufficient to further its charitable goals. Petitioner further contends that it qualifies for exemption because it is organized and operated to perform services that are integral to the exempt purposes of RHS, its tax-exempt parent, and Redlands Hospital, its tax-exempt affiliate.

II.   Applicable Legal Principles

* * *

B.   Promotion of Health as a Charitable Purpose

* * *

The promotion of health for the benefit of the community is a charitable purpose. . . . As applied to determinations of qualification for tax exemption, the definition of the term "charitable" has not been static. [ ] Suffice it to say that, in recognition of changes in the health-care industry, the standard no longer requires that "the care of indigent patients be the primary concern of the charitable hospital, as distinguished from the care of paying patients". Sound Health Association v. Commissioner, *supra* at 180. Rather, the standard reflects "a policy of insuring that adequate health care services are actually delivered to those in the community who need them." [ ] Under this standard, health-care providers must meet a flexible community benefit test based upon a variety of indicia, one of which may be whether the organization provides free care to indigents. * * * To benefit the community, a charity must serve a sufficiently large and indefinite class; as a corollary to this rule, private interests must not benefit to any substantial degree.

Discussion of the proscription against private benefit omitted. The issue is discussed later in this chapter.]

* * *

III.   *Petitioner's Claim to Exemption on a "Stand–Alone" Basis*

Applying the principles described above, we next consider whether petitioner has established that respondent improperly denied it tax-exempt status as a section 501(c)(3) organization.

A.   *The Relevance of Control—The Parties' Positions*

Respondent asserts that petitioner has ceded effective control over its sole activity—participating as a co-general partner with for-profit parties in the partnerships that own and operate the Surgery Center—to the for-profit partners and the for-profit management company that is an affiliate of petitioner's co-general partner. Respondent asserts that this arrangement is indicative of a substantial nonexempt purpose, whereby petitioner impermissibly benefits private interests.

Without conceding that private parties control its activities, petitioner challenges the premise that the ability to control its activities determines its purposes. Petitioner argues that under the operational test, "the critical issue in determining whether an organization's purposes are noncharitable is not whether a for profit or not for profit entity has control. Rather, the critical issue is the sort of conduct in which the organization is actually engaged."

* * *

We disagree with petitioner's thesis. It is patently clear that the Operating Partnership, whatever charitable benefits it may produce, is not operated "in an exclusively charitable manner". As stated by Justice Cardozo (then Justice of the New York Court of Appeals), in describing one of the "ancient principles" of charitable trusts, "It is only when income may be applied to the profit of the founders that business has a beginning and charity an end." Butterworth v. Keeler, 219 N.Y. 446, 449–450, 114 N.E. 803, 804 (1916). The Operating Partnership's income is, of course, applied to the profit of petitioner's co-general partner and the numerous limited partners.... It is no answer to say that none of petitioner's income from this activity was applied to private interests, for the activity is indivisible, and no discrete part of the Operating Partnership's income-producing activities is severable from those activities that produce income to be applied to the other partners' profit.

Taken to its logical conclusion, petitioner's thesis would suggest that an organization whose main activity is passive participation in a for-profit health-service enterprise could thereby be deemed to be operating exclusively for charitable purposes. Such a conclusion, however, would be contrary to well-established principles of charitable trust law. . . .

Clearly, there is something in common between the structure of petitioner's sole activity and the nature of petitioner's purposes in engaging in it. An organization's purposes may be inferred from its manner of operations; its "activities provide a useful indicia of the organization's purpose or purposes." [ ] The binding commitments that petitioner has entered into and that govern its participation in the partnerships are indicative of petitioner's purposes. To the extent that petitioner cedes control over its sole activity to for-profit parties having an independent economic interest in the same activity and having no obligation to put charitable purposes ahead of profit-making objectives, petitioner cannot be assured that the partnerships will in fact be operated in furtherance of charitable purposes. In such a circumstance, we are led to the conclusion that petitioner is not operated exclusively for charitable purposes.

Based on the totality of factors described below, we conclude that petitioner has in fact ceded effective control of the partnerships' and the Surgery Center's activities to for-profit parties, conferring on them significant private benefits, and therefore is not operated exclusively for charitable purposes within the meaning of section 501(c)(3).

B. Indicia of For–Profit Control Over the Partnerships' Activities

1. No Charitable Obligation

Nothing in the General Partnership agreement, or in any of the other binding commitments relating to the operation of the Surgery Center, establishes any obligation that charitable purposes be put ahead of economic objectives in the Surgery Center's operations. . . .

After the General Partnership acquired its 61–percent interest, the Operating Partnership—which had long operated as a successful for-profit enterprise and never held itself out as a charity—never changed its organizing documents to acknowledge a charitable purpose. . . .

2. Petitioner's Lack of Formal Control

a. Managing Directors

Under the General Partnership agreement, control over all matters other than medical standards and policies is nominally divided equally between petitioner and SCA Centers, each appointing two representatives to serve as managing directors. (As discussed *infra*, matters of medical standards and policies are determined by the Medical Advisory Group, half of whom are chosen by the General Partnership's managing directors.) Consequently, petitioner may exert influence by blocking actions proposed to be taken by the managing directors, but it cannot initiate action without the consent of at least one of SCA Center's appointees to the managing directors. . . .

The administrative record shows that petitioner has successfully blocked various proposals to expand the scope of activities performed at the Surgery

Center. Petitioner's ability to veto expansion of the scope of the Surgery Center's activities, however, does not establish that petitioner has effective control over the manner in which the Surgery Center conducts activities within its predesignated sphere of operations. Nor does it tend to indicate that the Surgery Center is not operated to maximize profits with regard to those activities. . . .

In sum, the composition of the managing directorship evidences a lack of majority control by petitioner whereby it might assure that the Surgery Center is operated for charitable purposes.[ ] Consequently, we look to the binding commitments made between petitioner and the other parties to ascertain whether other specific powers or rights conferred upon petitioner might mitigate or compensate for its lack of majority control.

b.   *Arbitration Process*

[The court notes that although the General Partnership agreement provides for an arbitration process in the event that the managing directors of the General Partnership deadlock, the ground rules for the arbitration process are minimal and provide petitioner no assurance that charitable objectives will govern the outcome and the arbitrators are not required to take into account any charitable or community benefit objective. It concludes that the arbitration process does not significantly mitigate petitioner's lack of majority control.]

c.   *The Management Contract*

[The court observes that the management contract between the Operating Partnership and SCA Management confers broad powers on SCA Management to enter into contracts, to negotiate with third-party payers and state and federal agencies, and to set patient charges. The court also notes that, as a practical matter, the Operating Partnership is locked into the management agreement with SCA Management for at least 15 years.]

[N]either the General Partnership agreement, the Operating Partnership agreement, nor the management contract itself requires that SCA Management be guided by any charitable or community benefit, goal, policy, or objective. Rather, the management contract simply requires SCA Management to render services as necessary and in the best interest of the Operating Partnership, "subject to the policies established by [the Operating Partnership], which policies shall be consistent with applicable state and Federal law."

* * *

Respondent asserts, and we agree, that this long-term management contract with an affiliate of SCA Centers is a salient indicator of petitioner's surrender of effective control over the Surgery Center's operations to SCA affiliates, whereby the affiliates were given the ability and incentive to operate the Surgery Center so as to maximize profits. This surrender of effective control reflects adversely on petitioner's own charitable purposes in contracting to have its sole activity managed in this fashion.

d. Medical Advisory Group

The Operating Partnership agreement delegates authority for making decisions about care and treatment of patients and other medical matters to the Operating Partnership's Medical Advisory Group. This group was inactive before the General Partnership became involved with the Operating Partnership, but there is no evidence to show what role, if any, petitioner played in reconstituting the Medical Advisory Group. * * *

e. Termination of Quality Assurance Activities

As required by the General Partnership agreement, on April 30, 1990, SCA Management entered into a quality assurance agreement with RHS. The term of the quality assurance agreement was conditioned on maintenance of a specified level of surgery activity in the Surgery Center. Petitioner concedes that the quality assurance agreement terminated after the first year. Although the agreement required the parties to negotiate a new quality assurance agreement in the event of such a termination, there is no evidence in the record that such negotiations ever occurred.

The termination of the quality assurance agreement vividly evidences petitioner's lack of effective control over vital aspects of the Surgery Center's operations. * * * The record does not reflect that petitioner performed any quality assurance work. Likewise, the record is silent as to how petitioner, in the absence of any operable quality assurance agreement, purports to assure itself that these vital functions will be discharged consistently with charitable objectives.

3. Lack of Informal Control

The administrative record provides no basis for concluding that, in the absence of formal control, petitioner possesses significant informal control by which it exercises its influence with regard to the Surgery Center's activities. Nothing in the administrative record suggests that petitioner commands allegiance or loyalty of the SCA affiliates or of the limited partners to cause them to put charitable objectives ahead of their own economic objectives. Indeed, until April 1992, petitioner was in a debtor relationship to SCA.

* * *

a. Provision for Indigent Patients

Petitioner concedes that as of December 31, 1993, Medi–Cal patients accounted for only 0.8 percent of total procedures performed at the Surgery Center. Petitioner argues that the type of services which the Service Center offers is not the type of services typically sought by low-income individuals. Petitioner notes that Redlands Hospital has negotiated certain provider agreements that designate the Surgery Center as a subcontractor to provide outpatient services for Medi–Cal patients, and that Redlands Hospital has caused the Surgery Center to increase its number of managed care contracts. Petitioner suggests that these efforts demonstrate petitioner's influence over the operations of the Surgery Center and evidence petitioner's charitable purposes.

We do not find petitioner's arguments convincing. The facts remain that the Surgery Center provides no free care to indigents and only negligible coverage for Medi–Cal patients. * * *

5. *Coordination of Activities of Redlands Hospital and the Surgery Center*

* * *

Although there may be cooperation between the Surgery Center and Redlands Hospital, nothing in the record suggests that these various cooperative activities are more than incidental to the for-profit orientation of the Surgery Center's activities. [ ]

C.　*Competitive Restrictions and Market Advantages*

By entering into the General Partnership agreement, RHS (petitioner's parent corporation and predecessor in interest in the General Partnership) not only acquired an interest in the Surgery Center, but also restricted its future ability to provide outpatient services at Redlands Hospital or elsewhere without the approval of its for-profit partner. Paragraph 16 of the General Partnership agreement, *supra*, prohibits the co-general partners and their affiliates from owning, managing, or developing another freestanding outpatient surgery center within 20 miles of the Surgery Center, without the other partner's consent. Moreover, Redlands Hospital may not "expand or promote its present outpatient surgery program within the Hospital." In fact, outpatient surgeries performed at Redlands Hospital decreased about 17 percent from 1990 to 1995, while those performed at the Surgery Center increased.

. . . Consequently, RHS effectively restricted its own ability to assess and service community needs for outpatient services until the year 2020. It is difficult to conceive of a significant charitable purpose that would be furthered by such a restriction.

* * *

Viewed in its totality, the administrative record is clear that SCA and petitioner derive mutual economic benefits from the General Partnership agreement. By borrowing necessary up-front capital from SCA, RHS (petitioner's predecessor in interest in the General Partnership), overcame a capital barrier to gain entry into a profitable and growing market niche. By forming a partnership with RHS, SCA Centers was able to benefit from the established relationship between Redlands Hospital and the limited partner physicians to acquire its interest in the Surgery Center at a bargain price.

By virtue of this arrangement, petitioner and SCA Centers realized further mutual benefits by eliminating sources of potential competition for patients, as is evidenced by the restrictions on either party's providing future outpatient services outside the Surgery Center, and by Redlands Hospital's agreeing not to expand or promote its existing outpatient surgery facility at the hospital. In light of the statement in the record that it is typical for national chains such as SCA to "shadow-price" hospitals in charging for services at outpatient surgery centers, it seems most likely that one purpose and effect of the containment and contraction of Redlands Hospital's outpatient surgery activities is to eliminate a competitive constraint for setting

Surgery Center fees (a matter delegated to SCA Management under the management contract, excluding charges for physicians' services).

* * *

There is no per se proscription against a nonprofit organization's entering into contracts with private parties to further its charitable purposes on mutually beneficial terms, so long as the nonprofit organization does not thereby impermissibly serve private interests. [ ] In the instant case, however, RHS relied on the established relationship between Redlands Hospital and Redlands physicians to enable RHS and SCA affiliates jointly to gain foothold, on favorable terms, in the Redlands ambulatory surgery market. Then, by virtue of their effective control over the Surgery Center, the SCA affiliates have been enabled to operate it as a profit-making business, with significantly reduced competitive pressures from Redlands Hospital, and largely unfettered by charitable objectives that might conflict with purely commercial objectives. [ ]

D. Conclusion

Based on all the facts and circumstances, we hold that petitioner has not established that it operates exclusively for exempt purposes within the meaning of section 501(c)(3). In reaching this holding, we do not view any one factor as crucial, but we have considered these factors in their totality: The lack of any express or implied obligation of the for-profit interests involved in petitioner's sole activity to put charitable objectives ahead of noncharitable objectives; petitioner's lack of voting control over the General Partnership; petitioner's lack of other formal or informal control sufficient to ensure furtherance of charitable purposes; the long-term contract giving SCA Management control over day-to-day operations as well as a profit-maximizing incentive; and the market advantages and competitive benefits secured by the SCA affiliates as the result of this arrangement with petitioner. Taken in their totality, these factors compel the conclusion that by ceding effective control over its operations to for-profit parties, petitioner impermissibly serves private interests.

[The Court goes on to reject petitioner's argument that it qualifies for exemption under the integral part doctrine.]

Notes and Questions

1. In an important affirmation of the analysis contained in Rev. Ruling 98–15, the Court of Appeals for the Fifth Circuit followed the *Redlands* Court's insistence on the centrality of control in evaluating a whole hospital joint venture. St. David's Health Care System v. United States, 349 F.3d 232 (5th Cir. 2003). St. David's Health Care System, a tax exempt entity operating an acute care hospital, entered into a limited partnership with HCA Inc. pursuant to which HCA would operate and manage the hospital in a whole hospital joint venture arrangement. The IRS subsequently revoked St. David's tax-exempt status retroactive to the partnership's formation finding that it was no longer engaged in activities that primarily furthered its charitable purpose. The court squarely rejected the hospital's contention, which the district court had endorsed, that the pivotal question was one of function, not control, i.e. exempt organizations that engage in activities via the joint venture that further their charitable purposes should retain their exempt status. Instead the court stressed that the operational test under 501(c)(3)

focuses on the purpose rather than the nature of an organization's activities. Thus, even though the court had "no doubt that St. David's via the partnership provides important medical services to the community," it found the hospital "cannot qualify for tax exempt status under 501(c)(3) if its activities under the partnership substantially further the private, profit-seeking interests of HCA." Where private parties or for-profit entities have either "formal or effective control," a presumption attaches "that the organization furthers the profit seeking motivations of those private individuals or entities." While remanding the case to the district court to determine whether control was effectively ceded to HCA, the court was openly skeptical of the claim that various protective measures were sufficient to save the day for St. David's. It questioned, for example, whether St. David's ability to appoint half the members of the board, its right to unilaterally remove the venture's CEO, assurances in the management services agreement that St. David's exempt status would not be endangered, and its right to compel dissolution, sufficed to establish control. Although on remand a jury held that St. David's should retain its exempt status, the IRS adheres to the view that the Fifth Circuit opinion "provided the proper framework for judging joint ventures between non-profits and for-profits ... [i.e.] a non-profit must have effective control in the joint venture." Fred Sokeld, IRS official Unfazed by Jury Decision in Joint Venture Case, 2004 Tax Notes Today 50 (May 12, 2004).

2. The succinct verdict of the commentators after Revenue Ruling 98–15 and the Tax Court's decision in *Redlands* is that "control is king." (This view was strongly reinforced by the *St. David's* decision). Why should that be so? Can you make an argument based on the language and history of the tax code that control should not be the ultimate touchstone for exemption? Can you imagine a compelling set of circumstances in which exemption is warranted even though the exempt organization lacked control over a partnership with a for-profit entity?

3. *Ancillary Joint Ventures.* The implications of *Redlands* & *St. David's* for "ancillary joint ventures" is somewhat uncertain. The IRS has approved dozens of such joint ventures involving medical office buildings, imaging centers, ambulatory surgical centers, treatment centers, physical therapy centers, hospital home care services, and nursing homes. See, e.g., Private Letter Ruling 200206058 (Nov. 16, 2001) (L.L.C. formed by hospital and physicians to provide new medical service); Private Letter Ruling 9517029 (acute care hospital and psychiatric hospital L.L.C. joint venture between an exempt university subsidiary and a for-profit company); 9645018 (outpatient dialysis service L.L.C. joint venture among an exempt hospital, an unrelated exempt health care system, and nephrologists). Private Letter Ruling 200118054 (Feb. 7, 2001) (proposed joint venture L.L.C. formed between a tax-exempt affiliate of a health care system and a group of local physicians); 200117043 (Jan. 30, 2001) (proposed joint venture between two tax-exempt health care entities). Note an important distinction between ancillary joint ventures and the whole hospital ventures involved in Revenue Ruling 98–15: in the former, the exempt hospital retains its separate existence, is subject to the community benefit standard, and often is contributing only a fraction of its assets. See Nicholas A. Mirkay, Relinquish Control! Why the IRS Should Change its Stance on Exempt Organizations in Ancillary Joint Ventures, 6 Nev. L. J. 21, 50 (2005). Whether the IRS is ready to move off the control standard for such ventures remains unclear. In a notable ruling the IRS approved an L.L.C. joint venture between a tax exempt university offering seminars to teachers to improve their skills and a for-profit entity that conducted interactive video training programs. Rev. Rul. 2004–51. Membership in the L.L.C. was divided equally between the for-profit and the university, but the latter retained "exclusive right to approve curriculum, training materials and instructors and determine stan-

dards" for the seminars. Noting that the venture did not constitute a substantial part of the University's activities, the IRS ruled that its participation in the venture would not jeopardize its exempt status. The fact that the ruling cited *St. David's* and Rev. Ruling 98–15, but did not explicitly apply those precedents or invoke the "control" standard and permitted a 50–50 venture to go forward has been interpreted by some to suggest that the test may be loosened in the future. See Mirkay supra at 57–59. But see id. at 59 (quoting IRS official reminding tax bar that Revenue Ruling 98–15 is "still on the books").

What alternative approaches might be applied to ancillary joint ventures? Professor John Colombo has proposed a framework that would employ the principles of UBIT to analyze distinct scenarios under which exempt organizations may engage in joint undertakings that involve businesses not in furtherance of their charitable purpose without losing their exempt status. See John D. Colombo, Commercial Activity and Charitable Tax Exemption, 44 Wm. & Mary L. Rev. 487 (2002). Others have proposed a bright-line quantitative rule that would also employ a UBIT analysis, but would impose a quantitative safe harbor (e.g. use of less than fifteen percent of the exempt organization's assets in the ancillary joint venture). Michael Sanders, Joint Ventures Involving Tax–Exempt Organizations For an excellent critique and proposed synthesis of these proposals see Mirkay, Relinquish Control supra at 70–72.

E. INUREMENT, PRIVATE BENEFIT AND EXCESS BENEFIT TRANSACTIONS: RELATIONSHIPS BETWEEN PHYSICIANS AND TAX–EXEMPT HEALTH CARE ORGANIZATIONS

Physicians and hospitals are highly interdependent both clinically and financially. In the language of economics, they jointly produce the end services provided to patients. As you have seen in the previous sections, hospitals may establish joint ventures with physicians for ancillary services both inside and outside the hospital or to provide care through free standing entities. Hospitals are motivated by both the desire to more efficiently use these resources and to cement their relationships with the physicians and thus assure themselves a steady flow of patients. For similar reasons hospitals and integrated delivery system also have frequently purchased physician practices or recruited physicians to establish a private practice in their geographic area, usually supplying some form of financial support provided to entice the doctor to relocate or open a practice.

These relationships between physicians and tax-exempt organizations raise issues for the tax-exempt provider. Several of these have been explored in the earlier sections of this chapter: IRS limitations on control in joint ventures; standards for unrelated trade or business income; and the achievement and protection of its charitable purposes.

In addition, the exempt organization must comply with three other major legal constraints on relationships between non-exempt (which includes physicians) and tax-exempt health care organizations. These are the proscriptions against private benefit and against private inurement (both of which flow from the language of Section 501(c)(3)) and the new statutory sanctions against excess benefit transactions (codified in IRC Section 4958). However, it appears that the excess benefit statute, which is discussed at the end of this section, will be the predominant tool for future enforcement by the IRS.

1. *Joint Ventures With Physicians*

GENERAL COUNSEL MEMORANDUM

39862 (Dec. 2, 1991).

[The Service reviews a physician-hospital agreement in which the hospital sold its future net income from certain departments to entities owned by physicians who admitted and treated patients at the hospital. Other excerpts from the GCM are included in the previous section on Joint Ventures.]

I. SALE OF THE REVENUE STREAM FROM A HOSPITAL ACTIVITY ALLOWS NET PROFITS TO INURE TO THE BENEFIT OF PHYSICIAN-INVESTORS

* * *

[Editors' Note: At the time of this GCM, the IRS took the position that all physician members of the medical staffs of hospitals—including those not employed by the hospital—have a such a close working relationship with and a private interest in the exempt hospital so as to be subject to the prohibition against inurement, which applies only to "insiders." The GCM stressed physicians' close professional working relationship with the hospitals, that "they largely control the flow of patients to and from the hospital and patients' utilization of hospital services while there", the binding effect of the medical staff bylaws, and that some may serve other roles at the hospital, such as that of part-time employee, department head, Board member, etc. As discussed in Section F, *infra*, the Service does not take the position that staff physician are "disqualified persons" with regard to application of the Excess Benefit statute, which will govern most inurement-type questions in the future. Whether it would adhere to the position taken in this GCM in future inurement cases involving staff member doctors is uncertain].

Even though medical staff physicians are subject to the inurement proscription, that does not mean there can be no economic dealings between them and the hospitals. The inurement proscription does not prevent the payment of reasonable compensation for goods or services. It is aimed at preventing dividend-like distributions of charitable assets or expenditures to benefit a private interest. This Office has stated "inurement is likely to arise where the financial benefit represents a transfer of the organization's financial resources to an individual solely by virtue of the individual's relationship with the organization, and without regard to the accomplishment of exempt purposes." ... [ ]

* * *

Whether admitted or not, we believe the hospitals engaged in these ventures largely as a means to retain and reward members of their medical staffs; to attract their admissions and referrals; and to pre-empt the physicians from investing in or creating a competing provider.... Giving (or selling) medical staff physicians a proprietary interest in the net profits of a hospital under these circumstances creates a result that is indistinguishable from paying dividends on stock. Profit distributions are made to persons having a personal and private interest in the activities of the organization and are made out of the net earnings of the organization. Thus, the arrangements confer a benefit which violates the inurement proscription of section 501(c)(3).

* * *

II. Sale of the Revenue Stream From a Hospital Activity Benefits Private Interests More Than Incidentally

[A] key principle in the law of tax exempt organizations is that an entity is not organized and operated exclusively for exempt purposes unless it serves a public rather than a private interest. Thus, in order to be exempt, an organization must establish that it is not organized or operated for the benefit of private interests such as designated individuals, the creator or his family, shareholders of the organization, or persons controlled, directly or indirectly, by such private interests. [ ] However, this private benefit prohibition applies to all kinds of persons and groups, not just to those "insiders" subject to the more strict inurement proscription.

* * *

In our view, some private benefit is present in all typical hospital-physician relationships. Physicians generally use hospital facilities at no cost to themselves to provide services to private patients for which they earn a fee. The private benefit accruing to the physicians generally can be considered incidental to the overwhelming public benefit resulting from having the combined resources of the hospital and its professional staff available to serve the public. Though the private benefit is compounded in the case of certain specialists, such as heart transplant surgeons, who depend heavily on highly specialized hospital facilities, that fact alone will not make the private benefit more than incidental.

In contrast, the private benefits conferred on the physician-investors by the instant revenue stream joint ventures are direct and substantial, not incidental. If for any reason these benefits should be found not to constitute inurement, they nonetheless exceed the bounds of prohibited private benefit. Whether viewed as giving the physicians a substantial share in the profits of the hospital or simply as allowing them an extremely profitable investment, the arrangements confer a significant benefit on them. Against this, we must balance the public benefit achieved by the hospitals in entering into the arrangements. The public benefit expected to result from these transactions—enhanced hospital financial health or greater efficiency achieved through improved utilization of their facilities—bears only the most tenuous relationship to the hospitals' charitable purposes of promoting the health of their communities. Obtaining referrals or avoiding new competition may improve the competitive position of an individual hospital, but that is not necessarily the same as benefiting its community.

* * *

2. *Physician Recruitment*

REVENUE RULING 97–21

1997–13 I.R.B. 8.

* * *

Situation 1

Hospital A is located in County V, a rural area, and is the only hospital within a 100 mile radius. County V has been designated by the U.S. Public Health Service as a Health Professional Shortage Area for primary medical care professionals (a category that includes obstetricians and gynecologists). Physician M recently completed an ob/gyn residency and is not on Hospital A's medical staff. Hospital A recruits Physician M to establish and maintain a full-time private ob/gyn practice in its service area and become a member of its medical staff. Hospital A provides Physician M a recruitment incentive package pursuant to a written agreement negotiated at arm's-length. The agreement is in accordance with guidelines for physician recruitment that Hospital A's Board of Directors establishes, monitors, and reviews regularly to ensure that recruiting practices are consistent with Hospital A's exempt purposes. The agreement was approved by the committee appointed by Hospital A's Board of Directors to approve contracts with hospital medical staff. Hospital A does not provide any recruiting incentives to Physician M other than those set forth in the written agreement.

In accordance with the agreement, Hospital A pays Physician M a signing bonus, Physician M's professional liability insurance premium for a limited period, provides office space in a building owned by Hospital A for a limited number of years at a below market rent (after which the rental will be at fair market value), and guarantees Physician M's mortgage on a residence in County V. Hospital A also lends Physician M practice start-up financial assistance pursuant to an agreement that is properly documented and bears reasonable terms.

Situation 2

Hospital B is located in an economically depressed inner-city area of City W. Hospital B has conducted a community needs assessment that indicates both a shortage of pediatricians in Hospital B's service area and difficulties Medicaid patients are having obtaining pediatric services. Physician N is a pediatrician currently practicing outside of Hospital B's service area and is not on Hospital B's medical staff. Hospital B recruits Physician N to relocate to City W, establish and maintain a full-time pediatric practice in Hospital B's service area, become a member of Hospital B's medical staff, and treat a reasonable number of Medicaid patients. Hospital B offers Physician N a recruitment incentive package pursuant to a written agreement negotiated at arm's-length and approved by Hospital B's Board of Directors. Hospital B does not provide any recruiting incentives to Physician N other than those set forth in the written agreement.

Under the agreement, Hospital B reimburses Physician N for moving expenses as defined in § 217(b), reimburses Physician N for professional liability "tail" coverage for Physician N's former practice, and guarantees Physician N's private practice income for a limited number of years. The private practice income guarantee, which is properly documented, provides that Hospital B will make up the difference to the extent Physician N practices full-time in its service area and the private practice does not generate a certain level of net income (after reasonable expenses of the practice). The amount guaranteed falls within the range reflected in regional or national surveys regarding income earned by physicians in the same specialty.

Situation 3

Hospital C is located in an economically depressed inner city area of City X. Hospital C has conducted a community needs assessment that indicates indigent patients are having difficulty getting access to care because of a shortage of obstetricians in Hospital C's service area willing to treat Medicaid and charity care patients. Hospital C recruits Physician O, an obstetrician who is currently a member of Hospital C's medical staff, to provide these services and enters into a written agreement with Physician O. The agreement is in accordance with guidelines for physician recruitment that Hospital C's Board of Directors establishes, monitors, and reviews regularly to ensure that recruiting practices are consistent with Hospital C's exempt purpose. The agreement was approved by the officer designated by Hospital C's Board of Directors to enter into contracts with hospital medical staff. Hospital C does not provide any recruiting incentives to Physician O other than those set forth in the written agreement. Pursuant to the agreement, Hospital C agrees to reimburse Physician O for the cost of one year's professional liability insurance in return for an agreement by Physician O to treat a reasonable number of Medicaid and charity care patients for that year.

Situation 4

Hospital D is located in City Y, a medium to large size metropolitan area. Hospital D requires a minimum of four diagnostic radiologists to ensure adequate coverage and a high quality of care for its radiology department. Two of the four diagnostic radiologists currently providing coverage for Hospital D are relocating to other areas. Hospital D initiates a search for diagnostic radiologists and determines that one of the two most qualified candidates is Physician P.

Physician P currently is practicing in City Y as a member of the medical staff of Hospital E (which is also located in City Y). As a diagnostic radiologist, Physician P provides services for patients receiving care at Hospital E, but does not refer patients to Hospital E or any other hospital in City Y. Physician P is not on Hospital D's medical staff. Hospital D recruits Physician P to join its medical staff and to provide coverage for its radiology department. Hospital D offers Physician P a recruitment incentive package pursuant to a written agreement, negotiated at arm's-length and approved by Hospital D's Board of Directors. Hospital D does not provide any recruiting incentives to Physician P other than those set forth in the written agreement.

Pursuant to the agreement, Hospital D guarantees Physician P's private practice income for the first few years that Physician P is a member of its medical staff and provides coverage for its radiology department. The private practice income guarantee, which is properly documented, provides that Hospital D will make up the difference to Physician P to the extent the private practice does not generate a certain level of net income (after reasonable expenses of the practice). The net income amount guaranteed falls within the range reflected in regional or national surveys regarding income earned by physicians in the same specialty.

* * *

ANALYSIS

When a § 501(c)(3) hospital recruits a physician for its medical staff who is to perform services for or on behalf of the organization, the organization meets the operational test by showing that, taking into account all of the benefits provided the physician by the organization, the organization is paying reasonable compensation for the services the physician is providing in return. A somewhat different analysis must be applied when a § 501(c)(3) hospital recruits a physician for its medical staff to provide services to members of the surrounding community but not necessarily for or on behalf of the organization In these cases, a violation will result from a failure to comply with the [requirements that] ... the organization ... not engage in substantial activities that do not further the hospital's exempt purposes or that do not bear a reasonable [or]in activities that result in inurement of the hospital's net earnings to a private shareholder or individual; [or] engage in substantial activities that cause the hospital to be operated for the benefit of a private interest rather than public; [or]engage in substantial unlawful activities.

Situation 1

... Hospital A has objective evidence demonstrating a need for obstetricians and gynecologists in its service area and has engaged in physician recruitment activity bearing a reasonable relationship to promoting and protecting the health of the community ... [The hospital's payments and loans] .. are reasonably related to causing Physician M to become a member of Hospital A's medical staff and to establish and maintain a full-time private ob/gyn practice in Hospital A's service area....

Situation 2

Like Hospital A in Situation 1, Hospital B has objective evidence demonstrating a need for pediatricians in its service area and has engaged in physician recruitment activity bearing a reasonable relationship to promoting and protecting the health of the community [and the incentives provided] are reasonably related to causing Physician N to become a member of Hospital B's medical staff ...

Situation 3

In accordance with the standards for exemption. ... Hospital C admits and treats Medicaid patients on a non-discriminatory basis. Hospital C has identified a shortage of obstetricians willing to treat Medicaid patients. The payment of Physician O's professional liability insurance premiums in return for Physician O's agreement to treat a reasonable number of Medicaid and charity care patients is reasonably related to the accomplishment of Hospital C's exempt purposes. Because the amount paid by Hospital C is reasonable and any private benefit to Physician O is outweighed by the public purpose served by the agreement, the recruitment activity described is consistent with the requirements for exemption as an organization described in § 501(c)(3).

Situation 4

Hospital D has objective evidence demonstrating a need for diagnostic radiologists to provide coverage for its radiology department so that it can promote the health of the community. The provision of a reasonable private practice income guarantee as a recruitment incentive that is conditioned upon Physician P obtaining medical staff privileges and providing coverage for the radiology department is reasonably related to the accomplishment of the charitable purposes served by the hospital. A significant fact in determining that the community benefit provided by the activity outweighs the private benefit provided to Physician P is the determination by the Board of Directors of Hospital D that it needs additional diagnostic radiologists to provide adequate coverage and to ensure a high quality of medical care. . . .

Notes and Questions

1. Note the key differences between private inurement and private benefit. The former is akin to a per se rule, requiring revocation or denial of exempt status, with no de minimis exception. Moreover, it applies only to "insiders," defined as private shareholders or individuals having a personal and private interest in or opportunity to influence the activities of the organization from the inside. Treas. Reg. § 1.50(a)–1(c). The private benefit limitation applies to transactions with "outsiders" to the exempt organization and entails a broader inquiry, weighing private benefits against community benefits. See Sonora Community Hosp. v. Commissioner, 46 T.C. 519 (1966). What goals of the two proscriptions explain the different approaches? What factors did the Service take into account in evaluating each of the scenarios in Rev. Ruling 97–21? Why did the balance tip against the hospital in GCM 39862? Who is considered an insider for inurement purposes? Might a prominent donor and fundraiser for a tax exempt hospital qualify even if she holds no formal office with the hospital? An influential consultant under contract to give management advice?

2. The core of the analysis of private benefit and private inurement is the relationship between what the exempt organization pays and the value, to its achievement of its exempt purposes, of what it receives. Might not-for-profit entities behave differently than for-profits in acquiring physician practices, recruiting physicians or structuring physician compensation and investment? Do a tax-exempt hospital's relationships with physicians require more careful scrutiny than its contracts with third party vendors? The IRS's view that staff physicians were in a position to influence administrators of tax exempt hospitals led to treating them as "insiders" for inurement purposes, a position that it may no longer adhere to. See Charles F. Kaiser and Amy Henchey, Valuation of Medical Practices, CPE Technical Instruction Program Textbook, 95 Tax Notes Today 168–69 (Aug. 28, 1995)(arms-length negotiation would ordinarily produce a purchase price that equates to fair market value in other transactions, but that in the purchase of practices by hospitals from physicians, especially those currently on the staff of the hospital, this assumption may not be valid). Compare the prohibition on private inurement to the approach to insider transactions contained in the Intermediate Sanctions on Excess Benefits law discussed in the next section of this chapter.

3. The requirement that the § 501(c)(3) organization pay no more than fair market value for the physician practice or for physician compensation or for services received in a joint venture is a clear and understandable goal. It is hard to monitor, however, in the absence of functioning markets. The valuation of

physician practices in particular presents substantial problems. Appraisal of the future income potential of the practice itself is particularly difficult and subject to differences among professional appraisers. Furthermore, although the IRS wants to assure that the § 501(c)(3) organization pays for no more than it receives in value, the Medicare and Medicaid programs prohibit payment for the value of future referrals by the doctors to the hospital. Thus, the parties might lean toward inflating the value of certain intangibles or certain allowable items (such as copy expenses for patient records) to bear the value of the referrals to the hospital. Does GCM 39862 indicate that the Service does not consider future referrals a value received? What issues arise when a system decides to divest itself of unprofitable physician practices and decides to sell the practices back to the physicians at a much lower price than it originally paid?

4. Inurement and private benefit issues frequently arise in a variety of other contexts, such as joint ventures involving hospitals and physicians. For example, in the *Redlands* case, reproduced earlier in this chapter, the Tax Court dealt with private benefit arising out of the arrangement:

> There is no per se proscription against a nonprofit organization's entering into contracts with private parties to further its charitable purposes on mutually beneficial terms, so long as the nonprofit organization does not thereby impermissibly serve private interests. [ ] In the instant case, however, RHS relied on the established relationship between Redlands Hospital and Redlands physicians to enable RHS and SCA affiliates jointly to gain foothold, on favorable terms, in the Redlands ambulatory surgery market. Then, by virtue of their effective control over the Surgery Center, the SCA affiliates have been enabled to operate it as a profit-making business, with significantly reduced competitive pressures from Redlands Hospital, and largely unfettered by charitable objectives that might conflict with purely commercial objectives. The net result to the SCA affiliates is a nonincidental "advantage; profit; fruit; privilege; gain; [or] interest" that constitutes a prohibited private benefit. See American Campaign Academy v. Commissioner, 92 T.C. 1053, 1065 (1989).

See also Anclote Psychiatric Ctr., Inc. v. Commissioner, T.C. Memo 1998–273, aff'd 190 F.3d 541 (11th Cir. 1999)(upholding IRS revocation of converting hospital's exemption based on inurement where sale of its assets to for profit entity owned by its former board members was for consideration less than fair market value).

5. Many other issues raised in the purchase of physician practices, physician recruitment and hospital-physician joint ventures are covered elsewhere in this text. For example, issues of self-referral and fraud and abuse are discussed in Chapter 11; antitrust concerns are covered in Chapter 12; and physician contracts are discussed in Chapter 9.

F. EXCESS BENEFIT TRANSACTIONS: PROTECTING HOSPITALS AND OTHER TAX EXEMPT ORGANIZATIONS FROM EXPLOITATION BY INSIDERS

In 1996 Congress adopted the Taxpayer Bill of Rights II (26 U.S.C.A. § 4958), an important new law designed to clarify the obligations of insiders in exempt organizations and to provide an alternative sanction for violations. The basic concept of the law is straightforward: it imposes an excise tax on insiders ("disqualified persons") engaged in "excess benefit transactions." But, as we've seen, nothing in tax law is simple. In January 2002, following four years of comment and revision, the Department of the Treasury issued final regulations which supply guidance concerning the numerous new concepts contained in § 4958. 26 C.F.R. § 53.4958–1—53.4958–8. Some key terminology and concepts must be mastered to apply the supposedly simple, "bright line" approach of the statute.

Scope. Congress intended § 4958 to be the exclusive sanction unless the conduct arises to such an extreme level (evidenced by the size and scope of the excess benefit and the organization's efforts to prevent the conduct) that the tax exempt organization can no longer be regarded as "charitable" and hence revocation is the appropriate sanction.

Excess Benefit Transactions. The statute defines an "excess benefit transaction" (EBT) as any transaction in which an economic benefit is provided by a tax exempt organization directly or indirectly to or for the use of a "disqualified person" where the value of the economic benefit provided by the organization exceeds the value of the consideration (including the performance of services) received for providing the benefit. 26 U.S.C.A. § 4958(c)(1). The core prohibited transactions are those in which the disqualified person engages in a *non-fair market transaction*, such as a bargain sale or loan; *unreasonable compensation arrangements*; or proscribed *revenue sharing arrangements*. The revenue sharing provisions have been reserved for future rulemakings which will give additional guidance as to the scope of permissible arrangements. The regulations give some additional guidance, such as indicating that compensation is reasonable only if its an amount that ordinarily would be paid for like services by like enterprises under like circumstances existing at the time the contract was made. Treas. Reg. 534958–4(b)(3). Further, compensation includes all forms of deferred income if earned and vested and fringe benefits (even if not taxable); however, payments must be intended as compensation by the tax exempt entity. Treas. Reg. 534958–4(c).

Disqualified Persons. "Disqualified persons" (DQPs) include "any person who was, at any time during the 5–year period ending on the date of such transaction, in a position to exercise substantial influence over the affairs of the organization, a member of the family of [such] an individual and, a 35–percent controlled entity [an entity in which such persons own more than 35% of the combined voting power if a corporation or of the profits interest if a partnership or of the beneficial interest of a trust or estate]." I.R.C. 4958(f)(1)(A).

Among those included in the category of DQPs are: officers, directors, and their close relatives. However, the detailed regulations make clear that persons with titles are not to be so regarded if their position is honorary or they have no powers or ability to exercise substantial influence. Treas. Reg. 534958–3(c). On the other hand, those with "substantial influence" are covered regardless of whether they hold a formal position with the exempt organization.

An important issue for hospitals has been whether staff physicians will automatically be considered to have substantial influence. Although the IRS had previously indicated that they would be considered "insiders" for inurement purposes, it has reversed its position for excess benefit analysis, as the following excerpts from the regulations indicate.

Example 10. U is a large acute-care hospital that is an applicable tax-exempt organization for purposes of section 4958. U employs X as a radiologist. X gives instructions to staff with respect to the radiology work X conducts, but X does not supervise other U employees or manage any substantial part of U's operations. X's compensation is primarily in the form of a fixed salary. In addition, X is eligible to receive an incentive award based on revenues of the radiology department. X's compensation is greater than the amount referenced for a highly compensated employee in section 414(q)(1)(B)(i) in the year benefits are provided. X is not related to any other disqualified person of U. X does not serve on U's governing body or as an officer of U. Although U participates in a provider-sponsored organization [ ] X does not have a material financial interest in that organization. X does not receive compensation primarily based on revenues derived from activities of U that X controls. X does not participate in any management decisions affecting either U as a whole or a discrete segment of U that represents a substantial portion of its activities, assets, income, or expenses. Under these facts and circumstances, X does not have substantial influence over the affairs of U, and therefore X is not a disqualified person with respect to U.

Example 11. W is a cardiologist and head of the cardiology department of the same hospital U described in Example 10. The cardiology department is a major source of patients admitted to U and consequently represents a substantial portion of U's income, as compared to U as a whole. W does not serve on U's governing board or as an officer of U. W does not have a material financial interest in the provider-sponsored organization (as defined in section 1855(e) of the Social Security Act) in which U participates. W receives a salary and retirement and welfare benefits fixed by a three-year renewable employment contract with U. W's compensation is greater than the amount referenced for a highly compensated employee in section 414(q)(1)(B)(i) in the year benefits are provided. As department head, W manages the cardiology department and has authority to allocate the budget for that department which includes authority to distribute incentive bonuses among cardiologists according to criteria that W has authority to set. W's management of a discrete segment of U that represents a substantial portion of its income and activities (as compared to U as a whole) places W in a position to exercise substantial influence over the affairs of U. Under these facts and circumstances, W is a disqualified person with respect to U.

Treas. Reg. 534958–3(g), Examples 10 and 11. What generalizable principles emerge from these examples that can be applied in other factual settings?

Organization Managers. Importantly, besides imposing penalties on the individuals receiving the benefits (see below), the act also levies a separate excise tax of 10 per cent on "organization managers," whose participation in the transaction was knowing, willful and not due to reasonable cause. The regulations define organization managers to include directors, trustees or officers and administrators with delegated or regularly exercised administrative powers, but not independent contractors such as lawyers and accountants, investment advisors or middle managers with power to make recommendations but not to implement decisions. See Treas. Reg. 534958–3(d)(2)(i). Where the organizational manager makes full disclosure of all facts to a professional advisor and relies on that advisor's reasoned, written legal opinion, no penalty will be imposed; the advisor may be a lawyer, accountant or independent valuation firm with expertise. Treas. Reg. 534958–1(d)(4)(iii).

Rebuttable Presumption of Reasonableness. A key element of the intermediate sanctions statutory scheme is a rebuttable presumption of reasonableness applicable to compensation arrangements and transfers of property with a disqualified person where specified procedural steps are followed. To qualify for the presumption, the terms of the transaction must be approved by a board of directors or committee thereof composed entirely of individuals who have no conflicts of interest with respect to the transaction and who have obtained and relied upon appropriate comparability data prior to making their determination and have adequately documented the basis for the determination. See Treas. Reg. 534958–6. The IRS may rebut the presumption with evidence that the compensation was not reasonable or the transfer was not at fair market value, such as by contesting the validity of comparables. The regulations give detailed instructions on standards for comparability determinations and give some relief for small organizations as to the data that must be used. Id. In its first advisory on compensation, the IRS found reliance by an independent board on a five-year old consultant report and the board's failure to separately evaluate compensation to comparable CEOs and consultants inadequate to establish the rebuttable presumption under Section 4958. Internal Revenue Service, Technical Advice Memorandum 200244028 (June 21, 2002).

Penalties and "Correction". Sanctions, in the form of an initial tax of 25 per cent of the excess benefit, are imposed on individuals who benefited from the transaction; the excess benefit is calculated as the amount by which a transaction differs from fair market value. Disqualified persons are subject to an additional tax of 200 per cent of the excess benefit unless the transaction is "corrected" promptly (generally meaning that the disqualified person must undo the transaction and compensate the exempt organization for any losses caused by the transaction). Notably, no sanctions are imposed on the exempt organization (however, as described above, organizational managers who knowingly and willfully participate are subject to a 10 per cent tax). Abatement of penalties is possible where the violation is due to reasonable cause and not willful neglect. In the notorious Bishop Estate case, one of the first uses of § 4958, the IRS imposed sanctions against the trustees of an estate in Hawaii who paid themselves exorbitant salaries for its management. See Carolyn D. Wright, IRS Assesses Intermediate Sanctions Against Bishop Estate Incumbent Trustees, 2001 Tax Notes Today 405 (January 5, 2001).

Caracci v. Commissioner. Caracci v. Commissioner, 118 T.C. 379 (2002), rev'd 456 F.3d 444 (5th Cir. 2006), the Tax Court took on for the first time the task of applying the intermediate sanctions provisions to a health care organization and, in a major setback, was reversed by the Fifth Circuit. The Caracci family had operated their tax-exempt home health businesses, known as the Sta–Home Health Agency, very much as a family business. Family members were the sole members of the board of each of the tax exempt entities and also held all key employment positions. For these services, the Caracci family paid themselves what the tax court characterized as "executive level" compensation. After experiencing operating losses for three years, and facing the prospect that Medicare, the principal payer for Sta–Home patients, would shift from cost reimbursement to prospective payment, the Caracci's undertook to convert the entities to for-profit status by selling their assets to three closely held corporations which were controlled and operated by the Caracci family. Concluding that the corporations paid inadequate consideration for the assets of the tax exempt entities, the Service asserted that the transaction resulted in an excess benefit transaction under § 4958. In a 71–page opinion the Tax Court upheld the IRS's assessment of excise taxes but rejected revocation of the Sta–Home entities' tax exempt status. It also concluded that the total excess benefit to the disqualified persons was approximately $5 million.

The Fifth Circuit's reversal contained a blistering criticism of the IRS's valuation analysis. It emphasized the lack of qualifications of the IRS's appraiser and his lack of direct exposure to the specific circumstances of the home healthcare market in Mississippi. Although the Caracci's tax advisor rendered an opinion at the time of the transaction and the family later obtained an appraisal from an expert appraiser with greater experience, the Tax Court had sided with the Internal Revenue Service. Indeed, the Sta–Home entities had lost money and had a negative cash flow, but the Tax court found value in the entities' intangible assets. For an analysis of *Caracci* and its implications for future disputes over valuation, authored by the taxpayers' expert witness, see Allen D. Hahn, Caracci and the Valuation of Exempt Organizations, 40 J. Health L. 267 (2007)(valuation models and reliance on comparables must be sensitive to the characteristics of the exempt organization and the regulatory policies affecting reimbursement).

Problems: Excess Benefit Transactions

1. Analyze whether the excess benefit law would apply in the following situations:

- Expenditures by a tax exempt hospital to recruit an obstetrician, currently practicing at a nearby hospital, to relocate his office nearby and obtain staff privileges. The expenditures (free rent, moving allowances, malpractice insurance subsidies) exceed payments customarily made and there is no documentation of a community shortage of obstetricians.

- Payment by a tax exempt hospital to certain Department Chairs, a fixed percentage of all revenues of the department.

- C, a tax exempt hospital, contracts with Y, a management company, which will provide a wide range of services for a management fee of 7% of C's adjusted gross revenues, as specifically defined in the contract. Y will also receive payments for any expenses it incurs including legal, consulting or accounting throughout the term of the contract.

2. Larry Levy, CEO of Exempt Hospital (EH) has received an offer from a for-profit system in another state that will pay him $2.2 million per year; provide him with a loan of $1 million; and give a performance bonus of $500,000 per year if he meets revenue targets. This package amounts to 50% more than EH currently pays him. It is believed to be in line with compensation at for-profit systems but is about 20% more than comparable nonprofit hospital systems pay. What should the Board of EH do and why?

3. EH currently pays Dr. Brady, an independent staff physician who serves as its Department Chair of Oncology (with responsibility for hiring staff, supervising credentialing, and handling administrative duties of hospital but no role in budgetary matters), a sum of $1000 per month. Dr. Brady has requested a new

compensation arrangement pursuant to which EH would pay him an additional $1000 for each new patient he or any member of the staff admits to EH who incurs total bills greater than $10,000. The EH Board approved this arrangement after a short briefing from its CEO who stressed that EH would have to shut down its oncology department if they didn't accede to Dr Brady's demand. What excess benefit tax liability and for whom? What steps should the parties take?

Review Problem: St. Andrew's Medical Center, Part Two

The Board of tax-exempt St. Andrew's voted against selling the hospital to for-profit Health Care Enterprises. Instead, it has chosen to follow an aggressive strategic plan to achieve the following objectives:

To develop closer working relationships with compatible health care institutions in our region in order to create a comprehensive system of health care delivery that will allow St. Andrew's to better respond to the needs of the purchasers of health care and the patients themselves;

To establish more effective collaborative and mutually beneficial relationships with the physicians who currently hold privileges at St. Andrew's and to develop new alliances with physicians who do not currently admit patients to St. Andrew's;

To develop new, more efficient and more accessible forms of delivery for our services.

St. Andrew's has served primarily an urban and suburban population, but its home city is actually located in a rural state. There is a very small for-profit, free-standing hospital called Parkdale Hospital, located about 50 miles southwest of St. Andrew's. It was originally established by the lead mining company located in that town, but is now owned by a group of three physicians. The physicians are finding the hospital management business terribly trying these days as they do not have the capital that is needed to renovate and improve Parkdale; and St. Anthony's sees Parkdale as a very low-cost facility that has a strong patient census for its size and that, most importantly, can "feed" St. Andrew's those patients who need a higher level of care. St. Andrew's has proposed a number of arrangements that might serve the interests of both Parkdale and St. Andrew's. St. Andrew's has asked you to advise them on the tax implications in light of St. Andrew's § 501(c)(3) status. If you see problems in the transactions, describe how you would remedy them to allow the transaction to go forward and achieve its essential purposes.

1. St. Andrew's has offered Parkdale a Management Services Agreement, in which St. Andrew's agrees to manage and administer Parkdale, providing it with all administrative services, including personnel management, financial planning, quality assurance and so on. The agreement would include a base price of approximately $150,000 per year plus 1% of Parkdale's net revenues. In coming to the price, St. Andrew's did consider its hope that the relationship with Parkdale will develop over time.

2. Alternatively, St. Andrew's has proposed that Parkdale and St. Andrew's establish a new entity called Rural Healthcare Partners. Partners would be structured as a limited partnership, with Parkdale and St. Andrew's as general partners and the three physician-owners of Parkdale as limited partners. St. Andrew's will provide 80% of the capital for the entity. Parkdale and St. Andrew's will share equally in decision making through a management committee. Profits

will be distributed in proportion to the contribution to capital, although it is understood that any excess of revenue over expenses will be re-invested in Partners during its first years. Much of it will be passed through to Parkdale for essential improvements. It is not clear exactly what Partners will do eventually. It is being established now as a vehicle for the development of future joint ventures between St. Andrew's and Parkdale. It will begin by doing physician recruitment for Parkdale, and perhaps later for rural hospitals outside of the area, and providing public relations for the Parkdale–St. Andrew's affiliation.

3. Dr. Simpson is a member of St. Andrew's board with strong professional and personal contacts in the medical community in and around Parkdale Hospital. He was instrumental in originating the contacts which gave rise to the discussions resulting in the preceding proposals. St. Andrew's plans to reward Dr. Simpson with a one year consulting contract for a sum of $100,000 for his past and future liaison efforts with Parkdale.

4. Recently, twenty obstetricians/gynecologists in the suburban area near St. Andrew's have formed an organization through which they operate as an entity even though they still practice in their own offices. Although these doctors currently admit patients both to St. Andrew's and to the other private hospital in town, they have been approached with an offer by the other hospital, Memorial, which is owned by a for-profit organization. Memorial Hospital has offered the entity below-market-value space in the doctors' office building attached to the hospital; free administrative services in the management of their practices including free use of the hospital's management information system; and the opportunity to become limited partners in the "Birthing Center," a special area which will be developed on the OB floor at the hospital and which will be the subject of an intense media campaign. The doctors will receive a proportionate share of the net revenue of the Center. In exchange, the doctors would agree to take any patient who wishes to receive OB/GYN services at Memorial as long as they have the requisite skills to care for the patient and as long as the patient has the ability to pay. Memorial has several contracts with health maintenance organizations for hospital services to their enrollees, and this arrangement between the OBs and Memorial would require the physicians to contract with and take patients covered by those HMOs. The physicians will not become employees of the HMO. A large number of the physicians' patients are located near the suburban Memorial Hospital, and fewer are located in the more urban area in which St. Andrew's is located, so the attraction to Memorial is strong despite the doctors' distrust of its for-profit structure.

Although obstetrics is not a very "profitable" service for St. Andrew's, OB patients are highly desirable to a hospital because they represent a potential stream of patients from the family. St. Andrew's wants to maintain active OB and neonatal services and requires a minimum number of patients to do so. There are a few OBs who are not members of this new entity, but they tend to be older and tend to practice in less desirable geographic areas, though no one spot in town is more than twenty minutes away from any other spot.

St. Andrew's plans to match Memorial's offer. In addition, it intends to further strengthen its ties to Parkdale by offering the physicians a generous income guarantee if they will establish an office near Parkdale where there is only one OB practicing part time. St. Andrew's will also require that the physicians agree to provide back-up services and consultation for high-risk pregnancies referred to it by Parkdale. The doctors will also be paid for any services they actually provide under this arrangement.

Chapter 11

FRAUD AND ABUSE

———————

Health care providers are subject to a large body of law governing their financial arrangements with each other and with payors. These state and federal laws cover many practices that amount to fraud, bribery, or stealing. In addition, they prohibit many contractual relationships, investments, and marketing and recruitment practices that are perfectly legal in other businesses. As will be seen, these laws are well-intentioned: they seek to rectify a number of serious flaws in the health care financing system, save the government money, and prevent conflicts of interest that taint the physician-patient relationship. Indeed, they have been used to bring to justice a large number of providers, including some major corporate entities, that have engaged in systematic fraud. Unfortunately, the particular statutes (and the regulations, cases and interpretative rulings and guidelines they have spawned) are also bewilderingly complicated and have generated confusion and cynicism in the health care industry. Further, some aspects of these laws may prove anachronistic under evolving payment systems. Nevertheless, they continue to have a profound impact on the health care industry and generate an enormous amount of work for health care lawyers designing organizational structures that must comply with their strictures.

I. FALSE CLAIMS

According to some estimates, Medicare and Medicaid fraud and abuse costs federal and state governments tens of billions of dollars per year. The Centers for Medicare & Medicaid Services (CMS) estimated that in 2005 Medicare overpaid $9.8 billion in fee-for-service payments, a sum that amounts to over four per cent of its fee-for-service reimbursement. Centers for Medicare & Medicaid Services, Improper Medicare FFS Payments Long Report for November 2006. Much of this problem undoubtedly can be traced to the structure and complexities of Medicare and Medicaid payment systems which give incentives and opportunities to engage in fraud or to "game the system" to maximize reimbursement. See Alice G. Gosfield, Medicare and Medicaid Fraud and Abuse § 1:2 (2007). The term "fraud and abuse" is a broad one, covering a large number of activities ranging from negligent or careless practices that result in overbilling, to "self-referral arrangements" that are seen as improperly enriching providers and encouraging overutilization, to outright fraudulent schemes to bill for services never rendered. Indeed, the "fraud" aspects of "fraud and abuse" prosecutions have involved overtly criminal schemes, sometimes with elements of racketeering and the involvement of organized crime. Recently federal prosecutors have sought to expand the reach of the anti-fraud laws to reach deficiencies in quality of care or products and the provision of misleading information by providers. This section deals with the law of false claims, which is designed to protect the government from paying for goods or services that have not been provided or were not provided in accordance with government regulations. Specific problems addressed by the law include: provider charges or claims for unreasonable costs, services not rendered, services provided by unlicensed or unapproved personnel, excessive or unnecessary care, and services not in compliance with CMS regulations, cost reports or other requirements.

There are a number of federal civil and criminal statutes that deal with false claims. In addition to the Medicare and Medicaid fraud and abuse law (discussed in the next section), the following criminal penalties may attach to false claims: federal and state false claim statutes, which make it a felony to knowingly and willfully make or cause to be made a false claim or statement under the Medicare program or a state health program including Medicaid, 42 U.S.C. § 1320a–7b(a); the mail fraud statute, 18 U.S.C. § 1341; laws prohibiting persons from knowingly making or presenting false or fraudulent claims to the United States government, 18 U.S.C. § 287; statutes prohibiting the making of false or fraudulent statements or representations, 18 U.S.C. § 1001; money laundering, 18 U.S.C. § 1956–57 and wire fraud, 18 U.S.C. § 1343. Secondary offenses such as aiding and abetting, 18 U.S.C. § 2, conspiracy, 18 U.S.C. § 371, and theft of government property, 18 U.S.C. § 1961–68 are also sometimes included in government charges. In addition, the submission of multiple false claims by an "enterprise" engaged in interstate commerce may constitute a violation of the Racketeer Influenced and Corrupt Organizations statute, 18 U.S.C. § 1961. Among the most important civil claims statutes are the Civil False Claims Act, 31 U.S.C. §§ 3729–33, which permits the federal government to recover from individuals who knowingly submit false claims civil penalties of $5,500 to $11,000 per claim plus three times the amount of damages sustained by the federal government, 31 U.S.C. § 3729, and private "qui tam" actions which enable private individuals to bring actions to enforce the False Claims Act, 31 U.S.C. § 3730(b).

Finally, spurred by incentives contained in the Deficit Reduction Act (DRA) of 2005, a number of states have adopted laws that closely follow the federal False Claims Act (FCA) and qui tam statutes. The DRA provided that for federal fraud cases which involve Medicaid funds recoveries, a state's share of damages will include an additional ten percent bonus if the state has adopted a statute that meets certain requirements including: liability provisions modeled on those found in the Federal FCA; provisions that "are at least as effective in rewarding and facilitating qui tam actions"; and a civil penalty that is not less than that authorized in the Federal FCA. Thus, if the state provides forty percent of the funding to its Medicaid program, it would actually be able to retain fifty percent of a FCA recovery. A second significant provision of the act requires any entity that receives or makes annual payments of $5 million or more under a state Medicaid plan to educate its employees about federal and state false claims laws by establishing written policies for all employees, contractors and others and providing "detailed information" regarding state and federal false claims acts and other antifraud laws including qui tam and whistleblower protection acts. See HHS Office of Inspector General, State False Claims Act Reviews, http://www.oig.hhs.gov/ fraud/falseclaimsact.html (as of Nov. 3, 2007). As of the end of 2007, thirteen states have applied to HHS for certification of having satisfied the DRA's requirements, but and only 8 have met the statutory criteria.

A. GOVERNMENTAL ENFORCEMENT

UNITED STATES v. KRIZEK

United States District Court, District of Columbia, 1994.
859 F.Supp. 5.

SPORKIN, DISTRICT JUDGE.

MEMORANDUM OPINION AND ORDER

On January 11, 1993, the United States filed this civil suit against George O. Krizek, M.D. and Blanka H. Krizek under the False Claims Act, 31 U.S.C. §§ 3729–3731, and at common law. The government brought the action against the Krizeks alleging false billing for Medicare and Medicaid patients. The five counts include claims for (1) "Knowingly Presenting a False or Fraudulent Claim", 31 U.S.C. § 3729(a)(1); (2) "Knowingly Presenting a False or Fraudulent Record", 31 U.S.C. § 3729(a)(2); (3) "Conspiracy to Defraud the Government"; (4) "Payment under Mistake of Fact"; and (5) "Unjust Enrichment". In its claim for relief, the government asks for triple the alleged actual damages of $245,392 and civil penalties of $10,000 for each of the 8,002 allegedly false reimbursement claims pursuant to 31 U.S.C. § 3729.

The government alleges two types of misconduct related to the submission of bills to Medicare and Medicaid. The first category of misconduct relates to the use of billing codes found in the American Medical Association's "Current Procedural Terminology" ("CPT"), a manual that lists terms and codes for reporting procedures performed by physicians. The government alleges that Dr. Krizek "up-coded" the bills for a large percentage of his patients by submitting bills coded for a service with a higher level of reimbursement than that which Dr. Krizek provided. As a second type of misconduct, the government alleges Dr. Krizek "performed services that should not have been performed at all in that they were not medically necessary." []

Given the large number of claims, and the acknowledged difficulty of determining the "medical necessity" of 8,002 reimbursement claims, it was decided that this case should initially be tried on the basis of seven patients and two hundred claims that the government believed to be representative of Dr. Krizek's improper coding and treatment practices. [] It was agreed by the parties that a determination of liability on Dr. Krizek's coding practices would be equally applicable to all 8,002 claims in the complaint. A three week bench trial ensued.

Findings of Fact

Dr. Krizek is a psychiatrist. Dr. Krizek's wife, Blanka Krizek was responsible for overseeing Dr. Krizek's billing operation for a part of the period in question. Dr. Krizek's Washington, D.C. psychiatric practice consists in large part in the treatment of Medicare and Medicaid patients. Much of Doctor Krizek's work involves the provision of psychotherapy and other psychiatric care to patients at the Washington Hospital Center.

Under the Medicare and Medicaid systems, claims for reimbursement are submitted on documents known as Health Care Financing Administration ("HCFA") 1500 Forms. These forms are supposed to contain the patient's identifying information, the provider's Medicaid or Medicare identification number, and a description of the provided procedures for which reimbursement is sought. These procedures are identified by a standard, uniform code number as set out in the American Medical Association's "Current Procedural Terminology" ("CPT") manual, a book that lists the terms and codes for reporting procedures performed by physicians.

* * *

The government in its complaint alleges both improper billing for services provided and the provision of medically unnecessary services. The latter of these two claims will be addressed first.

Medical Necessity

The record discloses that Dr. Krizek is a capable and competent physician. * * * The trial testimony of Dr. Krizek, his colleagues at the Washington Hospital Center, as well as the testimony of a former patient, established that Dr. Krizek was providing valuable medical and psychiatric care during the period covered by the complaint. The testimony was undisputed that Dr. Krizek worked long hours on behalf of his patients, most of whom were elderly and poor.

Many of Dr. Krizek's patients were afflicted with horribly severe psychiatric disorders and often suffered simultaneously from other serious medical conditions.* * *

The government takes issue with Dr. Krizek's method of treatment of his patients, arguing that some patients should have been discharged from the hospital sooner, and that others suffered from conditions which could not be ameliorated through psychotherapy sessions, or that the length of the psychotherapy sessions should have been abbreviated. The government's expert witness's opinions on this subject came from a cold review of Dr. Krizek's notes for each patient. The government witness did not examine or interview any of the patients, or speak with any other doctors or nurses who had actually served these patients to learn whether the course of treatment prescribed by Dr. Krizek exceeded that which was medically necessary.

Dr. Krizek testified credibly and persuasively as to the basis for the course of treatment for each of the representative patients. The medical necessity of treating Dr. Krizek's patients through psychotherapy and hospitalization was confirmed via the testimony of other defense witnesses. The Court credits Dr. Krizek's testimony on this question as well as his interpretation of his own notes regarding the seriousness of each patients' condition and the medical necessity for the procedures and length of hospital stay required. The Court finds that the government was unable to prove that Dr. Krizek rendered services that were medically unnecessary.

Improper Billing

On the question of improper billing or "up-coding," the government contends that for approximately 24 percent of the bills submitted, Dr. Krizek used the CPT Code for a 45–50 minute psychotherapy session (CPT Code 90844) when he should have billed for a 20–30 minute session (CPT Code 90843). The government also contends that for at least 33 percent of his patients, Dr. Krizek billed for a full 45–50 minute psychotherapy session, again by using CPT code 90844, when he should have billed for a "minimal psychotherapy" session (CPT 90862). These two latter procedures are reimbursed at a lower level than 90844, the 45–50 minute psychotherapy session, which the government has referred to as "the Cadillac" of psychiatric reimbursement codes.

The primary thrust of the government's case revolves around the question whether Dr. Krizek's use of the 90844 CPT code was appropriate. For the most part, the government does not allege that Dr. Krizek did not see the patients for whom he submitted bills. Instead, the government posits that the services provided during his visits either did not fall within the accepted definition of "individual medical psychotherapy" *or*, if the services provided *did* fit within this definition, the reimbursable service provided was not as extensive as that which was billed for. In sum, the government claims that whenever Dr. Krizek would see a patient, regardless of whether he simply checked a chart, spoke with nurses, or merely prescribed additional medication, his wife or his employee, a Mrs. Anderson, would, on the vast majority of occasions, submit a bill for CPT code 90844—45–50 minutes of individual psychotherapy.

[Documents sent to providers by Pennsylvania Blue Shield, the Medicare carrier for Dr. Krizek's area, explained the services in the 90800 series of codes as involving "[i]ndividual medical psychotherapy by a physician, with continuing medical diagnostic evaluation, and drug management when indicated, including insight oriented, behavior modifying or supportive psychotherapy" for specified periods of time.]

* * *

The government's witnesses testified that as initially conceived, the definition of the CPT codes is designed to incorporate the extra time spent in its level of reimbursement. It was expected by the authors of the codes that for a 45–50 minute 90844 session a doctor would spend additional time away from the patient reviewing or dictating records, speaking with nurses, or prescribing medication. The government's witnesses testified that the reimbursement rate for 90844 took into account the fact that on a 45–50 minute session the doctor would likely spend twenty additional minutes away from the patient. As such, the doctor is limited to billing for time actually spent "face-to-face" with the patient.

Dr. and Mrs. Krizek freely admit that when a 90844 code bill was submitted on the doctor's behalf, it did not always reflect 45–50 minutes of face-to-face psychotherapy with the patient. Instead, the 45–50 minutes billed captured generally the total amount of time spent on the patient's case, including the "face-to-face" psychotherapy session, discussions with medical staff about the patient's treatment/progress, medication management, and other related services. Dr. Krizek referred to this as "bundling" of services, all of which, Dr. and Mrs. Krizek testified, they reasonably believed were reimbursable under the 90844 "individual medical psychotherapy" code.

Defendant's witnesses testified that it was a common and proper practice among psychiatrists nationally, and in the Washington, D.C. area, to "bundle" a variety of services, including prescription management, review of the patient file, consultations with nurses or the patients' relatives into a bill for individual psychotherapy, whether or not these services took place literally in view of the patient. Under the defense theory, if a doctor spent 20 minutes in a session with a patient and ten minutes before that in a different room discussing the patient's symptoms with a nurse, and fifteen minutes afterwards outlining a course of treatment to the medical staff, it would be entirely appropriate, under their reading and interpretation of the CPT, to bill the 45 minutes spent on that patients' care by using CPT code 90844.

The testimony of the defense witnesses on this point was credible and persuasive. * * * The CPT codes which the government insists require face-to-face rendition of services never used the term "face-to-face" in its code description during the time period covered by this litigation. The relevant language describing the code is ambiguous.

The Court finds that the government's position on this issue is not rational and has been applied in an unfair manner to the medical community, which for the most part is made up of honorable and dedicated professionals. One government witness testified that a 15 minute telephone call made to a consulting physician in the patient's presence would be reimbursable, while if the doctor needed to go outside the patient's room to use the telephone—in order to make the *same* telephone call—the time would not be reimbursable. * * *

The Court will not impose False Claims Act liability based on such a strained interpretation of the CPT codes. The government's theory of liability is plainly unfair and unjustified. Medical doctors should be appropriately reimbursed for services legitimately provided. They should be given clear guidance as to what services are reimbursable. The system should be fair. The system cannot be so arbitrary, so perverse, as to subject a doctor whose annual income during the relevant period averaged between $100,000 and $120,000, to potential liability in excess of 80 million dollars[1] because telephone calls were made in one room rather than another.

The Court finds that Doctor Krizek did not submit false claims when he submitted a bill under CPT Code 90844 after spending 45–50 minutes working on a patient's case, even though not all of that time was spent in direct face-to-face contact with the patient. * * * The Court finds that the defendants' "bundled" services interpretation of the CPT code 90844 is not

---

1. The government alleges in the complaint that overbills amounted to $245,392 during the six-year period covered by the lawsuit. Trebling this damage amount, and adding the $10,000 statutory maximum penalty requested by the government for each of the 8,002 alleged false claims, results in a total potential liability under the complaint of more than $80,750,000. Dr. Krizek is not public enemy number one. He is at worst, a psychiatrist with a small practice who keeps poor records. For the government to sue for more than eighty million dollars in damages against an elderly doctor and his wife is unseemly and not justified. During this period, a psychiatrist in most instances would be reimbursed between $48 and $60 for a 45–50 minute session and $40 or less for a 20–30 minute session. This is hardly enough for any professional to get rich.

inconsistent with the plain, common-sense reading of the "description of services" listed by Pennsylvania Blue Shield in its published Procedure Terminology Manual.

Billing Irregularities

While Dr. Krizek was a dedicated and competent doctor and cannot be faulted for his interpretation of the 90844 code, his billing practices, or at a minimum his oversight of his wife's and Mrs. Anderson's billing system, was seriously deficient. Dr. Krizek knew little or nothing of the details of how the bills were submitted by his wife and Mrs. Anderson. * * *

The basic method of billing by Mrs. Krizek and Mrs. Anderson was to determine which patients Dr. Krizek had seen, and then to assume what had taken place was a 50–minute psychotherapy session, unless told specifically by Dr. Krizek that the visit was for a shorter duration. Mrs. Krizek frequently made this assumption without any input from her husband. Mrs. Krizek acknowledged at trial that she never made any specific effort to determine exactly how much time was spent with each patient. Mrs. Krizek felt it was fair and appropriate to use the 90844 code as a rough approximation of the time spent, because on some days, an examination would last up to two hours and Mrs. Krizek would still bill 90844.

Mrs. Anderson also would prepare and submit claims to Medicare/Medicaid with no input from Dr. Krizek. Routinely, Mrs. Anderson would simply contact the hospital to determine what patients were admitted to various psychiatrists' services, and would then prepare and submit claims to Medicare/Medicaid without communicating with Dr. or Mrs. Krizek about the claims she was submitting and certifying on Dr. Krizek's behalf. * * *

The net result of this system, or more accurately "nonsystem," of billing was that on a number of occasions, Mrs. Krizek and Mrs. Anderson submitted bills for 45–50 minute psychotherapy sessions on Dr. Krizek's behalf when Dr. Krizek could not have spent the requisite time providing services, face-to-face, or otherwise. * * * The defendants do not deny that these unsubstantiated reimbursement claims occurred or that billing practices which led to such inaccurate billings continued through March of 1992.

While the Court does not find that Dr. Krizek submitted bills for patients he did not see, the Court does find that because of Mrs. Krizek's and Mrs. Anderson's presumption that whenever Dr. Krizek saw a patient he worked at least 45 minutes on the matter, bills were improperly submitted for time that was not spent providing patient services. Again, the defendants admit this occurred. []

At the conclusion of the trial, both parties agreed that an appropriate bench-mark for excessive billing would be the equivalent of twelve 90844 submissions (or nine patient-service hours) in a single service day. [] Considering the difficulty of reviewing all Dr. Krizek's patient records over a seven-year period, Dr. Wilson's testimony as to having submitted as many as twelve 90844 submissions in a single day, and giving full credence to unrefuted testimony that Dr. Krizek worked very long hours, the Court believes this to be a fair and reasonably accurate assessment of the time Dr. Krizek actually spent providing patient services. *See Bigelow v. RKO Radio Pictures, Inc.*, 327 U.S. 251, 264, 66 S.Ct. 574, 579, 90 L.Ed. 652 (1946) (permitting factfinder to make "just and reasonable estimate of damage based on relevant data" where more precise computation is not possible). Dr. and Mrs. Krizek will therefore be presumed liable for bills submitted in excess of the equivalent of twelve 90844 submissions in a single day.

Nature of Liability

While the parties have agreed as to the presumptive number of excess submissions for which Dr. and Mrs. Krizek may be found liable, they do not agree on the character of the liability. The government submits that the Krizeks should be held liable under the False Claims Act, 31 U.S.C. § 3729, *et seq.* By contrast, defendants posit that while the United States may be entitled to reimbursement for any unjust enrichment attributable to the excess billings, the Krizeks' conduct with regard to submission of excess bills to Medicare/Medicaid was at most negligent, and not "knowing" within the definition of the statute. In their defense, defendants emphasize the "Ma and Pa" nature of Dr. Krizek's medical practice, the fact that Mrs. Krizek did attend some Medicare billing seminars in an effort to educate herself, and the fact that Mrs. Krizek consulted hospital records and relied on information provided by her husband in preparing bills.

By its terms, the False Claims Act provides, *inter alia*, that: Any person who—

(1) knowingly presents, or causes to be presented, to [the Government] . . . a false or fraudulent claim for payment or approval;

(2) knowingly makes, uses, or causes to be made or used, a false record or statement to get a false or fraudulent claim paid or approved by the Government;

(3) conspires to defraud the Government by getting a false or fraudulent claim allowed or paid;

* * *

is liable to the United States Government for a civil penalty of not less than $5,000.00 and not more than $10,000.00, plus three times the amount of damages which the Government sustains because of the act of that person.
* * *

31 U.S.C. § 3729(a). The mental state required to find liability under the False Claims Act is also defined by the statute:

For the purposes of this section, the terms "knowing" and "knowingly" mean that a person, with respect to information—

(1) has actual knowledge of the information;

(2) acts in deliberate ignorance of the truth or falsity of the information; or

(3) acts in reckless disregard of the truth or falsity of the information, and no proof of specific intent is required.

31 U.S.C. § 3729(b). The provision allowing for a finding of liability without proof of specific intent to defraud was a feature of the 1986 amendments to the Act.

* * *

The Court finds that, at times, Dr. Krizek was submitting claims for 90844 when he did not provide patient services for the requisite 45 minutes. The testimony makes clear that these submissions were made by Mrs. Krizek or Mrs. Anderson with little, if any, factual basis. Mrs. Krizek made no effort to establish how much time Dr. Krizek spent on a particular matter. Mrs. Krizek and Mrs. Anderson simply presumed that 45–50 minutes had been spent. There was no justification for making that assumption. In addition, Dr. Krizek failed utterly in supervising these agents in their submissions of claims on his behalf. As a result of his failure to supervise, Dr. Krizek received reimbursement for services which he did not provide.

These were not "mistakes" nor merely negligent conduct. Under the statutory definition of "knowing" conduct, the Court is compelled to conclude that the defendants acted with reckless disregard as to the truth or falsity of the submissions. As such, they will be deemed to have violated the False Claims Act.

Conclusion

Dr. Krizek must be held accountable for his billing system along with those who carried it out. Dr. Krizek was not justified in seeing patients and later not verifying the claims submitted for the services provided to these patients. Doctors must be held strictly accountable for requests filed for insurance reimbursement.

The Court believes that the Krizeks' billing practices must be corrected before they are permitted to further participate in the Medicare or Medicaid programs. Therefore an injunction will issue, enjoining the defendants from participating in these systems until such time as they can show the Court that they can abide by the relevant rules.

The Court also will hold the defendants liable under the False Claims Act on those days where claims were submitted in excess of the equivalent of twelve (12) 90844 claims (nine patient-treatment hours) in a single day and where the defendants cannot establish that Dr. Krizek legitimately devoted the claimed amount of time to patient care on the day in question. The government also will be entitled to introduce proof that the defendants submitted incorrect bills when Dr. Krizek submitted bills for less than nine (9) hours in a single day. The assessment of the amount of overpayment and penalty will await these future proceedings.

Other Observations

While the Court does not discount the seriousness of the Krizeks' conduct here, this case demonstrates several flaws in this country's government health insurance program. The government was right in bringing this action, because it could not countenance the reckless nature of the reimbursement systems in this case. While we are in an age of computers, this does not mean that we can blindly allow coding systems to determine the amount of reimbursement without the physician being accountable for honestly and correctly submitting proper information, whether by code or otherwise.

Nonetheless, the Court found rather troubling some of the government's procedures that control reimbursements paid to providers of services. Here are some of these practices:

1) The government makes no distinction in reimbursement as to the status or professional attainment or education of the provider. Thus, a non-technical person rendering a coded service will be reimbursed the same amount as a board-certified physician.

2) The sums that the Medicare and Medicaid systems reimburse physicians for services rendered seem to be so far below the norm for charges reimbursed by non-governmental insurance carriers. Indeed, the amount could hardly support a medical practice. As the evidence shows in this case, Board certified physicians in most instances were paid at a rate less than $60 per hour and less than $35 per 1/2 hour. The government must certainly review these charges because if providers are not adequately compensated, they may not provide the level of care that our elderly and underprivileged citizens require. What is more, the best physicians will simply not come into the system or will refuse to take on senior citizens or the poor as patients.

3) The unrealistic billing concept of requiring doctors to bill only for face-to-face time is not consistent with effective use of a doctor's time or with the provision of good medical services. Doctors must be able to study, research, and discuss a patient's case and be reimbursed for such time.

4) When Medicare dictates that a physician must report each service rendered as a separate code item, the physician is entitled to believe that he will be reimbursed for each of the services rendered. In actuality, the system pays for only one of the multitude of services provided. If this were done by a private sector entity, it would be considered deceitful. Because the government engages in such a deceitful practice does not make it right.

These are the lessons learned by this Court during this case. Hopefully, HCFA will reexamine its reimbursement practices to see what, if any, changes should be made.

UNITED STATES v. KRIZEK

United States Court of Appeals, District of Columbia Circuit, 1997.
111 F.3d 934.

SENTELLE, CIRCUIT JUDGE.

This appeal arises from a civil suit brought by the government against a psychiatrist and his wife under the civil False Claims Act ("FCA"), 31 U.S.C. §§ 3729–3731, and under the common law. The District Court found defendants liable for knowingly submitting false claims and entered judgment against defendants for $168,105.39. The government appealed, and the defendants filed a cross-appeal. We hold that the District Court erred and remand for further proceedings.

[The Court held that the district court erred in changing its benchmark for a presumptively false claim from 9 hours billed in any given day to 24 hours because it did not afford the government the opportunity to introduce additional evidence. It also agreed with the Krizeks cross-appeal that the District Court erroneously treated each CPT code as a separate "claim" for purposes of computing civil penalties instead of treating the government form 1500 which contained multiple codes as the "claim."

The court questioned the fairness of the government's definition of claim because it "permitted it to seek an astronomical $81 million worth of damages for alleged actual damages of $245,392."

* * *

[W]e turn now to the question whether, in considering the sample, the District Court applied the appropriate level of scienter. The FCA imposes liability on an individual who "knowingly presents" a "false or fraudulent claim." 31 U.S.C. § 3729(a). A person acts "knowingly" if he:

(1) has actual knowledge of the information;

(2) acts in deliberate ignorance of the truth or falsity of the information; or

(3) acts in reckless disregard of the truth or falsity of the information,

and no proof of specific intent to defraud is required.

31 U.S.C. § 3729(b). The Krizeks assert that the District Court impermissibly applied the FCA by permitting an aggravated form of gross negligence, "gross negligence-plus," to satisfy the Act's scienter requirement.

In Saba v. Compagnie Nationale Air France, 78 F.3d 664 (D.C.Cir. 1996), we considered whether reckless disregard was the equivalent of willful misconduct for purposes of the Warsaw Convention. We noted that reckless disregard lies on a continuum between gross negligence and intentional harm. In some cases, recklessness serves as a proxy for forbidden intent. Such cases require a showing that the defendant engaged in an act known to cause or likely to cause the injury. Use of reckless disregard as a substitute for the forbidden intent prevents the defendant from "deliberately blind[ing] himself to the consequences of his tortuous action." Id. at 668. In another category of cases, we noted, reckless disregard is "simply a linear extension of gross negligence, a palpable failure to meet the appropriate standard of care." Id. In *Saba*, we determined that in the context of the Warsaw Convention, a showing of willful misconduct might be made by establishing reckless disregard such that the subjective intent of the defendant could be inferred.

The question, therefore, is whether "reckless disregard" in this context is properly equated with willful misconduct or with aggravated gross negligence. In determining that gross negligence-plus was sufficient, the District Court cited legislative history equating reckless disregard with gross negligence. A sponsor of the 1986 amendments to the FCA stated,

Subsection 3 of Section 3729(c) uses the term "reckless disregard of the truth or falsity of the information" which is no different than and has the same meaning as a gross negligence standard that has been applied in other cases. While the Act was not intended to apply to mere negligence, it is intended to apply in situations that could be considered gross negligence where the submitted claims to the Government are prepared in such a sloppy or unsupervised fashion that resulted in overcharges to the Government. The Act is also intended not to permit artful defense counsel to require some form of intent as an essential ingredient of proof. This section is intended to reach the "ostrich-with-his-head-in-the-sand" problem where government contractors hide behind the fact they were not personally aware that such overcharges may have occurred. This is not a new standard but clarifies what has always been the standard of knowledge required.

132 Cong. Rec. H9382–03 (daily ed. Oct. 7, 1986) (statement of Rep. Berman).

While we are not inclined to view isolated statements in the legislative history as dispositive, we agree with the thrust of this statement that the best reading of the Act defines reckless disregard as an extension of gross negligence. Section 3729(b)(2) of the Act provides liability for false statements made with deliberate ignorance. If the reckless disregard standard of section 3729(b)(3) served merely as a substitute for willful misconduct—to prevent the defendant from "deliberately blind[ing] himself to the consequences of his tortuous action"—section (b)(3) would be redundant since section (b)(2) already covers such struthious conduct. Moreover, as the statute explicitly states that specific intent is not required, it is logical to conclude that reckless disregard in this context is not a "lesser form of intent," [ ] but an extreme version of ordinary negligence.

We are unpersuaded by the Krizeks' citation to the rule of lenity to support their reading of the Act. Even assuming that the FCA is penal, the rule of lenity is invoked only when the statutory language is ambiguous. Because we find no ambiguity in the statute's scienter requirement, we hold that the rule of lenity is inapplicable.

We are also unpersuaded by the Krizeks' argument that their conduct did not rise to the level of reckless disregard. The District Court cited a number of factors supporting its conclusion: Mrs Krizek completed the submissions with little or no factual basis; she made no effort to establish how much time Dr. Krizek spent with any particular patient; and Dr. Krizek "failed utterly" to review bills submitted on his behalf. Most tellingly, there were a number of days within the seven-patient sample when even the shoddiest record keeping would have revealed that false submissions were being made—those days on which the Krizeks' billing approached twenty-four hours in a single day. On August 31, 1985, for instance, the Krizeks requested reimbursement for patient treatment using the 90844 code thirty times and the 90843 code once, indicating patient treatment of over 22 hours. Outside the seven-patient sample the Krizeks billed for more than twenty-four hours in a single day on three separate occasions. These factors amply support the District Court's determination that the Krizeks acted with reckless disregard.

Finally, we note that Dr. Krizek is no less liable than his wife for these false submissions. As noted, an FCA violation may be established without reference to the subjective intent of the defendant. Dr. Krizek delegated to his wife authority to submit claims on his behalf. In failing "utterly" to review the false submissions, he acted with reckless disregard.

* * *

Notes and Questions

1. Exactly what conduct by Dr. Krizek did the government charge violated the False Claims Act? For what conduct and on what basis was he exonerated by the district court? Did the court's liability finding rest on the actions of Dr. Krizek or those of his subordinates?

2. The United States introduced expert evidence that the CPT codes 90843 and 90844 (individual psychotherapy) envisioned face-to-face therapy with the

patient for the entire time for which the service was billed (either 25 or 50 minutes). The Krizeks admitted they received reimbursement for time spent other than in face-to-face therapy, and introduced evidence from other physicians that "bundling" was common practice in obtaining reimbursement for private payors. What was the legal basis for absolving Dr. Krizek of liability for "upcoding"?

3. What hurdles does the government face in proving that services provided by a physician were not "medically necessary?" Do the patient's medical records and the physician's notes supply persuasive evidence on this issue? What reform efforts would assist the government in proving a knowing violation of the law? Does requiring providers to sign a certification attesting that they have reviewed each claim, that the service was medically necessary, and that the service was actually provided resolve all problems? See U.S. ex rel. Mikes v. Straus, the next case in this chapter. How do electronic claims submissions affect the proof problem?

4. Does the opinion of the Court of Appeals in *Krizek* clarify the boundary between reckless disregard and willful misconduct? Between reckless disregard and gross negligence? What evidence did it rely upon to reach its conclusion that the Krizeks had run afoul of that standard? Can you explain at what point evidence of shoddy record keeping and submission of implausible claims would constitute "reckless disregard" under the False Claims Act?

5. Following the Court of Appeals' determination that each 1500 Form constituted a "claim," the district court faced on remand the question of how many of the multiple forms, which taken together exceeded 24 hours in a single day, constituted separate "claims." Absent proof as to which specific claims were submitted beyond the 24–hour limit, the district court chose to count only the number of days (three) exceeding the 24–hour benchmark rather than the total number of claims exceeding that benchmark (eleven). United States v. Krizek, 7 F.Supp. 2d 56 (D.D.C. 1998). Judge Sporken voiced continued frustration with the government's case: "The Government's pursuit of Dr. Krizek is reminiscent of Inspector Javert's quest to capture Jean Valjean in Victor Hugo's Les Miserables . . . [T]here comes a point when a civilized society must say enough is enough." Id. at 60. Evaluate this and Judge Sporkin's "other observations." Do they betray a judicial sympathy toward medical professionals that is not customarily afforded to other defendants charged with violating statutory directives? Are they persuasive? Has the government brought this criticism on itself by "piling on," i.e., using all the weapons in its arsenal? The Krizek case became a cause celebre for some in the provider community who felt the government was overreaching in its prosecution of false claims against providers. Mrs. Krizek testified before a congressional committee relating her views on the case and the government's conduct. Administrative Crimes and Quasi Crimes: Hearing Before the Subcomm. on Commercial and Admin. Law of the H. Comm. on the Judiciary, 105th Cong. (1998), available at http://commdocs.house.gov/committees/judiciary/hju59925.000/hju59925_0. HTM.

6. How should the "reckless disregard" standard be applied in practice? Consider the following situations:

A defendant continues to submit claims despite having had similar claims rejected in the past by the Medicare carrier and receiving explicit warnings that such claims would not be reimbursed in the future. The defendant is able to point to advice by a consultant that, notwithstanding the above, his billing was proper. See United States v. Lorenzo, 768 F.Supp. 1127 (E.D. Pa. 1991).

A defendant who is charged with improperly billing Medicare for services asserts that the HCFA Provider Handbook (which sets forth general billing guidelines for physician services) contains no specific instructions concerning the services that the government claims were improperly billed. In addition, the defendant sought to clarify his obligations by making inquiries through the Freedom of Information Act to HCFA. However, language in HCFA's Carrier Manual suggests that the billing may be improper. Expert testimony establishes that physicians are generally familiar with the provisions of the Carrier Manual, but it dictates whether carriers should pay claims and is not intended to guide the physician's decision to submit a claim for reimbursement. Finally, in internal discussions with other defendants, the doctor stated his concern that the billings were "on uncertain ground." See United States ex rel. Swafford v. Borgess Medical Center, 98 F. Supp. 2d 822 (W.D. Mich. 2000). But see In re Cardiac Devices Qui Tam Litig., 221 F.R.D. 318, 340 (D. Conn. 2004) (government's allegations that hospital's billing for procedures involving non-FDA approved cardiac devices in contravention of payment policy set forth in the Hospital Manual provided to all hospitals by HHS sufficiently pleaded scienter under FCA).

A nursing home bills Medicaid for skilled nursing care services rendered to a patient who had entered into a continuing care contract with that facility under which he had no responsibility to pay for skilled nursing care services if he ever needed them. The nursing home administrator assumed that the patient's prior payments under the contract were implied payments for subsequent skilled nursing services and therefore he could legally bill Medicaid. Medicaid regulations make it clear he could not. The administrator never sought a legal opinion as to whether the home could bill Medicaid under such a theory even though it was a significant potential source of revenue for his facility. See United States ex rel. Quirk v. Madonna Towers, Inc., 278 F.3d 765 (8th Cir. 2002).

7.   What steps would you advise a provider client to take to guard against false billing? What internal safeguards, billing practices or supervision should the provider implement?

8.   The combined effect of the Health Insurance Portability and Accountability Act of 1996 (HIPAA), the Balanced Budget Act of 1997 (BBA), and the Deficit Reduction Act of 2005 (which created a new, generously funded "Medicaid Integrity Program") has been to vastly increase federal and state resources devoted to prosecuting false claims against the government. These acts increased funding for federal government prosecutions and data collection programs and added new prosecutorial tools to pursue claims against providers. They have resulted in major new investigative initiatives and litigation and have produced significant governmental recoveries. For fiscal year 2006, the Department of Health and Human Services Office of Inspector General (OIG) reported that its enforcement efforts resulted in $1.6 billion in funds returned to federal programs. The OIG also excluded 3,425 individuals and entities from participation in federal health care programs and took part in 472 criminal actions related to crimes against HHS programs. During that period, it also brought 272 civil actions, obtaining more than $1.3 billion in False Claims Act civil and administrative settlements or civil judgments related to the Medicare and Medicaid programs. Office of Inspector General, Dep't of Health and Human Services, Semiannual Report to Congress: April–September 2006, available at http://www.oig.hhs.gov/publications/docs/semiannual/2006/SemiannualFinalFY2006.pdf. The OIG's semi-annual report provides detailed descriptions of recommended and implemented fund-saving efforts for HHS administered programs. Id. at App. A–C. Government officials claim that these prosecutions are having an important "sentinel effect."

That is, Medicare audits showing decreases in improper claims and declines in the average Medicare case mix demonstrate that enhanced efforts to prosecute fraud and abuse has resulted in improved compliance and lower costs for federal programs. D. McCarty Thornton, Perspectives on Current Enforcement: "Sentinel Effect" Shows Fraud Control Works, 32 J. Health L. 493 (1999).

The Department of Justice and CMS have undertaken a number of investigative initiatives targeting specific areas of concern. Pharmaceutical manufacturers have been the subject of considerable attention. One prominent case involved TAP Pharmaceutical Products, which paid $875 million to settle charges of improperly marketing its prostate cancer drug, Lupron. Among the practices alleged were inducements given to prescribing physicians and HMOs (and in some cases billing for those inducements) which took the form of travel, entertainment, debt forgiveness, consulting services, free televisions, VCRs and free samples. See Kathleen McDermott, The Aftermath of United States v. TAP Pharmaceuticals, 6 Health Lawyers News 4 (April, 2002). In addition, AstraZeneca Pharmaceuticals LP paid $355 million to resolve criminal and civil claims that it improperly set its Average Wholesale Price for its prostate cancer drug Zoladex, paid illegal remuneration to induce the purchase of the drug, and failed to pay rebates owed to States under the Medicaid drug rebate program. Likewise, Bayer Corporation and GlaxoSmithKline entered into $257 million and $88 million settlements respectively in cases in which the government alleged they underpaid Medicaid rebates to state programs. See generally, Nicole Huberfeld, Pharma on the Hot Seat, 40 J. Health L. 241 (2007).

The government has also conducted a number of regional and nation-wide investigations involving suspect practices. For example, the Physicians at Teaching Hospitals Audit Program (PATH) concerned abuses of Medicare and Medicaid requirements that attending physicians must be present and directly supervise the provision of services by residents in teaching hospitals. The government has also focused its attention on certain providers whose practices have raised red flags. See, e.g., Office of Inspector General, Special Fraud Alert: Fraud and Abuse in Nursing Home Arrangements With Hospices, 63 Fed. Reg. 10, 415 (1998); Special Fraud Alert on Physician Liability for Certifications in the Provision of Medical Equipment and Supplies and Home Health Services, 64 Fed. Reg. 1813 (1999); Fraud Alert: Providers Target Medicare Patients in Nursing Facilities, 61 Fed. Reg. 30, 623 (1996). Future targets for government scrutiny are likely to include manufacturers of medical devices and technology, payors, and intermediaries. See James G. Sheehan & Jesse A. Goldner, Beyond the Anti-kickback Statute: New Entities, New Theories in Healthcare Fraud Prosecutions, 40 J. Health L. 167 (2007). Criticisms of the government's enforcement record focus on its use of enforcement initiatives in lieu of formal rulemaking, and its failure to give adequate guidance to the industry, see Gary Eiland, A Call for Balancing of Agency Sentinel Priorities, 32 J. Health L. 503 (1999). See generally, Timothy S. Jost and Sharon L. Davies, The Empire Strikes Back: A Critique of the Backlash Against Fraud and Abuse Enforcement, 51 Ala. L. Rev. 239 (1999); Lewis Morris and Gary W. Thompson, Reflections on the Government's Stick and Carrot Approach to Fighting Health Care Fraud, 51 Ala. L. Rev. 319 (1999).

UNITED STATES EX REL. MIKES v. STRAUS

United States Court of Appeals, Second Circuit, 2001.
274 F.3d 687.

CARDAMONE, CIRCUIT JUDGE.

On this appeal we review a complaint asserting violations of the False Claims Act (Act) [ ] brought by a plaintiff employee against her former employers, who are health care providers. The appeal raises issues of first impression in this Circuit concerning the applicability of medical standards of care to the Act.

* * *

BACKGROUND

A. Facts

In 1991 defendants Dr. Marc J. Straus, Dr. Jeffrey Ambinder and Dr. Eliot L. Friedman, physicians specializing in oncology and hematology, formed a partnership called Pulmonary and Critical Care Associates to extend their practice to include pulmonology, the branch of medicine covering the lungs and related breathing functions. In July of that year defendants hired plaintiff Dr. Patricia S. Mikes, a board-certified pulmonologist, to provide pulmonary and critical care services in defendants' offices in Westchester and Putnam Counties, New York. In September 1991 Mikes discussed with Dr. Straus her concerns relating to spirometry tests being performed in defendants' offices. Three months later, plaintiff was fired.

The parties dispute the reason for Mikes' termination. Plaintiff says she was fired because she questioned how defendants conducted their medical practice. Defendants declare that Mikes' employment agreement provided she was terminable-at-will, and that plaintiff had difficulty procuring privileges at area hospitals.

On April 16, 1992 Mikes commenced the instant litigation against defendants in the United States District Court for the Southern District of New York. asserting not only causes of action for retaliatory discharge and unlawfully withheld wages, but also a *qui tam* suit under the False Claims Act. She served the complaint on the United States Attorney who, on April 19, 1993, notified the district court that it declined its statutory right to substitute for Mikes in the prosecution of this litigation. [ ]

B. Prior Proceedings

Plaintiff's qui tam cause of action under the Act alleged that defendants had submitted false reimbursement requests to the federal government for spirometry services. Plaintiff contended that defendants' failure to calibrate the spirometers rendered the results so unreliable as to be "false" under the Act. In addition, Mikes averred that spirometry is an eligible service under the Medicare statute, and that defendants submitted Medicare claims for reimbursement during the period relevant to this dispute—now said to be 1034 claims from 1986 through 1993—for a total Medicare payout of $28,922.89.

After the government declined to take over as plaintiff, Mikes served defendants with her complaint on December 22, 1993. [After the initial complaint was dismissed, Mikes filed an amended complaint which added the claim that that defendants improperly received Medicare reimbursement for referrals to Magnetic Resonance Imaging (MRI) facilities in which they held a financial interest which violated the anti-kickback provision of the Medicare statute and also violated the False Claims Act. Eventually the district court granted summary judgment in favor of defendants and, finding the MRI claim vexatious, awarded attorneys fees to defendants.]

C. *Spirometry*

Before turning to a discussion of the law, it will be helpful to define spirometry—a subject that lies at the heart of this case—and plaintiff's allegations regarding defendants' performance of this diagnostic test. Spirometry is an easy-to-perform pulmonary function test used by doctors to detect both obstructive (such as asthma and emphysema) and restrictive (such as pulmonary fibrosis) lung diseases. The type of spirometers used by defendants measures the pressure change when a patient blows into a mouthpiece, thereby providing the doctor with on-the-spot analysis of the volume and speed by which patients can exhale. The spirometry equipment consists of readily transportable lightweight machines, and defendants apparently used at least one in each of their several offices.

Plaintiff's expert stated that spirometers are susceptible to inaccuracy through time and usage because they become clogged, causing false readings. Erroneous measurements may also arise from damage to the instrument through cleaning or disturbance during transport, or from variations in barometric pressure, temperature or humidity. Mikes claims that guidelines ... published ... by the American Thoracic Society (ATS guidelines), [which] set out the generally accepted standards for spirometry ... recommend daily calibration of spirometers[.]* * * Mikes maintains further that defendants' performance of spirometry did not conform to the ATS guidelines and thus would yield inherently unreliable data. She argues that defendants allowed medical assistants to perform spirometry tests when they were not trained in its proper administration. * * *

Defendants insist that after plaintiff raised her concerns regarding the spirometer and its use in their practice, they told her to review exam results for inaccuracy, and to train the medical assistants in proper spirometric administration. Dr. Straus reports that plaintiff did not apprise the practice of any false readings in response to this directive, nor did she supervise the medical assistants. With this factual background, we turn to the law.

DISCUSSION

* * *

II. "LEGALLY FALSE" CERTIFICATION THEORY

The thrust of plaintiff's qui tam suit is that the submission of Medicare reimbursement claims for spirometry procedures not performed in accordance with the relevant standard of care, that is, the ATS Guidelines—violates the False Claims Act. Mikes relies principally on the "certification theory" of liability, which is predicated upon a false representation of compliance with a federal statute or regulation or a prescribed contractual term. See Lisa Michelle Phelps, Note, Calling Off the Bounty Hunters: Discrediting the Use of Alleged Anti–Kickback Violations to Support Civil False Claims Actions, 51 Vand. L. Rev. 1003, 1014–15 (1998). This theory has also been called "legally false" certification. [ ] It differs from "factually false" certification, which involves an incorrect description of goods or services provided or a request for reimbursement for goods or services never provided.

Although the False Claims Act is "not designed to reach every kind of fraud practiced on the Government," United States v. McNinch, 356 U.S. at 599, 78 S.Ct. 950, it was intended to embrace at least some claims that suffer from legal falsehood. Thus, "a false claim may take many forms, the most common being a claim for goods or services not provided, or *provided in violation of contract terms, specification, statute, or regulation.*" S. Rep. No. 99–345, at 9, *reprinted in* 1986 U.S.C.C.A.N. 5266, 5274 (emphasis added).

Just as clearly, a claim for reimbursement made to the government is not legally false simply because the particular service furnished failed to comply with the mandates of a statute, regulation or contractual term that is only tangential to the service for which reimbursement is sought. Since the Act is restitutionary and aimed at retrieving ill-begotten funds, it would be anomalous to find liability when the alleged noncompliance would not have influenced the government's decision to pay. Accordingly, while the Act is "intended to reach all types of fraud, without qualification, that might result in financial loss to the Government,"[ ] it does not encompass those instances of regulatory noncompliance that are irrelevant to the government's disbursement decisions.

We join the Fourth, Fifth, Ninth, and District of Columbia Circuits in ruling that a claim under the Act is legally false only where a party certifies compliance with a statute or regulation as a condition to governmental payment. See United States ex rel. Siewick v. Jamieson Sci. & Eng'g, Inc., 214 F.3d 1372, 1376 (D.C. Cir. 2000) ("[A] false certification of compliance with a statute or regulation cannot serve as the basis for a qui tam action under the [False Claims Act] unless payment is conditioned on that certification."); Harrison, 176 F.3d at 786–87, 793; United States ex rel. Thompson v. Columbia/HCA Healthcare Corp., 125 F.3d 899, 902 (5th Cir. 1997); United States ex rel. Hopper v. Anton, 91 F.3d 1261, 1266–67 (9th Cir. 1996).

We add that although materiality is a related concept, our holding is distinct from a requirement imposed by some courts that a false statement or claim must be material to the government's funding decision.[ ] A materiality requirement holds that only a subset of admittedly false claims is subject to False Claims Act liability. [ ] We rule simply that not all instances of regulatory noncompliance will cause a claim to become false. We need not and do not address whether the Act contains a separate materiality requirement.

A. *Express False Certification*

We analyze first plaintiff's argument that defendants' claims contained an express false certification. An expressly false claim is, as the term suggests, a claim that falsely certifies compliance with a particular statute, regulation or contractual term, where compliance is a prerequisite to payment.

Plaintiff contends that by submitting claims for Medicare reimbursement on HCFA–1500 forms or their electronic equivalent, defendants expressly certified that they would comply with the terms set out on the form. Form HCFA–1500 expressly says: "I certify that the services shown on this form were medically indicated and necessary for the health of the patient and were personally furnished by me or were furnished incident to my professional service by my employee under my immediate personal supervision." Both the form, which further provides "No Part B Medicare benefits may be paid unless this form is received as required by existing law and regulations," and the Medicare Regulations, see 42 C.F.R. § 424.32, state that certification is a precondition to Medicare reimbursement. We agree that defendants certified they would comply with the terms on the form and that such compliance was a precondition of governmental payment. Cf. United States ex rel. Piacentile v. Wolk, Civ.A.No. 93–5773, 1995 WL 20833, at *2–*3 (E.D. Pa. Jan. 17, 1995) (finding False Claims Act violation where defendant altered Medicare Certificates of Medical Necessity without doctor's authorization, because the forms contained a certification that the claims represented the physician's judgment).

Yet plaintiff's objections to defendants' spirometry tests do not implicate the standard set out in the HCFA–1500 form that the procedure was dictated by "medical necessity." The term "medical necessity" does not impart a qualitative element mandating a particular standard of medical care, and Mikes does not point to any legal authority requiring us to read such a mandate into the form. Medical necessity ordinarily indicates the level—not the quality—of the service. * * *

This approach to the phrase "medically necessary"—as applying to *ex ante* coverage decisions but not *ex post* critiques of how providers executed a procedure—would also conform to our understanding of the phrase "reasonable and necessary" as used in the Medicare statute, 42 U.S.C. § 1395y(a)(1)(A) (1994) (disallowing payment for items or services not reasonable and necessary for diagnosis or treatment). * * *

Moreover, the section of the Medicare statute setting forth conditions of participation has separate provisions governing the medical necessity of a given procedure and its quality. [ ]This statutory design supports the conclusion that the medical necessity for a procedure and its quality are distinct considerations.

Inasmuch as Mikes challenges only the quality of defendants' spirometry tests and not the decisions to order this procedure for patients, she fails to support her contention that the tests were not medically necessary. * * * Thus, plaintiff's cause of action insofar as it is founded on express false certification is without merit.

B. Implied False Certification

1. Viability of Implied Certification Theory

Plaintiff insists that defendants' submissions to the government for payment were impliedly false certifications. An implied false certification claim is based on the notion that the act of submitting a claim for reimbursement itself implies compliance with governing federal rules that are a precondition to payment. See Phelps, *supra*, at 1015. Foundational support for the implied false certification theory may be found in Congress' expressly stated purpose that the Act include at least some kinds of legally false claims, see S. Rep. No. 99–345, at 9, *reprinted in* 1986 U.S.C.C.A.N. 5266, 5274, and in the Supreme Court's admonition that the Act intends to reach all forms of fraud that might cause financial loss to the government, see Neifert–White Co., 390 U.S. at 232, 88 S.Ct. 959.

* * *

But caution should be exercised not to read this theory expansively and out of context. The *Ab–Tech* rationale, for example, does not fit comfortably into the health care context because the False Claims Act was not designed for use as a blunt instrument to enforce compliance with all medical regulations—but rather only those regulations that are a precondition to payment—and to construe the impliedly false certification theory in an expansive fashion would improperly broaden the Act's reach. Moreover, a limited application of implied certification in the health care field reconciles, on the one hand, the need to enforce the Medicare statute with, on the other hand, the active role actors outside the federal government play in assuring that appropriate standards of medical care are met. Interests of federalism counsel that "the regulation of health and safety matters is primarily, and historically, a matter of local concern." Hillsborough County v. Automated Med. Labs., Inc., 471 U.S. 707, 719, 105 S.Ct. 2371, 85 L.Ed.2d 714 (1985).

Moreover, permitting qui tam plaintiffs to assert that defendants' quality of care failed to meet medical standards would promote federalization of medical malpractice, as the federal government or the *qui tam* relator would replace the aggrieved patient as plaintiff. * * * For these reasons, we think a medical provider should be found to have implicitly certified compliance with a particular rule as a condition of reimbursement in limited circumstances. Specifically, implied false certification is appropriately applied only when the underlying statute or regulation upon which the plaintiff relies *expressly* states the provider must comply in order to be paid. See Siewick, 214 F.3d at 1376 (holding that court will "infer certification from silence" only when "certification was a prerequisite to the government action sought"). Liability under the Act may properly be found therefore when a defendant submits a claim for reimbursement while knowing—as that term is defined by the Act, see 31 U.S.C. § 3729(b)—that payment expressly is precluded because of some noncompliance by the defendant.

2. *Plaintiff's Allegations Under the Implied Theory*

Mikes asserts that compliance with § § 1395y(a)(1)(A) and 1320c–5(a) of the Medicare statute is a precondition to a request for federal funds and that submission of a HCFA–1500 form attests by implication to the providers' compliance with both of those provisions.

a. § 1395y(a)(1)(A). Section 1395y(a)(1)(A) of the Medicare statute states that "no payment may be made under [the Medicare statute] for any expenses incurred for items or services which ... are not *reasonable and necessary* for the diagnosis or treatment of illness or injury or to improve the functioning of a malformed body member." 42 U.S.C. § 1395y(a)(1)(A) (emphasis added). Because this section contains an express condition of payment—that is, "no payment may be made"—it explicitly links each Medicare *payment* to the requirement that the particular item or service be "reasonable and necessary." The Supreme Court has noted that this section precludes the government from reimbursing a Medicare provider who fails to comply.[ ] Since § 1395y(a)(1)(A) *expressly* prohibits payment if a provider fails to comply with its terms, defendants' submission of the claim forms implicitly certifies compliance with its provision.

Yet, Mikes' insistence that defendants' performance of spirometry was not reasonable and necessary is without support. As set forth in our discussion of express certification, the requirement that a service be reasonable and necessary generally pertains to the selection of the particular procedure and not to its performance. [ ] While such factors as the effectiveness and medical acceptance of a given procedure might determine whether it is reasonable and necessary, the failure of the procedure to conform to a particular standard of care ordinarily will not. [ ] Since plaintiff contends only that defendants' performance of spirometry was *qualitatively* deficient, her allegations that defendants falsely certified compliance with § 1395y(a)(1)(A) may not succeed.

b. § 1320c–5(a). Plaintiff's implied false certification claims rely more heavily upon § 1320c–5(a). That section does mandate a qualitative standard of care in that it provides

It shall be the obligation of any health care practitioner ... who provides health care services for which payment may be made ... to assure, to the extent of his authority that services or items ordered or provided by such practitioner ...

(1) will be provided economically and only when, and to the extent, medically necessary;

(2) *will be of a quality which meets professionally recognized standards of health care;* and

(3) will be supported by evidence of medical necessity and quality ... as may reasonably be required by a reviewing peer review organization in the exercise of its duties and responsibilities.

42 U.S.C. § 1320c–5(a) (emphasis added).

Mikes avers that the ATS guidelines comprise a "professionally recognized standard of health care" for spirometry, and that defendants' failure to conform to those guidelines violates the Medicare statute. She believes defendants, by submitting HCFA–1500 forms for spirometry tests that did not comply with the ATS guidelines, engaged in implied false certification. But plaintiff's allegations cannot establish liability under the False Claims Act because—unlike § 1395y(a)(1)(A)—the Medicare statute does not explicitly condition payment upon compliance with § 1320c–5(a).

Instead, § 1320c–5(a) simply states that "[i]t shall be the obligation" of a practitioner who provides a medical service "for which payment may be made ... to assure" compliance with the section. Hence, it may be seen that § 1320c–5(a) acts prospectively, setting forth obligations for a provider to be eligible to participate in the Medicare program.* * *

The structure of the statute further informs us that § 1320c–5(a) establishes conditions of participation, rather than prerequisites to receiving reimbursement. The statute empowers peer review organizations to monitor providers' compliance with § 1320c–5(a). See 42 U.S.C. § 1320c–3(a) (1994). If a peer review organization determines that a provider has "failed in a substantial number of cases" to comply with the requirements of § 1320c–

5(a) or that the provider has "grossly and flagrantly violated" the section, the organization may—after reasonable notice and an opportunity for corrective action—recommend sanctions. See id. § 1320c–5(b)(1) (1994 & Supp. V 1999). If the Secretary agrees that sanctions should be imposed, and further finds the provider unwilling or unable substantially to comply with its obligations, the Secretary may exclude the provider from the Medicare program. [ ]

The fact that § 1320c–5(b) permits sanctions for a failure to maintain an appropriate standard of care only where a dereliction occurred in "a substantial number of cases" or a violation was especially "gross[ ] and flagrant[ ]" makes it evident that the section is directed at the provider's continued eligibility in the Medicare program, rather than any individual incident of noncompliance. [ ] This conclusion is reinforced by the ultimate sanction provided by § 1320c–5(b)(1): exclusion of the provider from Medicare eligibility. Further, the section explicitly provides that the Secretary may authorize an alternate remedy—repayment of the cost of the noncompliant service to the United States—"as a condition to the continued eligibility" of the health care provider in the Medicare program. 42 U.S.C. § 1320c–5(b)(3). Accordingly, § 1320c–5(a) is quite plainly a condition of participation in the Medicare program.

Since § 1320c–5(a) does not expressly condition *payment* on compliance with its terms, defendants' certifications on the HCFA–1500 forms are not legally false. Consequently, defendants did not submit impliedly false claims by requesting reimbursement for spirometry tests that allegedly were not performed according to the recognized standards of health care.

Finally, our holding—that in submitting a Medicare reimbursement form, a defendant implicitly certifies compliance with § 1395y(a)(1)(A), but not § 1320c–5(a)—comports with Congress' purpose as discussed earlier in this opinion. Section 1395y(a)(1)(A) mandates that a provider's choice of procedures be "reasonable and necessary"; it does not obligate federal courts to step outside their primary area of competence and apply a qualitative standard measuring the efficacy of those procedures. The quality of care standard of § 1320c–5(a) is best enforced by those professionals most versed in the nuances of providing adequate health care.

III. WORTHLESS SERVICES CLAIM

The government in its *amicus* brief and plaintiff at oral argument argue that the district court erred by not considering whether the defendants' submission of Medicare claims for substandard spirometry essentially constituted requests for the reimbursement of worthless services. An allegation that defendants violated the Act by submitting claims for worthless services is not predicated upon the false certification theory. Instead, a worthless services claim asserts that the knowing request of federal reimbursement for a procedure with no medical value violates the Act irrespective of any certification.

The Ninth Circuit's recent decision in United States ex rel. Lee v. SmithKline Beecham, Inc., 245 F.3d 1048 (9th Cir. 2001), is the leading case on worthless services claims in the health care arena. In *Lee*, the relator alleged that defendant, an operator of regional clinical laboratories, falsified laboratory test data when test results fell outside the acceptable standard of error. Id. at 1050. The Ninth Circuit held that the false certification theory ... was only one form of action under the Act, and that the district court should have considered the distinct and separate worthless services claim. Lee, 245 F.3d at 1053. As the Ninth Circuit explained, "[i]n an appropriate case, knowingly billing for worthless services or recklessly doing so with deliberate ignorance may be actionable under § 3729 [of the False Claims Act], regardless of any false certification conduct." Id.

We agree that a worthless services claim is a distinct claim under the Act. It is effectively derivative of an allegation that a claim is factually false because it seeks reimbursement for a service not provided. In a worthless services claim, the performance of the service is so deficient that for all practical purposes it is the equivalent of no performance at all.

We nevertheless find no liability in the instant case because plaintiff makes no showing that defendants knowingly—as the Act defines that term—submitted a claim for the reimbursement of worthless services. We have adopted the Ninth Circuit's standard that the "requisite intent is the knowing presentation of what is known to be false" as opposed to negligence or innocent mistake.

Plaintiff fails to substantiate that defendants knew their Medicare claims for reimbursement were false. At best, plaintiff urges that defendants submitted Medicare claims knowing they did not conform to the ATS guidelines. This allegation alone fails to satisfy the standard for a worthless services claim. The notion of presenting a claim known to be false does not mean the claim is incorrect as a matter of proper accounting, but rather means it is a lie. See id. Defendants have presented such overwhelming evidence of their genuine belief that their use of spirometry had medical value, we conclude as a matter of law they did not submit their claims with the requisite scienter.

* * *

Defendants have thus proffered ample evidence—most of which derives from disinterested non-party witnesses—supporting their contention that they held a good faith belief that their spirometry tests were of medical value. In light of this evidence, plaintiff's unsupported allegations to the contrary do not raise a triable issue of fact sufficient to bar summary judgment. [ ]

* * *

Notes and Questions

1. The *Mikes* opinion does not address the materiality of defendants' false claims. A number of courts have held that plaintiffs should be required to prove that a false statement contained in a Medicare cost report would have affected the likelihood of payment. See United States v. Intervest Corp., 67 F.Supp.2d 637 (S.D.Miss. 1999) (false statements about safe and sanitary conditions of housing units not material where government agency engaged in a pattern of making payments despite receiving reports of unsatisfactory conditions). See also Luckey v. Baxter Healthcare Corporation, 183 F.3d 730 (7th Cir. 1999) (failure to perform tests on blood plasma does not give rise to false certification claims in the absence of evidence that the tests were material to the government's decision to purchase plasma); United States ex rel. Pogue v. Diabetes Treatment Ctrs. of Am., Inc., 238 F.Supp.2d 258 (D.D.C.2002) (characterizing Mikes as the "most parsimonious

application of the implied certification theory" and finding that the case law does not reject the theory). An excellent analysis of the interrelationship of materiality and causation issues in the false certification cases is found in Joan H. Krause, Health Care Providers and the Public Fisc: Paradigms of Government Harm Under the Civil False Claims Act, 36 Ga L. Rev. 121 (2001).

2. Courts have split over whether the False Claims Act requires a showing of outcome materiality (that a falsehood or misrepresentation affects the government's ultimate decision to pay a claim) or claim materiality (that the misrepresentation is material to a defendant's claim of right). See generally United States v. Southland Management Corp., 288 F.3d 665, 675–6 (5th Cir. 2002) (outcome materiality requires showing of actual impact on whether government would pay a claim while claims materiality asks only if the falsehood is of the kind likely to influence a "reasonable agency"). Luckey v. Baxter Healthcare, supra, embraces an outcome materiality definition, holding that the omission must be "material to the government's buying decision." 183 F.3d at 733. Applying the outcome materiality standard in a qui tam case the district court, U.S. ex rel. Bidani v. Lewis, 264 F.Supp.2d 612 (N.D. Ill. 2003), addressed the important question of whether failure to disclose a violation of the anti-kickback statute (discussed in the next section of this chapter) will support a false claims case under a false certification theory. AMS, a corporation selling medical supplies paid Abbot Laboratories and Baxter Healthcare Corporation to provide supplies and equipment to dialysis patients and then submitted claims to Medicare for reimbursement. Abbot and Baxter gave AMS discounts and rebates from the list prices it charged for supplies and AMS did not report receiving these discounts in its claims to Medicare. The district court framed the issue before it as follows:

> [W]hether compliance with the AKS [anti-kickback statute] was so important to the Medicare reimbursement process or so central to Medicare reimbursement agreements that compliance with the AKS was a condition of reimbursement so that failure to disclose non-compliance resulted in wrongful payments.

Id. at 615. Finding the AKS "critical" to the Medicare reimbursement scheme, based on the criminal penalties, exclusion penalties and other sanctions under the law imposes, the court concluded:

> Compliance with the AKS is thus central to the reimbursement plan of Medicare. To state otherwise would be to allow participation and reimbursement for supplies purchased illegally only because the claimant had the luck of not being caught and convicted in the first place. Reimbursing a claimant for the supplies would put the government in the position of funding illegal kickbacks after the fact.

Id.

3. Courts applying the rule in *Mikes* have had to draw fine distinctions at times. In U.S. ex rel. Woodruff v. Hawaii Pacific Health, 2007 WL 1500275 (D. Haw. 2007), the court found that the defendants' false or fraudulent conduct in signing a Medicaid provider agreement when they knew nurses were performing procedures they were not licensed to perform only alleged violations of conditions of participation, not conditions of payment, and hence neither an FCA claim premised on false certification or a related claim of promissory fraud could be maintained. However, where a false claim action rested on the fact that a hospital had submitted claims for devices deemed not reasonable and necessary in the Hospital Manual, a district court found that *Mikes* did not bar an action under the FCA. In re Cardiac Devices Qui Tam Litig., 221 F.R.D. 318, 336 (D. Conn. 2004) ("This is not a case where the allegedly false claims are premised solely on a

regulatory violation that was not a condition to payment. The Government is challenging the claims because they allegedly violated the underlying condition to payment, that the services must have been reasonable and necessary.")

4. Especially controversial has been the use of the implied certification theory to support False Claims Act challenges to quality deficiencies in rendering care. The spectrum of fact situations runs from those in which providers provide no care or "worthless services," see United States ex rel. Lee v. SmithKline Beecham, Inc., 245 F.3d 1048 (9th Cir. 2001), and United States v. NHC Healthcare Corp., 115 F. Supp. 2d 1149, 1153 (W.D. Mo. 2000) (government claim allowed to proceed where defendants' nursing home "was so severely understaffed that it could not possibly have administered all of the care it was obligated to perform" under government program standards and could amount to claims for services not actually performed), to scenarios in which severe quality deficiencies lead to the conclusion that the care provided does not amount to the kind of care for which the government was billed. See United States ex rel. Aranda v. Community Psychiatric Ctrs., 945 F.Supp. 1485, 1487 (W.D. Okla. 1996) (denying motion to dismiss False Claims Act case involving a psychiatric hospital that allegedly failed to comply with Medicaid regulations requiring that facilities afford patients a "reasonably safe environment"); cf. United States ex rel. Bailey v. Ector County Hosp., 386 F.Supp.2d 759, 766 (W.D. Tex. 2004) (FCA "should not be used to call into question a health care provider's judgment regarding a specific course of treatment").

What problems do you anticipate might be associated with extending the False Claims Act to reach quality of care concerns? Do such cases offer benefits that regulation and malpractice law cannot achieve? See Joan Krause, Medical Error As False Claim, 27 Am. J.L. & Med. 181 (2001)(quoting federal prosecutor explaining "what I want to show [in quality of care cases] is the entire idea that the [defendant] is providing care to these people is a fraud . . ."); John R. Munich & Elizabeth W. Lane, When Neglect Becomes Fraud: Quality of Care and False Claims, 43 St. Louis U. L.J. 27, 42–46 (1999); John T. Boese, When Angry Patients Become Angry Prosecutors: Medical Necessity Determinations, Quality of Care and the Qui Tam Law, 43 St. Louis U. L.J. 53, 56–57 (1999) (explaining why managed care is likely to generate suits based on deficiencies in quality of care); Pamela H. Bucy, Fraud By Fright: White Collar Crime By Health Care Providers?, 67 N.C. L. Rev. 855, 920–24 (1989).

Is the next step to use the False Claims Act as a weapon to deal with the problem of medical error? Given the Institute of Medicine's attribution of cause for persistently high rates of error to systemic failures in health care institutions, an argument could be made that the Act would be an effective and efficient tool for challenging providers' systemic and long-term failures to meet the community's standard of care. For a thoughtful analysis of this issue, ultimately concluding that the balance tips against using the Act to challenge medical error, see Joan H. Krause, Medical Error as False Claim, *supra.*

5. How effectively do the enormous resources devoted to prosecuting fraud serve patients' interest? Fraud recoveries go to state and federal government or qui tam relators while patients usually receive no compensation. Are there identifiable harms to *patients* from fraudulent billing schemes? Recall that Medicare and Medicaid often impose co-payment requirements. Further, may there be physical and intangible harms from unnecessary or improper treatments or from procedures fraudulently billed but never rendered? How might prosecutors structure settlements with providers to arrange for compensation to patients? What keeps them from doing so? For a thorough analysis of this issue, see Joan Krause,

A Patient–Centered Approach to Health Care Fraud Recovery, 96 J. Crim. & Criminology 579 (2006). See also, William M. Sage, Fraud and Abuse Law, 282 J. Am. Med. Ass'n 1179 (1999) ("[the] central, unresolved question is whether the principal purpose of fraud and abuse law is to protect financial integrity or patient welfare"); Pamela H. Bucy, Crimes By Health Care Providers, 1996 U. Ill. L. Rev. 589, 660–61; Roger Feldman, An Economic Explanation for Fraud and Abuse in Public Medical Care Programs, 30 J. Leg. Stud. 569, 574 (2001). Other criticisms of doctrinal developments in false claims litigation point to adverse effects on consumers and health care delivery. See Dayna Bowen Matthew, An Economic Model to Analyze the Impact of the False Claims Act on Access to Healthcare for the Elderly, Disabled, Rural and Inner–City Poor, 27 Am. J.L. & Med. 439 (2001) (use by government and qui tam plaintiffs of false certification claims to fight against fraud is likely to have a disproportionately negative impact on the availability of healthcare to the poor); Joan H. Krause, "Promises to Keep:" Health Care Providers and the Civil False Claims Act, 23 Cardozo L. Rev. 1363 (2002) (magnitude of penalties and imprecisely-defined concept of abuse may result in unchecked prosecutorial discretion which may expand the FCA to encompass legitimate transactions); Patrick Hooper, It's Time to Tone Down Rhetoric in "War" Against Fraud, 4 Health Care Fraud Rep. (BNA) 307 (2000) ("[t]he current health care environment is not unlike the politically charged investigations of other periods of our history").

6. Under the so-called "reverse false claims" provision of the Act, § 3729(a)(7), anyone who "knowingly makes, uses, or cause to be made or used, a false record or statement to conceal, avoid or decrease an obligation to pay or transmit money or property to the government" may be subject to liability under the Civil False Claims Act. Plaintiffs invoked this subsection to claim that Columbia/HCA had concealed potential obligations to the government arising from its violation of the fraud and abuse laws when it filed annual cost reports that did not mention these abuses. See United States ex rel. Thompson v. Columbia/HCA Healthcare Corp., 20 F.Supp.2d 1017, 1049 (S.D. Tex. 1998). For a critical assessment of the theory and its application in this case, see Boese & McClain, *supra*, 51 Ala. L. Rev. at 50–55. See also United States ex rel. Hunt v. Merck–Medco Managed Care, 336 F.Supp.2d 430 (E.D. Pa. 2004) (actions by pharmaceutical benefit company to cover up its failure to meet performance guarantees in order to avoid contractual penalties with government "are efforts that conceal, 'avoid or decrease an obligation' to pay to the government").

Note on Corporate Fraud and Abuse

Despite decades of strenuous enforcement efforts by state and federal agencies, large corporate entities continue to run afoul of fraud and abuse laws. The egregiousness of the abuses by some of the nation's largest health care providers (including some not-for-profit entities) and manufacturers leads one to question the effectiveness of the current regime of sanctions, detailed and pervasive as they are. Some examples of the most recent prosecutions illustrate the magnitude of the problem:

- Tenet Healthcare Corporation, operator of the nation's second largest hospital chain, entered into a global civil settlement to resolve allegations of unlawful billing practices, improper outlier payments, kickbacks, and other conduct. Tenet agreed to pay the Government $900 million plus interest and enter into a 5–year CIA to resolve its liability under the False Claims Act and other statutes. The settlement covers government claims that Tenet billed the government for outlier payments that were based on inflated charges, paid kickbacks to physicians for patient referrals, and for billing Medicare for services that were ordered or referred by a physician with whom Tenet had a financial relationship. Press Release, OIG News, OIG Executes Tenet Corporate Integrity Agreement, Unprecedented Provisions Include Board of Directors Review (Sept. 28, 2006), available at http:// oig.hhs.gov/fraud/docs/press/TenetČIApressrelease.pdf.

- Lovelace Health System, based in Albuquerque, agreed to pay $24.5 million to settle charges of submitting false Medicare cost reports. Mark Taylor, Fraud record: Effect of Lovelace Case Uncertain, 32 Modern Healthcare 15 (Dec. 9, 2002).

- A large number of the nation's leading pharmaceutical corporations and pharmaceutical benefit management companies, including Bayer, Merck, GlaxoSmithKline, Serono Corp., AstraZeneca Pharmaceuticals, Schering–Plough, and TAP Pharmaceuticals have settled civil and criminal cases involving allegations of false claims and a variety of other efforts to defraud government payment systems. Together settlements involving the top ten pharmaceutical corporations exceed $3 billion. Taxpayers Against Fraud, Top False Claims Act Cases, available at http://www.taf.org/top100fca.htm.

- Even academic medical centers have become enmeshed in fraudulent schemes. In a case exposing extraordinary lapses in governance, financial management, legal advice, and ethical standards, the University of Medicine and Dentistry of New Jersey (UMDNJ) entered into a deferred prosecution agreement with the United States Department of Justice and submitted to supervision by a federal monitor. The alleged conduct at issue included behavior seemingly modeled on The Sopranos: awarding extremely lucrative no-show faculty positions to local cardiologists for patient referrals, double billing and false claims, award of no-bid contracts to avoid board review, self-dealing by board members who were doing business with the university or using their relationship to obtain university jobs or $1/year leases for friends and family. The investigation also involved FBI raids to prevent destruction of evidence, mistreatment of whistle-blowers, and other questionable practices. News Release, U.S. Attorney's Office, New Jersey, UMDNJ Deferred Prosecution Agreement (Dec. 29, 2005), http://www.usdoj.gov/usao/nj/press/files/pdffiles/UMDNJFINALDPA.pdf.

The government's allegations in some of these and other notorious cases reveal a shocking disregard for the law and a pattern of systematic abuse that permeated large corporations. What do they suggest about the need for criminal sanctions and specifically about the advisability of seeking jail terms for responsible individuals? What remedies are needed to assure that higher-ups in corporations do not simply adopt a "hear no evil" approach and neglect to monitor the activities of those under their supervision? Do they raise questions about the efficacy of the fiduciary duties of corporate officers and directors in ensuring compliance with the law in large corporations? Recall that the fiduciary duties of Caremark's corporate officers and directors to uncover wrongdoing were the subject of a shareholder's derivative suit, set forth in Chapter 10 of this book. Does the duty to monitor enunciated in that case seem likely to reduce the incidence of abuse? Note also the increasing importance of corporate compliance plans for both mitigating potential penalties and preventing violations. What kinds of compliance programs would be most effective? See Health Attorneys See Rapid Growth in Adoption of Compliance Plans, 5 Health L. Rep. (BNA) (Aug. 15, 1996) (citing survey results viewing codes of conduct, though widely used, as ineffective compared to employee training and hot-lines). Consider as you read the following sections whether the need for both detection and prevention of abuse justifies the multiplicity of legal remedies.

B. QUI TAM ACTIONS

31 U.S.C. § 3730. Civil actions for false claims

* * *

(b) Actions by private persons.—(1) A person may bring a civil action for a violation of [the False Claims Act] for the person and for the United States Government. The action shall be brought in the name of the Government. The action may be dismissed only if the court and the Attorney General give written consent to the dismissal and their reasons for consenting.

(2) A copy of the complaint and written disclosure of substantially all material evidence and information the person possesses shall be served on the Government * * * The complaint shall be filed in camera, shall remain under seal for at least 60 days, and shall not be served on the defendant until the court so orders. The Government may elect to intervene and proceed with the action within 60 days after it receives both the complaint and the material evidence and information.

* * *

(4) Before the expiration of the 60–day period or any extensions obtained under paragraph (3), the Government shall—

(A) proceed with the action, in which case the action shall be conducted by the Government; or

(B) notify the court that it declines to take over the action, in which case the person bringing the action shall have the right to conduct the action.

* * *

(c) Rights of the parties to qui tam actions.—(1) If the Government proceeds with the action, it shall have the primary responsibility for prosecuting the action, and shall not be bound by an act of the person bringing the action. Such person shall have the right to continue as a party to the action, subject to the limitations set forth in paragraph (2).

* * *

(d) Award to qui tam plaintiff. If the Government proceeds with an action brought by a person under subsection (b), such person [shall receive between 15 and 25 percent of the proceeds of the action or settlement of the claim, depending on the extent to which the person contributed to the prosecution, plus attorneys' fees and costs. If the government does not proceed the person may receive between 25 and 30 percent plus attorneys' fees and costs. If the action was brought by a person who planned and initiated the violation of the statutes, the court may reduce the person's share of proceeds and if the person is convicted of a crime for his or her role that person may not share any proceeds.]

(e) Certain actions barred.

* * *

(3) In no event may a person bring an action under subsection (b) which is based upon allegations or transactions which are the subject of a civil suit

or an administrative civil money penalty proceeding in which the Government is already a party.

(4)(A) No court shall have jurisdiction over an action under this section based upon the public disclosure of allegations or transactions in a criminal, civil, or administrative hearing, in a congressional, administrative, or Government Accounting Office report, hearing, audit, or investigation, or from the news media, unless the action is brought by the Attorney General or the person bringing the action is an original source of the information.

(B) For purposes of this paragraph, "original source" means an individual who has direct and independent knowledge of the information on which the allegations are based and has voluntarily provided the information to the Government before filing an action under this section which is based on the information.

* * *

(h) Any employee who is discharged, demoted, suspended, threatened, harassed, or in any other manner discriminated against in the terms and conditions of employment by his or her employer because of lawful acts done by the employee on behalf of the employee or others in furtherance of an action under this section, including investigation for, initiation of, testimony for, or assistance in an action filed or to be filed under this section, shall be entitled to all relief necessary to make the employee whole. Such relief shall include reinstatement with the same seniority status such employee would have had but for the discrimination, 2 times the amount of back pay, interest on the back pay, and compensation for any special damages sustained as a result of the discrimination, including litigation costs and reasonable attorneys' fees. An employee may bring an action in the appropriate district court of the United States for the relief provided in this subsection.

Notes and Questions

1. What advice would you have given to a hypothetical assistant working for Mrs. and Dr. Krizek in United States v. Krizek, supra, if she had approached you for legal advice before any investigation had begun of her employer? How would you have handled discussions with the U.S. Attorney's Office concerning her involvement in the matter? Could she continue to perform her job responsibilities for Dr. Krizek if she became a whistleblower or would it be necessary for her to quit? Before advising her, you may want to consult Luckey v. Baxter Healthcare Corp., 183 F.3d 730 (7th Cir. 1999), discussed in the preceding section of this chapter. In a portion of the opinion not reprinted above, Judge Easterbrook rejected the relator's claim for whistleblower protection under § 3730(h). Baxter had fired Ms. Luckey before her qui tam suit was unsealed and the court concluded that Baxter was not aware of the pending action. The court rejected the claim that because the employer knew of her strongly-held feelings about its testing practices, it should have been on notice of the possibility of her "assistance in" a suit. Likewise, despite Luckey's statements to co-workers that she planned to "shut down" the lab and "get rid" of her supervisors, the court concluded that Baxter was not prohibited from firing her: "Sabre-rattling is not protected conduct. Only investigation, testimony, and litigation are protected, and none of these led to Luckey's firing." 183 F.3d at 733.

2. If you represented Dr. Krizek and the matter went to trial, how would you seek to impeach the testimony of the assistant who became a qui tam relator?

As a lawyer for the Department of Justice (assuming it has entered and taken over the lawsuit), how would you insulate against this cross-examination or mitigate it? Suppose instead that it is Mrs. Krizek who decided to become the qui tam "relator." Would your advice change? What information would you need to elicit before advising her?

3. The constitutionality of the qui tam statute has come under attack on several grounds. In Vermont Agency of Natural Resources v. United States ex rel. Stevens, 529 U.S. 765, 120 S.Ct. 1858, 146 L.Ed.2d 836 (2000), the Supreme Court laid one question to rest, holding that, as partial assignees of the claim of the United States, qui tam relators satisfy the "case or controversy" requirements of Article III. In *Vermont Agency* the Supreme Court also held that states and state entities could not be subject to qui tam liability. 529 U.S. at 727–28. See Donald v. University of California Bd. of Regents, 329 F.3d 1040 (9th Cir. 2003) (denying share of settlement to relator who filed qui tam action regarding state university teaching hospital's billing practices). However, case law establishing that state employees and states may be qui tam relators remains undisturbed. See United States ex rel. Wisconsin v. Dean, 729 F.2d 1100 (7th Cir. 1984); United States ex rel. Fine v. Chevron, U.S.A., Inc., 72 F.3d 740 (9th Cir. 1995). See also Dorthea Beare, Are Government Employees Proper Qui Tam Plaintiffs?, 14 J. Leg. Med. 279 (1993); Gosfield, *supra*, § 5:13. Should a discharged employee who has signed an agreement with her employer releasing the employer of all claims and agreeing not to sue be able to pursue a qui tam action? What public policy arguments can be raised in favor of and against allowing such an action to proceed?

4. A significant obstacle for qui tam relators is statute's bar on actions in which there has been "public disclosure" of the allegations or transactions, which includes government hearings, investigations, or media reports. However the law provides an exception where the relator is the "original source" of the information, defined in 3730(e)(4)(B) as "an individual who [1] has direct and independent knowledge of the information on which the allegations are based and [2] has voluntarily provided the information to the Government before filing an action under this section which is based on the information." The Supreme Court has taken a strict view of the knowledge the relator must have, requiring fairly precise information about the state of affairs, the laws at issue and the false statement actually made. Rockwell Int'l Corp. v. United States, 127 S.Ct. 1397, 167 L.Ed.2d 190 (2007). There is a circuit split concerning the test as to whether a lawsuit is "based upon" publicly available information. The majority of circuits apply the standard that "a qui tam action is 'based upon' a public disclosure when the supporting allegations are 'the same as those that have been publicly disclosed...regardless of where the relator obtained his information,'" while the minority holds that "a lawsuit is based upon publicly disclosed information when it both depends essentially upon publicly disclosed information and is actually derived from such information." United States ex rel. Fowler v. Caremark RX, LLC, 496 F.3d 730 (7th Cir. 2007). See also In United States ex rel. Hays v. Hoffman, 325 F.3d 982 (8th Cir. 2003) (letter from whistleblower prompted state health agency to conduct a field audit of defendant's nursing home practices, which produced an audit report relator used to file a qui tam suit; because relator must be "more than a catalyst," relator held not an original source).

5. Qui tam actions have become the principle means by which the government uncovers fraud as over 80 percent of all government false claims actions are initiated by whistleblowers. Recoveries in cases involving health care fraud were $1.2 billion in 2003, $474 million in 2004 and $906 million in 2005. Taxpayers Against Fraud, Qui Tam Statistics, available at www.taf.org/fcastatistics2006.pdf.

Although the Department of Justice declines to intervene in most qui tam actions and the large majority of those in which it does not intervene are unsuccessful, most of the largest health care fraud cases in recent years have been the result of qui tam actions. In recent years, over 60 percent of all qui tam actions involved the health care industry, with the pharmaceutical industry drawing particular attention. Financial Impacts of Waste, Fraud, and Abuse in Pharmaceutical Pricing: Hearing Before the H. Comm. On Oversight, 110th Cong. (2007) (testimony of Lewis Morris, Chief Counsel to the Inspector General of HHS, and James Moorman, President of Taxpayers Against Fraud) (2006 FCA recoveries involving pharmautical industry total $4 billion; $60 billion in additional potential liability in pending cases), available at http://oversight.house.gov/story.asp?ID=1168. For the view that "privatization" of public law enforcement through the qui tam statute creates incentives to over-enforce the False Claims Act, see Dana Bowen Matthew, The Moral Hazard Problem with Privatization of Public Enforcement: The Case of Pharmaceutical Fraud, 40 Mich. J.L. Ref. 281 (2007). Does the fact that the government has on several occasions obtained large settlements from corporations only to later fail to obtain criminal convictions against individuals responsible for the alleged fraud suggest that incentives under the FCA are out of kilter? See id. at 309–17 (discussing the TAP litigation and other pharmaceutical industry settlements under the FCA).

What is the justification for qui tam actions? Do they advance legitimate law enforcement objectives? Might they create undesirable incentives that poison the employer-employee relationship? In evaluating the effectiveness of the qui tam law in enhancing the deterrent effect of the FCA, consider the need to assure that damages are set at levels that take into account the likelihood of detection and the total social costs imposed by the violator. See Gary Becker, Crime and Punishment: An Economic Approach, 76 J. Pol. Econ. 169 (1968); Robert Lande, Optimal Sanctions for Antitrust Violations, 50 U. Chi. L. Rev. 652 (1983).

OIG has also established a "Provider Self–Disclosure Protocol" that gives guidance to providers and suppliers making disclosures to the government regarding potential violations of Federal laws (as distinguished from innocent mistakes that may have resulted in overpayments). 63 Fed. Reg. 58,399 (October 30, 1998). Under the protocol, after making an initial disclosure, the provider or supplier is expected to undertake a thorough internal investigation of the nature and cause of the matters uncovered and make a reliable assessment of their economic impact (e.g., an estimate of the losses to the Federal health care programs). The OIG declines to make "firm commitments" as to what leniency disclosing providers can expect, but states that "full disclosure at an early stage generally benefits the firm or individual."

II. MEDICARE AND MEDICAID FRAUD AND ABUSE

A. THE STATUTE: 42 U.S.C. § 1320a–7B

* * *

(b) Illegal remunerations

(1) Whoever knowingly and willfully solicits or receives any remuneration (including any kickback, bribe, or rebate) directly or indirectly, overtly or covertly, in cash or in kind—

(A) in return for referring an individual to a person for the furnishing or arranging for the furnishing of any item or service for which payment may be made in whole or in part under a Federal health care program, or

(B) in return for purchasing, leasing, ordering, or arranging for or recommending purchasing, leasing, or ordering any good, facility, service, or item for which payment may be made in whole or in part under a Federal health care program,

shall be guilty of a felony and upon conviction thereof, shall be fined not more than $25,000 or imprisoned for not more than five years, or both.

(2) Whoever knowingly and willfully offers or pays any remuneration (including any kickback, bribe or rebate) directly or indirectly, overtly or covertly, in cash or in kind to any person to induce such person—

(A) to refer an individual to a person for the furnishing or arranging for the furnishing of any item or service for which payment may be made in whole or in part under a Federal health care program, or

(B) to purchase, lease, order, or arrange for or recommend purchasing, leasing, or ordering any good, facility, service, or item for which payment may be made in whole or in part under a Federal health care program,

shall be guilty of a felony and upon conviction thereof shall be fined not more than $25,000 or imprisoned for not more than five years, or both.

* * *

[Subsection (c) prohibits knowing and willful false statements or representations of material facts with respect to the conditions or operation of any entity in order to qualify such an entity for Medicare or Medicaid certification. Subsection (d) prohibits knowingly and willfully charging patients for Medicaid services where such charges are not otherwise permitted.]

(f) "Federal health care program" defined

For purposes of this section, the term "Federal health care program" means—

(1) any plan or program that provides health benefits, whether directly, through insurance, or otherwise, which is funded directly, in whole or in part, by the United States Government [other than the federal employees health benefit program]; or

(2) any State health care program, as defined in section 1320a–7(h) of this title.

B. PROBLEMS: ADVISING UNDER THE FRAUD AND ABUSE LAWS

Do any of the following transactions violate the fraud and abuse laws? Is there anything else wrong with them from a legal, ethical, or public policy perspective?

1. Starkville Community Hospital is located in a rural area in a distant corner of a large mid-western state. Recently, Dr. McPherson, the hospital's only obstetrician, announced his retirement. Few new physicians have settled in Starkville in recent years, and the community and hospital are very concerned about the loss of obstetric services. The hospital has decided, therefore, to implement a plan to attract a new obstetrician. It is offering to provide any board-certified obstetrician who will settle in Starkville and obtain privileges at Starkville Memorial the following for the first two years

the physician is on staff at the hospital: (1) a guaranteed annual income of $110,000, (2) free malpractice insurance through the hospital's self-insurance plan, and (3) free rent in the hospital's medical practice building. The new obstetrician would not be required to refer patients to Starkville Community, though the closest alternative hospital is 60 miles away. The obstetrician would also be expected to assume some administrative duties in exchange for the compensation package Starkville is offering. Starkville Community is currently engaged in negotiations with a young doctor who has just finished her residency and appears likely to accept this offer. There is a potential problem, however. Dr. Waxman, who came to Starkville two years ago and is the hospital's only cardiologist, has threatened that he will leave unless he gets the same terms.

2. Dr. Ness, a successful ophthalmologist, advertises in the weekly suburban shopping newspaper, offering free cataract examinations for senior citizens. He in fact does not charge those who respond to the offer for the Medicare deductible or co-insurance amounts, but bills Medicare for the maximum charge allowable for the service.

3. Managed care organizations are insisting that Samaritan Hospital offer wider geographic coverage in order to bid on contracts. A market study reveals that Samaritan is receiving few admissions from Arlington, a rapidly growing affluent suburb eight miles to the northwest. To remedy this problem, Samaritan has formed an MSO and has entered into negotiations to purchase the Arlington Family Practice Center, a successful group practice containing five board-certified family practitioners. The MSO has offered a generous price for the practice, which would be renamed Samaritan–Arlington Family Practice Center and its doctors would become salaried employees of the MSO entity. They would thereafter be required to admit patients only at Samaritan and to refer only to specialists who have privileges at Samaritan. The five doctors, who are weary of the administrative hassles of private practice, are eager to sell.

4. MegaPharma, a leading pharmaceutical manufacturer, plans to roll out several new drugs next year. Once it receives approval from the FDA, it plans to market these drugs aggressively to physicians. MegaPharma's marketing director intends to have her "detailers"—representatives who visit doctors' offices to market pharmaceutical products and explain their benefits—upgrade the quality of lunches they supply to the doctors and staff when they visit, offer large amounts of free samples, and give each doctor a souvenir IPOD inscribed with the MegaPharma logo and the names of the new drugs. In addition, MegaPharma will offer a $5000 honorarium and free travel to 50 physician "opinion leaders" from around the country to attend an annual educational seminar it sponsors. MegaPharma also hopes that many physicians will prescribe pezophine, one of its new drugs, for a use not approved by the FDA. (Such "off-label" prescribing is not in itself illegal, but FDA law forbids the manufacturer from marketing or advertising for that purpose). MegaPharma plans to offer honoraria to academics who have produced research about the off-label uses of pezophine and who themselves prescribe pezophine for off-label uses; it will offer honoraria for any talk or paper published regardless of whether other sources are also funding the academics' work.

5. Twenty-three small rural hospitals in a mid-western state have entered into a contract with a group-purchasing agent to purchase medical equipment and supplies for them. The agent will take advantage of volume discounts and of careful market research to significantly lower the cost of supplies and equipment purchased for the hospitals. The agent obtains, on average, a 5% rebate from suppliers for all goods it purchases.

6. Intermodal Health System, an integrated delivery system, has suffered losses averaging $100,000 per year per doctor on the physician practices it acquired five years ago. It has developed a plan to terminate the contracts of half of the physicians it now employs. Pursuant to their employment contract, each physician will receive a severance fee of $50,000. Intermodal will also waive covenants not to compete contained in contracts with terminated physicians. In addition, Intermodal plans to offer to its "most valued" terminated physicians lease agreements to continue to occupy the medical office space owned by an Intermodal subsidiary.

C. PENALTIES FOR FRAUD AND ABUSE

As we have seen, false billing, illegal remuneration (bribes and kickbacks), misrepresentation of compliance with conditions of participation, and a variety of other abuses involving federal health care plans are federal crimes and in most instances felonies. Of equal concern to providers, however, are the civil penalty and exclusion powers of the Office of Inspector General (OIG) of the Department of Health and Human Services (HHS). For providers dependent on Medicare and Medicaid for a large share of their business, exclusion from these programs can be effectively a death warrant, at least as serious as a felony conviction. Civil sanction proceedings are administrative in nature, criminal intent need not be shown, and the standard of proof is a preponderance of the evidence rather than beyond a reasonable doubt.

The list of behaviors for which HHS can assess civil money penalties is long and grows with every annual budget reconciliation act. For example, civil penalties of up to $10,000 per item or service plus three times the amount claimed can be assessed for an item or service that a person "knows or should know" was "not provided as claimed." 42 U.S.C. § 1320a–7a(a). The array of additional sanctions includes: civil money penalties against any person who provides false or misleading information that could reasonably be expected to influence the decision of when to discharge a Medicare beneficiary from a hospital, 42 U.S.C. § 1320a–7a(a)(3); penalties against Medicare or Medicaid HMOs that fail substantially to provide medically necessary services with a substantial likelihood of adversely affecting beneficiaries, or that impose premiums in excess of permitted amounts, 42 U.S.C. § 1395mm(i)(6)(A)(i)-(iii); penalties against hospitals that make direct or indirect payments to physicians as incentives for reducing or limiting services provided to beneficiaries or against physicians who accept such payments, 42 U.S.C. § 1320a–7a(b); and penalties of up to $2000 per violation may be imposed on doctors who fail to provide diagnosis codes on non-assigned Medicare claims, 42 U.S.C. § 1395u(p)(3). Finally the government may seek an injunction to enjoin any person from "concealing, removing, encumbering, or disposing" of its assets when seeking a civil monetary penalty. 42 U.S.C. § 1320a–7a(k).

Exclusion from participation in Federal health care programs is a potent and widely used weapon in the arsenal of those combating fraud. Nearly 3500 providers were excluded from the Medicare program in fiscal year 2006; 850 of those exclusions resulted from criminal convictions for program-related crimes, 295 for patient abuse and neglect, and 1868 were based on license revocations. Department of Health and Human Services and Department of Justice, Health Care Fraud and Abuse Control Program Annual Report for FY 2006 (2007), available at http://oig.hhs.gov/publications/docs/hcfac/hcfacreport 2006.pdf. The OIG must exclude individuals or entities for at least five years in four circumstances: conviction of a criminal offense related to the delivery of Medicare or state health care program services; conviction of a crime relating to neglect or abuse of patients; any federal or state felony conviction with respect to any act or omission in any health care program financed by any Federal, state or local government agency or involving fraud, theft, embezzlement, breach of fiduciary responsibility or other financial misconduct; or felony conviction of unlawful manufacture, distribution, prescription or dispensing of controlled substances. 42 U.S.C. § 1320a–7(a). See also Travers v. Sullivan, 791 F.Supp. 1471 (E.D. Wash. 1992) (no contest plea constitutes conviction of program-related crime and requires mandatory exclusion).

The OIG also has discretion to exclude providers for numerous other categories of offenses, including loss of professional license, submission of bills substantially in excess of usual charges or costs, substantial failure of an HMO to provide medically necessary services, substantial failure of a hospital to comply with a corrective plan for unnecessary admissions or other inappropriate practices to circumvent PPS, or default by health professionals on student loans. 42 U.S.C. § 1320a–7(b). An important amendment to the law allows for permissive exclusions of (1) persons who have direct or indirect ownership or control interests in a sanctioned entity and have acted in deliberate ignorance of the information; and (2) officers or managing employees, even if the individual did not participate in the wrongdoing. 42 U.S.C. § 1320a–7(b)(8). The law also fixes minimum periods of exclusion ranging from 1 to 3 years depending on the basis for exclusion. 42 U.S.C. § 1320a–7(b)(c)(3). However, in determining the length of permissive exclusions, the agency may consider other factors such as the availability of alternative sources of health care in the community. Exclusion or criminal conviction frequently results in disciplinary action by state professional licensure boards, and can thus end the professional career of even a professional who sees few Medicaid and Medicare patients. For a comprehensive review of the law governing exclusions, see Gosfield, supra, §§ 4:1–4:7. See also Pamela H. Bucy, The Poor Fit of Tradition Evidentiary Doctrine and Sophisticated Crime: An Empirical Analysis of Health Care Fraud Prosecutions, 63 Fordham L. Rev. 383 (1994).

D. TREATMENT OF REFERRAL FEES UNDER FRAUD AND ABUSE LAWS

Sharing the profits of collective economic activity is common throughout the economy generally. Landlords rent commercial properties under percentage leases, agents sell goods and services produced by others on commission, merchants grant discounts to those who use their services or encourage others to do so. Such activity has, however, long been frowned upon as it relates to health care. It is widely believed that patients lack the knowledge and information (or even the legal right, in the case of prescription drugs) to make health care decisions for themselves (choosing appropriate drugs or specialists, for example). Therefore, providers have a fiduciary obligation to recommend goods and services for patients considering only the patient's medical needs and not the provider's own economic interest. With the advent of government financing of health care, this concern has been supplemented by another: that financial rewards to providers for patient referrals might drive up program costs by encouraging the provision of unnecessary or inordinately expensive medical care.

For these reasons, the fraud and abuse statutes reproduced above prohibit paying or receiving any remuneration (directly or indirectly, overtly or covertly) for referring, purchasing, or ordering goods, facilities, items or services paid for by Medicare or Medicaid. Interpreted broadly, however, these provisions seem to proscribe a wide variety of transactions that might encourage competition or efficient production of health care. Indeed, many of the arrangements undertaken in connection with forming or operating PHOs, MSOs or integrated delivery systems discussed in Chapter 10 might, under a literal reading of the fraud and abuse statute, be felonies under the federal law. Considerable attention has been focused recently on the question of whether the statute and the judicial and administrative interpretations thereof successfully distinguish beneficial and detrimental conduct in the current market environment.

UNITED STATES v. GREBER

United States Court of Appeals, Third Circuit, 1985.
760 F.2d 68, cert. denied, 474 U.S. 988, 106 S.Ct. 396, 88 L.Ed.2d 348.

WEIS, CIRCUIT JUDGE.

In this appeal, defendant argues that payments made to a physician for professional services in connection with tests performed by a laboratory cannot be the basis of Medicare fraud. We do not agree and hold that if one purpose of the payment was to induce future referrals, the Medicare statute has been violated. * * *

After a jury trial, defendant was convicted on 20 of 23 counts in an indictment charging violations of the mail fraud, Medicare fraud, and false statement statutes. Post-trial motions were denied, and defendant has appealed.

Defendant is an osteopathic physician who is board certified in cardiology. In addition to hospital staff and teaching positions, he was the president of Cardio–Med, Inc., an organization which he formed. The company provides physicians with diagnostic services, one of which uses a Holter-monitor. This device, worn for approximately 24 hours, records the patient's cardiac activity on a tape. A computer operated by a cardiac technician scans the tape, and the data is later correlated with an activity diary the patient maintains while wearing the monitor.

Cardio–Med billed Medicare for the monitor service and, when payment was received, forwarded a portion to the referring physician. The government charged that the referral fee was 40 percent of the Medicare payment, not to exceed $65 per patient.

Based on Cardio–Med's billing practices, counts 18–23 of the indictment charged defendant with having tendered remuneration or kickbacks to the referring physicians in violation of 42 U.S.C. § 1395nn(b)(2)(B) (1982).

* * *

The proof as to the Medicare fraud counts (18–23) was that defendant had paid a Dr. Avallone and other physicians "interpretation fees" for the doctors' initial consultation services, as well as for explaining the test results to the patients. There was evidence that physicians received "interpretation fees" even though defendant had actually evaluated the monitoring data. Moreover, the fixed percentage paid to the referring physician was more than Medicare allowed for such services.

The government also introduced testimony defendant had given in an earlier civil proceeding. In that case, he had testified that ". . . if the doctor didn't get his consulting fee, he wouldn't be using our service. So the doctor got a consulting fee." In addition, defendant told physicians at a hospital that the Board of Censors of the Philadelphia County Medical Society had said the referral fee was legitimate if the physician shared the responsibility for the report. Actually, the Society had stated that there should be separate bills because "for the monitor company to offer payment for the physicians . . . is not considered to be the method of choice."

The evidence as to mail fraud was that defendant repeatedly ordered monitors for his own patients even though use of the device was not medically indicated. As a prerequisite for payment, Medicare requires that the service be medically indicated.

The Department of Health and Human Services had promulgated a rule providing that it would pay for Holter-monitoring only if it was in operation for eight hours or more. Defendant routinely certified that the temporal condition had been met, although in fact it had not.

* * *

I. MEDICARE FRAUD

The Medicare fraud statute was amended by P. L. 95–142, 91 Stat. 1183 (1977). Congress, concerned with the growing problem of fraud and abuse in the system, wished to strengthen the penalties to enhance the deterrent effect of the statute. To achieve this purpose, the crime was upgraded from a misdemeanor to a felony.

Another aim of the amendments was to address the complaints of the United States Attorneys who were responsible for prosecuting fraud cases. They informed Congress that the language of the predecessor statute was "unclear and needed clarification." H. Rep. No. 393, Part II, 95th Cong., 1st Sess. 53, *reprinted in* 1977 U.S. CODE CONG. & AD. NEWS 3039, 3055.

A particular concern was the practice of giving "kickbacks" to encourage the referral of work. Testimony before the Congressional committee was that "physicians often determine which laboratories would do the test work for their medicaid patients by the amount of the kickbacks and rebates offered by the laboratory.... Kickbacks take a number of forms including cash, long-term credit arrangements, gifts, supplies and equipment, and the furnishing of business machines." Id. at 3048–3049.

To remedy the deficiencies in the statute and achieve more certainty, the present version of 42 U.S.C. § 1395nr(b)(2) was enacted. It provides:

"whoever knowingly and willfully offers or pays any remuneration (including any kickback, bribe or rebate) directly or indirectly, overtly or covertly in cash or in kind to induce such person—

(B) to purchase, lease, order, or arrange for or recommend purchasing ... or ordering any ... service or item for which payment may be made ... under this title, shall be guilty of a felony."

The district judge instructed the jury that the government was required to prove that Cardic–Med paid to Dr. Avallone some part of the amount received from Medicare; that defendant caused Cardio–Med to make the payment; and did so knowingly and willfully as well as with the intent to induce Dr. Avallone to use Cardio–Med's services for patients covered by Medicare. The judge further charged that even if the physician interpreting the test did so as a consultant to Cardio–Med, that fact was immaterial if a purpose of the fee was to induce the ordering of services from Cardio–Med.

Defendant contends that the charge was erroneous. He insists that absent a showing that the only purpose behind the fee was to improperly induce future services, compensating a physician for services actually rendered could not be a violation of the statute.

The government argues that Congress intended to combat financial incentives to physicians for ordering particular services patients did not require.

The language and purpose of the statute support the government's view. Even if the physician performs some service for the money received, the potential for unnecessary drain on the Medicare system remains. The statute is aimed at the inducement factor.

The text refers to "any remuneration." That includes not only sums for which no actual service was performed but also those amounts for which some professional time was expended. "Remunerates" is defined as "to pay an equivalent for service." Webster Third New International Dictionary (1966). By including such items as kickbacks and bribes, the statute expands "remuneration" to cover situations where no service is performed. That a particular payment was a remuneration (which implies that a service was rendered) rather than a kickback, does not foreclose the possibility that a violation nevertheless could exist.

In United States v. Hancock, 604 F.2d 999 (7th Cir.1979), the court applied the term "kickback" found in the predecessor statute to payments made to chiropractors by laboratories which performed blood tests. The chiropractors contended that the amounts they received were legitimate handling fees for their services in obtaining, packaging, and delivering the specimens to the laboratories and then interpreting the results. The court rejected that contention and noted, 'The potential for increased costs to the Medicare–Medicaid system and misapplication of federal funds is plain, where payments for the exercise of such judgments are added to the legitimate cost of the transaction. . . . [T]hese are among the evils Congress sought to prevent by enacting the kickback statutes. . . ." Id. at 1001.

Hancock strongly supports the government's position here, because the statute in that case did not contain the word "remuneration." The court nevertheless held that "kickback" sufficiently described the defendants' criminal activity. By adding "remuneration" to the statute in the 1977 amendment, Congress sought to make it clear that even if the transaction was not considered to be a "kickback" for which no service had been rendered, payment nevertheless violated the Act.

We are aware that in United States v. Porter, 591 F.2d 1048 (5th Cir.1979), the Court of Appeals for the Fifth Circuit took a more narrow view of "kickback" than did the court in *Hancock*. *Porter's* interpretation of the predecessor statute which did not include "remuneration" is neither binding nor persuasive. We agree with the Court of Appeals for the Sixth Circuit, which adopted the interpretation of "kickback" used in *Hancock* and rejected that of the *Porter* case. United States v. Tapert, 625 F.2d 111 (6th Cir. 1980).

We conclude that the more expansive reading is consistent with the impetus for the 1977 amendments and therefore hold that the district court correctly instructed the jury. If the payments were intended to induce the physician to use Cardio–Med's services, the statute was violated, even if the payments were also intended to compensate for professional services.

A review of the record also convinces us that there was sufficient evidence to sustain the jury's verdict.

* * *

Having carefully reviewed all of the defendant's allegations, we find no reversible error. Accordingly, the judgment of the district court will be affirmed.

Notes and Questions

1. What is controversial about the *Greber* decision? What kinds of salutary or benign practices might it affect?

2. Other courts dealing with arrangements that have multiple purposes have generally followed *Greber's* holding that the purpose to induce referrals need not be the dominant or sole purpose of the scheme in order to fall within the anti-kickback law's prohibition. See, e.g., United States v. McClatchey, 217 F.3d 823, 834–35 (10th Cir. 2000). However, several decisions have introduced variations on that theme. For example, one court has required proof of a "material purpose" to obtain money for the referral of services to support a conviction under the statute. United States v. Kats, 871 F.2d 105, 108 (9th Cir. 1989). Another, more demanding approach holds that proof that a "primary purpose" of the payment was to induce future referrals is required. United States v. Bay State Ambulance and Hosp. Rental Serv., 874 F.2d 20, 30 (1st Cir. 1989). Not surprisingly, the OIG has chosen to follow the *Greber* standard. 42 C.F.R. § 1001.951(a)(2)(i) (exclusion applies "irrespective of whether the individual or entity may be able to prove that the remuneration was also intended for some other purpose . . ."). For criticism of *Greber*, see Eugene E. Elder, The Hypocrisy of the One Purpose Test in the Anti–Kickback Enforcement Law, 11 Medicare Rep. (BNA) 802 (July 28, 2000).

3. What purposes does the anti-kickback legislation serve? Does it advance or impede the provision of quality medical services? What economic or efficiency

arguments might be made in support of the law? Can it be argued that the law sweeps too broadly given the dynamics of today's market? At the time the legislation was passed, providers were almost uniformly paid on a cost-based, fee-for-service basis. With much of the private sector comprised of managed care or capitated provider payments, should a less restrictive rule be devised? See James Blumstein, The Fraud and Abuse Statute in an Evolving Health Care Marketplace: Life in the Health Care Speakeasy, 22 Am. J. L. & Med. 205 (1996). For the regulatory response to this problem, see the statutory exception applicable to risk-sharing arrangements, discussed *infra*.

4.   With the defendant's intent to obtain referrals in exchange for remuneration as the central issue in most criminal prosecutions under the anti-kickback statute, courts often must evaluate circumstantial evidence regarding defendant's mental state. The widely noted *McClatchey* case, United States v. McClatchey, 217 F.3d 823 (10th Cir. 2000), involved the appeal from conviction under the act by Dennis McClatchey, Chief Operating Officer of Baptist Medical Center. McClatchey oversaw negotiations with doctors Robert and Ronald LaHue who were principals in Blue Valley Medical Group, a medical practice providing care to nursing home patients. Prior contracts between Baptist and the LaHues had provided for payment of $75,000 per year to the doctors for serving as co-directors of gerontology services at Baptist; however, the LaHues performed almost no services and circumstances strongly suggested that the payments were made in return for their providing patient referrals to Baptist. 217 F.3d at 828–30. The evidence at trial showed that McClatchy directed negotiations which resulted in a revised contract that was legal and that McClatchy sought and received legal advice throughout the process. Weighing competing inferences regarding defendant's intent, the Tenth Circuit upheld a jury verdict convicting McClatchy. The court found that his knowledge that the LaHues had not performed substantial services under prior contracts, that the hospital staff did not want the LaHues' services, and that McClatchey stressed the importance of maximizing admissions from BVMG patients constituted sufficient evidence to sustain the jury's findings. Id. at 830. Concerning McClatchey's reliance on counsel, the court held as follows:

> McClatchey also argues that his actions throughout the negotiation process cannot give rise to an inference of his criminal intent because they were entirely directed and controlled by legal counsel. McGrath [a subordinate directly involved in the negotiations with the LaHues] testified however, that he and McClatchey told the lawyers what services to include in the contracts, not visa versa. Thus, the jury could reasonably attribute to McClatchey and McGrath both the decision to remove a minimum hour provision from the contract after the LaHues objected to such a requirement and the inculpatory inference of intent that can be drawn therefrom. Moreover, it was not the attorneys but McClatchey, Anderson, and McGrath who made the important decision to negotiate a new contract rather than ending Baptist's relationship with BVMG. Finally, McClatchey did not always heed the attorneys' advice.... The evidence, therefore, permitted the jury to reasonably reject McClatchey's good faith reliance on counsel defense and instead find he harbored the specific intent to violate the Act.

Id. at 830–31. The advice of counsel "defense" in this context really amounts to a claim that the government did not establish that the defendant "knowingly and willfully" engaged in unlawful kickback activities. To avail oneself of this defense, however, the defendant must establish that he disclosed all relevant facts to his attorneys and that he relied in good faith on that advice and acted in strict accordance with it. See Gosfield, *supra*, § 2:67. What problems do you foresee for a defendant wanting to invoke this defense at trial? The district court acquitted two attorneys indicted for their role in the scheme finding they did not cover up fraud with sham agreements, had "attempted to advise their clients to engage in legal transactions," and relied on clients' representations as to their conduct. See Osteopathy, Former Hospital Executives Convicted by Kansas Jury in Bribery Scheme, 8 Health L. Rep. (Apr. 18, 1999). What implications do these holdings have for attorney-client communications? The government also named several prominent attorneys as unindicted co-conspirators. Joan Burgess Killgore, Comment: Surgery with a Meat Cleaver: The Criminal Indictment of Health Care Attorneys in United States v. Anderson, 43 St. Louis U. L.J. 1215 (1999). A court subsequently held that the government had violated the due process rights of these individuals by identifying them in a pre-trial motion.

5. *Greber* dealt with the issue of whether defendant's evidence of purpose satisfied the statutory standard that remuneration be given or received "in return for" an item or service reimbursable under Medicare or Medicaid. A second and distinct *mens rea* requirement concerns whether defendant knew that the transaction was unlawful. In Hanlester Network v. Shalala, 51 F.3d 1390 (9th Cir. 1995), the Ninth Circuit held that the statute's "knowing and willful" language requires the government to prove not only that the defendant intentionally engaged in conduct prohibited by the statute, but that the defendant did so with the knowledge that his conduct violated the law. Under this standard, the government must show not only that the defendant intentionally entered into a referral arrangement later determined to violate the statute, but also that when the defendant entered into the arrangement, or while the defendant benefited from it, he or she knew the arrangement violated the dictates of the anti-kickback law.

The Supreme Court's decision in Bryan v. United States, 524 U.S. 184, 118 S.Ct. 1939, 141 L.Ed.2d 197 (1998), went a long way toward clarifying the general principles of intent applicable in criminal cases, but did not fully resolve the issue with respect to the Medicare and Medicaid Fraud and Abuse Statute. First, the Court made it clear that "willfully" will be construed in the criminal context to require proof of knowledge of some law or legal standard: "As a general matter, when used in the criminal context, a 'willful' act is one undertaken with a 'bad purpose.'" 524 U.S. at 191, 118 S.Ct. at 1945. This standard, however, may be satisfied by showing that the defendant acted with "an evil-meaning mind," which the Court defined as acting "with knowledge that his conduct was unlawful." 524 U.S. at 193, 118 S.Ct. at 1946. At the same time, *Bryan* lowered the standard of proof necessary to satisfy its test by accepting an accused's knowledge of general illegality unless the relevant statute is "highly technical." See Sharon L. Davies, Willfulness Under the Anti–Kickback Rules—Lessons from Bryan v. United States, 10 Health Lawyer 14 (July 1998). In a vigorous dissent, Justice Scalia argued that the majority's approach in *Bryan* might allow convictions where the defendant's knowledge of the illegality of his conduct went to issues peripheral to the conduct with which he was charged. For example, the dissenters posited that the defendant in *Bryan* might be guilty of the offense of selling firearms without a license even if he did not know of the license requirement but was aware that some other aspect of his conduct, such as filing serial numbers off the guns, was prohibited. 524 U.S. at 202, 118 S.Ct. at 1950. The following case applies *Bryan* to the anti-kickback law.

UNITED STATES v. STARKS

United States Court of Appeals, Eleventh Circuit, 1998.
157 F.3d 833.

BIRCH, CIRCUIT JUDGE:

Defendants Angela Starks and Andrew Siegel seek to overturn their convictions under the anti-kickback provision of the Social Security Act, 42

U.S.C. § 1320a–7b ("the Anti–Kickback statute"). Specifically, Starks and Siegel argue that the district court erred by refusing to instruct the jury concerning the relevant mens rea. In addition, Starks and Siegel contend that the Anti–Kickback statute is unconstitutionally vague.* * * We AFFIRM IN PART, REVERSE IN PART, and REMAND.

BACKGROUND

In 1992, Andrew Siegel was both the president and the sole shareholder of Future Steps, Inc., a corporation that developed and operated treatment programs for drug addiction. On April 22, 1992, Future Steps contracted with Florida CHS, Inc. to run a chemical dependency unit for pregnant women at Florida CHS's Metropolitan General Hospital ("the Hospital"). In return, Florida CHS promised to pay Future Steps a share of the Hospital's profits from the program. As a Medicaid provider, the Hospital performed medical services for indigent and disabled persons and received payment for these activities through Consultec, the fiscal intermediary for the Florida Medicaid program. Before executing the Future Steps–Florida CHS contract, Siegel initialed each page of the agreement, which included a provision explicitly forbidding Future Steps from making any payment for patient referrals in violation of the Anti–Kickback statute.

At the time Siegel signed this contract, Angela Starks and Barbara Henry had just become community health aides in the employ of the State of Florida Department of Health and Rehabilitative Services ("HRS"). Although Starks and Henry were employees of HRS, they actually worked in a federally-funded research project in Tampa, Florida known as "Project Support." As part of their duties, Starks and Henry advised pregnant women about possible treatment for drug abuse. Upon beginning their work at HRS, Starks and Henry learned from their supervisor both that they could not accept any outside employment that might pose a conflict of interest with their work at HRS and that they were obligated to report any outside employment to HRS.

During the spring of 1992, Future Steps had difficulty attracting patients. One of Future Steps's salaried "liaison workers," Robin Doud–Lacher, however, identified Project Support as a potential source of referrals because of its relationship with high-risk pregnant women. When Doud–Lacher's initial efforts to establish a referral relationship between Future Steps and Project Support failed, Siegel suggested to Doud–Lacher that she spend more time at Project Support, give diapers to Project Support, take Project Support workers to lunch, and otherwise build a relationship with Project Support's employees.

During one of her subsequent visits to Project Support, Doud–Lacher learned from Starks and Henry that cuts in federal spending threatened to reduce their work hours. When Starks and Henry asked if Doud–Loucher knew of other available work, she promised to inquire for them about opportunities at Future Steps.

After discussing Starks and Henry's interest with her immediate supervisor, Doud–Lacher spoke directly with Siegel about hiring the two women. Despite Starks and Henry's extant employment with HRS, Siegel told Doud–Loucher that he would pay Starks and Henry $250 for each patient they referred: $125 when a referred woman began inpatient drug treatment with

Future Steps and $125 after each such woman had stayed in Future Steps's program for two weeks.[2] After accepting Siegel's terms, Starks and Henry did not report their referral arrangement to anyone at Project Support or HRS.

At the outset of their work for Future Steps, Starks and Henry received checks written on Future Steps's account and signed by Siegel. Before issuing these checks, Siegel verified that the referred patients had actually entered the Future Steps program; he did not, though, verify that the referrals were legal. Although the checks Siegel signed were coded variously as payments for aftercare, counseling, and marketing expenses, Siegel was actually only paying Starks and Henry for their referrals. In fact, Siegel did not at any time pay Starks and Henry for any of their time, effort, or business expenses, or for any covered Medicare service.

When Doud–Lacher left Future Steps, Siegel had Michael Ix, another liaison worker, assume responsibility for the Starks and Henry referral arrangement. Generally, either Starks or Henry would call Ix and ask him to pick up a referral directly from the Project Support clinic. When Ix arrived at Future Steps with the referred patient, Siegel would give Ix a check for Starks and Henry. Later, after Henry told Ix that she did not want anyone at Project Support to see her receiving checks from Future Steps, Ix agreed to deliver the checks to Starks and Henry either in the Project Support parking lot or at a restaurant. Between June 1992 and January 1993, Future Steps wrote checks payable to Starks totaling $2750 and to Henry totaling $1975.

At the end of 1992, Future Steps began paying Starks and Henry in cash. To make these payments, Ix would withdraw cash from his personal bank account and meet Starks and Henry either at a restaurant or at a twelve-step program; Siegel and Future Steps would then reimburse Ix. On one occasion, Siegel accomplished this reimbursement by meeting Ix in a restaurant restroom and giving him $600. In total, Ix paid Starks and Henry approximately $1000 to $1200 in cash.

Beyond the impropriety of Starks and Henry's acceptance of referral payments from Siegel, the referral arrangement directly affected Starks and Henry's counseling of the pregnant women who relied on them and Project Support for help. At trial, several of Future Steps's clients testified that Starks and Henry threatened that HRS would take away their babies if they did not receive treatment for their drug addictions; in some instances, Starks and Henry threatened women with the loss of their babies if they did not go specifically to Future Steps. According to these women's testimony, Starks and Henry informed them only about Future Steps's program (eschewing discussion of alternative treatments), and most waited with Starks and Henry at the Project Support clinic until someone from Future Steps arrived to take them to the Hospital. Starks and Henry's physician supervisor also testified that she told the two HRS employees to be more evenhanded in their advice to Project Support's patients, after the number of women going to Future Steps from Project Support increased substantially.

2. Although Starks and Henry had suggested limiting their referrals to patients living outside the area surrounding Project Support and/or restricting their recruiting for Future Steps to their non-HRS hours, Siegel imposed no bounds on the nature of their referral efforts.

In total, Starks and Henry referred eighteen women from Project Support to Future Steps. From these referrals, the Hospital received $323,023.04 in Medicaid payments.

On July 29, 1994, a federal grand jury indicted Siegel, Starks, Henry, and Doud–Lacher on five counts related to the referrals. Count One charged all four defendants with conspiring against the United States, in violation of 18 U.S.C. § 371, by offering to pay remuneration for referral of Medicare patients, in violation of 42 U.S.C. § 1320a–7b(b)(2)(A), and by soliciting and receiving such referral payments, in violation of 42 U.S.C. § 1320a–7b(b)(1)(A). Counts Two and Three charged Siegel and Doud–Loucher with paying remuneration to Starks and Henry to induce referrals of Medicaid patients, in violation of 42 U.S.C. § 1320a–7b(b)(2)(A). Finally, Count Four charged Starks and Count Five charged Henry with soliciting and receiving referral payments, in violation of 42 U.S.C. § 1320a–7b(b)(1)(A).

* * *

DISCUSSION

On appeal, defendants Starks and Siegel renew two contentions from their trial. First, they claim that the district court committed reversible error when it refused to instruct the jury that, because of the Anti–Kickback statute's mens rea requirement, Starks and Siegel had to have known that their referral arrangement violated the Anti–Kickback statute in order to be convicted. Second, Starks and Siegel argue that the Social Security Act's prohibition on paid referrals, when considered together with the Act's safe harbor provision, 42 U.S.C. § 1320a–7b(b)(3) ("the Safe Harbor provision"), is unconstitutionally vague. We address each of these arguments before turning to the government's cross-appeals concerning Siegel's sentence.

I. Starks and Siegel's Appeals

A. The "Willfully" Instruction

Starks and Siegel argue that the district court erred in its instruction concerning the mens rea required under the Anti–Kickback statute. According to 42 U.S.C. § 1320a–7b(b), it is illegal for a person to "knowingly and willfully solicit[ ] or receive[ ] any remuneration" for referrals for services covered by the federal government. At trial, the district court gave our circuit's pattern instruction regarding the term "willfully":

> The word willfully, as that term is used from time to time in these instructions, means the act was committed voluntarily and purposely, with the specific intent to do something the law forbids, that is with a bad purpose, either to disobey or disregard the law.

In reviewing the district court's charge, we determine whether the court's instructions as a whole sufficiently informed the jurors so that they understood the issues and were not misled.

In support of their claim, Starks and Siegel rely heavily on United States v. Sanchez–Corcino, 85 F.3d 549 (11th Cir.1996), and Ratzlaf v. United States, 510 U.S. 135, 114 S.Ct. 655, 126 L.Ed.2d 615 (1994). Since we heard oral argument on this case, however, the Supreme Court has issued an opinion in

Bryan v. United States, 524 U.S. 184, 118 S.Ct. 1939, 141 L.Ed.2d 197 (1998), that clearly refutes Starks and Siegel's position.

In *Sanchez–Corcino*, a panel of this court held that the term "willfully" in 18 U.S.C. § 922(a)(1)(D) (requiring license for firearms), meant that the government had to prove that a defendant "acted with knowledge of the [§ 922(a)(1)(D)] licensing requirement." Id. at 553, 554 ("[k]nowledge of the general illegality of one's conduct is not the same as knowledge that one is violating a specific rule"). In *Bryan*, though, the Supreme Court explicitly rejected our decision in *Sanchez–Corcino*. See Bryan, 524 U.S. at 193, 118 S.Ct. at 1946. According to the *Bryan* Court, a jury may find a defendant guilty of violating a statute employing the word "willfully" if it believes "that the defendant acted with an evil-meaning mind, that is to say, that he acted with knowledge that his conduct was unlawful." Id. at 193, 118 S.Ct. at 1946. Further, the Supreme Court distinguished tax or financial cases, such as *Ratzlaf*, that "involved highly technical statutes that presented the danger of ensnaring individuals engaged in apparently innocent conduct." Id.[3] Because "the jury found that [the defendant] knew that his conduct was unlawful," the *Bryan* Court wrote, "[t]he danger of convicting individuals engaged in apparently innocent activity that motivated our decisions in the tax cases and *Ratzlaf* is not present here." Id. (footnote omitted). Thus, the Court held that "the willfulness requirement of [the firearms statute] does not carve out an exemption to the traditional rule that ignorance of the law is no excuse; knowledge that conduct is unlawful is all that is required." Id.[4]

Analogously, the Anti–Kickback statute does not constitute a special exception. Section 1320a–7b is not a highly technical tax or financial regulation that poses a danger of ensnaring persons engaged in apparently innocent conduct. Indeed, the giving or taking of kickbacks for medical referrals is hardly the sort of activity a person might expect to be legal; compared to the licensing provisions that the *Bryan* Court considered, such kickbacks are more clearly malum in se, rather than malum prohibitum. Thus, we see no error in the district court's refusal to give Starks and Siegel's requested instruction.[5]
[ ]

B. Vagueness

Starks and Siegel also argue that the Anti–Kickback statute is unconstitutionally vague because people of ordinary intelligence in either of their positions could not have ascertained from a reading of its Safe Harbor

---

3. In *Ratzlaf*, the Court reviewed a gambler's conviction for illegally structuring his banking transactions so as to avoid technical reporting requirements.

4. The *Bryan* Court thus upheld a jury instruction strikingly similar to the district court's "willfully" charge in this case:

A person acts willfully if he acts intentionally and purposely and with the intent to do something the law forbids, that is, with the bad purpose to disobey or to disregard the law. Now, the person need not be aware of the specific law or rule that his conduct may be violating. But he must act with the intent to do something that the law forbids. [ ]

5. Starks and Siegel also claim that the evidence was not sufficient to prove that they acted "willfully." Given that the government only had to show that they knew that they were acting unlawfully, however, this claim is unpersuasive. The government produced ample evidence, including the furtive methods by which Siegel remunerated Starks and Henry, from which the jury could reasonably have inferred that Starks and Siegel knew that they were breaking the law—even if they may not have known that they were specifically violating the Anti–Kickback statute.

provision that their conduct was illegal.[6] Under the Safe Harbor provision, the Anti–Kickback statute's prohibition on referral payments shall not apply to ... any amount paid by an employer to an employee (who has a bona fide employment relationship with such employer) for employment in the provision of covered items and services.... According to Starks and Siegel, this provision is vague because ordinary people in their position might reasonably have thought that Starks and Henry were "bona fide employees" who were exempt from the Anti–Kickback statute's prohibition on remuneration for referrals.

Starks and Siegel are correct that a criminal statute must define an offense with sufficient clarity to enable ordinary people to understand what conduct is prohibited. [ ] Both the particular facts of this case and the nature of the Anti–Kickback statute, however, undercut Starks and Siegel's vagueness argument. First, even if Starks and Siegel believed that they were bona fide employees, they were not providing "covered items or services." As the government has shown, Starks received payment from Siegel and Future Steps only for referrals and not for any legitimate service for which the Hospital received any Medicare reimbursement. At the same time, persons in either Siegel's or Starks's position could hardly have thought that either Starks or Henry was a bona fide employee; unlike all of Future Steps's other workers, Starks and Henry did not receive regular salary checks at the Hospital. Instead, they clandestinely received their checks (often bearing false category codes) or cash in parking lots and other places outside the Project Support clinic so as to avoid detection by other Project Support workers.

Furthermore, beyond these particular facts, we see no reason to view the Anti–Kickback statute as vague. In Village of Hoffman Estates v. The Flipside, 455 U.S. 489, 498–499, 102 S.Ct. 1186, 1193, 71 L.Ed.2d 362 (1982), the Supreme Court set out several factors for a court to consider in determining whether a statute is impermissibly vague, including whether the statute (1) involves only economic regulation, (2) provides only civil, rather than criminal, penalties, (3) contains a scienter requirement mitigating vagueness, and (4) threatens any constitutionally protected rights. As two of our sister circuits have already concluded, these factors militate against finding the Anti–Kickback statute unconstitutional. [ ] Indeed, the statute regulates only economic conduct,[7] and it does not chill any constitutional rights. Moreover, although the statute does provide for criminal penalties, it requires "knowing and willful" conduct, a mens rea standard that mitigates any otherwise inherent vagueness in the Anti–Kickback statutes's provisions. [ ] In sum, we agree with the district court that the Anti–Kickback statute gave Starks and

---

6. Starks and Siegel offer a variety of arguments to the effect that persons working in the medical field cannot anticipate what is prohibited under the Anti–Kickback statute and what is protected by that statute's Safe Harbor provision. They do not, and cannot, challenge, however, the government's contention that, since this is not a First Amendment case, we must evaluate their claim of vagueness only on an as-applied basis. [ ] Thus, we consider Starks and Siegel's claim in light of the facts of this individual case, looking only to the constitutionality of the Anti–Kickback statute as the government has applied it to Starks and Siegel. [ ]

7. In *Hoffman Estates*, the Court explained that "economic regulation is subject to a less strict vagueness test because its subject is often more narrow, and because businesses, which face economic demands to plan behavior carefully, can be expected to consult relevant legislation in advance of action." 455 U.S. at 498, 102 S.Ct. at 1193 (footnote omitted).

Siegel fair warning that their conduct was illegal and that the statute therefore is not unconstitutionally vague.

* * *

CONCLUSION

* * * With regard to Starks and Siegel's appeal, we hold that the district court did not err when it refused to give their requested instruction, and that the Anti–Kickback statute is not unconstitutionally vague as applied to Starks and Siegel. Therefore, we AFFIRM these parts of the district court's judgment. * * *

Notes and Questions

1. What aspects of the anti-kickback law does the Eleventh Circuit rely upon in *Starks* in holding that specific knowledge of that statute is not required? Are you satisfied that this approach does not run a risk of "ensnaring persons engaged in apparently innocent conduct" under the test set out in *Bryan*? What evidence going to the defendant's intent was available to satisfy the government's burden of showing that the defendants knew they were acting unlawfully? Were the inferences drawn from the defendants' conduct sufficient in this case? See generally Gosfield, *supra*, § 2:66. Sharon L. Davies, The Jurisprudence of Willfullness: An Evolving Theory of Excusable Ignorance, 48 Duke L. J. 341 (1998).

2. Defendants claimed that they qualified as bona fide employees under the statutory exception, 42 U.S.C. § 1320a–7b(b)(3), and safe harbor regulations, 42 C.F.R. § 1001.952, governing the anti-kickback law. The latter regulations, which are discussed in the next section of this chapter, shelter certain arrangements from legal challenge. The employment exception excepts remuneration paid to "bona fide" employees, defined in accordance with Internal Revenue Code, 36 U.S.C. 3121(d)(2), and excludes independent contractor relationships. Why did Starks and Siegel not qualify for the exception? As a general matter, what policy or rationale supports allowing an entity to hire a person who may solicit Medicare-related business to that entity? Don't such arrangements pose the same risks as other forms of remuneration in exchange for referrals?

3. An area of continuing controversy is whether violation of the anti-kickback provisions can be prosecuted as a false claim under the False Claims Act. As discussed above, implicit certification of compliance prohibitions against kickbacks and self-referrals raises issues of materiality under the FCA. See *supra* Section IA. See generally, Marc Raspanti & David Largaie, When Does Economic Credentialing Violate the Anti–Kickback Statute?, Health Law Handbook, § 6–12 (Alice Gosfield, ed., 2002). See also United States ex rel. Thompson v. Columbia/HCA Healthcare Corp., 125 F.3d 899 (5th Cir. 1997) (rejecting the argument that an illegal kickback taints the provider's claim for reimbursement so as to bring it within the FCA but finding that a hospital could be liable for submitting false claims and making false statements if it explicitly certified compliance with program regulations and payment was conditioned on such certification.) For critical analyses of these developments see John T. Boese & Beth C. McCain, Why Thompson is Wrong: Misuse of the False Claims Act to Enforce the Anti–Kickback Act, 51 Ala. L. Rev. 1 (1999); Pamela H. Bucy, Growing Pains: Using the False Claims Act to Combat Health Care Fraud, 51 Ala. L. Rev. 57, 78–79 (1999); Robert Salcido, Mixing Oil and Water: The Government's Mistaken Use of the Medicare Anti–Kickback Statute in False Claims Act Prosecutions, 6 Annals Health L. 105 (1997). Another issue is whether the government has suffered any injury where no

overcharge, upcoding or false billing occurred. On remand the district court in *Thompson* noted that it was not necessary for the government to prove that it had sustained damages, but also found that the government had incurred administrative and costs as a result of the false claim. United States ex rel. Thompson v. Columbia/HCA Healthcare Corporation, 20 F.Supp.2d 1017, 1047 (S.D. Tex. 1998). Is the use of the False Claims Act to enforce violations of the anti-kickback statute and regulations an example of government overreaching? Should qui tam relators be permitted to use the statute in this way as well, even when the government has elected not to pursue technical violations of the anti-kickback law?

Problem: Enforcement of the Fraud and Abuse Law by Private Parties

Several years ago, Drs. Vaughn, Canseco and Clemens leased space from Yawkey Community Hospital. The hospital gave each doctor discounts from prevailing market rates in the rent it charged them. Although the leases allowed for periodic increases based on the Consumer Price Index, the hospital did not enforce this provision on a regular basis. The doctors' testimony reveals a lack of awareness that the rents were below market rates and all deny having any understanding that referrals would be expected of them. Testimony of members of the hospital's board indicates that they believed that physicians located in nearby offices were more likely to refer to Yawkey Hospital; that the hospital's decision not to raise rents was based on a desire to increase physician "loyalty;" and that below-market rental rates were established in order to encourage patient referrals.

Accepting as true the testimony of all parties, has the hospital violated the fraud and abuse laws? Assume now that Fenway Health System has acquired Yawkey Community Hospital. Can Fenway Health Systems walk away from the leases arguing they are invalid because they violate federal and state anti-kickback laws?

E. STATUTORY EXCEPTIONS, SAFE HARBORS AND FRAUD ALERTS

The fraud and abuse statute contains several common sense exceptions. For example, discounts or reductions in price obtained by providers of services, literally proscribed by the language of the statute, are permitted if properly disclosed and reflected in the claimed costs or charges of the provider. Likewise, amounts paid by employers to employees and rebates obtained by group purchasing organizations are exempted under specified circumstances. (The employment exception is discussed in Note 2 following U.S. v. Starks, supra.) The Health Insurance Portability and Accountability Act of 1996 added an important new exception for "risk-sharing" arrangements. As described below, this exception is designed to answer criticisms that the law unreasonably deters arrangements such as capitated payments that foster delivery of cost-effective care and pose no substantial risk of overutilization, the key concern of the anti-kickback rules.

In addition to these statutory exceptions, the Secretary of HHS, acting pursuant to Congressional directive, has promulgated so-called "Safe Harbor" regulations to describe conduct that is not criminal under the fraud and abuse laws. This is a somewhat unusual provision in that it permits an administrative agency to designate conduct otherwise illegal under federal law as not subject to prosecution by the Justice Department. 42 C.F.R. § 1001.952. The total number of safe harbors now stands at twenty-five. Among the more important of the safe harbors are the following:

Rental, Personal Services, and Management Contracts

Three safe harbors for space and equipment rentals and for personal services and management contracts have very similar standards. Leases for space or equipment must be in writing and signed by the parties; must identify the space or equipment covered; must specify when and for how long space or equipment will be used and the precise rental charge for each use if the lease is not for full time use; and must be for at least one year. The amount of rent must be set in advance, must not take into account the volume and value of any referrals or business generated, and, most importantly, must reflect the fair market value of the space or equipment. Fair market value is defined as the value of the property for "general commercial purposes," or "the value of the equipment when obtained from a manufacturer or professional distributor," and cannot take into account the proximity or convenience of the equipment or space to the referral course. The requirements for personal services or management contracts are nearly identical to the rental provisions.

Personal Services and Management Contracts

This provision excepts payments made by a principal to an agent as compensation for the agent's services for written agency agreements of at least one year, provided the agreement specifies and covers all the services that the agent provides during that period. The aggregate compensation for the services must be set in advance, consistent with fair market value in an arms-length transaction, and not take into account the volume or values of any referrals or business otherwise generated between the parties. An agent is defined as any person other than an employee of the principal who has an agreement to perform services for or on behalf of the principal.

Sale of Practice

A limited safe harbor exists to protect sales of practices by retiring physicians. The sale must be completed within one year from the date of the agreement, after which the selling practitioner must no longer be in a professional position to refer Medicare or Medicaid patients or otherwise generate business for the purchasing practitioner. Sale options are not permitted unless they are completely performed within a year. The increasingly common practice of hospitals and MSOs purchasing the practices of physicians who thereafter are retained on staff is explicitly not protected by this rule, though a separate safe harbor for physician recruitment currently under consideration may protect some of these activities, and buying out a physician for a flat payment and then later employing the physician may be permissible.

Practitioner Recruitment

A practitioner recruitment safe harbor protects recruitment efforts by hospitals and entities located in government-specified health professional shortage areas (HPSAs). It permits payments or other exchanges to induce practitioners relocating from a different geographic area or new practitioners (in practice within their current specialty for less than one year) provided nine conditions are met. Among those conditions are that the agreement be in writing; that at least 75 per cent of the business of the relocated practice come from new patients; that at least 75 per cent of the new practice revenue be generated from the HPSA or other defined underserved areas; that the practitioner not be barred from establishing staff privileges with or referring to other entities; and that benefits and amendments to the contract may not be based on the value or volume of practitioners' referrals.

Safe Harbor for Price Reductions Offered to Eligible Managed Care Organizations

After a lengthy negotiated rulemaking process, the OIG announced two interim final rules to implement the statutory exception governing certain Eligible Managed Care Organizations (EMCOs). The two safe harbors apply to (1) financial arrangements between managed care entities paid by a federal health care program on a capitated basis and individuals or entities agreeing to provide to the manage care entity items or services under a written agreement and (2) financial agreements that, through a risk sharing arrangement, place individuals or entities at "substantial financial risk" for the cost or utilization of the items or services which they are obligated to provide. Recognizing that EMCOs having risk contracts which operate on a capitated rather than fee-for-service basis present little risk of overutilization and increased health program costs, the safe harbor protects price reductions (and other exchanges or remunerations) between eligible MCOs and individuals and entities. The second part of the price reduction safe harbor regulation addresses financial arrangements (subcontracts) between first tier contractors and other individuals or entities, known as downstream contractors.

Referral Agreements for Specialty Services

This safe harbor is designed to reduce any untoward effects that the anti-kickback laws may have on continuity of care and patient access to specialists. It protects any exchange of value among individuals and entities if one provider agrees to refer a patient to another provider for the rendering of a specialty service in exchange for an agreement by the other party to refer that patient back at a later time, as long as neither party may pay the other for the referral, although members of the same group practice may share revenues of the group practice.

Ambulatory Surgery Centers

This safe harbor provides a detailed regulatory scheme that protects returns on an investment interest, such as dividend or interest income, in four kinds of Ambulatory Surgery Centers (ASCs): surgeon-owned ASCs, single-specialty ASCs, multi-specialty ASCs, and hospital/physician ASCs. It does not apply to an ASC located on a hospital's premises that shares operating or recovery room space with the hospital for treatment of the hospital's inpatients or outpatients. Advisory Opinion 03–05, set forth following this note, deals with this Safe Harbor.

Investment Interests

This complex safe harbor provides that there is no violation for returns on "investment interests" including both equity and debt interests in corporations, partnerships and other entities held directly or indirectly through family members or other indirect ownership vehicles. It covers, first, investments in large, publicly-traded entities registered with the SEC and having $50 million in net tangible assets. The investment must also be obtained on terms equally available to the public, the entity must market items and services in the same way to investors and non-investors, and must comply with other requirements. Second, certain investments in small entities are permitted provided no more than 40 percent of the value of the investment interests in each class of investment is held by persons who are in a position to make or influence referrals to, furnish items or services to, or otherwise generate business for the entity. Moreover, no more than 40 percent of the gross revenue of the entity may come from referrals, items or services from investors. A number of other requirements apply including several that are different for active investors and passive investors. The 1999 amendments to this safe harbor allow for higher investment percentages in medically underserved areas. The importance of this safe harbor is limited by the fact that it does not shelter arrangements covered by the Stark Law (discussed in the next section of this chapter) which applies different standards to investments. However, for services not covered by Stark, the safe harbor has continuing importance.

Group Practices

A safe harbor shelters payments (such as dividend or interest income) received in return for investment interests in group practices. 42 C.F.R. § 1001.952(p). It covers business arrangements having centralized decision-making, pooled expenses and revenues, and profit distribution systems "not based on satellite offices operating substantially as if they were separate enterprises or profit centers." Modeled on the Stark exception, it adopts that statute's definition of "group practice" and provides that income from ancillary services must meet the Stark definition of "in-office ancillary services."

Electronic Health Records Arrangements and Electronic Prescribing

Two safe harbors adopted in 2006 establish conditions under which hospitals and certain other entities may (1) donate to physicians interoperable electronic health records (EHR), software, information technology, and training services and (2) provide physicians with hardware, software, or information technology and training services necessary and used solely for electronic prescribing. Substantially identical standards were adopted as exceptions to the Stark Law discussed in the next section.

The electronic prescribing safe harbor covers items and services that are necessary and used solely to transmit and receive electronic prescription information and requires that donated technology comply with standards adopted by the Secretary of HHS. Protected donors and recipients are: (1) hospitals to members of their medical staffs; (2) group practices to physician members; (3) Prescription Drug Plan sponsors and Medicare Advantage organizations to network pharmacist and pharmacies, and prescribing health care professionals. There is no limit on the value of donations but donors may not select recipients using any method that takes into account the volume or value of referrals from the recipient or other business generated between the parties.

The EHR safe harbor protects arrangements involving electronic health records software or information technology and training services necessary and used predominately to create, maintain, transmit, or receive electronic health records. While neither hardware nor software with a core functionality other than electronic health records is covered, software packages may include functions related to patient administration such as clinical support. Protected donors are individuals and entities that provide covered services to any Federal health care program and health plans. Donors may not select recipients using any method that takes into account directly the volume or value of referrals from the recipient or other business between the parties and while there is no limit on the aggregate value of technology that may qualify for safe harbor protection, recipients must pay 15 percent of the donor's cost for the donated technology.

A wide variety of other arrangements are covered by safe harbors, including subsidies for obstetrical malpractice insurance subsidies, and waivers of copayments and deductibles for inpatient hospital care and group purchasing organizations. Many of these safe harbors are narrowly drawn and afford only limited protection despite sometimes broader coverage sometimes implied by their titles. Moreover, safe harbor protection requires compliance with every requirement of all applicable safe harbors and the OIG has refused to adopt a standard of "substantial compliance" or to declaim intention to pursue "technical" or de minimis violations. See 56 Fed. Reg. 35,953, 35,957 (July 29, 1991). At the same time however, the safe harbors are not standards; conduct falling outside their boundaries may still pass muster under the intent-based statutory standard.

Another important source of guidance in this area are the fraud alerts issued by the Office of Inspector General of HHS. Dep't of Health & Human Services, Office of the Inspector General, Fraud Alerts, available at http://www.oig.hhs.gov/fraud/fraudalerts.html#1. These alerts set forth the OIG's interpretation of the statute as applied in certain situations and are intended to encourage individuals to report suspected violations to the government. Most notable among these is the Special Fraud Alert on Joint Venture Arrangements issued in 1989. The alert identified "questionable features" of certain joint ventures such as where investors chosen are potential referral sources; the investment shares of physician investors are proportionate to the volume of referrals; physicians are encouraged to refer to the entity or to divest their interest if referrals fall below an acceptable level or if physicians become unable to refer; the joint venture is structured as a "shell;" or the amounts of the investment are disproportionately small and returns disproportionately large. See also Response to Request for Guidance Regarding Certain Physician Investments in Medical Device Industries (Oct. 6, 2006) (confirming that 1989 Joint Venture alert is current guidance and noting application to investments in entities manufacturing medical devices). In a Special Advisory Bulletin, the OIG supplemented its 1989 Alert and identified what it termed "suspect contractual joint ventures" as an area of concern. 68 Fed. Reg. 23,148 (Apr. 30, 2003). The OIG's concern focuses on questionable contractual arrangements in which a health care provider in one line of business (the "Owner") expands into a related health care business by contracting with an existing provider of a related item or service (the "Manager/Supplier") to provide the new item or service to the Owner's existing patient population, including federal health care program patients. The Manager/Supplier not only manages the new line of business, but may also supply it with inventory, employees, space, billing, and other services. In other words, the Owner contracts out substantially the entire operation of the related line of business to the Manager/Supplier—otherwise a potential competitor—receiving in return the profits of the business as remuneration for its federal program referrals. Two examples given in the Bulletin:

- A hospital establishes a subsidiary to provide DME. The new subsidiary enters into a contract with an existing DME company to operate the new subsidiary and to provide the new subsidiary with DME inventory. The existing DME company already provides DME services comparable to those provided by the new hospital DME subsidiary and bills insurers and patients for them.

- A DME company sells nebulizers to federal health care beneficiaries. A mail order pharmacy suggests that the DME company form its own mail order pharmacy to provide nebulizer drugs. Through a management agreement, the mail order pharmacy runs the DME company's pharmacy, providing personnel, equipment, and space. The existing mail order pharmacy also sells all nebulizer drugs to the DME company's pharmacy for its inventory.

In what way might these arrangements facilitate conduct prohibited by the anti-kickback laws?

Other alerts have covered topics such as physician-to-hospital referrals, identifying as "suspect incentive arrangements" the payment of incentives for each referral; free or discounted office space, equipment or office staff training; minimum income guarantees; low interest loans or loans subject to forgiveness based on referrals; payment of physicians' travel expenses to conferences; payment of physicians' continuing education; disproportionately low health insurance rates for physicians; payment for services at above-market rates; prescription drug marketing schemes, nursing home reimbursement and arrangements with hospices, and rental of space in physician offices. An important source of guidance for attorneys is the Advisory Opinions issued by the Office of the Inspector General at HHS. While these opinions disclaim having any binding effect, they occasionally signal the agency's posture on controversial arrangements.

RE: OIG ADVISORY OPINION NO. 03–5

(Issued February 6, 2003).

Dear [name redacted]:

We are writing in response to your request for an advisory opinion regarding an ambulatory surgery center (an "ASC") that would be jointly owned by a hospital and a multi-specialty group practice that has a substantial number of physician members who would not personally use the ASC (the "Proposed Arrangement"). Specifically, you have inquired whether the Proposed Arrangement would constitute grounds for the imposition of sanctions under the exclusion authority at section 1128(b)(7) of the Social Security Act (the "Act") or the civil monetary penalty provision at section 1128A(a)(7) of the Act, as those sections relate to the commission of acts described in section 1128B(b) of the Act.

* * *

I. FACTUAL BACKGROUND

[Company X] (the "Surgical Center") is an [state redacted] ("State") limited liability company formed for the purpose of planning, developing, and operating an ASC that will be certified by Medicare under 42 C.F.R. part 416. [Company Y], an acute care hospital (the "Hospital"), owns 49% of the Surgical Center, and [Company Z], a multi-specialty clinic (the "Group") owns 51% of the Surgical Center.[8] For each investor, the return on the Surgical Center investment will be directly proportional to the amount of capital that the investor contributed. The Surgical Center will maintain an open medical staff. It will be located on land owned by the Hospital and leased to the Surgical Center pursuant to a written lease.

The Group has fifty-two shareholders (the "Group Shareholders"), each of whom is a licensed physician and an employee of the Group. Each Group Shareholder owns one share of the Group's stock, and any dividends paid by the Group are divided equally among the Group Shareholders. In addition, the Group employs other physicians who do not own Group stock (the "Group Associates") and other health care professionals, such as physical therapists, optometrists, and licensed nurse practitioners. Group Shareholders and Group Associates are collectively referred to herein as "Group Physicians." Some Group Physicians are surgeons; however, most are not. For example, there are fourteen family practitioners, eleven internists, six pediatricians, five obstetricians/gynecologists, two general surgeons, three orthopedic surgeons, and two ophthalmologists. The Surgical Center has certified that the salaries, bonuses, and any other forms of employment-related remuneration payable to Group Physicians will not take into account the physicians' referrals of patients to the Surgical Center or the volume of surgical procedures performed by the physicians at the Surgical Center or elsewhere.

The Hospital is wholly owned by a nonprofit corporation that is also the sole owner of two other hospitals. The Hospital employs forty-two physicians, including eight family practitioners, twelve internal medicine practitioners, eight obstetricians/gynecologists, and two pediatricians. Currently, the Hospital has eight operating suites for both inpatient and outpatient surgery, and physicians employed by the Group perform approximately 25% of all surgeries performed at the Hospital.

II. LEGAL ANALYSIS

A. Law

* * *

The Department of Health and Human Services has promulgated safe harbor regulations that define practices that are not subject to the anti-

---

8. The Surgical Center has two classes of members: the voting, Class A Members, consisting solely of the Hospital and the Group and the non-voting, Class B Members, each of whom must be either a State-licensed physi-

cian eligible for credentialing at the Surgical Center or a State legal entity with a majority of its owners being physicians who meet the foregoing requirements. No Class B memberships have been sold.

kickback statute because such practices would be unlikely to result in fraud or abuse. *See* 42 C.F.R. § 1001.952. The safe harbors set forth specific conditions that, if met, assure entities involved of not being prosecuted or sanctioned for the arrangement qualifying for the safe harbor. However, safe harbor protection is afforded only to those arrangements that precisely meet all of the conditions set forth in the safe harbor.

The safe harbor for investment interests in ambulatory surgical centers jointly owned by hospitals and physicians, 42 C.F.R. § 1001.952(r)(4), is relevant to the Proposed Arrangement.[9] One condition of the hospital-physician ASC safe harbor is that investing physicians who are in a position to refer patients to the ASC can only invest as individuals who meet the requirements for surgeon-owned ASCs, single-specialty ASCs, or multi-specialty ASCs set forth at 42 C.F.R. § 1001.952(r)(1), (r)(2), or (r)(3), as applicable, or as group practices composed of such physicians or surgical group practices.[10] Since the Surgical Center's investing physicians are investing through a multi-specialty group practice, for safe harbor protection the group practice (*i.e.*, the Group) must meet all the requirements of the group practice safe harbor at 42 C.F.R. § 1001.952(p) and the group practice must be composed of physicians who meet both the one-third practice income test at 42 C.F.R. § 1001.952(r)(3)(ii) and the one-third practice test at 42 C.F.R. § 1001.952(r)(3)(iii).[11]

B. Analysis

Surgical center joint ventures that include physician-investors in a position to generate surgical business are susceptible to fraud and abuse. Notwithstanding, in recognition that some physician-owned ASC ventures may be beneficial to the federal programs and their beneficiaries, the Department issued a narrow safe harbor for physician-owned ASCs that meet criteria carefully tailored to mitigate the risks of fraud and abuse. With respect to physician-investors, the safe harbor is carefully circumscribed to apply only to physicians who are unlikely to use the investment as a vehicle for profiting from their referrals to other physicians using the ASC. Accordingly, safe harbor protection is limited to physician-investors who actually use the ASC on a regular basis as part of their medical practices or who practice the same specialty as other physician-investors and are therefore unlikely to refer substantial business to "competing" physician-investors when they can earn the fees themselves.

9. In cases, such as the instant case, where the ASC is located in space owned by the hospital, the space rental safe harbor, 42 C.F.R. § 1001.952(b), is also relevant.

10. The terms "group practice" and "surgical group practice" are defined at 42 C.F.R. § 1001.952(r)(5).

11. Under the one-third practice income test, 42 C.F.R. § 1001.952(r)(3)(ii), at least one-third of each physician investor's medical practice income from all sources for the previous fiscal year or previous 12–month period must be derived from the physician's performance of procedures. Under the one-third practice test, 42 C.F.R. § 1001.952(r)(3)(iii), at least one-third of the procedures performed by each physician investor for the previous fiscal year or previous 12–month period must be performed at the investment entity. The term "procedures" is defined at 42 C.F.R. § 1001.952(r)(5).

The majority of the Group Physicians fit neither category. Since the Group is a multi-specialty group, there is a substantial likelihood of cross-specialty referrals for services performed in the ASC. Moreover, few of the Group Physicians will actually use the Surgical Center on a regular basis as part of their medical practice. In other words, the Proposed Arrangement would allow those Group Physicians for whom the Surgical Center is not an extension of their office practices to profit from their referrals to the Surgical Center or to their partners who perform procedures there. In this respect, the Proposed Arrangement poses the same risks as an ASC owned directly by surgeons and primary care physicians in the same community. In these circumstances, the fact that the ownership of the ASC is held indirectly through a group practice whose membership includes both surgeons and other potential referring physicians does not reduce the risk that the venture may be used to reward referrals.

Accordingly, we cannot conclude that the Proposed Arrangement poses a minimal risk of fraud and abuse.

III. CONCLUSION

Based on the facts certified in your request for an advisory opinion and supplemental submissions, we conclude that the Proposed Arrangement could potentially generate prohibited remuneration under the anti-kickback statute and that the OIG could potentially impose administrative sanctions on [Company X] under sections 1128(b)(7) or 1128A(a)(7) of the Act (as those sections relate to the commission of acts described in section 1128B(b) of the Act) in connection with the Proposed Arrangement. Any definitive conclusion regarding the existence of an anti-kickback violation requires a determination of the parties' intent, which determination is beyond the scope of the advisory opinion process.

IV. LIMITATIONS

[This advisory opinion has no application to, and cannot be relied upon by, any other individual or entity; may not be introduced into evidence in any matter involving an entity or individual that is not a requestor of this opinion; is applicable only to the statutory provisions specifically noted above and will not bind or obligate any agency other than the U.S. Department of Health and Human Services; is limited in scope to the specific arrangement described in this letter and has no applicability to other arrangements, even those which appear similar in nature or scope. No opinion is expressed herein regarding the liability of any party under the False Claims Act or other legal authorities for any improper billing, claims submission, cost reporting, or related conduct.]

Sincerely,

/s/

Lewis Morris, Chief Counsel to the Inspector General

Notes and Questions

1. Can you identify the risks associated with physician ownership and operation of ASC's? What are the potential benefits? How do the Safe Harbors attempt to strike a balance between these considerations?

2. The OIG issued 120 advisory opinions between January 1, 2001 and October 31, 2007. Dep't of Health and Human Services, Office of Inspector General, Advisory Opinions, available at http://www.oig.hhs.gov/fraud/advisory opinions/opinions.html. These opinions usually conclude that the proposed conduct falls within a safe harbor, determine that the activity can be undertaken with certain qualifications, or find prohibited remuneration but decline to subject the requester to sanctions. Many involve "white hat" issues that may involve prohibited remuneration but are deemed not to present significant risk to Medicare program objectives. See, e.g., Advisory Opinion No. 01–19 (Nov. 14, 2001) available at: http://www.oig.hhs.gov/fraud/docs/advisoryopinions/2001/ao01–19.pdf (involving a donation of free office space to an entity that provides free end-of-life services to patients with terminal illnesses). Although the vast majority of advisory opinions address whether a violation of the anti-kickback statute is present, a few discuss possible inducements to reduce or limit services. Waivers of co-payment are among the most frequently addressed topics, followed by proposed donations (including restocking of ambulance supplies), and joint ventures.

Note on Gainsharing and the Anti–Kickback Laws

An area of continuing controversy involving fraud and abuse laws has been hospital "gainsharing" programs. Broadly defined, the term refers to "an arrangement in which a hospital gives physicians a share of any reduction in the hospital's costs attributable in part to the physicians' efforts." Hearing on Gainsharing Before the Subcomm. on Health of the H. Comm. on Ways and Means, 109th Cong. (2005) (testimony of Lewis Morris, Chief Counsel to the Inspector General, U.S. Dep't of Health and Human Services)[hereinafter Morris Testimony], available at http://waysandmeans.house.gov/hearings.asp?formmode= view & id=3828. Some gainsharing practices are narrowly-targeted, such as those giving physicians a financial incentive to reduce the use of specific medical devices and supplies, to switch to specific products that are less expensive, or to adopt specific clinical practices or protocols that reduce costs. More comprehensive—and legally problematic—arrangements include those that offer the physician payments to reduce total average costs per case below target amounts. Of special concern for the government have been "black box" gainsharing arrangements that give physicians money for overall cost savings without knowing what specific actions physicians are taking to generate those savings. See Office of Inspector General, Dep't Health & Human Services, Special Advisory Bulletin: Gainsharing Arrangements and CMPs for Hospital Payments to Physicians to Reduce or Limit Services to Beneficiaries (July 1999), available at http://oig.hhs.gov/fraud/docs/ alertsandbulletins/gainsh.htm.

It can readily be seen that gainsharing arrangements may help align physician incentives with those of a hospital and thereby promote hospital cost reductions. Indeed, as discussed in Chapter 8, prospective payment under Medicare provides a strong impetus for hospitals to find a way to induce independent physicians to adopt practices that reduce costs. See Richard Saver, Squandering the Gain: Gainsharing and the Continuing Dilemma of Physician Financial Incentives, 98 Nw. U.L. Rev. 145, 146 (2003). At the same time, such payments may encourage physicians to use a particular provider, implicating concerns that underlie the anti-kickback law and the Stark Law (discussed in the next section of this chapter). Finally, gainsharing arrangements may serve as an inducement to deny services that are medically necessary. This risk is directly addressed by the Civil Monetary Penalty Law (CMP), 42 U.S.C. § 1320a–7a(b), which prohibits a hospital from "knowingly making a payment, directly or indirectly, to a physician as an inducement to reduce or limit items or services" furnished to Medicare or Medicaid beneficiaries under a physician's direct care.

The Office of Inspector General has been extremely wary of gainsharing arrangements, but has recently issued a series of favorable advisory opinions in which it indicated it would not challenge certain carefully-tailored proposals. Office of Inspector General, Dep't Health & Human Services, Advisory Opinions 05–01 through 05–06 (2005), available at http://oig.hhs.gov/fraud/advisoryopinions/opinions.html. Notably, the OIG's General Counsel has cautioned that despite these rulings, "absent a change in law, it is not currently possible for gainsharing arrangements to be structured without implicating the fraud and abuse laws." Morris Testimony, supra. In each letter the OIG stressed the significance of safeguards and characteristics of the arrangement that alleviated its concerns. Three important factors guide the OIG's analysis: accountability, quality controls and safeguards against payments for referrals. To ensure accountability, OIG favors transparent arrangements that "clearly and separately identify the actions that will result in cost savings," thus permitting both objective reviews by the government (and by the malpractice system) and a more complete understanding by patients and their doctors. Morris Testimony, supra. To ensure that quality of care is not impaired, the OIG deems it important to have qualified, outside, independent parties "perform a medical expert review of each cost-savings measure to assess the potential impact on patient care" and to establish baseline thresholds based on historic data that set limits on reductions of service so they do not impair patient safety. Where product standardization incentives are involved, the OIG looks favorably on assurances that individual physicians will still have available the same selection of devices and can make a case-by-case determination of the most appropriate device for the patient.

Finally, the OIG's advisory opinions insist on certain safeguards to prevent gainsharing from being used to reward or induce patient referrals. Consider the following limitations on how payments are calculated and distributed to physicians contained in the advisory opinions:

- Limiting participation to physicians already on the hospital's medical staff;
- Limiting the amount, duration, and scope of the payments;
- Distributing the gainsharing profits on a per capita basis to all physicians in a single-specialty group practice;
- Basing cost sharing payments on all surgeries, regardless of payor, with procedures not being disproportionately performed on Medicare or Medicaid patients.

What policies of the anti-kickback law does each safeguard serve and how does it do so?

While many support steps to legalize gainsharing on a wider scale, there is still considerable uncertainty about the circumstances in which gainsharing should be permitted and what regulations are needed to assure quality and avoid the risks inherent in payment for referrals. The DRA 2005 mandated that HHS establish a qualified gainsharing demonstration program under which the Secretary shall approve up to six demonstration projects to test and evaluate methodologies and arrangements between hospitals and physicians. See DRA 5007 Medicare Hospital Gainsharing Solicitation, http://www:cms.hhs.gov/DemoProjectsEval Rpts/downloads/DRA 5007 Solicitation.pdf. What information would you recommend be gathered to determine whether new regulations governing gainsharing arrangements are needed?

Problem: Sorting It Out

When you have completed your analysis of the problems at the beginning of this section, reconstruct the arrangements there presented to accomplish as substantially as possible the legitimate goals of the parties to the transaction without offending the fraud and abuse laws.

Next, consider the following problems affecting the formation of integrating organizations discussed in Chapter 10. For each of the scenarios below, explain how the anti-kickback law and any relevant safe harbor might apply and what steps should be taken to reduce legal risks.

- A hospital-controlled MSO provides staff, administrative services and equipment rentals to member physicians at "cost" or at levels below the fees it charges to non-members.

- An Integrated Delivery System purchases the tangible assets and patient records of a physician practice and pays on a five-year installment arrangement. The physicians work as employees at the hospital.

- A hospital-controlled MSO leases office space to its member physicians pursuant to a signed, written agreement for a five-year term. The lease terms reflect the fair market value of the leased space. In each of the first three years, the MSO has lost money.

- A PHO is jointly owned (50–50 equity split) by a hospital and its physicians. The hospital contributes 80% of the PHO's capital.

III. THE STARK LAW: A TRANSACTIONAL APPROACH TO SELF–REFERRALS

An alternative approach to dealing with fraud and abuse is to list and describe exhaustively transactions that are alternatively legitimate or illegitimate under the law. The Ethics in Patient Referrals Act (commonly referred to as the Stark Law in recognition of the legislation's principal sponsor, Rep. Fortney "Pete" Stark) does just that with respect to physician referrals for certain Medicare-financed services in which the physician (or immediate family member) has a financial interest. Besides making it illegal for physicians to make such referrals, Stark also prohibits any billings for services provided pursuant to illegal referrals. As originally enacted, Stark only applied to referrals for clinical laboratory services. Its reach was significantly expanded by the 1993 Omnibus Budget Reconciliation Act. As a result Stark now applies to services paid for by Medicaid as well as by Medicare and covers eleven "designated health services" (DHS): clinical laboratory services; physical therapy services; occupational therapy services; radiology, including MRI, CAT and ultrasound services; radiation therapy services and supplies; durable medical equipment and supplies; parenteral and enteral nutrients, equipment, and supplies; prosthetics, orthotics, and prosthetic devices; home health services and supplies; outpatient prescription drugs; and inpatient and outpatient hospital services. No payment can be made by Medicare or Medicaid for referrals for such services where the referring physician or member of his family has a financial interest. Any amounts billed in violation of the section must be refunded. Any person knowingly billing or failing to make a refund in violation of the prohibition is subject to a civil fine of $15,000 per item billed and to exclusion.

The Stark legislation responded to increasing evidence that "self-referrals" had become quite common, and quite costly. An OIG study issued in 1989 found that of 2690 physicians who responded to its study, 12 percent had ownership interests and 8 percent had compensation arrangements with businesses to which they referred patients. Office of Inspector General, Financial Arrangements Between Physicians and Health Care Businesses: Report to Congress (1989). It further determined that nationally 25 percent of independent clinical laboratories (ICLs), 27 percent of independent laboratories, and 8 percent of durable medical equipment suppliers were owned at least in part by referring physicians. Beneficiaries treated by physicians who owned or invested in ICLs received 45 percent more clinical laboratory services and 34 percent more services directly from ICLs than beneficiaries in general, resulting in $28 million in additional costs to the Medicare program. Do studies finding high rates of self-referral patterns establish that the additional services provided were unnecessary? Is strong and consistent empirical evidence of higher utilization among self-referring physicians sufficient to justify legislative decisions to broadly proscribe the practice?

Note that, subject to the exceptions discussed below, Stark adopts a "bright line" test. Unlike Medicare fraud and abuse laws, there is no requirement that the conduct involve the knowing and willful receipt of a kickback: if no exception applies, the law has been violated. However, as we will see, CMS has promulgated numerous exceptions and the Federal Register contains hundreds of pages of detailed regulations and commentary purporting to clarify or simplify compliance with the law.

A. SCOPE OF THE PROHIBITION

Stark I and II prohibit physicians who have (or whose immediate family member has) a "financial relationship" with a provider of designated health services from making "referrals" of Medicare or Medicaid patients to such providers for purposes of receiving any of the eleven "designated health services." The key terms are defined in 42 U.S.C. § 1395nn as follows:

(a) Prohibitions of certain referrals

* * *

(2) Financial relationship specified

For purposes of this section, a financial relationship of a physician (or an immediate family member of such physician) with an entity specified in this paragraph is—

(A) except as provided in subsections (c) and (d) of this section, an ownership or investment interest in the entity, or

(B) except as provided in subsection (e) of this section, a compensation arrangement (as defined in subsection (h)(1) of this section) between the physician (or an immediate family member of such physician) and the entity.

An ownership or investment interest described in subparagraph (A) may be through equity, debt, or other means and includes an interest in an entity that holds an ownership or investment interest in any entity providing the designated health service.

* * *

(h) Definitions and special rules

For purposes of this section:

(1) Compensation arrangement; remuneration

(A) The term "compensation arrangement" means any arrangement involving any remuneration between a physician (or an immediate family member of such physician) and an entity other than an arrangement involving only remuneration described in subparagraph (C).

(B) The term "remuneration" includes any remuneration, directly or indirectly, overtly or covertly, in cash or in kind.

* * *

(5) Referral; referring physician

(A) Physicians' services

Except as provided in subparagraph (C), in the case of an item or service for which payment may be made under part B of this subchapter, the request by a physician for the item or service, including the request by a physician for a consultation with another physician (and any test or procedure ordered by, or to be performed by (or under the supervision of) that other physician), constitutes a "referral" by a "referring physician."

* * *

(6) Designated health services

The term "designated health services" means any of the following items or services:

(A) Clinical laboratory services.

(B) Physical therapy services.

(C) Occupational therapy services.

(D) Radiology services, including magnetic resonance imaging, computerized axial tomography scans, and ultrasound services.

(E) Radiation therapy services and supplies.

(F) Durable medical equipment and supplies.

(G) Parenteral and enteral nutrients, equipment, and supplies.

(H) Prosthetics, orthotics, and prosthetic devices and supplies.

(I) Home health services.

(J) Outpatient prescription drugs.

(K) Inpatient and outpatient hospital services.

Notes and Questions

1. Note several things about these provisions. First, recall that the principal problem identified by academic studies that led to the enactment of Stark I was excessive and perhaps inappropriate referrals by physicians to entities in which they had an ownership interest. Why did Congress extend the law's reach beyond "ownership and investment interests?" Was this a necessary or wise policy choice? Second, Stark II reaches arrangements in which the flow of money is reversed from the normal self-referral pattern, i.e., the physician pays the entity for services provided. Why should such arrangements be outlawed? Third, consider the broad sweep of the term "referral" as used in the Act. Suppose Dr. Gillespe requests a consultation from Dr. Demento who in turn orders a lab test and physical therapy for the patient. For what referrals is Dr. Gillespe responsible?

2. Complying with the Stark law may pose problems for integrated organizations. Consider a joint venture PHO entity which is owned by staff physicians and a hospital in which the PHO will negotiate and administer managed care contracts for the physicians and the hospital. Assume the physicians have been given 50 percent ownership in the entity even though the bulk of the start-up costs were paid by the hospital. Do the physicians have an ownership or investment interest in the hospital? Is there a compensation arrangement? The answer is that no ownership or investment interest is present because the participating physicians have an ownership interest in the PHO, not the hospital to which they refer, and the PHO has no ownership interest in the hospital. A compensation arrangement may well exist because physicians may receive an indirect form of remuneration when, after an HMO contract is secured by the PHO, they begin to refer patients to the hospital. While conceivably certain exceptions might apply, the arrangement is obviously risky. See Leonard C. Homer, How New Federal Laws Prohibiting Physician Self–Referrals Affect Integrated Delivery Systems, 11 HealthSpan 21 (Apr. 1994).

3. Strong criticisms have been lodged against Stark. Organized medicine argues that the law is too complex and needlessly duplicative of other laws affecting self-referrals. Moreover, opponents assert that the law goes far beyond prohibiting physician ownership of facilities and invites governmental "micromanagement" of evolving network structures. Even Representative Stark has asked the Institute of Medicine to study ways to improve and simplify the statute. Medicare: Stark Asks Institute of Medicine to Form Working Group on Self–Referral Laws, Health Care Daily (BNA) (July 28, 1998). On the other side, the law has been defended as a pragmatic legislative choice that avoids the pitfalls of case-by-case litigation over issues of intent or reasonableness while unambiguously barring the most risk-prone referrals and permitting the most efficiency-enhancing arrangements. One proposal, vetoed by President Clinton in 1995, would have eliminated the law's ban on "compensation arrangements." Would confining Stark Law's coverage to ownership and investment interests capture the most problematic relationships, or as Representative Stark has opined, would it create a "loophole you can drive an Armored Division through?"

B. EXCEPTIONS

The Stark anti-referral law is an example of what is sometimes called an "exceptions bill." It sweepingly prohibits self-referrals but then legitimizes a large number of specific arrangements. Stark's exceptions are of three kinds: (1) those applicable to ownership or investment financial relationships; (2)

those applicable to compensation arrangements; and (3) generic exceptions that apply to all financial arrangements.

Many of the exceptions cover self-referral arrangements that pose little risk of abuse. For example, the statute rules out liability where referring physicians' incentives are controlled in some way, as with prepaid health plans; or where other circumstances reduce the risk of excess utilization, such as where the physician is an employee of the entity to which the referral is made, has a personal services contract or a space or equipment rental that meets commercial reasonableness tests or engages in isolated, one-time transactions with the entity. One notable exception, the "whole hospital exception," 42 U.S.C. 1395nn(e)d(3) which allows referring physicians who are "authorized to provide services at a hospital" to invest in that hospital, (but not "in a subdivision" thereof), gave ruse to the specialty hospital phenomenon discussed in Chapter 10. Perhaps the most important category, however, involves situations in which the physician is part of a group practice that is directly involved in providing the service. These latter provisos, the ancillary services and group practice exceptions, which do not necessarily involve circumstances that reduce the threat of overutilization, seem primarily designed to encourage the integration of practice among physicians.

Problem: Space and Equipment Rentals, Physician Recruitment

The Stark Law covers much of the same conduct as the bribe and kickback prohibition, but the legislation has its own exceptions that are worded somewhat differently. How does your analysis of problems 1 and 4 at pages 703–704 change under the exceptions reproduced below?

42 U.S.C. § 1395nn.

(e) Exceptions relating to other compensation arrangements

The following shall not be considered to be a compensation arrangement described in subsection (a)(2)(B) of this section:

(1) Rental of office space; rental of equipment

(A) Office space

Payments made by a lessee to a lessor for the use of premises if—

(i) the lease is set out in writing, signed by the parties, and specifies the premises covered by the lease,

(ii) the space rented or leased does not exceed that which is reasonable and necessary for the legitimate business purposes of the lease or rental and is used exclusively by the lessee when being used by the lessee, * * *

(iii) the lease provides for a term of rental or lease for at least 1 year,

(iv) the rental charges over the term of the lease are set in advance, are consistent with fair market value, and are not determined in a manner that takes into account the volume or value of any referrals or other business generated between the parties,

(v) the lease would be commercially reasonable even if no referrals were made between the parties, and

(vi) the lease meets such other requirements as the Secretary may impose by regulation as needed to protect against program or patient abuse.

* * *

(3) Personal service arrangements

[Certain personal service contracts are permitted if they meet certain conditions, including the condition that compensation not be related to the volume or value of referrals.]

* * *

(5) Physician recruitment

In the case of remuneration which is provided by a hospital to a physician to induce the physician to relocate to the geographic area served by the hospital in order to be a member of the medical staff of the hospital, if—

(A) the physician is not required to refer patients to the hospital,

(B) the amount of the remuneration under the arrangement is not determined in a manner that takes into account (directly or indirectly) the volume or value of any referrals by the referring physician, and

(C) the arrangement meets such other requirements as the Secretary may impose by regulation as needed to protect against program or patient abuse.

Note on Fair Market Value

The meaning of "fair market value" is often critical for determining the legality of business arrangements under both Stark and the Anti–Kickback law. For example, in United States ex rel. Goodstein v. McLaren Regional Med. Ctr., 202 F. Supp. 2d 671 (E.D. Mich. 2002), a qui tam action in which the government intervened, the issue was whether the defendant medical center had paid physicians illegal remuneration disguised as a lease agreement for the office building owned by the physicians' limited liability company. Because the physician defendants referred Medicare patients to the medical center and operated their practice out of the leased offices, and the payments allegedly violated both Stark and the anti-kickback statutes, the government asserted that false claims were involved. The court rejected the contention that the amount of rent paid was excessive, concluding that the lease agreement was an arms length transaction and that the lease rate set forth in the agreement was consistent with fair market value. Id. at 675. The court reasoned that defendants' expert testimony was sufficiently grounded on facts or data, was a product of reliable principles and methods, and reliably applied those principles to the facts in evidence. Id. at 679. Despite the fact that their appraisals were prepared in response to litigation, defendants won the "battle of experts" because of defects in the government's case, including the failure of its witnesses to consider certain comparables and their inconsistent application of valuation methodology. Moreover, the court held that the lease rate was not determined in a manner that took into account the value of potential patient referrals. Id. at 686. Do you find this holding controversial in view of the fact that the medical center had insisted on non-compete provisions and retained the right to vacate the leased space if the physician group ever moved out of the building (which the government had claimed "could have deprived [the medical center] of capturing a 'steady flow' of patient referrals)"? What if an arrangement satisfies the fair market value test, but the arrangement was nevertheless "influenced by the value or volume of referrals," e.g., a hospital chooses to enter into a lease with physicians at FMV, but decided to do so because it would result in referrals. For a discussion of this aspect of *McClaran*, see David M. Deaton, What is "Safe" about the Government's Recent Interpretation of the Anti–Kickback Statute Safe Harbors? . . . And Since When Was Stark an Intent–Based Statute?, 36 J. Health L. 549 (2003).

In the context of hospitals acquiring physician practices, the future revenue stream from referrals by the acquired physicians is almost invariably an important factor for a hospital deciding whether it will buy the practice. Yet the anti-kickback law squarely prohibits any excess payment that could be considered "remuneration" for such referrals. Hence, it is necessary to separate out the value of referrals before ascertaining the fair market value of the practice. In United States ex rel. Obert–Hong v. Advocate Health Care, 211 F. Supp. 2d 1045, 1049 n.2 (N.D. Ill. 2002), a district court acknowledged the difficulty in doing so:

> We note that fair market value here may differ from traditional economic valuation formulae. Normally, we would expect the acquisition price to account for potential revenues from future referrals. Because the Anti–Kickback Act prohibits any inducement for those referrals, however, they must be excluded from any calculation of fair value here. See 42 C.F.R. §§ 1001.952(b) and (c). There is, nonetheless, some value that would be considered fair and would comply with the statute.

The court went on to find the complaint failed to allege any facts such as what assets were acquired, their purported value, or the amount actually paid, from which it could draw such an inference that the hospital's payment exceeded fair market value. Id. at 1049. What, then, is the value of the practice to the hospital?

The court also rejected the claim that the requirement (in their employment contracts) that the doctors selling their practices refer their patients to defendant hospitals was, by definition, an inducement. It noted that both "[t]he Stark and Anti–Kickback statutes are designed to remove economic incentives from medical referrals, not to regulate typical hospital-physician employment relationships . . . [and] [b]oth statutes explicitly include employee exceptions." Id. at 1050.

Problem: Group Practices

Drs. Chung, Snyder, Williams, Mendez, Patel, and Jones each operate independent solo practices. All have offices within a three square mile area, but none share offices with each other. Several years ago, they formed a joint venture to provide a variety of laboratory services to their patients. Their attorney has now informed them that their joint venture violates the prohibitions of the Stark legislation. He has suggested that they consider forming a group practice to operate the laboratory. What steps must they take to form a group practice that will permit them to operate a laboratory together under the relevant language of revised 42 U.S.C. § 1395nn?

42 U.S.C. § 1395nn:

(b) General exceptions to both ownership and compensation arrangement prohibitions

[The self-referral prohibitions] of this section shall not apply in the following cases:

(1) Physicians' services

In the case of physicians' services * * * provided personally by (or under the personal supervision of) another physician in the same group practice (as defined in subsection (h)(4) of this section) as the referring physician.

(2) In-office ancillary services

In the case of services (other than durable medical equipment (excluding infusion pumps) and parenteral and enteral nutrients, equipment, and supplies)—

(A) that are furnished—

(i) personally by the referring physician, personally by a physician who is a member of the same group practice as the referring physician, or personally by individuals who are directly supervised by the physician or by another physician in the group practice, and

(ii)(I) in a building in which the referring physician (or another physician who is a member of the same group practice) furnishes physicians' services unrelated to the furnishing of designated health services, or

(II) in the case of a referring physician who is a member of a group practice, in another building which is used by the group practice—

(aa) for the provision of some or all of the group's clinical laboratory services, or

(bb) for the centralized provision of the group's designated health services (other than clinical laboratory services), unless the Secretary determines other terms and conditions under which the provision of such services does not present a risk of program or patient abuse, and

(B) that are billed by the physician performing or supervising the services, by a group practice of which such physician is a member under a billing number assigned to the group practice, or by an entity that is wholly owned by such physician or such group practice, * * *

* * *

(h)(4)

(A) Definition of group practice

The term "group practice" means a group of 2 or more physicians legally organized as a partnership, professional corporation, foundation, not-for-profit corporation, faculty practice plan, or similar association—

(i) in which each physician who is a member of the group provides substantially the full range of services which the physician routinely provides, including medical care, consultation, diagnosis, or treatment, through the joint use of shared office space, facilities, equipment and personnel,

(ii) for which substantially all of the services of the physicians who are members of the group are provided through the group and are billed under a billing number assigned to the group and amounts so received are treated as receipts of the group,

(iii) in which the overhead expenses of and the income from the practice are distributed in accordance with methods previously determined,

(iv) except as provided in subparagraph (B)(i), in which no physician who is a member of the group directly or indirectly receives compensation based on the volume or value of referrals by the physician,

(v) in which members of the group personally conduct no less than 75 percent of the physician-patient encounters of the group practice, and

(vi) which meets such other standards as the Secretary may impose by regulation.

(B) Special rules

(i) Profits and productivity bonuses

A physician in a group practice may be paid a share of overall profits of the group, or a productivity bonus based on services personally performed or services incident to such personally performed services, so long as the share or bonus is not determined in any manner which is directly related to the volume or value of referrals by such physician.

Note on Stark Regulations

Complex as the statute might seem, it is only the beginning. Practitioners must master hundreds of pages of detailed regulations and commentary that interpret and explain the law. The first wave of regulations came in 1995, a full six years after the passage of Stark I, with the issuance of the final rule governing physician self-referrals under that Act. 60 Fed. Reg. 41,914 (Aug. 14, 1995)(codified at 42 C.F.R. § 411.350). To give one important example, one section clarifies the requirement in the "group practices" exception that "substantially all" of the services of the physicians in the group be provided through the group and that these services be billed under a billing number assigned to the group so that amounts so received are treated as receipts of the group. 42 U.S.C. § 1395nn(h)(A)(ii). The Stark I regulations fix the "substantially all" requirement at 75 percent of all patient care services, as measured by time spent (rather than the dollar value of physician services provided) and as an average for all of the group members during a specific 12–month period. Notably, time spent on physician care services includes time devoted to consultation, diagnosis or "any tasks performed ... that address the medical needs of specific patients." The regulations also define group members as "physicians, partners and full-time and part-time physician contractors and employees during the time they furnish services to patients of the group practice...." 42 C.F.R. § 411.351. Why might these provisions be important to physicians?

In March 2004, CMS published its Stark II "Phase II Regulations" which interpreted many statutory provisions, clarified some of the provisions of the "Phase I Regulations" issued in 2001, and added some new exceptions to the law. 69 Fed. Reg. 15,932 (Mar. 26, 2004). A summary of the changes is found in Sonnenschein Nath & Rosenthal, Stark II, Phase II—Highlights and Preliminary Analysis, 13 Health Law Rep. (BNA) 481 (Apr. 1, 2004). Among the more important provisions are those that define or explain a host of terms including the meaning of "fair market value," "referral," "indirect financial relationship," and, the most vexing of technical terms, "to." Critically important is what falls within the definition of certain designated health services, e.g., are PET scans within the statutory definition of "radiology services, including [MRI and CAT] scans and ultrasound services?" Can CMS include it by adopting a regulation?

Exceptions. The Phase I Regulations added six new exceptions governing compensation arrangements and five new all-purpose exceptions. Phase II added six more compensation exceptions and one all-purpose exception, while deleting one all-purpose exception and clarifying some of the 16 exceptions that preceded Phase I. Among the more important are exceptions for: non-monetary compensation to physicians up to a maximum of $300 per year; incidental benefits, such as free parking, for members of a hospital's medical staff; charitable donations by physicians; compliance training given by a hospital to its medical staff; hospital purchases of medical malpractice insurance for OB–GYNs practicing in a physician shortage area; DHS furnished by academic medical providers (subject to many requirements); risk sharing arrangements involving compensation between managed care organizations or IPAs and physicians furnishing services to enrollees in a plan; free or reduced fee services extended as professional courtesy to members of a physician's office staff; arrangements that have "unavoidably and temporarily fallen out of compliance" with an exception; physician recruitment payments permitted for physicians' "relocation" (defined in the regulations) and isolated transactions, defined now to permit certain installment payments. See Sonnenschein, supra. More recently exceptions have been added allowing entities furnishing DHAs to provide hardware or software used solely for electronic prescription systems and for interoperable electronic health records. These exceptions closely parallel the safeharbors established under the antikickback law described supra at pp. 1070–75. Do these exceptions seem justified? Do they undermine the overarching purposes of the Stark law or are they pragmatic accommodations?

On August 27, 2007, CMS posted the third phase of the final Stark II regulation (Phase III). Though lengthy and replete with detailed prescriptions, the Phase III regulations made relatively few major changes to Phase II and do not create any new exceptions. In the preamble to the final rule, CMS emphasized that it continues to interpret the self-referral prohibition narrowly and the exceptions broadly. Only two of the many modifications—an expanded "stand in the shoes" provision for purposes of applying the rule describing direct and indirect compensation arrangements and a modified physician recruitment exception—are viewed as major changes. The first rule provides that a physician is deemed to stand in the shoes of his or her "physician organization" and have the same compensation arrangements with the same parties and on the same terms as does the physician organization. Phase III changes in the physician recruitment rules revise the definition of "geographic area served by the hospital" and add a special optional rule for rural hospitals that expands the geographic area into which a rural hospital may recruit a physician. See also 42 C.F.R. § 411.357(e)(4)(iii), 42 C.F.R. § 411.357(e)(4)(vi) (loosening rules affecting recruitment to rural areas and allowing physician practices to impose practice restrictions on a recruited physician such as reasonable liquidated damages provisions and nonsolicitation clauses as long as they do not unreasonably restrict the recruited physician's ability to practice medicine in the geographic area served by the hospital).

In-Office Ancillary Services. Perhaps the most significant and controversial exception for physicians allows them to benefit from referrals for ancillary services when they are furnished in an office of the referring physician or his or her group. 42 C.F.R. § 411.355(b). As illustrated by the problem preceding this section, this exception allows DHS to be furnished to patients in the same building where the referring physicians provide their regular medical services, or, in the case of a group practice, in a centralized building provided certain conditions are met. On July 2, 2007, as one of several contemplated and potentially far-reaching changes to the Stark regulations, CMS evidenced its frustration with what it regards as abuses of this exception. Although not proposing specific changes to the in-office ancillary services exception, the announcement signaled that it may in the future attempt to curtail use of this and other exceptions that have permitted a "migration of sophisticated and expensive imaging or other equipment to physician offices" that was not intended by the law or the drafters of the exception. 72 Fed. Reg. 38,122, 38,181 (July 12, 2007). Explaining that the purpose of the inoffice exception was to allow a limited range of services to be provided in physicians' offices when "necessary to the diagnosis or treatment of the medical condition that brought the patient to the physicians' office," CMS asked for comments on ways to ensure that the DHS qualifying for the exception are truly ancillary to the physician's core medical office practice and are not provided as part of a separate business enterprise. The Agency gave the following illustration of a problematic arrangement that "appears to be nothing more than enterprises established for the self-referral of DHS":

> [A] group practice provides pathology services furnished in a centralized building that is not physically close to any of the other group's other offices, and in some cases, the technical component of such services is furnished by laboratory technologists who are employed by an entity unrelated to the group. The professional component of the pathology services may be furnished to contractor pathologists who have virtually no relationship to the group practice.

72 Fed. Reg. at 38,181. Further, even when ancillary services are furnished in the same building as the group practice's office, CMS apparently is concerned that there may be little interaction between the physicians who are treating the patients and the staff who provide the ancillary services.

A closer examination of the regulations governing this exception reveals how CMS's fine-tuned distinctions defining the scope of the exception allow considerable leeway for physicians to self-refer. To qualify for the exception, the services must be provided either in a "centralized building" used by a group practice to furnish DHS or in the "same building" in which the referring physician (or his or her group) furnishes physician services "unrelated to the furnishing of DHS." CMS has been wary of the potential that the prospect of lucrative ancillary services will prompt physicians to abuse this exception. By way of illustration, the regulations describe a group practice that leases space at an imaging center away from their practice office, provides physician services there one day a week, and then provides imaging services for the rest of the week with no involvement or presence of the group physicians. 69 Fed. Reg. 16,054, 16,072 (Mar. 26, 2004). Consequently, CMS has set very specific limits on what constitutes the "same building" under this exception.

The Phase II regulations specify three situations as the exclusive circumstances that will satisfy the test:

- Where the office is open to patients at least 35 hours per week and is regularly used by the referring physician or group to practice medicine and the referring physician or group provide physician services for at least 30 hours per week (including "some" services that are non-DHS).

- Where the office is open to patients at least 8 hours per week and regularly used by the referring physician or group to practice medicine and furnish physician services for at least 6 hours per week. However, services provided by the referring physician's group practice do not count toward the 6–hour requirement, and the building must be one in which the patient receiving the DHS usually sees the referring physician or a member of his group for physician services.

- Where the office is open to patients at least 8 hours per week and regularly used by the physician or group to practice medicine and furnish physician services for at least 6 hours per week. Under this provision the referring physician must be present and order the DHS in connection with the patient's visit or the physician must be present when the DHS is furnished.

Is there a logic to these detailed rules? Why should there be an exception for in-office ancillary services in the first place? Can you explain to Doctors Chung, et al.

(in the problem on p. 736) what options they have if they want to offer ancillary services? What factors will likely influence their decision on which option to choose?

The Stark Law issues also arise in physician joint ventures and contractual arrangements with hospitals. CMS has expressed concern about abuse of exceptions permitting some of these arrangements, and has also announced proposed rules aimed at dealing with areas of concern involving a number of arcane (but potentially lucrative) arrangements, such as "per click" leases, percentage compensation arrangements and "under arrangements" joint ventures. 72 Fed. Reg. at 38,182–83. As hospitals elicit the assistance of their physician staffs in improving quality and efficiency, payments for those services may pose Stark Law problems. The following problem deals with an important exception designed to permit such arrangements.

Problem: Medical Directors

Facing declining admissions and rampant administrative inefficiency, Jeff Lewis, the CEO of Alta Bonita Central Hospital ("ABC") decided to create six new medical directorship positions effective January 1, 2007. Medical directors are typically independent staff physicians who enter into contracts with hospitals to perform certain administrative functions such as assisting in the development and implementation of standards of care, ensuring compliance with JCAHO standards and those of other regulatory bodies, providing consultations on high risk cases, and participating in the work of various hospital committees. The following chart indicates the specialty and number of referrals to ABC for each of its six medical directors for 2006, the year preceding their appointments, and for 2007.

Physician	Specialty	2007 Referrals	2006 Referrals
Dr. Singh	Orthopaedics	80	68
Dr. Kaur	Nephrology/Dialysis	78	46
Dr. LaCombe	OB/GYN	40	38
Dr. Hicks	Cardiology	62	46
Dr. Russell	Surgery	45	45
Dr. Anderson	Geriatrics	50	27

These physicians were all among the top ten referring physicians at ABC, collectively accounting for 65% of the hospital's admissions before they became medical directors. The agreements delineated specific requirements that each medical director was to fulfill, including a requirement that he or she work 16 hours per month and document the number of "actual hours" worked, and specified a monthly stipend. Doctors LaCombe, Hicks and Russell were given stipends of $1500 per month and Doctors Singh, Kaur and Anderson were paid $2500 per month

Recently, the new outside counsel for ABC conducted a compliance audit and found the following in the reporting records of the doctors. Dr. Russell reported 4 hours in March 2007, 3 hours in April 2007, 0 hours in May 2007, and 0 hours in June 2007. Dr. Russell turned in these timesheets in December 2007. Dr. Hicks turned in her timesheets for April, May, June, July, and August 2007 in September 2007, reporting on each timesheet 8 hours of work. Regardless of when the timesheets were turned in or how they were filled out (hours worked, duties completed), all the medical directors were paid their full monthly stipend at the end of every month.

What issues are raised under the Stark Law by the way ABC established its medical directorships and the way it has implemented its agreements? Using the following exception and guidance, how should ABC have proceeded in contracting with its medical directors?

The Personal Services arrangements exception to compensation arrangements, 42 USC § 1395nn(e)(3)(A), provides:

Remuneration from an entity under an arrangement (including remuneration for specific physicians' services furnished to a nonprofit blood center), if—

(i) the arrangement is set out in writing, signed by the parties, and specifies the services covered by the arrangement,

(ii) the arrangement covers all of the services to be furnished by the physician (or an immediate family member of such physician) to the entity,

(iii) the aggregate services contracted for do not exceed those that are reasonable and necessary for the legitimate business purposes of the arrangement,

(iv) the term of the arrangement is for at least 1 year.

(v) the compensation to be paid over the term of each arrangement is set in advance, does not exceed fair market value, and except in the case of a physician incentive plan, is not determined in a manner that takes into account the volume or value of any referrals or other business generated between the parties,

(vi) the services to be performed under the arrangement do not involve the counseling or promotion or a business arrangement or other activity that violates any State or Federal law, and

(vii) the arrangement meets such other requirements as the Secretary may impose by regulation as needed to protect against program or patient abuse.

42 C.F.R. § 411.351 provides in pertinent part:

Fair market value means the value in arm's-length transactions, consistent with the general market value. "General market value" means the price that an asset would bring as the result of bona fide bargaining between well-informed buyers and sellers who are not otherwise in a position to generate business for the other party; or the compensation that would be included in a service agreement as the result of bona fide bargaining between well-informed parties to the agreement who are not otherwise in a position to generate business for the other party, on the date of acquisition of the asset or at the time of the service agreement. Usually, the fair market price is the price at which bona fide sales have been consummated for assets of like type, quality, and quantity in a particular market at the time of acquisition, or the compensation that as been included in bona fide service agreements with comparable terms at the time of the agreement, where the price or compensation has not been determined in any manner that takes into account the volume or value of anticipated or actual referrals.

The Phase III Regulations, *supra* state:

Nothing precludes parties from calculating fair market value using any commercially reasonable methodology that is appropriate under the circumstances and otherwise fits the definition [in the Act] and § 411.351. Ultimately, fair market value is determined based on facts and circumstances. The appropriate method will depend on the nature of the transaction, its location, and other factors. Because the statute covers a broad range of transactions, we cannot comment definitively on particular valuation methodologies.

Note on State Approaches to Kickbacks and Referrals and Fee Splitting

Most states have enacted laws that prohibit kickbacks or deal in some way with the specific problem of referrals. These laws vary considerably in scope and detail. For example, most states prohibit Medicaid fraud, but some rely on more general statutes outlawing fraud or theft by deception or false statements to public officials; some impose both criminal and civil penalties for kickbacks; many apply regardless of whether government or private payment plans were involved; and a few have broadened federal anti-kickback laws, e.g., by prohibiting the provision of unnecessary care.

Among the states adopting self-referral legislation, most track with either the Medicare fraud and abuse or Stark legislation. However, some states have enacted disclosure statutes that do not prohibit physician ownership interests in facilities to which they refer, but require that the referring provider reveal such interests to her patients. Finally, a few states allow physician investment where there is a demonstrated "community need." Is mandating disclosure of providers' financial conflicts of interest a realistic solution? Are patients capable of evaluating the risks they face in accepting referrals from a doctor with a financial interest in the referred product or service? What kind of verbal disclosure can be expected from an interested physician? What effect would such disclosures have on the physician-patient relationship? What predictions would you make about the operation of a disclosure requirement based on your knowledge of informed consent? See E. Haav Morreim, Conflicts of Interest: Profits and Problems in Physician Referrals, 262 JAMA 390 (1989); Marc A. Rodwin, Physicians' Conflicts of Interest, The Limitations of Disclosure, 321 New Eng.J.Med. 1405 (1989). Finally, how valid are the premises of state community need laws? Are physicians likely to invest in facilities in areas where private investors are lacking? If so, why? Do these statutes create regulatory processes that may themselves be subject to abuse? This approach may be contrasted with the Stark law, which includes an exception for self-referrals of designated health services if provided in a rural area (using metropolitan statistical areas for delineating regions) and if substantially all the services are furnished to persons who reside in the rural area. 42 U.S.C. § 1395nn(d)(2). What are the pros and cons of the demonstrated community need approach as compared to the Stark exception?

Another source of law governing physician referral practices are the state medical practice acts. Such laws commonly provide that paying referral fees or "fee-splitting" constitutes grounds for revocation or suspension of a physician's license. See, e.g., Mass. Gen. L. ch. 112 §§ 12AA, 23P (1991). These statutes have sometimes been construed to prohibit arrangements that go beyond simple sharing of fees in connection with referral arrangements. See, e.g., in Lieberman & Kraff v. Desnick, 244 Ill.App.3d 341, 185 Ill.Dec. 245, 614 N.E.2d 379 (1993). Florida's fee-splitting statute has called into question the legality of many physician practice management arrangements whereby a physician pays a large organization a percentage of profits in exchange for management, marketing, and networking services. See Gold, Vann & White, P.A. v. Friedenstab, 831 So.2d 692 (Fla. Dist. Ct. App. 2002) (service agreement between physicians and medical management company providing management company a percentage of revenue constituted a illegal fee splitting arrangement). See Richard O. Jacobs & Elizabeth Goodman, Splitting Fees or Splitting Hairs? Fee Splitting and Health Care—The Florida Experience, 8 Annals Health L. 239 (1999); 1 Furrow et al., Health Law § 5–10(d).

Chapter 12

ANTITRUST

INTRODUCTION

Antitrust law has played a pivotal role in the development of institutional and professional arrangements in health care. Following the Supreme Court's decision in Goldfarb v. Virginia State Bar, 421 U.S. 773, 95 S.Ct. 2004, 44 L.Ed.2d 572 (1975), which held that "learned professions" were not implicitly exempt from the antitrust laws and found the Sherman Act's interstate commerce requirement satisfied with regard to legal services, extensive antitrust litigation spurred significant changes in the health care industry. Most importantly, cases following *Goldfarb* helped remove a series of private restraints of trade that had long inhibited competition. Antitrust enforcement has come to assume a somewhat different, albeit equally important, focus in today's market. The law has emerged as a powerful overseer of institutional and professional arrangements and ideally helps assure the evolution of market structures that will preserve the benefits of a competitive marketplace.

At the same time, however, applying antitrust law to the health care industry entails some special problems. In particular, the peculiarities and distortions of health care markets often necessitate a sophisticated analysis in order to reach economically sound results. A host of questions arise: What place is there for defenses related to the quality of health care in a statutory regime designed to leave such issues to the market? Does the behavior of not-for-profit health care providers conform to traditional economic assumptions about competitors? If not, should they somehow be treated differently? What impact do the widespread interventions by state and federal government have on the application of federal antitrust law? Do "market failures" in health care, particularly imperfect information, suggest more restrained approaches to applying antitrust law? Perspectives on these and other questions underlying antitrust's role are found in a number of academic writings. See, e.g. Peter J. Hammer & William M. Sage, Antitrust, Health Care Quality, and the Courts, 102 Colum. L. Rev. 545 (2002) (empirical study of case law finding "no cogent theory of nonprice competition has been developed to guide courts" and that decisions "divorce quality from competition rather than factoring it into a competitive mix"); Thomas L. Greaney, Chicago's Procrustean Bed: Applying Antitrust Law in Health Care 71 Antitrust L.J. 857 (2004) (courts' pervasive neglect of market failures in health care antitrust cases systematically biases outcomes); Thomas Rice, The Economics of Health Care

Reconsidered (1998) (questioning whether market forces will produce efficient or socially desirable outcomes); Sara Rosenbaum, A Dose of Reality: Assessing the Federal Trade Commission/Department of Justice Report in an Uninsured, Underserved, and Vulnerable Population Context, 31 J. Health Pol. Pol'y & L. 657 (2006).

The Statutory Framework

The principal antitrust statutes are notable for their highly generalized proscriptions. Rather than specifying activities that it deemed harmful to competition, Congress vested the federal courts with the power to create a common law of antitrust. This chapter will not deal with all of the antitrust laws applicable to the health care industry. The following introduction summarizes portions of the three principal federal statutes: the Sherman Act, the Federal Trade Commission Act, and the Clayton Act. It should be noted that most states have enacted antitrust statutes that are identical to or closely track these federal laws.

Sherman Act § 1: Restraints of Trade

Section One of the Sherman Act prohibits "every contract, combination ... or conspiracy in restraint of trade." 15 U.S.C. § 1. This broad proscription establishes two substantive elements for finding a violation: an agreement and conduct that restrains trade. The concept of an agreement—the conventional shorthand for Section One's "contract, combination or conspiracy" language—limits the law's reach to concerted activities, i.e., those that are a result of a "meeting of the minds" of two or more independent persons or entities. The second requirement of Section One, that the agreement restrain trade, has generated extensive analysis by the courts. Recognizing that all commercial agreements restrain trade, the Supreme Court has narrowed the inquiry to condemn only "unreasonable restraints" and has developed presumptive ("per se") rules to simplify judicial inquiries in particular circumstances. Among the restraints of trade that are reached by Section One are: price fixing (the setting of prices or terms of sale cooperatively by two or more businesses that do not involve sharing substantial risk in a common business enterprise); market division (allocating product lines, customers, or territories between competitors); exclusive dealing (requiring that a person deal exclusively with an enterprise so that competitors are foreclosed or otherwise disadvantaged in the marketplace); group boycotts (competitors collectively refusing to deal, usually taking the form of denying a rival an input or something it needs to compete in the marketplace); and tying arrangements (a firm with market power selling one product on the condition that the buyer buy a second product from it).

Sherman Act § 2: Monopolization and Attempted Monopolization

Section Two of the Sherman Act prohibits monopolization, attempted monopolization, and conspiracies to monopolize. 15 U.S.C. § 2. Unlike Section One, it is primarily directed at unilateral conduct. Monopolization entails two elements: the possession of monopoly power, defined as the power to control market prices or exclude competition, and the willful acquisition or maintenance of that power as distinguished from growth or development as a consequence of a superior product, business acumen, or historic accident.

Clayton Act § 7: Mergers and Acquisitions

Section Seven of the Clayton Act prohibits mergers and acquisitions where the effect may be "substantially to lessen competition" or "to tend to create a monopoly." 15 U.S.C. § 18. To test the legality of a proposed merger or acquisition, courts emphasize market share and concentration data but also take other factors into consideration to determine whether a merger makes it more likely than not that the merged firm will exercise market power.

Federal Trade Commission Act § 5: Unfair Methods of Competition

Section Five of the Federal Trade Commission Act prohibits "unfair methods of competition" (which the courts have interpreted to include all violations of the Sherman Act and Clayton Act), and "unfair or deceptive acts or practices." 15 U.S.C. § 45(a)(1). The Act empowers the FTC to enforce the provisions of the Sherman Act in civil suits, as well as by administrative procedures. Although the FTC Act covers only the activities of a corporation "organized to carry on business for its own profit or that of its members," courts have found that non profit associations whose activities provide substantial economic benefit to their members are within the FTC's jurisdiction.

Defenses and Exemptions

There are numerous statutory and judicially-crafted defenses to antitrust liability, several of which are of particular importance to health care antitrust litigation. The state action doctrine exempts from antitrust liability actions taken pursuant to a clearly expressed state policy to restrict free competition, where the challenged conduct is under the active control and supervision of the state. The high degree of state regulation of health care has spawned state action defenses in staff privileges cases, for example, when state law authorizes public hospitals to undertake mergers that lessen competition and supervises their conduct. The McCarran–Ferguson Act generally exempts the "business of insurance" from antitrust enforcement to the extent that the particular insurance activities are regulated by state law. 15 U.S.C. § 1011. (This should not be taken to mean, however, that "insurance companies" are exempt from antitrust scrutiny). The Noerr–Pennington doctrine protects the exercise of the First Amendment right to petition the government, so long as the "petitioning" is not merely a "sham" to cover anti-competitive behavior. This defense is relevant to lobbying efforts on health care issues and to participation in administrative proceedings, such as certificate-of-need applications, each of which may lead to an outcome that lessens competition. The most recent statutory defense relevant to health care is the Health Care Quality Improvement Act, 42 U.S.C. §§ 11101–11152, enacted by Congress in 1986, which grants limited immunity for peer review activities.

Interpretive Principles

The Law's Exclusive Focus on Competitive Concerns

There has long been widespread agreement in the case law that antitrust inquiries should focus exclusively on competitive effects and should not take into account purported non-economic benefits of collective activities such as advancing social policies or even protecting public safety. See National Society of Professional Engineers v. United States, 435 U.S. 679, 98 S.Ct. 1355, 55 L.Ed.2d 637 (1978) (rejecting as a matter of law a professional society's safety justifications for its ban on competitive bidding). This self-imposed boundary is based on the judiciary's skepticism about its competence to balance disparate social policies and the judgment that such concerns are more appropriately addressed to the legislature. Importantly, then, under Section One of the Sherman Act, courts will not consider justifications other than those asserting that a practice, on balance, promotes competition. As discussed *infra* in Section IA2, this constraint is in obvious tension with justifications by professionals that their collective activities have the purpose of advancing the quality of patient care.

An important corollary to the foregoing is the often-repeated maxim that antitrust law seeks to "protect competition, not competitors." Brown Shoe Co. v. United States, 370 U.S. 294, 82 S.Ct. 1502, 8 L.Ed.2d 510 (1962). This tenet serves to emphasize the distinction between harm to competitors who lose out in the competitive struggle due to chance or their own inadequacies and harm resulting from the impermissible conduct of rivals. Only the latter are cognizable under the federal antitrust laws. Courts have fashioned rules regarding standing and antitrust injury for private plaintiffs as well as substantive doctrines that serve to preserve this distinction. See e.g., Todorov v. DCH Healthcare Authority, 921 F.2d 1438 (11th Cir. 1991); see generally, 2 Barry R. Furrow, et al., Health Law § 14–3 (2d ed. 2000).

Per Se Rules and The Rule of Reason

Traditionally, judicial analyses of conduct under Section One of the Sherman Act have employed two approaches to testing the "reasonableness" of restraints. Some activities, such as price fixing, market allocations, and certain group boycotts have been considered so likely to harm competition that they are deemed illegal "per se." That is, if a plaintiff can prove that the defendant's conduct fits within one of these categories, the inquiry ends; the agreement itself constitutes a violation of the statute. In effect, then, the per se categorization establishes a conclusive presumption of illegality.

Activities not falling within the per se rubric are subject to broader examination under the rule of reason. Under this form of analysis, defendants escape liability if they prove that the pro-competitive benefits of the challenged activity outweigh any anticompetitive effects so that competition, the singular policy concern of the statute, is strengthened rather than restrained. In theory, courts undertaking a full-blown rule of reason analysis will balance competitive harms against competitive benefits. For example, if a large number of hospitals collectively assembled and shared information about the utilization practices of physicians on their staffs, a court might balance the potential collusive harm resulting from lessened inter-hospital competition against the market-wide competitive benefits of dispensing such information—assuming the information was shared with payors.

In practice, however, such balancing is rarely done. Courts usually truncate the process in one of several ways. For example, they may find that an alleged restraint has no possibility of harming competition where the colluding parties lack "market power." As a proxy for market power, which is defined as the ability profitably to raise price (or reduce quality or output), courts estimate the market shares of the colluding parties and examine other market conditions. (A firm's market share is the ratio of its volume of business in a market to that of all of its competitors.) Doing this, of course, requires that the factfinder define the dimensions of the geographic and product markets—determinations that require the exercise of considerable judgment. Even where a party has a high market share and there are relatively few competitors, however, market power still may be lacking. For example, the colluding parties may be unable to raise price because entry by others is easy or because buyers would quickly detect such an increase and cease dealing with the parties.

Indeed, in recent years, a series of Supreme Court decisions have shifted antitrust analyses away from a rigid per se/rule of reason dichotomy, treating the approaches instead as "complementary" and essentially establishing a continuum of levels of scrutiny. See California Dental Association v. FTC *infra* Section B1, this chapter. Thus, the modern approach allows courts to undertake threshold examinations of purported justifications and competitive effects before characterizing the conduct as governed by the per se rule. By the same token, courts may need only a "quick look" to condemn conduct under the rule of reason; they may dispense with prolonged factual inquiries when the truncated review reveals that purported efficiency benefits are lacking or an anticompetitive effect is obvious.

Joint Ventures and Ancillary Restraints

Among the most difficult and most important issues facing antitrust courts and enforcers today is the treatment to be accorded joint ventures. As a general matter, the rather elastic concept of the joint venture embraces agreements between separate business firms to jointly provide a service or produce a new product. When two or more competing entities are members of a joint venture, the arrangement may raise antitrust concerns because of the prospect that the venture may enable the parties together to exercise market power. At the same time, however, joint ventures have the propensity to improve the efficiency (i.e., lower the costs) of the participants.

True joint ventures are evaluated under the rule of reason. In contrast, "sham" arrangements—e.g., cartels that produce no integrative efficiencies but adopt the joint venture label—are treated under the per se rule. Legitimate joint ventures are characterized by some meaningful level of economic integration that allows the ventures to offer a new or improved product or significant efficiencies. Because such legitimate joint ventures entail restraints of trade among participants (e.g., price agreements or market allocations), they do not escape scrutiny entirely. For the joint venture with valid efficiency justifications, further examination of its competitive effect is required under the rule of reason.

The methodology for evaluating joint ventures derives from a seminal opinion by Judge Taft in United States v. Addyston Pipe & Steel Co., 85 F. 271 (6th Cir. 1898), *aff'd as modified*, 175 U.S. 211, 20 S.Ct. 96, 44 L.Ed. 136 (1899). The so-called "ancillary restraints doctrine" first inquires into the purpose of the arrangement to determine whether it is a "naked" restraint, i.e., one having no objective other than suppressing competition; if so, summary condemnation is usually appropriate. Where the joint venture possesses sufficient integration or efficiency justifications to escape per se classification, the analysis turns on three questions: (1) are possible restraints of trade subordinate and collateral to a legitimate joint undertaking? (2) are they necessary to the success of that joint undertaking? and; (3) are they no more restrictive of competition than necessary to accomplish the pro-competitive ends?

Scope and Sources

Antitrust reaches the full gamut of business practices—mergers; agreements between input suppliers and those "downstream;" joint ventures; and agreements among competitors; for example. It also has touched all levels of health care delivery and financing. Consequently it is not possible to cover the full range of issues raised by antitrust in health care in this chapter. There are a number of exceptional sources for students looking to review the widespread influence the law has had in health care. A good starting point is a joint report written by the FTC and Department of Justice, published in July, 2004, entitled Improving Health Care: A Dose of Competition (2004), available at http://www.ftc.gov/reports/healthcare/040723healthcarerpt.pdf. A valuable collection of essays commenting on some of the issues in this report was published in Special Issue: Federal Trade Commission Report on Health Care and Competition, 31 Health Pol., Pol'y. and L. (2006). The federal government has also issued guidance for health law attorneys practicing in this area. See, for example, the Statements of Antitrust Enforcement Policy in Health Care, 4 Trade Reg. Rep. (CCH) para. 13, 153 (August 18, 1996) ("Policy Statements"), released jointly by the Department of Justice and the Federal Trade Commission. These statements, which are discussed throughout this chapter, apply the joint venture analysis set forth above in a variety of health industry contexts. Other important sources of information include the numerous "advisory opinions" of the Federal Trade Commission and "business review letters" of the Department of Justice, which are prospective statements of each agency's enforcement intentions regarding proposed conduct in specific situations.

I.   CARTELS AND PROFESSIONALISM

A.   CLASSIC CARTELS

IN RE MICHIGAN STATE MEDICAL SOCIETY

101 F.T.C. 191 (1983).

OPINION OF THE COMMISSION

BY CLANTON, COMMISSIONER:

I.   INTRODUCTION

This case involves allegations that direct competitors, acting through a professional association, conspired to restrain trade by organizing boycotts and tampering with the fees received from third party insurers of their services. Of particular antitrust significance is the fact that the competitors are medical doctors practicing in Michigan, the association is the Michigan State Medical Society ["MSMS"], and the insurers are Blue Cross and Blue Shield of Michigan ("BCBSM") and Michigan Medicaid.

More specifically, the complaint in this matter charges, and the administrative law judge found, that the medical society unlawfully conspired with its members to influence third-party reimbursement policies in the following ways: by seeking to negotiate collective agreements with insurers; by agreeing to use coercive measures like proxy solicitation and group boycotts; and by actually making coercive threats to third party payers. . . .

* * *

Becoming frustrated in its negotiations with BCBSM on [issues regarding reimbursement], MSMS authorized its first proxy solicitation. Reacting to what it perceived to be the recalcitrant attitude of Blue Shield on the subjects of regionalization of fees and physician profiles, coupled with what appears to be a total lack of willingness to cooperate with MSMS in the development of a uniform claim form or even consider the use of the CPT procedural code, the Negotiating Committee recommended that the House of Delegates urge MSMS members to write letters to BCBSM withdrawing from participation but mail them to the Negotiating Committee to be held as "proxies." The House of Delegates authorized the committee to collect the proxies, but to use them only at the discretion of the Council, with prior notice to the members who submitted them, "if a negotiating impasse develops with Michigan Blue Cross/Blue Shield."

* * *

Each member of MSMS was urged by letter to resist "so-called cost-containment programs that in effect reduce reimbursement to physicians or place the responsibility for the reduction of costs solely on the practicing physician." The letter, from the Council chairman, referred pointedly to the fact that a threshold percentage of physicians must formally participate in order for BCBSM to operate under its enabling legislation. It enclosed two blank "powers of attorney," one for BCBSM and one for Medicaid, empowering the Negotiating Committee to cancel the signer's participation in either program if such action was deemed warranted by the Council. These powers of attorney were revocable at any time. . . .

As a result of this response, [a] dispute over radiologists' and pathologists' reimbursement was resolved in MSMS' favor with the status quo being preserved and BCBSM withdrawing its proposal. [ ] As explained below, these proxies also played a role in MSMS' dealings with Medicaid.

[In response to additional efforts by BCBSM to reduce utilization of physician services, the leadership of MSMS advised members to react to new reimbursement policies by writing letters threatening departicipation or actually withdrawing from participation. In addition, MSMS representatives protested cuts of approximately 11% in physician reimbursement under the Medicaid program by "waving" the departicipation proxies during meetings with the Governor and Medicaid officials. Although evidence suggested that physician participants in the Medicaid program fell off markedly after the MSMS collective action, the Commission did not find that state officials had been coerced by these actions.]

* * *

Conspiracy Allegations

The threshold issue here is whether MSMS' importunings with BCBSM and the Medicaid program amounted to conspiratorial conduct of the kind alleged in the complaint or simply represented nonbinding expressions of views and policy, as argued by respondent.... As discussed previously, the evidence quite clearly reveals that MSMS members, acting through their House of Delegates, agreed in 1976 to establish a Division of Negotiations for the purpose of working out differences with third party payers. The Division was specifically empowered, *inter alia*, to coordinate all negotiating activities of MSMS, collect "non-participation" proxies and obtain a negotiated participation agreement with third party payers that would obviate the need for physician non-participation. It also was specifically contemplated by MSMS that the Division of Negotiations would obtain authorization of all members to serve as their "exclusive bargaining agent." The debate in the House of Delegates clearly indicated that, although the Division would not negotiate specific fees, it would have authority to negotiate the manner by which fees or reimbursement levels would be established. [ ]

Thus, at the outset we find that the very creation of the Division of Negotiations reveals a collective purpose on the part of MSMS and its members to go beyond the point of giving advice to third party payers; in fact, it reveals a purpose to organize and empower a full-fledged representative to negotiate and resolve controversies surrounding physician profiles, screens and other similar matters. [ ] There is, in fact, considerable additional evidence that the Negotiating Division not only had the authority to reach understandings with third party payers but also utilized that authority (acting as agent for its members) in soliciting, collecting and threatening to exercise physician departicipation proxies, as well as in other negotiations with third party payers.

* * *

Turning to the boycott issue, the law is clear that the definition of that term is not limited to situations where the target of the concerted refusal to deal is another competitor or potential competitor. As the Supreme Court indicated, ... a concerted refusal to deal may be characterized as an unlawful group boycott where the target is a customer or supplier of the combining parties.... In the instant case, the alleged boycott involves concerted threats by MSMS and its members to refrain from participating in BCBSM and Medicaid unless the latter modified their reimbursement policies. Although BCBSM and Medicaid—the targets of the boycott—are not in competitive relationships with MSMS, that fact alone does not preclude a finding of a boycott.

Respondent, however, argues that the proxies were not exercised and, in the case of the departicipation letter campaign, that there was no adverse effect on BCBSM. As to the latter contention, MSMS points out that more physicians signed up to participate in BCBSM during the relevant period than withdrew from the program as a result of the campaign. The success [or] failure of a group boycott or price-fixing agreement, however, is irrelevant to the question of either its existence or its legality. Whether or not the action succeeds, "[i]t is the concerted activity for a common purpose that constitutes the violation." ... Furthermore, an agreement among competitors affecting price does not have to be successful in order to be condemned.

It is the "contract, combination ... or conspiracy in restraint of trade or commerce" which § 1 of the [Sherman] Act strikes down, whether the concerted activity be wholly nascent or abortive on the one hand, or successful on the other. [ ] Moreover, even if less than all members of an organization or association agree to participate, that fact does not negate the presence of a conspiracy or combination as to those who do participate. [ ]

As for the collection of proxies that were never exercised, the law does not require that a competitor actually refuse to deal before a boycott can be found or liability established. Rather, the threat to refuse to deal may suffice to constitute the offense. [ ] The evidence indicates that the threat implicit in the collection of departicipation proxies and the attendant publicity can be as effective as the actual execution of the threatened action. Indeed, it may be assumed that parties to a concerted refusal to deal hope that the announcement of the intended action will be sufficient to produce the desired response. That appears to be precisely what happened here, and there are contemporaneous testimonials by MSMS officials confirming the success of that strategy. For example, Dr. Crandall suggested that MSMS' "waving the proxies in the face of the legislature" persuaded the state attorney general that if he sued MSMS the state would have "orchestrated the demise of the entire Michigan Medicaid program." Also, as noted above, the Negotiations Division credited the members' response to the proxy solicitation with the favorable outcome of the dispute between the radiologists and BCBSM. And, as further evidence, there is the fact that MSMS reached a formal agreement with BCBSM which included the implementation of a statewide screen.

* * *

B. Legality of the Concerted Action

* * *

[I]t would appear that respondent's conduct approaches the kind of behavior that previously has been classified as per se illegal. Nevertheless, since this conduct does not involve direct fee setting, we are not prepared to declare it per se illegal at this juncture and close the door on all asserted procompetitive justifications.

To briefly recap, respondent has offered the following justifications for its behavior: (1) the practices had no effect on fee levels and, in any event, BCBSM and Medicaid took independent action to correct the perceived problems; (2) MSMS simply sought to insure that physicians were treated fairly especially in view of BCBSM's bargaining power; (3) the actions were, in part, an effort to counter BCBSM's violations of its charter and Michigan law in connection with its modified participation program; and (4) MSMS was striving to correct abuses of the Medicaid system and the poor perpetrated by "Medicaid mills."

With respect to respondent's first contention, MSMS claims that the conduct never led to uniform fees or prevented individual physicians from deciding whether to participate in BCBSM or Medicaid. We believe that these arguments miss the point with respect to the likely competitive effects of the restrictive practices. Where horizontal arrangements so closely relate to prices or fees as they do here, a less elaborate analysis of competitive effects is required. [ ] The collective actions under scrutiny clearly interfere with the rights of physicians to compete independently on the terms of insurance coverage offered by BCBSM and Medicaid. Moreover, the joint arrangements directly hamper the ability of third party payers to compete freely for the patronage of individual physicians and other physician business entities. . . .

* * *

On the question of whether the proposed policies of BCBSM and Medicaid were fair to physicians, respondent would apparently have us become en-meshed in weighing the comparative equities of the different parties to these transactions. In fact, considerable portions of the record are devoted to an assessment of the relative merits of MSMS' bargaining position. For us to consider whether the terms offered by the third party payers were fair or reasonable would lead us into the kind of regulatory posture that the courts have long rejected. . . . It would be analogous to the Commission serving as a quasi-public utility agency concerned with balancing interests unrelated to antitrust concerns. We believe that it is undesirable and inappropriate for us to step in and attempt to determine which party had the better case in these dealings. [The Commission found that the objective of correcting violations of law cannot justify a group boycott because alternative means of seeking redress were available.]

* * *

Respondent also suggests that its activities were motivated by concern for the welfare of its members' patients, especially in the case of Medicaid where, it is alleged, reductions in reimbursement levels might lead to lower physician participation rates and force low-income patients to seek less reputable providers (the so-called Medicaid mills). We concluded there that the relation-ship between such reimbursement mechanisms and health care quality was simply too tenuous, from a competitive perspective, to justify the broad restrictions imposed. . . . While we are not addressing ethical standards in this case, many of the quality and patient welfare arguments asserted here have a ring similar to those advanced in [In re AMA, discussed infra, in which the FTC rejected a ban on advertising justified by defendants as protecting informed consumer choice and a prohibition on contract-based reimbursement which defendants claimed resulted in harm to the public and inferior quality of medical service]. Even in the case of Medicaid reductions, where an argument might be made that arbitrary cuts could be counter-productive by impairing physicians' economic incentives to treat the poor, it is difficult to see how concerted agreements and refusals to deal can be sanctioned as a means of fighting proposed payment cutbacks. While granting MSMS' lauda-ble concerns about the effects of physician withdrawal from Medicaid, we observe that respondent clearly had public forums available to it to correct perceived mistakes made by the state legislature or the administrators of Medicaid; it could have expressed its views in ways that fell well short of organized boycott threats.

Finally, we find no suggestion among MSMS' justifications that the concerted behavior here enhanced competition in any market by injecting new elements or forms of competition, reducing entry barriers, or facilitating or broadening consumer choice. The price-related practices in question here are not ancillary to some broader pro-competitive purpose, such as a joint venture, an integration of activities, or an offer of a new product or service.…

* * *

In fact, we believe there are less anti-competitive ways of providing such information to insurers. The order that we would impose upon respondent allows it to provide information and views to insurers on behalf of its members, so long as the Society does not attempt to extract agreements, through coercion or otherwise, from third party payers on reimbursement issues. In allowing respondent to engage in non-binding, non-coercive discussions with health insurers, we have attempted to strike a proper balance between the need for insurers to have efficient access to the views of large groups of providers and the need to prevent competitors from banding together in ways that involve the unreasonable exercise of collective market power.

Notes and Questions

1. Does a decision by competing physicians to deal collectively in their negotiations with third party payers constitute price fixing? If so, why didn't the FTC treat this as a per se offense?

2. Consider the justifications offered by the Michigan State Medical Society physicians for their actions. Do any meet the requirement discussed in the introduction to this chapter that justifications must concern pro-competitive benefits arising from the restraint? Could collective negotiations be viewed as a market-improving step if they corrected market imperfections? Did they here? See Thomas E. Kauper, The Role of Quality of Health Care Considerations in Antitrust Analysis, 51 L. & Contemp. Probs. 273 (Spring, 1988); Thomas L. Greaney, Quality of Care and Market Failure Defenses in Antitrust Health Care Litigation, 21 Conn. L. Rev. 605, 650–52 (1989).

3. Boycotts traditionally have been subject to per se analysis, although the Supreme Court has cautioned in recent years that only certain collective refusals to deal will be summarily condemned. In Northwest Wholesale Stationers, Inc. v. Pacific Stationery, 472 U.S. 284, 105 S.Ct. 2613, 86 L.Ed.2d 202 (1985), the Court noted somewhat elliptically that, in order to merit per se treatment, some of the following factors must be present: (1) cutting off access to a supply, facility, or market necessary to enable the boycotted firms to compete; (2) market power in the boycotting firms; and (3) no plausible efficiency justifications. Only a few years later, however, the Court applied the per se rule to a boycott by lawyers serving as court-appointed counsel for indigent defendants and strongly defended presumptive treatment as administratively efficient and as a means of discouraging individuals from attempting inherently dangerous conduct. FTC v. Superior Court Trial Lawyers Ass'n, 493 U.S. 411, 110 S.Ct. 768, 107 L.Ed.2d 851 (1990). While the exact boundaries of the doctrine remain murky, plausible pro-competitive justifications for collective refusals to deal will remove conduct from per se classification. Lower courts have readily applied rule of reason analysis to alleged boycotts where, for example, providers were excluded from an IPA based on valid cost containment objectives. Hassan v. Independent Practice Associates, P.C., 698 F.Supp. 679 (E.D. Mich. 1988); Hahn v. Oregon Physicians' Service, 868 F.2d 1022 (9th Cir.1988).

4. The federal agencies have successfully challenged scores of provider cartels that engaged in a wide variety of practices designed to raise prices, thwart

competition from other providers, or stymie cost containment efforts of managed care organizations. For example, the FTC entered into a consent decree with Montana Associated Physicians, Inc. (MAPI), an organization of 115 physicians practicing in over 30 independent physician practices and constituting 43% of all the physicians in Billings, Montana. In re Montana Associated Physicians, Inc. and Billings Physician Hospital Alliance, Inc., FTC Docket No. C–3704, 62 Fed. Reg. 11,201 (1997). According to the FTC's complaint, physicians formed MAPI to present a "united front" when dealing with managed care plans in an attempt to "resist competitive pressures to discount fees" and forestall entry of HMOs and PPOs into the area. Individual members of MAPI told HMOs that they would negotiate only through their organization, and no individual MAPI member contracted with HMOs. See also United States v. North Dakota Hospital Association, 640 F.Supp. 1028 (D.N.D. 1986) (hospitals' joint refusal to extend discounts in bidding for contracts); American Medical Association, 94 F.T.C. 701 (1979) (final order and opinion), aff'd, 638 F.2d 443 (2d Cir. 1980), aff'd by an equally divided court, 455 U.S. 676, 102 S.Ct. 1744, 71 L.Ed.2d 546 (1982) (ethical rules barring salaried employment, working for "inadequate compensation," and affiliating with non-physicians); Medical Staff of Holy Cross Hospital, 114 F.T.C. 555 (1991) (consent order) (conspiracy by medical staff to obstruct development of Cleveland Clinic's multi-specialty group practice by denying staff privileges to clinic doctors). Collective bargaining undertaken by "sham" networks or purported physician unions are discussed *infra*.

5. In a very few instances, criminal charges have been filed against providers who have engaged in price fixing or price-affecting boycotts. In United States v. Alston, 974 F 2d 1206 (9th Cir. 1992), the Justice Department had indicted a group of dentists who allegedly conspired to fix co-payment fees received from insurers. The Ninth Circuit affirmed a jury verdict based on circumstantial evidence of meetings, discussions of mutual dissatisfaction and parallel conduct that the dentist entered into a price fixing conspiracy; however, the court upheld a motion for a new trial based on the contention that defendants lacked the necessary *mens rea* because they believed the payor had proposed the revised fee schedule. *Alston* was the first federal criminal prosecution involving health care providers since American Medical Ass'n v. United States, 130 F.2d 233 (D.C.Cir. 1942), aff'd, 317 U.S. 519, 63 S.Ct. 326, 87 L.Ed. 434 (1943), in which the AMA and an affiliated society were convicted of violating the Sherman Act by engaging in a variety of efforts to suppress HMOs. These efforts included expulsion from the medical society and the circulation of "white lists" to encourage boycotts of those doctors cooperating with HMOs. As will be discussed, in recent years the FTC has uncovered numerous cartelizing schemes by physicians organizing "sham" networks or undertaking other strategies to insulate themselves from competition fostered by managed care. However, no criminal charges have been brought by the Department of Justice. We have seen no similar reluctance by DOJ to bring criminal charges in cases involving anti-kickback schemes. What may explain the different treatment? See Thomas L. Greaney, Thirty Years of Solicitude: Antitrust Law and Physician Cartels, 7 Hous. J. Health L. & Pol. 101 (2007) (discussing the political, bureaucratic, and doctrinal forces making DOJ reluctant to pursue criminal enforcement in antitrust health care cases).

Note: Cartelizing Schemes in the Pharmaceuticals Industry: "Reverse Payments" by Brand Name Drug Manufacturers

Some of the most significant litigation in the history of antitrust law (measured by the dollars at stake) has been brought by the FTC, private plaintiffs, and state attorneys general challenging payments made by brand-name drug manufacturers to potential-rival generic manufacturers often accompanied by understandings that delay entry by the generic into the market. These payments typically occur in the context of settling patent disputes. They are referred to as "reverse payment" cases because the flow of the monetary settlement—from patentee to alleged infringer—is in the opposite direction of that typically expected in a patent settlement case.

The complex interplay of patent law and food and drug regulatory law has created strong financial incentives to violate the antitrust laws. Studies indicate that the first generic competitor typically enters the market at a price that is 70 to 80 percent of its brand-name counterpart and gains substantial share from the brand-name product in a short period of time. Subsequent generic entrants discount even further, prompting earlier generic entrants to reduce their prices. Price competition typically enables generic sellers to capture anywhere from 44 to 80 percent of branded sales within the first full year after launch of a lower-priced generic product. See Richard G. Frank & David S. Salkever, Generic Entry and the Pricing of Pharmaceuticals, 6 J. Econ. & Mgmt. Strategy 75, 89 (1997). Patent law gives the patent holder the legal right to exclude rivals. However, the patent process allows for the grant of patents without close review of their merits and many are overturned once challenged. According to an FTC study, generics manufacturers prevailed in 73 percent of all patent challenges between 1992 and 2000. See Jon Leibowitz, Comm'r, FTC, Anticompetitive Patent Settlements in the Pharmaceutical Industry: The Benefits of a Legislative Solution, Prepared Statement of the FTC Before the Committee on the Judiciary of the United States Senate 23–25 (Jan. 17, 2007), www.ftc.gov/speeches/leibowitz/070117anticompe titivepatentsettlements_ senate.pdf. For this reason commentators emphasize the "probabilistic" nature of the patent grant. Recognizing the potential for substantial consumer savings, Congress enacted the Hatch–Waxman law in 1984 to encourage generic drug manufacturers to challenge questionable patents. That law provides that the first generic manufacturer to make certain certifications before the Food and Drug Administration will have 180 days of marketing exclusivity, during which the FDA may not approve another generic applicant even if the first generic does not begin to market its drug. Though highly successful in inducing generic entry, Hatch–Waxman contained a serious flaw: it created an incentive for brand and generic manufacturers to conspire to delay entry and divide the profits of the extended period of monopoly of the branded drug.

Four courts of appeals have ruled on the legality of reverse payments in the context of settlements of pharmaceutical patent disputes. In two cases, both of which involved partial settlements, the agreements were ultimately found to violate Section 1 of the Sherman Act. Schering–Plough Corp. v. FTC, 402 F.3d 1056 (11th Cir. 2005), cert. denied, 548 U.S. 919, 126 S.Ct. 2929, 165 L.Ed.2d 977 (2006); See also, Valley Drug Co. v. Geneva Pharm., Inc., 344 F.3d 1294 (11th Cir. 2003) (agreement held illegal on remand in In re Terazosin Hydrochloride Antitrust Litig. (Terazosin II), 352 F. Supp. 2d 1279 (S.D. Fla. 2005)). In two other cases courts upheld final settlements involving reverse payments. In re Cardizem CD Antitrust Litig., 332 F.3d 896 (6th Cir. 2003); In re Tamoxifen Citrate Antitrust Litigation, 466 F.3d 187 (2d Cir. 2006). Much is disputed about these cases. Some, including the FTC, have suggested that *Cardizem* applies a per se analysis to reverse payments and contend that there is a split among the circuits; others, including the Department of Justice, dispute the existence of a circuit split and call for a more nuanced approach than one presumptively condemning all such payments. (This divergence in views led to the unusual specter of the FTC and DOJ lining up on opposite sides of whether the Supreme

Court should grant certiorari in the *Schering Plough* case). See Christopher M. Holman, Do Reverse Payment Settlements Violate the Antitrust Laws?, 23 Santa Clara Computer & High Tech. L.J. 489 (2007). Underlying the debate about whether and under what circumstances a presumptive rule should apply are such issues as: the weight to be afforded to the parties' risk aversion, the significance of policies encouraging settlements, the implications to be drawn from the size of payments and scope of the agreements, the "probabilistic" nature of patents, and the scope of exclusionary power that the law should attribute to patents. Over twenty-five law review articles have addressed this subject. See e.g., Herbert Hovenkamp, Mark Janis & Mark A. Lemley, Anticompetitive Settlement of Intellectual Property Disputes, 87 Minn. L. Rev. 1719, 1720–21 (2003); Carl Shapiro, Antitrust Limits to Patent Settlements, 34 RAND J. Econ. 391, 391 (2003); James Langenfeld & Wenqing L., Intellectual Property and Agreements to Settle Patent Disputes: The Case of Settlement Agreements with Payments from Branded to Generic Drug Manufacturers, 70 Antitrust L.J. 777 (2003).

The FTC has argued strenuously that its efforts to stop reverse payments have promoted competition and have significantly lowered pharmaceutical costs without endangering the patent settlement process. It points out that after its initial victories in litigation, parties essentially stopped making reverse payments for five years, but patent settlements continued to occur without imposing limitations on generic entry. However, soon after the decision of the Eleventh Circuit in *Schering Plough*, reverse payments reappeared: in 2006 fifty percent of the final settlement agreements between brandname and generic companies included both an agreement to defer generic entry and some form of payment from the brand-name firm to the generic challenger. See Jon Leibowitz, supra. The FTC has indicated that it it intends continue to pursue litigation challenging reverse payments and that it supports legislation designed to "fix" the Hatch–Waxman problem. Id. Legislation designed to establish a bright line rule regarding exclusionary payments has been introduced in Congress. Preserve Access to Affordable Generics Act, S.316, 110th Cong. (2007).

B. COLLECTIVE ACTIVITIES WITH JUSTIFICATIONS

1. *Restrictions on Advertising and Dissemination of Information*

CALIFORNIA DENTAL ASSOCIATION v. FEDERAL TRADE COMMISSION

Supreme Court of the United States, 1999.
526 U.S. 756, 119 S.Ct. 1604, 143 L.Ed.2d 935.

JUSTICE SOUTER delivered the opinion of the Court.

There are two issues in this case: whether the jurisdiction of the Federal Trade Commission extends to the California Dental Association (CDA), a nonprofit professional association, and whether a "quick look" sufficed to justify finding that certain advertising restrictions adopted by the CDA violated the antitrust laws. We hold that the Commission's jurisdiction under the Federal Trade Commission Act (FTC Act) extends to an association that, like the CDA, provides substantial economic benefit to its for-profit members, but that where, as here, any anticompetitive effects of given restraints are far from intuitively obvious, the rule of reason demands a more thorough enquiry into the consequences of those restraints than the Court of Appeals performed.

I

[Petitioner CDA, a nonprofit association of local dental societies to which about three-quarters of the State's dentists belong, provides desirable insurance and preferential financing arrangements for its members and engages in lobbying, litigation, marketing, and public relations for members' benefit. Members agree to abide by the CDA's Code of Ethics, which, *inter alia*, prohibits false or misleading advertising. The CDA has issued interpretive advisory opinions and guidelines relating to advertising. The FTC claimed that in applying its guidelines so as to restrict two types of truthful, nondeceptive advertising (price advertising, particularly discounted fees, and advertising relating to the quality of dental services), the CDA violated § 5 of the FTC Act. In its administrative proceedings, the Commission held that the advertising restrictions violated the Act under an abbreviated rule-of-reason analysis. In affirming, the Ninth Circuit sustained the Commission's jurisdiction and concluded that an abbreviated or "quick look" rule of reason analysis was proper in this case.]

The dentists who belong to the CDA ... agree to abide by a Code of Ethics (Code) including the following § 10:

> "Although any dentist may advertise, no dentist shall advertise or solicit patients in any form of communication in a manner that is false or misleading in any material respect. In order to properly serve the public, dentists should represent themselves in a manner that contributes to the esteem of the public. Dentists should not misrepresent their training and competence in any way that would be false or misleading in any material respect."

The CDA has issued a number of advisory opinions interpreting this section, and through separate advertising guidelines intended to help members comply with the Code and with state law the CDA has advised its dentists of disclosures they must make under state law when engaging in discount advertising.[1]

Responsibility for enforcing the Code rests in the first instance with the local dental societies, to which applicants for CDA membership must submit copies of their own advertisements and those of their employers or referral services to assure compliance with the Code. The local societies also actively seek information about potential Code violations by applicants or CDA members. Applicants who refuse to withdraw or revise objectionable advertisements may be denied membership; and members who, after a hearing, remain similarly recalcitrant are subject to censure, suspension, or expulsion from the CDA. [ ]

* * *

1. The disclosures include:

1. The dollar amount of the nondiscounted fee for the service[.]

2. Either the dollar amount of the discount fee or the percentage of the discount for the specific service[.]

3. The length of time that the discount will be offered[.]

4. Verifiable fees[.]

5. [The identity of] [s]pecific groups who qualify for the discount or any other terms and conditions or restrictions for qualifying for the discount. Id., at 724.

II

[The Court interpreted the FTC Act, which gives the Commission authority over a "corporatio[n]" that is "organized to carry on business for its own profit or that of its members," 15 U.S.C. §§ 44, 45(a)(2), as conferring jurisdiction over nonprofit associations whose activities provide substantial economic benefits to their for-profit members. The Court declined to predicate FTC jurisdiction on a showing that a supporting organization devoted itself entirely to its members' profits or that its activities focused on raising members' bottom lines.]

III

The Court of Appeals treated as distinct questions the sufficiency of the analysis of anticompetitive effects and the substantiality of the evidence supporting the Commission's conclusions. Because we decide that the Court of Appeals erred when it held as a matter of law that quick-look analysis was appropriate (with the consequence that the Commission's abbreviated analysis and conclusion were sustainable), we do not reach the question of the substantiality of the evidence supporting the Commission's conclusion.[2]

In National Collegiate Athletic Assn. v. Board of Regents of Univ. of Okla.[ ] we held that a "naked restraint on price and output requires some competitive justification even in the absence of a detailed market analysis." [ ]. Elsewhere, we held that "no elaborate industry analysis is required to demonstrate the anticompetitive character of" horizontal agreements among competitors to refuse to discuss prices. [ ] In each of these cases, which have formed the basis for what has come to be called abbreviated or "quick-look" analysis under the rule of reason, an observer with even a rudimentary understanding of economics could conclude that the arrangements in question would have an anticompetitive effect on customers and markets.... As in such cases, quick-look analysis carries the day when the great likelihood of anticompetitive effects can easily be ascertained....

The case before us, however, fails to present a situation in which the likelihood of anticompetitive effects is comparably obvious. Even on Justice Breyer's view that bars on truthful and verifiable price and quality advertising are prima facie anticompetitive, and place the burden of procompetitive justification on those who agree to adopt them, the very issue at the threshold of this case is whether professional price and quality advertising is sufficiently verifiable in theory and in fact to fall within such a general rule. Ultimately our disagreement with Justice Breyer turns on our different responses to this issue. Whereas he accepts, as the Ninth Circuit seems to have done, that the restrictions here were like restrictions on advertisement of price and quality generally, it seems to us that the CDA's advertising restrictions might plausibly be thought to have a net procompetitive effect, or possibly no effect at all on competition. The restrictions on both discount and nondiscount advertising are, at least on their face, designed to avoid false or deceptive advertising[ ] in a market characterized by striking disparities between the

---

2. We leave to the Court of Appeals the question whether on remand it can effectively assess the Commission's decision for substantial evidence on the record, or whether it must remand to the Commission for a more exten- sive rule-of-reason analysis on the basis of an enhanced record.

3. That false or misleading advertising has an anticompetitive effect, as that term is customarily used, has been long established. []

information available to the professional and the patient.[4] [] In a market for professional services, in which advertising is relatively rare and the comparability of service packages not easily established, the difficulty for customers or potential competitors to get and verify information about the price and availability of services magnifies the dangers to competition associated with misleading advertising. What is more, the quality of professional services tends to resist either calibration or monitoring by individual patients or clients, partly because of the specialized knowledge required to evaluate the services, and partly because of the difficulty in determining whether, and the degree to which, an outcome is attributable to the quality of services (like a poor job of tooth-filling) or to something else (like a very tough walnut). See Leland, Quacks, Lemons, and Licensing: A Theory of Minimum Quality Standards, 87 J. Pol. Econ. 1328, 1330 (1979); 1 B. Furrow, T. Greaney, S. Johnson, T. Jost, & R. Schwartz, Health Law § 3–1, p. 86 (1995) (describing the common view that "the lay public is incapable of adequately evaluating the quality of medical services"). Patients' attachments to particular professionals, the rationality of which is difficult to assess, complicate the picture even further. [] The existence of such significant challenges to informed decisionmaking by the customer for professional services immediately suggests that advertising restrictions arguably protecting patients from misleading or irrelevant advertising call for more than cursory treatment as obviously comparable to classic horizontal agreements to limit output or price competition.

[The Court of Appeals] brushe[d] over the professional context and describe[d] no anticompetitive effects. Assuming that the record in fact supports the conclusion that the CDA disclosure rules essentially bar advertisement of across-the-board discounts, it does not obviously follow that such a ban would have a net anticompetitive effect here. Whether advertisements that announced discounts for, say, first-time customers, would be less effective at conveying information relevant to competition if they listed the original and discounted prices for checkups, X-rays, and fillings, than they would be if they simply specified a percentage discount across the board, seems to us a question susceptible to empirical but not a priori analysis.... Put another way, the CDA's rule appears to reflect the prediction that any costs to competition associated with the elimination of across-the-board advertising will be outweighed by gains to consumer information (and hence competition) created by discount advertising that is exact, accurate, and more easily verifiable (at least by regulators). As a matter of economics this view may or may not be correct, but it is not implausible, and neither a court nor the Commission may initially dismiss it as presumptively wrong.[5]

* * *

4. "The fact that a restraint operates upon a profession as distinguished from a business is, of course, relevant in determining whether that particular restraint violates the Sherman Act. It would be unrealistic to view the practice of professions as interchangeable with other business activities, and automatically to apply to the professions antitrust concepts which originated in other areas. The public service aspect, and other features of the professions, may require that a particular practice, which could properly be viewed as a violation of the Sherman Act in another context, be treated differently." Goldfarb v. Virginia State Bar, 421 U.S. 773, 788–789, n. 17, 95 S.Ct. 2004, 44 L.Ed.2d 572 (1975).

5. Justice Breyer suggests that our analysis is "of limited relevance," because "the basic question is whether this ... theoretically redeeming virtue in fact offsets the restrictions'

The Court of Appeals was comparably tolerant in accepting the sufficiency of abbreviated rule-of-reason analysis as to the nonprice advertising restrictions. The court began with the argument that "[t]hese restrictions are in effect a form of output limitation, as they restrict the supply of information about individual dentists' services." Although this sentence does indeed appear as cited, it is puzzling, given that the relevant output for antitrust purposes here is presumably not information or advertising, but dental services themselves. The question is not whether the universe of possible advertisements has been limited (as assuredly it has), but whether the limitation on advertisements obviously tends to limit the total delivery of dental services. The court came closest to addressing this latter question when it went on to assert that limiting advertisements regarding quality and safety "prevents dentists from fully describing the package of services they offer," adding that "[t]he restrictions may also affect output more directly, as quality and comfort advertising may induce some customers to obtain non-emergency care when they might not otherwise do so," ibid. This suggestion about output is also puzzling. If quality advertising actually induces some patients to obtain more care than they would in its absence, then restricting such advertising would reduce the demand for dental services, not the supply; and it is of course the producers' supply of a good in relation to demand that is normally relevant in determining whether a producer-imposed output limitation has the anticompetitive effect of artificially raising prices.[6] ...

Although the Court of Appeals acknowledged the CDA's view that "claims about quality are inherently unverifiable and therefore misleading," it responded that this concern "does not justify banning all quality claims without regard to whether they are, in fact, false or misleading." As a result, the court said, "the restriction is a sufficiently naked restraint on output to justify quick look analysis." The court assumed, in these words, that some dental quality claims may escape justifiable censure, because they are both verifiable and true. But its implicit assumption fails to explain why it gave no weight to the countervailing, and at least equally plausible, suggestion that restricting difficult-to-verify claims about quality or patient comfort would have a procompetitive effect by preventing misleading or false claims that distort the market. It is, indeed, entirely possible to understand the CDA's

anticompetitive effects in this case." He thinks that the Commission and the Court of Appeals "adequately answered that question," but the absence of any empirical evidence on this point indicates that the question was not answered, merely avoided by implicit burden-shifting of the kind accepted by Justice Breyer. The point is that before a theoretical claim of anticompetitive effects can justify shifting to a defendant the burden to show empirical evidence of procompetitive effects, as quick-look analysis in effect requires, there must be some indication that the court making the decision has properly identified the theoretical basis for the anticompetitive effects and considered whether the effects actually are anticompetitive. Where, as here, the circumstances of the restriction are somewhat complex, assumption alone will not do.

6. Justice Breyer wonders if we "mea[n] this statement as an argument against the anticompetitive tendencies that flow from an agreement not to advertise service quality." But as the preceding sentence shows, we intend simply to question the logic of the Court of Appeals's suggestion that the restrictions are anticompetitive because they somehow "affect output," presumably with the intent to raise prices by limiting supply while demand remains constant. We do not mean to deny that an agreement not to advertise service quality might have anticompetitive effects. We merely mean that, absent further analysis of the kind Justice Breyer undertakes, it is not possible to conclude that the net effect of this particular restriction is anticompetitive.

restrictions on unverifiable quality and comfort advertising as nothing more than a procompetitive ban on puffery. . . .

The point is not that the CDA's restrictions necessarily have the procompetitive effect claimed by the CDA; it is possible that banning quality claims might have no effect at all on competitiveness if, for example, many dentists made very much the same sort of claims. And it is also of course possible that the restrictions might in the final analysis be anticompetitive. The point, rather, is that the plausibility of competing claims about the effects of the professional advertising restrictions rules out the indulgently abbreviated review to which the Commission's order was treated. The obvious anticompetitive effect that triggers abbreviated analysis has not been shown.

In light of our focus on the adequacy of the Court of Appeals's analysis, Justice Breyer's thorough-going, de novo antitrust analysis contains much to impress on its own merits but little to demonstrate the sufficiency of the Court of Appeals's review. The obligation to give a more deliberate look than a quick one does not arise at the door of this Court and should not be satisfied here in the first instance. Had the Court of Appeals engaged in a painstaking discussion in a league with Justice Breyer's (compare his 14 pages with the Ninth Circuit's 8), and had it confronted the comparability of these restrictions to bars on clearly verifiable advertising, its reasoning might have sufficed to justify its conclusion. Certainly Justice Breyer's treatment of the antitrust issues here is no "quick look." Lingering is more like it, and indeed Justice Breyer, not surprisingly, stops short of endorsing the Court of Appeals's discussion as adequate to the task at hand.

Saying here that the Court of Appeals's conclusion at least required a more extended examination of the possible factual underpinnings than it received is not, of course, necessarily to call for the fullest market analysis. Although we have said that a challenge to a "naked restraint on price and output" need not be supported by "a detailed market analysis" in order to "requir[e] some competitive justification," . . . The truth is that our categories of analysis of anticompetitive effect are less fixed than terms like "per se," "quick look," and "rule of reason" tend to make them appear. We have recognized, for example, that "there is often no bright line separating per se from Rule of Reason analysis," since "considerable inquiry into market conditions" may be required before the application of any so-called "per se" condemnation is justified. As the circumstances here demonstrate, there is generally no categorical line to be drawn between restraints that give rise to an intuitively obvious inference of anticompetitive effect and those that call for more detailed treatment. What is required, rather, is an enquiry meet for the case, looking to the circumstances, details, and logic of a restraint. The object is to see whether the experience of the market has been so clear, or necessarily will be, that a confident conclusion about the principal tendency of a restriction will follow from a quick (or at least quicker) look, in place of a more sedulous one. And of course what we see may vary over time, if rule-of-reason analyses in case after case reach identical conclusions. For now, at least, a less quick look was required for the initial assessment of the tendency of these professional advertising restrictions. Because the Court of Appeals did not scrutinize the assumption of relative anticompetitive tendencies, we vacate the judgment and remand the case for a fuller consideration of the issue.

It is so ordered.

JUSTICE BREYER, with whom JUSTICE STEVENS, JUSTICE KENNEDY, and JUSTICE GINSBURG join, concurring in part and dissenting in part.

I . . . agree that in a "rule of reason" antitrust case "the quality of proof required should vary with the circumstances," that "[w]hat is required . . . is an enquiry meet for the case," and that the object is a "confident conclusion about the principal tendency of a restriction." But I do not agree that the Court has properly applied those unobjectionable principles here. In my view, a traditional application of the rule of reason to the facts as found by the Commission requires affirming the Commission—just as the Court of Appeals did below.

= * *

I

The Commission's conclusion is lawful if its "factual findings," insofar as they are supported by "substantial evidence," "make out a violation of Sherman Act § 1." [ ] To determine whether that is so, I would not simply ask whether the restraints at issue are anticompetitive overall. Rather, like the Court of Appeals (and the Commission), I would break that question down into four classical, subsidiary antitrust questions: (1) What is the specific restraint at issue? (2) What are its likely anticompetitive effects? (3) Are there offsetting procompetitive justifications? (4) Do the parties have sufficient market power to make a difference?

= * *

A

The most important question is the first: What are the specific restraints at issue? [ ] Those restraints do not include merely the agreement to which the California Dental Association's (Dental Association or Association) ethical rule literally refers, namely, a promise to refrain from advertising that is " 'false or misleading in any material respect.' "[ ] Instead, the Commission found a set of restraints arising out of the way the Dental Association implemented this innocent-sounding ethical rule in practice, through advisory opinions, guidelines, enforcement policies, and review of membership applications. As implemented, the ethical rule reached beyond its nominal target, to prevent truthful and nondeceptive advertising. In particular, the Commission determined that the rule, in practice:

(1) "precluded advertising that characterized a dentist's fees as being low, reasonable, or affordable,"

(2) "precluded advertising . . . of across the board discounts," and

(3) "prohibit[ed] all quality claims."

Whether the Dental Association's basic rule as implemented actually restrained the truthful and nondeceptive advertising of low prices, across-the-board discounts, and quality service are questions of fact. The Administrative Law Judge (ALJ) and the Commission may have found those questions difficult ones. But both the ALJ and the Commission ultimately found against the Dental Association in respect to these facts. And the question for us—

whether those agency findings are supported by substantial evidence, is not difficult.

The Court of Appeals referred explicitly to some of the evidence that it found adequate to support the Commission's conclusions. It pointed out, for example, that the Dental Association's "advisory opinions and guidelines indicate that ... descriptions of prices as 'reasonable' or 'low' do not comply" with the Association's rule; that in "numerous cases" the Association "advised members of objections to special offers, senior citizen discounts, and new patient discounts, apparently without regard to their truth"; and that one advisory opinion "expressly states that claims as to the quality of services are inherently likely to be false or misleading," all "without any particular consideration of whether" such statements were "true or false." [ ]

The Commission itself had before it far more evidence. It referred to instances in which the Association, without regard for the truthfulness of the statements at issue, recommended denial of membership to dentists wishing to advertise, for example, "reasonable fees quoted in advance," "major savings," or "making teeth cleaning ... inexpensive." It referred to testimony that "across-the-board discount advertising in literal compliance with the requirements 'would probably take two pages in the telephone book' and '[n]obody is going to really advertise in that fashion.' "And it pointed to many instances in which the Dental Association suppressed such advertising claims as "we guarantee all dental work for 1 year," "latest in cosmetic dentistry," and "gentle dentistry in a caring environment."

* * *

B

Do each of the three restrictions mentioned have "the potential for genuine adverse effects on competition"? I should have thought that the anticompetitive tendencies of the three restrictions were obvious. An agreement not to advertise that a fee is reasonable, that service is inexpensive, or that a customer will receive a discount makes it more difficult for a dentist to inform customers that he charges a lower price. If the customer does not know about a lower price, he will find it more difficult to buy lower price service. That fact, in turn, makes it less likely that a dentist will obtain more customers by offering lower prices. And that likelihood means that dentists will prove less likely to offer lower prices. . . .

The restrictions on the advertising of service quality also have serious anticompetitive tendencies. . . . [I]t is rather late in the day for anyone to deny the significant anticompetitive tendencies of an agreement that restricts competition in any legitimate respect, let alone one that inhibits customers from learning about the quality of a dentist's service.

Nor did the Commission rely solely on the unobjectionable proposition that a restriction on the ability of dentists to advertise on quality is likely to limit their incentive to compete on quality. Rather, the Commission pointed to record evidence affirmatively establishing that quality-based competition is important to dental consumers in California. [The dissent goes on to summarize evidence that advertising concerning quality will bring in more patients and that restrictions adversely affected dentists who advertise.]

C

We must also ask whether, despite their anticompetitive tendencies, these restrictions might be justified by other procompetitive tendencies or redeeming virtues. [ ] This is a closer question—at least in theory. The Dental Association argues that the three relevant restrictions are inextricably tied to a legitimate Association effort to restrict false or misleading advertising. The Association, the argument goes, had to prevent dentists from engaging in the kind of truthful, nondeceptive advertising that it banned in order effectively to stop dentists from making unverifiable claims about price or service quality, which claims would mislead the consumer.

The problem with this or any similar argument is an empirical one. Notwithstanding its theoretical plausibility, the record does not bear out such a claim. The Commission, which is expert in the area of false and misleading advertising, was uncertain whether petitioner had even made the claim. It characterized petitioner's efficiencies argument as rooted in the (unproved) factual assertion that its ethical rule "challenges only advertising that is false or misleading." Regardless, the Court of Appeals wrote, in respect to the price restrictions, that "the record provides no evidence that the rule has in fact led to increased disclosure and transparency of dental pricing." With respect to quality advertising, the Commission stressed that the Association "offered no convincing argument, let alone evidence, that consumers of dental services have been, or are likely to be, harmed by the broad categories of advertising it restricts." Nor did the Court of Appeals think that the Association's unsubstantiated contention that "claims about quality are inherently unverifiable and therefore misleading" could "justify banning all quality claims without regard to whether they are, in fact, false or misleading."

With one exception, my own review of the record reveals no significant evidentiary support for the proposition that the Association's members must agree to ban truthful price and quality advertising in order to stop untruthful claims. The one exception is the obvious fact that one can stop untruthful advertising if one prohibits all advertising. But since the Association made virtually no effort to sift the false from the true, [ ] that fact does not make out a valid antitrust defense. [ ]

In the usual Sherman Act § 1 case, the defendant bears the burden of establishing a procompetitive justification. [ ] And the Court of Appeals was correct when it concluded that no such justification had been established here.

D

I shall assume that the Commission must prove one additional circumstance, namely, that the Association's restraints would likely have made a real difference in the marketplace. The Commission, disagreeing with the ALJ on this single point, found that the Association did possess enough market power to make a difference.... These facts, in the Court of Appeals' view, were sufficient to show "enough market power to harm competition through [the Association's] standard setting in the area of advertising." []

II

In the Court's view, the legal analysis conducted by the Court of Appeals was insufficient, and the Court remands the case for a more thorough application of the rule of reason. But in what way did the Court of Appeals fail? I find the Court's answers to this question unsatisfactory—when one divides the overall Sherman Act question into its traditional component parts and adheres to traditional judicial practice for allocating the burdens of persuasion in an antitrust case.

* * *

The upshot, in my view, is that the Court of Appeals, applying ordinary antitrust principles, reached an unexceptional conclusion. It is the same legal conclusion that this Court itself reached in *Indiana Federation*—a much closer case than this one. There the Court found that an agreement by dentists not to submit dental X rays to insurers violated the rule of reason. The anticompetitive tendency of that agreement was to reduce competition among dentists in respect to their willingness to submit X rays to insurers, [ ]—a matter in respect to which consumers are relatively indifferent, as compared to advertising of price discounts and service quality, the matters at issue here. The redeeming virtue in Indiana Federation was the alleged undesirability of having insurers consider a range of matters when deciding whether treatment was justified—a virtue no less plausible, and no less proved, than the virtue offered here. The "power" of the dentists to enforce their agreement was no greater than that at issue here (control of 75% to 90% of the relevant markets). It is difficult to see how the two cases can be reconciled.

* * *

Notes and Questions

1. On remand, the Ninth Circuit ordered dismissal finding the FTC had failed to show that the CDA's restrictions had a net anticompetitive effect and that the evidence of anticompetitive intent was ambiguous. 224 F.3d 942 (9th Cir. 2000). While acknowledging that the Supreme Court had not mandated a full blown rule of reason inquiry, the Ninth Circuit "opt[ed] for a particularly searching rule of reason inquiry in light of the plausibility and strength of the procompetitive justifications" supplied by expert testimony that advertising restrictions tend to protect the public from false or misleading information or unscrupulous providers. In view of the Supreme Court's decision and the Ninth Circuit's prior findings, do you find this approach surprising? If you do, you are in good company; see Stephen Calkins, California Dental Association: Not a Quick Look but Not the Full Monty, 67 Antitrust L.J. 495 (2000); William J. Kolasky, California Dental Association v. FTC: The New Antitrust Empiricism, 14 Antitrust 68 (Fall 1999). Equally controversial was the Ninth Circuit's decision not to remand to the FTC for further proceedings. The Court concluded that the FTC had ample opportunity to present evidence under a rule of reason theory but had failed to do so.

In finding the FTC's proof of net anticompetitive effect wanting, the Ninth Circuit parsed a number of economic studies advanced by the Commission in support of the proposition that restrictions on advertising tend to raise prices and do not materially improve quality of services. Ultimately it declined to rely on empirical studies which dealt with complete bans on advertising (in contrast to the partial restrictions imposed by the CDA) or with professions other than dentistry, such as optometry or law. How exacting should a court's proof requirements be when dealing with empirical economic evidence? Does the expertise of the FTC as an administrative agency charged with combating misleading advertising supply a basis for decreasing the role of the courts as arbiters of competing economic studies? For a useful survey of the evidence concerning the effects of advertising, concluding that evidence not in the record before the Supreme Court "overwhelmingly demonstrates that the fears of the CDA majority [were] unjustified," see Timothy J. Muris, The Rule of Reason After California Dental, 68 Antitrust L J. 527 (2000). See also Viazis v. American Association of Orthodontists, 314 F.3d 758 (5th Cir. 2002) (applying *California Dental* and concluding that orthodontist suspended for violating association's advertising rules had failed to proffer "relevant data").

2.   In FTC v. Indiana Federation of Dentists, 476 U.S. 447, 106 S.Ct. 2009, 90 L.Ed.2d 445 (1986), the FTC examined an agreement among dentists to refuse to submit x-rays used for diagnosis and treatment of patients to insurers. Insurers required x-rays to carry out review of the necessity of treatment pursuant to dental insurance plans limiting payment to the "least expensive set adequate treatment." While not employing the per se rule, the Court adopted the form of analysis described in CDA as a "quick look."

> Application of the Rule of Reason to these facts is not a matter of any great difficulty. The Federation's policy takes the form of a horizontal agreement among the participating dentists to withhold from their customers a particular service that they desire—the forwarding of x-rays to insurance companies along with claim forms. "While this is not price fixing as such, no elaborate industry analysis is required to demonstrate the anti-competitive character of such an agreement." ... A refusal to compete with respect to the package of services offered to customers, no less than a refusal to compete with respect to the price term of an agreement, impairs the ability of the market to advance social welfare by ensuring the provision of desired goods and services to consumers at a price approximating the marginal cost of providing them.

Id. at 459. Is there a significant difference between the conduct in *California Dental* and *Indiana Federation of Dentists*? Didn't both cases involve actions by a sizable majority of dentists to withhold information from purchasers on the grounds that they could not adequately evaluate it? Note the absence of direct proof of the restraint's effect on consumers in either case. Has the Court changed the requirements for "quick look" evaluations? What does *California Dental* suggest about the way courts should evaluate restrictions involving professionals in the future? Are the problems associated with asymmetry of information so pronounced in health care markets that professionals should be free from antitrust scrutiny? See Marina Lao, Comment The Rule of Reason and Horizontal Restraints Involving Professionals, 68 Antitrust L.J. 499 (2000). For an insightful analysis of how antitrust might evaluate restraints of trade that improve overall welfare by overcoming market imperfections, see Peter J. Hammer, Antitrust Beyond Competition: Market Failures, Total Welfare, and the Challenge of Intramarket Second–Best Tradeoffs, 98 Mich. L. Rev. 849 (2000).

3.   Under what circumstances would competing providers sharing information on fees or other competitively sensitive topics pose a significant threat? Should it ever be deemed per se illegal? See United States v. Burgstiner, 1991–1 Trade Cas. (CCH) ¶ 69,422 (S.D. Ga. 1991) (consent decree) (exchange of information about fees among twenty-two OB/GYNs after local businesses announced their intention to form a PPO; fees for normal deliveries and caesarean sections increased by $500 after the exchange). However, in some circumstances, joint provision and dissemination of data may improve competitive conditions and should be evaluated under the rule of reason. The federal enforcement agencies' enforcement guidelines allow providers to collectively provide factual information

concerning fees provided they adopt "reasonable safeguards" against anticompetitive activities. See U.S. Dept. of Justice & Federal Trade Commission, Statement of Antitrust Enforcement Policy in Health Care, Stmt. 5 (1996).

4.   How should antitrust law treat price surveys by business coalitions or other buyers of health services? When might buyer power (monopsony) pose competitive problems? See Clark C. Havighurst, Antitrust Issues in the Joint Purchasing of Health Care, 1995 Utah L. Rev. 409 (1995); Frances H. Miller, Health Insurance Purchasing Alliances: Monopsony Threat or Procompetitive Rx for Health Sector Ills, 79 Cornell L. Rev. 1546 (1994). The FTC and DOJ have issued numerous advisory opinions and business review letters approving such arrangements. Information exchange constitute a Section One violation or must there be an implicit agreement to fix prices? See United States v. Utah Society for Healthcare Human Resources, 1994–2 Trade Cas. (CCH) ¶ 70,795, 1994 WL 729931 (D. Utah 1994) (consent decree) (defendant hospital associations and eight individual hospitals charged with conspiring to restrain wage competition among themselves through a series of telephone calls and wage surveys that resulted in smaller wage increases than defendants would otherwise have paid). See also Letter from Charles A. James, Assistant Attorney General, U.S. Dept. of Justice to Jerry Edmonds (Sept. 23, 2002), available at www.usdoj.gov/opa/pr/2002 and Letter from Jeffrey Brennan, Bureau of Competition, FTC to Gregory G. Binford, (Feb. 6, 2003), available at www.ftc.gov/bc/adops. Despite evidence that physicians intended to use the results to increase their fees—in one case explicitly planning a campaign to "inform and educate the general public" about the "ill effects and other consequences of the policies and procedures, including depressed reimbursement, of third party payors," the agencies approved both plans. The letters cite a variety of factors that reduced risks that the data would foster collusion, such as the fact that survey data would not identify individual provider information and the physician markets were not concentrated. Does the result surprise you? Should the parties' intent to use the data for "advocacy" purposes offset the weight afforded to mitigating factors?

Note: The Nurse Wage Cases

A series of nearly identical class action complaints have been filed alleging that hospitals conspired to depress wages of registered nurses and to exchange information on nurse compensation, in violation of Section 1 of the Sherman Act. See e.g., Clarke v. Baptist Memorial Healthcare Corp., No. 06–2377–SHM-dkv, (W.D. Tenn. May 17, 2007) (denying motion to dismiss). Reed v. Advocate Health Care, Nos. 06–C–3337 & 06–C–3569, 2007 WL 967932, 2007–1 Trade Cas. ¶ 75,667 (N.D. Ill. March 28, 2007)(refusing to grant summary judgment based on labor exemption). See also United States v. Arizona Hospital and Healthcare Association, No. 2:07–cv–1030–PHX (D. Ariz. filed May 22, 2007), available at http://www.usdoj.gov/atr/cases/azhha.htm (settling claim that hospital association used "registry" to fix prices for the purchase of temporary nursing services from nurse staffing agencies). See Jeff Miles, The Nursing Shortage, Wage Information Sharing Among Hospitals, and the Antitrust Laws: The Nurse Wage Cases, 7 Hous. J. Health L. & Pol. 305 (2007). The complaints allege that the hospitals agreed to exchange detailed, non-public information regarding both current and future compensation paid to nurses, agreed not to compete with respect to nurse compensation, paid nurses at nearly identical rates, and recruited jointly at job fairs in order to avoid competing with each other.

The nurse wage cases allege that hospitals conspired to fix prices. A long line of antitrust precedent holds that interdependent, "parallel" pricing does not amount to a conspiracy. Something further must be proved, and information sharing may help supply that additional proof. See Todd v. Exxon Corp., 275 F.3d 191, 198 (2d Cir. 2001) ("Information exchange is an example of a facilitating practice that can help support an inference of a price-fixing agreement"). Note that the ultimate question on the conspiracy issue is whether there was a "meeting of the minds" to engage in collusive wage-setting. If a conspiracy is established, would this be a per se violation? Is it likely to be ancillary to some other procompetitive agreement?

The class action cases also raise the analytically distinct claim that the information sharing practices resulted in lower wages. Note that because the rule of reason would apply in assessing whether this constituted a violation under Section 1 of the Sherman Act, plaintiffs will have to either supply direct evidence of an anticompetitive effect or prove effect indirectly by establishing that the defendants possessed market power. Direct proof would likely entail either econometric studies estimating the "competitive" wage level and then comparing that level to the prevailing wage level in plaintiffs' market, or alternatively, wage comparisons with similar markets in which collusion did not occur. See Miles, supra, for an excellent analysis of the complexities inherent in using these methodologies. The alternative approach, establishing effect by indirect evidence requires requires plaintiffs to prove a relevant market. In alleging an effect on the market for hospital RNs, the class action plaintiffs exclude non-RNs (such as licensed practical nurses and nurses' aids) who may perform some of the same functions as RNs, as well as RNs who provide services outside of hospitals, such as in physicians' offices or ambulatory care facilities. What facts might support such a narrow market definition? As we will see, the critical question in defining a market is: what effect will a price change have on market participants? That is, would price-lowering effects of hospital collusion likely cause RNs to shift to non-hospital employment?

2. Private Accreditation and Professional Standard–Setting

One of the most challenging problems posed by the application of antitrust law to health care concerns the activities of private organizations of health professionals designed to promote high standards of professionalism and advance scientific learning through the promulgation of standards, guidelines, and ethical norms. Although antitrust analysis explicitly considers only the competitive effects of an association's challenged activities, evidence of quality goals frequently enters the picture, sometimes appropriately and sometimes not.

WILK v. AMERICAN MEDICAL ASSOCIATION

United States Court of Appeals, Seventh Circuit, 1990.
895 F.2d 352, cert. denied, 498 U.S. 982, 111 S.Ct. 513, 112 L.Ed.2d 524 (1990).

MANION, CIRCUIT JUDGE.

The district court held that the American Medical Association ("AMA") violated § 1 of the Sherman Act, 15 U.S.C. § 1, by conducting an illegal boycott in restraint of trade directed at chiropractors generally, and the four plaintiffs in particular. The court granted an injunction ... requiring, among other things, wide publication of its order.... The AMA appeals the finding of liability, and contends that, in any event, injunctive relief is unnecessary.... We affirm.

I.

[Plaintiffs, licensed chiropractors charged that the AMA violated sections 1 and 2 of the Sherman act by engaging in a conspiracy to eliminate the chiropractic profession by refusing to deal with plaintiffs and other chiropractors. After recounting the history of the AMA's opposition to and actions against chiropractic, the Court applies the rule of reason and finds sufficient evidence to conclude that the AMA possessed market power in the "health care services market" and that in any event the district court correctly found substantial evidence of adverse effects on competition caused by the boycott.]

* * * Moving on, the AMA argues that even if market power existed, it escapes liability under the rule of reason because [the AMA rule against associating with chiropractors] had overriding pro-competitive effects. The AMA's argument is not unpersuasive in the abstract; but unfortunately it relies on evidence which the district court rejected as "speculative." * * * Essentially, the AMA argues that the market for medical services is one where there is "information asymmetry." In other words, health care consumers almost invariably lack sufficient information needed to evaluate the quality of medical services. This increases the risk of fraud and deception on consumers by unscrupulous health care providers possibly causing what the AMA terms "market failure": consumers avoiding necessary treatment (for fear of fraud), and accepting treatment with no expectation of assured quality. The AMA's conduct, the theory goes, ensured that physicians acquired reputations for quality (in part, by not associating with unscientific cultists), and thus allowed consumers to be assured that physicians would use only scientifically valid treatments. This in effect simultaneously provided consumers with essential information and protected competition.

Getting needed information to the market is a fine goal, but the district court found that the AMA was not motivated solely by such altruistic concerns. Indeed, the court found that the AMA intended to "destroy a competitor," namely, chiropractors. It is not enough to carry the day to argue that competition should be eliminated in the name of public safety. * * *

* * *

[W]e agree with the district court that the AMA's boycott constituted an unreasonable restraint of trade under § 1 of the Sherman Act under the rule of reason. Therefore, the district court's findings that the AMA's boycott was anti-competitive, and was not counter-balanced by any pro-competitive effects were not erroneous. * * *

C. *Patient Care Defense*

In the AMA's first appeal, ... we explained that if plaintiffs met their burden of persuasion on remand by showing that [the rule against chiropractic] and the implementing conduct had restricted competition rather than promoting it, the burden of persuasion would shift to the defendants to show:

> (1) that they genuinely entertained a concern for what they perceive as scientific method in the care of each person with whom they have entered into a doctor-patient relationship; (2) that this concern is objectively reasonable; (3) that this concern has been the dominant motivating factor in defendants' promulgation of [the rule] and in the conduct intended to implement it; and (4) that this concern for scientific method in patient

care could not have been adequately satisfied in a manner less restrictive of competition.

* * *

The district court held that the AMA failed to meet the defense's second and fourth elements: that its concern for scientific method in patient care was objectively reasonable, and that the concern for scientific method in patient care could not have been satisfied adequately in a manner less restrictive of competition, respectively. While only those two rulings are at issue, it is useful to summarize the district court's treatment of the entire defense.

Although doubting the AMA's genuineness regarding its concern for scientific method in patient care, the district court concluded that the AMA established that element. While it was attacking chiropractic as unscientific, the AMA simultaneously was attacking other unscientific methods of disease treatment (e.g., the Krebiozen treatment of cancer), and, as the district court noted, the existence of medical standards or guidelines against unscientific practice was relatively common. * * * The court, however, found that the AMA failed to carry its burden of persuasion as to whether its concern for scientific method in patient care was objectively reasonable.

The court acknowledged that during the period that the Committee on Quackery [an AMA committee focusing on practices of providers of alternative medicine] was operating, there was plenty of material supporting the belief that all chiropractic was unscientific. But, according to the court (and this is unchallenged), at the same time, there was evidence before the Committee that chiropractic was effective, indeed more effective than the medical profession, in treating certain kinds of problems, such as back injuries. The Committee was also aware, the court found, that some medical physicians believed chiropractic could be effective and that chiropractors were better trained to deal with musculoskeletal problems than most medical physicians. Moreover, the AMA's own evidence suggested that at some point during its lengthy boycott, there was no longer an objectively reasonable concern that would support a boycott of the entire chiropractic profession. Also important was the fact that "it was very clear" that the Committee's members did not have open minds to pro-chiropractic arguments or evidence. * * *

Next, the court found that the AMA met its burden in establishing that its concern about scientific method was the dominant motivating factor for promulgating [the rule] and in the conduct undertaken and intended to implement it. * * * But even so, the court acknowledged there was evidence showing that the AMA was motivated by economic concerns, as well.

Finally, the court concluded that the AMA failed to meet its burden in demonstrating that its concern for scientific method in patient care could not have been satisfied adequately in a manner less restrictive of competition. The court stated that the AMA had presented no evidence of other methods of achieving their objectives such as public education or any other less restrictive approach. * * *

* * *

Notes and Question

1. The Supreme Court addressed the defendants' quality of care justifications in *Indiana Federation of Dentists*, 476 U.S. at 462–463:

> The gist of [defendant's] claim is that x-rays, standing alone, are not adequate bases for diagnosis of dental problems or for the formulation of an acceptable course of treatment. Accordingly, if insurance companies are permitted to determine whether they will pay a claim for dental treatment on the basis of x-rays as opposed to a full examination of all the diagnostic aids available to the examining dentist, there is a danger that they will erroneously decline to pay for treatment that is in fact in the interest of the patient, and that the patient will as a result be deprived of fully adequate care.

> The Federation's argument is flawed both legally and factually. The premise of the argument is that, far from having no effect on the cost of dental services chosen by patients and their insurers, the provision of x-rays will have too great an impact: it will lead to the reduction of costs through the selection of inadequate treatment.... The argument is, in essence, that an unrestrained market in which consumers are given access to the information they believe to be relevant to their choices will lead them to make unwise and even dangerous choices. Such an argument amounts to "nothing less than a frontal assault on the basic policy of the Sherman Act." [ ]

> Moreover, there is no particular reason to believe that the provision of information will be more harmful to consumers in the market for dental services than in other markets. Insurers deciding what level of care to pay for are not themselves the recipients of those services, but it is by no means clear that they lack incentives to consider the welfare of the patient as well as the minimization of costs. They are themselves in competition for the patronage of the patients—or, in most cases, the unions or businesses that contract on their behalf for group insurance coverage—and must satisfy their potential customers that they will not only provide coverage at a reasonable cost, but also that the coverage will be adequate to meet their customers' dental needs....

Does the Supreme Court's holding in *Indiana Federation of Dentists* overrule the Seventh Circuit's "patient care defense" in *Wilk*? The *Wilk* "patient care defense" requires that a court evaluate whether the defendant's "concern" was "objectively reasonable." How is the court to do this? Do you agree with the opinion's assumptions about the insurers' capacity and incentive to monitor quality?

2. Is it possible to present evidence of patient care and quality-improving benefits under the rationale that such proof demonstrated that a professional restraint counteracts market imperfections? Under a "market failure defense," in balancing the anticompetitive and procompetitive effects of a restraint, courts would analyze the functioning of the market in which the restraint operates. Defendant would be allowed to prove that the challenged restraint improved competition by offsetting a market failure. See Thomas L. Greaney, Quality of Care and Market Failure Defenses in Antitrust Health Care Litigation, 21 Conn. L. Rev. 605 (1989). For example in Koefoot v. American College of Surgeons, 652 F.Supp. 882 (N.D. Ill. 1986), plaintiff challenged a bylaw of the American College of Surgeons (ACS) that proscribed "itinerant surgery," which prohibited surgeons from delegating post-operative care to physicians other than surgeons. Could being designated as a Fellow in the ACS be regarded as a seal of approval? How might it help patients or managed care organizations in choosing surgeons? The

health care market suffers from market imperfections, such as problems with information, and from market failures such as a comparatively higher incidence of natural monopolies. Jonathan E. Fielding & Thomas Rice, Can Managed Competition Solve the Problem of Market Failure, 12 Health Aff. 216 (Supp. 1993).

3.   Can denial of accreditation or membership in a prestigious professional society constitute a valid antitrust injury claim? Marrese v. American Academy of Orthopaedic Surgeons, 1991–1 Trade Cas. (CCH) ¶ 69,398 (N.D.Ill. 1991), aff'd, 977 F.2d 585 (7th Cir. 1992) (unpublished opinion), is instructive in this regard. Dr. Marrese claimed that his rejection by the AAO amounted to an illegal boycott that harmed his reputation and denied him important professional benefits including patient referrals and access to the professional orthopaedic society of surgeons continuing medical education services. The Seventh Circuit's basis for upholding the trial court's decision rested on plaintiff's failure to prove that denial of membership caused a restraint of trade. Noting that membership was not necessary to practice medicine, obtain a staff appointment or receive referrals, the court found no restriction of output in any market. Moreover, it rejected the claim that withholding membership, which plaintiff analogized to a "seal of approval," stigmatized Dr. Marrese. Besides questioning whether such a stigma was significant (because plaintiff continued to receive referrals), the Court of Appeals stated that the loss of referrals would not be sufficient absent evidence that the Academy had prevented others from dealing with the doctor. See also, Viazis v. American Ass'n of Orthodontists, 314 F.3d 758 (5th Cir. 2002) (no concerted action in disciplinary action by association).

Note: Physician Staff Privileges

Hundreds of physicians who have been denied staff privileges at hospitals or had their privileges revoked, suspended or limited have brought suit under the antitrust laws against the hospital or its staff or both. These cases—aptly termed the "junk food of antitrust health care litigation"—have been almost uniformly unsuccessful. See 2 John J. Miles, Health Care and Antitrust Law § 10–1; Hammer & Sage, Antitrust, Health Care Quality and the Courts, *supra*. For a rare example of a successful challenge to a staff privileges determination, see Boczar v. Manatee Hospitals & Health Systems, Inc., 993 F.2d 1514 (11th Cir. 1993) (upholding a jury finding of anticompetitive intent and effect based on the hospital's pretextual explanations defending its actions, the plaintiff doctor's involvement in bringing to light deficiencies of other physicians, and the hospital's economic concerns about threatened loss of admissions from competing physicians who were opposed to plaintiff's membership on the staff). See also Brown v. Presbyterian Healthcare Servs., 101 F.3d 1324 (10th Cir. 1996).

Aggrieved physicians typically employ one of three antitrust theories. First, many assert that the denial of privileges is an anticompetitive boycott, usually instigated by rivals on the hospital's medical staff. See Oltz v. St. Peter's Community Hospital, 861 F.2d 1440 (9th Cir. 1988) (upholding nurse anesthetist's claim that a group of anesthesiologists had acquired an exclusive contract with a hospital by coercing it to terminate the anesthetist's contract; after plaintiff left the hospital each of the defendant anesthesiologists experienced a forty to fifty percent increase in earnings). Courts have dismissed or granted summary judgment in almost all such cases on one of several grounds with virtually all decisions applying the rule of reason. See, e.g., Flegel v. Christian Hosp., 4 F.3d 682 (8th Cir. 1993). Recall that under the Sherman Act, defendants engaged in a collective refusal to deal must advance a procompetitive justification in order to avoid per se treatment. Why is this requirement so readily met with respect to staff privileges determinations?

Under the rule of reason, plaintiff must establish that defendants have market power (unless, as in *Oltz* there is direct proof of effect), which is generally not present if there is a number of alternative hospitals at which the physician may practice. Robinson v. Magovern, 521 F.Supp. 842 (W.D.Pa. 1981), aff'd 688 F.2d 824 (3d Cir. 1982). Second, plaintiffs often cannot meet the conspiracy requirement under Section 1 of the Sherman Act because, where the hospital is the ultimate decision-maker on the grant of staff privileges, there is no plurality of actors. Under an alternative theory—the claim that the hospital has conspired with its medical staff—the courts are sharply divided. Compare Weiss v. York Hospital, 745 F.2d 786 (3d Cir. 1984) with Bolt v. Halifax Hosp. Medical Center, 891 F.2d 810 (11th Cir. 1990). See James F. Blumstein & Frank A. Sloan, Antitrust and Hospital Peer Review, 51 L. & Contemp. Probs. 7 (1988); William S. Brewbaker III, Antitrust Conspiracy Doctrine and the Hospital Enterprise, 74 B.U.L. Rev. 67 (1994). For a representative case surveying many of the defenses available to hospitals in staff privileges cases, see Oksanen v. Page Memorial Hospital, 945 F.2d 696 (4th Cir. 1991) (concluding with the observation "the antitrust laws were not intended to inhibit hospitals from promoting quality patient care through peer review nor were the laws intended as a vehicle for converting business tort claims into antitrust causes of action").

Many challenges involve exclusive contracts, pursuant to which certain medical services such as radiology, pathology, and anesthesiology are provided in a hospital by a single group of physicians. Plaintiffs challenging these contracts on antitrust grounds have attempted to characterize the contracts as "tying" arrangements which are per se illegal. This claim requires the plaintiff to prove that a seller with market power in one product (the tying product) has forced a buyer to purchase another product (the tied product) that the buyer ordinarily would prefer to purchase separately. Plaintiff doctors have been uniformly unsuccessful in challenging exclusive contracts as illegal tying arrangements. See Jefferson Parish Hospital Dist. No. 2 v. Hyde, 466 U.S. 2, 104 S.Ct. 1551, 80 L.Ed.2d 2 (1984); Collins v. Associated Pathologists, Ltd., 844 F.2d 473 (7th Cir. 1988).

Exclusive contracts may also be challenged as "exclusive dealing arrangements" under Section 1 of the Sherman Act. Staff privilege determinations are frequently challenged on a number of other grounds including due process, equal protection, and statutory civil rights claims. See generally Chapter 9 *supra*. Finally, an important factor further limiting the viability of these lawsuits is the Health Care Quality Improvement Act, 42 U.S.C. §§ 11101–11152, discussed in Chapter 9, which affords immunity to individuals involved involved in making staff privileges determinations in certain circumstances. Note however how the Act's "four reasonables" might in some cases prevent defendants from invoking HCQIA immunity. For example, how would a showing that defendant physicians involved in making an evaluation for staff privileges purposes were expressed concerns about a plaintiff's willingness to discount his fees be interpreted under the "reasonable belief" standard?

Problem: Quick Stop Clinics

Drug World, a pharmacy chain operating a large number of retail pharmacies in the upper Midwest, has announced plans to open 24–Hour "Quick Stop Clinics" at all its locations. The clinics will be staffed by RNs and PAs depending on state licensure and scope of practice laws. These providers will perform routine exams, take cultures, and prescribe medications within the scope of practice permitted under state law. Each clinic will enter into referral agreements with one or more local hospitals to assure direct access to physicians when the need presents. Good Samaritan Hospital (GSH) has entered into such an arrangement with a local Quick Stop Clinic. Under their partnership agreement, all doctors providing back up to Quick Stop RNs will have admitting privileges at GSH, and the clinics will be able to "streamline" a patient's journey to a specialist or through the emergency room at GSH, when medically appropriate.

A number of doctors holding staff privileges at GSH became quite upset when they got wind of this agreement. The group, though small (fewer than 5% of all doctors with privileges at the hospital), includes both primary care physicians who are concerned about losing current patients to the doctors to whom the clinic refers and several prominent specialists who feel they will lose established lines of referrals from primary care physicians. Some doctors believe that patients will come to them in worse shape, with missed diagnoses, and inadequate follow up. They have posted a notice at the hospital calling for an emergency meeting to discuss options to counter GSH's plan. The doctors intend to propose three possible courses of action, asking colleagues to:

- Agree that no doctors will serve as a supervisory physician to Quick Stop Clinic RNs or PAs or or accept referrals from the Clinic;

- Sign a letter to GSH adminstrators announcing plans to change their admitting practices so as to reduce the number of patients they admit to GSH; or

- Send a letter to all GSH physicians supplying academic studies and historical evidence of potential risks to patients from receiving care from nonphysicians under arrangements such as are proposed.

The CEO of GSH has approached you for advice on the legality of each action contemplated by the staff physicians. She says she wants to fight them vigorously and that she is willing to consider filing an antitrust lawsuit, complaining to the Department of Justice, terminating the staff privileges of the ringleaders of the group, or undertaking any other steps you recommend.

II. HEALTH CARE ENTERPRISES, INTEGRATION AND FINANCING

As discussed in Chapter 10, *supra*, the integration and consolidation of the health care industry spawned countless networks, health plans, alliances, and other business enterprises. These entities and contractual relationships often entail cooperation or outright mergers between previously competing providers or health plans. As such, they also raise the full spectrum of antitrust issues. For health care attorneys counseling clients forming such organizations, these issues are often the subject of close attention because many entities are quite openly seeking to acquire the maximum leverage they can in the competitive fray.

A. PROVIDER–CONTROLLED NETWORKS AND HEALTH PLANS

ARIZONA v. MARICOPA COUNTY MEDICAL SOCIETY

Supreme Court of the United States, 1982.
457 U.S. 332, 102 S.Ct. 2466, 73 L.Ed.2d 48.

JUSTICE STEVENS delivered the opinion of the Court.

The question presented is whether § 1 of the Sherman Act [ ] has been violated by agreements among competing physicians setting, by majority vote, the maximum fees that they may claim in full payment for health services provided to policyholders of specified insurance plans. The United States Court of Appeals for the Ninth Circuit held that the question could not be answered without evaluating the actual purpose and effect of the agreements at a full trial. [ ] Because the undisputed facts disclose a violation of the statute, we granted certiorari, and now reverse.

* * *

II

The Maricopa Foundation for Medical Care is a nonprofit Arizona corporation composed of licensed doctors of medicine, osteopathy, and podiatry engaged in private practice. Approximately 1,750 doctors, representing about 70% of the practitioners in Maricopa County, are members.

The Maricopa Foundation was organized in 1969 for the purpose of promoting fee-for-service medicine and to provide the community with a competitive alternative to existing health insurance plans. [ ] The foundation performs three primary activities. It establishes the schedule of maximum fees that participating doctors agree to accept as payment in full for services performed for patients insured under plans approved by the foundation. It reviews the medical necessity and appropriateness of treatment provided by its members to such insured persons. It is authorized to draw checks on insurance company accounts to pay doctors for services performed for covered patients. In performing these functions, the foundation is considered an "insurance administrator" by the Director of the Arizona Department of Insurance. Its participating doctors, however, have no financial interest in the operation of the foundation.

The Pima Foundation for Medical Care, which includes about 400 member doctors, [ ] performs similar functions. For the purposes of this litigation, the parties seem to regard the activities of the two foundations as essentially the same. No challenge is made to their peer review or claim administration functions. Nor do the foundations allege that these two activities make it necessary for them to engage in the practice of establishing maximum-fee schedules. * * *[7]

The fee schedules limit the amount that the member doctors may recover for services performed for patients insured under plans approved by the foundations. To obtain this approval the insurers—including self-insured employers as well as insurance companies[8]—agree to pay the doctors' charges up to the scheduled amounts, and in exchange the doctors agree to accept

7. The parties disagree over whether the increases in the fee schedules are the cause or the result of the increases in the prevailing rate for medical services in the relevant markets. There appears to be agreement, however, that 85–95% of physicians in Maricopa County bill at or above the maximum reimbursement levels set by the Maricopa Foundation.

8. Seven different insurance companies underwrite health insurance plans that have been approved by the Maricopa Foundation, and three companies underwrite the plans approved by the Pima Foundation. The record contains no firm data on the portion of the health care market that is covered by these plans. The State relies upon a 1974 analysis indicating that insurance plans endorsed by the Maricopa Foundation had about 63% of the prepaid health care market, but the respondents contest the accuracy of this analysis.

those amounts as payment in full for their services. The doctors are free to charge higher fees to uninsured patients, and they also may charge any patient less than the scheduled maxima. A patient who is insured by a foundation-endorsed plan is guaranteed complete coverage for the full amount of his medical bills only if he is treated by a foundation member. He is free to go to a nonmember physician and is still covered for charges that do not exceed the maximum-fee schedule, but he must pay any excess that the nonmember physician may charge.

The impact of the foundation fee schedules on medical fees and on insurance premiums is a matter of dispute. The State of Arizona contends that the periodic upward revisions of the maximum-fee schedules have the effect of stabilizing and enhancing the level of actual charges by physicians, and that the increasing level of their fees in turn increases insurance premiums. The foundations, on the other hand, argue that the schedules impose a meaningful limit on physicians' charges, and that the advance agreement by the doctors to accept the maxima enables the insurance carriers to limit and to calculate more efficiently the risks they underwrite and therefore serves as an effective cost-containment mechanism that has saved patients and insurers millions of dollars. * * *

III

The respondents recognize that our decisions establish that price-fixing agreements are unlawful on their face. But they argue that the *per se* rule does not govern this case because the agreements at issue are horizontal and fix maximum prices, are among members of a profession, are in an industry with which the judiciary has little antitrust experience, and are alleged to have pro-competitive justifications. . . .

= * *

B

Our decisions foreclose the argument that the agreements at issue escape *per se* condemnation because they are horizontal and fix maximum prices. [The cases] place horizontal agreements to fix maximum prices on the same legal—even if not economic—footing as agreements to fix minimum or uniform prices. [ ] The per se rule "is grounded on faith in price competition as a market force [and not] on a policy of low selling prices at the price of eliminating competition." * * * In this case the rule is violated by a price restraint that tends to provide the same economic rewards to all practitioners regardless of their skill, their experience, their training, or their willingness to employ innovative and difficult procedures in individual cases. Such a restraint also may discourage entry into the market and may deter experimentation and new developments by individual entrepreneurs. It may be a masquerade for an agreement to fix uniform prices, or it may in the future take on that character.

= * *

We are equally unpersuaded by the argument that we should not apply the *per se* rule in this case because the judiciary has little antitrust experience in the health care industry. [ ] The argument quite obviously is inconsistent with U.S. v. Socony–Vacuum Oil Co., 310 U.S. 150 (1940). * * * [Y]et the Court of Appeals refused to apply the *per se* rule in this case in part because the health care industry was so far removed from the competitive model.[9] Consistent with our prediction in Socony–Vacuum [ ] the result of this reasoning was the adoption by the Court of Appeals of a legal standard based on the reasonableness of the fixed prices, [ ] an inquiry we have so often condemned. [ ] Finally, the argument that the *per se* rule must be rejustified for every industry that has not been subject to significant antitrust litigation ignores the rationale for per se rules, which in part is to avoid "the necessity for an incredibly complicated and prolonged economic investigation into the entire history of the industry involved, as well as related industries, in an effort to determine at large whether a particular restraint has been unreasonable—an inquiry so often wholly fruitless when undertaken." [] ...

The respondents' principal argument is that the *per se* rule is inapplicable because their agreements are alleged to have pro-competitive justifications. The argument indicates a misunderstanding of the *per se* concept. The anticompetitive potential inherent in all price-fixing agreements justifies their facial invalidation even if pro-competitive justifications are offered for some. [ ] Those claims of enhanced competition are so unlikely to prove significant in any particular case that we adhere to the rule of law that is justified in its general application. Even when the respondents are given every benefit of the doubt, the limited record in this case is not inconsistent with the presumption that the respondents' agreements will not significantly enhance competition.

The respondents contend that their fee schedules are pro-competitive because they make it possible to provide consumers of health care with a uniquely desirable form of insurance coverage that could not otherwise exist. The features of the foundation-endorsed insurance plans that they stress are a choice of doctors, complete insurance coverage, and lower premiums. The first two characteristics, however, are hardly unique to these plans. Since only about 70% of the doctors in the relevant market are members of either foundation, the guarantee of complete coverage only applies when an insured chooses a physician in that 70%. If he elects to go to a nonfoundation doctor, he may be required to pay a portion of the doctor's fee. It is fair to presume, however, that at least 70% of the doctors in other markets charge no more than the "usual, customary, and reasonable" fee that typical insurers are willing to reimburse in full. [ ] Thus, in Maricopa and Pima Counties as well as in most parts of the country, if an insured asks his doctor if the insurance coverage is complete, presumably in about 70% of the cases the doctor will say "Yes" and in about 30% of the cases he will say "No."

It is true that a binding assurance of complete insurance coverage—as

---

9. "The health care industry, moreover, presents a particularly difficult area. The first step to understanding is to recognize that not only is access to the medical profession very time consuming and expensive both for the applicant and society generally, but also that numerous government subventions of the costs of medical care have created both a demand and supply function for medical services that is artificially high. The present supply and de-

mand functions of medical services in no way approximate those which would exist in a purely private competitive order. An accurate description of those functions moreover is not available. Thus, we lack baselines by which could be measured the distance between the present supply and demand functions and those which would exist under ideal competitive conditions." 643 F.2d at 556.

well as most of the respondents' potential for lower insurance premiums[10]—can be obtained only if the insurer and the doctor agree in advance on the maximum fee that the doctor will accept as full payment for a particular service. Even if a fee schedule is therefore desirable, it is not necessary that the doctors do the price fixing. The record indicates that the Arizona Comprehensive Medical/Dental Program for Foster Children is administered by the Maricopa Foundation pursuant to a contract under which the maximum-fee schedule is prescribed by a state agency rather than by the doctors. [ ] This program and the Blue Shield plan challenged in Group Life & Health Insurance Co. v. Royal Drug Co., 440 U.S. 205, 99 S.Ct. 1067, 59 L.Ed.2d 261 (1979), indicate that insurers are capable not only of fixing maximum reimbursable prices but also of obtaining binding agreements with providers guaranteeing the insured full reimbursement of a participating provider's fee. In light of these examples, it is not surprising that nothing in the record even arguably supports the conclusion that this type of insurance program could not function if the fee schedules were set in a different way.

The most that can be said for having doctors fix the maximum prices is that doctors may be able to do it more efficiently than insurers. The validity of that assumption is far from obvious,[11] but in any event there is no reason to believe that any savings that might accrue from this arrangement would be sufficiently great to affect the competitiveness of these kinds of insurance plans. It is entirely possible that the potential or actual power of the foundations to dictate the terms of such insurance plans may more than offset the theoretical efficiencies upon which the respondents' defense ultimately rests.[12]

* * *

IV

Having declined the respondents' invitation to cut back on the per se rule against price fixing, we are left with the respondents' argument that their fee

---

10. We do not perceive the respondents' claim of procompetitive justification for their fee schedules to rest on the premise that the fee schedules actually reduce medical fees and accordingly reduce insurance premiums, thereby enhancing competition in the health insurance industry. Such an argument would merely restate the long-rejected position that fixed prices are reasonable if they are lower than free competition would yield. It is arguable, however, that the existence of a fee schedule, whether fixed by the doctors or by the insurers, makes it easier—and to that extent less expensive—for insurers to calculate the risks that they underwrite and to arrive at the appropriate reimbursement on insured claims.

11. In order to create an insurance plan under which the doctor would agree to accept as full payment a fee prescribed in a fixed schedule, someone must canvass the doctors to determine what maximum prices would be high enough to attract sufficient numbers of individual doctors to sign up but low enough to make the insurance plan competitive. In this

case that canvassing function is performed by the foundation; the foundation then deals with the insurer. It would seem that an insurer could simply bypass the foundation by performing the canvassing function and dealing with the doctors itself. Under the foundation plan, each doctor must look at the maximum-fee schedule fixed by his competitors and vote for or against approval of the plan (and, if the plan is approved by majority vote, he must continue or revoke his foundation membership). A similar, if to some extent more protracted, process would occur if it were each insurer that offered the maximum-fee schedule to each doctor.

12. In this case it appears that the fees are set by a group with substantial power in the market for medical services, and that there is competition among insurance companies in the sale of medical insurance. Under these circumstances the insurance companies are not likely to have significantly greater bargaining power against a monopoly or doctors than would individual consumers of medical services.

schedules involve price fixing in only a literal sense. For this argument, the respondents rely upon Broadcast Music, Inc. v. Columbia Broadcasting System, Inc., 441 U.S. 1, 99 S.Ct. 1551, 60 L.Ed.2d 1 (1979).

In *Broadcast Music* we were confronted with an antitrust challenge to the marketing of the right to use copyrighted compositions derived from the entire membership of the American Society of Composers, Authors and Publishers (ASCAP). The so-called "blanket license" was entirely different from the product that any one composer was able to sell by himself. [ ] Although there was little competition among individual composers for their separate compositions, the blanket-license arrangement did not place any restraint on the right of any individual copyright owner to sell his own compositions separately to any buyer at any price. [ ] But a "necessary consequence" of the creation of the blanket license was that its price had to be established. [ ] We held that the delegation by the composers to ASCAP of the power to fix the price for the blanket license was not a species of the price-fixing agreements categorically forbidden by the Sherman Act. The record disclosed price fixing only in a "literal sense." [ ]

This case is fundamentally different. Each of the foundations is composed of individual practitioners who compete with one another for patients. Neither the foundations nor the doctors sell insurance, and they derive no profits from the sale of health insurance policies. The members of the foundations sell medical services. Their combination in the form of the foundation does not permit them to sell any different product. [ ] Their combination has merely permitted them to sell their services to certain customers at fixed prices and arguably to affect the prevailing market price of medical care.

The foundations are not analogous to partnerships or other joint arrangements in which persons who would otherwise be competitors pool their capital and share the risks of loss as well as the opportunities for profit. In such joint ventures, the partnership is regarded as a single firm competing with other sellers in the market. The agreement under attack is an agreement among hundreds of competing doctors concerning the price at which each will offer his own services to a substantial number of consumers. It is true that some are surgeons, some anesthesiologists, and some psychiatrists, but the doctors do not sell a package of three kinds of services. If a clinic offered complete medical coverage for a flat fee, the cooperating doctors would have the type of partnership arrangement in which a price-fixing agreement among the doctors would be perfectly proper. But the fee agreements disclosed by the record in this case are among independent competing entrepreneurs. They fit squarely into the horizontal price-fixing mold.

The judgment of the Court of Appeals is reversed.

It is so ordered.

JUSTICE BLACKMUN and JUSTICE O'CONNOR took no part in the consideration or decision of this case.

JUSTICE POWELL, with whom THE CHIEF JUSTICE and JUSTICE REHNQUIST join, dissenting.

The medical care plan condemned by the Court today is a comparatively new method of providing insured medical services at predetermined maximum costs. It involves no coercion. Medical insurance companies, physicians, and patients alike are free to participate or not as they choose. On its face, the plan seems to be in the public interest.

* * *

II

This case comes to us on a plaintiff's motion for summary judgment after only limited discovery. Therefore, ... the inferences to be drawn from the record must be viewed in the light most favorable to the respondents. * * * This requires, as the Court acknowledges, that we consider the foundation arrangement as one that "impose[s] a meaningful limit on physicians' charges," that "enables the insurance carriers to limit and to calculate more efficiently the risks they underwrite," and that "therefore serves as an effective cost-containment mechanism that has saved patients and insurers millions of dollars." The question is whether we should condemn this arrangement forthwith under the Sherman Act, a law designed to benefit consumers.

Several other aspects of the record are of key significance but are not stressed by the Court. First, the foundation arrangement forecloses *no* competition. Unlike the classic cartel agreement, the foundation plan does not instruct potential competitors: "Deal with consumers on the following terms and no others." Rather, physicians who participate in the foundation plan are free both to associate with other medical insurance plans—at any fee level, high or low—and directly to serve uninsured patients—at any fee level, high or low. Similarly, insurers that participate in the foundation plan also remain at liberty to do business outside the plan with any physician—foundation member or not—at any fee level. Nor are physicians locked into a plan for more than one year's membership. Thus freedom to compete, as well as freedom to withdraw, is preserved. The Court cites no case in which a remotely comparable plan or agreement is condemned on a per se basis.

Second, on this record we must find that insurers represent consumer interests. Normally consumers search for high quality at low prices. But once a consumer is insured [ ]—i.e., has chosen a medical insurance plan—he is largely indifferent to the amount that his physician charges if the coverage is full, as under the foundation-sponsored plan.

The insurer, however, is not indifferent. To keep insurance premiums at a competitive level and to remain profitable, insurers—including those who have contracts with the foundations—step into the consumer's shoes with his incentive to contain medical costs. Indeed, insurers may be the only parties who have the effective power to restrain medical costs, given the difficulty that patients experience in comparing price and quality for a professional service such as medical care.

On the record before us, there is no evidence of opposition to the foundation plan by insurance companies—or, for that matter, by members of the public. Rather seven insurers willingly have chosen to contract out to the foundations the task of developing maximum-fee schedules. [ ] Again, on the record before us, we must infer that the foundation plan—open as it is to insurers, physicians, and the public—has in fact benefitted consumers by "enabl[ing] the insurance carriers to limit and to calculate more efficiently the risks they underwrite." Nevertheless, even though the case is here on an incomplete summary judgment record, the Court conclusively draws contrary inferences to support its per se judgment.

* * *

IV

The Court acknowledges that the *per se* ban against price fixing is not to be invoked every time potential competitors literally fix prices. One also would have expected it to acknowledge that *per se* characterization is inappropriate if the challenged agreement or plan achieves for the public pro-competitive benefits that otherwise are not attainable. The Court does not do this. And neither does it provide alternative criteria by which the *per se* characterization is to be determined. It is content simply to brand this type of plan as "price fixing" and describe the agreement in *Broadcast Music*—which also literally involved the fixing of prices—as "fundamentally different."

In fact, however, the two agreements are similar in important respects. Each involved competitors and resulted in cooperative pricing. [ ] Each arrangement also was prompted by the need for better service to the consumers. [ ] And each arrangement apparently makes possible a new product by reaping otherwise unattainable efficiencies. [ ] The Court's effort to distinguish *Broadcast Music* thus is unconvincing.[13]

Notes and Questions

1. *Maricopa* has been criticized for its wooden application of the per se rule. See, e.g., Peter M. Gerhart, The Supreme Court and the (Near) Triumph of the Chicago School, 1982 Sup. Ct. Rev. 319 (1984). Can you detect, notwithstanding the opinion's more sweeping pronouncements, an attempt to evaluate the nature and necessity of the price agreements and the justifications offered? Consider how the ancillary restraints doctrine would apply in this case: what, for example, is the plurality's assessment of the "reasonable necessity" of the price agreement? See 1 Furrow, et al., Health Law § 10–27. Another notable feature was the fact that the foundations adopted maximum, rather than minimum, fee schedules. Commentators contend that the dangers of maximum price fixing are not sufficiently large to

---

13. The Court states that in Broadcast Music "there was little competition among individual composers for their separate compositions." This is an irrational ground for distinction. Competition *could* have existed, [ ], but did not because of the cooperative agreement. That competition yet persists among physicians is not a sensible reason to invalidate their agreement while refusing, similarly to condemn the Broadcast Music agreements that were *completely* effective in eliminating competition.

The Court also offers as a distinction that the foundations do not permit the creation of "any different product." But the foundations provide a "different product" to precisely the same extent as did Broadcast Music's clearinghouses. The clearinghouses provided only what copyright holders offered as individual sellers—the rights to use individual compositions. The clearinghouses were able to obtain these same rights more efficiently, however, because

they eliminated the need to engage in individual bargaining with each individual copyright owner.

In the same manner, the foundations set up an innovative means to deliver a basic service—insured medical care from a wide range of physicians of one's choice—in a more economical manner. The foundations' maximum-fee schedules replace the weak cost containment incentives in typical "usual, customary, and reasonable" insurance agreements with a stronger cost control mechanism: an absolute ceiling on maximum fees that can be charged. The conduct of the insurers in this case indicates that they believe that the foundation plan as it presently exists is the most efficient means of developing and administering such schedules. At this stage in the litigation, therefore, we must agree that the foundation plan permits the more economical delivery of the basic insurance service—"to some extent, a different product." []

justify per se treatment. See, e.g., Frank H. Easterbrook, Maximum Price Fixing, 48 U. Chi. L.Rev. 886 (1981). Is it possible that the foundation may have adopted its pricing policies with an eye to limiting the risk of entry by HMOs? In that case wouldn't the arrangement be objectionable for its propensity to preserve supra-competitive prices, albeit at a lower level than existed before the foundations were formed? See Keith B. Leffler, Arizona v. Maricopa County Medical Society: Maximum–Price Agreements in Markets with Insured Buyers, 2 Sup.Ct. Econ. Rev. 187 (1983). For an economic analysis contending that the competitive significance of physician controlled networks depends on the structure of both the demand side and the supply side of the market for physician services, see Roger Blair & Jill Boylston Herndon, Physician Cooperative Bargaining Ventures: An Economic Analysis, 71 Antitrust L.J. 989 (2004) (physician bargaining power can sometimes be benign or even procompetitive under conditions of bilateral monopoly, i.e. where physicians face insurers with market power).

2. *Maricopa* left open many questions about when integration among providers would be permissible, especially those involving PPOs having little financial integration. The FTC/Department of Justice Policy Statements, which have been revised several times since their original promulgation in 1994, give guidance on several important issues. Compare the agencies' analysis in the following Policy Statement and Advisory Opinion with *Maricopa's* treatment of issues such as risk sharing, market power and efficiencies.

U.S. DEPARTMENT OF JUSTICE AND FEDERAL TRADE COMMISSION, STATEMENTS OF ANTITRUST ENFORCEMENT POLICY IN HEALTH CARE

4 Trade Reg. Rep. (CCH) para. 13,153.
(August 18, 1996).

8. Statement of Department of Justice and Federal Trade Commission Enforcement Policy on Physician Network Joint Ventures

* * *

A. *Antitrust Safety Zones*

This section describes those physician network joint ventures that will fall within the antitrust safety zones designated by the Agencies. The antitrust safety zones differ for "exclusive" and "non-exclusive" physician network joint ventures. In an "exclusive" venture, the network's physician participants are restricted in their ability to, or do not in practice, individually contract or affiliate with other network joint ventures or health plans. In a "non-exclusive" venture, on the other hand, the physician participants in fact do, or are available to, affiliate with other networks or contract individually with health plans. * * *

1. Exclusive Physician Network Joint Ventures That The Agencies Will Not Challenge, Absent Extraordinary Circumstances

The Agencies will not challenge, absent extraordinary circumstances, an exclusive physician network joint venture whose physician participants share substantial financial risk and constitute 20 percent or less of the physicians [ ] in each physician specialty with active hospital staff privileges who practice in the relevant geographic market. [ ] In relevant markets with fewer than five physicians in a particular specialty, an exclusive physician network joint venture otherwise qualifying for the antitrust safety zone may include one physician from that specialty, on a non-exclusive basis, even though the inclusion of that physician results in the venture consisting of more than 20 percent of the physicians in that specialty.

2. Non–Exclusive Physician Network Joint Ventures That The Agencies Will Not Challenge, Absent Extraordinary Circumstances

The Agencies will not challenge, absent extraordinary circumstances, a non-exclusive physician network joint venture whose physician participants share substantial financial risk and constitute 30 percent or less of the physicians in each physician specialty with active hospital staff privileges who practice in the relevant geographic market. In relevant markets with fewer than four physicians in a particular specialty, a non-exclusive physician network joint venture otherwise qualifying for the antitrust safety zone may include one physician from that specialty, even though the inclusion of that physician results in the venture consisting of more than 30 percent of the physicians in that specialty.

3. Indicia of Non–Exclusivity

* * * [T]he Agencies caution physician participants in a non-exclusive physician network joint venture to be sure that the network is non-exclusive in fact and not just in name. The Agencies will determine whether a physician network joint venture is exclusive or non-exclusive by its physician participants' activities, and not simply by the terms of the contractual relationship. * * *

4. Sharing Of Substantial Financial Risk By Physicians In A Physician Network Joint Venture

To qualify for either antitrust safety zone, the participants in a physician network joint venture must share substantial financial risk in providing all the services that are jointly priced through the network. [ ] The safety zones are limited to networks involving substantial financial risk sharing not because such risk sharing is a desired end in itself, but because it normally is a clear and reliable indicator that a physician network involves sufficient integration by its physician participants to achieve significant efficiencies. [ ] Risk sharing provides incentives for the physicians to cooperate in controlling costs and improving quality by managing the provision of services by network physicians.

The following are examples of some types of arrangements through which participants in a physician network joint venture can share substantial financial risk: [ ]

(1) agreement by the venture to provide services to a health plan at a "capitated" rate; [ ]

(2) agreement by the venture to provide designated services or classes of services to a health plan for a predetermined percentage of premium or revenue from the plan;

(3) use by the venture of significant financial incentives for its physician participants, as a group, to achieve specified cost-containment goals. Two methods by which the venture can accomplish this are:

(a) withholding from all physician participants in the network a substantial amount of the compensation due to them, with distribution of that amount to the physician participants based on group performance in meeting the cost-containment goals of the network as a whole; or

(b) establishing overall cost or utilization targets for the network as a whole, with the network's physician participants subject to subsequent substantial financial rewards or penalties based on group performance in meeting the targets; and

(4) agreement by the venture to provide a complex or extended course of treatment that requires the substantial coordination of care by physicians in different specialties offering a complementary mix of services, for a fixed, predetermined payment, where the costs of that course of treatment for any individual patient can vary greatly due to the individual patient's condition, the choice, complexity, or length of treatment, or other factors. * * *

B. The Agencies' Analysis Of Physician Network Joint Ventures That Fall Outside The Antitrust Safety Zones

Physician network joint ventures that fall outside the antitrust safety zones also may have the potential to create significant efficiencies, and do not necessarily raise substantial antitrust concerns.

* * *

1. Determining When Agreements Among Physicians In A Physician Network Joint Venture Are Analyzed Under The Rule Of Reason

Antitrust law treats naked agreements among competitors that fix prices or allocate markets as per se illegal. Where competitors economically integrate in a joint venture, however, such agreements, if reasonably necessary to accomplish the pro-competitive benefits of the integration, are analyzed under the rule of reason. [ ] In accord with general antitrust principles, physician network joint ventures will be analyzed under the rule of reason, and will not be viewed as per se illegal, if the physicians' integration through the network is likely to produce significant efficiencies that benefit consumers, and any price agreements (or other agreements that would otherwise be per se illegal) by the network physicians are reasonably necessary to realize those efficiencies. [ ]

Where the participants in a physician network joint venture have agreed to share substantial financial risk as defined in Section A.4. of this policy statement, their risk-sharing arrangement generally establishes both an overall efficiency goal for the venture and the incentives for the physicians to meet that goal. The setting of price is integral to the venture's use of such an arrangement and therefore warrants evaluation under the rule of reason.

Physician network joint ventures that do not involve the sharing of substantial financial risk may also involve sufficient integration to demonstrate that the venture is likely to produce significant efficiencies. Such integration can be evidenced by the network implementing an active and ongoing program to evaluate and modify practice patterns by the network's physician participants and create a high degree of interdependence and cooperation among the physicians to control costs and ensure quality. This program may include: (1) establishing mechanisms to monitor and control utilization of health care services that are designed to control costs and assure quality of care; (2) selectively choosing network physicians who are likely to further these efficiency objectives; and (3) the significant investment of capital, both monetary and human, in the necessary infrastructure and capability to realize the claimed efficiencies.

* * *

Determining that an arrangement is merely a vehicle to fix prices or engage in naked anti-competitive conduct is a factual inquiry that must be done on a case-by-case basis to determine the arrangement's true nature and likely competitive effects. However, a variety of factors may tend to corroborate a network's anti-competitive nature, including: statements evidencing anti-competitive purpose; a recent history of anti-competitive behavior or collusion in the market, including efforts to obstruct or undermine the development of managed care; obvious anti-competitive structure of the network (e.g., a network comprising a very high percentage of local area physicians, whose participation in the network is exclusive, without any plausible business or efficiency justification); the absence of any mechanisms with the potential for generating significant efficiencies or otherwise increasing competition through the network; the presence of anti-competitive collateral agreements; and the absence of mechanisms to prevent the network's operation from having anti-competitive spillover effects outside the network.

* * *

[The Statement sets forth the methodology for balancing anticompetitive and procompetitive effects under the rule of reason: assessing the market power of the network in each physician services relevant market; evaluating effects by considering incentives for anticompetitive conduct and whether "there are many other networks or many physicians...available to form competing networks;" evaluating the risks of "spillover" effects on contracts outside the networks; and weighing the offsetting efficiency benefits uniquely achievable through the networks.]

Notes and Questions

1. The Statements repeatedly emphasize that merely because a physician network joint venture does not fall within a safety zone does not mean that it is unlawful under the antitrust laws. Many arrangements outside the safety zones have received favorable business review letters or advisory opinions from the agencies. See, e.g., Letter from Anne K. Bingaman, Assistant Attorney General, to John F. Fischer (Oklahoma Physicians Network, Inc.)(Jan. 17, 1996) (approving non-exclusive network with "substantially more" than 30% of several specialties, including more than 50% in one specialty). What facts might be particularly persuasive in mitigating the agencies' concerns about a network whose size exceeded safety zone thresholds? In a Business Review Letter to the Sante Fe Managed Care Organization, the Department of Justice considered a proposed physician-controlled network that would combine physicians practicing in numerous specialties, which, with some exceptions, constituted separate relevant markets for analysis. Letter from Joel I Klein, Assistant Attorney General, Antitrust Division, U.S. Dept. of Justice to David Marx (Feb. 12, 1997). While most of the concentration totals fell within the Policy Statement 8 threshhold for non-exclusive networks, several did not. For example although SFMCO included 70% of all pediatricians in the relevant market, the Department observed that pediatricians were a small minority of all family practice physicians in the network and were unlikely to be able to extract supracompetitive prices given that they would

share a risk pool with so many other doctors. Notably, the opinion allows for the possibility that SFMCO could subcontract with other non-network physicians to expand their network further. Essentially, if SFMCO "created a diversity of interest between the subcontracting physicians and member physicians so that members had an incentive to control the network's costs," they could add to their network, even up to 100 per cent of each specialty market. Can you explain the economic rationale for this loophole? The FTC and Department of Justice have issued over 100 advisory opinions concerning the health care industry, a large proportion of which concern provider-controlled networks. DOJ business review letters and FTC advisory opinions may be found on the Internet at http://www. usdoj.gov and http://www.ftc.gov. Additional helpful guidance is found in the several hypothetical scenarios and analysis contained in the Policy Statements.

2. *Messenger Model Arrangements.* Another section of the 1996 Policy Statements created a relief valve for physicians wanting to form networks but unwilling to undertake risk sharing or clinical integration. Under so-called "messenger model" networks agreements, physicians may use a common agent to convey information to and from payors about the prices and price-related terms they are willing to accept. Policy Statements, supra, Statement 9. However, the messenger must communicate individually with each network physician and not act as a conduit for information sharing or agreements among members. The model is violated when:

> the agent coordinates the providers' responses to a particular proposal, disseminates to network providers the views or intentions of other network providers as to the proposal, expresses an opinion on the terms offered, collectively negotiates for the providers, or decides whether or not to convey an offer based on the agent's judgment about the attractiveness of the prices or price-related terms. Id.

In essence, the 1996 Policy Statements establish a presumption that physicians complying with the model's parameters have not collectively agreed upon prices, but instead have determined their prices individually. Central to the concept, of course, is the integrity of the messenger—he must function solely as a conduit for offers and exchanges between payors and individual providers. One commentator has suggested that the messenger model operates under such unrealistic assumptions that it may be the case that the government "purposely created a gray area of enforcement" to allow physicians to share the economic rewards of networks despite restrictions imposed by the case law. Jeffrey L. Harrison, The Messenger Model: Don't Ask, Don't Tell?, 71 Antitrust L.J. 1017, 1017 (2004). Other factors may include political pressures faced by the antitrust agencies and the increasingly regulatory role the agencies have assumed. See Thomas L. Greaney, Thirty Years of Solicitude: Antitrust Law and Physician Cartels, 7 Hous. J. Health L. & Pol. 101 (2007).

In an astounding number of cases, physician networks have engaged in blatant violations of the messenger model. See Id.; Jeff Miles, Ticking Antitrust Time Bombs: A Message for Messed–Up Messenger Models, AHLA Health Lawyers News, Nov. 2002, at 5. The FTC has brought over 60 administrative actions challenging these, typically branding them as per se price fixing schemes. For the most part these cases involve noncompliance with obvious prohibitions of the model, such as polling members on desired prices and using those prices to negotiate on behalf of members. Yet violations have continued apace, a practice likely attributable to the fact that the FTC typically only imposes injunctive prohibitions ("go forth and sin no more") consent decrees.

3.   Do recognized areas of specialization constitute a distinct market for analysis under the Policy Statements? Compare Letter from Anne K. Bingaman, Assistant Attorney General, Antitrust Division, to Steven J. Kern and Robert J. Conroy (March 1, 1996) (concluding that family practitioners and other primary care physicians who treat children were not widely accepted substitutes for pediatricians) with Letter from Anne K. Bingaman, Assistant Attorney General, Antitrust Division to James M. Parker (Oct. 27, 1994) (board-certified pulmonologists are not exclusive providers of pulmonology-type services; merger of two pulmonology groups allowed to proceed because of significant competition from surgeons, family practitioners and other primary care physicians). What facts would you gather and what witnesses would you interview to decide whether a given specialty constitutes a relevant market?

4.   Statement 9 of the Policy Statements analyzes the competitive implications of "multiprovider networks," i.e., ventures such as physician-hospital organizations (PHOs), whereby providers who offer both competing and complementary services may jointly market their services. Because many such networks are controlled by competing providers, much of the analysis about horizontal restraints of trade contained in Statement 8 is directly applicable and is repeated and elaborated upon in Statement 9. A PHO, it should be noted, might raise competitive concerns in any of a number of markets: the various services markets in which its physicians compete; inpatient and outpatient hospital services markets; and the market for multiprovider networks themselves. Multiprovider networks may raise vertical issues as well. Where a network establishes vertical exclusive arrangements that restrict providers from dealing with other networks or other providers, the effect may be to exclude those providers or networks (or impair their ability to compete). For example, a network may enlist such a large proportion of the market's general surgeons that competition from rival networks or hospitals may be inhibited. These concerns arise only where the other networks have few alternatives to which they may turn and they are unable to recruit needed providers from outside the market. For a discussion of the circumstances under which exclusive contracting may constitute an anticompetitive clog on the market, see Section C infra. For cases settling charges that dominant hospitals established PHOs with large percentages of area physicians in order to retard the growth of managed care by foreclosing the development of new networks, see United States and State of Connecticut v. Healthcare Partners, 60 Fed.Reg. 52014 (Oct. 4, 1995) (notice of proposed final judgment) and U.S. v. Health Choice of Northwest Missouri, 60 Fed. Reg. 51808 (Oct. 3, 1995) (notice of proposed final judgment).

FEDERAL TRADE COMMISSION, ADVISORY OPINION IN RE MEDSOUTH, INC.

(February 19, 2002).

* * *

DESCRIPTION

MedSouth is an independent practice association (IPA) that includes competing primary care and specialist physicians who practice in the "South Denver/Arapahoe County" area of Denver, Colorado. It is a for-profit corporation owned by the physician practices of its members. All MedSouth physicians have a practice location in South Denver, and staff privileges at one of the three hospitals located in that area.

As we understand the facts based on the information you have submitted, MedSouth currently includes approximately 432 physicians in 216 practices.

One hundred one of the physicians are primary care practitioners (PCPs) (family practitioners, general internists, and pediatricians); and 331 are specialists in 39 specialties and subspecialties. In general, the specialists in MedSouth are those to whom MedSouth PCPs most frequently refer. Until the year 2000, MedSouth had capitated risk contracts with payers that required most referrals to be made to other physicians in MedSouth. The referral patterns established under those contracts largely have continued. MedSouth estimates that its PCPs make 90% to 95% of their referrals to specialty physicians in MedSouth. MedSouth's specialists, however, also receive a large number of referrals from doctors outside the IPA.

MedSouth expects that a number of its current members will terminate their membership in the organization before it fully implements the proposed program and attempts to negotiate contracts, so that it will represent fewer physicians in negotiations with payers than currently are members.

* * *

Contractual relationships between physicians and payers in the Denver area have undergone significant change in the past several years. Beginning in 1998 or 1999, Denver physicians established a number of financially-integrated IPAs that entered into capitated contracts with local HMOs. Many of these groups experienced significant financial difficulties under those contracts, and a number of the organizations declared bankruptcy. In the wake of this experience, payers and most physician groups, including Med-South, terminated their capitated contracts.[15] Some MedSouth physicians, however, wish to continue to practice on a partially-integrated basis with other members of the IPA.

The Proposed Integration Program

MedSouth proposes to implement a program that it believes will result in lower costs, higher quality, and more efficient delivery of its members' services.... According to your letter, the proposed program has three major goals:

1. to integrate the provision of primary and specialty services so they are delivered in a coordinated fashion;[16]

2. to integrate these coordinated physician services with a clinical resource management program that involves sharing of patient clinical information, development and implementation of practice protocols, and oversight and reporting of physicians' performance relative to preestablished benchmarks, so as to improve patient outcomes, decrease use of physician resources, and provide MedSouth with a competitive advantage with respect to other physician practices in the area; and

15. Our understanding is that when these capitated contracts were terminated, MedSouth members were in fact willing to contract with payers on an individual basis at prevailing market prices.

16. MedSouth's operating philosophy is that the quality and efficiency of patient care are maximized when the services of primary care and specialist physicians are integrated so that patients are cared for in a coordinated manner. In accordance with this outlook, primary and specialty care physicians are equally represented on MedSouth's Board of Directors. Also, two of MedSouth's four officers must be primary care doctors, while the other two must be specialists.

3. to offer payers a network in which all physicians have agreed to participate and in which the physicians will work together to improve care and to compete with other physicians and physician groups.

... [T]he proposed program ... will have two major parts: (1) a web-based electronic clinical data record system that will permit MedSouth physicians to access and share clinical information relating to their patients; and (2) the adoption and implementation of clinical practice guidelines and performance goals relating to the quality and appropriate use of services provided by MedSouth physicians. All physicians contracting through MedSouth will be required to participate in these activities. With these systems, MedSouth believes it will be able to improve and standardize members' treatment of specific diagnoses and their fulfillment of standards of care; reduce medical errors and improve patient care outcomes; permit its members to provide their services more efficiently and to reduce the aggregate long-term cost of physician services; and demonstrate to payers, employers, and others that the integrated and coordinated delivery of services by primary care and specialist physicians can improve the quality and delivery of physician services.

* * *

You stated that MedSouth also is developing: (1) clinical protocols covering the majority of MedSouth physicians' patient population; and (2) measurable performance goals relating to the quality and appropriate utilization of services that are linked to those protocols. The IPA proposes to secure members' commitment to adhere to those protocols in their office and hospital practices; review the performance of MedSouth physicians individually and collectively with respect to those goals; assist members in meeting the goals; and, if necessary, expel physicians who cannot or will not meet the goals. The physician participation agreement will specify the physicians' commitment to participate in all the network's programs; to adhere to the IPA's standards and protocols; and to implement the technology that permits MedSouth to report performance information to members and to third parties.

* * *

NEGOTIATION OF CONTRACTS

MedSouth proposes to offer the medical services of its participating members pursuant to this program to commercial third-party payers, and to negotiate and execute contracts under which MedSouth members would provide services to health plan enrollees. Thus, the IPA will seek to negotiate price and other contract terms on behalf of physician members of the network. It will retain a consultant to develop fee proposals for use in contract negotiations and, if necessary, to gather information from MedSouth physicians. The consultant will not disclose competitively sensitive information received from MedSouth physicians to other physicians in the network. Physician services will be paid for on a fee-for service basis. In addition, MedSouth intends to charge a network access fee to payers purchasing the package of services, that will support its operating and administrative costs. MedSouth will not be involved in claims processing or payment. ...

While MedSouth seeks to offer its members' services to payers as a package, you represent that it is intended to be, and will actually be, a non-exclusive network. The MedSouth Physician Participation Agreement will specifically state that physicians are not precluded from participating in other physician contracting organizations, or from contracting with payers independently. You have represented that customers not wishing to purchase the network services will be able to negotiate and contract with MedSouth physicians individually . . .

ANALYSIS

Form of Analysis

Standing alone . . . joint negotiation of price terms by non-integrated, competing physicians would constitute an agreement among the physicians not to compete on price, and would be illegal per se. Per se treatment is inappropriate, however, and more elaborate analysis under the rule of reason is warranted, when the joint negotiation of price is reasonably related to an efficiency-enhancing integration of the participants' economic activity and is reasonably necessary to achieve the procompetitive benefits of that integration. How detailed that analysis should be depends, of course, on the circumstances. . . .

Efficiency-enhancing integration typically involves joint performance of one or more business functions of the participants in a way that potentially benefits consumers by expanding output, reducing price, or enhancing quality, service or innovation, and that could not reasonably be achieved by the participants individually. The integration must likely generate procompetitive benefits that enhance the participants' ability or incentives to compete, and thus offset any anticompetitive tendencies of the arrangement. Joint negotiation of prices is not "reasonably necessary" if the participants could achieve an equivalent or comparable efficiency-enhancing integration through practical means that provide significantly less restriction on competition.

We conclude that MedSouth's overall proposed course of conduct, as described in the information you have supplied, should not be accorded per se treatment. The program in which MedSouth proposes to engage appears to be capable of creating substantial partial integration of the participating physicians' practices, and to have the potential to produce efficiencies in the form of higher quality or reduced costs for patient care services rendered by network physicians. More elaborate analysis under the rule of reason, therefore, is warranted.

INTEGRATION AND LIKELY EFFICIENCIES

Taken as whole, the proposed program is designed to facilitate and increase communication and cooperation among MedSouth physicians, both in the treatment of individual patients and in modifying the regular practice patterns of members of the IPA. The collective development and implementation of the protocols and benchmarks has the potential to create significant integration and interdependence among the physicians in their rendering of medical services. The physicians have pooled their resources and expertise to identify common standards of care. Through their agreement to abide by those standards, the physicians have subjected themselves, to some extent, to the collective judgment of the group with respect to their patterns of practice; and they have agreed to make themselves individually and collectively accountable for their performance by making information about their achievement of goals, which are linked to those standards, available to customers.

* * *

The computer system facilitates both dissemination and implementation of these common standards and communications among MedSouth doctors relating to the care of particular patients. The system is intended thereby to reduce duplicative tests and procedures, promote better coordination of treatment, and speed up provision of referral services. Computerized prescribing and other data entry systems have the potential to reduce errors and adverse events. While any physician could achieve some of these benefits by investing in his/her own information system, adoption of the same system by a group of physicians who maintain referral relationships with one another can provide a number of additional benefits. Having compatible systems permits physicians in different practices who are caring for the same patients to communicate and share clinical information more easily. . . . The existence of the system is likely to further cement referral relationships within the network and lead to closer working relationships among network physicians in the future, thus amplifying the benefits that result from the physicians' participation in the program. We note, however, that mere adoption of a common clinical information system by itself, without the other programs that MedSouth intends to implement, would not suffice to establish that otherwise competing members of a physician network have integrated their practices in a manner or to an extent that joint negotiation of prices could be deemed ancillary to an efficiency-enhancing joint venture.

THE RELATIONSHIP OF JOINT CONTRACTING TO THE PRODUCTION OF EFFICIENCIES

The extent to which collective negotiation of prices is ancillary to this integration is a crucial question. Generally speaking, an agreement is ancillary to a competitor collaboration to the extent that it is subordinate to and reasonably necessary to accomplish the goals of the integration, unless the parties could have achieved similar efficiencies by practical, significantly less restrictive means. It may be possible to develop an arrangement, apart from payment for the professional services of the network physicians, under which those physicians could be appropriately compensated for the costs entailed in providing programs of the type MedSouth intends to undertake. In this instance, however, we conclude that the price agreement bodied in joint negotiation of contracts for services to be provided subject to the entire proposed program appears to be reasonably related to the integration among MedSouth members, and reasonably necessary for MedSouth to achieve the procompetitive benefits it seeks.

In order to establish and maintain the on-going collaboration and interdependence among physicians from which the projected efficiencies flow, the doctors need to be able to rely on the participation of other members of the group in the network and its activities on a continuing basis. This does not appear to be possible if contracting for the sale of services is done individually. The price for professional services rendered under health plan contracts needs to be established, and if it is done through individual negotiation and contracting, then no one can count on the full participation of the group's members. Whatever value the program has for consumers, beyond what would result from individual doctors computerizing their records and determining to follow particular guidelines, is significantly dependent on the doctors being able to function as a group within which patients are commonly referred.[17] In the absence of the group being able to assure continuing participation of its members in its contracts, some of the benefits are likely to go unrealized.

In addition, joint contracting may permit the network to allocate the returns among members of the network in a way that creates incentives for the physicians to make appropriate investments of time and effort in setting up and implementing the proposed program. According to your letter, it is important for MedSouth to be able to assure that the rewards from the program flow to the doctors in an equitable manner, so that some are not able to charge disproportionately high prices relative to other members, and thereby capture an excessive proportion of the value of the network's programs. . . .

COMPETITIVE EFFECTS

The fundamental concern of antitrust analysis is whether a given arrangement may have a substantial anticompetitive effect and, if so, whether that potential effect is offset by any procompetitive efficiencies resulting from the conduct. The central question is whether, taking into account both potential procompetitive and anticompetitive effects, the arrangement is likely to harm competition by increasing the ability or incentive of the participants to raise price above—or reduce output, quality, service, or innovation below the level that likely would prevail in the absence of the agreement. The ability and incentive of the participants to compete individually with one another and with their joint undertaking is an important part of the analysis.

Because the proposed program is yet to be implemented, it appears to be impossible at this point to predict the magnitude of anticompetitive or procompetitive effects that will flow from its actual operation. . . . [T]he information available to us indicates that the MedSouth membership as presently constituted likely would be able to exercise significant market power, and thus to extract higher prices, if the doctors coordinate their actions outside the integrated group.

MedSouth currently has a large number of participating doctors who are concentrated in a distinct area of the city. In a number of specialties, they constitute half or more of the physicians with admitting privileges at the three hospitals in south Denver. Of particular significance with respect to the

---

17. The situation here differs from that in Arizona v. Maricopa County Medical Society, 457 U.S. 332 (1982), where the decision of each doctor whether to accept the "maximum fee" as payment in full was essentially unrelated (except to the extent that the common agreement on prices eliminated competition among the participating doctors) to the decision of any other physician to do the same thing. While the organization performed some "peer review" of the necessity and appropriateness of care rendered to patients, it made no claim that the challenged agreement on prices was reasonably necessary to the efficient functioning of the review process. [ ]Moreover, it is highly unlike- ly that the type of peer review performed by the foundations for medical care in Maricopa created any significant interdependence or on-going cooperation among foundation members with respect to their clinical practices. The foundations for medical care of that era were community-wide organizations sponsored by local medical societies and designed to have broadly inclusive memberships. The peer review they performed was claims-based, retrospective review in order to determine whether the claim should be paid, reduced, or denied; the standards they used generally were designed simply to detect deviations from local community norms of practice. [ ]

needs of local health plans that contract for physician services, MedSouth contains a substantial proportion of the internists and family practitioners in the south Denver area. For example, MedSouth's current members are 51% of the internists and 33% of the family practitioners at Swedish Hospital, and from 50% to 100% of the specialists in 19 other practice areas at that hospital. * * * As noted above, however, we do not know how many of these physicians will remain members of MedSouth after the venture is launched. A significant decrease in the number of MedSouth participating physicians would lessen the risk of anticompetitive harm.

It appears that access to some significant number of MedSouth doctors is necessary for health plans to have adequate networks to support a marketable product and to have enough conveniently located doctors to care for their current enrollees. [M]any practices in that area are full and some are closed to new patients. . . . To date, however, in spite of that shortage, there appears to have been little new entry by physicians.

Doctors in other areas of the city do not appear to be realistic alternatives to many of the doctors located in south Denver, especially the PCPs. * * * Consequently, individual contracts with MedSouth members appear to be a principal alternative to a contract with the group as a whole. . . .

In spite of MedSouth's explicit policy of "nonexclusivity," MedSouth members may have the incentive and the ability to agree not to contract independently of the venture. They have incentives to seek higher fees to recoup their investments in developing and implementing the proposed program. Negotiation of fee-for-service rates for the group will involve identification of price levels that could become the focal point for collusion on individual contracts. To the extent that the program creates greater communication and interdependence among the doctors, the easier it likely would be for them to coordinate their activities. Particularly in light of the doctors' existing referral arrangements, MedSouth members may be able to discipline members of the IPA who might be inclined to break ranks and contract independently. We cannot conclude with certainty that MedSouth's physicians actually will contract outside the IPA; nor can we conclude, at this early stage, that MedSouth's operation will restrict competition unreasonably. MedSouth plans to take steps to ensure that its physicians will in fact be available to contract independently with health plans.

In addition, we cannot now determine the extent to which the group will achieve the efficiencies that it expects. . . . The information we have obtained in analyzing physician markets suggests that, in actual practice, it is often difficult to change physicians' established patterns of practice. Doing so does not result simply from the adoption of guidelines and benchmarks. Rather, the effectiveness of such programs depends upon a number of intangible factors, including the degree of commitment to the process by the members of the group and the effectiveness of its leadership. To change practice patterns requires an ongoing commitment of time, effort, and expertise, and it can be difficult to accomplish even when there are significant external incentives to do so. The experience of other physician groups indicates that it is harder to achieve implementation of this type of program in a large group, in the absence of direct financial risk relating to achievement of network goals, or where the physicians are not already closely connected to one another, and that each physician needs to have a significant number of patients subject to the system before it has an actual impact on his or her practice patterns.

* * *

CONCLUSIONS

We conclude, on balance, that the proposed program appears to have the potential to improve the quality and effectiveness of health care services that are delivered to patients, and thus to provide important benefits to consumers. Given the prospective nature of the analysis inherent in an advisory opinion, we do not have any direct evidence of either efficiencies or competitive effects. Based on all the factors discussed above, we have concluded that we would not recommend a challenge to MedSouth fully implementing the program and then offering it to payers on a collective basis. As long as doctors are, in fact, willing to deal individually on competitive terms with payers who do not want the package product, as you represent will be the case, significant anticompetitive effects appear unlikely. If final physician participation in the group is significantly smaller than MedSouth's current membership, significant anticompetitive effects, likewise, may be unlikely. If, however, Med-South's member physicians are able to use collective power to force payers to contract with the network or to pay higher prices, then absent evidence that substantial efficiency benefits outweighed likely anticompetitive effects, we likely would recommend that the Commission bring an enforcement action. As your letter recognizes, members of the network face an increased antitrust risk to the extent that they do not actually agree to contract with health plans independent of the network and at competitive prices, either when a payer prefers as an initial matter not to purchase the group product or when it has done so and then desires to return to individual contracting. Of course, concerted refusal by some or all of MedSouth's members to deal with payers outside of the IPA would appear to be unrelated to the joint venture presented in your request, and, thus, to be illegal per se. This office will monitor MedSouth's operations and the behavior of its physician members for indications that the proposed conduct is resulting in significant anticompetitive effects.

Notes and Questions

1. Should clinical integration be treated on a par with financial integration for purposes of avoiding per se analysis? Is there a sufficiently precise definition of clinical integration contained in the FTC policy statements or the MedSouth decision to assure that physicians will align their efforts in a manner that improves efficiency and not direct them to raising prices? Does MedSouth adequately answer the question, required under Rule of Reason analysis, of why the price agreement is reasonably necessary to accomplish the procompetitive objectives of the plan?

2. Fulfilling the promise in the MedSouth advisory opinion to closely monitor the group's activities, the FTC staff issued a follow-up letter to the organization in June, 2007. Letter from Markus H. Meier, Esq., FTC, to John J. Miles, Esq. (June 18, 2007), http://www.ftc.gov/bc/adops/070618medsouth.pdf. Based on information provided by MedSouth concerning various aspects of its operation, the staff concluded that MedSouth had continued efforts to integrate and that there was no indication it has exercised or increased its market power. Responding to

the fact that MedSouth has lost 32.5 percent of its physicians since the issuance of the 2002 letter, the staff stated that the reduction may well be indicative that a program of clinical integration requires very serious commitment and effort by physicians to engage in the activities that are necessary to achieve the beneficial objectives of such a program, as well as physicians' weighing of the economic costs and benefits of participating in such a program. This may be instructive for other provider networks, particularly ones involving large numbers of physicians, regarding the practical realities and potential difficulties inherent in coordinating and clinically integrating the care provided to numerous enrollees through a network comprising many independent physicians. Id. at 8.

3.   In a staff advisory opinion to Suburban Health Organization (SHO), the FTC found that the proposal involved some potentially beneficial integration among the participants, but concluded that the reasons given for collective bargaining did not justify that elimination of competition. Advisory Opinion Letter from David R. Pender, Esq., FTC, to Clifton E. Johnson, Esq., Hall, Render, Killian, Heath & Lyman (Mar. 28, 2006), http://www.ftc.gov/opa/2006/03/shor31. shtm. SHO was to act as a "super PHO," serving as the exclusive bargaining and contracting agent with most insurers for 192 primary care physicians employed at eight independent hospitals in the Indianapolis, Indiana, suburbs. When selling their employed physician's services to insurers under the proposed arrangements, member hospitals would deal only through SHO and do so only at prices set by the group. Finding that the program eliminated price competition that would otherwise exist among the hospitals for the employed physician's services, the letter concluded the arrangement likely violated the antitrust laws. SHO attempted to rely on clinical integration benefits arising from development of practice protocols and disease-specific treatment parameters, data collection for use in monitoring physician behavior and outcomes, production of educational materials, and use of a bonus pool to reward financially-desirable behavior and results. While conceding that the integration had the potential to improve care and create efficiencies, the letter stressed the program's limited nature and scope. For example, SHO only represented hospitals' employed primary care physicians, and thus did not reach the full range of medical services. Moreover employees, the letter noted, can be expected to be responsive to their employers' requirements and thus the need for the programs incentives seemed attenuated. Because most of the program's integration and efficiencies were informational in character and did not involve integration or interdependence among the participating physicians in *actually providing* their medical services, they were less likely to provide significant benefits. Finally, the letter stated that the price agreement was not reasonably necessary to achieve any of the potential efficiencies or consumer benefits.

4.   Many of the details of clinical integration analysis require further elaboration and justification. See, e.g., Thomas B. Leary, The Antitrust Implications of "Clinical Integration:" An Analysis of the FTC Staff's Advisory Opinion in MedSouth, 47 St. Louis U. L.J. 227 (2003) (questioning whether counting physicians is an adequate measure of market power, given differentiation among physicians and the nature of the services they provide and expressing doubts that efficiencies can be effectively measured using conventional antitrust tools). Does a decrease in output necessarily reflect less competition; might it indicate an improved use of resources (i.e., fewer unnecessary tests and services)? Further, does the MedSouth letter implicitly favor non-exclusive arrangements? Isn't there an unacknowledged tension between the advisory letter's conclusions as to the necessity of joint contracting to promote efficiency (i.e., the need to assure that physicians are tightly bound to the plan) and its endorsement of the non-exclusive nature of the arrangement as lessening anticompetitive risks? Finally, in giving

detailed advice on what constitutes clinical integration, have antitrust enforcers assumed a regulatory role, perhaps one that detracts from their ability to prosecute violations of the law in litigation? Some academic commentators have criticized antitrust doctrine for failing to explicitly account for quality. See William M. Sage & Peter J. Hammer, A Copernican View of Health Care Antitrust, 65 L. & Contemp. Probs. 241 (2002). A more radical critique of antitrust is provided by an economist who emphasizes the market imperfections endemic in health care and suggests that government control may yield better outcomes for consumers than reliance on competition. See Thomas Rice, The Economics of Health Care Reconsidered (1998).

5. *Physician Unions.* Fewer than 10 percent of practicing doctors in the United States are members of labor unions and approximately 20 percent of those who are in unions are residents employed at hospitals. Attracted by promises that unions will enable them to "level the playing field" in contractual bargaining with managed care entities, some physicians began to form unions in the 1990s and lobby for laws that would grant independent physicians the right to enjoy immunity from antitrust law under collective bargaining. See Robert L. Lowes, Strength in Numbers: Could Doctor Unions Really Be the Answer? 75 Med. Econ. 114 (1998); Steven Greenhouse, Angered by H.M.O.'s Treatment, More Doctors Are Joining Unions, N.Y. Times, Feb. 4 1999. See generally William S. Brewbaker III, Physician Unions and the Future of Competition in the Health Care Sector, 33 U.C. Davis L. Rev. 545 (2000). Because the antitrust labor exemption enables only physicians who are employees and occupy non-supervisory positions to collectively bargain through labor unions and courts have interpreted the labor exemption not to apply to physicians in independent practice, see American Med. Ass'n v. United States, 317 U.S. 519, 63 S.Ct. 326, 87 L Ed. 434 (1943); FTC v. Indiana Federation of Dentists, 101 F.T.C. 57 (1983), rev'd on other grounds, 745 F.2d 1124 (7th Cir. 1984), legislation was proposed that would extend some protection to independent physicians contracting with MCOs. Richard M. Scheffler, Physician Collective Bargaining: A Turning Point in U.S. Medicine, 24 J. Health Pol. Pol'y & l. 1071, 1073–74 (1999). One bill, which passed the House of Representatives in 2000 but was not considered by the Senate would have legalized per se conduct such as collective negotiations by physicians on both price and non-price issues when undertaken in compliance with the legislation. Quality Health–Care Coalition Act of 1999, H.R. 1304, 106th Cong. (1999). The FTC and Department of Justice strongly opposed the proposed legislation arguing that it would not improve quality of care and that it would enable physicians to negotiate in their self-interests, e.g. for higher fees and less restrictive managed care controls. Several states have adopted laws granting physicians immunity for collective bargaining in narrowly defined circumstances. Tex. Ins. Code §§ 29.06 (a) & 29.09 (b). See also N.J. Stat. § 52:17B–196 (2002).

The government has challenged several attempts to organize physician unions that did not meet the prevailing standard for an exemption under the antitrust laws In FTC and the Commonwealth of Puerto Rico v. College of Physicians–Surgeons of Puerto Rico, 5 Trade Reg. Rep. (CCH) § 335 (D.P.R.1997), the FTC alleged that the College, a quasi-public organization consisting of all physicians in Puerto Rico, engaged in an illegal boycott when it held a 72–hour action in which members refused to provide services except on an emergency basis to protest health reform legislation that had a capitation rate that was too low in the view of members. See also United States v. Federation of Physicians and Dentists, Inc., No. 98–475 available at www.usdoj.gov/atr/cases/f200600/200654 (final judgement) (settling civil action charging a physician union consisting of nearly all orthopedic surgeons in Delaware with organizing a boycott and jointly terminating contracts with Blue Cross of Delaware in order to resist fee reductions). In 2002, there were numerous physician strikes or other work stoppages in protest of rising medical malpractice costs. Should these be regarded as boycotts under the antitrust law? Does the fact that these actions have a "political" objective immunize them from antitrust scrutiny? For an interesting parallel, see FTC v. Superior Court Trial Lawyers Association, 493 U.S. 411, 110 S.Ct. 768, 107 L.Ed.2d 851 (1990), in which the Supreme Court upheld the FTC's challenge to a group boycott by lawyers representing indigent clients in criminal matters in the District of Columbia. See also Charles Taylor, Over the Line? Feds Watch Doc Walkouts with Antitrust Concerns, Mod. Healthcare, at 12, available in 2003 WL 9135214.

B. PAYORS WITH MARKET POWER

KARTELL v. BLUE SHIELD OF MASSACHUSETTS, INC.

United States Court of Appeals, First Circuit, 1984.
749 F.2d 922, cert. denied, 471 U.S. 1029, 105 S.Ct. 2040, 85 L.Ed.2d 322 (1985).

BREYER, CIRCUIT JUDGE.

Blue Shield pays doctors for treating patients who are Blue Shield health insurance subscribers, but only if each doctor promises not to make any additional charge to the subscriber. The basic issue in this case is whether this Blue Shield practice—called a "ban on balance billing"—violates either Sherman Act § 1 forbidding agreements "in restraint of trade," 15 U.S.C. § 1, or Sherman Act § 2 forbidding "monopolization" and "attempts to monopolize," [ ]. The district court, [] held that the practice constituted an unreasonable restraint of trade in violation of section 1. We conclude that the practice does not violate either section of the Sherman Act; and we reverse the district court.

. . . Blue Shield provides health insurance for physician services while its sister, Blue Cross, insures against hospital costs. The consumers of Blue Shield insurance, at least those who buy "full service" prepaid medical benefits, can see any "participating doctor," *i.e.*, a doctor who has entered into a standard Participating Physician's Agreement with Blue Shield . . . Under the standard agreement, a participating doctor promises to accept as payment in full an amount determined by Blue Shield's "usual and customary charge" method of compensation. * * * Blue Shield pays this amount directly to the doctor; the patient pays nothing out of his own pocket and therefore receives no reimbursement.

The district court also found that Blue Shield provides some form of health insurance to about 56 percent of the Massachusetts population . . . [or] about 74 percent of those Massachusetts residents who *privately* insure against health costs. * * * Virtually all practicing doctors agree to take Blue Shield subscribers as patients and to participate in its fee plan.

The district court found that, because of the large number of subscribers, doctors are under "heavy economic pressure" to take them as patients and to agree to Blue Shield's system for charging the cost of their care. The court believed that the effect of this payment system, when combined with Blue Shield's size and buying power, was to produce an unreasonably rigid and unjustifiably low set of prices. In the court's view, the fact that doctors cannot charge Blue Shield subscribers more than the Blue Shield payment-schedule amounts interferes with the doctors' freedom to set higher prices for more expensive services and discourages them from developing and offering patients more expensive (and perhaps qualitatively better) services. For these and related reasons, the district court held that Blue Shield's ban on "balance billing" unreasonably restrains trade and thereby violates Sherman Act § 1. Blue Shield appeals from this holding. The plaintiff doctors cross-appeal from other rulings of the district court in Blue Shield's favor.

* * *

I

We disagree with the district court because we do not believe that the facts that it found show an unreasonable restraint of trade. . . .

A

We disagree with the district court's finding of "restraint." To find an unlawful restraint, one would have to look at Blue Shield as if it were a "third force," intervening in the marketplace in a manner that prevents willing buyers and sellers from independently coming together to strike price/quality bargains. Antitrust law typically frowns upon behavior that impedes the striking of such independent bargains. The persuasive power of the district court's analysis disappears, however, once one looks at Blue Shield, not as an inhibitory "third force," but as itself the purchaser of the doctors' services. * * * Antitrust law rarely stops the buyer of a service from trying to determine the price or characteristics of the product that will be sold. Thus, the more closely Blue Shield's activities resemble, in essence, those of a purchaser, the less likely that they are unlawful.

Several circuits have held in antitrust cases that insurer activity closely analogous to that present here amounts to purchasing, albeit for the account of others. And, they have held that an insurer may lawfully engage in such buying of goods and services needed to make the insured whole. The Second Circuit has held lawful a Blue Shield plan requiring pharmacies to accept Blue Shield reimbursement as full payment for drugs they supply to Blue Shield subscribers. [ ] The Third Circuit has allowed a hospital cost insurer (Blue Cross) to reimburse hospitals directly (and apparently completely) for services to subscribers. [ ] * * *

At the same time, the facts before us are unlike those in cases where courts have forbidden an "organization" to buy a good or service—cases in which the buyer was typically a "sham" organization seeking only to combine otherwise independent buyers in order to suppress their otherwise competitive instinct to bid up price. [ ] No one here claims that Blue Shield is such a "sham" organization or anything other than a legitimate, independent medical cost insurer. But cf. Virginia Academy of Clinical Psychologists v. Blue Shield of Virginia, 624 F.2d 476 (4th Cir. 1980) (Blue Shield found to be a combination not of policyholders, but of physicians), *cert. denied,* 450 U.S. 916, 101 S.Ct. 1360, 67 L.Ed.2d 342 (1981).

Once one accepts the fact that from a commercial perspective, Blue Shield in essence "buys" medical services for the account of others, the reasoning underlying the Second, Third, and Seventh Circuit views indicates that the ban on balance billing is permissible.

* * *

[T]he doctors seek to distinguish these precedents by pointing to an important district court finding either not present or not discussed in depth in these other cases. The district court here found that Blue Shield is a buyer with significant "market power"—*i.e.,* the power to force prices below the level that a freely competitive market would otherwise set. They argue that Blue Shield's "market power" makes a significant difference. We do not agree.

At the outset, we note that Blue Shield disputes the existence of significant "market power." It points out that the district court relied heavily upon participation by 99 percent of all Massachusetts doctors in Blue Shield's program, as "prov[ing] * * * Blue Shield's economic power." But, Blue Shield says, this by itself proves little. Participating in Blue Shield's program does not stop doctors from taking other patients or from charging those other patients what they like. As long as Blue Shield's rates are even marginally remunerative, 99 percent of all doctors might sign up with Blue Shield if it had only ten policyholders or ten thousand instead of several million.

Blue Shield adds that the record does not prove the existence of the single harm most likely to accompany the existence of market power on the buying side of the market, namely lower seller output. [ ] Indeed, here the district court found that the supply of doctors in Massachusetts has "increased steadily during the past decade." Blue Shield also claims that whatever power it possesses arises from its ability as an "expert" to prevent doctors from charging unknowledgeable patients *more* than a free (and informed) market price. [ ]

On the other hand, several doctors testified that low prices discouraged them from introducing new highly desirable medical techniques. And, they argue that fully informed patients would have wanted to pay more for those techniques had they been allowed to do so.

To resolve this argument about the existence of market power—an issue hotly debated by the expert economists who testified at trial—would force us to evaluate a record that the district court described as "two competing mountains of mostly meaningless papers." Rather than do so, we shall assume that Blue Shield possesses significant market power. We shall also assume, but purely for the sake of argument, that Blue Shield uses that power to obtain "lower than competitive" prices.

We next ask whether Blue Shield's assumed market power makes a significant legal difference. As a matter of pure logic, to distinguish the examples previously mentioned one must accept at least one of the following three propositions: One must believe either (1) that the law forbids a buyer with market power to bargain for "uncompetitive" or "unreasonable" prices, or (2) that such a buyer cannot buy for the account of others, or (3) that there is some relevant difference between obtaining such price for oneself and obtaining that price for others for whom one can lawfully buy. In our view, each of these propositions is false, as a matter either of law or of logic.

First, the antitrust laws interfere with a firm's freedom to set even uncompetitive prices only in special circumstances, where, for example, a price is below incremental cost. Such a "predatory" price harms competitors, cannot be maintained, and is unlikely to provide consumer benefits. [ ] Ordinarily, however, even a monopolist is free to exploit whatever market power it may possess when that exploitation takes the form of charging uncompetitive prices. As Professor Areeda puts it, "Mere monopoly pricing is not a violation of the Sherman Act." [ ] * * *

The district court did not suggest here that the prices subject to the "balance billing" ban were "predatory." Nor (with one possible exception, see [*infra*]) do the parties point to evidence of any price below anyone's "incremental cost." [ ] Rather, the district court suggested that Blue Shield's prices were "uncompetitively low," "unreasonably low," lower than the doctors might have charged to individual patients lacking market power. That is to say, Blue Shield obtained prices that reflected its market power. For the reasons just mentioned then, if Blue Shield had simply purchased those services for itself, the prices paid, in and of themselves, would not have amounted to a violation of the antitrust laws. [ ]

Second, as we previously mentioned, there is no law forbidding a legitimate insurance company from itself buying the goods or services needed to make its customer whole. The cases that we have cited are unanimous in allowing such arrangements. The rising costs of medical care, the possibility that patients cannot readily evaluate (as competitive buyers) competing offers of medical service, the desirability of lowering insurance costs and premiums, the availability of state regulation to prevent abuse—all convince us that we ought not create new potentially far-reaching law on the subject. And, the parties have not seriously argued to the contrary.

Third, to reject the first two propositions is, as a matter of logic, to reject the third. If it is lawful for a monopoly buyer to buy for the account of another, how can it be unlawful for him to insist that no additional charge be made to that other? To hold to the contrary is, in practice, to deny the buyer the right to buy for others, for the seller would then be free to obtain a different price from those others by threatening to withhold the service. This reasoning seems sound whether or not the buyer has "market power."

In essence, then, the lawfulness of the term in question stems from the fact that it is an essential part of the price bargain between buyer and seller. Whether or not that price bargain is, in fact, reasonable is, legally speaking, beside the point, even in the case of a monopolist. As Blue Shield stresses in its brief, health maintenance organizations, independent practice associations, and preferred provider organizations all routinely agree with doctors that the doctors will accept payment from the plan as payment in full for services rendered to subscribers. We can find no relevant analytical distinction between this type of purchasing decision and the practice before us—even on the assumption that Blue Shield possesses market power.

B

We now consider more closely the specific arguments raised by the district court and the parties to show that Blue Shield's "balance billing ban" is anti-competitive in practice. The [plaintiffs'] brief sets forth in summary form the following allegedly harmful effects of the ban:

(1) Price competition among physicians for services covered by Blue Shield's service benefit policies is "virtually eliminated."

(2) Doctor's prices have tended to cluster around Blue Shield's "maximum price levels."

(3) Doctors wanting to compete by offering innovative or "premium" services are inhibited from doing so because Blue Shield's pricing structure assumes that physicians' services are fungible and mandates the same price ceilings for virtually all physicians.

(4) Doctors just entering practice are discouraged from doing so by particularly low levels of Blue Shield reimbursement.

(5) Blue Shield's low prices lead doctors to charge higher prices to others.

(6) Blue Shield discourages doctors from charging others low prices by insisting that its subscribers be given the benefit of any such low prices.

(7) Blue Shield's pricing system discourages doctors from trying out more expensive services that could bring about lower total medical costs, *e.g.,* a "colonoscopy with polypectomy," an expensive service that is nonetheless cheaper than the surgery that would otherwise be needed to cure the patient.

(8) Blue Shield, by reason of its pricing practices, has been able to attract more subscribers, extending its "competitive edge" over other health insurers, and increasing its dominance in the health insurance business.

The first seven of these arguments attack the price term in the agreement between Blue Shield and the doctors. To argue that Blue Shield's pricing system is insufficiently sensitive to service differences, or that it encourages high costs, or does not give the patients what they really need, or to claim that the buyer is making a bad decision is like arguing that the buyer of a fleet of taxicabs ought to buy several different models, or allow the seller to vary color or horsepower or gearshift because doing so either will better satisfy those passengers who use the fleet's services, or will in the long run encourage quality and innovation in automobile manufacture. The short—and conclusive—answer to these arguments is that normally the choice of what to seek to buy and what to offer to pay is the buyer's. And, even if the buyer has monopoly power, an antitrust court (which might, in appropriate circumstances, restructure the market) will not interfere with a buyer's (nonpredatory) determination of price.

* * * A legitimate buyer is entitled to use its market power to keep prices down. The claim that Blue Shield's price scheme is "too rigid" because it ignores qualitative differences among physicians is properly addressed to Blue Shield or to a regulator, not to a court. There is no suggestion that Blue Shield's fee schedule reflects, for example, an effort by, say, one group of doctors to stop other doctors from competing with them. [ ] Here, Blue Shield and the doctors "sit on opposite sides of the bargaining table" [ ]. And Blue Shield seems simply to be acting "as every rational enterprise does, *i.e.,* [to] get the best deal possible" [ ]. The first seven adverse consequences to which appellees point are the result of this unilateral behavior.

Plaintiffs' eighth argument focuses on the health insurance business: Blue Shield's "ban on balance billing," by attracting more subscribers, augments its share of the health insurance business, thereby enabling it to secure still lower doctor charges. This argument, however, comes down to saying that Blue Shield can attract more subscribers because it can charge them less. If Blue Shield is free to insist upon a lower doctor charge, it should be free to pass those savings along to its subscribers in the form of lower prices. * * *

Finally, the district court rested its decision in large part upon the Supreme Court's recent case, Arizona v. Maricopa County Medical Society. [] *Maricopa,* however, involved a *horizontal* agreement among competing doctors about what to charge. A horizontal agreement among competitors is typically unlawful because the competitors prevent themselves from making *independent* decisions about the terms as to which they will bargain. * * * [T]he antitrust problems at issue when a single firm sets a price—whether, when, and how courts can identify and control an individual exercise of alleged market power—are very different from those associated with agreements by competitors to limit independent decision-making. A decision about the latter is not strong precedent for a case involving only the former. *Maricopa* is simply not on point. * * *

C

Three additional circumstances militate strongly here against any effort by an antitrust court to supervise the Blue Shield/physician price bargain. * * *

First, the prices at issue here are low prices, not high prices. [ ] Of course, a buyer, as well as a seller, can possess significant market power; and courts have held that *agreements* to fix prices—whether maximum or minimum—are unlawful. [ ] Nonetheless, the Congress that enacted the Sherman Act saw it as a way of protecting consumers against prices that were too *high,* not too low. * * *

Second, the subject matter of the present agreement—medical costs—is an area of great complexity where more than solely economic values are at stake. * * * This fact, too, warrants judicial hesitancy to interfere.

Third, the price system here at issue is one supervised by state regulators. [ ] While that fact does not automatically carry with it antitrust immunity, [ ] it suggests that strict antitrust scrutiny is less likely to be necessary to prevent the unwarranted exercise of monopoly power. * * *

These general considerations do not dictate our result in this case. They do, however, counsel us against departing from present law or extending it to authorize increased judicial supervision of the buyer/seller price bargain. * * *

* * *

Notes and Questions

1. Is the Court's skepticism about Blue Shield's market power warranted? After all, it did control 74 percent of the private insurance market in Massachusetts and had provider contracts with 99 percent of the state's physicians. On the

other hand, is market share data alone a reliable indicator of market power? See Ball Memorial Hospital, Inc. v. Mutual Hospital Insurance, Inc., 784 F.2d 1325 (7th Cir. 1986) (absence of entry barriers in health insurance refuted possibility that insurer with large market share possessed market power); see also Frank H. Easterbrook, Maximum Price Fixing, 48 U. Chi. L. Rev. 886, 904 (1981) ("[health insurer] monopsony power is inconceivable in most instances"). For a telling refutation of Easterbrook's position, see Mark V. Pauly, Competition in Health Insurance Markets, 51 Law & Contemp. Probs. 237 (1988). Pauly argues that brand loyalty and switching costs undermine the assumption that ease of entry always obviates concerns about insurer market power. He also demonstrates that monopsony insurers may well profit from pushing provider prices "too low" so that consumers do not receive an adequate level of service and quality.

Noting that *Kartell* has frequently been cited by courts rejecting challenges to health insurers' alleged exercise of market power on the grounds that insurers were merely acting as aggressive purchasing agents "thus implying that their actions are welfare-enhancing for consumers," Professors Hammer and Sage expose the opinion's flawed assumptions regarding the market for health insurance. Peter J. Hammer and William M.Sage, Monopsony as an Agency and Regulatory Problem in Health Care, 79 Antitrust L.J. 949 (2004). They argue that the treatment of "health insurers as proxies for end-users collapses a three-level model of industrial production—comprised of provider-suppliers, insurer-producers, and patient-consumers—into a single buyer-seller dyad... [and] thereby sidesteps an inquiry into the competitive conditions of resale that is central to the traditional antitrust analysis of producer monopsony." Id. at 950. Can you explain, based on your knowledge of how health insurance is organized and purchased and physicians' relationships to insurers, why the court's simplified "dyad" is inadequate? Hammer and Sage also provide a thorough analysis of the economic and regulatory context in which Blue Shield operated, concluding that several factors not identified by the court constrained the exercise of monopsony power.

2. Section 2 of the Sherman Act does not make illegal the possession of monopoly power or even the charging of monopoly prices. Rather, plaintiff must prove willful acts that helped defendant obtain or preserve market power "as distinguished from growth or development as a consequence of a superior product, business acumen or historic accident." United States v. Grinnell Corp., 384 U.S. 563, 570–71, 86 S.Ct. 1698, 16 L.Ed.2d 778 (1966). Did the Court adequately analyze whether the balance billing ban contributed to preserving Blue Shield's market power, such as by excluding rivals? Were the long-run effects of driving price below market levels explored? See Frances H. Miller, Vertical Restraints and Powerful Health Insurers: Exclusionary Conduct Masquerading as Managed Care? 51 Law & Contemp. Probs., 195, 220–24 (1988). How satisfactory is the court's analysis of the effects of the ban on the physician market? Does the fact that physicians were not leaving Massachusetts in droves prove the absence of monopsonistic effects? Aren't there a host of other variables affecting the total supply of physicians over time? See Herbert Hovenkamp, Antitrust Policy After Chicago, 84 Mich. L. Rev. 213 (1985) (faulting the reasoning of the court in *Kartell* for its "static market fallacy").

Some courts may have been too quick to dismiss the possibility that a dominant insurer might exercise market power. In Travelers Insurance Company v. Blue Cross of Western Pennsylvania, 481 F.2d 80 (3d Cir. 1973), cert. denied, 414 U.S. 1093, 94 S.Ct. 724, 38 L.Ed.2d 550 (1973), a commercial insurer charged that a Blue Cross plan's favorable contracts with hospitals (enabling it to pay 15 percent less for hospital services than other insurers) assured it of lower premium rates and market dominance. Applying reasoning later echoed by the *Kartell* court, the Third Circuit observed that the defendant was doing "no more than conduct[ing] its business as every rational enterprise does, i.e., to get the best deal possible." 481 F.2d at 84. A close examination of the facts in *Travelers*, however, suggests that Blue Cross was engaged in strategic behavior that rings a strikingly anticompetitive note. The most plausible explanation for the discounts lies in the appreciation by the hospitals and Blue Cross of their mutual, anticompetitive interest in the arrangement. By granting the largest insurer a standard discount, the hospitals could reduce pressures to grant other discounts because there would be no other formidable buyers in the market. At the same time, the absence of competition at the payer level was assured because no rival could match the low hospital costs incurred by Blue Cross. See Clark C. Havighurst, The Questionable Cost–Containment Record of Commercial Health Insurers in Health Care in America: The Political Economy of Hospitals and Health Insurance, 221 (H.E. Frech III ed., 1988). The foregoing analysis is a good example of the impact on antitrust of new economic models demonstrating the possibility of exclusion through vertical contracting and "raising rivals' costs." In cases such as this, "Post–Chicago" economic analysis demands closer investigation of arrangements that would easily pass muster under conventional "Chicago School" principles. See Thomas G. Krattenmaker & Steven C. Salop, Anticompetitive Exclusion: Raising Rivals' Costs to Achieve Power Over Price, 96 Yale L.J. 209 (1986).

3. Government antitrust enforcers have devoted considerable attention to "most favored nations" (MFN) clauses in provider contracts with health plans. These clauses typically stipulate that the health plan will not pay the provider any more than the lowest discounted price the provider gives to any other payor. The limited case law on the subject is mixed.

Ocean State Physicians Health Plan, Inc. v. Blue Cross & Blue Shield of Rhode Island, 883 F.2d 1101 (1st Cir. 1989) involved an MFN imposed by a Blue Cross/Blue Shield plan that controlled 80% of the Rhode Island private health insurance market. When Ocean State, a new HMO, began to make significant inroads into its market, the Blue plan insisted that participating physicians grant them the same discount they granted Ocean State. Thereafter about 350 of Ocean State's 1200 participating physicians left the plan. A jury found the Blue plan guilty of violating Section 2 and of tortious interference with Ocean State's contractual relationships and awarded Ocean State $3.2 million. Citing *Kartell*, the First Circuit affirmed a judgment notwithstanding the verdict, finding that the "most favored nations" clause was a legitimate competitive strategy to assure that the Blue plan could get the lowest price for services rather than an attempt to monopolize the health insurance market. See also Blue Cross & Blue Shield of Michigan v. Michigan Association of Psychotherapy Clinics, 1980 WL 1848 (E.D.Mich. 1980) (rejecting per se price fixing claim against insurer's "non-discrimination clause"); but cf., Willamette Dental Group, P.C. v. Oregon Dental Service Corp., 130 Ore. App. 487, 882 P 2d 637 (1994) (criticizing *Ocean State* and rejecting defendants' argument that an MFN can never constitute predatory pricing); Reazin v. Blue Cross and Blue Shield of Kansas, Inc., 899 F.2d 951 (10th Cir. 1990), cert. denied, 497 U.S. 1005 110 S.Ct. 3241, 111 L.Ed.2d 752 (1990) (MFN is evidence that insurer possessed monopoly power and MFN contributed to that power).

Most of the MFN cases have involved insurers with substantial market shares. However, in United States v. Delta Dental of Rhode Island, 943 F.Supp. 172 (D.R.I. 1996), 1997–2 Trade Cas. ¶ 71,860 (1997) (consent decree), the government alleged that the defendant's MFN amounted to an illegal agreement under § 1 of the Sherman Act even though it insured only 35–45% of all persons with dental insurance in the market while having provider contracts with over 90% of all dentists. How can an MFN harm competition in such circumstances? If a health plan is not dominant in its market, what conditions are necessary before it can have an exclusionary effect on other plans by using an MFN? Note that, in addition to "raising rivals' costs," MFNs can cause several other kinds of anticompetitive harm. For example, they can facilitate collusion by eliminating the dynamic mechanisms whereby prices are effectively ratcheted down and they can "dampen competition" by reducing the aggressiveness of competitors. See Jonathan B. Baker, Vertical Restraints with Horizontal Consequences: Competitive Effects of "Most–Favored–Customer" Clauses, 64 Antitrust L.J. 517 (1996); Arnold Celnicker, A Competitive Analysis of Most Favored Nations Clauses in Contracts Between Health Care Providers and Insurers, 69 N.C. L.Rev. 863 (1991).

4. The McCarran–Ferguson Act provides a limited exemption for the "business of insurance" if the state regulates those activities and they do not constitute "boycott, coercion or intimidation." 15 U.S.C. §§ 1011–15. Two cases, Group Life and Health Insurance Co. v. Royal Drug Co., 440 U.S. 205, 99 S.Ct. 1067, 59 L.Ed.2d 261 (1979) rehearing denied, 441 U.S. 917, 99 S.Ct. 2017, 60 L.Ed.2d 389 (1979) and Union Labor Life Insurance Co. v. Pireno, 458 U.S. 119, 102 S.Ct. 3002, 73 L.Ed.2d 647 (1982), have interpreted the term "business of insurance" very restrictively, limiting the meaning of that term to activities involving risk-spreading and transferring the policyholders' risk; relationships between insurers; and usually only parties in the insurance industry. This leaves many cost-containment activities of insurers subject to antitrust oversight. The Insurance Antitrust Handbook (M. Horning & R. Langsdorf, eds. 1995). At the same time, the McCarran–Ferguson Act shields a wide range of obviously anticompetitive conduct. Agreements among insurers to fix subscriber premiums or actions of a dominant insurer regarding the types of policies it will sell or the conditions attached thereto are exempt. See *Royal Drug,* Klamath–Lake Pharmaceutical Ass'n v. Klamath Medical Service Bureau, 701 F.2d 1276 (9th Cir. 1983). In *Ocean State,* the court found that the McCarran–Ferguson Act immunized defendants' marketing and pricing policies in its HMO coverage and the imposition of higher rates on employers that offered a competing HMO option.

Note on Exclusion of Providers by Managed Care Organizations

In contrast to the extensive attention paid to provider-controlled networks that are overinclusive or engage in price fixing, discussed *supra,* little antitrust concern has been raised about the exclusion of physicians or hospitals from plans or networks that are controlled by independent insurers or HMOs. As a general matter, antitrust law has regarded exclusion, deselection, and exclusive panel arrangements as legitimate marketplace decisions and any adverse consequences to excluded physicians are thus seen as a normal consequence of competition. Glen Eden Hospital, Inc. v. Blue Cross & Blue Shield of Michigan, Inc., 740 F.2d 423 (6th Cir. 1984); Barry v. Blue Cross, 805 F.2d 866 (9th Cir. 1986). Indeed, government agencies and commentators have generally extolled the benefits of "selective contracting." See, e.g., Department of Justice/FTC Policy Statement 9 ("selective contracting may be a method through which networks limit their provider panels in an effort to achieve quality and cost containment goals and enhance their ability to compete against other networks"). Courts have upheld actions by insurers or HMOs to reject or deselect providers from their panels as unilateral decisions because they lack elements of concerted action under Section 1 of the Sherman Act. See e.g., Continental Orthopedic Appliances, Inc. v. Health

Ins. Plan of Greater New York, 956 F.Supp. 367 (E.D. N.Y. 1997) (noting that "[g]enerally, a health maintenance organization has the right to determine the companies it chooses to recommend to its customers, if it does not do so as a result of an illegal conspiracy to restrain trade"). Likewise, monopolization claims under Section 2 against insurer decisions as to the composition of their panels have been unsuccessful because of the insurers' lack of market power and the absence of anticompetitive purpose arising from vertical decisions involving selecting physicians.

However, as discussed in the previous section, where the payer or a network of payers is provider-controlled, the plan is treated as a combination among those who control it, and decisions to exclude competing physicians are considered horizontal agreement. While older cases involving physician controlled Blue Shield plans and contemporary cases involving physician controlled networks may fall in the horizontal category, they too are almost always unsuccessful. Courts have uniformly applied the rule of reason where the rationale for exclusion from a provider-controlled IPA or PPO has been the providers' incompetence or overutilization of services. See, e.g., Levine v. Central Florida Medical Affiliates, Inc., 72 F.3d 1538 (11th Cir. 1996); Hassan v. Independent Practice Associates, 698 F.Supp. 679 (E.D.Mich. 1988). On the other hand, defendants bear the burden of coming forward with a plausible rationale for excluding an entire class of providers. See Hahn v. Oregon Physicians' Service, 868 F.2d 1022 (9th Cir. 1988), (denying defendants' motion for summary judgment where excluded podiatrists rebutted justifications based on overutilization of services). Once the rule of reason is applied to provider deselection or exclusion, the often dispositive threshold question is whether the plan had market power. An illustrative case is Capital Imaging Associates, P.C. v. Mohawk Valley Medical Associates, Inc., 996 F.2d 537 (2d Cir. 1993), in which the plan had less than three per cent of the market's HMO subscribers and contracted with only seven per cent of the area's physicians.

At what level of concentration would a problem arise? Should a court look only to the market share of the defendant plan or should it consider the overall concentration of plans in the market? Is the percentage of total physicians participating in the plan a better surrogate for the plan's market power? These difficult questions have not been definitively answered by the courts, but the Department of Justice/FTC Policy Statements offer the following guidance:

> Where a geographic market can support several multiprovider networks, there are not likely to be significant competitive problems associated with the exclusion of particular providers by particular networks.... [E]xclusion may present competitive concerns if providers are unable to compete effectively without access to the networks, and competition is thereby harmed.

Policy Statements, *supra*, Statement No. 9. Plaintiffs need not prove market power, however, if they can demonstrate that their exclusion has had actual detrimental effects on competition, such as higher prices to consumers. Establishing such effects is usually not possible. See Levine v. Central Florida Medical Affiliates, Inc., 72 F.3d 1538 (11th Cir. 1996) (no "actual detrimental effect" because plaintiff was able to establish a profitable solo practice and defendants' conduct did not raise the price of service in the market).

Problem: Mountain Health Care

Mountain Health Care (MHC), the largest managed care company in its market, sells nearly seventy percent of all private health insurance policies. MHC, which began as a nonprofit association of hospitals, owns hospitals that deliver 60 per cent of all inpatient health care services in that market. A group of forty-nine optometrists have filed suit against MHC claiming that it has violated Section 1 and 2 of the Sherman Act by conspiring with ophthalmologists on its managed care panels (who also have staff privileges at MHC hospitals) to exclude optometrists from being placed on the preferred panels of MHC managed care plans. Plaintiffs claim that in exchange for MHC's agreement not to panel optometrists, the conspiring ophthalmologists agreed to refer their patients to MHC's hospitals and surgical facilities instead of those operated by MHC's competitors.

Optometrists sell optical hardware (glasses and contact lenses) and are licensed to perform the full scope of nonsurgical eye care (NSEC) and to prescribe prescription drugs. Ophthalmologists also perform NSEC but also are licensed to perform surgical eye care, and usually have staff privileges at hospitals to perform those procedures. The local ophthalmologists' trade association has long sought to limit the ability of optometrists to compete, having lobbied against legislation that was adopted ten years ago allowing the latter to perform the full range of NSEC. More recently, prominent ophthalmologists on staff at MHC hospitals have repeatedly urged managers of MHC's managed care subsidiary not to panel optometrists, arguing that only those practicing under the supervision of ophthalmologists should be accepted "in order to maintain the high quality of care provided by MHC." The optometrists are prepared to prove that they provide NSEC at lower cost than do ophthalmologists and have come upon one internal MHC study showed that its managed care plans could save $400,000 per year by adding optometrists to its panels.

MHC has recently amended its plans' provider agreements to permit it to engage in economic credentialing including terminating any providers "based on business or competitive reasons" or on "under-utilization of MHC related providers and facilities." MHC has terminated at least one ophthalmologist for failure to direct his patients to MHC surgical facilities. MHC's accounting records suggest that it saves money on implementing peer review, quality control, and credentialing for its health plans when it contracts with providers who have staff privileges at its hospitals, as contrasted with optometrists who cannot have staff privileges. In addition, administrators of the MHC plans believe they save costs and improve quality by selective contracting and do not need additional providers of NSEC at this time.

What antitrust claims might be brought under Section 1 and 2 of the Sherman Act? What additional evidence would be of importance to evaluating each theory? Your preliminary legal research has uncovered the following:

In order to present enough evidence for a jury to infer an antitrust conspiracy, something more than "mere complaints" from a distributor to a manufacturer are necessary. Other "plus factors" such as evidence that alleged conspirators were acting contrary to their independent interest when taking action can give rise to an inference of a conspiracy. See Monsanto Co. v. Spray–Rite Serv. Corp., 465 U.S. 752 at 764, 104 S.Ct. 1464, 79 L.Ed.2d 775 (1984). See also Matsushita Elec. Indus. Co. v. Zenith Radio Corp., 475 U.S. 574, 588, 106 S.Ct. 1348, 89 L.Ed.2d 538 (1986). ("Antitrust law limits the range of permissible inferences from ambiguous evidence in a Section 1 case.")

C. MERGERS AND ACQUISITIONS

1. *Hospital Mergers*

HOSPITAL CORPORATION OF AMERICA

106 F.T.C. 361 (1985).

CALVANI, COMM'R.

I. INTRODUCTION TO THE CASE

A. *The Acquisitions*

In August 1981, Respondent Hospital Corporation of America ("HCA"), the largest proprietary hospital chain in the United States, acquired Hospital Affiliates International ("HAI") in a stock transaction valued at approximately $650 million. [ ] At the time of the acquisition, HAI owned or leased 57 hospitals and managed 78 hospitals nationwide. Prior to its acquisition by HCA, HAI owned or managed five acute care hospitals in the general area of Chattanooga, Tennessee, and HCA acquired ownership or management of these hospitals through the transaction. Some four months later HCA acquired yet another hospital corporation, Health Care Corporation ("HCC"), in a stock transaction valued at approximately $30 million. At the time of the acquisition, HCC owned a single acute care hospital in Chattanooga. These two transactions provide the genesis for the instant case.

As a result of the HCA–HAI acquisition, Respondent increased its hospital operations in Chattanooga and its suburbs from ownership of one acute care hospital to ownership or management of four of the area's eleven acute care hospitals. Within the six-county Chattanooga Metropolitan Statistical Area ("Chattanooga MSA"), HCA changed its position from owner of one hospital to owner or manager of six of fourteen acute care hospitals. With the acquisition of HCC, HCA obtained yet another acute care hospital in Chattanooga. Thus, HCA became owner or manager of five of the eleven acute care hospitals within the Chattanooga urban area and seven of the fourteen in the Chattanooga MSA.

* * * Administrative Law Judge Parker found that the acquisitions violated Section 7 of the Clayton Act and Section 5 of the Federal Trade Commission Act, and ordered HCA to divest two of the hospitals of which it had acquired ownership. Judge Parker also ordered that HCA provide prior notification to the Commission of certain of its future hospital acquisitions. HCA appeals the Initial Decision on several grounds; Complaint Counsel appeal certain of Judge Parker's findings as well.

* * * We affirm Judge Parker's finding of liability and modify his opinion only as stated below.

* * *

III. THE PRODUCT MARKET

An acquisition violates Section 7 of the Clayton Act "where in any line of commerce in any section of the country, the effect of such acquisition may be substantially to lessen competition, or to tend to create a monopoly." 15 U.S.C. Sec. 18 (1982). Accordingly, we now turn to the definition of the relevant "line of commerce" or "product market" in which to measure the likely competitive effects of these acquisitions. In measuring likely competitive effects, we seek to define a product or group of products sufficiently distinct that buyers could not defeat an attempted exercise of market power on the part of sellers of those products by shifting purchases to still different products. Sellers might exercise market power by raising prices, limiting output or lowering quality. * * *

Complaint Counsel argued below that the product market [ ] was properly defined as the provision of acute inpatient hospital services and emergency hospital services provided to the critically ill. [ ] This definition would exclude non-hospital providers of outpatient services, e.g., free standing emergency centers, as well as non-hospital providers of inpatient services, e.g., nursing homes, from the product market. It would also exclude the outpatient business of hospitals, except for that provided to the critically ill in the emergency room. The rationale for excluding outpatient care is that inpatient services are the reason for being of acute care hospitals; inpatient services are needed by and consumed by patients in combination and therefore can be offered only by acute care hospitals. Inpatients in almost all cases will purchase a range of services and not just one test or procedure; they will typically consume a "cluster" of services involving 24–hour nursing, the services of specialized laboratory and X-ray equipment, the services of equipment needed to monitor vital functions or intervene in crises, and so forth. An acutely ill patient must be in a setting in which all of these various services can be provided together. * * * According to this reasoning, outpatient services are not an integral part of this "cluster of services" offered by acute care hospitals, and therefore must be excluded.

Respondent, on the other hand, urged that the market be defined to include outpatient care as well as inpatient care. Respondent's expert witness, Dr. Jeffrey E. Harris, testified that outpatient care is growing rapidly for hospitals, as well as for free-standing facilities such as emergency care and one-day surgery centers, which compete with hospitals for outpatients. Moreover, because of substantial changes in medical technology, there are a growing number of procedures that can be provided on an outpatient basis that previously could have been done on only an inpatient basis.

Judge Parker agreed that the market should include outpatient services provided by hospitals but excluded outpatient services provided by non-hospital providers, holding that only hospitals can provide the "unique combination" of services which the acute care patient needs. He defined the relevant product market to be the cluster of services offered by acute care hospitals, including outpatient as well as inpatient care, "since acute care hospitals compete with each other in offering both kinds of care and since . . . acute care outpatient facilities feed patients to the inpatient facilities."

Neither HCA nor Complaint Counsel appeal Judge Parker's product market definition.[ ] Accordingly, for purposes of this proceeding only, we accept Judge Parker's finding on this issue. [ ]

However, we do note that Judge Parker's definition does not necessarily provide a very happy medium between the two competing positions; the evidence in this case tended to show *both* that free-standing outpatient facilities compete with hospitals for many outpatients and that hospitals offer and inpatients consume a cluster of services that bears little relation to outpatient care. If so, it may be that defining the cluster of hospital inpatient services as a separate market better reflects competitive reality in this case. * * * Certainly, it is clear that anti-competitive behavior by hospital firms could significantly lessen competition for hospital inpatients that could not be defeated by competition from non-hospital outpatient providers. Our analysis will hence proceed with primary reference to the cluster of services provided to inpatients.

IV. THE GEOGRAPHIC MARKET

* * * Because we are concerned only with an area in which competition could be harmed, the relevant geographic market must be broad enough that buyers would be unable to switch to alternative sellers in sufficient numbers to defeat an exercise of market power by firms in the area. * * * If an exercise of market power could be defeated by the entry of products produced in another area, both areas should be considered part of the same geographic market for Section 7 purposes, since competition could not be harmed in the smaller area. That is the geographic market should determine not only the firms that constrain competitors' actions by currently selling to the same customers, but also those that would be a constraint because of their ability to sell to those customers should price or quality in the area change. * * *

* * *

HCA would have us adopt Hamilton County, Tennessee, together with Walker, Dade and Catoosa counties in Georgia, the "Chattanooga urban area." as the relevant geographic market. HCA predicates its conclusion largely on an analysis of evidence concerning physician admitting patterns.

* * * With few exceptions, every physician who admitted to Chattanooga urban area hospitals admitted exclusively to other hospitals in the Chattanooga urban area. Conversely, physicians admitting and treating patients at hospitals outside the Chattanooga urban area rarely admitted and treated patients at hospitals in the Chattanooga urban area.

* * *

Additionally, the weight of the evidence concerning patient origin suggests that patients admitted to Chattanooga urban area hospitals who live outside of the Chattanooga urban area are, with few exceptions, in need of specialized care and treatment unavailable in their own communities. * * * Hospitals in outlying communities do not always provide quite the same product that the urban area hospitals provide such patients, and therefore patient inflows are not necessarily indicative of the willingness of patients to leave their home areas for services that are available in those areas. Judge Parker agreed with HCA that the Chattanooga urban area is the relevant geographic market in this case. [ ]

On appeal, Complaint Counsel agree that the Chattanooga urban area is an appropriate geographic area in which to assess the competitive effects of these acquisitions. However, they claim that a much more appropriate geographic market is the federally designated Metropolitan Statistical Area that includes Chattanooga. In effect, Complaint Counsel would have us add the Tennessee counties of Marion and Sequatchie to the market proffered by HCA and adopted by Judge Parker. By adding this area, three additional hospitals—South Pittsburgh Municipal Hospital, Sequatchie General Hospital, and Whitwell Community Hospital—would be included in the relevant market. Both South Pittsburgh and Sequatchie were acquired by HCA from HAI, and Complaint Counsel seek divestiture by HCA of its long-term lease arrangement with South Pittsburgh. [ ]

* * *

* * * Geopolitical designations such as "MSA" may reflect a host of considerations that do not concern the issue of competition between hospitals. * * * Nor do we find any evidence that MSA designations were ever intended to reflect an economic market for purposes of Section 7. We do not here conclude that an MSA will never accurately reflect the relevant geographic market in a hospital merger case. But where, as here, the MSA designation excludes important sources of potential competition, it must be rejected. * * *

* * *

V.   The Effect on Competition

A.   *The Effect of HCA–Managed Hospitals*

One of the major dimensions of HCA's purchase of HAI was the acquisition of some 75 to 80 hospital management contracts. * * * Two of these were management contracts HAI had with two hospitals in the Chattanooga urban area—Downtown General Hospital and Red Bank Community Hospital. * * * HCA argues, and Judge Parker agreed, that Downtown General and Red Bank hospitals should be treated as entities completely separate from HCA, incapable of being significantly influenced by HCA in its role as administrator. * * *

We conclude that treating the two managed hospitals as entities completely independent of HCA is contrary to the overwhelming weight of the evidence in this case. As manager, HCA controls the competitive variables needed for successful coordination with the activities of HCA-owned hospitals in Chattanooga. Moreover, as manager it knows the competitive posture of managed hospitals so well that the likelihood of any anti-competitive behavior HCA wished to engage in is greatly increased.

* * *

Indeed, the very reason that a management firm is hired, as reflected in the management contracts, is to direct the competitive operations of the managed hospital. The evidence shows clearly that management recommendations, including proposed rate increases, are almost invariably followed by the boards of directors of Downtown General and Red Bank. * * *

* * *

* * * The evidence compels us to consider the market shares of Downtown General and Red Bank as part of HCA's market share in considering the effect on competition in this case. [ ] Even were the evidence not as compelling, we would consider HCA's management of the two hospitals to greatly enhance the likelihood of collusion in this market. [ ]

* * *

B.   The Nature of Competition Among Chattanooga Hospitals

Traditionally, hospitals have competed for patients in three general ways: first, by competing for physicians to admit their patients; second, by competing directly for patients on the basis of amenities and comfort of surroundings; and third, by competing to a limited degree on the basis of price. The first two constitute "non-price" or "quality" competition, and by far have been in the past the most important of the three.

[The court explains that although nonprice competition has been the primary form of rivalry among hospitals, price competition is growing in the hospital industry and Chattanooga hospitals are now "far more likely to present themselves to insurers, employers and employee groups as less costly than their competitors as one method of attracting business."]

. . . We do not here conclude that price has been the prime arena in which hospitals in Chattanooga compete. However, we do think it clear that even though rates are not constantly adjusted due to a changing price structure, they have been periodically set with some reference to what the market will bear in face of the prices of other hospitals.

It is clear that Section 7 protects whatever price competition exists in a market, however limited. * * *

* * *

C.   Respondent's Market Share and Concentration in the Chattanooga Urban Area

Three ways to measure a hospital's share of the acute care hospital services market are by using: (1) bed capacity; (2) inpatient days; and (3) net revenues. Bed capacity and inpatient days measure a hospital's position with regard to the cluster of inpatient services, the heart of hospital care. Net revenues, on the other hand, account for both inpatient and outpatient services.

Naturally, because of their proposed market definitions, Complaint Counsel advocate use of inpatient measures, while HCA urges net revenues as the preferable measure since it accounts for outpatient services. We conclude, however, that the three measures are so similar in this case that they yield the same result whatever measure is used.

* * *

[The court concludes that HCA's market share increased significantly and that it considered "an increase in concentration in an already concentrated market to be of serious competitive concern, all other things being equal."]

[A]ll other things being equal, an increase in market concentration through a reduction in the absolute number of competitive actors makes interdependent behavior more likely. * * * These acquisitions decreased the number of independent firms in the market from 9 to 7. [ ] The costs of coordination or of policing any collusive agreement are less with fewer participants, and the elimination of competitive forces in this market facilitates joint anti-competitive behavior.

In sum, evidence of the increased concentration caused by these acquisitions points toward a finding of likely harm to competition, all other things being equal. [ ] HCA's acquisitions have made an already highly concentrated market more conducive to collusion by eliminating two of the healthiest sources of competition in the market and increasing concentration substantially. But all other things are not equal in this market, and statistical evidence is not the end of our inquiry. In the absence of barriers to entry, an exercise of market power can be defeated or deterred by the entry or potential entry of new firms regardless of the structure of the existing market. * * * We now turn to the issue of entry barriers and conclude that they confirm and even magnify the inference to be drawn from the concentration evidence in this case.

D. Barriers to Entry

* * *

* * * [T]here is hardly free entry into the acute care hospital industry in either Tennessee or Georgia. Indeed, the CON [certificate of need] laws at issue here create a classic "barrier to entry" under every definition of that term. In *Echlin Manufacturing Co.*, we defined a "barrier to entry" to include "additional long-run costs that must be incurred by an entrant relative to the long-run costs faced by incumbent firms." * * * We explained that "[t]he rationale underlying this definition is that low-cost incumbent firms can keep prices above the competitive level as long as those prices remain below the level that would provide an incentive to higher-cost potential entrants."

If a potential entrant desires to build a new hospital in Chattanooga, he must incur all the costs in time and money associated with obtaining a CON. The cost of starting a new hospital includes not only the start-up costs that any firm would incur to enter the market but also the costs of surviving the administrative process. Incumbents in this market, however, did not incur such costs during initial construction. They have only had to incur those costs for additions made to bed capacity since the enactment of the CON laws a decade ago. [ ] Incumbents thus have a long run cost advantage over potential entrants. The result is that market power could be exercised by incumbents without attracting attempts at entry as long as supracompetitive profits are not high enough for a potential entrant to justify incurring all the ordinary costs of starting a hospital *plus* the significant costs of obtaining a CON.

The evidence is clear that those costs are significant in this market. We agree with Judge Parker that because incumbent hospitals can oppose new entry, even an unsuccessful opposition to a CON application may delay its disposition by several years. * * *

Thus the CON process provides existing hospitals in the Chattanooga urban area ample opportunity to significantly forestall the entry of a new hospital or the expansion of an existing hospital within the area. Indeed, the evidence shows that existing hospitals frequently oppose CON applications when they feel competitively threatened. * * *

* * *

In sum, it is not merely the costs of obtaining a CON that a potential entrant faces, but the significant risk of being denied entry once those costs have been incurred. This risk, which incumbents did not have to face when building their hospitals, in effect raises the costs of entry a significantly greater amount. As a result, many potential entrants may decide not to even attempt entry. Indeed, the evidence shows that CON regulation has had a deterrent effect in the Chattanooga market.

* * *

E. The Nature and Likelihood of Anti-competitive Behavior in the Chattanooga Hospital Market

1. The Nature of Anti-competitive Behavior

* * *

Some of the most likely forms of collusion between hospitals would involve collective resistance to emerging cost containment pressures from third-party payors and alternative providers. For example, joint refusals to deal with HMOs or PPOs may occur, or perhaps joint refusals to deal on the most favorable terms. Conspiracies to boycott certain insurance companies that are generating price competition may occur. Utilization review programs may also be resisted. Hospitals could concertedly refuse to provide the information desired by third-party payors—information that would otherwise be provided as hospitals vie to attract the business of those payors and their subscribers. The result of any such boycott would be to raise prices, reduce quality of services or both. [ ]

* * *

Quality competition itself might also be restricted. For example, the group of hospitals in a relevant market might agree to staff their wards with fewer nurses yet continue to maintain current rates for inpatient services. Patients would be harmed by the resulting drop in quality of services without any compensating reduction in price of services. Colluding hospitals in the market, however, would profit from their agreement by cutting costs without cutting revenues. Again, hospitals could accomplish anti-competitive ends not only by fixing staff-patient ratios but by agreeing on wages or benefits to be paid certain personnel—for example, laboratory technicians. Indeed, wage and salary surveys are common in this market. The result would be the same—to hold the cost of inputs down with probable harm to the quality of output of health care services. [ ] Hospitals could also agree not to compete for each other's personnel or medical staff. Indeed, some Chattanooga urban area hospital firms have already engaged in such behavior.

Moreover, under certificate of need legislation, the addition of new services and purchases of certain kinds of new equipment require a demonstration of need for the expenditure, and the existence of need is determined in part by the facilities already provided in the community. It would thus be to the advantage of competing hospitals to enter into agreements among themselves as to which competitor will apply for which service or for which piece of equipment. * * * Such market division by private agreement would save hospitals the expense of applying for numerous CONs but may harm the quality of care that would be available to patients were CON approval sought independently by each hospital with reference to its own merits and expertise.

Concerted opposition to the CON application of a potential new entrant is yet another manner in which Chattanooga hospitals could successfully collude. * * *

Anti-competitive pricing behavior could also take several forms. For example, hospitals could work out agreements with respect to pricing formulas. * * * Hospitals could also successfully collude with respect to price by agreeing not to give discounts to businesses, insurers and other group purchasers such as HMOs and PPOs. * * *

In sum, we conclude that hospitals compete in a myriad of ways that could be restricted anti-competitively through collusion. [ ] Thus, it appears that a merger analysis in this case need be no different than in any other case; market share and concentration figures, evidence of entry barriers and other market evidence taken together appear to yield as accurate a picture of competitive conditions as they do in other settings. Nevertheless, although HCA concedes that many of the above described forms of collusion *could* occur, the heart of HCA's case is that collusion in this market is inherently unlikely, and to that contention we now turn.

2. *The Likelihood of Anti-competitive Behavior*

Section 7 of the Clayton Act prohibits acquisitions that may have the effect of substantially lessening competition or tending to create a monopoly. Because Section 7 applies to "incipient" violations, actual anti-competitive effects need not be shown; an acquisition is unlawful if such an effect is reasonably probable. * * *

The small absolute number of competitors in this market, the high concentration and the extremely high entry barriers indicate a market in which anti-competitive behavior is reasonably probable after the acquisitions. The fact that industry members recognize the enormity of entry barriers makes collusion even more probable. In addition, hospital markets have certain features that evidence a likelihood of collusion or other anti-competitive behavior when they become highly concentrated.

First, price elasticity of demand for hospital services is very low, which makes anti-competitive behavior extremely profitable and hence attractive. * * * Second, because consumers of hospital services cannot arbitrage or resell them as is often possible with goods, discrimination among different groups of consumers is possible. That is, collusion may be directed at a certain group or certain groups of consumers, such as a particular insurance company, without the necessity of anti-competitive behavior toward other groups. Third, the traditions of limited price competition and disapproval of advertising provide an incentive for future anti-competitive restrictions of those activities. Fourth, and in the same vein, the advent of incentives to resist new cost containment pressures may create a substantial danger of hospital collusion to meet pressures. Fifth, the hospital industry has a tradition of cooperative problem solving which makes collusive conduct in the future more likely. Hospitals have historically participated in voluntary health planning in a coordinated manner, and along with other professional organizations, such as medical societies, have participated in developing joint solutions to industry problems.

* * * The most convincing evidence of the facility with which such collusion could occur is a blatant market allocation agreement executed in 1981 between Red Bank Community Hospital and HCC. The parties actually *signed a contract* under which Red Bank agreed that for a period of three years it would not "file any application for a Certificate of Need for psychiatric facilities or nursing home facilities." Moreover, the parties agreed that they would not compete for each other's personnel and medical staff during that time period, and that they would not oppose each other's CON applications in certain areas. Such an overt agreement to refrain from competition at the very least demonstrates the predisposition of some firms in the market to collude when it is in their interest; at worst it shows a callous disregard for the antitrust laws. [ ]

* * *

Furthermore, a basis for collusion is provided by the exchanges of rate, salary and other competitively sensitive information that occur in this market. * * *

* * *

* * * It is true that the undisputed evidence shows that more vigorous competition, including more direct price competition, is emerging in the health care industry, but it is a fallacy to conclude that growing competition in health care markets means that these acquisitions pose no threat to that competition. In fact, it is just that emerging competition that must be protected from mergers that facilitate the suppression of such competition. * * *

a. Non-profit Hospitals and the Likelihood of Collusion

HCA contends that the most fundamental difference between hospitals in Chattanooga is that several of the hospitals are "non-profit" institutions. Economic theory presumes that businesses in an industry are profit-maximizers and that output will be restricted in pursuit of profits. Non-profit hospitals, the argument goes, have no incentive to maximize profits, rather, they seek to maximize "output" or the number of patients treated. HCA contends that non-profit hospitals may have other goals as well, such as providing the most sophisticated and highest quality care possible, or pursuing religious or governmental goals. In short, HCA argues that collusion would not occur because the "for-profit" and "non-profit" competitors have no common goal.

We disagree that non-profit hospitals have no incentive to collude with each other or with proprietary hospitals to achieve anti-competitive ends. First, we note that non-profit status of market participants is no guarantee of competitive behavior. * * *

* * *

In addition, administrators of non-profit hospitals may seek to maximize their personal benefits and comfort through what would otherwise be known as profit-seeking activity. * * *

* * *

[T]wo major non-profit hospitals, Erlanger and Tri–County, have a tremendous incentive to participate in price collusion. Erlanger has sole responsibility for unreimbursed indigent care in Hamilton County. * * * Because it must subsidize unreimbursed care out of the rates charged to paying customers, Erlanger cannot compete effectively through price cutting. Erlanger's rates are 50 dollars per day *or 10%* higher than they would be if such cross-subsidization between paying and non-paying patients were not necessary. Because it cannot price below a level that covers the direct costs it incurs for indigent care, Erlanger would in fact benefit from a decrease in price competition through interdependent behavior. The same analysis applies to Tri–County, which must provide care for indigent residents of Walker, Dade and Catoosa counties in Georgia, and shift costs from non-paying to paying patients. * * *

* * *

b. *Purported Obstacles to Successful Coordination*

... HCA argues that even if hospitals in Chattanooga were inclined to collude, the administrators of those hospitals would find it difficult to reach anti-competitive agreements or understandings, or to sustain them if they ever were reached. This is so because the ideal market circumstances for collusion are not present, i.e. where manufacturers are selling "some simple, relatively homogeneous good, well characterized by a single price." HCA contends that hospital services are heterogeneous and influenced by a variety of complicating factors. Hospitals provide a large number of varied medical tests and treatments and each patient receives unpredictable personalized service the extent of which is determined by physicians. Moreover, HCA claims costs and demand vary between hospitals. And because the dominant avenues of competition relate to the quality of medical care and patient amenities, hospitals would have to agree on a whole host of things to eliminate competition in a manner sufficient to earn monopoly returns, it is alleged.

* * *

HCA's analysis of the likelihood of collusion distorts competitive reality. HCA would have us believe that the world of possible collusion is limited to complicated formulae concerning every aspect of hospital competition—that market power can only be exercised with respect to the entire cluster of services that constitutes the acute care hospital market through a conspiracy fixing the overall quantity or quality of treatment running to each patient in the market. Rather than focus on the likely avenues of collusion among hospitals, HCA assumes into existence a world in which collusion is infeasible.

* * *

HCA offers an additional reason why the acquisitions allegedly create no risk that Chattanooga hospitals will collude to eliminate price competition, arguing that price collusion is unlikely because of the role of Blue Cross in this market. * * *

We cannot accept HCA's claims that Blue Cross has both the omniscience and market power to halt successful collusion by Chattanooga hospitals. First, under the current Blue Cross charge approval system, collusion could be difficult to detect. If all the hospital firms in Chattanooga attempt to raise prices a similar amount in the review process, coordinated pricing could be overlooked; there is no *a priori* reason why Blue Cross would consider this to be the result of collusion rather than a rise in costs. * * *

Furthermore, even if detected, we do not think such collusion could be easily deterred by Blue Cross. HCA ignores the fact that Blue Cross has a contract not only with participating hospitals but also with its subscribers. Blue Cross must serve its subscribers in the Chattanooga area, and HCA does not explain how Blue Cross could reject a concerted effort by the hospitals there even if it wanted to; certainly, Blue Cross could not ask its subscribers to all go to Knoxville for hospital care if Chattanooga urban area hospitals colluded. * * *

* * *

VII. CONCLUSION

We hold that HCA's acquisitions of HAI and HCC may substantially lessen competition in the Chattanooga urban area acute care hospital market in violation of Section 7 of the Clayton Act and Section 5 of the Federal Trade Commission Act.

Notes and Questions

1. The Seventh Circuit reviewed and upheld the decision of the Federal Trade Commission in Hospital Corporation of America v. FTC, 807 F.2d 1381 (7th Cir. 1986). Calling the FTC's decision a "model of lucidity," Judge Posner reviewed the Commission's analysis of the merger:

> When an economic approach is taken in a section 7 case, the ultimate issue is whether the challenged acquisition is likely to facilitate collusion. In this perspective the acquisition of a competitor has no economic significance in itself; the worry is that it may enable the acquiring firm to cooperate (or cooperate better) with other leading competitors on reducing or limiting output, thereby pushing up the market price. *Hospital Corporation* calls the issue whether an acquisition is likely to have such an effect "economic," which of course it is. But for purposes of judicial review, as we have said, it is a factual issue subject to the substantial evidence rule.

Judge Posner discussed HCA's arguments that collusion is unlikely because of the heterogeneity of hospital markets, the rapid technological and economic change experienced by the hospital industry, and the size of third party payers. He concluded: "Most of these facts do detract from a conclusion that collusion in this market is a serious danger, but it was for the Commission—it is not for us—to determine their weight." This analysis is directed at the risk of "coordinated effects" resulting from a merger—that is, an enhancement of the ability of the merged entity to exercise market power by acting in coordination with others competitors in a market. Compare this kind of harm with the "unilateral effects" analysis in the Evanston Hospital case *infra*. For an explication of the overall methodology followed by the federal enforcement agencies in evaluating mergers see U.S. Department of Justice and Federal Trade Commission, Merger Guidelines (1992), 57 Fed. Reg. 41552 (Sept. 10, 1992).

2. Note that the enforcement agencies, affirmed by the courts, have identified as the relevant product market in hospital merger cases a "cluster market" consisting of most inpatient services and some outpatient services for which there are no practical alternatives. A factor complicating product market definition is the fact that the numerous services in the "cluster" have widely differing geographic market dimensions. For some sophisticated tertiary care services like organ transplants, the geographic market is certainly regional or perhaps national, while the markets for emergency care and many routine acute care services are obviously very local. Almost all litigated hospital merger cases have settled on a product market definition that encompasses primary and secondary services, but excludes tertiary care which has a wider geographic market but usually does not impact the competitive dynamics among local hospitals. Might it be better to refine the analysis further by delineating those portions of the product market which are predominantly local and not subject to substitution by distant hospitals? Should each DRG be a separate product market? See, FTC v. Butterworth Health Corp., 946 F.Supp. 1285 (W.D.Mich. 1996).

Antitrust enforcement has reached mergers involving numerous other segments of the health care industry besides hospitals. For example, state and federal enforcers have challenged mergers of physician groups (Maine v. Cardiovascular & Thoracic Assocs., P.A., 1992–2 Trade Cas. (CCH) ¶ 69,985 1992 WL 503594 (Maine Sup. Ct., Kennebec Cnty., 1992) (consent decree); Maine v. Mid Coast Anesthesia, P.A., 1991–2) Trade Cas. (CCH) ¶ 69,683 (Maine Sup. Ct., Kennebec Cty., 1992) (consent decree), and Letter from Charles F. Rule, Assistant Attorney General, Antitrust Division, to William L. Trombetta (Aug. 28, 1987) (Business Review Letter to Danbury Surgical Associates)); rehabilitation hospitals (Healthsouth Rehabilitation Corp., 60 Fed. Reg. 5,401–01 (Dept. of Justice, 1994) (consent order); hospitals providing inpatient psychiatric care (Charter Medical and National Medical Enterprises, 59 Fed. Reg. 60,804–01 (Dept. of Justice, 1994); skilled nursing facilities (United States v. Beverly Enterprises, 1984–1 Trade Cas. (CCH) ¶ 66,052 (M.D. Ga. 1984) (consent decree); retail pharmacy services (THC Corp., 59 Fed. Reg. 46,438 (Dept. of Justice, 1994)); HMOs (In the Matter of Harvard Community Health Plan, Inc. and Pilgrim Health Care, Inc., No. 95–0331 (Suffolk Superior Ct. Mass. 1995)); and an "innovation market" in gene therapy techniques (Ciba–Geigy Ltd., 62 Fed. Reg. 409 (1997) (consent decree). See also FTC v. Cardinal Health, Inc., 12 F. Supp. 2d 34 (D.D.C. 1998) (enjoining two mergers involving wholesale drug distributors and rejecting defendants' argument that the relevant market should include self-distribution by large pharmaceutical chains that purchased and warehoused their own pharmaceuticals directly from manufacturers). Market definition poses difficult questions in these cases. For example, how would you go about determining the geographic market for skilled nursing home services? Who is the "buyer" of these services?

FEDERAL TRADE COMMISSION v. TENET HEALTH CARE CORPORATION

United States Court of Appeals Eighth Circuit, 1999.
186 F.3d 1045

Beam, Circuit Judge.

Tenet Healthcare and Poplar Bluff Physicians Group, Inc., doing business as Doctors' Regional Medical Center (collectively, Tenet) appeal the district court's order enjoining the merger of two hospitals in Poplar Bluff, Missouri.

After a five-day hearing, the district court granted a motion for a preliminary injunction filed by the Federal Trade Commission (FTC) and the State of Missouri. The district court found a substantial likelihood that the merger would substantially lessen competition between acute care hospitals in Poplar Bluff, Missouri, in violation of section 7 of the Clayton Act, 15 U.S.C. § 18. We reverse.

I. BACKGROUND

* * *

Tenet Healthcare Corporation owns Lucy Lee Hospital in Poplar Bluff, a general acute care hospital that provides primary and secondary care services 201 licensed beds ... and operates ten outpatient clinics in the surrounding counties. Doctors' Regional Medical Center in Poplar Bluff is presently owned by a group of physicians, ... has 230 licensed beds ... and also operates several rural health clinics in the area. Though profitable, both hospitals are underutilized and have had problems attracting specialists to the area. Tenet recently entered into an agreement to purchase Doctors' Regional which it will operate as a long-term care facility, consolidating inpatient services of the two hospitals at Lucy Lee. It plans to employ more specialists at the merged facility and to offer higher quality care in a comprehensive, integrated delivery system that would include some tertiary care.

* * *

The evidence adduced at the hearing shows that Lucy Lee and Doctors' Regional are the only two hospitals in Poplar Bluff, other than a Veteran's Hospital. The combined service area of these hospitals covers eight counties and an approximate fifty-mile radius from Poplar Bluff.*

Market participants, specifically, employers, healthplans and network providers testified that they had negotiated substantial discounts and favorable per diem rates with either or both Lucy Lee and Doctors' Regional as a result of "playing the two hospitals off each other." These managed care organizations and employers testified that if the merged entity were to raise its prices by 10 percent, the health plans would have no choice but to simply pay the increased price. They testified that they perceive it is essential for the plans to include a Poplar Bluff hospital in their benefit packages because their enrollees would not travel to other towns for primary and secondary inpatient treatment. They stated that their employees and subscribers find it convenient to use a Poplar Bluff hospital; are loyal to their physicians in Poplar Bluff and would not be amenable to a health benefit plan that did not include a Poplar Bluff hospital.

The evidence shows that patient choice of hospitals is determined by many variables, including patient/physician loyalty, perceptions of quality, geographic proximity and, most importantly or determinatively, access to hospitals through an insurance plan. Managed care organizations have been able to influence or change patient behavior with financial incentives in other healthcare markets. This practice is known as "steering." Representatives of

---

* A "service area" is generally defined as the area from which a hospital derives ninety percent of its inpatients.

Poplar Bluff managed care entities testified, however, that they did not believe such efforts would be successful in the Poplar Bluff market. They testified it would be unlikely that they could steer their subscribers to another hospital, or could exclude the merged Poplar Bluff entity in the event of a price increase, in spite of the fact that such tactics had been successful in other markets. They did not regard the Cape Girardeau hospitals as an alternative to Poplar Bluff hospitals because the Cape Girardeau hospitals were more costly. Witnesses conceded, however, that employees had been successfully "steered" to other area hospitals in the past. Several employers testified that they could successfully steer their employees to Missouri Delta Hospital in Sikeston, Missouri. The representative of one large employer testified that the large employers could prevent price increases through negotiation based on their market power and that the merged entity would provide better quality healthcare.

Lucy Lee and Doctors' Regional obtain ninety percent of their patients from zip codes within a fifty-mile radius of Poplar Bluff. In eleven of the top twelve zip codes, however, significant patient admissions-ranging from 22% to 70%-were to hospitals other than those in Poplar Bluff. There is no dispute that Poplar Bluff residents travel to St. Louis, Memphis, and Jonesboro for tertiary care. The evidence also shows, however, that significant numbers of patients in the Poplar Bluff service area travel to other towns for primary and secondary treatment that is also available in Poplar Bluff.

* * *

II. Discussion

* * *

A geographic market is the area in which consumers can practically turn for alternative sources of the product and in which the antitrust defendants face competition. Market share must be established in a well-defined market. [ ] A properly defined geographic market includes potential suppliers who can readily offer consumers a suitable alternative to the defendant's services. [ ] Determination of the relevant geographic market is highly fact sensitive. [ ] The proper market definition can be determined only after a factual inquiry into the commercial realities faced by consumers.

The government has the burden of proving the relevant geographic market. [ ] To meet this burden, the FTC must present evidence on the critical question of where consumers of hospital services could practicably turn for alternative services should the merger be consummated and prices become anticompetitive. [ ] This evidence must address where consumers could practicably go, not on where they actually go. [ ] *Bathke*, 64 F.3d at 346 (articulating the test as the distance "customers will travel in order to avoid doing business at [the entity that has raised prices]" rather than the distance customers would travel absent a price increase); [ ].

The FTC proposes a relevant geographic market that essentially matches its service area: a fifty-mile radius from downtown Poplar Bluff. It is from this service area that the two hospitals obtain ninety percent of their patients. A service area, however, is not necessarily a merging firm's geographic market for purposes of antitrust analysis.

* * *

The question before us is whether the FTC provided sufficient evidence that the proposed merger will result in the merged entity possessing market power within the relevant geographic market. Because we conclude that the FTC produced insufficient evidence of a well-defined relevant geographic market, we find that it did not show that the merged entity will possess such market power.

The district court found that statistical evidence did not establish either the geographic market proposed by the FTC or the market proposed by Tenet. It nonetheless found, relying on anecdotal evidence, that the merger would likely be anticompetitive. Our review of the record convinces us that the district court erred in several respects. The evidence in this case falls short of establishing a relevant geographic market that excludes the Sikeston or Cape Girardeau areas. The evidence shows that hospitals in either or both of these towns, as well as rural hospitals throughout the area, are practical alternatives for many Poplar Bluff consumers.

In adopting the FTC's position, the district court improperly discounted the fact that over twenty-two percent of people in the most important zip codes already use hospitals outside the FTC's proposed market for treatment that is offered at Poplar Bluff hospitals. The district court also failed to fully credit the significance of the consumers who live outside Poplar Bluff, particularly those patients within the FTC's proposed geographic market who actually live or work closer to a hospital outside that geographic market than to either of the Poplar Bluff hospitals. If patients use hospitals outside the service area, those hospitals can act as a check on the exercise of market power by the hospitals within the service area. [ ] The FTC's contention that the merged hospitals would have eighty-four percent of the market for inpatient primary and secondary services within a contrived market area that stops just short of including a regional hospital (Missouri Delta in Sikeston) that is closer to many patients than the Poplar Bluff hospitals, strikes us as absurd. The proximity of many patients to hospitals in other towns, coupled with the compelling and essentially unrefuted evidence that the switch to another provider by a small percentage of patients would constrain a price increase, shows that the FTC's proposed market is too narrow.

We question the district court's reliance on the testimony of managed care payers, in the face of contrary evidence, that these for-profit entities would unhesitatingly accept a price increase rather than steer their subscribers to hospitals in Sikeston or Cape Girardeau. Without necessarily being disingenuous or self-serving or both, the testimony is at least contrary to the payers' economic interests and thus is suspect.* In spite of their testimony to the contrary, the evidence shows that large, sophisticated third-party buyers can do resist price increases, especially where consolidation results in cost savings to the merging entities. The testimony of the market participants

---

* We add that, in making this observation, we do not question the district court's assessment of the credibility of these witnesses. Although the witnesses may have testified truth- fully as to their present intentions, market participants are not always in the best opinion to assess the market long term. [ ]

spoke to current competitor perceptions and consumer habits and failed to show where consumers could practicably go for inpatient hospital services.

The district court rejected the Cape Girardeau hospitals as practicable alternatives because they were more costly. In so doing, it underestimated the impact of nonprice competitive factors, such as quality. The evidence shows that one reason for the significant amount of migration from the Poplar Bluff hospitals to either Sikeston, Cape Girardeau, or St. Louis is the actual or perceived difference in quality of care. The apparent willingness of Poplar Bluff residents to travel for better quality care must be considered. As the district court noted, healthcare decisions are based on factors other than price. It is for that reason that, although they are less expensive, HMOs are not always an employer's or individual's choice in healthcare services. *See* Blue Cross and Blue Shield United of Wisconsin v. Marshfield Clinic, 65 F.3d 1406, 1412, 1410 (7th Cir. 1995) (Posner, J.) (noting "[g]enerally you must pay more for higher quality" and "the HMO's incentive is to keep you healthy if it can but if you get very sick, and are unlikely to recover to a healthy state involving few medical expenses, to let you die as quickly and cheaply as possible."). Thus, the fact that Cape Girardeau hospitals are higher priced than Poplar Bluff hospitals does not necessarily mean they are not competitors. [ ] The district court placed an inordinate emphasis on price competition without considering the impact of a corresponding reduction in quality.

We further find that although Tenet's efficiencies defense may have been properly rejected by the district court, the district court should nonetheless have considered evidence of enhanced efficiency in the context of the competitive effects of the merger. The evidence shows that a hospital that is larger and more efficient than Lucy Lee or Doctors' Regional will provide better medical care than either of those hospitals could separately. The merged entity will be able to attract more highly qualified physicians and specialists and to offer integrated delivery and some tertiary care. [ ] The evidence shows that the merged entity may well enhance competition in the greater Southeast Missouri area.

In assessing the "commercial realities" faced by consumers, the district court did not ... consider the impact of the entry of managed care into the Cape Girardeau market. The evidence shows that managed care has reduced prices in Poplar Bluff and in other markets. A similar downward pressure on prices is now being felt in Cape Girardeau, with the recent entry of managed care into that market. The district court also relied on the seemingly outdated assumption of doctor-patient loyalty that is not supported by the record. The evidence shows, and the district court acknowledged, that the issue of access to a provider through an insurance plan is determinative of patient choice. Essentially, the evidence shows that patients will choose whatever doctors or hospitals are covered by their health plan. Undeniably, although many patients might prefer to be loyal to their doctors, it is, unfortunately, a luxury they can no longer afford.... As much as many patients long for the days of old-fashioned and local, if expensive and inefficient, healthcare, recent trends in healthcare management have made the old healthcare model obsolete.

The reality of the situation in our changing healthcare environment may be that Poplar Bluff cannot support two high-quality hospitals. Third-party payers have reaped the benefit of a price war in a small corner of the market for healthcare services in Southeastern Missouri, at the arguable cost of quality to their subscribers. Antitrust laws simply do not protect that benefit when the evidence shows that there are other practical alternatives for healthcare in the area. We are mindful that competition is the driving force behind our free enterprise system and that, unless barriers have been erected to constrain the normal operation of the market, "a court ought to exercise extreme caution because judicial intervention in a competitive situation can itself upset the balance of market forces, bringing about the very ills the antitrust laws were meant to prevent." [] This appears to have even more force in an industry, such as healthcare, experiencing significant and profound changes. Under the circumstances presented in this case, the FTC has not shown a likelihood of success on the merits of its section 7 complaint and we find the district court erred in granting injunctive relief.

Notes and Questions

1. The geographic market determination turns on the question of where customers could practicably turn in the event that prices were increased as a result of enhanced market power (or in the terminology of the Merger Guidelines, there was a "small but significant increase in price"). In the context of hospital mergers, patient origin data (usually compiled using the zip code of the residence of each patient) has traditionally been used to calculate the inflow and outflow of patients to hospitals from a geographic region. This data, however, is at best a starting point for analysis, as the Eighth Circuit points out. Courts must ask where buyers (patients) or their health plans or employers would turn in the event of a price increase resulting from the merger. What evidence did the FTC and the State of Missouri rely on to answer this question? Do you agree with the reasons supplied by the court to dispute the government's analysis? Given the speculative nature of the question, what evidence would you regard as most reliable? Does the fact that some individuals are willing to travel some distance to receive hospital services necessarily imply that others will also do so if prices are increased? For the view of economists branding these assumptions as fallacious because individuals have highly heterogeneous preferences regarding traveling for hospitals care based on the availability of family support, their place of employment, convenience, and because hospitals are highly differentiated in their services, amenities, reputations, and so forth, see Cory Capps et al., The Silent Majority Fallacy of the Elzinga Hogarty Criteria A Critique and New Approach to Analyzing Hospital Mergers. Natl'l Bureau of Econ. Research, Working Paper No. 8216, 2001. See also, Kenneth Danger & H.E. Frech, Critical Thinking about "Critical Loss" in Antitrust, 46 Antitrust L. Bull. 339 (2001); James Langenfeld & W. Li, Critical Loss Analysis in Evaluating Mergers, 46 Antitrust Bull. 299 (2001). But see Barry Harris & Joseph J. Simon, Focusing Market Definition: How Much Substitution is Enough?, 12 Research L. & Econ. 207 (1989).

2. The government lost seven consecutive hospital merger cases in the 1990s, most on the issue of whether the government had correctly defined the geographic market. See e.g., FTC v. Freeman Hospital, 69 F.3d 260 (8th Cir. 1995); California v. Sutter Health System, 84 F. Supp. 2d 1057 (N.D.Cal. 2000). See Thomas L. Greaney, Chicago's Procrustean Bed, *supra* (analyzing cases and noting courts' failures to acknowledge market failures and product differentiation as cause of overestimating size of hospital markets). Does the court's opinion in *Tenet* suggest a hostility toward managed care or skepticism about the benefits of hospital competition in general? See id. (suggesting that the "managed care backlash" may have subtlety influence courts in certain antitrust cases).

Responding to their lack of success in court, the FTC and DOJ produced a lengthy report on competition policy in health care, and conducted retrospective studies of the impact of horizontal hospital mergers in selected markets around the country, including some that were the subject of unsuccessful litigation by the government. See FTC & Department of Justice, Dose of Competition *supra.* The FTC ultimately brought an administrative complaint challenging one already consummated merger, between the Evanston Northwestern Healthcare Corporation and Highland Park Hospital, which is discussed in the following section.

3. *Overcoming the Presumption of Illegality: Nonprofit Status and Other Factors.* If the government establishes a prima facie case of illegality based on market share and market concentration data, defendants may overcome that presumption by showing that the merger is not likely to have anticompetitive effects. They may do this by proving that market conditions or special characteristics of the merging firms make it unlikely that they will exercise market power after the merger is consummated. See Merger Guidelines, § 2; 2 Furrow, et al., Health Law § 14–58. A number of courts have refused to find that the not-for-profit status of the merging hospitals constitutes sufficient grounds to rebut the government's prima facie case. See, e.g., U.S. v. Rockford Memorial Corp., 898 F.2d 1278 (7th Cir. 1990) A district court closely examined the issue with novel results in FTC v. Butterworth Health Corporation and Blodgett Memorial Medical Center, 946 F.Supp. 1285 (W.D.Mich. 1996), aff'd 121 F.3d 708 (6th Cir. 1997). The court found that not-for-profit hospitals do not operate in the same manner as profit-maximizing businesses, especially when their boards of directors are comprised of community business leaders who have a direct stake in maintaining high quality, low cost hospitals.

Do you agree that such hospitals are, as the court suggested, more likely to behave in the interests of their consumers (akin to "consumer cooperatives") rather than acting as profit maximizers? What assumptions does this finding make about the role of board members in directing the affairs of a hospital? What limits are placed on them by their fiduciary duties as board members? In this connection, the *Butterworth* court also relied on a number of voluntary "community commitments" made by the merging hospitals, including a freeze on prices or charges, commitments to limit profit margins, and promises to serve the medically needy. Do such assurances provide a sufficient guarantee that the parties will not exercise market power? See FTC & Dept. of Justice, A Dose of Competition, ch. 4 at 33 ("nonprofit status should not be considered as a factor in predicting whether a hospital merger is likely to be anticompetitive"); Barak K. Richman, Antitrust and Nonprofit Hospital Mergers: A Return to Basics, ___ U. Penn L. Rev. ___ (criticizing courts' analysis of nonprofit status and arguing the issue has diverted attention from the core concerns of antitrust merger doctrine); Thomas L. Greaney, Antitrust and Hospital Mergers: Does the Nonprofit Form Affect Competitive Substance? 31 J. Health Pol. Pol'y & L. 511 (2006) (rejecting FTC/DOJ preemptive approach and suggesting that systematic differences between nonprofit and for-profit hospital behavior may warrant consideration in some cases).

4. Other factors sometimes advanced to rebut the presumption of illegality include the financial weakness of one of the merging firms and the relative strength of buyers in the market. Entities claiming protection under the "failing firm" defense face high proof burdens, see Merger Guidelines § 5.1, but the defense was successfully asserted in California v. Sutter Health System, 84 F. Supp. 2d 1057 (N.D.Cal. 2000). In FTC v. Cardinal Health, Inc., 12 F. Supp.2d 34 (D.C. 1998), the court carefully analyzed the defendants' rebuttal claims that ease of entry into the wholesale drug distribution market should obviate competitive

concerns. The court found that, despite a few examples of successful entry by new drug wholesalers, the defendants had failed to demonstrate that significant and effective entry was likely given various barriers that had impeded or slowed new competitors' effectiveness in the market. The court also rejected the defendants' claim that powerful buyers would likely counteract the defendants' market power.

5. *Efficiencies.* The law on efficiencies as a defense to an otherwise anticompetitive merger is somewhat unclear. Although Supreme Court case law and the legislative history of the Clayton Act does not seem to support an efficiencies defense, see Alan A. Fisher & Robert Lande, Efficiency Considerations in Merger Enforcement, 71 Cal. L.Rev. 1580 (1983), a number of lower courts have explicitly considered potential cost-savings and other efficiencies associated with mergers both as an absolute defense and as a factor to be considered in evaluating the merger's likely competitive effects. See, e.g., FTC v. University Health, Inc., 938 F.2d 1206 (11th Cir. 1991). The Merger Guidelines and most of the litigated cases require that the parties show that the claimed efficiencies cannot be realized by means short of a merger and that the efficiencies be "merger specific", i.e. attributable to and causally related to the combination of the two firms. Merger Guidelines, § 4. Inability to clear these hurdles is often decisive in cases in which courts reject the efficiencies defense. The court in *Tenet* followed the approach of considering potential efficiencies resulting from the merger in the context of analyzing the merger's overall impact. Does this form of analysis permit a more speculative standard? Should the potential to enhance quality of care be folded into the competitive analysis of efficiencies? See Kristin Madison, Hospital Mergers in an Era of Quality Improvement, 7 Hous. J. Health L. & Pol. 265 (2007).

6. A number of state attorneys general have settled antitrust challenges to hospital mergers and other affiliations by allowing the merger to go forward subject to various commitments and payments by the hospitals. For example, in Commonwealth of Pennsylvania v. Capital Health System Services, 1995–2 Trade Cas. (CCH) ¶ 71,205, 1995 WL 787584 (M.D. Pa. 1995) (consent decree), the Pennsylvania Attorney General entered into a consent decree approving the merger of two Harrisburg, Pennsylvania hospitals subject to the condition that they pass on to the community $56 million (of a projected $70 million in cost savings attributable to the merger) in the form of various free or low cost services such as child immunization, mammograms and substance abuse programs. In addition, the merged hospitals agreed to hold price increases for five years to changes in the Consumer Price Index plus two percent. See also, Pennsylvania Attorney General, Attorney General Corbett Negotiates Two Agreements in University of Pittsburgh Medical Center's Acquisition of Mercy Hospital (May, 2007) http://www.attorneygeneral.gov/press.aspx?id=2531 (announcing settlement of merger investigation resolving antitrust concerns by requiring UPMC to extend existing health plan contracts and pricing for eight years; negotiate "in good faith" and submit to binding arbitration in certain circumstances where negotiations break down; and maintain an open medical staff). What are the advantages and disadvantages of entering into "regulatory" consent decrees of this kind? Is the public better served than by employing the conventional relief afforded in antitrust merger cases, namely an injunction prohibiting the merger?

IN THE MATTER OF EVANSTON NORTHWESTERN HEALTHCARE CORP.

Federal Trade Commission, August 6, 2007.

OPINION OF THE COMMISSION

I. INTRODUCTION

In 2000, Evanston Northwestern Healthcare Corporation ("Evanston") merged with Highland Park Hospital ("Highland Park"). Prior to the merger, Evanston owned Evanston Hospital and Glenbrook Hospital.

The Commission issued an administrative complaint challenging Evanston's acquisition of Highland Park under Section 7 of the Clayton Act four years after the transaction closed. Given that the merger was consummated well before the Commission commenced this case, we were able to examine not only pre-merger evidence, but also evidence about what happened after the merger.

There is no dispute that ENH substantially raised its prices shortly after the merging parties consummated the transaction. There is disagreement about the cause of those price increases, however. Complaint counsel maintains that the merger eliminated significant competition between Evanston and Highland Park, which allowed ENH to exercise market power against health care insurance companies. Respondent argues that, during the due diligence process for the merger, ENH obtained information about Highland Park's prices that showed that Evanston had been charging rates that were below competitive levels for a number of years. Respondent contends that most of ENH's merger-related price increases simply reflect its efforts to raise Evanston Hospital's prices to competitive rates. Respondent also maintains that some portion of the merger-related price increases reflects increased demand for Highland Park's services due to post-merger improvements at the hospital.

Chief Administrative Law Judge Stephen J. McGuire ("ALJ") found in his Initial Decision that the transaction violated Section 7 of the Clayton Act and ordered ENH to divest Highland Park. We affirm the ALJ's decision that the transaction violated Section 7 of the Clayton Act. Considered as a whole, the evidence demonstrates that the transaction enabled the merged firm to exercise market power and that the resulting anticompetitive effects were not offset by merger-specific efficiencies. The record shows that senior officials at Evanston and Highland Park anticipated that the merger would give them greater leverage to raise prices, that the merged firm did raise its prices immediately and substantially after completion of the transaction, and that the same senior officials attributed the price increases in part to increased bargaining leverage produced by the merger.

The econometric analyses performed by both complaint counsel's and respondent's economists also strongly support the conclusion that the merger gave the combined entity the ability to raise prices through the exercise of market power. The economists determined that there were substantial merger-coincident price increases and ran regressions using different data sets and a variety of control groups that ruled out the most likely competitively-benign explanations for substantial portions of these increases. The record does not support respondent's position that the merger-coincident price increases reflect ENH's attempts to correct a multi-year failure by Evanston's senior officials to charge market rates to many of its customers, or increased demand for Highland Park's services due to post-merger improvements.

We do not agree with the ALJ, however, that a divestiture is warranted. The potentially high costs inherent in the separation of hospitals that have functioned as a merged entity for seven years instead warrant a remedy that restores the lost competition through injunctive relief.

* * *

Notes and Questions

1.   In challenging a merger that had been completed over six years prior to its final decision in the case, the FTC faced both challenges and opportunities. On the plus side, the Commission could look at the actual outcome of the merger, examining whether the anticompetitive effects associated with a facially anticompetitive acquisition actually occurred. On the other hand, it was forced to deal with the difficult dilemmas concerning relief: would it be feasible to insist on "structural relief" (i.e. order divestiture of Highland Hospital)? If not, what alternative remedy would restore the competitive conditions the market enjoyed before the merger? To the surprise of many, the Commission's order required the hospital to "establish separate and independent negotiating teams—one of Evanston and Glenbrook Hospitals and another for Highland Park." The FTC explained its remedy as follows:

> While not ideal, this remedy will allow MCOs to negotiate separately again for these competing hospitals, thus re-injecting competition between them for the business of MCOs....[In future cases involving consummated mergers], where it is relatively clear that the unwinding of a hospital merger would be unlikely to involve substantial costs, all else being equal, the Commission would likely select divestiture as the remedy.

With the FTC having conceded that the hospitals have significantly merged operations, what benefit will separate negotiations serve? For example, will the two hospitals be able to "compete" on the basis of cost, service or reputation? In view of the remedy adopted, was *Evanston* a Pyrrhic victory for the Commission or a strategic move designed to reverse the course of hospital merger doctrine?

2.   Note the following differences between the theories advanced by the FTC in *Evanston* and those employed in prior litigation.

- The FTC rejected patient origin data as a useful tool in defining the relevant geographic market. Instead it relied on the actual effects in the market place to prove the existence of a market.

- The FTC's theory of harm to competition from the merger rested on "unilateral effects" analysis. That is, the two merging hospitals were able to raise prices because each was the next best alternative of the other in the eyes of a significant number of patients and thus were able to raise prices after the merger without regard to the actions of other area hospitals.

- Although the majority of the Commission found it unnecessary to address the theory, complaint counsel alleged, and two commissioners agreed, that it would not be necessary to prove a geographic market in the case because anticompetitive effect was established independently.

3.   The principal basis on which the FTC relied to find proof of harm to competition was its economic analysis of post-merger price increases by Evanston

Hospital. Underlying the econometrics presented by experts are some common-sense factors that must be accounted for before one can attribute the price increases to enhanced market power resulting from the merger. What factors do you think were considered to test whether price actually increased? Remember that nonprice variables affecting costs may influence the price of any product or service. See Peter J. Hammer, Competition and Quality as Dynamic Processes in the Balkans of American Health Care, J. Health Pol. Pol'y & L. 473 (2006).

In fact, experts for both sides *agreed* that the ENH had significantly increased the prices of one of the hospitals it previously owned, Evanston Hospital, after its acquisition of Highland Park Hospital. Given this fact, what factors might explain that increase *other than* the exercise of market power? Defendants advanced one unprecedented explanation for the price increases: the "learning about demand" defense. They claimed that ENH raised price at only at Evanston Hospital and did so there only because it discovered through the merger that it was underpricing its services. It learned that the acquired hospital, Highland Park, a somewhat less sophisticated hospital than Evanston Hospital, had been receiving higher reimbursement from third party payers in the area. The FTC rejected this explanation on several grounds; for example, after the merger, ENH terminated the executive responsible for managed care contracting at Highland, and retained his counterpart from Evanston Hospital.

Although the Commission relied heavily on the economic evidence regarding price increases, it noted a number of pre- and post-acquisition internal documents that supported its theory. Several of these documents indicated that ENH thought that Highland Park was its chief competitor and that after the merger it would be easier to increase prices. Other documents suggested that managed care entities played Evanston Hospital and Highland Park off against each other. The Commission also examined the testimony of managed care executives which to some degree supported its theory of unilateral effects, but also provided some evidence that the merging hospitals faced competitive pressures from a number of other area hospitals. (Note that the Evanston hospitals are located in a small, affluent and densely populated area less than 20 miles from Chicago). Does the FTC's discounting of this testimony conflict with its insistence in *Tenet* and other cases that factfinders should credit the views of third party payors with respect to geographic market definition? Did the FTC even need to rely on testimony other than that of the economists?

Problem: Evaluating A Hospital Merger in Your Community

Suppose the largest and third largest hospitals (or hospital systems) in your community proposed to merge. What will the key issues be? What facts would you gather in seeking to defend this transaction against antitrust challenge? What testimony from payors, employers, expert witnesses, or parties to the transaction would be helpful?

2. Managed Care Mergers

The health insurance industry has witnessed a rapid succession of major mergers. According to the AMA there have been over 400 mergers involving health insurers over the past decade and the largest remaining companies, Aetna, Cigna, United Healthcare, Foundation Health Systems, and Wellpoint Health Networks, control a large share of the nation's private insurance business. See Edward Langston, "Statement of the American Medical Association to the Senate Committee on the Judiciary United States Senate: Examining Competition in Group Health Care," Sept. 6, 2006, http://www.ama-assn.

org/ama1/pub/upload/mm/399/antitrust090606.pdf (study finding more than 95% of Metropolitan Statistical Areas (MSAs) had at least one insurer in the combined HMO/PPO market with a market share greater than 30% and more than 56% of MSAs had at least one insurer with market share greater than 50%). This data may overstate the risks of high concentration, however, as it does not include self insurance by large corporations and the degree of actual concentration in well defined insurance markets is disputed. See A Dose of Competition, ch. 6 at 7 (noting testimony that "health insurance markets in most geographic areas enjoy robust competition"). See also, David A. Hyman & William E. Kovacic, Monopoly, Monopsony and Market Definition: An Antitrust Perspective on Market Concentration Among Health Insurers, 23 Health Affs. 25 (2004). Although the Department of Justice has challenged several mergers involving large national organizations, these cases resulted in limited divestitures in a small fraction of the markets in which the firms did business. For example, Aetna's buyout of Prudential Health Care was settled by consent decree filed jointly by the U.S. Department of Justice and the Texas Attorney General's Office. U.S. and State of Texas v. Aetna Inc., No. 3–99 CV 1398–H (N.D Tex.), 64 Fed. Reg. 44946–01 (1999). As a condition of obtaining approval of the merger, the decree requires that Aetna divest certain HMOs operated by a subsidiary in Texas. The government's complaint contended that the proposed merger would have made Aetna the dominant provider of health-maintenance-organization and HMO-point-of-service plans in Houston and Dallas, with 63 percent and 42 percent of enrollees in those areas. A few years later, the government changed its view of the relevant market for analysis and challenged mergers alleging a product market consisting of both HMO and PPO products, observing that the line had blurred considerably between the characteristics of these kinds of plans. However, the government limited the market in one case to to markets for small group insurance on the theory that these groups cannot self-insure and have fewer alternatives. U.S. v United Health Group Incorporated and PacificCare Health Systems, No. 1:05–cv–02436 (D.D.C. filed Jan. 20, 2005), *available at* www.usdoj.gov/atr/cases/unitedhealth.htm

As an alternative theory of harm in these cases, the government alleged that the merger would reduce competition in the market for physician services. For example, the government's complaint in Aetna stated "the proposed acquisition will give Aetna the ability to depress physicians' reimbursement rates in Houston and Dallas, likely leading to a reduction in quantity or degradation in quality of physicians' services." Assuming that physicians in the relevant markets are reimbursed by non-HMO and HMO–POS plans (including Medicare and Medicaid) and that such reimbursement constitutes, say, three-quarters of total reimbursements in the markets, how might the government prove its theory of competitive harm? For critical analyses of the government's theory in this case, see Robert E. Bloch, Scott P. Perlman & Lawrence Wu, A New And Uncertain Future For Managed Care Mergers: an Antitrust Analysis of The Aetna/Prudential Merger, Antitrust Rep. 37 (Dec. 1999); Thomas L. Greaney, Antitrust and the Healthcare Industry: The View from the Three Branches, 32 J.Health L. 391 (1999). The government's economic analysis is set forth in Marius Schwartz, Buyer Power Concentration and the Aetna–Prudential Merger (Oct. 20, 1999) http://www.usdoj.gov/atr/public/speeches.

3. *Physician Mergers*

Antitrust attention has only occasionally focused on physician mergers. In the only case thus far decided by the courts, HTI Health Services, Inc. v. Quorum Health Group, Inc., 960 F.Supp. 1104 (S.D. Miss. 1997), the district court refused to enjoin a merger of the two largest physician clinics in Vicksburg, Mississippi with one of two hospitals in town. Notably, the court held that plaintiff had properly alleged four distinct physician service markets: primary care, general surgery, urology, and otolaryngology; in addition, it accepted a primary care sub-market for pediatrics. However, the court rejected plaintiff's argument that a distinct market for managed care purchasers could be established based on discounting practices. The case is notable for its treatment of the competitive implications of the merger in these markets notwithstanding the extremely high market shares held by the parties. For example, with respect to urology, the court noted there were only two urologists in the market and concluded that it was inconceivable that Congress had intended for the Clayton Act to prohibit the two physicians from practicing together under the same roof and characterized the market as a "natural monopoly." With respect to primary care services in which the merged entity would control between 58% and 70% of the market (which it defined to include general practitioners, family practitioners and internists, but not ob/gyns), the court emphasized that the absence of barriers to entry effectively obviated concerns about the defendant's potential exercise of market power. Id. at 1133. In this connection, the court relied upon the fact that the plaintiff hospital (Columbia/HCA) had a highly successful record in recruiting new physicians into the market to serve its facility.

The antitrust enforcement agencies have reviewed several physician mergers. A threshold question is whether a combination of competitors actually constitutes a bona fide merger. In its challenge to a transaction involving two surgical groups that had formed a for-profit LLC, the FTC alleged that the groups had not agreed to share profits, centralize control or take other steps so as to be considered a single entity; hence their attempt to negotiate with managed care companies through this entity constituted an illegal conspiracy. In re Surgical Specialists of Yakima (2003) (consent order) www.FTC.gov. See also State v. Maine Heart Surgical Assocs., P.A., 1996 WL 773330 (ME Super. CT. 1996) (consent decree) (state attorney general settling challenge to merger of physician specialty practices conditioned on entity accepting all contracts offered at or above reference price and not entering into exclusive contracts). Because these investigations involved acquisitions of groups practicing in certain specialty areas, analyses of market definition and entry were critical. For example, in examining a proposed merger between a group of cardiovascular thoracic surgeons and a group of vascular surgeons, the Justice Department reviewed the specific vascular procedures that the two groups performed and defined the relevant product markets based on sixty or more overlapping procedures common to specialists. In clearing the merger, the Department emphasized the fact that payers needed to include only a very few peripheral vascular surgeons (the relevant market) in a managed care network and that there were sufficient independent providers of such services who were not a part of the merging groups to obviate competitive concerns raised by the high market shares of the merging parties. In addition, it noted that sponsored entry or expansion by existing competing groups would defeat attempts to raise prices. Letter from Joel I. Klein, Assistant Attorney General, Antitrust Division, U.S. Department of Justice to Bob D. Tucker (Re: CVT Surgical Center and Vascular Surgery Associates) (Apr. 16, 1997). By contrast, in another business review letter, the Department indicated that there was a substantial likelihood that it would challenge a proposed merger of two physician groups of board certified gastroenterologists in Allentown, Pennsylvania. Letter from Joel I. Klein, Assistant Attorney General, Antitrust Division, U.S. Department of Justice to Donald H. Lipson (Gastroenterology Associates Limited, et al.) (July 7, 1997). The Department concluded that although there was some overlap in the procedures performed by gastroenterologists and other physician specialties, gastroenterologists could probably collectively raise prices because managed care organizations required gastroenterologists on their panels as a "critical selling point." The Department also concluded that the service market was highly localized because of patients' "psychological barriers" to traveling even a small distance for treatment.

Review Problem: The Heart Specialty Hospital

Heart-of-the-Midwest Orthopedic Surgical Hospital (HOTMOSH) has applied to its state health planning agency for a certificate of need (CON) to open a new acute care hospital in Bedrock Kansas. It will offer facilities for inpatient and outpatient orthopedic surgery and related procedures and a variety of outpatient services including radiology and laboratory services. The hospital is owned by an LLC controlled by two groups of orthopedic surgeons each of which own 40 percent of the membership interest; the remaining ownership is held by other Bedrock physicians.

The three community hospitals in Bedrock are very concerned about the impact HOTMOSH will have on their revenues. Freda Fieldstone, CEO of Bedrock Community Hospital (BCH), has called a meeting with the other hospitals to discuss formulating a "joint response" to the CON application. Besides urging the other hospitals to ask the planning commission to reject the application, she hopes to enlist their support in a campaign to elicit help from managed care organizations. One idea is to have each hospital commit to contacting one managed care organization MCO (its "dancing partner") to urge that company not to contract with HOTMOSH and, if necessary, to "intimate" that the other hospitals in the market would probably be very unhappy if the MCO chose to include the specialty hospital in its network.

Because BCH is the largest orthopedic hospital in the area and other hospitals are not at risk for losing nearly as much business, Ms. Fieldstone believes she must come up with a strategy to ensure she will have the support of the other hospitals. Because St. Lucas Hospital has filed a CON application to add 20 new oncology beds to its campus, Ms Fieldstone believes that if she "hints" that BCH might oppose this CON application unless St. Lucas supports her on the HOTMOSH issue, she will "get their attention." If that doesn't work she plans to hint that BCH may also be thinking of opening a new oncology service.

Finally, Ms. Fieldstone has several "backup" plans:

- Terminate the staff privileges of every doctor at BCH who has an ownership interest or who refers more than five patients per year to HOTMOSH.
- Create a "super PHO" to bargain with MCOs on behalf of the other hospitals performing orthopedic services in town. If that is not possible, to

"clinically integrate" the orthopedic surgeons on her staff who do not have an ownership in HOTMOSH so that they can negotiate as a unit with MCOs.

- If all else fails, negotiate a merger or joint venture with HOTMOSH once it establishes that it is successful in the market.

Recognizing that these ideas may raise some antitrust concerns, Ms. Feldstone has solicited your counsel. Advise on the possible antitrust risks you see for each strategic option and what might be done to reduce legal risk.

Index

References are to Pages

†